P9-CLB-222

LEGAL PROBLEM SOLVER

READER'S DIGEST

LEGAL PROBLEM SOLVER

A Quick-and-Easy Action Guide to the Law

The Reader's Digest Association, Inc.
Pleasantville, New York • Montreal

The editors would like to thank the following people and organizations for their help in preparing this book:
Malcolm Davis
Bruce Silverglade
National Resource Center for Consumers of Legal Services
U.S. Railroad Retirement Board
U.S. Department of Health and Human Services

Printed in the United States of America

Library of Congress Cataloging in Publication Data

Legal problem solver: a quick-and-easy action guide to the law.
p. cm.
Includes index.
ISBN 0-89577-550-6
1. Law — United States — Popular works. I. Reader's Digest Association.
KF387.L44 1994
349.73 — dc20
[347.3] 93-27340

▪ Contents ▪

About This Book

Knowledge is power, goes an old saying, and nowhere is that truer than in the field of law. Armed with the right facts, you can avoid legal pitfalls, bail yourself out of trouble, minimize potential losses, become a wiser consumer, and take full advantage of the rights and benefits you are entitled to as a citizen. LEGAL PROBLEM SOLVER shows you how to do all these things.

Throughout this book you will find valuable information on hundreds of law-related topics, as well as advice on how to deal with the kinds of legal problems that an average person is likely to encounter in daily life. With nearly 700 major entries encompassing virtually every area of everyday law, this legal action guide is one of the most comprehensive—and comprehensible—books of its kind. It contains reliable information and sound advice on everything from pawnbrokers to stockbrokers, from dating to divorce, from false advertising to false arrest.

This book is not intended to be a substitute for a lawyer, but it can serve as a trusted legal adviser. For instance, it will help you determine whether you need a lawyer in the first place. Fighting a traffic ticket or getting a document notarized may not require an attorney, while buying real estate or signing an important contract usually should not be undertaken without one.

If you do hire a lawyer, LEGAL PROBLEM SOLVER will make you a better-informed client. Before consulting a lawyer, first see what this book has to say about your particular situation. Chances are, it will answer some of your questions, help you formulate others, and give you a sense of how serious or complex your problem is. Then, when you do meet with an attorney, these few minutes of preparation will have saved you both time and money (most lawyers bill by the hour). More important, you will be better equipped to understand the attorney and better able to help him serve you effectively.

LEGAL PROBLEM SOLVER is a user-friendly reference tool. Entries are arranged in alphabetical order, and the information you need is readily accessible. If you don't see the topic you're looking for, check the comprehensive index at the back of the book.

The typical LEGAL PROBLEM SOLVER entry begins with a clear definition of the topic. It then goes into a fuller explanation of how the subject can affect your life. It assesses the relative risks you assume by taking certain actions, and it explains how the law affects different people in different situations. In most entries, straightforward examples give the reader a clear idea of how legal principles apply in circumstances familiar to all of us.

Often, hypothetical problems are introduced to illustrate a topic. In many articles numbered "Steps to Take" outline specifically what you need to do to resolve the issue. When a topic is related to other entries, cross-references are included to help you locate them. You will also find cross-references to the *Everyday Legal Forms* that appear at the back of the book.

Special supplementary features add to the reader's understanding of a given subject. Convenient *Checklists* serve as reminders about what not to overlook when you must take action or need to solve a problem. *ABC's* boxes simplify and summarize the essentials of a topic. And the features called *Real Life, Real Law* offer pertinent examples of how the law has been applied in actual court cases in the real world.

As you dip into LEGAL PROBLEM SOLVER, you will notice that it is refreshingly free of legal jargon. No matter how lofty or abstract the principles involved, you will find no turgid, technical legalese in this book. Instead, you will find clear, concise explanations of the facts, written in plain English and illustrated with concrete, down-to-earth examples. On the few occasions when legal terminology must be used, it is clearly defined. In addition, the *Glossary* defines and clarifies more than 300 legal terms.

Of course, no book—no matter how large—can cover every aspect of the law or answer every conceivable question. LEGAL PROBLEM SOLVER provides neither the last word on every subject nor the only word. Although every effort has been made to ensure that the information provided is as complete, accurate, and up-to-date as possible (including last-minute changes made at press time), the reader must keep in mind that laws change over time, and they often vary from state to state and from town to town.

LEGAL PROBLEM SOLVER is first and foremost an action guide. Its purpose is to help you help yourself. But without doubt some situations call for a lawyer, not a layman. So if you are going to take any legal action that you believe may have serious consequences, be sure to consult an attorney first.

—The Editors

FROM
ABANDONED PROPERTY
TO
AUTOPSY

Abandoned Property

You are on the way to the bus stop when you see it—a beautiful blue bicycle, the very kind your daughter wants. But it's not in the window of a bicycle shop; it's piled atop the trash set at the curb for pickup. You see that the bike has a flat tire and a broken chain but otherwise is in good condition. Is it all right to take it home?

The answer depends on whether or not the bike has been abandoned.

In order to be considered abandoned, a piece of property must have been left on purpose by the owner, who must have no intention of claiming it. (The law involved here applies only to personal property, not to real estate. For a discussion of abandoned real estate, see ADVERSE POSSESSION.)

In this instance, the bicycle seems to be abandoned. The trash pile is where much abandoned property ends up, and the bicycle's condition suggests that it has been thrown away.

Before claiming the bike, however, you should consider a couple of other possibilities. First, the bike may have been stolen and left with the trash by the thief. If that is so, the true owner has not voluntarily given up ownership, and you have no right to take it.

Second, even if the bike was not stolen, the owner may not have intended it to go out with the trash. In that event, the bicycle is considered lost, not abandoned. Fortunately, there is a solution to your problem.

STEPS TO TAKE

1. If you have any doubt about whether the bicycle was truly abandoned, try to find out whether someone living in a nearby building abandoned it.

2. If this proves futile, take the bicycle to the police station. State and local governments may take charge of lost or stolen property and dispose of it after enough time has passed for the owner to claim it. Ask for a receipt for the bicycle. If it remains unclaimed for the period provided for by law (usually about 90 days), you can claim it as your own.

Abandonment

When lawyers use the word *abandonment*, it has the dictionary meaning of "relinquishing" or "giving something up completely." However, laws are very specific about what a person must do in order to abandon something.

A person may abandon a legal claim, for example, by failing to bring a lawsuit within the time prescribed by law. See STATUTE OF LIMITATIONS.

A tenant may abandon her apartment before her lease is up by leaving it vacant and allowing the landlord to reclaim it. See TENANT'S RIGHTS.

If you forget your umbrella in a restaurant, you have not abandoned it. But if you leave your shoes at the shoe repair shop for six months, the owner can assume that you have abandoned them. See ABANDONED PROPERTY.

If a wife disappears and fails to communicate with her husband within a reasonable period of time, she is said to have abandoned her spouse. But if she keeps in touch by telephone and regularly sends money to take care of the children, she is not considered to have legally abandoned her family. See DIVORCE.

Abortion

Abortion, the deliberate miscarriage of an embryo or fetus, is subject to both state and federal laws. Since 1973, when the Supreme Court of the United States decided the case of *Roe v. Wade*, the Court has limited the states' authority to regulate an adult woman's right to have an abortion.

RIGHT OF PRIVACY

In that ruling the Supreme Court held that a woman's decision to terminate a pregnancy is protected by the Constitution's guarantee of the right of privacy. However, the Court did not find that privacy is an absolute right or that a woman has the right to an abortion under any circumstances. The Court recognized that the individual states have a legitimate interest in regulating abortions to ensure that they are performed safely.

STATE GUIDELINES

In the *Roe* v. *Wade* case the Court set specific guidelines for state regulation of abortion.

◇ During the first three months of pregnancy (the first trimester), the states cannot interfere with a doctor's decision, made in consultation with a patient, to end a pregnancy.

◇ The states may pass laws regulating the performance of abortions in the second three months of the pregnancy (the second trimester), provided that they are for the protection of the woman. For example, a state might (and many do) require that second-trimester abortions be performed in a clinic that meets state standards for proper equipment and trained personnel.

◇ Under *Roe* v. *Wade* the states may prohibit all abortions after a fetus becomes viable (able to live outside the mother's womb).

CHALLENGES TO ROE V. WADE

In recent years some states have passed laws challenging the Supreme Court's 1973 abortion decision. In 1989 the Court upheld a Missouri law requiring a doctor to determine if the fetus is viable before performing an abortion, if he believes the patient is 20 or more weeks pregnant. If the fetus is viable, the doctor cannot perform the abortion. Twenty weeks is in the second trimester, when, under *Roe* v. *Wade*, abortion can be regulated.

Many states also passed laws requiring parental consent before an abortion can be performed on a minor, and some enacted laws requiring the husband's notification or consent before his wife can have an abortion. In 1992, the Supreme Court upheld provisions of a Pennsylvania law that required a woman under the age of 18 to obtain the consent of one parent or the permission of a state judge. In doing so, the Court reasoned that states may regulate abortion procedures if they do not create an undue burden on a woman's decision to have an abortion, and that the parental consent requirement does not create such a burden.

At the same time, however, the Court struck down as unduly burdensome another provision of the law that required a married woman to notify her husband of her decision to obtain an abortion or face imprisonment. In a 5-4 decision, the Supreme Court, refusing to overturn its decision in *Roe* v. *Wade*, reaffirmed that the right to obtain an abortion was protected by the U.S. Constitution.

In 1988, the federal government imposed regulations that prohibited staff members at federally funded family-planning clinics from mentioning abortion to patients as an alternative. Later the Department of Health and Human Services modified this so-called gag rule to permit doctors to discuss abortion with their patients at these clinics. In November of 1992 a federal Court of Appeals ruled that the department had failed to follow procedural guidelines when it changed the regulation; as a result neither the modification nor the gag rule could be enforced.

In the early 1990's several states passed laws either banning abortion or limiting it to cases of rape and incest and situations in which an abortion is necessary to save the mother's life. But at the end of the Court's 1992-93 term, *Roe* was still the law of the land.

ABUSIVE LANGUAGE

If someone showers you with unflattering words, tells you where to go, or otherwise berates you, you might want to see her arrested and fined or imprisoned. Objectionable as it is, however, abusive language is not a crime and does not usually provide sufficient cause for a civil lawsuit.

Suppose, however, that a neighbor repeatedly curses you and your family in an outrageous manner over a period of time. As a result, you suffer mental anguish, become ill, and miss work. You may be able to sue your neighbor for inflicting emotional distress, and if you win, you may be able to collect both your lost wages and additional money as punishment.

When combined with lies, racial slurs, or sexual innuendo,

abusive language enters an entirely different realm of the law, and lawsuits may be appropriate. See DEFAMATION; HATE CRIME; LIBEL AND SLANDER; SEXUAL HARASSMENT.

ACCESSORY

A person who helps someone else commit a crime but is not present while the crime is being committed is known as an accessory. There are two kinds of accessories:

◇ An *accessory before the fact* helps plan or prepare for a crime—for example, he supplies a gun to a bank robber but does not participate in the robbery itself.

◇ An *accessory after the fact* helps the criminal avoid capture and trial after the crime has been committed. For example, a person who throws the robber's gun into the river or who allows him to hide from the police in the attic is an accessory after the fact.

In most states an accessory before the fact is considered as responsible for the crime as the person who actually commits it, and the two frequently receive the same punishment. An accessory after the fact is treated more leniently because his actions relate more to the obstruction of justice than to the crime itself. See also ACCOMPLICE.

ACCIDENTS

The word *accident* has no special legal meaning. Life insurance policies, laws regarding workers' compensation, disability insurance policies, and the like often provide their own definitions of what constitutes an accident. Laws and lawyers focus on who is responsible for causing the accident or allowing it to happen. For more on your legal responsibility in preventing accidents and your rights if you are an accident victim, see ACCIDENTS AT WORK; ACCIDENTS IN THE HOME; ACCIDENTS IN PUBLIC PLACES; ACCIDENTS ON GOVERNMENT PROPERTY; ACCIDENTS ON PUBLIC TRANSPORTATION; AUTOMOBILE ACCIDENTS; BOATING.

ACCIDENTS AT WORK

Every year, thousands of Americans are injured in work-related accidents. Whether the injury is as minor as a dislocated finger or is permanently disabling, a worker is entitled by law to receive compensation for injuries caused by someone else's action or negligence. Workers' compensation laws require most employers to buy accident insurance to cover medical expenses and to compensate injured workers for lost wages. In return, employers are assured that an employee who suffers an injury will not be allowed to sue. See WORKERS' COMPENSATION.

Self-employed workers are excluded from coverage, however, as are many farm workers, household workers, volunteers, employees of companies with a limited number of workers, and employees of nonprofit organizations. If your job is not subject to workers' compensation laws, you should buy a disability insurance policy to provide income in case you are unable to work. See DISABILITY INSURANCE.

If you should happen to be injured on the job, notify your employer immediately. Notification will help to protect your legal rights and will also protect other employees from a potentially dangerous condition. If your employer does not respond, seek legal advice.

ACCIDENTS IN THE HOME

Suppose a guest in your home sits in a wobbly chair and it collapses, injuring her back. Or suppose the plumber slips on your freshly mopped kitchen floor and hurts his knee. Can you be held responsible? The answer depends on the circumstances. Generally, if visitors are clearly warned about existing dangers, such as a weak chair or a slippery floor, the homeowner will not be held responsible.

HOMEOWNER'S OBLIGATION

The law recognizes that no home is 100 percent accident-proof, but it does require the occupant to take certain precautions to be sure that visitors are not hurt. Such phrases as "duty of care" and "reasonable care" are used to describe a homeowner's obligation to protect visitors from harm, and the amount of care required depends on the visitor's reason for being in the home.

THREE TYPES OF VISITORS

Most states recognize three categories of visitors to your home—invitees, licensees, and trespassers. The amount of reasonable care that you must show toward each varies.

Invitees are people who come into your home for both their own benefit and yours. They include babysitters, plumbers, repairmen, potential home buyers, and letter carriers. You owe invitees the greatest duty of care. For example, to prevent your babysitter from tripping over a loose floorboard, either repair it or temporarily cover it with boxes, perhaps with a note attached, and clearly warn the sitter of the danger in advance.

Licensees enter your home for their own benefit or convenience. They include salesmen, people asking for directions, relatives, guests, and in some states, fire fighters and police. The duty of care you owe to licensees varies from state to state, but is generally less than that owed to invitees. If a cosmetics saleslady visits your home, for example, you don't have to cover your loose floorboard with boxes, but you should warn her of the danger.

Trespassers enter a property without permission—for example, burglars and mischievous children. Understandably, they are owed the least amount of protection by homeowners. If a burglar trips over your loose floorboard, he gets what he deserves. One exception to the law's unsympathetic view of trespassers involves children who harmlessly walk on your property. If you are aware of a hazardous condition, such as a broken swing or rickety tree house on which they might hurt themselves, you must correct the condition or, at least, warn about the danger. See also ATTRACTIVE NUISANCE; TRESPASS.

STEPS TO TAKE

Preventing accidents that can injure visitors also prevents costly lawsuits. Here are a few tips on using "reasonable care":

1. Inspect your property for hidden dangers (wobbly railings, rotten stairs, and the like) and make appropriate repairs.

2. If repairs cannot be made before visitors come into your home, warn them explicitly about the dangers.

3. When someone is on your property, take extra care when performing dangerous tasks, such as moving ladders or using power tools.

4. Put signs up to warn trespassing children (or adults) of any hazards that exist on your property, and if possible, remove the danger.

ACCIDENTS IN PUBLIC PLACES

Stores, restaurants, theaters, and other businesses have a responsibility to their patrons to protect them from accidents. But by law, they are not expected to ensure the complete safety of people who enter their premises, which are regarded as public places.

REASONABLE CARE

According to law, shop owners must exercise "reasonable care" in seeing that no one gets hurt. To fulfill this obligation, the owner should take the following precautions:

◇ Inspect his property periodically to eliminate potential risks to customers.

◇ Make sure that floors are not slippery and rugs are not torn, wrinkled, or loose.

◇ See that entrances and exits are not blocked and are easy to find.

◇ Mark clear glass doors in some way to keep people from walking into them.

◇ Keep rooms well lighted.

◇ Post warnings about hazards that are not easily noticeable, such as unexpected steps.

HIDDEN DANGERS

The duty to warn is not limited to dangers that the proprietor is aware of. For example, if a customer in a lighting store gets a shock from a defective lamp, the owner may be responsible even if she did not know the hazard existed. The assumption is that if the owner had shown reasonable care by periodically inspecting the premises, she would have been aware of the danger.

The duty to use reasonable care also applies to establishments that maintain parking lots, garages, and restrooms for customers, but not to storerooms, kitchens, and other areas closed to the public.

MERCHANDISE DISPLAYS

A store must display merchandise in a way that minimizes the risk of injury. Because displays are designed to attract the customer's attention, they may become a hazard. If a customer walking down an aisle is distracted by a motorized cardboard clown waving a tube of toothpaste back and forth, and as a result trips over a case of sardines left in the aisle, the store may be responsible. In most situations, however, the person who tripped over an obvious obstruction would have no complaint.

ROLLER COASTERS AND FOUL BALLS

Owners and managers of amusement parks, stadiums, ski resorts, golf courses, zoos, and other recreational areas are also subject to the duty of reasonable care and must warn patrons of dangers that are not apparent. People who visit a pony ride at a country fair, for example, should be warned about a pony that kicks.

In amusement parks, rides that have a potential for serious injury, such as roller coasters, require more care, warnings, and inspections than safer rides like merry-go-rounds. In ballparks all seats must be inspected periodically for safety, and screens must be put up around home plate to protect spectators from being hit by foul balls and flying bats.

Sometimes the behavior of other patrons creates hazards that could lead to injuries. If a gang of reckless teenagers at a skating rink is not kept under control by supervisory personnel, for example, the management may be responsible for any injuries that result.

REAL LIFE, REAL LAW

The Case of the Snow-Covered Stairs

On a snowy January afternoon, Sarah was climbing the stairs to a second-floor gift shop when she lost her footing and fell. She filed a lawsuit against the owner of the business to recover for her injuries, claiming that the owner had been negligent in failing to keep the steps free of snow.

The court disagreed. In handing down the decision, the judge pointed out that a shopkeeper cannot be expected to keep an outside stairway snow-free at all times, especially while snow is still falling. Because the proprietor had regularly swept the stairs and had not allowed a significant amount of snow to accumulate, the court ruled that she was not negligent in failing to remove the freshly fallen snow Sarah had slipped on.

STEPS TO TAKE

If you are injured in a public place, do the following:

1. Report the accident to the management right away.

2. If the person in charge writes a report of the accident, get a copy of it. If he does not, write a letter to the management yourself, outlining the details of the accident.

3. Get the names and addresses of witnesses.

4. Ask your physician to document all of your injuries in writing.

5. Obtain photos of your injuries if possible.

6. The management or its insurer may ask you to sign a release. Do not sign anything until you have talked to your lawyer. He will probably advise you to wait until you know the full extent of your injuries and how much they have cost you. What at first seems like a minor injury may get worse later.

7. If your injury is clearly due to the owner's negligence, he may be willing to settle out of court. If not, you can file a lawsuit seeking compensation for medical bills, disability or disfigurement, lost wages, and pain and suffering.

8. If you are injured in a publicly owned place, such as a city park, municipal building, or sidewalk, you must sue the city, state, or federal government. See ACCIDENTS ON GOVERNMENT PROPERTY.

ACCIDENTS ON GOVERNMENT PROPERTY

As you are cruising along the highway on a gorgeous day in spring, a pothole the size of a small crater appears in the road ahead. You swerve, but your wheel hits it anyway. Afterwards, you realize an ominous shimmy has developed in your car. Can you sue the state for the damage to your car?

At one time a private individual could not sue a government for injuries and damages. Now, however, most governments can be sued—provided that the circumstances are appropriate and the correct procedures are followed.

City, state, and federal property must be kept in reasonably safe condition. For example, floors in government buildings must not be slippery, public roads must have a well-maintained surface, and trees in public parks must be kept free of rotting branches that could fall and hit someone. If you are injured as a result of the government's failure to meet these standards, you can file a lawsuit. But you should be aware that the procedures differ somewhat from other lawsuits.

SPECIAL RULES

In most situations, before you can file suit against the city, state, or federal government, you have to file a claim with the appropriate government office. For example, if you are hurt by a falling branch in a city park, you can file a claim with the city clerk's office. If you are hurt on state or federal property, you must file your claim with the agency responsible for that particular building, park, or other property.

Usually you have a very short period of time after the accident to file your claim. If it is rejected, you have another short period of time to file your lawsuit. These times may be extended if you can show that an injury or circumstances beyond your control prevented you from filing on time.

If your claim is relatively small, you can file suit in small-claims court. But if it is large, you should seek the help of an attorney experienced in filing claims against the government. That way you will be sure to meet all the requirements necessary to keep your claim alive.

LIMITATIONS ON AWARDS

If you suffered greatly as a result of government negligence, you may not be able to collect an amount proportionate to your damages even if you win your lawsuit. The federal government and some states and cities have laws that place limits on the awards they must pay to private citizens. For example, Colorado limits its liability for injuries and damages to $250,000 per person. See also SOVEREIGN IMMUNITY.

ACCIDENTS ON PUBLIC TRANSPORTATION

The companies that run buses, taxis, trains, planes, and ferries, which charge money to take people from one place to another, are called common carriers. Since the accidents that can occur are potentially serious, common carriers are required to use what the law calls the highest degree of care for their passengers' safety. This means that they are responsible for any injuries resulting from even the slightest carelessness on their part. In addition, responsibility for such carelessness may rest not only on the common carrier but also on the person who operates the vehicle—the driver, engineer, pilot, or captain.

The high degree of care expected of common carriers begins when passengers are boarding and ends when they are safely off. Buses, trains, and taxis, for instance, must stop long enough to allow passengers to get in and out safely. Suppose a woman is getting out of a cab and the driver, miffed at the size of the tip she gave him, takes off suddenly and injures her arm. The driver and the cab company can be held responsible for her injury.

Common carriers must provide help in boarding and getting off when (1) a passenger is disabled or frail, (2) the stopping place is unsafe, or (3) the step to the vehicle is high.

Common carriers and their employees must also use the highest degree of care in selecting, maintaining, and operating vehicles. When passengers are on board, the aisles and floors must be kept clear, and baggage must be carefully secured in racks. Drivers must obey all traffic, navigation, and aviation laws and must not make sudden starts or stops.

PASSENGERS' RESPONSIBILITIES

Common carriers must warn passengers of dangers they are not likely to see for themselves, such as unexpected steps. But they cannot be expected to warn about hazardous situations that appear out of nowhere. For example, if an elderly man suddenly goes berserk on a train and whacks a fellow passenger with his umbrella, the railroad is not to blame. But if the man had been waving the umbrella madly and bellowing threats toward other passengers, and the train crew did nothing to stop him, the railroad would most likely be held responsible.

Passengers have a duty to be reasonably careful too. Suppose a passenger on a speeding train ignores signs warning people not to stand between cars and is injured as a result. Because he was largely responsible for the injury, he probably could not win a suit against the carrier. However, if a passenger and a carrier share responsibility for an accident, the passenger may be partially compensated for his injuries.

PLATFORMS AND WAITING ROOMS

A common carrier's responsibility for its buildings and other facilities, such as stations, platforms, and waiting areas, is one of reasonable care (not the highest degree of care). The same standard applies to carriers as to stores and restaurants. See ACCIDENTS IN PUBLIC PLACES.

STEPS TO TAKE IF YOU ARE INJURED

If you are the victim of an accident on public transportation, follow the steps outlined in the entry ACCIDENTS IN PUBLIC PLACES, plus the following:

1. If you are injured on a bus or taxi, get the driver's name, license plate number, and the vehicle identification number.

2. If a written report of the accident is made by anyone other than the common carrier, such as the police or coast guard, make every effort to obtain a copy of that report.

See also AIRLINE ACCIDENTS.

ACCOMPLICE

An accomplice is someone who helps another person commit a serious crime. Many times an accomplice is considered just as accountable for the crime as the person who actually committed it.

The accomplice may or may not be present at the scene of the crime, and his assistance may be provided before, during, or after the crime itself. An "accessory before the fact" is one type of accomplice. This person provides assistance before the crime but is not at the scene while it is being committed. See ACCESSORY.

An accomplice who is present while a crime is being committed is usually referred to as an aider and abettor. Such a person may, for example, serve as a lookout while a burglar breaks into a store. Or he may assist a mugger by watching for potential victims and signaling when one is near.

A person is not an accomplice simply because he witnesses a crime. Suppose you are browsing in a jewelry store and you see a stranger steal a watch. Even if you fail to report the crime, you are not an accomplice since you do not know the thief and have gained nothing from the crime.

ACKNOWLEDGMENT

Sometimes a court requires that the person who wrote a will or other legal document make a formal declaration that the document is authentically his. This declaration, called an acknowledgment, is usually made in the presence of a notary public or officer of the court, such as a lawyer. A form (also called an acknowledgment) is then completed as evidence. For an example of an acknowledgment, see EVERYDAY LEGAL FORMS, beginning on page 552.

ACT OF GOD

When the usually punctual Meadowlark String Quartet failed to show up for a concert in Topeka, Kansas, the audience and concert promoters were understandably angry. But it was later learned that as the quartet was driving into town, a tornado blew their van off the road and into a ditch. The quartet was released from the legal consequences of not showing up because they were prevented from doing so by an act of God.

Flash floods, tidal waves, earthquakes, hurricanes, incapacitating disease, and death are all considered acts of God—accidents of nature that cannot be foreseen or prevented in any way. In such circumstances standard legal obligations do not apply.

Sometimes insurance policies contain clauses that exclude payment for damages caused by acts of God. For example, your insurance company may not reimburse you for your car if it is destroyed by a falling tree.

ACTUAL CASH VALUE

The fair price on the open market for any kind of property—such as a house, car, land, or furniture—is known as its actual cash value. The term means the same as fair market value, market value, market price, cash value, and the like, but it is quite different from book value. See BOOK VALUE.

Actual cash value is the amount a buyer would be willing to pay in the normal course of business. It is not, for example, the price paid when the buyer has an urgent need to buy or the seller has to raise money quickly.

The term *actual cash value* also refers to the value of property after allowing for depreciation. Insurance companies, for instance, consider the actual cash value of property in determining how much they will reimburse a policyholder.

ADOPTION

Adoption is a legal proceeding that severs a person's legal ties to his or her biological parents and substitutes new parents.

Anybody can be adopted as the child of someone else. Stepparents can adopt stepchildren, an aunt and uncle can adopt a niece or nephew, an adult can adopt another adult, and, of course, a couple (or a single adult) can adopt a child unrelated and previously unknown to them.

The new parents have the same rights, duties, and responsibilities toward the adopted child that they would have toward a child born to them. When an adoption is complete, a new birth certificate is prepared and filed, reflecting that the child has the same legal standing as a biological child of the adoptive parents.

METHODS OF ADOPTION

The traditional way of adopting an infant or child is through an adoption agency, but increasingly people are finding and adopting children through private placement.

Private placement
When the child's biological parents (also known as the birth parents) choose the adoptive parents for their child, the adoption process is referred to as private placement.

Every state allows parents to place a child with a relative, such as a sister or brother. In many states parents can let nonrelatives adopt their child. In such adoptions a third person, such as a doctor or lawyer, usually acts as an intermediary between the birth parents and adoptive parents. However, in Delaware private placements are completely prohibited, and in Massachusetts, Michigan, and Minnesota private placements are allowed only with persons related to the family.

In private placements the adoption process is relatively uncomplicated. It merely requires following the proper legal steps, described in the box on page 17.

Agency adoption
Every state licenses agencies to place children for adoption. Such agencies may be private or a part of the state government, but all are strictly regulated by the state in which they operate.

A couple or an individual applying to an agency to adopt a child must undergo rigorous screening and must be prepared to present evidence of personal stability, adequate financial resources, and an understanding of the special circumstances that adoptive families must deal with.

Private agencies may also have their own specific requirements regarding such factors as age, race, or religion. Some agencies may work only with particular groups—children with special needs, nonwhite children, or children from foreign countries, for example.

When you are dealing with an adoption agency, remember that its rules are supported by state law, and you have to obey the rules.

ADOPTING THROUGH AN AGENCY

Whether you adopt a child through a state agency or a private one, you can expect to go through a process similar to the following:

◇ *Application*. You will be asked to complete a written application. Some applicants are rejected solely on the basis of this initial screening.

◇ *Intake interview.* This interview is the first face-to-face meeting between the applicant and the agency staff. It can last several hours.

◇ *Family study.* This was formerly the notorious "home study," in which a social worker came to the applicant's home to see whether there was dust on the furniture or a skeleton in the closet. Today this in-depth study of prospective adoptive parents is called a family study and may consist of several office interviews in addition to a home meeting. Applicants who reach the family study stage are considered good prospects by agencies.

◇ *Approval by agency.* Following the family study, the agency accepts or rejects the applicants as prospective adoptive parents. Some agencies have procedures for appealing the decisions, and in some states the decision can be appealed to the state department in charge of adoptions. Names of approved parents are placed on a waiting list.

◇ *Placement of child.* How long it takes for a couple to be offered a child after they have been approved depends on what they want. A white couple who want to adopt a white infant might be discouraged from adopting via an agency in the first place, because few white babies are available for adoption. Older children are more available, no matter what their race. And parents who adopt a child with a disability may receive a subsidy.

◇ *Period of supervision.* After the child comes to live in his new home, a period of time must elapse before the adoption can be made final, to ensure that the match is suitable.

◇ *Legal adoption.* Following a number of legal procedures, outlined in the box at left, a judge signs the adoption papers, and a new birth certificate is issued.

CHECKLIST

Legal Steps in an Adoption

Although adoption is often a complicated and somewhat time-consuming procedure, the formal legal steps are straightforward and relatively simple.

❏ **NOTICE.**
Notice of adoption proceedings is given to everyone legally interested in the case, except the child himself. When the child is illegitimate, the father must usually be notified as well as the mother.

❏ **PETITION.**
The prospective parents must ask the court to be allowed to adopt the child. This petition gives the names and addresses of the adopting parents, of the child, and of the natural parents, if known, as well as the child's sex and age.

❏ **WRITTEN CONSENT.**
The written consent of the child's natural parents or of the adoption agency must accompany the petition.

❏ **HEARING.**
A hearing is held during which the court examines the qualifications of the prospective parents and grants or denies the petition accordingly. Because adoption proceedings are confidential, the hearing takes place in a closed courtroom, and records of it are usually available for examination only by court order.

❏ **PROBATION.**
Most states require a period of supervision or probation, during which the child lives with the adopting parents while a state agency watches the family to see how the relationship develops. If everyone is happy with the situation, the court issues a permanent adoption decree.

❏ **BIRTH CERTIFICATE.**
A new birth certificate is issued for the child, giving his new family name, the date and place of his birth, and the ages of his adopting parents at the time of his birth. The old birth certificate is sealed and filed away, after which it can usually be opened only by someone who has obtained a court order.

INTERNATIONAL ADOPTION

Sometimes, for humanitarian reasons or to get a baby or young child, couples decide to adopt a child from overseas. The availability of these children varies—one year children from Korea are easy to adopt; at another time children from

ADOPTEES' RIGHTS

The rights of adoptees to obtain information about their birth parents depend upon the laws of the state where the adoptions took place.

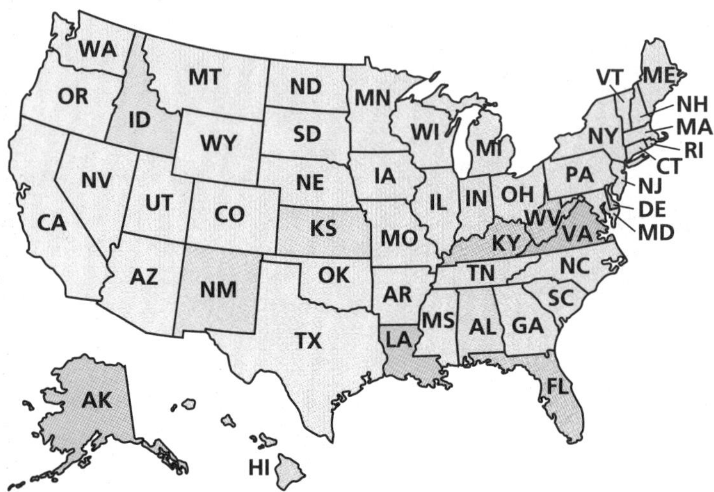

Allow adult adoptees to receive identifying information about birth parents only with their consent

Allow adult adoptees to seek a court order to obtain identifying information in cases of medical necessity

Allow adult adoptees to examine original birth certificate without birth parents' consent

Prohibit the release of identifying information, although these states may have "mutual consent registries"

Central America are available. Overseas adoptions involve more red tape than local adoptions do. Couples must comply not just with the laws of their state but also with the laws of the child's country of origin and with U. S. laws. American law requires that one of the following conditions apply: the child has been abandoned; he is an orphan; or the biological parents cannot provide for him.

One route for foreign adoption is through U.S. agencies affiliated with foreign adoption agencies. They can help you with the legal requirements and paperwork, and you may not have to leave the country.

You can also work directly with a child-placement agency in a foreign country or directly with the child's family, but you will be on your own in complying with state, federal, and foreign laws. You will also have to travel to the foreign country either to complete the adoption process or to begin it there and finalize it in the United States. Many couples who complete the adoption process abroad complete it again according to their own state's laws once they return home.

HOW NOT TO ADOPT A CHILD

Because agency adoption is a slow process and infants are in short supply, couples may wittingly or unwittingly participate in adoptions that are illegal.

Black-market babies

In legal private adoptions, the adopting parents usually pay for the mother's medical expenses as well as for all legal expenses. Most states limit the amount of medical expenses that adopting parents can pay for. If they pay more, they may find themselves charged with buying a black-market baby.

Let us say that Judy and Michael have decided to adopt a child privately. A friend refers them to a lawyer who is known to find babies quickly. The lawyer tells them that his fee will be $5,000 and that they will have to pay $25,000 for the mother's expenses. If the expenses appear reasonable, they should ask to see the bills. If the lawyer refuses to show them the bills, they should leave.

But suppose that Judy and Michael receive a call from their family doctor, who knows that they want to adopt a baby. The teenage daughter of a patient has just given birth, and she has decided not to keep the child. The father is also willing for the child to be adopted. Judy and Michael could safely explore this possibility for adoption, but not without a lawyer's advice.

Newspaper ads

Sometimes people advertise for children in the classified sections of newspapers. This step requires caution and in some states is illegal. Anyone who advertises for a child and gets a response should make sure that the child really belongs to the mother, obtain both parents' consent, and thoroughly examine the child's and the parents' medical histories.

WHO MUST CONSENT TO AN ADOPTION

In order for a legitimate child to be eligible for adoption, his or her parents must have died or given up their rights as parents, either by consent or because a court order has legally deemed them to be unfit parents. Every state defines unfitness in its own way, but generally abandonment of a child makes a parent unfit, as does severe neglect or abuse or a parent's chronic mental illness.

Even when a child is adopted by a stepfather or stepmother, the biological father or mother must either be dead or have given up parental rights. When a child reaches a certain age—10 to 14, depending on the state—he must consent to his own adoption.

Whether both parents of a child born out of wedlock must consent to his adoption depends on the circumstances. Suppose Linda becomes pregnant with John's child, even though John is married to someone else. John is happy that they are to have a child together, and when the baby is born, he signs a paternity agreement acknowledging his fatherhood. He provides regular financial support and visits as often as he can. Linda cannot put the child up for adoption without John's consent.

But if John never visits his child, refuses to help support him, and never acknowledges the child, he has effectively given up his parental rights and his consent is not necessary.

If a child was conceived as a result of rape or incest, the father's consent is not required.

If the birth parent has a change of heart after consenting to an adoption, whether her child will be returned depends on the state in which the adoption proceedings take place. Many states allow a birth parent to revoke consent only if it was obtained by fraud or while under duress. Other states allow the birth parent to withdraw consent for any reason within a specified time, usually a matter of days or weeks. Still other states permit revocation within a specified time period, but only if the biological parents can show that the revocation is best for the child.

ADOPTEES' RIGHTS

Recently much attention has been given to the adult adoptee who is searching for her roots and wants to reunite with her birth parents. Previously, most states made adoption records confidential, thus leaving many adoptees without even basic information about their parents' medical history. Today the old laws are being replaced with less restrictive laws, which allow the flow of information.

Medical records
All states require that medical and hereditary data, as well as the social histories of both the birth parents and their child, be filed at the time of the adoption. In most states such data must be "non-identifying"—that is, no one must be able to determine from the information who the parents are.

Although all states also provide that adoption records be sealed, or confidential, most of them allow the adoptive parents or an adult adoptee access to non-identifying medical information. In this way a child can find out whether his mother had a hereditary disease without learning who she is.

In some states the courts can provide an adult adoptee with identifying information if the biological parents consent. In others an adult adoptee has the right to examine his or her original birth certificate without their permission. And in others an adult adoptee can request the release of identifying information in the event of medical necessity or other extraordinary circumstances.

Mutual consent registries
Many states now have "mutual consent registries," which allow adult adoptees and birth parents to register their names, addresses, and other information if they wish to reestablish contact with each other.

ADULTERY

Voluntary sexual intercourse between a married person and a person other than his or her spouse constitutes adultery, and is still a crime in a number of states, punishable by a fine or imprisonment or both. In practice, however, few prosecutions for adultery take place, both because it is usually difficult to prove and because prosecutors are faced with so many other crimes, such as homicide and drug trafficking, that can cause greater harm to society at large.

ADVERSE POSSESSION

It is possible for someone to gain ownership of your property simply by occupying or using it. This process is called adverse possession. The theory behind adverse possession is that by failing to challenge another person's use and possession of your property, you abandon your own claim to ownership.

Even a homeowner can lose title to (that is, ownership of) his property by adverse possession. Suppose your neighbor has built a circular driveway that juts onto your land for several feet. To keep the peace, you have said nothing. When he sells the property, you plan to hire a lawyer and notify the new owner that part of the driveway is yours. But depending on how long you have let the situation continue, you could lose title to that piece of property forever.

ELEMENTS OF POSSESSION

Fortunately for the true owner, a number of important elements must be present before another person can successfully claim ownership by adverse possession.

◇ Possession must be, in legal terminology, "open" and "notorious"—that is, it must be obvious to the other members of the community.

◇ The person claiming ownership by adverse possession must also show that he has actual possession of the property. In the case of real estate, actual possession could be shown by erecting a fence around the property, building a road or driveway on it, planting crops, or building a house on the land and occupying it. In the case of personal property, the neighbor with whom you stored some furniture could show possession of it by furnishing her living room with it for all to see, or by wearing the ring you gave to her for safekeeping and telling people that it is hers.

◇ The possession must be hostile to the owner's interest. A tenant who pays rent has open, notorious, and actual possession of your property, but he does not dispute your right of ownership. Therefore he cannot claim ownership by adverse possession.

◇ The possession must be uninterrupted and continue for a period specified by state law—from 5 years to 30 years or more. If the true owner retakes possession of the property during this period, however, the adverse possession comes to an end.

Suppose Jim owns a piece of land in the country, to which he used to drive every fall to go hunting. His interests changed, however, and he stopped going there. One day a concerned neighbor calls to tell Jim that a stranger has been camping on the land several weekends every fall. Will the stranger be able to claim the land by adverse possession?

Because the camper's "possession" is only intermittent, Jim need not fear losing his land to him. He does not even need to visit his property to restate his claim. But he should recognize the possibility that someone else might take open, notorious, hostile, and continuous possession of his land if he is not more watchful.

STEPS TO TAKE

If you think you are in danger of losing your property by adverse possession, this is what you can do:

1. Determine the length of time the person has been occupying or using your property.

2. Find out how long your state's law says that adverse possession must exist before you lose title to your property.

3. Notify the occupant in writing that he is trespassing and demand that he end the trespass.

4. If he refuses, or if the state law's time limit is near, contact a lawyer immediately.

AFFIDAVIT

An affidavit is a written statement of facts, signed and sworn to before a notary public or other official authorized to take oaths. Generally an affidavit is made voluntarily.

Often someone with knowledge of facts that are pertinent to a business transaction or a lawsuit is asked to write an affidavit of what he knows. For example, if you were the accountant for a boutique whose owner put it up for sale, you might be asked to make an affidavit attesting to the accuracy of the store's financial records. Or if you witnessed an accident, you might sign an affidavit in which you described what you saw. If you make a statement that you know to be untrue in an affidavit, you are guilty of perjury.

A sample affidavit is included in EVERYDAY LEGAL FORMS, beginning on page 552. See also DEPOSITION; OATH AND AFFIRMATION; PERJURY.

AFFIRMATIVE ACTION

The federal Civil Rights Act of 1964 prohibited job discrimination on the basis of race, color, national origin, religion, or sex. But the law merely prevented further discrimination against minorities; it did not correct inequities that resulted from past discrimination.

In 1965 President Lyndon B. Johnson issued an executive order requiring all contractors working for the federal government to take "affirmative action" to ensure that members of minorities were hired. (Women were included as a minority by legislation passed in 1972.) In the years that followed, affirmative action—that is, positive steps to compensate minorities for past discrimination—became a commonplace employment practice as a result of state and federal legislation and court decisions.

Not every company must have an affirmative action plan. Those which show no pattern of discrimination need not have one, nor must companies with less than 15 employees. But federal law requires many firms to have such plans, including those that do business with the federal government. Similarly, states have laws requiring affirmative action programs for companies that provide goods and services to state and local governments.

In 1972 federal law required colleges and universities to institute affirmative action programs. They were required to admit more minority students and faculty, especially to graduate and professional schools.

Critics of affirmative action say the practice is actually a form of reverse discrimination, claiming that members of minority groups get jobs even though they are less qualified than white or male applicants. As a result these plans have been challenged in court. While some of the challenges have proved successful, most affirmative action plans have been upheld. See also CIVIL RIGHTS.

AGE DISCRIMINATION

The boss comes bearing bad news. Because of cutbacks at the company, you are being let go, even though your performance on the job has always been more than satisfactory. This is tough news to take at the age of 50, and it gets even worse when you find out two months later that you have been replaced by a person 15 years younger, and at half your salary. If this should in fact ever happen to you, you may have been a victim of age discrimination—a practice prohibited by law in most instances.

DISCRIMINATION IN EMPLOYMENT

In this instance your former employer may have violated the federal Age Discrimination in Employment Act (ADEA) of 1967. This law makes it illegal for government agencies and companies with 20 or more employees to discriminate in hiring, employment, or promotion against workers who are 40 years old or older on the basis of age. It also prohibits age-based discrimination in job benefits, such as health or life insurance.

Many states, too, have laws prohibiting age discrimination by employers. These laws are usually enforced by the state's department of labor or human rights commission.

MANDATORY RETIREMENT

Since 1986 federal law has also prohibited employers covered by the ADEA from establishing mandatory retirement ages, except in certain cases.

A company can establish a mandatory retirement age for its executives, for example, provided they are entitled to retirement benefits of $44,000 or more per year, exclusive of Social Security. And some

REAL LIFE, REAL LAW

The Case of the Discharged Driver

John worked for an interstate bus company that required its drivers to retire when they reached age 60. When John had to retire, he brought a complaint under the federal Age Discrimination in Employment Act. He argued that his job performance had always been excellent and that there was no indication that he lacked the skills necessary to continue working.

The court, however, found that forcing John to retire was not a violation of the ADEA, because the bus company's statistics showed that older drivers were involved in more accidents than younger ones. Because the bus company had to provide safe transportation to its customers, it could legitimately consider a driver's age as a qualification for continuing employment.

kinds of jobs—such as those of police officer, fire fighter, and airline pilot—can be subject to mandatory retirement because age usually decreases a person's ability to perform the duties such jobs require.

CREDIT DISCRIMINATION

Another federal law, the Equal Credit Opportunity Act, prohibits banks, loan companies, and other credit grantors from denying credit on the basis of the applicant's age.

STEPS TO TAKE

If you believe your employer has discriminated against you because of your age, here are some things you can do:

1. Register a complaint with your company's human resources department.
2. File a formal complaint of age discrimination with your state's office of human rights or department of labor.
3. Call or write the federal Equal Employment Opportunity Commission (EEOC) for information about the requirements for filing a formal complaint of age discrimination. You may have to wait 60 days after you file your claim with a state agency before the EEOC will accept a claim from you.
4. Consult a lawyer experienced in employment-discrimination law. The federal Age Discrimination in Employment Act (ADEA) allows you to file a private suit 60 days after you file a claim with the EEOC. The various deadlines for filing a claim are complicated, however, and you may lose your claim if you are not careful to comply with them exactly.

AGENT

A person who is authorized to act on behalf of another person or for a business is an agent. An agent is more than a mere employee, because he often is required to exercise independent judgment in the performance of his duties. Unlike an employee, he can make agreements with others that legally bind the party he serves (the principal); for example, he can enter into contracts or manage property.

However, an agent is always under the control of the principal, even if it is not always used. Let us say you have hired an agent to manage a rental house that you own. You can tell the agent not to rent to Ms. X, because you do not think she is reliable. But if you do not give him those instructions, and he thinks her credentials are satisfactory, you cannot object if he rents your house to her.

When a principal discharges his agent, he is no longer bound by the agent's actions. See INDEPENDENT CONTRACTOR; INSURANCE AGENT AND BROKER; POWER OF ATTORNEY; REAL ESTATE AGENT AND BROKER.

AGE OF CONSENT

The minimum age at which a person may legally marry or enter a sexual relationship is called the age of consent. In most states the age of consent is 18, although in a few it is as low as 15. A young man or woman who wants to marry before reaching the age of consent must obtain his or her parents' consent and, in some states, court approval before the marriage can take place.

An adult who has sex with a person under the age of consent may be convicted of statutory rape. See STATUTORY RAPE.

AIDS

Acquired immune deficiency syndrome, or AIDS, is a fatal disease caused by infection with a virus known as HIV, the human immunodeficiency virus. In the decade after the disease was first identified in 1981, more than 100,000 Americans died of AIDS, and about 1 million more tested HIV-positive—that is, they were infected with HIV.

AIDS is a communicable disease, usually transmitted by sexual contact or by injection into the bloodstream. The latter type of infection often results from contaminated needles that are shared by intravenous drug users.

Understandably, a disease as deadly as AIDS causes widespread fear. Many people believe they have the right to know if they are being exposed to the virus. On the other hand, because the disease is fatal and is associated with male homosexuals and intravenous drug users, people with AIDS are often reluctant to admit it for fear of being stigmatized.

AIDS AND THE LAW

In the 1990's, well over a decade after AIDS was identified, laws were still inconsistent in regard to the disease. Although both the federal and state governments want to protect the public from AIDS, they also have a duty to protect persons infected with the disease from unwarranted discrimination. For example, the U.S. Immigration and Naturalization Service may deny admission to persons who are HIV-positive, but the federal Fair Housing Act considers people with AIDS handicapped and prohibits discrimination against them when they apply for housing.

State laws are inconsistent too. Every state requires that AIDS cases be reported to either the state or the local health department, but only a few states require that persons who test HIV-positive be reported. About half the states require that the sexual partners of persons who carry the AIDS virus be notified of their exposure to the virus. In other states the law strictly protects the identity of anyone who tests positive for HIV in order to prevent discrimination in employment, education, and housing. All states permit insurance companies to test applicants for HIV before issuing life and health insurance policies, and to reject applicants who test positive for the virus.

Because AIDS itself has no symptoms, it has been difficult for federal and state governments to categorize it as a disability for social service programs and Social Security disability payments. However, many AIDS-related diseases, such as cancer, tuberculosis, and heart disease, are considered disabilities, and those who suffer from them may be eligible for government-subsidized medical services and disability payments. In 1993 the definition of AIDS was expanded in order to make more of those who test HIV-positive eligible for those benefits.

States also provide assistance to AIDS patients, who in many instances are rendered destitute by the disease.

INDIVIDUAL PRIVACY VERSUS PUBLIC HEALTH

Federal and state laws have been proposed that would require doctors and other health-care workers to tell patients whether they were infected with HIV. In 1993, Maryland's Supreme Court imposed this duty on physicians under certain circumstances.

A number of states have criminally prosecuted people who knew they were infected with HIV but did not tell their sexual partners. One state filed attempted murder charges against an infected prison inmate who bit a prison guard. In addition, hundreds of civil lawsuits have been filed against HIV sufferers by people whom they have allegedly exposed to the virus.

The laws concerning AIDS are in a state of flux. How they will finally take shape depends to some extent on whether medical science finds a cure.

AID TO FAMILIES WITH DEPENDENT CHILDREN

When George's wife died, he was left alone to care for his two young children, Sue and

Tim. Then, to compound the tragedy, he broke his back while trying to repair the roof and is now unable to earn a living. Since George has no insurance or other means of support, how can he and his family cope?

Such cases of misfortune and need are what inspired the federal welfare program called Aid to Families With Dependent Children, or AFDC. The program is designed to help provide children and their families with the basic necessities of life while also trying to ensure that the families it supports stay together.

Although the federal government supplies the money and the basic guidelines for the program, it is administered at the state and local levels. It is the child or children who determine whether a family is eligible for AFDC. The child must be under 18 and live in the home of a parent or other relative who cannot support him. A child may be considered deprived of parental support if the family's principal wage earner is (1) dead, (2) absent from the home, (3) physically or mentally disabled, or (4) unemployed. In the example above, Sue and Tim are deprived of George's support because of his disability.

HOW BENEFITS ARE DETERMINED

Each state determines not only whether a family is eligible for benefits but also what amount it should receive. In doing so, the AFDC office compares the family's financial resources to the amount that state has decided a family of that size requires in order to live.

Applicants must provide the AFDC office with accurate information about family wages and other sources of income. From time to time, families that receive benefits may be reevaluated to confirm that they are still eligible. Families must also cooperate with the AFDC office in other ways—for example, by revealing the whereabouts of an absent parent.

One of the goals of the AFDC program is to help families to become self-supporting again. To accomplish this, the state may require parents to take part in job training or employment search programs to remain eligible for benefits.

HOW TO APPLY

If your family is having trouble making ends meet for reasons beyond its control, you have a right to seek AFDC assistance. To do this, simply fill out an application at the local office of your state's welfare agency.

AIRLINE ACCIDENTS

Although the risk of being killed in a plane crash is less than one-tenth the risk of being killed in an auto accident, when airline accidents do occur, the consequences are often dire. The extent to which an airline can be held financially responsible, or liable, depends to a large degree on whether the flight is domestic or international. If a flight begins and ends within the United States, the airline can be held responsible for all damages that result from injuries or death due to a plane crash.

If an international flight begins or ends in the United States, or stops at an airport in the United States, the airline's liability is strictly limited. The maximum amount that can be awarded is $75,000, including legal fees. If the lawsuit is filed in a state that awards legal fees to the winner of the lawsuit, then the maximum is $58,000, plus legal fees. This limited liability was established by an international treaty known as the Warsaw Convention.

If the flight does not touch down within the United States, the extent of an airline's liability depends on which version of the Warsaw Convention its country of origin ratified. If the country follows the original treaty of 1929, the maximum liability is $10,000. If it follows the amended version of 1955, liability is limited to $20,000. And if it follows the 1975 treaty, the maximum is $140,000.

You may, however, be able to sue for amounts that exceed these limits. If the accident was due to gross negligence or willful misconduct by the airline or its employees—for example, if the ground crew failed to secure and lock the doors or if the pilot was not qualified to fly that particular aircraft—the Warsaw Convention limitations do not apply and you can sue for greater amounts.

Some credit card companies provide automatic flight insurance as an incentive for people to use their cards to purchase tickets. If someone dies in a plane crash, his or her next of kin should find out how the ticket was paid for. Insurance benefits of $100,000 or more may be payable to the person's estate. See also ACCIDENTS ON PUBLIC TRANSPORTATION.

AIRLINE CHARTER

You spot an ad in the travel section of the Sunday paper offering a bargain-basement price for a flight to Honolulu. Somewhat incredulous, you call the number listed. The person who answers confirms the low price but informs you that the flight is a charter, rather than a flight on a regularly scheduled airline. You have never heard of the charter company, but the low price is hard to resist. Is it too good to be true?

Most charter flights are arranged by charter operators, who buy a number of seats from an air carrier at a heavily discounted price and then resell them to the public. Charter companies try to keep their prices below rates offered by regularly scheduled airlines, but you cannot assume that a charter is always the cheapest way to fly.

Still, a charter flight can save you money, and it could be the only way to fly to your destination nonstop. But you may have to sacrifice some comfort and convenience. It is possible, for example, that the flight will be (1) on a carrier you have never heard of, (2) scheduled at an inconvenient time, (3) on a plane with tight seating arrangements, or (4) preceded by long check-in lines at the airport.

In the past some charter operators have either failed to provide the services promised or suddenly gone out of business. To protect consumers, the U.S. Department of Transportation now requires operators to set up escrow accounts for all charter payments made by passengers. This ensures that customers will receive refunds if the operator cancels the flight or goes out of business.

STEPS TO TAKE

Before you fly on a charter, be sure to do the following:

1. Shop around for the lowest air fares to make sure the charter price is really a bargain.
2. Contact the Department of Transportation's Regulatory Analysis Office to find out whether the charter operator has established the required escrow account.
3. Ask the Department of Transportation's Consumer Affairs Division and your local Better Business Bureau whether any complaints have been filed against the charter operator and the air carrier.
4. Be sure that you understand your rights and obligations as a passenger before you sign a contract with a charter operator.

AIRLINE PASSENGER RIGHTS

You are one of those people who hate to fly—but for reasons that have nothing to do with safety. In the past you have been bumped from flights, the airlines have lost your luggage, and you have missed connecting flights. What are your rights?

BUMPING

Being bumped, or not being allowed to board the flight you booked, is the result of the airlines' traditional practice of accepting reservations for more seats than are on the plane. It is not against the law, and the airlines state they must overbook because many travelers who make reservations for flights never show up.

When a flight is overbooked, the airline is legally required to ask for volunteers who are willing to give up their seats and take a later flight. As an inducement, the airline usually offers some kind of compensation, such as a free round-trip ticket to a destination of one's choice. If not enough volunteers come forward, some passengers will have to stay behind against their will. Usually, the passengers who checked in last are bumped.

If you are bumped, you may be angered and inconvenienced, but you still have certain rights:

◇ Usually the airline must put a passenger who has been bumped on the next available flight to his destination, even if it means reserving a seat for him on another airline.

◇ If a bumped passenger arrives at his destination between 1 and 2 hours late, the airline must pay him either the price of a one-way ticket or $200, whichever is less.

◇ If the passenger arrives

more than 2 hours late, the amount to be paid is doubled.

◇ The airline must pay this compensation to the passenger within 24 hours.

◇ Although the airline is not required to reimburse a bumped passenger for meals, hotels, and other expenses, it may on occasion do so.

LOST OR DAMAGED LUGGAGE

Many of the complaints about air travel concern lost or damaged luggage. An airline's responsibility to compensate you for luggage is limited. At present, airlines do not have to pay you more than $1,250 for luggage lost on domestic flights and $9.07 per pound for international flights, even if your luggage is worth more.

Moreover, an airline will reimburse you only for the depreciated value of your luggage and its contents. For example, if you bought a suitcase for $125 and used it for a year, you might get only half that amount from the airline.

Some airlines limit their liability even further. For example, one airline refuses to take responsibility for damage to soft luggage or for the loss of wheels from suitcases. The same airline demands that passengers file a written claim within 4 hours of arrival, and provide written documentation of the contents of lost baggage within 45 days. People who do not follow these rules forfeit any claims for reimbursement.

The way to protect yourself against baggage losses is to pack your luggage so that you can carry it on board or to buy some form of insurance. You may buy "excess valuation" insurance directly from the airline, or your homeowners insurance policy may provide "off-premises" coverage for lost or damaged items. In addition, some credit card companies provide baggage insurance if you use their card to purchase your ticket.

SMOKING

Since 1990, smoking has been prohibited on all domestic flights of less than six hours in the United States. On international flights it is allowed only in certain rows, and not in the aisles or restrooms. Note that restrooms have smoke detectors; those who try to disable them can be fined up to $1,000.

CONDITIONS OF CARRIAGE

The conditions that govern the legal relationship between an airline and its passengers are spelled out in each airline's contract of carriage.

These conditions, which vary from one airline to the next, relate to canceled flights, missed connections, reservations, check-in times, and restrictions on which kinds of passengers they will accept. For example, an airline may refuse to accept a passenger who is sick, on drugs, behaving erratically, or unable to fasten his seat belt.

This information may not appear on the ticket and is not always made readily available. To get a copy of an airline's "conditions of carriage," as these rules are called, write to

REAL LIFE, REAL LAW

The Case of the Bumped Businessman

Bill bought a plane ticket to Richmond, Virginia, with the understanding that it could not be refunded or exchanged. When he got to the airport, Bill learned that the airline had substituted a much smaller plane for the one originally scheduled and that he was being bumped as a result. The airline offered Bill an alternative flight, but it would not arrive until 6 hours after the first flight, and at another airport. As far as the airline was concerned, it had fulfilled its duty.

But Bill refused the alternate flight and rescheduled his trip for 2 weeks later. He also sued the airline in state court, charging it with bad faith. He claimed that the nonrefundable ticket limited his right to change his plans but did not prevent the airline from making changes without informing ticket holders. Bill eventually won his case and was given a significant award by the court.

Federal law only requires airlines to provide bumped passengers with an alternate flight and limited compensation. But, as Bill found out, passengers sometimes have additional rights under unusual circumstances.

the airline's office of consumer affairs or to the Air Transport Association of America, 1709 New York Avenue NW, Washington, DC 20006.

STEPS TO TAKE

Here are a few suggestions on how to resolve a problem with an airline:

1. Ask for the address and phone number of the airline's office of consumer affairs at the ticket counter or call the airline's central reservation number.

2. Make your complaint in writing. Be sure that you include the flight number, the flight time, and a clear description of the problem and what you want done about it. Include copies of boarding passes and ticket receipts if you can.

3. If you feel the airline has not resolved your problem in a fair way, you can file a complaint with the government. For information write to the U.S. Department of Transportation, Office of Consumer Affairs, 400 7th Street SW, Washington, DC 20590.

ALCOHOL

Both federal and state laws regulate the manufacture and sale of alcoholic beverages.

The federal government regulates liquor by issuing permits to manufacturers and wholesalers, supervising imports, and enforcing standards for safety and quality. For example, federal law requires that labels include not only the alcohol content of each beverage but also warnings about the hazards of its use by drivers and by pregnant women. The law also prohibits brewers and distillers from making any claims about the intoxicating effects of their products.

The legal age for alcohol possession and consumption is 21 in every state. Other state laws vary: some restrict the number of bars in a given area, or the number that can serve drinks to people who are standing up, or the number that can serve drinks without serving food as well. In some states you can buy beer in grocery stores but not wine and spirits (hard liquor). In others, alcoholic beverages can be sold only in special state-run stores.

Some states allow local communities to decide for themselves how to regulate alcohol, as long as their ordinances do not conflict with state law. The result is that a "dry" county, whose citizens have banned the sale of liquor, for example, may be situated next to a county where liquor can be sold in "package" stores but not in restaurants.

UNDERAGE DRINKING

An adult who gives alcohol to a minor may be subject to prosecution, fines, and imprisonment, and a liquor store that sells alcohol to a minor may have its license revoked.

Some states prohibit minors from drinking at home, with or without the permission of their parents. Under some circumstances, even when there is no such law, a parent who lets his child consume alcohol to excess may be prosecuted for child abuse.

DRUNKEN BEHAVIOR

Alcohol and the law often rub elbows when crimes are committed by people under the influence. Suppose a man, after leaving a party, goes on a rampage and smashes all the glass windows on a city street. Can he be held responsible?

It depends. If he deliberately got drunk, he would probably have no case, because voluntary intoxication is not considered an acceptable defense. However, if the man is a teetotaler who never touches alcohol because it makes him go berserk, and he was told that the punch he was drinking contained only fruit juice, there is a good chance he would not be held responsible for the damage he did.

Some state laws hold the owners of bars, restaurants, and liquor stores responsible for injuries inflicted by their patrons as a result of drunkenness. These laws, called dram shop acts, apply only if the person selling the liquor knew the patron was already drunk.

But what about hosts of private parties who continue to serve drinks to guests who are already under the influence? The states are split on this issue. Some apply the same standards expected of bars and liquor stores, while others do not hold private individuals responsible.

STEPS TO TAKE WHEN YOU ARE A HOST

If you are hosting a party at which liquor will be served, it will be worth your while to take the following precautions:

REAL LIFE, REAL LAW

The Case of the Holiday Host

When Harold left his employer's Christmas party, he was obviously drunk. While driving home he ran a red light and knocked down a pedestrian, whose leg was broken in the accident. She decided to sue Harold's employer.

The employer argued that under his state's law, the host of a social gathering is not responsible for the actions of a guest who drinks too much at his party. But the fact emerged that in this case the employer was not merely hosting a social gathering; he was also using the party to advance his business, and therefore had the same responsibilities as a bar or restaurant to stop serving alcohol to Harold after he was noticeably drunk.

Courts in some other states would not have ruled against the employer, but keep in mind that it is wise to err on the side of caution when serving people alcohol.

1. Try to limit the amount of alcohol being served. Offer a variety of soft drinks and fruit juices as well as beer, wine, and hard liquor.

2. Close the bar an hour or so before the party ends.

3. Serve snacks and coffee or nonalcoholic beverages to give people time to sober up before they drive home.

4. If a guest appears to be under the influence, do not let him drive. If necessary, have someone drive him home or offer him a bed for the night. See also ALCOHOLISM; DRUNK DRIVING.

ALCOHOLISM

The problems associated with alcoholism are many, but those that concern the law center primarily on the workplace. In recent years increasing numbers of employers are requiring employees to submit to alcohol and drug testing, especially when their jobs affect the safety of others.

Although the law in this area is far from settled, the trend is to permit such testing, except when it is discriminatory—for instance, if only employees that belong to a minority are tested.

Because an employer has a duty to maintain the safety of his workplace, he can usually discipline or fire employees who abuse alcohol in a way that threatens the general safety.

Sometimes, however, an employee may be able to challenge an employer's hasty actions. Let us say that Jack is frequently late to work or absent altogether. His eyes are bloodshot and his hands often tremble, but this does not seem to affect his work. One day Jack shows up late for the third time in one week, and his employer tells him he is fired.

If Jack's company normally warned employees before firing them, or if it usually referred workers to an employee assistance program or some other counseling program aimed at rehabilitation, Jack might be able to have his dismissal reversed because the company failed to follow standard procedures. See also DRUG TESTING; EMPLOYEE ASSISTANCE PROGRAM.

ALIEN

A person who is not a citizen of the United States either by birth or by naturalization is considered an alien. Aliens can visit, study, work, or make their home in this country, but only with the permission of the federal government.

The conditions aliens must meet in order to enter the United States are determined by Congress, and the laws that apply to their admission and residency are enforced by the Attorney General of the United States and the Immigration and Naturalization Service (INS).

Not everyone who wants to enter the United States is allowed to do so. For example, the INS refuses to admit people who are mentally ill, who have been convicted of serious crimes, and who carry certain diseases, such as AIDS. Also, aliens who want to work in this country may do so only if they are not depriving American citizens of job opportunities.

ALIENS' RIGHTS AND RESPONSIBILITIES

Although aliens are not permitted to vote in federal, state, or local elections, they have most of the other constitutional rights U.S. citizens enjoy. An alien who is accused of a crime, for example, must be informed of the charges against him and of his right not to incriminate himself. If he cannot afford an attorney, one will be provided, and he is presumed innocent until proven guilty. The children of aliens can attend public schools.

Along with these rights and privileges come certain responsibilities. Aliens must pay taxes on income they earn in the United States and on property they own. Aliens who have applied for U.S. citizenship can be compelled to serve in the military in times of war.

Aliens must obey the laws of this country, even when those laws clash with the customs of their native land. For example, among some communities of Laotian aliens in the United States it is not uncommon for a man to "steal" a bride from the home of her family. Although this custom is legal in Laos, it is considered kidnapping here, and Laotians have been prosecuted in a number of cases.

There is no federal law preventing aliens from buying property and operating businesses in the United States. Some states prohibit aliens from owning real estate, but these laws are rarely enforced.

DEPORTATION

Aliens who do not comply with the immigration laws can be sent back to the country from which they came. Grounds for deportation include entering the country without permission, telling lies in order to gain entry, staying longer than permitted, and violating the terms of admission. For example, an alien admitted to this country to attend college may be deported if he stops attending classes or if he takes a job without getting permission.

Before being deported, an alien is entitled to a hearing before an officer of the INS. He also has the right to hire an attorney, call witnesses, present evidence, and testify on his own behalf. If the hearing officer orders deportation, the decision can be appealed to the Board of Immigration Appeals and then to federal court. However, unless the hearing officer was arbitrary or failed to follow the law, the deportation order will be allowed to stand.

UNDOCUMENTED ALIENS

Since the 1970's the United States has been faced with the problem of thousands of people entering the country illegally across the Mexican border. They have come in search of jobs—often as migrant farm workers and household help—that pay many times what they could earn in their home countries. Immigrants from Europe and Asia have often entered the country as tourists or students and remained illegally.

Over the years, many of these undocumented aliens settled into American society. They raised families, started businesses, and bought homes, but lived with the fear of discovery and deportation. Although the sheer numbers of undocumented aliens threatened to overburden state and federal welfare programs, it seemed unfair to deport those who had been in the United States for a long time and had made strong investments in the country despite their lack of citizenship.

To deal with the problem, the federal government granted undocumented aliens a period of amnesty in 1987-88. Those who came forward and registered with the INS during the amnesty period were allowed to remain, even though they had entered the country illegally. Those who failed to register, or who came into the country during or after the amnesty period, are still subject to deportation. However, a 1990 law established a new lottery system that annually grants permanent legal residence to the first 40,000 applicants from 34 designated countries. See also CITIZENSHIP; IMMIGRATION; VISA.

ALIMONY

When a couple separates or divorces, the payments made by one spouse to support the other are called alimony. In the past, courts made men responsible for family support upon divorce or separation. Husbands paid alimony to their former wives and child support for their children.

Today, with women providing an increasing share of family income, the delegation of financial responsibility when a marriage breaks up has changed (with women often assuming a greater share than previously) and so has the terminology. The word *alimony* is being replaced in legal usage by the terms *spousal support* and *maintenance*. See DIVORCE; PALIMONY.

ALLEGATION

An accusation that serves as the basis for a civil lawsuit or criminal prosecution is called an allegation. In order for the accuser to win his case, he must prove his allegation. For example, in a suit for damages resulting from an auto accident, the claim that the driver's carelessness caused the plaintiff's injuries is an allegation that must be proved before the plaintiff can be compensated for injuries suffered.

In referring to cases in which allegations have been made but not proved, reporters, attorneys, and others must use the word *alleged* to avoid defaming people who have been accused but not found guilty—for example, "the alleged robber was found a block from the scene of the crime."

ALTERNATIVE DISPUTE RESOLUTION

Hoping to save yourself time and trouble, you buy an expensive tractor-mower to cut your lawn. But what you get instead is trouble of another kind: the machine digs up the lawn, will not shift into reverse, and repeatedly conks out. The company refuses to replace it, and you cannot afford an expensive, time-consuming lawsuit. Do you have another choice?

You certainly do. More and more consumers these days are using alternative dispute resolution (ADR), which bypasses the clogged and costly courts and may well be the wave of the future.

ADR is an umbrella term that encompasses several different ways of resolving disputes: negotiation, conciliation, mediation, and arbitration. In negotiation, the two parties try to come to an agreement by themselves. Conciliation and mediation rely on an impartial third party, or referee, to find a fair solution. Arbitration employs a referee too, but it is a more formal process, in which the decision of the third party is usually legally binding. See also ARBITRATION; CONCILIATION; MEDIATION.

ADR is generally cheaper, faster, and less stressful than litigation, and it is often more effective. Used for years in labor disputes, it is now a common way of resolving neighborhood disputes and consumer battles with manufacturers, insurers, doctors, home contractors, and others.

STEPS TO TAKE

To find out whether your dispute is one that ADR can help settle, and which of the several types is best for you, do one or more of the following:

1. Call your Better Business Bureau and ask their advice. They may direct you to a mediator or arbitrator.

2. Look in the Yellow Pages under "Arbitration" or "Mediation" for the name of a local company, lawyer, or retired judge who practices ADR.

3. The American Bar Association Standing Committee on Dispute Resolution publishes a directory of ADR organizations. For names of ADR practitioners, write to the committee at 1800 M Street NW, Suite 290 FN, Washington, DC 20036.

AMNESTY

In granting amnesty a government provides a large number of people with immunity from prosecution for a criminal offense. From that time forward, however, those who were given amnesty must obey the law.

Amnesty is usually invoked when it presents the most workable solution to a problem that has gotten out of hand. For example, in 1977 President Jimmy Carter granted amnesty to draft evaders in an effort to heal the nationwide bitterness caused by the war in Vietnam. And in the 1980's the government granted amnesty to aliens who had entered the country illegally, provided that they came forward and registered with the Immigration and Naturalization Service.

Any level of government can offer some type of amnesty to those who have violated its laws. For example, public libraries may offer amnesty from fines to borrowers who return long-overdue books.

ANIMALS

Although animals provide us with food, clothing, transportation, hard work, and companionship, they are also capable of creating a nuisance, destroying property, causing injury, and even taking people's lives. As a result, laws have been enacted to protect the public from animals. And since animals are often on the receiving end of injury and harm, other laws have been passed to protect animals from people.

Animals are divided into two categories by law: (1) wild animals, which cannot be completely tamed, such as lions, tigers, bears, and alligators; and (2) domestic animals, which are tame by nature or have been tamed by humans. Sheep, cattle, horses, chickens, and other farm animals, as well as pets such as cats and dogs, are domestic animals. See Dog Law; Pets.

FARM ANIMALS

Local zoning laws often prohibit keeping farm animals in residential neighborhoods. Some ordinances limit the number of chickens, ducks, and pigeons one may keep on one's property. Since raising pigeons is a popular hobby in some cities, laws may restrict not only the number of pigeons one can keep but also where the pigeon coop can be located in relation to neighbors.

Large farm animals are usually forbidden within city limits, but in one California community, a property owner was allowed to keep a goat during the summer for the purpose of controlling the weeds in his lawn.

UNWANTED VISITORS

When an animal wanders onto your property, you are entitled to take reasonable measures to remove it. If you cannot simply shoo it away, you can try calling the owner.

If you do not know who the owner is, you can call your local animal control department, which will send someone to remove it. Unless the animal is vicious, you cannot kill it. If you do, the owner can sue you for the animal's value and possibly extra compensation too.

ANIMAL OWNERS' RESPONSIBILITIES

If your neighbor's sheep, cow, or other domestic animal dines on the flowers in your garden or traipses across your freshly cemented patio, the animal's owner is responsible for the damage, whether or not he knew the animal was likely to do such mischief.

Oddly enough, however, if a domestic animal kicks, bites, pecks, or otherwise injures you—whether on your property or anyone else's—its owner cannot be sued, unless he knew the beast had a history of inflicting such injuries.

Different laws apply to wild animals. The owner of a wolf, bear, tiger, monkey, alligator, or other wild animal is responsible for any injuries it may cause—even if the owner did his best to keep the animal from doing any harm. Even a zoo or circus, where animals are caged, can be sued if people are injured as a result of getting too close to an animal.

REAL LIFE, REAL LAW

The Case of the Pampered Pig

An animal lover who lived in the suburbs bought a pig from a farmer. He was so fond of the pink, squealing animal that he kept it in the house and treated it like a dog or other pet. Not surprisingly, the pig grew larger and larger until it became a hog (a pig that weighs more than 120 pounds).

Since the animal was no longer suitable for the house, the owner built a pen in the backyard, where the hog lived quite happily. After a while, however, the neighbors complained that it attracted swarms of flies, gave off unpleasant odors, and emitted loud, grunting noises.

The owner claimed the hog was a pet and should not be subject to the zoning laws that prohibit keeping farm animals in a residential area. But because the neighbors found the animal both offensive and a threat to their property values, the hog was declared a nuisance. The owner, rather than part with his pet, chose to move to a place where hogs were permitted.

CRUELTY TO ANIMALS

Although beatings come to mind first, domestic animals may be victims of many forms of mistreatment: failing to provide enough food or water; keeping an animal in unhealthy surroundings; not caring for an animal when it is sick; or abandoning it to the elements. Cock fighting and dog fighting are also considered forms of cruelty and are against the law in most places. A person who is convicted of cruelty may have his animal taken from him and may also be subject to fines or imprisonment.

FAIR AND UNFAIR GAME

Laws strictly regulate the hunting and capturing of wild animals. The federal Endangered Species Act, for example, protects many animals that are declining in numbers from being killed, captured, or otherwise threatened.

Deer and other game animals are protected by state laws that require hunters to be licensed. They also restrict the equipment hunters can use and limit the times and the places they can hunt.

ANNUITY

One way for a person to have money available after retirement is through an annuity, which is a type of investment typically obtained from an insurance company. An annuity is a contract by which you pay an amount of money (either in a lump sum or over a period of years) to the insurance company, which invests the money. In return, the company agrees that on a specified date it will begin to pay you a regular sum each month, usually for the rest of your life.

The payment is actually a repayment of the amount you contribute, plus earnings such as interest. Depending on your contract, the annuity may end when you die, or the balance may be paid to someone you name as a beneficiary.

Like any other contract, an annuity can be broken—but not without a price. If you decide to terminate an annuity you will probably have to pay a penalty, most likely a percentage of the amount of money that you have already paid into the annuity. The exact terms of the penalty are spelled out in your contract. To avoid an unpleasant surprise, read it carefully and be sure you understand it before you sign on the bottom line.

ANNULMENT

An annulment is a legal action that declares a marriage void. Unlike a divorce, which legally ends a marriage, an annulment asserts that the marriage never existed in the first place.

How can it be, you may ask, that a marriage never existed if a hundred people watched the couple get married? Just as divorce recognizes flaws in a marriage that caused it not to work, annulment recognizes flaws that existed prior to a marriage which, if known, would have prevented a legal marriage from taking place.

WHY AN ANNULMENT?

Annulments are far less common than they were in the past, largely because divorces are easier to obtain. Even so, in some cases annulment may be faster and cheaper than divorce. In addition, some states make it hard for a person to remarry after a divorce, whereas annulment presents no such obstacle.

The Catholic Church considers annulment the only way to end a marriage. If a couple are granted a church annulment, a legal annulment or divorce is nevertheless required before either may remarry.

Sometimes annulment may be the only choice, because the union was considered void to begin with—for instance, a marriage between a boy and girl who are underage.

GROUNDS FOR ANNULMENT

If Jane and John meet on vacation in Hawaii, get married after a quick courtship, and within a week have second thoughts, they probably will not be able to have the marriage annulled. The grounds for annulment are many, but a hasty marriage is not one of them.

Laws vary from one state to another, but the following are the most common circumstances that enable two parties to get an annulment:

◇ If one or both were underage when they married.

◇ If one or both were forced to marry because of some threat, as in the classic "shotgun wedding."

◇ If one or both were mentally ill, drunk, or otherwise unable to understand the implications of the wedding.

◇ If one party hid some important fact from the other, such as a criminal record, a serious disease, sexual impotence, a previous marriage, or even a lack of intention to have children.

ANTIQUE

When does something that is old become an antique? What is the difference between junk and collectibles? In law, there is no cut-and-dried definition and no set age at which an object becomes an antique. Virtually anything that is old—whether a rug, a statue, a piece of china, a car, or a doll—can be called an antique.

EVALUATING ANTIQUES

Putting a value on antiques can be as hard as defining what they are. An item's worth depends on its scarcity, its condition, who made it, the materials used, the quality of the workmanship, its historical significance, and its current popularity as a collectible item.

One way to find out what an antique is worth is by consulting collectors' guides, which list the prices of similar items sold at auction. Another way is to consult an appraiser, dealer, or other expert who knows the current market price.

If you hire an appraiser, make sure that he is a specialist in the kinds of items you are having appraised—Turkish rugs, 18th-century Chippendale furniture, or early American quilts, for example.

To make the appraisal go more smoothly, gather together in advance all the documents that relate to your antique, such as bills of sale and previous appraisals. If you have a lot of items, provide an inventory for the appraiser.

Appraisers bill you for their services in different ways. Some charge a flat fee, some an hourly rate, and some a percentage of the value of the collection. To avoid an unpleasant surprise, be sure you understand in advance how the appraiser will charge you. See also APPRAISAL.

LET THE BUYER BEWARE

Suppose you go to an auction and pay a high price for a musket used during the Revolutionary War. At home, while cleaning your new acquisition, you find the words "Made in Taiwan" on the stock. Will you be able to sue the auction house? The answer depends on how the item was represented at the time of purchase.

Dealers often provide a written description of the piece they are selling. It includes the age of the item, its condition, the materials used in its manufacture, and the name of the artisan. Antiques of great value or historical significance usually come with a *provenance*—a document that includes the names of all of the item's previous owners. These documents serve as the dealer's warranty that the item is genuine.

If these documents are provided, and the item later turns out to be a reproduction or forgery, as was the case with the musket, the dealer could be held responsible for breach of warranty or for fraud. However, if no documents or guarantees are provided at the time of sale, the buyer must assume the risk of his purchase.

APPEAL

A court trial usually ends with a winner and a loser. The loser may have lost only temporarily, however, if he is able to file an appeal—a procedure in which he claims the lower court made the wrong decision and asks a higher court to review the case in hopes of a ruling that is more favorable to him.

Usually an appeal can be made twice—once to an intermediate court and once to the highest court. In the state court systems, intermediate courts are usually called appellate courts, and the highest court is usually the state supreme court. The intermediate courts of the federal court system are the U.S. Courts of Appeals. The highest court of the land is the Supreme Court of the United States. For more information on the different kinds of courts, see COURTS.

LIMITATIONS ON APPEALS

Not every decision of a lower court may be appealed, or challenged. Most often, appeals are based on the claim that some sort of legal error was made by the lower court—for example, the judge gave the wrong instructions to the jury. The simple introduction of new evidence or disputes about matters of fact cannot serve as the basis for an appeal.

Decisions that may be appealed to a higher court often involve important questions of law or knotty constitutional issues.

Whether the decision is reviewable may also depend on the amount of money awarded by the court or the value of property related to the case. In some states, only lawsuits that involve a specified minimum amount of money are allowed to be appealed.

HOW AN APPEAL IS MADE

An appeal usually begins when the appellant (the person who brings the appeal) files a notice of appeal. This notice, which states that some aspects of the lower court decision were in error, is sent to the appellate court and to the appellee (the person against whom the appeal is brought). Both the appellant and appellee then file documents, called briefs, with the appellate court.

The briefs present the facts of the case, the questions which the appellate court is being asked to consider, and the arguments about these questions. The purpose of the appellant's brief is to point out the errors he claims were made by the lower court. The appellee's brief tries to show that the decision of the lower court was correct. The appellate court reviews these briefs along with the record of the lower court. No trial takes place, and neither new evidence nor witnesses are allowed.

Sometimes the attorneys for both sides are permitted to present short oral arguments that allow them to address questions outlined in the briefs and the appellate judges to inquire about either side's position.

POSSIBLE OUTCOMES

After hearing the oral arguments and reviewing the trial court record and briefs, the appellate court renders its decision. Appellate court decisions are of four kinds:

◇ The appellate court may affirm the lower court's decision, having found that no errors were made during the original trial.

◇ It may reverse the lower court's decision—the loser in the lower court is declared the winner.

◇ It may modify the lower court's decision by agreeing with parts of the decision but disagreeing with others.

◇ It may remand the case—that is, send it back to the lower court for a new trial—because it finds that some facts were not resolved.

APPRAISAL

The determination of the value of a home, furniture, antiques, jewelry, art, or other property is called an appraisal. It should be done by a professional appraiser who has no personal interest in the property.

An appraisal of real estate is usually required when you apply for a mortgage. The most common method for gauging the worth of a house or land is by comparing it with similar properties.

There are also occasions when you may want personal property appraised. Insurance companies, for example, need appraisals to determine how much coverage to offer for most household items of value.Very expensive items, however, may require more coverage than provided by a standard homeowners policy. For a few extra dollars, an owner can buy additional coverage based on the property's appraised value. See ANTIQUE.

Federal law requires states to license real estate appraisers, but other kinds of appraisers are unregulated; almost anyone can claim to be one. Check an appraiser's experience and credentials before you hire him. If you suspect he is not impartial, get another opinion. (For example, do not ask the jeweler from whom you plan to buy a diamond ring to recommend an appraiser.)

If you need an appraisal for mortgage purposes, check with the lender to be sure he approves of the appraiser whom you are considering.

ARBITRATION

You bought a beautiful and expensive new car six months ago. However, it has been in the repair shop four times already, and you want a new car. The dealer does not want to give you one. You don't want to file a lawsuit and the amount is too big for small-claims court. What can you do?

One thing you can do is to take your dispute to arbitration. Arbitration, along with mediation and conciliation, is a way to solve disputes without going to court.

In mediation and conciliation the two parties in a dispute turn to a third person, who serves as an adviser and helps them settle their difference. In arbitration, the disputing parties place the decision entirely in the hands of a third person or persons. The decision of the arbitrator is final and binding. One exception to this rule is a court-ordered arbitration, which can be appealed. See also COLLECTIVE BARGAINING; CONCILIATION; MEDIATION.

HOW ARBITRATION WORKS

Arbitration begins when the parties to a dispute agree to present the controversy to one or more impartial persons who will decide the matter. Each side appoints an arbitrator and together the arbitrators appoint a third arbitrator (also called an umpire), who actually hears and decides the case.

In a matter of weeks a hearing is scheduled. The arbitrator listens to the facts and examines documents and other evidence presented by both sides. Although he may be (and often is) a lawyer, he does not have to base his decision on legal considerations. He may use fairness or common business practice as a basis for his decision, called an award.

Once the award is made, usually in a matter of days or weeks, it may be confirmed in a court. Confirmation converts the award into a judgment, or decision of the court. This means that the winning party can use legal means to collect the money or otherwise enforce the award. In some cases, to avoid going to court to collect, each party posts a bond for the amount in dispute.

ADVANTAGES

Arbitration is usually cheaper than court proceedings ($300 to $400 for a small commercial dispute and less than $2,000 for a dispute involving $100,000) and you can put limits on the amount you will spend. Arbitration is also much faster, as lawsuits can take months or years to resolve.

TYPES OF DISPUTES

Almost any dispute can be arbitrated—divorce and custody disputes, medical malpractice, insurance claims, accident cases, contract disputes, sales agreements, to name a few. Many types of contracts, such as auto sales agreements, have arbitration clauses. If yours does not, and a dispute arises, ask an arbitration service (discussed below) for a standard arbitration agreement.

Some industries, including auto and major household appliance makers, moving companies, stockbrokerage firms, and funeral homes, have their own arbitration systems. The arbitrator's decision is usually not binding on the consumer.

ARBITRATION SERVICES

Numerous nonprofit and for-profit organizations offer arbitration services to the consumer. The American Arbitration Association (with headquarters at 140 West 51st Street, New York, NY 10020-1203) has offices nationwide. Most states have alternative dispute resolution systems, which frequently offer arbitration services.

STEPS TO TAKE

Let us say you have bought a $3,000 dining room set, and it was delivered to you with the upholstery in the wrong color. You claim you chose another color in the same pattern; the furniture dealer says the existing color is close enough. What do you do?

1. Get the furniture dealer to agree to arbitration.

2. Select an arbitrator. Look in the Yellow Pages or get references from lawyers, from businessmen, or from the arbitration service if you are using one. Try to find out if the arbitrator has decided similar cases in a way that would be favorable to you.

3. Obtain the rules of arbitration from the arbitrator and make sure you understand them. You and your opponent can usually agree to change them if you wish.

4. When you present the facts of the case at the arbitration hearing, explain the applicable law as you understand it and traditional business or professional practices in your area. For instance, it may be customary for merchants to provide buyers with a swatch of the material they ordered.

5. Be ready to supply eyewitnesses or expert witnesses. Perhaps a friend came along when you placed your order and heard you say you wanted pink, not peach.

6. Find out whether the other side will be represented by a lawyer. If so, consider hiring your own.

7. Even though arbitration hearings are less formal than court proceedings, be businesslike in your dress and overall demeanor.

Armed Services

In many ways the armed services represent a world different from that of civilians. They have their own customs and codes of behavior—even their own laws and courts.

WHO THEY ARE

The U.S. armed services consist of the U.S. Army, Navy, Marine Corps, and Air Force. The U.S. Coast Guard, which in peacetime is a part of the Department of Transportation, is under the Navy Department in wartime or when the president so directs. Each branch of the military is headed by a civilian secretary, who reports to the secretary of defense, a member of the president's Cabinet. At the top is the president himself, who is commander-in-chief of the armed forces.

Nowadays the armed services are made up entirely of volunteers, but young men are nevertheless required by law to register with the Selective Service when they reach the age of 18. See also SELECTIVE SERVICE.

A person must also be 18 (or 17 with parental consent) in order to enlist. Men and women over 35 are not eligible, but exceptions have been made for former military personnel who want to resume their careers or people with special skills.

OBLIGATIONS AND RESTRICTIONS

Most people who enlist are obligated to serve for two years. While they are in military service, they are entitled to their rights as citizens, but they must also obey orders. Thus their rights are somewhat limited in order to maintain strict order and discipline.

Civilians have the right to travel freely throughout the country, but members of the armed forces have restrictions placed upon them. For example, if they leave their assigned locations without prior permission, they may be subject to arrest, trial, and punishment. The trial is conducted by a court-martial, a military court used to try military offenses. See COURT-MARTIAL.

WOMEN IN THE ARMED SERVICES

In the past, women in military service were usually assigned to units made up of other women. Today, however, men and women serve side by side. And although Congress still bans women from serving in most combat units, women pilots may now fly combat missions. In 1991, when troops were sent overseas for Operation Desert Storm, many women who previously would have been considered noncombatants found themselves in battle zones.

THE RESERVES AND NATIONAL GUARD

In addition to the regular full-time military establishment, Army, Air Force, and Naval Reserve and National Guard personnel serve on a part-time basis. Members of these units spend most of their time as civilians—they are called together only for routine training and for emergencies.

The National Guard functions on both the state and federal levels. Some units are directed by the United States Army and others are directed by the Air Force. During such emergencies as earthquakes and riots, units may be called up by the governor to assist police in keeping the peace or to perform other tasks in the public interest. In the event of a national emergency, the president may order National Guard units to go on active duty.

FINANCIAL PROTECTION

When members of the Reserve or the National Guard are summoned to active duty by the president, they must, of course, leave their jobs. Their pay on active duty often falls far short of civilian pay, but they still owe rent, mortgage and car payments, and other bills of civilian life. To help protect military personnel on active duty from losing their homes and ruining their credit, Congress passed the Soldiers and Sailors Relief Act in 1940, and it remains in force today.

This act protects personnel in a number of ways: It prohibits the eviction of military families who fall behind in rent.

It limits the amount of interest creditors can charge during the period of active service. It also prevents creditors from enforcing judgments against military personnel who cannot appear to defend themselves.

But the law protects military personnel only from debts incurred before their active duty, and the failure to pay the debt must be a direct result of being called into service.

LEAVING THE ARMED SERVICES

At the conclusion of their enlistment period, military personnel may be offered the opportunity to reenlist, but this is not guaranteed. Those who complete their enlistment and want to leave usually receive an honorable discharge.

If the discharge is to be less than honorable, there must be a hearing before a military board of review. Those who do not receive an honorable discharge may be ineligible for veterans' benefits. See also UNIFORM CODE OF MILITARY JUSTICE; VETERANS BENEFITS.

ARMS, RIGHT TO BEAR

The right of American citizens to bear arms is guaranteed by the Second Amendment to the U.S. Constitution, which reads: "A well regulated Militia, being necessary to the security of a free State, the right of the people to keep and bear Arms, shall not be infringed."

This amendment focuses on the group rather than the individual, suggesting that a community at large has a right to defend itself against harm. State constitutions, on the other hand, focus on the individual in that they guarantee the private ownership of guns.

The right to bear arms has restrictions. For example, federal law and some state laws require a handgun purchaser to wait a period of time between buying a gun and taking possession of it. This waiting period allows police to investigate the purchaser's background. It also provides a cooling-off period that may prevent an angry person from becoming violent in the heat of the moment.

Many states require that purchasers of guns be licensed or fingerprinted, and some do not allow convicted felons to own guns for a specified period of time. Some state laws forbid people to own semiautomatic weapons, and federal laws ban the importation of certain types of assault weapons. See also WEAPON.

ARRAIGNMENT

At an arraignment a person accused of a crime appears before the court to hear the charges against him, to be informed of his constitutional rights, and to enter a plea of not guilty, guilty, or no contest.

If the accused person enters a plea of not guilty, a trial date is set. If the accused pleads guilty or no contest, a sentence will be imposed. If the crime is a minor one, the judge may impose the sentence right away, but if the crime is more serious, he will have to set a later date for the sentencing.

Depending on the state and the severity of the crime, some aspects of an arraignment may occur at an initial court appearance or at a preliminary hearing. For the steps in a criminal proceeding, see CRIMINAL PROCEDURE. See also PRELIMINARY HEARING.

ARREARS

A debt is in arrears when part of the amount due remains unpaid. For example, suppose you take out a loan for $500 in January and agree to make payments of $60 a month to pay off the principal and interest. You make your payments in February and March, but miss the one for April. In May you are $60 in arrears. Depending on the terms of the loan, you may be charged a penalty based on both the amount owed and the length of time you are in arrears.

ARREST

An arrest occurs when a police officer detains a person and takes him into custody to answer for a crime. In most cases an arrest is made with a warrant, an order issued by a magistrate or judge that directs a police officer to take someone into custody. A copy of the warrant is given to the accused at the time of the arrest.

ARREST WARRANTS

Warrants serve to protect the rights of innocent people. Before the warrant is issued, a judge or magistrate (such as a justice of the peace) reviews the evidence against the accused person to ensure that he or she is not arrested on insufficient evidence or for arbitrary reasons. The magistrate or judge must be assured that there is some reasonable ground for believing that a crime has been committed and that the person named has committed it.

Let us say a police officer wants to obtain a warrant to arrest a man for holding up a liquor store. Although the man was masked at the time of the crime, the store owner reported that he had a crescent-shaped scar on his left hand, just like one on the hand of a notorious neighborhood thug. When the police officer presents this evidence to the judge, he is issued a warrant for the man's arrest.

ARRESTS WITHOUT WARRANTS

Police officers can arrest a person without a warrant only under special circumstances. For example, an officer may arrest a person who commits an offense right before his eyes, if he believes a crime is about to be committed, or if he believes a person has committed a crime and there is no time to procure a warrant.

ARRESTING THE WRONG PERSON

If a police officer arrests the wrong person for a crime as a result of misidentification, he will usually not be responsible for false arrest. As long as he acts in good faith, the police

CHECKLIST

What To Do If You Are Arrested

If you are a solid citizen, being arrested is probably the least of your worries. But in the unlikely event that you are arrested, here are a few things to remember:

❑ **DO NOT RESIST ARREST.**
You do not have the right to resist a lawful arrest. Resisting arrest is a criminal offense in itself and will only make things worse. Even if you are ultimately acquitted of the charge that prompted the arrest, you may still be convicted of resisting arrest.

❑ **ASK FOR A COPY OF THE ARREST WARRANT, OR ASK WHAT CHARGES HAVE BEEN FILED AGAINST YOU.**
If there is a warrant for your arrest, the police officer should have it with him. The warrant states the charges against you, and you are entitled to a copy of it. If you are being arrested without a warrant, the police officer must tell you what crime he is arresting you for.

❑ **IDENTIFY YOURSELF.**
The police officer will ask for your name and address. If you refuse to identify yourself, you will not be able to make bail and will be kept in custody until your trial.

❑ **DO NOT MAKE ANY OTHER STATEMENTS TO THE POLICE UNTIL YOU SPEAK TO A LAWYER.**
You have the right to remain silent. Your natural impulse may be to tell your side of the story, and you may even believe that remaining silent gives the impression that you have something to hide. This is not the case. Resist the temptation to defend yourself by speaking up, because you may inadvertently implicate yourself in a crime.

If the police attempt to question you, tell them you want to speak with a lawyer before making any comment. You will then be allowed to call your lawyer. If you do not have a lawyer, you will be given one, but this could take several days. In the meantime, continue to remain silent.

❑ **CALL A FRIEND, RELATIVE, OR LAWYER TO HELP YOU PUT UP BOND.**
You will probably be able to be released until trial by "making bail," or "putting up bond." The bail or bond is money you provide to ensure that you show up at the trial. After you appear, the money will be returned to you.

You may not have to put up cash or property for a bond, however. You may be allowed to sign a recognizance bond, which is a written promise to appear.

If you are told to put up cash but do not have it, you may hire a bondsman to post the bond.

❑ **OBEY ALL CONDITIONS OF YOUR BOND.**
A bond is a conditional release. The condition might be that you abstain from alcohol or stay away from certain individuals until your trial. Follow the conditions to the letter, or your bond could be revoked, and you will have to await your trial in jail.

department cannot be sued for a simple mistake. See also CITIZEN'S ARREST; SEARCH WARRANT.

ARSON

Arson is the act of intentionally setting fire to a building or other property. At one time, when the penalty for arson was death, the definition of the crime was strictly limited. The fire had to be set with the intention of causing harm, and the building had to belong to someone else.

Today arson is defined differently in the various states, but the type of property that is burned and the intention of the person who set the fire are common factors associated with the crime. Setting off an explosive that causes a fire also qualifies as arson.

Arson is no longer limited to setting fire to someone else's house. You have committed arson if you intentionally set fire to your own home (and you may also be found guilty of defrauding your insurance company), a public or commercial building, or in some states, a bridge, a boat, woods, or an open field.

Usually the building has to be occupied. Setting fire to a building that is abandoned, under construction, or being demolished may not be arson (but it is a crime).

The extent to which a building must burn before arson can be established also varies—from only a small portion in some states to the entire building in others. The law may also specify that damage must exceed a specified dollar amount.

Originally the person who started the fire had to mean to destroy the building completely. Today when states prosecute someone for arson, they no longer have to prove such an intent. Partial damage, such as smoke damage or charring, is sufficient evidence that arson was intended.

Arson is a felony, punishable by imprisonment. The length of the sentence depends on the extent of damage and is usually longer if the building is one in which people live.

ARTIFICIAL INSEMINATION

When a couple cannot conceive a child because the husband is not fertile, they may rely on artificial insemination in order to have a child. In this procedure sperm is collected from a donor, who is usually anonymous. A doctor then inserts the sperm into the woman's uterus to fertilize her egg and produce a child.

BIOLOGICAL VERSUS LEGAL FATHERHOOD

Sometimes a relative provides the sperm for fertilization, but more often the donor is anonymous, and the sperm is obtained from a sperm bank. Even though the donor is the biological father of a child conceived by artificial insemination, he gives up all the rights and responsibilities of parenthood before the procedure begins. For example, he cannot be asked to provide financial support for the child, nor is he permitted visitation rights. Usually, the donor never knows whether a child was conceived from his sperm or even whether the sperm was used.

The husband of the woman who has been artificially inseminated is considered the legal father of the child, provided that he consents to the procedure in writing. Neither the adoption process nor other legal proceedings are required, and the husband's rights and responsibilities as a parent are the same as they would be if the child were his own. See also IN VITRO FERTILIZATION.

SURROGATE MOTHERS

When the wife is unable to conceive, a couple may decide to use the husband's sperm to impregnate another woman, who agrees to serve as a surrogate mother. When she bears the child, she turns it over to the couple with whom she made the arrangement. See SURROGATE MOTHER.

ASSAULT AND BATTERY

Although the two terms are often used together, assault and battery are actually two separate acts.

Assault is a deliberate act that puts another person in fear of immediate physical harm. Even if no attack follows, the reasonable belief that an attack was intended is all that is necessary to constitute an assault. No actual physical contact is required in committing an assault, but there must be the justified fear that some sort of attack is about to take place.

For example, a man who raises his hand and threatens to strike someone is guilty of assault. But a person who says something like, "If I had a gun, I'd shoot you," is not guilty of assault since there is no threat of immediate harm.

Battery is intentional physical contact committed by one person against another. Accidental contact, like bumping against a fellow passenger in a crowded subway car, is not battery. However, slight contact that is offensive and intentional can be considered battery. For example, the manager of a Texas hotel was found guilty of battery because he snatched away a patron's plate in a "loud and offensive" manner, even though the contact did not result in the diner's suffering any physical injury.

Assault and battery are civil wrongs (torts) as well as criminal acts. You can sue for injuries you suffer as the result of an assault or battery. See TORT.

ASSEMBLY, RIGHT OF

The First Amendment to the U.S. Constitution protects your right to assemble peaceably, and many states have similar provisions in their own constitutions. As with most rights, however, the right of assembly has some limits.

A government can regulate the use of public places under its control. Therefore, a city or county may legally require a group to obtain a permit before holding a meeting or demonstration in a public place.

The size of the group is an important factor in granting permits, as the government has to deal with such tangles as traffic flow problems. If 60,000 people want to protest in midtown Manhattan during rush hour, for example, they are sure to cause traffic problems.

But there are no set rules for how many people constitute a crowd, or assembly. Three people do not need a permit to gather at a street corner, but if those three people start a party and the number swells to 30, the police might consider the gathering a disturbance rather than an exercise in the right of assembly.

The government, however, cannot deny a permit because of the nature of the meeting or the kind of group. It cannot, for example, refuse a permit to a group that wants to remove the mayor from office or a group composed of left-wing radicals. Also, if the government denies the use of a public place to one particular group, it must do so to all groups.

Governments can impose reasonable requirements for granting permission to assemble. For example, a city may deny permission to hold a demonstration on the busiest downtown street at the height of rush hour. The city may require a bond or charge a fee to help defray the costs to the public of additional police, clean-up, and other expenses it incurs because of the meeting. Any conditions placed on one group must be applied to all.

ASSIGNMENT

The transfer of property, rights, or responsibilities from one person to another is called an assignment. You could assign the rent you receive from a house you own to your daughter, for example.

Generally you can assign duties and responsibilities you assume, but contracts often specifically prohibit such assignments. Suppose you have agreed to write an article for a magazine. As the deadline nears, you have all the research done, but you suddenly have writer's block and you cannot complete the article on time. Whether you can ask your friend who is a journalist to do it for you depends on the terms of your contract with the magazine's publisher.

ASSIGNMENT OF LOANS

A common form of assignment is the assignment of debts, such as mortgages and other types of loans. Many financial institutions assign their loans, including mortgages, to other companies; the debtor is then obligated to pay the new holder of the loan.

If the lender from whom you received your loan assigns it to another financial institution, he will inform and will also notify you of the new lender's name and address. You will then be required to make payments to the new holder of the loan.

The new holder cannot change the terms of the mortgage.

See the EVERYDAY LEGAL FORMS section, beginning on page 552, for an example of a general assignment.

THE MORTGAGE ASSIGNMENT SCAM

In the 1980's, criminals developed a highly successful scam that took this form: Homeowners were sent official-looking letters informing them that their mortgages had been assigned to the authentic-sounding institution named on the letterhead. The letters directed the homeowners to begin sending their mortgage payments to the new lender's address.

Many homeowners did so, only to learn months later from the original lenders that no assignment had ever taken place. As a result, the homeowners had become delinquent in their mortgages and were in danger of losing their homes.

STEPS TO TAKE

1. If you receive a notice of assignment of a loan, and you suspect that it is not authentic, inform your current lender.

2. If no assignment was made, notify the attorney general.

ATTACHMENT

Attachment is a legal procedure that brings the property of a debtor under the control of a court while he is being sued by his creditor. Attachment is used to keep the debtor from destroying, hiding, or otherwise disposing of property that could be used to satisfy a judgment, or court decision, that the creditor might win against the debtor.

Suppose Joseph files a lawsuit to collect a debt of $5,000 that Miles owes him. Miles has a bank account of $15,000. To prevent Miles from giving the money to his mother and thus putting it out of Joseph's reach, Joseph can ask the court to attach Miles's bank account for the amount of $5,000.

The word *attachment* is sometimes used erroneously to describe a garnishment (a court order that lets the creditor obtain his money). See GARNISHMENT.

ATTORNEY

An attorney is an agent, a person authorized to act on another's behalf. An *attorney-at-law* is an officer of the court, licensed by the state, who can be appointed by others to act on their behalf in legal matters. See LAWYER.

An *attorney-in-fact* is someone authorized by a power of attorney to act for another person in conducting business matters, in transferring property, or for other purposes. The actions of an attorney-in-fact are binding on the person who gave him the power of attorney (the principal). See POWER OF ATTORNEY.

ATTRACTIVE NUISANCE

An attractive nuisance is an object or condition on someone's property that is both potentially hazardous and attractive to children—something that might entice children to wander onto the property and become exposed to danger. A swimming pool, a tree house, or a concrete foundation could each be considered an attractive nuisance.

In general, a property owner is not legally responsible if an adult is injured while trespassing on her property. But if the trespasser is a child, the so-called attractive-nuisance doctrine in most states holds a landowner responsible for injuries suffered. To prevent an accident—as well as to avoid possible prosecution—the owner must try to minimize any risks to children playing on his or her property.

PONDS VERSUS SWIMMING POOLS

The states take different views on what constitutes an attractive nuisance. In some states, for example, ponds, trees, boulders, streams, and other naturally occurring features do not fall into this category. But manmade objects such as swimming pools, swings, see-saws, electrical towers, and heavy equipment are almost always attractive nuisances.

DETERMINING A PROPERTY OWNER'S RESPONSIBILITY

In deciding whether a property owner is to blame for a trespassing child's injuries, the courts consider several factors.

◇ Did the landowner know that children might trespass on the property? If, for example, she had previously asked children to leave, she would more likely be held responsible.

◇ Did the owner know that the object presented a risk of serious injury? No landowner can make her property completely safe for children. Nor can an owner be held responsible for certain conditions, such as cliffs or fires, that create obvious dangers.

◇ What is the child's age? The younger a child is, the less likely he is to understand the risks he may be taking, and the more likely an owner is to be held responsible for the child's injuries. Children 12 years old and under have a better chance of being financially compensated for their injuries than do teenagers. In some states 14 years is the maximum age to which the attractive-nuisance doctrine applies.

◇ What is the likelihood of injury compared to the effort needed to prevent it? A house under construction in a secluded area, for example, is not likely to be noticed by many children, and injuries received from playing around the building site would probably not be serious. Therefore, it would be unfair to expect the landowner to fence in the site. Electrical towers, in contrast, are very hazardous. If they are located in a populated area, it would not be unreasonable to expect the power company to erect fences around the towers.

AUCTION

An auction is a public sale at which items are sold by competitive bidding. Although auctions are popular with collectors and bargain hunters alike, they can present pitfalls for those who are ignorant of the basic procedures.

EXAMINING THE GOODS

Most of the time, items to be auctioned are on view before the auction takes place. If you are going to bid on an item, you should first look it over to determine its value. In the case of real estate, the auctioneer usually announces a time and date prior to the auction for inspection of the property.

TERMS OF THE AUCTION

By law, the rules and conditions that apply to an auction must be published in newspaper ads and announced at the sale before the bidding begins. An auctioneer may require that payment be in cash only, or the seller may offer no guarantees about the quality or authenticity of the property being sold. The high bidder must honor those terms, even if he was not aware of them at the time that he made his bid.

A seller can refuse to sell an item below a certain minimum price, called the upset price. He can even bid on his own property, as long as the other bidders are notified before the bidding begins. But if an auction is "without reserve," the seller can neither withdraw an item because bids are too low nor drive them up by bidding on his own property.

THE BIDDING PROCESS

Bidding may be by voice, in writing, or by a nod or hand signal. Secret signals between bidder and auctioneer are not permitted, but an auctioneer may be on the alert for a particular bidder's signal, which may be so discreet that it is not apparent to other bidders.

When offers appear to have stopped, the auctioneer usually warns bidders of their last chance to bid by saying: "Going once, going twice. . ." before he strikes a block with his hammer and says, "Sold!"

Once a high bid has been accepted, both buyer and seller are bound by the agreed price. The seller cannot accept a higher price from someone else after the auction, and the buyer cannot withdraw the bid. In some states a buyer who defaults must make up the difference between his bid and a lower resale price.

Although by law anyone can bid at an auction, the auctioneer may exercise discretion. For example, he does not have to accept bids from minors, people who are not mentally competent, or people he thinks will not honor a bid.

AUCTION SCAMS

At an auction the seller wants the highest price, while the bidders are looking for a bargain. These two opposing interests sometimes prompt unscrupulous behavior.

It is illegal for a seller to fraudulently inflate bids. Suppose a seller, determined to get the highest possible price for his Mission-style furniture, hires two people to make bids. These two accomplices, or "puffers," understand that they will not be bound by their offers, and as the auction proceeds, cast a higher bid whenever there is a lull in the bidding. When a bona fide buyer finally does win the bid, he may pay much more than the item is worth. If the buyer later discovers the scam, a court may void the sale and order the buyer's money returned.

In another common scam a potential buyer who wants to get a good deal at an auction pretends to represent a charity. The other buyers, believing they are performing a public service by letting the charity pay a lower price, are reluctant to outbid the impostor, who then gets a bargain price. If the seller discovers the buyer's ruse, he can void the sale.

For a discussion of real estate auctions, see FORECLOSURE.

AUTOMOBILE ACCIDENTS

Some automobile accidents are unavoidable, and no one can be blamed. But when the owner or operator of a motor vehicle is negligent, he will be held liable, or legally responsible, for any damages resulting from the accident.

WHAT NEGLIGENCE MEANS

With regard to automobile accidents, negligence means the failure to use ordinary or reasonable care in operating a vehicle. Under ordinary conditions, just obeying all traffic and safety laws would constitute ordinary care. But sometimes obeying the law is not enough. For example, when the roads are wet or icy, extra caution is required. The same is true when someone drives through a residential area or a school zone.

SHARED RESPONSIBILITY

Suppose an accident is due to the negligence of both drivers. For example, Jane backs out of her driveway carelessly and runs into Judy, who has just run a red light. While both drivers are at fault, Judy is more at fault than Jane. Because of situations like this, all states have what are called comparative-fault laws, which relate the amount of money a person can receive to the degree to which he was at fault. In this instance, Jane receives more compensation than Judy, because the court figured her to be only 25 percent at fault, in contrast to Judy's 75 percent. Comparative-fault laws vary, so be sure to check those in your state.

PEDESTRIANS AND PASSENGERS

The amount of care drivers must show toward pedestrians depends on who the pedestrians are. Drivers must use more care around a child, for example, and the younger the child the greater the care, because a child may not understand the dangers associated with moving vehicles. Adults and older children generally require less caution—a driver can reasonably expect that they will not step off the curb into traffic. But if the person is aged or handicapped in some way, a driver must use special care.

A driver is also obligated to the passengers in his car. The degree of care often depends on whether the passenger is an invited guest or is paying.

Many states have guest statutes that define the extent of a driver's responsibility toward nonpaying passengers. Under these laws an invited guest can recover damages (compensation for his injuries) only if the driver was grossly negligent—if he was drunk, for example.

If a passenger shares expenses with the driver, as in a car pool, he may be considered a paying passenger, in which case the guest statute would not apply. The driver may then be held financially responsible for the passenger's injuries if he failed to use ordinary care. In states without guest statutes, however, the standard of ordinary care applies to all passengers, paying or nonpaying.

CAR OWNER'S RESPONSIBILITY

Although the driver of a car can always be held responsible for negligence, the owner may be at fault too, even if he was not in the car at the time of the accident. Since cars are often shared by family members, some states have adopted a "family car," or "family purpose," doctrine. This law imposes liability on the owner when a family member causes an accident—but only if the car is being used for a family purpose. For example, if your teenage son has an accident while driving to the supermarket to buy groceries, you can be held responsible.

An owner may also be responsible for an accident if he allows a questionable person to drive his car. For example, lending a car to someone who has been drinking or who does not have a driver's license is considered negligent. See also DAMAGES; FAMILY CAR DOCTRINE; NEGLIGENCE.

SEAT BELTS

An issue that is often debated by the courts is whether your right to be compensated for injury in an automobile accident should be affected by whether you were wearing a seat belt. In some states, not wearing a seat belt may prevent you from receiving the full compensation for injuries. In other states, however, this is not the case. See also SEAT BELT LAWS.

STEPS TO TAKE IF YOU ARE IN AN ACCIDENT

It is not easy to think clearly right after an auto accident. But if you remember these steps, you may avoid trouble later on:

1. Do not move injured people until medical help arrives. Moving them can make their injuries worse.
2. If no one is injured, move the cars out of traffic to prevent another accident.
3. Call the police. They will make out a report describing how the accident happened.
4. Get the other driver's name, address, phone number, license number, and the name of his insurance company.
5. Get the names, addresses, and telephone numbers of witnesses.
6. Do not say anything to the other driver about how the accident happened, such as "Oh, it was all my fault." Such a statement may not be true, and more important, it may be used against you in court.
7. If the other driver offers to give you a check for the damages to your car in exchange for your not telling the police, say no. The amount offered may not cover the damages, or the check may bounce. In addition, by keeping silent you may be breaking a state law requiring damages over a specified amount to be reported.
8. Call your insurance agent. He will start processing your claim, and if you are out of town he may be able to get you a rental car and a place to stay.
9. If you are injured, do not sign anything until the full extent of your injuries is known. Some serious injuries do not show up until later.

AUTOMOBILE INSURANCE

Automobile accidents account for thousands of deaths and injuries each year, and the resulting medical costs, property damage, and lost wages add up to billions of dollars. An auto insurance policy is an agreement between you and an insurance company stating that, in return for a specific amount of money (the premium), the insurance company will pay for certain types of damages you sustain or cause with your automobile.

Most states require you to have a specified minimum amount of insurance coverage. If you get into an accident and you do not have insurance, you may lose your license for a year or more, and you may also be fined. Several states demand proof of coverage when your car is registered.

INSURANCE POLICIES

Insurance companies offer various kinds of auto insurance, including collision insurance; comprehensive insurance; and liability insurance, which many states require owners to have. Check your state's insurance laws before buying a policy.

No-fault insurance

In states that have no-fault insurance laws, an auto owner (as well as any other authorized driver or any passenger) who is injured in an accident collects up to a certain limit for personal injury from the owner's insurance company, no matter who was at fault. In some states, the owner may also be compensated up to a specified limit for damage to his car.

The driver applies first to his insurance company for compensation for medical expenses and lost wages. Depending on the state, if the accident was serious enough, he may also be able to sue the driver at fault for negligence. Suppose Bob speeds through a red light and smashes into the driver's side of Mary's car, paralyzing her. Bob is only slightly injured. Both Bob's and Mary's insurance companies automatically pay each of them for their injuries up to the policy limits—for example, $25,000 each. But since Mary's injuries cost her $250,000 and she was not negligent, she can sue Bob for the remaining $225,000.

Liability insurance

Most states also require liability coverage. When you are "liable," or responsible, for an accident, and you have a liability policy, your insurance company is obligated to pay for any claims made against you arising from the other driver's personal injuries and damages to his car—up to the limit of the policy. The company must also pay if an accident occurs while someone else is driving your car with your permission (but not for business purposes).

The states requiring liability insurance set low limits for coverage, and many people buy only the lowest coverage required to avoid paying higher premiums. But such frugality is ill-advised. Suppose, for example, that John hit Carol as she was crossing the street, and her resulting hospital bills total $50,000. If John's low-cost liability policy does not pay for bills amounting to more than $30,000 per person, Carol can sue John personally for the remaining $20,000 in medical expenses.

The way to avoid such a situation is to buy at least enough insurance to cover your assets. If they exceed the limits of a standard policy (usually from $300,000 to $500,000) an umbrella policy will give you an additional $1 million or more over the limit of your regular liability protection.

Some states allow members of your household to claim payment from the insurance company if they are injured in an accident that you cause. Other states specifically prohibit such payments.

If you have an accident, your insurance company will provide legal defense if you are sued for damages. But if you think your policy coverage is lower than your potential liability, you should hire your own attorney to protect your personal interests.

Collision and comprehensive insurance

Collision insurance covers the repair of your car if it is damaged in a collision with another vehicle or object, even if the collision was your fault or was intentionally caused by the other driver. For example, if someone with a grudge against you purposely crashes into your car as you pull out of your driveway, collision insurance will compensate you for any damage to your car.

Comprehensive coverage protects you against incidents not covered by collision insurance—from theft and from property damage caused by falling objects, vandalism, riots, earthquakes, fires, floods, tornadoes, hurricanes, lightning, and explosions.

Many comprehensive policies specifically exclude personal items stolen from a car, such as jewelry or important documents. But a car stereo is

REAL LIFE, REAL LAW

The Case of the Uncooperative Defendant

Ralph was three times over the legal limit for intoxication and driving approximately 100 miles an hour when he struck Ethel from behind. Ethel sued Ralph, but on the day of trial, Ralph did not appear, even though the lawyer provided by his insurance company had notified him of the time and place of the trial and the need for his presence. He had also warned Ralph that failure to cooperate could result in a loss of coverage.

The case went to trial without Ralph. The jury found in favor of Ethel and awarded her a substantial amount of money. When she tried to collect from Ralph's insurance company, the company refused to pay, citing Ralph's failure to cooperate. The company claimed that this failure relieved it of its obligations under the insurance policy, and that Ralph was personally responsible for compensating Ethel.

Your insurance company will provide your legal defense in a lawsuit resulting from an accident that was your fault, but you have an obligation to cooperate with the lawyers. If you fail to do so, the company may refuse to pay any compensation it owes to the injured person, leaving you stuck with the bills.

different; it is often considered equipment that is part of the car, and so may be covered by the policy.

Both collision and comprehensive coverage include a "deductible" clause, which specifies an amount, usually $250 or $500, that you must pay before the insurance company will pay compensation. If the cost of your broken windshield is $279 and the deductible is $250, your insurance company will give you only $29 to pay for the windshield; the rest comes out of your own pocket.

Uninsured and underinsured motorist coverage
With uninsured motorist coverage, a driver or a member of his family will be compensated for bodily injury inflicted by an uninsured or a hit-and-run driver. In some states this coverage may also include underinsured motorists, such as those who have only the required minimum liability insurance. Your insurance company will pay what the other driver's did not cover. In no-fault states this coverage may not be necessary.

Medical payments insurance
Medical payments insurance provides compensation for medical expenses to you, your family members, and your passengers, regardless of fault. You and your family are also covered while walking or riding in another car. The policy may also cover injuries suffered by someone who is getting in or out of your car—for example, when a passenger accidentally slams the door on his finger.

Personal injury protection
Generally more extensive than medical payments insurance, personal injury protection (PIP) insurance guarantees payment up to the limit of the policy for medical bills resulting from an accident, even if it was due to the owner's own negligence. Depending on the state, coverage may also include lost wages and may pay the salary of someone who performs the injured person's duties—for example, a nursemaid who takes care of an injured mother's children. If an accident causes serious injury or death and the owner was not at fault, he (or his heirs) may usually collect from the PIP policy and then sue the other driver for damages beyond the PIP coverage. In no-fault states, whether the owner has the right to sue the other driver is determined by law. PIP is required in states with no-fault laws; it is an option in others.

DETERMINING INSURANCE RATES

When fixing rates for drivers, insurance companies consider such factors as: (1) their age and marital status; (2) the make, model, and year of the car; (3) the ages of additional drivers (especially teenagers); (4) driving records of the persons to be insured; (5) how the car will be used; and (6) the owner's place of residence.

Insurance rates are higher or lower according to the driver's "risk group" and how much protection is desired. A $50,000 liability policy for a male teenager costs much more than the same coverage for a 50-year-old woman, because statistical data show that the male teenager is much more likely to have an accident.

Insurance companies may raise their rates after a claim is filed, even if the insured was not at fault. They base their rate increases on the number of claims filed by the driver, not just the dollar amounts they might have to pay out. The insurance rates for someone who has had five "fender benders" will probably be raised more readily than those of a person who has made a claim for only one serious accident.

AUTOMOBILE PURCHASE

Buying an automobile, whether new or used, usually means spending a lot of money. For this reason and because a number of things can go wrong in the process, you should know your legal rights.

BUYING A NEW CAR

When you buy a new car, you enter into a contract. As is the case with any other contract, the best time to prevent a problem is before you put your signature on the dotted line.

Financing
Determine in advance how much you can afford to pay. Most lenders will help you figure out this amount. The rule of thumb they use is that your total monthly debt payments should amount to no more than 20 percent of your income after taxes. Many lenders preapprove car loans so that you know before you shop how

much you can pay. A dealer, knowing what your limits are, may decide to give you a better price on the car.

Never take the automobile before you have arranged the financing. If your financing falls through and you have to return the car, your purchase contracts may require you to pay a fee for each day you have possession of the car plus an additional amount for each mile you have driven it. If this happens, you could lose a considerable amount of money.

Taking delivery

Before you accept a car, be sure to inspect it and take it for a test drive. Do this even if you have already driven the same or a similar model before, because every single automobile is different.

Be particularly careful if your car was specially ordered from the factory. If you notice any defects, or if the car you receive is not exactly what you ordered, you have the right to reject it. But the dealer has the right to modify the car to the proper specifications within a reasonable time, and if he does so, you must accept it.

It is the dealer's duty to deliver your car within a "reasonable time" after the delivery date specified on the purchase order. For example, a reasonable time for delivering a standard inexpensive car might be a week after the date specified but much longer for a limited-production import.

If the dealer does not deliver in a reasonable time, you may have the right to cancel the order and get back your down payment. If the dealer knew when he took your order that he could not deliver the car on time, you may be able to sue him for fraud as well.

The warranty

Every new car sold in the United States comes with a manufacturer's warranty, which the dealer must give you. A typical manufacturer's warranty covers defects in materials and workmanship for 12 months or 12,000 miles, with a longer period of coverage for such major components as the engine, the transmission, and the power train.

Most states have laws stating that new cars come with an implied (unwritten) "warranty of merchantability." This type of warranty assures a consumer that the product he is buying meets certain minimum standards of quality and safety. If it does not meet these standards, the dealer or manufacturer may be held responsible. See WARRANTY AND GUARANTY.

Both federal and state laws protect car buyers from getting stuck with a "lemon"—a new car with recurring problems. See LEMON LAW.

ABC's OF ILLEGAL AUTO DEALER PRACTICES

Consumer protection laws prohibit new- and used-car dealers from making certain claims and engaging in fraudulent practices. It is illegal for an auto dealer to:

- ❑ Refuse to show you a car that has been advertised at a low price unless it has already been sold; or substitute a car that has less equipment than the advertised car.
- ❑ Knowingly conceal the fact that a car has been repainted, repaired, rebuilt, or damaged in shipment.
- ❑ Advertise a car it does not have in its possession, unless the ad clearly states when the car will become available.
- ❑ Sell a used car that does not display the federally required warranty information sticker on the window.

BUYING A USED CAR

You should handle the purchase of a used car differently from that of a new car.

Inspection

Before you agree to buy a used car, arrange for an independent inspection of it. A reputable dealer will not object to such a request. If the dealer does object, you can assume he has something to hide.

Have the car inspected by a mechanic you trust. He may see mechanical problems that would otherwise have been overlooked. The dealer may then correct minor problems or lower the price. If the problems affect the engine, transmission, or other major components, look for another car.

Other precautions

If the dealer tells you that major work was done on the car, such as installing a new engine, ask to see the receipts. Give these to your mechanic so that he can make certain that the work was actually completed.

Although the practice is illegal, a dishonest used-car dealer may set back the odometer on a car to lower the mileage, thus increasing its apparent value. Ask your mechanic to check to see if the car's overall condition seems to match the mileage on the odometer. If you have any reason to believe the odometer has been adjusted, you would be well advised to look for another dealer and another car.

Another protection against odometer tampering is provided by federal law—namely, a form that includes a signed statement verifying the mileage. The odometer form must be filled out by the seller of the car (whether a dealer or a private individual) and presented to the buyer.

Used car warranties
Federal law requires used-car dealers to display a sticker in the window of each car indicating what kind of warranty it has. If there is no warranty, the sticker must clearly state that the car will be sold "as is"—without a warranty.

If a warranty is offered, the dealer must indicate on the sticker whether it is a full warranty or limited warranty, how long it will last, and what parts and systems are covered. If the buyer will have to pay part of the repair costs, the sticker must indicate the amount. For example, the warranty might cover only half the cost of transmission repairs for a certain period of time. If it should break within that period, the dealer will repair it, but the owner will have to pay 50 percent of the bill.

Used car dealers sometimes offer optional warranties, but these are often expensive, cover things that rarely go wrong, and have a short duration. If you are tempted to buy an optional warranty just to be safe, read it carefully so that you don't spend good money for something that is essentially worthless.

Buying a car from the owner
Buying a used car from a private individual poses a different problem. Unless he sells cars on a regular basis, an owner is not considered a dealer and will not be bound by the standard laws that protect consumers. If the car falls apart even one day after you buy it, you may have no recourse. However, many good bargains are to be found from private car owners, who would rather sell their cars quickly than spend the time and effort trying to get higher prices.

Be sure to have the car inspected by a mechanic you know and trust. Don't be afraid to ask pointed questions about the car's problems. Most private individuals would rather tell the truth and risk losing a sale than be accused of misrepresentation later.

PUTTING IT IN WRITING

Whether you are buying a new or a used car and whether from a dealer or a private individual, it is essential to get any oral promises from the seller included in a written contract. For example, if the salesperson at a dealership promises to include stereo speakers in the back as well as the front of the car or to provide rustproofing at no extra cost, you may not be able to collect on these promises unless they are written into your contract. See also CONSUMER PROTECTION.

AUTOMOBILE REGISTRATION

The purpose of automobile registration is to give the state some measure of control over the cars that operate on its roads and highways. Through registration, automobiles and their owners are identified in public records, and this enables car sales, thefts, and accidents to be monitored.

In all states you must obtain a registration certificate and license plates in order to drive your car on public roads. In a number of states you must also carry your registration certificate whenever you drive.

Other requirements for registration vary from state to state. Some states require vehicles to pass emissions tests or safety inspections, while others do not.

If you move to another state, you are usually allowed a grace period of 10 to 30 days to register your car in that state. A similar grace period is sometimes allowed between the expiration date of a registration and the date it must be renewed.

If your vehicle is not properly registered, you can be fined, and your vehicle may be towed and impounded if it is parked on a public street. You may

CHECKLIST

How to Sell Your Car

The easiest way to sell your car is to take it to a dealer and accept whatever price he offers. If you want the best price, however, you will have to sell it privately, and that means doing a little work. These guidelines will help you through the process:

❑ **FIND OUT WHAT YOUR CAR IS WORTH.**
Before you set a price, find out the approximate value of your car. Look in one of the used-car price books, called "blue books," or take your automobile to used-car dealers and ask what they would give you.

❑ **MAKE YOUR CAR LOOK ITS BEST.**
People tend to judge a book by its cover, so wash and wax your car, clean the inside, and be sure the horn, lights, and doors work.

❑ **BE SURE THE CAR WILL PASS INSPECTION.**
A car that meets your state's standards for safety and emissions is a much more attractive buy than one that needs work.

❑ **ADVERTISE.**
Place a classified ad in your local newspaper and post ads on community bulletin boards, such as the ones in supermarkets. The ad should include the car's make, model, year, options, condition, mileage, and your asking price. State that the sale is "by owner" and give your phone number. Also place a for-sale sign in the window of the car, with your phone number and the price.

❑ **GET THE PAPERS TOGETHER.**
Ask your state motor vehicle department what forms to use and what procedure to follow when you transfer ownership of your car. Be sure you have the car's title, registration, warranties, and service records on hand.

❑ **PREPARE A BILL OF SALE.**
The bill of sale should include the following: your name and address and that of the buyer, the date of sale, a description of the automobile, the vehicle identification number, the license plate number, the odometer reading, and the price. Also, state that the car is being sold "as is" (without any guarantees).

❑ **DON'T LIE TO THE BUYER.**
In most states, you are not legally required to tell the buyer about your car's defects, but if he asks, you must either tell him the whole truth or decline to say anything at all. If you lie or tell only half the truth, the buyer may sue you.

❑ **ALLOW A TEST DRIVE.**
Test drives are customary, but be sure the buyer has a valid driver's license before he gets behind the wheel. Ride along with him to be sure he does not steal your car.

❑ **DON'T TAKE RISKS WHEN GETTING PAID.**
Ask the buyer to pay you with a certified check, cashier's check, money order, or cash. If he pays by personal check, keep the automobile until the check clears.

have to pay the towing and storage charges in order to reclaim your car.

AUTOMOBILE RENTAL

Rental car companies are allowed to make their own rules about who can rent a car. Some of their restrictions seem discriminatory, but they are not against the law.

Most companies will not rent to a person under 21 years of age, and some charge higher rates for drivers under 25. One common requirement is that renters must present at least one major credit card, even though the company will accept payment by cash or traveler's check when the car is returned.

COLLISION INSURANCE

When renting a car, you will be offered the chance to buy collision insurance, often called a collision-damage waiver or loss-damage waiver, usually costing $10 or more per day. This insurance will protect you from financial responsibility for any damage to the rental car.

In most states, if you refuse collision coverage you can be held responsible for damage up to the full value of the car, no matter how the damage was caused—even if a drunken driver hit the automobile while it was parked or a police car hit it while running a red light.

ALTERNATIVE COLLISION INSURANCE

If you have an automobile insurance policy, you may find that it automatically extends collision coverage to include a rented car. Be sure to read your policy, however, as some policies exclude this coverage.

Many credit card companies provide free collision insurance if you use their card when you rent a car. But you may be required to seek reimbursement from your primary insurer before they will pay a claim, or to pay the damages out of your own pocket before they will reimburse you.

AUTOMOBILE REPAIR

Few things are anticipated with as much dread as having to take your car to the repair shop. For one thing, you expect it will cost twice or 10 times what it should. And what will you do if the car still does not run properly?

Most of the problems that come with auto repairs can be avoided by simply taking a few precautions. For example, if a dispute arises about the work that was done or the cost of the repairs, you are in a better position when you can offer written documents as evidence of your agreement with the repair shop. The most important documents are the written estimate and the work order.

THE WRITTEN ESTIMATE

In many states a repair shop is legally required to provide a written estimate. The estimate should list the cost of each part and note whether the parts being installed are used, reconditioned, or rebuilt. A separate list should indicate the estimated cost of labor. Ask for a written estimate even if your state does not require it and, if possible, get two or more additional estimates from different repair shops.

Having a written estimate on hand can be important if the final bill is higher than the estimate. Although it is not unusual for the estimate to be less than the final bill, a wide gap between the two raises some questions about the repair shop's reliability.

Some repair shops stoop to the unscrupulous practice of giving an extremely low estimate to attract a customer, while knowing that the final bill will be much higher. This is called lowballing and is a type of fraud. If you are a victim of lowballing, you can file a lawsuit to recover the cost of the repairs. With a written estimate it is much easier to prove in court that lowballing occurred. The court may award you extra money—called punitive damages—in addition to the cost of repairs, to discourage the shop from repeating the practice in the future.

THE WORK ORDER

As important as the estimate is the work order—the document you sign authorizing the repair work. In most states a repair shop can legally charge a customer only for the work that appears on the work order. It is important, though, that you have the repair shop indicate the price of the work to be done as specifically as possible on the order. In the case of a lowball, for example, the mechanic may tell you the work will cost $200, write out a work order with no specific price, and then charge you $800. In this situation, if you refuse to pay, the repair shop can legally put a lien on your car. The best thing to do is pay the bill and then take the case to small-claims court.

In a dispute, the work order,

ABC's OF AUTO REPAIR RIP-OFFS

The relatively few "rotten apples" in the auto repair business have managed to give the whole industry a bad name. Some of their most common schemes and the ways to avoid them include:

❑ Claiming that certain repairs must be done when they are not necessary. (Get a second opinion from another repair shop.)

❑ Using old parts and charging for new ones. (Ask for written proof that the parts are new or have them inspected by another mechanic.)

❑ Failing to give the removed parts to the customer for his inspection. (Stipulate in the work order that you must be given the old parts.)

❑ Making repairs that the customer never requested or charging for work that was never done. (Make sure all work to be done is itemized on the work order. If possible, watch the mechanic while he does the work.)

which is a contract, can be used by either party as evidence for its claims. Because it has such legal importance, you should fully understand what you are signing. Make sure that any vague or incorrect items on a work order are clarified and corrected. Never sign a blank work order, since it gives the repair shop the authority to make whatever repairs it wants and charge for them.

WARRANTIES AND PARTS

Before you choose a repair shop, find out what kinds of warranties, or guarantees, the shop provides for parts and labor. The warranties should be included on the work order or put in writing somewhere else. You will need to know about these documents in the event that the work has not been done to your satisfaction.

Another way to safeguard your interests is to request that any parts removed from your car be saved and returned to you. These parts could be useful evidence if a dispute develops over the work performed. Unless the parts are under warranty and have to be returned to the manufacturer, you have a right to keep them. If necessary, have them checked by another mechanic to see if they really needed to be replaced. See WARRANTY AND GUARANTY.

UNSATISFACTORY WORK

If you are dissatisfied with the repair work on your car, you can respond in several ways. You can give the repair shop the chance to redo the job, or if that does not work, you can take the car to another place.

Although you will have to pay another repair bill by taking your car elsewhere, the second bill can be used to show that the work was not done properly by the first shop. You may then be able to get the original shop to give you a refund. If they will not do so, you can file a lawsuit in small-claims court to recover your loss or try to resolve the dispute through arbitration.

RIGHTS OF THE REPAIR SHOP

Just as you have the right to expect proper repair work, the shop has the right to be paid for work well done. If the customer does not pay, most states will give the shop a mechanic's lien, which allows the shop to keep the car until payment has been made. In some states the lien is automatically created when the repair work is completed—the shop owner does not have to file a document with the court.

While a lien is in effect, the shop may charge a customer fees for storing the car until the repair bill is paid. To avoid the lien and the additional storage cost, you should consider paying a contested bill first and then look into other legal alternatives that may be able to resolve the dispute. See also ALTERNATIVE DISPUTE RESOLUTION; ARBITRATION; MECHANIC'S LIEN; SMALL-CLAIMS COURT.

AUTOPSY

When a person dies, a dissection of the body is sometimes performed to find out the cause of death. This procedure is called an autopsy and is legally required only when a coroner decides it is necessary.

A coroner usually requests an autopsy when a death is unexplained, unexpected, suspicious, or violent. For example, if a body is discovered in a car at the bottom of a river, an autopsy is needed to establish the cause of death. It is important to know whether the death was caused by a heart attack, for instance, or by a malicious act committed before the automobile entered the water. The results of an autopsy are kept on file in the coroner's office and can be used as evidence in a trial.

A family may object for religious or other personal reasons to having their loved one's body subjected to an autopsy. But when one is required by law, it must be performed regardless of family objections.

Usually the family would rather have an autopsy performed than remain ignorant about the cause of death. If the cause of death proves to be a physical ailment, such as an unsuspected heart condition, family members can benefit by knowing about it. Such knowledge may put them on the alert to seek treatment for the same condition in themselves. On the other hand, if murder is suspected, the family can be satisfied that the police will have information that is necessary to pursue justice.

If an autopsy is performed without the family's permission and for reasons that do not conform to state law, the family will have substantial grounds to initiate a lawsuit.

FROM BABYSITTER TO BUYERS CLUB

BABYSITTER

Someone who is temporarily entrusted with the care of another person's child—usually just for an evening but sometimes for a few days or more—is known familiarly as a babysitter. The sitter must follow the parents' instructions in regard to meals, bedtimes, and the like, and is legally required to use reasonable precautions to protect the child's safety.

But if your child gets sick or is injured while in the care of a sitter, the sitter does not have the legal authority to obtain medical treatment. Suppose your child starts vomiting and has a fever and the sitter takes him to the hospital. The medical staff will not treat him without your permission unless they consider his condition a medical emergency.

Such a situation has obvious risks, especially if you leave your child in the care of a babysitter for an extended period of time—for example, while you attend an out-of-town wedding. One way to protect your child is to grant the babysitter medical power of attorney, authorizing her to consent to treatment if it becomes necessary. In such a situation the babysitter must be an adult, because power of attorney cannot be granted to minors.

If you are leaving your child in the care of a minor, consider giving special power of attorney to a neighbor or a relative who lives nearby. A sample form for special power of attorney is included in the section titled EVERYDAY LEGAL FORMS, beginning on page 552. See also DAY CARE.

BAD FAITH

Fraud or dishonesty in dealing with another person, either by misleading him or by refusing to fulfill a contractual obligation, is known as bad faith. When a dealer sells a reconditioned television set, claiming it is new, he is acting in bad faith.

Although acting in bad faith is not a crime, it can affect the opinion of a judge or jury that is deciding a lawsuit. Because our society values fairness (good faith), a person who is found to have acted in bad faith is unlikely to win his suit.

The concepts of good faith and bad faith apply equally to buyers and sellers. A shopper who buys a party dress can expect that its quality is reasonably good and that she will not have to return it because of defects. The retailer can assume that the customer is honestly buying the dress and does not plan to return it once the party is over.

BAIL

In the American system of justice, a person accused of a crime is considered innocent until proved guilty. Bail is the release of an accused person awaiting trial in return for his promise that he will appear in court on the trial date.

BAIL BOND

Although sometimes a court may release an accused person on his own recognizance (his written promise to appear), most situations require the posting of a sum of money, also called bail.

The amount of bail depends on the nature of the crime and the accused person's links to the community, such as steady employment, property ownership, and family ties. Each of these factors helps a court assess the likelihood that a defendant will appear for trial and not "jump bail." If the accused shows up as required, the bail is returned to the person who put it up.

When bail is granted, a court may impose restrictions that will also help to ensure the appearance of the accused in court. For example, a court may restrict his freedom to travel, the kind of people with whom he associates, or his living arrangements. Failure to observe such conditions imposed by the court constitutes a separate violation of the law.

The accused may find his bail revoked, and he may have to spend additional time in jail.

THE BAIL BONDSMAN

Although excessive bail is forbidden under the Constitution, bail is ineffective unless the amount is set high enough to discourage forfeiture—usually more money than most defendants can afford on their own. Money for bail can be obtained from bail bondsmen, moneylenders who will, for a fee, guarantee to pay the full amount of bail if the accused jumps bail. The bondsman's fee is usually about 10 percent of the bail amount. He does not have to lend the money if he considers the defendant a poor risk.

Suppose John is accused of burglary and bail is set at $5,000, which John cannot afford. John's attorney locates a bail bondsman, who for a $500 fee posts a bond with the court guaranteeing payment if John does not appear. John is then released until the trial date. For his own protection, the bondsman may also require John to provide collateral such as jewelry, securities, or written guarantees of payment signed by relatives or friends.

If John does appear at the trial, the bondsman gets his $5,000 back and also keeps the $500 John paid him. If John does not appear at his trial (having decided to leave town rather than face charges), the bail bondsman forfeits the $5,000, but gets to keep the collateral (if any) that John provided. The bondsman also has the right to personally pursue and arrest John.

HOW TO FIND A BONDSMAN

Most bail bondsmen have their offices near the local courthouse or police station, and many advertise their services in the Yellow Pages. The police and lawyers in the community are the best sources of information on bail bondsmen. Should you or a member of your family be arrested, you will certainly need to find an experienced attorney, who will take care of arranging bail.

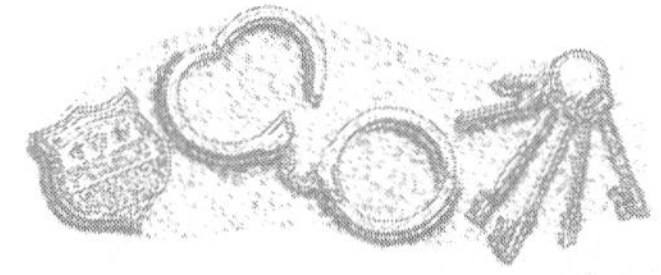

BAILMENT

When you lend your lawn mower to your neighbor, have your car parked by a lot attendant, or take your VCR to the shop for repair, you have created a type of contract known as a bailment. In each of these and many other situations, property, and the responsibility for it, passes from the hands of one person (the bailor) to another (the bailee). Every consumer who makes such a transaction should know when a bailment is created and the responsibilities of the parties concerned.

HOW BAILMENT IS CREATED

Three steps are required for a bailment to exist. First, the property must be delivered to the bailee, who then has charge of it. This happens, for example, when you let your neighbor borrow your lawn mower.

Sometimes the property itself may not actually be delivered to the bailee, but the bailee may obtain possession and control of it. This kind of delivery, called constructive delivery, occurs when a bank gives a customer the key to a safe-deposit box. Although the box remains with the bank, the customer has control because he has the key.

Second, the bailee must know that the property is being delivered and agree to receive it. If you deliver your VCR to the repair shop without informing a clerk that you are doing so, the shop will not be responsible if someone steals it.

Third, because bailment is a type of contract, there must be some "consideration"—something of value given or relinquished by one person to induce the other to agree to the contract. The bailor's temporary loss of possession of his property in exchange for the bailee's promise to return it later is all the consideration required for a bailment.

THREE KINDS OF BAILMENT

The person to whom you entrust your property has varying degrees of responsibility for it, depending on the type of bailment. Three kinds of bailment can be created.

◇ When you deliver your VCR to the repair shop and the owner agrees to repair it for a price, you have created a bailment for mutual benefit. Your benefit is getting the machine fixed; the shop owner benefits by getting paid. In this type of bailment, the bailee must exercise ordinary care while the property is in his possession. If he leaves the VCR on the edge of the table and he accidentally knocks it off, the bailee is responsible for damage to the VCR. But if an armed robber stole the machine at gunpoint, the shop owner would not be responsible.

◇ When you leave your wristwatch in the safe provided by your athletic club, you have created a bailment for the sole benefit of the bailor, you. The club is therefore not responsible for loss or damage to your watch unless its employees are grossly negligent. If the safe alarm fails suddenly and someone walks in and takes your watch, the club will not be responsible. But if the safe keeper simply leaves the door open and goes out for coffee, the club will be responsible.

◇ Lending your lawn mower to your neighbor creates a bailment for the sole benefit of the bailee. You gain nothing by relinquishing your property to her. In this situation your neighbor must be very careful not to lose or damage the lawn mower. If she runs your mower over a metal sprinkler head and destroys the mower blade, she is responsible for repairing it.

Bait-and-Switch

The ad in the Sunday newspaper sounds tempting. Steaks, roasts, and chops are all priced below your local supermarket's prices for ground beef. When you arrive at the store to take advantage of the bargain, the clerk seems less than eager to sell you the advertised special. "That meat's tough and fatty," she tells you. "Why not consider our Executive Special? It costs more, but the quality is good."

When you find that the Executive Special is twice what you had expected to pay, you tell the clerk you will take your chances with the advertised special. "Sorry," she says, "but the special is all sold out."

If this happens, you have been subjected to a technique known as bait-and-switch, in which an item (the bait) is advertised at a bargain price to lure you into the store. Once there, you are told that the advertised item is inferior or unavailable, and you are urged to buy the more expensive version (the switch).

When confronted with this kind of sales tactic, your best step is out the door. You should also consider filing a complaint with your state's department of consumer affairs. The bait-and-switch technique is illegal in every state, and merchants who engage in it can be fined and required to make restitution to victimized consumers.

Balloon Loan

In a balloon loan, the final payment is significantly larger than each of the previous payments. If not properly understood, a balloon loan can cause trouble for the unwary buyer.

Balloon mortgages are often used when a seller finances the purchase of his home for the buyer. The buyer makes monthly payments of principal (the money borrowed) and interest as though the loan extended over a 15- or 30-year period. However, the principal becomes due as a lump sum much earlier—for instance, after three or five years—and at that time the buyer must pay off the balance (the balloon payment). Because the monthly payments on the loan usually consist primarily of interest, very little principal is repaid before the balloon payment becomes due. The buyer may therefore owe almost as much as he did originally. See also MORTGAGE.

Bank Account

When you have a bank account, you have an agreement with the bank whereby you can deposit money with it and the bank, in return, will pay you interest or let you draw checks against the money, or both.

Holders of bank accounts today have a number of advantages not available in the past. Many of these are the result of the deregulation of the banking industry that took place in the 1980's. For example, restrictions affecting minimum balances and interest rates were eliminated, and savings banks can offer interest-bearing checking accounts, called NOW (negotiable order of withdrawal) accounts. If you have a bank account, your rights and responsibilities, and those of the bank, are determined by the type of account you open. Deposits fall primarily into two categories: general and special.

GENERAL DEPOSITS

Most bank accounts—including checking, savings, money market accounts and certificates of deposit—consist of what are called general deposits. When you make a general deposit, you transfer ownership of your money to the bank, which can use it to make loans or investments or to help run the bank.

When you make a general deposit, you are essentially giving the bank a loan. The bank gives you a deposit slip as proof of the loan and creates a credit in your account against which you can withdraw funds. As your debtor, the bank is legally obligated to pay out money from your account according to your instructions.

SPECIAL DEPOSITS

Unlike general deposits, special deposits do not become the property of the bank. The bank merely holds the money and, upon the depositor's demand, returns the money to the depositor or pays it to someone else. The most common types of special deposits are money held in escrow (for example, a deposit on a home), items placed in a safe-deposit box, and money put in a trust fund.

Special deposits represent a kind of bailment—that is, you have delivered your personal property to the temporary custody of another person or organization. You retain ownership of the property and the bank must either return it to you or deliver it to someone else according to your instructions. See also Bailment; Escrow; Safe-Deposit Box; Trust.

WHAT THE DIFFERENCE MEANS TO YOU

Knowing the differences between general and special deposits is important, because the way your money is deposited can affect you legally and financially.

Loss of funds
Since funds in a general deposit are under the control of the bank, the bank must bear the responsibility for any loss. If the bank pays $500 to a thief who has stolen your passbook, it must replace your money.

But if a special deposit is lost, stolen, or destroyed, and the bank has exercised reasonable care over the money, the bank will not be held responsible for the loss. Suppose a bank holds a trust account for Paul, with Paul's nephew Earl as the trustee. Earl withdraws $500 from the account, ostensibly to benefit Paul, but uses it to buy himself a suit. The bank is not responsible for the loss, and Paul must seek repayment from the trustee.

Loans
General and special deposits are treated differently with respect to loans. Suppose you take out a loan at the bank where you have your savings account, which is a general-deposit account. If you are unable to pay the full amount of the loan when it falls due, the bank is allowed to dip into your savings account to make up the difference. However, the bank is forbidden to take money from a special-deposit account.

TIME DEPOSITS AND DEMAND DEPOSITS

If you have a certificate of deposit, Christmas Club account, or vacation-fund account, you have what is known as a time deposit. You lend your money to the bank for a specified length of time and you cannot withdraw money from the account before the time has gone by. The advantage of time deposits is that the bank usually gives you a higher return. The disadvantage is that your money is tied up for the specified time and you have to pay substantial penalties if you withdraw your money prematurely.

Most general-deposit accounts are demand-deposit accounts: you can withdraw some or all of your money at any time. Checking and savings accounts are demand-deposit accounts, but are subject to federal regulations regarding the availability of funds.

GETTING AT YOUR MONEY

The Expedited Funds Availability Act (EFAA) requires banks to give you next-day access to certain funds deposited in a demand-deposit account. These include cash deposits, automatic deposits, and funds from government checks, certified checks, cashier's checks, checks drawn on other accounts at the same bank, and the first $100 of a day's check deposits to the account.

You must be given access to funds deposited from local checks within two business days, and you must have access to funds from nonlocal checks within five business days. In at your bank, ask the customer service department.

CHECKLIST

Tips for Safe Banking

A simple trip to the bank can sometimes be more dangerous than you might think. Here are a few ways to protect yourself:

❑ **DO NOT ENDORSE CHECKS YOU ARE TAKING TO THE BANK FOR DEPOSIT.**
If you do, add the words "for deposit only" next to your signature. A check with only your signature on the back is a blank endorsement. In other words, anyone can cash the check if you happen to lose it.

❑ **FOLLOW YOUR BANK'S INSTRUCTIONS WHEN YOU DEPOSIT CASH IN A DEPOSIT BOX OR AN AUTOMATIC TELLER MACHINE (ATM).**
Your money could disappear if, for example, the envelope in which you place your deposit is not sealed properly, does not contain a deposit slip, or is put in the wrong slot.

❑ **WHEN YOU GET CASH FROM A TELLER, COUNT IT RIGHT AWAY.**
Be sure to count your cash with your hands on top of the counter, so that they are in full view of the teller. Then, if you are shortchanged, it will be much simpler to prove.

❑ **DO NOT LEAVE THE BANK WITH CASH IN YOUR HAND.**
Put it out of sight first, and be wary of anyone who is watching you, who jostles you, or who follows you. If you are robbed even while inside the bank, the bank is not responsible because the money was in your possession when it was taken.

❑ **BE CAUTIOUS WHEN YOU USE AN ATM.**
Do not use an ATM in a dark or isolated area, and be on the lookout for people loitering nearby. Also, when using an ATM, shield your personal identification number (PIN) from people standing behind you, and do not walk away until you have put away your money.

addition, on the day that money from deposited checks has registered in your account, up to $400 of it must be made available to you for cash withdrawal after 5:00 P.M.

There are a few exceptions to these EFAA rules. The bank is allowed to deny you access to your money temporarily if your demand-deposit account is less than 30 days old, or if you have a history of bounced checks. However, the bank must tell you why it is denying access to your funds and when they will be available.

States may also have laws determining how long a bank can hold your deposit before making the funds available to you, and often these laws make the funds available sooner than the EFAA requires. Some banks, however, grant customers access to funds sooner than either state or federal law requires. To find out the policy

JOINT ACCOUNTS

Bank accounts can be set up for one person or more. The signature card of the account indicates who is entitled to withdraw the funds. Unless the terms of the account state otherwise, each person listed on the signature card owns the funds in the account and has access to them. If one person dies, the funds belong to the surviving owner or owners. Heirs of the deceased owner will have no claim to the money unless they are owners of the account.

Sometimes joint accounts are set up for the convenience of one of the owners during his lifetime, and not to give the other person ownership. Suppose you want to name another person on your account so that she can make deposits and withdrawals for you, but you do not want the money to become her property in the event of your death. In order for the bank to understand your intentions, you must include careful instructions on the signature card when you open the account.

POD ACCOUNTS OR TOTTEN TRUSTS

If the account is in your name only, you are the only one who can withdraw funds from it. When you die, the account will be passed on to your heirs as part of your estate. However, if you want to avoid having the account included as part of your estate for probate, you can arrange for a person of your choice to receive it upon your death. By doing so, you have created a payable-on-death (POD) account, which is also called a Totten trust. See PROBATE; TOTTEN TRUST.

YOUR BANK STATEMENT

Your bank is required to provide you with a periodic statement—a document that shows the status of your account. You should check the statement carefully and report any errors as soon as possible. If you do not, you may not be able to recover any money you lose owing to a bank error.

But if the bank makes a mistake in your favor and credits your account with $5,000, for example, you must report the error to the bank. If you withdraw the money you may have to face criminal charges. See also CHECK; ELECTRONIC FUNDS TRANSFER ACT.

STEPS TO TAKE

Here are some suggestions that might be useful to you if you have a problem with your bank account:

1. Talk to a bank officer or someone in the bank's customer service department. Most banks will make an effort to resolve your problem as quickly as possible.

2. If the problem cannot be resolved to your satisfaction, write or call your state banking department. You can get the address and telephone number from your local library.

3. If your bank is a member of the Federal Reserve System, call or write the Federal Reserve office in your area and explain your problem.

BANK FAILURE

An unexpected side effect of federal bank deregulation became evident in the late 1980's, when banks began to fail at an alarming rate, owing to unwise and sometimes dishonest investments by banks. In fact, more banks failed between 1987 and 1991 than during the entire Great Depression. In 1990 banks and savings and loan institutions closed at the rate of one per day.

Consumers became concerned about the safety of their deposits, even though since 1934 accounts in commercial banks have been insured by the Federal Deposit Insurance Corporation (FDIC) and in savings banks by the Federal Savings and Loan Insurance Corporation (FSLIC). (In 1989 the FSLIC became a division of the FDIC.) Although all national and state banks belonging to the Federal Reserve System must be insured by the FDIC, depositors nevertheless feared that the insurance money available for compensating the customers of closed banks would run out because of the sheer number of failures.

The FDIC insures each account in its member banks to a maximum of $100,000. If a bank fails, depositors receive the full amount of their deposits up to this amount. If you have more than $100,000 to deposit, you should divide the amount into several different accounts of less than $100,000 each. Keep each account in a different bank. You can maintain several accounts in the same bank under different names, but doing so is risky.

Some states also provide insurance coverage for state banks and other financial institutions, but these insurance funds have often proved inadequate to protect depositors after a large bank failure. Customers of failed banks in Colorado and Rhode Island that were covered only by state insurance have received settlements that were far less than the amounts that were deposited. Most state-chartered, state-insured banks have now acquired FDIC protection.

IF YOUR BANK FAILS

When a bank fails, the FDIC first tries to find a buyer to take over the bank. Often a larger, stronger institution assumes the accounts of a failed bank. For most customers, very little of consequence changes when their bank fails. While accounts are being transferred, access to funds is limited for a day or two, but soon the new bank issues account information and checks to customers.

If the FDIC cannot find a buyer for a troubled bank and the bank closes, depositors receive payment up to the insured maximum of $100,000 within 10 business days of the closing. The payment may be in the form of a check, or the depositor's account may be transferred to another bank.

STEPS TO TAKE

If you have a question, concern, or complaint about the business practices of your bank, write for help as indicated:

1. If your bank is nationally chartered, write to the Comptroller of the Currency, Consumer Affairs Division, Washington, DC 20219. A bank is nationally chartered if it says "National Bank of . . ." or if the letters "N.A." follow its name.

2. If your bank is a member of the Federal Reserve System, write to the Board of Governors, Federal Reserve System, Division of Consumer Affairs, Washington, DC 20551.

3. If your bank is insured by the FDIC, write to: Federal Deposit Insurance Corporation, Office of Bank Customer Affairs, Washington, DC 20429.

4. If your bank is state chartered, there should be an office of bank supervision in your state capital. You should be able to obtain its official name and address from the local office of a state legislator.

See also Bank Account; Check; Credit Union; Federal Deposit Insurance Corporation (FDIC); Savings and Loan Association.

BANKRUPTCY

Federal bankruptcy laws provide a legal procedure by which a debtor obtains relief from the demands of his creditors. The Constitution gives Congress full authority to make bankruptcy laws, and the federal courts administer them.

Although bankruptcy was once considered a source of personal shame, changes in the bankruptcy laws and a shift in public sentiment have made it more common and acceptable. Nevertheless, you should consider bankruptcy only as a last resort, since it can remain in your credit history for up to 10 years. During that period, it may be very difficult to obtain credit. Not only creditors, but potential employers avoid bankrupts. You should look into the available alternatives before filing for bankruptcy.

ALTERNATIVES TO BANKRUPTCY

If your financial troubles are only temporary, get in touch with your creditors first and try to renegotiate payments until your financial circumstances improve. The creditor may be willing to accept a smaller total amount to settle the outstanding debt.

The Consumer Credit Counseling Service, a nationwide nonprofit organization listed in local telephone directories, also can help you negotiate with creditors and create a budget that will avoid future overspending and indebtedness.

If neither alternative works, look for a lawyer experienced in bankruptcy law. Bankruptcy laws are complicated, and filing bankruptcy is not a do-it-yourself job.

BANKRUPTCY BY THE NUMBERS

Different types of bankruptcy are referred to by the chapter numbers of the Federal Bankruptcy Code. The most common bankruptcies used by individuals are Chapters 7 and 13.

Chapter 7 bankruptcy is often called straight bankruptcy. In a Chapter 7 proceeding, most of the debtor's property is sold, and the proceeds are used to pay back creditors' claims. Consumers who have a lot of unsecured debts (such as credit card debts, which are incurred without giving collateral in exchange), own little property, and are not steadily employed generally file Chapter 7 bankruptcies.

Chapter 13 bankruptcy is known as the wage earner's plan. The debtor negotiates a new repayment plan with creditors, either by reducing the amount owed to each or extending the payments over a three- to five-year period. However, debtors who have more than $100,000 in unsecured debts and more than $350,000 in secured debts (debts incurred with collateral, such as a mortgage or a car loan) are not eligible to use Chapter 13. They can use Chapter 11.

Although Chapter 11 bankruptcy is used primarily by businesses, it is also available to individuals with too many assets to qualify for a Chapter 13 bankruptcy. Under a Chapter 11 proceeding, the debtor negotiates with his creditors to reduce the amount he owes them or to extend the amount of time he has to repay them. While the plan is being put together, all efforts to collect money from the debtor are prohibited, and once the plan is approved, all the creditors named in the bankruptcy petition are bound to it.

Chapter 12 of the Bankruptcy Code is for farmers. Special provisions of this chapter allow bankrupt farmers to avoid foreclosures on their land by pledging a portion of their future crops to pay their debts.

WHAT YOU CAN KEEP

In a Chapter 7 bankruptcy the debtor's property is divided up among the creditors, who take their share according to law. Both Congress and the states have passed laws listing certain items of property (or their equivalent in money) that cannot be repossessed or sold to pay creditors in a bankruptcy proceeding. This exempt property generally consists of items a person needs for survival, plus some kinds of personal property.

Under the Bankruptcy Code, a person filing for bankruptcy is allowed to keep the following:

◇ Up to $7,500 of equity (what you actually own, not what you owe) in a personal residence—such as a house, a condominium, or a mobile home—or in a burial plot. If your house is worth $50,000, for example, and you owe a mortgage balance of $45,000, your exemption is limited to the $5,000 of equity you own. The holder of your mortgage can still foreclose if you are behind in your payments.

◇ Up to $1,200 of equity in a motor vehicle.

◇ Up to a total of $4,000 in household furnishings, household goods, clothing, appliances, books, animals, crops, and musical instruments that are for your personal use or that of your dependents. The value of any one of these items cannot exceed $200.

◇ Up to $500 in jewelry.

◇ Up to $400 of equity in real estate other than your residence, as well as an additional $3,750 of any amount not used in the home equity exemption.

◇ Up to $750 in books or other tools used in your trade or profession or that of your dependent.

◇ Rights to life insurance death benefits under a policy

CHECKLIST

Six Bad Reasons for Filing Bankruptcy

Bankruptcy has become an increasingly common way for Americans to get out from under the burden of debt and the problems that come with it, but bankruptcy is not always the best solution for credit problems. Filing for bankruptcy may not be necessary or advisable under the following circumstances:

❑ **IF YOU ARE THREATENED WITH GARNISHMENT OR A WAGE ASSIGNMENT.**
By law, only 25 percent of your wages can be used to satisfy a court judgment, except for alimony and child support.

❑ **IF YOUR DEBTS ARE PRIMARILY FOR UNPAID TAXES, ALIMONY, OR CHILD SUPPORT.**
Bankruptcy does not relieve you of these obligations, although you may not have to pay some taxes that are more than three years overdue.

❑ **IF YOUR DEBTS ARE SECURED BY YOUR HOME OR OTHER PROPERTY.**
To eliminate a secured debt, such as a mortgage, through bankruptcy, you usually are required to allow your creditor to repossess the property and sell it. You may be better off trying to renegotiate your payment schedule with the creditor, or selling the property yourself and paying off the debt before the property is repossessed.

❑ **IF YOU ARE BEING HARASSED BY COLLECTION AGENCIES.**
A federal law, the Fair Debt Collection Practices Act, prohibits bill collectors from harassing you by telephone or approaching you in person. Among other provisions, it limits the hours during which collection agencies can call you, prohibits them from using obscene or threatening language, and prohibits them from calling you if they have the name of your attorney.

❑ **IF YOU RECENTLY INCURRED A LOT OF DEBT.**
Bankruptcy proceedings will not allow you to avoid paying debts you ran up in expectation of declaring bankruptcy to wipe them out.

❑ **IF YOU RECENTLY TRANSFERRED PROPERTY TO ANOTHER PERSON.**
If you put your house in your mother's name, for example, so that it would be beyond the reach of your creditors, you have committed a fraud.

you own, as well as a maximum of $4,000 of a life insurance policy's cash surrender value, dividends, or interest. This means you will probably have to give up a policy that has a cash value. See CASH SURRENDER VALUE.

◇ Prescribed health aids used by you or your dependent.

◇ Social Security payments, veterans' benefits, and disability, sickness, and unemployment compensation, regardless of value. Alimony or spousal support, pensions, profit-sharing payments, stock bonus payments, and annuities are also exempt, but only up to an amount approved by the bankruptcy court.

◇ State compensation payments for crime victims, proceeds from a wrongful-death lawsuit, and other payments for personal injury or loss of life are also subject to limitations by the bankruptcy court.

State exemptions are not always the same as federal exemptions. In Connecticut, Hawaii, Massachusetts, Michigan, Minnesota, New Jersey, New Mexico, Pennsylvania, Rhode Island, Texas, Vermont, Washington, and Wisconsin, debtors can choose between the two. Other states allow the state exemptions only, but they may offer an advantage: Texas and Florida, for example, have large exemptions for home equity.

Most states will double the amount of each exemption when a husband and wife jointly file for bankruptcy.

DEBTS YOU CANNOT DISCHARGE

Although the purpose of bankruptcy is to give the debtor a fresh start by eliminating the pressure of debts he cannot pay or by stretching out the debts in a repayment plan, the following debts cannot be dismissed by filing bankruptcy:

◇ Most federal, state, and local taxes.

◇ Student loans made or insured by the government.

◇ Debts for criminal fines or penalties.

◇ Alimony and child support payments.

◇ Debts denied or waived in a previous bankruptcy petition.

◇ Debts arising from larceny or embezzlement, from the debtor's willful and malicious injury of someone else, or from the debtor's drunken driving.

◇ Debts incurred by fraud.

It is considered fraud (itself a crime for which you can be prosecuted) to incur debts on a last-minute spending spree before you file for bankruptcy, with the expectation that these debts will be discharged. To avoid having to prove that the spending was done in anticipation of bankruptcy, federal law says that debts for luxury items (a fur coat, for example, but not a refrigerator) over $500 incurred within 40 days of filing the bankruptcy petition, or cash advances of $1,000 or more obtained within 20 days of filing, cannot be discharged.

If a debt is not listed on the bankruptcy petition, or if the creditor is not given adequate notice of the bankruptcy filing, the debt will not be discharged.

CHAPTER 7 BANKRUPTCY

A Chapter 7 proceeding begins with the filing of a bankruptcy petition in a federal bankruptcy court. There is a filing fee of about $120. If you, the debtor, file the petition, the bankruptcy is said to be voluntary. If a creditor or a group of creditors files a petition, the bankruptcy is involuntary.

The bankruptcy petition is a form that asks you to divulge what property you own, your income, your living expenses, debts, exempt property, and any purchase or sale of property in the previous two years. Once the petition is filed, a trustee appointed by the bankruptcy court assumes legal control of your nonexempt property. The trustee is usually a lawyer with experience in handling bankruptcy property. His principal job is to obtain as much of your property as possible to satisfy creditors' claims. The trustee is also required to challenge claims that are unjustified. As a fee for his service, the trustee is paid some percentage of the money he recovers for creditors.

The court sends notices of the petition to all the creditors named in it. From this time forward, all collection efforts, foreclosures on your home mortgage, and garnishments of wages are stopped by a procedure known as the automatic stay. But you will probably lose your home anyway and keep only the amount of your equity in it, up to $7,500.

A date is set for you to meet with creditors, usually several weeks after the petition is filed. At this meeting, you are questioned about your debts, assets, and other facts relating to the bankruptcy. If a creditor wants to raise an objection to having his debts discharged, he must do so at this meeting.

Finally, the court will discharge (wipe out) all the debts listed in your bankruptcy petition. You cannot file another Chapter 7 bankruptcy for six years.

CHAPTER 13 BANKRUPTCY

The procedures for filing for a Chapter 13 bankruptcy are essentially the same as those for Chapter 7, but the results are different. Under Chapter 13 you get to keep most of your property, and you present the court with a plan to repay most creditors within three to five years. The total of the repayments must be about the same as the value of your nonexempt property, so if the value of your nonexempt property is $10,000, your payments would be about $2,000 a year in a five-year plan. But if you are in default on your mortgage payments, you will probably still lose your home. See FORECLOSURE.

Although Chapter 13 is often referred to as the wage earner's plan, just about any steady source of income can be used to repay creditors, including self-employment income or earnings from investments. If your source of income dries up after your repayment plan is approved, you can either modify the plan or convert to the Chapter 7 plan that discharges your debts.

SPOUSES AND COSIGNERS

If you are married, it is usually best to file a joint bankruptcy petition. Otherwise, the spouse who does not file will be completely responsible for any joint debts. Similarly, a person who has cosigned (guaranteed) a loan for you can be held responsible for repaying the loan if you file for bankruptcy. Before you file, you should consider how your bankruptcy will affect any relatives or friends who may end up paying the debt that you are having discharged. See also COSIGNING.

STEPS TO TAKE TO AVOID BANKRUPTCY

Although the bankruptcy laws are designed to give an overextended debtor a fresh start, it is better to avoid the problems of bankruptcy altogether. These are some ways to help keep your debts under control:

1. Make a realistic budget. Be sure to include a fund for emergency expenses, such as sickness, home repairs, or unemployment, so that you will not have to rely on expensive credit to meet them.

2. Keep your mortgage or rent payments at no more than one-third of your monthly gross income.

3. Keep your monthly payments on personal debt at no more than 20 percent of your take-home pay.

4. When you do need credit, shop for the best terms and interest rates available. Interest rates on bank credit cards can vary by as much as 8 percent, depending on the issuer.

5. If you have a savings account at a bank or with a credit union, you may be able to obtain a better interest rate by financing purchases through those institutions.

BAR ASSOCIATION

A bar association is an organization of lawyers at the local, state, or national level. The word *bar* comes from the traditional wooden railing that separates the general public from those concerned with the trial. A bar association usually makes rules that govern the professional conduct of its members and the procedures for disciplining them for misconduct, which are generally enforced by the state's highest court. If you have dealings with a lawyer who you think is behaving unethically, you should report the problem to the local bar association.

In most states lawyers may choose whether to become members of the state bar association, but a few states require bar membership in order to practice law.

BARGAIN AND SALE DEED

In real estate, deeds of various kinds are used to transfer title, or ownership, from one person to another. They include warranty deeds, grant deeds, quitclaim deeds, and bargain and sale deeds. In a number of states (such as Florida, New Jersey, and Wyoming) the bargain and sale deed is commonly used. This type of deed does not contain any explicit guarantees that the property is free and clear of liens or mortgages. Even so, courts have held that the seller is responsible for any actions that he has knowingly taken to cause title problems (such as allowing a lien to be placed on the property). To protect yourself against such actions, you should make sure there is a clause in the deed, called a covenant against the grantor's acts, that holds the seller responsible for them.

To protect yourself further, you should have a title search conducted or buy a title insurance policy. In addition, since courts have placed different interpretations upon the seller's responsibility when using a bargain and sale deed, you may want to consult a lawyer who is familiar with the real estate laws in your state. See also FULL COVENANT AND WARRANTY DEED; GRANT DEED; LIEN; QUITCLAIM DEED; REAL ESTATE; TITLE INSURANCE.

BATTERED WOMEN

Four million reported cases of domestic violence each year make battery the No. 1 cause of injuries to women in the United States. This high number contributes to even gloomier statistics: one-third of all the women murdered in the United States each year are killed by a husband or boyfriend.

For a long time, court and law enforcement officials ignored violence in the home. Indeed, until this century, laws in some states permitted men to "chastise" their wives by beating them. Even when those laws changed, ingrained attitudes about family privacy and the role of women did not. Police were often reluctant to get involved in domestic disputes, and victims hesitated to prosecute their attackers.

Today many women still decline to press charges against their abusers for fear of retribution or social stigma or for economic reasons. If an arrest is made, they may urge the prosecutor to drop the charges.

DOMESTIC VIOLENCE: AN OFFENSE

Every victim of spousal abuse is the victim of a crime, just as if she had been assaulted by a stranger. Any woman who is subjected to physical abuse, whether from her spouse or from anyone else, has the right to call the police and demand the arrest and prosecution of the offender.

MANDATORY ARREST

To address the problems of reluctant victims and escalating violence, some communities and states have instituted policies that require the arrest of the offender in any domestic assault. By transferring the responsibility of pressing charges from the victim to the state, these laws relieve victims from any pressure they may feel to drop charges against their attackers. If officers are called to the scene of domestic violence, they must arrest the offender. After charges are filed, the prosecutor may proceed with the case even if the victim does not want to do so.

Once an arrest is made, the victim has the right to be kept informed about developments in the case, such as court hearings and the prosecutor's plans to plea-bargain or drop the charges. See PLEA BARGAINING.

ORDERS OF PROTECTION

One way the victim of domestic violence can help herself is to obtain a court order that forbids the offender from further harassing or abusing her. Depending on where she lives, these orders are known as adult-abuse orders, orders of protection, temporary restraining orders, or protection from abuse orders. In most states they give the victim temporary possession of the family residence and require that the offender stay away from her home, place of business, or anywhere else she may be. If the couple has children, the court can award temporary custody and child support.

After a civil order of protection is imposed, the court sets a hearing at which the accused can give his side of the story. If the victim fails to appear at this hearing, or if the judge finds that no abuse has occurred, the temporary order will be voided. However, if the judge is convinced that abuse has taken place, he can extend the order for a period of six months to a year, depending on the law in that state.

A person who violates a civil order of protection may be found guilty of contempt of court. See CONTEMPT OF COURT.

SHELTERS

Many battered women feel that a restraining order will not prevent the abuser from returning to harm them further, and sometimes their concerns are justified. For women who have nowhere else to turn, a nationwide network of shelters and safe houses exists, the locations of which are kept secret. The telephone numbers of these shelters can be obtained from the police, courts, and workers at victim-advocacy programs.

The shelters provide temporary housing and counseling for women and children fleeing abusive homes. They may also offer the services of court advocates, who help women acquire civil orders and appear with them in court to give emotional support during the criminal prosecution.

STEPS TO TAKE IF YOUR SPOUSE OR COMPANION BEATS YOU

1. Call the police for help, and be ready to give the details of the incident. Ask them to make a report.

2. Get medical help if you need it. Tell the doctor truthfully what happened. She will understand that you are not to blame for the abuse: your partner is.

3. Save all evidence of the abuse, such as torn clothing. Take photos of injuries and damaged property if you can.

4. Move out with your children. If you do not have a place to go, call the police for the name of a battered women's shelter near you.

5. Take all important documents with you. You should have your driver's license; birth certificates and Social Security cards for you and your children; school records; utility bills, for establishing identity; credit cards; passports; and any other documents that will take time to duplicate. If you cannot leave your abuser right away, store the documents and some money in a safe place where you can get them quickly once you do decide to leave.

BETTER BUSINESS BUREAU

The Council of Better Business Bureaus is a voluntary association of business people that provides various free or low-cost services to consumers. Headquartered in Washington, D.C., it has offices in virtually every American city, which provide the following services:

Reliability reports. The Better Business Bureau (BBB) maintains records on thousands of companies across the country, on the basis of which the firms are rated "satisfactory" or "unsatisfactory." A satisfactory rating means that a firm has responded to all complaints brought by the bureau or has no record of complaints against it. An unsatisfactory rating may mean that the company fails to answer complaints, uses questionable business practices, or refuses to discontinue deceptive advertising. In most cities these reports are free, but in some consumers must call the BBB using a 900 telephone number at a cost of 95 cents per minute.

Consumer complaint services. Written complaints about businesses are forwarded to companies by the bureau, which asks for a written response from a company official.

Arbitration. Consumers and companies may be able to have the bureau arbitrate certain disputes. The arbitrations are conducted by specially trained volunteers. No attorneys are required. See also ARBITRATION.

Autoline. This service handles consumers' disputes with auto manufacturers through mediation or arbitration.

Although the bureau has no legal authority, it reports any illegal activities it finds to law enforcement officials. It provides referrals to other organizations and agencies that deal with matters the BBB does not handle. See also CONSUMER PROTECTION.

BEYOND A REASONABLE DOUBT

The standard of proof that is required to convict a person of a crime is very high. It is called proof beyond a reasonable doubt and amounts to almost absolute certainty.

Because punishment is much more severe for crimes than for civil wrongdoings (such as breach of contract or fraud), the law requires that there be no "reasonable doubt" that the accused is guilty of committing the offense. The facts in the case must be such that any other explanation for the crime is extremely unlikely. See also BURDEN OF PROOF; EVIDENCE.

BIGAMY

A woman in Florida was sentenced to serve 60 days in jail and had to divorce two of her three husbands. The woman's crime was bigamy, or willfully being married to more than one person at a time. Every state prohibits this behavior, and thus any bigamous marriage is invalid.

When you enter into a marriage, it remains valid until the death of your spouse or until the marriage has been dissolved by divorce or legal annulment. You cannot marry someone else unless your first marriage has ended for one of these reasons.

Bigamy is a crime. If you marry someone who you know is already married, you too might be charged with bigamy.

IF YOU THOUGHT YOU WERE DIVORCED

If you thought you were legally divorced when you remarried, most states would allow you to use this as a defense against a bigamy charge and would not convict you.

Even so, it is important to pay special attention to your state's divorce laws so that you do not inadvertently commit bigamy. For example, in many states a divorce decree is not final on the day when the last proceedings took place, but only after a waiting period of 30 to 60 days.

IF YOU THINK YOUR SPOUSE IS DEAD

If your spouse has disappeared and has not been in touch with you or other family members for a long while, you may have good reason to think that she is dead. If you really believe that your spouse is dead when you enter into another marriage, you have a valid defense against bigamy charges.

It is important to know your state's laws regarding waiting periods. In most states five to seven years must pass before a person can be presumed dead, and a spouse cannot remarry until that time has elapsed. See also DEATH.

IF YOUR RELIGION PERMITS BIGAMY

Some religious groups have traditionally allowed marriages to more than one partner, but the Supreme Court has rejected this as a defense against the charge of bigamy, and permits states to prosecute even when the persons involved were practicing their religion.

BILL OF LADING

A bill of lading is the contract used when goods are transported from one location to another. Moving companies and railroads, as well as other shipping companies, write a bill of lading as proof of their agreement with the owner of the property. The bill of lading also serves as a receipt, listing the goods or personal property that is being shipped.

BILL OF RIGHTS

The first 10 amendments to the U.S. Constitution are referred to as the Bill of Rights. The backbone of American civil liberty, these amendments list the basic rights, freedoms, and protections of every United States citizen.

THE RIGHTS IN BRIEF

Five of the amendments are of particular importance. The First Amendment guarantees freedom of religion, speech, press, assembly (the right to meet peacefully in groups), and petition (the right to ask the government for fair treatment). See ASSEMBLY, RIGHT OF; PRESS, FREEDOM OF; RELIGION, FREEDOM OF; SPEECH, FREEDOM OF.

The Fourth Amendment forbids unreasonable searches and seizures. In most cases, the police must obtain a warrant before they can search your home or place you under arrest. See PROBABLE CAUSE; SEARCH AND SEIZURE.

The Fifth Amendment, famous for its guarantee against self-incrimination during a criminal trial, enumerates other rights as well, such as due process of law, fair compensation for property taken for public use, and protection against double jeopardy (being tried twice for the same crime). See CONDEMNATION; DOUBLE JEOPARDY; DUE PROCESS OF LAW; FIFTH AMENDMENT.

The Sixth Amendment champions the right to a fair trial, and the Eighth Amendment

The Bill of Rights

AMENDMENT I
Congress shall make no law respecting an establishment of religion, or prohibiting the free exercise thereof; or abridging the freedom of speech, or of the press; or the right of the people peaceably to assemble, and to petition the Government for a redress of grievances.

AMENDMENT II
A well regulated Militia, being necessary to the security of a free State, the right of the people to keep and bear Arms, shall not be infringed.

AMENDMENT III
No Soldier shall, in time of peace be quartered in any house, without the consent of the Owner, nor in time of war, but in a manner to be prescribed by law.

AMENDMENT IV
The right of the people to be secure in their persons, houses, papers and effects, against unreasonable searches and seizures, shall not be violated, and no Warrants shall issue, but upon probable cause, supported by Oath or affirmation, and particularly describing the place to be searched, and the persons or things to be seized.

AMENDMENT V
No person shall be held to answer for a capital, or otherwise infamous crime, unless on a presentment or indictment of a Grand Jury, except in cases arising in the land or naval forces, or in the Militia, when in actual service in time of War or public danger; nor shall any person be subject for the same offence to be twice put in jeopardy of life or limb; nor shall be compelled in any criminal case to be a witness against himself, nor be deprived of life, liberty, or property, without due process of law; nor shall private property be taken for public use, without just compensation.

AMENDMENT VI
In all criminal prosecutions, the accused shall enjoy the right to a speedy and public trial, by an impartial jury of the State and district wherein the crime shall have been committed, which district shall have been previously ascertained by law, and to be informed of the nature and cause of the accusation; to be confronted with the witnesses against him; to have compulsory process for obtaining witnesses in his favor, and to have the Assistance of Counsel for his defence.

AMENDMENT VII
In Suits at common law, where the value in controversy shall exceed twenty dollars, the right of trial by jury shall be preserved, and no fact tried by a jury shall be otherwise re-examined in any Court of the United States, than according to the rules of the common law.

AMENDMENT VIII
Excessive bail shall not be required, nor excessive fines imposed, nor cruel and unusual punishments inflicted.

AMENDMENT IX
The enumeration in the Constitution, of certain rights, shall not be construed to deny or disparage others retained by the people.

AMENDMENT X
The powers not delegated to the United States by the Constitution, nor prohibited by it to the States, are reserved to the States respectively, or to the people.

prohibits excessive bail, excessive fines, and cruel and unusual punishment. The issue of how to interpret the phrase *cruel and unusual punishment* has affected important decisions by the Supreme Court about the constitutionality of the death penalty. See CRUEL AND UNUSUAL PUNISHMENT; DEATH PENALTY.

BEFORE AND AFTER THE 14TH AMENDMENT

At the time when it was originally drafted, the Bill of Rights applied only to the federal government, not to the individual states—that is, the states were free to restrict the rights of their citizens as they wished. For example, a state could set its own limits on bail and punishment or censor the contents of newspapers and other publications.

Things changed dramatically after the adoption of the 14th Amendment in 1868. It specified that "no State shall make or enforce any law which shall abridge the privileges or immunities of citizens of the United

States; nor shall any State deprive any person of life, liberty, or property, without due process of law." The Supreme Court has interpreted those words to mean that the Bill of Rights applies as much to the individual states as to the federal government. See also ARMS, RIGHT TO BEAR; CIVIL RIGHTS; CONSTITUTION, U.S.; RIGHTS, INDIVIDUAL.

BILL OF SALE

A bill of sale is a document that transfers ownership of a piece of personal property from one person to another in exchange for money.

Suppose that your neighbor wants to buy your lawn mower. Once you agree on a price, you should prepare a bill of sale identifying the buyer, the seller, and the lawn mower, and stating the price. After you receive full payment, you turn the mower over to your neighbor, along with the bill of sale, which is his proof of ownership.

If a bill of sale is prepared properly, it can prevent the buyer from claiming that the seller misrepresented the item he purchased. If you state on the bill of sale that the mower is being sold "as is," you have proof that you made no special claims regarding its condition.

Not everything you sell requires a bill of sale, but you should write one up for valuable items, such as video and audio equipment, antiques, automobiles, and jewelry. Rules for selling special items such as guns and automobiles vary from state to state.

A sample bill of sale is provided in the EVERYDAY LEGAL FORMS section of this book, beginning on page 552.

BINDER

A binder is a written agreement used in some kinds of transactions until a final contract is prepared.

INSURANCE

An insurance binder provides temporary protection until a formal policy is issued. For example, when Clara applies for a homeowners policy, the insurance agent covers her with a binder while the company reviews her application to determine the value of the house, its susceptibility to fire, and other risks the insurance will cover. If Clara's home is damaged while the binder is in effect, the insurance company must pay any legitimate claims she makes, even if her insurance application is ultimately rejected. See also HOMEOWNERS INSURANCE; INSURANCE.

REAL ESTATE

In real estate a binder between the buyer and seller of property indicates that the buyer has paid a sum of money, called an earnest money deposit, in return for the right to purchase the property. The binder serves as a preliminary agreement until the fully detailed formal sales contract is completed.

Suppose Ralph wants to buy a house in a new development and makes an offer that is accepted. Ralph and the owner sign a simple paper identifying them as buyer and seller, describing the property and stating its price, and specifying the amount (usually from $100 to

REAL LIFE, REAL LAW

The Case of the Hesitant Home Buyers

Mike and Laurie Conway signed a binder to purchase a home and made an earnest money deposit of $500. The terms of the binder gave the Conways 10 days to arrange for a home inspection and to sign a final purchase agreement.

Three days later, the Conways found a home they liked better at a lower price. They notified the seller of the first house that they had changed their minds, and requested that their $500 be refunded. When the seller refused to return their money, the Conways sued him in small-claims court for their deposit.

The court turned down the Conways' claim. It found that the seller had complied with all the terms contained in the binder. The fact that the Conways had changed their minds was not enough to invalidate the binder.

Although a binder is not the final contract for the purchase of a home, it is a legally enforceable document.

$1,000) that Ralph is paying as proof of his serious intention. Ralph gives the money to the owner, who then takes the property off the market.

A binder is not a purchase agreement (a legal obligation to buy the house), nor is it a down payment (a percentage of the price of the property payable at the closing). With a binder, Ralph can choose not to buy the house after he has paid the fee, but in many cases his money will not be returned. For a sample binder, see the EVERYDAY LEGAL FORMS section, beginning on page 552. See also HOME BUYING AND SELLING.

BIRTH CERTIFICATE

A birth certificate is an official record of a person's birth—the time, date, and place of birth, and the parents' names and ages. It is recorded in the county where the child is born.

There is no legal requirement that a child be given his father's last name, and the choice of another last name does not affect the father's rights or duties.

It is important to have a copy of your child's birth certificate. You may be asked to present it when he first enters school, and he will need it when he applies for a driver's license, financial aid for college, or any type of government assistance.

ADOPTION

When an adoption is granted by a court, copies of the adoption decree are forwarded to the bureau of vital statistics in the state where the adopted child was born. The bureau then prepares a new birth certificate with the adoptee's new name, the names of the adoptive parents, and their ages when the adoptee was born. Information about the adoptee's natural parents becomes confidential and does not appear on the new birth certificate.

ILLEGITIMACY

When a child is born out of wedlock, the mother often gives the child her last name. If later the father acknowledges the child as his, or if the parents marry, the name on the birth certificate can usually be changed. Some states allow the birth certificate to be changed if the mother marries another man and he agrees to have his name put on the child's birth certificate.

If requested, most states will eliminate any reference to illegitimacy (such as the mother's marital status when the child was born) from the new birth certificate. As in the case of a certificate altered by an adoption, the history of the child is kept confidential.

NAME CHANGES

If, as an adult, you decide to change your name, you can do so in a court proceeding and have your birth certificate amended to reflect your new legal name. See NAME CHANGE.

HOW TO OBTAIN YOUR BIRTH CERTIFICATE

To request a copy of your birth certificate, call the bureau of vital statistics in the state of your birth and be ready to provide the following information:

◇ Your name as it appears on the birth certificate.

◇ Your date of birth.

◇ Your place of birth.

◇ Your mother's maiden name.

◇ Your father's name.

In some states you have to make your request in writing and pay a fee. The bureau of vital statistics will tell you what the charges are and where to write for your copy.

BIRTH CONTROL

In 1965 the U.S. Supreme Court held that a Connecticut law prohibiting the use of contraceptives, even by married couples, violated the Fourth Amendment of the U.S. Constitution, under which Americans have a basic right to privacy. Several years later, the Court struck down another law that banned the prescription or sale of contraceptives to unmarried persons.

Today the use of birth control and contraceptives is widespread, but several related issues continue to spark controversy and litigation.

MINORS

Medical personnel usually will not treat minors or give them medical advice without parental consent, except in emergencies. However, some states have laws that allow minors to obtain birth control counseling and even prescriptions without parental consent. In recent years schools in Los Angeles, Chicago, and Miami began to dispense condoms to students who had parental consent. New York City schools have taken that idea one step further: their students do not need parental consent.

Whether a minor should be required to have parental consent before obtaining an abortion has been a source of much conflict. But in 1992 the Supreme Court held that states may pass laws requiring an underage girl to obtain her parents' consent. If she does not want to ask them or if they refuse to consent, she may ask a judge for permission.

CONTRACEPTIVE FAILURES

Contraceptives do not provide 100 percent protection against pregnancy or disease. The statistical chances for the failure of a particular type of contraceptive are available from the doctor who prescribes it or the pharmaceutical company that makes it. If a woman becomes pregnant as a result of the failure of a contraceptive device or medicine, she has no cause for suing her doctor or the pharmaceutical company.

Vasectomy, a surgical procedure that sterilizes a man, has a near-zero failure rate. However, sometimes the operation is performed incorrectly, and pregnancy results. In such a case the couple can file a lawsuit for negligence. Generally, they can only recover the expenses of prenatal care and birth and the costs of raising the child. The courts usually will not award money to the child for wrongful life. See WRONGFUL LIFE.

SIDE EFFECTS

The side effects of contraception have become a major area of litigation. One of the most famous cases involved the Dalkon Shield, an intrauterine birth control device (IUD). By 1991 nearly 100,000 claims had been filed against the A. H. Robins Company by women injured by the device. The injuries were due to a design flaw that caused infections resulting in pelvic inflammation, sterility, and sometimes death. Because of the large number of claims, the manufacturer filed for bankruptcy, and claims against the company are being settled through a trust fund established for that purpose.

MANDATORY BIRTH CONTROL

Contraceptives have recently become a part of sentencing techniques in some courts. For example, a California woman found guilty of child abuse was sentenced to a year in jail and three years of probation. Upon her release from prison, she was ordered to use Norplant, a long-acting contraceptive that is implanted under the skin and is effective for up to five years. In Florida a teenager who was convicted of killing her newborn child was sentenced to remain on birth control for 10 years after her release from prison. Requiring contraception as part of a sentence has been questioned constitutionally, however, and the future of this practice remains in doubt.

Birth control can be ordered for persons who are unable to care for themselves and have been declared legally incompetent. If a woman has been declared incompetent, her legal guardian must consent to the prescription of contraceptives for her. Guardians of both men and women can sometimes authorize sterilization procedures. However, the U.S. Supreme Court has struck down state laws that mandated sterilization for mentally impaired men and women.

BLACKLISTING

Dan Watson, an employee at the Big Brass Button factory, is fired after reporting a safety violation to the Occupational Safety and Health Administration (OSHA). He sues his company for a handsome sum and wins. The company's executives then place Dan's name on a list of former employees who have caused problems. Five years later, when Dan applies for work with a manufacturer in the same town, he is turned down.

Dan is the victim of blacklisting, the practice of making a list of certain people who are to be denied some opportunity, usually employment. Blacklisting is most commonly done by employers to prevent former employees from obtaining jobs elsewhere. Sometimes employers exchange blacklists or buy them from companies who compile lists of undesirable workers, such as employees who have filed for workers' compensation.

Although blacklisting has been outlawed in a number of states, these laws can be hard to enforce. The former employee may be required to show that the employer's actions were willful or malicious or that the employer misrepresented the truth. Blacklisting laws in some states do not prevent an employer from giving information about a former employee's performance or qualifications if the information is true.

If an employee does win a lawsuit against an employer who blacklisted him, he may collect double or triple damages from the employer, that is, two or three times the amount of his actual money losses. To discourage the employer from further blacklisting, the court may award the employee additional money, called punitive damages. See also REFERENCE, EMPLOYEE; WHISTLE-BLOWER.

LABOR UNIONS

Labor unions have also practiced blacklisting, circulating lists of employees who refused to join the union or of members who did not take part in a strike or refused to follow union rules. They have also blacklisted subcontractors with whom they have had a dispute, passing the list to the general contractors who employ them.

LEGAL BLACKLISTING

Not all blacklisting is illegal. For example, federal law allows the comptroller general to provide federal agencies with lists of companies that have failed to meet the conditions of their government contracts. A company placed on these lists cannot be awarded another government contract for a period of three years.

BLACKMAIL

The crime of illegally exacting money from someone by using a threat is called blackmail. The blackmailer typically threatens to destroy property, cause injury, or reveal a damaging secret unless money or something else of value is given to him. See EXTORTION.

BLOOD-ALCOHOL TESTING

A police officer who suspects you of driving under the influence of alcohol may ask you to take a blood-alcohol test, which measures the amount of alcohol present in your blood. A breath test, blood test, or urine test may be used. You only have to take one of the three tests, and usually you can choose which one you take. See also BREATH TEST.

In most states a blood-alcohol content of .001, or one-tenth of 1 percent, is enough for a driver to be considered legally intoxicated. Most people are surprised at how little they have to drink to reach that percentage. For example, a person who weighs 150 pounds may become legally drunk just by consuming two or three beers in an hour.

A driver's ability to operate a car safely after drinking is not a defense against a drunk-driving charge based on a blood-alcohol test. Suppose you have had a few beers and are pulled over by the police because you have a broken tail light. The officer questioning you smells alcohol on your breath, asks you to take the blood-alcohol test, and you fail. Even though you were driving safely and obeying the traffic laws, you will not be able to use these facts as a defense.

REFUSING A BLOOD-ALCOHOL TEST

The police cannot force you to take a blood-alcohol test, but failing to do so can have serious consequences. Every state has so-called implied-consent laws making the driver's consent to blood testing a condition of keeping his driver's license. If you refuse to take a blood-alcohol test, your license may be suspended immediately, but usually the officer has to so inform you and give you another chance to take the test. If you still refuse, your license may be suspended for as long as a year, and you can be prosecuted for drunk driving anyway. See also IMPLIED CONSENT.

In Alaska, Iowa, and Minnesota, you have a constitutional right to consult a lawyer before deciding whether to submit to a blood-alcohol test. In most states, however, you do not.

CHOOSING WHICH TEST TO TAKE

Assuming you are allowed to choose the test you take, your wisest choice is probably the breath test. The results of this test are known immediately, so that if you pass, you will be released right away. Furthermore, these results do not hold up in court as well as the results of the other tests. The test that is hardest to challenge in court is the blood test.

FAILING A BLOOD-ALCOHOL TEST

If a blood-alcohol test reveals that you are legally intoxicated, you will be charged with drunk driving. The legal terminology for the offense varies slightly from state to state. It may be called driving under the influence (DUI) or driving while intoxicated (DWI).

After you are booked, your car may be impounded. You will be allowed to telephone a friend, a family member, or a lawyer to arrange for your release from police custody and to take you home.

The results of the test will be forwarded to the local district attorney's office, along with any other evidence against you. If the district attorney decides to prosecute, you should find a lawyer with experience in drunk-driving cases. See also DRUNK DRIVING.

BLOOD TESTING

Blood testing is required in a variety of legal circumstances. You may have to take a blood test before you get married or if you are a man involved in a paternity suit. Blood tests are used more and more often to screen people for the AIDS virus. In addition, if you happen to be stopped for drunk driving, you may be required to take a blood-alcohol test.

MARRIAGE LICENSES

Before issuing a couple a marriage license, most states require them to take a blood test to determine whether either is infected with a venereal disease, such as syphilis. If the test is positive, the license is withheld. At one time, Illinois required a prospective bride and groom to submit to a blood test for AIDS, but this law was repealed in 1992.

PATERNITY SUITS

In a lawsuit for child support, a man may claim he is not responsible for the child's support since he is not his father. To establish paternity, a court may require him, as well as the child, to take a blood test.

Until recently the only blood test available for helping to prove paternity could determine merely that a man was *not* a particular child's father. The test used, the ABO test, was based on the fact that children inherit their blood types from their parents. If Mary and John both have type A blood, their children will never have type B blood. Therefore, if Mary has a child with type B blood, John (and the courts) can be sure that it is not his. However, this does not mean that Jack, who also has type B blood, and who has been living with Mary and John, is the father. Any man with type B blood could be the father.

The newer, human leukocyte antigen (HLA) test is more telling than the ABO test. The test is based on the fact that these antigens, which are present in every person's blood cells, are inherited and unique to that person (except for identical twins). Some experts believe that the test is more than 95 percent accurate. In some states when an HLA test is positive, the only way a man can disprove paternity is to show that he was not around when conception took place.

AIDS TESTING

Because of the rise of AIDS, many insurance companies require applicants for health or life insurance policies to submit to blood tests for the human immunodeficiency virus (HIV). Although some states once outlawed these tests, the law in every state now permits them. See also AIDS.

DRUNK DRIVING

If a police officer suspects you of driving while intoxicated, he can ask you to take a test to measure your blood's alcohol content. See BLOOD-ALCOHOL TESTING; BREATH TEST; DRUNK DRIVING.

BLUE LAW

A law that forbids certain kinds of businesses to be open on Sunday is called a blue law. Blue laws are also called Sunday or Sabbath Day laws, but their primary purpose is not religious. It is rather to give workers a day of rest and to promote the general welfare of the community.

For example, many states

ban the sale of liquor on Sunday. This prohibition is meant to ensure that at least one day of the week will see a reduction in the purchase (and perhaps the consumption) of alcohol. Other blue laws prohibit the sale of most goods, but not necessities such as food.

In recent years the trend has been against the enactment or enforcement of blue laws.

BLUE-SKY LAW

State laws that regulate the sale of securities such as stocks and bonds in order to protect consumers from fraud are referred to as blue-sky laws. In order to offer securities for sale within a state, a company must reveal the risks related to the purchase of its stocks and bonds, and the company is not allowed to overstate the potential return on an investment. The term *blue-sky law* is supposed to have originated when a judge ruled that a particular stock "had as much value as a patch of blue sky." The sale of stocks and bonds in interstate commerce is regulated by the Securities and Exchange Commission. See SECURITIES AND EXCHANGE COMMISSION; STOCKS AND BONDS.

BOATING

Just as drivers must obey the rules of the road, boaters must follow the laws that pertain to boating. Speed limits, safety equipment, proper lighting, and right-of-way rules are some of the subjects the laws cover.

Failure to observe the nautical "rules of the road" can lead to lawsuits as well as criminal charges. If your boat does not have the proper lights and, as a result, you have a collision, you can be held responsible for injuries and damages. You can also be held responsible for accidents that occur if you operate a boat under the influence of drugs or alcohol; fail to keep a proper lookout for other boats, water-skiers, or swimmers; or neglect to warn of approaching danger.

You should never allow your boat to be used by someone who is not qualified to operate it. If an accident occurs, you can be held responsible even if you were nowhere near the scene of the accident.

You can obtain specific information about the laws governing the safe operation of boats from the U.S. Coast Guard office closest to you or from your state's department of recreation. The Coast Guard Auxiliary and many state recreation departments sponsor classes that teach safe boating techniques.

BOND

There are many types of bonds but they all have the same general purpose: they are documents that represent a promise by one party to pay (or do something for) another party after a specified length of time. Some bonds, such as savings and corporate bonds, are used to borrow money. Others, such as bail bonds and performance bonds, serve as a guarantee that money will be paid if a certain promise—to appear in court or to complete a job, for example—is not kept. See also BAIL; CONTRACTOR; STOCKS AND BONDS.

BOOK VALUE

If you own stock in a corporation, you may hear a reference to the stock's "book value." This is the value of a share of stock, as determined by subtracting the company's liabilities from its assets and then dividing that amount by the total number of shares that the company has issued.

For example, suppose there are 1,000 shares of Wonderful Widget Works, Inc. The company's assets, including its factory, its office equipment, and the money owed to it, equal $1 million. The company's liabilities, such as unpaid invoices from suppliers, transportation costs, and salaries, amount to $200,000. The company's theoretical worth—its assets minus its liabilities—equals $800,000.

Dividing this amount by the 1,000 shares of ownership in the company, the book value of each share is $800. It is important to compare a stock's book value with its price to determine whether the stock is sound or overpriced.

BORROWED PROPERTY

Your car refuses to start, and you need to get to a crucial appointment. Your neighbor, seeing your predicament, offers to

REAL LIFE, REAL LAW

The Case of the Wobbly Ladder

When Louise borrowed her next-door neighbor Max's stepladder to change the light bulb in her kitchen, Max told her that one of the ladder's support braces was loose. Louise decided to borrow it anyway. The ladder collapsed with Louise on it and she fell, breaking her arm and bruising two ribs. Louise was unable to work for several weeks.

Louise sued Max to recover money for her injuries and the time she lost from work. Her attorney argued that because Max knew the ladder was dangerous, he should have refused to lend it. The court disagreed, and held that Max's warning about the ladder was enough. Louise assumed the risk that the ladder would collapse when she decided to borrow it in spite of the warning she had received.

Someone who borrows another person's property cannot be compensated for injuries suffered while using it unless the owner knew of a hazardous condition and failed to warn the borrower about the danger.

let you borrow his car for the morning. You accept his generous offer.

Borrowing a car or any other kind of personal property creates what is known as a bailment. As the borrower, you become a bailee of your neighbor's property. Because your neighbor does not gain anything of value in allowing you to borrow his car, this bailment is considered to be for your sole benefit. As a result, you are legally required to exercise extraordinary care while using the car, and you must return it on demand in the same condition in which you received it. If someone sideswipes the car and scratches the fender while you are borrowing it, you are responsible for the damage despite the fact that you were not at fault.

But suppose your neighbor lends you his car knowing that it needs a brake job. If you have an accident because you cannot stop the car in time to avoid a collision, your neighbor could be held at least partially responsible for the accident. See also BAILMENT.

BOUNCED CHECK

The day before your car payment is due you realize that you do not have enough money to pay it. But since your paycheck is due at the end of the week, you write a check and mail it to the loan company. You are sure that by the time the company presents the check to your bank, you will have received and deposited your paycheck. As luck would have it, however, the check you wrote reaches the bank first. In other words, your check has "bounced," or been returned to the loan company. Now you are in legal trouble as well as financial trouble.

Unless you have arranged for overdraft protection, the bank has no obligation to honor a check written on an account with insufficient funds. Writing a check on an account that you know has insufficient funds to cover the check is a crime and may be punishable by fine or imprisonment.

Even if the overdraft was unintentional and you escape criminal prosecution, the cost of this mistake can mount up considerably. Unless you have an agreement with the bank permitting overdrafts (a service that has become increasingly popular in recent years), the bank usually imposes a service charge on your account to compensate it for the added cost of handling.

In some states a person or company that receives a bad check can sue for up to three times the amount of the check and can collect attorney's fees, court costs, and other expenses related to collection of the money. One Colorado man who wrote a check for less than $30 against insufficient funds found himself obligated to repay nearly $1,000 after all the costs of collection were added up. See also CHECK.

BOUNDARY LINE

The border where one piece of real estate ends and another begins is known as a boundary line. Boundary lines may be imaginary lines that exist only on maps, or they may be indicated by objects like stakes, stone monuments, fences, rivers, trees, cliffs, or any other physical markers.

Most property owners have only a rough idea where their boundary lines are because most of the time it is not necessary to know the exact location. However, if you or your neighbor wants to chop down a tree, put up a fence, or build a new garage near the edge of your property, you need to know precisely where your boundary line is in order to avoid possible legal troubles.

WHEN BOUNDARY LINES ARE IN DOUBT

Your deed should describe your boundary lines, or you should be able to find them on the town map. If neither of these documents divulges their location, you may have to call a surveyor to make a survey of your property. Unfortunately, a survey can be expensive, ranging from several hundred dollars to more than $1,000. If nothing more is at stake than a bed of shrubbery, you and your neighbor may be able to agree on where the boundary is.

In some states a court will determine the location of your boundary line, but the process can be time-consuming and expensive, especially if the end result is that the court orders a survey anyway.

WHEN OTHERS BUILD ON YOUR LAND

But suppose you come home from work one day and see a bulldozer clearing a strip of your land to make way for your neighbor's tennis court. What should you do?

Take action right away. Most of the time you can solve the problem on the spot by explaining to your neighbor that he is on your property. If he does not cooperate, you can threaten to call the police or sue. If he still refuses, your lawyer can have a judge order him to stop work until you can bring a suit against him for trespassing on your property.

If you do not take action, the consequences can be worse than you might think. First, if you wait until your neighbor completes his tennis court before you sue, the judge will be reluctant to have it destroyed. Second, if you try to sell your house, the insurance company may not insure your land as long as a neighbor is occupying part of it. Third, if the neighbor uses your land long enough, he may obtain a permanent right to do so. See ADVERSE POSSESSION; EASEMENT; FENCE BUILDING; TRESPASS.

BOYCOTT

If you refuse to patronize a company or attempt to prevent others from doing so, you are imposing a boycott. For example, some civil rights groups encouraged the boycott of a shoe manufacturer whose products were targeted for the African-American market but who had few minority employees. Consumer groups may urge a boycott of products that they feel are overpriced in an effort to bring the prices down. In 1992 the Communication Workers of America urged consumers to boycott AT&T by switching their long-distance service to other carriers. See also LABOR UNION.

BREACH OF CONTRACT

The colors have been picked, the contract has been signed, the advance payment made. But on the appointed day your house painter fails to show up. When he does arrive, three days later, the paint he applies is not the one you had chosen. Then, halfway through the job, he demands an extra $100 to finish. When you refuse, he stomps out of the house, never to return. Each of these actions is a breach of the painter's contract with you. Breach of contract occurs when, without any justification, one of the parties fails to complete his or her part of the bargain.

WAYS A CONTRACT CAN BE BREACHED

You can breach a contract by not keeping your promises; by not paying for the work done; by delivering defective merchandise; by not completing a job; or by not doing it correctly.

Preventing the other person from fulfilling his side of the

bargain, such as refusing to let in the painter on the day he is scheduled to work, is a breach of contract, as is canceling your paint job the day before the painter is due to begin.

SUBSTANTIAL PERFORMANCE

Not every broken promise is a breach of contract. Suppose the painter told you he was going to use the Blue Giant brand, but you notice that the cans are labeled Mighty Midget. He assures you that the quality and color of the substituted paint are equal to the one specified. If this is true, he has given you essentially the same product that you agreed to accept. This is known as substantial performance, and you have no grounds for legal complaint.

MONEY DAMAGES

When you suffer loss resulting from a breach of contract, you can sue to be compensated. For example, in the case of the unreasonable painter, the three-day delay in itself would probably not have caused you any real loss. But you can sue for the cost of buying paint to cover the poorer-quality coat he applied and for any additional expenses you incur by hiring another painter to finish the job. These money losses to you are known as damages.

But note that when you sue, a court will expect you to show that you tried to minimize your loss and the resulting damages. Let us say that on the day the painter was supposed to arrive you missed a day of work and were docked for it. Your mother-in-law was at home with you, however, and could have called you when the painter arrived. In this instance, you would probably not be entitled to receive reimbursement for your lost wages from the painter.

SPECIFIC PERFORMANCE

Sometimes money is neither what you want nor what you are entitled to when you suffer a breach of contract. Suppose you find the silver coffee service you have always wanted in a secondhand silver shop. You pay for it but leave it behind to be cleaned. When you come to pick it up, the owner tells you that in the meantime he has learned it is worth much more money and offers you a refund. You have a right to demand the coffee set at the price you paid. This is called specific performance and is the remedy you would sue for.

One very important exception to the specific performance remedy is personal services. Let us say you sign a contract with an interior decorator to redo your living and dining room. Just before her first scheduled visit, she tells you she is too busy and cannot do your work. You cannot ask a court to force her to decorate your home. The law considers this a violation of the 13th Amendment, which prohibits "involuntary servitude."

STEPS TO TAKE FOR A BREACH OF CONTRACT

If you believe you are the victim of a breach of contract, here are some steps to take:

1. In writing, notify the person with whom you have the contract of the breach. Tell him what you expect him to do to correct it. Give him a firm deadline for taking action (such as 10 days or 2 weeks).

2. Send the letter by certified mail, return receipt requested. Keep a copy of the letter, along with the written contract, if there is one.

3. If you do not receive a satisfactory response by your deadline, you may want to take legal action. If the amount in question is relatively small, your best bet may be to go to small-claims court. But if the amount is large, if money damages alone will not compensate you adequately, or if the offender lives in some other state, you may have to file a lawsuit. In this event, you should hire an attorney for advice on and assistance in pursuing your claim.

4. Try to keep things in perspective. If the breach is insignificant, consider whether the matter is worth pursuing legally. For example, suppose your contract called for you to receive three hand-painted china figurines. If you find that one of them has a minor blemish, you must decide if the cost, in time and money, of pursuing your right to a perfect figurine will exceed the amount that a court would award you. See also CONTRACT.

BREACH OF PROMISE

The right to sue for breach of promise or, more precisely, breach of marriage promise, was a time-honored way for a jilted fiancée (or fiancé) to be avenged. Suppose that Tom and Wanda become engaged and set a date. During the following months Wanda makes the wedding preparations—buying gowns, hiring a hotel and caterer, ordering flowers. But when the big day comes, Tom is nowhere to be found.

Legally, Tom is guilty of breach of promise. At one time nearly every state would have allowed Wanda to sue Tom solely for failing to honor his promise to marry her. If she had taken the matter to court, she would have been awarded money to compensate her for her injured feelings and suffering. Today, however, the courts in states that recognize breach of promise will order Tom only to pay Wanda part or all of her expenses relating to the wedding preparations. See also ENGAGEMENT, BROKEN.

BREACH OF THE PEACE

Anything that violates the order and tranquillity of a community may be considered a breach of the peace. For example, setting off fireworks, playing very loud music, or using obscene language in public have all been considered to be breaches of the peace.

A person who breaches the peace can be charged with disorderly conduct or disturbing the peace, depending on local law. These offenses are usually considered misdemeanors, punishable by fine or by imprisonment of up to a year in some states. See DISORDERLY CONDUCT; DISTURBING THE PEACE.

BREATH TEST

If a police officer suspects you of driving under the influence of alcohol, he can ask you to take a sobriety test on the spot, or he can take you to the police station to take one of three kinds of blood-alcohol tests: blood, urine, or breath.

If you agree to take a breath test, you will be told to blow into a tube connected to a Breathalyzer, a device that measures the concentration of blood alcohol in your breath. You can refuse to take the test, but if you do, your license will almost certainly be suspended.

WHAT YOU SHOULD KNOW

If the machine registers a blood-alcohol level over the legal limit (.001 or one-tenth of 1 percent in most states), you will be arrested for drunk driving. The law in some states requires the police to give you two Breathalyzer tests, which must register levels within .02 percent of one another. In these states if the police do not provide this opportunity, or if the test results are too far apart, they cannot be used as evidence against you.

YOUR OPTIONS IF YOU FAIL

Breath tests are the least accurate method of measuring blood-alcohol concentration, and are often successfully challenged in court. A lawyer who is experienced in defending drunk-driving cases can be very helpful if you are arrested for failing a Breathalyzer test. See also BLOOD-ALCOHOL TESTING; DRUNK DRIVING.

BRIBERY

Ed, who has been barreling down the highway at 85 miles per hour, meekly pulls over to the curb when his rearview mirror reveals a police car gaining on him, rooftop lights flashing. When the officer comes forward and announces that he is ticketing Ed for speeding, Ed pulls out a $100 bill and offers it to the officer if he will "just forget the whole thing." The officer counters with a charge of attempted bribery. But if the officer accepted Ed's offer, he too would be guilty of bribery.

In legal terms bribery is a gift—money, trips, merchandise, or tickets to sporting events—offered to a public official in exchange for favors within the scope of the official's duties. The list of persons who qualify as public officials is long and includes sheriffs and other peace officers, jurors, witnesses, school-board members and school officials, federal narcotics agents, U.S. attorneys, and IRS inspectors.

If a public official seeks payment for taking an official action, he is guilty of soliciting a bribe, which is also a felony in most states.

BRIEF

No matter what kind of lawsuit you pursue, you or your lawyer may be required to prepare a written statement for the court to support your case. This brief, as it is called, usually contains a summary of the facts of the case, cites the law that you believe governs the dispute, and explains how the law should be applied. The brief concludes with a statement of the decision you are requesting from the court.

BROKER

In general, a broker is a person who is retained to arrange sales for other people. Unlike agents who represent either the buyer or the seller, the broker serves as a middleman in the transaction, bringing the parties together and helping them reach a mutual agreement.

For example, an insurance agent generally represents a single company and offers only the products of that company. An insurance broker offers the products of several companies and can therefore provide clients with a selection of insurance products.

For discussions of the responsibilities of various types of brokers and agents, see also INSURANCE AGENT AND BROKER; REAL ESTATE AGENT AND BROKER; STOCKBROKER.

BURDEN OF PROOF

You have brought a lawsuit against the manufacturer of a hair dryer that caught fire while you were using it, burning your hands and face. Efforts to settle the suit have failed, and the case is set for trial. It is up to you (the plaintiff) or your attorney to convince the court to rule in your favor.

To do so, you will have to meet the "burden of proof." This means that it is your responsibility to prove that the facts of the case weigh in your favor. Because you have begun the lawsuit, the initial burden of proving that the hair dryer was defective falls on you.

If the manufacturer claims that the injuries you suffered were the result of your own negligence, the manufacturer will have to bear the burden of proving its allegation that you were negligent.

Courts use one of three different standards in determining whether a party has met its burden of proof:

◇ *Preponderance of the evidence*. This standard is the easiest to meet and is used in most lawsuits, as for breach of contract and personal injury. It involves weighing the evidence of both parties to see which side is more believable. If the evidence is found to be even, the party bearing the burden of proof cannot win. But if the evidence is slightly more convincing toward the party who has the burden of proof, that side will prevail.

◇ *Clear and convincing proof*. Some civil suits require stronger evidence than preponderance of evidence, but not absolutely conclusive evidence. This is called clear and convincing proof. The clear and convincing standard applies in a fraud claim, in a lawsuit that tries to establish the provisions included in a lost contract or will, or when family members want to withdraw life support from a terminally ill patient.

◇ *Beyond a reasonable doubt*. This last standard is required in criminal cases. A person cannot be convicted of a crime unless the judge or jury is convinced of the defendant's guilt beyond a reasonable doubt. If there is any reasonable uncertainty about the defendant's guilt based on the evidence presented, no conviction can take place.

BURGLARY

Someone enters your home and stealthily moves around the living room. You call the police, who take him away. Will the prowler be charged with burglary?

Burglary, also known as breaking and entering, originally meant that a culprit forcibly entered a home at night with the intention of committing a felony, usually theft. Today, however, state laws include commercial buildings, kennels, stables, and barns in their definitions of burglary, and do not limit the act to nighttime.

The statutes in some states have also eliminated the need for a "breaking," which means some part of the structure, such as a lock or a window, has been broken, moved, or removed. Formerly, if the intruder entered through a partially opened door or window, he could not be convicted of burglary. But many current laws state that picking a lock, opening a latch, or even turning a doorknob is enough to qualify the offense as burglary.

REAL LIFE, REAL LAW

The Case of the Bad-Luck Burglar

Jeff Andrews died while attempting to burglarize a warehouse. The warehouse owner, who had been the victim of burglary more than a dozen times in the previous two years, had booby-trapped his building with a shotgun wired to the front door. When Jeff broke the lock and opened the door, the gun went off, killing him instantly.

The warehouse owner was charged with manslaughter. His attorney argued that he was entitled to protect his property. But the court held that the use of deadly force was unjustified, and the warehouse owner was found guilty and sentenced to prison.

Although burglary is a crime, property owners are limited in the kinds of steps they can take to protect their homes and businesses from intruders.

To be considered a burglar, someone must enter a house with the intent to commit a crime. Under the law a person who breaks and enters but does not intend to steal or commit some other felony is not guilty of burglary. But he could be guilty of trespass. If someone intending to steal is frightened away or changes his mind, he can still be found guilty of burglary. See also TRESPASS.

BUSINESS TAXES

Operating a business involves paying taxes and fees to local, state, and federal governments.

If you operate your business as a sole proprietorship (that is, as a single owner), you are required to pay a self-employment tax to cover Social Security contributions. If you have employees, you must contribute to their Social Security accounts and pay state and federal unemployment premiums. You may also have to buy workers' compensation insurance.

If you sell goods, you will probably have to collect and pay sales taxes to your state and local governments. In most states the department of revenue collects all sales taxes and disburses them to the local authorities. Some states now require certain service businesses to collect sales taxes.

If your business is a partnership or corporation, it must file state and federal income tax returns, and the partners must pay taxes on their income from the partnership. Your business may also be subject to state and local licensing fees.

The Small Business Administration, a federal agency that was formed to promote and assist the development of small businesses, can help guide you through the maze of business taxes, and the IRS offers free publications and assistance with federal taxes. You can find the nearest offices of these agencies in the federal government listings in your telephone directory. See also CORPORATION; LIMITED-LIABILITY COMPANY; PARTNERSHIP; SMALL BUSINESS.

BUYERS CLUB

The postcard in the mailbox bears good news. You are being offered a chance to join a buyers club, with the promise of big savings every time you purchase merchandise through the club's catalog. Although the membership fee sounds a bit high, the convenience of catalog shopping and the substantial discount offered by the club seems to more than offset the expense. But does it really save you money?

Some clubs do offer merchandise or services at reduced prices and charge reasonable membership fees, but other clubs cost their members more in time, money, and delay than they will ever save through lower prices.

Some buyers clubs give members the opportunity to shop in warehouselike stores for discounted household goods and food, which must be purchased in large quantities. Usually the membership fee is modest, and the savings can be considerable. If you have enough storage space at home to accommodate buying in bulk, this type of buyers club may be worth considering.

Other clubs do not have stores but instead offer members discounted shopping through catalogs or with coupons. The coupons are redeemable for goods or services at certain stores. But one should be wary of coupon clubs. The coupons may be valid under limited circumstances or totally useless because the stores have gone out of business.

Both coupon and catalog buyers clubs tend to have high membership and renewal fees. In the case of catalog clubs, the products and brands that are listed in the catalog may not be exactly what you are looking for. Some clubs actually stock little or no merchandise, and club members must shop around in retail stores to find the merchandise they want. Then they must provide the club with the brand names and model numbers of items they want to buy. Only then will the buyers club place the order with the manufacturer. Weeks or months may pass before the merchandise is delivered.

To determine whether a buyers club will actually save you money, do some comparison shopping in local stores. Check to see whether the buyers club imposes additional charges for freight and handling. Also, take into account the high membership and renewal fees. For example, an initial membership fee can be as high as $500. Even if you save 25 percent on each item purchased, you will have to spend $2,000 during the first year before you begin to realize any savings.

If you do decide to join a particular buyers club, first check their record with your local Better Business Bureau or consumer protection agency.

CALENDAR

When lawyers refer to the calendar, they mean the court calendar—a list of cases awaiting a trial or a hearing in court.

In discussing your case your lawyer may also refer to a "calendar call." This is a court session during which the judge determines the progress of cases awaiting trial—depositions that must be taken and motions that must be made before trial. Sometimes the judge sets the date for a trial at that time. See also DEPOSITION.

CAPITAL GAINS TAX

The tax you pay on the profit you make from the sale of a capital asset is called a capital gains tax. The Internal Revenue Service considers just about anything you own a capital asset. Your house, car, boat, jewelry, and stocks and bonds are all capital assets. In 1992 the federal government was taxing capital gains at almost the same rate as other income, but at other times they were taxed at much lower rates.

HOW THE TAX WORKS

Suppose you bought a 1976 Cadillac convertible several years ago for $10,000. Because the car is now a collector's item, and because you have kept it in mint condition, you are able to sell it for $35,000 today. Your capital gain is $25,000, and your tax on the gain, if you are in the 28 percent tax bracket, is $7,000.

When you pay your federal income taxes, you report your capital gains on Schedule D and on Form 1040. You can deduct any costs associated with selling the car, such as advertising fees and sales commissions. These deductions will reduce the amount of your capital gain and you will probably pay less tax.

SELLING YOUR HOME

A capital gains tax is due on the sale of real estate just as it is on the sale of other capital assets. But the law makes an exception if the property is your own home—your principal residence. You may defer payment of the tax for up to two years, and if you buy a new principal residence before the two-year period expires, you may not have to pay the tax at all.

To avoid payment of the capital gains tax, the purchase price of your new home must equal or exceed the selling price of your former house. If you sell your residence for $80,000 and your new house costs $80,000 or more, you will owe no tax.

You do not have to put all the money you received from the sale into your new purchase in order to avoid the tax. For example, suppose you sell your house for $120,000 and make an overall profit of $40,000 from the sale. If you buy a new house for $121,000, you can make a minimum down payment of $6,050 (5 percent), and put the remainder of the $40,000 to some other use. You will not have to pay capital gains tax on the balance.

ONE-TIME $125,000 EXEMPTION

Another kind of relief from the capital gains tax was designed for older people. If you are over 55 and have lived in your home for three of the past five years, you may take a one-time exemption of up to $125,000 of your capital gain when you sell your principal residence.

Let us say that three decades ago you bought a home costing $12,000, and over the years you spent $10,000 on renovations. Because of rising real estate values the house is now worth $200,000. You plan to sell it and buy a condominium in Florida for $60,000, and you will pay $14,000 in realtor's and attorney's fees and closing costs. See CLOSING, REAL ESTATE.

When you figure your capital gain, you are permitted to subtract from the $200,000 not only the original price of your old house but also the expenses for renovations and closing costs. This leaves a capital gain of $164,000. When you subtract the $60,000 for the condo, the balance is $104,000—less than $125,000. If you elect to take your one-time exemption, you will owe no tax.

Suppose you are a homeowner over 55 and are engaged to marry another homeowner over 55. Each of you plans to sell your old house and move into a new one together. Once you marry, you will be entitled to only one exemption between you. To come out on top financially, both of you should sell your houses before you marry.

CASHIER'S CHECK

A check issued by a bank against its own account and signed by a bank officer is known as a cashier's check. Because it is drawn against the bank itself and not against a private depositor's account, a cashier's check often is accepted by a party (such as an auction house or an antiques dealer) that will not take a personal check. You can buy a cashier's check from your bank either with cash or by having money transferred to the bank from your account.

CASH SURRENDER VALUE

If you decide to cancel your life insurance policy, you may receive a sum of money from your insurance company. This is called the cash surrender value—the amount of money you receive when you surrender, or give up, the policy.

Not all life insurance policies have a cash value when they are surrendered. Your policy (which is a contract) states whether you are entitled to cash it in before your death. See LIFE INSURANCE.

Whole-life insurance policies and endowment policies both accumulate cash values. The premiums you pay on these policies include not only the cost of the actual life insurance (the death benefit) but an additional amount invested by the insurance company. This investment, plus the money it earns, is considered the cash value of the policy.

One advantage of a policy that accumulates cash value is that you can borrow against it at a relatively low interest rate. Many policies also contain a provision that allows you to use the cash value to pay past due premiums. In both cases, if you do not repay the loan, the amount you borrowed is deducted from the death benefit, and what remains is paid to the beneficiary.

CASUALTY INSURANCE

Automobile collision insurance, homeowners insurance, and business insurance are some of the various kinds of casualty insurance. It provides financial protection against injuries or loss you cause someone else, as well as injuries or loss suffered by you and by others covered by the policy. For example, a business casualty policy provides liability coverage for another person's loss or injury due to the negligence of the business or its employees. It may also protect a business against loss due to theft or damage by its own employees. See also AUTOMOBILE INSURANCE; FLOOD INSURANCE; HOMEOWNERS INSURANCE.

CAUSE OF ACTION

Your neighbor slipped on the icy sidewalk in front of your house, and now she has started a lawsuit against you in order to be compensated for her injuries. The legal papers you have been served state that she is charging you with negligence for failing to keep the sidewalk safe. Your alleged negligence is the cause of action—the claim that serves as the basis for filing a lawsuit.

Failure to come up with a legitimate cause of action usually leads to the dismissal of a lawsuit. Suppose your neighbor dropped a banana cream pie on your sidewalk and slipped on that—instead of on the ice. Although the accident happened on your property, it was caused by her negligence rather than yours. In this event, she would have no cause of action—in other words, no legally acceptable reason to initiate a lawsuit against you.

CENSORSHIP

Suppose you write a pamphlet describing the corruption you have discovered at a government agency. Just as the pamphlet is about to be published, the agency goes to court and asks for an injunction to halt its publication.

You have become the victim of attempted censorship, an effort to prevent information from reaching the public. It is a violation of freedom of speech and freedom of the press, both of which are guaranteed by the First Amendment. Censorship is also known as prior restraint because the information is suppressed before it has a chance to reach the public.

WHEN CENSORSHIP IS LEGAL

The Supreme Court has permitted some censorship during the time of war. For example, factory workers, scientists, soldiers, and other people connected with the war effort can legally be prevented from talking or writing about the work they do. Also during wartime, newspaper, radio, and television reporters may not be allowed to give out information about troop movements and locations and the kinds of weapons that are being used in combat.

CONTROVERSIAL MATERIAL

The issue of censorship has come up in relation to the government's sponsorship of controversial works of art. In the early 1990's several artists were denied grants from the National Endowment for the Arts (NEA) when Congress passed legislation requiring that the NEA consider "general standards of decency" in making its awards. In 1992 a federal judge found that this requirement violated the artists' First Amendment rights, and the next year the government paid a substantial financial settlement to the artists who had challenged the NEA standards.

Decisions made by book publishers have also created controversy. When the manuscript of Bret Easton Ellis's novel *American Psycho* was delivered to his New York publisher in 1991, the editors found it highly offensive and halted publication. Although there were shouts of censorship, the editors were within their legal rights, because the author was free to find another publisher (as, in fact, he did). See also PRESS, FREEDOM OF; PRIOR RESTRAINT; SPEECH, FREEDOM OF.

CERTIFIED CHECK

Sometimes, to be sure that a check will be honored, a person will ask for payment with a certified check, which you can get from your bank. By certifying the check, the bank guarantees to the person who is to be paid (payee) that the money needed to pay the check is in your bank account. This amount is frozen in your account until the payee collects it from the bank. Unlike a cashier's check, which is written on the bank's account, a certified check is written on your own account. See CASHIER'S CHECK.

To certify a check, a word such as *certified* or *accepted* is usually stamped on it, along with the signature of a bank officer.

Because the bank has guaranteed payment, you cannot stop payment on a certified check. The bank also must honor the check; if it does not, you can sue for wrongful conduct. See also CHECK.

Certified Public Accountant

In order to become a certified public accountant (CPA), an accountant must pass an examination administered by the state in which he practices. The certification exam varies from state to state, but it is based on a national model written by the American Institute of Certified Public Accountants (AICPA). Once an applicant has passed the exam, he is licensed by the state, and becomes a member of the institute.

Aside from doing regular accounting work such as preparing tax returns and auditing, CPA's may examine and report on the financial records of corporations and individuals. Unlike a noncertified accountant, a CPA has a fiduciary relationship (one of trust) with his client and must hold his client's business in strict confidence. For example, if he is hired by the board of directors of a corporation to examine its books, he is responsible to them and not to the management of the corporation. He is also obligated to report erroneous information in financial statements that he reviews.

If a CPA fails to meet the standards of his profession, which are spelled out in state law and by the AICPA, he may have his license suspended or revoked and may be expelled from the institute. In addition, he may be held responsible for any financial loss he has caused his client.

Change of Venue

When a trial is moved from one district or county to another, the move is called a change of venue, or location. The most common reason for a change of venue is bias. For example, attorneys may claim that they cannot find an impartial jury because of media publicity about a case in the original locale. But the fact that the media have covered a case does not mean that the trial will inevitably be moved. It will probably remain in its original location if the court is convinced that jurors will decide the case solely on the evidence presented in court and not on what is reported by the media.

Bias on the part of the judge presiding over the case is another reason to move a trial, if another judge in the same district is not available. For example, a change of venue may be ordered if the judge has a financial interest in the case, or if the judge happens to be a friend, relative, or even just an acquaintance of one of the parties in the case.

Sometimes a trial is moved to promote the cause of justice. For instance, moving the trial to another location may enable the jury to view the scene of the crime or accident, or may bring the trial closer to important documents and witnesses.

Character Evidence

Evidence presented during a trial about a person's traits and overall conduct is called character evidence. It is used to help the judge and jury decide if the person's alleged actions as they relate to the case are consistent with his behavior in the past. Usually offered by a "character witness," the evidence may be the statement of a close friend or of someone familiar with the person's reputation in the community.

Character evidence is not a substitute for factual proof. A judge will allow it only if a person's character has some bearing on the case—for example, in a child-custody suit.

After a conviction in criminal cases, character witnesses are sometimes called to help the court decide what sentence should be imposed. For example, a person convicted of embezzlement may call witnesses to testify that the crime was out of character for him—that it resulted from a nervous breakdown, devastating financial loss, or some other difficulty—and that he was otherwise a model citizen. The purpose of this kind of character evidence is to convince the court to impose a more lenient sentence. See also EVIDENCE; EXTENUATING CIRCUMSTANCES.

CHARITABLE DONATION

Thousands of charitable organizations in the United States help the poor, the sick, the elderly, and the homeless. Funds may also be raised for many other causes, ranging from sports to the arts.

Because charitable organizations relieve the government of some of its burden, the Internal Revenue Service and most states give charities special treatment. Charities often pay a lower rate of income tax or sometimes no tax at all, and may be exempt from state and local property taxes.

For the taxpayer, donations to qualified charities are deductible from income tax, as long as deductions are itemized on the return. If you do not know whether a charity qualifies for tax-exempt status, you can ask the organization or the Internal Revenue Service.

WHAT YOU CAN DEDUCT

The amount of money you can claim as a contribution depends on whether you got anything in return. If you make a $50 contribution to your local public television station, you can claim a $50 deduction. But if you attend a benefit concert, you must deduct the amount of money you would have paid for tickets at the box office. Or suppose you attend a benefit auction and pay $300 for a camel hair coat donated by a local boutique. If the coat costs $300 in the shop, you cannot claim the $300 as a deduction. But if you pay $450 for the coat, the extra $150 is a tax-deductible contribution.

If you give clothes, furniture, toys, or other personal property to a tax-exempt charitable organization, you can include the fair market value as a tax deduction. (The fair market value is what a willing buyer would pay a willing seller, and it is usually much less than the original cost.) Get a receipt to serve as proof of your donation if your tax return is audited. See also INCOME TAX AUDIT.

CHARITY SCAMS

Most charities are legitimate, but some are scams run by people who put the money they collect into their own pockets. By the time the authorities find out about the deception, the bogus charities have vanished from the community, only to start up again somewhere else.

STEPS TO TAKE

To protect yourself from charity scams, be sure to keep the following precautions in mind:

1. Be suspicious of an organization with a name resembling that of a well-known charity. For example, the "Salvation Union" could be a fraudulent outfit trading on the name of the Salvation Army.

2. If an unknown charity claims to be affiliated with a recognized one, call the latter to confirm the relationship.

3. Be wary of solicitations made over the telephone or

CHECKLIST

When a Charity Telephones

Although many legitimate charities solicit contributions by telephone, some callers who claim to represent charities are confidence artists who seek donations (often to fake organizations) in order to fill their own pockets. Below are some tips to help minimize troubles when a fund-raiser calls.

❑ **NEVER GIVE YOUR CREDIT CARD NUMBER TO A FUND-RAISER WHO CALLS YOU.**
Always make contributions by check, payable to the charity only—not to the name of an individual.

❑ **DON'T ALLOW YOURSELF TO BE PRESSURED TO MAKE AN ON-THE-SPOT CONTRIBUTION.**
Legitimate charities will be as happy to take your money tomorrow as today. If the caller intimidates you, report the call to the police and the state attorney-general's office.

❑ **ASK HOW MUCH OF YOUR DONATION WILL ACTUALLY GO TO THE CHARITY.**
Some telephone fund-raising organizations keep as much as 90 percent of the contributions that they solicit.

❑ **IF YOU ARE IN DOUBT ABOUT THE CHARITY, ASK FOR WRITTEN INFORMATION.**
This will not only give you more time to think, it will also enable you to make a more informed judgment.

door-to-door. (See the checklist at left.)

4. Beware of any appeal disguised as an invoice or a bill.

5. Before sending money to an unfamiliar charity, call the consumer affairs division of your state attorney general's office. Most states require charities to register with the attorney general. If the charity is not legitimate, your call may help him put an end to its activities.

6. If a charity sends you a gift that you did not request, you are not obligated to make a donation or to return the item.

Chattel Mortgage

A chattel is an item of personal property—a car, boat, bond, or any other property except real estate. A chattel mortgage is a loan that is guaranteed by pledging the borrower's chattel as collateral. He keeps the item that he puts up as collateral, while the lender files an agreement with a local public office specifying the amount of the debt and the property used as collateral. If the borrower does not repay the loan as agreed, the lender can take the property and sell it to satisfy the amount of the loan.

In recent years most chattel mortgages have been replaced by documents that are known as security agreements. They are regulated by the Uniform Commercial Code (UCC), a body of laws relating to commerce that have been adopted at least in part by all states. See SECURITY AGREEMENT; UNIFORM COMMERCIAL CODE.

Check

Every day, millions of checks change hands, transferring money from one party to another. Most of us write checks routinely, unaware that their use and misuse have a number of legal consequences.

The basic process is simple: the person who writes a check (the drawer) directs his bank (the drawee) to pay a specified sum of money from his account to a third party (the payee).

CASHING CHECKS

Banks are usually required to cash a check when the payee presents it to the drawer's bank, provided the payee is one of its customers. If he is not, the bank may refuse to cash the check. The payee then may take the check to his own bank or to a business that offers check-cashing services.

The reason a bank may be reluctant to cash a check when the payee is not one of its depositors is that the bank has no protection if the drawer's account does not have sufficient funds to cover the check. In contrast, when one of its own depositors presents a check, the bank can protect itself by putting a temporary hold, or lien, on that person's account until the check clears.

INSUFFICIENT FUNDS

If a check "bounces"—if it is returned by the bank because of insufficient funds—the payee must try to collect the money from the person who wrote the check. For example, suppose someone buys a television set from you at a garage sale and pays with a check that bounces. You should first try to talk to the purchaser and attempt to arrange for payment in cash. If your attempt at negotiation fails, you can always take the case to small-claims court in order to get your money or recover the set. See also BOUNCED CHECK.

STOP-PAYMENT ORDERS

Suppose you suddenly realize you do not have enough money in your account to cover a check, or for some reason you do not want a certain check to be paid by the bank—a check to a charity that you subsequently find is bogus, for example. What can you do? One solution is to tell your bank to stop payment on the check.

The bank will ask for your account number, the number of the check, the amount, the date, and the name of the payee. You can stop payment by telephone, but the bank will generally require written authorization within a few days. Unless the check was certified or was already paid, a bank usually honors a stop-payment order. It does, however, charge a fee to cover the cost of the paperwork involved.

FORGED CHECKS

If you discover that a check has been forged in your name, notify your bank immediately. Since it has your correct signature on file, the bank is responsible if it allows the forged check to go through and must replace the money taken from your account to pay it. It is the bank's responsibility to recover the money from the forger.

However, if your own negligence contributes to the forgery, the responsibility may be placed on you. For example, if you do not notify the bank when your checkbook is lost or stolen, you may not be able to recover the money that is lost to a forger.

If you notice a forged check when you review your bank statement, report it to the bank right away, or you could lose your right to get back the money from the bank. Remember that each month you have the responsibility to examine your statement and canceled checks to be sure your records agree with those of the bank.

ALTERED CHECKS

Another way a crook may tamper with your check is by altering the amount. Suppose you write a check for $5 to Harvey Potts, an unscrupulous antiques dealer. By adding two zeros and the word *hundred* to your check, he collects $500 from your bank account. Are you responsible for the loss of the money?

It depends. If you wrote the check in such a careless way that Harvey could easily alter it, you could be considered negligent and responsible for the full amount. But if you made the check out in the proper manner, your bank is the unlucky party. It can still deduct from your account the $5 you intended to pay in the first place, but it will have to get the other $495 from Harvey Potts.

By following a few simple rules you can discourage people from altering your checks:

◇ When writing the amount of the check in numerals, don't leave any space between the dollar sign printed on the check and the numbers you enter to the right of it. Write the cents numbers raised above the line and underline them twice.

◇ When writing the amount of the check in words, use capital letters (they are much harder to alter than script) and draw a straight line between the amount and the word *dollars* printed on the check.

◇ Never give anyone a "blank check" (one you have signed without filling in the amount), even if you trust him to fill in the correct amount later. If he loses the check or if he turns out to be untrustworthy and fills in a higher amount, you cannot complain to the bank. When you sign a blank check, you assume the risk.

ENDORSING CHECKS

Be careful when endorsing checks for deposit. If you sign your name on the back without any other statement, you have made a "blank endorsement," authorizing the bank to pay the funds to anyone who presents the check—even a thief who steals it after you endorse it. (But the bank is responsible if it cashes a check on which your endorsement was forged, because it has a duty to verify each depositor's signature.)

To avoid the risk of a blank endorsement you can instruct the bank to deposit funds directly into your account. To do this, simply write the words "for deposit only" on the back of the check next to your signature. This prevents anyone else from cashing the check.

You can also direct the bank to cash the check not for you but for a third party. For example, if the endorsement reads "Jane Witherspoon—pay only to Derek Davis," the bank can give the money only to Derek Davis unless Derek in turn endorses the check to another person. However, some banks will not honor checks with such third-party endorsements.

If you want to endorse a check over to a third person, but you do not want to be responsible if the check should bounce, you can protect yourself by the way you write the endorsement. Suppose you owe Bob $200 and Abe has just given you a check for that amount. You sign the check over to Bob, but you include the words "without recourse" in the endorsement. Now if the check is no good, Bob cannot hold you responsible for the money. He will have to seek it from Abe, who initially wrote the check. See also Bank Account; Cashier's Check; Certified Check; Electronic Funds Transfer Act; Float; Kiting.

Child Abuse and Neglect

Under normal circumstances, parents have the right to the custody of their children, the right to control and discipline them, and the right to make decisions with regard to their health and welfare.

But if parents abuse or neglect their children, they may forfeit some or all of these rights. Sometimes the state through its juvenile or family courts must step in and assume the parents' responsibilities.

CHILD ABUSE

State laws define child abuse and declare when the state may take action to protect the child.

Corporal punishment

In most states parents have the right to use corporal punishment as long as it is not excessive. For example, the average spanking (though many experts contend it is wrong) does not legally constitute child abuse. But 50 blows with a leather belt definitely does.

Any injury requiring medical attention that a parent or other adult inflicts is child abuse. So are actions that, although they produce no visible wounds, amount to torture, such as holding a child's head under water or confining a child to a closet or basement. Increasingly, courts are holding parents responsible if their child is harmed by another person, such as a boyfriend.

Sexual abuse

Sexual behavior toward a child, including intercourse, fondling for a sexual purpose, or making a child watch sexual acts, calls for legal action when discovered. But hugging, kissing, and touching a child in an affectionate, nonsexual way is not sexual abuse, nor is taking photos of your child nude in the bathtub, as long as the pictures are not suggestive or provocative.

Emotional abuse

Physical and sexual abuse cause emotional damage, but emotional abuse can also be inflicted by itself. For example, if a mother dresses her young son in skirts and parades him around as a girl, or a father repeatedly calls his teenage daughter a slut, the humiliation the child suffers amounts to emotional abuse. Such actions may constitute legal grounds for removing the child from the custody of the parents.

CHILD NEGLECT

Extreme neglect of a child is a crime that warrants court intervention. It can take a number of forms.

Abandonment

When a parent leaves his or her children without making arrangements for their supervision, care, or support, the parent is guilty of abandonment. If the abandonment continues for a long time, the child may be taken from the parent and put up for adoption.

Failure to provide

Not giving a child adequate food, shelter, supervision, or medical care is also considered neglect. But whether the state can intervene depends on the circumstances.

In general the state cannot remove children from their homes if their parents' failure to provide for them is due solely to poverty. For example, if a family is living in a camper with no electricity, and local service agencies have no shelter to provide them, the state does not have grounds to remove the children from the family home against the parents' will.

If resources are available to the family, however, and they refuse to take advantage of them, the state may intervene to protect the children. For example, if low-income housing is available to a single mother, but she insists on living in a public park with her infant child, she could be charged with neglect and her child placed in a foster home.

The failure of parents to provide their children with adequate medical care is usually grounds for court intervention, but many states make an exception for parents who hold strong religious beliefs. For instance, parents who believe in the healing power of faith may not be charged with child neglect if they fail to take their daughter to the doctor when she is sick. However, if her life is at risk, the court may intervene and appoint a guardian to authorize medical treatment.

Mental disorders

If a parent cannot care for a child owing to a long-term mental illness, the court may make alternative custodial arrangements for the child.

MANDATORY REPORTING

In an effort to stop child abuse many states have enacted mandatory reporting laws. They require that professionals such as doctors, nurses, teachers, social workers, therapists, and police officers report any suspected child abuse to the state child-protection service.

Professionals who fail to report the suspected abuse may be charged with a crime. Those who do report child abuse are granted immunity in the event that they make an honest mistake. For example, a doctor who discovers multiple bruises on a child suspects child abuse and files a report. Later it turns out the bruises were due to a fall. The child's parents cannot sue the doctor for making a false report—nor can they sue her for slander, libel, breach of confidentiality, or invasion of privacy.

VOLUNTARY REPORTING

Even if you are not a professional legally required to report child abuse, you should report abuse if you have a good (preferably concrete) reason for suspecting it. Although you may be wrong in your suspicions, it is better to put the interests of the child first. Do not assume that someone else will report the abuse, or that it is none of your business. The child could be suffering great harm and have no way to protect himself. Do not worry about retaliation, because your report will be kept confidential.

Many areas of the country have child-abuse hotlines you can call. If you do not have this service where you live, you can call your local police, who will forward your report to the proper authorities for investigation. For a child in immediate danger of serious injury or death, call 911, the police emergency number.

CHILD-ABUSE INVESTIGATIONS

When a local child-welfare agency receives a report of child abuse or neglect, it is required by law to conduct a prompt investigation. The kind of action taken depends on the severity of the abuse.

In cases of serious abuse or neglect, the child is removed from the custody of his parents immediately. If crimes such as rape or beating have been committed, the parents may be arrested and charged. The child-welfare agency then makes arrangements for the child to stay with relatives, a foster family, in a shelter, or, if necessary, a hospital. Within a few days a court hearing is held and a judge decides whether it is necessary to remove the child from his parents' custody permanently.

In less serious situations, when the child is not in immediate danger, he cannot be removed from the family home. The court may, however, require the parents to undergo counseling or take parenting lessons. If they refuse to cooperate or the situation gets worse, the court may remove the child from the home.

If the abuse or neglect is minor or is unlikely to recur—for example, if a parent left her child unattended in the park for five minutes—the welfare agency and the parents may agree to work together informally. Sometimes the investigation produces no evidence of wrongdoing, and the case is closed.

COURT PROCEEDINGS

Cases of serious abuse or neglect are referred to the juvenile court or the family court, which determines who should have jurisdiction, or authority, over the child—the parents or the court. If there is sufficient evidence that the child is in danger, the court assumes authority and may take any one of a number of measures for his protection. The court may:

◇ Allow the child to remain at home under the supervision of the child-protection agency.

◇ Order the child to be placed in a foster or group home until the family situation has improved.

◇ Temporarily suspend all contact between the parents and the child.

◇ In extreme cases, take away the parents' rights to the child and have the child placed in an adoptive home or in long-term foster care.

Removing a child from the custody of his parents, whether temporarily or permanently, is a drastic move. Most of the time, therefore, when the family cooperates with the court to rectify the problems that led to the abuse or neglect, the child will be returned to the family home. See also FAMILY COURT; JUVENILE OFFENDER.

CHILD CUSTODY

Child custody means much more than having your children live in your home. It also includes the right to guide and discipline them and the right to make important decisions about their education, religious training, and medical care.

Every parent has the right to the custody of his or her children, unless that right has been restricted or taken away by a court. Typical circumstances under which a parent must give up custody are these:

◇ When a juvenile or family court finds that the parent has neglected or abused his child. See CHILD ABUSE AND NEGLECT.

◇ When a parent voluntarily gives his custodial rights to another person in an adoption proceeding. See ADOPTION.

◇ When a parent loses some or all of his custodial rights in a divorce. See DIVORCE.

Most legal questions that affect child custody arise in cases of divorce. While the parents are married, they have equal custody of their children. But when they separate, hard decisions must be made. The parents must try to agree on a custody arrangement that is in the best interests of their children. If they cannot agree, the divorce court must make the decision for them.

JOINT CUSTODY

In many states the courts must grant the parents joint custody by law unless there is good reason not to. Joint custody means that the parents share responsibility when it comes to important decisions such as education and medical care. It does not necessarily mean that the children spend half their time in their mother's home and half in their father's.

The physical custody of the children can be handled in a number of ways. Usually children live with one parent most of the time and regularly visit the other. Sometimes parents who live in the same school district switch the children's residence every few months, or the children spend part of the week with each parent. Whatever physical arrangements are made, joint custody is most successful when the parents cooperate to do what is best for their children.

SOLE CUSTODY

Sole custody resembles joint custody on the surface because the parent who does not have custody is usually permitted visitation rights—even for extended periods of time, such as the Christmas holidays or the entire summer. The main difference is that in sole custody only one parent carries the full responsibility for making important decisions about the children's lives.

Sometimes the court may limit visitation rights. If the judge knows that a father is likely to do harm to his son if they are left alone, she can order that a third person be present during the visit. If she feels that a mother may try to abduct her children, she may order that the visit take place within the city limits. If the judge finds that a parent is often too drunk to care for a child overnight, she can order that visits be arranged during the day. In extreme cases, such as when a parent is known to

JOINT CUSTODY

Joint custody is the shared responsibility of a divorced couple for raising their child. It is viewed differently in the various states, as indicated on this map.

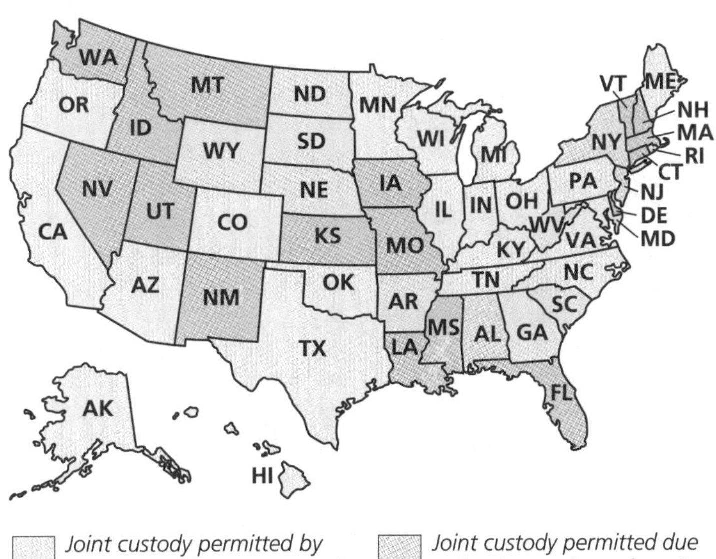

Joint custody permitted by law, but neither encouraged nor discouraged

Joint custody permitted by either law or legal precedent, and encouraged

Joint custody permitted due to legal precedent of previous court decisions, but a court decision is preferred for each case

Joint custody not permitted or not encouraged

be a constant danger to the children, the judge can deny visitation rights altogether.

SPECIAL CIRCUMSTANCES

A number of factors may affect the court's decision in awarding custody.

Tender-years doctrine
In the past, most courts presumed that young children (children of "tender years") belonged with their mother. In a contest between parents for custody, they awarded custody to the mother unless she was shown to be unfit. The modern trend, however, is to regard both parents as equally fit and to award custody to the parent who can provide the better care for the children.

Wishes of the child
Many courts consider the wishes of the child in making a custody determination, especially if he is a teenager. However, the judge has the authority to go against those wishes if they are not in the child's own best interests.

Third-party custody
If the judge determines that neither parent is fit to have custody of the children, she may award custody to someone else, such as a grandparent or other relative. Parents may also agree between themselves to place their children with another person.

Grandparents' rights
State law may allow grandparents to file a petition during the divorce proceedings in order to arrange for their own visitation rights. This ensures that their opportunities for seeing their grandchildren are not subject to the whims of the custodial parent. See also GRANDPARENTS' RIGHTS.

Modification
A custody order can always be modified by the court if circumstances warrant the change. For example, a judge may alter a custody arrangement if the custodial parent interferes with the other parent's visitation rights, makes plans to move out of state, or suffers from a debilitating illness that makes caring for the child virtually impossible.

CHILD EMPLOYMENT

Both the federal and state governments have strict laws to protect children from overwork, hazardous jobs, and dangerous, unhealthful, or immoral working conditions. The federal Fair Labor Standards Act sets minimum ages for doing certain kinds of work and prohibits other kinds of work altogether. States may have laws setting stricter standards than federal laws, and when they do state laws apply.

Minors are also protected by federal and state minimum-wage laws, and by federal and state laws regulating the number of hours they may work.

TYPES OF EMPLOYMENT

Under the Fair Labor Standards Act no child under the age of 18 may be employed in hazardous occupations such as coal mining, logging, excavating, roofing, slaughtering, and meat packing, or in jobs that involve handling explosives, exposure to radiation, or the operation of power-driven machinery.

A 16- or 17-year-old may work at almost any job as long as it does not involve any of these tasks. For example, a boy may take a summer construction job provided he does not operate a bulldozer. Or he may work in a hospital but not around the X-ray machinery.

Children under 16 must usually get a permit from the local office of the state department of labor in order to be employed. The jobs states allow them to hold include office work, cashiering, bagging groceries, cleaning, and working in fast-food establishments. The employer is responsible for asking the minor to show a permit before letting him work.

Newspaper delivery and odd jobs such as shoveling snow, lawn mowing, and babysitting do not require a permit and are open to young people of all ages. In addition, under federal law, there are no age restrictions for theatrical employment.

WORK HOURS

Under federal law, minors under 16 may not work during school hours. While school is in session, they can work up to three hours a day on school days and eight hours a day on nonschool days between 7 A.M. and 7 P.M. In summer they may work as late as 9 P.M. The maximum number of hours they can work each week is 18 when school is in session and 40 at other times.

State laws also regulate children's working hours. When a state law is stricter than the federal law, the state law applies. You can get more information about these laws from the local or regional office of your state's labor department.

WAGES

To encourage the employment of young people, federal and state laws sometimes exempt jobs related to school vocational-training programs from minimum-wage requirements. In the late 1980's Congress enacted a law that allowed employers to pay below-minimum wages to teenagers receiving job training in stores, fast food restaurants, and certain kinds of agricultural occupations. The law, which permitted paying 85 percent of the minimum wage, expired in March 1993.

State minimum-wage laws apply only to employers who are not engaged in interstate commerce. For example, a regional grocery store chain must pay the federal minimum wage while a roadside stand that sells home-grown produce must pay only the state minimum wage, which is often lower.

EMPLOYER VIOLATIONS

Employers who violate the federal Fair Labor Standards Act are subject to penalties of up to $10,000 for each offense. The court may also issue an injunction to prohibit the employer from continuing the illegal employment of children. Any employer failing to comply with the injunction can be found in contempt of court. Repeated, willful violations may result in fines up to $10,000, imprisonment up to six months, or both.

REAL LIFE, REAL LAW

The Case of the Underage Actor

From his first appearance as a five-year-old with Charlie Chaplin in the silent film *The Kid,* Jackie Coogan was one of America's favorite child stars. During the next 13 years, he earned hundreds of thousands of dollars as one of the motion-picture industry's highest-paid actors.

But when Jackie Coogan became an adult, he found that the fortune he had earned had been spent by his parents or wasted on bad investments. And Coogan was not alone; many other underage actors found that the money they had earned was in their parents' bank accounts.

To protect these children's earnings, California passed the law that came to be known as the Coogan Act. Under this legislation, most of the earnings of child actors and entertainers are placed in trust until they reach the age of majority.

While Jackie Coogan himself received no financial benefit from the Coogan Act, the law has helped countless Hollywood child stars over the years, protecting them from the kind of financial loss that he suffered.

FARM LABOR

Exceptions to child labor laws are made for farm labor. Minors from 16 to 18 years old may operate certain hazardous farm machinery on their family farm or on any farm if they are student learners or have passed tests in operating machinery.

CHILDREN'S RIGHTS

Because of their immaturity, children do not have the same rights as adults. Our laws are written to protect children from the consequences of their acts and to prevent them from doing things that require greater maturity. Except for those activities specifically prohibited by law, however, children are under the control and protection of their parents.

A child becomes an adult when she reaches the age of majority—18 to 21 years old, depending on the state. A child may also be considered an adult for some purposes, such as driving, but not for others, such as voting.

MEDICAL DECISIONS

Parents not only have the duty to provide medical care for their children but also have the right to make the decisions relating to this care.

A universal exception to this

right is made when a child's life or health is in danger. If neither parent is available to give his or her consent in an emergency, medical care can be provided without it. If a child's life is endangered because parents refuse to provide medical treatment or provide inappropriate treatment, the state will intervene, and a court can appoint a guardian to make medical decisions for the child.

Some states allow minors to obtain birth control information, contraceptives, and abortions, as well as treatment for venereal disease and drug and alcohol abuse, without the consent of their parents. See also ABORTION.

ADOPTION

In some states children over a certain age, usually 14, must give their consent before they can be adopted.

A minor who has a child may consent to the child's adoption without parental approval. Many states require the minor to obtain independent legal advice regarding the consequences of surrendering her rights to the child. See also ADOPTION.

MARRIAGE AND SEX

A minor usually may not marry without the consent of at least one parent. If she does, the marriage may later be declared void and annulled. Some states allow minors to petition the court for permission to marry if parents refuse to grant it.

Except for sexual relations with a spouse, minors under a certain age—which is usually 18 but varies with the state—cannot legally consent to a sexual act. If the person with whom the minor has sexual relations is an adult, the adult can be prosecuted for statutory rape. In some states a minor who has sexual relations with another minor may also be prosecuted. See also AGE OF CONSENT; STATUTORY RAPE.

DRIVING AND WORKING

Minors can apply for a driver's license when they reach the age specified by state law, but some states require the parent's consent. See also DRIVER'S LICENSE.

Children under 14 have no right to work except in "casual employment," such as delivering newspapers and babysitting. Federal and state laws regulate the types of employment open to minors who are 14 and over and the number of hours they may work. Parents have the right to keep the money earned by their minor children unless they have become emancipated (see next page) or unless state law protects the child's earnings. See CHILD EMPLOYMENT.

CONTRACTS

If an adult enters into a contract with a minor, the adult can be held to the contract but the minor cannot. Suppose 16-year-old Johnny signs an agreement to buy a television on an installment plan. If, after making only one payment, he calls the dealer and tells him to pick up the television, there is nothing else the dealer can do. Furthermore, if the television should be destroyed in a fire, Johnny, unlike an adult, could not be required to make any additional payments, and the dealer would be out of luck.

In most states the legal age for making a contract is 18. But most states allow minors to enter into binding contracts for "necessaries," such as food, clothing, and medical care. Some states let them contract for automobile insurance and educational loans. See also CONTRACT.

DRINKING, SMOKING, AND PORNOGRAPHY

Every state prohibits the sale of alcohol to anyone under 21 and tobacco to persons under 18. Most states also have laws that prohibit the sale of obscene or pornographic materials to minors. Both the minor using the alcohol, tobacco, or obscene material and the adult who supplies it face criminal prosecution. See also ALCOHOL.

INHERITANCES AND WILLS

Minors may inherit property but cannot manage or dispose of their inheritance until they reach the age of majority. Most states require a person to be 18 or 19 in order to make a valid will. If a minor dies and has property, it will be distributed according to state laws, generally to the next of kin. See DYING WITHOUT A WILL; WILL.

JUVENILE COURT

Children who have been accused of crimes are tried in juvenile court, a distinct and separate system from adult criminal courts. Children generally do not have a right to trial by jury, and the juvenile court proceedings are closed and confidential so that they will not stigmatize a child in later life.

Nevertheless, children do have many of the same rights as adult criminal defendants, including the right to be represented by a lawyer, to confront their accusers in open court, to cross-examine the witnesses against them, to remain silent, and to be presumed innocent until found guilty. See also JUVENILE OFFENDER.

EMANCIPATION

When a child is emancipated, he is freed of parental control and his parents no longer have any legal duties toward him. He has the right to be employed, to keep his wages, and to live apart from the family home. He can also make contracts, write a will, and get a driver's license without his parents' consent.

Emancipation occurs automatically when a child reaches the age of majority—18 or 19, depending on the state—but it can take place earlier if, for example, he gets married or enters military service.

EXPANDED RIGHTS

Recently, public attention has been focused on the expanded rights that some courts have given to children. In 1992, a court in Florida allowed a 12-year-old boy to petition for termination of his natural parents' custody rights, allowing him to be adopted by his foster parents. Since then, similar cases have been filed in other states.

Weeks later, in New York, a state judge further expanded the concept of children's rights when he allowed an 11-year-old boy to fire the court-appointed attorney who was representing the youth in his parents' divorce case.

CHILD SUPPORT

With so many children living in homes headed by single parents, child support has become a national issue. According to one study, single parents with two children in some areas received support payments ranging from $51.60 to $200 per month. By contrast, parents eligible for welfare payments from Aid to Families With Dependent Children received $321 per month. In the 1980's Congress enacted legislation to help ensure that children of divorced parents receive the money they need for food, clothing, shelter, medical care, and other necessities from the absent parent.

HOW CHILD SUPPORT IS CALCULATED

When parents divorce or separate, they can agree between themselves on a fair amount for the absent, or noncustodial, parent to pay the parent with whom the child is living. If they cannot agree, or if the noncustodial parent just does not contribute, the custodial parent must go to court to obtain a child support order. This is a legal judgment, or decision of the court, which directs the absent parent to pay the custodial parent a certain sum for the child's support, usually on a monthly basis.

Until recently most states did not have established guidelines to help the courts arrive at the amount of child support that should be awarded. A judge either determined the amount case by case or approved a figure suggested by the parents. As a result, awards of support were often inadequate and inconsistent.

To help correct this situation, Congress passed the Child Support Amendments of 1984, which required the states to adopt uniform statewide child support guidelines by October 1987. Another federal law, the Family Support Act of 1988, strengthened the 1984 law by making minimum-support guidelines mandatory and effective by October 1989.

Although each state uses its own method for calculating minimum child support payments, the amount of support is usually based on the child's needs, the resources of the parent with whom he lives, and the absent parent's ability to pay. The courts also consider the child's customary standard of living in setting the amount of support. You can find out the guidelines in your state from the clerk of the county court or any law library.

If you are the noncustodial parent, in addition to making support payments you may be required to pay for (1) health insurance to cover your child's medical and dental costs (or part or all of the expenses if no insurance is available); (2) the child's education; and (3) child care expenses if the custodial parent works. You may also have to buy life insur-

CHECKLIST

Tracking Down a Deadbeat Dad (or Mom)

The Uniform Reciprocal Enforcement of Support Act (URESA) makes it easier to collect support from a parent who has moved out of state, but the parent must first be located. Here are some steps you can take to find a parent who has moved away.

❑ **CALL OR WRITE HIS MOST RECENT EMPLOYER.**
The former employer may have obtained a forwarding address in order to send a W-2 form at the end of the year. Or, a new employer may have asked for a reference, making the parent traceable to the new company.

❑ **CHECK WITH UNIONS OR SOCIAL ORGANIZATIONS TO WHICH THE PARENT BELONGED.**
The former spouse may have left a forwarding address for benefit statements or asked about the organization's affiliate in another state. You can ask the organization in the new state if the parent is on its roster.

❑ **CALL THE PARENT'S FORMER UTILITY AND PHONE COMPANIES.**
Ask if he left a forwarding address to receive a refund of overpayments or deposits.

❑ **MAKE INQUIRIES OF FORMER BUSINESS ASSOCIATES, RELATIVES, OR FRIENDS.**
Do not assume that they will all assist the parent in hiding out. You need only one person who is angry enough about the parent's neglected responsibility to put you on the right track.

❑ **CONSULT YOUR STATE'S PARENT LOCATOR SERVICE.**
This organization is usually part of the division of family services or the social services office. If you can provide the missing parent's name and Social Security number, the locator service will ask the state department of motor vehicles, the unemployment insurance office, and the department of revenue for leads on the missing parent. The parent locator service can also contact its counterparts in other states where you suspect the parent may be living. In addition, it can work with the Federal Locator Service, which has access to data from the Social Security Administration, Department of Defense, Veterans' Administration, and Internal Revenue Service.

❑ **DON'T GIVE UP.**
You have a right to receive support ordered by the court. Keep calling the district attorney's office in your area. In this situation, it is often the squeaky wheel that gets the grease.

ance, naming the custodial parent as beneficiary.

Generally the courts do not consider having a lot of debt a good reason to lower your support payments (or for you not to make them on time). But they may consider a reduction if you have other children to support, and if you are not working they may have you pay an amount based on the supposition that you are making the minimum wage.

MODIFYING CHILD SUPPORT PAYMENTS

If your circumstances (or those of your former spouse) change substantially, you (or your spouse) may be able to change the amount of the support payments. Suppose you become disabled and cannot work. Or your former spouse, with whom the child lives, returns to work and gets a job with a fabulous salary. In both instances the court might consider your request for a reduced child support payment.

Changing the amount of child support requires a court order. To get one, you must file a motion and present evidence of the need for modification at a court hearing. You will usually need a lawyer's assistance, but a few states—among them California, New York, and Vermont—now offer simplified proceedings that you can handle on your own.

For more information on what course of action to take, you can consult the clerk at the county court or the librarian at the county law library, who will be able to give you the particulars on these proceedings.

HOW COURTS ENFORCE SUPPORT ORDERS

Although it is not difficult for the custodial parent to get a support order from the court, collecting the support is another matter. In the 1980's, as the number of single-parent families increased, evasion of child support payments became so widespread that it became a national scandal. The federal Family Support Act addressed this problem by requiring every state to have laws by October 1994 that authorize the automatic withholding of support payments from the noncustodial parent's wages or other regular source of income, such as a pension or a trust fund.

If mandatory withholding is not yet being enforced in your state, you may be required to send payments to the court, which, in turn, will pay the custodial parent. It is also possible that if you began making support payments prior to the enforcement of the Family Support Act in your state, you will be able to continue making them as before, either directly to the parent or to the court.

WHEN PAYMENTS ARE IN ARREARS

When the noncustodial parent fails to make a payment on time, he is said to be in arrears. There are a number of steps the custodial parent can take when this happens. She will have to go to court, but she will find judges sympathetic to families left to their own devices by a delinquent parent.

Garnishment
The court may issue an order to the employer of the delinquent parent to withhold money from the employee's wages and send it to the court. Suppose Mary's former husband, Sam, is two months in arrears in his support payments, which total $700. The judge, who expects Sam to resume making his regular $350 monthly payments, issues an order for $100 to be garnisheed (withdrawn) from Sam's weekly paycheck until the $700 is paid. If Sam continues not sending his regular monthly payment, Mary will have to get another order from the court.

If Sam had other assets, such as stocks or savings, the judge might decide to attach those funds instead of garnisheeing his wages. Employers do not like to be responsible for garnisheeing wages, and they often do not look kindly on an employee who appears to be neglecting his parental duties.

Contempt of court
A child support order is an order of a civil court and must be obeyed. If Sam has the resources to pay and simply refuses to do so, whether out of anger, stubbornness, or irresponsibility, Mary can go to court and obtain an order for Sam to appear in court and give the reason—"show cause," in legal terminology—why he cannot make his payments. If Sam's reasons are not valid, the judge will order him to pay. If he still refuses, the judge may hold him in contempt of court.

Contempt of court is punishable by imprisonment. The judge may order Sam to be jailed until he pays the child support he owes. In many states it is also a crime to fail to support your children if you are able to do so.

Interception of funds
Many children who are not being supported by a parent are helped out by funds from the Aid to Families with Dependent Children program. If the delinquent parent is due to receive a federal income tax refund, the district attorney may ask the Treasury Department to send all or part of the refund to the welfare agency that supplied the aid to the children. Some states also intercept state tax refunds. See also AID TO FAMILIES WITH DEPENDENT CHILDREN.

A custodial parent who is not receiving welfare may also ask the district attorney to intercept the delinquent parent's tax refunds.

Credit bureau reports
When payments are in arrears by $1,000 or more, child support enforcement agencies are required by federal law to report this information to credit bureaus. Some agencies routinely make such reports, regardless of the amount owed.

SUPPORT ACROSS STATE LINES

Enforcing a child support order when the parent who owes it has left the state has always been more difficult, because the court in one state has no authority in another. Usually it is financially as well as personally impractical for the custodial parent to hire a lawyer and file a suit in another state.

To remedy the situation, every state has adopted the provisions of the Uniform Reciprocal Enforcement of Support Act (URESA) or its successor, known as RURESA (Revised Uniform Reciprocal Enforcement of Support Act). These acts allow for a court order of child support to be issued in the state where the custodial parent lives and then transferred to the noncustodial parent's state for enforcement.

The procedure is relatively simple. Suppose Bob, who is divorced from Samantha, moves to Montana from New York, the state in which Samantha lives with their child. Soon after, Samantha stops receiving child support payments from Bob. Samantha asks the court that originally issued the support order to help her out; officials get in touch with the district attorney's office in Montana and provide a copy of the original support order. The Montana district attorney takes this order to the appropriate court, which orders Bob to resume the support payments. Should Bob refuse, he may face a contempt of court charge in Montana. Bob gets the point, and Samantha starts to receive her payments again.

In theory, both URESA and RURESA should be useful laws. In practice, however, this is not always the case. Overburdened courts, with backlogs of local cases, may give low priority to out-of-state cases. A custodial parent may also find that the support order is reduced if the second state has guidelines lower than the one in which the order was issued.

Nevertheless, URESA and RURESA should not be overlooked as a way to enforce a support order when your former spouse moves to another state. The clerk of the court responsible for enforcing your support order will give you specific information about implementing URESA, and the lawyer who handled your divorce should also be able to advise you. See also DIVORCE.

STEPS TO TAKE IF YOUR SPOUSE FAILS TO MAKE SUPPORT PAYMENTS

If you have a support order for a child in your custody but are not receiving your payments, the following steps may help you secure the payments:

1. Get the help of an attorney or state agency. You may either hire your own lawyer or use the services of your local welfare office or child support enforcement unit. In some states the district attorney's office will help you; in others a court trustee is authorized to monitor and help collect child support payments.

2. Determine the precise amount you are owed. Since most support payments are made through the clerk of the court, his records may show how much has been paid and how much is owed. If no such records exist, review your bank statements or deposit slips to find out what has been paid.

3. Make copies of important documents. Your lawyer will need to see the original court order setting the amount of child support and any further orders that have altered that amount. If payments have come through the court, she must have a copy of the current court ledger to see how much has been paid.

4. Be ready to supply information about the other parent. If your lawyer intends to issue garnishment orders, she must know a few things about the noncustodial parent, such as where his bank is, who owes him money, and where he works. Other helpful information is his Social Security number, last address, and last employer. Some courts ask for a photograph and fingerprints, if available.

CHURNING

Just about every week, the stockbroker Louise hired six months ago calls her with investment advice, which is usually about the same. A stock she bought last month is about to go down, but another is poised to skyrocket. Now is the time to sell the old stock and buy the new one.

Louise follows her broker's advice, but in spite of all the buying and selling, she never seems to make any money. Whatever profit she realizes gets eaten up by the broker's commissions.

It is possible that Louise is the victim of churning—the practice of a broker's making excessive transactions in an investor's account without adequate justification, usually to generate commissions.

A stockbroker is considered a fiduciary, which means that he must act in the best interest of his client. Churning is a violation of this duty, and a broker who is found guilty of this activity may have his license suspended or revoked.

STEPS TO TAKE

If you think your broker may be churning your account, you should do the following:

1. Call or write the nearest office of the Securities and Exchange Commission (SEC), which licenses most stockbro-

kers. The SEC has authority to investigate both individual brokers and brokerage firms.

2. If your broker is not licensed by the SEC, ask your state attorney general's office to investigate your claim. Brokers who sell only mutual funds may not be licensed.

3. Write the National Association of Security Dealers. Most brokers belong to this voluntary organization, which investigates claims and may revoke the membership of a broker who engages in fraud or questionable practices.

See also SCAMS AND SWINDLES; STOCKBROKER; STOCKS AND BONDS.

CIRCUMSTANTIAL EVIDENCE

Facts that indirectly establish other facts, or from which other facts can be inferred, are known as circumstantial evidence. When Evelyn disappeared from home one day, her husband, Jack, called the police to report her as a missing person. Weeks later the police found Evelyn's body; she had been fatally shot.

In investigating Evelyn's death, the police discovered that Jack had recently purchased a large insurance policy on his wife's life, and that he had also bought an automatic pistol, which he told the police he had lost. In addition they learned that Jack had been having an affair with a coworker. Although no one saw Jack shoot Evelyn, and the police never found the gun used to kill her, Jack was charged with the murder of his wife, based on the circumstantial evidence.

In this situation, the facts that (1) Jack owned a pistol, (2) had insured his wife's life, and (3) was having an affair with his coworker could all be proved. These facts were enough to lead the police to the conclusion that Jack had murdered his wife. In this case, the circumstantial evidence also convinced the jury that convicted him.

Circumstantial evidence is just as useful in court as direct evidence. Its strength lies in its logic. It can be used in civil lawsuits—such as those involving contracts and wills—as well as in criminal cases.

CITIZEN'S ARREST

Private citizens have the right to make an arrest of any person who commits a crime in their presence. For example, if you are in an auto accident with another driver who is obviously intoxicated, and the driver tries to leave the scene, you may legally detain him until the police arrive. Although the police will take the driver into custody and make the formal charge of drunk driving, your action in holding him for the police constitutes an arrest.

Before you make a citizen's arrest, however, you should be very sure that the person you are arresting has committed a crime. The law grants the police immunity from civil lawsuits if they make an honest mistake when arresting a person, but no such immunity is granted to private citizens. The exception to this rule is in cases of suspected shoplifting in certain states. See also FALSE ARREST; FALSE IMPRISONMENT; SHOPLIFTING.

CITIZENSHIP

The 14th Amendment to the U.S. Constitution states that "all persons born or naturalized in the United States, and subject to the jurisdiction thereof, are citizens of the United States and of the State wherein they reside." This means that anyone born in the 50 states or the District of Columbia is automatically an American citizen, even if born to parents who are not citizens. Generally children born in Puerto Rico, the Virgin Islands, and Guam are U.S. citizens.

If you were not born in the United States or any of its possessions, you may still have citizenship depending on your date of birth and your parents' status as citizens. If you were born:

◇ *Before May 24, 1934,* you are a citizen if your father was an American citizen, unless he never lived in the United States.

◇ *Between May 24, 1934, and January 12, 1941,* you are a citizen if one of your parents was a citizen and lived in the United States at some time before your birth.

◇ *Between January 13, 1941, and December 23, 1952,* you are a citizen if one parent was a citizen and lived in the United States or its possessions for one year sometime before your birth.

◇ *After December 24, 1952,* you are a citizen if both your parents were citizens and one parent was a national (lived in the United States or its outlying possessions) before you were born. If one parent was a citizen and the other an American national, the citizen must have lived in the United States or its possessions for one year sometime before your birth. If one parent was a citizen and the other an alien, the citizen must have lived in the United States or its territories for at least 10 years before your birth, including 5 years after his or her 14th birthday.

ABC's OF YOUR RIGHTS ABROAD

A U.S. citizen's right to travel abroad is guaranteed by the Fifth Amendment, but this right is not without restrictions. Once abroad, you are protected to some extent by the U.S. consulate in the country you are visiting, but you will not have the same rights there that you have at home. Listed below are some legal rights and restrictions to keep in mind when you travel abroad.

❑ You must have a passport to leave the United States, unless you are traveling to Canada, Mexico, a U.S. possession (such as Puerto Rico or the Virgin Islands), or a country whose treaty with the United States does not require a passport.

❑ You may be denied a passport if your conduct abroad is likely to cause damage to national security or foreign policy; if a federal warrant has been issued for your arrest on a felony charge; if a criminal court order prohibits your departure; or if a court has ordered you committed to a mental institution.

❑ The State Department can prohibit travel to a country engaged in armed hostilities with the United States or to a country where U.S. citizens are in imminent danger.

❑ While abroad, you must obey the laws of the country you are visiting; if you do not, you will be subject to the same procedures and penalties that apply to the local citizens.

❑ The American embassy can take steps to see that the laws of the country you are visiting are properly applied to you; protect your estate and property rights in court; and appear on your behalf in court.

❑ The American embassy can't obtain for you any special rights other than those belonging to the local citizens, or exempt you from that country's laws.

❑ When you return from your stay abroad, you cannot be denied readmission to the United States, even if you do not have a passport.

NATURALIZATION

To acquire citizenship if you are not a citizen by birth, you must satisfy the following requirements, as stipulated by the U.S. Constitution and the Immigration and Nationality Act of 1952:

◇ You must be at least 18 years old, but the age requirement may be waived if you served honorably on active duty in the U.S. Armed Forces during a time of conflict.

◇ You must have lawfully entered the United States for permanent residence.

◇ You must have had a residence in the United States for five consecutive years and lived here for at least half that time. If you are married to a U.S. citizen, you may apply for naturalization after three years of continuous residence as long as you have been married for the entire time.

◇ You must have lived in the state where you apply for citizenship for at least six months.

◇ You must be a person of good moral character, measuring up to the standards of the community. (Conviction for a traffic violation, for example, does not bar citizenship, but being found guilty of fraud or theft does.)

◇ You must be "attached to the principles of the Constitution of the United States, and well disposed to the good order and happiness of the United States."

◇ You must prove your ability to read, write, and speak English—except if you have a learning disability or are over 50 and have lived in the United States for at least 20 years.

◇ You must be able to answer fundamental questions about the U.S. government.

◇ Finally, you must file a petition for naturalization and attend a hearing to examine your qualifications, after which you must take the oath of allegiance to the United States.

RIGHTS AND OBLIGATIONS OF CITIZENSHIP

Naturalized citizens have essentially the same legal rights, privileges, and obligations as American-born citizens except that they cannot become president of the United States. They cannot become representatives in Congress until they have been citizens for seven years or senators until they have been citizens for nine years.

American citizens must obey the laws of the United States and of the state in which they reside, and must pay federal and state taxes. In time of war men may be drafted into the armed forces. Citizens are obligated to be loyal to their country, but this loyalty does not mean they cannot criticize the government or must approve of every law or action. See BILL OF RIGHTS; CIVIL RIGHTS; DUE PROCESS OF LAW; EQUAL PROTECTION OF THE LAWS; MIRANDA WARNINGS; RIGHTS, INDIVIDUAL.

DUAL CITIZENSHIP

It is possible to be a citizen of the United States and of another country. For example, a child born in the United States to parents who are not U.S. citizens or a child born abroad to U.S. citizens may be considered a citizen of both countries. An American citizen can become a citizen of another country as long as he is not required to renounce his American citizenship when doing so.

LOSS OF CITIZENSHIP

A naturalized citizen may lose his citizenship if he obtained it illegally or through fraud, or if within five years of naturalization he establishes a permanent residence abroad or joins an organization that advocates the violent overthrow of the U.S. government.

Certain actions, called expatriating acts, can result in loss of citizenship for both naturalized citizens and citizens by birth. These actions include:

◇ An act of treason or sedition against the United States. See TREASON.

◇ Swearing or declaring allegiance to a foreign state.

◇ Serving in the armed forces of, or accepting other employment from, a foreign country that requires an oath of allegiance to that country.

◇ Renouncing U.S citizenship in writing.

See also ALIEN; IMMIGRATION.

CIVIL RIGHTS

The term *civil rights* refers to the rights every individual is entitled to have while living in the United States. The Constitution gives citizens a measure of civil rights when it refers to the "privileges and immunities" of the citizens of the "several states." The Bill of Rights, enacted in 1791 as the first 10 amendments to the Constitution, first spelled out the civil rights of Americans. Since then many laws have been passed to clarify and expand them.

The civil rights of Americans are many, including the freedom to worship as one pleases and the right to bear arms. This article discusses a right that has developed over time—the right not to be discriminated against. For discussions of other rights, see ARMS, RIGHT TO BEAR; BILL OF RIGHTS; DUE PROCESS OF LAW; EQUAL PROTECTION OF THE LAWS; PRESS, FREEDOM OF; RELIGION, FREEDOM OF; SPEECH, FREEDOM OF.

CIVIL RIGHTS ACTS OF THE 1860'S

For nearly a century after its adoption, the Bill of Rights remained unchanged, even though adult white men were the only citizens it truly protected. At the end of the Civil War, in 1865, the nation adopted the 13th Amendment, which outlawed slavery and other forms of involuntary servitude.

In the years immediately following the war, Congress enacted a series of civil rights acts aimed directly at securing the rights of former slaves. The first of these guaranteed equal rights for all people in the United States; another assured every citizen of an equal right to own, inherit, rent, or buy and sell real estate or personal property; a third act made it a crime to use "force, intimidation, or threat" to deny anyone equal protection of the laws.

In 1868 the far-reaching 14th Amendment was adopted. It

guaranteed that no state could interfere with the civil rights of a citizen or deny him due process of law. Although the citizens Congress had in mind were black people, the phrase chosen was "all persons." In 1870 the 15th Amendment was adopted to allow all citizens to vote without regard to "race, color or previous condition of servitude." Despite these laws, blacks and others continued to suffer racial, religious, and other forms of discrimination. It was not until 1920 that women finally gained the right to vote when the 19th Amendment was adopted.

In the late 1950's and 1960's civil rights once again received widespread attention. In 1957 Congress established the federal Civil Rights Commission to investigate the issue of racial discrimination and race relations and to report back to the president and Congress. During the 1960's, Congress, in response to a grass-roots civil rights movement, enacted a number of laws to afford equal rights to everyone.

THE 1960'S CIVIL RIGHTS MOVEMENT

After activists like Rosa Parks and Martin Luther King, Jr., brought the injustice suffered by blacks and other minorities to the public eye and conscience, national sentiment for new civil rights legislation grew. The Civil Rights Act of 1960 established that states cannot prevent qualified voters from registering to vote and stipulated that anyone, even a government official, who tries to prevent a qualified voter from registering can be sued.

In 1964 President Johnson signed into law the most far-reaching piece of federal civil rights legislation in American history. The Civil Rights Act of 1964 declared that public education, public facilities (public parks and swimming pools, for example), and public accommodations (such as restaurants, hotels, and motels) must be equally available to all persons. Furthermore, all federally funded social programs were required to comply with the antidiscrimination measures of the act. Four years later the Civil Rights Act of 1968 prohibited discrimination in housing based on race, color, religion, or national origin.

These federal laws prohibiting discrimination in public facilities or places of public accommodation apply to any business that is in some way a part of interstate commerce. If a private facility is located in a place of public accommodation, it cannot discriminate. For example, a privately owned diner in a bus terminal or a fast-food restaurant at a turnpike rest stop must treat all customers equally. The same principle prohibits state and local governments from discriminating in such facilities as hospitals, nursing homes, state parks, and prisons.

Not all discrimination is illegal or unconstitutional, however. Private individuals may choose the people with whom they associate, and private-membership clubs may also be exempt from federal antidiscrimination laws. But state and local governments can (and often do) establish ordinances that require equal access to these clubs. See AGE DISCRIMINATION; DISABLED AMERICANS; ELECTION LAWS; JOB DISCRIMINATION; SEXUAL HARASSMENT.

CIVIL SERVICE

The nonmilitary employees of a national, state, or municipal government who carry out its day-to-day operations are called the civil service. A police officer in St. Louis is a civil servant, as is a secretary to the lieutenant governor of Florida or an expert on political developments in East Africa at the State Department. The rules under which civil servants are hired, paid, promoted, and dismissed constitute the civil service system.

Civil service systems were established in the U.S. to ensure that government workers were qualified for their jobs. Originally most government jobs were filled by the friends and political supporters of elected officials, and their relationship with the official was often the only qualification they had. As a result many important government functions were performed incompetently or not at all. Even if a government worker was competent, his job was secure only as long as his benefactor remained in office.

In 1883 an act of Congress established the Civil Service

Commission to enforce objective standards for recruiting, compensating, and dismissing federal employees. Since then, applicants have been required to take competitive exams to prove that they are qualified.

Once hired, civil servants can generally be fired only if they do not adequately perform their work. In most situations, they are not allowed to strike, since their work involves public welfare and safety, and they may not take an active, public role in partisan politics. However, they can vote and debate political issues privately.

The Civil Service Commission was dissolved in 1978. Its functions were split between the Merit Systems Protection Board, which is responsible for safeguarding the rights of federal workers, and the Office of Personnel Management (the OPM), which recruits and manages government employees.

You can obtain information about available federal civil service jobs and how to apply for them by calling or visiting the OPM office in your area or the Federal Information Center. See also FEDERAL INFORMATION CENTER.

State civil service systems follow the federal model, and state civil service jobs are listed with the civil service commission of each state.

CLASS ACTION

Normally anyone who is involved in a lawsuit must have a chance to appear in court and present her side of the case. This is a sensible rule for most lawsuits, but in a case that involves hundreds or thousands of plaintiffs, allowing each one to appear would quickly exhaust court officials and cause unnecessary delays in the resolution of the suit.

To overcome this problem, a judge may allow one or more plaintiffs to bring a lawsuit on behalf of many others who have the same claim against the defendant. Such a class-action suit, as it is called, permits all similar claims to be heard in a single trial.

For example, a recent class-action suit was started on behalf of all the airline passengers who had used a common reservations system operated by some of the major airlines. In filing the suit the plaintiffs claimed that the airlines conspired to keep customers from receiving the lowest possible fares. Because each of these customers could have started a separate lawsuit, the judge authorized a class action to resolve the issue for all possible plaintiffs and so relieve the burden on the court system.

Anyone who is a member of the class is bound by the ruling of the court, even if she has no actual knowledge of the lawsuit. In this case anyone who had bought a ticket from any airline served by the reservations system was automatically a member of the class. If a person qualifies for the class but does not want to be included in the suit, she must notify the court of her decision.

When a judge agrees to hear a case as a class action, the attorneys for the plaintiff place class-action notices in newspapers and other publications that are likely to be read by the members of the class. The ads notify readers that the class has been certified and states how members can be excluded from the lawsuit if they wish. In this case, ads were placed in *USA Today*, the *Wall Street Journal*, and major city newspapers likely to be read by people who travel on airlines.

When the case is settled, notices are again placed in publications and sometimes aired on television. Those who can provide proof of their membership in the class (in this case by completing a claim form provided by the court or by providing old airline tickets) are paid out of a fund established by the defendant. Anyone who is eligible for a settlement must make her claim within the allotted time or forfeit her rights. Funds that are unclaimed revert to the defendant.

CLEMENCY

Clemency is a power given to the president of the United States and the governors of the 50 states to reduce a convicted criminal's sentence. An act of clemency recognizes that although a crime was committed, mitigating factors justify reducing the severity of the court's sentence. Some examples of clemency include reducing fines, shortening prison terms, and granting pardons.

But clemency is not a right. Even if there are mitigating circumstances, a governor or the president is not obligated to grant it. See also PARDON.

Closing, Real Estate

The final step in the sale and purchase of a house or other real estate is known as the closing. The closing usually takes place at a meeting at which the buyer pays the seller, the seller gives the deed to the buyer, and the final mortgage transactions take place.

Buyers are often apprehensive about closings because they must pay large sums of money, sign imposing documents, deal with attorneys and bankers, and be sure that all the cumbersome paperwork is done correctly. Some of these fears are exaggerated, however, because the buyer's lawyer or financing representative (or both) usually take care of most of the paperwork, and they have as great a stake in seeing that nothing goes wrong as does the buyer.

BEFORE THE CLOSING

In the weeks or months before the closing, the buyer must arrange for financing, have the property inspected, and have a title search made to ensure that the seller truly owns (has title to) the property and that it is free of liens. When these things have been taken care of, the buyer is ready to complete (close) the transaction.

The closing date is set in the sales contract. If either party is not ready to close the sale on that date, he must arrange for a postponement and may have to pay a penalty. Not showing up for a closing can mean forfeiting the deposit and being sued for the value of the property.

In many states, closings are held in the office of the buyer's mortgage lender. Although not all closings require a lawyer, it is a good idea to hire an experienced real estate attorney to review the closing documents.

TRANSFER OF OWNERSHIP

At the closing, the seller and buyer, their real estate agents, and the bank's representative meet to complete the transaction. After all the documents are signed, the seller gets his money and the buyer gets the deed and keys to the house.

The buyer should make sure that the deed is signed by all the owners, dated, and certified by a notary public. If a corporation (such as a real estate development company) owns the property, appropriate documents must be submitted showing that the company has the authority to sell it.

CHECKLIST

Your Real Estate Closing

When you buy a house or other real estate, you will have to examine a number of documents, including the ones listed below, when ownership of the property is finally transferred from the seller to you.

❑ **SALES CONTRACT.**
You should see both the original sales contract and any changes made in it subsequently.

❑ **CLOSING STATEMENT.**
Be sure the items in it agree with the sales contract, and that any changes made to it are correct.

❑ **DEED TO THE PROPERTY.**
This is the document that transfers title (or ownership) from the seller to you, the buyer.

❑ **SELLER'S AFFIDAVIT.**
This document proves that no liens or mortgages are outstanding on the property.

❑ **MORTGAGE DOCUMENTS.**
These will depend on the nature of your mortgage agreement.

❑ **PRORATING AGREEMENTS.**
These documents specify how you and the seller will divide such ongoing expenses as property taxes, insurance, and utilities.

❑ **HOMEOWNERS INSURANCE.**
You and the seller must both have proof that the property is insured.

❑ **SELLER'S WARRANTIES.**
Be sure to obtain warranties on the roof, plumbing, heating system, and appliances.

❑ **OTHER DOCUMENTS.**
These may include a property survey; a bill of sale for personal property being transferred to you from the seller (such as furniture or appliances); and a termite inspection report.

CLOSING COSTS

What complicates a closing and puts dread in the heart of a prospective buyer are the closing costs, or settlement costs. They consist of the costs beyond the actual price of the property: appraisal fees, notary fees, lender's fees, attorney's fees, plus money for insurance, taxes, and other miscellaneous expenses. Generally, the closing costs amount to about 5 percent of the purchase price, but they can be higher. It is best to add them up ahead of time to be sure you have the cash on hand to cover them at the closing.

Help to buyers struggling with closing costs is provided by the federal Real Estate Settlement Procedures Act (RESPA), passed in 1974. The law requires that, within three days after you apply for a real estate loan, the lender must provide you with two items designed to protect you against unfair practices and eliminate unpleasant surprises at closing. One is a booklet called *Settlement Costs: A HUD Guide,* prepared by the Department of Housing and Urban Development. The other is an itemized estimate of your closing costs. (Note that the law does not apply to refinancing or to assumed mortgages.)

At least one day before the closing, you must be given a copy of the closing statement, which will contain a detailed list of your final closing costs.

CLOSING STATEMENT

Both parties receive copies of the closing statement—a complete financial accounting of the real estate transaction. It lists the purchase price, the amount already paid toward it, any outstanding mortgages on the property, how the money paid by the buyer is to be applied to those mortgages, and the closing costs. The closing statement also indicates how the insurance costs and real estate taxes will be apportioned between the buyer and seller, and what part of the purchase price has been applied to the seller's obligations, such as real estate commissions, mortgage taxes, surveying costs, and outstanding utility bills.

Finally, the closing statement shows the total balance due to the seller after all payments have been deducted. Both parties should review this document carefully to be sure that the money paid for the property is distributed according to the terms of the contract.

AFTER THE CLOSING

As soon as possible after the closing, the buyer (or his representative) should record his deed to the property, usually at the local courthouse. If the seller has not already done so, he should apply for refunds on his insurance and make sure that arrangements have been made regarding the transfer or cancelation of his mortgage. See also HOME BUYING AND SELLING.

COBRA

Under a federal law enacted in 1986, companies with 20 or more employees must give them the opportunity to continue their group health insurance coverage when their employment ends. The name of the law is the Consolidated Omnibus Budget Reconciliation Act (COBRA). The purpose of the act is to protect workers and families of workers from losing their medical insurance if the worker quits, is fired, divorces his or her spouse, or dies. Most of the time the continued coverage can be obtained for 18 months, but in certain situations it can continue for as long as three years. Only employees who are fired for gross misconduct are ineligible for this continuation of coverage.

Although insurance under COBRA is better than finding yourself suddenly without health insurance, it can be costly. Your premium will be up to 102 percent of the group rate that you and your company paid for your coverage. Suppose you have been paying $60 a month for your company-sponsored health insurance plan, and the company pays $140 toward your coverage each month. If you leave the company and continue your coverage under COBRA, you can be charged up to $204 per month for the same coverage.

There is another significant disadvantage of COBRA. If you happen to develop a serious medical problem during the continuation of your coverage, you may not be able to obtain health insurance at a later time on your own. Rather than waiting until your COBRA coverage expires, start looking for other health insurance as soon as possible.

For specific details on how COBRA protects your own insurance coverage, ask your employer's personnel or human resources department. See also HEALTH INSURANCE.

CODICIL

A legal document that changes or amends a person's last will and testament is known as a codicil. For instance, if your will names your uncle as an executor and he dies, you can write a codicil naming a new executor, rather than writing a new will. To be valid, a codicil must be drawn up with the same formalities as the will itself. For example, if the law in your state requires three persons to witness a will, the codicil also must be witnessed by three persons.

Many lawyers advise their clients not to use codicils because as separate documents, they can become lost or separated from the will, which would then be carried out without the changes in the codicil. And today, with modern computer technology, it is just as easy to rewrite your will to incorporate the changes you want to make. See also ESTATE PLANNING; WILL.

COHABITATION

Living together as husband and wife without being married is known legally as cohabitation. Some states have criminal laws against "notorious" cohabitation—openly living together without being married. While these laws are rarely enforced, some communities do enforce zoning laws that prohibit unrelated persons from living together in a single-family home. See COMMON-LAW MARRIAGE; LIVING TOGETHER; ROOMMATES; ZONING.

COLLATERAL

Collateral is property pledged to ensure that a debt will be paid. Suppose you want to apply for a bank loan in order to expand your business. The bank may ask you to pledge your accounts receivable (the money owed to you for your goods or services) as collateral for the loan. Or if you need a loan in order to send your child to college, you might pledge stocks and bonds you own as collateral or take out a second mortgage on your home. If you fail to repay the loan, you will have to forfeit, or give up, the collateral. See also MORTGAGE; SECURITY AGREEMENT.

COLLECTION AGENCY

A collection agency is a company hired by creditors to collect overdue debts. For providing this service, the agency receives a percentage of the amount it recovers, which can run from 10 percent to more than 50 percent.

By the time a business gives your overdue bill to a collection agency, you will have received several letters or telephone calls requesting payment. You may be frightened, particularly if you cannot pay the bill and you do not want your neighbors or employer to know about your financial position. At one time bill-collecting agencies were able to play on these fears. They made threatening phone calls in the middle of the night and at your job, and burly collectors claiming to be law enforcement officers might have knocked on your door demanding payment.

To counter such practices, in 1977 Congress passed the Fair Debt Collection Practices Act (FDCPA), which clearly states what an agency may and may not do. The checklist on page 103 spells out these nefarious and prohibited practices.

WHAT A COLLECTION AGENCY MUST DO

The FDCPA requires collection agencies to follow certain procedures when they call or write you about a debt. Within five days of its first telephone call or letter to you, the collection agency must send you a notice in writing that states the amount of the debt and the name of the creditor to whom you owe it. The notice will inform you that you have 30 days after receipt of the notice to dispute the debt and to ask for a written verification of it. These rules apply only to consumer debts, not to business debts or to collection efforts made directly by the creditor to whom you owe the debt.

CHECKLIST

Illegal Collection Agency Practices

Under the Fair Debt Collection Practices Act of 1977, a bill collector representing a collection agency may not do any of the following:

- ❑ Communicate with your neighbors, employer, or anyone else for any reason except to ask where you live.
- ❑ Tell anyone that he is trying to collect a bad debt from you.
- ❑ Send you a postcard or mail a letter in an envelope that reveals the sender is a collection agency.
- ❑ Phone you before 8 A.M. or after 9 P.M.
- ❑ Phone you at work if you or your employer objects to your receiving calls there.
- ❑ Use obscene, profane, or threatening language.
- ❑ Make your name public as a person who fails to pay his bills.
- ❑ Fail to identify himself as a bill collector when he calls you or pretend to be a lawyer, law enforcement officer, or other government official.
- ❑ Obtain information by claiming that he is taking a survey or that you have committed a crime.
- ❑ Write or call you personally if you have told him that you are represented by an attorney.
- ❑ Communicate with you in any manner once you notify the agency in writing that you do not want to hear from him.

COLLECTION AGENCY PRACTICES

Once a collection agency receives a bill to collect, its chief goal is to get from you as much money as possible, as quickly as possible. As a result, despite FDCPA and state laws that also regulate collection agencies, bill collectors continue to use a variety of unethical, even illegal, collection tactics. For example, a bill collector might tell you that the original creditor will accept a partial payment to settle the account in full. You make the payment, only to find later that you are being sued for the remainder of the debt. If a collection agency makes such an offer, beware. Be sure that the original creditor has agreed to the terms.

Another common practice among unethical collectors is to ask you to write a series of postdated checks to pay off the debt. The collector promises not to deposit the checks until the dates written on them, and assures you that your bank cannot cash the checks ahead of time. Don't fall into this trap. Checks are now processed electronically, and there is a good chance that no human being will ever see what date you have written. The agency will deposit the checks immediately, and you may end up with an overdrawn account, bank fees, bounced checks, and a lot more trouble than you started with. If the collection agency agrees to accept payment in installments, do not send them before they are due.

STEPS TO TAKE

If you think a collection agency has been acting illegally, you can take the following steps:

1. Notify the collection agency in writing (by certified mail, return receipt requested) that you do not wish to hear from them anymore. Their next step must be to take you to court.

2. Write the Federal Trade Commission, Bureau of Consumer Protection, Pennsylvania Ave. at Sixth St. NW, Washington, DC 20580, or call (202) 326-2222. You may also contact the nearest regional office of the FTC and file a complaint. A collection agency that violates the FDCPA can be sued.

3. Call or write the consumer protection division of your state attorney general's office. States also have laws regulating collection agencies.

COLLECTIVE BARGAINING

Collective bargaining is the legal process of negotiating an agreement between an employer and his employees' authorized representative (usually a labor union) on wages, hours, and other conditions of employment. The rules that regulate collective bargaining were established by the National Labor Relations Act of 1935 (NLRA).

Employees have the right to bargain collectively through their union, and an employer must enter negotiations when the employees' representative requests them. Bargaining, however, does not mean that the parties must come to an agreement. Both sides may stick to their positions until the negotiations reach an impasse. See also LABOR UNION.

Under federal law both sides must negotiate in good faith—that is, with the desire to reach an agreement. But they can use such tactics as filing unfair labor practice charges or calling a strike to further their purposes. The NLRA defines unfair labor practices. Included among them are work slowdowns, refusing to negotiate, and refusing to abide by a negotiated contract. Filing an unfair labor practice charge can delay the bargaining, since once a charge is filed, the National Labor Relations Board conducts an investigation. If the NLRB does not dismiss the charge and a settlement cannot be reached, the matter can go to a hearing before a judge—a process requiring the presentation of evidence and witnesses.

Neither party is relieved of its mandate to bargain because of legal pressures from the other side, such as a boycott, strike, or lockout. See also BOYCOTT; STRIKE.

In order for the union to be able to negotiate effectively, the employer must give its representatives information about the general operation of the business—including information relating to wages, working hours, job standards, factors used to evaluate employees, seniority, and safety and health conditions.

When an agreement is finally reached, the terms and conditions are spelled out in writing, and the agreement becomes an enforceable contract. Failure to comply with the contract can lead to action by the National Labor Relations Board. See NATIONAL LABOR RELATIONS BOARD.

COLLEGE ADMISSIONS

No one has a legal right to a college education, and colleges can set their own standards for admission. They can require that students have a specified high school grade average and a specified score on college entrance exams, such as the Scholastic Aptitude Test (or SAT). They may also choose to admit someone based on other kinds of achievements, as in sports, extracurricular activities, the arts, or community service. The school is not required to tell applicants why they have been rejected.

Although state-supported colleges, like private institutions, have admission standards, they are often required to admit every student who meets them. Your high school guidance counselor will know the admissions policies for the university system in your state.

No college or university that receives federal funding (and this includes most schools) can discriminate against students on the basis of race, religion, or ethnic origin. In fact, many schools have adopted affirmative action programs to provide increased educational opportunities to students from racial and ethnic minorities. See also AFFIRMATIVE ACTION.

Colleges usually charge a nonrefundable application fee to offset the cost of examining the applicant's qualifications. This practice is legal, as long as you are told when you pay the fee that it will not be refunded. Some colleges waive the application fee for students who can show financial hardship.

COLLEGE SCHOLARSHIP

A scholarship is an amount of money awarded to a student for his support or to pay his tuition while he studies. Students may be selected for college scholarships on the basis of ability, previous school record, or financial need, but in recent years the vast majority of scholarships have been need-based.

Scholarship money may be available through colleges and universities, corporations, private individuals, foundations, labor unions, and the federal and state governments. Public funds are usually reserved for students who have financial need, while scholarships from private sources may be given to students who show academic promise and may or may not have financial need.

Whoever donates the funds,

whether a school, private individual, foundation, or corporation, usually sets the conditions for the scholarship. Once a student accepts a scholarship, it becomes an enforceable contract between the donor and the student. If the donor fails to pay, the student may go to court to enforce the contract and obtain his money. Similarly, the student must live up to the terms of the scholarship. For example, a track athlete may receive a scholarship with the understanding that she will participate on the track team while maintaining at least a B average. If she drops out of the team or gets only a C+ average, she may lose her scholarship. See also STUDENT LOAN.

STEPS TO TAKE WHEN APPLYING FOR A SCHOLARSHIP

Listed below are a few things to do if you are applying for a college scholarship:

1. If you are a high school student, talk to your guidance counselor. She will be able to help you get information about both scholarships in general and those that are available in your chosen field.
2. If you are employed, ask about company-sponsored scholarships. Many large firms offer scholarships to employees or their children.
3. Ask your librarian for the most recent and comprehensive sources on scholarships. Publications such as *Arco's College Financial Aid*, *Barron's Complete College Financing Guide*, *Lovejoy's Guide to Financial Aid*, and *Peterson's College Money Handbook* have up-to-date information.
4. Write the college of your choice and ask for information on scholarships. Find out their policy on both need-based and merit scholarships.
5. Apply for any scholarships for which you might qualify on merit. Do this regardless of your family income. Apply early, so that you are not denied funding simply because the money ran out.
6. Be wary of companies that charge a fee to help you locate what they call "hidden scholarships." You can probably obtain the same information on your own for free.

COLLUSION

A secret agreement between two or more parties to break the law or defraud a third party is known as collusion.

Suppose you bought a new car last year, which has turned out to be a lemon with multiple problems that no mechanic seems able to correct. The car is also heavily insured. You make an agreement with your friend Steve to take your car and dispose of it in the river. You report the car as stolen, collect the theft insurance, and split it with Steve. You and he are guilty of collusion.

Or suppose several construction companies are bidding for a contract to build an office building. Alpha Corporation, the lowest bidder, makes a secret pact with Beta Corporation, the second-lowest bidder, to withdraw from the competition if the Beta Corporation promises to award lucrative subcontracts to Alpha. The two companies would be guilty of collusion.

COMMERCIAL PAPER

Commercial paper is a document that represents one person's obligation to pay money to someone else. The most important thing about commercial paper is that it is negotiable. For a document to be negotiable, it must be in writing and signed by the person making the promise to pay. The promise to pay must be unconditional and for a specific sum. The money is either payable on demand or at a time stated in the document. The four types of commercial paper are checks, bank drafts (such as cashier's checks), promissory notes, and certificates of deposit. See also BANK ACCOUNT; CASHIER'S CHECK; CHECK; PROMISSORY NOTE.

COMMON CARRIER

Bus lines, airlines, railroads, taxicabs, moving companies, and trucking lines—businesses that transport the general public or personal property for hire (for a fee)—are called common carriers. They are distinguished from private carriers, such as charter bus companies and air cargo companies, which transport people or property only by special arrangement.

By publicly declaring themselves to be in the transportation business, common carriers are legally required to carry any and all passengers or freight, assuming space allows and the fee has been paid. If they do not, they could face a lawsuit. For more information on the responsibilities of common carriers, see ACCIDENTS ON PUBLIC TRANSPORTATION; MOVING; TAXICAB.

Common carriers are regulated by the state or the federal government, depending on where they operate. Intrastate companies (those that stay entirely within one state) are subject to state laws, while interstate companies and those that do business abroad are regulated by federal law.

COMMON LAW

The legal system of the United States consists of three kinds of law: the U.S. Constitution, the statutes passed by legislative bodies such as Congress, and common law. Unlike the laws created by legislative bodies, common law is made by judges when they apply previous court decisions (called precedents) to new cases. If no precedent or other law exists, the judge can make a new law to fit the situation. Since common law evolves case by case, it is often referred to as case law.

American common law is based on the English common-law system, which originated in the 12th century. At that time judges made their decisions on the basis of accepted social customs, common sense, and what they regarded as fairness. Such rulings then became the law for similar cases in the future. Many state laws in the United States evolved from English common law. Modern laws relating to arson, burglary, trespass, and property ownership, for example, are based on English common law. Unless a state has enacted a statute that differs from the common law, the common law still applies.

Today, common law is used in cases that involve contracts, property ownership, and personal injury, because for the most part, states have not passed laws on these subjects. Common law is a part of the legal system of every state except Louisiana. Louisiana's system, based on the Napoleonic Code, limits the power of judges to affect the law.

COMMON-LAW MARRIAGE

Henry has lived with his girlfriend June for three years. Now they are breaking up, and June is threatening to sue Henry for alimony. She claims that although they never got a marriage license or had a wedding ceremony, they have a common-law marriage. Is she right?

It depends. Contrary to common belief, living together for a certain number of years does not automatically create a common-law marriage. The couple must both agree that they are married, and their relationship must meet other criteria too.

WHERE COMMON-LAW MARRIAGES ARE LEGAL

Henry and June must live in a state that permits common-law marriages. Only 14 states now do: Alabama, Colorado, Georgia, Idaho, Iowa, Kansas, Montana, Ohio, Oklahoma, Pennsylvania, Rhode Island, South Carolina, Texas, and Utah. However, some states that ban common-law marriages recognize those legally entered into elsewhere.

HOW A COMMON-LAW MARRIAGE IS FORMED

Even in those states that permit them, common-law marriages have to meet certain requirements:

◇ Both of the people must be qualified to marry—that is, they must be single, sane, competent, able to understand the meaning of the marital relationship, and in most states, of legal age to marry.

◇ Both parties must agree that they are married, although the agreement does not have to be in writing. A future plan to marry does not constitute a common-law marriage.

◇ The parties must also present themselves to the public as husband and wife, and they must live together. To demonstrate that they are married, Henry and June can, for example, own a house together, share the same last name, or name each other as beneficiaries on their insurance policies.

RIGHTS AND RESPONSIBILITIES

Once a common-law marriage is formed, the couple have all the rights and responsibilities that belong to conventionally married people. For example, Henry and June must support each other and any children born during the marriage (who are considered legitimate). If either partner dies, the other is entitled to Social Security survivor benefits and to pension or other benefits normally awarded to a surviving spouse.

ENDING A COMMON-LAW MARRIAGE

Although there are no formalities when a common-law marriage begins, legal divorce proceedings are necessary to end it. Someone who has been in a common-law marriage cannot marry again until he or she has obtained a divorce. See also Annulment; Divorce; Marriage.

Community Property

Nine states recognize the concept of community property: Arizona, California, Idaho, Louisiana, Nevada, New Mexico, Texas, Washington, and Wisconsin. In those states all the property a couple acquire during their marriage belongs to each spouse in equal shares. Even if one partner earned all the money during the marriage, each is legally assumed to have made equal contributions and therefore has equal rights to the couple's property.

Property owned by each spouse before the marriage and property given solely to one spouse, such as an inheritance, belong exclusively to that partner and are called separate property.

Depending on the state and the circumstances, fine distinctions are sometimes applied to determine whether a particular type of property is separate or community property.

Insurance payments
Awards paid by insurance companies for damaged property are considered community property, but only if the damage is to community property.

Personal-injury awards
Awards for personal injury become separate property in all of the community-property states except Wisconsin and California. In California personal-injury awards are deemed community property if the injury occurred during the marriage.

Workers' compensation
Workers' compensation benefits, severance pay, and disability benefits are community property if they replace income that would have been earned during the marriage. For instance, when Steve marries Ellen, he is receiving severance pay from his former employer. The severance pay continues for six months after their marriage. That six months' pay is community property.

Education
A professional license or degree is not considered property, but if one spouse contributes to the education of the other, he or she may be entitled to some reimbursement.

Life insurance
Money received from a life insurance policy bought during the marriage is considered community property. Half of it goes to the surviving spouse even if that spouse was not named as the beneficiary. For example, Jim buys a life insurance policy with a death benefit of $100,000, naming his daughter from his first marriage as beneficiary. When Jim dies, his second wife, Nancy, will be entitled to half the proceeds of his policy. If Jim buys the policy before he marries Nancy, it is considered separate property, but if he uses community-property funds to pay the premiums after their marriage, Nancy will be entitled to a refund of half the premiums paid during the marriage.

DIVORCE IN COMMUNITY-PROPERTY STATES

How property is divided upon divorce in a community-property state varies with the state. In California, Louisiana, and New Mexico all community property must be equally divided. In Arizona, Idaho, Nevada, Texas, Washington, and Wisconsin the court may decide how to divide it. The division does not have to be exactly even, but it must be fair. Suppose that Florence earned $90,000 a year during her marriage to Hal, while Hal, who is disabled, earned only $10,000. The court may award Hal more of the community property because he is less able to be self-supporting.

In Washington the divorce court may divide separate property. In Texas separate property always remains in the hands of the one who initially owned it. Courts in Nevada, Louisiana, and New Mexico can use one spouse's separate property if there is not enough community property to provide support to the other. For example, the court may decide to give Michele the income from a house her husband, Philip, inherited, so that she can use it for her support.

In California, Idaho, and Arizona, separate property can be neither divided nor given to the other spouse for support, but the court may take it into consideration in making the distribution. And if the spouse who owns the separate property owes alimony or child support, the court can place a lien on it until he pays up. See also EQUITABLE DISTRIBUTION.

INHERITING FROM YOUR SPOUSE

In a community-property state, when one spouse dies, half of the community property is considered to belong to the surviving spouse. The other half is distributed according to the will prepared by the deceased spouse. If no will was made, the remaining half is subject to the laws of the state. See DYING WITHOUT A WILL.

COMPETENCY

In law, a person is deemed to be competent if he is legally qualified to perform a specific function and meets all of the requirements for doing so. If a person is declared incompetent, he cannot take part in any legal proceedings or be legally bound to a contract. Incompetent people include children, senile or mentally retarded persons, and in some cases, drug addicts and alcoholics.

COURT PROCEEDINGS

Before a criminal case can be tried, the judge must make sure that the defendant understands why he is being brought to court and what will happen there. The defendant should be able to cooperate with his attorney and assist in his own defense. If the defendant does not understand his situation and cannot participate at his trial, he is considered incompetent and cannot be tried for the offense.

The issue of competency also arises in court when a person is called as a witness. Before being allowed to testify, the witness must show that he comprehends the significance of taking the oath to tell the truth and is reasonably able to answer questions about what he saw or heard.

WILLS

In order for a will to be valid, the testator, or person who makes it, must be competent: he must understand what it means to make a will, realize what property he has, be able to identify the people who could benefit from property he might leave them, and be able to dispose of his property according to a plan.

Many wills are contested on the basis of the testator's competency, which is hard to

REAL LIFE, REAL LAW

The Case of the Widow's Will

When Mrs. McKinley wrote her last will and testament, she included provisions disposing of property that had belonged to her late husband, which he had placed in a trust. Under the terms of his will, Mrs. McKinley was entitled to name someone to receive the trust property, and in her will she left it to her grandson, Peter. If she had not named anyone, the property would have gone to Mr. McKinley's daughters (who were Mrs. McKinley's stepdaughters).

Eighteen months after writing her will, Mrs. McKinley was judged incompetent, and she died three months later. Her will was admitted into probate and challenged by her stepdaughters. They argued that because Mrs. McKinley was incompetent at the time of her death, the provision in her will distributing the trust property to her grandson was invalid, and that they should receive it as provided for in their father's will.

The court rejected their argument and upheld Mrs. McKinley's will. It reasoned that the time to inquire into Mrs. McKinley's competency was not the time of her death, but the time when the will was written. Since no one disputed the competency of Mrs. McKinley at the time she wrote her will, the court refused to set the will's provisions aside.

establish after he dies. If you suspect that a senile relative has made a will, you should see a lawyer before he dies. See also INCOMPETENCY.

COMPLAINT

The document that initiates a civil lawsuit is called the complaint. It serves as notice to the defendant that he is being sued; it sets forth the facts that the person suing him (the plaintiff) will use to support his lawsuit; and it states the remedy that the complainant seeks from the defendant.

COMPOSITION WITH CREDITORS

An agreement in which a debtor agrees to pay a portion of what he owes and his creditors accept his partial payment as a full settlement of the debt is called a composition with creditors. Suppose Jim owes $10,000 to a rug company and $3,000 to a computer dealer. He gets into financial trouble and cannot pay his debts. Instead of filing for bankruptcy, he arranges a deal with the two companies to pay a percentage of the original debt.

The two companies agree to accept 40 cents for every dollar Jim owes them and to forgive the rest. Jim ends up paying $4,000 to the rug company and $1,200 to the computer dealer. He will not have to pay the balance of the debt. See also BANKRUPTCY.

THE CONTRACT

A composition with creditors is a contract, and its terms must be met exactly. The contract must state the total settlement agreed upon and the payment plan to be implemented. The money can be due immediately or at a specified later date, and it may be paid in a lump sum or in installments. Jim should make sure that the contract also has a clause stating that the agreed amount will satisfy the debts completely.

RIGHTS OF EACH SIDE

If Jim makes a payment late, both the rug company and the computer dealer can sue for breach of contract and make a claim for all of the original debt. In addition, when he obtained the composition, he forfeited the right to file for bankruptcy.

Once the contract has been signed, Jim's creditors cannot claim any more money than the amount stated. For example, the rug company cannot accept the $4,000 from Jim and then put a lien on his car for the remaining amount.

COMPROMISE AND SETTLEMENT

A compromise and settlement is an agreement by which two disputing parties settle for less than what is specified in the contract. Suppose the contractor whom you hired to put a new roof on your house has finished the job, but you are not satisfied with the work. Some shingles are already coming loose and the gutters are poorly fastened. The roofer, however, thinks the job is fine and wants to be paid for it. You could take this dispute to court and possibly end up spending more money than it would cost to hire someone to finish the job properly. But you might do better if you proposed a compromise and settlement.

For example, after discussing the problem with the contractor, you might agree not to pursue any further claims against him for his poor workmanship. In return, he forgives the final payment due him under the terms of the contract.

The agreement can be either written or verbal, but it is better to put it in writing. Your written proof will be important if the contractor later sues you for not making the final payment on the roof.

CONCEALED WEAPON

Most states have laws that make it a crime to carry a concealed weapon without government permission. "Carrying" includes holding the weapon in your hand or having it in a pocket, purse, or briefcase. To be concealed, the weapon must be legally prohibited and intentionally hidden from public view. In some states, the law states "weapons," "arms," or "firearms" in general; in others, the weapons are explicitly listed: machine guns, billy clubs, blackjacks, razors, brass knuckles, sawed-off shotguns. Unless you are carrying a weapon that is specified in the law, you are not likely to be convicted.

A major aspect of the crime is intent. You must know that you are carrying a concealed weapon. If you can prove that someone slipped a revolver into your shopping bag, for example, you are not guilty of carrying a concealed weapon.

One exception to the crime in some states is carrying the weapon in your home or place of business. In these states, for example, a shopkeeper wearing a pistol in a holster under his coat cannot be found guilty of carrying a concealed weapon unless he leaves the shop while wearing it.

You may also be allowed to carry a concealed weapon if you routinely transport large amounts of cash, precious gems, or negotiable securities or if you have received death threats. Your local police department can provide information about the requirements that you must meet in order to obtain a permit to carry a concealed weapon. See also ARMS, RIGHT TO BEAR; WEAPON.

CONCILIATION

Conciliation is one of several ways to solve a dispute without going to trial. In court, just before a trial is about to begin, the parties may try to hammer out a compromise that will avert the need for a long and costly trial. This process is called conciliation. The term is often used interchangeably with mediation, but the two are not the same. See also ALTERNATIVE DISPUTE RESOLUTION; MEDIATION.

CONDEMNATION

You have just made the final payment on your mortgage when you receive a letter from the state government informing you that your house is being condemned, or taken from you for public use. The government plans to build a raw-sewage pipeline through your property to a treatment plant. After you calm down, you call your attorney and ask him how to handle the situation.

The right to condemn and appropriate private property for public use, known as eminent domain, is one of the powers vested in the government. Both the federal and state governments have the power of eminent domain, although in many instances they delegate it to cities and towns, to government agencies, or to private corporations that provide a public utility, such as natural gas or electricity.

The right of eminent domain means that the government can force a property owner to cede his land to the government. However, both federal and state constitutions restrict the government's right to take private property. For example, the Fifth Amendment to the U.S. Constitution states: "nor shall private property be taken for public use, without just compensation."

PROPERTY THAT CAN BE TAKEN

Private property can be condemned only for some public use. It may be taken over completely as a site for a government building, for a public service (such as a railroad, bridge, road, or port), for urban development, or because it is a risk to the public health and safety.

Sometimes the landowner is not completely deprived of his property, but his use of it is partially restricted or disturbed. For example, a government may plan to put a natural gas pipeline, electric-power and telephone lines, or electrical towers on your private property. Or land may be partially flooded to create a dam. Or a shoreline may be altered so that the property is no longer on the waterfront. In all of these instances you have the right to contest the plan and to be compensated for the loss of your use of the property.

Condemnation does not always mean that your property is physically taken from you. If its value is diminished because of nearby activity or because your ability to use it is restricted, you are entitled to be compensated. For example, a government airport may disturb the operation of a dairy farm, or a private road to property may no longer be accessible because the government regraded a highway.

WHAT HAPPENS IN A CONDEMNATION PROCEEDING

If a government decides to exercise its right of eminent domain, it must follow certain steps. First, it must attempt to negotiate in good faith an acceptable price for your land. Condemnation proceedings are held only in the event that no agreement can be reached.

Condemnation proceedings determine whether the government's reason for taking your property is justifiable and if so, what you should receive as compensation. You have the right to appear at the proceeding and express your views on the reason for the taking and the amount of compensation. You have the right to present your own evidence and to cross-examine witnesses.

At the end of the proceeding the court decides on the just compensation. This figure is typically based on the fair market value of the property—what a willing buyer would pay a willing seller. Other considerations include the price you originally paid for the property, depreciation, replacement value, and any buildings, crops, or minerals located on your land. In some states, the government may not appropriate your property until it pays the compensation.

Not all condemnation proceedings are alike. In some states there is only one hearing; in others, several. Procedures also vary according to the type of property that is being condemned (land for a road or for access to electric-power lines) and the organization that is condemning it (the federal government or a state-chartered utility, for instance).

If the government is not following proper procedure, your attorney can petition the court to make sure that all legal requirements are being met. If they are not, you may be able to halt proceedings with an injunction (a court order to prevent someone from taking certain actions). In some states, you can sue to protect your property rights.

PROPERTY THAT CANNOT BE TAKEN

Not all property is available for condemnation. Some state laws prohibit condemnation of property used for such purposes as orchards, cemeteries, factories, or gardens. However, the property must be actively used for that purpose when condemnation proceedings begin. After the proceedings have begun, you cannot convert your property to one of the exempt uses as a way of preventing the government from taking your land.

CONDOMINIUM

A condominium, or "condo," may be a multiple-unit building (an apartment house) or complex (a group of townhouses) in which each unit is separately owned. If you buy a unit in a condominium, not only do you own the unit you purchased, but you become a part owner of the common areas, such as sidewalks, elevators, gardens, laundry rooms, swimming pools, and parking areas. Together with the other condo owners, you are financially responsible for maintaining these common areas. The larger your unit is, moreover, the greater the percentage of common area that you will likely be responsible for maintaining.

As a condominium owner, you are a member of the condominium association, which consists of the owners of the individual units. You and the other members pay a monthly fee to provide common-area maintenance. You also elect the association's officers and directors, who make the day-to-day decisions on the maintenance of the condominiums.

FINANCING

A mortgage obtained to finance the purchase of your condominium is like the mortgage on a single-family house. It becomes a lien against your property until you have made all the required payments. If you should default, the bank or other lender can foreclose on your property, just as it would on a house. See FORECLOSURE; MORTGAGE.

OWNERSHIP

When you buy a condominium, you will receive three important documents: a deed, a declaration of condominium, and a copy of the bylaws.

Condo deed

The deed, which is recorded at the county courthouse, includes a detailed description of your condominium unit, with the apartment number, size, location, and any other pertinent information. It also states the dollar value of your unit at the time of purchase, the percentage amount of your responsibility for maintaining the common areas, and a list of these common areas. It includes any covenants that dictate the ways in which you can use your condominium. The deed should not have any provisions that contradict either the declaration of condominium or the condominium bylaws.

CHECKLIST

For Condominium Buyers

If you are thinking of buying a condominium, you will want to take these steps before you sign a purchase contract.

❑ **REVIEW THE CONDOMINIUM DEVELOPER'S PROSPECTUS.**
This document should contain information about the developer's background and financial history, the plans for the condominium project and timetables for completion, and the amount of interest the developer will keep in the project once it is completed. A call to your local consumer protection agency can tell you if there are any complaints outstanding against the developer.

❑ **EXAMINE THE OPERATING BUDGET OF THE COMPLEX .**
You will want to know how monthly assessments for the maintenance of common areas are computed, as well as the amount of reserves that the condominium has set aside to cover major building repairs.

❑ **READ THE CONDOMINIUM ASSOCIATION'S DEED, COVENANTS, AND BYLAWS.**
What restrictions are there on the way you can use your condominium? Will you be prohibited from placing a flower box on your windowsill, or will you be limited in the number and kind of pets you may keep? Some condo associations enforce their rules very strictly, right down to such items as how large a flag you can display on the Fourth of July.

❑ **TALK TO THE PEOPLE WHO LIVE IN THE COMPLEX.**
Current residents should be able to tell you if they are happy with their purchase, if common areas are kept clean and maintained properly, if noise or traffic is a problem, and if security and police protection are adequate.

❑ **CHECK THE STABILITY OF THE CONDO WITH LOCAL REAL ESTATE AGENTS.**
If there is a high turnover of residents, or if many units are rented out by their owners, the building may not be well run.

❑ **EXAMINE THE PUBLIC RECORDS AT THE COUNTY OFFICE OF THE RECORDER OF DEEDS.**
The recorder of deeds can tell you the value of units that have recently been purchased in the condo. If the value of the condominium is not rising as fast as other real estate in the area, you may want to reconsider buying.

Declaration
The declaration of condominium contains information required by state law. It must include a physical description of the whole condominium complex; the exact details of each unit; a description of the common areas; and the rules, restrictions, and responsibilities that apply to the owners.

The declaration of condominium may specify the number of votes that each unit wields in the association, the procedures for assessing and paying maintenance fees, and the procedures for assessing payments for major repairs or improvements.

Bylaws
The bylaws give the procedures for the election of association officers and directors and for meetings. They also cover rules for routine maintenance and insurance. A condominium owner must adhere to his association's bylaws. See also Cooperative Apartment; Home Buying and Selling.

CONFESSION

A confession is a voluntary admission of guilt by a person accused of a crime and his description of the events and circumstances under which he committed it. To be admissible in a criminal trial, a confession must be made voluntarily and not as the result of force or coercion. If a confession occurred during questioning by the police, the accused must have been advised of his rights against self-incrimination. See also Criminal Law; Miranda Warnings.

CONFESSION OF JUDGMENT

A confession of judgment is a clause in a financing contract for items such as automobiles, houses, or television sets. The clause states that if you, the buyer, miss a payment, even for a legitimate reason, the seller can go to court and obtain a judgment against you. The judgment could be for as much as the entire amount due or perhaps for the property itself, depending on the terms of the contract. You will not be permitted to defend yourself. Moreover, you will have to pay the seller's lawyer for representing you.

If you find a clause in a contract that sounds like a confession of judgment, do not sign the contract. Confessions of judgment are illegal or highly restricted in many states.

CONSENT FORM

The occasions when you are asked to give your consent—that is, to agree actively and voluntarily to someone else's action—are becoming increasingly numerous. Consent forms are a part of daily life. You will be asked to sign one before you receive medical treatment, when you request payment from your health insurer, and under certain other special circumstances.

RELEASE OF CONFIDENTIAL INFORMATION

Doctors, lawyers, and other professionals, as well as such institutions as hospitals, drug treatment centers, and psychiatric facilities must keep all their records confidential. Anyone who attempts to secure your confidential records or releases them without your permission is violating federal and state laws. If you want to have confidential information divulged—for example, if your insurance company wants to examine your hospital records before it reimburses you for medical expenses—you must sign a written consent to that effect. Your medical insurance claim form includes a "blanket release," a type of consent form that allows the release of all records pertinent to your medical condition.

In other situations, such as when you want to provide medical records to your attorney, you can create your own consent form. The form should do the following:

◇ Identify precisely which records you want released.

◇ Name the person or persons who are authorized to receive the records.

◇ Specify the period of time for which the release will remain in effect.

AGENTS

In order to designate someone to sign a contract for you as your agent, you must execute a consent form called a power of attorney. Suppose your company wants to transfer you to another city, and you do not have time to sell your house. Your best friend, Alma, agrees to run ads in the local paper for you, look after your house, and sell it at a price you set. If she finds a buyer, Alma cannot sign a contract to sell your house unless she has your written authorization. The form in this situation should identify Alma as your agent, limit her authority to the sale of your house, and spell out any other terms, such as a minimum price and the fact that payment is due in full before the new owner moves in. See POWER OF ATTORNEY.

SPOUSES' WILLS

In many states probate laws specify that a portion of an estate must be set aside for a surviving spouse—no matter what the will says. Originally, these laws were meant to prevent widows from becoming destitute and wards of the state. But today many people are marrying for the second time and discovering that their state probate laws are not appropriate for them.

Suppose that Elizabeth, a widow, remarries and becomes the stepmother to three grown children. Both she and her new husband, David, have accumulated savings and property before their marriage. David wants to leave half his estate to Elizabeth to use during her lifetime, but would like his children to receive those assets after her death. Elizabeth would like her own property to go eventually to her nieces and nephews rather than to David's children after his death.

David's and Elizabeth's wills might not be valid under the laws of their state unless each of them signs a written consent to the other's will. See also PRENUPTIAL AGREEMENT; WILL.

MEDICAL TREATMENT

A doctor may not treat you without your permission, and your permission must be based

REAL LIFE, REAL LAW

The Case of the Concertgoers' Consent

When Sunnyside Elementary School arranged for its third grade to attend a children's concert at a nearby city, the school district required each child's parents to sign a consent form. The form released the district from any responsibility in the event the child was injured on the trip.

The bus driver who arrived to take the group appeared intoxicated, but the principal nevertheless allowed her to make the trip. Several miles out of town, she lost control and drove into a ditch, seriously injuring a number of children.

When the injured children's parents sued the school district, the district defended itself by pointing to the consent forms the parents had signed. But the court held the school district responsible. Since the principal knew of the driver's condition, he was negligent in letting her drive the school bus.

on an understanding of the essential facts. This is called informed consent, and it is the cornerstone of your rights as a patient, whether in a hospital or other medical facility or in the doctor's office. Although you should always understand what is written in the consent form (or what you are agreeing to verbally—for example, if you are being given a prescription), hospitals and physicians are still responsible for giving you the appropriate medical advice and treatment. See INFORMED CONSENT; PATIENT'S RIGHTS.

The only time that a patient's informed consent is not required is in an emergency. If you are in a train wreck and rescuers rush you unconscious to the nearest hospital, the law assumes that you would like to have whatever medical procedures are needed to save your life. You cannot object later on religious or other grounds.

WHEN CONSENT IS NOT VALID

It is essential for anyone who signs a consent form to be fully aware of the relevant facts and understand the consequences. For this reason, consent given by minors and incompetent people or consent forms signed as the result of a trick or fraud have no legal effect. You cannot claim fraud easily or arbitrarily, however, as the courts presume that a competent adult who signs a form has read and understood it. Make sure you read any consent form carefully; never rely on someone else to tell you what it says.

A consent form signed under duress or coercion is not enforceable. If a father gives consent to the adoption of his child because the mother has threatened to bring false charges against him for child abuse, his consent is not valid.

CHILDREN'S ACTIVITIES

Parents are often asked to sign consent forms for their children so that they are able to participate in certain activities. Generally these forms release the school district, church, scout troop, or other organization from liability if a child is injured in an accident. But many courts will not allow such consents to be used to bar a lawsuit, and hold that no person can, by means of a consent form, release another party from liability for negligence that has not yet occurred. Permitting this type of release removes incentives for caretakers to act responsibly. See also LIABILITY; NEGLIGENCE.

IMPLIED CONSENT

Sometimes written consent is not practical or possible, as in a medical emergency such as the train wreck mentioned above. In such situations, consent is said to be implied. Suppose a passerby sees a dog threatening your child before you do and rushes onto your property to protect her. In this instance the law assumes you want him to do this—that is, that he has your implied consent—and you will not be able to accuse him of trespassing.

CONSIGNMENT

When you ask a merchant to sell goods for you in exchange for a commission, you have entered into a consignment sales agreement. You retain ownership of the articles until they are sold, and the merchant becomes your agent. She is obligated to get the best deal possible, account for the merchandise, and forward payment for any goods that are sold within a reasonable time, after first deducting her commission.

Consignment is a time-honored practice for wholesalers and manufacturers; and individuals also sell personal items such as antiques, artwork, rare books, and stamp collections on consignment, as well as ordinary clothing and furniture.

Be careful when you sign a consignment agreement. Most merchants have standard forms that serve their own interests. The merchant may be allowed to reduce the price of your merchandise without your consent, for example. Be sure that your agreement clearly states the amount of the merchant's commission and allows you to reclaim unsold goods whenever you like. If you cannot convince the merchant to change her standard agreement, look for someone who will agree to your terms. For a sample consignment sales agreement, see EVERYDAY LEGAL FORMS, page 352.

CONSPIRACY

When two or more people or groups agree to commit an illegal act or to accomplish a legal objective by illegal means, they are guilty of conspiracy. Suppose Simon, an official at the state lottery office, and his next-door neighbor, Irma, agree that Simon will forge winning numbers on losing lottery tickets and pay out winnings to Irma, who will turn over half the money to Simon later on. In addition to being charged with the crime of fraud, Simon and Irma can be charged with conspiracy to commit fraud, which is a separate crime. If convicted, they would each receive two sentences.

CONSTITUTION OF THE UNITED STATES

When it had been adopted by 11 of the original 13 states, the U.S. Constitution became the foundation of America's political and legal system and the "supreme law of the land" in 1788. It established the three branches of the federal government: the legislative branch, which makes the laws; the executive branch, which administers and enforces the laws; and the judicial branch, which interprets the laws. Neither the Congress nor the state legislatures can pass laws that contradict constitutional principles or provisions. The U.S. Supreme Court ultimately determines whether any given law is unconstitutional.

Although the Constitution has proved to be a remarkably workable document, its framers knew that they could not foresee all the possible changes that might be needed. Thus they included among its provisions the means for amending it. Article Five provides that an amendment must be proposed either by a vote of two-thirds of the Congress or by a convention of two-thirds of the states, and that it must be ratified by three-fourths of the state legislatures. This provision ensures that a constitutional amendment will not be passed in the heat of the moment and will have broad public support.

To date there have been 27 amendments to the U.S. Constitution, the first 10 of which are the Bill of Rights. The Bill of Rights limited only the powers of the federal government, leaving the states free to deprive a citizen of a right guaranteed in the Bill of Rights. For that reason, many legal scholars consider the 14th Amendment, proclaimed in 1868, to be the most important of all the other constitutional amendments. It says that the states cannot deny their citizens the equal protection of the laws and the due process guaranteed by the Fifth Amendment.

The amendment has broad applications. For example, on the basis of it, the courts were able to nullify state laws that enforced racial segregation. For more information about the provisions of the U.S. Constitution, see BILL OF RIGHTS; CIVIL RIGHTS; DUE PROCESS OF LAW; EQUAL PROTECTION OF THE LAWS; FULL FAITH AND CREDIT; RIGHTS, INDIVIDUAL.

CONSTITUTIONS, STATE

Each of the 50 states has enacted its own constitution, and each state constitution contains a bill of rights to protect citizens from unnecessary governmental intrusion into individual liberties. State constitutions may go further than the

U.S. Constitution in the rights they extend to state residents. For example, the U.S. Constitution does not explicitly give citizens the right to use obscene speech and print obscene literature, but Oregon's constitution specifically protects obscenity as free speech.

While a state can give its citizens broader rights than those in the U.S. Constitution, it cannot be more restrictive. A state constitutional provision that banned all firearms, for example, would be struck down by the Supreme Court as a violation of the Second Amendment's guarantee of the right to bear arms.

State constitutions also have provisions that determine the way in which a state exercises its police power—its right to pass laws that protect public morals, health, safety, and well-being. For example, a state is exercising its police power when it regulates schools and hospitals and sets licensing requirements for professionals, health and safety standards for restaurants and theaters, and vaccination requirements for school children.

Like the U.S. Constitution, the state constitutions contain provisions specifying how they may be amended.

CONSUMER PROTECTION

Years ago the American consumer had little choice but to be guided by the old Latin saying *Caveat emptor* ("Let the buyer beware"). Buyers had very few options when a product turned out to be unsafe, defective, or unsatisfactory in some way.

CONSUMERS' RIGHTS

During the 1960's, however, the rights of consumers were championed by the federal government, which outlined four objectives that came to be known as the Consumer Bill of Rights. These were:

◇ The right to be sure that whatever you buy is safe. See PRODUCT SAFETY AND LIABILITY.

◇ The right to be told the truth about the products you buy, and to be protected from fraudulent or misleading information (such as false advertising or improper labeling). See FALSE ADVERTISING.

◇ The right to choose from a variety of products that are acceptable in both quality and price. Antitrust laws and the government's promotion of small business further this goal.

◇ The right to complain to and be heard by the government, which must develop policies that respond to the needs of consumers.

Inspired by these guidelines, proconsumer legislation has gained wide support over the years. Although no uniform law covers all aspects of consumer protection, a large number of federal, state, and local laws establish consumers' rights, and some of them are tailored to special kinds of transactions. See also MAIL-ORDER SALES; TELEPHONE CALL.

Largely because of these relatively recent laws and enlightened attitudes toward consumer protection, the phrase *caveat emptor* has been re-

CHECKLIST

Where to File Consumer Complaints

Below are some familiar consumer complaints and the federal agencies that handle them:

❑ **COMPLAINTS ABOUT FOODS, DRUGS, AND COSMETICS.**
Food and Drug Administration
Consumer Complaints Division
5600 Fishers Lane
Rockville, MD 20857
(301) 443-1240.

❑ **COMPLAINTS ABOUT MAIL FRAUD.**
U.S. Postal Inspection Service
Public Affairs Branch
475 L'Enfant Plaza SW
Washington, DC 20260-0010
(202) 268-4293.

❑ **COMPLAINTS ABOUT UNSAFE PRODUCTS.**
Consumer Product Safety Commission
5401 Westbard Avenue
Bethesda, MD 20207
(301) 492-6580.

❑ **COMPLAINTS ABOUT ADVERTISING, LABELING, WARRANTIES, DOOR-TO-DOOR SALES, CREDIT AND COLLECTION PRACTICES.**
Federal Trade Commission
Bureau of Consumer Protection
Pennsylvania Ave. at Sixth St. NW
Washington, DC 20580
(202) 326-2222.

❑ **COMPLAINTS THAT DO NOT FIT THE ABOVE CATEGORIES.**
Call your regional office of the Federal Information Center listed in your local directory.

placed by the more reassuring concept that the customer has legal rights. Now, in fact, it is often the seller, rather than the consumer, who must beware.

Sometimes, however, even reputable businesses fall short of their usual standards. For example, a salesperson may make false or misleading statements about a product in the hope of getting you to buy it, or the product itself may not be up to standard quality.

STEPS TO TAKE

If you have a complaint about a product or the person who sold it to you, follow these steps:

1. Tell the merchant as soon as possible. In most cases he will try to resolve your problem right away for the sake of his own reputation and of customer satisfaction.

2. If you have to repeat your complaint more than once, put it in writing. You will then have a record that can be shown in court if a lawsuit becomes necessary. Your letter should clearly state the nature of your complaint, the action you want taken, and the date by which you expect a response. If you have already talked to someone at the company about your problem, mention his name, the date of your talk, and the action he promised to take.

3. If you return a product by mail, insure the package and follow the company's mailing instructions. If you do not get your anticipated refund, repairs, or replacement within a reasonable time, write another letter asking for an explanation, and send it by certified mail, return receipt requested.

4. Keep copies of all correspondence between you and the company. The more documentation you have, the stronger your case will be if you need to take further action.

5. If your complaint is not resolved to your satisfaction, you may want to consider filing a lawsuit in small-claims court or entering into mediation or arbitration. See ARBITRATION; SMALL-CLAIMS COURT.

See also BETTER BUSINESS BUREAU; DAMAGED MERCHANDISE; FEDERAL TRADE COMMISSION; FOOD AND DRUG LAWS; WARRANTY AND GUARANTY.

CONTEMPT OF COURT

Any action that undermines the court's authority, dignity, or ability to administer justice is contempt of court.

Someone who ignores a subpoena or insults a judge in the courtroom will be held in contempt of court. Parties to a lawsuit who destroy court records or open documents that the court has ordered sealed can be held in contempt. So can witnesses who commit perjury, courtroom observers who carry a weapon, anyone who refuses to obey a court order, and jurors who ignore court instructions not to discuss the case with the press. Attorneys show

REAL LIFE, REAL LAW

The Case of the Mudslinging Motorist

Willard appeared in traffic court to answer a speeding ticket. The police officer who gave Willard the ticket took the stand, and Willard (who was representing himself) began to cross-examine her.

Rather than simply disputing her testimony, Willard proceeded to attack her personal reputation and character. In coarse and rude language, he accused her of promiscuity, which was not relevant to his case. The judge warned Willard to stop being offensive and vulgar.

But Willard merely accused the judge of trying to deprive him of his right to a fair trial and continued to attack the police officer. The judge cited Willard for contempt of court and fined him $200. As Willard cursed the judge under his breath, the judge heard his words and sentenced Willard to five days in jail.

When the five days were up, Willard was required to appear in court to apologize to the judge and to the police officer. The judge then found Willard guilty of speeding and fined him the maximum amount permitted under state law.

contempt of court when they make disrespectful comments, assist a client in evading trial, or violate the rules of the court.

CIVIL VERSUS CRIMINAL CONTEMPT

Contempt of court is classified as either civil or criminal. You commit civil contempt when you fail to obey a court order—for example, by not appearing when subpoenaed, refusing to pay child support or alimony, or failing to testify before a grand jury after being granted immunity from prosecution.

You commit criminal contempt, a more serious offense, when your action undermines the court's authority. Some examples of criminal contempt include carrying a weapon in the courtroom, destroying evidence, and bribing a witness.

PUNISHMENT FOR CONTEMPT

Punishment for contempt may consist of a fine, imprisonment, or both. For civil contempt, you may be confined to jail until you agree to comply with the court's wishes. For example, if Harold has refused to pay the child support he owes, he may be jailed until he pays up.

If you are sent to jail for criminal contempt, you will receive a sentence for a fixed term, just as you would for any other criminal offense.

CONTINGENT FEE

When an attorney agrees to be paid for his services only if he succeeds in winning an award or settlement in the case, the money he gets is called a contingent fee. It is figured as a percentage of the amount obtained in the lawsuit. The contingent fee has been called the "key to the courthouse" for people who have a legitimate case but cannot afford to pay a lawyer an hourly fee.

Contingent fees are used only in civil—not criminal—cases, and most commonly in cases involving personal injuries. Today, many lawyers who seek personal-injury cases on a contingent-fee basis advertise their services in newspapers and magazines.

Every state allows contingent-fee arrangements, but with restrictions. For some kinds of cases they are not permitted at all. For example, a lawyer may not represent a client in a divorce case in return for a percentage of the alimony payments or a share of the property that his client receives.

In many states, contingent-fee agreements between a lawyer and his client must be in writing. Even in states where a written agreement is not required by law, however, you should always ask the lawyer to provide one. If he is not willing to do so, you would be wise to look for another lawyer.

Contingent fees range between one-quarter and one-half of the monetary settlement obtained, but most are figured at one-third. The fee also may depend on how much work the lawyer has done. Most lawyers will take a reduced percentage if the case is settled before a trial begins, a somewhat larger percentage if it is settled after a trial has begun, and the largest percentage if the trial is completed.

Courts have the power to review contingent-fee agreements, and they may reduce the fee if it seems unfair. Also, some state laws set limits on the amount that an attorney can charge in certain cases, such as those involving workers' compensation and medical malpractice.

In addition to the lawyer's fee, the client is responsible for paying court costs (for filing fees, depositions, and the like). One way to reduce the total amount is to have an agreement whereby the court costs are deducted from the amount of the settlement before the lawyer's fee is calculated.

Suppose your lawyer's fee is 30 percent. You win an award of $20,000, and your court costs amount to $5,000. If you calculate the fee before deducting court costs, you will have to pay your lawyer 30 percent of $20,000, or $6,000, plus court costs of $5,000, for a total of $11,000. But if you deduct court costs before calculating the fee, you will pay your lawyer 30 percent of $15,000, or $4,500, plus the court costs, for a total of $9,500. By deducting court costs first, you save yourself $1,500.

Keep in mind that you may be responsible for paying court costs whether you win or lose. If you win, these costs can usually be deducted from your award or settlement, but if you lose, the money will come out of your own pocket. See also LAWYER.

CONTINUANCE

When a trial or part of a trial is postponed, the procedure is called a continuance. It is up to the presiding judge to decide whether to grant a continuance, but he will usually do so if it is requested in good faith. Suppose the prosecuting attorney in a criminal case wants to call a crucial witness, but she is in the hospital recovering from an appendectomy. In this case the prosecutor's request for a continuance will be granted. But if a lawyer asks for a continuance merely to delay the trial, it will be refused.

A continuance is automatically granted when a trial cannot be held as scheduled. For example, if a lawsuit comes before a court near the end of its term and, because of delays in other cases, it cannot be heard before the current term expires, it will simply be continued into the court's next term. See also COURTS.

CONTRACT

Whether we realize it or not, most of us enter into contracts every day. Whenever you buy lunch at a restaurant, subscribe to a magazine, take a ride in a taxi, or get a haircut, you are making a contract.

A contract is a legally enforceable agreement between two or more people. It can be implied (with the terms of the contract evident from the circumstances, as when you order a pizza) or express (with the terms specifically laid out orally or in writing, as when you agree to buy a camera from a friend). Not all contracts are enforceable, however, because the law requires some to be in writing.

CONTRACTS THAT MUST BE IN WRITING

In 17th-century England a law known as the Statute of Frauds required that certain kinds of contracts (especially those subject to fraud) must be in writing. Today some version of the Statute of Frauds is on the books in all 50 states. Usually the kinds of contracts that must be in writing include:

◇ Contracts for the sale of goods worth more than about $500 (the amount varies from state to state).

◇ Contracts for the sale of real estate.

◇ Contracts that cannot be completed within a year of being made, such as a lease that lasts longer than a year.

◇ Contracts promising to pay another person's debts, such as an executor 's agreement to pay the debts of an estate out of his own pocket.

◇ Contracts made in consideration of marriage, such as prenuptial agreements. See PRENUPTIAL AGREEMENT.

WHAT MAKES A CONTRACT ENFORCEABLE

Almost any adult can enter into a contract, but certain requirements must be met before a contract can be enforced in a court of law. These include:

Mutual agreement

The parties must have a "meeting of the minds" regarding the details of the contract, so that they are clearly understood. This mutual agreement is the result of an offer by one party and its acceptance by another.

Suppose a coworker offers to sell you his stereo system for $350, and you agree to buy it. He delivers a CD player, a cassette deck, and a receiver, but does not include the speakers that you assumed were part of the deal. If you decide not to go through with the purchase and your coworker sues you in small-claims court for breach of contract, you can legitimately argue that there was no contract in the first place, since the two of you made different assumptions about a key part of it, and therefore had no mutual agreement.

In written contracts, clear and precise wording is important. If a contract happens to contain wording that is confusing or ambiguous, it probably cannot be enforced. Furthermore, the contract would probably be interpreted by a court in favor of the person who did not write it.

Consideration

Consideration is a legal term that refers to something of value that each person hopes to get out of the contract. In the example above, the consideration for your coworker's stereo is the sum of $350. The consideration for your $350 is the stereo itself.

A promise without consideration is unenforceable. Suppose your coworker had said, "I'm going to deliver my stereo to you on Sunday," and then failed to show up. Without consideration you could not require him to deliver it. But if you had said, "Great, and I will give you $350 for it," there would be consideration—and an oral contract.

Competence

The parties to a contract must be legally competent—that is, they must be considered by law to be capable of handling their own affairs. This excludes people who are underage, intoxicated, or mentally unsound.

For example, suppose Oscar, who has Alzheimer's disease, enters into a contract for two years' worth of dance lessons. When he does not pay, the dance studio sues Oscar for the money. Oscar's lawyer can use the defense that the contract is not valid because of Oscar's incompetence.

Legality

The purpose of the contract must be legal. A hired killer cannot go to court to demand payment from the person who hired him to commit the murder. In some states, gambling debts fall into the category of contracts that cannot be enforced. See GAMBLING.

Time limit

A contract must specify a time period for completion. If you enter into a contract to plant trees on a neighbor's farm but fail to indicate when the job will be done, your contract may not be enforceable.

Proper form

As discussed above, certain types of contracts must be in writing. If they are not, they will not be enforceable.

BREAKING A CONTRACT

If you fail to meet any of the terms of a legally enforceable contract, you are breaking, or breaching, the contract. Selling defective merchandise, not doing work that was promised, and not paying someone the money you owe him are all breaches of contract.

A breach of contract can be partial (as when you move out of an apartment a month before your lease is up without making the last rent payment) or total (deciding not to move in after you have signed the lease).

The victim of a breach of contract is entitled to seek reimbursement. The amount of money that can be awarded will depend on both the nature of the contract and the nature of the breach. For further discussion, see BREACH OF CONTRACT.

REAL LIFE, REAL LAW

The Case of the Confusing Contract

When Nick joined the Holistic Health Club, he signed a three-year membership contract. One clause in the contract said that the annual membership fee was guaranteed not to increase during those three years. But another clause gave the club the right to raise its rates whenever circumstances warranted.

After the first year, Nick received a notice from the club informing him that, because of new equipment purchases and other improvements, he would have to pay an additional $200 a year to continue as a member. When he refused to pay, the club refused to admit him to its facilities.

Nick sued the club, claiming that the fee he had paid was guaranteed by his contract and could not be raised. The club owners responded by pointing to the clause that gave them the right to raise rates whenever they deemed it necessary.

The court ruled in favor of Nick. It held that because the two clauses pertaining to fees contradicted each other, the contract was ambiguous. When a contract is ambiguous, the ambiguity is interpreted in favor of the party who did not write the contract. Nick was able to continue his membership without having to pay the additional fee.

See also CONTRACTOR; DAMAGES; HOME BUYING AND SELLING; HOME IMPROVEMENT AND REPAIR; SCAMS AND SWINDLES.

CONTRACTOR

As commonly used, the term *contractor* refers to a person who is in the business of home building, home improvement, and home repair. Contractors are usually hired by homeowners, and the work they agree to do is laid out in a legal contract (hence the term).

HIRING A CONTRACTOR

Although most contractors are honest and reputable, many are not. It therefore pays to be cautious when hiring a contractor. Ask friends and neighbors who have had work done on their homes for recommendations, and interview several contractors before you decide on the one you want.

Be sure to ask the contractors you interview for references from satisfied customers, and follow up on the information by talking to the customers themselves. Also, ask the contractor (or one of his customers) if you can see a recently completed job.

If your state law requires contractors to be licensed or certified, make sure that the contractors you are considering have obtained the proper credentials.

Request a written bid from each contractor, and be sure that all the bids call for the same quality and the same kinds of construction materials.

THE CONTRACT

Have your agreement with the contractor put in writing and make sure it is as specific as possible. For major jobs, such as an addition to your home or an in-ground swimming pool, the contract should be reviewed by your lawyer.

At the minimum, the contract should describe the work to be done, the materials that will be used, the proposed completion date, the warranties provided on the work, and the schedule for the contractor's payments.

The payment schedule should specify that, when the job is done, you will withhold 10 to 20 percent of the final payment until the contractor has cleaned up the work area, you have written proof that you are no longer subject to mechanic's liens from suppliers and subcontractors, and you are assured that the job has been done right. In addition, ask for a provision (called liquidated damages) in your agreement that penalizes the contractor if he misses the completion date by more than a week or two.

Insist that the contractor give you a list of the suppliers and subcontractors, such as plumbers and electricians, who will be working with him. Then you will know who can file a lien against your home if the contractor does not pay them. You should also ask for proof that the contractor is covered by workers' compensation and liability insurance. See also MECHANIC'S LIEN.

Since most cities now require permits for remodeling work as well as for building jobs, your contract should require the contractor to obtain these permits and give you copies of them. If inspections are required, you should also receive copies of the inspectors' reports.

MONITORING THE WORK

Keep an eye on the work as it progresses, and don't be afraid to ask questions about anything that does not seem right or match your expectations. It is a lot easier, for example, to correct a plumbing mistake before the drywall goes up than after the job is done.

Suppose you change your mind in the middle of a project. You want a picture window where an ordinary-size window has just been installed; or you decide you want flagstones on your patio rather than the brick you specified at first. In such a case, you should submit a written request, called a change order, to the contractor. He, in turn, will give you the adjusted cost and the revised completion date in writing.

Make the payments as required by your contract, but do not make them earlier than scheduled. When the job is done, make a list of any items that you find unsatisfactory or incomplete and give it to the contractor. Do not make the final payment until they are corrected.

WHEN SOMETHING GOES WRONG

Suppose that the new tile floor in your kitchen has begun to crack, or the wooden beams in your new family room already show signs of warping. Most reputable contractors provide warranties on their materials and workmanship and will correct the situation without cost to you. If you hired a contractor without demanding written warranties, however, you may have to rely on a court to decide whether the contractor was at fault and you are therefore entitled to compensation.

Or suppose the contractor you hired works for two days and then disappears after you have given him a substantial down payment. Or the contractor's helper trips over a small end table, sending an expensive vase crashing to the floor. Predicaments like these have spurred a number of states and cities to require contractors to be licensed and to post a bond. If the contractor does not finish the job or pay for the damage, the bond can be used to satisfy your claims.

STEPS TO TAKE

If a dispute develops between you and your contractor that you cannot resolve, here is what you can do:

1. Call your local consumer protection agency to report the problem. In many parts of the country, this agency will talk to the contractor and try to work out a solution.

2. Check the terms of your contract; they may include a clause that requires arbitration. If your contractor is a member of the Better Business Bureau or a trade organization such as the National Association of the Remodeling Industry, you may be able to resolve your dispute by mediation or arbitration. See ARBITRATION; MEDIATION.

3. If your contractor refuses to cooperate with you in an effort to settle the dispute, you may have to sue him. If you do, be sure to hire a lawyer who has experience in disputes with contractors. See also HOME IMPROVEMENT AND REPAIR.

COOLING-OFF PERIOD

It sounds good when the salesman appears at your door. He promises that just for letting him demonstrate his central-vacuuming system, you will receive a set of steak knives and a chance to win a trip to Hawaii. Three hours later you find yourself agreeing to buy the system for $500—just to get him to leave. You're finally free to go to bed.

In the light of morning, however, you realize you don't need a central-vacuuming system for your studio apartment. But you have signed a contract. Is there anything you can do?

In this situation, there is. Under rules established by the Federal Trade Commission, you have a three-day grace period, or cooling-off period, to cancel the contract. In fact, the salesman is required to give you the forms and instructions for cancellation at the time you sign your contract.

This federal regulation applies to most sales made outside a store or other regular place of business—especially sales made by door-to-door salesmen. It does not apply to the following:

◇ Sales of real estate, insurance, or securities.

◇ Contracts for emergency home repairs.

◇ Sales of less than $25.

◇ Sales made by telephone or mail.

Some states provide cooling-off periods for telephone sales, health-club memberships, and other types of sales where the customer is a captive audience. But don't assume that a contract is covered by these laws. If you have any doubt, call your local department of consumer affairs. See also HEALTH CLUB; TELEPHONE CALL.

For a sample Door-to-Door Sales Three-Day Cancellation Notice, see EVERYDAY LEGAL FORMS, beginning on page 552.

STEPS TO TAKE

This is the procedure to follow if the three-day cooling-off period applies to a contract you have signed:

1. Mail in the cancellation form provided by the salesman. You have until midnight of the third business day after the sale to cancel your contract.

2. Send it by certified mail, return receipt requested. That gives proof that you mailed the form and gives you an acknowledgment from the postal service that it was delivered.

3. If the salesman did not give you a form, your right to cancel the contract is extended indefinitely, but you must still write the company to let them know that you want to cancel. You should also inform your local department of consumer affairs that you were not given the required forms.

COOPERATIVE APARTMENT

In some parts of the country, especially in eastern cities, many apartment buildings are run as cooperatives. When you buy an apartment in a cooperative building (called a co-op for short), you enter into a form of ownership different from that of either a house or a condominium. See CONDOMINIUM.

When you own a house, you usually own the entire structure and the land. When you own a condominium, you own the space your apartment occupies. When you own a co-op, you own shares in a corporation. The corporation is the cooperative, which owns the building and all the apartments in it. When you "buy" a cooperative, you are not buying the apartment itself. You are buying shares in the corporation, which gives you the right to occupy your apartment.

Your monthly payments, called maintenance, will ordinarily include your share of the building's mortgage payments, its property taxes, and a building maintenance fee, which helps pay for such expenses as doormen, gardeners, and repairs. If one of your fellow co-op owners does not make his maintenance payments, the remaining owners (including you) are responsible for them. Your maintenance might be increased or you might have to pay a special assessment to make up for the default.

Buying a co-op presents a unique set of problems. Financing is sometimes more difficult to obtain than for a home, because a co-op loan is secured by shares in a corporation rather than by real estate. In addition, co-ops have rules, called bylaws, that you agree to obey when you buy. You may find, for example, that you cannot have a pet or a washing machine in your apartment. You may also find that the co-op's board of directors has veto power if you decide to move and want to sell your shares.

Given these potential problems, it is essential that you consult a lawyer who knows your local real estate law. Ask him to review the purchase agreement before you buy. See also HOME BUYING AND SELLING; REAL ESTATE.

COPYRIGHT

Copyright is the protection given by federal law to people who create original works of various kinds, such as books, magazines, plays, poems, movies, songs, records, tapes, paintings, sculptures, dances, computer programs, and board games. The holder of a copyright has the primary right to market, distribute, display, perform, or reproduce a work. By copyrighting his work, the creator guards himself against theft—that is, he protects his work from those who would reproduce it for their own gain without compensating him.

WHAT CAN BE COPYRIGHTED

Only an original work can be copyrighted. This does not mean that everything about it must be brand-new, but the work must include some form of original expression. Originality is necessary because copyright laws protect the expression of ideas, not the ideas themselves or the facts underlying the ideas.

For example, suppose you intend to write a western novel, and you do some time-consuming research on posses and cattle rustlers in the Old West. Then you concoct a plot in which the main character is saved from lynching by a band of gun-toting barmaids. Neither your painstaking research (which consists of facts) nor your wonderful plot (which consists of ideas) can be copyrighted. Only your novel itself can be copyrighted, because it alone qualifies as an expression of ideas.

In order to be copyrighted, a work must also be put down on paper, film, magnetic tape, canvas, or another "tangible medium." For example, a songwriter who never records her songs on tape or on paper cannot claim any copyright.

WHAT CANNOT BE COPYRIGHTED

Suppose you decide to write an article analyzing the Battle of the Bulge and obtain a copyright for it. This does not prevent someone else from writing his own article on the subject, using the same facts. Historical facts and statistics, which are available to the general public, cannot be copyrighted.

Other examples of things that cannot be copyrighted are:

◇ Names, titles, and symbols (except trademarks).

◇ Ideas, systems, processes, devices, and discoveries. But note that these may qualify for patent protection. See PATENT.

◇ Blank forms and blank checks, address books, tape measures, height and weight charts, and score cards.

◇ Works created by the U.S. government.

FAIR USE

There are some instances when a work may be reproduced—in whole or in part—without violating a copyright. This is called fair use. The main purpose of fair use is to allow people engaged in educational pursuits to quote part of a work without paying a fee or laboring to obtain permission. Such users include people who are involved in research, teaching, news reporting, and criticism. For example, a journalist who writes a book review for a newspaper or magazine is allowed to quote passages from the book without getting permission.

For other kinds of users, where the line falls between fair use and copyright infringement usually depends on the ratio of the amount of material used to the amount contained in the work as a whole. For example, if the author of a book on how to write short stories quotes no more than a few sentences from a published story, the quotation would be considered fair use. But if she quoted several pages, she would have to obtain permission.

INFRINGEMENT

The violation of a copyright holder's exclusive right to publish and distribute his work is known as infringement. To sue for infringement, the copyright holder must be able to demonstrate that the infringer had access to his work and that there is a substantial similarity between the copyrighted piece and the work of the alleged infringer. In addition, the copyright holder must file his lawsuit within three years of the date of the infringement.

If the copyright holder wins his case, the court may order the defendant to stop further infringement. The judge (or jury) may also award the owner compensation for his loss.

Copyright infringement is a criminal offense, and the punishment may include both fines and imprisonment. Special criminal penalties have been established for infringement involving sound recordings and motion pictures.

U.S. COPYRIGHT LAWS

The copyright laws in this country have been revised several times over the years. Under the Copyright Act of 1909, an author's published work was protected for 28 years and could then be renewed for another 28 years. To receive protection, the work had to bear a copyright notice (a one-line statement that appears on the back of the title page) and be registered with the Copyright Office in Washington, D.C. Failure to include the copyright notice on a single copy of a published work could destroy the copyright. Unpublished work was not fully protected.

In 1978 a new version of the Copyright Act went into effect. As of that date, both published and unpublished works are protected, and the protection is not lost if proper notice is omitted from the work. However, the copyright must be registered with the Copyright Office within five years of its first publication, and works published before March 1, 1989, must contain a copyright notice. Works published after that date are not required to bear a copyright notice, but to ensure complete protection, it is still strongly recommended that they do.

For most works created after the 1978 law was enacted, the copyright will last for the life of the creator plus 50 years. Un-

REAL LIFE, REAL LAW

The Case of the Borrowing Beatle

In the early 1970's, Beatle George Harrison wrote and recorded a song entitled "My Sweet Lord." The song was an international hit, and was played on radio stations around the world.

But to the composers of the 1960's hit "He's So Fine," Harrison's composition sounded a little too familiar. They filed suit against Harrison for violating their copyright, pointing out that the melodies of the two songs were similar. They asked for compensation from Harrison, who argued that he had not intentionally used their song as a basis for his own.

The court found that although Harrison had not consciously stolen the melody of "He's So Fine," he did have access to and familiarity with the tune—factors that weigh heavily in copyright infringement cases. Because of this, and the substantial similarity between the two songs, the court found that Harrison had violated the song's copyright and ordered him to compensate its composers.

like the 1909 law, there is no renewal. When the designated period of time expires, the copyright no longer exists and the work is part of the "public domain." This means that anyone can use the material for any purpose without obtaining permission from the author or paying for its use.

UNPUBLISHED MATERIAL

An original work does not have to be published to have copyright protection, because protection begins automatically when the work is created. Nor does a copyright notice have to appear on unpublished work in order for it to be protected. However, it is advisable to put a copyright notice on work that is being released to the public, simply because it shows that the author is aware of his rights and wants to deter possible infringement.

STEPS TO TAKE TO OBTAIN A COPYRIGHT

If you have produced a work for which you wish to have copyright protection, here are the steps you should take:

1. Place a copyright notice on the work. The notice consists of three pieces of information: the copyright symbol (©); the name of the person who owns the copyright; and the year the work was produced—for example: "Copyright © John Smith 1995." The copyright notice must be legible and easily seen. If you are publishing a book with a reputable publisher, all you need to do is put this notice on the manuscript. The publisher will take care of the steps that follow.

2. Send for a copyright application by writing to the Copyright Office, Library of Congress, Washington, DC 20559, or calling the Federal Information Center, at one of the numbers given on page 225.

3. The next step in securing a copyright is to register your work with the Copyright Office. This means submitting a completed application form, the required fee, and one or more copies of the work. Some kinds of materials, such as sculptures, scientific research, stationery, and greeting cards are exempt from this requirement.

Although you have five years to complete the registration process, it is wise to do it as soon as possible. Doing so provides additional evidence of your ownership if a lawsuit becomes necessary.

4. Once the Copyright Office has received your application and other materials, and it has determined that the work can be copyrighted, you will get a Certificate of Registration.

CORPORAL PUNISHMENT

Corporal punishment usually refers to the kinds of bodily discipline, such as spanking or paddling, sometimes administered in schools. Whether a public school may discipline its students with corporal punishment is a matter of state and local law. Some states, such as Maine and Massachusetts, and many local school districts strictly prohibit any form of corporal punishment. But other states and school districts allow teachers and school officials to use it.

Even those states that permit corporal punishment, however, place restrictions on it. The punishment inflicted must be reasonable, and it must not be out of proportion to the offense or to the child's age. Some state statutes describe in detail how much force can be used; others require that the parents be notified and give their approval before a student can be physically punished.

ABUSE OF PUNISHMENT

The right to administer corporal punishment is sometimes abused. Suppose seven-year-old Bobby disrupts his class by making animal noises, and he continues to do so after his teacher, Mr. Dawson, asks him to stop. Mr. Dawson loses his temper, and instead of giving Bobby a light spanking with a wooden paddle as prescribed by state law, he beats the boy across the back with a wire coat hanger, drawing blood.

Bobby's parents can both file a lawsuit and bring criminal charges of assault and battery against Mr. Dawson and the school. A teacher who oversteps the legal bounds on corporal punishment may be disciplined or even fired.

STEPS TO TAKE

If your child has been subjected to corporal punishment at school that you believe was unjust or excessive, you can take these steps:

1. Arrange a meeting with the school principal.

2. Ask the principal what legal authority the school used

REAL LIFE, REAL LAW

The Case of the Paddled Pupil

When 10-year-old Jimmy bounced a basketball off the blackboard, his teacher took him to the front of the class and gave him three hard whacks on the rear end with a paddle. Jimmy told his parents, who called the principal and expressed their outrage. She informed them that the teacher was within her rights to use corporal punishment, because it was permitted by state law. Not mollified, Jimmy's parents sued both the school and the teacher for assault and battery. The suit argued that Jimmy's spanking was a form of "cruel and unusual punishment," which is prohibited by the U.S.Constitution.

The court ruled in favor of the school. Under the laws of Jimmy's state, corporal punishment is permitted as long as it is reasonable and not excessive. The court ruled that Jimmy's punishment fell within state guidelines, and that since he had suffered only momentary pain and embarrassment, his constitutional rights had not been violated.

to validate the decision to administer the punishment.

3. If he will not tell you, or if you suspect there is no justification for the punishment, consult an attorney to help you decide what legal action to take against the school.

CORPORATION

A corporation is a business or organization formed by a group of people, and it has rights and liabilities separate from those of the individuals involved. It may be a nonprofit organization engaged in activities for the public good; a municipal corporation, such as a city or town; or a private corporation (the subject of this article), which has been organized to make a profit.

In the eyes of the law, a corporation has many of the same rights and responsibilities as a person. It may buy, sell, and own property; enter into leases and contracts; and bring lawsuits. It pays taxes. It can be prosecuted and punished (often with fines) if it violates the law. The chief advantages are that it can exist indefinitely, beyond the lifetime of any one member or founder, and that it offers its owners the protection of limited personal liability.

LIMITED LIABILITY

If you own shares in a corporation that cannot pay its debts and is sued by its creditors, the assets of the company may be seized and sold. But although you can lose your investment, the creditors cannot attach your personal assets (such as cars, houses, or bank accounts) to satisfy their claims.

There are some important exceptions to this rule, however. If the business affairs of a corporation and its shareholders are so entangled that they are, in effect, one and the same, an opponent in a lawsuit may be able to convince a court to "pierce the corporate veil" and impose personal liability, or responsibility, on the active shareholders. Personal liability may also be imposed if the corporation does not comply with required legal formalities or fails to keep proper records.

FORMING A CORPORATION

If you want to form a corporation, you must obtain a state charter. Here are some things to do before you apply:

◇ Choose the state in which you want to incorporate. This will usually be the state where your company has its headquarters or where it conducts most of its business. Some people prefer to incorporate in states that impose few regulations or no corporate income tax, such as Delaware, Nevada, and Wyoming.

◇ Decide whom you want as officers. Although many states require at least two or three parties to form a corporation, they need not all be shareholders. You may want to ask friends or family members to serve as the initial officers. If you remain the sole shareholder, you alone will control the corporation's activities.

◇ Choose a name for your corporation. This is not as simple as it sounds. If the name you propose is identical to or resembles that of an existing corporation, your state's secretary of state may refuse to issue a charter under that name. To avoid this problem, search the corporate records in your state for similar names before submitting your application. If you plan to operate nationwide, you will have to find out whether corporations in other states have similar names. If this seems like too much trouble, you can seek the help of a company that specializes in corporate services. It will make a search for you, usually for a reasonable fee.

Now you are ready to apply for a charter by submitting to the secretary of state a document called the articles of incorporation, along with the required fees. Each state's incorporation laws dictate the contents of the articles, but generally they must contain the corporation's name and address, its purpose, the number and type of shares being issued, and the names and addresses of the incorporators.

You can buy books that tell you how to form your own corporation, but they may not cover all the steps required in your state. It is best to get the help of a lawyer when you incorporate or at least have him review your articles of incorporation for potential problems before you file. Most lawyers will do this for a few hundred dollars or less, and the fee is deductible from the corporation's income tax.

FORMING A CHAPTER S CORPORATION

If your business is small, you may want to consider forming a Chapter S corporation. Its advantage is that the federal government does not consider it a taxable entity, and only its shareholders are taxed on their profits. To qualify, the corporation must be a domestic corporation, not a foreign one, and have no more than 35 stockholders. Only persons, trusts, or estates (not other corporations) can own stock in an S corporation, and it may issue only one class of stock. To obtain S corporation status, the corporation must file Form 2553 with the Internal Revenue Service and receive IRS approval. Failure to meet the requirements (as by having too many stockholders) automatically ends S corporation status.

PROFESSIONAL CORPORATIONS

A professional corporation, or P.C., is formed much like a regular corporation but can have only one stockholder, who must be a licensed professional, such as a doctor or engineer. A professional who has incorporated as a P.C. cannot use the corporation to shelter himself from a charge of malpractice, but otherwise receives the same protection from personal liability as any other corporate shareholder. For example, Jane, a patient of Dr. Grimes, who is a P.C., breaks her ankle when she trips on the waiting room carpet and sues. She is awarded $5 million in compensation because she happens to be a prima ballerina. But Jane can collect only from the assets of Dr. Grimes's practice, not from him personally—even if he is worth $10 million personally, but his practice has only $2 million in assets.

MAINTAINING A CORPORATION

Once your corporate charter is issued, the incorporators must meet to elect directors and pass the corporation's bylaws, the rules by which the corporation is run. The directors then become responsible for managing the corporation, although they can appoint officers to supervise day-to-day operations. In small corporations, the incorporators, directors, and officers are often the same people.

A corporation needs money to operate, and its initial financing generally comes from the sale of stock. In many small corporations, the incorporators, family, and friends buy and own most of the stock. This type of corporation is called a closed corporation because its stock is not for sale to the general public. Other companies raise money by selling shares through a public offering. Since public offerings are closely regulated by federal and state governments, incorporators should obtain competent legal advice before offering shares for public sale.

TYPES OF SHARES

Shares in a corporation usually fall into one of two classes, common and preferred. Most common stock entitles owners to vote at the company's annual meeting, although some common stock can be nonvoting. If you own common stock, you will receive dividends from the corporation whenever it declares them. The corporation

REAL LIFE, REAL LAW

The Case of the Corporate Veil

The AAA Corporation owed more than $500,000 to various creditors when it filed for bankruptcy. The creditors filed suit against the single shareholder, John, asking that he be held personally responsible for the debts of the corporation. John argued that the debts in question were those of the corporation, and he could not be held responsible for them.

But the creditors showed that the AAA Corporation had failed to hold annual meetings, elect officers, or pass corporate resolutions as required by state law. The evidence also showed that John deposited checks made to the corporation directly into his personal bank accounts, and that he often paid for alleged corporate expenses with his personal credit card.

As a result, the court held that the AAA Corporation was merely an alter ego that John used to escape responsibility for his debts. The court "pierced the corporate veil" that protects shareholders from personal liability and ordered John to repay the creditors from his personal holdings.

Owners of a corporation that fails to keep its records in order or operates in a manner that makes it indistinguishable from those who own it can find themselves personally liable for the corporation's debts.

---

does not have to declare a dividend on common stocks.

Owners of preferred stock are usually entitled to vote at corporate meetings, and they receive a fixed dividend payment every year, whether the company earns a profit or not.

State laws require corporations to keep adequate records and make them available to shareholders. Officers and directors who unreasonably refuse a shareholder's request to see company records can be fined. See STOCKS AND BONDS.

DISSOLVING A CORPORATION

Most corporations are set up to exist indefinitely. However, a majority of the shareholders can vote to dissolve the corporation (some states require a two-thirds majority). If a minority of the shareholders think a corporation is being mismanaged, they can bring a lawsuit to dissolve it. And the company's creditors can petition to have it dissolved in bankruptcy court if they are not being paid.

If a corporation is dissolved, it first goes through a "winding-down" period. It collects whatever assets it has (such as bills that are owed to it), pays off the legitimate claims of its creditors, and distributes any money left over to the shareholders. Once this process is complete, the corporation files a certificate of dissolution with the secretary of state, and the corporation's existence ends.

COSIGNING

When you sign a contract, you may be required to have it cosigned (signed by someone else) in order to guarantee that the terms of the contract will be met. For example, when Dick decided to buy a new car, he was told he could not qualify for an auto loan unless he had a cosigner. He asked his cousin Elmer to cosign his loan, and Elmer agreed out of a sense of family loyalty. Six months later Elmer received a notice from Dick's bank. Dick had failed to make the required payments on the car, and now the lender wanted payment in full from Elmer. When Elmer called Dick for an explanation, he found out that his cousin had moved away without leaving a forwarding address. Elmer ended up having to pay off Dick's sizable car loan.

The cosigner of a loan agreement or any other contract assumes the same legal responsibilities as the original signer. If you are ever asked to cosign someone else's loan, remember that there is more involved than just helping a friend to borrow some money. You will be legally committed to pay the entire sum if your friend cannot, and the lender can file a lawsuit against you to collect what is owed. Moreover, in most states the lender can collect the debt from you without first trying to collect it from the borrower. You should also be aware that most lenders do not require a cosigner unless they lack confidence in the borrower's ability to repay.

STEPS TO TAKE

If you do decide to act as a cosigner, you should be sure to:

1. Get a copy of the loan agreement.
2. Make sure you receive a separate document that identifies the debt being guaranteed and explains the cosigner's rights and obligations. Federal Trade Commission rules and the law in most states entitle you to such a document.
3. If the borrower has not kept up the payments, and the lender demands payment in full from you, contact the lender immediately. You may be able to arrange a repayment plan, rather than having to pay the total amount as a lump sum.
4. Get the help of a lawyer with experience in consumer credit cases. If the lender has failed to give you all the documents required by state and federal law, you may not have to repay the debt.

COUNTERFEIT MONEY

Making a false copy of something for the purpose of passing it off as the real thing is the crime known as counterfeiting. While almost anything can be illegally duplicated, from stamps to theater tickets, the word *counterfeiting* most often applies to money.

KINDS OF PHONY MONEY

Counterfeit money is of two kinds—forged bills that were printed illegally by someone other than the U.S. government, and legitimate currency that has been altered in order to change its value. The altered kind is produced when, for example, a counterfeiter cuts out the corners of a $20 bill and pastes them over the corners of a $1 bill. At a busy sales counter, the altered bill is presented as payment for a small purchase. If the clerk is distracted and fails to look closely at the bill, the counterfeiter will receive change for the larger bill. He then can usually replace the larger bill that he mutilated, since a damaged bill can be exchanged for a new one as long as more than half of the damaged one remains.

The kind of counterfeit money we hear about most often is the printed kind. In the past, counterfeiters used engraved metal plates to print money. But with the recent advances in photographic reproduction techniques, their job has been made much simpler. In fact, the new color processing machines are making it easier for criminals to counterfeit not only currency but stock and bond certificates, tickets to high-priced events, valuable stamps, and travelers' checks.

IF YOU HAVE A BOGUS BILL

What should you do if you find that you have a counterfeit bill?

CHECKLIST

How to Spot a Counterfeit Bill

Counterfeit bills vary widely in quality, from crudely printed imitations to expert forgeries. Here are some tips on how to spot them:

❑ **SCRUTINIZE THE PAPER.**
Authentic U.S. currency is printed on paper that contains tiny red and blue threads.

❑ **LOOK CLOSELY AT THE TREASURY SEAL.**
The Treasury seal is printed just to the right of the portrait. In most cases it is bright green, indicating the bill is a Federal Reserve Note. (A few U.S. Notes, with red seals, and Silver Certificates, with blue seals, are still in circulation.) The points on the seal of an authentic bill should be sharply defined and evenly spaced.

❑ **CHECK THE SERIAL NUMBER.**
The digits should be evenly spaced, well aligned, and the same color as the Treasury seal. If you are accepting a number of bills at once, see if the serial numbers differ. Most counterfeiters will use only one serial number.

❑ **LOOK AT THE PORTRAIT.**
On authentic currency the portrait is sharp and clear, and is composed of finely etched lines.

❑ **RUB THE BILL AGAINST A SHEET OF WHITE PAPER.**
If the ink smears off, you probably have a counterfeit bill.

Once money is recognized as counterfeit, the last person to possess it before the discovery will suffer the loss. So if you try to deposit the bill in your bank account and the bank notices that it is counterfeit, the deposit will not be credited to your account (and the bank is required by law to inform the police). However, if you make a withdrawal and the bank inadvertently gives you a counterfeit bill it accepted from another customer, you are entitled to reimbursement from the bank. To be on the safe side, examine all bills as soon as you receive them.

Suppose Jill has a counterfeit bill and, rather than get stuck with it, she passes it along to someone else, such as the cashier in a grocery store. One of several things may happen. If the cashier fails to notice the phony bill, Jill will probably get away with it. But if he does notice it, he may call the police and have Jill arrested.

Now, suppose that after getting caught trying to pass the bogus bill, Jill claims she didn't know it was counterfeit. Can she be prosecuted? It depends. If the bill is an obvious forgery, one the average person would be likely to notice, she may be in trouble. Moreover, even if Jill offers to take it back when she is caught, her offer will not remove the possibility of her being prosecuted.

If, on the other hand, Jill receives and passes along counterfeit money that she believes is genuine, and it also looks genuine to the average person, she cannot be convicted of violating the law.

COURT-MARTIAL

As its name suggests, a court-martial is a court established under military law to hold trials and to punish military personnel for criminal activity. Behavior that is not criminal in civilian law, such as being absent without leave, may violate military regulations and make a serviceman or woman subject to a court-martial. The punishments a court-martial may impose include reduction in rank, imprisonment, dishonorable discharge, or any combination of these.

Defendants in a court-martial do not have a right to a jury trial. They are usually judged by one or three military officers, but in the most serious cases a panel of five presides.

Aside from a jury trial, military personnel have most of the same rights as civilian defendants, including the right to legal counsel, to call defense witnesses, and to confront and cross-examine accusers. If convicted, a defendant may appeal a verdict to a special court, the U.S. Court of Military Appeals, whose decision is final. Since 1950, courts-martial have been conducted under rules set out in the Uniform Code of Military Justice. See also UNIFORM CODE OF MILITARY JUSTICE.

COURTS

Courts serve as impartial forums to which opposing parties can bring their disputes for resolution. The role of the courts is to interpret and apply the law to the facts of each case in order to bring about justice.

Courts are of all different kinds: state and federal courts, criminal and civil courts, small-claims and supreme courts, and many others. Which type of court hears a particular case depends on its jurisdiction.

JURISDICTION

A court's authority to hear certain cases and not others, as determined by law, is known as its jurisdiction. Jurisdiction may be based on one or more things, such as geographical area, the subject of the case (taxes or juvenile law, for example), civil versus criminal matters, or the amount of money at stake in a lawsuit.

The broadest of all the divisions that determine jurisdiction is the division between the state and the federal court systems, which are separate but have much in common. For a discussion of the criteria that determine whether a federal or a state court has authority over a case, see FEDERAL COURTS.

State courts

State courts are organized in levels. Most have three such levels: the lowest, where cases are tried; the middle, where cases are appealed; and the highest, where cases are further appealed. (Some states do not have the middle level.)

At the lowest level are the trial courts, also known as courts of original jurisdiction, because they are where cases begin. A trial court will hear the evidence, decide the facts of the case, and apply the law to those facts. Depending on local custom, trial courts may be called district courts, circuit courts, superior courts, county courts, or courts of common pleas. They are said to have general jurisdiction, because they hear all types of cases.

Also at this level are special courts, which hear cases involving specific areas of law. Probate courts, juvenile courts, and family courts are examples of special courts.

Many state systems also have municipal courts, which hear disputes that involve limited amounts of money and petty crimes. These include small-claims courts, traffic courts, and magistrates' courts.

At the middle level of state courts are the appellate courts (sometimes called intermediate appellate courts, since the state supreme court is also, strictly speaking, an appellate court), where cases from the lower courts may be appealed. An appellate court does not decide the facts of a case. It accepts the facts as decided by the trial court but looks at the applicable law and procedural rules to see if they were properly applied. The appellate court may affirm the lower court's decision, reverse it, or modify it. In some instances, the case will be remanded, or given back, to the trial court for further proceedings.

A party who is dissatisfied by the ruling of an appellate court may appeal his case to the state's highest court, often called the state supreme court.

Federal courts

Like most state court systems, the federal court system is also composed of three levels. The lowest, where cases are actually tried, includes the district courts, which hear various kinds of cases within a certain geographical area, as well as more specialized courts such as bankruptcy courts, Tax Court, the Court of Claims, and the Court of International Trade.

The middle level, where cases from the lower courts are appealed, consists of the circuit courts of appeals and the Court of Customs and Patent Appeals. These operate in a manner similar to state appellate courts.

The highest federal court is the U.S. Supreme Court, consisting of nine justices appointed by the president. Only a small fraction of the cases that are appealed to the Supreme Court can be heard. Therefore, the Court most often chooses cases that affect many people, that could affect the way the Constitution is interpreted, or whose outcome could ultimately change the law itself.

HOW COURTS ARE RUN

The purpose of the courts is to settle disputes. How they go about doing so varies somewhat from court to court, but the general procedures are often similar.

Court rulings

If the case is tried before a jury, the jury must decide on the facts in the case, based on the evidence. It must then, according to the judge's instructions, apply the law to those facts to arrive at a verdict. If there is no jury, the judge (or panel of judges) decides what the facts are, applies the law to those facts, and renders a judgment.

The decisions of the panel of judges on an appellate court are generally determined by a simple majority vote, although some rules specify that a certain number of judges—known as a quorum—must be present to render a valid judgment. By requiring less than a unanimous decision, the court can function even when a judge dies, resigns, or is temporarily absent for any reason.

When an appellate court makes a decision on a case, its explanation for reaching that decision is called the court's opinion. When the judges agree on the outcome of the case but base their decisions on different reasons, the reasoning that has been adopted by the majority is given first, and other judges write what are called concurring opinions. Judges who disagree with the decision may write dissenting opinions.

Court records

A record of the court's proceedings is made by the clerk of the court. Written opinions are often published in bound volumes that become part of law libraries. They are used by lawyers in preparing cases and by other courts for guidance in deciding similar cases.

Access to court records is not restricted to people involved in a case. Court records are public records, but the right to inspect them is governed by law. Requests to examine or copy court records may be granted to people with a legitimate interest in the case, but requests made simply out of curiosity, or for the purpose of publishing embarrassing infor-

Federal Court System

The federal court system is headed by the U.S. Supreme Court. Below the Supreme Court are a dozen appeals courts and, beneath them, about 90 district courts. The arrows in the chart below show how cases are appealed from the lower to the higher federal courts.

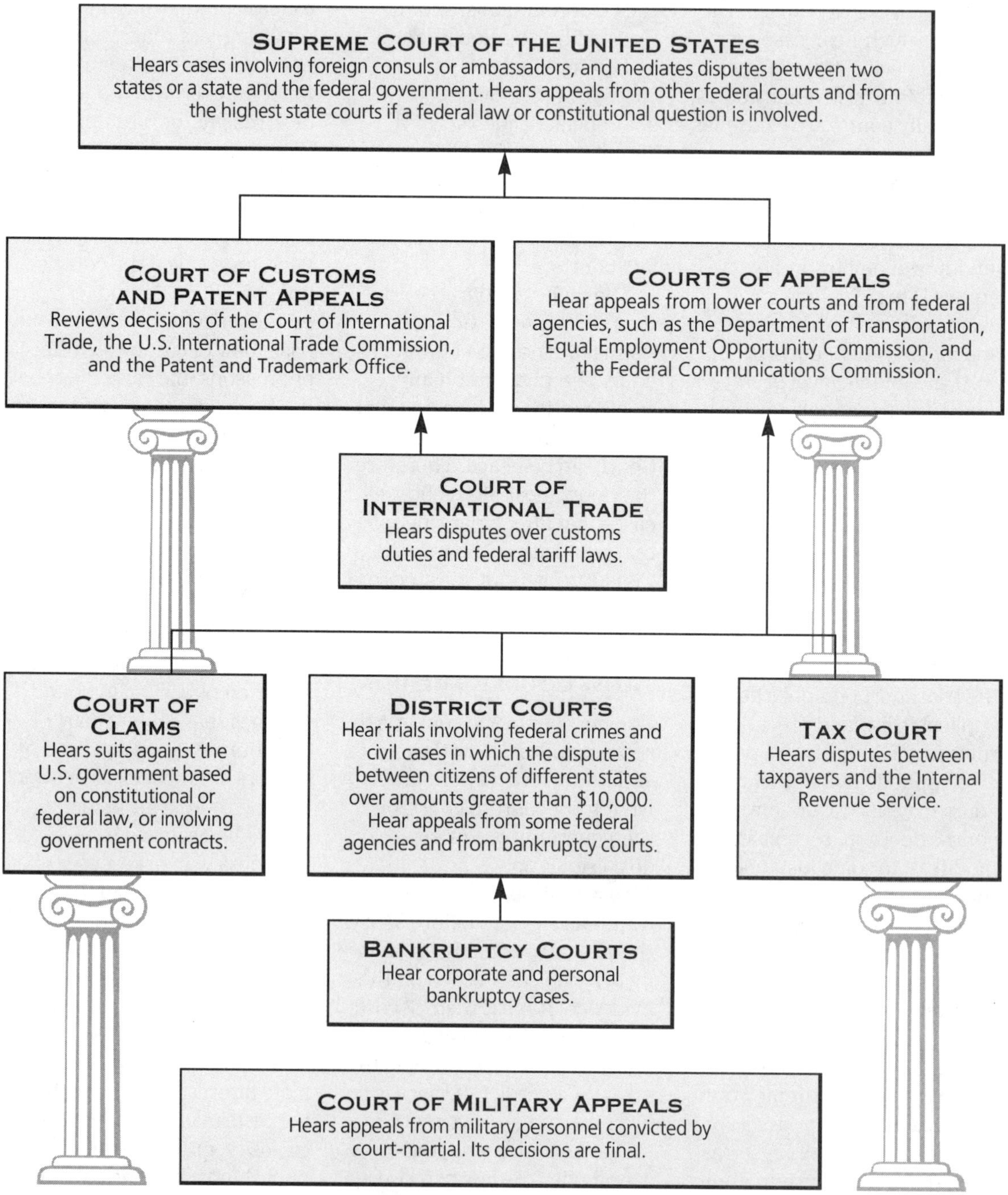

Supreme Court of the United States
Hears cases involving foreign consuls or ambassadors, and mediates disputes between two states or a state and the federal government. Hears appeals from other federal courts and from the highest state courts if a federal law or constitutional question is involved.

Court of Customs and Patent Appeals
Reviews decisions of the Court of International Trade, the U.S. International Trade Commission, and the Patent and Trademark Office.

Courts of Appeals
Hear appeals from lower courts and from federal agencies, such as the Department of Transportation, Equal Employment Opportunity Commission, and the Federal Communications Commission.

Court of International Trade
Hears disputes over customs duties and federal tariff laws.

Court of Claims
Hears suits against the U.S. government based on constitutional or federal law, or involving government contracts.

District Courts
Hear trials involving federal crimes and civil cases in which the dispute is between citizens of different states over amounts greater than $10,000. Hear appeals from some federal agencies and from bankruptcy courts.

Tax Court
Hears disputes between taxpayers and the Internal Revenue Service.

Bankruptcy Courts
Hear corporate and personal bankruptcy cases.

Court of Military Appeals
Hears appeals from military personnel convicted by court-martial. Its decisions are final.

State Court Systems

The court system of each of the 50 states is headed by a supreme court (which is not always called by that name). Below the high court may be appeals courts and, below them, trial courts, local courts, and special courts. The arrows in the chart show how cases are appealed from lower to higher state courts.

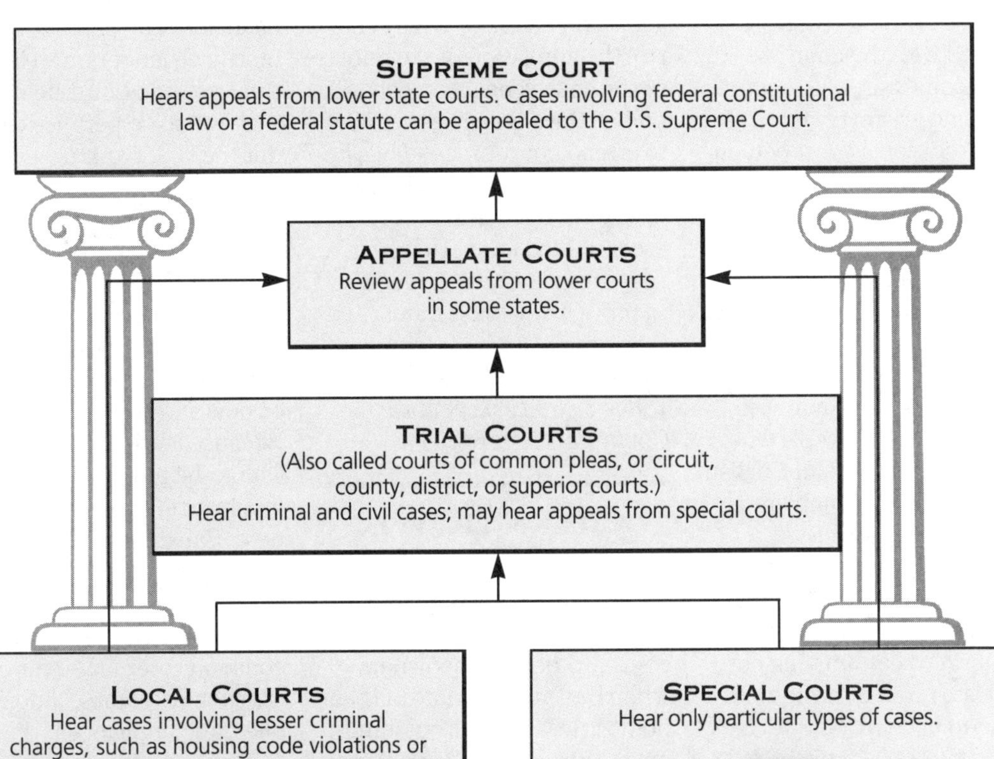

Local Courts

Hear cases involving lesser criminal charges, such as housing code violations or creating a nuisance, as well as claims for small amounts of money. The names and functions of these courts vary from state to state.

TRAFFIC COURTS
Try cases involving minor traffic violations.

POLICE COURTS
Hear cases involving violations of local ordinances.

MAGISTRATE'S COURTS
Hear cases involving minor offenses, such as traffic violations.

JUSTICE (JUSTICE OF THE PEACE) COURTS
Similar to magistrate's courts.

MUNICIPAL (CITY) COURTS
Hear minor criminal cases and lawsuits for small amounts.

Special Courts

Hear only particular types of cases.

PROBATE (SURROGATE) COURTS
Hear cases involving adoption, conservators, guardians, incompetency, and estates.

JUVENILE (FAMILY) COURTS
Hear paternity and child-support suits and cases involving abused, delinquent, or neglected children.

SMALL-CLAIMS COURTS
Hear cases involving sums of money up to a set dollar limit. (May be separate courts or part of another state or local court.)

CRIMINAL COURTS
(in some states)
Try cases involving minor crimes.

COURTS OF CLAIMS
(in some states)
Hear claims against the state.

mation, may be refused. Some records may be sealed by the court—for example, to protect the identities of juveniles or victims of sexual assault.

Court personnel
The clerk of the court makes notes about the proceedings in each case and receives all papers filed with the court, which then become part of the court record and are reviewed by the judge. Additional court personnel include law clerks (who do legal research for the judge), court attendants or bailiffs (who maintain order in the courtroom), and stenographers (who take down a word-for-word record of court proceedings). Interpreters may be available to assist people who do not fully understand English or who are hearing-impaired.

Terms and sessions
By law, a court is authorized to perform its judicial functions, including the conduct of trials, only during a certain time period. This is often referred to as the "term of court." The U. S. Supreme Court, for example, has only one term of court each year, which begins on the first Monday in October and concludes in June or July of the following year. The Court then reconvenes in October for the start of another term.

Within a given term, sessions are held. These are the times during which the judge or judges actually hear cases.

Court procedure
Specific rules and procedures must be followed in presenting a case in court. The federal and state court systems have their own rules of procedure regarding jurisdiction, parties, pretrial motions, evidence, judgments, and appeals.

Courts also have the authority to control all judicial proceedings and to ensure that the dignity of the court is maintained. For example, a court may prohibit photographs of an accused person, or it may control the admission of the public to the courtroom. As a general policy, the public has the right to attend court proceedings because public access is designed to assure that a hearing or trial is conducted fairly. However, a judge may limit public access to protect a witness's identity, to maintain order, or to assure that the proceedings are just.

See also APPEAL; FEDERAL COURTS; JURISDICTION.

CRAMDOWN

A cramdown is a procedure used especially by bankruptcy courts to help homeowners when the current value of their home is less than its outstanding mortgage. Here is an example of how it works:

Suppose you lost your job six months ago and are having trouble paying your bills. You took out a $100,000 mortgage on your home, but because of a depressed economy, the most you can get for your house now is $80,000. Your mortgage is a secured loan, with your house as collateral. Even if you were to declare bankruptcy and your house were sold, the bank still could demand the remaining $20,000 you owe.

With a cramdown, the bankruptcy court reduces ("crams down") the amount of your mortgage to the home's current market value, or $80,000. The remaining $20,000 is converted into an unsecured debt, which can be discharged in a bankruptcy proceeding. See BANKRUPTCY.

Needless to say, cramdowns have not been popular with mortgage lenders, and in 1993 the Supreme Court held that they were not permissible under the U.S. Bankruptcy Code.

CREDIT

Your credit is your ability to borrow money now and pay it back later, or to make purchases now and pay for them later. Because lenders collect interest on the money they provide in advance, credit is big business. Banks, savings and loan associations, and merchants extend hundreds of billions of dollars of credit every year to consumers for major purchases, such as homes, automobiles, and appliances.

To decide whether you are a good credit risk, lenders need information about your income, expenses, and bill-paying history. Rather than spending the time and money to conduct their own investigations, lenders turn to credit bureaus for this information. See CREDIT BUREAU AND CREDIT RATING.

Establishing credit can be a study in frustration. Suppose you have never had a credit card or taken out a loan, and now you want to establish credit. To do so, you go to a bank to take out a small loan, well within your means, which you expect to repay month by month.

You find out, however, that you cannot get a loan until you have established some kind of credit record. What can you do?

One way that you can begin to establish a credit record is to apply for a credit card at a local department store. Always pay your bills on time, and after a few months apply for another card at another store. After another few months apply for a national credit card, such as Visa or Mastercard. Once you have a national card, you are considered a good credit risk.

Another way to establish credit is to take out a secured loan at your bank. With this kind of loan, you pledge a bank savings account as collateral for a personal loan. Until the loan is repaid in full, you are prevented from making withdrawals from your savings account that would reduce its value below the amount of money you still owe. If you make the scheduled payments on time, the bank will report you to credit bureaus as a reliable customer, and you will have established a credit record that lenders can look to when you apply for loans in the future.

Credit Bureau and Credit Rating

A credit bureau is a private company that collects data about your employment, earnings, and debts. It sells this information to banks, credit card companies, department stores, and other institutions that want to find out whether you are a good financial risk.

Contrary to popular belief, your credit history (the information collected by a credit bureau) does not contain a judgment about your character or your general reliability as a person. A credit bureau reports facts, not judgments, and those facts include statistical information received from stores, banks, and other sources. It is up to an individual lender to review your record and decide whether you are a good risk.

What Your Credit File Contains

Although your credit file does not contain moral judgments, it probably contains more information than you would like. In addition to your name, address, and Social Security number, it lists your employment history, marital history, liens (claims) against your property, lawsuits, arrests, and convictions. But most of the information in your credit file is financial: whom you owe money to; how long you take to pay your debts; balances in your bank accounts; debts that have been turned over to collection agencies; and any recent bankruptcy.

The term *credit rating* derives from the fact that credit bureaus use a point system, on a scale from 0 to 9, to describe your payment history. For a given debt, 0 indicates "paid within 30 days," the most favorable rating. Things get worse the higher the number goes. For example, an 8 means the debt was sent to a collection agency, and a 9 means it was discharged by bankruptcy.

ABC's Of Your Credit Rights

A number of federal laws protect your rights as a consumer when you receive or apply for credit. Listed below are some of these laws and what they do.

- The Equal Credit Opportunity Act forbids lenders from discriminating against you on the basis of race, color, national origin, religion, age, sex, or marital status when you apply for credit.
- The Fair Credit Reporting Act and the Fair Credit Billing Act set forth procedures that let you inspect your credit report and correct errors in it.
- The Truth-in-Lending Act requires lenders to tell you how much it costs to borrow money: the interest rate, the annual percentage rate, and the amount of each payment if the loan is for a fixed period.
- The Fair Debt Collection Practices Act regulates debt collectors and forbids them to use collection methods that are unreasonable or abusive.

These laws are enforced by the Federal Trade Commission (FTC), which also investigates consumer complaints. For more information, or to file a complaint, call or write the Federal Trade Commission office in your area. You will find the address and phone number listed in your local telephone directory.

Often credit bureaus do, however, report information that is incorrect. According to the Federal Trade Commission, mistakes made by credit bureaus have prompted more consumer complaints than any other issue brought to their attention. For example, your report may contain information about someone with a name similar to yours, or it may say that a loan you repaid is still outstanding. You may be denied a credit card, a mortgage, insurance, or even employment because of such mistakes.

YOUR LEGAL PROTECTIONS

According to the federal Fair Credit Reporting Act of 1971, a lender who denies you credit must give you the reason. If the rejection was due to information in your credit record, you have a right to receive a free copy of that information if you ask for it within 30 days of being turned down. If the adverse information is incorrect, you should ask to have the record changed.

When the credit bureau investigates and it discovers that the information is wrong, it must remove the error from your file. If the bureau still believes the information is correct, you can enter into your file a 100-word statement contesting or explaining the information and demand that the credit bureau give your statement to anyone who has asked for a copy of your credit report during the last six months.

Another benefit ensured by the Fair Credit Reporting Act is that negative information must be removed from your credit record after a specified time, usually seven years. A bankruptcy, however, can stay in your file for as long as 10 years.

ASKING TO SEE YOUR FILE

Many financial advisers think that it is a good idea to review your record at one of the large credit bureaus at least once a year. Old inaccuracies can keep reappearing as a result of computer errors, and you may be able to head off potential problems if, for example, you are planning to apply for a loan. If your credit record is wrong at one bureau, you should not only have it corrected there but also find out if it is wrong at other credit bureaus by obtaining copies of their records.

The three largest credit bureaus in the United States are Trans Union, Equifax, and TRW. All three have toll-free telephone numbers to handle consumer complaints. To get a copy of your credit record, first call to find out how much it will cost (if it is not free, it will usually be less than $10) and what information will be needed to locate your file (usually your name, address, and Social Security number). Then write to the credit bureau requesting a copy of your file.

TRW offers consumers one free credit report annually. To get one, write TRW Consumer Assistance, P.O. Box 2350, Chatsworth, CA 91313. Include your name (and your spouse's name if you are married); your current address and any others you have had for the last five years; date of birth; and Social Security number. Enclose a photocopy of your driver's license or other verifiable identification. Your credit report should arrive within two or three weeks.

CREDIT CARD AND CHARGE ACCOUNT

Credit cards and charge accounts are handy ways to purchase items now and pay for them over time, but using them can be costly. Many of the nationally recognized cards (the ones stores want to see when they ask for a "major" credit card), carry interest rates that hover around the 20 percent mark, as do the charge accounts offered by department stores and other merchants.

The interest rate is not important if you pay your credit card bill in full each month. But if you make only partial payments, finding a card with a lower interest rate can save you hundreds of dollars each year. Furthermore, since 1991, the interest on credit cards and personal loans is no longer deductible on your income tax return, making a lower rate even more important.

By shopping around, you can find institutions that will issue a card to a good credit risk at a rate 5 or 6 percent less than that charged by other issuers.

But check the annual fee for the card; some banks charge as much as $75.

HOW TO HANDLE DISPUTED BILLS

If you use a credit card, always look carefully at your monthly statement as soon as it arrives. If you see a charge for an item you did not buy or an amount that is greater than what you actually paid for a particular purchase, tell the issuer right away. The federal Fair Credit Billing Act requires you to notify the issuer in writing within 60 days after the erroneous bill was sent to you. In your letter, include your name, address, and account number; identify the item you are questioning; and give the reason you believe it is wrong.

The lender then has 30 days to acknowledge receipt of your letter. While it investigates your claim, the lender cannot ask you to pay the disputed amount and cannot report you as delinquent to a credit bureau. However, the lender can subtract this amount from your credit limit. For example, if your credit limit is $1,000 and a disputed charge of $750 appears on your bill, your credit limit will be reduced to $250.

Within two billing periods or 90 days, whichever comes first, the lender must either correct your bill or explain to you in writing why it believes the original bill was correct. If you were billed by mistake, the amount will be removed from your account, along with any interest that accrued while the error was being investigated. But if the original bill was correct, you will have to pay the disputed amount plus interest.

Suppose you still believe the charge is a mistake, and the lender does not. For the time being, until the dispute is resolved, you should pay the required amount—for two good reasons: (1) interest charges will accumulate further, and (2) the lender may report you to a credit bureau as delinquent and thus damage your credit rating. If the dispute continues unresolved, you should consult a lawyer. She may advise you to file a lawsuit and let a judge settle the matter. See also CREDIT BUREAU AND CREDIT RATING.

CHARGE BACKS

The Fair Credit Billing Act also protects you when you buy defective goods or when your purchase is never delivered. Suppose you use a major, or national, credit card to buy a dishwasher at your local appliance store. The dishwasher does not work, and the store will not replace it. What can you do?

You are legally entitled to have the credit card company remove the charge from your account. This is what is known as a "charge back." It is similar to the "stop payment" order you ask your bank to make after writing a check you do not want to be cashed. See CHECK.

When you request a charge back, the credit card company investigates the problem. If it finds that your complaint is legitimate and that you have made a reasonable effort to resolve your dispute with the merchant, it will remove the charge from your account. If the company has already paid the merchant, it will deduct the amount from any future payments to the merchant or take some other action to have the money returned. This provision of the Fair Credit Billing Act proved especially valuable for travelers who held unused tickets on airlines that went out of business.

When you use a national bank card, you are subject to restrictions on charge backs. You have charge-back protection only if:

◇ The amount in question is more than $50.

◇ The sale took place within your home state.

◇ The sale took place less than 100 miles from your home.

When you use a credit card issued by the seller, such as a department store credit card, you are not required to pay for defective or undelivered merchandise, no matter what the amount of the sale or where it took place.

LOST OR STOLEN CREDIT CARDS

Are you responsible for unauthorized charges when your credit card or charge card is lost or stolen? If you notify the card issuer as soon as you discover your card is missing, you will not be responsible for any charges made after you reported the loss. If charges were made on your card before you reported it missing, you are liable only for the first $50.

The first thing to do when you find that your card has been lost or stolen is to call the card issuer. Get the name and address of the person you are speaking to and follow up your telephone call with a letter. Since the credit card company is responsible for any unauthorized charges over $50, you can be sure your problem will be treated expeditiously. The company will cancel your present account right away and issue you a new card.

If your credit card company sends you a letter urging you to buy "credit card protection," a kind of insurance against unauthorized use of your card, think twice about it. After a couple of years, the fees you pay for this "protection" will probably exceed the $50 you might have forfeited after a loss or theft.

UNAUTHORIZED USE BY SOMEONE YOU KNOW

Under the terms of your credit card agreement, you are not responsible for unauthorized charges, no matter who makes them. Suppose your teenage daughter uses your credit card to buy a portable compact disc player. If you did not authorize the charge, you are not obligated to pay it. But your daughter must return the machine, and she may also face charges of theft by fraud. Furthermore, if you have allowed her to use your card in the past, you may have a hard time convincing the credit card issuer that the charge was unauthorized. Your cooperation in their investigation of your daughter's actions will probably be required in order to give substance to your claim of unauthorized use. This does not mean you will have to watch your child go to jail, but more likely that you will have to make sure that the item is returned, and perhaps compensate the merchant for wear and tear on the machine.

CREDIT COUNSELING

You have been unable to keep up with your debts—your car has been repossessed, your credit cards have been canceled, and now you are getting strongly worded letters from collection agencies. Friends suggest that you file for bankruptcy, but you find the idea too humiliating. What can you do? You may want to consider the alternative provided by credit counseling.

A nonprofit organization called the Consumer Credit Counseling Service (CCCS) offers help to consumers who are having difficulty paying their debts. The CCCS has hundreds of offices from coast to coast, and they are listed in the telephone directories of most major cities. If you cannot locate the office nearest you, call the main office at (800) 388-2227, or write to CCCS, 8701 Georgia Avenue, Suite 507, Silver Springs, MD 20910.

The CCCS will help you negotiate an extended repayment plan with your creditors. It will also help you establish a budget and develop responsible spending habits to avoid future money problems. Although your creditors may still report your tardy payment record to credit bureaus, this negative information will stay on your credit record for no more than seven years. In contrast, if you had chosen to file for bankruptcy, it would remain on your record for 10 years. See CREDIT BUREAU AND CREDIT RATING.

A word of caution: a number of organizations with names similar to the Consumer Credit Counseling Service claim to provide debt counseling or debt-consolidation services. But most of these companies do little more than offer new loans to troubled debtors. The new loans are supposed to allow you to pay off existing loans with a single payment to the consolidator.

Unfortunately, many people who take out these loans end up deeper in debt than they were before, because the single loan payment owed to the consolidator, along with application fees and other charges, may be greater than the combined payments on their previous debts. Moreover, without help in budgeting, they may run up their credit card balances all over again. See also BANKRUPTCY; COMPOSITION WITH CREDITORS.

CREDIT UNION

A credit union is a nonprofit cooperative that functions much like a bank or savings and loan association. It receives deposits from and makes loans to its members, who usually share some common bond, such as working at the same company or belonging to a particular labor union.

Because credit unions are nonprofit, tax-exempt, and conservative in their lending policies, they tend to offer their members a better deal than banks and savings and loan associations. Because they know their customers better, they have fewer losses from bad loans and thus can pay higher interest rates on deposits. They may also charge lower interest rates for loans. Many credit unions are now competing more directly with banks, offering such services as money market accounts, credit cards, and automatic teller machines.

Most credit unions are members of the National Credit Union Administration (NCUA), an agency of the federal government that insures credit union deposits. They offer the same protection as FDIC-insured commercial banks—that is, they insure accounts up to $100,000.

Other credit unions are protected by programs administered by the individual states. See also BANK ACCOUNT; SAVINGS AND LOAN ASSOCIATION.

CRIMINAL LAW

You look in the rearview mirror and see the flashing red lights of a police car. Pulling over to the side of the road, you wait for the police officer to approach the car. He tells you that you were speeding, asks for your license and proof of insurance, and returns to his patrol car to check whether there is a warrant for your arrest.

Several minutes pass before the police officer returns, gun drawn, and orders you out of the car. Before you know what has happened, you are being searched, handcuffed, and placed in the back of the patrol car. The officer tells you that you are wanted for armed robbery in another state, and that you will be held for extradition. You know you are innocent, but how will you convince the police, a judge, or a jury?

If, as in this alarming scenario, you find yourself charged with a crime, you have certain basic rights that are designed to protect you from being convicted of an offense you did not commit. These rights, as guaranteed by the Constitution, are fundamental to American justice. However, they are subject to interpretation, and many federal and state statutes have been enacted to help define them more clearly.

RIGHT TO DUE PROCESS OF LAW

The 5th and 14th Amendments to the Constitution guarantee you due process of law. If you are accused of a crime, you must be notified of the charges and be given a reasonable opportunity to defend yourself. You must be given a public trial by a competent, impartial court that follows the rules of criminal procedure and observes the standards of fundamental fairness. See also CRIMINAL PROCEDURE; DUE PROCESS OF LAW.

Over the years, many cases have been brought before the courts to determine what constitutes fundamental fairness. For example, in one case the Supreme Court found that the standards of fundamental fairness were violated when a criminal defendant had to appear at his trial wearing prison clothes. In a case in which the proceedings were dominated by a mob and the jury was swayed by intimidation, the Supreme Court ruled that the trial was fundamentally unfair.

RIGHT TO EQUAL PROTECTION OF THE LAWS

The law may not be enforced in a way that discriminates against you on the basis of race, religion, or national origin. All criminal statutes must be applied evenhandedly, with no one group being singled out for prosecution.

This does not mean that prosecutors do not have some latitude in deciding whom to prosecute; you cannot use equal protection of the laws as a defense simply because another person who committed an identical crime was not charged. See also EQUAL PROTECTION OF THE LAWS.

RIGHT TO A SPEEDY TRIAL

The Sixth Amendment guarantees you the right to a speedy trial. What is meant by a speedy trial is not precisely defined in the amendment, so a number of states have set their own time limits. If you are not given a speedy trial as defined by state law, the charges against you will be dismissed.

Suppose John is indicted for car theft. In his state, the law specifies that he must be tried within one year. When the year is up and he has still not been brought to trial, his lawyer petitions the court claiming John's right to a speedy trial has been violated. The charges are then dismissed.

RIGHT TO A TRIAL BY JURY

Both the Sixth Amendment and Article Three of the Constitution give you the right to a trial by jury. You may waive this right, but if you want a jury trial and it is denied, any conviction that results is invalid. This right does not usually apply to traffic infractions and other petty crimes, but in some jurisdictions (state, county, or municipal) you can request a jury trial even for such minor offenses.

The jury must be drawn from a cross-section of the community where the trial is being held, and neither the prosecution nor the defense may intentionally exclude any group. But a jury need not proportionally represent all the racial groups in a given area. In cases that may call for capital punishment, the prosecution cannot exclude all potential jurors who oppose the death penalty.

In order to be fair and impartial, the jury must remain free of outside influences. Members should not be subjected to excessive pretrial publicity (what is considered excessive is determined case by case) or to publicity during the trial, and they should not communicate with witnesses.

Contrary to popular belief, the Constitution does not require that a jury be made up of 12 people, but most states require that juries have either 6 or 12 members. Nor does the Constitution require that the jury's verdict be unanimous, even though most states do. See also JURY.

RIGHT TO BE PRESENT AT YOUR TRIAL

You have the right to be present at any stage of the trial that will affect you. This includes the selection of the jury, presentation of evidence, arguments by attorneys, judge's instructions to the jury, announcement of the verdict, and judge's sentence. If you do not show up for your trial, you have waived your right to be present, and the court may try the case without you.

RIGHT NOT TO INCRIMINATE YOURSELF

According to the Fifth Amendment, if you are charged with a crime you cannot be compelled to testify against yourself. This right extends to other situations as well. For example, you cannot be required to testify about something that might lead you to be accused of a crime, nor can you be forced to produce documents containing evidence that will implicate you in a crime.

However, the U. S. Supreme Court has held that other kinds of evidence, such as fingerprints, blood type, and physical appearance, do not fall within the scope of Fifth Amendment protection. Therefore, you can be legally compelled to provide a sample of your handwriting, submit to blood tests, have your fingerprints taken, and appear in a lineup.

The right against self-incrimination is often called the right to remain silent. This right has been extended to protect people even during the early stages of a criminal investigation, before any charges have been filed. For example, you have

REAL LIFE, REAL LAW

The Case of the Video Witness

In a child-abuse case in Maryland, the trial judge heard testimony from experts that the alleged victim of abuse would experience severe emotional and psychological suffering and would be unable to communicate if forced to testify in the physical presence of the defendant. The court agreed to allow the witness to testify outside the defendant's presence through the use of one-way closed-circuit television. The defendant was convicted.

He appealed, arguing that his right to confront his accuser had been violated. But the U.S. Supreme Court upheld the conviction. The Court held that in this case, it was not necessary for the jury to observe the victim in the defendant's presence, and that the trial judge was not required to explore a less restrictive alternative before allowing the closed-circuit testimony.

Although a person accused of a crime has the constitutional right to confront his or her accuser, this case demonstrates that the right is not absolute.

the right to refuse to speak with the police about a crime you may be accused of. Once the trial is underway, the prosecution may not make comments to the jury suggesting that your failure to talk to the police or to testify at the trial implies that you are guilty. See also MIRANDA WARNINGS.

RIGHT TO COMPEL WITNESSES

If accused of a crime, you have the right to use the subpoena power of the courts; that is, you can compel witnesses to come forward to give testimony.

You cannot, however, force a witness to incriminate himself. Suppose Al is being tried for a robbery committed by Bob, in which Jack drove the getaway car. Al cannot force Jack to testify on Al's behalf because that would cause Jack to incriminate himself.

RIGHT TO CONFRONT ACCUSERS

The Sixth Amendment gives you the right to hear and cross-examine witnesses who testify against you. If one of your witnesses cannot be present at the trial, you may in some cases be able to introduce testimony that was recorded previously. See DEPOSITION.

In recent years some states have passed laws that permit children who have been the victims of crime to testify without being in the presence of the accused. The reason for this is to protect the children from being traumatized. Some states also allow the hearsay statements (statements of what the witness heard someone else say) of children to be admitted as evidence, but in other states this is considered a violation of the right to confront one's accusers. See also HEARSAY.

RIGHT TO ASSISTANCE OF COUNSEL

Under the Sixth Amendment, if you are charged with a crime, you have the right to be represented by a lawyer. If you cannot afford one, the court must appoint one for you. In some courts, public defenders represent people who cannot afford a lawyer. In others, lawyers in private practice are appointed for this purpose.

The right to assistance of counsel means that your lawyer must meet with you, advise you of your rights, and propose various defenses. If you are being held in jail before or during your trial, you have the right to communicate freely and privately with your lawyer.

No court will force a lawyer on a defendant who does not want one. In addition to having the right to an attorney, you also have the right to dispense with one and represent yourself. If you do, the court may appoint an attorney to help you prepare and present your own case, even if you don't use him.

RIGHT TO PRESUMPTION OF INNOCENCE

If you are accused of a crime, under the law you are presumed innocent until proved guilty. The burden of proof is on the prosecution, which must establish your guilt beyond a reasonable doubt in order to obtain a conviction. See also BURDEN OF PROOF.

CRIMINAL PROCEDURE

Every state has its own rules to ensure the orderly prosecution of criminal charges. These procedures vary somewhat from state to state, and they may also differ depending on whether the crime is a misdemeanor (a crime punishable by a year or less in jail) or a felony (a more serious crime punishable by a year or more in prison). Generally, however, criminal procedure follows the same basic pattern. Once the preliminary investigation ends and a suspect has been identified, the prosecution begins—usually with an indictment or a complaint.

INDICTMENT, INFORMATION, OR COMPLAINT

If the prosecutor believes you have committed a crime, he can begin the process against you in one of several ways, depending on the law in the state where you live.

Indictment

Often the prosecutor begins by seeking an indictment from a grand jury—a group of 12 to 24 people who are assembled to hear the evidence against you. If they believe there is enough evidence to begin a prosecution, they will indict you, or charge you with the crime.

You do not have the same rights in a grand jury proceeding that you do in a trial. For example, you do not have the right to be present during the proceedings and to cross-examine witnesses—in fact, you may not even be aware that the grand jury is hearing evidence against you.

A grand jury indictment is required in certain cases to set a prosecution in motion. For example, a federal crime that may be punished by more than a year in prison or by death cannot be prosecuted unless an indictment is returned by a federal grand jury.

Information or complaint When an indictment is not called for, the prosecutor can initiate the process by filing an "information" or "complaint." These have the same effect as an indictment.

The indictment, information, or complaint must, at the minimum, state the nature of the offense and the date and time of occurrence—enough information to let you know the crime you are charged with.

After the grand jury returns the indictment or the prosecutor files the information or complaint, you will be summoned to appear in court on a given date for a "first appearance," or you may be arrested. If arrested, you will either be jailed until the first appearance or given the opportunity to post bail and be released until then. See ARREST; BAIL.

FIRST APPEARANCE

At your first appearance, the court will make sure that you have received a copy of the charges against you and that you understand them. The court will also inform you of your right to have an attorney and will ask if you can afford one. If you cannot, the court will appoint one for you.

At this time the court will also set your bond. If the bond has already been set and you have been bailed out, the court might impose conditions on it, such as ordering you not to leave town. If you are unable to put up the money for your bond, the court may reduce it.

If you have been charged with a felony, your first appearance is also the time when the court will set a date for your preliminary hearing.

PRELIMINARY HEARING

At the preliminary hearing, the prosecution must present enough evidence to convince the court that a crime has occurred and that there is "probable cause" to believe that you committed it. Probable cause is not as strict a standard as "beyond a reasonable doubt," which represents the level of proof required for a conviction.

You have the legal right to be present at your preliminary hearing, where you can cross-examine witnesses and present your own evidence. If the court is not convinced that there is probable cause that a crime occurred or that you committed it, the charges will be dismissed. However, charges that are dismissed at the preliminary hearing stage can sometimes be refiled if additional evidence later comes to light.

If the court does find probable cause to believe that you committed the crime, you will be required to stand trial. Before your trial, you will have to appear for an arraignment.

ARRAIGNMENT

At the arraignment you will enter your plea: guilty, not guilty, or no contest (or *nolo contendere).* A plea of no contest does not constitute an admission of guilt but is an admission that the prosecution has sufficient evidence to obtain a conviction if the case goes to trial. A plea of guilty or no contest does not require a trial; the court simply proceeds to sentencing. If you plead not guilty, your case will be set for trial. For most criminal cases you may choose to have either a jury trial or a trial by the court. In the latter case, the judge will decide your guilt or innocence.

TRIAL

If you choose a jury trial, the proceedings will begin with the selection of a jury. Far more jurors than necessary will be summoned, and the defense and prosecution will then pick a jury from those called. They will question the potential jurors to find out whether they know any facts about the case, have any particular prejudices about it, are acquainted with you or any of the witnesses, or are in some way unlikely to be fair and impartial.

Once the jury has been chosen, the trial can proceed. The prosecution presents evidence and questions witnesses, and your lawyer cross-examines those witnesses and tries to show that they are mistaken or are not telling the truth. You may testify on your own behalf, but you cannot be forced to testify, because it would violate your Fifth Amendment rights. If you choose not to testify, the jury is told not to assume that your silence is a sign of guilt. See also CRIMINAL LAW; FIFTH AMENDMENT.

When both sides have presented their case, the judge instructs the jury on the law. For example, in a first-degree murder case, the judge will inform the jury about which elements (such as willful killing and premeditation) must be proved in order to obtain a murder conviction.

The jury then retires to a separate room, where it must try to determine what happened on the basis of the evidence alone. When the jury decides what the facts are, it must apply the law to them, as instructed by the judge, and determine if you committed the crime. In some states, all 12 jurors must agree, but in others only 10 must agree. When the jurors reach their verdict, they return to the courtroom and announce it to the court.

If the jury finds you are not guilty, you will be let go. If it finds you guilty, the judge will set a date for sentencing. If the jury cannot agree on a verdict, it is called a "hung jury"; the judge will declare a mistrial, and the prosecution will have to decide whether to start over again. See MISTRIAL.

SENTENCING

Before your sentence is determined, the court may order an investigation of your background, education, work history, criminal record, and family situation. The investigators may also consult the victims of the crime to find out the impact it had on them and the sentence they would recommend. The court will review this report as part of the process of arriving at an appropriate sentence. See also VICTIMS' RIGHTS.

The sentence must be within the guidelines set by law for your particular crime. You may be fined, sent to prison, or both. Or if you are lucky, you may be released on probation, which means you will not go to jail as long as you follow certain rules. See PROBATION.

Someone who is sentenced to death (in those states that permit capital punishment) will not be executed immediately. Lengthy appeal processes are currently required by law before an execution can be carried out. See DEATH PENALTY.

APPEAL

If you believe that certain mistakes were made during your trial—for example, if you believe the judge did not instruct the jury properly—and that this resulted in your conviction, you can file an appeal.

In the appeals process, a higher court reviews the proceedings of the trial court to find out if mistakes were made and if those mistakes justify a reversal of the trial court's decision. While awaiting a decision about your appeal, you may either be free on bond or start serving your sentence. If the appeals court reverses your conviction, you must be released or given a new trial.

If you are found not guilty, the prosecution may also appeal the verdict if it believes that mistakes in the trial led to an unjust acquittal. However, if the appeal is successful, you cannot be retried, as this would violate the constitutional prohibition against double jeopardy. The decision of the appeals court would merely clarify the law in the future and prevent the courts from making a similar mistake. See APPEAL.

CROSS-EXAMINATION

Cross-examination, the process of questioning the opposing party's witness in a court proceeding, is a mainstay of courtroom dramas. A lawyer calls a witness to the stand. After a few minutes of testimony that makes the defendant look hopelessly guilty, the lawyer turns smugly from the witness stand and says, "No further questions, Your Honor." Then his opponent rises to cross-examine the witness and, with a series of deftly phrased questions, pummels what moments ago had seemed like rock-solid evidence into a fine dust of half-truths, hazy memories, and pitiful lies.

PURPOSES

Although cross-examination is rarely so dramatic in real-life courtrooms, it is fundamental to our judicial system. In typical court procedure, the cross-examination follows the initial questioning—the "direct examination"—of a witness by the party that has called him. The opposing attorney may then cross-examine the witness for a number of reasons: to clarify testimony given previously; to discredit the witness; to test whether the witness is telling the truth; or to develop points that will be helpful to the attorney's client.

A judge cannot deny the right of cross-examination in either civil or criminal cases, because this would be a denial of the right to a fair trial. If a witness is unavailable for cross-examination for some reason, such as illness, the testimony he gave during direct examination may be removed, or stricken, from the record. Or if a witness refuses to answer questions during cross-examination, the court may strike the testimony that he gave on direct examination. If the case is being heard by a jury, the members of the jury are instructed to ignore anything the witness said during direct examination.

LIMITATIONS

As a general rule, neither a witness in a civil case nor a party to the lawsuit can refuse to answer questions during a cross-examination. In criminal cases, however, there is one exception to this rule: a defendant or witness may refuse to answer a question if it violates his Fifth Amendment right against self-incrimination. See also FIFTH AMENDMENT.

The majority of states limit cross-examination to topics that were brought up during direct examination. Questions may be asked to get more details from a particular witness or to point out inconsistencies or weaknesses in his testimony. For example, the exchange may go something like this:

ATTORNEY: Under direct examination, didn't you say that you saw the defendant strike Mr. Smith?

WITNESS: Yes.

ATTORNEY: And where were you when you saw this take place?

WITNESS: At the end of the alley.

ATTORNEY: What time did you say it was?

WITNESS: Just after midnight.

ATTORNEY: Wasn't it awfully dark out?

WITNESS: Well, yes.

ATTORNEY: So let me ask you how you can be so sure the defendant was the person who struck Mr. Smith?

WITNESS: Well, I guess I'm not sure, but I think it was him.

The only exception to limiting the topics of cross-examination to those brought up during the direct examination occurs when the attorney for one side is trying to discredit a witness for the opposing side. For example, the attorney may be permitted to ask questions that show the witness has an interest in the outcome of the case or that reveal the witness to be biased because he has a personal relationship with the person on whose behalf he is testifying.

LEADING QUESTIONS

Leading questions are prohibited during direct examination. However, they are allowed during cross-examination to enable the opposing lawyer to get the answers he wants from a witness. A leading question is usually worded so that the witness need only answer yes or no—for example, "Didn't you see the defendant strike his wife?" Such questions enable the attorney to limit what a witness can say and thus to shape the testimony to fit his case.

While the court must give each side the chance to cross-examine witnesses called by the other side, in some cases the lawyer chooses not to do so. If a witness's story is airtight and unassailable, cross-examination might do more harm than good. Or an attorney may forgo cross-examination in order to indicate to the jury that a witness has nothing to say that is of importance to the case. See also CRIMINAL PROCEDURE.

CRUEL AND UNUSUAL PUNISHMENT

The Eighth Amendment to the Constitution prohibits the government from using "cruel and unusual punishment." This is usually defined as punishment that is grossly out of proportion to the crime or that shocks the moral sensibility of reasonable people. For example, in American prisons, the torture of prisoners is prohibited because it is considered cruel and unusual punishment. So are harsh sentences for minor crimes and substandard prison conditions caused by overcrowding.

Imposition of the death penalty for murder and for other extremely serious crimes, such as drug dealing that results in someone's death, has not been held to violate the Eighth Amendment, however, as long as clear guidelines prevent judges and juries from arbitrarily sentencing convicted criminals to death.

Even so, the issue remains controversial. The law regarding what constitutes cruel and unusual punishment is still evolving more than 200 years after its prohibition. See also DEATH PENALTY.

CUSTOMS, U.S.

If you buy merchandise in another country and want to take it home, it must first be cleared by the U.S. Customs Service. In many cases, the things you bought will be subject to tariffs, or duties—extra charges collected by the government. These duties are imposed to raise the price of foreign goods so that they will not adversely compete with goods produced in this country.

Suppose you buy a cashmere coat in Ireland for $600, but a similar coat made here costs $1,000. To protect U.S. clothing companies, the federal government may impose a duty on the foreign coat to narrow the gap between the two prices. The amount of the tariff will probably not raise the Irish coat's price to that of the American coat, but it will make the foreign purchase less attractive financially.

The kinds of goods subject to duties and the amounts owed for each kind of item are listed in federal tariff schedules. The amount to be paid not only varies from item to item, but also depends on the country from which the item is being imported.

EXEMPTIONS

When you return from a trip abroad with items you purchased there, you are entitled to an exemption of $400 (per person) on most articles you bought for personal use, for household use, or for gifts. When the total exceeds $400, however, you must prepare an itemized list of everything you bought and pay the appropriate duty on the excess amount.

Family members traveling together can consolidate their purchases to avoid paying duty. For example, suppose that during their trip to Italy, Mr. Hopkins bought $550 worth of merchandise and Mrs. Hopkins bought only $200 worth. They can combine their purchases for a total of $750 ($50 less than their combined limit) and pay no duty. Otherwise, Mr. Hopkins would be subject to a duty on the $150 that exceeded his personal exemption.

Children are entitled to the exemption as well. If the Hop-

REAL LIFE, REAL LAW

The Case of the Sensitive Smuggler

In their effort to stop drug smuggling across American borders, U.S. Customs agents created a "smugglers' profile" of women who were typically found to be carrying illegal drugs into the country at Miami International Airport. According to the profile, these women were usually young, clean-looking, and traveling alone on flights from Bogotá. They wore loose-fitting dresses to conceal the drugs carried underneath and carried only one suitcase, with no items to declare, in order to clear customs quickly.

When Susan arrived at Miami, she fit this profile. She was referred to two female customs inspectors, who took her to a private room and asked her to remove her dress and slip. When she did, the inspectors found seven packets of cocaine in her girdle. She was placed under arrest and convicted of violating federal laws against importing cocaine.

Susan appealed her conviction, claiming that the search was both illegal (because there was no probable cause for it) and unreasonable (because it required her to undress in front of the customs agents).

The U.S. Court of Appeals disagreed and upheld the conviction. It noted that, unlike other kinds of searches for which the government must show probable cause, border searches require only suspicion of illegal activity. Also, the court found nothing unreasonable about Susan's search, because she was examined by other women in a dignified way and in a private place.

kinses were traveling with their two daughters, they would be entitled to four exemptions of $400 each, and the exemptions could be consolidated for a total family allowance of $1,600.

RESTRICTIONS AND PENALTIES

Certain kinds of items—such as farm products, seeds, or animals—have the potential for causing harm to the nation's agriculture, public health, or ecological balance. Therefore, the Customs Service may require you to obtain a permit before bringing them into the United States. Some items are banned altogether, such as potted plants, narcotics, dairy products, and merchandise from countries that are considered unfriendly to the United States. Other kinds of items that may be subject to restrictions include cigarettes, guns, and alcoholic beverages.

If you fail to declare items you purchased abroad, or if you intentionally declare an amount that is lower than the item's actual price, you will be subject to penalties. At the very least, you will have to pay the appropriate duty, and you may also be fined an amount equal to the cost of the item in the United States. In addition, depending on the severity of the circumstances, the Customs Service may decide to seize your undeclared purchase, and you may be subject to criminal prosecution.

FROM DAMAGED MERCHANDISE TO DYING WITHOUT A WILL

DAMAGED MERCHANDISE

Sometimes when you make a purchase, you end up with damaged merchandise. What you do with it—and how you go about getting a refund or replacement—depends in large part on how you bought it and the way it was sent to you.

MAIL-ORDER PURCHASES

When you receive damaged goods that you bought by mail order, keep the shipping carton and all the packing materials, as they may be needed to substantiate the cause of the damage. For example, a dented box indicates the package was damaged in transit. If the merchandise was broken because the seller packed it improperly or the delivery company mishandled it, you are entitled to a replacement from the company.

Check the company's catalog for instructions on returning damaged goods. Or call the customer service department to find out how they want you to return the merchandise and whether you will be reimbursed for postage or shipping costs.

If the company used a private delivery service, such as United Parcel Service (UPS), it may arrange for the delivery service to pick up the damaged merchandise at no cost to you. This is a common practice with mail-order companies. Companies that send merchandise through the U.S. Postal Service will probably require you to pay the shipping costs when you send something back.

If you return the merchandise by mail, insure the package and keep the receipt as proof that you sent it. If you return it by using a private service, your package will probably be automatically insured up to a certain amount. You can buy additional coverage for more expensive items.

IN-STORE PURCHASES

Before you buy an item at a store and take it home, be sure to ask about the store's return policy. Does the store accept returns of damaged goods? Is there a time limit? If you can, watch the person who is packing the item and inspect the package before leaving the store. If the merchandise arrives in a sealed manufacturer's carton, do not accept a carton that looks poorly wrapped, badly dented, or otherwise damaged. Some stores specifically state that your only recourse when merchandise is damaged this way lies with the manufacturer.

Some stores sell floor models or slightly damaged merchandise at reduced prices. If you buy such merchandise, be careful. Although you can sometimes get a bargain, damaged goods are usually sold "as is," which means that you probably cannot get a refund or replacement under any circumstances.

If a salesperson assures you that "We guarantee all our merchandise," ask her to put the promise in writing. Be sure she indicates the extent of any repairs the store will make, as well as how long this guarantee will last.

GOODS THAT BREAK AFTER YOU RECEIVE THEM

Often merchandise proves inferior or defective only after you have had it at home for a while. In such circumstances, you will have to go either to the store owner or the manufacturer for repair or replacement. Many merchants will not accept responsibility after you have kept an item for a certain length of time.

In the case of small appliances (such as toasters and clock radios), the responsibility for repairing or replacing damaged merchandise usually belongs to the manufacturer, not the merchant, and you must contact the manufacturer directly. For more information, see MAGNUSON-MOSS WARRANTY ACT; WARRANTY AND GUARANTY.

If neither the seller nor the manufacturer will take responsibility for the damaged goods, you may have to initiate an action in small-claims court to recover your money. See also SMALL-CLAIMS COURT.

DAMAGES

The money awarded in a lawsuit to someone who has been harmed or injured because of another person's wrongful conduct (whether in the form of some action or of negligence), is known as damages. If Mary's fall, caused by Harry's leaving a brick on the path to his house, left her with a slight limp, Harry cannot make her leg straight again. If Mary sues Harry for negligence and wins, the jury will award her damages that express in money the extent of the harm Harry's act did to her. The award is not intended to make Mary so rich that she will be able to hire limousines to carry her around, nor to punish Harry by leaving him so poor he will have to sell his house.

You are entitled to damages only for particular types of injury or loss that are recognized by law. For example, you may win damages if someone destroyed your property, caused you personal injury, or caused you financial loss by breaking a contract. But the law does not give you the right to collect damages for hurt feelings, for a single trespass (a neighbor's use of your yard once for a shortcut), or for your lack of sleep (due to noise from a nearby railroad line). Successful lawsuits may result in an award of one or more of three categories of damages: compensatory, nominal, and punitive.

COMPENSATORY DAMAGES

Compensatory damages consist of money that will repay someone for a loss or injury. Suppose the transmission of Ray's auto was ruined when he drove over a large pothole on a city road. Ray also broke his hand when he drove over the hole. Ray sued the city and won, and the jury ordered the city to reimburse him for the cost of the transmission and the medical expenses associated with his broken hand, nothing more. These are called compensatory damages.

But suppose Ray is a carpenter and cannot work for six weeks after the accident. His loss of wages is a direct consequence of the accident, and he could therefore expect to be reimbursed for this loss as part of his compensatory damages.

Some forms of personal injury, such as pain and suffering, or mental anguish, are real and merit compensation, but attaching specific dollar amounts may be difficult. Suppose you suffer a minor injury in an accident, and as a result you become nervous, irritable, and have trouble sleeping. Your suffering is obviously very real, but it may be impossible to place an exact monetary value on it, especially if you are able to work at your regular job and do not incur a loss of income.

Breach of contract
Compensatory damages are also awarded when there has been a breach of contract. If you have a contract with Country Landscapers to plant your yard for $3,000 and they never

ABC's
Of Compensatory Damages

Damages awarded to a plaintiff in a civil lawsuit are of three kinds: nominal, punitive, and compensatory. Compensatory damages—the most common kind—represent the amount of money that will compensate the plaintiff for his loss. Some damages, such as those for medical bills, are easy to calculate because they have precise dollar values. Other amounts, such as those for mental suffering, are not easily measured, and require the judge or jury to make the fairest possible decision given the circumstances of the case.

DAMAGES THAT ARE EASILY MEASURED:

- ❑ Medical bills (including money for doctors, hospital care, and medication).
- ❑ Lost employment income (based on wages or fees).
- ❑ Costs to repair or replace damaged property.
- ❑ Increased living costs (such as remodeling a home to accommodate a wheelchair).

DAMAGES THAT ARE NOT SO EASILY MEASURED:

- ❑ Loss of future income (based on the injured person's age, job history, and education).
- ❑ Physical disfigurement or impairment.
- ❑ Loss of memory or other mental impairment.
- ❑ Physical pain and suffering.
- ❑ Mental pain and suffering.

show up, your damages would be the difference between the $3,000 and any higher amount you had to pay another contractor for the job. Therefore, if you had to pay another landscaper $3,500, your damages would be $500.

Responsibilities of the injured person

When you are harmed or injured as a result of someone else's wrongful act or breach of contract, you have a duty to minimize your loss or suffering. Suppose Nancy's upstairs neighbor Jerry went out late one night and left the sink faucets running. The sink overflowed and the water dripped into Nancy's living room. Nancy was at home, but because she was angry with Jerry, she did not call the superintendent to enter Jerry's apartment and turn off the water; nor did she put a bucket under the drip. Instead she sued Jerry not only for the damage to her ceiling, but for a new carpet. Because Nancy did nothing to mitigate, or lessen, her damages, she would probably be reimbursed only for repairs to her ceiling.

NOMINAL DAMAGES

Nominal damages, a small sum awarded as recognition of a defendant's wrongful act, is the law's way of recognizing that a person's rights have been violated, even when he has not suffered any real loss.

When a judge (or jury) imposes nominal damages, which can be as low as $1, he symbolically places blame on the defendant (the person sued). For example, a trespasser was ordered to pay $1 in damages to a neighbor for repeatedly using his lawn as a shortcut.

If a person suffers damage to himself or his property, nominal damages may be awarded when he does not demonstrate the exact extent of his loss. For example, if Ray failed to document the cost of the repairs to his auto or the medical costs for his broken hand, the judge or jury would have no basis for deciding the extent of his loss, leaving no alternative but to award nominal damages.

Nominal damages are also awarded in civil liberties cases. For example, a person who is arrested in a case of mistaken identity may receive only nominal damages, especially if he was in custody only briefly and he was released as soon as the mistake was discovered.

PUNITIVE DAMAGES

A plaintiff may be given punitive (also known as presumptive, or exemplary) damages in order to punish a defendant for his actions. Punitive damages also serve to warn others that certain conduct will not be condoned. They are typically awarded in lawsuits where a defendant has acted in a willful, wanton, or malicious way, or has otherwise demonstrated a total indifference or reckless disregard for the consequences of his act. If Ray's reckless driving caused him to hit and injure a bicyclist, for instance, he might be required to pay both compensatory and punitive damages. This award is meant to send Ray and others like him a strong message to drive more carefully.

ASSESSING DAMAGES

Typically, it is the judge who determines the types of damages a plaintiff may recover. A court may also decide that damages should be limited, because the plaintiff could have avoided a loss or injury. For example, suppose that Ray lost control of his car and drove it through the window of a local liquor store. If the owner fails to board up the window or post a guard after the incident, Ray cannot be held responsible for losses the store incurs when looters enter it later that night and steal the merchandise.

In jury trials, the jury will decide how much money should be awarded, although a judge usually has the discretion to increase or reduce the amount of a jury award.

In some contract cases, it may be difficult to determine the exact amount of damages caused by one party's failure to fulfill its part of the bargain. Suppose a company makes an agreement with a law firm to provide legal services to its employees as a benefit. If the law firm decides to back out of the agreement and the matter is brought to court, a judge or jury might not be able to decide how much extra the company would have to pay to replace the law firm's services—and as a result it might not award any damages. To avoid such a situation, contracts often include a "liquidated damages" clause that specifies how one party is to be compensated if the other breaks the contract.

DATE RAPE

Date rape, or *acquaintance rape,* is the term used for rape committed by a man whom the victim knows socially. It also covers nondating situations, such as rape by a coworker, neighbor, or classmate. Estimates are that date rape accounts for 80 percent of all rapes—that is, only 20 percent are committed by strangers.

For victims, prosecution of such rapes presents a distinctive set of problems. Because the rapist knows the victim, he may try to coerce her into not reporting the crime. If the rapist is a boyfriend, the victim may feel guilty about subjecting him to prosecution. In addition, she may be afraid of being accused of having seduced the rapist, having consented to sexual relations and later claiming she was raped, or of bringing rape charges as a retaliation because she was jilted.

Because women realize that if they are raped their behavior will be scrutinized and their character may be questioned, many victims decide not to report the crime or do not report it right away. Because a delay in reporting the crime may also be due to psychological trauma, some courts allow the prosecution to present expert evidence to that effect in order to give the victim the opportunity to explain the delay. See also RAPE; STATUTORY RAPE.

DATING

Even the ritual of dating can lead to legal problems. As high school proms grow more and more elaborate and expensive, young women who have been "stood up" by their dates on prom night have started filing lawsuits, usually in small-claims court, against the young men. In one such case filed in California, the young man who failed to show up was ordered to reimburse his prom date for the cost of her dress, shoes, and hairstyling, even though he claimed to have suffered a broken ankle that made it impossible to attend the prom. Some courts—in California, New York, and Illinois, for example—have agreed that the women should be compensated, while others have not. In many ways these cases resemble the breach of promise suits brought by jilted fiancées. See BREACH OF PROMISE.

A much more serious consequence of dating is rape, when the woman is sexually assaulted by a man whom she knows and has no reason to fear. See DATE RAPE.

Another area of concern is the workplace. When male and female coworkers date, the potential for sexual harassment increases, especially if one of them is a supervisor or manager and it is the subordinate who wishes to end the romance or stop further advances. To avoid this possibility, some companies prohibit dating between supervisors and subordinates and sometimes between coworkers too. See SEXUAL HARASSMENT.

DAY CARE

Of the 21 million children in the United States under the age of six, 54 percent of them have mothers who work outside the home. Of these children, 46 percent are cared for in their own home, mainly by relatives; 23 percent are in family day care, meaning they are cared for in the caregiver's home; 14 percent are in day-care centers; 9 percent are in nursery school; and 8 percent accompany a parent to work.

REGULATION

Standards for both day care and child care are determined by state law. These standards and their enforcement vary widely from state to state.

Most day-care providers who take children into their home are unlicensed and, therefore, unregulated. Even when they do have licenses, they are rarely monitored by licensing authorities.

Day-care centers are more closely regulated, but government regulations and periodic inspections do not provide sufficient guarantees that a child will be properly cared for in a clean and safe environment or offered a variety of stimulating, healthy activities. You can help ensure your child's well-being by following the suggestions listed in the "ABC's of Choosing Day Care," on page 151.

CHILD CARE IN YOUR HOME

If you plan to hire someone to come into (and perhaps live in) your home to care for your children, you will have to make certain special arrangements. For example:

◇ You may be required to contribute to her Social Security account, and to withhold and remit federal and state income taxes from her pay.

◇ You should be sure that your home insurance policy covers the caregiver for any injuries she may incur in your home or while in your employ.

◇ If she will be using your car, be sure that your automobile insurance will cover her as a member of your household.

◇ If your caregiver is not a citizen, make sure she has the proper work authorization.

See also HOMEOWNERS INSURANCE; HOUSEHOLD HELP.

DAY-CARE TAX CREDIT

Working parents are entitled to claim day care as an "employment-related expense" on their federal income tax returns. Your state may have a similar tax credit. In 1993 the federal credit per child was 20 percent of the cost of day care up to an annual maximum of $2,400. Thus, the maximum credit for one child was $480 per year, $960 for two children, and so on.

DAY CARE AS A JOB BENEFIT

Under federal law, an employer that offers a flexible benefit plan (sometimes called a cafeteria plan) for its employees may include a day-care benefit as part of it. If the plan is qualified by the IRS, this benefit is tax-free to the recipient and allows the employer to take a tax deduction for the cost of administering the benefit. You can obtain information about a day-care benefit (or about the possibility of beginning one) from your company's human resources department. See FLEXIBLE BENEFITS.

LEGAL PROTECTION

Although each state has its own laws regulating day care, most address the following concerns.

Number of children
Each state limits the number of children allowed at a day-care center or in family day care.

Training
Some states require a caregiver to receive some kind of training in order to be licensed. The training may include attending child-care workshops, taking college courses, or satisfying reading requirements in child development. Some states may require that day-care centers have a program director with appropriate academic credentials and teaching experience.

Health tests
Day-care providers must prove that they have been vaccinated against tuberculosis and other communicable diseases.

Physical facilities
For safety, some states require day-care centers to have the following: at least 25 square feet of play space per child; an adequate number of toilets and sinks in proportion to the number of children; fire extinguish-

ABC's OF CHOOSING DAY CARE

In trying to find the best day care for your child, you should gather all the information you can about the available options and investigate each one before entrusting your child to someone else.

❑ Look for a center or provider whose location, hours, and fees match your needs.

❑ Investigate the provider's reputation. Get recommendations from friends, coworkers, and relatives if possible. If the provider has not been personally recommended, ask for references from both former and current clients, and talk to them by telephone. Be sure to ask former clients why they left. If you get even a whisper of negative feedback, look elsewhere.

❑ Visit every provider you are considering. Make sure the premises are clean, spacious, and safe. Take a close look at toys, bathroom facilities, playground equipment, and conditions for daytime naps. Ask to see fire exits, extinguishers, and smoke detectors.

❑ Determine the staff-to-child ratio. A rule of thumb is that each adult caregiver can be responsible for no more than four infants, five preschoolers, or six older children. Make sure the caregivers are knowledgeable in child development.

❑ Ask how long the staff has been working there. Child care is a low-paying job with a high turnover. The longer the workers have been employed by the center, the more certain you can be that it is well managed.

❑ Ask the day-care operator how employees are screened and how carefully workers' backgrounds are investigated. Observe staff interactions with children. Do they get on the floor and engage in activities? Do they speak directly to the children and seem to enjoy being with them?

❑ Find out how medical needs and emergencies are handled. The day-care provider should maintain medical records of the children in her care, as well as consent forms from parents so that the provider can make medical decisions if parents cannot be reached. Be sure that emergency procedures are posted and that at least one caregiver who is trained in CPR and first aid is always present .

❑ Spend some time observing daily activities. Are meals, naps, and playtimes well organized? Do the children look happy? Is there regular activity, or do the children (and staff) simply sit around watching television?

❑ Ask if you can visit at any time when your child is there. If the provider tells you that there are certain times when parents are not allowed to visit or that you must request permission to visit in advance, look for another provider. Day-care facilities are not schools and should not restrict parental visits.

ers and smoke alarms; covered garbage containers; guards on stairways, heating elements, and electrical outlets; an accessible telephone with emergency numbers posted nearby; bathrooms with doors that unlock from both sides; a refrigerator; and locked storage cabinets for medications.

Activities
Some states require all caregivers to provide a specified number of hours of supervised outdoor play per day, as well as rest periods and snacks. A few states require day-care providers to prepare written activity plans to develop children's creativity, self-confidence, physical coordination, and intellectual growth.

Consent forms
Most states require caregivers to obtain health data on each child, as well as medical consent forms in case a child needs medical care and neither parent is available to consent.

Child abuse registry
Some states require caregivers to report the name, address, and birthdate of every person who works in a day-care facility or lives in a provider's home, so that those names can be screened for reports or convictions of child abuse or neglect.

Emergency plans
Centers may be required to develop and post emergency plans for fires, storms, tornadoes, and floods, and to practice and record fire drills.

Admissions
A day-care center may be required to have a written, nondiscriminatory admission policy, and it should let parents know whether religious train-

ing is included in the day care.

To obtain more specific information about the laws regulating day care in your state, call or write your state's child welfare agency.

DEATH

Death is the cessation of life; but the medical community has not formulated any precise definition of when life ends, and courts have been forced to define for themselves the moment of death. The definition is important, because medical advances enable life-support systems to sustain a person's bodily functions for extended periods of time. The growing demand for organ transplants has further focused the need for objective standards regarding the moment of death. The sooner the heart, kidneys, liver, and other vital organs are taken from the donor after death, the better the chance for a successful transplant. The moment of death must be clearly defined to prevent a terminally ill person from being declared dead prematurely.

CRITERIA

Criteria that the states use to establish death include the following: a permanent vegetative state (when a person is unconscious and cannot perform such vital activities as eating); absence of movement, breathing, or reflexes; no response to stimuli; a flat electroencephalogram (a recording of brain waves that shows no brain activity); and the failure of a vital organ. The Uniform Determination of Death Act, which was adopted by 26 states by 1992, defines death as the cessation of all brain activity and respiratory and circulatory functions.

RIGHT TO DIE

Advances in medical technology make it possible to sustain life when there is no hope of a cure or improvement. The question therefore arises as to whether a patient or his family has the right to refuse medical treatment under these circumstances. Resolving this issue involves balancing the patient's right to die with the state's interest in preserving life. The state's interest is evident from laws against not only murder but also euthanasia and suicide. See EUTHANASIA.

The state is obligated to seek the extension of life, unless there is clear and convincing evidence that doing so would violate the sick person's wishes. Allowing a person to die, even when desired by the sick person, challenges the integrity of the medical profession; asking a doctor or nurse to withhold medical treatment can amount to asking her to violate her professional ethics—to "do no harm." In addition, innocent third parties, such as family members, must be protected when such a decision is made.

Therefore, a competent adult generally has the right to refuse medical treatment only if he clearly expresses his wishes orally or in writing, and does not do so under duress. He can write, or complete, a form called a "living will" to state the circumstances under which he wants no extraordinary measures taken to preserve his life. Or he can execute a durable power of attorney for health care, which designates a third party to make medical decisions for him if he is unable to do so. See LIVING WILL; POWER OF ATTORNEY.

PRESUMPTION OF DEATH

Sometimes it is not known whether a person is alive or dead, because he is missing. If someone has disappeared, it is often essential that he be declared dead, since without such a declaration, his property cannot be distributed to his heirs, nor can they receive benefits from his life insurance. Also, his spouse cannot remarry.

In most states the courts will make the presumption that a person is dead after seven years of continued and unexplained absence. If there is evidence that the person was seen or heard from within that seven-year period, he cannot be presumed dead.

If some event or incident in a missing person's life might explain his disappearance, the court is less likely to declare him dead. For example, if he was wanted by the police, if he had an unhappy marriage or family situation, or if a threat had been made against his life, then his continued absence can be reasonably explained.

Before declaring a missing person dead, courts want proof

that his family or others made a "diligent search" for him. After a search has been conducted, the court will examine the evidence and decide whether to issue an order declaring the person dead.

When a court declares a missing person dead, the official date of death is usually set at seven years from the date of disappearance. In some cases, however, it is important to presume that death took place earlier. For example, death benefits or inheritance may be contingent on an earlier date of death. Suppose Enoch disappeared in 1989, and his father dies in 1992. The father's will left everything to Enoch, but it also provided that if Enoch died before his father, everything would go to Enoch's cousin Elizabeth. Elizabeth has evidence that Enoch may have died soon after his disappearance. She could ask the court to declare the date of Enoch's death as occurring before his father's, so that she would receive the estate right away.

Courts are sometimes willing to presume an earlier date of death if the missing person was exposed to some danger that makes his death likely, such as fire, war, or hazards at sea.

See also FUNERAL AND BURIAL; DYING WITHOUT A WILL; WILL.

STEPS TO TAKE IF YOUR SPOUSE HAS DISAPPEARED

Suppose your husband or wife has mysteriously disappeared, and you wonder whether your partner is living or dead. Here are a few suggestions about what to do:

1. Tell your friends and family members about the disappearance and ask them to let you know if they hear anything from your spouse.

2. File a missing person's report with your local police department. You will need to provide them with a recent picture of your spouse, a physical description, and the names of people he or she may contact.

3. Check with hospitals to see if they have admitted any unidentified accident victims.

4. Contact the issuers of your spouse's credit cards and ask whether any meals, hotel rooms, or other purchases have been charged to the cards.

5. Call your local Social Security office, which may be able to provide you with leads about where your spouse is working.

6. Call the Passport Services office of the State Department at 202-647-0518 to see if a passport was recently issued to your spouse.

7. If much time has elapsed and your search has failed, find an attorney who can help you to petition the probate court for a declaration of death.

DEATH PENALTY

Although the Eighth Amendment to the U. S. Constitution prohibits "cruel and unusual punishment," the death sentence, or capital punishment, is not in itself unconstitutional. In 1972, however, the Supreme Court held that a Georgia state law permitting judges and juries to impose the death penalty was unconstitutional, because without any guidelines the jury had too much discretion. Death penalty laws in other states that were similar to the law in Georgia were therefore unconstitutional too. In 1976 the Supreme Court held that states could impose the death penalty if their statutes were carefully drafted to prevent inconsistent, arbitrary, and capricious sentencing practices.

It is up to each state to enact laws pertaining to capital punishment. In general, death penalty laws have been upheld if the punishment is imposed for specific crimes, such as:

◇ Murder committed for monetary gain (including an armed robbery, a murder for hire, or a murder for inheritance or insurance).

◇ Murder committed while under sentence of imprisonment (such as a murder committed in prison, during or after an escape, or while on parole).

◇ Murder committed in conjunction with heinous, cruel, or depraved behavior (such as a murder committed after the physical torture or sexual abuse of the victim).

By 1993, 39 states had enacted death penalty laws. Only the following states had not: Iowa, Kansas, Maine, Massachusetts, Michigan, Minnesota, New York, North Dakota, Rhode Island, Vermont, and West Virginia. The federal government also imposes capital punishment for certain kinds of offenses.

Although the death penalty is on the books in most states, death sentences are rarely imposed and even more rarely carried out. National statistics

REAL LIFE, REAL LAW

The Case of the Callous Killer

John, a neighbor of Guy and Debra, knocked on their trailer door one night, accompanied by a man named Rick. When Guy let them in, John pulled a gun and Rick taped both their hands behind their backs. A few minutes later, their roommate Robin and her friend Shawn arrived, and they too were bound.

After searching the home for valuables, John and Rick forced Robin, Shawn, and Guy into Robin's car. John returned to the trailer and killed Debra. Then John and Rick drove the others into the desert, where they forced their victims to lie face down on the ground. Rick first shot Guy in the back of the head; then John shot and killed both Shawn and Robin.

Believing Guy to be dead, Rick and John left, but Guy survived the shooting and was able to call for help. He later testified that while Shawn and Robin were still alive, Rick had ordered John to shoot, saying, "Hurry up, hurry up, ain't no tongue-waggin' from dead tongues."

John later killed himself during a gun battle with the police, and Rick was convicted and sentenced to death for the murders of Robin and Shawn on the grounds that the murders were committed in a cruel, heinous, and depraved manner.

Rick appealed the sentence, maintaining his crimes did not fit this classification, but the supreme court of Arizona upheld the sentence. It found that the unimaginable stress and fear experienced by the victims as they witnessed each successive murder met the state's definition of cruelty.

The court also found the murders met the definition of heinous and depraved, since they were not necessary to accomplish the robbery, but solely to eliminate witnesses. All these factors combined to convince the court that the imposition of the death penalty was justified in Rick's case.

indicate that the death penalty is imposed in only three percent of all murder convictions. Moreover, death sentences are subject to numerous appeals, which, even when eventually denied, lengthen the average time between the imposition of the penalty and the actual execution to seven years. Supporters of the appeals process point to the number of death-row inmates who were subsequently found to be innocent, while opponents point out that the cost of the appeals is generally borne by the public. In 1992 the Supreme Court ruled that placing arbitrary limits on the number of appeals a convicted murderer can make violates his constitutional rights.

State governors—and in some cases, parole board officials—have the discretion to grant clemency to condemned prisoners by imposing less severe sentences, such as life imprisonment. Such a decision to commute a sentence cannot be set aside by a court.

DEBT

Most Americans have debts of some kind. Debt in the form of consumer loans and mortgages enables most people to own a home and a car. And credit card debt allows people to buy from department stores, gas stations, restaurants, and other retail outlets and pay for their purchases later.

TYPES OF DEBT

Debts fall into two categories: secured and unsecured. Secured debts, such as auto loans and home mortgages, are those in which the borrower offers collateral to the lender; that is, the borrower gives the lender an interest in the house or the car until he pays his debt. Unsecured debts, such as credit card purchases, are ones in which the lender depends entirely on the borrower's promise to pay him back. See COLLATERAL; CREDIT CARD AND CHARGE ACCOUNT; MORTGAGE.

If you owe money that you cannot repay, the type of debt you have incurred affects the lender's ability to collect. For example, if you default on your mortgage, which is secured by your home, the lender has the right to go to court, seek foreclosure, obtain ownership of your house, and sell it. If your debt is unsecured, the lender must ask the court for permission to appropriate any assets you have, such as your wages or money in your bank account, which can be used to satisfy the debt. See COLLECTION AGENCY; FORECLOSURE; GARNISHMENT.

UNMANAGEABLE DEBT

If you are unable to reduce the balance on your credit cards, or if you are using cash advances on your credit cards to pay your everyday living expenses, you are probably living beyond your means. If so, you may want to seek the help of the Consumer Credit Counseling Service, which maintains local offices across the country. The CCCS advises debtors on ways to reduce their debts and manage their finances. See CREDIT COUNSELING; GARNISHMENT.

If your debts are completely unmanageable, you may have to do what 900,000 Americans did in 1992: file for personal bankruptcy. See BANKRUPTCY.

DEED

The written document that transfers title to (ownership of) real estate is called a deed. A deed must accurately identify the property being transferred, the name of the persons or organization making the transfer, and the names of those receiving ownership. Typically, the deed must be signed by the person making the transfer in the presence of witnesses who can attest to the fact that the transferer's signature is valid and that he or she transferred it voluntarily.

In most states, certain other formalities must be observed. The deed must be delivered to the new owner, he must accept it, and the deed must be recorded. Recording the deed involves delivering it to the recorder's office in the county where the property is located. The deed is then photocopied, and the copy is inserted into a chronological record of property transfers. In this way, an official record exists, putting the public on notice of the transfer of property and of the new owner.

If you fail to record a deed, you will have difficulty transferring ownership when you want to sell the property. With modern real estate closing procedures, however, it is unlikely that a deed would not be recorded. Further protection of your ownership is provided by a title insurance policy. See also CLOSING, REAL ESTATE; TITLE INSURANCE.

After the deed is copied and recorded, it will be returned to you. Keep it in a safe place, such as a bank safe-deposit box or a fireproof box in your home. Before the era of photocopying, a lost deed meant trouble if you wanted to sell or mortgage the property it covered. These days, however, it is a relatively simple matter to obtain a certified copy of a deed from the recorder's office.

For sample deeds, see the EVERYDAY LEGAL FORMS section of this book, beginning on page 552. For more detailed information on the various kinds of deeds, see BARGAIN AND SALE DEED; FULL COVENANT AND WARRANTY DEED; GRANT DEED; QUITCLAIM DEED.

DEED IN LIEU OF FORECLOSURE

A deed in lieu of foreclosure is a means to allow a mortgage lender to take title to property without going through foreclosure proceedings in the event that the owner cannot make his mortgage payments. The procedure requires the owner to surrender the deed to his home to the mortgage lender. A deed in lieu of foreclosure has certain advantages: the lender saves on foreclosure costs and can resell the house to another buyer, while the debtor avoids the stigma of a foreclosure or bankruptcy.

No lender is legally required to agree to the use of a deed in lieu of foreclosure, and some lenders refuse to take part in the procedure. See also BANKRUPTCY; FORECLOSURE.

DEED OF TRUST

In some states—for example, California, Colorado, and Wyoming—a deed of trust is used instead of a mortgage on real estate. It transfers ownership of the property not to the buyer but to one or more trustees—for instance, a title insurance company or an official known as a public trustee—who hold the property as security until the debt is paid in full. When the entire debt is paid, the deed is transferred to the debtor, who only then becomes the owner of the property. If the debt is not paid, the trustees may sell the property and pay the debt with the proceeds of the sale. See also FORECLOSURE; MORTGAGE; TRUSTEE.

DEFAMATION

Frank and Mary had worked together at the Jimson Company for many years when they had a falling out. Afterward, Mary learned that Frank had been saying things behind her back—not only that she was incompetent as an accountant but also that she probably was not above dipping her hands into the petty cash. Mary, feeling hurt and indignant, wants to sue Frank for defamation. Will she win her suit?

Perhaps. Making a false statement that harms someone's good name or reputation and holds that person up to ridicule or contempt is defamation. Mere criticism is not. If Frank had said that in his opinion Mary was not meticulous enough to be a good accountant, Mary could not claim defamation. But even given Frank's outrageous comments about Mary, she might not win a lawsuit for defamation.

PROVING DEFAMATION

Each state has its own laws of defamation, but in most states Mary would be able to win her suit only if she could prove that Frank's statement embodied all of the following elements:

◇ The statement was truly defamatory, containing words (such as "thief," "untrustworthy," or "incompetent") that could ruin Mary's good name.

◇ Frank denigrated Mary to other people, such as her coworkers (who need not believe Frank for his words to be considered defamatory). If Frank merely ranted and raved at Mary in private and no one else heard him, Mary's feelings may have been injured but her reputation was not. If someone inadvertently overheard the conversation, it would not be considered defamation, because Frank did not intend his words to be overheard.

◇ The statement established that the person whom Frank accused of incompetence and theft was indeed Mary. If Frank told a coworker that the redheaded woman who reports to Jane had been stealing, and Mary is the only person who fits this description, the identification of Mary is sufficient.

◇ Frank's defamatory statement truly harmed Mary. Suppose that no one listens to Frank because he is known to be jealous and petty, and Mary even got a raise not long after Frank's accusation. Under such circumstances, she would not be able to prove defamation.

In some states Mary would not have to show that she suffered harm if Frank accused her of committing a crime, being unchaste, or having a loathsome disease; nor would she have to show she suffered harm if the defamatory statement could affect her in her trade or profession.

LIBEL AND SLANDER

Proving defamation becomes more complicated in cases involving the media. When a defamatory statement is written or otherwise permanently recorded — as in the newspapers or on television — it is called libel. If the statement is merely spoken but is heard by a third person, it is called slander.

Sometimes the distinction between libel and slander is hard to make. Some courts consider statements made on radio and television to be slander while others consider them libel. The distinction becomes important when the courts award damages (money to compensate for the harm the defamed person suffered), because some kinds of slander may not be considered to cause the kind of lasting damage that libel does.

DEFAMATION OF PUBLIC FIGURES

Public figures (such as politicians or celebrities) are normally expected to withstand more criticism than private persons are. Therefore, if a public person sues for libel or slander, the court requires not only proof of the elements discussed above but also evidence that the defamer acted "falsely and maliciously" in making the defamatory remarks. Thus, for instance, if Frank and Mary happened to be politicians who were running against each other for a Senate seat and Frank accused Mary of being dishonest because she did not keep her earlier campaign promises, he would probably not be held liable for defamation. However, if Frank were to accuse Mary publicly of adultery or bribery, simply as a smear tactic with no basis in fact, Mary would have a good case.

DAMAGES

If Mary wins her suit for defamation, Frank will be required to pay damages—that is, to compensate her with money. If Mary establishes that his statement was made with malice, Frank might have to pay her an additional amount, called punitive damages. See DAMAGES.

DEFAULT

The failure to perform a duty imposed by law or keep a contractual promise is known as a default. A father who fails to make child support payments as required by his divorce decree is in default. So is a person who does not make a minimum payment on his credit card.

The law prefers to see people make good on their obligations, rather than forcing them to go to court. As a result, most contracts, and even some court orders, include procedures for correcting a default. Suppose you have a contract with a gardening company to mow your lawn every two weeks. If the mowers fail to show up, the company would, strictly speaking, be in default. However, most contracts have a clause giving the company a chance to avoid default by working on a later day, subject perhaps to a small financial penalty.

DEFAULT JUDGMENT

When one of the parties to a lawsuit fails to appear in court, the opposing party may ask the judge to issue a default judgment. Suppose you file a suit in small-claims court against a dry cleaner for damaging an expensive evening dress. If the day for hearing your case arrives and the cleaner does not show up, you can request the judge to order a default judgment against him. You must then notify the dry cleaner that you have won a default judgment and that he must pay you what the court ordered.

However, judges prefer to decide lawsuits on their merits, and therefore try to avoid issuing default judgments. Consequently, if the dry cleaner can show a good reason (such as illness or an accident) for missing the trial, the judge might withdraw (or "vacate") the default judgment and set a new date for trial.

DEFICIENCY JUDGMENT

When Cora could no longer make her car loan payments, the loan company repossessed the car and sold it to satisfy the loan. Although Cora owed $7,000 for the car, the sale brought only $4,500. To satisfy the loan, the lender went to court and obtained a judgment against Cora for the remaining $2,500. This type of judgment is called a deficiency judgment. With it, the lender can garnishee Cora's wages, put a lien on her house, or attach other property she owns, such as a bank account.

Not all states allow a lender or mortgagee to obtain a deficiency judgment. But if you are notified that someone to whom you owe money is seeking a deficiency judgment for repossessed property, be sure to get a lawyer's advice immediately. You may be able to have the court void the judgment, if you can show that the lender did not try to get the best possible price for your property or that he failed to follow the proper legal procedures, which vary from state to state. See also SECURITY AGREEMENT; UNIFORM COMMERCIAL CODE.

DEPOSITION

If you are ever involved in a lawsuit—as a plaintiff, a defendant, or a witness—you may be called upon to give a deposition. A deposition is the sworn testimony of a witness taken out of court by a lawyer, weeks or sometimes months before the trial. Depositions are used to gather information as well as to obtain testimony from a witness who will not be available at the trial.

WHAT HAPPENS AT A DEPOSITION

In many respects, giving a deposition is similar to testifying at a trial, except that no judge or jury is present. If you give a deposition (in which event you will be called the "deponent"), you will be asked by the attorney for one of the parties to appear at a designated time and place. If you refuse, you could be subpoenaed by the court. The deposition usually takes place in a lawyer's office. When you arrive, you will first be placed under oath. Then you

ABC's
OF GIVING A DEPOSITION

If you are called on to give a deposition, try to do the following:

- ❑ Tell the truth. When you give a deposition you are placed under oath, just as if you were in court. If you lie, you may face penalties for perjury.
- ❑ Obey any subpoena. If you do not appear for a deposition voluntarily, the lawyers in a case can have a subpoena served on you, which legally compels you to appear. A subpoena is an order of the court, and if you do not obey it you may be found in contempt of court. Once found in contempt, you could be fined or put in jail.
- ❑ Bring any necessary documents. The lawyers in a case may request that you bring documents with you when you appear for your deposition. If these documents are listed in the subpoena, you must bring them along. You should take the original documents, but it is a good idea to take photocopies too.
- ❑ Listen to the questions carefully and answer them to the best of your ability. Do not volunteer information that you are not asked for.
- ❑ If you have a good legal reason for not wishing to appear at a deposition or for not producing documents, consult an attorney. In some cases, you may be able to get the subpoena "quashed," or set aside. Never simply ignore a subpoena. You must go through the proper legal channels and have a judge determine whether or not you must appear.

will be asked a series of questions by the lawyer taking your deposition.

Lawyers for both plaintiff and defendant may be present. Each lawyer will have a chance to question you. Just as they would in a trial, the lawyers may object to a question, claiming that it should not be answered. Because no judge is present and objections cannot be ruled on at the time they are made, you must answer the question anyway. Later on, the judge will decide if the answer should be disclosed in court.

The questions asked and the answers given at your deposition will be recorded by a court reporter.

THE PURPOSE OF DEPOSITIONS

When lawyers use depositions to gather information, it is part of the pretrial process known as discovery, during which fact-finding and investigating take place. See DISCOVERY.

Lawyers prefer to obtain information from a witness by deposition, even if the same witness will testify at the trial. Because the witness is under oath, the lawyer can prepare his case with the confidence that the witness will not tell a different story at the trial. If at the trial the witness does alter her testimony, the lawyer can use the deposition to cast doubt on her reliability.

Lawyers also use depositions when a witness cannot be present at the trial—for example, if she is ill, planning to move out of state, or lives far away. If the lawyer has the deposition at the trial, it can be read to the judge or jury in place of testimony. Sometimes depositions are recorded or videotaped, and the recording or video is played at the trial. The court regards such depositions to be just as valid as testimony that is given in person.

DEPRECIATION

As property ages and is used, its value diminishes; this loss of value is called depreciation. Just about any kind of property used in business—from filing cabinets and word processors to automobiles and apartment buildings—depreciates in value solely because of age, use, and ordinary wear and tear. For example, by 1994, a computer bought as recently as 1993 will have depreciated through use. Its value may also diminish owing to advances in computer technology.

Depreciation is important when you borrow money to pay for a car, because you may end up owing more on the car than it is worth. Suppose you owe $6,000 on an automobile you bought for $7,000. You can no longer afford to make the payments, and the lender repossesses the car. Its value has depreciated to $5,000 and that is all he can sell it for. You will still owe the lender $1,000. See DEFICIENCY JUDGMENT.

The depreciated value of certain income-producing property entitles taxpayers to income tax deductions, provided the value of the property is depreciated in accordance with Internal Revenue Service depreciation schedules. You can obtain information and IRS depreciation schedules at your local IRS office, at most libraries, or by calling the IRS Tax Forms Distribution Center at 800-829-3676 and requesting Publication 534 (*Depreciation*) and Form 4562 (*Depreciation and Amortization*).

DISABILITY INSURANCE

According to statistics from the Insurance Information Institute, a 35-year-old man or woman is nearly four times as likely to become disabled as to die in the coming year. Yet relatively few Americans buy disability insurance to provide income for themselves and their families in case they are disabled and cannot work.

SOCIAL SECURITY DISABILITY INSURANCE

Although the Social Security Administration provides protection for persons who become disabled, the payments are relatively small and the benefits often difficult to claim.

In order to obtain Social Security disability payments, you must have a severe impairment that is expected either to result in death or to last for a year or more and prevent you from doing any gainful employment. Conditions that the Social Security Administration considers disabling include severe arthritis, loss of function of both arms or both legs, blindness, mental illness, serious heart disease, or cancer that is progressive and has not been controlled or cured.

The disability must prevent you from engaging in "any gainful employment," not just in your current line of work. If you are capable of working at all, you are ineligible for disability coverage from Social Security. For example, if you were making $100,000 a year as a real estate agent but are now unable to drive, you can be denied disability payments if you are able to be employed as a clerical worker for $5 per hour.

HOW DISABILITY BENEFITS ARE CALCULATED

Even if your disability meets Social Security guidelines, you must still have worked long enough and recently enough at a job covered by Social Security in order to receive benefits. See also SOCIAL SECURITY.

Under Social Security rules, you must accumulate a certain number of "work credits," or "quarters," in order to receive disability benefits. In 1993 a person earned one credit for each $590 in earnings, to a maximum of four credits per year (this is why the credits are also called quarters).

The number of work credits you need to qualify for disability benefits depends on your age at the time you become disabled. For example, if you become disabled before age 24, you must have six credits in the three-year period immediately preceding your disability. If you are 24 to 31 years old, you must have accumulated credits for working half the time between age 21 and the onset of your disability. If you are over 31 when you become disabled, you will need from 20 to 40 credits, depending on your age at the time of disability. You must usually have earned at least 20 of those credits in the 10-year period before you became disabled.

HOW TO APPLY FOR BENEFITS

If you should become disabled, you should apply for disability benefits immediately at your local Social Security office. You may apply by mail or over the telephone if you cannot make the trip; and a spouse, relative, or friend can complete the application for you if you cannot do so yourself. Look in your local telephone directory under "U.S. Government" or "Social Security Administration" for the office nearest you.

To process your application, the Social Security Administration will require the following information:

◇ Your Social Security number and proof of age, such as a

CHECKLIST

Shopping for Disability Insurance

Not all private disability insurance is alike, and the amount of coverage is not the only consideration. When you look for an affordable policy, try to find one with as many of the following features as possible.

❏ **PAYMENTS TILL RETIREMENT.**
Your policy should pay full benefits up to your retirement age, when you will become eligible to receive Social Security benefits.

❏ **COST OF LIVING ADJUSTMENTS.**
Disability policies that provide cost of living adjustments (known as COLA's) are more expensive than fixed-benefit policies but provide better coverage. For example, if you become disabled when you are young and only have fixed benefits, inflation will severely reduce the value of your policy over time.

❏ **RENEWABILITY AND NONCANCELABILITY.**
A disability insurance plan should be guaranteed renewable or, even better, noncancelable by the insurer. A guaranteed renewable plan assures you of your right to renew the policy, though the rates may increase. A noncancelable plan prevents the insurer from raising premiums or canceling your coverage because your medical condition changes.

❏ **ABILITY TO BE EMPLOYED WHILE DISABLED.**
Make sure that the policy defines disability as the inability to work at your chosen occupation and will not reduce your disability benefit if you earn income from another job while disabled.

❏ **CHOICE OF WAITING PERIOD.**
Since most disability insurance policies call for a waiting period before benefits begin, try to find a plan that lets you choose how long the period will be. In general, it can vary from 30 to 180 days or more. Typically, the longer the waiting period, the lower the premium. If your employer provides short-term coverage, you may want to time the waiting period so that your personal policy benefits begin when your company's short-term coverage ends.

❏ **DISCOUNT.**
You may be able to purchase a plan through a professional organization, union, or other membership association. Such organizations often offer insurance at a substantial discount.

birth certificate or passport.

◇ The names, addresses, and telephone numbers of the doctors and hospitals that have treated you for your disability, as well as the dates when treatments took place.

◇ A summary of your work record over the last 15 years or from the time you began working, whichever is less.

◇ A description of the kinds of work you did.

◇ A copy of your most recent W-2 form if you are an employee, or a copy of your most recent income tax return if you happen to be self-employed.

◇ Dates of military service, if any.

◇ Dates of prior marriages, if any.

◇ The claim number of any other benefits you receive because of your disability, such as workers' compensation.

After you make your application, a medical doctor and an evaluation specialist will review it. When this process (which may also include a medical examination) has been completed, a decision will be made to award or deny the Social Security benefits. If your claim is approved, you will receive written notice from the Social Security Administration showing the amount of your monthly benefit and the date of your first payment. If your claim is denied, you have the right to appeal this decision within 60 days of being notified. Specific information about your appeal rights is included with the notice of denial that you receive from the Social Security Administration.

Before applying for Social Security disability insurance benefits, you should obtain a copy of the SSA Publication 05-10029, entitled *Disability*, available from your local Social Security office.

PRIVATE DISABILITY INSURANCE

Most people who have private disability insurance obtain coverage through their employee benefits program, but the coverage is usually for short-term disabilities only. For longer periods of disability, you will probably have to purchase a policy from a private insurer. The features you should look for in a policy are outlined in the checklist on page 160.

Many insurance companies limit the amount of disability coverage you can obtain, to discourage people from applying for or continuing to receive disability payments. Try to buy a policy that will pay at least 60 to 75 percent of your gross income from work. Although you may require all of your current income to live on, you do not need a policy that pays 100 percent of your income because benefits from a disability policy that you paid for are tax-free.

DISABLED AMERICANS

Congress has estimated that more than 43 million Americans have a disability. While many disabled people are capable of holding a job and living independently, they often encounter discrimination, particularly in employment, housing, and education. To ensure that disabled Americans have an even chance at succeeding in society, Congress— starting in the mid-1960's— passed several key laws, culminating in the Americans With Disabilities Act (ADA) in 1990. Although the ADA mandates sweeping changes for the disabled, especially in the private sector, it does not alter previous federal laws, such as the Urban Mass Transportation Act of 1964, which requires that all transportation projects receiving federal funds accommodate the disabled (by making buses accessible to people in wheelchairs, for example). Another federal act, the Architectural Barriers Act of 1968, requires that federal buildings and federally financed housing be accessible to the disabled.

Prior to the ADA, the Rehabilitation Act of 1973 was one of the first acts aimed at outlawing discrimination in employment of the disabled at the federal level. Section 501 of this act prohibits discrimination in federal employment. Section 503 requires businesses who are awarded federal contracts for $2,500 or more to demonstrate affirmative steps to hire people with disabilities and accommodate the needs of disabled workers in the workplace. Section 504 prohibits federally funded programs or activities from discriminating against disabled individuals.

AMERICANS WITH DISABILITIES ACT

The Americans With Disabilities Act, a far-reaching piece of legislation, forbids discrimination against the disabled in all parts of the public sector and, for the first time, in the private sector as well. This means that state and local agencies, as well as most privately owned concerns, must comply with the provisions of the act or demonstrate why they cannot.

Under the Americans With Disabilities Act, the definition of disability was broadened to include chronic conditions, injuries, and diseases (including AIDS) that cause the physical or mental impairment of one or more major life activities, such as walking, learning, or seeing.

The ADA has several major goals. First, it establishes the guidelines for hiring and accommodating the disabled in the workplace. Beginning in July 1992, private and public employers with 25 employees or more could no longer discriminate against people with disabilities when hiring, firing, or promoting. An employee who is otherwise qualified for a job except for his disability henceforth must be "reasonably accommodated" by the employer unless doing so creates an "undue burden" on the employer. Companies with as few as 15 employees must comply by July 1994. Reasonable accommodation might include providing a blind worker with job instructions in braille or installing ramps for employees who use wheelchairs. (Some changes can earn the company tax credits.)

Second, starting in 1992, the Americans With Disabilities Act mandates that public buildings and services be accessible and adequate for the disabled population. Public schools must, therefore, be barrier-free and must reasonably accommodate the educational needs of disabled children. Public transportation, such as local buses and subways, must be made physically accessible for the disabled and have designated seating areas that are adequate for them. If local governments cannot comply, they must provide alternate means of transportation. Similarly, public buildings, such as libraries, post offices, and city halls, must be made barrier-free.

Third, the ADA requires private companies that do business with the public to provide the disabled with equal access to goods, services, and facilities. This means that stores, private schools, restaurants, and hotels, for example, must make "reasonable" changes so that their facilities are accessible to the disabled. (Churches and private clubs are exempt, but many have voluntarily complied.)

A store, for instance, must make its entrances accessible to people in wheelchairs unless it claims that such changes would be too costly. However, the store is still required to offer an alternate means of serving disabled customers, such as having salespeople bring products to the door. All new construction with an occupancy date on or after January 26, 1993, must have accommodations for the disabled that comply with specific standards of the act.

The Americans With Disabilities Act also provides for the needs of those whose hearing, speech, or sight is impaired. For example, to accommodate the deaf, a hotel might be required to provide signing interpreters as well as telecommunications devices for the deaf (also known as TDD's).

QUESTIONS AND COMPLAINTS

If you think your employer has violated your rights under the ADA, and you wish to sue, you must first file a complaint with the Equal Employment Opportunity Commission (EEOC), 2401 E Street NW, Washington, DC 20506. The EEOC is required to investigate all job-related complaints.

For information about access to public transportation and facilities, write the Department of Justice, Constitution Avenue and 10th Street NW, Washington, DC 20530.

Because the ADA is new, many of its regulations and requirements have yet to be tested in the courts. If you have concerns about how the ADA affects you—as an employer, merchant, or disabled person—ask any local organization for the disabled or see a lawyer.

DISBARMENT

Once an attorney is admitted to the bar—that is, allowed to practice law—he usually retains this right for life. However, if he engages in serious professional misconduct, a lawyer can be disbarred, which means that his license to practice law can be taken away, usually for good.

State law determines the circumstances under which a disbarment may occur, but in general, it is prompted by one or more of the following:

REAL LIFE, REAL LAW

The Case of the Lamentable Lawyer

Al had been practicing law for nearly 20 years when Gregory retained him, for a fee of $5,000, to file a lawsuit against Gregory's former employer. Several months went by, and Gregory heard nothing from Al. When he called Al's office, Al told him he was conducting an investigation and had written Gregory's former employer to demand payment of damages.

Many more months went by, and Gregory still had heard nothing from Al. He again called Al's office, only to learn that Al had never contacted Gregory's former employer. Even worse, Al had allowed so much time to go by that Gregory had lost the right to pursue his claim in court.

Gregory filed a complaint against Al with the attorney disciplinary commission of the state supreme court. At the hearing, Al argued in his defense that he had been under terrible pressure due to the death of his partner and that he was also suffering from alcoholism. He pointed out that he had paid Gregory a substantial amount in restitution for his lost lawsuit.

The disciplinary commission refused to excuse Al's unprofessional behavior—especially his lying to Gregory. Because other clients of Al's had filed similar complaints, the commission concluded that his behavior was unlikely to change and recommended that he be disbarred. The state supreme court agreed and ordered the disbarment.

◇ The attorney violated the trust and confidence of his clients.

◇ The fees he charged were excessive or the way he charged them was deceptive.

◇ He represented two or more parties whose interests conflicted.

◇ He conducted himself in a manner that offended judges or obstructed justice.

Disbarment is usually permanent. Although most states allow a disbarred attorney to petition the court for reinstatement after a specified period of time, the petition is generally denied. See also LAWYER.

DISCOVERY

Television courtroom dramas often include scenes in which an unexpected witness is called to the stand, or new evidence is introduced, surprising everyone in the courtroom and also bringing about a dramatic turn in the case. In real life, however, such surprises rarely happen—on the contrary, they are deliberately avoided.

This lack of surprise is largely due to a process known as discovery. It includes a variety of procedures that are used by both sides to learn as much about the case as possible before the trial begins. For example, the two sides may want to confirm certain facts, exchange pertinent documents, examine property, or share testimony that has been recorded by witnesses who are unable to appear at the trial.

The purpose of discovery is to provide a faster and fairer trial by allowing access to information that is possessed by the opposing party. It permits lawyers on both sides to prepare their cases more thoroughly by enabling them to learn what evidence exists and which facts are already agreed upon. While discovery is used in both civil and criminal cases, its use is much more extensive in civil lawsuits.

TYPES OF DISCOVERY

A number of different methods for obtaining information are used in the discovery process:

◇ *Depositions.* A deposition is oral testimony given outside the court. It is made under oath, usually in the office of the lawyer who requested it, and is recorded by a court reporter. For example, in a lawsuit filed against a department store by a man who was injured while riding a store escalator, depositions may be requested from witnesses to the mishap who were also riding the escalator, from escalator repair personnel, and from the store management. See also DEPOSITION.

◇ *Interrogatories.* Unlike depositions, which are given orally, interrogatories are written questions that must be answered under oath and in writing by the opposing party.

◇ *Admissions.* One party may request that the opposing party admit an important fact about the case or affirm that a document that will be used at the trial is authentic. Obtaining an admission from the opposing party beforehand saves time and expense at the trial because it eliminates the need to prove those issues that are not actually in dispute.

In the case described above, for example, the injured man may ask the store to admit that the escalator was vibrating badly at the time of the mishap. Or the store may request that the man admit he was taking a type of medication that made him feel dizzy.

◇ *Other requests.* Information is not always obtained by asking people questions. Sometimes a party may ask to look at objects such as documents, photos, or other property that is under the opposing party's control. A physical or mental examination may be ordered by the court if a person's condition is relevant to the lawsuit.

In the department store case, the injured man may ask to have the escalator inspected, and the store's attorney—perhaps suspecting the man may have had some medical condition that contributed to the accident—may request that he be examined by a doctor.

LIMITATIONS ON DISCOVERY

While discovery is often extensive, it does not permit each side to obtain any and all information from the opposing one. If one party objects to a request made by the other, for example, she may not want to cooperate by giving a deposition. In this event, the court will decide whether the party must supply the requested information.

Discovery will be denied if the information (such as that shared between an attorney and client) is privileged—that is, private and confidential, by law—or if it violates the right of a citizen to protect himself against self-incrimination. A judge will also deny discovery if the information is irrelevant, or if it is used simply to annoy, embarrass, or oppress the opposing side or its witnesses.

DISCRIMINATION

Many laws have been enacted and constitutional decisions handed down that prohibit discrimination in this country—in housing, schools, the workplace, and elsewhere. However, not all forms of discrimination are illegal. Landlords, for example, may discriminate against potential tenants on the basis of their income and their past records as tenants. See EQUAL PROTECTION OF THE LAWS; TENANT'S RIGHTS.

Employers are free to discriminate against job applicants and employees on the basis of age, provided that the worker is not over the age of 40—an age group protected by the federal Age Discrimination in Employment Act (ADEA). That is, a company could dismiss a worker who is 35 years old in favor of one who is only 25 without violating federal law, but state or local laws may prohibit the practice. See AGE DISCRIMINATION; JOB DISCRIMINATION.

Discrimination based on sex, race, national origin, religion, or disability is generally prohibited and can lead to a lawsuit if you engage in it. See CIVIL RIGHTS; DISABLED AMERICANS; SEX DISCRIMINATION.

DISINHERITANCE

To disinherit someone is to state in your will that you want to deprive an heir of the right to receive any share of your estate. For example, a mother may want to disinherit a son who has abandoned the family, or a tormented husband may want to disinherit his wife.

Under the law in every state, you have no obligation to leave any part of your estate to your children. But you do not have the right to disinherit your husband or wife. If you do, the disinherited spouse has the option of "electing against" your will after you die. This means that your spouse may take the share of the estate that he or she would have received if you had died intestate (without a will).

In a number of states you cannot disinherit a child just by leaving him out of your will. You must state specifically that you do not want him to receive anything and then name the persons you do want to be your heirs. If you want to remove your child from your will, consult a lawyer experienced in estate planning. See ADOPTION; HEIR; WILL.

DISORDERLY CONDUCT

What constitutes disorderly conduct is determined by local law, but it usually involves offenses such as disturbing the peace or endangering the public health, safety, or morals. Fighting or swearing in public, vagrancy, loitering, and other similar behavior is usually considered disorderly conduct.

Often the circumstances determine whether an activity amounts to disorderly conduct. For example, picketing may be acceptable in front of a manufacturing plant but not in front of the company president's home, where it may disturb the peace in the neighborhood.

Disorderly conduct is usually a minor offense, punishable by a fine, imprisonment, or both. See also BREACH OF THE PEACE; DISTURBING THE PEACE.

DISORDERLY HOUSE

A disorderly house is a place where people routinely engage in conduct that is criminal, poses a threat to public health or safety, corrupts public morals, or encourages a breach of the peace. A disorderly house can be a house of prostitution, a shop where drugs are sold from the back room, or a grocery store where liquor is sold without a license. A disorderly house need not be a house; it can be a boat where illegal gambling is going on, a garage where stolen merchandise is received, or even a parking lot where bets are taken.

You can commit the offense of maintaining a disorderly house even if you do not own the premises. As long as you are part of the management and know that people are breaking the law there, you can be found guilty of maintaining a disorderly house. The penalty is generally a fine, but if you have several offenses, you may lose your license to operate your parking lot, for example, or other business. See also BREACH OF THE PEACE.

DISTURBING THE PEACE

If you willfully create a disturbance in a public area, or interfere with the peace and quiet of a family or an individual, you are said to be disturbing the peace. Playing your electric guitar raucously in the middle of the night so that your neighbors can hear it is disturbing the peace. So is drag racing on public streets or engaging in a shouting match on the main street of your town.

Exactly what kinds of actions constitute disturbing the peace is determined by state and local laws. In most areas disturbing the peace is considered a misdemeanor and can be punished by a fine, imprisonment, or both. See also BREACH OF THE PEACE; DISORDERLY CONDUCT.

DIVIDEND

The portion of its profits that a corporation passes on to its stockholders is called the dividend. The corporation's board of directors decides how much the allocation for dividends will be, and the rest of the company's profit is reinvested in the business.

Corporations often issue two kinds of stock, common and preferred. The dividends on shares of common stock can vary in amount.When business is good, dividends may be high. But when business is bad, or when the company needs to invest in expensive new equipment or property, dividends can be very low or nonexistent.

When companies issue preferred stock, they guarantee payment of a specified dividend. Owners of the stock usually have the right to receive their dividends before any are paid to owners of common stock. Moreover, most preferred stocks have cumulative rights. This means that if the corporation cannot pay dividends as scheduled, they continue to build up. When the company becomes profitable again, the late dividends must be paid, along with current preferred dividends, before any are paid to owners of common stock. See also STOCKS AND BONDS.

DIVORCE

One of every two marriages in the United States ends in divorce. But though divorce is commonplace, it is rarely easy or smooth. Besides dealing with emotional strain, the family and the court must address a number of difficult tasks:

◇ Dissolving the marriage.

◇ Providing for child custody and child support.

◇ Making arrangements for spousal support.

◇ Dividing the property.

◇ Resolving the debts.

Each party to a divorce has his or her own concerns, and the nature of a couple's disagreements varies widely with the circumstances. Therefore, many possible approaches may be taken to getting a divorce.

SEPARATION AGREEMENT

In most states, divorce proceedings will go more quickly and smoothly if the couple can agree on such issues as the division of property, spousal support (alimony), child custody, and child support. If these matters can be settled early, fewer decisions will have to be left to the court. To provide a framework for their agreement on these issues, a couple may choose to draw up a formal separation agreement — a document that can be presented to the divorce court and made a part of the divorce decree. See SEPARATION.

For most couples, however, major areas of disagreement call for another approach. Suppose Kevin and Connie both want a divorce, but Kevin feels that Connie wants too much money for spousal support (and for too long a time), and Connie feels that Kevin is not offering enough child support. If they cannot arrive at an agreement, Kevin and Connie will each have to present their case to the divorce court and ask it to rule on these important issues.

GROUNDS FOR DIVORCE

Kevin and Connie do not have to blame each other for the failure of their marriage. At one time the states required a person to prove that his or her spouse was at fault in some way, but times have changed, and this is no longer true.

No-fault divorce

Today every state has no-fault divorce laws. One spouse (or both) simply shows the court that the two are incompatible, that they have "irreconcilable differences," or that the marriage is irretrievably broken. But a judge will not grant a divorce without a good reason, and he must be shown that the marriage should be dissolved. Although no-fault laws do not set out conditions that render a marriage broken, judges examine each case individually and consider the following:

◇ Whether the spouses are separated, and the length of the separation.

◇ Whether one spouse has left home and refuses to return.

◇ If there are profound and abiding conflicts over such important issues as religion, finances, sex, or child rearing.

◇ If the spouses' personalities conflict in such a way that living together is impossible.

◇ If the spouses have tried to reconcile their differences.

◇ If one party refuses to take steps toward reconciliation.

◇ Whether both parties consider the marriage to be irretrievably broken.

However, it is not necessary that both parties agree to no-fault divorce. One spouse may obtain a no-fault divorce over the objections of the other if the court finds that the marriage is irretrievably broken.

Fault

Despite their no-fault laws, about three-quarters of the states also still allow divorces based on fault: cruelty, adultery, abandonment, or some other misdeed that will serve as grounds for divorce. In some states, a spouse may be able to have alimony reduced or eliminated if the other spouse is found to be at fault. But fault grounds often lead to long and unpleasant divorce proceedings, with one or both of the spouses trying to find damaging evidence against the other.

Separation

In about half of the states, separation is a basis for no-fault divorce. If the couple has lived apart for a specified period of time (usually from six months to three years), the spouse seeking the divorce may give this as the reason for the divorce petition. In some states a period of separation is a requirement for a no-fault divorce. See also SEPARATION.

COUNSELING

No-fault statutes make it much easier for a couple to end a marriage, but even so, a judge may refuse to grant a divorce if he believes the marriage can be saved. Many states allow courts to order the parties to receive counseling before the judge decides to grant a divorce.

Sometimes one partner does not want a divorce and will ask the judge to order the other partner to go into counseling. Once the counseling has been completed, however, the partner who opposes the divorce can do very little to prevent it.

HIRING A DIVORCE LAWYER

Because of their differences over spousal and child support, Kevin and Connie each hired a lawyer for the divorce. Although some lawyers can handle the proceedings for both parties, it is rarely a good idea. It is difficult for a lawyer to represent each party fairly and with equal loyalty when they are in dispute.

When you hire an attorney, whether for a divorce or other legal proceeding, be sure to obtain a written fee agreement before work begins. You should also demand a periodic accounting of work being done on your case and the amount you owe. If you cannot afford an attorney, you may be able to obtain one through a government-funded legal aid program. See also LAWYER; LEGAL AID.

THE DIVORCE PROCESS

In Kevin and Connie's case, the legal proceedings for their divorce begin when Connie's attorney files a divorce petition (sometimes called a divorce complaint, or petition for dissolution). In the petition, Connie asks that the court grant a divorce based on the couple's irreconcilable differences.

The petition states that the court has jurisdiction (authority) over the divorce because Connie has been a resident of the state for the length of time required by law. Normally, a petition also asks the court to make decisions regarding child custody, child support, spousal support, the division of property, and the resolution of debts. But since Kevin and Connie have already agreed on everything except child support and spousal support, the court must address only these issues.

Once Connie's lawyer has

CHECKLIST

Getting Through a Divorce

Getting through a divorce means enduring a series of traumatic changes in your life, so try to take them one step at a time. Listed below are a few suggestions on how to make the divorce process go a little more smoothly—for you, your spouse, your children, and even your lawyer.

❑ WORK OUT AN ACCEPTABLE CUSTODY AGREEMENT.
Unless you have a good reason to believe that contact with your spouse will be harmful to your children, try to work together to create a custody and visitation arrangement that will allow the children to maintain a loving relationship with both parents.

Don't pull the children into your conflict by belittling your spouse in front of them, enlisting them as spies, or using them as messengers. If you do, your children are bound to build up long-term resentments.

❑ TRY TO GET A HANDLE ON YOUR FINANCES.
In many marriages, one spouse is in charge of the checkbook, the bill paying, and other financial matters. If you are the other spouse, you may have to educate yourself about your finances.

Find out, for example, how much is in your bank accounts, the cash value of your insurance policies, the amount in your IRA or profit-sharing accounts, the value of your stocks and bonds, and the location of your deeds and titles to property. Determine the value of your furniture, antiques, art, jewelry, and special collections (such as stamps) by getting an appraisal.

Take an inventory of your debts, including mortgages on your real estate, liens on your vehicles, or money owed on credit cards. Determine the amount of each debt, the name of the creditor, and the terms of repayment.

Your lawyer may ask to review your income tax returns for the last few years, as earning power is an important factor in figuring alimony, child support, and the division of property and debts.

❑ COMPLY WITH ALL DISCOVERY REQUESTS AND OBEY ALL TEMPORARY ORDERS.
During your divorce, you and your spouse will probably engage in a great deal of "discovery"—a legal term that means asking each other to produce financial records and other documents and to account for each other's assets and debts.

Do not try to hide assets from your spouse. If the court later finds out that you did so, your case could be reopened and you might be penalized.

Note that, before a full divorce hearing, the court often gives special temporary orders. It might allow one partner the use of the family home, arrange for child custody and support, or restrain the partners from harassing each other. You should obey temporary orders to the letter. If you do not, the judge could find you in contempt of court.

❑ KNOW WHAT YOUR DIVORCE IS COSTING YOU.
Whether you are making support payments or receiving them, you should expect to have less money to spend than you had before. When your household breaks up, you will have many of the same expenses but fewer resources to pay them, so plan ahead.

You also have to pay your divorce lawyer. Be certain to get a written fee agreement from him, and don't hesitate to ask for an itemized record of his time and expenses. If you have a question about an item you have been billed for, ask your lawyer about it as soon as possible.

❑ BEHAVE YOURSELF.
Even if fault is not an issue in your divorce, your conduct may be when it comes to child custody. If you want the court to find that you are a responsible parent, you must act like one. For example, if you are engaged in a dispute over child custody, don't host a series of wild parties in your home. Assume that your social life is being monitored and will be reported to the court.

❑ DON'T TRY TO GO IT ALONE.
Share your feelings with friends and family. If they can't help, find a professional counselor or support group. Divorce is difficult, but other people can ease you through the process. Although your lawyer will be sympathetic and supportive, talking to a friend will be less expensive; talking to a professional counselor might be a good idea too.

filed the petition, the next step is to serve Kevin with a summons and a copy of the divorce petition. Generally, a neutral party must deliver the papers in person, but in some states the papers may be sent by mail. If the spouse's whereabouts are unknown, notice of the petition may be published in the local newspaper.

If the person from whom the divorce is sought (called the respondent or the defendant) wishes to contest the divorce, he must respond to the court within a specified number of days. If he does not, the court may grant the divorce whether or not he wants it. In Kevin's case, since he wants to dispute the demands Connie made for herself and their children, Kevin's attorney files an answer, and a date for the hearing is scheduled.

Before the hearing, Kevin and Connie hold several settlement conferences during which each side proposes compromises. In each instance, however, the other party rejects them. It is then up to the court to decide about child support and spousal support. Before doing so, it must consider a number of criteria.

CHILD CUSTODY AND CHILD SUPPORT

Since Kevin and Connie have no disagreement about custody, the court will probably go along with their wishes. If the parties cannot agree on who should get custody, or if the judge does not believe that their agreement is in the best interests of the children, the judge will have to make the decision. In doing so, he considers which parent is more emotionally stable, which has the stronger bond with the children, which is more nurturing, and which is better suited to provide discipline, moral guidance, religious training, and a safe environment.

Often the court awards parents joint custody, meaning that both share in decisions about such important matters as the children's education and medical treatment. However, the court usually instructs that minor children live with one parent most of the time and have regular visits with the other. See CHILD CUSTODY.

In determining child support, which is usually paid by the noncustodial parent to the parent who has physical custody, the judge considers the financial resources of each parent, the medical and educational needs of the children, the family's standard of living, and the tax burden for either parent as altered by the support order. Such factors were weighed by the judge in Kevin and Connie's case, and his decision was presented in the divorce decree (see next page).

As long as the children are minors, the court's custody and support decisions are subject to review. If circumstances change, the court may modify a previous order. See CHILD SUPPORT; GRANDPARENTS' RIGHTS; GUARDIAN AD LITEM.

SPOUSAL SUPPORT

While they are married, a husband and wife have the duty to support each other financially. When the marriage ends, the court may order one spouse to keep supporting the other. The husband is usually ordered to support his former wife, but sometimes the reverse is true.

When deciding whether (and to whom) to order spousal support, or alimony—as well as how much and for how long—the court balances many factors: the length of the marriage; the age of each partner; the spouses' education, job skills, and earning potential; their accustomed standard of living; and the independent financial resources of each. The courts may even consider whose behavior caused the divorce and may, for example, refuse to grant alimony to an adulterous spouse.

Some states have laws that limit the number of years alimony may be paid—usually from three to seven years. In many cases, the court awards payment for whatever length of time it deems is necessary for the recipient to get on his or her feet.

The obligation to pay alimony ends when the spouse receiving it dies, remarries, or begins to live with someone else. If the spouse who is paying the alimony dies, payments may continue if the spousal support agreement stipulated that the surviving spouse be named a beneficiary on the other's insurance policy or be allowed to make a claim against his estate. See also ALIMONY.

DIVISION OF PROPERTY AND DEBTS

Marriages are a bit like businesses. Each partner usually brings some property to the marriage, and they both acquire property along the way. They incur debts too. When they get divorced, the court must decide how to distribute the property and must give instructions for the payment of the couple's debts.

Property

If a couple lives in one of the community-property states, the court's job is relatively simple. It determines what property is community property (that is, belongs to both partners) and divides it equally between them. See COMMUNITY PROPERTY.

In other states the court is not required to make an equal division — just a fair division, or an "equitable distribution," based on such factors as the length of the marriage and the contributions of each spouse during the marriage. See EQUITABLE DISTRIBUTION.

Debts

The division of debts is as important as the division of property, and sometimes the two are related. For example, if the wife is awarded the couple's new car, the court might direct her to assume responsibility for the payments on it. However, the court will also consider which spouse has more money. The judge might direct that the wife, who has fewer financial resources, receive the family home, but that the husband continue to make the mortgage payments. The court may also require one partner to pay the other's legal fees incurred in the divorce.

One problem divorced couples often face is that creditors are not bound by the decision of the divorce court. If both husband and wife signed a promissory note while they were married, they are both still obliged to pay the creditor. Suppose the court assigned the wife responsibility for the debt, but she fails to pay it or declares bankruptcy. The creditor can then look to the husband for payment. Likewise, if the husband fails to pay one of his assigned debts, the wife could be sued by creditors.

Prenuptial agreements

Many people, especially those who have been married once and are about to marry again, choose to enter into a prenuptial (or antenuptial) agreement— a legal contract made before marriage that assigns property rights to each spouse. The agreement usually states that whatever property each partner held prior to the marriage will remain his or hers alone. Property acquired during the course of the marriage is usually considered the couple's joint property, subject to division by the court or the laws of the state.

Courts will usually enforce a prenuptial agreement, unless it appears that the agreement was not voluntary or was made with insufficient information. If one spouse hid his or her true wealth from the other, for example, the court may invalidate the agreement and divide the property some other way. See also PRENUPTIAL AGREEMENT.

THE DIVORCE DECREE

After hearing the evidence, the divorce court judge usually enters a decree of divorce. In Kevin and Connie's case, which involved a dispute about child and spousal support, the court tried its best to be fair. It ordered Kevin to pay a bit more than he wanted to for spousal support, but instructed that the payments extend for a shorter period of time than Connie had asked for. The court gave Kevin liberal visitation rights and ordered him to pay child support according to the state's mandatory support guidelines.

In a number of states, a period of time (usually only a few months) must elapse between the date when the divorce decree is issued and the date it becomes final. During this time, the parties are prohibited from marrying anyone else.

Once the divorce decree has been issued by the court, the only way to prevent the divorce from becoming final is by appealing the court's decision. Such appeals are quite rare, however, and those that succeed are even rarer.

Nor can the parties who obtained the divorce resume the relationship of husband and wife. To be married again, they must go through another marriage ceremony.

QUICK AND EASY DIVORCES: A WORD OF WARNING

If you are thinking about getting a divorce, you may have come across the so-called do-it-yourself divorce kits sold in bookstores. These kits claim to contain all the forms necessary to obtain a legally valid divorce, and they promise to save you hundreds or even thousands of dollars in legal fees.

In reality, the long-term cost of using one of these kits can far exceed the money you save. For example, a kit cannot give specific advice about a couple's unique situation, help you determine that your spouse is being honest about disclosing his or her assets, or inform you about the subtle differences in court procedures from one state to another.

Using the forms supplied with these kits can lead to unnecessary delays if they do not meet local standards or if, later on, you or your spouse decides to seek a modification of support orders.

Similarly, you should be cautious about lawyers who advertise low-cost divorces. In most cases, you will find that these prices cover only the simplest situations and that costs can mount if you and your spouse disagree on important issues.

Some states, however, offer various forms of "expedited divorce." These procedures can reduce costs, eliminate the need for an attorney, and speed the process of obtaining a divorce. But if disputes need to be resolved, these procedures will not work. Only if you and your spouse are in total agreement about the most sensitive and potentially troublesome issues—the division of property, child custody, the amount and duration of spousal and child support, and the resolution of debts—will these simplified procedures be worth investigating. See ANNULMENT.

DNA FINGERPRINT

DNA (deoxyribonucleic acid) is present in the cells of every living thing and carries each individual's unique genetic code. The likelihood of correctly identifying a person on the basis of an analysis of that person's DNA sample is generally thought to be very high. The possibility of two people having DNA with exactly the same structure (except for identical twins) may be as low as 1 in 135 million. Thus DNA identifications can help prosecutors identify criminal suspects.

A DNA "fingerprint" is obtained by performing a laboratory analysis of a sample of a suspect's cells—usually from his blood, semen, hair, or skin. If the DNA fingerprint matches the DNA found in similar matter discovered in a criminal investigation—for example, if the skin found under a murder victim's fingernails matches the DNA of the accused person—a prosecutor has powerful evidence for winning her case.

DNA fingerprints are especially useful as tools in prosecutions for crimes such as rape, which are often committed without witnesses and are followed by the contradictory testimony of two individuals. Indeed, between 1987 and 1990, over 1,000 criminal investigations in the United States relied upon incriminating DNA fingerprints, resulting in hundreds of convictions.

DNA fingerprinting nonetheless has its detractors. Some scientists challenge the reliability of DNA tests, contending that the likelihood of similar DNA results is closer to 1 in 24 than 1 in 135 million. To some, DNA fingerprints are no more reliable than lie detector tests, which were once considered scientific but are now widely discredited. As a result, courts in a number of states refuse to allow DNA fingerprinting to be used as evidence or limit statements to jurors about the accuracy of DNA testing.

DOG LAW

You may think of your dog as a member of your family, but the state thinks of him as part of your personal property. This is one reason state and local governments regulate your dog ownership, by requiring you to do things like pay a fee and obtain a license for your dog, have him vaccinated against certain dangerous diseases, such as rabies and distemper, or keep him on a leash when you walk him in public.

If your dog happens to be one of the breeds believed to be especially dangerous, such as a pit bull or Doberman pinscher, the government may impose even stricter laws. For example, in some states the owners of certain breeds must prove that they have liability insurance to pay for any injury caused by their pets. Moreover, a number of communities across the country have gone so far as to ban certain kinds of dogs altogether, such as pit bulls or hybrids between dogs and wolves.

REAL LIFE, REAL LAW

The Case of the Costly Canine

When Elaine's roommate, Joyce, backed out of the driveway of their house, she did not see Elaine's elderly dog sleeping in the car's path. The dog, Winston, was severely injured, and had to be destroyed. Elaine sued Joyce in small-claims court, asking $1,000 in damages to compensate her for the loss of Winston, for the veterinarian's fee, and for her pain and suffering.

In court, the evidence showed that Joyce had been negligent. She knew that Winston often slept in the driveway and that he would not hear an approaching car's engine because he was deaf. As a result, the judge held Joyce responsible for Winston's death. She permitted Elaine to recover the cost of having the veterinarian put Winston to sleep, but she could not place a monetary value on Elaine's attachment to Winston. And since Elaine had not actually seen her dog injured, she could not receive damages for emotional distress under her state's laws.

Although most dog owners think of their pets as invaluable, in many states the law treats them like any other kind of personal property when determining compensatory damages.

DOG BITES

Many people wrongly believe there is a "one-bite rule" protecting them from responsibility the first time their dog bites someone. In about half the states, however, all dog owners are held strictly responsible when their dogs bite someone. In most of the other states, an owner will be held responsible for his dog biting others if he knew of the dog's dangerous tendencies—for example, if it growls and barks or tries to escape from restraints when people pass by.

An owner may, however, be able to escape responsibility for dog bites if he can show that the dog bit because it was provoked, or that the person the dog bit was a trespasser. Nevertheless, if the dog presents a real danger to the public because it is consistently vicious, it may be taken away by the local animal control department. See ANIMALS; LIABILITY; NEGLIGENCE; PETS; TORT.

BARKING

If Fido barks loudly and consistently, he may be a nuisance in law as well as in fact. If someone complains about your dog's barking and you fail to silence him, you may have to pay a fine or be forced to get rid of him. Of course, in many communities the police are busy with more serious crimes and may not have time to follow up on complaints. But if your neighbor cannot get the police to help, she may choose to bring a civil lawsuit. In some communities, the local animal control department will help mediate a dispute about a dog's bad behavior. See also NEIGHBORS; NUISANCE.

DOMICILE

Your domicile is your permanent place of residence, even if you live elsewhere part of the time. For example, if you own a home in Illinois, and you vote and file taxes in Illinois, your legal domicile is Illinois, even though you may spend part of each summer at the vacation cottage you own in Wisconsin. The concept of domicile can be important when deciding in which court a case should be brought to trial, where a will should be administered after a death, and whether a state or foreign country can tax one's income. See LAWSUIT; RESIDENCY LAW; WILL.

DOUBLE JEOPARDY

A clause in the Fifth Amendment to the U.S. Constitution, commonly known as the double jeopardy clause, guarantees that no person shall "be subject for the same offense to be twice put in jeopardy of life or limb." Most state constitutions have a similar guarantee.

The double jeopardy clause means that once a person has been found not guilty of a crime, he can never be tried for it again, even if evidence is later obtained that proves his guilt. Although this sounds relatively straightforward in theory, in practice it is not always easy to determine whether double jeopardy applies or not.

WHAT "TWICE" MEANS

Double jeopardy protects a person only after a court has issued a final judgment in a case. Thus if a judge declares a mistrial (because of a procedural or other problem during trial), or if there is a hung jury (meaning the jury cannot decide on a verdict), double jeopardy usually does not apply, because the court was not able to issue a final judgment. If a defendant appeals a case, and the appeals court reverses the lower court and orders that the case be tried again, the double jeopardy clause does not apply.

WHAT "OFFENSE" MEANS

The double jeopardy clause says that a person may not be "put in jeopardy" twice for the same offense. However, it is important to understand that *offense* has a strict legal meaning. An offense is not necessarily the same as the criminal act itself. Suppose Bob breaks into Jessica's home, forces her into his car, and rapes her. Bob may be tried for burglary, kidnapping, and rape, even though all the offenses occurred at about the same time and appear to be part of the same act. If Bob is tried for burglary and acquitted, he can still be prosecuted for rape and kidnapping.

Or suppose that Bob kidnaps Jessica in Ohio and then transports her through Pennsylvania, New York, and New Jersey before he is caught. He may be prosecuted in all four states on the grounds that his actions may have violated the laws of all four states. But if Bob is found not guilty of kidnapping in Ohio, the constitutional prohibition against double jeopardy would not prevent him from being prosecuted by the other states— or by the federal government— on kidnapping charges. Let us say he stole the car in which he kidnapped Jessica. The verdict on the kidnapping charge would not prevent him from being prosecuted for auto theft, because theft is a different criminal act from kidnapping.

REAL LIFE, REAL LAW

The Case of the Too-Careful Court

Frank, Joe, and Mike were all charged with burglary and larceny following two break-ins during which valuable jewelry was stolen. Toward the end of the trial, the prosecutor asked an assistant, in a voice loud enough for the jury to hear, "Is the man with the info on their records here?"

The trial judge was concerned that this comment could result in possible prejudice against the defendants, because it might lead the jury to believe that the defendants had criminal records. He called the lawyers to the bench and told them that he would declare a mistrial. This meant that there would be a new trial, with a new jury.

The defendants objected. They assured the court that if the jury found them guilty, they would not claim that the jury had been prejudiced by the remark. But the judge refused to allow the trial to continue, declared a mistrial, and sent the jury home. Later, the defendants were put on trial again and convicted.

The defendants appealed the conviction. They claimed that the second trial placed them in double jeopardy, since the first trial should not have ended in a mistrial.

The state supreme court agreed. It stated that a judge's discretion to discharge a jury before it has reached a verdict should be exercised only under extraordinary circumstances because of the prohibition against double jeopardy.

The court said that during the first trial, since the evidence was almost complete and the defendants wanted to have their guilt or innocence determined without further delay, the judge made a mistake by declaring a mistrial. As a result, the second prosecution and subsequent convictions were declared invalid under the double jeopardy clause.

DOWER AND CURTESY

Under English common law, a married person had a right to a part of his or her spouse's property at the time of death. A widow's right to part of her husband's property was known as her dower; the widower's right to a share of his wife's property was known as curtesy.

Today, dower and curtesy have been replaced in most states by statutes that provide for the spouse of a deceased person if he or she dies without a will or fails to provide for the spouse adequately in the will. See also DISINHERITANCE; DYING WITHOUT A WILL.

DRINKING AGE

In 1989 the legal drinking age in every state in the country became 21. The adoption of a uniform drinking age nationwide followed a unique set of circumstances.

Although concern about alcohol abuse and drunk driving had led to a growing movement among the populace for a uniform national drinking age of 21, the federal government could not order all the states to observe a specified drinking age without passing a constitutional amendment.

In lieu of this complicated procedure, Congress pressured the states by enacting legislation to withhold federal highway funds if they did not set the legal drinking age at 21. This strategy worked, and in 1989 Wyoming became the last state to adopt a law prohibiting the sale of alcohol to any person under age 21.

Stores, taverns, and restaurants that sell alcoholic beverages to persons under 21 may be fined, and their licenses to do business may be suspended or revoked. Minors who are guilty of consuming alcoholic beverages may be placed under court supervision. See also ALCOHOL; DRUNK DRIVING.

DRIVER'S LICENSE

The main reason driver's licenses are issued is to enable state governments to guarantee the health and safety of their citizens. Each state sets its own requirements for obtaining a driver's license, including age, knowledge of the basic rules of the road, and passing a driving test. In some states, the applicant has to pass an eye test and show that he does not have any physical or mental disability that might impair his ability to drive.

SPECIAL LICENSES

A special license—such as one issued to drive a school bus or a truck—usually requires the driver to meet higher than normal standards. Thus a person with frequent traffic violations will probably not be able to obtain a bus driver's license.

Restricted licenses or learner's permits may be issued to minors before they reach the state's minimum age for obtaining a regular license. Restrictions may include limiting the occasions when a minor uses the vehicle (such as driving to and from school) or requiring a licensed driver to be in the car.

MOVING TO ANOTHER STATE

Because each state has different licensing requirements, whenever you move to a new state you should be sure to find out what you need to do to drive in that state. Some states allow residents to use out-of-state licenses for a short period of time, while others require residents to obtain a license for that state almost immediately.

RENEWAL AND REEXAMINATION

Driver's licenses expire after a specified number of years. In most states you must simply complete a new application form, which may include questions about your health and criminal record. In some states you must take a vision test to determine whether you need to wear glasses or contact lenses for driving. If you do not renew the license before the expiration date, you may have to begin the application process all over again.

If you have been involved in certain types of accidents or cited for particular traffic violations, you may be required to take your driver's tests again. Failure to comply could lead to revocation of your license.

As a driver, you should always remember that driving is a privilege, not a right. The laws of every state permit state authorities to suspend or revoke a driver's license if a person commits many traffic violations. Generally, state laws punish "moving violations" (driving offenses made while a car is in motion) much more severely than they punish nonmoving violations (such as illegal parking). In recent years most states have established especially harsh penalties for drunk driving. See DRUNK DRIVING.

Many states employ a point system to determine when a license should be suspended or revoked. Different point values are assigned to the various traffic violations. If a driver accumulates a specific number of points in a designated period of time, the state may act to suspend or revoke his license.

DRUG

In everyday usage, the word *drug* refers either to medicine prescribed by physicians or to illegal substances such as marijuana, cocaine, or heroin. But the federal government and most states classify many other substances as drugs. Under federal law, for example, drugs are defined as substances used in the "diagnosis, cure, mitigation, treatment, or prevention of disease in man or other animals." Thus laxatives, antacids, hypodermic needles, and even horse liniments are defined as drugs. The fact that a product is labeled "nutritional" as opposed to "medicinal" does not prevent it from being regulated as a drug. Such medical devices as surgical pins and breast implants are also regulated by the government.

The Food and Drug Administration (FDA) is the federal agency that regulates the manufacture and sale of drugs in the United States to ensure that they are safe, effective, and carry labels with the appropriate warnings on side effects and contraindications. The FDA also ensures that the availability of potentially harmful drugs is limited to prescription by physicians. Most prescription drugs sold to consumers do not need to carry warnings, but the manufacturer must provide them for the pharmacist. If you ask, your pharmacist will show you all the information he receives from the manufacturer, including the warnings.

At one time, when a doctor prescribed a medication by its brand name, a pharmacist was legally bound to provide that drug, even if a lower-priced generic equivalent was available. Today, however, state laws generally allow a pharmacist to substitute the generic drug in order to reduce the cost of prescription medication. In some states the law actually requires pharmacists to offer consumers the option of purchasing lower-cost generics, and in at least one state, New York, pharmacists must give the generic drug unless the doctor has specifically ordered the name-brand. See also FOOD AND DRUG LAWS.

DRUG ABUSE

The law regulates the use of both illegal drugs (such as marijuana, heroin, and cocaine) and prescription medicines (such as codeine, diazepam, and demerol), which are both identified as "controlled substances." *Drug abuse* refers to the illicit use of an illegal drug or the improper use of a legal prescription drug—for example, relying excessively on the painkiller your doctor has prescribed for you.

CONTROLLED SUBSTANCES

In order to determine penalties for drug abuse (or "substance abuse"), most state laws classify drugs into categories established by the federal Uniform Controlled Substances Act. These categories (or "schedules") group dangerous drugs on the basis of their potential for harm in relation to their possible medical benefits.

Schedule I includes drugs that are considered most dangerous and that have virtually no medical benefit. Their use carries the harshest punishment. Among the Schedule I drugs are heroin and hallucinogens, such as LSD. Although marijuana is also a Schedule I drug, its status has been controversial. Many physicians claim it has been effective in the treatment of both glaucoma and the symptoms of nausea associated with chemotherapy.

Schedule II drugs have important medical uses but are also widely abused. They include cocaine, opium, and amphetamines, along with other very strong stimulants and depressants. Schedule III and IV drugs include milder forms of stimulants and depressants, while Schedule V consists of drugs that are medically useful but still pose a minimal danger, such as cough syrups that contain codeine.

PENALTIES FOR DRUG POSSESSION

Most laws penalize people for the purchase or possession of drugs, not the actual use (or abuse) of them. The penalties vary with state law—from stiff prison sentences to parole on the condition that the convicted abuser seek rehabilitation.

Because many medical professionals view drug abuse as a disease, some states emphasize rehabilitation. However, as public concern about the use of drugs has grown, so have the penalties in many states. For example, several states that had previously reduced penalties for possession of marijuana have reinstated severer punishment in recent years.

Criminal penalties for buying and possessing illegal drugs often depend on the accused's age, past history, and the type of drug purchased. For example, a minor caught with marijuana in her possession may be put into the custody of the family courts, placed in a juvenile detention center or group home, and required to attend drug counseling sessions. See also JUVENILE OFFENDER.

For an adult, different penalties apply. In some states a first-time conviction for possession of any kind of controlled substance may carry a penalty of one year in prison and a $5,000 fine, while in others a conviction for a small amount of marijuana may bring little more than a fine and an order to attend counseling. Repeat offenses will prompt increasingly severe sentences, and in a few states may lead to charges that the accused is a habitual criminal and should be imprisoned for life.

If a person is caught with large quantities of drugs in his possession, many states presume the drugs are intended for sale and will prosecute the offender for drug dealing. The federal government and many states also have civil forfeiture laws that allow the government to seize the property of a person charged with drug possession. In many cases, property owned by others (such as a borrowed car in which illegal drugs are found) has also been forfeited as a result of a drug arrest, even when the owner was unaware of its illicit use. See also DRUG DEALING; DRUG TESTING; FORFEITURE.

DRUG DEALING

The term *drug dealing* usually refers to the unauthorized and illicit manufacture, sale, or possession (in large quantities) of "controlled substances," or drugs. See DRUG ABUSE.

Depending on state law, and also depending on the drug involved, a first conviction for manufacturing or selling a controlled substance can bring a penalty of up to 15 years in prison and a fine of up to $25,000 for each offense. Repeat offenders may see their sentences and fines doubled.

Under federal law, drug dealers may receive the death penalty for the crime of conducting activities that result in another person's death. Some of those convicted have been sentenced to death under this law, but so far no one has been executed. See also DEATH PENALTY.

DRUG TESTING

Irene has been asked to submit to a drug test at her job, and she is concerned that this may be a violation of her privacy. Can she refuse to take the test? Irene's rights will depend very much upon the kind of job she has and the state where she lives. Although drug tests remain controversial, they are used by many public and private employers to identify workers who use drugs.

TESTS BY PRIVATE COMPANIES

If Irene works for a private company that has no connection with the federal government, she may not have to take a drug test. Concern about invasion of privacy and the harm that incorrect test results can cause has led legislatures in at least 12 states to enact laws limiting drug tests. In some of these states, for example, drug testing can be conducted only if the employer has "probable cause" to suspect drug use or "reasonable suspicion" that it has occurred. However, the random testing of employees may be permissible under certain specified conditions—for example, if the employee is a bus or taxi driver, operator of heavy equipment, or other worker with the potential to do harm to himself or others. Companies have the right in most states to test prospective employees. Irene can at least take comfort from the fact that, by law, the test must be performed in a manner that protects her privacy and dignity. See also EMPLOYEE HIRING AND FIRING.

In some states, laboratories that process test results must be licensed or certified. Positive test results must be confirmed by a second test, and confidentiality and privacy must be observed both during testing and in recording test results. A few states require employers to allow the employee to explain or refute test results. An employer who violates state drug testing laws may be faced with a civil lawsuit filed by the employee.

TESTS AND THE FEDERAL GOVERNMENT

If Irene's job is with the federal government, she can be asked to take a drug test, particularly if she is in a sensitive position, such as one that requires top security clearance. She may be required to submit to drug testing if she has an accident or if her employer has some other reason to believe that she is using drugs.

Irene can also be required to submit to drug testing if she performs a job regulated by the government. For instance, the Department of Transportation authorizes drug testing for most transportation-related workers, including pilots, flight attendants, mechanics, airport security clearance personnel, truck drivers, and railroad and other mass-transit workers.

If Irene is required to take a drug test and refuses, or takes a test and the results are positive, disciplinary action may result. The penalty will vary depending on the circumstances. A written reprimand may be issued, or she may be temporarily suspended or even fired. If she tests positive, she may be referred to drug counseling and rehabilitation centers. If she refuses such referrals, she may be fired.

Some employees who object to drug testing have challenged the tests in court, but the right to test has generally been upheld. For example, the Department of Transportation's concern with transportation safety has been ruled to outweigh any intrusion into employee privacy. Also, according to the Supreme Court, drug testing is not unlawful search and seizure under the Constitution.

DRUNK DRIVING

Driving or operating a motor vehicle while intoxicated is a crime in every state. The law refers to drunk driving as driving while intoxicated (DWI) or driving under the influence (DUI). A person will be found guilty of DWI if a prosecutor can establish beyond a reasonable doubt that the accused was: (1) driving (2) a motor vehicle (3) on a public road or highway or other area under state jurisdiction (4) while under the influence of an intoxicating beverage or liquor.

It is not always easy to prove these conditions. Take the first one — driving. Suppose that Oliver was found asleep at the wheel of his car on the shoulder of the road. The key was in the ignition, but the engine was not running. Whether this constitutes driving depends on the wording of the statute. In some states the law says that a person is guilty of drunk driving only if he was actually operating a motor vehicle at the time he was discovered. But in other states the fact that Oliver could easily wake up and drive off at any time might be enough to satisfy the condition that he was driving.

The second requirement for establishing DWI, that the accused be operating a "motor vehicle," usually means that a person has to be found behind the wheel of a car, truck, or motorcycle, or in some states, a moped or snowmobile. In some instances people have been convicted for drunk driving while riding a bicycle.

The third condition — that the drunk driving has to occur in an area governed by state law — is defined variously by the individual states. If Oliver was found driving on an abandoned road, in a trailer park, on a farm, or on the grounds of a factory, for example, he might not be guilty of DWI in some states, because these areas are private property. But in other states the DWI statute may cover private roads, driveways, and parking lots.

The final requirement, that the driver must be under the influence of an intoxicating beverage or liquor, is also defined differently throughout the country. In some states a conviction may be obtained only when the defendant's driving ability has been significantly impaired. In others only the slightest impairment of driving ability constitutes driving "under the influence." In these states Oliver could be convicted if he had been weaving from side to side, driving at night with no lights, or bouncing off the curb.

Some states have a crime called "driving while impaired," the standards for which are lower than for driving while intoxicated. For example, the testimony of an officer that the driver's speech was slurred during a field sobriety test may be sufficient for a conviction. Driving while impaired is usually easier to prove than drunk driving and may carry less severe penalties.

One of the drawbacks of drunk-driving laws has been the absence of an objective standard by which to measure whether a person is intoxicated. That is why many states have enacted laws that designate a specific alcohol content in the blood as legal proof of the inability to drive. The standard for DWI is usually .10 percent blood-alcohol content, while the standard for driving while impaired may be only .05 percent. See BLOOD-ALCOHOL TESTING.

ABC's

OF DRUNK-DRIVING PENALTIES

The time when police officers and courts were likely to let a drunk driver off with a fairly light penalty is gone. Today a drunk-driving charge can bring heavy fines and prison sentences. The penalties outlined here (one or more of which may be applied for each offense) are typical of many state laws. Most states have similar laws for driving under the influence of alcohol.

FIRST OFFENSE

- ❑ A fine of not less than $100 or more than $500.
- ❑ Mandatory screening for substance abuse at the defendant's own expense.
- ❑ Up to 12 days of community service.
- ❑ Up to 90 days in jail.
- ❑ Driver's license suspended from six months to two years, although a restricted license may be available.
- ❑ Six points charged against the defendant's license.

SECOND OFFENSE

- ❑ A fine of up to $1,000.
- ❑ Mandatory screening for substance abuse at the defendant's own expense.
- ❑ Up to 12 days of community service.
- ❑ Up to one year in jail.
- ❑ Driver's license revoked for a minimum of one year.
- ❑ Six points charged against the defendant's license.

THIRD AND SUBSEQUENT OFFENSES

- ❑ A fine of up to $5,000.
- ❑ Mandatory screening for substance abuse at the defendant's own expense.
- ❑ Up to 12 days of community service.
- ❑ A felony conviction with a penalty of up to five years in jail.
- ❑ Driver's license revoked for a minimum of five years.

MAKING A DRUNK-DRIVING ARREST

A police officer has the right to stop Oliver if there is reason to believe that he is drunk—for example, if he is driving erratically, without lights, or in some other way that indicates his judgment may be impaired.

The officer may ask Oliver to perform a field sobriety test if he seems intoxicated or if the officer smells alcohol. He may ask Oliver to perform some physical test, such as walking a straight line or placing a finger on his nose with eyes closed—actions that will show whether someone's reflexes have been impaired by alcohol. If Oliver fails the field sobriety test, the officer may ask him to take a medical test to determine the level of alcohol in his bloodstream. A Breathalyzer test may be given on the spot, or a urine or blood test may be taken after Oliver is brought to a police station or medical facility. See BREATH TEST.

IMPLIED CONSENT TO BE TESTED

Most states have enacted driving laws that employ the principle of implied consent. These laws state that when a person gets a driver's license, he is presumed to have consented to submit to a test to gauge his blood-alcohol level if the circumstances justify doing so. If Oliver refuses to take the test, for example, his license may be suspended or revoked.

The right to consult an attorney before taking such a test varies from state to state. In some states drivers have the right to do so as long as the delay is not too long. Long delays can affect test results, because blood-alcohol levels change as the body absorbs and eliminates alcohol. In other states the courts have found that the constitutional right to an attorney does not apply to taking blood-alcohol tests.

PUNISHMENT

State penalties for drunk driving are tough. Fines, imprisonment, suspension of driving privileges, community service, and driver reeducation classes are some of the penalties that can be imposed on convicted drunk drivers. If the driver's actions lead to someone's injury or death, the driver may be charged for such crimes as felony drunk driving, second-degree murder, vehicular homicide, or manslaughter.

STEPS TO TAKE

If you are stopped by a police officer who suspects you of drunk driving, here are a few points worth keeping in mind:

1. Don't be hostile or belligerent. Comply with the officer's requests.

2. Ask the officer if you may consult with an attorney before submitting to a breath, blood, or urine test.

3. If he says no, take the test. Refusing to submit to the test may result in automatic suspension of your driver's license, even if you are later found not to have been under the influence of alcohol.

4. If you are charged with drunk driving and are placed under arrest, call a lawyer as soon as possible to arrange for your release from custody. Or call a friend or family member to make these arrangements for you.

5. Don't make any statements to the police until you have consulted an attorney. Admissions you make can and will be held against you in court. If you are placed in a holding cell with other prisoners, do not make any statements to them about your drinking habits, either. Some inmates may try to trade this information to the prosecutor in an attempt to obtain a lesser sentence or a reduced charge for themselves.

DRY CLEANER

When you leave your clothes with a dry cleaner, you have created what is known in the law as a bailment. That is, you leave your property with the dry cleaner for servicing, and do so for your mutual benefit: your clothes are cleaned, he is paid, and he returns the clothes to you.

The cleaner is required by law to use "ordinary care" in handling and safeguarding your property while it is in his possession. Nevertheless, you as a customer should do whatever you can to protect your clothes against any loss or damage that might occur.

To begin with, get a receipt for the clothing you leave. The receipt should account for each item of clothing, and it may include special instructions for cleaning (as when you request that a grease spot be removed). Be sure to look for any conditions printed on the receipt. Cleaners often state that they will not be responsible for clothing left beyond a certain period of time, usually 90 days. Although courts do not always enforce such provisions, you should pick up items within a reasonable time to help avoid the potential for loss or damage to your garments.

When you leave your clothes, the cleaner is expected to handle them responsibly. He must not lose them or clean an item that he knows will be damaged in the process. For instance, if a garment carries a label saying "Hand Wash Only—Do Not Dry Clean," the dry cleaner should not clean it. If he does so and the garment is ruined, he will be obliged to reimburse you for the actual cash value—its original cost minus an amount based on the garment's age and wear and tear.

A dry cleaner usually has a right to try to repair damage to a garment before reimbursing you for its value. Before letting him do so, however, have another professional look at it. Then, if the dry cleaner does not repair the damage, you will be able to prove the harm that was done.

Occasionally a garment is damaged because of a flaw in the fabric or because the garment was incorrectly labeled. If this happens, many dry cleaners ask the Fabricare Institute of America (12251 Tech Road, Silver Spring, MD 20904), a trade association, to analyze the garment. If the damage was due to a manufacturing flaw or improper labeling, the cleaner is not responsible for compensating you, although the manufacturer may be.

You are not obliged to have the garment tested, but if you do not do so, and you subsequently sue the dry cleaner for negligence, your case against him will not be as strong. See also BAILMENT; NEGLIGENCE; WARRANTY AND GUARANTY.

DUE PROCESS OF LAW

Due process refers to the constitutional guarantees that the government cannot take away the basic rights of life, liberty, and property in an arbitrary and unreasonable manner. In practical terms this means, for example, that if the government intends to raze Robert's house in order to use the land for a new highway, he must be notified and must have the chance to state his objections to the government's plans and propose alternatives. See also CONDEMNATION.

Due process derives from two clauses in the U.S. Constitution. The first, part of the Fifth Amendment, states that no person shall "be deprived of life, liberty, or property, without due process of law." This guarantee is understood to apply only to the federal government. The second clause, part of the 14th Amendment, provides that no state shall "deprive any person of life, liberty, or property, without due process of law." Because of these two provisions, all the branches of federal, state, and local government must respect the due process guarantees.

Actions by private persons do not have to comply with due process of law. Suppose Xavier were renting an apartment in a private housing complex and the owner wanted to move Xavier to another apartment in order to make room for a parking garage. Xavier would not have the same due process rights against his landlord. He might, however, have contractual rights that could prevent this from happening.

TO WHOM DUE PROCESS APPLIES

The guarantee of due process applies to American citizens, residents of possessions of the United States, aliens (people from foreign countries who have not become U.S. citizens),

CHECKLIST

Choosing a Dry Cleaner

When it comes to dry-cleaning problems, an ounce of prevention is worth a pound of cure. Before you risk taking your most valued clothes to a new dry cleaner, find out the following:

❑ **HOW LONG THE DRY CLEANER HAS BEEN IN BUSINESS.**
A number of cleaners come and go, but the good ones stay in business for many years.

❑ **WHETHER THE CLEANING IS DONE ON THE PREMISES OR IS SENT OUT TO A PLANT.**
Although large plants often do a better job, they may not offer the personalized attention your clothes require. They also lose garments more frequently.

❑ **WHETHER THE DRY CLEANER BELONGS TO THE LOCAL BETTER BUSINESS BUREAU.**
Membership in the Better Business Bureau indicates that the cleaner may be more responsive to consumers. In addition, if a dispute arises, you may be able to settle it by arbitration.

❑ **WHAT KINDS OF SERVICES ARE PROVIDED.**
Ask whether the cleaner gives special attention to stains, checks buttons, and does tailoring.

❑ **WHETHER THE FEES ARE THE SAME FOR WOMEN'S AND MEN'S CLOTHING.**
Cleaners often charge women twice as much as men for the same type of garment. If the cleaner does this, go elsewhere. You may also want to register a complaint with your state attorney general's office or local consumer affairs department.

members of the armed forces, prisoners, and corporations.

PROCEDURAL DUE PROCESS

Lawsuits asserting the denial of due process rights have become a familiar feature of our political landscape, and can take two forms. If Robert was not notified that his house was going to be razed to the ground in order to make way for a new highway, he could bring a lawsuit charging denial of procedural due process. That is, Robert could argue that the government had not followed the appropriate steps that had been set up to protect people's property. Because procedural due process focuses on the rights of the individual citizen, it is often referred to as giving a person the opportunity to "have his day in court."

SUBSTANTIVE DUE PROCESS

Substantive due process, in contrast, focuses on the government and its authority to make or enforce certain kinds of legislation. For example, if the government properly notified Robert but he is convinced that his house and those of his neighbors are being destroyed for reasons that are suspect, he may bring a lawsuit claiming that his substantive due process rights have been violated.

Substantive due process means that the government cannot enact legislation that is unreasonable and arbitrary. Thus, for example, if Robert can prove that the government is destroying his home to benefit a private real estate company that owns nearby property, he may have a valid due process lawsuit. Similarly, if the government wants to tear down Robert's house because he uses it for gambling, but gambling is not illegal in his state, he may challenge the law as arbitrary and unreasonable, and therefore a violation of substantive due process.

Laws must be definite and clear enough that a person of ordinary intelligence does not have to guess at their meaning. This requirement is especially important in the area of criminal statutes, such as those that apply to loitering and vagrancy. A law that is vaguely worded—for example, "A person cannot be in the street without a purposeful intention"—cannot pass a due process analysis. The courts deem such statutes "void for vagueness" because they give no clear or fair indication what activity is prohibited.

If they are not to violate substantive due process, laws as well as the means provided for their enforcement must have a legitimate government purpose. Suppose that a city government wants to contain the spread of AIDS among its citizenry. If it passes a law setting up a plan to educate the public about the disease, this would not violate substantive due process. But a law requiring each new resident to take an AIDS test would both exceed the state's authority and invade individual privacy to such a degree that it would constitute a violation of substantive due process.

If a particular statute affects only a certain portion of the population, the law will meet due process requirements as long as it applies equally to all persons who are in a similar situation—for example, a law requiring that all drivers over age 75 take a driving test every two years.

If a law discriminates between individuals in similar situations, courts apply one of two tests to determine whether due process was violated. Courts apply the "compelling state interest" test when constitutionally "suspect" classifications such as age, race, or sex are involved, or when the law affects a fundamental right such as the freedom of religion. This test requires the court to determine whether the classification is needed to further a compelling state interest. For example, the law requiring frequent driving tests for those over 75 has highway safety as its compelling state interest. Therefore, in this situation the age classification specified in the law does not violate due process.

The other test, called the "rational basis" test, is applied to classifications that are not suspect. This test requires the court to determine whether a law is reasonably related to a legitimate government interest. For example, a state law requiring all drivers and passengers to wear seat belts while they are riding in automobiles applies to the classification of drivers and passengers. But unlike the driving test law mentioned above, it does not discriminate on the basis of age or any other constitutionally suspect classification (such as sex or race). Since it serves the legitimate government interest of highway safety as well, it passes the rational basis test. See also FIFTH AMENDMENT.

DURESS

Duress is the use of pressure or intimidation by one person against another, causing the other person to do something she would not ordinarily do. For example, if Lisa threatens to harm her elderly mother unless she changes her will, leaving all of her property to Lisa and her boyfriend, Lisa is guilty of duress.

When signed legal documents such as wills, deeds, or contracts are involved, proof of duress may result in the documents' being invalidated.

DYING DECLARATION

A dying declaration is a statement made by a dying person, who is mentally competent and aware of his imminent death, about a crime or other wrong that has been done by or to him — for example: "Jeremy is the man who shot me," or "I'm the one who stole Meg's ring," or even "I have another wife and family in Arizona."

Dying declarations are assumed to be truthful because people who know they are dying usually have no reason to lie. Therefore, a dying declaration, whether oral or written, may be used as evidence in court, provided its authenticity can be proved or witnesses can confirm it.

DYING WITHOUT A WILL

If you die without leaving a valid last will and testament, your property will be distributed to your heirs under your state's laws of descent (who will inherit) and distribution (what they will inherit). These laws are also referred to as laws of intestate succession.

Descent and distribution laws are meant to give your property to the people whom the law thinks you would most likely have chosen if you had executed a will. As a result, descent and distribution laws are written on the assumption that you would rather leave your property to your immediate family than to more distant family or friends.

These laws vary from state to state, but inherited property usually goes first to the surviving spouse. Next in line are living children, then parents, brothers and sisters and their direct descendants, and finally grandparents and their direct descendants.

The spouse does not inherit everything, however. For example, if you are married, have a child, and die without a will, in many states your spouse will inherit only one-third to one-half of your property, with the remainder going to your child. If you are a widow and you die without a will, all your property will go to your children (or to grandchildren if your own child has died leaving offspring). If you have adopted a child, he or she is entitled to share equally in your estate, but stepchildren you have not legally adopted may not receive anything.

If you die without a spouse and have no children or grandchildren, your parents, if living, will usually receive your property, although some states also distribute a share to any living brothers or sisters. If your parents die before you, your brothers and sisters will share equally in your estate. And if there are no closer survivors, your cousins, nieces, nephews, and even aunts and uncles may receive your property.

If none of these relatives survives you, your property goes to your nearest living blood relative. If no blood relative can be found, your property may "escheat," or revert to the state. In short, descent and distribution laws are the state's way of writing a will for you when you neglected to do so yourself.

When a state applies its laws of descent and distribution, there is the risk that the persons nearest and dearest to you, such as your spouse and children, will not receive the share you would want them to have and that they might need for their financial security. To guarantee that your wishes for distributing your property are met, a valid last will and testament, preferably prepared by a lawyer, is a must. See WILL.

Earned Income

The money or other compensation you receive from an employer for work you have done is known as earned income. In contrast, money you do not work for—such as money you win, inherit, or obtain from investments—is not considered earned income. Salaries, commissions, bonuses, tips, stocks, bonds, and even merchandise that is received in exchange for work are considered earned income for tax purposes.

Earned-Income Credit

The earned-income credit is one of the most overlooked tax deductions available to low-income families. If you have children and your salary is relatively low, you can claim an earned-income credit on your federal tax return if you meet the following criteria:

◇ You must have earned income in the United States during the taxable year.

◇ Your tax return must cover a full year, and if you are married, you must file jointly with your spouse.

◇ Your adjusted gross income must not exceed the legal limit. (In 1993 that amount was $22,370.)

◇ You must have a "qualifying child"—either your own son or daughter, or an adopted child, grandchild, stepchild, or foster child—who is under age 19 (under age 24 if a full-time student). A child of any age who is permanently and totally disabled also qualifies. The child must have lived with you in the United States for more than six months, except for a foster child, who must have lived with you for a full year. A child who was born or who died during the year qualifies if he lived with you.

◇ You yourself are not listed as the child of someone who is taking an earned-income credit on his or her tax return.

If you meet these criteria, you could be eligible for a basic credit, a health insurance credit, and an extra credit for a qualifying child born during the tax year. The dollar amounts of these credits are subject to change annually. In 1993 the maximum basic credit was $1,324 for a taxpayer with one child; the maximum health insurance credit was $451; and the maximum extra credit was $376. The Internal Revenue Service (IRS) can calculate the amounts you are entitled to receive.

Beginning in 1994, changes in federal law increase the maximum amount of earned income credit and loosen the requirements for eligibility, making childless workers with incomes below $9,000 eligible to receive credit. For detailed information on the new law, see the instructions accompanying your income tax forms.

Earnest Money

A deposit given to a seller by a buyer as evidence of his intention to follow through with a purchase is called earnest money. In return, the seller promises not to sell the property to someone else.

For important purchases, such as automobiles or real estate, earnest money, together with a document called a binder, takes the property off the market while the buyer obtains financing and investigates the property before signing the final sales contract.

Earnest money need not be a large sum, and buyers usually negotiate to make it as small as possible. The accompanying binder should state the amount and purpose of the deposit and clearly specify the circumstances under which it will be refunded. Reasons for a refund include the failure to obtain suitable financing or the discovery of structural flaws or other serious problems during an inspection of the property. A buyer may forfeit an earnest-money deposit if she fails to abide by the terms of the binder. See BINDER; HOME BUYING AND SELLING.

EASEMENT

The right to use another person's land for a specific purpose is called an easement. For example, if Maud's property does not extend all the way to the street, her neighbor may grant her an easement, affording her access to the street by allowing her to use a strip of his own land. Easements may also be established for the benefit of either the general public or the government—as when a municipal utility company runs sewer lines under private property.

TYPES OF EASEMENTS

Easements are categorized in several ways. An *easement appurtenant* benefits the person who has received it and becomes part of his estate. It is permanent and can be inherited. The easement Maud acquired through her neighbor's land is an easement appurtenant. An *easement in gross* allows someone to use another's property for an activity such as harvesting crops or cutting timber. This type of easement is a personal privilege; it cannot be inherited by or assigned to another person.

Easements may be either affirmative or negative. An *affirmative easement* permits someone else to do something on your property; a *negative easement* prohibits you from doing something on your property. For example, if you buy land from an adjacent homeowner who enjoys a scenic view from her backyard, she may insert a negative easement into the sales contract that prohibits you from building anything on your land that would obstruct her view.

CREATING AN EASEMENT

One way of creating an easement is through a provision in a deed, contract, or will. Such an *express easement* is enforceable because the document satisfies the Statute of Frauds, which specifies that easements must be in writing.

An *easement by implication*, in contrast, is not in writing. Such an easement may be created when, for example, property is divided into smaller lots and sold. If Ben installs a water pipeline so that he can water his livestock, and he later sells part of his land to Evelyn, Ben retains the right to use the pipeline that runs through Evelyn's property, even though this was not specified in their sales contract.

An *easement by prescription* is also an implied easement. It is created by one's continual use of another's land for a specific purpose, even though nothing has been put in writing and the owner has not expressly stated that he agrees to the activity. Suppose Farmer Brown and Farmer Green own two neighboring farms. Farmer Brown's land does not extend to the county road, and he reaches the road by crossing over a small corner of Farmer Green's acreage. If Brown creates a well-worn, visible path across Green's land and continues to use it for a number of years, he may have created an easement by prescription. If he has, Green cannot suddenly decide, after several years (the exact length of time varies with state law), to prevent Brown from using the path . The rules that apply to easement by prescription are similar to those governing adverse possession. See also ADVERSE POSSESSION.

LOSING AN EASEMENT

Farmer Brown and others who enjoy express or implied easements should not assume that they can never be taken away. People can lose their easements if they abuse them. For example, if you have allowed your neighbor to cross a piece of your land to get to a public road, but he later sets up a business that results in numerous customers tracking back and forth over your property, you can take the easement away from him.

ELDER LAW

Older Americans have special needs and unique legal problems. Many attorneys and other professionals who offer services to the elderly make a special study of the laws affecting them. Areas of the law identified as being of major concern to older people are abuse and neglect, age discrimination, guardianships and conservatorships, money management, estate planning, long-term health care, and the right to die. If you think you need a lawyer, but are not sure how to find a good one, see LAWYER.

ABUSE AND NEGLECT

Some experts estimate that every year some 1.5 million adults over age 60 are neglected or physically, emotionally, or sexually abused, often by family members or professional caretakers.

Most states have enacted laws to protect the elderly against such crimes. In some states, older persons can seek orders of protection similar to those granted to battered women. All but a few states have mandatory reporting laws that require health care workers and other professionals to report suspected cases of abuse or neglect. Some state laws impose fines and prison sentences on caretakers who are convicted of such wrongdoing. See also NURSING HOME; ORDER OF PROTECTION.

If you suspect that an older person is the victim of abuse or neglect, report the situation to your local social services office or police department. They will investigate the matter, and your name will be kept confidential. If the abuse or neglect occurs in a hospital or nursing home, notify your state board of health.

AGE DISCRIMINATION

The federal Age Discrimination in Employment Act (ADEA) prohibits employers from firing, refusing to hire, or withholding benefits or in-house training from employees because of their age. The act also prohibits lenders, such as credit card companies, banks, and mortgage companies, from denying credit to elderly persons solely on the basis of age.

If, however, you become frail and are often out sick or have difficulty getting to work on time, the ADEA does not protect you from being fired. Employers can fire anyone, young or old, for chronic lateness or absenteeism. For more information, see AGE DISCRIMINATION; EMPLOYEE HIRING AND FIRING.

MONEY MANAGEMENT AND ESTATE PLANNING

Some older people have difficulty managing their finances and handling their everyday affairs. If age or illness has impaired someone to the point that she cannot make rational decisions about medical care, finances, and other issues, a relative or a close friend may apply to the court for a guardianship or conservatorship. A guardianship enables someone to make all decisions regarding the older person's care, while a conservatorship enables him to handle the older person's financial affairs. If the court agrees that the older person cannot manage her affairs and that the person to be appointed is both able and trustworthy, the judge will make the appointment. See GUARDIAN AND WARD.

Because a guardianship deprives the ward of making most of the important decisions in her life, and a conservatorship denies her the right to have a say in her financial affairs, they should be used only when absolutely necessary. Several alternatives exist that make it possible for an older person to transfer responsibilities to someone else while otherwise remaining in control of her life. She can, for instance, petition the court to appoint a conservator or execute a power of attorney authorizing a friend or relative to write checks and make sure that bills are paid on time. If she chooses, she can execute a durable power of attorney, which will remain in effect if she subsequently becomes incompetent or incapacitated. Another option is a "springing" power of attorney, which becomes effective only when a specified event takes place, such as a hospitalization. For a complete discussion of these options, see POWER OF ATTORNEY.

Another important area of elder law is estate planning. Judicious estate planning not only helps a person avoid paying taxes unnecessarily but relieves her of the need to be concerned with the management of her property. For example, she can place her assets in a revocable living trust, with herself as the beneficiary and an adult child or another reliable person as cotrustee. See ESTATE PLANNING; LIVING TRUST; NURSING HOME.

A major concern of many elderly people and their families is that their life savings, and especially their homes, will go to the government if they should require long-term nursing-home care. The federal law has provisions that allow citizens to avoid this eventuality, at least in part. See MEDICAID.

HEALTH CARE AND LIVING WILLS

Older people have special concerns about the costs and complexities of long-term health care. For instance, filling out claim forms for benefits and going through a formal appeals process if a claim is denied can be arduous. While some storefront offices make high-flown claims that they can secure Medicare benefits, these businesses should be avoided. If you need help filling out your insurance claims, ask a trusted friend or a qualified social worker at a senior center or local office for the aging.

A number of "Medigap" insurance policies are advertised as "picking up where Medicare leaves off." But before you buy such a policy, carefully evaluate what it covers and make sure you understand what it does not cover. See HEALTH INSURANCE; MEDICARE.

Many people do not want their lives to be extended when drastic measures such as respirators and feeding tubes are required; nor do they want to pass on to their families the burden of deciding when to end artificial life support. As a result, most states have enacted laws that allow persons of all ages to leave living wills—written instructions to withdraw or withhold life-support systems if they should become terminally ill and unable to make their wishes known. For a full discussion, see LIVING WILL.

ELECTION LAWS

Fundamental to any democracy is its citizens' right to vote. In the United States, national elections are regulated by Congress, within the guidelines set by the Constitution. Also within constitutional guidelines, the individual states have wide latitude in regulating state and local election procedures, such as the location of polling places, qualifications for voting, and restrictions on absentee balloting. See ABC'S OF YOUR RIGHT TO VOTE on page 186.

THE FREEDOM TO VOTE

If elections are truly to reflect the will of the people, no qualified voter should be prevented from voting. Both the federal Civil Rights Act and the Voting Rights Act guarantee all qualified persons the right to vote regardless of race, color, or national origin. These acts prohibit the use of intimidation or coercion against citizens to keep them from voting and allow the federal government to bring lawsuits to end discriminatory voting laws and practices. The following guidelines are the direct result of these acts:

◇ Literacy tests may legally be given to prospective voters, but anyone who has completed the sixth grade is presumed to be literate and need not take a literacy test. The Civil Rights Act requires that copies of literacy tests and their answers be made available on request.

◇ Voters are entitled to absolute secrecy. An election that is conducted in such a way that an individual's vote is identifiable can be invalidated.

◇ If it is proved that a candidate won an election through fraud, bribery, or coercion, he cannot assume office.

◇ Most states prohibit electioneering within a specified distance from a polling place, because this practice may intimidate voters.

◇ If any violence or intimidation of voters takes place in a district, all the votes in that district can be invalidated.

EQUALITY OF VOTES

The right to vote has no real meaning if the votes are not weighed equally. "One person, one vote" has long been a basic tenet of our democracy.

Each state's legislature or a commission designated by the legislature is authorized to divide the state into districts whose voters elect members to the U.S. House of Representatives and the state legislatures. Because the Constitution requires that electoral districts have substantially similar populations, the states must redraw the districts periodically to reflect population changes.

To prevent "gerrymandering"—the practice of redrawing district lines to give an advantage to a particular candidate or party—most state laws require that legislative districts have a compact and undivided territory. Through gerrymandering, a party in power could, for example, cause a U.S. congressman or a state representative from a rival party to lose his seat by redrawing his district so that its boundaries include fewer voters belonging to the party that elected him and more from the opposing party. If gerrymandering is suspected, the courts are authorized to look into the matter, and a lawsuit may be initiated by the state's attorney general or by individual voters. The

ABC's
Of Your Right to Vote

At the first elections held in the fledgling United States of America, the only people allowed to vote were white males. Since then, a series of amendments to the Constitution has vastly extended voting rights, but the individual states still maintain certain restrictions.

STATE RESTRICTIONS:

❑ States may establish residency laws and objective literacy standards. They may also specify a minimum age for voters within constitutional guidelines.

❑ States can deny the vote to people who are mentally incompetent or who have been convicted of a serious crime.

❑ States may require that all voters be citizens, but must not discriminate between natural and naturalized citizens.

❑ Most states allow absentee voting, but with certain limitations. Absentee ballots are usually granted to people who have an important reason for being away from their local district on election day, who are too ill to leave their home, or who have a physical disability that prevents them from making the trip to the polling place.

FEDERAL RIGHTS:

❑ In 1870 the 15th Amendment forbade the disqualification of any voter due to his race, color, or former status as a slave.

❑ In 1920 the 19th Amendment enfranchised women by prohibiting any statute that denies the right to vote based on sex.

❑ In 1964 the 24th Amendment declared that the failure to pay a poll tax could not disqualify someone from voting in a federal election.

❑ In 1971 the 26th Amendment lowered the voting age to 18.

court may order reapportionment within a specified time, and if the legislature fails to act, the court itself can reapportion the electoral districts. In 1993 the U.S. Supreme Court overturned a redistributing plan designed to increase representation of minority voters on the grounds that it was unconstitutional.

THE BALLOT

A candidate for public office may be nominated either by his political party or by petition. Some states require that political parties hold primary elections to choose their nominee. Before you can vote in a primary election, your state law may require you to declare yourself as a member of the party holding the primary—that is, you may not be able to vote in a Democratic primary unless you are a registered Democrat. It is for this reason that voting officials are allowed to ask you about your party affiliation when you register to vote. A few states, however, allow voters to "cross over" from one political party to another during primary elections—Republicans may vote for Democratic primary candidates and Democrats for Republicans.

A candidate who is not nominated by a political party may be placed on the ballot if a petition with the number of signatures required by state law is filed with the board of elections or secretary of state. Some states permit voters to cast their vote for a candidate who is not on the official ballot simply by writing the candidate's name on a form at the polls. These are called write-in votes. States are not obliged by the U.S. Constitution to recognize write-in votes, however.

CAMPAIGN SPENDING

A number of laws now regulate campaign spending and financial contributions to candidates. The amounts that individuals and groups (often called political action committees, or PAC's) may contribute are limited by law. In national elections, a voter may contribute up to $1,000 per candidate. A PAC may contribute $5,000 to a single candidate (or to several if it is qualified by the Federal Election Commission as a multicandidate PAC). Candidates are usually required to file public statements listing contributions that they have received.

In the past, federally elected representatives who decided not to run again for office could keep any PAC surplus that they had. A new law prohibits those who retired after 1992 from doing so. See also POLITICAL ACTION COMMITTEE.

CONTESTED ELECTIONS

In some states candidates or voters may request a recount of the votes after they have been tallied, and in most states they may contest election results in court. Legal grounds for recounts or challenges include the violation of election laws (for example, through bribery), the rejection of legal votes, the acceptance of illegal votes (votes by unregistered voters or multiple votes by the same voter), the improper preparation of ballots (such as misstating party affiliation), and violation of the rules of secrecy.

ELECTRONIC FUNDS TRANSFER ACT

No one who opened his first bank account 20 or more years ago could possibly have predicted the kinds of services and conveniences that modern technology has made possible. Today paychecks and Social Security checks are deposited electronically into individual bank accounts. And by inserting a plastic card and punching in a personal identification number (PIN) into an automated teller machine (ATM), you can withdraw cash from your bank account at convenient locations around town whether your bank is open or not.

On the negative side, such options increase the likelihood of error and even theft. Suppose you authorize your bank to send the Southfork Savings Bank $500 each month to pay off your mortgage. If the computer operator mistakenly pushes the zero key one more time than she should, Southfork would receive $5,000 of your money. Furthermore, if you are ever foolish enough to keep your PIN number with your ATM card and a thief steals your wallet, he can withdraw all the money from your account. For this reason, it is best to memorize your PIN number. Choose one that is easy to remember and hard for someone else to guess, such as your mother's date of birth.

Fortunately, you have some important rights under the Electronic Funds Transfer Act, which Congress passed in 1978 to protect consumers who use cash dispensers, automated teller machines, and other electronic systems for crediting or debiting their bank accounts. The act sets forth the rights and responsibilities of consumers who authorize electronic transfers, the parties that initiate them (such as employers or government agencies), and the financial institutions (such as banks, savings and loan associations, and credit unions) that execute the transfers.

TRANSACTIONS COVERED BY THE ACT

The Electronic Funds Transfer Act regulates the automatic deposit or withdrawal plans by which a financial institution is authorized to credit or debit a customer's account electronically, via telephone, computer, magnetic tape, or other instrument. The act does not apply to transactions involving cash, checks, money orders, or credit cards. Nor does it apply if you use an automated teller machine to transfer funds from one of your bank accounts to another.

YOUR RIGHTS AS A CONSUMER

If you sign an agreement for an electronic funds transfer service, the bank must give you the following basic information:

◇ The types of transfers you can make (typically, automatic monthly payments and ATM transactions).

◇ Fees and charges for the transfers.

◇ How to stop payment on a preauthorized transfer.

◇ Your responsibility (or the liability you have) for unauthorized transfers.

◇ Your right to receive documentation of transfers.

◇ A summary of your rights under the act, including an explanation of the procedures for resolving errors.

LIABILITY

If someone gains access to your bank account and transfers funds from it without your permission, do you bear the loss? Not entirely. If the bank did not supply you with a card or other means of access to your account, along with proper identification of you as the owner (such as a signature or photograph), you are not liable for an unauthorized transfer.

If the bank complied with that requirement, your liability is still limited, but it increases with the amount of time that elapses before you report the matter to the bank. For example, if you report a lost or stolen card before it is used, your liability is zero. If you report the loss within two business days after you discover an error on your bank statement (whether or not you noticed at first that your card was missing), your liability is limited to $50. If you report the matter between 2 and 60 days after you notice a problem, your liability is $500. After 60 days, you are responsible for all unauthorized uses that you failed to report.

STOPPING AUTOMATIC WITHDRAWALS

To stop payment on an automatic withdrawal—for example, if you no longer want to buy shares in a mutual fund that you have authorized to make monthly debits from your account, you should notify the bank, orally or in writing, three business days in advance of the date the withdrawal is usually made. If you give notice on the telephone, the bank may ask you to confirm your instructions in writing within two weeks. Your written notice should include the name of the person you spoke with at the bank and the date.

DOCUMENTATION

You are entitled to documentation of every transfer on your account. The bank statement must list the amount, date, and type of the transfer; the account from which or to which the funds were transferred; the party forwarding or receiving the funds; and the location and identification of the terminal that was used if the transaction was on an ATM.

If you are receiving automatic deposits at regular intervals of 60 days or less, the bank can choose either to notify you when each deposit arrives or to notify you only if the expected deposit was not made. In addition, you should receive a statement every one to three months, depending on the type of account and the transfers being made. The statement must contain your opening and closing balances, a summary of the transfers, any fees the bank has charged during that period, and an address and telephone number for inquiries.

If you have authorized automatic withdrawals and the amounts vary (as they would with a monthly utility bill, for instance), the bank must notify you of the dates and amounts of the withdrawals.

RESOLVING ERRORS

If you notice an error, such as an incorrect debit—either on your bank statement or on an ATM receipt—you must notify the bank orally or in writing within 60 days if you want the mistake corrected. The bank must look into the matter and report its findings to you within 10 days. If it needs more time, the bank may provisionally recredit your account with the amount in question. It then has 45 days to complete its investigation of your error.

If the bank finds that an error was indeed made, it must correct the error within one business day. If it concludes that it did not make an error, the bank must notify you within three business days.

STEPS TO TAKE

If you do not agree with the bank's findings about an error, take the following steps:

1. Write to the manager of the bank. At your request, the bank must show you the documents that were used in its investigation.

2. If you are still not convinced, write to the Division of Consumer and Community Affairs, Board of Governors of the Federal Reserve System, 20th Street and Constitution Avenue NW, Washington, DC 20551. The Federal Reserve will try to resolve problems over which it has authority.

3. If still in doubt, you can call or write your state attorney general's office or state banking commission.

4. As a last resort, you can sue the bank.

EMBEZZLEMENT

Embezzlement differs from other types of theft in that it involves the violation of a trust. Unlike fraud or swindling, for example, embezzlement does not entail obtaining another's property illegally through false pretenses. Rather, the embezzler has the property lawfully in his possession before he misappropriates (takes) it. The property is misappropriated if the embezzler conceals, converts (sells), or makes away with it without the knowledge of the owner. The difference between ordinary theft and embezzlement is best illustrated by the following two examples, which are based on actual cases.

A used-car salesman told his boss that he had a cash customer for a car on the lot, even though he did not. The dealer entrusted his car to the salesman, who sold it, pocketed the cash, and never showed up for work again. When the salesman was eventually arrested and brought to trial, he was found guilty of grand larceny, not embezzlement, because he took the car illegally, under false pretenses.

In the second example, the legal circumstances are somewhat different. Mary accepted Edward's proposal of marriage. When he apologetically told her he could not afford to buy her an engagement ring, she gave him her diamond cocktail ring so that he could have the diamonds removed and reset. But the couple quarreled and broke off their engagement, and Edward sold the ring and kept the money. He was found guilty of embezzlement. Although he received the ring legally, he acted illegally when he sold it for his own gain.

Many states have replaced embezzlement statutes with a single law that covers all types of theft.

EMPLOYEE

Generally speaking, an employee is anyone who works for someone else. But in the legal sense, you are an employee only if you work in a specified place during specified hours, or if you are provided with tools, supplies, or a place to work by your employer.

Sometimes, an unethical employer will ask you to sign a form stating that you agree not to be considered an employee, but to work instead as an "independent contractor." The employer does this to avoid making payments for Social Security, unemployment insurance, and workers' compensation. If you wish, you can place an anonymous call to the IRS and inform them of your company's dubious practice. The tax authorities use a checklist of factors to determine whether an employer-employee relationship exists, the most important of which is "control."

If you are truly an independent contractor or freelance worker—that is, if your employer does not dictate where you work and when, and does not provide you with a place to work—you are not legally an employee. Therefore, your employer is not required to pay for the above-mentioned government benefits or any company benefits that he offers to employees, such as vacation time. See also INDEPENDENT CONTRACTOR.

EMPLOYEE ASSISTANCE PROGRAM

As employers have come to realize that the well-being of their employees contributes strongly to company productivity, they have adopted programs for helping employees with their problems. One of these is the employee assistance program, or EAP, now offered by many larger employers and a growing number of smaller ones.

The typical EAP helps employees get assistance for personal, medical, legal, and other problems. By contacting an EAP counselor, usually by means of a toll-free telephone number, an employee can be directed to private and community resources that offer drug counseling, legal advice, marriage counseling, and other services, such as help in obtaining care for an elderly or ill parent. Ask your company's department of human resources for information about your company's EAP.

CONFIDENTIALITY

A primary concern of employees who are offered an EAP is confidentiality. Many employees are hesitant to take advantage of these services for fear that their problems will be revealed to other employees, or worse, to their employer.

Generally, however, these fears are unfounded. EAP's scrupulously safeguard the identity of the employees who use the program. Medical professionals and attorneys who participate in EAP's are ethically bound by the same confidentiality requirements that would be extended to any of their private patients or clients. No information can be disclosed to anyone without the employee's consent.

EMPLOYEE HIRING AND FIRING

Employers are governed by a variety of federal and state laws regarding the hiring and firing (or "termination") of employees. For example, the Civil Rights Act of 1964, the Americans With Disabilities Act of 1990, and the Age Discrimination in Employment Act of 1967 prohibit discrimination based on race, color, religion, sex, national origin, disability, or age. These federal laws apply to employers involved in interstate commerce and with a specified number of employees (generally 15 to 20). Government employers are subject to similar prohibitions. See also AGE DISCRIMINATION; CIVIL RIGHTS; DISABLED AMERICANS.

JOB ADVERTISEMENTS AND JOB APPLICATIONS

The prohibition against discrimination applies equally to job advertisements and job applications. Therefore, an advertisement or application cannot state a preference for candidates of a particular race, color, sex, or age. For example, an employer who ran a newspaper ad that said "Help Wanted, White Male" or "Help Wanted, Asian Female," or employed language such as "recent high school graduate" (suggesting that only younger people apply) may be subject to discrimination charges.

Advertisements or applications that express a preference based on age, national origin, religion, sex, or the absence of a disability are allowed only if they reflect a legitimate qualification for the job. For instance, a Catholic church may require that applicants for a position as a church administrator or spokesperson be Roman Catholic. Similarly, inquiries about age are legal if the employer can demonstrate that the skills needed for a particular job make it necessary to restrict applicants by age. Courts have recognized that jobs such as firefighter and police officer, for example, require younger people with the physical stamina to perform the job.

JOB INTERVIEWS

Alice, who is young and wears a wedding ring, was interviewed for a job as a sales representative. At the interview she was asked whether she intended to have children. The employer was concerned because the job required the employee to be on the road a lot. He was afraid that if Alice started having children, she might quit.

No matter how innocent the employer's intentions, this sort of question, while not necessarily prohibited by law, may lead to charges of unfair hiring practices. So may questions about a job candidate's age, marital status, possible pregnancy, number of children, national origin, height, weight, or handicap (except when the handicap might affect job performance). The basic rule is that an employer should only ask questions that are relevant to the applicant's qualifications for the job.

CRIMINAL RECORDS

In some parts of the country, inquiries about arrests or convictions are illegal or may be asked only under limited circumstances. However, in most states employers may inquire about convictions (through a question on the application form or a personal interview) if past criminal activity could interfere with a person's ability to perform a job. For example, if Alice is applying for a job as a bank teller, that bank may ask on its application form whether prospective employees have criminal convictions and refuse to hire her if she does. Applicants do not have to make known arrests that did not lead to convictions.

TESTING JOB APPLICANTS

Alice was asked to take a personality test for the sales representative job. Psychological tests of this kind are permitted if they have been shown to be valuable in predicting job performance. However, tests that are used to discriminate on the basis of race, color, religion, sex, age, or national origin are illegal. For instance, a test full of questions containing American slang might be found to discriminate on the basis of national origin.

Drug tests

Employers can test job applicants for drugs provided that the applicant agrees to the test. Usually the employer's intention to test for drugs is expressed on the job application form, and the applicant agrees to it by signing the form. The circumstances under which drug testing may be performed are quite different once an applicant becomes an employee. See DRUG TESTING.

Polygraph tests

A polygraph, or lie detector, test attempts to measure a person's truthfulness by using an electronic device to monitor bodily changes as the person is being asked various questions. As a general rule, private employers cannot give polygraph tests to applicants or employees or ask them about polygraph test results obtained elsewhere. Nor can an applicant be denied employment simply because he refuses to take a polygraph test.

Federal law provides a few exceptions to these rules. Companies with federal government contracts relating to national security operations are allowed to conduct polygraph tests, as are companies that provide security services or manufacture or distribute controlled substances such as drugs. Polygraph tests may also be given to employees suspected of stealing money, property, or confidential trade secrets.

Employers who violate the polygraph testing law may be sued by employees or job applicants wrongly asked to take a polygraph test. See also LIE DETECTOR TEST.

TERMINATION OF EMPLOYMENT

Suppose that, nine months after beginning her job as a sales representative, Alice and her boss have a major disagreement and he fires her. Alice is furious and wants to sue. Does she have a right to her job? The answer is probably not.

Firing at will

Unless Alice has a written contract with her employer stating the terms of her employment and reasons for termination, she does not have a right to a job and can be fired at will for no reason at all. However, federal and state antidiscrimination laws prevent employers from firing workers due to reasons such as their sex, race, religion, or national origin. And other state laws now further restrict or limit an employer's ability to discharge employees. Under these laws, an employee who is terminated without a good reason or in violation of public policy can file suit claiming "wrongful discharge" and seek reinstatement and recovery of lost wages and benefits. It is a violation of public policy, for example, to fire an employee for refusing to give false testimony in a lawsuit in which the company is involved.

It is discriminatory to fire an employee for his conduct when other employees who engaged in similar conduct were not fired. For example, if a black employee and a white employee were both equally responsible for damaging company property, and only the black employee was fired, the company could be sued for racial discrimination.

Whistle-blowers and others

Workers may not be fired from their jobs for exercising their legal right to report hazardous or unhealthy working conditions to the Occupational Safety and Health Administration (OSHA) or to other agencies that monitor the workplace. See OCCUPATIONAL SAFETY AND HEALTH ADMINISTRATION (OSHA); WHISTLE-BLOWER.

The courts have also refused to uphold an employee's termination when he has reported illegal activity or when his wages have been garnisheed for the first time. By federal law, employees cannot be fired for serving on a federal jury, and most states have similar laws that apply to jury duty in state courts.

Challenging a termination

If the reason given for termination is unsatisfactory work, but the employer or immediate supervisor has never shown any dissatisfaction with the employee's job performance, the worker may have a basis for challenging the dismissal. Some courts have found that it is unfair for an employer to fire an employee without giving him any warning that his job performance is not up to par and without making any suggestions about how he might improve.

A few states have laws requiring employers to give employees reasons for their dismissal. If your employer fires you without giving a reason, check the laws in your state. If you learn that the dismissal was based on false information, you may be able to file a complaint with your state department of labor, and you may be able to sue him for defamation. See DEFAMATION.

Even in states where the employer does not have to tell the employee why he was dismissed, the reason may be learned through other sources.

For example, if you have the right to see your personnel files, you may uncover the reason by looking carefully at your employment records. Or you may learn why you were fired if you apply for unemployment compensation; an employer is required by law to give a reason for firing you if he disputes your eligibility for workers' compensation, and the state must tell you what that reason is. See EMPLOYEE PERSONNEL RECORDS; WORKERS' COMPENSATION.

Constructive discharge
The resignation of an employee in order to avoid intolerable working conditions or illegal activities is known as constructive discharge. Suppose Alice's boss touches her "accidentally" at every opportunity and asks her if she really is happily married. Her complaints about his behavior go unheeded, and she sees no way out except to resign. She would then have good reason to sue her employer and would also be eligible for unemployment benefits.

Payment on termination
In every state, a discharged employee must be given a termination check on the last day of work or on the next regular payday, and the check must include all the wages due him up to that time. An employer cannot refuse to pay an employee on the grounds that his work was unsatisfactory. See also JOB DISCRIMINATION.

EMPLOYEE PAYCHECK DEDUCTIONS

The gross amount of money you earn as an employee is your salary or wage. However, unless you are an independent contractor, your paycheck will be subject to deductions—for Social Security, income taxes, and other purposes. Some of these deductions are determined by law, and others are left up to you. See also INDEPENDENT CONTRACTOR.

Deductions vary because of the types of benefits (such as health insurance and pension programs) offered by the employer and because each state or locality has different tax rates. Your state department of labor can provide information about what payroll deductions are required for taxes in your state.

There is no limit on the types of deductions that can be made from an employee's paycheck. However, the law places limits on the amounts of some deductions, such as wage garnishments or deductions to cover cash register shortages. See GARNISHMENT; SOCIAL SECURITY.

CASH SHORTAGES AND MISAPPROPRIATED FUNDS

Some employers require employees to reimburse the company when a cash register has a shortage at the end of the day, when inventory is missing, or when merchandise is damaged. State laws differ as to the amount an employer may recover as a result of such losses. Generally speaking, the deduction cannot reduce an employee's pay below the minimum wage, and some state laws require an employee to give written permission for a payroll deduction.

The situation is handled differently when an employee wrongfully takes money—or misappropriates funds—from a company. His net pay may be reduced to an amount below the minimum wage until the money is repaid. However, this action can be taken only if the employee has been found guilty in court of taking the money.

An obvious question to ask is why such an employee would not simply be fired for taking money. The answer is that some small employers (and a few large ones too) may want to give a long-time employee a second chance, especially if his previous record was a good one. The employer may also believe that payroll deductions are the most convenient and dependable way to recover the lost money.

CASH ADVANCES AND LOANS

An employer sometimes makes a cash advance or loan to an employee. In such a case, both the employer and the employee must sign an agreement stating that the money will be repaid through payroll deduction. If the amount of the payroll deduction is not specified in the agreement, a reasonable deduction is allowed. Deductions that are earmarked to repay the principal are permitted to reduce the employee's pay below the minimum wage, but deductions for interest, loan processing, or other fees must not do so.

EMPLOYEE PERSONNEL RECORDS

Arthur suspects that his supervisor has put some negative job-performance evaluations in his file. He asks to see his file, but his request is denied. Arthur is furious. He argues that it is, after all, his personnel file, and he should be able to see it.

Unfortunately for Arthur, an employee is not automatically entitled to examine his personnel file. Employees are generally not given access to their files because unlimited access might inhibit superiors from making frank evaluations of job performance. In fact, the right to inspect a personnel file is generally available only when established by law. Since your file could contain everything from your job application and performance evaluations to medical records, letters of reference, and other personal information, you may want to find out whether the law permits you to examine it.

GOVERNMENT EMPLOYEES

Federal government employees and employees of states that have enacted record-access laws usually have the right to see their personnel files. This often means the employee can not only read the file but also make copies of documents and dispute information contained in it. For example, if Arthur is a federal employee and an insurance company wants certain information from his personnel file, Arthur has the right to inspect it first. If he finds any inaccuracies, he can request that they be corrected. If they are not, his employer must give him a reason.

PRIVATE EMPLOYEES

As of 1993, employees of private businesses and corporations have had the right to inspect their personnel files in the following states: Alaska, Arkansas, California, Connecticut, Delaware, Illinois, Maine, Massachusetts, Michigan, Minnesota, Nevada, New Hampshire, Oregon, Pennsylvania, Rhode Island, Washington, and Wisconsin. But even in these states, the right is often limited. For example, in some states an employee cannot see letters of reference or criminal investigative reports. In others, an employee can examine letters of reference only after the identifying names and information have been deleted.

Some other states are far more permissive: in Connecticut, Delaware, Illinois, Massachusetts, Michigan, Minnesota, New Hampshire, Washington, and Wisconsin, an employee may not only inspect the material in the personnel file but also insert a rebuttal.

PRIVACY

Just because Arthur may not be able to examine his file does not mean that the information is never disclosed. For example, employers must report certain biographical and statistical data to government agencies, such as the Equal Employment Opportunity Commission. The information that can be disclosed to a government agency, however, is generally not of a personal nature.

Because of the sensitive nature of medical records, some states require employers to implement procedures for maintaining their confidentiality. For example, the employer may be required to obtain the employee's written permission before disclosing medical data contained in his file. See also CONSENT FORM; PRIVACY RIGHTS.

EMPLOYEE RETIREMENT INCOME SECURITY ACT (ERISA)

In 1974 Congress enacted the Employee Retirement Income Security Act, or ERISA, a comprehensive statute that lays out the rules for employee benefit plans. ERISA dictates the kinds of information that must be included in such plans, the criteria for administering them, and penalties for failure to follow ERISA's rules. Despite its name, the Employee Retirement Income Security Act does not apply just to retirement income plans. It also covers a wide range of employee benefits, including certain kinds of health insurance plans.

Suppose the Acme Trucking Company decides to create an employee benefit plan. As a commercial enterprise, it must

REAL LIFE, REAL LAW

The Case of the Padded Pension

In 1988 Glenn and several of his coworkers were offered an early retirement plan by their company. The company gave them such an attractive estimate of their monthly pension benefits that Glenn and his colleagues chose to retire early. Each of them received the promised benefits for more than a year.

Then in May of 1990, the company informed the retirees that a mistake had been made in calculating their benefits, resulting in overpayments that varied from $200 to $1,000 a month. The company then began paying the lower benefits.

Glenn and his fellow retirees sued, arguing that the company had misled its employees in an effort to induce them to take early retirement. For example, on several occasions Glenn had asked the company for a copy of the benefit plan, which would have allowed him to investigate it carefully. The company refused his request.

The court ruled in favor of Glenn and his fellow employees. It held that since ERISA requires a company to disclose complete and accurate information about its pension plan to covered employees, Glenn's company had violated federal law. The court ordered the company to pay the retirees their promised benefits, as well as attorney fees and court costs.

follow the rules established by ERISA. (Noncommercial entities, such as religious or governmental bodies, are not subject to these regulations.) ERISA guidelines apply to both welfare benefit plans (which provide vacation, medical, accident, death, or disability benefits) and pension benefit plans (which provide employees with retirement income). Pension benefit plans, however, must meet certain requirements for funding, participation, and vesting that do not apply to welfare benefit plans.

PENSION PLAN RULES

A pension plan is a program established by an employer to provide income to its employees upon their retirement. It may be funded entirely by the employer, or employees may make contributions as well. See Pension Plan.

Because employers must follow ERISA's guidelines, the Acme Trucking Company must make sure that most of its employees (usually about 70 percent) will be eligible for its pension plan and that the plan does not discriminate against any of them. For example, if Acme's officers, executives, or shareholders meet eligibility requirements but the company's lower level employees do not, the plan would be discriminatory.

Eligible Acme employees must be allowed to participate in the pension plan after they have completed one full year of service with the company or have reached the age of 21, whichever comes later. However, if a new employee is within five years of the plan's normal retirement age, he may have to work for a specified number of years before he can receive benefits when he retires. For example, if Norman comes to work at Acme at age 62, and the retirement age is 65, Norman may have to work for, say, five years before becoming eligible for the plan. He could then retire at 67 and receive a pension.

If Acme's plan is set up so that an employee is fully vested as soon as he is a participant, then the plan can require three years of service before the employee is eligible to participate.

VESTING

An important aspect of any pension plan is the provision called vesting. Vesting refers to that point in time—usually after a number of years of service in the company—when an employee acquires a right to his pension benefits. Contributions to an employee's pension fund are usually made by both the employee and the company. Those made by the employee belong to him (are vested to him) immediately. But those made by the company are not available to the employee until he is vested in them.

ERISA requires that a company set up vesting in one of two ways. An employee may either become 100 percent vested after five years, or vested by increasing percentages over three to seven years. For example, if Acme decides to use the latter plan, and an employee has worked there three years, he may be 20 percent vested. After six years, he will be 80 percent vested, and after seven years he will be 100 percent vested. (If Acme's plan began before 1989, however, different kinds of schedules may apply.)

FIDUCIARIES

ERISA requires Acme to appoint one or more fiduciaries to administer its pension and welfare benefit plans. A fiduciary is a trusted administrator of funds, and is responsible for investing pension and other benefit funds according to rules endorsed by the Treasury Department. The basic requirements are that the assets be managed prudently and that the investment portfolio be diversified. The funds cannot be transferred to Acme or to the fiduciary for their own benefit. See FIDUCIARY; TRUSTEE.

SUMMARY PLAN DESCRIPTION

When Tracy, an Acme employee, becomes eligible to participate in Acme's benefit plan, the company must give her a document called a summary plan description, which outlines the benefit plan in plain English. In addition, every year Acme must provide Tracy with a summary annual report on the plan's finances.

If Acme changes its plan in any way after Tracy becomes a participant, the changes must be given to her in writing. It is, in fact, not easy for a company to change the terms of its plan once the plan has been established. If Acme decides to alter the terms of its plan, or if it decides to eliminate the plan entirely, the company may do so, provided that it follows the legally required steps.

DISTRIBUTION OF BENEFITS

Some pension plans provide benefits in the form of a lump-sum distribution—that is, a one-time payment, which can be transferred to an Individual Retirement Account without incurring taxes. Others provide pension benefits as annuities, or regular, usually monthly payments. ERISA requires annuities to be "joint and survivor" annuities—that is, if an employee dies before his spouse, she will continue to receive benefits.

EMPLOYEE RIGHTS

Your rights as an employee are largely determined by the legal restrictions placed on your employer — and they are often few in number. Essentially, employers cannot discriminate in hiring, firing, or promoting employees on the basis of race, color, national origin, religion, sex, age, or disability. But otherwise, the employer-employee relationship is a matter of contract law. Unless your employment agreement (or union contract) lists special rights that you are entitled to as an employee, or unless you are employed by the government and thus have certain protections spelled out by law, your employer is generally free to set whatever policies he wishes as conditions of employment, even if these policies seem unreasonable. If you are what is known in legal language as an employee at will (one who may terminate his employment at any time)—and most employees are—your employer in turn can fire you at will and does not even have to give a reason for firing you.

EMPLOYEE PRIVACY

You probably regard your privacy as sacred, but your employer may not, depending on the circumstances.

Searching employees
Unreasonable searches and seizures are forbidden by federal and state laws, but these laws apply only to government activities; private employers are not bound by them. Employers often maintain that because they are burdened with increasing employee theft and use of illegal drugs in the workplace, they must resort to searches in order to control these problems. In general, employers have the right to search employees' lockers, work stations, briefcases, purses, lunchboxes, and other items that could be used to conceal stolen company property or illegal drugs. Cars parked on company lots may also be searched.

Use of company phones
Employers have the right to limit or prohibit the use of company telephones by employees for private calls. Today, some companies even "audit," or monitor, employees' phone

calls, and employers can make it a condition of employment that you permit them to do so.

Candid cameras

Employers may also conduct surveillance of workers by observing them at their desks and installing video cameras that show selected areas of the workplace. As long as the employer does not create an unnecessary invasion of privacy, such as installing video cameras in the restrooms, this monitoring activity is permissible.

PROHIBITED ACTIVITIES

Remember that although all of these actions are generally permitted when used for legitimate and legal business purposes, the situation becomes different when the employer exceeds certain limits. For example, an employer may not make physical threats toward an employee or refuse to allow him to leave the premises. Such actions could amount to assault and false imprisonment, and the employer could be sued.

An employer cannot single out employees for search or surveillance or similar activities on the basis of their race, religion, sex, and the like. If, for example, an employer searches the purses and briefcases only of Korean-American workers, the searches would be considered discriminatory and therefore illegal. But if the searches are applied to all employees, they will most likely be allowed.

YOUR BEHAVIOR OUTSIDE THE WORKPLACE

You may think that what you do when you are not at work is strictly your own business, but your employer may think otherwise. Employers have been permitted to fire people who were involved in illicit activities or who were discovered to be moonlighting at another job. They have also been allowed to fire employees for engaging in conduct that had a negative impact on the employer's reputation or business. For example, one company's decision to fire a member of the Ku Klux Klan was upheld by the court after the company showed that it faced business losses due to the employee's Klan-related activities. See also AGE DISCRIMINATION; EMPLOYEE HIRING AND FIRING; EMPLOYEE WORKING CONDITIONS; JOB DISCRIMINATION; PRIVACY RIGHTS; REFERENCE, EMPLOYEE; SMOKING.

EMPLOYEE WORKING CONDITIONS

Employers have an obligation to provide employees with a healthy and safe environment in which to work. In addition, they must provide special protection to workers subject to unique hazards. For example, a health-care company may be required by law to provide protective clothing and headgear to technicians who use radioactive materials. An assembly plant whose employees operate heavy machinery may be required to install special safety devices to prevent injuries. And workers at a noisy construction site may be required to wear protective ear coverings.

OSHA AND OTHER FEDERAL LAWS

Health and safety conditions in the workplace are governed primarily by federal law. The most important federal law protecting workers from job-related hazards is the Occupational Safety and Health Act (OSHA), which is administered by the Occupational Safety and Health Administration (also known as OSHA). If you suspect a violation of OSHA's safety rules, you should report it to the agency immediately. OSHA will investigate the matter, and if the violation is confirmed, the agency can impose penalties on the employer.

Most types of businesses fall under the jurisdiction of OSHA, except for family-owned farms and workplaces protected by other federal laws. Self-employed individuals are exempt from OSHA regulations, as are some businesses with very few employees. If you are unsure whether your employer is subject to OSHA regulations, look for a posted notice on workplace health and safety, which is required by OSHA, or contact your local OSHA office. For details on how to file a complaint with OSHA, see OCCUPATIONAL HEALTH AND SAFETY ADMINISTRATION (OSHA).

In addition to OSHA, there is other federal legislation designed to protect workers in industries such as nuclear power (the Atomic Energy Act), mining (the Federal Mine Safety and Health Act), airlines (the Federal Aviation Act), and railroads (the Federal Railroad Safety Authorization Act).

STATE LAWS

Because OSHA encourages states to develop their own health and safety standards, your state may have its own regulations governing the workplace. Since state plans must be approved by OSHA, they are usually equal to (or stricter than) federal standards. The important thing for workers to remember is that when workplace safety is regulated by a state agency, their complaints must be directed to the state agency, not to OSHA. Local or regional OSHA offices can tell you if a plan has been enacted in your state.

SMOKING IN THE WORKPLACE

Because of the growing concern about the adverse health effects of smoking, many workplaces limit the areas where employees may smoke, and some employers prohibit smoking entirely. In addition, many state and local governments are passing antismoking laws. See also SMOKING.

EMPLOYMENT AGENCY

The purpose of an employment agency is to bring job seekers and employers together. Employment agencies help job hunters by providing referral and counseling services, and they help employers by locating and screening job candidates. Agencies usually act on behalf of the employer, but they do provide a service to both parties, just as real estate agents do. Before you use an employment agency, you should be aware of your rights and your responsibilities.

SIGNING A CONTRACT

Employment agencies often require you to sign a contract before they will help you to find a job. You should read the contract carefully so that you will know whether you will owe the agency money, and if so, when.

Your contract should state the fee to be charged, who will have to pay it (you or the em-

CHECKLIST

Choosing the Right Employment Agency

Looking for a job is hard work, and finding the employment agency that can best help you is not easy either. Listed below are some questions you should ask before you register with an employment agency.

❑ HOW LONG HAS THE AGENCY BEEN IN BUSINESS?
Since a number of employment agencies go out of business fairly quickly, be careful to choose one that has a good reputation and a proven track record. To find out whether there have been any complaints about the agency you are considering, call your local Better Business Bureau.

❑ IS THE AGENCY EXPERIENCED IN PLACING PEOPLE WITH YOUR BACKGROUND?
Employment agencies are becoming more and more specialized. For example, an agency that primarily places engineers may not be able to help you find a job as a teacher.

❑ WILL THE AGENCY HELP YOU IMPROVE OR REFRESH YOUR JOB SKILLS?
Many agencies provide job seekers with access to word processors, computers, printers, and other facilities. If you need such services, find out whether the agency provides them.

❑ CAN THE AGENCY HELP ITS CUSTOMERS WITH RÉSUMÉS AND INTERVIEW SKILLS?
Many employment agencies will help you write a résumé and coach you on how to conduct yourself during a job interview. If you need this kind of help, find out how much you can expect before signing a contract. But beware of agencies that charge a fee up front for these services. They may offer little more than a poorly written résumé and a few photocopies.

❑ WHAT ARE THE TERMS OF THE CONTRACT?
Employment agencies will often ask you to sign a written contract before they will help you. Read it before you sign, and find out whether you have any financial obligation to the agency and whether the agency is entitled to a finder's fee even if you manage to locate a job on your own. Whether or not you will owe the agency money even if it fails to place you in a job is an important consideration.

ployer), and the conditions of payment. If you are responsible for the fee, as a rule you will have to pay it when you accept the job that the agency found for you. If you change your mind and never start work, the agency is usually entitled to its fee. You are responsible for paying the fee even if you quit the job soon after you take it.

If you start work and are later fired, some agencies may still require full payment; others may reduce the fee to a percentage of the original total. Some state laws restrict an employment agency's ability to collect full payment under these circumstances. At least one state, Pennsylvania, forbids an agency to collect its entire fee if the employee loses the job within 10 weeks after accepting it.

When you read your contract, check to see what happens if the agency was only partially responsible for finding you a job. Suppose that an agency sets up an appointment for you with an employer. Although you are not hired for that particular job, the company keeps your résumé and calls you later about another opening, for which you are hired. Even though the agency's role was indirect, its efforts to some degree resulted in your getting a job. Therefore, you may have to pay the agency's fee.

DISCRIMINATION BY EMPLOYMENT AGENCIES

Employment agencies cannot discriminate against job seekers. It is illegal, for instance, for an employment agency to refuse to refer an applicant to a prospective employer on the basis of age, sex, religion, race, color, national origin, or disability. Employment agencies are also prohibited from sending employers lists of job applicants that classify people according to one or more of these categories.

HEADHUNTERS

If you are in a management position, sometime during your career you may be contacted by an executive recruiter, or "headhunter." Headhunters use their contacts in the business world to learn about promising or successful managers, and then try to match these individuals with a company that is seeking employees with their qualifications.

Headhunters are generally legitimate business people, and some of them may be able to help you find a good job. But be wary of firms that claim to be executive recruiters but charge a fee. Many of these firms say they are able to "tap the hidden job market," providing access to personnel managers and top executives. In reality, however, they may offer little more than a résumé service and a list of telephone numbers for you to call. Any company that wants a big fee before it does any work for you should be viewed with caution. Consult your local consumer protection agency to find out whether a given firm has a questionable record.

OTHER CAUTIONS

Be careful, too, about dealing with firms that promise to find you a lucrative job in a foreign country. After the Gulf War in 1991, a number of companies began to advertise employment opportunities related to the rebuilding of Kuwait. They offered to obtain interviews and jobs in return for fees that sometimes ran into hundreds of dollars. In fact, no jobs were available for American workers, and in many cases these companies closed their doors and disappeared before any legal action could be taken against them.

Similarly, a number of companies provide information about federal government jobs, which you access by calling a 900 telephone number. There is nothing illegal about this service, but it is usually costly and unnecessary. You can learn about federal government jobs for free by calling or visiting the nearest federal Office of Personnel Management. You can learn about state government jobs by contacting your state's department of personnel or human resources.

ENGAGEMENT, BROKEN

After a long-distance courtship, Jessica agreed to marry Brian. To be with him, she quit her job in a large city and then moved to a small town, where she began working—without pay—as Brian's bookkeeper. Three months after the move, and a month before the wedding, Brian broke off the engagement, saying he did not love Jessica anymore. He asked her to return the engagement ring and leave.

A few days later, Jessica received the bill for their wedding invitations and wondered if she should sue Brian for what she felt he owed her. Does Jessica have any right to make Brian pay for a portion of the wedding expenses? Can she keep the ring? What about her moving costs and earnings from the job that she gave up?

BREACH OF PROMISE SUITS

Depending on the state she lives in, Jessica may be able to sue Brian for breach of promise (a form of breach of contract) and request damages, or compensation, for her monetary losses. For example, she may be able to recover her moving expenses, the earnings she forfeited by quitting her previous job, and even the salary she would have received from Brian as a paid bookkeeper. She may also recover the money she paid for her wedding gown and the deposits she paid for florists and caterers.

In some states, however, breach of promise suits for broken engagements (sometimes called heart-balm lawsuits) are not permitted. These states include Alabama, California, Colorado, Florida, Indiana, Maine, Massachusetts, Michigan, Nevada, New Hampshire, New Jersey, New York, Pennsylvania, and Wyoming. Maryland has abolished breach of promise suits except when the jilted woman is pregnant.

RETURN OF ENGAGEMENT GIFTS

Even in many of the states that prohibit heart-balm lawsuits, Jessica will probably be able to keep her engagement ring. In most states, because Brian broke the engagement, he has no right to expect the return of a gift he gave in contemplation of marriage. Jessica also has the right to ask Brian to return any gifts she gave him, since he broke the engagement. If Brian and Jessica had mutually agreed to break their engagement, they would each be obligated to return the gifts they received from each other. See also BREACH OF CONTRACT; BREACH OF PROMISE.

ENTRAPMENT

Entrapment takes place when law enforcement officers induce a person to commit a crime that he had not planned to commit and then prosecute him for the crime.

One day while walking down the street Karl was approached by Debbie, an undercover police officer. They started talking, and after a few minutes, Debbie said she had some marijuana if Karl wanted it. Karl had never thought of trying marijuana, but he liked Debbie and agreed to take some. Debbie pulled the marijuana out of her jacket and asked Karl to hold it for her. Then shortly after he accepted it, Karl was surrounded by policemen and arrested for possession of marijuana. At his trial, Karl used entrapment as his defense.

WHEN DECEPTION IS FAIR

On the issue of entrapment, the U.S. Supreme Court has stated: "A line must be drawn between the trap for the unwary innocent and the trap for the unwary criminal." Courts usually disapprove of trickery on the part of the police but allow it within certain limits. If someone already intends to commit a crime, and the police simply make it easier for the person to do so, their actions do not constitute entrapment.

Suppose the police send a female officer dressed in plain clothes into an area where several purse snatchings have occurred. If a man snatches her purse, there has been no entrapment because the police officer did not set up the crime or induce the man to commit it.

HOW THE COURTS DECIDE

To prove entrapment, the accused must usually show that the crime was planned by the police and that they used pressure, persuasion, trickery, or fraud to induce someone to commit it. The court must decide whether the police caught a real criminal or took advantage of an innocent person. In doing so, the judge considers how familiar the accused was with the type of crime in question and how likely he would have been to commit the crime without the entrapment.

Prosecuting attorneys in some states, for example, can introduce evidence of the defendant's previous crimes in order to demonstrate the intent to commit a similar offense. Other states, however, do not allow this kind of evidence, and the court's judgment is based only on whether the actions of the police would induce a normally law-abiding citizen to commit a crime.

ENVIRONMENTAL PROTECTION

Beginning in the 1960's, public awareness of the need to protect the environment led to important federal and state legislation, and the trend continues today. Acid rain, depletion of the ozone layer, hazardous wastes, and auto emissions are just a few of the environmental concerns of the 1990's.

The idea of protecting the environment is not new. The Federal Power Act of 1920 and the Fish and Wildlife Coordination Act of 1934 recognized the importance of maintaining an ecological balance. It was not until the 1960's, however, that federal and state legislatures began to enact laws that set standards for allowable levels of pollutants to preserve areas not yet threatened by pollution or contamination.

NATIONAL ENVIRONMENTAL POLICY ACT

The passage of the National Environmental Policy Act (NEPA) of 1969 signaled the federal government's recognition of the need to protect the environment. The act committed the federal government to working with state and local governments in monitoring the impact of proposed federal projects on the environment.

NEPA created the Council on Environmental Quality. Its role is to provide the president with annual reports on the state of the environment and to evaluate current and future federal efforts to protect it.

ENVIRONMENTAL PROTECTION AGENCY

As more laws and regulations were enacted, a central agency was needed to oversee all of the efforts to protect the environment. In 1970 President Richard M. Nixon issued an executive order establishing the Environmental Protection Agency (EPA) to administer most environmental laws and to coordinate environmental policies. The EPA establishes regulations, sets standards for emissions, determines whether chemicals are hazardous to the ecology or to human health, and oversees and enforces compliance from businesses and industries nationwide.

Although the Department of the Interior, the Department of Agriculture, and the Army Corps of Engineers bear some responsibility for protecting the environment, the major task belongs to the EPA. The following is a discussion of some of the laws and policies that the EPA enforces.

Clean Air Act

The Clean Air Act has undergone a number of revisions since it first became law in 1955. A major change occurred in 1970, when the responsibility for determining air-quality standards was transferred from the states to the federal government. The EPA was given the job of dealing with air pollution from all sources, including chemicals, motor vehicles, and industries.

Sulfur dioxide and nitrogen oxide, which are emitted from power plants, damage lakes, forests, and other ecosystems in the form of acid rain. The amendments to the Clean Air Act in 1990 mandate that emissions of these chemicals be reduced to control acid rain.

Scientific evidence shows that chlorofluorocarbons (or CFC's) and other chemicals are damaging the ozone layer. A possible association between CFC's and global warming has also added to the push for their regulation. The use of CFC's in aerosol cans was phased out by law in the 1980's, and the 1990 amendments call for a phase-out of the production and sale of all CFC's. Emphasis is placed on the recycling and disposal of existing CFC-producing chemicals, such as those used in air conditioners and refrigerators.

Motor vehicles are also major air polluters. The 1990 amendments to the Clean Air Act require gasolines that burn more cleanly and set stricter limits on auto emissions.

Federal Water Pollution Control Act

Enacted in 1948, the Federal Water Pollution Control Act initially focused on pollution caused by the discharge of waste from sewage-treatment plants, agricultural feedlots, and industrial plants. Subsequent amendments provide for the regulation of cleanup ef-

CHECKLIST

What You Can Do to Protect the Environment

Much of the job of protecting the environment is up to individuals like you. As a consumer, you can help in a number of ways:

❑ **BE ENERGY-CONSCIOUS.**
If you have energy-efficient appliances, a car that gets good mileage, and proper home insulation, you will save energy and a lot of money too.

❑ **RECYCLE.**
Glass, newspapers, cardboard, plastic containers, metal cans, and aluminum foil can all be recycled. If you don't have a recycling center in your community, try to get one started.

❑ **DISPOSE OF CHEMICAL WASTES WISELY.**
Never dispose of used motor oil, gasoline, or household chemicals by pouring them down a drain or into a sewer. Some communities provide for the pickup of hazardous wastes.

❑ **AVOID CONTAINER WASTE.**
Buy reusable containers and, when possible, choose products that are not overpackaged.

❑ **REPORT POLLUTERS.**
Report pollution violations to the EPA or your local environmental agency. If appropriate, file a lawsuit against a company or individual who is causing damage to the environment.

forts following spills of oil and other hazardous substances, and broaden the scope of the act to halt the discharge of pollutants and herbicides.

Safe Drinking Water Act
The Safe Drinking Water Act of 1974 gives the EPA the responsibility for finding out what chemicals and other pollutants contaminate public drinking water and for setting acceptable levels of bacteria, lead, radioactive substances, and other chemicals.

Lead Contamination Control Act
Concerns about lead in drinking water led to the 1988 Lead Contamination Control Act, which prohibits the manufacture of water coolers with lead-lined tanks. Coolers that had such tanks were recalled. The act also authorized federal grants to aid schools in reducing the levels of lead in their drinking-water systems.

Marine Protection, Research, and Sanctuaries Act
Ocean waters are protected under an act passed in 1972. One of its primary goals is to control the dumping of waste into the ocean. The act gives the EPA the authority to require companies to obtain a special permit for ocean dumping. It also allows the EPA to designate specific areas that can be used for dumping.

Federal Insecticide, Fungicide, and Rodenticide Act
Under the provisions of the Federal Insecticide, Fungicide, and Rodenticide Act, all pesticide products must be registered with the EPA before they can be sold. The manufacturer must show that these products do not cause an unreasonable risk to people or the environment and must test each pesticide to discover its potential for causing birth defects, cancer, and nerve damage.

Resource Conservation and Recovery Act
Provisions for the safe disposal of solid and hazardous wastes from both household and industrial sources are outlined in the Resource Conservation and Recovery Act. The act prohibits the disposal of a number of highly toxic chemicals. Anyone who generates, transports, or disposes of hazardous wastes is required to keep strict records of these activities, and any facility that stores or disposes of hazardous wastes must obtain a permit from the EPA.

Comprehensive Environmental Response, Compensation, and Liability Act
Hazardous-waste accidents are covered by CERCLA, which was passed in 1980. With its amendments the act, also known as Superfund, authorizes the EPA to require those responsible for hazardous-waste spills to clean up the damage. The EPA also has the option of cleaning up the hazardous-waste site itself and then suing those responsible for the costs involved.

Oil Pollution Act
Recent accidents involving oil spills, such as the *Exxon Valdez* disaster, resulted in the passage of the Oil Pollution Act of 1990. In an effort to minimize the likelihood of oil spills, the act requires oil tankers in U.S. territorial waters to have double hulls and calls for swift, effective action when

accidents occur. Penalties for oil spills have been increased dramatically.

Endangered Species Act
The Endangered Species Act of 1973, amended in 1988, gives the Department of the Interior the power to protect wildlife refuges and wildlife species whose survival is threatened. For example, it is a federal crime to buy, sell, possess, import, or export any animal or plant placed on the endangered-species list. As of 1992, the list included the grizzly bear, ocelot, ivory-billed woodpecker, Florida panther, red wolf, California condor, alligator, Florida golden aster, and Santa Cruz cypress.

Wilderness Act of 1964
A National Wilderness Preservation System was created by the Wilderness Act of 1964. As a result, more than 9 million acres of land were designated as national forests. The Alaska National Interest Lands Conservation Act of 1980 called for the protection of another 90 million acres from further economic development.

STATE AND LOCAL LAWS

Every state and many cities and towns have enacted environmental-protection laws, but they vary from place to place. Regulations that limit landfills or restrict the kinds of materials that can be added to a landfill, for example, are not the same in every state. A company that produces waste in one state may therefore try to ship it to one whose laws for disposal are more lenient. Conflicts that arise between states regarding their environmental laws may wind up in the federal courts, which have jurisdiction over disputes between states.

EQUAL PROTECTION OF THE LAWS

The 14th Amendment to the U.S. Constitution contains a clause prohibiting the governments of the individual states from denying any person the "equal protection of the laws." Under this clause, called the equal protection clause, the resident of any given state is entitled to the same rights as any other resident—insofar as those rights can be protected by the state.

Suppose that Marleen, an African-American businesswoman, has just moved to Middleton. As an ambitious newcomer, she would like to get to know the local business and community leaders, most of whom are members of the Willow Club. Marleen applies for a membership but is turned down. Because the club has no African-American members, Marleen suspects racial discrimination and files a lawsuit, claiming she has been denied equal protection of the laws.

If the Willow Club is funded and operated by the state and Marleen makes a good case that she was denied membership because of her race, she will probably win her lawsuit. However, if the Willow Club is privately run, her lawsuit will probably fail because equal protection of the laws does not apply to private organizations, no matter how discriminatory their rules may be.

Suppose the privately owned Willow Club conducts educational workshops and seminars for the Middleton business community, which are partially funded by the state. In this instance, Marleen's lawsuit would have a good chance of winning, because the equal protection clause prohibits discrimination by organizations supported or funded by the state. See also PRIVATE CLUB.

The equal protection clause is based on the premise that government should benefit everyone, not any particular group of people to the exclusion of others. The states may pass laws that apply to one group of persons only if doing so promotes legitimate state purposes. But a state may not classify people in an arbitrary way—the classification must have a rational basis and serve the interests of the public.

GOVERNMENT ACTION ON BEHALF OF SPECIFIC GROUPS

Equal protection does not require that all persons be treated in the same way. But it does require that when a state acts on behalf of a distinct group of people, it does so in order to promote a legitimate state purpose. For example, courts have found that minority job programs do not violate the equal protection clause because they serve to develop a state's human resources. Nor is the equal protection clause violated when wealthier individuals are taxed at a higher rate than others, because the increased revenue will be used to pay for government needs.

Conversely, if a person is denied his constitutional right to legal representation in a criminal proceeding because he cannot pay a lawyer, that person is being denied the equal protection of the laws. As a result, public defenders play an important role in courtrooms across the country.

PROHIBITED CLASSIFICATIONS

Under the current interpretation of the equal protection clause, certain groupings, or classifications, are almost always prohibited as violations of equal protection because they serve no legitimate state interest. Other classifications are frequently (but not always) prohibited.

Laws that classify people on the basis of race, color, national origin, or religion are almost always prohibited. Thus if Mary, a Baptist, becomes engaged to a Roman Catholic, but her application for a marriage license is denied because of a state statute against interdenominational marriage, that statute could be invalidated on equal-protection grounds. If Mary became engaged to another woman, however, and her marriage license was denied because of a state law prohibiting same-sex marriage, she would have no basis for a lawsuit because such laws apply equally to everyone and are deemed to serve a legitimate state interest.

Classifications based on sex are sometimes allowed, but only if they serve an important government objective. For example, suppose Tiffany, a police recruit, fails a demanding physical-agility test and is not appointed to the police force. Stating that women fail the test more often than men and that the test is therefore discriminatory, Tiffany sues the force, claiming that her rights to equal protection have been violated. Her lawsuit will probably fail, because courts have found that the physical demands of police work justify such tests. If, however, Tiffany and other women are passed over for promotions merely because they are women, their claims to being denied equal protection are justified.

Age is another classification that the court sometimes allows, but age-discrimination claims are always closely examined. For instance, it is not a violation of the equal protection clause to require people to reach a certain age before they can vote or serve in the military. This requirement is based on the grounds that a person must achieve a certain level of physical and mental development before he can intelligently elect a public official or undergo the strains of combat. Laws setting minimum-age requirements for drinking alcohol, driving, and receiving birth control information without parental consent have all been upheld for similar reasons.

The same kind of reasoning applies to classifications based on maximum age. For example, the equal protection clause is not violated by a state law that requires uniformed state police officers to retire when they reach the age of 50, nor by a statute that requires judges to retire at age 70. In cases challenging these laws, the courts have held that the state had a legitimate interest in assuring that its police officers possessed the physical strength and stamina of youth and that its judges possessed acute mental powers.

NO ARBITRARY CLASSIFICATIONS

For equal-protection analysis, it should be noted that a classification may never be arbitrary; it must always be rooted in a legitimate state interest. Thus it was found that a state university's retirement policy requiring that employees over 65 show "superior competence" as a condition of continued employment violated the equal protection clause. Similarly, a law that required the consent of the mother, but not the father, to the adoption of their illegitimate child was found to violate the clause. Both laws were deemed arbitrary and unrelated to any legitimate state interest. See also CIVIL RIGHTS; CONSTITUTION, U.S.; DISCRIMINATION; RIGHTS, INDIVIDUAL.

EQUITABLE DISTRIBUTION

Dorothy and Doug have been married for 15 years. While Doug was going to engineering school, Dorothy worked full time to help pay his tuition costs. Once he began working, however, she stayed at home, taking care of the house and their two children. Unfortunately, Dorothy and Doug have grown apart over the years and have recently agreed to get a divorce. But before their divorce is finalized, they must divide their property. In their state, as in most states, when a married couple divorces, their property is divided according to a set of guidelines known as equitable distribution.

ABC's OF EQUITABLE DISTRIBUTION

When you get a divorce, the court must divide your property according to the principles of equitable distribution (unless you live in a state where community-property laws apply). The court must try to divide the property as fairly as possible, taking into account such factors as these:

- ❑ You and your spouse's station in life and the standard of living you were accustomed to during the marriage.
- ❑ The particular needs of each of you, with consideration given to such factors as age, health, and earning skills.
- ❑ Evidence of fault or marital misconduct on the part of one or both of you that may have led to the divorce.
- ❑ How long you were married.
- ❑ The source of jointly held property (whether, for instance, it was originally acquired by or given to one spouse rather than both).
- ❑ The value of your separate property compared to the financial needs of your spouse.
- ❑ The earning capacity of you and your spouse, and whether at an earlier time one partner sacrificed his or her own education and career goals in order to support the other.
- ❑ The provisions for child custody and child support.
- ❑ Homemaking and child-rearing services rendered by one or both of you during the course of the marriage.
- ❑ Debts incurred or dissipation of assets by one or both of you while you were married.

EQUITABLE DISTRIBUTION VERSUS COMMUNITY PROPERTY

Property may be divided in one of two ways: through the principles of *equitable distribution* (which have been adopted in most states) or those of *community property* (which apply in just a few). In community-property states, the law assumes that husband and wife are each entitled to 50 percent of the marital property. By contrast, in equitable-distribution states, the law assumes only that each party has an interest in the marital assets—that is, in property owned by the marriage partners; the divorce court will decide what percentage is appropriate. For a list of community-property states, see COMMUNITY PROPERTY.

HOW MARITAL ASSETS ARE VALUED

Because Dorothy and Doug live in an equitable-distribution state, the law will assume that each of them has contributed to the accumulation of assets. While Dorothy has not worked outside their home for the last decade, her efforts in taking care of the home and caring for the children have a monetary value. In addition, Dorothy's work as a homemaker is recognized as contributing to Doug's ability to earn a salary and invest some of his earnings.

Even if Doug has title to the house, the car, and the savings bonds purchased during their marriage, equitable-distribution laws guarantee that Dorothy has an interest in that property. However, because state laws differ, the assets to which Dorothy is entitled will vary from state to state (and from judge to judge).

JOINT VERSUS SEPARATE PROPERTY

Dorothy and Doug must find out if their state makes a distinction between joint and separate property. If it does not, all of the property owned by both of them at the time of their divorce will be considered joint property and subject to division by the court, no matter when or how it was acquired.

If they happen to live in a state that does recognize a distinction between joint and separate property, the court will have to consider other matters, such as when the property was acquired and whether it was a gift or part of an inheritance. Suppose Dorothy owned a lakeside summer cottage before her marriage to Doug. If her state recognizes separate property, the court will not grant Doug any interest in the cottage. Similarly, if Doug's aunt died during their marriage, leaving him a brand-new car, the car would be considered his separate property. However, if his aunt was fond of both of them and specifically left the car to both Dorothy and Doug, the gift would be treated as joint property.

In some states gifts from one spouse to the other are considered separate property, while in other states they are treated as joint property. Wedding gifts, unless obviously intended for use by one party only, are usually assumed to be part of the family home, and so will be considered joint property.

Dorothy and Doug quickly realize that it is no easy matter to distinguish separate from joint property. For instance, before his marriage to Dorothy, Doug had a separate bank account. After their marriage he put that account into a joint fund used to buy their house. In most states, this money would probably be treated as joint property, because it would be almost impossible to separate Doug's contribution from Dorothy's after so many years had passed.

FUTURE INCOME

Before the divorce judge, Dorothy claims that she is entitled to some portion of Doug's future income. She points out that since she worked to put her husband through engineering school, his earning power was increased as a direct result of her efforts.

Unfortunately for Dorothy, in her state and most others, future income, enhanced earning capacity, professional licenses, and degrees from a college or university are not subject to equitable distribution in divorce.

Although most states do not recognize claims on future income, they will often compensate for this by awarding alimony. And the amount may be affected by the court's appreciation of the fact that one spouse gave up certain opportunities of her own in order to allow the other to pursue his educational and career goals. See also ALIMONY; COMMUNITY PROPERTY; DIVORCE.

EQUITY

The word *equity* has two different meanings that pertain to the law. The first and simplest refers to the value of property, minus any amount owed on or secured by that property. For example, suppose your home is worth $100,000, but you owe a mortgage balance of $85,000. Your equity in your home is $15,000.

The second meaning of equity, which will be discussed in more detail, concerns the fairness or impartiality of legal proceedings. It involves a complex set of rules first established in England and later adopted in American courts.

HISTORICAL ROOTS OF EQUITY

Originally, there were two different kinds of courts in England (and also in America until the 1930's)—courts of law and courts of equity (also known as courts of chancery). If a person wanted to receive a certain sum of money, he would bring his case to a court of law. If he wanted to right a wrong that could not be satisfied by a money payment, he would bring his case to a court of equity.

Suppose that a century ago Alexander, a famous impresario, signed Natalia, the most famous soprano of her day, to perform in concert. The day before the concert, the temperamental Natalia had a violent disagreement with Alexander and refused to sing. Alexander sued her in a court of law for the amount he lost in unsold and returned tickets. He also sued her in a court of equity. Although he could not force Natalia to sing, he could ask the court to issue an injunction—an equitable order preventing her from singing for anyone else until she fulfilled her contract with him.

Principles of equity require "clean hands," meaning that Alexander could not sue in a court of equity if he had not acted in a completely fair manner. Thus, if Natalia had canceled because Alexander had contracted to put her in a respected concert hall but at the last minute asked her to sing in a neighborhood pub, his hands would be considered "unclean" and he would be unlikely to get the injunction he requested.

EQUITY TODAY

At present, in most areas of the United States, the courts allow people to seek equitable claims and monetary claims at the same time. Equity awarded by the court can take the form of an *injunction* (a court ruling that is meant to prevent future harm to someone); a *declaratory judgment* (a ruling that declares what a person's rights are); *specific performance* (a ruling that directs one party to comply with the terms of a contract); or *restitution, reformation,* or *rescission* (actions taken by the court to remedy an unfair contract).

ESCALATOR CLAUSE

An escalator clause in a contract allows a party to receive more money if certain unpredictable circumstances occur.

Suppose Joe is a contractor who agrees to build an addition to your house. When the contract is signed, Joe estimates that construction will cost $10,000. Because construction estimates are notoriously unreliable, Joe asks for an escalator clause in his contract. If the cost of Joe's building materials suddenly and unaccountably increases, the escalator clause permits Joe to charge you more. It protects Joe's ability to make a profit under the terms of the contract despite unforeseen cost increases.

An escalator clause may lead to abuses. The best way to protect yourself is to refuse to sign a contract that contains one, or to sign it only if the escalation is limited to a reasonable percentage of the base amount. Although there are no legal limits on the increases called for in escalator clauses, the courts will not enforce those that are clearly unconscionable. See also CONTRACT.

ESCROW

Escrow means that money or documents are being temporarily held by a neutral third party until all the conditions of a contract are satisfied. Escrow is most often used in real estate transactions.

Suppose that Mary agrees to buy office space from Atlas Realty. Before the contract is signed, she agrees to put her down payment "in escrow," meaning that she gives the money to a third party (or escrow agent), who will hold it in a special account until the closing. Mary does this as a sign of good faith, and, in turn, Atlas lets the escrow agent hold the deed to the property. See HOME BUYING AND SELLING.

ESTATE PLANNING

Your estate is the sum total of what you own (including all your real estate and personal property) when you die. If you own a significant amount of property, you should have an estate plan. Even relatively small estates can benefit from wise planning, and for people who have estates in excess of $600,000, estate planning is an absolute must. Without it, a sizable chunk of the estate could end up in the hands of the government or in the pockets of lawyers. See ESTATE TAX; WILL.

THE NEED FOR ESTATE PLANNING

Estate planning is more than just writing a will and providing for your survivors after you are gone. It also involves taking steps to arrange for the transfer of property to your survivors in ways that are legal but will minimize high estate taxes. A sound estate plan will also reduce the costs of probate—the process by which the court distributes property to heirs. See PROBATE.

ESTATE-PLANNING OPTIONS

Here are some common estate-planning options that you can use to reduce probate expenses and delays, as well as help preserve your property:

Joint tenancy

You and your spouse (or someone else) can own your house as a "joint tenancy with right of survivorship." This means that when one of you dies, the house will automatically pass to the other person and will not be subject to probate. See JOINT TENANCY.

Totten trust

You can open a bank account "payable on death" to another

person. For example, the signature card of Marla's bank account might read "Marla Jones, owner, payable on death to Carl Jones." When Marla dies, Carl will become the sole owner of the account, which will not be treated as part of her estate. Savings bonds can also be purchased this way. See TOTTEN TRUST.

Life insurance
Be sure to name your spouse or other family member, not your estate, as the beneficiary on your life insurance policy. In this way, the policy is not considered a part of your estate for probate purposes, although the benefit still may be subject to state or federal estate taxes.

Living trusts
You can create a "living trust" payable to one or more persons. Because the property is held in a trust created during your lifetime, it passes outside your estate to those you have named, and so is not subject to probate and administration costs. See LIVING TRUST.

Cash gifts
You can avoid estate taxes and probate by giving cash gifts during your lifetime. You are allowed to give up to $10,000 per year to the person of your choice, and married couples can make a combined gift of up to $20,000 per year to anyone they choose without having to pay any gift taxes.

THE NEED FOR A WILL

Even if you have a comprehensive estate plan, you should still have a will. Most people have property that cannot be provided for by using the estate-planning options outlined above.

Suppose Abe's Aunt Helen dies and leaves her house to him in her will. Abe, a millionaire, dies before he can create a joint tenancy with a right of survivorship for himself and his sister, Diane. As a result, the house becomes a part of his estate, subject to the costs and delays of estate administration. See JOINT TENANCY.

But at least Abe had a will. If he had none, state law would determine who would inherit the house, and if he had children or other brothers and sisters, under the laws of most states Diane would not have received the house as Abe had wished. See also DYING WITHOUT A WILL.

PLANNING YOUR OWN ESTATE

It may be possible for you to put together a do-it-yourself estate plan, in that an abundance of self-help materials are currently available on the subject. However, you should keep in mind that the tax ramifications of estate planning are complex, and you may want to seek professional advice.

Also, proper estate planning requires formal legal documents. If the documents are not correctly completed, the consequences could be disastrous for your survivors. For example, if a trust document is incorrectly drafted, you could jeopardize the right of your survivors to receive trust income. If your will is vaguely worded or is not signed according to the requirements of the laws of your state, your estate could be subject to lawsuits challenging its terms.

GETTING PROFESSIONAL HELP

Even if you plan your own estate, you should have the plan reviewed by a lawyer with experience in estate planning.

Many insurance agents, financial consultants, and accountants also provide estate-planning services. If you use one of them, you should first find out whether the person has anything to gain by helping you. For example, an insurance agent earns a commission on each policy he sells. This does not mean that the policy he recommends is a bad idea, or that his advice is not helpful. It does mean, however, that the agent is less likely to give you unbiased advice. For this reason you should consult a lawyer, accountant, or other professional who has nothing to gain (except his fee) by examining your estate plan. See also FINANCIAL PLANNER.

ESTATE TAX

All of the property a person owns at the time of his death is known as his estate. Estates are subject to both federal and state taxes. Because state estate taxes vary, ask an attorney or accountant about your state's laws. See also INHERITANCE TAX.

On the federal level, you do not have to pay estate taxes unless your estate exceeds $600,000. A federal tax return must be filed for every estate that exceeds $600,000 in value. It usually must be filed within nine months of the date of death, but extensions may be allowed. The amount of tax is based on the value of the deceased's "gross estate," minus certain deductions and credits.

GROSS ESTATE

To calculate the gross estate, the executor—or the estate's administrator (a person or entity appointed by the court when there is no will)—must inventory the deceased's property, placing a value on each item. The gross estate includes all of a person's assets, from tangible personal property, such as furniture, clothing, jewelry, cars, and appliances, to cash, bank accounts, stocks, bonds, and other money assets. Real estate, partnerships, and other business interests must also be accounted for in an estate inventory, and life insurance policies may be included too. If the deceased held promissory notes, loans, or mortgages representing money owed to him, they are part of the estate.

DEDUCTIONS

Funeral and estate administration expenses cannot be deducted until the inventory is complete. Administration expenses include attorneys' and accountants' fees, appraisal costs, and the cost for conducting a sale of any estate property. Often an executor or administrator is required to carry out certain wishes of the deceased, such as forgiving debts, which are then deducted. Other deductions include mortgages on the deceased's property, gifts to charity, and losses resulting from fire, storm, or theft.

For most people, one of the most important deductions is the marital deduction. If the deceased was married at the time of death, the marital deduction allows an unlimited amount of property to be transferred to the surviving spouse without being taxed. In this way, jointly held marital property is taxed only once, on the death of the surviving spouse.

Special tax considerations apply to estates over $600,000 when you do not leave the entire amount to your spouse. Your tax adviser can explain in detail the tax consequences for the estate of a surviving spouse inheriting more than $600,000 via the marital deduction.

CREDITS

After the deductions from the gross estate have been subtracted, an estimated tax is computed. It is then necessary to determine what tax credits apply to the estate. Every estate is allowed a credit of $192,000, which is equal to the tax on the first $600,000 of an estate's value. If an estate is valued at less than $600,000, it will not usually be subject to federal estate tax.

Tax credits are also available for property that the deceased inherited from a person who died less than 10 years earlier if the inherited property was included (and taxed) in the donor's estate. In addition, death or inheritance taxes paid to any state or foreign country may be credited against any federal estate tax owed.

INCOME TAX

Suppose an estate consists largely of stocks, bonds, and savings accounts, and the assets continue to earn income after a person dies. From the date of death until the assets of the estate are distributed to heirs, any income earned by such assets is subject to federal income tax paid out of the assets of the estate.

Under federal law, taxable income earned by an estate must be reported annually on IRS Form 1041 (Fiduciary Income Tax Return) if the gross income amounted to more than $600. If the income was given to a beneficiary of the estate during the tax year, the beneficiary must pay the income tax.

If the deceased lived in a state that imposes individual income tax, the executor or administrator must also file a state income tax return.

REDUCING ESTATE TAXES

There are several ways to reduce estate taxes, but they require you to give up control of some of your property while you are still alive. For example, you can make annual cash gifts of up to $10,000 each to family members and friends without incurring gift taxes while you are alive, or estate taxes when you die. Or you can execute an irrevocable trust that gives complete control of some or all of your property to another. See also GIFT; TRUST.

ESTIMATE

Because Al's car has been acting up recently, he takes it to Sandy, his mechanic. Sandy listens to the motor for a minute or two but cannot pinpoint the problem. Al agrees to leave the car so that Sandy can examine it more thoroughly and give Al an estimate of the repair cost.

Sandy reports that the car's valves need replacing. She estimates that the job will cost $600. At Sandy's garage Al signs a work order authorizing her to begin work. The next week, however, when Al returns to pick up his car, Sandy hands him a bill for $660.

Can Sandy charge Al more than her estimate? Probably. Since any estimate, by definition, is not an exact figure, a merchant is not bound by it. In most states, Sandy can legally raise her bill, but only by a limited amount over her estimate. If after beginning the work she realizes that her estimate was especially low, or if the work required is more extensive than she first thought, Sandy must inform Al of the revised estimate and have him authorize it before she continues.

Sandy also sent Al a $30 bill for her estimate. Although many businesses offer free estimates as a courtesy, there is no law prohibiting Sandy from charging for her services. As always, the buyer should beware. Some companies take advantage of the widespread belief that estimates are free by offering an estimate for work that needs to be done; then they bill the unwary customer. Unless you have a definite understanding that an estimate is free, you may find yourself harassed by a collection agency and even faced with a lawsuit if you refuse to pay the bill.

To protect yourself, always find out in advance whether an estimate is free and get it in writing. You will then have evidence of your agreement in case the company later tries to charge you. If a company advertises free estimates and then tries to bill you, you have no obligation to pay.

EUTHANASIA

From the Greek word meaning "easy death," euthanasia, or mercy killing, has become an increasingly controversial topic in the past decade. Because modern medical procedures allow life to be prolonged—but not necessarily improved, and sometimes worsened—medical and legal experts have debated whether euthanasia is a valid and merciful method of ending suffering or whether it is a violation of society's prohibition against murder.

In the early 1990's the issue of euthanasia was brought into focus by Dr. Jack Kevorkian, a Michigan physician who invented a device that helps people commit suicide. Kevorkian was indicted by a Michigan grand jury for his role in the voluntary deaths of people who were chronically ill. The charges against Dr. Kevorkian were dropped, but in other cases the courts have tended to regard euthanasia as murder.

Several states, such as California, Maine, New Hampshire, and Washington, have proposed laws that would permit a mentally competent person with a terminal illness to obtain a doctor's assistance to speed death. But to date no state has passed such a law.

Euthanasia should not be confused with the withdrawal of life-support systems, which may be done at the request of a terminally ill patient or his family. See also Death; Living Will.

EVICTION

Sue is Arnold's tenant. In legal terms, Sue is said to be "in possession of" Arnold's premises. However, if Sue does not pay her rent (or otherwise violates the terms of her lease), Arnold may decide to begin eviction proceedings—the process by which a landlord acts to reclaim possession of his premises.

Eviction is of two kinds: actual and constructive. Actual eviction occurs when the landlord takes direct action to remove the tenant. Constructive eviction occurs when the landlord has willfully created such intolerable conditions that the tenant leaves on his own.

ACTUAL EVICTION

Actual eviction, the forcible removal of a tenant from a landlord's premises, may be lawful or unlawful. If Arnold changes the locks on Sue's apartment, he has broken the law in most states. More commonly, a landlord will begin legal eviction proceedings in state or local housing court.

The eviction process
Suppose Sue continues to pay Arnold rent but refuses to va-

cate her apartment after her lease expires, becoming a "holdover" tenant. Or suppose Sue still has her lease but fails to pay rent. In either case, Arnold may go to court and initiate what is called a summary proceeding to evict her from the building.

A summary proceeding (also known as summary ejectment, dispossessory warrant proceeding, forcible detainer, or simply landlord-and-tenant proceeding) is generally a simple and straightforward affair. The only issue before the court is whether Sue should be removed from the premises because she has failed to pay the rent or because she is a holdover tenant.

If other issues are at stake, such as Arnold's claim that Sue damaged his property, the situation is more complicated. Arnold will not be able to raise these issues in a summary proceeding. He will have to initiate a separate lawsuit, which is likely to take longer to resolve.

Eviction proceedings begin like other lawsuits. Arnold must file a petition, or complaint, with the court listing his grievances. He must then serve Sue with the petition and with a notice of petition informing her that he has initiated eviction proceedings and stating the time and place of the hearing. Sue has to answer the petition, including any defenses she has to Arnold's charges.

Defenses

In her answer to Arnold's charges, Sue may present the defense that she is not a holdover tenant because the lease promised her 12 months' occupancy and she was not able to move in until 10 months ago because Arnold was renovating the apartment. Or Sue may claim that she has not paid her rent because the heating system in Arnold's building is faulty and he refuses to fix it. In either situation, Sue will be more likely to convince the court if she can provide proof of her claims.

Suppose Sue agrees that she owes some but not all of the back rent. The court may allow her to pay Arnold and remain in the apartment. However, Sue may be obliged to pay Arnold's court costs for bringing the eviction proceedings.

If the court agrees with Arnold that Sue is unlawfully in possession of Arnold's premises, it will issue an eviction order. The order is used to obtain a warrant that is given to a sheriff or marshal, who will come to Sue's apartment and see that she gives up the premises. Prior to eviction, Sue will ordinarily be given several days' notice that a warrant has been issued in order to give her time to get out.

CHECKLIST

Steps Leading to an Eviction

Before a landlord can evict a tenant from a rented house or apartment, he must follow a series of legal steps. Although these steps vary both with the circumstances and with local laws, they tend to follow the same general pattern.

❑ **BREACH OF THE LEASE.**
First, you must have breached (violated the terms of) the lease by not paying rent, by remaining beyond the time specified in the lease, or by some other serious misconduct.

❑ **NOTICE OF THE BREACH.**
The landlord must then give you notice of the breach and an opportunity to remedy it (by paying the back rent, for example). The notice must also state that the landlord intends to evict you if the breach is not remedied within a specified number of days.

❑ **EVICTION ORDER.**
If you fail to remedy the breach, the landlord must go to court to get an eviction order.

❑ **COURT HEARING.**
You must be given the opportunity to be heard by the court and to raise defenses to the landlord's charges.

❑ **COURT DECISION.**
If you are found in breach of the lease, the court may allow yet another period of time for you to remedy the breach and remain in the house, or it may order you to move out within a specified period of time.

❑ **EVICTION.**
If you fail to do as the court orders, the landlord may ask the local sheriff to enter the premises and remove your possessions, allowing the landlord to regain control of the property.

If, after eviction, Sue remains convinced that Arnold wrongfully evicted her from his premises, she can bring a lawsuit against him. In addition to regaining possession, Sue might be able to recover her moving expenses, lost profits (if she happened to be a commercial tenant), and the costs of defending herself in the eviction proceeding.

CONSTRUCTIVE EVICTION

Suppose Arnold wants to tear down his building and sell the property to a developer for a princely sum. He deliberately does not repair the heating system and elevator when they break down, hoping to make life so uncomfortable for Sue and the other tenants in the building that they will have to move out. This is known as constructive eviction.

Constructive eviction is any action (or inaction) that violates the basic right of every tenant to have the normal use and "quiet enjoyment" of her property. A landlord's failure to provide heat, water, and lighting or to maintain elevators can also be constructive eviction. In such situations, however, the landlord must be notified, preferably in writing, and given a chance to repair the defect. The tenant should keep a copy of her letter.

Proving constructive eviction

To prove constructive eviction, Sue must show that Arnold intended to deprive her of the normal use and quiet enjoyment of her apartment. She can do this by documenting both his actions and her efforts to have him stop. In addition, she must show that the actions were so intolerable that she was forced to move out.

Surrender

Suppose Arnold tells Sue to move out and, without a word of protest, she does so. This is called surrender. Because Sue voluntarily gave up possession, she cannot later argue that Arnold evicted her. See also LANDLORD; LEASE.

EVIDENCE

Evidence consists of anything (such as records, objects, documents, or testimony from witnesses) that is presented in court to prove a point. The rules of evidence govern what kinds of information may be presented at a trial—that is, whether the evidence is admissible or inadmissible.

ADMISSIBLE EVIDENCE

Relevance determines whether evidence is admissible. Suppose Sam wrote a letter to his business partner, Ralph, saying that he intended to substitute sweaters made by another knitwear firm for the 100 jeweled sweaters ordered by Jan's Boutique. The letter would be relevant evidence in a breach of contract suit that Jan filed later over the substitution. However, a memo from Ralph to Sam urging him to increase production of jeweled sweaters would not be relevant.

Evidence of past crimes is frequently deemed inadmissible because it is irrelevant. Such evidence forces the defendant to defend himself against past charges, and it tends to divert the jury's attention from evidence relating to the current case.

Direct versus circumstantial evidence

All evidence is either *direct* or *circumstantial.* Direct evidence stands on its own. For example, at Frank and Kathy's divorce trial, Tod swears that he saw Frank having dinner with Monica and holding her hand across the table. Tod's testimony is direct evidence.

But suppose Tod testifies that Frank, who is always prompt at meetings, showed up at a board meeting one hour late, with his hair tousled and a pink smudge on his collar. In this case, Tod's testimony is circumstantial evidence. It may point to Frank's having an extramarital affair, but it does not establish that fact, and it especially does not prove that Monica was involved.

If enough circumstantial evidence accrues, however, it can in some cases decide the issue. Suppose another witness saw Frank and Monica in Frank's car, with Monica applying lipstick before stepping out and hailing a taxi. The jury might conclude that the total circumstantial evidence was enough to convince them.

Other categories of evidence

Admissible evidence can take a number of forms other than the testimony of witnesses under oath. It may be a document, an object, or a demonstration. The letter that Sam wrote to Ralph, for example, is termed *documentary evidence*. So is Frank and Kathy's marriage certificate, if introduced as evidence. But if Kathy found the keys to Monica's apartment in Frank's suit, the keys would be called *real evidence*.

If a chemist testified that the pink stain was salad dressing, not lipstick, and provided scientific evidence showing the difference between the stains, the evidence would be referred to as *demonstrative evidence*.

INADMISSIBLE EVIDENCE

Certain kinds of evidence are prohibited in court—that is, they are termed inadmissible.

Opinion and speculation
Suppose Tod is permitted to testify that he heard Frank and Kathy arguing and that Kathy had stormed out of the room looking very upset. He would probably not be permitted to say that he could tell from her appearance that Frank had just told her he loved Monica. Opinion and speculation are generally not allowed, unless a person testifies as an expert witness. See EXPERT WITNESS.

Character or reputation
Evidence that supports or casts doubt on a person's character or reputation is usually not admissible, since it may divert attention from the facts. If someone has a good reputation, it does not mean that he did not break the law, and vice versa. However, sometimes such evidence is allowed. For example, a witness might be called to testify that Tod, who says he often saw Frank with Monica, has a habit of lying.

Hearsay evidence
Hearsay evidence does not come from the direct personal knowledge of the witness. In the divorce proceeding of Frank and Kathy, if Tod says that Frank's friend Wally told Tod that Frank had told him that he was going to leave Kathy, the evidence would be hearsay and the judge would not allow it. Hearsay evidence is not admissible in a trial because it is considered unreliable. For example, Tod could have misunderstood Wally, and Wally himself could have wrongly interpreted Frank's words. See also HEARSAY.

EXCLUSIONARY CLAUSE

An exclusionary clause is the part of a contract that restricts what the parties can do to remedy the situation if their contract is broken. Suppose Jay, a dishware merchant, agrees to buy 10,000 coffee cups from Bob. Both sign a contract with an exclusionary clause stating that Jay cannot force Bob to sell if Bob changes his mind before shipping the goods. The day before Bob is to send the coffee cups to Jay, he pulls out of the deal. Because of the exclusionary clause, Jay cannot force Bob to deliver the cups, although other remedies may be available. See BREACH OF CONTRACT; CONTRACT; DAMAGES.

EXECUTOR AND ADMINISTRATOR

When you make out a will, you must name an executor who will handle your estate after your death. If you do not have a will, the court will appoint an administrator to handle your estate. Many states call executors and administrators "personal representatives."

CRITERIA

You should choose as your executor someone in whom you have absolute trust and confidence. An executor should be someone (or some institution, such as your bank) that is extremely well organized and reliable. After your death, he will be responsible for paying your debts (including estate taxes, if any) and for distributing, selling, or otherwise managing your property according to your wishes.

Your executor's actions will be reviewed by a judge or other officials of the probate court, which has the authority to invalidate an executor's decisions if they are found to be questionable or improper. If necessary, the probate court can revoke the executor's authority to act for the estate.

You can require an executor to be bonded to ensure against the possibility that he might take the property for his own personal gain. But because the cost of the bond is charged to the estate, the amount that the beneficiaries will receive is reduced. Therefore, most people choose to waive the bonding requirement. See also ESTATE PLANNING; ESTATE TAX; PROBATE; WILL.

NAMING AN EXECUTOR

Legally, you can name just about anyone you want to serve as executor for your estate, provided that you select someone of legal age who is competent to perform the necessary duties (see the checklist at right). Ideally, she should be familiar with your personal and financial affairs. For this reason, many married people name their spouses, adult children, or close personal friends. Although usually not required, it is wise to pick someone who lives nearby. This makes it easier for the executor to take care of such administrative details as settling the deceased's personal affairs, closing bank accounts, selling property, and appearing in court.

CO-EXECUTORS

Sometimes a testator (a person who makes a will) names two individuals, or an individual and a financial institution, as co-executors. Although most states permit such an arrangement, it is not usually advisable. If the co-executors disagree on how to administer the estate, they must go to court to have the dispute settled. This will delay the settlement and distribution of the estate. Naming co-executors also means extra fees that must be paid out of the estate.

Occasionally, however, naming a co-executor may be advisable. For example, if you want to name your niece executor because you trust her to carry out your wishes, but she is not experienced in financial matters, you can name a co-executor to assist her.

EXECUTOR'S CONSENT

Before naming a person as executor in your will, ask his per-

CHECKLIST

Your Duties as Executor of an Estate

If you are named as the executor of someone's estate, your list of chores may seem daunting, but keep in mind that you will be permitted to hire attorneys, accountants, and other professionals to help you with the more technical aspects of your duties. Even so, as the executor, you are the one who has the ultimately responsibility to do the following:

❑ **TAKE THE WILL TO PROBATE COURT.**
Here you will receive the court's authorization (called letters testamentary) to take control of the deceased person's property and proceed as executor.

❑ **OPEN A CHECKING ACCOUNT IN THE NAME OF THE ESTATE.**
Expenses of the estate will be paid out of this account, and all money owed to the estate will be deposited in it.

❑ **TAKE AN INVENTORY.**
Obtain an itemized appraisal of all the real estate and personal property in the estate.

❑ **MAKE THE PROPER ANNOUNCEMENTS.**
Notify all of the deceased person's known creditors of his or her death, and publish notices in local newspapers announcing your appointment as executor, noting the time limit for filing claims against the estate.

❑ **FILE CLAIMS.**
These include claims for life insurance, Social Security, and employee death benefits.

❑ **TRANSFER PROPERTY.**
This may involve transferring personal property to the estate's name and investing or selling assets as necessary to fulfill the terms of the will.

❑ **HANDLE UNRESOLVED LAWSUITS.**
You must pursue any claims or lawsuits that were pending at the time the person died.

❑ **PAY DEBTS.**
You must pay all of the estate's legitimate debts and contest any unjustified claims.

❑ **PAY TAXES.**
You will have to prepare state and federal income and estate tax returns and pay all taxes due out of the assets of the estate.

❑ **REPORT TO THE PROBATE COURT.**
Submit an accounting of your actions as executor to the probate court, along with a schedule for distributing the remaining assets to the beneficiaries named in the will.

❑ **DISTRIBUTE THE PROPERTY.**
Property must be passed to the beneficiaries, and any property placed in trust must be transferred to the designated trustees.

❑ **GET DISCHARGED.**
Petition the probate court for a final discharge of your duties as an executor.

mission to make sure that he is able and willing to serve. Similarly, carefully consider any request from someone asking you to serve as her executor. If you are not willing to take on the duties, it is better to say so.

In your own will, you should name an alternate executor, in case your executor cannot serve or refuses to do so at the time of your death. If this happens and you have not named an alternate, the court will appoint someone who may not be as scrupulous in carrying out your wishes or as diligent in preserving your assets as a relative or friend of your choice.

MAKING THE EXECUTOR'S JOB EASIER

After you name an executor, give him a copy of your will to let him know in advance what he will have to do, and give him the chance to discuss with you any questions he may have about your intentions. If you decide not to discuss these matters with him, either because you wish to keep your intentions private or because the executor is an heir to your estate, at least let him know where you keep your will.

Take note: never put a will in a bank safe-deposit box. This box may be sealed upon your death and can take months to open, thus slowing up the distribution of your estate.

SPECIAL RESPONSIBILITIES

If you become an executor, you are ultimately responsible for carrying out the terms of the will and for paying all taxes that are due. If you should neglect to pay taxes while you are administering the estate, you may find that you are personally responsible for paying them after the estate is settled. Similarly, if the beneficiaries decide that you did not act in the best interest of the estate—if you paid out claims that they thought were unjustifiable or made unwise investments, for example—they might sue you.

EXECUTOR'S FEES

State laws entitle an executor to get paid for administering an estate. In some states the fee is a percentage of the total value of the property. In others, the probate court sets a reasonable fee for the executor's services.

Because these fees are deducted from the estate, an executor with close ties to the estate (such as a family member) often waives the right to receive payment for his duties.

ADMINISTRATORS

Most of what has been said about executors also applies to administrators. The principal difference is that, because an administrator is court-appointed when a person dies without a will, and must follow the rules set out in state law, she might not distribute your estate as you would have liked. An administrator is also certain to receive a fee, payable from your estate. Thus it is in your best interest both to have a will and to name an executor.

EXPERT WITNESS

An expert witness is a person whose professional or occupational training entitles him to offer a judgment on what happened in a case, even if he or she did not witness it. An expert may provide only information within his knowledge or experience. For instance, in a trial involving a car accident, a mechanic may be used as an expert witness to testify regarding her knowledge of and experience with the reliability of the brake system of a particular model of car. Because expert witnesses are often paid for their testimony, the mechanic may be asked whether she will receive compensation for testifying, and if so how much. The reason for the questions is to bring to light any self-interest the witness may have in presenting a certain point of view. See also EVIDENCE.

EXTENUATING CIRCUMSTANCES

Certain facts that make a crime seem less serious or reprehensible are known as extenuating circumstances. For example, Brian, who has no previous criminal record, has been convicted of robbing a grocery store and faces five years in prison. Prior to sentencing, Brian's lawyer argues that Brian should be put on probation instead of serving his jail sentence. The lawyer explains that Brian, who has a wife and six children, recently lost his job and robbed the store in desperation. Brian's lawyer is asking the judge to be more lenient than usual, considering the extenuating circumstances.

Other types of extenuating circumstances that a judge may consider include the defendant's age, his physical and mental health, his family obligations, and his standing and reputation in the community.

EXTORTION

Extortion is the unlawful collection of money from someone through threat or the use of one's influence. Extortion usually applies to intimidation by public officials, but under the laws of some states private persons can also be found guilty of extortion. For example, a health inspector who threatens to close a restaurant unless the owner pays him $50 is guilty of extortion when the owner pays up. If the inspector threatens, but the owner does not pay, the inspector is nonetheless guilty of attempted extortion. See also BLACKMAIL.

EXTRADITION

Richard, who lives in Florida, has been charged in Illinois with smuggling thousands of pounds of illegal drugs, and Illinois wants to bring him to trial. In order to obtain custody of Richard, the Illinois authorities must ask the governor of Florida for Richard's extradition to Illinois. They are simply requesting that the state where Richard is living turn him over to the state of Illinois.

If officials in Florida agree to the extradition request, they may then arrest Richard. But the governor does not have to comply with it if he feels that Richard's safety will be endangered by his being sent to Illinois. If Richard is already under arrest in Florida for crimes committed there, the governor is not required to comply immediately with the Illinois request. He may first be tried and convicted for his Florida crimes, and he may serve a prison sentence in Florida before being returned to the authorities in Illinois. Furthermore, Richard himself may go to court in Florida and contest the extradition request.

If Richard lives abroad and authorities in the United States want him for trial, they will make a formal request to the government of that country for his extradition. If the two countries have no extradition treaty, the other country is not required to turn him over. However, in 1992 the U.S. Supreme Court ruled that federal agents could enter a foreign country, apprehend a person accused of crimes in the United States, and bring him back to this country to stand trial without making a formal extradition request—unless such actions are prohibited by an extradition treaty (between the United States and the country where the person was taken into custody) that bars kidnapping. See also HABEAS CORPUS.

FROM FALSE ADVERTISING TO FUTURE INTEREST

FALSE ADVERTISING

Americans are inundated by countless ads from radio, television, newspapers, magazines, the daily mail, and even the telephone. As a consequence, it is often difficult to differentiate between ads that are false and misleading and ads that merely exaggerate their claims.

Under federal and state law, false advertising—advertising that contains untrue statements—is strictly prohibited. Suppose an ad for a new cold remedy trumpets: "This amazing new discovery cures the common cold." If the manufacturer cannot substantiate this claim, the law could prohibit him from making the statement in an advertisement.

Although it is illegal for advertisers to make false statements, they are permitted to "puff," or make exaggerated claims, and they are allowed to express an opinion about their product. For instance, if the advertiser says that the cold remedy is "the most soothing relief on earth for the common cold," he is not guilty of false advertising, because no reasonable person would take it as a statement of fact.

Omitting vital information can sometimes violate false-advertising laws. For example, a muffler shop ad that claims to install mufflers "for the low, low price of $19.95" would be deceptive if it failed to disclose that the price quoted does not include the cost of clamps or pipes, which usually also need to be replaced. Thus the final price a consumer will pay is considerably more than the advertised figure.

FEDERAL LAWS

On the national level, the primary authority responsible for guarding against false advertising is the Federal Trade Commission (FTC). Suppose that Jeffrey, an ardent environmentalist, buys plastic garbage bags because they are marked "biodegradable." He later finds out that the bags degrade only if treated with special chemicals. Jeffrey might file a complaint with the FTC for false advertising, arguing that the manufacturer of the garbage bags made false and deceptive claims about its product. The FTC would then investigate Jeffrey's complaint. If it was found valid, the agency would first try to convince the manufacturer to alter the ad voluntarily. If that failed, the FTC would issue a cease and desist order requiring the ad to be corrected or withdrawn. The manufacturer might even have to run new ads admitting that the earlier ones were misleading.

Under federal law, an individual cannot file a civil suit against a manufacturer for false advertising. However, the FTC can sue on behalf of consumers who have been harmed.

STATE LAWS

Nearly every state has enacted laws to regulate advertising. They are usually called unfair and deceptive acts and practices statutes or consumer fraud acts, and they often bear a close resemblance to federal laws. The state laws apply to false advertising that takes place within the borders of a given state.

Unlike the federal government, many states allow consumers to file private lawsuits and collect money damages (compensation) from advertisers who make false or deceptive claims. For example, Jeffrey could either sue the bag manufacturer for a refund (in small-claims court) or join with others in a class-action suit to recover a larger sum of money. See also CLASS ACTION; CONSUMER PROTECTION; FEDERAL TRADE COMMISSION; FRAUD; MAIL; MAIL-ORDER SALES; SCAMS AND SWINDLES; TELEPHONE CALL.

FALSE ARREST

When a police officer, sheriff, marshal, or anyone else with legal authority unlawfully detains a person or interferes with her freedom of movement

REAL LIFE, REAL LAW

The Case of the Bogus Bust Developer

For nearly two decades, a product called the Mark Eden Bust Developer was advertised in women's magazines as "a sure way to make your bust grow right before your eyes." Purchasers of the device were instructed to do exercises with it and were guaranteed to see a three-inch increase in bust size the first week.

Because the magazines were sent through the U.S. mails, the U.S. Postal Service began a prosecution against the company for false advertising. As part of its case, the Postal Service presented scientific evidence that the bust developer did not do what its ads promised.

Undeterred, the company fought the Postal Service for more than 16 years before it finally agreed to settle out of court, pay a fee of more than $1 million to the Postal Service, and stop making claims about its product that it could not prove. The irony is that, by stalling in the courts for such a long period of time, the company was able to sell more than $40 million worth of bust developers before it was forced to stop its false advertising.

without just cause, he is guilty of false arrest.

Suppose Harry goes to the Department of Motor Vehicles to renew his driver's license. While Harry is waiting in line, a police officer enters the building, makes an unpleasant comment about his appearance, and arrests him. The officer refuses to tell Harry the reason for his arrest, and instead of taking him to the police station, the officer drops Harry off in a vacant lot on the edge of town.

It later turns out that the officer is on a personal crusade against people who, like Harry, have long hair. Because having long hair is not a crime, Harry's arrest was false, and he may be entitled to sue the police officer and the city for interfering with his right to freedom of movement. See also ARREST; FALSE IMPRISONMENT; TORT.

FALSE IMPRISONMENT

Putting someone in jail unlawfully is, as the phrase implies, false imprisonment. But the legal meaning is actually broader. False imprisonment occurs whenever one person restrains another, depriving that person of her freedom without the legal authority to do so.

RESTRAINING SUSPECTED SHOPLIFTERS

The issue of false imprisonment often arises when suspected shoplifters are detained by a merchant. Suppose Linda is shopping at the Mallmart drugstore and buys a lipstick, which she puts into her purse. A security guard named Bud sees her doing this and thinks she is stealing the lipstick. He approaches Linda, takes her to the store's security office, refuses to tell her why he is detaining her, and locks her in the room for an hour. In the meantime, a clerk tells Bud that Linda paid for the lipstick.

When Linda is finally allowed to go, Bud explains the mix-up and apologizes, but she is fuming and threatens to sue. Linda may indeed have a case against Bud and Mallmart for false imprisonment, because she was deprived of her freedom without sufficient reason or legal authority. If Bud had explained to Linda why he was detaining her and quickly proceeded with his investigation, Linda would not be able to claim false imprisonment.

All merchants have the right to take reasonable measures to protect their property, and these include detaining suspected shoplifters. But in Linda's case, the restraint was unreasonable and therefore unlawful. See also SHOPLIFTING.

FALSE IMPRISONMENT BY THE POLICE

Suppose Bud was a police officer. Although the police have a right to enforce the law when they think it is being violated, they cannot abuse their powers. For instance, even if Linda had taken the lipstick, she could sue Bud for false imprisonment if he locked her in his patrol car and left her there for hours without telling her the reason she was being detained.

Law enforcement officials must exercise their arrest powers in a reasonable fashion. For example, they cannot arrest someone outside of their own jurisdiction (area of authority), wrongfully deny someone the opportunity to make bail, or continue to hold someone who is entitled to be released.

The concept of false imprisonment has its limits, however. A criminal defendant who has been acquitted cannot claim that he has been falsely imprisoned merely because he was found not guilty. By the same token, a police officer who acts within the bounds of his lawful authority, even if he arrests an innocent person, cannot be charged with false imprisonment. See also FALSE ARREST.

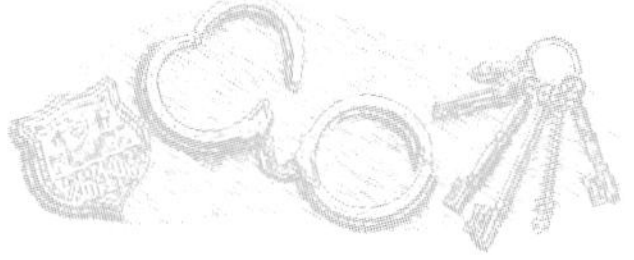

FALSE PERSONATION

Pretending to be someone you are not in order to defraud another is known as false personation. Suppose you answer your doorbell and a man in a business suit tells you that his name is John Bailey and that he is collecting donations for the Oakwood Orphans' Hospital, located in your town. You know the cause is worthy, so you give him $50. He thanks you and moves on to the next house.

The following day, you realize that you forgot to ask for a receipt for tax purposes. When you call the hospital to request one, you learn that the hospital has never heard of John Bailey, nor does it solicit door-to-door contributions. You are a victim of false personation.

The federal government and several states have laws against false personation. For example, federal law makes it illegal to impersonate a government employee (such as an FBI agent), a coroner, a U.S. citizen, or a representative of the American Red Cross or 4-H Club. Violators are subject to fines and imprisonment.

State laws prohibit the impersonation of police officers and other government officials, charity workers, and members of the clergy. For instance, the comedian Lenny Bruce was once charged with false personation for soliciting money while dressed in clerical garb.

To convict someone for false personation, the prosecution must show that the victim suffered a loss as a result of the crime. However, false personation of a government employee or someone in an official capacity may be punishable even if no one is harmed. For example, someone can be prosecuted for impersonating a police officer even if all he does is amble down the street and talk to people.

FALSE PRETENSE

The crime of false pretense (also known as false representation) involves misrepresenting facts or circumstances in order to defraud someone. Borrowing property with no intention of returning it, declaring that an item is an antique when it is really a reproduction, and paying someone with a check drawn on a defunct account are all typical examples of false pretense.

When Carol sold her car to Kevin, he specifically asked her if it had ever been in an accident. She knew very well that, six months earlier, she had crashed the car, damaging its frame. Nonetheless, she told Kevin that the car had never been in an accident. Kevin paid her $3,000, even though the car was worth only about $500. Carol therefore obtained $2,500 by false pretense.

GETTING PROMISES IN WRITING

To protect yourself against false pretense, you should always ask a seller (whether he is a private individual or a merchant) to put in writing any promises or claims about the merchandise he is trying to sell you. Should you decide to sue him for false pretense, the burden of proof will be on you, and if you do not have his claims in writing, the case will rest simply on your word against his. See also BURDEN OF PROOF.

CRIMINAL VERSUS CIVIL CASES

In most states, it is a crime to sell goods or obtain money by false pretense. However, most criminal courts are overburdened with what prosecutors consider to be more serious matters, and they may not give these cases the highest priority. Therefore, a victim of false pretense may be better off starting a civil lawsuit to recover his loss. See also FRAUD; LAWSUIT; SCAMS AND SWINDLES; WARRANTY AND GUARANTY.

FAMILY

There is no all-purpose legal definition of the term *family*, although it generally applies to a person's spouse, children, and parents. When necessary, a statute may define the word. For example, in some places zoning laws and restrictive covenants limit occupants of a home to "family members" and define *family* as persons related by blood, marriage, or adoption. By contrast, other localities have extended the definition to include unmarried and homosexual couples.

Most state laws recognize that family relationships are unique, and are therefore subject to special legal protections and restrictions. For example, spouses are generally not required to testify against each other.

Family relationships are of such importance that special family courts have been established across the country, and family law has become an important legal specialty. See also ADOPTION; CHILD CUSTODY; CHILDREN'S RIGHTS; FAMILY COURT; HOMOSEXUAL RIGHTS; INCEST; LIVING TOGETHER; ZONING.

FAMILY ALLOWANCE

Some states allow the family of a deceased person to collect money from his estate for living expenses before the estate has been settled. This is known as a family allowance.

For example, Jim had a valid will when he died, but because all the property he owned was in his name, his widow Marilyn faced the prospect of spending several months without funds to support herself and their children during the probate process. Luckily, Marilyn lived in a state that permitted family allowances. The court handling Jim's will authorized Marilyn and her children to receive a family allowance out of Jim's estate until the court proceedings related to his will were completed.

Not every state has this provision, however. To find out whether your state has a family-allowance statute, consult a lawyer who specializes in wills and estates, or visit your county law library and ask the librarian to help you look up your state probate code. See also PROBATE; WILL.

FAMILY-CAR DOCTRINE

The family-car doctrine, also known as the family-purpose or family-use doctrine, is a principle of negligence law used to impose financial responsibility on the head of a family who owns, provides, and maintains a car for his family's general use. Under this doctrine, if the owner of the car has given members of his family explicit or implied permission to use the car, and one of them causes personal injuries or property damage while driving that car, the owner will be responsible for the injuries and damages.

The owner can be held liable, or responsible, even if he was not in the car during the accident. For example, one day when Benjy was driving his father's car, he hit a woman on a bicycle, breaking her leg and ruining her bike. Under the family-car doctrine, Benjy's father would be responsible for compensating the woman for her medical bills and for replacing her bike.

When the family-car doctrine is applied in a lawsuit, in some instances the court may assign liability to the person who has title to the car, even when he is not actually making the payments or providing the upkeep. If a car is being paid for and used almost exclusively by your son, daughter, or other family member, but its title is in your name, you may want to transfer the title to that person—in order to avoid being sued as the official "owner."

Although the family-car doctrine typically applies to family members, it has been known to extend to situations in which a third party is driving with the permission of a family member. It has also been applied to motorcycles as well as automobiles, but not to bicycles. See also AGENT; NEGLIGENCE.

FAMILY COURT

In some states, special courts deal with family issues such as adoption, divorce, spousal support, guardianship, and juvenile crime. These so-called family courts represent an effort to give a single forum to various family-related legal problems.

MARRIAGE AND COHABITATION

Couples seeking a legal separation, annulment, or divorce are

REAL LIFE, REAL LAW

The Case of the Family Car

Seventeen-year-old Jeff was involved in a serious accident that injured another driver, named Shirley. When Shirley filed a lawsuit for the injuries she suffered, she sued not only Jeff but also his father, claiming that the family-car doctrine applied.

Jeff's father argued that he should not be held responsible for the accident his son caused. Jeff had been the actual purchaser of the car and was responsible for obtaining his own insurance and making the car payments. His father had no control over when or where Jeff drove the car.

However, the title to the automobile—the legal proof of its ownership—had Jeff's father's name on it. The court therefore held that regardless of the circumstances surrounding the use of the car, Jeff's father was the owner, and the family-car doctrine could be applied to hold him responsible for Shirley's injuries.

in some states required to go to family court, which also handles such related issues as alimony and child support. Cases involving unmarried partners, such as "palimony" lawsuits (in which one person seeks financial support after cohabiting with another), may also be heard in family court. In some states, if two people want to marry but one or both of them are not of legal age, they may apply to family court for permission. See also AGE OF CONSENT; PALIMONY.

CHILD CUSTODY AND SUPPORT

A divorced parent who wants to receive monthly child support payments from a former spouse, have the amount of support changed, or enforce a payment obligation previously ordered by a court generally presents the case in family court. Family courts may also be authorized to decide disputes over a child's legitimacy or parentage and to handle adoption procedures.

JUVENILE OFFENDERS

In districts without a separate juvenile court, the family court often decides cases involving minors who are in trouble at school or home, or with the law. Such cases involve children under a specified age (generally 16 or 18) who, for instance, cannot be controlled by their parents or who have been skipping school.

In some states, the family court may have authority to handle such criminal matters as shoplifting, running away from home, or loitering by juveniles. Assault, robbery, and other more serious crimes are not normally handled in family court. They are usually tried before a judge in criminal court, regardless of the age of the accused person. See also Juvenile Offender.

NEEDY AND ABUSED CHILDREN

Another important family court responsibility is to protect children. Child abuse and neglect cases, as well as those involving the treatment or placement of mentally ill children, are often handled by family court. The court may limit or terminate parents' rights to care for their children, or it may file charges against parents who desert, abandon, or fail to provide support for their children. See also CHILD ABUSE AND NEGLECT.

JUDICIAL POWERS

Although family courts address a limited range of issues, family court judges have many of the same powers as judges in courts of general jurisdiction. They can administer oaths, subpoena witnesses, grant continuances, and issue court orders. And if someone does not comply with a court order, a family court judge can punish him for contempt of court. See also COURTS.

FAMILY LEAVE

Until 1993 few employees who had to take extended time off from their jobs because of a family illness or the birth of a child could be sure that their jobs would remain secure. In that year, President Clinton signed into law the federal Family and Medical Leave Act.

FAMILY AND MEDICAL LEAVE ACT

The act allows employees to take a leave of absence from their job without pay in order to care for a sick spouse, child, or parent, or to care for a newborn, adopted, or foster child within a year of the child's arrival. In some instances, the law also allows workers to take time off because of their own medical conditions.

The law requires employers with more than 50 employees to provide up to 12 weeks of unpaid leave annually. Workers who put in less than 1,250 hours within a 12-month period (about 25 hours per week) and certain key employees whose salaries put them in the top 10 percent of the employer's work force are not covered. Employees are required to give at least 30 days' notice when the need is foreseeable.

The employer has the right to ask for a health-care provider's certification to verify a serious illness, and he may ask for a second medical opinion. The employer must continue health care coverage during leave, and when the employee returns, he is guaranteed either the same job or a comparable one.

STATE LAWS

Many states enacted family-leave laws before 1993, but the circumstances under which they apply vary. For example:

◇ Connecticut, Maine, Rhode Island, Vermont, and

Wisconsin, allow leave for the birth or adoption of a child and for the serious illness of the worker or a member of his family. In these states, the law applies to both private and state employees.

◇ Alaska and Georgia permit the leave described above for state employees only.

◇ California, New Jersey, Oregon, and Washington require state and private employers to provide leave for new parents and for the serious illness of a family member, but not for an illness suffered by the employee himself.

◇ Florida, Hawaii, Illinois, Maryland, North Dakota, Oklahoma, and West Virginia provide leave for new parents and for the serious illness of a family member, but the law applies only to state employees. In Hawaii, the law covers private employees beginning in 1994.

◇ Minnesota permits leave for both public and private employees upon the birth or adoption of a child, but not for illness. Virginia allows the same kind of leave, but restricts it to state employees.

The length of leave permitted varies from state to state. For example, in Alaska, state employees may take up to 18 weeks a year for the adoption or birth of a child, and 18 weeks every two years for illness. In Illinois, state employees may take up to a year of leave for the same purposes.

Even if you live in a state that has a family-leave law, it may not apply to you if you work for a small business. In Maine, for example, the law applies only to businesses with at least 25 employees, and in Rhode Island businesses must have at least 50 workers.

If you live in a state without a family-leave law, or if your state law and the federal Family and Medical Leave Act do not apply to you, check with your company's human resources department to see if it has voluntarily instituted a family-leave policy. If you are covered by a work contract or a collective-bargaining agreement, you may be entitled to some kind of family leave.

FAMILY LOAN

Sometimes when a person needs to borrow money—to buy a home or cover medical or funeral expenses, for example—he must turn to a relative or a friend because he cannot get a commercial loan. This type of loan presents its own hazards and, if not properly and legally arranged, can result in a family feud, broken friendship, or the lender's losing his money.

If you decide to lend money to a friend or member of your family, treat the loan as you would any other business transaction. Have the borrower execute a promissory note or even a mortgage, set an interest rate, and establish a repayment schedule. These arrangements not only protect your right to be repaid but prevent the Internal Revenue Service from considering the transaction a gift and possibly imposing gift taxes. See GIFT.

It is important that the interest rate you set for a family loan is reasonable—that is, close to current consumer rates. If not, the IRS may refuse the borrower deductions that it ordinarily allows on some kinds of business loans or mortgages, and the lender may not be able to take a deduction for a bad debt if the loan is not repaid. As a lender, you must declare any interest you have received on the loan as taxable income.

As with a commercial loan, a lender is legally entitled to take a delinquent debtor to court in order to obtain a judgment for an unpaid loan. See also JUDGMENT.

FEDERAL BUREAU OF INVESTIGATION

Created in 1908, the Federal Bureau of Investigation (FBI) is the primary investigative arm of the United States Department of Justice. It investigates most violations of federal law. These investigations involve locating witnesses and gathering evidence to support charges of criminal misconduct. The FBI concentrates on several areas of public concern. They are white-collar crime, illegal drugs, organized crime, terrorism, violent crime, and counterintelligence.

Other agencies sometimes work with the FBI. For example, the FBI and the Drug Enforcement Agency (DEA) often cooperate in the investigation of drug cases. If you become aware of a federal crime, such as counterfeiting or drug smuggling, you should call the FBI office in your area.

Federal Communications Commission

The Federal Communications Commission (FCC) was created in 1934 to establish and enforce rules and standards for interstate and international radio and wire communications. At present, its responsibilities include the regulation of television and radio broadcasts, satellite communications, telephone and telegraph operations, two-way radio operators, and, most recently, cable television.

The FCC's regulatory duties include monitoring electronic communications, granting licenses to broadcasters, enforcing rules that pertain to equal time, and dealing with consumer complaints.

LICENSING

Applications for broadcasting licenses are granted to radio and television stations by the FCC's Mass Media Bureau. In evaluating a station's qualifications, the bureau considers such criteria as the station management's financial viability, moral character, hours of broadcast, and willingness to provide programming that serves the community.

In general, applicants that meet these criteria are granted a license for a period of three years. When its license is up for renewal, each station must let the public know in order to permit the community to comment on whether the renewal should be granted.

EQUAL TIME

Another responsibility of the Mass Media Bureau is enforcing equal-time rules, which require stations to provide opposing political candidates with equal access to the airwaves. Equal-time rules do not always apply. For example, just because one candidate appears on a news program does not mean that the station must put an opposing candidate on the same program. But if a station sells advertising time to one candidate, it must offer it to others at the same rate.

If a candidate believes her right to equal time has been violated, she must notify the station of her desire for equal time within one week of the other candidate's appearance.

CONSUMER COMPLAINTS

Viewers and listeners sometimes voice complaints about television and radio stations. They may, for example, object to programs that show political bias or advertisements with offensive sexual content.

The best way to file such a complaint is to write a letter to the station and send a copy to the Federal Communications Commission, 1919 M Street, NW, Washington, DC 20554. If you are complaining about a particular program, note the time and date of the broadcast. If enough complaints are received, the FCC may not renew the station's license.

The FCC is not permitted to censor programs before they are broadcast. In 1991, for example, a number of affiliates of the Public Broadcasting System scheduled a television show about homosexual lifestyles that contained graphic sexual material. Although the FCC received a number of complaints about the program before it was shown, it could not prevent the show from being aired. See Prior Restraint.

Federal Courts

The United States has two court systems—federal and state. Federal courts hear cases involving federal or constitutional law, disputes between states or between the citizens of different states, controversies involving maritime affairs and foreign countries, and cases in which the United States government is either the plaintiff or the defendant.

The federal court system, which operates independently of the state court systems, derives its power from the U.S. Constitution and federal laws. It consists of three parts: (1) district courts, (2) courts of appeals, and (3) the Supreme Court. In addition, specialized courts, such as the Tax Court, the U.S. Claims Court, and the Court of International Trade, handle various kinds of cases.

STRUCTURE

The federal court system is set up in such a way that it resembles a pyramid, with more than

90 district courts at the base, 13 courts of appeals in the middle, and the Supreme Court at the top. The 50 states, the District of Columbia, Guam, the Northern Mariana Islands, Puerto Rico, and the Virgin Islands are divided into 12 judicial districts, or circuits. Each state is wholly within one judicial district, and every state has one or more district court.

District courts are the federal courts of original jurisdiction; thus, they are usually the first courts to hear cases involving federal law. Each district court typically has one to three judges.

In 1968 the Federal Magistrates Act was passed to help district court judges with their caseloads. It allows magistrates to perform a wide range of administrative, procedural, and scheduling functions.

Both federal judges and magistrates are nominated by the president. Their appointment must then be approved by the Congress. See also JUDGE; MAGISTRATE'S COURT.

AUTHORITY OF FEDERAL COURTS

Attorneys often spend a great deal of time and energy deciding whether they can or should take a case to a federal or state court. To be tried in federal court, a case must fill one of two requirements. The first is that the parties must show that the judge will have to decide a "federal question"—one that is governed by federal laws and treaties. For example, a $100,000 claim by an individual that alleges employment discrimination under the civil rights statutes would be considered a federal question.

The other category requires "diversity" among the parties—that is, the opposing parties must reside in different states, or one must be from a foreign country. For example, provided that at least $10,000 is in dispute, a New Jersey citizen can sue an Ohio corporation in Ohio federal district court, or a Dutch corporation can sue the state of Alabama in Alabama federal district court.

Federal courts also have the authority to hear cases involving federal criminal law and decide a number of specialized disputes, including admiralty (maritime) cases, bankruptcy cases, patent and trademark questions, and cases brought against the federal government by an individual, a business, or an organization. For a chart of the federal court system, see COURTS. See also CRIMINAL LAW.

APPEALING A FEDERAL CASE

The first appeal of a federal district court decision is to the U.S. Court of Appeals. There are 13 such Courts of Appeals. Twelve of these cover the district courts in the various states and territories and the District of Columbia. The 13th court, known as the Court of Appeals for the Federal Circuit, has nationwide jurisdiction. It has the authority to review selected cases—regardless of the location in which they originated—and it reviews decisions made by the U.S. Patent and Trademark Office, the U.S. International Trade Commission, the Secretary of Commerce, and the Court of Claims.

Unlike state appeals courts, the U.S. Courts of Appeals will hear all appeals from federal districts, regardless of merit. One reason for this openness is that for most cases the court of appeals is also the court of last resort, because the Supreme Court has the discretion to decide which cases it will hear.

Some of the cases heard by the federal Courts of Appeals are appeals of decisions made by such federal agencies as the Food and Drug Administration, the Social Security Administration, and the Environmental Protection Agency.

Appeals are usually heard by three judges, although in special cases (such as a case involving controversial issues of constitutional law), all of the judges assigned to a circuit will hear a case together.

APPEALS TO THE SUPREME COURT

If a party is dissatisfied with a decision by a federal appeals court, he can appeal to the nation's highest court—the U.S. Supreme Court. However, because the Supreme Court exists as much to rule on important questions of law and policy as to decide particular disputes, it chooses the cases it hears. The Supreme Court may also hear certain cases from the start, such as disputes between states or between a state and the federal government. See also SUPREME COURT, U.S.

SPECIAL FEDERAL COURTS

The federal court system also includes a number of special

courts, which hear and decide disputes involving technical subjects. The following are the most important of these federal courts.

Bankruptcy courts

In 1984 Congress revised the bankruptcy court system so that every district now has a bankruptcy court. The rules for initiating and appealing bankruptcy cases are different from those for other federal cases. Bankruptcy court cases are appealed to federal district courts. See BANKRUPTCY.

Claims Court

Under certain limited circumstances, such as alleged violations of federal laws or the Constitution, or claims involving government contracts or Indian lands, an individual or group can sue the federal government. These lawsuits are initially brought before the Claims Court. Any appeals from the Claims Court are heard by the Court of Appeals for the Federal Circuit. See also SOVEREIGN IMMUNITY.

Court of International Trade

Once known as the Customs Court, this special court primarily hears disputes over tariff rates and customs duties. See also CUSTOMS, U.S.

Tax Court

If a person feels that the government has taxed him unfairly, he may bring his case to the Tax Court. But before the Tax Court will hear a case, the taxpayer must have received a notice of deficiency—a formal statement from the Internal Revenue Service that demands payment of taxes, penalties, and interest regarding a disputed tax return. In some cases, the Supreme Court reviews Tax Court decisions. See also INCOME TAX.

FEDERAL DEPOSIT INSURANCE CORPORATION

Created by Congress in 1933 in response to the banking crisis, the Federal Deposit Insurance Corporation (FDIC) insures deposits in most banks and savings and loan associations. Depositors who keep their money in institutions with FDIC coverage are insured up to a maximum of $100,000.

If you have more in your account than $100,000, or if you have more than one account in the same name at the same bank, your insurance coverage is limited to $100,000 total. So if you have $50,000 in certificates of deposit, $50,000 in a passbook savings account, and an additional $20,000 in a checking account at the same bank, and if all the accounts are in the same name, $20,000 of the total $120,000 you have on deposit will not be insured.

To be certain that all of your money is protected, open accounts in several different banks insured by the FDIC. If you keep it in a single bank, the FDIC will provide separate coverage for one account in your name and one held jointly. Each account will be covered up to $100,000. Mutual funds and investment products sold by banks are not covered by the FDIC. See BANK FAILURE.

FEDERAL INFORMATION CENTER

The Federal Information Center helps individuals locate the federal agency that can provide information about a specific federal program. Whether you are in search of an application for a copyright, an answer to a consumer complaint, or information about U.S. Savings Bonds, the Federal Information Center will either answer your questions or direct you to the appropriate agency. To find out how to reach the Federal Information Center, see the checklist on the next page.

FEDERAL NATIONAL MORTGAGE ASSOCIATION (FANNIE MAE)

Fannie Mae is the nickname for a federally chartered but privately owned organization, the Federal National Mortgage Association, created to encourage home construction and mortgage lending. Fannie Mae works like this: Suppose you obtain a mortgage on your home from Acme Bank. Fannie Mae buys your mortgage and hundreds like it from Acme and other banks, savings and loan associations, mortgage companies, and insurance companies. It also buys mortgages insured by government agencies such as the Federal Housing Administration and the Department of

CHECKLIST

How to Talk to the Government

If you want to communicate with a government agency but do not know how to go about it, your first step should be to call the Federal Information Center, which will point you in the right direction. Listed below are the numbers to call (depending on where you live) along with other pertinent information:

❏ **EASTERN TIME ZONE.**
Call 800-347-1997 between 9 A.M. and 10:30 P.M.

❏ **CENTRAL TIME ZONE.**
Call 800-366-2998 between 9 A.M. and 9:30 P.M. Residents of Iowa, Kansas, Missouri, and Nebraska call 800-735-8004 between 9 A.M. and 5:30 P.M.

❏ **MOUNTAIN TIME ZONE.**
Call 800-359-3997 between 10:30 A.M. and 7:30 P.M.

❏ **PACIFIC TIME ZONE.**
Call 800-726-4995 between 10:30 A.M. and 7:30 P.M.

❏ **ALASKA.**
Call 800-729-8003 between 12:30 P.M. and 9:30 P.M.

❏ **HAWAII.**
Call 800-733-5996 between 1:30 A.M. and 10:30 P.M.

❏ **IF YOU ARE DEAF.**
If you use telecommunications devices for the deaf (TDD/TTY) call 800-326-2996.

❏ **IF YOU PREFER TO WRITE.**
Use the following address:
Federal Information Center
P.O. Box 600
Cumberland, MD 21502

Veterans Affairs. (When banks sell their mortgages to Fannie Mae, they have more money to lend to their customers.)

Fannie Mae in turn issues securities backed by the mortgages it has bought. Investors who buy the securities get monthly payments based on the principal and the interest paid on the mortgages owned by Fannie Mae. Most people who invest in Fannie Mae securities do so through mutual fund companies that purchase the securities in large numbers. See also GOVERNMENT NATIONAL MORTGAGE ASSOCIATION (GINNIE MAE); STOCKS AND BONDS.

FEDERAL TRADE COMMISSION

The Federal Trade Commission (FTC) is the government agency that enforces most federal consumer protection laws. The FTC investigates thousands of claims each year regarding issues as diverse as false advertising, credit practices, door-to-door sales, funeral home charges, and warranty claims for faulty products. See COLLECTION AGENCY; COOLING-OFF PERIOD; CREDIT BUREAU AND CREDIT RATING; FUNERAL AND BURIAL; WARRANTY AND GUARANTY.

The Federal Trade Commission seeks to protect the consumer's interest in a number of ways. For instance, the agency issues trade rules mandating the practices that must be followed in particular industries (such as requiring tobacco companies to put the Surgeon General's warnings on cigarette packages). Trade regulations have the same force of law as if they were created by statute.

The FTC also issues industry guidelines to help companies avoid actions that may later be deemed harmful or deceptive to the consumer. For instance, the FTC requires light bulb manufacturers to list the wattage and average expected life of the bulb on their packaging.

In addition, the FTC has the authority to file civil lawsuits on behalf of consumers who have been harmed by unfair or deceptive trade practices. These lawsuits consolidate claims and, as a result, save time and money. See also CONSUMER PROTECTION; FALSE ADVERTISING.

ENFORCEMENT PROCEDURES

If the FTC finds that a company is committing unfair or deceptive trade practices, the agency first notifies the company and gives it a chance to voluntarily correct its practices. If the company refuses to do so, the FTC issues a formal complaint against the company, whose representatives will have to attend a hearing held by an administrative-law judge.

An FTC administrative hearing is very much like a courtroom trial. After the evidence has been presented, the judge issues a decision. If the decision is in the FTC's favor, the judge will issue a cease and desist order against the company. The company has the right to appeal such an order, and the order will not be enforced until all possible appeals have been exhausted. This can take months or even years.

EFFECT OF FTC ORDER

Once an FTC order becomes final, it applies to all companies in the same industry. For example, an FTC order requiring one clothing manufacturer to print information about the fabric on the label would apply to all clothing manufacturers.

The FTC can also order a company to take corrective measures, such as changing its advertising to address previously made false claims. For example, a company that claimed its pills cured the common cold could be required to include a statement in future ads that "no medication cures the common cold."

FELONY

A felony is a serious crime, such as arson, burglary, kidnapping, rape, armed robbery, or murder. Unlike misdemeanors (less serious offenses), felonies are punishable by a prison sentence of one year or more in prison. A person who has been convicted of a felony is called a felon. See also FELONY MURDER RULE; PARDON; PAROLE.

FELONY MURDER RULE

The felony murder rule provides that a killing committed in the act of committing a felony, such as a robbery, will be punished as though it were intentional murder.

For example, when an oil company executive was kidnapped, one of the kidnappers shot and wounded him in the course of the abduction. Afraid to seek medical care, the kidnappers left the executive bound and gagged in an isolated storage room, where he died. As soon as the criminals were caught and the circumstances of the victim's death were revealed, a hue and cry arose for the alleged kidnappers to be charged with felony murder. Even though they had not intended to kill the oil executive, he had died in the course of their felony, which was the kidnapping.

Most states have adopted the felony murder rule, but many have limited its scope.

FENCE BUILDING

As a landowner, you have a legal right to erect a fence or other barrier (such as a hedge) anywhere on your property. However, before building a

REAL LIFE, REAL LAW

The Case of the California Killer

At midnight one evening, Frank went into a bar in Sacramento, California, and ordered a six-pack of beer. When the bartender returned from the cooler, he saw Frank pointing a gun at him. Frank made the bartender empty the cash register; then he left the bar, got into a car driven by his friend Arlin, and rode away.

A deputy sheriff who learned of the robbery drove to an intersection that he suspected the robbers would pass. When he saw the car, he followed it and signaled the driver to stop. Arlin stopped the car and ran into a nearby field, but Frank remained inside. A second deputy sheriff then arrived, drew his revolver, and approached the car. Frank shot and killed him.

Convicted of felony murder, Frank appealed his sentence to the California Supreme Court. He argued that the felony murder rule should not be applied to his case because the killing did not occur in the course of the actual robbery. The court disagreed with Frank's contention. Because the killing took place while Frank was "in hot flight with the stolen property," the robbery was in the escape stage and therefore still in progress. As a result, the killing was judged to be first-degree murder—punishable by death—under the felony murder rule.

fence, you should determine the exact location of your boundary line. Building a fence on another person's property, even by mistake, may be considered a trespass, or the fence may become the property of the owner on whose land it is built. See ADVERSE POSSESSION.

It is also worth checking your state, county, and municipal laws to find out whether any ordinances restrict the height, location, or type of fence you can build. In addition, some municipalities require you to obtain a building permit before constructing a fence. If you live in a planned community, find out if your deed restricts the type of material and style of fence you are allowed to build.

Before you build a fence, you should know the following:

◇ Fences that are permanently attached to the land (for instance, those with the fence posts sunk into the ground) may be considered fixtures, and therefore may legally become part of the property. If you move, you cannot take it with you.

◇ If you build a fence that is within your property boundary lines, you can alter or remove it whenever you wish.

◇ If you build a fence right on the boundary between your property and your neighbor's, it is known as a partition fence and is owned by both of you.

PARTITION FENCES

Adjoining property owners usually own partition fences as "tenants in common." In most states, tenants in common have equal responsibility for the construction and maintenance of partition fences, and one cannot alter or remove the fence without the other's permission. If you (or your neighbor) do not want to assume responsibility for the fence, you can make a private arrangement that gives sole ownership of the fence to the other person. Such an arrangement is essentially a contract for sale of real estate. It should be in writing and recorded in the county recorder's office, and it is binding on subsequent owners.

In some states, tenancy in common is established only when the fence is used by both property owners. Fence use can be difficult to establish; in some areas it may depend on whether you have completely enclosed your property with fences or whether there is a fence on only one side of your property. See TENANCY IN COMMON.

If you have a partition fence and want your neighbor to contribute to its repair, first notify her that you intend to repair the fence and expect her to split the cost. Include a written estimate, but be aware that if you do the work yourself you cannot ask for payment for your labor, only for any materials used. If she does not respond after a reasonable period of time, you can go ahead and do the work, then try to recover the cost from her. Eventually, you may have to take the case to small-claims court.

SPITE FENCES

If your neighbor builds a fence that serves no reasonable use, but was built simply to annoy you, it is referred to as a spite fence. Suppose Greg has a dispute with his neighbor Sam regarding the appearance of Sam's backyard, where Sam keeps old car parts and tools. Greg feels that the junk constitutes an eyesore. Fed up with Greg's repeated comments and complaints, Sam builds a fence that is nine feet high and made of rough, unpainted lumber. It blocks Greg's view of Sam's messy yard, but it also blocks out the light that fell on Greg's vegetable garden. Greg decides to turn to the courts to compel Sam to alter the fence, or to order Sam to compensate him for the loss of his vegetable garden and a reduction in his property's value.

Some states have laws that prohibit spite fences, but all such laws require you to show that your neighbor acted unreasonably by building the fence and that your property rights have been significantly affected.

STEPS TO TAKE

If you believe your neighbor is building a spite fence, here are a few things you can do:

1. First investigate the local laws that restrict fence height or appearance. Try to alert your neighbor to any regulations before the fence is built so that she has time to redesign it.

2. If the fence appears to comply with local restrictions, check to see if there are any spite-fence laws on the books.

3. If you live in a community that is governed by covenants, examine them for restrictions that may prohibit the fence.

4. Check with your homeowners association or local government representative to determine if mediation services are available. They can help you reach a compromise.

5. If mediation does not work or is not available, you will probably have to hire an attorney and take the case to court. The burden will be on you to prove malice on the part of your neighbor, as well as to prove that you are in some way harmed by the presence of the fence. See also BOUNDARY LINE; EASEMENT; MEDIATION; NEIGHBORS; NUISANCE; TRESPASS.

FIDUCIARY

Someone who voluntarily accepts the duty of acting on behalf of another, and in his best interest, is known as a fiduciary. Suppose that your elderly father is no longer capable of managing his money—paying his bills, looking after his bank accounts, or reinvesting his certificates of deposit. He asks you to manage his affairs for him, and you agree to do so. You have become your father's fiduciary.

The word *fiduciary* is often used to describe a relationship, such as the one above, in which one person manages money or property for another. But it also describes relationships in which one person trusts another to act in his best interest, such as an executor and the beneficiary of an estate, a guardian and ward, a real estate agent and the seller, an attorney and a client, a trustee and the beneficiary of a trust.

A trustee, for example, must manage the trust property wisely, follow all state and federal laws imposed on trusts, and administer the trust according to its terms. Failure to follow these procedures is considered a breach of fiduciary duty, and the trustee could be held responsible for losses suffered as a result of the breach. A fiduciary cannot use his position for personal gain, although he can be paid for performing his duties. See also EXECUTOR AND ADMINISTRATOR; GUARDIAN AND WARD; LAWYER; TRUST.

FIFTH AMENDMENT

The Fifth Amendment to the U.S. Constitution is the source of many of the personal rights for which the U.S. justice system is famous. The amendment applied only to federal law when it was written, but the Supreme Court extended many of its provisions to state law.

RIGHT TO A GRAND JURY

The Fifth Amendment begins by stating that "no person shall be held to answer for a capital, or otherwise infamous crime, unless on a presentment or indictment of a Grand Jury." A capital crime is one punishable by death; an "infamous crime" is a felony, such as rape or robbery. This part of the amendment applies only to federal crimes. See CRIMINAL PROCEDURE; FELONY; GRAND JURY.

DOUBLE JEOPARDY

The Fifth Amendment goes on to state: ". . . nor shall any person be subject for the same offence to be twice put in jeopardy of life or limb." This prohibition means that no person may be tried or punished a second time for the same crime. See DOUBLE JEOPARDY.

SELF-INCRIMINATION

The amendment continues: ". . . nor shall [any person] be compelled in any criminal case to be a witness against himself." The Fifth Amendment protects people from being forced to make a confession. It is the origin of the Miranda warnings, which the police must give to every suspect in custody before they can question him. Therefore, when a person is arrested, he is told that he "has a right to remain silent." Similarly, a witness who is being questioned may "take the Fifth"—typically by stating that he refuses to give a response "on the grounds that the answer may tend to incriminate me."

In short, the Fifth Amendment protects people from being forced to give testimony or from unwittingly making any statements that would subject them to criminal penalties. See also CRIMINAL LAW; MIRANDA WARNINGS.

LIFE, LIBERTY, AND PROPERTY: THE RIGHT TO DUE PROCESS

Next, the Fifth Amendment provides that no person shall "be deprived of life, liberty, or property without due process of law." Of these three elements, the meaning of the "right to liberty" has been most frequently debated in the courts. The right to liberty has been found to encompass not only freedom from physical restraint, such as imprisonment, but also freedom to enter into a contract, live and work where one chooses, pursue a lawful livelihood, acquire an education, and marry and raise children. This clause is one of the most far-reaching protections given by the Bill of Rights. For further discussion, see DUE PROCESS OF LAW.

JUST COMPENSATION FOR PROPERTY

The amendment ends with the statement: ". . . nor shall private property be taken for public use, without just compensation." This clause is a recognition that the government may reasonably regulate the use of, impose taxes on, and exercise its powers to appropriate private property. When the government does take property for public use, however, it must compensate the owner fairly. See CONDEMNATION; FORFEITURE.

FINANCE COMPANY

Like a bank, savings and loan association, and credit union, a finance company makes loans to consumers for a variety of purposes, including auto purchases, home improvements, vacation funds, and college expenses. However, finance companies usually charge higher interest rates than other lenders do because they often extend credit to people who, because of poor credit standing or another reason, cannot qualify for a loan elsewhere.

Like other lenders, finance companies must comply with the federal Truth-in-Lending Act, which requires lenders to disclose the interest charges, number of payments, the amount of each payment, total amount to be repaid, and total of all finance charges. Many states also have laws regulating finance companies. If you have a problem with, or want to inquire about, a finance company, your state's consumer protection agency or attorney general should be able to help. You can also write to the Credit Practices Division, Federal Trade Commission, Pennsylvania Avenue and Sixth Street NW, Washington, DC 20580. Or you can contact an FTC regional office. See also TRUTH-IN-LENDING ACT.

FINANCIAL PLANNER

You have recently left a company where you worked for 20 years, taking with you a hefty lump-sum payment from the company's profit-sharing plan. This is the largest amount you have ever had and you do not know what to do with it. A friend suggests that you go to a financial planner, but you are not sure what that means.

A financial planner is a person who offers personally tailored financial advice. He may make investment suggestions and help you with tax, estate, and retirement planning. A good financial planner can be extremely helpful to you in creating a budget, directing investments, and recommending adequate amounts of life and disability insurance. Ultimately, however, it is your responsibility to make decisions about your financial goals and your choice of investments. You should decide for yourself whether to take some risks in hopes of getting higher financial returns. Do not make the mistake of entrusting someone else with the complete authority to make all your financial decisions.

Because there are very few state or federal licensing requirements for financial planners, almost anyone can claim to be a financial planner, regardless of his background, education, or training. Thus, for example, many insurance agents, stockbrokers, and commodity traders call themselves financial planners, when they are in fact salespeople whose income depends on the commissions they receive from selling you policies and investments. Even though they are constrained by laws relating to negligence, fraud, and breach of contract, the policies and investments they offer you may not serve your best financial interests.

To avoid such pitfalls, consider using a fee-based financial planner, who receives his income from the fee he charges you for your financial plan, rather than from commissions on products he sells. Depending on your income, the kind of property you own, and the complexity of your financial situation, fees can range from several hundred to several thousand dollars. However, the fees you pay for financial-planning services may be deducted on your federal income tax return, provided that the services are related to your investments or to tax planning.

CHECKLIST

Choosing a Financial Planner

If you need the services of a financial planner, interview several candidates before hiring one. In addition to asking about their qualifications and fees, be sure to ask the following important questions:

❑ **WHAT IS YOUR EXPERIENCE WITH CUSTOMERS LIKE ME?**
Find out whether the planner has worked with people whose income and circumstances are similar to yours.

❑ **ARE YOUR INVESTMENT PLANS DIVERSIFIED?**
A good financial planner will recommend dividing your funds among several different kinds of investments, such as mutual funds, stocks, and investment-grade bonds. Be wary of a planner who favors one kind of investment too heavily—if his advice is wrong, your investment may be depleted or lost.

❑ **WHAT DO YOU CONSIDER A SOLID RATE OF GROWTH?**
If a planner promises you unusually high returns, you will almost certainly be taking higher risks. If you cannot afford to take chances with your money, consider settling for smaller returns from safer investments.

❑ **DO YOU SELL INSURANCE POLICIES OR INVESTMENTS?**
If so, find out what they are and what kind of commission the planner gets. If a planner has an interest in particular investments, you should ask what he might gain by recommending them.

❑ **MAY I SPEAK TO SOME OF YOUR CURRENT CLIENTS?**
A reputable planner will be happy to refer you to his other clients.

❑ **WILL YOU PERSONALLY BE AVAILABLE TO ADVISE ME?**
You should be aware that large financial-planning organizations may assign accounts to junior members of the firm. On the other hand, using a one-person operation with a large number of clients may mean that the planner will not be readily available.

❑ **DO YOU HAVE A BROCHURE AND A SAMPLE FINANCIAL PLAN TO SHOW ME?**
The more you are able to see in writing, the better you can judge a planner's qualifications. In addition to a brochure and a sample financial plan, ask to see a copy of the planner's Form ADV—a document that financial-planning firms use to report their operations to the Securities and Exchange Commission.

To find a financial planner, first ask friends and advisers, such as your attorney. You can also call the Institute of Certified Financial Planners (800-282-7526) or the International Association for Financial Planning (800-945-4237). These organizations maintain lists of financial planners who have satisfied certain educational requirements. For example, the College for Financial Planning in Denver offers correspondence courses that lead to the designation of Certified Financial Planner (CFP). The American College located in Bryn Mawr, Pennsylvania, certifies candidates as Chartered Financial Consultants (ChFC) after they have passed tests on estate planning, investments, taxes, and financial topics. If your planner has been certified by one of these organizations, you can have some confidence that she is qualified.

As an extra precaution, you should find out whether your prospective planner has ever been disciplined for financial impropriety by a regulatory body, such as your state insurance commission or real estate board or the Securities and Exchange Commission.

FINANCIAL RECORDS

Keeping financial records is a necessary chore, but it is often difficult to know which documents to keep and for how long. The following guidelines are designed to help you put your financial records in order and keep them that way:

TAX RECORDS

Because you must document your income for the Internal Revenue Service (IRS), keep a home file containing the W-2 and 1099 forms that report income. If you itemize deductions (or if there is a chance that you will), save all records of potential deductions, such as medical expenses, interest payments on your mortgage, charitable contributions, and any business expenses that are not reimbursed by your employer. Because the IRS keeps tax returns on file for seven years, you should do the same, saving copies of your tax returns and all supporting records in the event of an IRS audit. For the same reason, you should also keep your bank statements and your canceled checks for seven years. Store tax-related documents in a safe and accessible place, such as a metal file cabinet. See also INCOME TAX; INCOME TAX AUDIT.

CREDIT INFORMATION

Keep a list of all your credit card and Automated Teller Machine (ATM) account numbers and the telephone number of each issuer so that you can report a lost or stolen card quickly and avoid liability for unauthorized use. Put the list in a safe but accessible place in your home.

OTHER FINANCIAL RECORDS

Stock certificates, bonds, deeds, mortgages, and similar documents should be kept in a bank safe-deposit box for extra security. When you buy or sell stocks, bonds, or real estate, put the documents that relate to the sales—such as receipts, canceled checks, closing documents, and final statements—in your income tax files, because you will have to report any gains or losses you made on those sales to the IRS.

Keep utility bills only until you receive the subsequent bills, verifying that your accounts are up to date. Of course, if you are having a dispute with a company, keep all the bills until the dispute is resolved.

INVENTORY OF RECORDS

Prepare a list indicating where you have stored important financial records and documents. You will find a sample personal records inventory form in the EVERYDAY LEGAL FORMS section of this book, beginning on page 552. Tell trusted relatives and friends where they can find the list in case of emergency. See also PERSONAL RECORDS.

FINE

A fine is a financial penalty imposed on someone who has broken the law. Some offenses, such as parking violations, are usually punishable only by fines. More serious offenses may be punishable by fine or imprisonment or both.

Usually a fine is imposed as a judgment, or decision, of the court, and is determined either by the judge or the jury. When a fine is imposed by a court, you must pay it or appeal the sentence. The time given for payment is usually set by law; if not, the judge sets a reasonable amount of time for payment.

If the penalty for a crime is either a fine or imprisonment, and the law does not specify a period of time allowed for payment, the court has occasionally jailed those who were unable to pay right away. If the penalty is both a fine and imprisonment, the fine may be reduced or even eliminated after part of the jail term has been served.

If you do not pay a fine and are jailed as a result, local law usually limits the length of your imprisonment. Suppose you receive a $100 fine for not curbing your dog and refuse to pay because you feel the fine is outrageous. The judge can order you to be jailed. However, if your local ordinance says that every day you spend in jail reduces the fine by $10, you may have to spend 10 days in jail, but no more.

In some states unpaid fines result in a lien, or claim, by the local government upon your property. If you do not pay the fine, you may end up losing your car or house, for example.

If someone owes a fine and dies before paying it, his estate does not have to pay the fine. See also FORFEITURE; LIEN.

FIRE

The crime of setting fire to property (either yours or another person's) is called arson. See ARSON.

Other kinds of fires, although they may seem innocent, are also against the law. For example, many communities have laws making it an offense to burn leaves or trash in an open fire, even on your own property. In some states, if you build a fire on your property and it spreads to a neighbor's, you may be charged with a criminal offense called negligent burning. In addition, your neighbor can sue you for any damage your fire caused. See also NEGLIGENCE.

In some parts of the country, concerns about air pollution have led communities to ban or restrict the use of wood-burning fireplaces. Some communities offer financial assistance or tax incentives to homeowners who refrain from using their fireplaces or convert them into units that use only nonpolluting electricity or gas.

FIRE INSURANCE

Insurance against a fire that burns part or all of your home or business is usually part of a homeowners or business owners insurance policy, which includes insurance against a variety of other hazards as well. See HOMEOWNERS INSURANCE; INSURANCE.

If your home or business is damaged by fire, the insurance company will reimburse you, at least in part, for your loss, even if the damage is a result of your own negligence. Suppose you carelessly leave the fire screen open on your fireplace and a spark from the fire sets your rug ablaze. Your homeowners insurance should cover the loss. Such insurance usually pays for incidental fire damage as well, such as damage caused by smoke, water, and even firefighters who need to break through windows, doors, or walls to extinguish the fire. Most policies also pay for damage caused by lightning, even if there is no resulting fire.

FISHING RIGHTS

Fish, like other wildlife, are owned by the state when they are in their natural habitat, even if the fish are in waters on private property. For example, a state law that prohibits catching certain species of fish applies even to fish in a stream that passes through private property.

Under most circumstances, the right to catch fish depends on where the body of water is located. If there is a pond or lake that is entirely contained within the boundaries of your property, the right to fish in it is exclusively yours. The same is true for a river or stream that flows through your property—you have exclusive fishing rights on the portion that is on your land. A person who fishes on private property without the owner's permission is guilty of trespassing. When several persons own a lake or pond—because each has property along its shore—they all have fishing rights to the entire lake.

If you own property that adjoins a nonnavigable river or stream (one that cannot be used by a boat), you have exclusive fishing rights from the water's edge to the center of the river or stream. If a stream or river passes through your property, the fish still belong to the state, and although you can catch them, you cannot otherwise harm them or interfere with their movement (by building a dam, for example).

Everyone has a right to fish in rivers, ponds, and lakes that are navigable. If you own property on such a body of water, you have the same right to fish in it as anyone else. But, once again, you can prohibit anyone from fishing on your land.

The power to regulate fishing on public property rests with the states. They may, for example, require you to buy a fishing license; restrict the size, number, and species of fish you may catch; limit the times you can fish; restrict or prohibit the use of nets, spears, and lures; and prohibit the use of explosives or other devices to capture large numbers of fish.

Anyone who violates fishing laws is subject to a fine. A serious or repeated violation of fishing laws is punishable as a misdemeanor, that is, by a fine or imprisonment or both.

FIXTURE

A piece of property that is permanently attached to real estate (by being screwed or bolted into a floor or wall, for example) in such a way that it becomes part of the real estate is known as a fixture.

When you buy, sell, or rent a building, you should be clear about what constitutes a fixture. For example, if you are buying a house that has a den lined with built-in bookcases that you admire, be sure the sales contract states to whom these will belong. Similarly, if you are selling the house and plan to take the bookcases with you, be sure that this is spelled out in the contract.

If you are a tenant, you can usually take any fixtures you installed with you when you leave, provided you do not do great damage to the real estate. For instance, if you should be so foolish as to install central air conditioning in a house you rent, you could not remove it. You could, however, take out window air conditioners you install, even if you had nailed brackets into the walls to support them.

To be safe, check your lease before installing any fixtures. It may state that anything you nail or screw into the building, such as shelving, appliances, or cabinets, becomes the property of the landlord.

FLAG, U.S.

Because the American flag is a symbol of the nation, federal laws regulate the manner in which it can be displayed. No other flag should fly above the American flag on U.S. soil; the flag should not be allowed to touch the ground; it should not be flown in inclement weather; and it should not be flown at night unless illuminated.

In reality, many of these laws are ignored and they are not consistently enforced, but when political activists have desecrated the flag as a form of protest, they have sometimes been prosecuted under federal and state laws. In 1989 the federal Flag Protection Act was passed, making it a crime to mutilate, deface, physically defile, burn, maintain on the ground or floor, or trample upon the flag of the United States. The Supreme Court struck down this law in 1990, however, stating that the right to free speech and expression is even more important than the principle of protecting a national symbol. See also SPEECH, FREEDOM OF.

FLEXIBLE BENEFITS

More and more employers are offering benefit programs that allow employees to choose benefits that are tailored to their individual needs and personal preferences. These programs are sometimes referred to as flexible-benefits or "cafeteria" benefit plans. A flexible-benefits plan lets each employee choose among several benefits, which can include such traditional ones as group health, life, and disability insurance, or less traditional benefits, such as child care or care for elderly parents.

When an employee contributes to a flexible-benefits plan, her taxable income is reduced by the amount she contributes. Suppose Kathleen's employer offers a flexible-benefit plan that includes child care. Kathleen designates $250 of her monthly pretax salary of $2,500 for child care under the plan. The money is deducted from her salary, and she pays no income tax on it, reducing her salary for income tax purposes to $2,250. (Kathleen still pays the day care center or babysitter out of her pocket, but is reimbursed up to $3,000 per year by the plan.). Without the plan, she would be paying the $3,000 in after-tax dollars. If she does not use part or all of the $3,000 for child care, she cannot get her money back.

To qualify for this favorable tax treatment, a flexible-benefits plan must be in writing and include information about the following: the time period for which the benefits apply, rules for determining eligibility, descriptions of the various benefits offered to eligible employees, the method for choosing benefits, and the means by which employer contributions are made.

Not all employers offer a flexible-benefits program, but if they do, they must provide at least two benefits from which to choose. Your company's human resources department will tell you whether such benefits are available.

FLOAT

The period between the time a check is written or a credit card charge is made and the time the money is collected from an account is called the float. Suppose you write a check to the supermarket on Friday morning. The check remains in the cashier's drawer until the end of his shift. It is then turned over to the store's bookkeeper, who deposits it at the supermarket's bank on Saturday morning. The bank processes it on Monday and does not present it to your bank for collection until Tuesday morning. The "float" for your check has been four days.

Some people try to "play the float"—that is, even though they do not have enough money in their bank account to cover a check, they expect to make a deposit by the time the check reaches their bank. Playing the float on a checking account is a bad idea. If you miscalculate the time, your check will not be honored, resulting in financial penalties, administrative hassles, and perhaps even criminal charges. See also BOUNCED CHECK.

FLOATER

An insurance policy that supplements a standard homeowners policy and gives additional protection to personal property, especially certain valuables, is known as a floater. For example, standard homeowners insurance does not cover expensive antiques to the full extent of their value or insure your fur coat if it disappears from a restaurant's coatroom, but you can buy a floater that will.

Floaters can be comprehensive and cover all your personal property and the property of those who live with you, or they can be written for only specified items, such as computers, jewelry, cameras, and furs.

For the most part, floaters are "all risk" policies—that is, they cover property against everything except specific exclusions. A standard policy covers only what is specifically named in the policy.

The name *floater* means that the coverage "floats" with the item covered—that is, it applies whether the item is in the home, in storage, or in transit. Many homeowners insurance policies include off-premises coverage, but it is generally not as extensive as that provided by floaters. A review of your policy can help you determine the limitations of your present homeowners coverage. See also HOMEOWNERS INSURANCE.

FLOOD INSURANCE

Whether your homeowners insurance policy covers you in the event of a flood depends on the type of flood. Standard homeowners policies seldom pay for flood damage caused by severe rain or other natural causes. However, if you live in an area that has been subject to flooding, you may be able to obtain coverage through the federal National Flood Insurance Program (NFIP). This insurance is available in communities that have tried to minimize the potential for flood damage. Your insurance agent can tell you whether your community qualifies.

If your home is flooded as a result of a burst water pipe, standard homeowners policies often provide coverage. They will pay for all (or part) of your personal property loss and structural damage and may even provide for you to stay elsewhere until the pipe can be repaired and the water damage cleaned up. See also HOMEOWNERS INSURANCE.

FOOD AND DRUG LAWS

To protect American consumers, the U.S. Congress has enacted a series of laws over the years to ensure that the food, drugs, cosmetics, and medical devices that are sold to the public are safe and effective. Federal regulations set safety standards for everything from imported tea to microwave ovens, and a number of federal agencies are responsible for implementing these federal laws. For example, eggs, meat, and other agricultural products are inspected and graded by the Department of Agriculture; the Environmental Protection Agency sets standards for herbicides; the Department of Commerce regulates foods imported from other countries; the Bureau of Alcohol, Tobacco, and Firearms regulates labeling and additives in alcoholic beverages; and the Department of Defense oversees the foods supplied to the armed forces.

The primary responsibility for implementing federal food and drug laws, however, belongs to the Food and Drug Administration (FDA), an agency of the Department of Health and Human Services. Different divisions within the FDA—for example, the Drug

Labeling Compliance Division, the Animal Feeds Division, and the Product Quality Control Division—specialize in different kinds of operations.

FOODS

Federal legislation regulating foods and their ingredients began with the Tea Importation Act of 1897. It was one of the first laws designed to keep adulterated or misbranded food out of the marketplace, and it is still in effect today.

In 1957 the Meat Inspection Act and the Poultry Products Inspection Act mandated the inspection of livestock both before and after slaughter to screen out diseased animals and prevent the contamination of healthy meat and poultry during storage and processing.

In 1988 new laws were enacted to monitor pesticide residues in foods. The responsibility for setting regulations that pertain to these residues belongs to the Environmental Protection Agency (EPA). For a list of federal laws regulating food and other substances, see the checklist on page 236.

State and local regulation

Foods sold in the same state in which they are produced are generally exempt from federal control, since they are not sold through interstate commerce. Consequently, individual states and municipalities have established their own agencies to monitor the quality and safety of locally produced foods. They may also monitor pesticide labeling of packaged food, and expiration dates on canned food and fresh meat, fish, and poultry.

Labeling

A great deal of federal legislation has been aimed at improving product labeling. Ingredients are supposed to be listed clearly on packaged food in order of their quantity by weight, so that a consumer can see at a glance, for instance, whether a spaghetti sauce contains more corn syrup or water than tomatoes.

The nutritional content of most prepared foods must also be listed. For foods sold after May 1994, the labels must give both a reference daily intake (RDI) for vitamins and minerals and a daily value (DV) for substances like cholesterol and sodium that are associated with chronic diseases. Consumers can use this information to determine the amount of vitamins, minerals, fat, sodium, and cholesterol one serving of a prepared food contains.

The FDA is also authorized to ban false and misleading claims, and even false and misleading pictures on labels. For example, it has instructed manufacturers to remove illustrations of hearts and the claim "no cholesterol" from some high-fat products on the grounds that they are misleading. A salad dressing, margarine, jar of mayonnaise, or box of cookies may indeed contain no cholesterol, but if it contains high amounts of saturated fat, it will be useless in combating heart disease. See also FALSE ADVERTISING.

Note that products claiming to be "organic" or "natural" are not required to meet any legal requirements for such claims in about half the states.

Food additives

The FDA can require companies to conduct extensive laboratory tests to determine whether food additives—for instance, food coloring, preservatives, and flavor or texture enhancers—pose a risk to consumers. Under the Food Additives Amendment of 1958, the FDA has the right to prohibit the use of additives if they are found to be potentially harmful—even if only when given to laboratory animals. In 1977, for instance, the FDA banned the use of saccharin, a sugar substitute, as an additive after it was found to be carcinogenic to laboratory animals. The U.S. Congress has the power to override the FDA decisions, however, and has done so in this case.

Additives that are proved not to be harmful during such testing are given the classification GRAS ("generally recognized as safe"). Regulations that go into effect in 1994 require additives that were previously excluded, such as food dyes, to be listed on food labels.

Irradiation

Food is sometimes irradiated—exposed to radiation at specific frequencies—to destroy bacteria and prevent the growth of insects. The process has been approved for flour, spices, fruits, vegetables, and poultry.

Concern over the long-term effects of irradiation on food products has led some states to place temporary bans on the procedure. By law, foods that have been irradiated must display a symbol, known as a radura, and the words "treated with irradiation."

CHECKLIST

Important Food and Drug Laws

Since 1897, a number of federal laws have been passed to protect consumers and regulate the manufacture and distribution of foods and drugs. Here are some of the most important of these laws:

❑ **TEA IMPORTATION ACT OF 1897.**
Provides for the inspection of all imported teas.

❑ **MEAT INSPECTION ACT OF 1906.**
Gives the Department of Agriculture the authority to inspect meat-processing facilities.

❑ **FOOD, DRUG, AND COSMETIC ACT OF 1938.**
Ensures that all such items are safe, and sets standards for manufacture and labeling.

❑ **PUBLIC HEALTH SERVICE ACT OF 1944.**
Sets safety standards for blood, vaccines, and serums, as well as for shellfish, pasteurized milk, and food that is sold on public transportation.

❑ **AGRICULTURAL MARKETING ACT OF 1946.**
Gives the guidelines for regulating the processing of fruits and vegetables.

❑ **POULTRY PRODUCTS INSPECTION ACT OF 1957.**
Allows the USDA to inspect all poultry production.

❑ **DRUG AMENDMENTS OF 1962.**
Require the FDA to approve new drugs before they are marketed. (Amend the Food, Drug, and Cosmetic Act of 1938.)

❑ **FAIR PACKAGING AND LABELING ACT OF 1966.**
Gives the FDA more authority to regulate labeling of net weights. (Further amends the Food, Drug, and Cosmetic Act of 1938.)

❑ **FEDERAL MEAT INSPECTION ACT OF 1967.**
Prohibits meat from being imported from those countries in which certain animal diseases have been reported.

❑ **WHOLESALE MEAT ACT OF 1967.**
Ensures that meat is properly marked, labeled, and packaged, and that it is wholesome.

❑ **WHOLESALE POULTRY PRODUCTS ACT OF 1967.**
Regulates the storage and handling of poultry.

❑ **EGG PRODUCTS INSPECTION ACT OF 1970.**
Governs the processing and labeling of egg products.

❑ **MEDICAL DEVICE AMENDMENTS OF 1976.**
Regulate the testing and marketing of medical devices. (Further amend the Food, Drug, and Cosmetic Act of 1938.)

❑ **FOOD LABELING ACT OF 1990.**
Requires nutrition information on most food labels and sets standards for health claims.

Food supplements
Powders, pills, and liquids that can be used to supplement or replace normal meals must list their contents and nutritional value. In addition, they cannot make health claims that are not substantiated.

Plant inspections
The Department of Agriculture has the primary responsibility for inspecting meat- and poultry-processing plants. The department sends inspectors to factories, warehouses, and other places where food is produced, processed, packed, or held for interstate commerce. These inspections are ongoing—in some cases the inspectors are on the site all the hours the business is in operation.

RADIATION

Public concern about the possible health hazards of radiation from medical and household appliances prompted the passage of the Radiation Control for Health and Safety Act in 1968. In 1990 the FDA was given the responsibility to enforce the act, which sets safety standards for products and medical equipment that emit radiations, such as X-ray machines, microwave ovens, and television sets.

DRUGS

The best known and most comprehensive federal legislation regulating drugs is the Food, Drug, and Cosmetic Act, which helps ensure that prescription drugs, medical devices, infant formulas, food additives, and vaccines are safe and effective.

To obtain FDA approval for a new drug, manufacturers must

follow rigorous testing procedures and demonstrate that the drug is being manufactured under safe and sanitary conditions. They must show that the drug (1) does what it is supposed to do, (2) is not toxic in normal doses, and (3) has benefits that outweigh its side effects. When the drug is approved for sale, the manufacturer must include adequate information about its uses, contraindications, and dangers on the package label.

Moreover, the FDA must separately approve each purpose for which a drug is used. For example, if a drug has been approved for treating heart ailments and is later found to help baldness, the manufacturer must seek FDA approval a second time before marketing the drug for baldness prevention.

In some cases, foods are also classified as drugs, depending on the manufacturer's claims. For example, if a cookie manufacturer claimed that its product cures heart disease, the FDA would consider it a drug.

Before a manufacturer can bring a single new drug to the market, years may elapse and many millions of dollars may be spent on research and testing. Because the FDA has been criticized by the public for taking too long to approve drugs for certain life-threatening illnesses, it has started to allow some experimental drugs, such as those used to treat AIDS, to reach the public sooner. See also AIDS; DRUG; DRUG ABUSE.

ENFORCEMENT

To ensure that contaminated, unwholesome, or misbranded products do not reach consumers, the FDA may ask the manufacturer to issue a recall. If that request is not acted upon, the FDA may ask the U.S. Attorney General to seize the product, file a criminal complaint against the violator, or seek an injunction to prevent further distribution of the product.

STEPS TO TAKE

If you have bought a food, drug, medical device, or cosmetic that you think is unsafe, you should report your concern.

1. If the item was locally produced, notify your state or city consumer protection agency.

2. If the item came from another state, consult your telephone directory for the number of the FDA field office nearest you, or write to the agency's headquarters: 5600 Fishers Lane, Rockville, MD 20857. (For meat and poultry, contact the local office of the Department of Agriculture.)

3. If you bought the item as a result of misleading advertising, write to the Federal Trade Commission, Pennsylvania Avenue and Sixth Street NW, Washington, DC 20580, or your state attorney general. See also CONSUMER PROTECTION; FALSE ADVERTISING.

F.O.B.

F.O.B., or "free on board," is a contractual term meaning that a seller will deliver merchandise at no charge to a particular shipping point. For example, a shipment of California wines going to New York might be sent F.O.B. from the winery to a trucker (or other carrier) in Los Angeles. This means that the seller is responsible for getting the wines onto the truck in Los Angeles at his expense and without breakage. However, once the wine is on the truck, the buyer becomes the owner of the wine, and the seller pays no more delivery charges and is no longer responsible for breakage. The terms of an F.O.B. contract usually specify that the buyer will pay for the goods either before or at the same time that the seller turns them over to the carrier. See also CONTRACT.

FORECLOSURE

Losing one's home through foreclosure (the forced sale of a home in order to pay back the financer) can be a nightmare. Foreclosure takes place when a homeowner cannot repay his loan according to the terms of the agreement with the lender. The lender may begin legal proceedings to have the borrower's property sold. Then the proceeds from the sale are used to pay off the outstanding debt. Although foreclosure is a realistic threat to a delinquent borrower, only about 1 percent of homeowners actually experience it. In fact, most lenders try to avoid foreclosure because it is costly, takes a long time, and does not guarantee

ABC's

Of Buying a Foreclosure Property

You may have heard that it is easy and inexpensive to buy a foreclosed home, but actually a good deal of hard work and expense is involved. If you want to undertake such a venture, here are some practical suggestions to guide you:

❑ To find out about foreclosure properties, contact a real estate agent or banks and savings and loan associations in your area. For Fannie Mae (Federal National Mortgage Association) foreclosure properties, write to Fannie Mae Properties, Box 13165, Baltimore, MD 21203. They will send you a list of current properties. Properties that have been foreclosed on by the Departments of Housing and Urban Development or Veterans Affairs will be listed in the real estate section of your local newspaper.

❑ If you are interested in a particular property, visit it before you bid on it at auction, but keep in mind that it may be occupied. You can ask the owners to let you inside, but they have the right to refuse. If the house is vacant, the real estate broker handling the foreclosure may be able to let you in.

❑ Conduct a title search in the county records to find out if there are any other liens against the property besides the mortgage, since in some states you will have to pay these off if you are the winning bidder.

❑ Before deciding how much to bid, ask a real estate broker about the prices of comparable homes in the area.

❑ Keep in mind that you may have to make extensive repairs to the house. Sometimes people whose properties have been sold through foreclosure damage the property out of spite, ripping out appliances and knocking holes in plaster walls.

❑ Ask about bidding procedures and how to make payment. In most cases you will need to pay about 10 percent down with a cashier's check, and you will have a limited time to obtain financing.

❑ Do not believe books and television shows that claim to show you how to buy foreclosed properties with no deposit and then resell them for big profits. Lenders who have foreclosed on a home will expect a down payment from you just as from any other buyer. Also, do not count on a bargain basement price for the property. Expect to pay only about 5 or 10 percent less than you would normally pay for a similar property.

❑ Finally, be aware that many state laws give the former owner the right to redeem his property, or buy it back, within 6 to 12 months. If the owner can come up with the money to redeem the property, you will get your money back, but you will have to give up the house.

complete recovery of the loan.

Foreclosure laws vary from state to state, but proceedings generally follow a series of steps similar to those described below.

FIRST MISSED PAYMENT

When you took out your loan, you signed a promissory note and a mortgage. Both documents contain clauses that set forth your rights regarding payments and the lender's rights.

If you miss a payment, the lender is usually required to send you a letter of reminder along with an imposed late fee of about 5 percent of the amount due.

If you still fail to pay, the lender has to send you a formal "notice of default," which informs you that you can "cure" your default within a specified time by making your payments and paying any additional fees that have accrued. The notice should specify the exact amount you owe as well as the last day on which it can be paid.

The lender is obliged to send this notice to your last known address; it is up to you to be sure that he has your current address. If you pay what you owe within the time limit and then keep up with your payments, the lender can take no further action against you. If you cannot make the payments, you can still avoid foreclosure by selling your house yourself—although you may have to reduce its price for a quick sale.

THE LAWSUIT

If you do not pay the amount you owe by the date due, the

lender may initiate foreclosure proceedings. He will start by suing you for the unpaid balance of your loan, and asking a court to foreclose the mortgage—that is, bar you from redeeming it, or paying it off—and order your property to be sold. You will be named as a defendant in the lawsuit, along with any third parties who may have an interest in your property (such as other creditors who want your property sold to repay them or government agencies that have claims for unpaid taxes). The lender will have a foreclosure petition delivered to you, either by the sheriff or by certified mail.

If you receive a foreclosure petition, consult a lawyer immediately. If you have a valid defense, such as that you have made all the necessary payments, your lawyer may be able to have the action stopped. If you do not, she may be able to come to some agreement with the lender. Finally, she can advise you whether to seek the protection of bankruptcy court (which will temporarily stop foreclosure proceedings), especially if you are having trouble paying your other bills. See BANKRUPTCY.

If you are in default by at least three payments, but your mortgage is insured by the Federal Housing Administration (FHA), you may be able to avoid foreclosure by means of the mortgage assignment program administered by the Department of Housing and Urban Development (HUD). You can obtain more specific information about this program from your mortgage company.

JUDGMENT AND JUDICIAL SALE

If the lender proves his case (that he has lived up to his contractual obligations and that you have defaulted on your mortgage), the court will give him a judgment for the amount due and order your property to be sold. This sale is known as a judicial sale or sheriff's sale—a public auction usually held at the local courthouse. Most states have laws that determine how the notice of a judicial sale is given; often it is published in the local newspaper.

After the notice is published, and before the sale takes place, most lenders will give you one last chance to make good on your loan by paying the amount due plus penalties (assuming interest rates have not gone up). Thus you may be able to save your home even at this late date. If you still cannot pay the lender, your property will be sold to the highest bidder.

TIME LIMIT TO REDEEM PROPERTY AFTER FORECLOSURE

Although the time limit for redeeming real estate after a foreclosure sale in some states depends on the size and type of property and the amount of debt involved, the limits indicated on this map apply in most cases.

DEFICIENCY JUDGMENT

After the sale, the lender will ask the court to grant approval of the sale and to calculate any "deficiency judgment"—the amount remaining if the sale price of the house does not cover the amount you owe the lender. Armed with this judgment, the lender may then garnishee your wages or seize your assets to redeem his money. See DEFICIENCY JUDGMENT.

On the other hand, if your property is sold for more than you owe, the court determines where the excess funds will go. Usually, other parties who have a lien, or claim, on your property, are repaid, and if there is any money remaining, it is given back to you. See LIEN.

REDEMPTION

In order to give you every possible opportunity to keep your home, most states allow you a period of time (usually 6 to 12 months) after the foreclosure and sale during which you can redeem your home, or buy it back. During this time you can continue to live in your home. If you pay the entire amount you owe the lender within this period, including the foreclosure costs, you have redeemed your property. The person who bought your home at the foreclosure sale will be refunded his money. See also MORTGAGE.

FOREIGN BANK ACCOUNT

People who travel abroad, invest in foreign markets, or seek financial privacy sometimes open a bank account in a foreign country. The process of opening a foreign bank account is not complicated.

CHOOSING A BANK

For a possible source of banks that do business with foreign depositors, contact the embassies of the countries that interest you. Embassies are located in Washington, D.C., and some countries have consulates in major U.S. cities.

As with an American bank, you should inquire about a foreign bank's services, fees, interest rates, and minimum deposit requirements. Ask how often funds can be transferred out of an account; whether taxes are withheld on interest paid to nonresident accounts; whether you can conduct transactions by mail, telephone, or wire; and whether the account representatives speak English.

GREATER PRIVACY

A primary reason for opening a foreign bank account is privacy. Some U.S. government agencies (including the Internal Revenue Service, the Federal Deposit Insurance Corporation, and the Treasury Department) have access to information about bank accounts in the United States, but not to foreign accounts, except under special circumstances. For example, Switzerland will only provide information to a foreign government that is investigating a crime that is also a crime under Swiss law.

In some countries—including Austria, Switzerland, and the Cayman Islands—banks allow accounts to bear a number in place of the owner's name. In Switzerland the identity of the account holder is known only to a few senior bank officials; all other personnel, including the tellers, know only the number. The procedures for setting up numbered accounts vary. Generally, the depositor must visit the bank and show reliable identification, such as a passport.

TAXES AND DISCLOSURE LAWS

Some countries withhold taxes on interest and dividends paid to nonresidents. Income from foreign investments is also taxable in the United States, but you can reclaim foreign taxes you paid. To do so, you must apply for a tax credit on your federal income tax return. It is illegal not to disclose this income on your income tax return. Other IRS tax forms ask for information about foreign trust accounts with balances of $10,000 or more.

TRANSFER OF FUNDS

If you transfer $10,000 or more from the United States to a foreign country, whether to a bank or elsewhere, you must give written notice to the U.S. Customs Service, which provides a disclosure form for this purpose. If you are going to transfer funds by mail, wire, or telephone, send the form to the U.S. Customs Service, 1301 Constitution Avenue NW, Washington, DC 20229. If you are taking the money abroad personally, you should complete the form and give it to a customs officer at your U.S. point of departure.

FORENSIC MEDICINE

Forensic medicine is a medical specialty that focuses on legal problems—especially those involving crime, medical malpractice, and personal injury. (Forensic means "concerned with courts and the law.")

CRIMINAL CASES

Perhaps the best-known use of forensic medicine is in criminal law. Forensic pathologists (doctors who are trained in the various techniques that are necessary for crime detection) often are important witnesses in criminal cases.

A forensic pathologist is specially trained in autopsy techniques. In the case of a suspected murder, he will try to determine the cause of the victim's death, the age and cause of any wounds, the time of death, and other circumstances surrounding the death. In some cases he may be able to determine the identity of both the victim and the murderer if they are not known.

In addition to conducting autopsies, a forensic pathologist may visit crime scenes, interview witnesses, and perform laboratory experiments. He examines the victim's clothing as well as the body itself and analyzes the hairs, fluids, and body tissues found on a crime victim or at the scene. From such evidence, the forensic pathologist can, for example, tell whether a particular tissue type matches that of the victim or any of the suspects.

FORENSIC PSYCHIATRY IN CRIMINAL CASES

Forensic psychiatrists are often asked to determine whether a particular defendant has the mental ability to distinguish right from wrong, or whether she was unable to control her behavior. Forensic psychiatrists may also determine whether a defendant is mentally able to assist in her defense.

Such questions are important, since a person who cannot distinguish right from wrong or who is suffering from delusions cannot be held legally accountable for her crimes. A person unable to assist in her own defense will not be put on trial until able to do so.

CIVIL CASES

Forensic medicine is used in civil cases too. In medical malpractice and personal-injury cases, juries may have to decide whether the defendant met a "reasonable standard of care" or was negligent. In order to prove negligence or malpractice, the plaintiff may have to present expert opinions from medical professionals.

FORFEITURE

To forfeit is to lose or be deprived of something because of an offense or failure to act. Fines and penalties are forfeits. Forfeiture also occurs when the government—usually a law enforcement agency—takes possession of property used in illegal activities, without compensating the owner. For example, the proprietor of a popular bar lost his business when the state bureau of investigation arrested one of his employees for running an illegal betting operation at the bar. The skipper of a charter fishing service lost a boat he had rented to some weekend sportsmen when federal agents intercepted it off the Florida coast and found that it was carrying five pounds of cocaine. The state government sold the bar, and the Drug Enforcement Administration now uses the boat for undercover operations. Although the two businessmen broke no laws themselves, and were unaware of the illegal activities by the bartender and the sportsmen, the government was able to take their property through forfeiture proceedings.

PUNISHING THE INNOCENT AS WELL AS THE GUILTY

Laws permitting these kinds of forfeits are criticized when they affect innocent parties, such as the two businessmen described above. Although forfeiture laws have been challenged as violating the 5th and 14th Amendments to the Constitution, which prohibit the seizure of private property without due process of law and without just compensation, they have generally been upheld. However, some state and federal courts have often declared forfeiture laws illegal.

Some state forfeiture laws do, however, protect innocent owners. In Florida, for example, if an automobile owner (or the finance company from whom he borrowed the money) can prove that he did not know his car was being used for illegal purposes, he will not lose the car. In some other states, a lender or person holding a lien on property that has been seized will be called upon to establish that he investigated the debtor and discovered no reason to suspect illegality.

The U.S. Supreme Court has declared that "forfeitures are not favored," and for this reason forfeitures are unlawful unless clearly authorized by a specific law—most often one that regulates hunting, gambling, drugs, or alcohol. A 1993 Supreme Court decision held that federal officials cannot seize property purchased with drug-trafficking profits if it was subsequently given to an innocent party. The innocent party must have a chance to defend her right to that property.

REAL LIFE, REAL LAW

The Case of the Forfeited Ford

Bob was so proud of his nephew, Jeff, for graduating from college that as a graduation gift he lent his vintage Ford Mustang to Jeff for a trip to Florida. As Jeff was returning home through another state, he picked up a hitchhiker carrying a large backpack. Just a few miles down the road, Jeff was stopped by a highway patrolman, who demanded that both men get out of the car. Despite the hitchhiker's protests, the officer searched the backpack and found several thousand dollars' worth of cocaine. He arrested the hitchhiker and impounded Bob's car.

Bob was sure that once the official realized that he had nothing to do with the cocaine, his property would be returned. He was wrong. The state forfeiture law contained no provision to protect innocent owners. Even though the charges against the hitchhiker were ultimately dismissed because the search by the highway patrolman was held to be illegal, the county attorney persisted in the forfeiture proceeding.

After many months and thousands of dollars in legal fees, Bob's forfeiture case was tried before a jury. The government was merely required to show that the cocaine was being transported in Bob's car. It did so, and the jury awarded a forfeiture.

Unlike most cases of this type, Bob's ultimately had a happy ending. Bob applied to the state's governor for a remission, and under intense pressure from the press and public opinion, the governor ordered the car returned.

ABUSES OF FORFEITURE

Some local laws allow a person who has provided information that forms the basis of a forfeiture to claim a percentage of the value of the property as a reward. State governments that confiscate property and turn it over to the federal government may be entitled to keep as much as 85 percent of its value. Furthermore, federal laws tend to make it harder for an owner to recover confiscated property than some states do. Therefore, state law enforcement agencies may transfer property to federal officers. Forfeiture laws are criticized when they are used primarily to provide an easy source of revenue for law enforcement agencies. Some agencies have been censured for using such proceeds for inappropriate acquisitions.

WHERE FORFEITURE LAWS APPLY

The federal government has many laws regarding forfeiture of property, and 47 states have forfeiture laws of some kind. Some cities have also passed laws that allow the forfeiture of property that is used in violation of city codes.

COURT PROCEEDINGS

Although forfeitures are often linked to crimes and criminal prosecutions, forfeiture proceedings are usually viewed as civil. In some states, such as Florida, they may proceed independently of any criminal prosecution or its outcome. Suppose Jim lent his car to his best friend Carl, who was arrested for speeding while driving it and was found to be carrying bootleg whiskey in the trunk. The state seized the car and started forfeiture proceedings. Even if Carl is acquitted of bootlegging, or is never even charged, Jim could still end up losing his car.

In other states, such as Oregon, the property that has been

forfeited must be returned to its owner if a criminal defendant is acquitted. And a few states prohibit forfeiture proceedings if the owner has been convicted of the related crime, maintaining that forfeiture would constitute double jeopardy. See DOUBLE JEOPARDY.

Most forfeiture proceedings are "show cause" hearings. This means an owner must prove to the court why his property should not be forfeited. Since forfeiture is a civil proceeding, the government only has to prove its case by a "preponderance of the evidence"—a much easier task than proving guilt beyond a reasonable doubt, as is required in criminal cases. See also BURDEN OF PROOF; RICO; SEARCH AND SEIZURE.

REMISSION

If the forfeiture is allowed by the court, the property owner may be able to have his forfeited property returned by obtaining a "remission" from the governor of a state, the courts, a federal official, or the president of the United States, depending on the circumstances.

AVOIDING FORFEITURE

As long as forfeiture laws remain on the books, anyone can be a victim of unfair practices. Reduce your risk by allowing only people you know well to use your property, especially those items you cannot afford to lose.

FORGERY

Creating a false document or substantially altering a genuine one with the intent to defraud is forgery. Someone creates a false document, for example, if he steals a checkbook, fills in all the blanks, and cashes the checks. If a person changes a provision in another's will, he is guilty of forgery by altering an otherwise genuine document.

A forgery does not have to be handwritten. Engraving, printing, stamping, or typing with an intent to defraud is forgery. In some states, fraudulently obtaining a legitimate signature is also forgery. Suppose Jim has his elderly father sign a form that Jim claims is needed by the Internal Revenue Service. The father later discovers the form was a quitclaim deed to his own home, transferring the ownership to his son. Jim is guilty of forgery.

ESTABLISHING FORGERY

For a person to be convicted of forgery, three things must be established: (1) a document must have been created or altered, (2) the document must be able to deceive someone, and (3) there must have been an intent to defraud.

Creation and alteration

Creating a document such as a check, deed, or promissory note can constitute forgery. So can making changes that substantially alter the meaning or legal effect of a document. Inserting zeroes into the amount of a check, so that $10 becomes $100, is a common example, although not every state considers this forgery.

Revising dates on a contract, receipt, or other legal document is another form of alteration. For example, a contract may specify that the Cunningham Crumpet Company will pay all of salesman Barry's expenses through June 15. If Barry changes the date to cover expenses incurred through July 15, he is a forger.

For an alteration to be considered a forgery, it must be "material"—that is, it must substantially change the meaning. Adding a middle name to someone's name in a contract would not be a forgery if it served to further identify that person.

Deceptiveness

To be a forgery a document must look realistic enough to deceive people into believing it is genuine. Someone who photocopied a $20 bill and crudely colored it green, for example, would not be likely to be charged with forgery. See COUNTERFEIT MONEY.

Intent to defraud

The most important element of forgery is the intent to defraud, which must be proved beyond a reasonable doubt by the prosecuting attorney.

Some actions that appear to be forgery are not, because there is no attempt to defraud. Suppose Harold wants to deposit his wife Harriet's paycheck into her account while she is away. He signs her name to endorse the check and deposits it into her account. Because he has Harriet's permission to act as her agent, Harold is not guilty of forgery. Or suppose you want to make certain numbers in a contract more legible. If you misread a number and mistakenly change a 3 to an 8, you are not guilty of forgery because you did not intend to defraud anyone.

PUNISHMENT

Forgery is a felony, and the penalty increases with the seriousness of the crime. A forger may also be financially responsible for the loss his forgery caused, as in the case of an altered check. See also CHECK.

FOSTER HOME

When parents cannot or will not provide proper care for a child, the courts can temporarily transfer custody to a state child-welfare agency. The agency may then place the child in a foster home—a private residence that provides a structured, caring environment for the child. Sometimes children are placed in foster homes when their parents have voluntarily given them up for adoption. The length of time that a child stays in a foster home can be as short as one night or as long as several years.

Foster care is not the same as adoption; a foster child's parents usually retain their parental rights, and the child will eventually be either returned to them or adopted by someone else. In some cases, foster parents adopt their foster children, and in certain states they are given adoptive preference if the child becomes available for adoption. See also ADOPTION.

THE FOSTER HOME LICENSE

A foster home must be sanctioned by a state child-welfare agency. Every state has its own standards for approving and licensing foster homes, but the procedure for licensing is similar in most states.

Physical inspection
If you have called your local child-welfare agency and indicated that you are interested in becoming a foster parent, you will be visited by a social worker from the agency. She will make certain that your home is well kept, that it contains sufficient space for a foster child or children, and that it meets the agency's minimum standards for health and safety. Typically, homes are required to have smoke detectors, fire extinguishers, and separate beds for each foster child.

Physical exams
Because children who are placed in foster homes often can be exceptionally demanding, their foster parents should be in good health. You may therefore be asked to provide a statement from your family physician concerning your health and to undergo testing for certain communicable diseases, such as tuberculosis.

Background screening
The agency will conduct a background check on all adults in your household. Certain criminal convictions or recorded complaints of child abuse or neglect will rule you out as a prospective foster parent.

Personal evaluation
In the last 20 years the profile of a typical foster home has changed. Increasingly, single women and men become foster parents, and some states provide day care for children whose foster parents work outside the home. As the needs of foster children vary, a social worker will help you determine what type of child would be best suited for your home.

Training
As a prospective foster parent, you are usually required to undergo state-sponsored training to learn how to deal with children who have suffered neglect or abuse. If you will be caring for a child with great emotional or physical needs, you will be taught the specialized skills required. The training should also help you to understand the legal system and the social workers with whom you will be dealing.

FOSTER PARENTS' RESPONSIBILITIES

As a foster parent, you should receive a contract from the agency that spells out your duties and responsibilities to the child and to the agency—as well as those of the agency toward you and the child. Your primary obligation will be to care for and nurture the child who has been placed in your care. You will also be required to ensure that your foster child attends school and keeps necessary appointments. Although foster parents are responsible for disciplining the foster child, agencies strictly forbid physical punishment.

You will receive a stipend for your foster child's basic needs, including food, clothing, and toiletries. The agency is usually responsible for making medical, dental, and counseling services available, as well as providing special educational services. However, you should be forewarned that the stipend rarely if ever covers all of a child's needs; foster care is never a lucrative career.

You will be in frequent contact with the social worker assigned to monitor you and your child, reporting to her on the child's development. The social worker should be able to answer your questions and offer guidance, and she should keep you informed of your foster child's legal status and any future plans for her.

You should not expect that a child living with you will be there forever. The child must return to a permanent living situation, and you will be expected to assist with the process of reintegration.

In some cases, it is not advisable or possible to return a child to her family—for example, if she was severely abused by her parents, if they abandoned her, or if they are chronically mentally ill. The social workers may then want to build a case in order to terminate the parents' rights to the child. In such an instance, you might be asked to report to the court whether the parents visited the child, how they interacted with her, and any other observations you have made about the child.

FOSTER PARENTS' RIGHTS

Foster parents have fewer legal rights than anyone else in the foster-care system. A child in foster care is usually in the legal custody of the state (or in some cases a private, nonprofit agency). Although there are exceptions, foster parents do not participate in court proceedings relating to their foster child, and a foster child may be removed from the home at any time. In some states, however, a foster parent who has had custody of a child for a significant period of time will be given notice before the child is removed. See also CHILD CUSTODY; CHILDREN'S RIGHTS.

FRANCHISE

A franchise is a special privilege that is granted or sold. There are two basic types. The first is a government franchise, whereby the government gives an individual or corporation a privilege unavailable to the rest of the population. Set up primarily for the benefit of the public, government franchises authorize such bodies as utility companies, taxi and bus companies, and corporations responsible for building and maintaining bridges, tunnels, and ferries.

The second type of franchise is the grant of a privilege by a company to an individual or another company. This grant is usually made by a contract or the sale of a license, and almost always involves the payment of a fee to the company that grants the privilege.

PRIVATE BUSINESS FRANCHISES

In a private franchise the "franchisor" sells the right to do business using a certain trade name or set of business practices to a "franchisee." This arrangement is especially popular in businesses where a certain level of quality or service is associated with a particular product, such as automobile sales and leasing, fast food, and "brand-name" clothing. Although franchise agreements can be elaborate, they generally specify the methods and procedures a franchisee must follow in exchange for the right to operate the franchised business. This can mean as much as having to rely on the franchisor for all goods and services or as little as promising to maintain a specified level of quality. In any event, the franchisee is solely responsible for the debts, taxes, insurance, and other expenses of the business.

OWNING A FRANCHISE: WHAT YOU SHOULD KNOW

Charlotte has always wanted to run a family-style restaurant. But because she has little experience in managing a business, she decides to look into buying a franchise. This way, she reasons, she will have the benefit of a well-established name, as well as the experience, skills, advertising, and reputation of a national enterprise. Charlotte's reasoning is supported by statistics: While 40 percent of newly established businesses fail within one year, fewer than 5 percent of franchised businesses suffer the same fate. And whether your dream is to own a family-style restaurant, a video outlet, or a clothing store, there is a wealth of franchising opportunities from which to choose. About 2,000 franchisors of businesses are in operation in the United States today.

The pros and cons

As with any other business, operating a franchise has both advantages and drawbacks. Franchisors usually provide training programs and will help with site selection and other important issues—a definite plus for novices who are looking for guidance and structure.

On the negative side, many franchisors have strict policies governing hours of operation, customer service, use of the company logo, and other business practices. Furthermore, franchise contracts often contain specific guidelines governing a range of concerns from cleanliness to how merchandise is displayed, which are meant to ensure the uniformity of the franchise operations. Although franchisees must be given time to correct problems, noncompliance with these mandatory guidelines can result in the cancellation of the franchise contract.

The cost to you

Starting a franchise requires capital. Franchisees are almost always required to pay an initial fee, usually payable upon signing the contract; this fee can range from less than $1,000 to over $100,000. Ideally, in exchange for the initial fee, the franchisee receives a business package developed by an established organization.

In addition to the start-up fee, the franchisor may charge a royalty of up to 10 percent of sales (not profits): for every dollar the franchisee takes in, the franchisor may be entitled to receive 10 cents. Many businesses operate on a profit margin of less than 5 percent, so it can be hard to turn a profit if the royalty charged by the franchisor is high.

Most franchisors charge an advertising fee to help pay for the cost of local and national advertising in newspapers and on radio and television. Like the royalty, this fee is usually

CHECKLIST

Evaluating a Franchise Opportunity

Before signing an agreement to buy a franchise, carefully read the franchisor's Uniform Franchise Offering Circular (UFOC) and note how the following points have been covered:

❑ **EXCLUSIVE RIGHTS.**
Some franchisors offer exclusive rights to territories, while others will grant many franchises within the same area. Sometimes the franchise company may crowd franchisees by operating its own stores nearby.

❑ **WRITTEN CONFIRMATION.**
Make sure that any spoken promises or agreements made by the franchisor are stated in the UFOC and in the contract.

❑ **COST OF TRAINING.**
If your franchisor requires a training program, find out whether the cost of travel and other expenses are included in your initial investment fee.

❑ **ADDITIONAL SERVICES.**
Find out exactly what services are provided as a part of your franchise agreement—for instance, marketing advice or accounting help, or other assistance.

❑ **SUPPLIES AND INVENTORY.**
If the agreement states that you must purchase all equipment, supplies, and inventory from the franchisor or a specified supplier, ask for the reason. For instance, is the franchisor or supplier able to give you the best price, or are the goods unavailable elsewhere?

❑ **OTHER FRANCHISEES.**
The franchisor must supply you with the names, addresses, and phone numbers of at least 10 franchisees in your area. It is important to visit these investors, both to see their day-to-day operations and to check on claims made by the franchisor.

❑ **SELLING YOUR FRANCHISE.**
In general, your rights to sell or transfer your franchise may be subject to the franchisor's approval. In some cases the franchisor has the right of first refusal to buy the franchise if you later wish to sell it, or if you become disabled or die while you own it.

❑ **TERMINATION OF THE FRANCHISE AGREEMENT.**
Make sure any clauses pertaining to the termination of the franchise agreement are consistent with the laws of your state. You can find out laws regarding termination by contacting your state consumer protection agency.

calculated as a percentage of sales (generally 1 or 2 percent) and is charged on a regular basis. An advertising fund has a distinct advantage for franchisees, since it allows for far more advertising than most small-business owners could afford on their own.

The franchisor's prospectus should provide you with the basic information to make a reasonable business decision. However, it is also wise to carefully consider your own personality and professional goals before signing any agreement. For example, if you have years of experience or are bothered by having others tell you how to use your time and set up your operation, you may not want to buy a franchise.

PROTECTING THE FRANCHISEE

To help protect prospective franchisees, federal and state laws have been enacted to regulate franchise sales.

Federal regulations
Issued by the Federal Trade Commission (FTC), federal regulations require full disclosure of the terms and conditions of franchise operation. These include the fees, royalties, expiration date of the franchise license, and any other obligations or restrictions that the franchisee ought to know about in advance of the sale.

This information is contained in the franchisor's Uniform Franchise Offering Circular (UFOC). In addition, the UFOC must include the franchisor's audited financial statement, complete information about the franchisor's personal and business background (including any previous bankruptcies or litigation), short biographies of any other people affiliated with the franchisor (such as partners, managers, and trustees), and a list of current franchisees.

Moreover, any claims that the franchisor has made about actual or projected sales or potential profits must be substantiated in the UFOC. Penalties can be imposed on companies that fail to follow statutory requirements.

State regulations
About one-third of the states also have franchise regulations. All of these states require franchisors to register with the proper state authority before offering franchises—this applies to out-of-state companies as well as to those located in the state.

In addition, many regulated states require franchisors to establish an impoundment account, which allows you to recover your initial fee if you feel that the franchisor has not met his obligations and promises. Regulations in some states also require that the franchisor's advertisements be reviewed and approved by a state agency.

WAITING PERIOD

Both state and federal regulations require a waiting period of 10 business days between the time a potential purchaser receives the UFOC and the time he signs the franchise agreement.

If you have been pressured into signing a contract before the 10-day waiting period has come to an end, you are not bound by the contract. See also Federal Trade Commission; Trademark.

FRAUD

Fraud is the intentional misrepresentation of the truth in order to induce another person to part with something of value or surrender a legal right. Conviction for fraud requires proof that the victim relied on the misrepresentation to his detriment. A victim can sue to recover money that he lost as a result of fraud, but proving fraud can be difficult.

PROVING FRAUD

At a minimum, the following must be proved in order to convict someone of fraud:

Misrepresentation
"Intentional misrepresentation" is the legal terminology for telling a lie. Suppose you are planning to buy a house and its owner tells you that the foundation is in perfect condition when she knows that the basement walls are on the verge of collapse. The owner has made an intentional misrepresentation. However, if she honestly does not know that the foundation is crumbling, the owner is not guilty of intentional misrepresentation.

Material fact
An intentional misrepresentation must be of a "material

fact," or one that is important and relevant. Suppose the owner of the house tells you she replaced the roof five years ago. After you buy the house, you discover that the roof is actually 10 years old. If the roof is sound, the fact that it is five years older than you believed is not a material fact that would have influenced your decision to purchase that property.

Reliance upon the fact

Proof of fraud requires that the buyer relied on the intentional misrepresentation of a material fact. Suppose you take a tour of the basement, and see for yourself that the foundation is collapsing and that the cellar is full of water. You cannot later say that you relied on the owner's representation that the foundation was in top condition. Even if you did not see the damage, the fact that a reasonable and expected amount of diligence on your part would have disclosed it may be enough to invalidate a claim of fraud.

Detriment or harm

Finally, a victim of fraud must suffer some detriment or harm. If you buy the house and it collapses, you can be compensated only if you were damaged by the collapse. For example, if an appraisal shows that without the house the property is worth more than what you paid for it, you cannot win your lawsuit claiming fraud.

CRIMINAL LIABILITY

Some fraudulent acts are criminal. State and federal laws define the fraudulent acts that can be punished by fines or imprisonment or both. Among them are false advertising and medical quackery, making a false odometer statement, selling bogus securities, and collecting insurance premiums but not forwarding them to the insurer. See also CONSUMER PROTECTION; FALSE ADVERTISING; ODOMETER STATEMENT; SCAMS AND SWINDLES; WARRANTY AND GUARANTY.

FREEDOM OF INFORMATION ACT

The Freedom of Information Act (FOIA) requires that federal agencies allow public access to their records. For instance, if you as a private citizen want to know about asbestos contamination, you would seek information from the Environmental Protection Agency (EPA); and if you want to find out about companies that use live animals for cosmetic testing, you would write to the Food and Drug Administration (FDA).

FOIA requests can be made to agencies that belong to the executive branch of government only (not the judicial or legislative branches). In addition, some types of information are not subject to public disclosure. They include:

◇ National defense and foreign policy secrets.

◇ Trade secrets and other commercial information.

◇ An agency's personnel rules and practices.

◇ Interagency legal and policy documents.

◇ Personnel files, medical files, and other information that, if disclosed, would constitute an invasion of privacy.

◇ Some law enforcement investigation files.

◇ Documents concerning financial institutions.

◇ Some geological surveys.

If the information you asked for has already been made public, the agency does not have to supply it again.

MAKING A FOIA REQUEST

If you want to obtain information from the federal government but do not know whom to contact, call the Federal Information Center, which will steer you in the right direction. For information on how and when to call, see FEDERAL INFORMATION CENTER.

Once you know what the proper agency is, write a concise letter requesting, as specifically as possible, the information you want. Follow the form presented in the EVERYDAY LEGAL FORMS section of this book, beginning on page 552.

Within 10 business days of receiving your request, the agency must tell you whether or not it will be granted.

IF AN AGENCY DENIES A REQUEST

If an agency denies your FOIA request, it must give you the reason for doing so and inform you of your right to appeal the denial. An agency cannot deny a request because part of the requested document is exempt from disclosure, but must make whatever deletions are needed to prevent the disclosure of exempt information. You can appeal any denial to the agency, and you can file suit in federal district court if your appeal is denied. The court will review the agency's reasons for denying disclosure and either uphold that decision or order the requested documents be sent to you. But courts are reluctant to question an agency's judgment, and filing a lawsuit may therefore be a waste of time and money.

STATE LAW

Many states now have laws similar to the FOIA requiring state agencies to disclose information and documents. To find out what kinds of information must be made available and how to make your request, ask your librarian for help or call your state attorney general's office. See also GOVERNMENT RECORDS; SUNSHINE LAW.

FRIVOLOUS SUIT

A lawsuit that has no legal merit is called a frivolous suit. Suppose Barney is the owner of Barney's Widgets. His principal competitor, Ace Widgets, has been cutting into his market recently, and Barney is getting worried. He decides to file a lawsuit against Ace, alleging unfair trading practices. Even though Barney knows that Ace has not engaged in any unfair trading practices, he hopes that the lawsuit will cost Ace time and money, thus eating into Ace's profits. Barney also hopes that Ace will be forced to disclose some of its trade secrets in the course of the suit.

Barney's lawsuit is frivolous. A lawsuit should be started only if some factual and legal basis warrants it. It should not be based on false or irrelevant claims. And it should not be filed if the plaintiff, or his lawyer, knows (or can easily find out) that similar suits have been rejected by the courts.

Sometimes lawsuits are filed just to harass or embarrass the other party. For example, creditors are notified when a debtor has been declared bankrupt, and they are no longer entitled to pursue him for the debt. If a creditor then files a suit to collect the debt or seeks garnishment of the debtor's wages, he is filing a frivolous suit.

If a plaintiff and his lawyer bring a frivolous lawsuit, they may both be subject to sanctions by the court. In the example above, Barney may have to pay Ace's attorneys' fees, as well as any other expenses Ace incurred in having to defend against Barney's claim. Barney's lawyer may be subject to serious disciplinary action by the local bar association, and both Barney and his lawyer can be sued by Ace.

FULL COVENANT AND WARRANTY DEED

Title to (ownership of) real estate is transferred by means of a legal document called a deed. As evidence of ownership, a seller may give a buyer one of three types of deeds: (1) a full covenant and warranty deed, (2) a bargain and sale deed, or (3) a quitclaim deed. For a discussion of these types of deeds, see BARGAIN AND SALE DEED; QUITCLAIM DEED.

Of the three kinds of deeds, a full covenant and warranty deed offers a buyer the greatest protection because it guarantees that no other person owns any of the property, and that no claims (such as liens or unacknowledged easements) will be made against the property. If the seller gives a full covenant and warranty deed, and a third person subsequently appears claiming access or title to the property, the buyer can sue the seller. Similarly, if someone appears with a lien against the property that was imposed before the sale, the buyer can seek compensation from the seller for the amount of the lien. See also DEED; EASEMENT; HOME BUYING AND SELLING; LIEN; TITLE INSURANCE.

FULL FAITH AND CREDIT

Article 4, Section 1, of the U.S. Constitution provides that "Full Faith and Credit shall be given in each State to the public Acts, Records, and judicial Proceedings of every other State." The main purpose of this clause is to prevent litigation that has already been concluded in one state from being pursued in another state—that is, when a person obtains a valid legal decision in one state, he can expect that it will be recognized in all other states.

Suppose that Bruce wins a personal-injury lawsuit against Susie, whose broken doorstep caused Bruce to break his leg. Because of the full faith and credit clause, if Susie moves from Ohio to Arizona and refuses to pay the compensation to Bruce, he would not have to start a new personal-injury suit in an Arizona court in order to get his money. He would, however, have to file a suit asking Arizona to recognize the Ohio court's decision. If Bruce had lost his lawsuit against Susie, she would be protected against his suing her again in the Arizona courts.

Under certain circumstances, full faith and credit does not apply—for example, when the court that heard the case did not have the proper jurisdiction (authority). Also, child-custody decisions are sometimes exempt from the full faith and credit clause because they are never final and can be modified at a future date to protect the child's interests.

FUNERAL AND BURIAL

When you die, decisions will have to be made about your funeral and burial. These decisions include such details as the time, place, and manner of your funeral and burial and the choice of a marker or monument for your grave or tomb. If you have definite ideas about how your funeral and burial should take place, you should make them clear to your family and friends. The more you do to communicate your wishes, and the more explicit your instructions, the more likely it is that they will be carried out.

It is best to put your wishes in writing, but do not put them in your will. A will is a legal document for the disposition of property, and it is usually not read until after funeral arrangements have been completed or the deceased has been buried. See also EXECUTOR AND ADMINISTRATOR; PROBATE; WILL.

LETTER OF LAST INSTRUCTIONS

To communicate your wishes, you should prepare a letter of last instructions—a private document (as compared to a will, which becomes public when it is filed with the court) detailing the funeral and burial arrangements you desire for yourself.

A letter of last instructions can be as specific as you wish. It may tell how you want your body disposed of (cremation, burial, or donation to medical science) and whether you want flowers at your funeral or contributions to your favorite charity. If you decide to donate your organs, you should complete a Uniform Anatomical Gift Form. Copies of letters of instruction for burial and cremation are included in the EVERYDAY LEGAL FORMS section beginning on page 552.

Give copies of your letter of last instructions (which can be changed and updated as you wish) to family members or friends who may ultimately have the responsibility for handling your funeral arrangements. Put the original in a safe place where it can easily be found upon your death. Do not put it in a safe-deposit box, since the box may be sealed for a period of time after your death until a tax official inventories its contents.

Writing a letter of last instructions does not guarantee that your wishes will be carried out. The letter is not a binding legal document, and your family or the executor of your estate may handle funeral arrangements as they see fit. However, some states have laws recognizing the right of each person to decide on the disposal of his body. If you ask for a burial, your family cannot decide to cremate your body.

If you do not express your wishes prior to death, the right to make decisions about your funeral and burial arrangements may be given to your surviving spouse or other family members; some states specify who has these rights. If no one comes forward to claim a body, state or local laws will determine how the body will be disposed of.

FINANCIAL RESPONSIBILITY

Unless you pay in advance for your funeral and burial, the expenses incurred are generally deducted from your estate before any other assets are distributed.

If your estate does not have enough money to cover the cost of a funeral and burial, your next of kin may be held responsible for the cost in some states. If no family member or other person can be identified and made to pay for these expenses, the cost may be assumed by your local government, but you may be buried in a pauper's cemetery.

THE FUNERAL RULE

No matter how explicit your funeral instructions, it will be up to family or friends to carry them out. To prevent the funeral industry from taking advantage of grieving survivors, the Federal Trade Commission (FTC) issued the Funeral Rule. It requires funeral homes and mortuaries to give prices and provide information about services over the telephone. When your family visits the facility, they must be given a list detailing the price of each service and each item offered. In addition, the funeral home is obligated to tell which services are required by law and which are optional. Finally, everything selected—from the casket and obituary notices to the clergy and pallbearers—must be accounted for on an itemized statement.

The FTC's Funeral Rule also requires cemeteries to provide a written statement detailing the cost of the plot as well as any additional expenses, such as upkeep. Some cemeteries have rules governing headstones, markers, flowers, and other decorations. Before signing a contract, the family should make sure that the cemetery's rules do not conflict with their wishes or those of the deceased.

PREPAYMENT OPTIONS

To spare your family the burden of planning and paying for your funeral, you may decide to make advance arrangements.

Burial societies

One option is to join a burial or memorial society. These cooperative organizations charge members a one-time fee, and at the time of your death they make all the arrangements according to your instructions. Since these organizations work with local funeral directors, they receive substantial discounts on funerals and burials.

Burial insurance

Another option is to buy burial insurance, which covers the cost of your funeral and burial or cremation. Burial insurance may cost more than a term life insurance policy for the same benefits. If you buy a term life insurance policy instead of burial insurance, make sure that the beneficiary understands that he is to use the policy proceeds for your funeral expenses. Do not name your estate as the beneficiary, because the benefits may be held up during the process of probate. See also Life Insurance.

Pre-need plans

Many funeral homes offer a variety of "pre-need" arrangement plans. Under these, you arrange and pay for your funeral and burial in advance. Usually the money is placed in a trust fund or a life insurance policy, with the funeral director as the beneficiary. However, in a few states the funeral director is allowed to turn your payments over to a private investment firm, a practice that can lead to problems. In a recent case, an investment firm mismanaged funeral funds, forcing several funeral homes into bankruptcy and leaving consumers with nothing.

Before investing in such a pre-need plan, find out where the money is to be invested. If it is not going into a trust fund regulated by the state, you should probably choose another policy. Also find out whether you can transfer your arrangements to another funeral home if you move. If you are paying on an installment plan, ask whether your agreement will be good if you die before making all of your payments. Some contracts state that the prearranged price is not locked in until you have paid in full.

Finally, be sure your family or friends know that you have paid for your funeral and burial. In some cases, families have paid for a loved one's funeral only to discover that a prepaid plan was already in place with another funeral home.

You may also prepay for a cemetery plot, but first consider whether you will still be living in the same place at the time of your death.

EMBALMING

The rules relating to embalming, which preserves a corpse from rapid deterioration after death, vary from state to state. Embalming is one of the costliest items on a funeral bill and it is not always necessary. There are three situations in which embalming may be required by law: (1) when the body is to be transported across state lines, (2) when burial will be delayed, or (3) when the deceased died of a communicable disease. In addition, a funeral home is likely to suggest embalming for open-casket viewing.

CREMATION

State or local law may set requirements regarding cremation. For example, it may not be necessary to buy a casket; an approved cremation container may be sufficient. State or local law may also restrict the right to scatter the ashes of a deceased person following his cremation.

OUT-OF-STATE DEATHS

It is sometimes necessary to transport a body across a state line—to bring someone home for burial, for instance. State laws or municipal ordinances may impose certain requirements before a body can be moved into or out of a state. Funeral homes can usually get the necessary permits to transport the body.

DISINTERMENT

Once a body is buried, it is considered to be in the custody of the law and cannot be disinterred—that is, removed from its grave or tomb—without court approval. The courts will not allow a body to be moved except out of necessity or for a justifiable family purpose. For example, disinterment may be necessary if the cemetery has been abandoned or the land is needed for a public improvement. A change in burial place may also be approved if a family wishes to buy a larger cemetery plot to accommodate all of its members.

The courts allow a body to be disinterred for the purpose of performing an autopsy to gather evidence about the cause of death. But before a court will give its permission, the judge must be satisfied that disinterment is needed and that there is a reasonable likelihood that evidence will be gained by doing so. For more information about determining the cause of death, see AUTOPSY.

MISCONDUCT

Anyone who disturbs a grave site or disinters or destroys a corpse may be held in violation of state or local laws. In addition, performing an unauthorized embalming or an unauthorized autopsy or improper burial may entitle the heirs of a deceased person to sue for money damages.

FUTURE EARNINGS

Future or potential earnings are often at issue in lawsuits when damages or other monetary awards are being assessed. Cases in which future earnings are disputed often involve personal injury.

For example, suppose Gene, a 35-year-old construction worker, is injured in an automobile accident and is permanently paralyzed from the waist down. If Gene could have been reasonably expected to work in construction for another 25 years, a court might award damages based on the loss of 25 years of his average future earnings as a construction worker. However, Gene must produce evidence of his probable future income (adjusted for inflation) and his potential for earnings in a different field of endeavor. If he can get work as a telephone operator or a bookkeeper, for instance, his probable salary as an office worker will be calculated over the same time period and subtracted from the total award. See also DAMAGES.

FUTURE INTEREST

A right to property you do not currently hold but will obtain at some future time is known as a future interest.

Suppose your father dies and leaves his home to "my friend, Rita, during her lifetime, and thereafter to my children." Rita has a present interest in the home, which is known as a life estate. You and your siblings have a future interest in the property.

Because of your future interest (or "remainder"), Rita is prohibited from selling the home or doing anything that intentionally diminishes its potential value to you. When Rita dies, your future interest becomes a present interest. At that point, you and your siblings will be entitled to occupy, sell, lease, or otherwise dispose of the home. Until then, however, you have no legal right to do anything with it.

Another kind of future interest involves a temporary gift of property. Suppose your father gives his home to Rita for 10 years but reserves the right to occupy it at the end of that period. He has what is known as a reversionary future interest. See also LIFE ESTATE; WILL.

GAMBLING

Since many states have realized that legalized gambling is a means by which they can obtain additional revenue, they have relaxed some of the prohibitions against various forms of gambling. The proceeds from lotteries and other gambling ventures are considered "voluntary taxes" and are used to increase state revenues. See also LOTTERY.

Games such as blackjack and roulette can now be played legally at casinos in many places other than Atlantic City and Las Vegas. For instance, in both Illinois and Iowa, casino gambling is now permitted on riverboats. State-run lotteries and racetrack betting are found throughout the country, and in New York and Connecticut you can even place an off-track bet by telephone. And because Indian reservations are covered by special rules under the 1988 Indian Gambling Act, many reservations hold bingo games and other forms of gambling.

Operating a gambling enterprise is a crime unless permitted by state or local law. Where it is legal, a license is required. In areas where gambling is permitted, local governments typically control where and how it takes place. For example, although a slot machine is legal at the Glory Hole Saloon in Central City, Colorado, it is not legal in Denver. Therefore, if you are planning to set up even a small gambling enterprise, such as a bingo game or raffle, for fund-raising or any other purpose, be sure to consult your local law. See also LICENSE.

States prohibit certain types of people from gambling, such as minors and incompetents. In most places you must be at least 18 years old to gamble in a lottery or at a racetrack and 21 years old to gamble in a casino. In a recent case, a 17-year-old hit the $100,000 jackpot on a slot machine in Las Vegas. But because he was not legally old enough to gamble in the casino, he could not collect the money, nor was his father able to collect it on his behalf.

Winnings from legal and illegal gambling are subject to federal, state, and sometimes local taxes. However, the Internal Revenue Service (IRS) allows you to deduct gambling losses up to the amount of your winnings. Suppose you win $5,000 at blackjack, but lose $10,000 playing poker. You can take a $5,000 deduction on your income tax form. For this reason save all the receipts that you get for your bets and keep accurate records of your winnings and losses.

Casinos, racetracks, and other gambling establishments must report to the IRS any individual's winnings that are in excess of $600 at one time (by filing Form W2-G). If a person's winnings exceed $1,000, the establishment is generally required to withhold 20 percent for the IRS. If your winnings are small, and you are tempted not to declare them on your tax return, note that tipsters often inform the IRS about winning gamblers, and criminal investigations are conducted to expose illegal gamblers. See also SWEEPSTAKES.

GARAGE SALE

If your basement and garage are overflowing with old dishes, appliances, and knickknacks that have accumulated over the years, you can sell them by holding a garage or yard sale. Before going ahead, however, take a few precautions to avoid violating any laws.

◇ Find out if your local law requires you to obtain a permit to hold a sale. Some communities limit the number of garage sales you can hold in a single year, and you can be fined if you exceed that number.

◇ If you live in an area that is controlled by a homeowners association (such as a private housing development or apartment complex), call the management office to ask if there are any restrictions on garage sales. For example, you may be required to conduct the sale only during certain hours or on specified days so that the crowds and traffic that the sale attracts are less likely to be disruptive to your neighbors.

◇ Inquire about any restrictions your local government has placed on the size or position of signs advertising the sale. For example, some communities prohibit posting signs on utility poles or require that signs be removed within a certain time after the sale ends.

◇ Ask your accountant or local tax office whether money you earn at your garage sale is considered taxable income. Generally, it is not, since you do not make a profit when you sell merchandise for less than you paid for it. You are not usually required to collect sales tax unless you conduct garage sales as a regular business.

◇ Familiarize yourself with the condition of all the items you plan to sell, and state their condition honestly. If a neighbor buys a toaster that you claim is in working condition, he is entitled to a refund if it is not. It is a good idea to put "as is" signs on any items that are damaged or that do not work.

◇ Be ready to give your customers a bill of sale for more expensive items in case of later disputes. See BILL OF SALE.

GARNISHMENT

Garnishment is a legal measure that a creditor can use to collect money owed to him. But rather than getting the money directly from the debtor, the creditor collects it from a third party, such as the debtor's employer. Suppose Ed borrowed $5,000 from his cousin Francine, giving her a promissory note in which he agreed to repay the money in one year. After two years Francine had not been able to collect any money from Ed. Her lawyer, Dee, suggested that Francine seek to have Ed's wages garnisheed. Dee's first step was to obtain a court judgment authorizing the garnishment. With this in hand, Dee was able to contact third parties (garnishees) who owed Ed money or had possession of his property. Likely garnishees included the bank that held his savings, and his employer, whom Dee chose as the most likely garnishee. Ed's employer was required to pay the amount specified in the court order directly to Francine from Ed's wages until the full debt was repaid. The order can be terminated only if Ed's circumstances change—if he loses his job, for example, or if he repays the money.

ATTACHMENT

Only Ed's property that is held by a third party can be taken. Thus, if Ed wears an expensive watch, Francine cannot force him to sell it through garnishment. She can, however, make him sell the watch through an attachment proceeding. See ATTACHMENT.

STATE LAW RESTRICTIONS

State law restricts who can be a garnisher and the amount and type of property or assets that can be garnisheed—particularly if the garnishment is of the debtor's wages. For example, most states do not allow pensions to be garnisheed. In some states garnishment of wages is prohibited, and in others garnishment is allowed only to collect back child support.

FEDERAL LAW RESTRICTIONS

The Federal Consumer Credit Protection Act also restricts the amount that Francine can garnishee from Ed. He must be allowed to keep 75 percent of his weekly net wages (after deductions) or 30 times the federal minimum hourly wage, whichever is greater. Suppose Ed's net weekly income is $500, and the minimum hourly wage is $4.25. Therefore, 75 percent of his net income is $375, while 30 times the minimum wage is $127.50. As 75 percent of his income is the greater amount, Francine may garnishee only the remainder of his weekly net income, or $125.

Restrictions on the amounts that can be garnisheed do not apply if the debt is for federal or state taxes, if a bankruptcy court ordered the garnishment, or if the garnishment is for back child support.

PROTECTIONS

Ed's employer cannot fire him from his job because his wages are being garnisheed. In fact, employers who violate this law are subject to criminal penalties. If you are involved in a garnishment proceeding, you should consult your state's law for any other requirements for, or protections against, a garnishment, or you should ask your attorney. See also BANKRUPTCY; CREDIT; INCOME TAX.

GIFT

A gift is the voluntary transfer of property from one person (known as the donor) to another (known as the donee). In order for such a transfer to be a true gift, the donee does not promise anything of value in exchange. The law distinguishes between a gift made while living, or a gift *inter vivos,* and a gift made while dying, or a gift *causa mortis*. This distinction is important primarily for tax and estate-planning purposes.

GIFTS INTER VIVOS

Three legal requirements must be met for a gift *inter vivos* to be valid. First, the donor must intend to make the gift—that is, to transfer ownership permanently to the donee. For instance, if you tell your nephew that he can use your car for his honeymoon in Niagara Falls, you have not made a gift, because you expect him to return the car to you afterward.

Second, the property must be delivered. A mere promise does not constitute a legal gift. If you promise your niece that you will give her a video player and you change your mind, she cannot require you to turn the player over to her. Delivery can be actual or symbolic. Actual delivery would occur if you put the video player in your niece's hands. But the delivery would be considered symbolic if you transferred the title to your car to your nephew.

Third, a gift *inter vivos* is complete only if the donee accepts it. If you decide to leave a kitten on your neighbor's doorstep, she does not have to accept it, even if you intend it as a gift. But if she takes the kitten and begins to feed and care for it as her own, she cannot later force you to take it back. Conversely, if your neighbor takes the kitten and you later decide you want it back, she does not have to return it to you.

Gifts in the mail

If you receive merchandise in the mail that you did not order, you are not required to pay for it. The law considers merchandise sent to you unsolicited to be a gift. See also UNORDERED MERCHANDISE.

GIFTS CAUSA MORTIS

Gifts *causa mortis,* or those gifts given in contemplation of death, also require intention, delivery, and acceptance. However, gifts *causa mortis* can be made only of personal property, not of real estate. Therefore, if your great-uncle Louis, who is on his deathbed with a case of pneumonia, turns to you and says, "I want to give you the whole 500-acre ranch," his statement does not fulfill the requirements for a valid gift (he must actually deed the property to you or leave it to you in his will). However, if he says, "I want you to have my prize saddle and tack," he has made a valid gift *causa mortis.*

A gift *causa mortis* should be made orally (so it is helpful to have a witness). If the donor writes down that he intends to give you a gift, such instructions may be considered a will and thus subject to the strict requirements necessary for a will to be valid. A gift *causa mortis* may also be invalid if the donor was contemplating suicide at the time. See WILL.

A gift *causa mortis* becomes the property of the donee only when the donor dies. If Uncle Louis changes his mind before he dies, or if he recovers from his pneumonia and does not give you the saddle, you have no right to claim it. But if you are promised a gift *causa mortis* and do not receive it when the donor dies, you can file a claim against his estate.

GIFTS AND TAXES

Under federal law, one person can give up to $10,000 per year as a gift to another without incurring any gift tax. So a married couple can give their son and daughter-in-law a total amount of $40,000 each year—$10,000 from each parent to both children. This sort of gift-giving is commonly used to minimize death taxes. Before giving gifts of money, check with your accountant, lawyer, or other estate-planning professional to determine how to take maximum advantage of the federal and state gift-tax laws. See also ESTATE PLANNING; ESTATE TAX; TRUST.

GIFTS TO MINORS

All the requirements of gift-giving apply when the donee is a minor, but certain gifts—such as real estate and stocks—must be managed until the minor becomes an adult. See UNIFORM TRANSFERS TO MINORS ACT.

GOOD FAITH

Good faith means honest and fair dealing, with no intent to take advantage of or defraud another person. A seller is acting in good faith when she has no knowledge of facts that would make a transaction unfair or illegal. If you sell your car to someone without knowing that it has a faulty transmission, you are selling it in good faith. But if you misrepresent the condition of the transmission or try to disguise it, you have not acted in good faith and may be guilty of fraud.

If you deal with a seller who is not acting in good faith, you may have to take the matter to court. Suppose James buys a computer from Chips, a computer store. James specifically asks the salesman, George, if the computer has sufficient memory to run his accounting program, and George assures him that it does. When James tries to run the program on his computer, however, he discovers that he will require extra memory components. If Chips refuses to exchange the computer or to give James a refund, James can take the matter to small-claims court to obtain the money for the components he needs, provided the amount is no greater than the maximum for such courts (usually about $2,000). However, James will have to prove that George knew that the computer was inadequate for James's needs. If James wants to have the sale rescinded (that is, to return the computer and get his money back), he may have to seek the services of a lawyer. See also BAD FAITH; FRAUD; SMALL-CLAIMS COURT.

GOOD SAMARITAN LAWS

While skating on a local pond, Tina falls through the ice. Hal, a stranger, sees her struggling to get out and throws a rope to her. Unfortunately, Tina cannot reach the rope and, thinking that he cannot save her by himself, Hal runs to a nearby house for help. Meanwhile, Tina manages to crawl out of the water on her own. Later she sues Hal for negligence in his rescue attempt. Can she win her case?

Probably not. Every state now has some form of "Good Samaritan" law. These laws protect people from liability for acts they commit while providing assistance to someone in distress.

Although state Good Samaritan laws vary, they usually offer immunity from responsibility if the rescuer exercises ordinary or reasonable care. However, in most states a rescuer like Hal could be found responsible if his actions were grossly negligent or if he acted in a willful or wanton way. For instance, if Hal had left the

REAL LIFE, REAL LAW

The Case of the Surgeon Samaritan

A woman who had been in an automobile accident was brought to an Ann Arbor hospital in critical condition. The emergency-room physician examined her and decided that she required an operation. Because the surgeon on duty was not available, the emergency-room physician asked another surgeon who was off duty to come to the hospital to treat the accident victim. When the surgeon arrived, he conducted additional tests and determined that surgery was needed. Before he could perform the operation, however, the woman died of cardiac arrest.

The woman's husband filed a lawsuit against the off-duty surgeon and the hospital. The surgeon filed a motion to be dismissed from the suit, claiming that he was immune from liability under Michigan's Good Samaritan statute, which provides that off-duty medical practitioners are immune from civil liability when they respond to a request for emergency assistance.

The court upheld the surgeon's argument. It further stated that one purpose of a Good Samaritan law is to encourage medical personnel to respond to emergencies even though they are not obligated to do so. Allowing the lawsuit to proceed would have had a negative effect on other medical personnel, who might refuse to provide assistance for fear of a malpractice claim.

scene without intending to call for help or made Tina's situation worse by entangling her in the rope, he might be found guilty of negligent conduct and be ordered to compensate her.

Good Samaritan laws often contain provisions that exempt off-duty members of certain occupations—such as firefighters and police officers, who ordinarily have a legal obligation to come to the rescue even when not on duty—from liability. Suppose an off-duty paramedic is nearby when you slump to the pavement with chest pains and she administers CPR until help arrives. You probably could not sue her if she broke one of your ribs. Even so, Good Samaritan laws often state that aid must be given only if immediately needed to save a life.

In some states, Good Samaritan laws do not apply to emergency aid given in hospitals or other health-care facilities. In addition, many statutes specify that assistance must be provided without expectation of payment. Suppose you suffer an asthma attack in your doctor's office and the emergency care she gives you is not adequate. Her state's Good Samaritan law may not protect her—even if she claims she did not demand payment—because you were in her office as a paying patient.

Good Samaritan laws generally do not exempt owners or occupiers of land from their duty to protect certain classes of people—such as children, salespeople, and repair personnel—who are on their property. Because these laws vary, proceed cautiously if you plan to sue, or are being sued, on the basis of a Good Samaritan law. See also ACCIDENTS IN THE HOME; NEGLIGENCE; TORT; TRESPASS.

GOVERNMENT NATIONAL MORTGAGE ASSOCIATION (GINNIE MAE)

The Government National Mortgage Association is a federal organization that trades in the secondary mortgage market; that is, it buys and sells home mortgages from the banks and other financial institutions that originally hold them. Ginnie Mae deals only in home mortgages that are insured by either the Department of Veterans Affairs or the Federal Housing Administration.

The nickname "Ginnie Mae" is also used to refer to the securities that are backed by those mortgages. Because Ginnie Mae securities are sold in minimum amounts of $25,000, most individuals invest in Ginnie Maes through a mutual fund, which can require as little as a $100 initial investment. See also FEDERAL NATIONAL MORTGAGE ASSOCIATION (FANNIE MAE); MUTUAL FUND.

GOVERNMENT RECORDS

There are any number of reasons why you might need to obtain such government records as a birth, death, or marriage certificate or a divorce decree. These records are usually available from one or more state or local offices. Although the names of these offices vary, you can generally obtain the records you want at the offices specified below :

◇ *For birth and death certificates,* which you may need in order to collect insurance benefits or to get a clear title to real estate, for example, write to the state's bureau of vital statistics (which may also be called the office of vital records or bureau of records and statistics), located in the state capital. Generally, you must make your request in person or in writing and pay a fee. See also ADOPTION; BIRTH CERTIFICATE.

◇ For marriage and divorce records, write to the vital statistics bureau or the county clerk in the county where the marriage or divorce took place.

◇ *For records regarding real estate* (including deeds or liens), call the recorder of deeds in the county where the real estate is located.

◇ *For records about criminal or civil court proceedings,* contact the clerk of the court where the trial took place. All you need to know is the name of one or more parties in the case, but the records will be found more quickly if you know the case file number. For transcripts of the trial or certified copies of documents used in the trial, a fee will be required in advance. Records of juvenile court proceedings are not available to the public.

Under the Freedom of Information Act, agencies of the federal government are required to make most of their records available to the public, though there may be some exceptions. Most states now have similar laws. To request information, write to the relevant agency. For a more detailed explanation of how to request government records, see FREEDOM OF INFORMATION ACT.

Another federal law, the Privacy Act, gives you the right to know what information government agencies keep about you and why they keep it. This act also permits individuals to find out about the transfer of their personal records from one government agency to another or to private organizations or other individuals.

Most agencies are supposed to use information only for the purpose for which they first obtained it. For instance, the U.S. Census Bureau collects information concerning people's income. This information is meant for statistical purposes only; it is not supposed to be passed along to the Internal Revenue Service to help the IRS find taxpayers who have underreported their income. You can sue an agency that fails to comply with the Privacy Act. See also PRIVACY RIGHTS.

GRANDFATHER CLAUSE

A provision in a law allowing someone to continue a practice that the law otherwise restricts or prohibits is called a grandfather clause. Such a clause usually applies only to a current activity and to a specific person or organization.

Suppose your state outlaws the incineration of old tires. The law may have a provision that allows a company already operating a tire incinerator to continue doing so, even though no one else can set up a new tire-incinerator business. If the owner of the existing incinerator sells his property or tries to open a new incinerator somewhere else, the clause would probably not apply either to the new owner or the new location.

To obtain a grandfather-clause exemption, contact the regulatory body that oversees the business, such as the zoning board, health department, or environmental agency.

GRAND JURY

The Fifth Amendment to the U.S. Constitution provides that no person may be tried for a serious criminal offense without first being indicted, or formally accused, at a grand jury hearing. This procedure was designed to protect individuals from unreasonable, abusive, or unwarranted prosecutions by the federal government. The Fifth Amendment applies only to federal criminal prosecutions. States are not required by the Constitution to provide grand juries, although many of them do. See FIFTH AMENDMENT.

POWERS AND DUTIES OF THE GRAND JURY

A grand jury is convened by the court to investigate crimes within the court's jurisdiction (the scope of its authority) and to determine whether there is sufficient cause to indict someone. The work of the grand jury is to bring an accusation, not to determine a person's guilt or innocence. This is done during a subsequent trial.

In some states, grand juries may be convened to investigate any suspected crime, while in others their powers are limited to issues submitted by the court or the prosecutor's office for the specific purpose of obtaining a grand jury indictment. Before the judge or prosecutor can ask for a grand jury investigation, he must have sufficient reason to suspect that it will reveal criminal conduct.

SELECTING A GRAND JURY

Grand jurors are selected from local residents over the age of 18 years. Prospective jurors are expected to be representative of their community—that is, they must not be drawn from any one economic, racial, or religious group. They must swear to be impartial and to keep the proceedings secret. In some states prospective jurors who have been convicted of a felony will not be allowed to serve on a grand jury.

Grand juries are usually composed of 12 to 23 people; in most states, grand juries can return an indictment if a majority of the members concur.

IF YOU ARE CALLED AS A WITNESS

A grand jury will summon witnesses, who may be required to bring documents or other evidence and who must answer all the grand jury's questions, except those that reveal privileged information or may be self-incriminating. Witnesses do not have the right to have an attorney present at a grand jury proceeding. However, federal courts and some states permit a witness's lawyer to stand outside the jury rooms and will let the witness consult him if she fears self-incrimination.

Because the grand jury is investigating the possibility of a crime, it may consider evidence that would be inadmissible at a criminal trial, such as evidence seized without a warrant in violation of the Fourth Amendment. See EVIDENCE; SEARCH AND SEIZURE.

SECRECY OF THE PROCEEDINGS

Unlike criminal trials, grand jury proceedings are held in private. This prevents witness tampering, encourages all witnesses to disclose information without fear of retaliation, and prevents the target of an investigation from fleeing. (In fact, he may not even be aware of the proceedings.) Unless they result in an indictment, the proceedings of a grand jury are not disclosed. Federal law and some state laws make such disclosure a criminal offense or a civil contempt of court. See CONTEMPT OF COURT.

GRANDPARENTS' RIGHTS

When their son was killed in an automobile accident, Mary Jane and Gene Parker took some comfort in the fact that he left behind two beautiful children. The Parkers offered emotional and financial support to their daughter-in-law, who politely but firmly declined.

In the months following their son's funeral, the Parkers saw their grandchildren less and less frequently, and only when they had initiated contact. The Parkers respected their daughter-in-law's need for a little distance, but called weekly to say hello to the children.

A year after their son's accident the Parkers received a letter from their daughter-in-law, explaining that she was moving out of state with the children, and she felt it was in their best interests to have no more contact with their grandparents.

The Parkers were stunned. Although they were not close to their son's wife, they never expected to be cut off from their grandchildren. Do they have any legal recourse?

RECOGNIZING GRANDPARENTS' RIGHTS

Yes, they do. As of 1993 most states had laws that allowed grandparents to petition the courts for visitation rights. National statistics suggest that the Parkers are far from alone in their dilemma. It is estimated that 20,000 to 50,000 grandparent-visitation cases are currently active in this country.

The right to petition varies among states, depending on the circumstances under which a grandparent may bring legal action. Grandparent-visitation statutes do not guarantee that a court will order visitation on request—they merely ensure that grandparents can petition a court. In fact, about one-half of the grandparent-visitation petitions filed are denied.

In determining whether to grant a grandparent's request for visitation, a judge is guided by what she perceives to be in the child's best interests. She considers many factors, including the relationship between the parties, their health, and the child's and parents' wishes. If you have seen your grandchild only occasionally and have been a minor influence in his life, you may not win a visitation order. If you do win, the court may revoke the visits if they are no longer in the child's best interests.

An order permitting visitation does not necessarily prevent the parent from moving out of state, although the court may rule that grandchildren be allowed to visit their grandparents during holidays.

In many states grandparents may appear in juvenile court proceedings to seek custody of their abused, abandoned, or neglected grandchildren, and they will often receive custodial preference. If a grandchild is placed in foster care, her grandparents may petition for visitation rights. However, if a grandchild is adopted by a stranger (other than a stepparent), her grandparents may lose visitation rights.

If you win visitation rights but the parents deny you time with your grandchild, you may seek a contempt of court citation against the parents.

GETTING HELP

Help for those grandparents seeking visitation rights, custody, or information concerning state laws on grandparents' rights is available through the

Grandparents' Rights Organization. Its address is 555 South Woodward Avenue, Suite 600, Birmingham, MI 48009, or call 313-646-7191.

GRANT

A grant is a gift of property or legal rights to property. Private organizations, foundations, the federal and state governments, and individuals can all be sources of grants.

Grants are offered for many purposes, including scientific research, educational opportunities, renovating real estate, and supporting the arts. Grant donors generally require that interested persons submit an application. The donor is under no obligation to award a grant if no applicant qualifies.

A grant can be conditional—for example, it may stipulate that the recipient use the money only for approved purposes, or that he submit a report at the end of the project for which funds were provided. If a recipient fails to meet the conditions of such a grant, the donor may revoke it and demand the return of grant funds.

For instance, Elisabetta, a wealthy patron of the arts, offered a grant for the purpose of setting up a dance studio for underprivileged children. A group of former dancers obtained the grant by promising that they would set up a studio and have the children stage a recital at the end of one year. When the year was up, Elisabetta was distressed to learn that not only was no recital scheduled, but the grant recipients had spent almost all the funds on a fact-finding trip to Italy. Elisabetta would be entitled to ask that the grant money be returned. See also COLLEGE SCHOLARSHIP; GIFT.

GRANT DEED

A grant deed is a form of deed in which a seller of real property warrants that he has not already conveyed the property to anyone else and that there are no undisclosed claims against it. Unlike a full covenant and warranty deed, a grant deed does not include a promise by the seller that he will defend the buyer against a third person's claims to the property. To the buyer of the property, a grant deed provides more protection than a quitclaim deed (which merely transfers whatever interest the seller might have) and about an equal level of protection as a bargain and sale deed with covenants against the grantor's acts. See also BARGAIN AND SALE DEED; FULL COVENANT AND WARRANTY DEED; QUITCLAIM DEED; TITLE INSURANCE.

GRIEVANCE PROCEDURE

A grievance procedure is a formal means for handling complaints and problems in the workplace. Most labor unions have negotiated grievance procedures as part of their master agreement, whereby the union steward or other intermediary transmits workers' complaints to management. The purpose of these procedures is to bring order to the workplace, promote communication, and minimize or prevent labor disputes. See also LABOR UNION.

GUARDIAN AD LITEM

Appointed by the court, a guardian ad litem ("guardian for the suit") acts on behalf of a minor or for an adult who has been declared physically or mentally incapable of assuming responsibility in a lawsuit. The guardian ad litem's authority extends only to matters pertaining to the lawsuit. See also GUARDIAN AND WARD.

A guardian ad litem's role is to safeguard the rights of the person she represents, who is known as the ward. However, she is not entitled to share any award won by the ward. Nor is she responsible if the ward is required to make any compensation or reparation.

CASES INVOLVING CHILDREN

If a lawsuit is started in a child's name, a guardian ad litem must be named in the suit, as well as the child. This guardian is often one of the child's parents but may be any competent adult. If the child is a defendant in a case, the plaintiff will ask the court to appoint a guardian ad litem. Most states require juvenile courts to appoint a guardian ad litem in cases of child abuse or neglect.

Sometimes in divorce proceedings involving child custody, the judge may find that the parents are unable to act in the best interests of their children, and he may appoint a guardian ad litem for the children to act as their advocate.

INCOMPETENT OR MISSING ADULTS

Any lawsuit with an incompetent adult as a defendant or plaintiff requires the appointment of a guardian ad litem.

In some instances a guardian ad litem may also be appointed to represent a missing party. For example, in adoption cases when one or both parents have disappeared, state law may require the court to appoint a guardian ad litem to protect the absent parents' interests. In mortgage foreclosures or certain lawsuits involving real estate, the court may appoint a guardian ad litem to represent parties who might have some claim to the property in question but cannot be found.

GUARDIAN AND WARD

Abandoned or orphaned children, as well as insane, elderly, or invalid persons who are unable to care for themselves or their property, are often entrusted by the court to the care of a guardian. The court will give this guardian the legal right and responsibility to care for the person (known as the ward) or his property or in some cases both.

GUARDIANS OF MINOR CHILDREN

A minor child's parents are considered his natural guardians. As such they have the right and responsibility to make important decisions on his behalf—such as where he should go to school, whether he should attend a church, and so on. If the parents are divorced, the custodial parent is considered the guardian. When parents have joint custody, they are both guardians. See also CHILD CUSTODY; CHILDREN'S RIGHTS.

Parents of minor children should draft wills designating a person to be appointed as guardian in the event that they both die. This is known as a testamentary guardianship. Generally, such a guardian will have custody of the children, as well as a duty to manage their property; however, you need not assign the same person both responsibilities. If you are naming a testamentary guardian, consider the following:

◇ Be sure that the person you have named is willing to take on the responsibility of raising your children. If possible, name one or two alternatives in the event that your first choice becomes unable to care for your children.

◇ Choose someone who is prepared to bring up your children in a way that is compatible with your own beliefs, customs, values, and religious practices.

◇ Speak with an estate planning professional about the

CHECKLIST

Naming a Guardian or Conservator

When appointing guardians or conservators, the courts consider a number of factors, some of which are listed below:

❑ **WISHES OF THE PARENT.**
When appointing a guardian for a minor, courts consider the wishes of the parents (such as those expressed in a will). However, courts are not bound by those wishes if they are not in the child's best interests.

❑ **WISHES OF THE CHILD.**
Some state laws provide that courts must consider the wishes of children who have reached a certain age (14 in many states) when designating a guardian.

❑ **RELATIONSHIP TO THE WARD.**
When naming guardians, courts prefer to appoint close blood relatives whenever possible.

❑ **AVAILABILITY OF SUITABLE CANDIDATES.**
If there are no suitable candidates among a ward's close relatives or associates, courts often appoint a bank trust department or government official as the conservator of the ward's property.

❑ **FITNESS.**
In determining a candidate's fitness, courts consider his moral character, business competence, stability, health, and age.

❑ **RELIGION.**
In appointing a guardian for a minor, courts prefer to name a person with the same religious background as the minor.

best way to provide for your children. For instance, you may wish to set up a trust for your teenage children so that they can receive money in small amounts at a time, rather than leaving them a lump sum that must be managed by their guardian in accordance with a court's directives.

A divorced parent with custody of minor children may try to cut off a former spouse's rights by designating another person to act as a testamentary guardian. However, the courts will not honor such a designation unless the former spouse agrees or is an unfit parent.

If you do not name a testamentary guardian in your will, any interested party—such as a grandparent or a social service agency—can initiate guardianship proceedings. A few states allow children to choose their own guardians if they are at least 14 years old, but the court must approve the choice.

CONSERVATORSHIP

In many states, a guardian is a person entrusted with the complete care of another, while a conservator is a person who is appointed to manage just the property and finances of another. Often parents are appointed as conservators of their minor children's inheritance.

Upon her death, 10-year-old Matt's grandmother left him a 75-acre farm and $250,000 in cash and securities. His parents want to sell Matt's farm to pay off their own mortgage and use the money to send their older son to college. Can they do so?

Probably not. Even though Matt's parents are the conservators of his property, they are not entitled to sell or dispose of property held in Matt's name, but must manage and conserve it for his benefit—not for that of his brother or themselves.

Courts have the authority to appoint conservators for people who are unable to manage their own affairs. However, being forgetful, foolish, naive, or unlucky in business matters is not enough to justify the appointment of a conservator. For example, somebody who invests his family's savings in a new computer software company that quickly goes bankrupt has made an unwise investment. That is not enough to warrant appointing a conservator. If the same person, however, sold the family business for a handful of magic beans, the family could ask a court to appoint a conservator.

If a person wishes, she may petition the court to appoint a guardian or conservator to manage her affairs, even if she is a competent adult. See also Power of Attorney.

POWERS AND DUTIES OF GUARDIAN AND CONSERVATOR

The guardian or conservator is usually responsible for such duties as paying the debts of the ward from her assets, suing to protect her property, taking out loans when necessary, entering into contracts for her, and collecting debts and settling claims relating to her property. Both guardians and conservators may employ accountants, attorneys, real estate agents, and others to manage the ward's estate.

A guardian or conservator must be reasonable and prudent in his decisions. He may be held responsible for losses if it can be shown that he was reckless or indifferent to his duties, or negligently acted contrary to the ward's interests, as by selling property at a loss. If there are funds to be invested, the guardian must make safe, nonspeculative investments that will produce an income for the ward. A court will judge whether a guardian or conservator has acted in the ward's best interests by applying to him the standard of reasonable and prudent behavior.

All guardians and conservators are subject to the supervision and direction of a court. They must provide the court with a regular accounting of their wards' estates and report actions taken on their behalf. Some states have laws requiring the guardian to obtain court approval for transactions involving the ward's property. If a guardian acts with court approval, he will not be responsible for any resulting losses.

A guardian or conservator may be removed from his post by the court for neglecting his duty to his ward, disobeying court orders, or misusing the ward's property and funds. If a guardian or conservator fails to put his ward's interests first when conducting the ward's business, the responsibility can be taken away from him.

FROM HABEAS CORPUS TO HOUSEHOLD HELP

Habeas Corpus

A Latin term meaning "you have the body," *habeas corpus* is a writ (court order) directing a warden or other official to produce a prisoner so that the court can decide whether he is being legally detained or imprisoned. The writ of habeas corpus is considered one of the great safeguards of personal liberty. Because it charges that a person is being deprived of his constitutional right to liberty, a writ of habeas corpus receives prompt attention from the court.

A writ of habeas corpus is available to someone who feels he has been illegally detained or imprisoned, but it may be filed only after all other means of redress have been exhausted—from both the state and federal authorities. For instance, an incarcerated robber or a prisoner on death row must have made either a motion for a new trial or an appeal to a higher court, and have been denied one of these, before asking for a writ of habeas corpus.

Although writs of habeas corpus are often filed by prisoners or their families, they can also be used under other circumstances. An alien who has been refused the right to enter the country may seek a writ of habeas corpus to challenge that decision. A soldier may obtain a writ to challenge his retention in the armed services. A person who thinks he is being wrongfully confined in a mental institution may try to seek a writ of habeas corpus as a way to force a court to review the legality of his confinement. See also APPEAL; ARREST; BAIL; DEATH PENALTY; IMMIGRATION.

Hate Crime

Legally, a hate crime is any crime committed solely because of the victim's gender, race, nationality, religion, political belief, or sexual orientation. Although hate crimes are always motivated by bigotry, they take many different forms—from vandalism (such as painting a swastika on a synagogue wall) to intimidation (such as making threatening phone calls to mosques) to outright physical assault.

A GROWING CONCERN

In April 1990, owing to concern about the growing number of hate crimes, Congress enacted the Hate Crimes Statistics Act. This act requires the U.S. Department of Justice to collect statistics about crimes to determine whether they are related to racial, ethnic, sexual, or religious bias. The information is meant to be used to increase public awareness about hate crimes, to help formulate law enforcement policies, and to teach officials how to recognize such crimes. Some states also have laws mandating collection of hate-crime data.

Hate-crime victims should report incidents to the police for investigation. If there is sufficient evidence, the district attorney will prosecute the person who committed the crime.

LEGISLATION

Many states have laws against hate crimes, and over 20 states have adopted model legislation prepared in 1981 by the Anti-Defamation League (ADL). Some states also prohibit specific hate crimes, such as painting racial slurs on property.

The ADL model legislation makes certain criminal acts more serious if they are motivated by bias, although it does not make bias itself a crime. For example, the legislation provides that persons who deface or damage schools, cemeteries, places of worship, and community centers will be subject to higher penalties if the vandalism was motivated by bias than if it was not. The legislation also sets higher penalties for acts of intimidation, such as telephone harassment and assault, when they are motivated by bias. Sentences for hate crimes can range from community service and property restoration to prison terms.

FREEDOM OF SPEECH

A unanimous 1992 decision by the U.S. Supreme Court found a St. Paul, Minnesota, hate-crime ordinance unconstitutional because it infringed upon the right to freedom of speech guaranteed by the FirstAmendment . The ordinance was challenged by a juvenile offender, who was convicted of burning a cross on the front lawn of a home owned by a black family. In challenging his conviction, he argued that the ordinance, which banned messages of racial, gender, or religious intolerance, was unconstitutionally vague and was prohibited by the First Amendment. The Supreme Court agreed, and held that the amendment prohibits governments from restricting speech and conduct solely because of the ideas they express.

In 1993, however, the Court upheld laws that sentence people who are convicted of criminal actions to extra prison time if they have targeted victims because of their race, religion, disability, or sexual orientation, since these laws punish conduct, not speech.

CIVIL LAWSUITS

Whether or not any criminal charges are filed, victims of hate crimes can sue for compensation for damage to their property or injuries from an assault. If an assault results in death, surviving family members can also seek damages for their loss by filing a wrongful-death action. See also ASSAULT AND BATTERY; WRONGFUL DEATH.

HEALTH CLUB

As summer approached, Ned decided to join a health club in an effort to shape up his body. A club near his office offered a "lifetime membership" for only $1,000, so Ned signed a contract in which he agreed to pay $50 monthly until his membership fee was paid up. Two months later, the club owners declared bankruptcy.

Unfortunately, that was not the end of the story. Not realizing that his financial obligation did not end when the club was closed, Ned stopped his payments. Now he is being hounded for the unpaid balance by a finance company to which the club sold Ned's contract before going into bankruptcy. Health clubs and other businesses sell their contracts to obtain immediate cash, rather than waiting for the members to pay all their installments. A contract that may be sold like this is called a "completely assignable" contract, and the finance company may collect any money due.

Ned's experience is not uncommon. As many others like him have discovered, health clubs and spas go in and out of business as quickly as promises to diet and exercise are made and broken. Even so, there are ways you can protect yourself from falling into the financial traps associated with them.

THE CONTRACT

You should never sign a long-term contract. Try to find a club that will let you join on a monthly basis, or ask for a two- or three-month trial membership. Even if the club stays in business, your enthusiasm may wane, your financial situation may change, or you may move to another neighborhood. To protect consumers from getting in over their heads, some states have passed laws prohibiting health clubs from offering memberships lasting longer than two years.

As Ned found out, it can be costly to sign a membership contract without reading the fine print—so scrutinize the contract thoroughly and make sure you understand all your obligations. Never rely on oral assurances from the staff. If a promise is not in writing, it is probably not enforceable.

Find out whether you will be allowed to sell the remainder of your membership or receive a refund if you move, change jobs, or simply lose interest.

CHOOSING A CLUB

If you are thinking of joining a health club or spa, do not yield to high-pressure sales pitches or offers that are good "today only." Instead, investigate the club. How long has it been around? Does it have a large membership? Does it make an effort to improve its facilities?

Ask to use the club once or twice to make sure that it does provide the facilities and services it has promised. Visit the club at the time of day you are planning to use it most often. During your visit, talk to other members and note the size of the crowd, the number of staff members, the supply of towels and lockers, and the general level of cleanliness.

CONSUMER PROTECTION

Many states have laws that offer some protection to health club members. For example, after signing a contract, you often have three days to cancel the membership and receive a full refund. In some states you must be allowed to put your membership "on hold" if you cannot use it for a while because of injury or illness. See COOLING-OFF PERIOD.

Some states require health clubs and spas to buy bonds to protect members from experiences like Ned's if the club goes out of business. If the facility closes, you may file for a refund with the bonding company, but the bond may not be adequate to cover all refund claims.

Your local consumer affairs office will be able to give you details on the laws relating to health clubs and spas in your state. See also BETTER BUSINESS BUREAU; CONSUMER PROTECTION.

HEALTH INSURANCE

An accident or illness, whether short- or long-term, can cause a temporary loss of income and leave a lot of bills. The role of health insurance is to protect people against the high cost of medical care. Both individuals and groups (groups may be composed of businesses, trade groups, or professional associations) can buy health insurance from private companies. In addition, two government-sponsored programs, Medicaid and Medicare, are available to those who qualify.

Some states have incorporated model health insurance benefits into their insurance laws, outlining certain mandatory and optional features. Health insurance coverage can vary widely, but in general, most private health insurance policies provide some combination of the following types of coverage: (1) basic medical; (2) hospitalization; and (3) catastrophic, or major medical. See also MEDICAID; MEDICARE.

PREMIUMS AND DEDUCTIBLES

Companies that provide health insurance operate by collecting regular payments (premiums) from their customers in exchange for a guarantee to cover certain health-care costs. The insurance company determines the amount of these premiums based on a number of factors, including whether the policy is for a group or an individual and the expectation of how much medical care the policyholders will require. See also INSURANCE.

Most insurers require policyholders to pay a certain part of their health-care costs annually before the company starts paying benefits. This amount, known as a deductible, varies with the amount and type of coverage you hold.

BASIC COVERAGE

Although policies differ, basic medical insurance covers physicians' fees (whether you are hospitalized or are treated in a doctor's office or a hospital outpatient department), laboratory and radiology services, and often prescription drugs.

Insurance companies conduct surveys to determine the reasonable, customary charge in a given area for a particular service or procedure. For example, if the usual price for having an appendix removed in Indianapolis is $2,000, an insurance company may consider that amount an appropriate reimbursement. If a local surgeon charges a patient more than $2,000, the patient will be required to pay the difference.

Then, most companies require the insured to pay a certain portion—usually 10 or 20 percent—of each reimbursable fee. This is called coinsurance.

Suppose you slip on your kitchen floor and break your wrist. Because your job requires long hours at a computer terminal, you decide to see a preeminent orthopedist in your town. He charges $1,200 to operate on your wrist, but your insurance company has determined that $800 is the allowable fee for this service. You are therefore responsible for the $400 difference. In addition, because your policy has a 20 percent coinsurance provision, the company will reimburse you only $640. (Note that some doctors may reduce their fees if you inform them of the limitation of your coverage.)

HOSPITALIZATION COVERAGE

Almost all health insurance plans pay for all or part of the costs of hospitalization for a certain number of days. Generally, insurance covers the hospital's daily rate for a semiprivate room (usually defined as one shared by two people).

You must pay the difference if you want a private room.

The number of days covered differs according to the plan. For instance, if an insurance company has determined that, on average, a patient requires three nights in the hospital for an uncomplicated appendix removal, the insurer will not reimburse a patient for a fourth night—unless complications have compelled the extra day. Thus health insurers can influence both health-care providers and consumers to keep the number of days spent in a hospital to a minimum.

In addition to covering the cost of room and board, hospitalization policies cover related expenses, such as nursing services, medications, intravenous solutions, oxygen therapy, X-rays, surgical dressings, and other hospital laboratory services. See also HEALTH MAINTENANCE ORGANIZATION; PREFERRED PROVIDER ORGANIZATION.

MAJOR MEDICAL COVERAGE

Major medical, also known as catastrophic, policies cover the costs of serious or prolonged illness, expensive surgery, or other costly treatments. After the annual deductible is met, these plans pay a part, typically 75 to 80 percent, of charges up to $2,000 and 100 percent after that until the policy's lifetime benefit maximum is reached. This limit is also known as a stop-loss provision. For example, if a plan's maximum coverage is $1 million, a policyholder is responsible for all his health-care fees over that amount.

Suppose that a patient's hospital stay results in a bill of $30,000, and the major medical policy covers 80 percent (after payment of a $500 deductible) of charges up to $2,000, then 100 percent to a lifetime maximum of $500,000. The insurer would pay $29,100, and the patient would have to pay the deductible plus $400 (20 percent of $2,000), or $900.

GROUP INSURANCE

Many people receive health insurance through a group plan provided by their employer, by a union, or by some other professional organization. Group policies offer much lower premiums than individual health plans do, in large part because the risks are spread out among the group.

Some employers pay the entire premium of the employee's health-care plan; such plans are known as noncontributory. Other companies deduct a part of the premium from each employee's paycheck; such plans are called contributory.

With group insurance, the insurance company prepares one master policy, or contract, which is signed by the insurer and the employer or organization taking it out. Each participant in the group receives a certificate and brochure outlining coverage in general terms. For more detailed information about health coverage, participants can refer to the policy summary, which is usually available from the company's employee benefits or human resources department.

Self-insurance

Some companies set up and fund their own medical insurance plan. This is known as self-insurance. In some instances, this type of plan offers more limited benefits and higher deductibles and copayments than those offered by insurance companies. Perhaps the most important drawback to self-insurance is that the company can reduce a participant's lifetime benefit after he contracts a catastrophic illness, such as cancer or AIDS.

Family coverage

Most group policies can be extended to cover a member's spouse and children. The premiums and deductibles are usually higher.

INDIVIDUAL POLICIES

Contract (freelance) or part-time workers, employees of small businesses, and others who cannot get health insurance through an employer or other group have the option of buying individual insurance for themselves and their families.

Because premiums are high and coverage is more limited under many individual plans, buyers should carefully review the terms of several insurance policies to see which one will provide the best protection at the most reasonable rate. For further information, consult the health division of your state insurance commission.

DENIAL OF COVERAGE

Insurance companies can deny policies to the ill and to anyone deemed to be a poor risk because of bad health, a previous history of a disease (such as cancer), or employment in a "rated" occupation (one that insurance companies consider dangerous, such as skydiving instruction or working with toxic chemicals). Many companies will, however, insure such people at higher rates.

Experimental treatment
In some cases experimental treatment may be the only option for certain life-threatening diseases. Some insurance companies may allow policyholders to pay an additional premium for coverage of specific experimental cancer treatments and transplant procedures, should they become necessary in the future. Coinsurance and benefit limits still apply.

Preexisting conditions
Most individual health insurance policies contain some provision that allows an insurer to deny coverage for a "preexisting condition" or to terminate coverage after a specified period. A preexisting condition is generally defined as a health problem that existed before (often one to five years before) the coverage was purchased.

In addition, any illness or injury that occurs after the policy was purchased, but which can be traced back to a preexisting condition, will likely be excluded from coverage. Suppose you experience nerve damage and atrophy resulting from a knee injury that was listed as a preexisting condition. Although the nerve damage occurs after you buy the policy, it relates back to the excluded preexisting condition and will probably not be covered.

No duplicate benefits
Most insurance policies include a provision requiring "coordination of benefits." Under this provision, no one can collect from more than one insurance company for the same illness or treatment.

Still, if you and your spouse are both covered by group health insurance provided by your employers, you may want to consider keeping both policies. In this way, you may be able to have complete coverage for illnesses or injuries (after your deductible is paid). For example, if a wife's policy covers 80 percent of a medical bill, her husband's policy will often pay the remaining 20 percent.

If you pursue this course of action, examine both policies to find out to which insurer you should submit bills first. Then submit a claim to the second company for whatever amount the first insurance company does not pay you. If both you and your spouse are insured by the same company, however, this strategy will not work.

There is another type of duplication that is never permitted. Suppose that Margaret was driving home from work, and as she made a legal turn onto a side street was hit broadside by an oncoming car. Her injuries put Margaret in the hospital for several days, and she also required physical therapy to restore full use of her legs. Margaret's insurance company paid her medical bills. In the meantime, the police determined that the other motorist was at fault, and in her settlement with the other driver's insurance company, Margaret was reimbursed for all her medical expenses. Can she keep the money? Probably not. Most policies contain subrogation clauses, which allow the injured person's insurance company to recover its expenses if they are paid by the person responsible for the injury or by his insurance company.

RENEWAL AND CANCELLATION

Some individual health insurance policies are "guaranteed renewable contracts," which means that the policyholder is entitled to renew the policy at the end of its term. If the policy contains a guaranteed renewable provision, you are assured of health protection up to a certain age, commonly 65 years. Guaranteed renewal provisions do not prevent the insurance company from raising its premiums at the beginning of the new term.

If your policy has a noncancellation clause, you are covered throughout the term of the contract at guaranteed rates. However, there are reasons for which any insurance policy can be canceled before its expiration. One common reason is the failure to pay premiums when they are due. If your policy lapses for this reason, you can be required to prove your insurability again.

Another ground for cancellation is the insured's failure to disclose a medical condition. When you fill out an insurance application, you do not have to reveal more than you are asked, but you should be honest about your personal, family, and medical history.

Individual members cannot be dropped from group plans; an insurance company can only cancel the policy for the entire group. Furthermore, when you leave the employment of an organization with 20 or more employees where you were insured by a group policy, federal law requires that you must be offered the option of continuing your coverage at your own expense for up to 18 months, unless you were fired for gross misconduct. Some states have similar laws extending this option to employees not covered by federal law. See COBRA.

Preauthorization

Some insurance policies require you to seek a second or third opinion for treatment of certain conditions or for certain procedures. In addition, you may be required to notify the insurance company for authorization in advance of hospitalization or within a certain period after entering the hospital for emergency reasons. If you do not follow these procedures, you may have to pay additional fees.

Travel

Some policies provide health insurance coverage only within the United States. If you are traveling to a foreign country, you should check with your insurer to find out whether you need to purchase additional insurance to cover any medical expenses you incur abroad.

STEPS TO TAKE

If your insurance company denies a claim you make for reimbursement, or if it pays you less than the amount you believe you should receive, take the following actions:

1. Call the insurer's claims department and ask for a written explanation for the denial of your claim and a statement of the precise policy terms that allow the company to deny it.

2. If you have an individual policy, get in touch with the agent who sold it to you. He may be willing to intercede on your behalf, especially if your claim is being denied on the basis of a questionable interpretation of the policy.

3. File a complaint with your state's department of insurance. The department will investigate your complaint and may be able to exert its influence on the insurer if it decides that your claim has been unreasonably denied.

4. See if your plan contains a clause that provides for compulsory arbitration to settle a dispute over a claim. Arbitration will avoid the expense and delays of legal action, although you will have to pay arbitration fees. See ARBITRATION.

5. For a large claim, you can hire an attorney to pursue the matter in court. If your insurer has acted in bad faith by refusing to cover a legitimate claim, you may receive compensatory damages. See also DAMAGES.

HEALTH MAINTENANCE ORGANIZATION

Established in the 1970's in response to the increasing cost of health care, health maintenance organizations (HMO's) are health plans whose members pay a fixed monthly premium for access to a range of medical services, including visits to physicians, hospitalization, and surgery. The biggest difference between HMO's and traditional health insurance is that the HMO patient pays few or no additional fees herself.

Health-care providers affiliated with HMO's receive a set fee for each patient no matter how often they treat her or how many tests they order for her. Therefore, the HMO staff has an incentive to contain costs, and to this end, most HMO's place an emphasis on early detection and preventive health care. Monthly premiums usually cover checkups and other preventive measures not often included in a traditional insurance plan.

A market for HMO's was assured in 1973 when Congress enacted the Health Maintenance Organization (HMO) Act. This law makes federal grants and loans available to groups that wish to develop HMO's, and requires employers with more than 25 employees to offer HMO's as an alternative health-care choice.

TYPES OF HMO'S

There are essentially two types of HMO's. Under the so-called staff model, HMO's directly employ staff physicians, who work together in one facility. The patient chooses her primary physician from among the staff. If she needs specialized care, the primary-care physician refers her to a specialist on staff. If the group lacks a particular specialist, the HMO may

CHECKLIST

Evaluating an HMO

Although an HMO can help reduce out-of-pocket costs for medical care, you should ask the following questions before you join one:

❑ **WHAT SERVICES AND PROCEDURES ARE COVERED?**
Does the HMO cover preexisting conditions, and are such services as psychological counseling or drug- and alcohol-abuse programs included?

❑ **WHERE DO I OBTAIN MEDICAL SERVICES?**
Is the provider's office nearby? If you become ill or suffer an injury while out of town, will the HMO pay for your medical care? Will you be assigned to a regular primary-care physician, or will you get whatever doctor is on duty when you need care?

❑ **HOW LONG DOES IT TAKE TO GET AN APPOINTMENT?**
Will you have to wait more than two weeks for an appointment? (Longer waits may mean that the HMO is understaffed.) If you have an emergency, what procedures will you need to follow to get authorization for an ambulance and emergency care?

❑ **HOW ARE COMPLAINTS HANDLED?**
What can the HMO do if you are unhappy with the care you receive or if you believe you need a second opinion from another physician?

contract with nonstaff physicians for those services.

Other HMO's, known as individual practice associations, contract with physicians to treat HMO patients in their own offices on a prepaid basis. Each patient enrolled in the program is provided with a list of participating doctors, from which she can choose her primary-care physician.

Advantages
HMO's offer members a number of advantages, including:

◇ *Fixed costs.* Members pay a monthly premium in exchange for virtually unlimited access to health care services, at no extra charge. (A few services may require an extra fee.)

◇ *Reduced paperwork.* All paperwork is handled by the HMO's staff. Patients do not have to file any claim forms.

◇ *Prompt attention to medical needs and easy access to treatment.* At well-run HMO's, members have access to health care 24 hours a day, 365 days a year. Moreover, because many HMO's employ specialists and have centers with laboratory and treatment facilities, members do not have to go from one office to another for treatment and tests.

Disadvantages
HMO's have certain drawbacks, however, including:

◇ *A limited choice of specialists.* Members are unable to choose their own specialists or seek outside opinions. In addition, emergency care at a nonaffiliated hospital may not be covered.

◇ *Treatment by medical personnel other than doctors.* To hold down costs, much of the basic treatment at HMO's may be provided by nurse practitioners or doctor's aides.

◇ *Limited service.* HMO's typically perform fewer tests and offer fewer services than non-HMO group practices.

SHOPPING FOR AN HMO

When choosing an HMO, be sure to ask the questions on the checklist at left. In addition, try to select an HMO that has been in business for a while and has a relatively low staff turnover. If you can, examine the credentials of each of the physicians who work there.

Find out what hospitals the HMO uses and whether they are accredited by the Joint Commission on Accreditation of Healthcare Organizations (JCAHO). Also, talk with current HMO members to see if they are satisfied with the service. Finally, check whether the HMO is a member of the the Group Health Association of America (GHAA). This association has strict criteria and will not accept an HMO for membership unless it conforms to association standards. See also Health Insurance; Preferred Provider Organization.

HEARING

Conducted much like a trial, a hearing is a proceeding during which evidence is heard for the purpose of deciding a matter of fact or a point of law. During a hearing, opposing sides appear in court or before a state or federal agency to present and offer arguments about evidence and about points of law pertaining to the case. Both sides will usually have attorneys present.

A judicial hearing is much like a regular trial, and the outcome can settle a lawsuit, even though the purpose of the hearing may be to decide a preliminary matter before the trial begins. Suppose a preliminary hearing finds that key evidence against the defendant was obtained without a search warrant. Because there is no other evidence sufficient to obtain a conviction, the charges are dismissed—there is no reason to proceed to a trial that will only find the defendant not guilty.

Public administrative agencies (such as housing authorities) and legislative committees (such as those of the U.S. Congress) hold hearings to investigate issues and resolve disputes. These kinds of hearings tend to be less formal than those conducted by a court of law, and the rules governing admissibility of evidence are not as stringent as the rules in a criminal or civil trial. See also CRIMINAL PROCEDURE; EVIDENCE.

HEARSAY

In legal terms, hearsay is secondhand information—something a witness heard another person say. Because the witness has no direct knowledge of the facts, and the original speaker is not under oath or subject to cross-examination, hearsay evidence is usually not admissible in court.

There are exceptions to the hearsay rule, with each state deciding what hearsay it will consider admissible in court. For example, deathbed confessions are generally considered reliable and admissible as evidence. Some states have enacted laws that allow as evidence the hearsay statements of children who are alleged victims of crimes. See also DYING DECLARATION; EVIDENCE.

HEAT OF PASSION

The term *heat of passion* is most often used in reference to a crime where mitigating circumstances obscured a person's judgment to the extent that she then acted impulsively. These circumstances may be considered to have so clouded the person's judgment that she cannot be judged according to the same standards as a person whose actions are deliberate and voluntary. As a result, for example, a charge of murder may be reduced to the lesser charge of manslaughter.

Suppose that, upon returning home from work, Lucy finds that a man who had previously assaulted her aged mother is waiting for her in the driveway. The man begins to taunt Lucy and threatens to "beat up" her poor mother "any time he feels like it." As a result of his incessant badgering, Lucy flies into a rage and strikes the man in the face with her heavy briefcase. He falls, hits his head, and later dies of his injuries. Lucy's impulsive act is considered to be a crime committed in the "heat of passion," and therefore she is charged not with murder, but with manslaughter. See also CRIMINAL LAW; MURDER.

HEIR

An heir is a person (often a relative) who is entitled by law to inherit another person's property. State laws (known as laws of descent and distribution, or intestate succession) control the distribution of assets if someone dies without a will . Thus, for instance, if your widowed grandmother dies without a will and you are her only surviving relative, you are most likely to be her heir.

A child who is not mentioned in a parent's will is known as a pretermitted heir, meaning one who is passed by or omitted. Usually the omission is not intentional and can be rectified. Suppose Jack has three sons, Harry, Barry, and Larry. When Jack wrote his will, Larry had not yet been born. Jack died without revising his will, which states that he is leaving everything to "my sons, Harry and Barry." Larry will probably be entitled to an equal share of Jack's estate even though he is not mentioned in the will.

Sometimes, however, a parent intends to disinherit a child by simply not mentioning his name in the will. That should work in states in which a pretermitted child statute protects only children born after the will is executed. But some states protect all omitted children. In those states, if it is your intention to disinherit one of your children, you must so specify in your will. Otherwise, the child could claim a share of your estate. See also DYING WITHOUT A WILL; INHERITANCE TAX; WILL.

HIT-AND-RUN DRIVER

A hit-and-run-driver is the operator of a motor vehicle (including motorcycles and recreational vehicles, or RV's) who strikes a pedestrian, bicyclist, or another vehicle and then leaves the scene of the accident. Every state has laws requiring persons involved in an accident to stop and identify themselves, and to remain at the scene of the accident until the extent of any damages and injuries can be assessed. Leaving the scene of an accident is a criminal act, and severe penalties will be imposed on the driver. A hit-and-run driver can be charged with vehicular manslaughter or other crimes.

To avoid prosecution as a hit-and-run driver, and to ensure that your insurance claims are settled without delay, you should remain at an accident in which you are involved. If someone has been injured, assist him as best as you can until emergency help arrives. See also AUTOMOBILE ACCIDENTS.

If you strike an empty vehicle and cannot locate the driver, leave a slip of paper under the windshield wiper with your name, telephone number (or your lawyer's telephone number), driver's license number, and information about your insurance coverage.

IF YOU ARE A VICTIM

If you are struck by a hit-and-run driver, try to track down any witnesses who may have noticed the vehicle's license plate number or anything else that could help to identify the driver. If you have collision coverage, your insurance company will compensate you for damage to your vehicle; if you have personal-injury protection, you will be compensated for medical expenses. See also AUTOMOBILE INSURANCE.

If your injuries are serious, or the damage to your vehicle is extensive, you may seek compensation beyond that provided by your insurance. In order to get sufficient evidence for a civil suit, you may have to get the help of the police or even hire a private investigator or an attorney to track down the hit-and-run driver.

REAL LIFE, REAL LAW

Crimes Ruled by Passion

When deciding whether to reduce a charge of murder to manslaughter, a judge considers the time that elapsed between any provocation and the killing, the weapon used, the manner of the killing, the relations of the parties, and whether the defendant acted in the heat of passion. Below are some cases in which heat of passion was claimed as a mitigating factor.

In Wisconsin, after discovering that his wife had been unfaithful, a husband agreed to a reconciliation. When he later caught her in a compromising position with her lover, he killed them both on the spot. The court found that the husband acted in the heat of passion and was guilty of manslaughter, not murder.

In Nebraska a man killed his boss after being fired. The court found that being fired was not adequate provocation to justify a charge of manslaughter; the employee was tried for murder.

In Massachusetts a woman on trial for killing her husband attempted to have her murder charge reduced to manslaughter on the basis that her husband had confessed to an adulterous past. The judge ruled that a past affair was not sufficient provocation to reduce the charge.

In South Carolina a man who had raped a woman later parked his truck in front of her home and shouted for her to come out. Her husband emerged from the house and shot him dead. Because the husband acted under extreme provocation, the court termed the killing manslaughter.

HITCHHIKING

Hitchhikers stand by the side of the road hoping to get a free ride from a driver going in the same direction. Hitchhikers and the motorists who pick them up sometimes become the victims of crimes ranging from robbery to assault. As a result, hitchhiking is illegal in most states, and a hitchhiker can be punished by a fine.

Holographic Will

A will that is handwritten and signed by the person making it, but not witnessed in accordance with state law, is called a holographic will. Only about half the states recognize holographic wills, and those that do have very strict definitions of what constitutes a valid one. Some states have refused to accept holographic wills that were not entirely written by hand—for example, when the date was typed in. To be safe, it is always better to have a formal will properly drawn up and witnessed. See also WILL.

Home Business

Many entrepreneurs begin their business by working out of their homes or apartments. If the business grows, they can then take on the larger commitment of office space and staff. Consulting firms, mail-order suppliers, caterers and bakers, crafts producers, and many other businesses can be run from a desk or kitchen table. Starting a business always involves up-front investment and planning. Yet by starting your business from home, you can minimize your expenses.

For instance, Sandra, who has a degree in graphic arts from a local college, has always enjoyed designing clothing for herself. Last Christmas she saved money on gifts by turning a room in her apartment into a small studio and making silk-screen scarves to give as Christmas presents. Her creations were so admired that several of her friends offered to pay her if she would make them some more. Excited by her early success, Sandra wonders whether she should leave her full-time job and start her own business at home. Before she hands in her notice, she ought to do some serious planning.

TAX AND FINANCIAL CONSIDERATIONS

If, like Sandra, you are thinking about starting a small business, first contact your local Small Business Administration for some basic advice on planning.

You should also talk to an accountant or tax specialist to find out the financial implications of running a business out of your home. You will have to make Social Security contributions and pay federal, state, and local taxes. The accountant will be able to tell you what type of bank account to open and what kinds of records you need to keep. For example, because federal law allows you to deduct a portion of your rent, utilities, and capital costs for equipment and furniture for the business, you should keep all your bills and receipts.

However, the Internal Revenue Service (IRS) will allow you to take these deductions only under certain conditions. Your home office must be the only or most important place of business, or the place where you regularly meet with clients. For example, in a recent case an anesthesiologist in Virginia was denied his home office deduction when the IRS determined that he used the office only for administrative activities—such as keeping patient records and sending bills—and not for his primary work, which was treating patients in hospi-

ABC's of Home Business Zoning Laws

Zoning laws that pertain to home businesses vary considerably from place to place, so be sure to find out what they are in your area. Typical zoning laws may:

- ❑ Prohibit retail sales or client visits to your home. If client visits are allowed, zoning laws may specify the number of parking spaces you need to provide.
- ❑ Ban signs advertising your business or limit their size, type, and location.
- ❑ Prevent you from hiring employees who are not members of your family.
- ❑ Prohibit or require a separate entrance for your business and your residence.
- ❑ Limit the square footage of your home that can be devoted to business purposes.
- ❑ Prohibit unusual or offensive odors or noises.
- ❑ Restrict the hours during which you can operate your business.

tals. Although the decision was overturned in Tax Court, in 1993 the Supreme Court ruled in favor of the original IRS decision. Because home office deductions are judged on an individual basis, you must be prepared to justify your deduction to the IRS.

Insurance

You will also need liability insurance protection beyond that of a usual homeowners policy, both for yourself and for any employees or visiting clients. And unless you are covered by your spouse's health insurance, you will need to buy an individual health insurance policy. Your insurance agent will be able to tell you what kind of coverage you should have. You may also wish to set up a retirement plan. See ACCIDENTS AT WORK; BUSINESS TAXES; HEALTH INSURANCE; INCOME TAX; INSURANCE; RETIREMENT PLANNING; SOCIAL SECURITY.

LOCAL RESTRICTIONS

Because local laws may affect your home business plans, you should check with your zoning board to find out whether any zoning restrictions will apply to you when you are working out of your home. Some zoning ordinances prohibit all home businesses, while others merely restrict the hours that you can conduct business with others in your home. If you are going to operate a mail-order business, you may have to obtain a post office box rather than ship and receive items from your home. If you fail to observe zoning laws, the local government can fine you and shut down your business. See also ZONING.

If you rent your home, look at your lease to see whether your home business is subject to any restrictions. If you own your home, check your deed or ask the administrator of your local homeowners association. If you start a home catering operation, for instance, and a restrictive covenant in your deed prohibits the operation of a home business, your neighbors may file a lawsuit against you and obtain an injunction forbidding you to continue doing business. See LEASE; RESTRICTIVE COVENANT.

If your business violates a local zoning ordinance, you can request a variance—special permission to operate your business despite the law. You should make a written request to the zoning board, which will review it and notify the surrounding property owners to see if they have any objections. You may be able to overcome such objections if you can show the zoning board that there are similar businesses operating in your neighborhood and that your business will not prove disruptive or create a nuisance for your neighbors.

BUSINESS OWNERSHIP

You should decide what form your business will take. The simplest type of ownership is a sole proprietorship, but an accountant or a lawyer may advise you to incorporate the business. If you do incorporate, the corporation, rather than you personally, is responsible for the business's debts and for any lawsuits filed against it. Suppose the dye in Sandra's scarves stained Susannah's $5,000 designer suit, Susannah sued her, and the court awarded Susannah $2,500 in damages. If Sandra's business is incorporated, Susannah could obtain her money only from the corporation. She could not garnishee Sandra's personal bank account or foreclose on her house to collect the money.

Despite its advantages, incorporation is not always recommended for a new business. Incorporating your business may cost you more in taxes (and fees charged by a lawyer or an accountant) than a sole proprietorship. Many businesses begin as sole proprietorships and incorporate when they start to grow. See also CORPORATION; SOLE PROPRIETORSHIP.

NAME AND TRADEMARK

You may also want to create a trademarked name and logo that reflect the type of product you are selling. However, you cannot duplicate another company's name if it infringes in any way on the company's conduct of its business. Suppose Sandra likes the name Sandra's Silks, but a nearby store already uses that name. This store can stop Sandra from using its trademark to prevent loss of business due to customers' confusion over the name. Avoid this problem by searching through your local and state trademark records for the trademark you propose to use, or by hiring a firm that specializes in searching trademark records to perform this service for you. You should also apply for patents to protect any original products or processes. See also PATENT; TRADEMARK.

CAUTIONS

Be cautious in your choice of suppliers, managers, sales representatives, and consultants. Suppose that Sandra is selling her scarves at a crafts show when she is approached by a man who claims to know retailers and distributors. He would be happy to sell her products if she gives him a percentage of the sales he arranges. Sandra should politely ask the man for his card and tell him that she will be in touch with him. Then she should call her local Better Business Bureau, which will let her know whether any complaints have been filed against the man for unscrupulous business practices. Sandra can also ask other clients or suppliers for recommendations.

Never enter into an arrangement with someone without a written contract that clearly spells out your relationship and each of your responsibilities. See also CONTRACT.

You should be wary of advertisements in magazines or on television offering good wages for simple work such as stuffing envelopes, clipping coupons, or assembling crafts or jewelry. Far from being legitimate ways to begin a home business, many of these companies charge you start-up fees for "materials" or "instructions" and then either fail to deliver the materials or send instructions containing so many restrictions that you will never make any money. Be suspicious of any scheme that charges start-up fees. If you suspect that a company may not be legitimate, check with your state attorney general or local Better Business Bureau. See PYRAMID SALES SCHEME.

PROFESSIONAL CONSIDERATIONS

Be sure to obtain from your local and state governments any licenses or permits required in your area, including a business license and a sales tax permit to exempt you from paying any sales tax on items that you will resell, such as the fabric used in making slipcovers or the clay for pottery. Any business that deals with food must meet food-handling and health regulations. A business such as a hair salon, an inn, or a day-care center will require licenses and safety inspections by the appropriate government agency. See also LICENSE.

If you decide to hire employees, ask your state department of labor about the responsibility you will have to the people who work for you. You will have to withhold taxes from your employees' paychecks and pay for Social Security taxes, workers' compensation, and unemployment insurance. If you hire only independent contractors or commissioned salespeople, you should give them written work-for-hire contracts and submit W-2 or 1099 forms to the Internal Revenue Service at the end of the year. See also EMPLOYEE PAYCHECK DEDUCTIONS; INDEPENDENT CONTRACTOR; SELF-EMPLOYMENT; WORKERS' COMPENSATION.

HOME BUYING AND SELLING

Housing is usually the single biggest cost in a family budget, and home ownership is one of the biggest financial responsibilities you will ever have. Even though individually owned single-family homes are still in the majority, you can own another type of home, such as a condominium (in which the owners of each unit also have an interest in a development's common facilities) or a cooperative (where ownership is of shares in a corporation). Whether you are buying or selling a house, condominium, or cooperative, a thorough understanding of the process is helpful. See also CONDOMINIUM; COOPERATIVE APARTMENT; MOBILE HOME.

PROFESSIONAL SERVICES

Many home buyers begin their search at a real estate agency. Typically, the agency will have listings of homes that are for sale. These listings may be exclusive to the agency or "open" listings shared by many agencies. With open listings, more people are likely to be looking at the same properties. If you are a seller, listing a property exclusively with one broker means that you will pay him a full commission. But if you sell the house yourself under an exclusive listing, you are not required to pay the broker.

With an "exclusive right-to-sell" listing, the seller has to pay the broker no matter who sells the house. Although this means that the seller must pay a commission no matter what, the broker has a greater incentive to sell the house.

Many brokers place properties on a special "multiple listing service" so that other brokers can offer the property. If another broker sells the property, she and the original broker split the commission.

If you are a buyer, keep in mind that the agent typically works for the seller (who pays the commission), and as such, represents the seller's interests. In many states, buyers who are concerned about this arrangement can engage the services of a "buyer's broker," who works only on their behalf.

As an alternative to a real estate agent, some sellers put their homes up for sale themselves, do their own advertising, and negotiate directly with the buyer. A seller who does this is commonly referred to as a FIZZBO (from "For Sale by Owner"). If you want to use the FIZZBO approach, you will not have to pay a real estate agent's fee. However, you will have to find potential buyers and show the house yourself, negotiate your own contract, and risk wasting time with buyers who are unqualified. See also REAL ESTATE AGENT AND BROKER.

OFFER TO PURCHASE

Whatever the procedure, the first step in a real estate transaction is for the buyer to make an offer to purchase. The form of the offer will vary according to local custom. One common approach is to make the offer with a "binder" (a document, usually in a standardized form, which is drawn up stating the amount the buyer is offering). If the offer is accepted by the seller, the binder becomes a sales contract. The binder also contains any contingencies that must be met before the sale is finalized. For instance, most sales are subject to the buyer's ability to obtain suitable financing and to sell his current property. The offer is usually also contingent on a satisfactory appraisal and inspection of the property. For a sample binder, see the EVERYDAY LEGAL FORMS section, beginning on page 552.

When the binder is drawn up, an "earnest-money deposit" is made by the buyer. This is a check (often for $1,000) made out to the real estate broker or to a "trust account" of the seller's attorney, proving that the buyer seriously intends to buy the house. State law varies on when and where this check can be deposited. In some states it must go into the broker's escrow account. While the money is in escrow, it belongs to the buyer; if the sale is canceled, a written agreement should specify whether the buyer or the seller receives the money. See EARNEST MONEY.

If you are negotiating a home sale yourself, the check should be made out to an impartial party known as the "escrow agent." This agent must hold the funds in trust until a formal contract is drawn up. A buyer should never make an earnest-

REAL LIFE, REAL LAW

The Case of the Haunted House

Jeff and Patrice found what they hoped would be their dream house and signed a contract to buy it. Only afterward did they discover that many in the community of Nyack, New York, thought that the Victorian house they were about to purchase was haunted. In fact, the seller had even had a magazine article published about the ghosts inhabiting her home.

Jeff and Patrice asked to have the contract canceled and their deposit returned. They claimed that the seller had failed to disclose the reputation of the house to them before the contract was signed and that its notoriety would diminish its value. The seller refused, so Jeff and Patrice took her to court.

Although a local trial court found in favor of the seller and refused to cancel the contract, that ruling was overturned when Jeff and Patrice appealed. In its decision, the appeals court ruled that because the seller had written about the ghosts and discussed them extensively with the media, the house was haunted "as a matter of law," and that the buyers were entitled to have its reputation disclosed before they signed the contract. The court ordered the contract canceled, and Jeff and Patrice's deposit was refunded.

money check payable to the seller. See also ESCROW.

When the seller receives an offer, he can either accept it, reject it outright, or propose a counteroffer. Then the buyer, in turn, can either reject the counteroffer or make one of her own. This process can be repeated until an agreement is reached. At that point the binder is signed by both parties and a formal contract is drawn up. If the buyer backs out once the binder is signed, she forfeits her deposit. If the seller changes his mind, the buyer's deposit is returned.

HIRING A LAWYER

Early in the process, both the buyer and the seller should hire lawyers who are experienced in real estate law. A good real estate lawyer can advise on negotiations, help conduct a title search, and represent the parties at the closing. She can also be of use if there are any problems with inspection, disclosure, and clearing the title. And if either one of the parties changes his mind about the sale, the lawyer will be able to protect her client's rights.

THE CONTRACT

Like the binder, a contract of purchase is usually a standard form. A typical contract states the price of the house, formalizes the deadlines for meeting the contingencies agreed to in the offer to purchase, and sets a date for closing the sale. To avoid disputes, the contract should also specify any furnishings, appliances, and fixtures that are included in the sale.

If the buyer has trouble getting a mortgage, the parties can agree to extend the contract. However, the seller can put the property back on the market if the buyer cannot get a mortgage within the specified time. See also MORTGAGE.

APPRAISAL

Mortgage lenders usually ask the buyer to pay for a professional appraiser to determine the market value of the property (which often differs from its tax assessment value). Every state now either requires that real estate appraisers obtain licenses or is in the process of developing some accreditation procedure. Meanwhile, national and regional organizations also set standards for appraisers. A good appraiser should charge a flat fee for the service and provide a full written report, indicating the method by which the property's value was appraised. See also APPRAISAL.

If the appraisal is significantly lower than the asking price, the lender may not want to give the buyer a mortgage for more than a percentage of the appraised value. The buyer can then try to renegotiate the contract based on the value given by the appraiser; obtain another appraisal and then try to renegotiate the price with the lender; or—as a final option—find financing elsewhere.

INSPECTION

The contract should not only give the buyer the right to have the house inspected; it should also provide that if the inspection finds any serious problems with the roof, house foundation, or the electrical, heating, or plumbing systems, the sale is canceled or the seller has the option of making repairs, after which the sale can proceed.

Newly built homes are usually inspected by the local building inspector. If the buyer of such a home suspects a problem not disclosed by the seller (who is usually a developer), he should have the house inspected privately. If a buyer is purchasing an older home, some mortgage lenders require him to obtain a certificate of noninfestation from a termite inspector and a radon test.

Your real estate agent, your lawyer, the local Better Business Bureau, or the local office of consumer affairs can help you find reputable home and termite inspectors. Although there are no state or federal guidelines for home inspectors, a good inspector will follow the guidelines established by the American Society of Home Inspectors (ASHI). A home inspector should state his fee in advance and provide a full written report of the inspection. However, most inspectors cannot be held liable for any defects that they fail to notice during an inspection.

DISCLOSURE

A problem sometimes arises in real estate transactions when the seller knows about a problem with the property but fails to disclose it. Most states have laws that require full disclosure by the seller. In such a state, if the seller hides a problem that substantially reduces the value of the home, the person who buys the home can file a lawsuit in order to get money for repairs or even to have the sale canceled. In a state that does not have a full-disclosure law, buyers should be diligent about discovering any flaws in the house, particularly those of a structural nature.

TITLE

One of the final steps the buyer must take is to determine that the title to (ownership of) the house is free of any liens, fraud, or error. If the seller owns the home in joint tenancy, if he is divorced, or if the house is part of a deceased person's estate, the buyer should make sure that anyone who had an interest in its ownership has relinquished it.

A title company usually conducts the title search. If any problems arise, the sale of the property may not be completed until the matter is resolved. See also TITLE INSURANCE.

Before taking title to the house, the buyer should decide with his lawyer what type of ownership he wants. The house may be owned by only one person, or it may be held in joint tenancy, tenancy by the entirety, or some other form of ownership. Finally, the buyer needs to apply for title insurance and homeowners insurance. See also JOINT TENANCY; TENANCY BY THE ENTIRETY.

CLOSING

If the buyer obtains financing, the title is clear, and the home and termite inspections show no defects, a closing will take place. At the closing the seller will transfer the deed to the buyer in exchange for the purchase price. Specific closing procedures vary from one place to another, but generally these steps are followed:

◇ Prepaid expenses, such as property taxes and utility bills, are apportioned between the buyer and the seller.

◇ Unless the buyer is paying the full purchase price in cash at the time of the sale, he will sign a mortgage agreement with his lender.

◇ The buyer gives a check to a closing agent, who makes the disbursements and gives the remainder to the seller.

◇ The buyer receives the deed and the keys to the house and may now take possession on the agreed date. See also CLOSING, REAL ESTATE; DEED.

HOME EQUITY LOAN

Mortimer's old jalopy is on its last legs, he has mortgage payments to meet, and his son will be going to college next year. Mortimer's savings will not cover all of these expenses, so he decides to borrow some money. However, his bank is charging 14 percent interest for personal loans, and the interest rate on his credit card is nearly 20 percent.

One solution Mortimer might consider is a home equity loan (sometimes known as a second mortgage), for which his home is used as collateral to secure the loan. Home equity loans, which are permitted in every state except Texas, are either for a fixed amount or for a revolving line of credit (in which the line of credit is restored as the principal is repaid).

ADVANTAGES

Home equity loans have several advantages over other loans:

◇ *Competitive interest rates.* Because the collateral is Mortimer's home, a home equity loan will probably have a lower interest rate than another kind of loan. The rates are lower because the borrower is more likely to repay the loan in order to keep his home, and because homes are assets with a fairly stable value.

◇ *Tax savings.* The interest on home equity loans is generally tax deductible up to $100,000, whereas the interest on credit card debt and personal loans is not deductible at all.

◇ *Low fees.* Mortimer may find a home equity lender who can offer low application fees and finance charges.

DISADVANTAGES

There are some disadvantages to home equity loans, however. First, just as with a regular mortgage, if Mortimer defaults on his payments, he could lose his home to the lender, since the loan will be secured by a lien against Mortimer's home. See also FORECLOSURE; LIEN.

Second, most lenders will let you borrow only up to 80 percent of the equity you have in your home. For example, suppose Mortimer's home is appraised at $150,000, and his mortgage balance is $120,000. Since his equity is $30,000, most lenders will give him no more than $24,000. Nonetheless, Mortimer may be able to combine a home equity loan with other kinds of loans to meet his financial needs.

STEPS TO TAKE

If you are thinking about taking out a home equity loan, first review these steps:

1. Examine your financial circumstances. If you are having difficulty meeting your current expenses, you should recognize that a home equity loan is not a quick fix. If you fall behind on your payments, you could lose your home.

2. Shop around for a lender. According to a 1991 survey conducted by the American Banking Association, some home equity lenders charged up to 17 different fees for processing a single loan, while others charged very few fees, or none at all.

3. Ask whether your interest rate is fixed or variable. A lender may advertise an "introductory" interest rate but then reserve the right to increase this rate after an introductory period expires. Find out if your interest rate will change during the lending period, and be sure to know the maximum rate that can be charged. These rates may be capped by state law. See also TRUTH-IN-LENDING ACT.

4. Compare the long-term cost of a home equity loan with other lending options. Most home equity loans offer low interest rates, but they stretch out payments over many years. Thus you can end up paying more in interest over the long haul than if you had settled for a shorter-term personal loan, even one with a higher interest rate. Because a long payment term has high interest costs, a home equity loan often makes the most financial sense if you can promptly repay it. You are unlikely to incur any penalties if you prepay a home equity loan. See also MORTGAGE.

HOME IMPROVEMENT AND REPAIR

This year Eileen plans to make some much-needed improvements and repairs to her house. Specifically, she wants to add a deck, install new carpeting all through the house, and reroute the driveway around the back of the house. Eileen hopes to install the carpet herself and hire someone to do the other jobs. No matter who does the work, there are some basics she should keep in mind.

PERMITS AND LICENSES

First, Eileen should check with her local government to determine what permits or licenses are required for these jobs. Tasks that do not require structural changes and that will not affect her neighbors, such as installing the new carpet, usually do not require a permit. However, the new deck and the major alterations to her driveway are likely to require a work or building permit.

In most communities any electrical, heating and cooling, or plumbing work must be done by a licensed professional. If Eileen hires an electrician to run wiring out to her new deck, she will need to have the wiring examined by an inspector, and she must get a certificate of approval (also called a certificate of occupancy) when the work has been completed.

Do not try to sidestep the procedures and costs of getting a permit or using licensed contractors where required by law. For instance, if Eileen installs a hot tub on her new deck without checking to see if it is in compliance with local building regulations, she may have to remove the hot tub later if the building inspector finds out about it. And if the work done on the hot tub is faulty, the consequences could be fatal.

FINANCIAL CONSIDERATIONS

Before you begin any work, check with your accountant. You may be able to use the cost of home improvements to reduce any capital gains taxes if you later sell the house. You may also discover that you do not have to pay sales tax on certain items used for construction purposes.

CONTRACTORS AND SUBCONTRACTORS

If, like Eileen, you are overseeing the work on your house, or are doing some of it yourself, you are serving as your own general contractor. But you may have to hire subcontractors to work for you.

Before hiring contractors or subcontractors, you should go through the following steps:

◇ Get several estimates from reputable contractors. An estimate that is too low often means that the subcontractor is underestimating the amount of work, and the final price may be significantly higher.

◇ Come to a clear understanding with subcontractors

about the work they are to perform and how it is to be done. You should have a contract with each subcontractor; if you are later dissatisfied with his work, you can prove that he failed to follow your instructions. See also CONTRACTOR.

◇ Check both the subcontractor's liability insurance and your own to see if you are covered for any injuries to a worker while he is on your property. If not, speak with your insurance agent about getting this coverage. See also INSURANCE; WORKERS' COMPENSATION.

◇ Go to your county law library to look into the lien laws in your state. If a subcontractor fails to pay his employees or suppliers, they may be able to make a claim against you. See also MECHANIC'S LIEN.

HOME REPAIR AND IMPROVEMENT SCAMS

Home repair and improvement is a big business, and unscrupulous people may try to swindle you. Be on the lookout for these common tactics:

Unsolicited work
One day when Eileen is out mowing her lawn, a man in a truck pulls up. He says that he noticed that she could use a new driveway coating. He says that, as it happens, he just finished a job down the block and has some extra materials available to redo her driveway at a discount for cash payment.

Eileen is a savvy consumer and refuses his offer. Had she agreed, she might have ended up with a driveway resurfaced in a thin coat of motor oil. If you are ever approached by someone under similar circumstances, do not confront him directly, but notify the police.

The material downgrade
Suppose Eileen had a subcontractor install her carpeting. She agreed to purchase a particular type, but the subcontractor put in an inferior one and then charged her for the more expensive item. Eileen should have checked the carpet before it was installed. After the fact, she may have to sue in small-claims court for the difference in price or to have the carpet exchanged.

Bait-and-switch tactics
Eileen sees an ad for bargain-priced patio tiles. Tempted by the offer (or "bait"), she calls the contractor, who pays her a visit but says that her job cannot be done at the advertised price. Instead he begins a hard sell to convince her that she should buy more expensive substitute tiles (the "switch"). Eileen insists that she will take the bargain tiles or nothing. See also BAIT-AND-SWITCH.

The fake inspector
A person claiming to be an inspector for the local public utility knocks on Eileen's door and demands entry to inspect her furnace. Eileen asks him for appropriate identification before allowing him inside. When he cannot show this, she closes the door and calls the police.

Impostors sometimes pose as government or utility inspectors to gain entry into homes. Once inside, the fake inspector examines the homeowner's furnace, plumbing, or wiring, and "warns" that they are dangerous. If repairs are not made immediately, the homeowner will have to pay a large fine and the utility company may disconnect service. Luckily, the inspector knows a contractor who can do emergency repairs. Frightened by the prospect of the fine and a service cutoff, the homeowner agrees to have repairs made. In this scam, the so-called inspector usually works for the contractor.

If anyone claiming to be an inspector comes to your door, ask for identification and call the government agency he claims to work for before allowing him in your home. A legitimate inspector will not object to being checked out, while a con artist will quickly disappear if you question his credentials. See also CONSUMER PROTECTION; SCAMS AND SWINDLES.

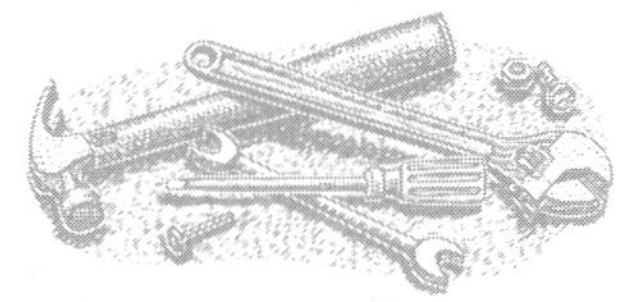

HOMEOWNERS ASSOCIATION

If you live in a planned development or subdivision, chances are that it has a homeowners association—a private nonprofit corporation whose purpose is to give residents a voice in how the community is maintained and to make sure that property values remain as high as possible. By 1992 one in six Americans lived in a planned development with a homeowners association, and by the year 2000 the ratio is expected to be one in three.

A homeowners association is generally organized in accordance with a document known as a community declaration, part of the developer's master plan. The officers and directors of the association are members of the community, elected by their fellow residents. In most planned communities a homeowners association performs one or more of the following functions:

◇ Enforces the covenants, conditions, and restrictions governing the use and development of community property.

◇ Provides maintenance and upkeep for community property, such as sidewalks, open spaces, and greenbelts.

◇ Manages and maintains community recreational facilities, such as swimming pools, playgrounds, and tennis courts.

To pay for these services, the homeowners in the community are assessed a fee. This fee will be stated in your property deed and adjusted according to the community's needs. If a homeowner fails to pay the fee, the association may be entitled to collect late charges and interest, sue the homeowner, and file a lien against his property.

COVENANTS AND RESTRICTIONS

Homeowners associations try to protect the value of all the property of the community by enforcing the covenants and restrictions in the property owners' deeds. Depending on the community, a homeowner may be required to obtain the association's approval before painting her house, replacing the roof, erecting a television antenna or satellite dish, building a garage, or installing solar panels. Other covenants may prohibit parking certain vehicles on the street. Homeowners may also be prevented from hanging laundry outside to dry, erecting fences, planting trees that interfere with a neighbor's view, or landscaping property in an unusual way.

DISPUTES BETWEEN NEIGHBORS

Homeowners associations in many communities provide mediation services as a way to help resolve disputes between neighbors. Suppose your next-door neighbor decides to work on his 1967 Dodge Dart in his driveway, and the car sits up on blocks with its parts scattered around for weeks. There is no covenant in his property deed that prohibits him from working on the car, but it is unsightly and you think it is dangerous to local children. You asked your neighbor to hurry up and finish, but to no avail. You may be able to sue him for creating a private nuisance, but first, if you live in a community with a homeowners association, ask the association to help mediate your dispute. In most instances the mediators will be members of your community who have received special training in resolving problems that arise between neighbors. Their role is not to make a binding ruling about the dispute, but to help you and your neighbor work out a solution to it. See also MEDIATION; NEIGHBORS.

DISPUTES WITH AN ASSOCIATION

Suppose you paint your house a color that is unacceptable to the homeowners association. The association should notify you in writing that you are in violation of the restrictions in your deed and give you a deadline to take corrective action.

You are entitled to a hearing before the association's board of directors. If you cannot resolve your dispute and do not comply with the board's instructions, the association may file suit against you and obtain a court order to require your compliance.

HOMEOWNERS INSURANCE

Homeowners insurance is purchased by individuals to protect their homes and possessions against certain risks, including fire, theft, and vandalism. In most cases, mortgage lenders insist that home buyers purchase this insurance when they buy the house. But you should also update your homeowners insurance policy as the value and replacement cost of your home rise.

Most policies contain several sections indicating the maximum amount of coverage you have for each type of loss. The real-property section covers the primary building and any other structures on the property (such as sheds or garages). The personal-property section covers possessions—furniture, rugs, and the like. Another section covers loss of use, indicating the amount the company will pay if your house is damaged and you cannot live in it. For example, if a fire causes major damage to your house, forcing you to move into a hotel while repairs are made, your policy may cover some of your additional living expenses.

Most homeowners policies also include liability insurance. It is usually divided into two categories: (1) personal liability insurance and (2) medical insurance. The first protects a homeowner if he is sued for having caused bodily damage to someone or for damaging another person's property. The second provides payment of medical expenses if someone is accidentally injured while on your property or as a result of your actions. See also NEGLIGENCE; TRESPASS; UMBRELLA INSURANCE.

BASIC COVERAGE

There are six common types of homeowners insurance, used in all states but Texas (which has slightly different categories, as established by the state board of insurance). The basic policy is designated by the industry as HO-1. This type of policy provides protection of the house and its contents from losses resulting from (1) fire, lightning, and smoke, (2) explosions, (3) windstorms and hail, (4) civil commotion and riot, (5) vehicles and aircraft, (6) vandalism and malicious mischief, (7) theft, (8) glass breakage, and (9) volcanic eruption. Losses resulting from an earthquake or a flood are not covered.

BROAD COVERAGE

For protection against other types of losses, a broad coverage, or HO-2, policy may be a better choice. In addition to the risks outlined above, HO-2 policies cover six other types of risks, including losses from (1) falling objects; (2) accidental leakage or flow of water or steam from plumbing, air conditioning, heating systems, or household appliances; (3) the weight of snow, ice, or sleet; (4) sudden accidental cracking, rupture, bulging, or burning of a hot-water or steam heating system, air conditioning system, or sprinkler system; (5) short circuits or other accidentally generated currents that damage wiring or electrical appliances, fixtures, or other devices; and (6) freezing of any part of a plumbing, heating, or cooling system, or of a household appliance.

SPECIAL COVERAGE

Under an HO-3, or special, policy, the house, but not its contents, is protected against all risks except those specifically excluded by the policy. Normal exclusions include loss resulting from war, nuclear accidents, floods, and earthquakes. Although the contents of the home are not covered from all risks under the HO-3 policy, an "endorsement" may be added (for an additional expense). It gives virtually the same protection to personal property as that provided for the house.

COVERAGE FOR TENANTS AND CO-OP OWNERS

People who live in rental units or cooperative apartments may also purchase home insurance policies. In a cooperative apartment building, the residents lease their apartments from the corporation in which they own shares. The building itself is owned, maintained, and insured by the corporation. Since renters and co-op owners do not own their dwellings, insurance companies have designed HO-4, or tenant, policies to provide coverage for the contents of the home but not for the actual building itself. The protection offered is exactly the same as that provided in an HO-2 broad-coverage policy. Renters and co-op owners can also buy liability insurance. See also COOPERATIVE APARTMENT.

COMPREHENSIVE COVERAGE

The most expensive type of homeowners insurance is the comprehensive, or all-risks, policy. Designated HO-5, it insures the dwelling and its contents against all risks except those specifically excluded by the policy. Typical exclusions include flood, war, nuclear accidents, and earthquakes.

CONDOMINIUM COVERAGE

The common areas of the building, such as the lobby, elevators, and lawns, are insured by the condominium corporation. Nevertheless, the owners of the individual units should buy insurance in the event of a fire, flood, or some other incident that destroys the contents of the unit. These homeowners can buy HO-6 policies, which will provide protection similar to that of the HO-4. See also CONDOMINIUM.

EXCLUSIONS

Most insurance policies contain exclusions or restrictions—

that is, specific conditions or items that the policy does not cover. Damage that is caused by a flood or an earthquake, for instance, will not be covered by most policies. Theft and vandalism coverage may be limited if you live in a high-crime area or if you are away from your home for more than 30 days at a time. And if you work from your home, you may need additional insurance to cover professional or business liabilities. See also HOME BUSINESS.

AMOUNT OF COVERAGE

How much insurance coverage should you buy? This depends upon how much you need and can afford. In general, most homeowners buy policies that insure between 80 to 100 percent of the replacement value of their property. Eighty percent coverage is sufficient in most cases, because even rebuilding a house from scratch rarely includes buying land or laying a new foundation.

Nevertheless, the cost of replacing a home often exceeds the price the owner paid for it or its current market value. For this reason, owners can buy replacement cost insurance that exceeds the value of their home. However, homeowners are not allowed to reap a bonus under the replacement cost policy. Let us say that you buy a house for the price of $85,000 and then buy replacement insurance for coverage of up to $100,000. If your home is destroyed and it costs you only $94,000 to rebuild, the insurance company is obligated to pay you just that amount. Even if you hold two separate policies on your house, you cannot collect twice for the same loss. See also FIRE INSURANCE.

Additional coverage

Although the homeowners policies described above will protect your possessions against basic losses (including, in most places, off-premises theft), some personal items should be insured separately because their value is greater than the limit of most homeowners policies. Jewelry, furs, musical instruments, antiques, artwork, cameras, coins, and other collectibles can be insured up to their full value—both in your home and elsewhere—with an additional policy called a "floater." See FLOATER.

Endorsements

You may also buy added protection in the form of an endorsement (addition to the policy) to cover the replacement cost of the contents of your home. Under standard insurance, the contents of a house are typically covered for their actual value—which is the replacement cost minus depreciation. A replacement cost endorsement provides for the full cost of replacing an item that is stolen from or damaged in your home, and sometimes for losses that occur away from your home.

High-crime areas

Insurers are reluctant to give policies to renters and homeowners who live in areas where burglaries and robberies are frequent. As a result, the Federal Crime Insurance Program subsidizes policies for residents who live in these areas. Recipients of this type of insurance are required to fulfill security requirements, such as installing deadbolt door locks, security bars, and other kinds of protective equipment.

Natural disasters

In some areas of the country, homeowners can purchase flood, earthquake, mudslide, tornado, or other insurance to protect against damage caused by rare but potentially catastrophic events.

In qualifying communities homeowners can turn to the federal government's National Flood Insurance Program for protection. Your insurance agent can tell you whether this program is available in your area. See FLOOD INSURANCE.

Earthquake insurance is needed more by homeowners on the West Coast than by those in the East. In fact, by law insurance companies in California must offer earthquake coverage—though homeowners are not obliged to purchase it. The cost of earthquake coverage is expensive and is calculated not only on the basis of the location of the home, but also on its construction. For instance, because a brick home is more likely to be damaged during an earthquake, the cost of an endorsement is higher than for a timber frame house.

Before buying extra hurricane insurance, double-check with your broker. Often damage from windstorms will be covered under your standard homeowners policy.

As you add endorsements to a policy, its cost increases. One way to decrease insurance costs is to buy a perpetual policy, in which all premiums are paid at once. These policies are hard to find, however. For more information on lowering your insurance costs, see the checklist on page 302.

Homeowners Warranty

Most builders of new homes today offer buyers a homeowners warranty against structural defects in the house. This type of warranty is almost always a marketing tool to assure the buyer of a home that the house builder and insurer will stand behind the home's quality.

SOME WARNINGS

In most instances homeowners warranties actually limit a builder's responsibility for construction defects. For example, a typical warranty may require a builder to repair "excessive" cracks in foundation floors or walls during the first year. The warranty may define "excessive" cracking so narrowly that your foundation would be on the verge of collapse before the warranty covered any repairs.

Similarly, many homeowners who felt secure because their homes were covered through companies such as the Home Owners Warranty Corporation (HOW) found that their claims were rejected when HOW simply denied that major structural defects existed. HOW's warranty defined major structural defects so strictly that the owners of houses that were built on landfills with no foundation footings or steel reinforcements (and which were finally condemned) had their claims rejected. And even when HOW ultimately was forced to honor warranty claims, months and even years passed while the company delayed payment.

STEPS TO TAKE

To protect yourself if you buy a home that is covered by a homeowners warranty, do the following:

1. Read the warranty carefully to be sure you know exactly what it covers.
2. Do not rely on a builder's oral assurances that he will correct problems not covered by the warranty. He should put all his promises in writing.
3. Have an independent inspector look at the house, rather than relying on the local building inspector. You may want higher standards of workmanship than are called for by your local building code.
4. If you think you have a claim under your homeowners warranty, file it with the warranty company as soon as possible and be persistent. Keep records of your phone calls and correspondence relating to the claim. Then if you are forced to take your claim to court, you can demonstrate that you tried to have the warranty enforced.
5. If your home purchase was financed by the Federal Housing Administration or the Department of Veterans Affairs, inform these agencies if you have any complaints about the way warranty claims are handled. They will investigate and can refuse to guarantee construction loans to a builder who fails to comply with the terms of his warranties. See also MORTGAGE; WARRANTY AND GUARANTY.

Home Schooling

Sarah's parents believe that the school curriculum in their district emphasizes secular values while undercutting biblical teachings. Jamal's father wants his son to learn more about his African heritage and the contributions of African culture. Peter and Ben's mother fears that public schools put a premium on conformity at the expense of creativity. Brittany's mother is concerned about violence in the local schools. Although they have different reasons, these parents have decided to educate their children at home.

Home schooling is gaining rapidly in popularity. Estimates suggest that from 300,000 to 500,000 school-age children are currently taught at home.

COMPULSORY EDUCATION LAWS

Because the state has a future interest in training its young people to be productive and good citizens, every state has compulsory education laws. These laws require that children who are taught at home receive an education comparable to one they would receive in public schools. For example, all states require students to have instruction in basic subjects such as mathematics, social studies, and English.

Parents who teach their children at home must comply with the compulsory education laws in their state, and state and local school boards may supervise home schooling. If a child's

ABC's

Of Home Schooling

Home schooling is legal throughout the country, but the requirements vary widely from state to state. If you are thinking of educating your children at home, here are a few things you should do:

- ❑ Check with your state department of education to find out what qualifications they require for home school instructors. Some states permit only someone with a teaching certificate to instruct children in the home. In other states a college degree or simply a high school diploma is necessary.
- ❑ Ask whether your local school board or state department of education must approve the curriculum you propose. You will have to teach certain standard subjects—a requirement that has been unsuccessfully challenged as a violation of religious freedom.
- ❑ Ask your local school board about the extent of supervision of home schooling in your area. Some boards require children schooled at home to be tested by an independent evaluator. In other areas a representative of the school board must review the students' work. And in some districts, students must take standardized tests.
- ❑ You may be able to obtain teaching materials from your school board or state department of education. Several private organizations also provide workbooks and other aids for course work, curriculum outlines, and computer software.

home schooling program does not meet requirements set by the government, his parents may be charged with violating truancy laws. For information on home schooling requirements, see the box above.

Homicide

Homicide is defined as the killing of a person as a result of another person's action or failure to act. But homicide is not always a crime. For example, justifiable homicide (killing someone while trying to protect your life) is not a crime. Nor is homicide committed to protect the life of someone else. See also MANSLAUGHTER; MURDER; SELF-DEFENSE.

Homosexual Rights

Although discrimination that is based on gender is prohibited under federal civil rights laws, discrimination based on a person's sexual orientation is not. Homosexuals are generally not afforded any special legal protection under federal law. In fact, in a number of states, laws still prohibit homosexual acts between consenting adults, even in their own homes.

However, at least five states and a number of cities have passed laws that extend some legal protection to homosexuals. Although these laws vary, in general they prohibit discrimination in housing, public accommodations, and employment. Criminal laws may also impose penalties on anyone who harasses or assaults someone because of their homosexuality. See also HATE CRIME.

Although no state recognizes marriages between homosexuals, several communities have enacted laws extending spousal benefit coverage to the partners of homosexual employees, including family-leave care for seriously ill homosexual partners. In a number of states, homosexuals have been allowed to adopt children. A homosexual is entitled to will his property to anyone he chooses, including another homosexual.

Until recently, homosexuals were not permitted to serve in the armed forces. However, due to recent changes in regulations, military recruiters may no longer ask potential recruits about their sexual orientation, and existing servicemen and women cannot be discharged unless they reveal their homosexuality. Further legislation is pending on this issue.

One area in which homosexuals have gained greater legal protection is that of child custody. At one time, courts generally refused to grant custody to parents who were admittedly homosexual. Increasingly, however, courts have awarded child custody to homosexual parents when they found it was in the child's best interest. See also AIDS; DISCRIMINATION.

HOSPITAL

Each state has the authority to regulate how many hospitals (whether public or private) may be established in a given area and how they must be maintained. State and federal laws and regulations affecting hospital operation cover a wide range of practices—including everything from billing procedures to the number of beds.

ACCREDITATION

Most hospitals seek accreditation by the Joint Commission on Accreditation of Hospitals (JCAH), an organization established by the American Hospital Association. Without this accreditation, hospitals cannot receive Medicare payments. Residents and interns at teaching hospitals only receive credit for their training if the hospital has JCAH accreditation.

ADMISSIONS

Not all hospitals are obligated to accept you as a patient, except in emergencies. Privately funded and profit-making hospitals in particular may turn away nonemergency patients. However, hospital bylaws, group health plan provisions, and local laws often restrict a hospital's right to refuse admission to patients who are not in need of emergency care.

Federal Medicare regulations state that participating hospitals cannot base eligibility for admission on the patient's race or ethnic background or on the fact that a person is disabled. The federal Hill-Burton Act, which funds hospital construction, places similar restrictions on hospitals that receive its funds.

Ability to pay

In many instances, a patient's ability to pay cannot be used as a factor for admission. For example, hospitals that receive Hill-Burton Act funding are required to provide services to those unable to pay. In addition, Hill-Burton requires hospitals to inform the public (by means of classified newspaper advertisements and notices posted in admissions areas and business offices) that they will treat persons unable to pay.

Emergency care

Generally, hospital emergency rooms, especially in hospitals that accept Medicare, are required to accept all patients who seek emergency care. A failure to provide such care could provide the grounds for a lawsuit against the hospital. See also MEDICARE.

In some instances, a hospital's emergency services may not be equipped to give certain types of care—such as for serious burns. In these situations, state law may allow the hospital to transfer patients to another facility if it can be done without jeopardizing the patient's condition. Often, cooperative arrangements exist among hospitals to coordinate specialized emergency care such as this.

DISCHARGES

A hospital may face legal penalties and may be sued if it discharges a patient who requires additional care. In fact, lawsuits for medical negligence and abandonment have been successful against hospitals that discharged patients too early. See also NEGLIGENCE.

Conversely, suppose that you want to leave the hospital, but your doctor feels that you still need medical care, or the hospital wants you to pay your bill before you leave. A hospital generally cannot hold you against your wishes, and doing so could lead to a lawsuit for wrongful detention. However, if you have a communicable disease or need further care, and leaving the hospital would endanger your well-being or the health and safety of the community, the hospital may be allowed to detain you. See FALSE IMPRISONMENT; PATIENTS' RIGHTS; PHYSICIAN AND SURGEON.

Your insurance company, Medicare, and Medicaid may give you coverage for a specific procedure only for a certain length of time. For more information, see HEALTH INSURANCE; MEDICAID; MEDICARE.

BILLING

Even if you have hospitalization insurance, your coverage may not pay all the bills you incur during a hospital stay. Because you are responsible for any bills your insurance does not cover, you should try to keep your costs as low as possible.

Be sure to discuss the need for suggested procedures and tests with your doctor beforehand, and see if any of them can be eliminated or performed on an outpatient basis. If your insurance company requires preauthorization before you are admitted to the hospital, get it; otherwise you may have to pay extra for treatment. Many of the personal bankruptcies filed each year are due to a patient's inability to pay hospital bills. See also BANKRUPTCY.

To avoid paying more than you owe, carefully review your hospital bill. A number of studies have shown that patients are often billed for services they did not receive. Most hospital bills have charge codes rather than plain English; ask the billing office to give you a list of these codes, along with explanations of vague or "miscellaneous" charges.

If you believe you have been overbilled and the hospital will not reduce your bill, call your insurer's claims department; it may intervene on your behalf.

HOTEL AND MOTEL

Special laws apply to the operation of hotels and motels (and other public accommodations, such as inns and guest houses), and these businesses must be licensed by the state in order to operate.

A hotel or motel may not turn away a guest because of her race, ethnicity, religion, or gender. Nonetheless, hotels and motels are not required to accept every potential guest. Thus a hotel may prohibit families with pets, for example, or require that its guests be at least 25 years old, have a major credit card, and pay a deposit. In addition, in most instances a hotel may, at its own discretion, request a guest to leave if he has been especially rowdy or difficult.

SAFETY STANDARDS

Operators of hotels and motels are obliged to keep their guests (and their guests' valuables) reasonably safe. Regulations that cover fire and building safety, cleanliness, and so on are enforced by the local fire, health, and building departments, which periodically inspect hotels and motels.

Hotels and motels have to ensure adequate security for guests in their rooms by providing doors that lock, changing keys or locks periodically or when keys are missing, responding to calls for assistance, and removing dangerous, suspicious, or unregistered persons from the hotel premises. Common areas such as lobbies, parking garages and lots, meeting rooms, and hallways must be well lighted and safe.

Most states also require hotels and motels to provide a secure vault for storing guests' valuables.

SUING A HOTEL FOR NEGLIGENCE

The laws in most states allow hotels to limit their liability for losses that their patrons incur. In some cases, however, you may be able to sue. For example, if a hotel knowingly hires an employee who has a criminal record, some courts would consider the hotel responsible for any loss you suffered from the employee's actions. Or, if you are assaulted in a hotel's dimly lit parking area, you may be able to sue if you can prove that the hotel knew about the potential danger.

In recent years the Motel 6 chain had a number of security problems. In 1988 two ex-con-

ABC's OF HOTEL AND MOTEL SAFETY

Although accommodations such as hotels and motels must ensure their guests' safety, there are some precautions a guest can take to avoid becoming the victim of a crime:

- ❑ Refuse to accept a room whose door has only a single lock or that has no peephole.
- ❑ Keep the room's doors and windows closed and locked.
- ❑ Don't open the door to anyone unless you know who he is. If someone claims to be from hotel maintenance or security, call the front desk to confirm his identity.
- ❑ If you are returning to your room late at night, use the building's main entrance and ask an employee to escort you to your room.
- ❑ Place your valuables in the hotel's safe. State laws limit the liability of hotels and motels for items missing from your room, and you may find yourself having to bear the cost of replacing expensive items stolen from your room.

victs raped a photographer who was staying at a Motel 6 in Fort Worth, Texas, and stole her car and cameras. The photographer's $10 million negligence suit against Motel 6 was settled in 1991 and helped to heighten public awareness about the importance of safety measures.

GUESTS WITH DISABILITIES

Under the Americans With Disabilities Act of 1990, hotels and motels must make reasonable efforts to accommodate guests with handicaps. This may mean taking such measures as installing ramps and elevators, widening doorways to make room for wheelchairs, adapting bathrooms for accessibility, and providing Braille notices of emergency procedures. See also DISABLED AMERICANS.

PAYING THE BILL

If you refuse to pay your bill, the laws in most states permit the hotel or motel to hold your luggage until the bill is paid. Also, since many hotels require you to give a credit card number when you register, any outstanding fees can be charged to your credit card. See also LIEN.

HOUSEHOLD HELP

Domestic employees, including child care providers, chauffeurs, gardeners, cooks, maids, and caretakers, are offered the same kind of federal and state protection as other workers.

If you hire someone to work in your home, you must follow certain procedures in order to comply with the regulations of the Internal Revenue Service (IRS) and the Immigration and Naturalization Service (INS). You must first obtain an employer identification number (EIN) by filing IRS form SS-4.

Tax requirements

Because you are considered an employer by the IRS, you are responsible for the following:

◇ If you pay more than $50 to a household worker during any calendar quarter, you are required to pay Medicare and Social Security (FICA) taxes. Failure to pay Social Security tax may result in a penalty equal to 100 percent of the tax, plus any interest owed. Any compensation that you give to your worker in the form of food, lodging, clothing, or other noncash items is not subject to these taxes.

◇ If you pay wages in excess of $1,000 per calendar quarter, you must pay federal unemployment insurance.

◇ You may also face state and local income tax withholding duties.

◇ Each year, you must give your employee a completed IRS form W-2 (Wage and Tax Statement).

◇ The employee is responsible for filing her own income tax return.

◇ If the household worker is sent to you by an agency or contractor to whom you make payments, then the agency or contractor (not you) is considered the worker's employer.

Your local tax office or your lawyer or accountant can tell you more about the tax regulations in your area.

Other obligations

To meet INS regulations, you must have any domestic worker complete INS form I-9, the Employment Eligibility Verification form, proving that she may work legally in the United States. If you do not complete this form, you may be fined. Keep the form on file in the event an INS or Department of Labor official requests it. You must also examine either a U.S. passport, a certificate of U.S. citizenship, a certificate of naturalization, or a resident alien card. If these documents are not available, you may establish verification from a combination of papers showing identity and authority to work. A common combination is the worker's driver's license and Social Security card.

In most states, you are not required to take out workers' compensation for your household help. Nonetheless, you may be financially responsible for injuries a worker suffers on your property. You should have enough liability insurance to pay for any claims made by employees in your home.

If you hire someone through an agency, make sure it is licensed, bonded, and insured. Then, if the worker steals or damages your property, the agency can be held liable if you can prove the employee's guilt. See also EMPLOYEE PAYCHECK DEDUCTIONS; HOMEOWNERS INSURANCE; IMMIGRATION; NEGLIGENCE; WORKERS' COMPENSATION.

ILLEGITIMACY

Children born to parents who are not married to each other are called illegitimate. The law once tended to treat illegitimate children as second-class citizens, partly because of society's belief in the sanctity of a marriage, and partly because blood relations were used as the basis for inheritance and property rights. Today illegitimate children are, for the most part, entitled to the same legal benefits as legitimate offspring.

THE PRESUMPTION OF LEGITIMACY

The following presumptions carry the force of law:

◇ Every person is now presumed legitimate until facts demonstrate otherwise.

◇ Children born to a married woman are presumed to be the children of her husband and are therefore legitimate—even if the child was conceived before the marriage took place.

◇ Children conceived during a marriage but born after its termination, whether by death, divorce, or annulment, are presumed to be the legitimate children of the husband.

LEGITIMATION

The reasons someone may want to prove a child's paternity are many, but the most common is to compel the father to assume financial responsibility for his offspring. Every state has laws regarding legitimizing children, but in general an illegitimate child is automatically legitimized if the child's parents marry, if the child's biological father admits his paternity in writing, or if the father openly acknowledges the child as his offspring.

Acknowledgment of paternity imposes a duty of support on the father and gives him visitation and custody rights. It also gives an illegitimate child the same status as an heir to his father's estate as his legitimate brothers and sisters have.

ESTABLISHING PATERNITY

Many states have adopted the Uniform Parentage Act, which outlines procedures for establishing paternity and enforcing support. If a father takes no voluntary action to legitimize his child or disputes paternity, the mother, the child, or state welfare authorities may sue him to establish paternity and enforce the child's right to support. Unless he can show that he was sterile or simply not near the mother at the time of conception, a presumed father may be required by the court to submit to DNA or blood tests that can establish a relationship between him and the child. Several of these tests are considered very accurate, although some fathers have tried to challenge them in court. See also Aid to Families With Dependent Children; Child Support; DNA Fingerprint.

IMMIGRATION

The term *immigration* refers to the process by which noncitizens (aliens) come to the United States to take up permanent residence. Permanent residents have the right to live and work in the United States, but they do not automatically become citizens. The Immigration and Naturalization Service, a division of the Department of Justice, exercises control over immigration. See also Alien; Citizenship, U.S.

QUOTAS AND PREFERENCES

Aliens who wish to enter the country for permanent residence must obtain an immigration visa. (Those aliens who intend to stay only for a limited period of time apply for a nonimmigrant visa.) The number of immigration visas issued each year is strictly controlled, and Congress has revised it several times in the last few years. Beginning in fiscal year 1995, up to 675,000 visas will be issued annually, to be distributed on the basis of family relationships (480,000), employment (140,000), or so-called diversity (55,000), as discussed below. See also VISA.

Family preference visas

There is no numerical limit on immediate relatives of U.S. citizens, defined as children, parents, and spouses. Any excess in this category is subtracted from another category. Family preference is given as follows:

◇ First preference is given to the unmarried children of U.S. citizens.

◇ Second preference goes to the spouses and the unmarried children of permanent residents.

◇ Third preference is given to the married children of U.S. citizens.

◇ Fourth preference goes to the adult siblings of citizens (those over 21 years of age).

Employment visas

Up to 140,000 immigrants are admitted to the country on the basis of their employment. In most cases, these immigrants must have an offer of permanent employment from a U.S. employer, and in many cases the Department of Labor must certify that no qualified U.S. workers are available to fill the position. It must also be shown that the employment of people in certain categories will not adversely affect the wages and working conditions of permanent residents who are similarly employed. For example, an employer cannot open an auto plant in Wyoming, then claim a shortage of qualified workers and bring in immigrant laborers who will work for minimum wages with no benefits. The employment-based visas are generally allocated as follows:

◇ 40,000 a year go to persons with extraordinary ability in the arts, sciences, education, business, or athletics; or who are outstanding researchers, professors, or multinational managers or executives.

◇ 40,000 visas a year may be given to professionals with graduate degrees and to people with exceptional ability in the arts, sciences, or business.

◇ 40,000 visas are available for professionals with bachelor's degrees and to skilled or unskilled workers who are coming to perform nonseasonal work. In this category, only 10,000 visas will be offered to unskilled workers (those who have less than two years' training or experience).

◇ 10,000 visas are reserved for persons classified as "Special Immigrants" under regulations set out by the INS. Genally, this means people with very specialized occupations.

◇ 10,000 visas are set aside for investors who will be creating employment in the United States. To qualify, the immigrant must be investing a minimum of $1 million (or $500,000 in a rural area) and creating at least 10 new jobs.

Diversity visas

For people in countries who have been underrepresented among immigrants to the United States in recent years, 55,000 visas are set aside. The attorney general determines allocations for these countries.

REFUGEES

Defined by the INS as persons who have been persecuted, or have a reasonable fear of persecution, because of their race, religion, nationality, social group, or political opinions, refugees are subject to a separate set of guidelines. The president fixes the number of refugees permitted to enter the United States each year.

IMMUNITY

Immunity is a special privilege or an exemption from a certain duty (such as paying taxes or serving on a jury) that other citizens are required to perform. In recent years many of the usual reasons for granting immunity have been rejected by the courts, including the principle of sovereign immunity (which prevented citizens from suing their government).

SUING SPOUSES

Traditionally, spouses could not sue one another for injuries inflicted either intentionally or negligently. For example, a wife could not file suit against her husband for injuries she suffered in a car accident while he was driving. The reason behind this rule was that such lawsuits disrupted "marital harmony" and created opportunities for fraud or collusion.

Some states will now allow spouses to sue for any injuries caused by intentional wrongful acts (such as assault) and for car accidents, but not for other kinds of negligence. States that favor abolishing interspousal immunity believe that questions of fraud and collusion are better determined by the judge or jury hearing the case.

PARENT-CHILD IMMUNITY

Parents were long immune from lawsuits brought by their

minor children. The courts did not want to jeopardize family peace or interfere with the parents' right to discipline their children. Issues of fraud and collusion were also a concern.

Today, in some states, children are allowed to sue their parents for any injuries caused deliberately or through negligence. Often these lawsuits are brought for financial reasons. For instance, if a mother's careless driving results in an accident that leaves her child with injuries, she will be responsible for the child's medical expenses. However, if the child is able to sue and wins his case, the mother's liability insurance will cover the cost of his injuries.

Cases in which minor children have sued their parents for bad parenting have not generally been successful. A child may, however, sue a parent who uses unreasonable punishment. The law considers that a spanking or sending a child to bed without supper is reasonable punishment. But withholding meals for several days or giving a beating that causes injury is considered unreasonable. In such cases the child can sue, and the state can prosecute for child abuse. See also CHILDREN'S RIGHTS.

SOVEREIGN IMMUNITY

The idea of sovereign immunity was adopted from English common law, which held that the "king can do no wrong." In the United States this has meant that the government could not be sued without its consent.

Today courts and lawmakers have waived sovereign immunity in a number of cases. For example, a person who is injured through the negligence of a government employee may sue that government department (as long as the employee was on duty at the time of the incident); persons injured on government or public property as a result of a dangerous condition may also sue. See also ACCIDENTS ON GOVERNMENT PROPERTY; SOVEREIGN IMMUNITY.

IMMUNITY FROM PROSECUTION

A participant in a crime may be granted immunity from prosecution in exchange for testimony given to a grand jury or during a trial. State and federal laws dictate when such immunity may be offered. In some instances the prosecutor is given complete discretion in making this decision; in others the court must be involved.

IMPLIED CONSENT

Actions, signs, or silence suggesting that a person has given his permission for something to happen is known as implied consent. Suppose you agree to let your teenage neighbor mow your lawn. For several months, you pay him weekly for his services. One week, after he has mowed the lawn, you refuse to pay him, claiming that you did not ask him to do the work. If he takes you to small-claims court, the court will probably find that your ongoing relationship was a form of implied consent to the mowing, and will order you to pay the bill.

Similarly, suppose that for years you and your family have used your neighbor's yard as a shortcut to the grocery store. Whenever he has seen you, your neighbor has always been quick with a smile and a wave. If he suddenly calls the police and accuses you of trespassing, you would be justified in claiming that his years of friendly acknowledgment implied his consent to the arrangement. See also ADVERSE POSSESSION.

In a slightly different vein, when you obtain a driver's license, most states consider that you give your implied consent to submit to blood-alcohol testing if you are stopped for suspicion of drunk driving. If you refuse to submit to this testing, your license may be automatically suspended or revoked. See also DRIVER'S LICENSE; DRUNK DRIVING.

INCEST

Incest—the act of sexual intercourse or marriage between people who are closely related by blood, or in some states, by marriage—is always a crime. All states have laws that prohibit sexual relations between parent and child, grandparent and grandchild, and brother and sister, including half brothers and half sisters. In addition, many states prohibit sexual relations between uncle and niece, aunt and nephew, and first cousins.

The incest statutes in some states prohibit sexual intercourse between persons who are related by adoption, but in other states the relationship must be a blood relationship.

Persons who are convicted of having an incestuous relationship are subject to fine or imprisonment or both.

INCOME TAX

Although federal income taxes have been collected for more than 80 years, Americans are always looking for ways to minimize the amount they owe. The legality of federal income tax, which was authorized in 1913 by the 16th Amendment to the U.S. Constitution, has been challenged many times, but never successfully. However, although taxes must be paid, there are legal ways of reducing your tax bill. In the words of the renowned federal judge Felix Frankfurter, "Nobody owes any public duty to pay more than the law demands: taxes are enforced exactions, not voluntary contributions." All taxpayers should know the laws concerning tax preparation, tax filing, and penalties for delinquency or fraud. See also INCOME TAX AUDIT.

WHO MUST FILE

Under the federal Internal Revenue Code, all U.S. citizens, all resident aliens, and those nonresident aliens and dual status aliens who are married to U.S. citizens or to permanent residents generally must file an income tax return if their gross income (that is, income before any deductions or exemptions have been calculated) exceeds a minimum amount. This figure depends on the taxpayer's status and is revised yearly. In 1993 the amount of gross income that necessitated filing a tax return was as follows:

◇ For single, divorced, or legally separated persons under the age of 65, the minimum was $6,050; for single filers 65 and older, $6,950.

◇ For a single person filing as a head of household or a married person with a dependent child who lived apart from her spouse, the minimum was $7,800 for those under 65 and $8,700 for those 65 and older.

◇ For a married couple filing jointly, the minimum was $10,900 if both were under 65. If one spouse was 65 or older, the amount was $11,600; if both spouses were 65 or older, it was $12,300.

◇ For a married person who was filing singly or who was not living with her spouse, the minimum was $2,350.

Special rules apply for widowed persons and for minor children who have incomes.

REPORTING INCOME

Although the income tax system is considered to be one of voluntary compliance, the federal government has a number of ways to verify income. For example, employers use W-2 forms to report the wages and salaries of all of their employees; money paid to independent contractors is reported on Form 1099-MISC; and interest income is reported by the bank to the IRS on Form 1099-INT. If the income that a taxpayer reports does not match up with what has been reported to the IRS, she is likely to receive an inquiry about her return.

An individual must file one of three tax forms, depending on his filing status (whether single or married) and whether the deductions or credits he can take are greater than the standard deduction for his filing status. Consult the IRS or the instruction booklet that comes with your annual tax packet for the latest information on which of the following forms to file:

◇ Form 1040EZ is for single taxpayers under 65 who have no dependents, whose taxable income is less than $50,000, and who do not itemize deductions or receive earned-income or other tax credits. See also EARNED-INCOME CREDIT.

◇ Form 1040A is for taxpayers whose taxable income is less than $50,000 but who are claiming certain credits or deductions, which include earned-income credit, deductions for IRA contributions, credits for child- and dependent-care expenses, and credit for the elderly or disabled.

◇ Form 1040 is for persons whose taxable income is $50,000 or more, who have income from such sources as foreign investments, interest income in excess of $400, capital gains distributions, or nontaxable dividends, or who want to itemize deductions.

As you may take deductions for many expenses—including some medical and dental fees, real estate property taxes and home mortgage interest, charitable contributions, and moving expenses (if the move is business related)—it is worth doing a trial calculation of deductions on Schedule A of the 1040 form before you file. See also CAPITAL GAINS TAX; MOVING.

TAX PREPARATION

Every taxpayer is personally responsible for the information on her tax return, even if the return was completed by a tax-preparation company or an accountant. When you sign the return, you are stating under penalty of perjury that all the information is true and correct to the best of your knowledge. See also TAX PREPARATION.

What happens when your tax return contains an error? If it results in an underpayment to the IRS, you will owe not only that amount but also any interest or penalties that may have accrued.

If you discover that you have underreported your income after you have sent off your return, you may be able to avoid paying a penalty if you immediately file an amended return listing the additional income. Similarly, if you discover that you failed to take a legitimate deduction or credit on your return, you can file an amended return and ask for a refund of the amount you overpaid.

TAX FILING

If you think you will be entitled to a tax refund, you will undoubtedly want to file your return as soon as possible. If you owe money, however, there is really no reason to file your return before the April 15 deadline.

The IRS now offers "Fast Filing," which allows taxpayers to file their federal returns by computer in anticipation of a speedy refund by direct deposit into their bank accounts. To do this, you must take your return to an IRS-authorized tax preparer, who will transmit your information for a fee. You will also have to complete Form 8453 (U.S. Individual Income Tax Declaration for Electronic Filing), which the tax preparer will send to the IRS, along with your W-2 and any other forms.

According to the IRS, electronic filing is more accurate and faster than mailing your return. You can use it even if you owe taxes, provided you mail your check by April 15.

Be wary of so-called fast refund or fast filing offers that are now made by some tax preparers and banks. In actual fact, these expedited refunds are nothing more than high-interest loans. Suppose you are due a refund of $300 and you are offered a "fast refund" for a fee of "only $30." If you would normally receive your refund from the IRS within a month, the fee for obtaining your money from the tax preparer ahead of time works out to an annual interest rate of about 120 percent!

ESTIMATED TAXES

If you are self-employed, or you usually owe more than $500 to the IRS at filing time (because of income that you received from investments), you should estimate your approximate taxable income for the upcoming year and file quarterly prepayments to the IRS based on this amount. These so-called estimated taxes are filed on Form 1040-ES. If you fail to file these forms and pay estimated taxes when required by the IRS, you may be subject to penalties for underpayment of taxes.

TAX EXTENSIONS

It is possible to receive an automatic four-month extension for filing your return. To do so, you must file Form 4868 by April 15, which will enable you to delay filing until August 15. If you can show a good reason for needing another extension, using Form 4868, the IRS may grant you one until October 15. However, you will not receive an extension for paying your taxes, which will still be due on April 15. By that date, you must make an estimated payment of what you owe. If your estimate is less than 90 percent of the tax owed on your return, you will be faced with penalty and interest charges on the balance you owe when you complete your return. If you overestimate your tax liability, you will receive a refund of the amount you overpaid (but no interest) once you file your tax return for the year.

PENALTIES AND INTEREST

Failure to file a federal income tax return or to pay taxes that are due can result in some very stiff financial penalties. If for some reason you cannot pay what you owe the IRS, file your return anyway and send in as much as possible. The penalty for not filing is usually 5 percent of the total amount due for each month that your return is late; however, the penalty cannot exceed 25 percent of the amount that you owe. In addition to penalties, you will have to pay interest, which will be assessed both on the amount you owe and on any penalties imposed by the IRS.

If you file your return but you fail to pay the amount due, the penalty is usually one-half of 1 percent of the unpaid balance for each month it is owed, up to 25 percent of the amount due. You will also be charged interest on late payments. In most cases it is cheaper to get a loan or take an advance on a credit card than pay IRS penalties and interest.

The IRS can charge penalties for frivolous returns, substantial understatement of taxes, fraudulent reporting, and negligence. Any taxpayer who is found guilty of deliberately failing to file, of tax evasion, or of making false statements on a return may be subject to criminal penalties as well.

If you are unable to raise the amount you owe, you should inform the IRS as soon as possible. Fill out Form 9465, asking the IRS for an installment payment agreement, and attach it to your return. You can expect to hear from the IRS within 30 days. Do not be surprised if the IRS takes a threatening stand and demands that you pay up. Remember that you are expected to do whatever it takes (including selling or refinancing your car or home) in order to pay your taxes. The Internal Revenue Service can seize bank accounts and real estate, and garnishee your wages if you ignore its demands for payment. See also GARNISHMENT.

RECORD KEEPING

Keeping careful records not only helps in tax preparation but will also be useful in the event you are audited. But what should you keep, and how long should you keep it? Every taxpayer needs a record of his income. For most people, this is the W-2 form on which their employers report their wages from the previous year. Other possible sources of income include taxable interest income, dividends, tips, and certain fellowships and scholarships.

Taxpayers who itemize their deductions should keep on file records of all the deductions they claim (including canceled checks or receipts for doctor visits, any charitable donations, and their unreimbursed business expenses, for example). The statute of limitations for most tax returns is three years from the date the return was due or filed, or two years from the date that you paid the tax, whichever is later. You should keep all of your records (including copies of your income tax returns) for at least that long, although experts often recommend that you keep all financial records, including your tax records, for up to seven years. See also FINANCIAL RECORDS.

RESOLVING PROBLEMS WITH THE IRS

If you have a tax problem that you cannot clear up through normal channels, you should contact the Problem Resolution Officer at the IRS district office for your area. The officer will try to clear up your case

REAL LIFE, REAL LAW

The Case of the Divorcée's Deductions

Beth was dissatisfied with the financial settlement she received when she was granted her divorce. To reopen the settlement case, she hired a lawyer, Gerry, to whom she agreed to pay a contingency fee of 35 percent of any additional settlement. After three years, Gerry was able to convince the judge to award Beth $500,000 in addition to her original settlement. Gerry's fee and disbursements came to almost $200,000.

When Beth tried to claim the $200,000 as a deduction on her income tax return, the IRS disallowed it. The agency gave two reasons: First, Gerry's fee was excessive; and second, provisions in the Internal Revenue Code make legal fees related to a divorce nondeductible.

Beth took her case to the Tax Court, which ruled in her favor. It held that the main purpose for which Gerry was hired was not to assist Beth with her divorce but to protect her right to taxable income from properties owned by her ex-husband. Under the tax code, legal fees incurred in order to produce or protect taxable income are tax deductible. The court also held that Gerry's fees were not excessive, as he had worked on the case for three years and would have received nothing had his efforts failed.

within five days, but if he cannot, you will be informed of the status of your complaint and the name and phone number of the officer who is handling it.

If you disagree with the tax examiner's findings from an audit, you can have your case reviewed by the IRS Appeals Office. If it rules against you, you can take your case to the U.S. Tax Court (which has a special small-claims division for cases that involve less than $10,000). Once you petition the Tax Court, the IRS cannot assess additional taxes or penalties while your lawsuit is in progress. But interest on taxes and interest you owe accrues until your case is concluded.

The Tax Court has other advantages. When you take your appeal to court, the IRS will generally try to settle the case quickly, thus reducing the interest you will owe if the judge decides against you. Furthermore, if the IRS raises other issues, the burden of proof will rest on the agency, not you.

You can appeal your case to District Court or to the U.S. Claims Court in Washington, D.C., but only after you have paid the disputed amount and have made an unsuccessful attempt to have your money refunded. If you take your case to either of these courts, you will need an attorney.

STATE AND LOCAL INCOME TAXES

Today most states impose an income tax on persons who live within the state's borders or who live elsewhere but are employed in the state. Some municipalities also impose income taxes. Generally these taxes are based on the adjusted gross income that a taxpayer reports to the federal government, with additional adjustments. State revenue departments demand prompt filing of tax returns. State income tax laws vary; if you have specific concerns, speak with an accountant or other tax professional in your state.

INCOME TAX AUDIT

An income tax audit is an official examination of individual or corporate financial records by the Internal Revenue Service (IRS) for the purpose of determining the accuracy of a tax return. Audits are the primary tool available to the IRS to enforce compliance with tax laws. If an audit reveals that you have taken some improper deductions, for instance, you may owe the IRS extra taxes, interest, and often a penalty as well. The IRS can do an audit within three years of a return being filed, but in specific circumstances, such as fraud, the time limit is seven years. Most audits are made within 18 months of filing a return.

WHO CAN BE AUDITED

Approximately one out of every 100 tax returns is audited, but there is a greater likelihood that some taxpayers will be audited than others. In particular, someone who has a large income or is self-employed may be subject to an audit. Often taxpayers who are to be audited are chosen by an IRS computer program that is designed to identify anything unusual in a tax return. For example, your return may be audited for one of the following reasons:

◇ Tax deductions (such as those for charitable contributions) that are disproportionate to your income.

◇ Failure to provide the appropriate information about certain expenses.

◇ Unusual expenses (such as large travel expenditures for a shoe-repair business).

◇ Income that varies widely from year to year.

◇ W-2 forms that do not match those that the IRS has received from your employer.

In addition, the Taxpayer Compliance Measurement Program randomly selects approximately 50,000 taxpayers each year and asks them to document every item on their tax returns—a particularly strict type of audit.

PREPARING FOR AN AUDIT

If you get an audit notice in the mail, do not panic—a notice does not always mean you have done something wrong. The IRS may have seen something unusual on your tax return.

Read the audit notice carefully; it may be a simple request for you to send additional documents to the IRS. Most audit notices specifically state the reason for the audit. Suppose you made very large charitable contributions in proportion to your income. The IRS might ask for proof that you made the contributions. Once you send sufficient documentation (such as canceled checks or receipts) the agency may be satisfied and the audit completed.

In other situations you may be asked to call an IRS office and make an appointment for the audit to be conducted in person. The IRS will decide where you will meet. An audit examiner, or auditor, will either meet you at his office or, if a "field" audit is called for, he will come to your office or that of your attorney or tax preparer. An auditor is not likely to come to your home unless you operate your business from there, or unless it is inconvenient for you to travel for some reason, such as a disability. An IRS office audit is preferable, since it prevents the auditor from looking through your records for additional information.

The audit notice usually requests that you bring specific documents that relate to the problem that was found with your return (for example, appraisals of property you gave to a charity, canceled checks, or receipts), as well as any general business records (such as bank statements, brokerage statements, or appointment books) that the auditor wishes to see. The IRS will allow you at least several weeks to prepare for the audit—plenty of time to collect the documents you need. Do not discuss the details of your audit with the auditor on the telephone. Wait until you have all your documents assembled and the examination begins. If you need more time to collect the information, ask that the audit be rescheduled.

THE AUDIT EXAMINATION

If you prepared your tax forms yourself, or even if you hired someone else, try to become familiar with the laws pertaining to your case by reading the publications produced by the IRS. If you had a preparer do your taxes, have her appear with you at the audit to explain how your return was done. In fact, if your tax return was prepared by an attorney, a certified public accountant (CPA), or an "enrolled agent" (a tax professional who has passed an IRS examination), she can appear in your place. The main advantage of having a professional represent you is that she should be familiar with tax laws and with IRS examination procedures. However, you will have to pay for her services, and audits can last for a full day or more. If you and your spouse filed a joint tax return, only one of you need attend the audit.

At the audit, the examiner will ask to see any documents he thinks are relevant. With a field audit, be prepared for him to ask questions based on what he sees. For instance, if you claimed that your business only paid you $20,000 last year but you have racing boat trophies on display in your office, an examiner may ask how you could afford such a boat on your salary. You can refuse to answer a question until you get further documentation, particularly if the question concerns an area of your return that was not specified on the original audit notice. Furthermore, an auditor must ask you for the information he needs; he cannot, for instance, go through your files without your permission.

Give the auditor your cooperation. If you do not, your resistance may prompt a further examination of your records. And if you lie outright, you can be charged with perjury.

Do not volunteer any information that the auditor has not requested. Simply supply him with the information he needs and answer his questions about it. If you feel that the auditor is unnecessarily rude or unpleasant, ask to speak to his supervisor. You are legally entitled to request another auditor to review your documents.

Some taxpayers receive a refund with interest at the conclusion of an audit, but it is far more likely that you will have to pay additional tax. If you owe additional federal taxes, you may also owe additional state taxes, as the federal government will notify your state tax department of the adjustment made to your tax return as a result of the audit (unless you live in a state with no income tax). If you disagree with the auditor's conclusion, you can make an immediate appeal to his supervisor and a further appeal, within 30 days, to the IRS Appeals Division. For information on appealing IRS decisions, see INCOME TAX.

If you have intentionally misrepresented your financial situation and made false statements on your return, the IRS or the Justice Department may decide to press charges against you. See also TAX PREPARATION.

INCOMPETENCY

A person is incompetent if he is mentally or otherwise unable to handle his own affairs. The standard test of competency is to determine whether a person can understand the nature and consequences of his actions.

Courts are sometimes asked to decide whether a person is incompetent, and their findings are important.

COMPETENCY TO STAND TRIAL

Among the fundamental rights afforded a defendant in criminal proceedings is the right to confront his accusers and to present evidence in his own defense. It is unfair to have someone stand trial if he is so mentally impaired, or suffers from mental illness to such a degree, that he cannot understand the nature of the proceedings, cannot communicate properly with his lawyers, and cannot assist in his own defense. Incompetency proceedings are usually started by the attorney who is representing the accused.

If a judge declares that the accused is incompetent, he will not be tried for the crime but will often be confined to a mental institution until he can be declared competent. If the condition is permanent or chronic, the trial may never take place.

A person who was found to be mentally disturbed at the time of an alleged crime may nevertheless be competent to stand trial later. For instance, a schizophrenic person may be required to go to court if at the time of the trial his symptoms are being controlled by medication. But his mental condition at the time of the crime may affect the verdict and his sentence. See also INSANITY PLEA.

COMPETENCY TO MANAGE ONE'S AFFAIRS

If a person has a mental illness or defect, or a physical infirmity that renders her unable to manage her daily affairs, a court may declare her incompetent and appoint a guardian to oversee her affairs or to represent her in a civil court case.

Family members usually initiate such incompetency proceedings, but any interested party may do so. Bad judgment, unusual behavior, or eccentricity does not necessarily render a person incompetent, nor does old age or poor health. However, habitual intoxication may do so, especially if the use of alcohol or drugs has permanently impaired a person's ability to reason.

A person who has been declared incompetent loses many rights, among them the right to decide where to live, to choose health care, to marry, to have a driver's license, or to vote. But the law prevents others from taking advantage of an incompetent person. For example, she cannot be held accountable for contracts she makes or for the transfer of property. See also BIRTH CONTROL; MARRIAGE.

NATURE OF INCOMPETENCY PROCEEDINGS

Incompetency proceedings usually take place in the district court where the person whose competence is questioned (the "proposed ward") lives. Anyone who wishes to have the proposed ward judged incompetent must file a petition to the court. The proposed ward must then be notified of the proceedings against her and, in many states, her close relatives must also be notified. She is entitled to have an attorney, and she has the right to a court-appointed attorney if she cannot afford a lawyer herself. In some states she is entitled to a trial by jury if she asks for one. She should probably go to the hearing, although her attendance is not required.

At the hearing, the proposed ward has the right to refute evidence of her incapacity and to present her own witnesses. Usually the court requires medical evidence of her incompetence, although other kinds of evidence may also be relevant.

If the judge finds that the proposed ward is incompetent, he will appoint a guardian or a conservator to assume her custody and manage her affairs. He will arrange for her to stay in her home or be placed in a mental institution, hospital, nursing home, group home, or other institution. The guardian has the legal authority to act for the ward in all matters and to manage the ward's property to ensure that it is preserved, if possible. In rare instances the ward may be restored to competency because the disability or illness is cured. See also GUARDIAN AND WARD.

An incompetency action is different from a proceeding for involuntary commitment, by which a mentally ill or disabled person is placed in an institution if a court rules that he is a danger to himself or to others.

INDEPENDENT CONTRACTOR

Not everyone who works for another person is an employee. An independent contractor (also called a freelance worker) provides a service or product for specific clients, but the clients do not directly control the work that is done. Independent contractors perform a service in exchange for money, according to the terms of a contract with the client. They must provide their own place to work, and they determine their own working hours. Some types of work lend themselves to independent contracting. Writers, translators, graphic designers, craftspeople, and other professionals often prefer the flexibility of freelance work.

EMPLOYERS' CONSIDERATIONS

A company that hires an independent contractor does not have to contribute to his Social Security, unemployment insurance, and workers' compensation insurance, or provide such benefits as health or disability insurance or a retirement plan. As a result, the Internal Revenue Service (IRS) may scrutinize an independent contractor's written agreements. An employer who tries to falsely characterize employees as independent contractors can be subject to financial penalties.

In addition, employers are responsible for the actions of employees in ways that do not apply to independent contractors. If an employee makes a mistake at work, the employer may bear the responsibility for lawsuits or claims filed against the company. As an example, even though defects in a car's safety belts can be traced to a single employee on the assembly line who made a mistake, the company has the responsibility to pay compensation to any customers who suffered injuries due to the faulty belts. Of course, the employee may end up losing his job because of his mistake or negligence.

Suppose, however, that a freelance carpenter makes cabinets for a decorating firm. Six months after the firm sells the cabinets to customers, complaints start coming in that the cabinets are warping. If the customers sue the firm, the firm can name the carpenter as a codefendant in the lawsuit.

INDEPENDENT CONTRACTORS' CONSIDERATIONS

As an independent contractor, you have obligations that differ from those of an employee.

Insurance and zoning
If you work out of your home, make sure that you have sufficient liability insurance and that you are not violating any local zoning laws and deed or lease restrictions. Because you are not eligible for unemployment insurance, you should try to provide for periods when you are out of work. Also, as an independent contractor, you will have to obtain health insurance for yourself unless you are covered by your spouse's benefits. See also HEALTH INSURANCE; HOME BUSINESS; INCOME TAX; INDIVIDUAL RETIREMENT ACCOUNT; KEOGH PLAN; SOCIAL SECURITY.

Tax consequences
An accountant can tell you the tax consequences of working as an independent contractor. You will have to pay Social Security and estimated income taxes, usually on a quarterly basis. However, you will probably be able to take deductions for business-related expenses, such as travel, entertainment, and certain household expenses if you work from your home.

If you claim business expenses, you must keep complete records. Some experts say that the tax returns of independent contractors are more likely to be audited, especially if they list home-office deductions.

Rights to your work
Sometimes freelance work that is done by professionals such as writers or translators is considered "work for hire," and the person who pays for the work obtains the copyright to it. Otherwise, an independent contractor retains the rights to her work (as is often the case with photographers). Your contract should specify who owns the rights to your work. See also CONTRACT; COPYRIGHT.

Getting paid
One of the most difficult tasks that faces an independent contractor is trying to collect payment from the companies and individuals for whom she has worked. Generally, independent contractors cannot afford to hire collection agencies to pursue unpaid bills. Furthermore, if the company for whom you were working goes into

bankruptcy, you may at best be considered an unsecured creditor. Once again, your best legal defense is a clear contract that spells out the payment terms. See also SELF-EMPLOYMENT.

INDICTMENT

An indictment is a formal charge, issued by a state or federal grand jury, accusing someone of a felony crime. Grand jury proceedings differ among states and the federal government. For instance, in federal law, a crime that is punishable by death cannot be prosecuted unless an indictment is issued by a federal grand jury.

Convened from time to time, grand juries are presented with cases by prosecuting attorneys. After reviewing the case and interviewing witnesses, the grand jury decides whether there is sufficient evidence for the case to be tried. If there is, it issues an indictment. Once the indictment is issued, the accused person may be arrested or arraigned (formally charged before a judge). Sometimes a prosecutor may file reduced charges if the defendant agrees to plead guilty. See also CRIMINAL PROCEDURE; GRAND JURY.

INDIVIDUAL RETIREMENT ACCOUNT

An Individual Retirement Account, or IRA, is a personal investment account authorized by the U.S. government under the Employee Retirement Income Security Act (ERISA) of 1974. IRA's are intended to stimulate private investment and encourage people to save money for retirement. They can be held by any qualified person who receives "earned" income from wages, a salary, commissions, or alimony. "Unearned income," such as dividends, interest, pensions, and capital gains, does not qualify for an IRA contribution.

IRA's offer certain tax benefits. First, an income tax savings occurs when you put your money into an IRA. For employees who have a retirement plan at work, a full tax deduction is allowed for couples filing jointly whose adjusted gross income is less than $40,000, and single people or heads of households with adjusted gross incomes under $25,000. A partial tax deduction is allowed for some higher-income taxpayers.

For taxpayers with no retirement plan at work, a full tax deduction is allowed for single taxpayers and heads of households. If a couple files jointly and one spouse has an employer-sponsored retirement plan, they get a full deduction only if their adjusted gross income does not exceed $40,000, and a partial deduction if it does not exceed $50,000.

Another tax savings occurs because the earnings from the IRA funds accumulate tax-free, unlike income from many investments, on which you must pay taxes annually. Also, because most people do not withdraw IRA funds until they have retired (and are usually in a lower tax bracket), the money they have deposited over the years is likely to be taxed at a lower rate when withdrawn.

OPENING AN IRA

An IRA is not an investment like a bond or share of stock; it is a vehicle for investments. You can open an IRA account with financial institutions such as banks, savings and loan associations, and trust, insurance, and mutual fund companies.

You may wish to invest your IRA money in a certificate of deposit (CD) or a bank savings account; in stocks or bonds in a stockbroker's account; or in a mutual fund account. However, IRA funds cannot be used to invest in real estate or in art, antiques, gems, stamps, and other collectibles (except for gold and silver coins).

You may open more than one IRA account, although you cannot contribute more to them than the allowable total annual limit. The advantage of having several different IRA's is that you can make different kinds of investments that have various rates of return and also hold varying degrees of risk. See also ANNUITY; MONEY MARKET ACCOUNT; MUTUAL FUND.

CONTRIBUTIONS

You can contribute annually to your IRA accounts up to a maximum of $2,000 (or 100 percent of earned income, whichever is less). This annual limit is absolute; you cannot deposit $1,500 into an IRA one year and then $2,500 the next year to make up the difference, although you can divide the $2,000 between different accounts (for example, you could deposit $500 into your mutual stock fund account and place $1,500 into a certificate of deposit).

Married couples may establish separate IRA's if they are both employed. A couple may contribute up to $4,000 ($2,000 each) annually. A nonworking spouse (or one who makes less than $250 a year) can still open an IRA; however, the couple's total annual contribution will be limited to $2,250: $2,000 for the working spouse and $250 for the nonworking one.

You can switch funds from one IRA to another (known as a rollover). If you roll over funds, you should know that there is a 60-day limit from the time you withdraw the money until you must deposit it in the new IRA. The IRS usually requires that 20 percent of the withdrawal be withheld unless it is rolled over directly into another IRA. Consult an accountant or the IRS about current rules on such withdrawals. See PENSION PLAN.

There is no lower age limit for IRA contributions (as long as you have earned the income you are contributing). But once you reach age 70½, you can no longer put money into an IRA.

WITHDRAWALS

Before you reach age 59½, if you withdraw funds from your IRA, you must pay a penalty of 10 percent of the amount you withdraw in addition to the normal income tax due on these funds. However, if you should die before you reach 59½, your estate or your heirs will not be penalized for withdrawing funds. The penalty also does not apply if you become totally and permanently disabled before age 59½.

Between the ages of 59½ and 70½, you can make IRA withdrawals if you want to. But once you reach the age of 70½ you must begin withdrawing money from your IRA by April 1 of the following year. Every year from then on, you must withdraw a minimum amount, which is calculated by the IRS based on your life expectancy. For more detailed information, send for IRS Publication 590.

INFORMED CONSENT

Every competent adult has the right to decide whether or not to seek medical care. That decision belongs to the patient, not the doctor, no matter how wise or skillful the doctor may be. Informed consent refers to a physician's duty to explain any treatment, medication, or surgical procedure to a patient beforehand and to obtain his permission to proceed with it.

When you go to the doctor's office or to the hospital, you are usually confronted with a stack of forms to read and sign. They may contain long lists of complications and side effects that are related to your proposed treatment, ranging from dizziness to death. When you sign these forms, indicating to the doctor that you understand all the information that pertains to your treatment, you are granting your informed consent. A doctor who fails to obtain this consent before treating you may be guilty of malpractice.

Suppose George is diagnosed with high blood pressure, and his doctor gives him information that compares the success rates of different kinds of drug treatments and lists the possible side effects and risks. She explains that no treatment can be effective unless George also modifies his diet and begins to exercise. Until George's doctor is sure that George understands this information, she will not proceed. See also CONSENT FORM; PATIENTS' RIGHTS.

Informed consent is also required from subjects who participate in experiments to test new drugs or procedures. The subjects must be informed of both the reason for the experiment and the possible consequences of participating in it.

EXCEPTIONS TO INFORMED CONSENT

Minors are not expected to give their consent for medical care. Their parents (or guardians) must give consent to medical treatment, except in emergencies. Exceptions are also made in some states so that minors may obtain counseling for birth control or abortion or seek treatment for sexually transmitted diseases and drug- and alcohol-related problems without their parents' knowledge.

If a physician believes that a child's life is in danger, but the parents will not allow the required treatment, a court may appoint a guardian who is then authorized to give his consent. Such a situation occurs when parents deny treatment to their child because of their religious beliefs. See ABORTION; CHILDREN'S RIGHTS.

In emergency situations, if a patient is unconscious and unable to communicate, or the parents or guardian of a minor cannot be reached, a doctor may provide treatment to save the patient's life or to preserve him from great bodily injury. The doctor presumes that the patient would have given his consent if he were able. Similarly, during the course of an operation, if a life-threatening or extremely serious complication or emergency arises, the surgeon may treat the patient's condition without obtaining his specific consent to do so.

In certain cases the disclosure of information necessary for a patient to give his informed consent can adversely affect his health or mental well-being. When a doctor withholds information from a patient on such grounds, he is exercising what is known as therapeutic privilege. In the past, for example, diagnoses of incurable cancer were withheld from patients because it was believed that their quality of life would be diminished (although the families may have been told). And in recent years, patients suffering from Alzheimer's disease are sometimes not told because that knowledge may promote stress or depression that can contribute to the progression of the disease. Furthermore, patients who suffer from diseases that cause impairment of their judgment or ability to reason are not always considered capable of giving informed consent to medical care.

INHERITANCE TAX

Twenty states have some kind of inheritance tax, which is a tax imposed on someone who receives property from another person's estate. Inheritance taxes differ from state and federal estate taxes, which are imposed on the deceased person's estate before the property is transferred to the heirs.

An inheritance tax is paid to the state in which the deceased person was a permanent resident. If, for example, you live in Colorado and your Uncle Oscar lived in Nebraska, you would pay tax on the property you inherited from him to the state of Nebraska.

In most instances, inheritance taxes are small, especially if the heir is a spouse or child of the deceased. However, if the heir is not related to the deceased, the inheritance tax may be as high as 32 percent of the value of the inheritance.

Call or write your state department of revenue to find out

INHERITANCE AND ESTATE TAXES

State inheritance and estate taxes can quickly deplete an estate. These taxes are subject to change; your state's department of revenue can tell you about any recent changes.

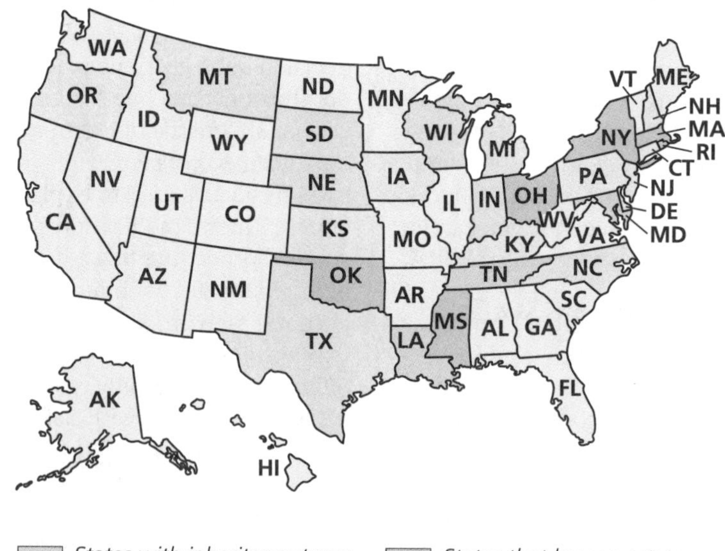

States with inheritance taxes of 10 percent or less.

States with a maximum rate of 12 to 16 percent.

States with a maximum rate of 16 to 32 percent.

States that levy an estate tax.

States that have neither estate nor inheritance tax.

the laws in your state. To minimize the inheritance tax on your heirs, consult an accountant or a lawyer who is an estate-planning expert. See also ESTATE TAX; PROBATE; WILL.

INSANITY PLEA

The insanity plea is a defense used in criminal trials. In legal usage, the term *insane* refers to someone who is mentally ill and is therefore incapable of distinguishing between right and wrong. An insanity plea will often be based on the M'Naughten rule, which holds that if a person who has committed a crime either could not tell the difference between right and wrong or simply did not know what he was doing, he cannot be found guilty.

In courts that do not accept the M'Naughten rule, a defendant can be considered insane if he lacked the ability to realize that his conduct was criminal or he was unable to conform his behavior to the law.

In other states a defendant can avoid criminal responsibility by proving that he gave way to an "irresistible impulse" —that he could not prevent himself from committing the act. This defense is used when a defendant has endured long-term abuse at someone else's hands or was driven by circumstances to a desperate act.

It is not necessary for a defendant to be insane at the time of his trial, and the nature of a person's insanity does not have to conform to a particular medical diagnosis, although medical testimony may be called upon at the trial to help determine the facts of an individual case.

A person can be considered "temporarily insane" due to illness, chronic drug or alcohol abuse, or extreme mental distress—anything that has led to mental impairment or diminishment of reason. However, voluntary intoxication is not a reasonable basis for a temporary-insanity plea.

A defendant who is declared not guilty by reason of insanity is usually committed to a mental institution. If he regains his sanity in the future, he will be set free. See also HEAT OF PASSION; INCOMPETENCY.

INSIDER TRADING

Buying or selling stock because you have information about the company that is not equally available to all stockholders is known as insider trading. Insider trading is illegal when it allows some people (whether employees, outside investors, or stockbrokers) to benefit at others' expense.

Executives of publicly traded companies (companies that are traded on a stock exchange, such as the New York Stock Exchange) often purchase their company's stock or they receive it as part of their compensation. Like other stockholders, they have the right to buy or sell the shares they own. However, they are in an advantageous position because they often know, before the public does, of situations that might affect the stock's price. When the company is in a bad situation, they can sell their stock before the price drops, and when things look good, they can buy more stock.

To inform the Securities and Exchange Commission (SEC) of any insider trading, "inside" stockholders are required to report their stock trading to the SEC every month. The SEC makes those reports available to the public. (You can get a report from the SEC or your library's business section.)

If convicted, inside traders stand to lose the profit from their transactions and can be fined by the SEC or even have federal criminal charges filed against them. See also STOCKS AND BONDS.

INSURANCE

Insurance is a way for individuals or groups to protect themselves against losses that could cause serious financial difficulties. In a contract of insurance (called a policy), an insurance company agrees to compensate you (or a beneficiary you have named in the policy) if a specified event, such as a fire or the death of the insured person, takes place. Insurance policies may also provide protection from property loss or lawsuits. A comprehensive automobile insurance policy, for example, will reimburse you if your car is damaged or stolen, and liability insurance will protect you from lawsuits if you have an accident. In return for this coverage, you pay to the insurance company regular amounts of money known as premiums.

The company providing the

insurance is called the insurer; the party who buys the insurance is known as the policyholder. Although many people buy insurance policies so that they can protect themselves from loss, far fewer will have to file claims for payment. Thus insurers profit by spreading out the risk of paying claims among all of their policyholders.

TYPES OF INSURANCE

The various types of insurance generally fall into three categories: personal insurance, by which a person's life or health is covered; property insurance, by which a person's home, car, or other personal belongings are covered; and liability insurance, by which the insured person is covered for any lawsuits filed against him by others.

The terms of the policy dictate the amount of reimbursement or compensation that the policyholder can receive from the insurer. In the case of life insurance, a specified beneficiary will receive the compensation upon the death of the policyholder. See AUTOMOBILE INSURANCE; CASUALTY INSURANCE; FIRE INSURANCE; FLOOD INSURANCE; HEALTH INSURANCE; HOMEOWNERS INSURANCE; INSURANCE AGENT AND BROKER; LIABILITY INSURANCE; LIFE INSURANCE.

CHECKLIST

Cutting Down Insurance Costs

When you add up the costs of all your insurance coverage, the total may be quite high. Ask your agent or broker about the following ways to reduce your costs:

❑ **CONSOLIDATE YOUR POLICIES.**
You may get a discount if you purchase your homeowners, auto, and other insurance policies through one company alone.

❑ **RAISE THE DEDUCTIBLE.**
By raising the amount you will pay out of pocket on your homeowners and auto insurance, you can reduce your premiums by 10 percent or more.

❑ **GET AUTO INSURANCE THAT FAVORS GOOD RISKS.**
You may get reduced premiums if you have an antitheft or safety device, if you drive less than 7,500 miles a year, or if you have a good driving record. School-age drivers who have good grades or have completed a driver training course can receive reductions, and drivers over 50 or 55 years old may also receive discounts on their premiums.

❑ **BUY "PARTICIPATING" LIFE INSURANCE POLICIES.**
Such policies entitle you to receive dividends, which you can use to pay your premiums. Although the premiums may be higher at first, you should save money in the long run.

❑ **ASK ABOUT "LIFESTYLE" DISCOUNTS.**
Nonsmokers pay lower rates for life and health insurance, and so may people who get regular exercise or who do not drink.

❑ **INVESTIGATE HOMEOWNERS SAFETY DISCOUNTS.**
Some homeowners insurance companies reduce premiums if you have protective devices such as smoke detectors, fire extinguishers, and security alarms, or if your house is built of materials that are fire-resistant.

❑ **COMPARISON SHOP.**
Call other companies for price quotes. If you tell your agent that you have been offered a lower rate elsewhere, he may match it. In addition, some companies give long-term policyholders a discount of 5 percent or more. Ask your agent or broker.

INSURANCE REGULATION

There are thousands of insurance companies in America. They are regulated by state insurance departments, which grant licenses to insurers, approve insurance claim forms, regulate rates, and try to protect policyholders' interests by investigating complaints made about specific insurers. Because state regulations vary, a policy that is approved for sale in one state may be prohibited in another, and rates for virtually identical policies may vary from one state to another.

Most states have insurance guaranty funds that pay claims if an insurer becomes insolvent. However, not every state provides the means to honor policies of insurers who fail, and the federal government generally does not provide any protection. Your state insurance department can tell you about protection in your state.

BUYING A POLICY

Before taking out a policy, particularly for life insurance, evaluate the financial health of your insurer. Several independent companies regularly rate insurance companies; their reports should be available in the business section of your library. A state insurance department can tell you whether it has received complaints about the way an insurer handles claims.

When discussing insurance with a sales agent or broker, ask him when your policy goes into effect. When you fill out an application, the agent sends it to the insurance company experts (called underwriters), who analyze it and determine the risk the company would assume by accepting it. You are insured only when the company approves your application. If an agent tells you that your policy is in effect from the time you complete the application, the insurance company can be held to this claim. For certain types of insurance, such as a homeowners policy, the agent who takes your application is authorized by his company to issue a "binder"—in essence, a temporary policy that serves to protect the applicant from loss while the application is being reviewed. See also INSURANCE AGENT AND BROKER.

CANCELLATIONS AND CHANGES

Read a new insurance policy thoroughly, including the cancellation provision. You should be able to cancel a policy whenever you like. Also find out how the company will return to you any premiums that you have paid in advance—for example, if you made a semiannual payment for your homeowners policy but you are moving after two months and must cancel it.

State laws establish the conditions under which your insurer can cancel or fail to renew your policy. Typical reasons for an insurer to cancel a policy are fraudulent or excessive claims, a failure to pay premiums, or lying on an application. If you tell a health insurance company that you do not smoke, for instance, the company could cancel your policy if it later discovers that you do smoke.

Most states require that policies include an incontestability clause, stating that the insurer cannot cancel your policy after it has been in effect for a certain period. Your state insurance department can tell you if your state has such a rule.

MAKING A CLAIM

Filing an insurance claim may be as simple as sending copies of your doctor's bills to the insurer. With property insurance, however, there are certain procedures you must follow.

If your property is damaged or lost, call your insurer as soon as possible. You must provide documentation for your claim, such as invoices for repairs, appraisals of property that has been lost, or a police report of a theft. In many cases the insurer will ask you to submit an estimate of repairs for damage to a car or other property, or it may want the damage to be appraised by a company representative. If the repairs exceed the amount authorized by your insurer, the company will probably not pay the difference.

A claims adjuster will investigate your claim and determine how much money you will get. The adjuster cannot reject a claim that is legitimate, and you should not feel obligated to accept the first offer she makes.

If a lawsuit is filed against you, you must gather any information regarding the lawsuit and forward it to your insurer.

STEPS TO TAKE IF YOUR CLAIM IS NOT HANDLED PROPERLY

If you are dissatisfied with the way a claims adjuster is handling your case, here are a few suggestions about what to do:

1. Speak to your adjuster's supervisor, who may be able to offer you additional money to settle your claim.

2. Hire your own appraiser or an independent adjuster to make an estimate of the damages or loss. The person you hire should be licensed in your state. (Your state insurance department can tell you their requirements for independent adjusters.) Send his appraisal to a supervisor at your insurance company.

3. You and your insurer can each hire trained arbitrators to hear your dispute and to propose a fair settlement of your claim. See also ARBITRATION.

4. File a written report with your state department of insurance. In some states this department will intercede for you.

5. If your claim is complicated, your attorney can negotiate with the insurer for you.

6. Ultimately, you may bring your insurer to small-claims

court or have an attorney file a lawsuit against the company. If it is found that the company or its representative acted in bad faith, you may be awarded money. Remember, however, that you may come out ahead by settling with your insurer, as a lawsuit can be expensive.

Insurance Agent and Broker

Most people purchase their insurance policies through an agent or a broker. In general, an insurance agent represents a particular insurance company, while an insurance broker acts as the customer's agent, seeking the best coverage and terms available from a variety of insurance companies. Sometimes a broker may act as an agent. To be sure you are getting impartial information, ask the person from whom you buy a policy about his relationship to the insurer.

Insurance agents and brokers are regulated by the state in which they conduct their business. To become licensed, they are usually required to pass a written examination and provide evidence of good character. Insurance agents and brokers have an obligation to conduct business in good faith both with their customers and with the insurance companies they represent.

◇ A broker or agent must try to get the terms and amount of coverage that you request. If he cannot do so, he should notify you immediately. Suppose you ask your insurance broker for a $1 million medical policy. He presents your application to several companies, all of whom reject you because of your previous health problems. Your broker must tell you the status of your application and your chances of obtaining coverage.

◇ If an agent or broker tells you he is obtaining insurance for you and then fails to do so, he may be responsible to you for any loss you suffer. Suppose you file an application for a homeowners policy and give the agent (or broker) a check for the first premium. Instead of sending it to the insurance company, he puts it in his filing cabinet. Weeks pass, and there is a small fire in your kitchen. You call the insurance company's claims department, only to learn that it has no record of your policy. In this situation the agent could be held liable for the loss you suffered.

◇ If a broker or agent misrepresents the terms, conditions, premiums, or coverage provided by the policy, and as a result you suffer a loss, you may be able to sue him. Written agreements are always easier to prove than oral promises.

◇ If an agent or broker does not properly identify the property, and as a result your claim is denied by the insurance company, he may be responsible for the loss. For instance, when writing a policy for car insurance, the agent must describe the car correctly. Read both your application and your policy to ensure that your property is accurately described.

◇ If the agent agreed to keep your coverage current and the policy expires or is canceled, he may be responsible for any resulting loss. If he does not forward a premium to the company and your policy is canceled for that reason, you can hold him responsible for any loss you suffer. Similarly, he must notify you when your policy is due to be renewed.

◇ If the insurance company becomes insolvent and fails to pay a claim, your agent or broker is generally not personally responsible to you financially—unless he knew that the company would not be able to honor its claims.

◇ An agent must cancel insurance, or lower or limit coverage, when instructed to do so by his company.

◇ When an agent leaves a particular company to work for another, he may solicit his previous customers unless he signed a contract that expressly prohibited him from doing so. See also Good Faith; Insurance; Negligence.

Intent

Intent is the state of mind a person has when he deliberately commits a criminal offense or a civil wrong. Suppose you get a check from someone who bought your son's rickety old bicycle for $10. The buyer mistakenly makes the check out for the sum of $100. If you see the mistake and cash the check knowing it was written in error, you have acted with intent. Intent is a necessary component of many criminal acts, and prosecutors must prove that there was intent on the part of the defendant in these cases.

Unless a statute says otherwise, prosecutors do not have to prove intent to obtain a conviction for a crime that is considered inherently wrong, such as homicide, rape, or arson. A person who committed such a crime was probably aware that he was doing something wrong. Other acts, such as avoiding taxes, are not inherently wrong but they are against the law. It is not necessary to have intent to do wrong or to know that an act is a crime to be found guilty in such cases. (This is what is meant by saying "ignorance of the law is no excuse.")

If a defendant committed an illegal act that he did not intend to commit, he may be convicted of a less serious crime. For instance, a homicide is considered murder if the prosecution can prove that the accused intended to kill the victim. If this cannot be proved, the accused may be convicted of a lesser charge, such as manslaughter.

If someone is insane or incapable of forming the criminal intent necessary to commit a crime, he may be found not guilty, but he may also be committed to a mental institution. See also INSANITY PLEA.

The law presumes that most children cannot form the criminal intent sufficient to commit many crimes. However, many youths and even children willfully and knowingly do so. For this reason, a system of juvenile courts has been established to deal with the problem of young lawbreakers. See also JUVENILE OFFENDER.

INTERLOCUTORY DECREE

An interlocutory decree is a temporary or provisional decree issued by a court. Suppose Adele had a dispute with her employer because she refused to relocate to another city. Her employer fired her, and Adele sued him for back wages and reinstatement of her pension and health benefits. Halfway through the trial, the judge issued an interlocutory decree that ordered Adele's employer to restore her health benefits to her while the court continued to hear the case on the subject of wages and pension benefits. If the court ultimately concluded that Adele indeed deserved to have her health benefits continued, the judge would restate the court's decision in the final decree he issued.

IN VITRO FERTILIZATION

In vitro fertilization is a means by which an infertile couple can conceive a child. Despite popular use of the phrase "test tube baby," the child's conception takes place in a petri dish (*in vitro* means "in glass"). The procedure involves extracting an ovum from a woman and fertilizing it in the dish. A resulting embryo is then implanted into her uterus (or that of another woman) so that the pregnancy can continue normally. The service is provided in a private fertility clinic, physician's office, or hospital, and it is usually very expensive.

In vitro fertilization first came to the public's attention when Louise Brown, the first child brought to term as a result of the method, was born in England in 1978. Since that time, this and other reproductive technologies have presented lawmakers and judges with challenging legal and ethical questions, for which there are often no clear-cut solutions.

The procedure often calls for repeated attempts at fertilization, and the chances that a healthy child will result are small. To attract customers, a few clinics have misled would-be parents by exaggerating their success rates. Also, because the overall success rate is so low, health insurance companies generally exclude in vitro procedures from their policies. In 1993 at least three states—Hawaii, Texas, and Maryland—required insurers to provide such coverage.

RIGHTS OF THE PARENTS

In vitro fertilization separates two biological aspects of pregnancy: the first is contributing the egg and the other is carrying the child to term. Thus the donor who is the genetic mother of the embryo is not always the same woman who undergoes the pregnancy and delivers the child. Usually only one of these two women becomes the legal mother of the child.

The donor of an egg is not necessarily always known to its recipient. When the donor and the recipient do not know one another, fertility clinics try to maintain a policy of strict confidentiality so that they will never meet. When the donor and the recipient do know one another, it is extremely important that the donor knows she will not be the child's legal parent. Usually, fertility clinics draw up separate contracts for each party, spelling out each of their responsibilities and stating their parental rights.

In addition to the contract, recipients may wish to consult an attorney about the possibility of obtaining the donor's consent to an adoption proceeding to further ensure that there are no disputes about who is the child's legal mother.

In one famous case a donor contributed an egg that was then fertilized in vitro with her husband's sperm. The fertilized egg was implanted in another woman, who had agreed in writing to carry the child and to relinquish her parental rights to the child. However, her relationship with the couple broke down during the course of the pregnancy, and before she had given birth, she tried to sue for custody of the child. The court ruled against the woman, holding that the couple were the genetic parents of the child, and that the woman who carried the baby was not its mother. See also SURROGATE MOTHER.

IF SOMETHING GOES WRONG

Although clinics try to screen donors for sexually transmitted diseases and genetic problems, mistakes can and do happen. In one recent case a couple who believed that their child was conceived with the husband's sperm in fact gave birth to a baby whose race was different from that of both parents. They sued the fertility clinic.

If a donor lies about a genetic defect that he or she has, and a child subsequently inherits the trait, the parents are more likely to sue the clinic than the donor.

IOU

An IOU, shorthand for "I Owe You," is a paper given by a borrower to a lender. An IOU will normally contain the amount to be repaid and the borrower's signature. However, a simple IOU may not be adequate proof of a debt if the lender is obliged to seek his repayment in court, as it does not have the characteristics of a proper contract.

In particular, an IOU does not specify what a lender has received in return for his loan or the date by which it must be repaid. Rather than lending money to someone in exchange for an IOU, you should execute a promissory note—a written promise by the borrower to repay you according to specific terms. See PROMISSORY NOTE.

REAL LIFE, REAL LAW

The Case of the Frozen Embryos

In order to have a child, a Tennessee couple underwent several in vitro fertilization procedures—without success. As is common practice among fertilization clinics, the embryos were kept frozen so that they would be available for successive attempts.

The couple's marriage eventually deteriorated. When they divorced, each of them sued for custody of the frozen embryos. The wife wanted to have the embryos implanted because she still wanted to have a child. The husband objected, arguing that he should not be forced to become a father against his will and be obligated to support the child until it reached adulthood.

The judge who heard the divorce case found in favor of the mother and ruled that it was in the best interest of the embryos to allow them the chance to develop. However, on appeal the decision was reversed, and the court ordered the embryos returned to the father, who had them destroyed. (Generally, the law does not consider that embryos have rights.)

Some attorneys suggest that a couple should express their wishes in writing about what should happen to the embryos in the event of death or divorce. However, there is no guarantee that a court would accept the couple's decision, or that one partner could enforce a written agreement against the wishes of the other partner. Therefore, the legal status of frozen embryos remains unclear.

JOB DISCRIMINATION TO JUVENILE OFFENDER

JOB DISCRIMINATION

A wide variety of federal and state laws prohibit employers from discriminating against job applicants and employees on the basis of race, color, gender, religion, national origin, disability, or age (over 40) in hiring, firing, and on the job. The major federal laws that address job discrimination are the Civil Rights Act of 1964 (and its subsequent amendments), the Age Discrimination in Employment Act of 1967, and the Americans With Disabilities Act of 1990.

Title VII of the Civil Rights Act is the most far-reaching of these laws, because it forbids job discrimination by federal and state government employers and all private employers with 20 or more workers. The law prohibits discrimination not only in hiring and firing, but in promotions, raises, leaves of absence, benefits, and most other aspects of employment.

Equally important for workers, state laws prohibit employers from discriminating on the basis of sex, age, race, national origin, color, religion, or disability. Many state laws are more explicit than the corresponding federal laws. Some states, for instance, prohibit discrimination against welfare recipients, homosexuals, the obese, or employees who engage in certain lawful activities—such as smoking or drinking—when they are not at work. See also AGE DISCRIMINATION; DISCRIMINATION; SEX DISCRIMINATION.

FILING A COMPLAINT WITH THE EEOC

An important result of Title VII of the Civil Rights Act was the creation of the Equal Employment Opportunity Commission (EEOC), which enforces antidiscrimination laws. Employees who feel they have been discriminated against may file a complaint with the EEOC, but a response is very likely to be delayed because the EEOC is overburdened with complaints. When the EEOC does respond, it may order your employer to do one or more of the following: cease the discrimination; hire, rehire, or promote you; award you back pay; or establish an affirmative action program.

Filing a complaint with the EEOC may bring results in other ways, too. Employers are reluctant to be accused of discrimination, since it can leave them with a bad reputation. Thus even if the EEOC does not act upon a complaint, the fact that it has been filed may prompt the employer to correct the discriminatory situation.

It is illegal for an employer to retaliate against an employee for filing a complaint with the EEOC. It is also illegal for an employer to retaliate against someone who cooperates with an ensuing investigation. If you are demoted or fired for your involvement with an EEOC complaint, you can bring a lawsuit against your employer for his wrongful treatment of you. See also WHISTLE-BLOWER.

WHEN DISCRIMINATION IS ALLOWED

Despite the wide range of legal prohibitions, some types of job discrimination are permitted. When hiring, an employer can claim that the job he is filling has a bona fide occupational qualification (BFOQ). For example, a nursing home administrator may want to hire a certain number of female nurses to attend to the personal needs of women patients. Similarly, a hospital obstetrics ward could employ only female nurses. Courts have upheld this kind of qualification based on gender out of recognition for the patients' personal privacy.

Sometimes national origin, religion, or age may also be a legitimate criterion—as when a casting company limits actors to certain age groups to cast roles for plays and movies. It would hardly be appropriate, for example, to cast an 80-year-old man as Dennis the Menace.

Neither are personal traits exempt from discrimination. A telephone operator who was dismissed from her job because her employer thought her voice sounded unpleasant claimed unlawful discrimination, as did a man who lost his position as host in a restaurant because his manager felt he was not sufficiently handsome to suit the restaurant's image. In both of these cases the dismissals were held to be lawful.

REVERSE DISCRIMINATION

Job discrimination against a Caucasian person may be harder to prove than discrimination against a member of a racial or ethnic minority. In one case in Texas, however, a white athletic coach who was fired by an African-American high school principal sued the school district for racial discrimination. When presenting his case, the coach showed that he was a member of a white minority within the school, was well qualified for the position, and was replaced by a less-than-qualified African-American coach. The coach won his case.

The issue of reverse discrimination has sometimes been invoked to criticize affirmative action programs, which were implemented by the federal government to encourage minority hiring. When tested in court cases, however, affirmative action programs have been upheld in the majority of cases. See also AFFIRMATIVE ACTION.

UNPROVED DISCRIMINATION

Occasionally what may appear to be discrimination can fail to meet the test under the scrutiny of the courts. For example, an African-American professor dismissed from his position at a major university was unable to win a job-discrimination claim when evidence showed that his dismissal was due to the unfavorable evaluations given to him by his students. And the firing of a Hispanic sales representative was upheld when the evidence showed that he was dismissed because of his inability to get along with customers. See also CIVIL RIGHTS; EMPLOYEE HIRING AND FIRING.

STEPS TO TAKE

If you think you have been the victim of job discrimination, you can do the following:

1. Before you file your complaint, gather together all the evidence you need. Save all relevant documents given to you by your employer (such as performance evaluations). Keep records of any incidents of discrimination that take place, noting names, dates, and any other pertinent information. Also, compare notes with other employees who may also have been discriminated against. If your information is well documented, your complaint will be taken more seriously.

2. To file a complaint, first find out if your state has some kind of equal-opportunity procedures. In some cases these may be more efficient than the procedures of the EEOC.

3. If it is not feasible to file a complaint with the state, call your local EEOC office, which is listed in the blue pages of the telephone book, to find out the proper procedure for filing a federal complaint and to obtain the necessary forms. Note that in most instances you must file your complaint within 180 days from the time of the most recent act of discrimination.

JOINT TENANCY

Joint tenancy is a form of ownership by which more than one person holds title to property. Upon the death of one owner, her share passes entirely to the other owner or owners. For example, if you and your brother own your property as joint tenants, you will become the sole owner when he dies, even if he has tried to leave his interest to someone else. See WILL.

Known more formally as "joint tenancy with right of survivorship" (often abbreviated on bank and real estate records as JTWROS), joint tenancy can be useful as an estate-planning tool. Property owned under joint tenancy does not need to pass through probate when one owner dies, thus enabling the surviving owner or owners to avoid probate costs and delays. See PROBATE.

Property that is held in joint tenancy is subject to estate taxes, but only for the share that belonged to the deceased. Suppose you and your brother each deposited $10,000 in a joint tenancy account. If your brother dies, you will receive the entire $20,000. But if you provide proof of the amount of your contribution, only $10,000 will be included in his taxable estate. See also ESTATE PLANNING; ESTATE TAX.

A word of caution: If you hold a bank account, stocks,

bonds, or other personal property in joint tenancy, you or the other owner—whoever holds proof of ownership (such as a passbook or stock certificate) —has access to the whole property. For example, if Jim and Jody jointly own $30,000 worth of bonds, and then have a falling out, one of them can cash in the bonds without the knowledge or approval of the other. See also BANK ACCOUNT; TENANCY BY THE ENTIRETY; TENANCY IN COMMON; TRUST.

JUDGE

A judge is a public officer who has been authorized to administer the law in a court. He presides over the court and applies the laws of the nation or of his district or state to each case. In cases where there is no jury, the judge decides the outcome.

Federal judges must be lawyers, but state judges may or may not be. Those state judges who are not lawyers usually preside over municipal courts. State laws may also set a minimum age for judges.

The procedure for choosing judges for state and local courts varies according to state law. The judges may be elected, or they may be appointed by state officials. Judges usually serve a specified term of office. They can be removed by impeachment or, if elected, by being voted out in general elections.

Federal judges are nominated by the president and must be approved by the Senate. Federal judges are appointed to lifetime terms, except for Bankruptcy Court judges, who serve for a length of time specified by law.

Even when a federal or state judge has been appointed for life, he may be impeached if he abuses his power or is convicted of a serious crime. Federal impeachment proceedings are conducted by the Senate after charges have been brought by the House of Representatives.

Judges are sometimes called justices. At the federal level, this term is reserved for members of the Supreme Court. On the local level, judges may also be called magistrates.

JUDGMENT

A judgment, the final decision rendered by a court after it has reviewed the evidence presented to it, resolves the issues in dispute and imposes the court's ruling on the parties involved. Unless a judgment is changed by an appeal, the parties have to obey it or face the possibility of a fine or imprisonment.

The judgment handed down to a defendant found guilty in a criminal trial may include a fine or a prison sentence. In civil cases the most common judgment in favor of the plaintiff is an award of compensation, or money damages. In fact, *judgment* and *money damages* are often used synonymously when referring to cases involving personal injury or property damage. See also DAMAGES.

COLLECTING YOUR JUDGMENT

It is one thing to get a court's judgment in your favor, and another to collect that judgment. When you receive a judgment of money damages, the person who lost the case (the judgment debtor) may not pay you right away. In some cases the court imposes a deadline for payment, such as 30 to 45 days after the judgment has been decided upon; in other cases it may only specify that the judgment be paid within a "reasonable time."

If the judgment debtor files an appeal, you may not receive your damages for some time. Some courts require that any money damages be placed in an escrow account while the appeal is being heard.

In some states, when you win a lawsuit, the clerk of the court sends the losing party a form known as a judgment debtor's statement of assets. Unless he has already paid the judgment, the debtor must complete this form and return it to you. On the form he is asked to state his place of employment and to list his assets, such as bank accounts, real estate, stocks, bonds, and personal property.

With this form you can go to court to ask for a writ of execution, which you can take to the county sheriff's office. The sheriff will formally deliver, or "serve," the writ on the judgment debtor's bank, brokerage house, or mortgage holder. He may even serve the writ on the debtor's employer in order to garnishee his wages. Since your judgment creates a claim, or lien, upon his property, you can seize the amount needed to pay off the judgment. Keep in mind, however, that there are limits on the amount of wages that can be subject to garnishment and that some states have a "homestead exemption," which prevents a judgment creditor from seizing a person's home to satisfy a judgment. See also GARNISHMENT.

If the judgment debtor fails to complete the statement of assets or claims that he has no assets with which to pay the judgment, you may have to subpoena him to appear at a postjudgment deposition. During the deposition, your attorney will question him about his income and assets and will require him to provide copies of bank statements, financial statements, tax returns, and other documents that may disclose the amount and nature of his assets.

If the judgment debtor cannot pay you in a lump sum, you can agree to receive the money in installments. Be sure to get the agreement in writing and have him sign it. Note that you are entitled to receive interest on the judgment from the date it is awarded until the date it is paid in full. The interest rate on court judgments is set by state law. The clerk of the court can tell you the rate in your state.

When the judgment debtor does pay up, he will ask you to sign a form known as a satisfaction of judgment, as proof of payment. Do not sign this form until you have actually received the payment. For example, if you take a personal check and it is later returned for insufficient funds, you will have to go back to court to have the judgment reopened. It is better to accept only cash, a money order, or a cashier's check.

OTHER KINDS OF JUDGMENTS

Not all judgments in civil cases result in money damages, nor are they necessarily made at the conclusion of a trial.

Summary judgment
When the evidence supporting the position of one of the parties is very clear from the outset, there may be no need for a trial. In such cases the court can issue a summary judgment. Either party to a case has the right to request such a judgment, and the judge will make a decision based on the motions and the supporting documents supplied by the parties.

Default judgment
A default judgment might be issued when one of the parties fails to appear in court or fails to follow court procedure. Because courts prefer to decide disputes on their merits, however, a default judgment can often be overturned if the party in default offers a good reason for the procedural mistake or the failure to appear—such as illness or an accident. See also DEFAULT JUDGMENT.

Declaratory judgment
A declaratory judgment determines the rights of the parties in a case or gives the court's opinion on a legal question. For example, if the language written in a contract is not clear, the parties may ask the court to decide on the meaning of the contract. They are not seeking money or other property from one another; they are just asking the court to settle a dispute before a wrong is committed.

See also COURTS; CRIMINAL LAW; LAWSUIT.

JURISDICTION

The term *jurisdiction* refers to the extent of a particular court's authority to hear a case and determine its outcome. If a court exceeds its jurisdiction, it cannot enforce its judgment, or decision, in a given case.

A court's jurisdiction is determined by such factors as geographical location, the type of case (such as divorce or bankruptcy), whether the case involves civil or criminal law, and whether the applicable laws are those of the district, the state, or the federal government. The categories that determine jurisdiction often overlap. For example, a small-claims court in Hartford, Connecticut, has several kinds of jurisdiction: (1) it is a civil (not criminal) court; (2) it serves one city, Hartford; and (3) it only handles disputes involving relatively minor sums of money. See COURTS.

JURY

A jury is a group of people selected from the community to inquire into the facts of a civil or criminal case and to make decisions about them. The people chosen to sit on a jury are called jurors. They are sworn to hear the evidence presented and to evaluate it according to the instructions that are given to them by the presiding judge.

There are two kinds of juries. A grand jury hears allegations of crimes, considers evidence, and decides whether or not to issue indictments. It consists of 12 to 23 members, depending on state law (federal grand juries have 16 to 23 members). A trial jury (sometimes called a petit, or small, jury because of its size) hears evidence at a trial and consists of 6, 8, or 12 members. When the word *jury* is used by itself, it refers to a trial jury.

Criminal defendants have the constitutional right to a jury trial in all cases except trials for petty crimes (such as vagrancy or littering). Once a criminal defendant is convicted, some states give the jury the right to determine the sentence or to recommend one. In other states, sentencing is strictly the duty of the judge.

The parties to certain kinds of civil actions, or lawsuits, are entitled to jury trials, including breach of contract and negligence cases. Some states do not allow jury trials in divorce cases or disputes over estates. See also GRAND JURY.

JURY DUTY

When you receive a notice in the mail summoning you to jury duty, it may raise questions in your mind: Why were you chosen? How long will you serve? Will your boss let you go? Will you have to stay in a hotel room for weeks on end? Will you be allowed to see your family?

Even though such questions concern those who are called to jury duty, they rarely become issues. Employers are usually understanding about absences for jury duty. In many states it is illegal for an employer to dismiss an employee because of an absence due to jury duty. Most cases are settled in days rather than weeks, and jurors are rarely sequestered (isolated) in hotel rooms.

A summons to jury duty represents one of the most important aspects of civil life, for the right to trial by jury is a cornerstone of American democracy. In most criminal cases and in many civil cases, the parties in U.S. courts have the right to have their cases decided by a group of their fellow citizens—a jury of their peers.

HOW PROSPECTIVE JURORS ARE SELECTED

The process of selecting those who will be called for jury duty generally works as follows:

◇ First, a court official determines how many names should be placed on the jury list.

◇ Other officials then find names—typically from voter-registration lists and from local tax records—and place them in a jury box. (Even though the terms *jury box* and *jury wheel* are still common, the process is often done by computer.)

◇ When the court issues an order for a jury to be selected, or "impaneled," a court official selects names at random.

◇ Those selected are mailed a summons to appear for jury duty at a given time and place.

A CIVIC DUTY

Suppose your summons comes during your employer's busiest time. Can you decline to serve? Probably not. In most places, however, you may have your service postponed for a while, and the postponement may be repeated a specified number of times. But sooner or later, unless you fall into one of the categories discussed in the section below, you must serve.

A summons for jury duty is an order from a court. If you do not obey it, a judge may order you to serve or find you in contempt of court (punishable by a jail sentence or fine).

Jury duty is every citizen's duty. No law requires the government to pay jurors, nor are employers required to pay their workers while they are serving on a jury. Nonetheless, the government usually gives jurors a nominal fee for each day of service, and many employers pay their employees during their absence from work.

WHO CAN BE EXCUSED

If you run your own business and have no employees, you may plead economic hardship and be excused from jury duty. You may also be excused if you take care of young children or you have a health problem that makes it hard for you to serve.

Some professionals are automatically excused, sometimes by law. Doctors, firefighters, and police officers are often excused because their jobs are essential to the public welfare. Lawyers and court officials may be excused because they have professional knowledge that may interfere with their ability to evaluate cases impartially. Depending on the court's rules and state law, others that may be excluded from jury service are convicted felons, noncitizens, persons who are incompetent, and persons who do not speak English. The states may decide upon their own guidelines for exclusion, as long as they do not discriminate on the basis of race, religion, sex, or national origin.

HOW JURORS ARE CHOSEN

When you appear for jury duty, there is no guarantee that you will serve on a jury. More people are summoned than will be needed because not all potential jurors will be qualified.

When jurors are needed for a case, a group is usually selected at random from the larger pool. Then begins the process of *voir dire*—choosing the jury. First, all the people who have been called will be sworn to answer truthfully any questions put to them by the judge and the lawyers. (The judge may leave all the questioning to the lawyers.) In any event some potential jurors will be weeded out because they are biased or there is some other factor that would make it difficult for them to decide the case strictly on the evidence. If a juror willfully conceals information or lies in order to serve on a jury, he may be guilty of perjury. See PERJURY.

Some jurors may be disqualified because of their profession. If you are an accountant being considered to serve as a juror in a tax-fraud case, a lawyer might feel that your expertise would hinder rather than help your judgment. The lawyer may therefore make a "challenge for cause," protesting that you are unable to serve impartially. If the judge agrees, you will be excused.

A juror may also be excused from a case for the following: a close friendship or kinship with one of the parties; knowledge of the case or some financial interest in it; or a preconceived opinion about the outcome.

After the parties are satisfied that no remaining jurors can be challenged for cause, each side may be allowed peremptory challenges, for which they are not required to give a reason. A peremptory challenge may not be allowed, however, if there is any suspicion that it is being used to exclude a juror solely on the basis of race.

BECOMING A JUROR

Once the jury selection is complete, the judge impanels the jury—that is, she swears in the jurors and informs them of their duties during the trial.

Often the judge will impanel one or two more jurors than are required, especially when the trial is expected to take a long time. These "alternate" jurors sit with the jury and hear the testimony but do not attend the deliberations unless a juror falls ill or is otherwise unable to complete his service.

HEARING THE CASE

After the jury has been sworn in and has received its preliminary instructions, the jurors listen to the lawyers' opening statements. The lawyers then call their witnesses and present evidence. The statements and portions of the evidence may be contradictory. In some courts the jurors may be allowed to take their own notes.

The jurors may not discuss the case among themselves while they are still hearing evidence, and they must avoid all media accounts of the case. In the rare cases that get a lot of press coverage, the jury may be sequestered (confined to a hotel or elsewhere until the proceedings are over).

INSTRUCTIONS FROM THE JUDGE

After all the evidence has been presented, and before the jury leaves to decide on an outcome, the judge instructs the jurors regarding laws that apply to the case. The judge might ask the jury to answer specific questions (for example, "Was the supermarket management negligent by failing to provide safety restraints for children in its shopping carts?"). Or she may ask them to return a general verdict (for example, "We find the defendant guilty.").

IN THE JURY ROOM

Although the procedure for selecting a foreperson varies, his role is always to preside over the jury's deliberations and announce the verdict. Once in the jury room, the jurors discuss the evidence presented during the trial.

When the discussion is over, the jury votes. If the judge has asked the jury to determine several questions (known as counts in criminal cases), the jury votes on each one separately. Even when the judge has asked for a general verdict, the jury may vote several times before it reaches a verdict.

For some cases, such as those that involve serious crimes, a unanimous verdict is needed. Other cases require a less than unanimous verdict.

When the verdict has been reached, the jury returns to the courtroom to announce it. The parties to the case may request that the jury be "polled"; that is, each juror must state whether he agrees with the verdict. If the jurors publicly confirm the verdict in this way, the parties can be more confident that no juror was pressured into voting against his conscience.

If the jury cannot decide on a verdict, it is said to be hung, or deadlocked. If the jury is hopelessly deadlocked, a new trial will be set (unless the plaintiff and defendant settle, or the prosecutor decides not to retry the case). Most judges urge the jury to deliberate longer, in hopes that the jurors will reach a decision, before declaring the jury deadlocked.

After the verdict is given, the judge gives a judgment (which may be a fine, prison sentence, or money damages). The jurors are now free to discuss the case with anyone and can resume their normal activities.

Jury Tampering

Jury tampering means trying to influence a juror with bribes, threats, suggestions, information, and the like—something other than the evidence that is presented in the courtroom. The crime of jury tampering is considered a form of obstruction of justice and is punishable by a fine or imprisonment.

Bribes and Threats

Perhaps the commonest form of jury tampering occurs when a person offers money, makes promises, or threatens jurors in order to influence the outcome of a case. A juror who solicits bribes in return for rendering a certain decision is also guilty of jury tampering.

Attempting to bribe a court officer who has contact with the jury also constitutes jury tampering. One officer who is often a target for bribery is the bailiff—the person who takes charge of the jury, communicates between the jury and the judge, and shields the jury from the outside while its deliberations are taking place.

Forbidden Communications

The jury is charged with reaching a decision based solely on the evidence that is presented in court. It is thus illegal to give information to a juror outside of courtroom proceedings. For example, giving a juror news accounts of the case before a decision has been reached constitutes jury tampering.

A nonjuror who tries to talk to a juror about the case during the course of the trial or a juror who discusses the case with another juror before the jury goes into deliberation are both considered to be guilty of jury tampering.

Justice of the Peace

A justice of the peace is a local or state judicial officer with limited authority. Popularly known for presiding over wedding ceremonies, justices of the peace also have other functions, such as presiding over trials for traffic offenses and other misdemeanors. Their rulings usually may be appealed, depending on state law.

In most states justices of the peace are elected. Some states require a justice of the peace to be a licensed attorney. See also Courts; Judge.

Juvenile Offender

An adult who is convicted of committing a crime is considered a criminal, but a minor is classified as a juvenile offender. In the United States, cases of minors accused of crimes are usually handled by the juvenile courts. The philosophy of the juvenile courts is that children who break the law should receive treatment rather than punishment.

The offenses with which a minor can be charged as a juvenile offender range from noncriminal acts such as truancy, to petty crimes such as shoplifting, to serious crimes such as rape, robbery, and murder.

Deciding How to Prosecute a Minor

Each state has its own laws to determine who will be treated as a juvenile offender. In some states any person under the age of 18 who has committed a crime is considered a juvenile offender. In others, the cutoff point is age 16.

Some states prosecute a minor as an adult in certain circumstances. For example, traffic offenses are almost always prosecuted in the adult courts. In addition, the more serious the crime, the lower the age at which a minor may be prosecuted as an adult. If a minor is accused of murder, for example, state law may require that he be punished as an adult if he is more than 14 years old.

Some states have additional criteria they use to determine whether to prosecute a minor as an adult rather than a juvenile—for example, if the minor has a history as a juvenile offender; if the minor has committed a crime that is especially heinous or violent; or if the juvenile justice system is not able to offer the appropriate kind of treatment and rehabilitation.

When such considerations arise, the juvenile court holds a hearing (attended by the juvenile, his parents or guardian, the judge, the prosecutor, the defense attorney, and in some instances a probation officer or social worker) to determine whether the minor will remain in the juvenile system or will be referred to an adult court.

REAL LIFE, REAL LAW

The Case of the Dangerous Delinquent

Steven was a 17-year-old on probation from juvenile court when he and his fellow gang members attacked a group leaving a restaurant on Christmas Eve. Steven stabbed at least two members of the group. He was taken into custody and charged with robbery, assault, and attempted murder.

Because of the seriousness of the crimes, the district attorney petitioned the juvenile court to allow Steven to be tried as an adult, as provided by state law. Steven's probation officer agreed that the juvenile justice system could not deal with Steven. Despite this, the juvenile court refused to release Steven from its authority, and Steven was sentenced to only 15 months in a juvenile detention facility for his crimes.

When the district attorney appealed the decision, the court of appeals reversed it, citing the severity of the crimes, the lack of evidence that Steven could be rehabilitated in the juvenile justice system, his previous record of violent behavior, and his lack of remorse. The court ordered that Steven be tried as an adult.

DETAINING JUVENILES

Juvenile offenders, technically speaking, are not "arrested," but are taken into custody by law enforcement officers or by a social worker. Once a juvenile is in custody, the court decides whether he should be held for further proceedings. The court bases its decision on the seriousness of the charge, whether detention is necessary for the protection of the juvenile (or the community), and the likelihood that he will show up for further hearings.

Unlike adults, juveniles have no right to bail. They are usually released into the custody of a parent or guardian. If the child is detained, he will be placed in a juvenile detention center or, if necessary, in jail—but segregated from adult prisoners.

CONSTITUTIONAL RIGHTS OF MINORS

Minors have many of the rights that adult defendants have. They may not be interrogated by law enforcement officers unless they have been informed of their rights to remain silent and to be represented by an attorney. Many states will not allow police officers to question a juvenile suspect unless a concerned and informed adult (a parent, the child's lawyer, or a juvenile officer) is present. See also MIRANDA WARNINGS.

Minors also have the right to have a trial, to be provided with a lawyer, to present and cross-examine witnesses, to testify in their own defense, and to avoid self-incrimination. However, they do not have the right to a trial by jury. To protect minors from publicity, juvenile court proceedings are closed to the public.

AFTER THE TRIAL

If a court has deemed a minor to be a juvenile offender, the judge has a variety of options.

Keeping in mind the ideal goals of treatment and rehabilitation, he may place the child on probation, leaving him in the custody of his parents or guardian, or he may place the child in a foster or group home—perhaps one that includes a drug and alcohol treatment program if needed. If the child is a threat to the community at large, he may be placed in a secure facility, commonly known as a detention center or juvenile hall.

Just as, technically speaking, minors are not "arrested," they are not "sentenced" either. Instead they are kept under court supervision until it is no longer necessary (as determined by the court and by the probation officer's report), or until they are too old for juvenile court jurisdiction. If no further difficulties arise, they are released.

The juvenile justice system cannot continue to supervise young people beyond the age specified by state law. In some states, for example, a juvenile who has killed another person intentionally cannot remain under juvenile court supervision past the age of 25. Knowing that juveniles are released sooner than adults charged with the same crime, gangs often use them to traffic drugs and commit other crimes.

Today, in an effort to reduce the danger to society posed by juvenile criminals, more and more prosecuting attorneys are trying to charge older juveniles as adults. If a juvenile who has murdered someone is charged as an adult, for example, he may receive a sentence of life in prison instead of being released after a short time.

CONFIDENTIAL RECORDS

Juvenile records may be examined only by the court and the parties involved. In many states all juvenile records are sealed unless a juvenile court orders them to be opened.

Often juvenile records are "expunged," that is, all records of the charges or judgments against a minor are destroyed and are considered never to have happened. Expungement usually takes place after a request has been made, or a petition filed, to the court by the juvenile offender (if now an adult) or by his guardian. Some states allow expungement after a specified period of time has passed with no further offenses. See also CHILDREN'S RIGHTS; FAMILY COURT.

STEPS TO TAKE IF YOUR CHILD IS IN CUSTODY

If your child is taken into custody, you should go to his aid immediately, but heed the following advice:

1. Hire an attorney.
2. Tell your child not to answer any questions until the attorney is present.
3. Do not volunteer information that could be used against your child in court. Generally speaking, it is best to say nothing until you talk to a lawyer.
4. Find out where your child is being held. A child must be placed in a juvenile detention facility, not in a cell with adult offenders.
5. Insist that your child be brought before a judge quickly to determine whether he must be held longer or can be released into your custody.

K — FROM KEOGH PLAN TO KITING

KEOGH PLAN

Suppose you own a store or operate a gas station, motel, or other small business. Because you are self-employed, you do not have a company-sponsored pension plan, and you would like to save more money for retirement than the $2,000 per year that you can put into an Individual Retirement Account (IRA). What should you do?

A Keogh plan is one solution. These plans have been available since 1962, when the Self-Employed Individuals Tax Retirement Act, or Keogh Act (named for the New York congressman who introduced the bill) was passed. Keogh plans are the best means for the self-employed to save money for retirement on a tax-sheltered and tax-deferred basis. The money you put into a Keogh account is deducted from your gross income in the year that you make the contribution, and

CHECKLIST

Choosing a Keogh Plan

There are four basic types of Keogh plans. Select the one that best suits your business and your plans for retirement.

❑ **PROFIT-SHARING PLAN.** This flexible plan allows you to make tax-deductible contributions up to 15 percent of your net self-employment earnings or $30,000, whichever is less. You can change the percentage of your earnings that you contribute each year. In a year that business is slow, for example, you can lower or cease your contribution.

❑ **MONEY-PURCHASE PLAN.** Designed for people who expect to have steady, large incomes, this plan allows you to make a larger, but constant, contribution of up to 20 percent of your net earnings or $30,000, whichever is less. If you specify that 12 percent of your income will be contributed the first year, you will have to contribute 12 percent in subsequent years or you will have to pay a penalty to the IRS.

❑ **PROFIT-SHARING AND MONEY-PURCHASE COMBINATION PLAN.** This hybrid plan lets you make the largest possible contribution while allowing you to pay less in low-profit years. For example, you might establish a money-purchase plan with a fixed contribution rate of 7 percent, and a profit-sharing plan to which you contribute another 13 percent of net earnings, up to a $30,000 maximum. If in later years your earnings go down, you will have to make the money-purchase contribution of 7 percent, but you can reduce or eliminate the profit-sharing contribution without incurring a penalty.

❑ **DEFINED-BENEFIT PLAN.** The defined-benefit plan allows you to pick the retirement benefit you want to receive and then contribute the amount of money that you will need in order to reach that goal. In 1993 the maximum annual benefit you could receive at age 65 was $115,641, (this figure is adjusted annually for inflation). This plan is the most complicated and the most costly to administer. It must be checked each year by an actuary (a professional who determines life expectancies) to see that it complies with any changes in the law and to ensure that you are contributing the proper amount. Before you set up a defined-benefit plan, get the advice of a financial planner.

the interest your account earns is not taxable until you begin withdrawing it. By then you will probably be retired and perhaps in a lower tax bracket.

A Keogh plan has the same purpose and tax status as an IRA, and you can make similar types of investments with both. However, the annual amount you can contribute to a Keogh plan is much higher than with an IRA, and you can contribute past the age of 70½.

ELIGIBILITY

Anyone who is self-employed, including independent contractors (freelance workers), persons who own an unincorporated business, or members of a professional partnership may set up a Keogh account. Even if you work for a company that offers a pension plan, you can open a Keogh with money you earn from self-employment.

Federal law requires employers who have Keogh plans for themselves to open Keogh accounts for their employees. For example, lawyers and doctors who work in solo practices must cover their secretaries, nurses, receptionists, and other staff after they have employed the workers for a certain length of time (normally 1 or 2 years).

CONTRIBUTIONS

A Keogh account must be opened by December 31 of the year for which you would like to claim it as a tax deduction (whereas you can open an IRA until April 15 of the following year to get the deduction). In subsequent years both IRA and Keogh contributions can be made up to April 15 of the following year.

If you are an employer who has a Keogh plan for yourself and your employees, you may contribute to your own account only if you have net earnings in the business for which the plan was established, even though you may have to contribute to your employees' accounts.

If you are an employee, the plan will usually be funded by your employer's contributions; however, you may also make contributions (up to 10 percent of your salary but not more than $30,000), but they will not be tax deductible.

SETTING UP A PLAN

You can establish a Keogh plan through your bank or through a financial services company, such as a brokerage firm or a mutual fund company. These institutions may set a minimum opening balance. For details about the types of Keogh plans, see the checklist on page 316. One of these, the profit-sharing and money-purchase combination plan, is like having two plans at once. Except for this case, a person may not have more than one Keogh plan.

Employees who establish a Keogh plan may choose from a wide variety of investments, including stocks and bonds, mutual funds, even gold U.S. coins. However, the law does not allow the purchase of collectibles, such as antiques, gems, paintings, or stamps.

WITHDRAWALS

As with an IRA, you cannot withdraw money from a Keogh plan before you are 59½ years old without paying a 10 percent penalty. Between the ages of 59½ and 70½, you can withdraw money or not, as you wish. But once you are age 70½, you must begin to withdraw your retirement funds by April 1 of the following year, even though you may still be contributing to the plan. You are allowed to withdraw the money in a lump sum or in installments, but you must withdraw a minimum amount, which is determined by the Internal Revenue Service. See also EMPLOYEE RETIREMENT INCOME SECURITY ACT (ERISA); INDIVIDUAL RETIREMENT ACCOUNT; PENSION PLAN.

KIDNAPPING

Kidnapping is broadly defined as the carrying away of someone against his will by means of force or fraud. It is similar to the crime of false imprisonment, but usually involves the threat that the victim will be taken from one place to another. See FALSE IMPRISONMENT.

State and federal laws define kidnapping in different ways. Under the Federal Kidnapping Act (which is also called the Lindbergh Act), a person must have been transported across a state line or to another country. (However, this is assumed to have occurred if the victim is not released within 24 hours.) Because kidnapping is a federal crime, the FBI may be involved in kidnapping cases.

Many states also make it a crime to interfere with the custody of a child (commonly known as child-snatching). See also MISSING CHILDREN.

Penalties for kidnapping vary greatly, depending on the law and the circumstances. If a kidnapper holds a person for ransom, the sentence is generally more severe. The use of a dangerous weapon may also call for a more severe punishment. The most stringent punishment is imposed if the kidnapping victim dies during the course of the abduction or before he has been safely returned.

KITING

Kiting is the writing of checks against a bank account that is closed or does not exist, or an illegal use of the "float" period between the time a check is written and the time it is presented for payment. See FLOAT.

Kiting is often used to swindle people out of their money. Suppose Guy writes a $1,000 check against an account that he knows does not contain that amount. He goes to a bank in a nearby town, where he opens an account by depositing the $1,000 check. He also asks the bank to give him $50 of the face value of the check. As a courtesy to its new customer, the bank honors Guy's request, only to have his check bounce. To the bank's misfortune, Guy has by now skipped town, leaving the bank $50 poorer.

Kiting schemes are also used to take advantage of merchants or individuals who are making a one-time sale. Suppose you advertise in the local newspaper to sell your canoe for $500. In response, Ernest appears at your door; he is well dressed and personable, and he offers to give you the full asking price for your canoe. But because he says he is short of cash, he offers to give you a check for $550 in exchange for the canoe and $50. You put in a call to Ernest's bank, where a teller informs you that Ernest has sufficient funds in his account to cover the check. Happy to have made the sale, you give Ernest his $50 along with the canoe and its paddles.

The next day you deposit Ernest's check, but within the week it has bounced. Between the time you called Ernest's bank and the time you deposited his check, dozens of other checks that Ernest wrote have passed through the account. Not only have you lost your canoe, you have given an extra $50 to a smooth-talking crook!

STEPS TO TAKE

To protect yourself against the various types of check kiting, follow these procedures when making a transaction:

1. Never accept a check that is drawn on an account with an out-of-town bank, unless it is from someone you know personally and trust.

2. Sell merchandise for its exact purchase price. Never give extra money to someone in exchange for a check.

3. Have your buyer go to the nearest bank to cash his check. Although banks are sometimes victims of kiting schemes, they have procedures for recognizing kiters.

4. Allow the buyer to take the merchandise only after his check has cleared. Also require him to give you identification so that you can find him if anything goes wrong.

5. If you suspect someone of trying to swindle you by kiting a check, notify your local police immediately. They can warn others in the community of the potential problem and attempt to locate the con artist. See also CHECK; SCAMS AND SWINDLES.

LABOR UNION

A labor union is an employee organization formed primarily to negotiate employment contracts on behalf of its members, using the process known as collective bargaining. Collective bargaining addresses various employee concerns, including wages, benefits, and working conditions. Labor unions provide other services to their members as well, such as insurance and pension plans, and they represent their members in disputes with employers. See also COLLECTIVE BARGAINING.

LEGAL AUTHORITY

Although workers in the United States have organized for generations, the union movement was given a significant boost in the 1930's, when Congress passed the National Labor Relations Act (NLRA). This act, also known as the Wagner Act, gave unions the legal authority to represent groups of workers—called bargaining units—in the collective-bargaining process. These units consist of groups of employees whose places of work, employers, or job tasks give them a common interest in such work-related issues as pay, working hours, working conditions, vacations, and health benefits.

Not all employees are covered by the NLRA. For example, management employees, government workers, and farm and household workers are not covered, but their right to bargain collectively may be covered by other laws.

The NLRA also created a federal agency, the National Labor Relations Board (NLRB), to be responsible for supervising and regulating the negotiating process between employers and unions. Federal labor laws enacted after the NLRA provide that collective-bargaining agreements are enforceable in court and establish procedures to assure that union leaders represent the interests of their members.

WHY UNIONS WORK

Labor unions achieve success because there is power in numbers. If collective-bargaining negotiations fail, organized workers can force employers to recognize their demands through strikes, slowdowns, and boycotts. These methods would have limited impact if only a few workers participated. See also BOYCOTT; STRIKE.

FORMING A UNION

When employees decide to form or be represented by a

union, they usually contact the local division or parent organization of a national union, such as the United Auto Workers or the Teamsters. The employees or the union petition the NLRB to hold an election in which employees can vote on union representation. Generally, a petition to form a union must be signed by at least 30 percent of the employees in the bargaining unit that is named in the petition—for example, 30 percent of the forklift operators at an appliance manufacturing plant.

If the NLRB decides that an election is in order, a vote is then taken by secret ballot. If a majority of employees vote in favor of the union, it is certified as their bargaining agent.

UNION MEMBERSHIP

In exchange for representation and benefits, union members have certain obligations.

Dues

Union members agree to have dues deducted from their paychecks. Dues are used for many purposes: to supply funds for organizing efforts; to provide a strike fund to pay employees if a strike is called; to pay lobbyists to promote legislation favoring issues the union supports; and to pay the union's administrative costs.

Union dues usually average about $50 per month for most workers, although those who are highly paid may be required to contribute more, and lower-paid workers less. New union members may be required to pay an initiation fee of several hundred dollars, which often can be paid in installments.

An employee may withhold part of his union dues under particular circumstances. For instance, if you disagree with your union's political stance, you are legally entitled to withhold the portion of your union dues that is put toward political purposes. If you have an objection to union policy and want to withhold your dues, you must inform your employer and the union in writing.

You cannot be forced to join a union if you have religious objections to membership; however, you may still have to pay union dues since every employee benefits in some way from union representation.

Union shops

Unions and employers in many states have negotiated agreements that require prospective employees to join a union as a condition of their employment. Companies covered by such agreements are known familiarly as union shops. There are two basic kinds of union shop: (1) a true union shop, which requires all employees to join the union (if an employee has not joined within a specified time, he will be dismissed); and (2) an agency shop, which does not require membership, but does require employees to pay union dues.

Right-to-work laws and open shops

Nearly half of the states have "right-to-work" laws. In these states you cannot be required to join the union at your workplace or to pay its dues. Moreover, at such "open shops" the union must represent you, even if you do not belong to it, and you have the right to file a complaint with the NLRB if you feel that the union has not been representing your interests. See also RIGHT-TO-WORK LAWS.

LANDLORD

Anyone who leases to another person an apartment, house, or other real estate that he owns is a landlord. Landlords have certain legal rights and responsibilities, some of which are prescribed by law. However, it is always best to have a written lease that spells out both the landlord's and the tenant's rights and duties. A sample residential lease is included in the EVERYDAY LEGAL FORMS section of this book, beginning on page 552. See also LEASE.

Whatever the terms of the lease, you as a landlord may not discriminate against potential tenants on the basis of sex, race, marital status, age, or religion. However, you may make decisions based on their past record as tenants, work history, or ability to pay the rent on time. You have the right to ask them for personal, credit, and income references, as well as pay stubs that verify their income. You may also have a credit reporting agency run a check on an applicant's credit.

SECURITY DEPOSITS

As a landlord you have a right to demand a security deposit from your tenants that, in many states, must not exceed one month's rent. The purpose of a security deposit is to protect the landlord's investment in the event of damages, and it is an incentive to the tenant to care for the place in which he lives. See SECURITY DEPOSIT.

WARRANTY OF HABITABILITY

A landlord's responsibilities are also defined by state law. In many states a landlord, simply by offering her premises for rent, provides an "implied warranty of habitability." This means that the property must be fit to live in. In some states that have this warranty, courts have ruled that defective wiring, leaky roofs, inadequate plumbing, or nonworking appliances violate the warranty. In others, however, the implied warranty of habitability obligates the landlord to provide only such basics as heat, electricity, and water.

If a landlord fails to uphold the warranty of habitability, a tenant may sue her. As a result, she may be required to return part of the tenant's rent, as well as to correct any violations and make necessary repairs.

Ask your local department of housing about landlord-tenant laws in your area.

PROPER USE

Landlords may expect tenants to use a property for its intended purpose. For example, if you rent out a house for residential use and your tenant operates a hair salon out of it, you can demand that he close up shop.

Although normal wear and tear can be expected, landlords can expect tenants to take reasonable care of their property. Standard leases contain clauses obligating tenants to pay for damages that are beyond the usual wear and tear. Other duties (such as mowing the lawn) may also be spelled out. All clauses and restrictions must comply with any state and local laws and regulations, and tenants who fail to meet them may be evicted. See also EVICTION; RENT STRIKE; TENANT'S RIGHTS.

MAKING REPAIRS

Landlords must make emergency repairs as soon as possible after being notified of the problem. Other repairs must be done within a "reasonable period." Many states now allow tenants to make repairs on their apartments and deduct the cost from the rent. First, however, they must notify the landlord in writing of the problems and of their intention to "repair and deduct" the expenses from the rent if the landlord does not make the repairs within a reasonable period of time. If a tenant does make repairs, he must give his landlord an accounting of his costs.

ACCESS TO THE APARTMENT

Landlords must give tenants their privacy. A landlord may enter the house or apartment only after giving the tenant a reasonable amount of notice (usually 24 hours) and only during normal business hours. A landlord may enter an apartment without permission to make emergency repairs. Of course, tenants and landlords may work out their own access arrangements, but a landlord who violates a tenant's privacy can be sued for damages.

Sometimes a landlord may require limited access to an apartment. For instance, if she is trying to sell or rent the property, she may include a clause in the lease specifying which hours she may enter the apartment and for what purpose. However, a clause that infringes unreasonably upon a tenant's right to privacy will probably not be enforceable. Suppose a clause in your lease permits your landlord to enter the apartment at any time to show the property to prospective buyers. Can your landlord then demand access at 6 A.M., or from 9 P.M. to midnight? Probably not. A court would likely find that such demands are unreasonable and in violation of your privacy.

LANDMARK

Local communities and state and federal governments have passed laws that make it possible to preserve historic buildings from destruction or major modification by having them designated as landmarks. To obtain landmark status, a property must meet certain criteria. For example, a building may be so designated because a person who was of historic significance lived or stayed there, or because it was the site of a historic event. Landmark status may also be granted to buildings that typify a style of architecture, such as houses that were designed by Frank Lloyd Wright. A group of buildings or an area of town may be worthy of the designation because they represent an era that the community wants to preserve.

Suppose your town has an old house in which your state's constitution was signed. The house needs some paint, but it is well constructed and has a distinctive character. A developer in the community wants to buy it and tear it down to make room for a parking lot. If you want to preserve the house, and if your community has a landmark law, you can petition the local landmark- or historic-preservation commission to designate the house as a landmark.

Upon receiving the petition, the commission will hold a hearing to determine whether the building has true historical value. At this point the owner has an opportunity to challenge the designation. One common objection is that landmarking the building will unfairly deprive him of his right to do what he likes with his property. Since citizens often seek to establish landmarks as much to prevent change as to preserve history, an owner may often prevail on these grounds. See also CONDEMNATION.

If landmark status is granted, the building's owner may be prevented from tearing down his building or altering it in any way that is inconsistent with the original structure. Any renovations must not affect the building's historical integrity. If you are renovating an older home, for example, a landmark law might prohibit the installation of false dropped ceilings or modern office partitions.

To obtain specific information about landmark designations and historic preservation in your community, ask your local housing or zoning department. See also ZONING.

LAST-CLEAR-CHANCE RULE

Negligence cases are often not clear-cut, particularly if the plaintiff (injured party) may have contributed to his own accident or injury. It is the court's job to determine who bears the responsibility in a case, and whether the plaintiff's own negligence was a factor. In cases where the court reaches such a conclusion, approximately one-third of the states apply the rule of contributory negligence. This rule states that if the judge or jury finds that the plaintiff's negligence contributed to the accident, he will not be able to recover monetary damages.

The last-clear-chance rule was developed to soften the effect of this rule. Suppose that late one afternoon, at dusk, Don's car began to make an odd sound. Don stopped it along a flat stretch of highway but neglected to turn on his hazard lights or take any other steps to warn oncoming cars that he had stopped. Suddenly, a truck hit Don's car in the rear, destroying it and injuring Don. Don sued the truck driver for negligent driving.

The trucker argued— and the court agreed— that Don was guilty of contributory negligence because he failed to warn oncoming traffic of his predicament, and he did not drive off the highway. Nonetheless, the judge ordered the truck driver to compensate Don. Had the driver been more vigilant, he would have seen Don's car and thus avoided the accident. The truck driver had a "last clear chance" to prevent the accident. See also NEGLIGENCE; TORT.

LAWSUIT

A lawsuit is a legal procedure begun by one party (an individual or a group) against another in order to rectify an injustice. Lawsuits are also called civil actions, to distinguish them from criminal actions, or prosecutions by the state. The goal of many lawsuits is to get compensation for damages, to stop someone from creating a nuisance, or to enforce a contract. See also CIVIL RIGHTS.

Lawsuits are won due to a preponderance of the evidence —that is, one party must have better evidence than the other. Suppose Sam and Diane have an oral agreement that Sam will sell Diane his microwave oven for $50. Sam later changes his mind, and Diane sues him to enforce the contract. If the only evidence is Sam's word against Diane's, and both are equally credible, Diane will not be able to prove her case. However, suppose Diane has a witness, Rebecca, who will testify that she heard Sam make the contract with Diane. Her testimony backs Diane up in every way, and she is a credible witness. Even though Sam denies that he made the agreement with

Diane, a court would probably rule in her favor because of the evidence supplied by Rebecca. See also EVIDENCE.

TYPES OF LAWSUITS

Some of the more familiar categories of lawsuits are contract actions, tort actions, and suits against private nuisances.

Contract actions

When a person fails to meet the terms of a contract, as in the example above, the other party to the contract may file a civil action claiming breach of contract. The lawsuit may ask the court to order the defendant to uphold the contract, to pay compensation for damages resulting from his failure to obey its provisions, or to void the contract, relieving both parties of their duties. See also BREACH OF CONTRACT; CONTRACT.

Tort actions

Tort actions are lawsuits that seek compensation for a civil wrong (as opposed to a crime) committed by someone against another person. Included are lawsuits for personal injury or property damage due to negligence, as well as suits for libel, false arrest, and other disputes.

Some incidents may result in both civil and criminal actions simultaneously. For example, someone who causes an accident because he drives recklessly not only may be sued by the injured party, but also may be prosecuted by the state for criminally negligent behavior. See also DAMAGES; TORT.

Private nuisances

A nuisance interferes with a person's enjoyment of her life or property. Suppose your neighbor's dog stands in the backyard howling all day and night. You have often asked the neighbor to keep his dog quiet, but he has ignored you. You can file a civil lawsuit in court to force your neighbor to do something about his dog. See also NUISANCE; PET.

THE STEPS IN A LAWSUIT

Civil procedure varies from state to state, but most lawsuits follow the same basic steps.

Demand and response

Before a lawsuit is filed, the plaintiff (the person filing the suit) makes a written demand on the defendant (the person he is suing), stating his claim, the response he is asking for, and a time limit for the defendant to respond. For example, suppose Jeff is suing Jennifer for injuries he suffered when he fell down her porch steps. He writes a demand stating his claim (that he fell on her steps, which were negligently maintained, and he suffered injuries as a result). His demand requests a response (payment of $20,000 for medical costs, lost wages, and pain and suffering), and it must be made within a time limit of 10 days.

If the defendant fails to respond in an acceptable manner (if he does not agree with the amount of money requested or offers a lower amount than the plaintiff might accept), then the plaintiff will file a complaint with the court. The complaint describes the dispute as the plaintiff sees it, the legal basis for filing the lawsuit, and the remedy the plaintiff is asking the court to grant. The complaint, along with a summons, is delivered by the sheriff (or a process server) to the defendant. The summons notifies the defendant that a suit has been filed and gives him a time limit (usually 10 to 30 days) to give a response, which is known as an answer. In his answer, the defendant may deny some or all of the charges, raise certain defenses, or file a counterclaim for damages that he feels the plaintiff owes him.

If the defendant does not answer the summons and complaint, the plaintiff can ask the court to grant a default judgment. If it is evident that the defendant was properly notified (called proof of service), the default may be granted. See also DEFAULT JUDGMENT.

Gathering evidence

Once the defendant's answer is received, the discovery process can begin. During this process, which takes place before the actual trial, each party can seek information from his opponent to help build and strengthen his case. See DISCOVERY.

In addition to conducting discovery, each side may file a variety of motions with the court asking it to rule on different issues, such as whether certain evidence is admissible at the trial, or whether a party must respond to a particular discovery request (for documents, for example) made by his opponent. Meanwhile, either side may approach the other with offers of settlement, hoping to avoid the added costs and delays of a trial. The court itself may try to help the opponents reach a settlement.

The trial

If no settlement is reached, a trial is held. Since lawsuits are civil cases, they may be tried with or without a jury, depending on the wishes of the parties and the provisions of the law.

The plaintiff's attorney may make an opening statement to the court, setting forth all the facts he intends to prove. The defendant's attorney may then make an opening statement, or he may choose not to make a statement until the plaintiff has presented his entire case.

Because the burden of proof is on him, the plaintiff presents his case first. He calls witnesses, who are sworn in and questioned, or examined, by his attorney. Then cross-examination by the defendant's attorney follows. When the plaintiff has fully presented his case, he is said to "rest his case." See also CROSS-EXAMINATION.

Now it is the defendant's turn. First his attorney may choose to make a motion for dismissal, claiming that the plaintiff has failed to make a case. If any evidence supports the plaintiff's claim, however, this motion will be refused. The defense now calls its witnesses and questions them under oath, after which the plaintiff may cross-examine them.

After the defense rests, the plaintiff gets a chance to conduct a rebuttal—an opportunity to present new evidence that contradicts that of the defense. Each side then makes closing statements, which reinforce the key points of its case.

The court's decision

At this point, if the case was tried without a jury, the judge retires to consider the evidence before announcing his decision. If the case was tried before a jury, the judge will instruct the members of the jury on the law and how it should be applied to the facts of the case. Then the jury retires to deliberate.

Once the jury's decision is announced, the losing side may ask the judge to grant a "judgment notwithstanding the verdict." This is a request that the judge overturn the jury's decision because it is clearly contradicted by the evidence and the law. Judgments of this type are frequently requested but rarely granted, and the losing side will either have to accept the judgment or file an appeal. See also COMPLAINT; COMPROMISE AND SETTLEMENT; JURY; SMALL-CLAIMS COURT; STATUTE OF LIMITATIONS.

LAWYER

Maggy, who is a professional singer, is preparing to sign a recording contract, but she does not understand the fine print. Julie and George are getting married, and they would like to have a prenuptial agreement. Sarah, who works as a cashier in a department store, has been accused of stealing money from the cash register. Although all of these situations are different, the people who are involved have one thing in common—they would be well advised to consult a lawyer.

DECIDING WHEN YOU NEED A LAWYER

Sooner or later you will probably need a lawyer to advise you about a problem or to settle a dispute. But you may not know whether or not your problem requires a lawyer. In general, you should consult a lawyer if your problem is complex, if it involves a lot of money, or if the consequences of not doing so could be severe.

Certain specific situations almost always call for a lawyer. In addition to those mentioned above, some of these are:

◇ When you are starting your own business.

◇ When you are buying or selling your home or are threatened with loss of your home.

◇ When you have suffered an injury or your property has been damaged, especially when the damage was due to someone else's negligence.

◇ When you must draw up a will or a trust.

◇ When you must sign a contract, lease, or other important document.

◇ When you are trying to get a divorce, separation, or annulment.

◇ When you adopt a child or would like to obtain custody of one.

◇ When you are accused of a crime or have been the victim of a crime.

FINDING A LAWYER

Waiting until a problem arises before finding a lawyer may mean that you are choosing one under extreme stress. This may be costly to you, both personally and financially. Therefore, it is worth your while to find a lawyer before you actually need one. Here are some tips for conducting your search:

◇ *Shop around.* Getting recommendations from family, friends, and others whom you trust is probably the best way to find a suitable lawyer. If that fails, call the bar association in your area. Be sure to ask how lawyers are selected for its list. In many places the bar association will accept any lawyer who applies, providing she is in good standing with the bar. It is important for you to realize that this screening process may not be particularly thorough, and a listing with the local bar is not necessarily a guarantee of a lawyer's quality. As a last resort, look under the "Lawyers" entry in the Yellow Pages of your telephone directory.

◇ *Interview before you hire.* Many attorneys will offer a free or low-cost initial consultation. Ask about this charge as well as about the fees for services at the time you schedule an interview. The goals of your interview should be to assess the lawyer's competence and to determine whether you find that her personality is compatible with your own. You will also want a lawyer with experience that matches your needs. For example, if you want to have a will drafted and you need help in estate planning, you do not want a lawyer who mainly handles divorce cases.

◇ *Get organized.* If you are hiring the attorney to help you with a specific problem, show her any useful documents or contracts. Be aware that the lawyer will probably want to give your papers a quick review during the first meeting. See also LEGAL AID.

LAWYERS' FEES

Be sure that you come to a clear understanding with your lawyer about her fees before you hire her. Ask specific questions about acceptable methods of payment. For example, some lawyers require a partial payment (called a retainer) before they begin, and will thereafter bill you at an hourly rate. Some lawyers accept credit cards or let you pay in installments. In personal-injury cases, many lawyers charge a contingent fee, which is based on the amount you are awarded as a result of a settlement or trial. See also CONTINGENT FEE.

Some lawyers will perform certain kinds of standardized legal work for a flat fee, such as preparing a simple will or representing you in an uncontested divorce. But if the matter becomes more complicated than the lawyer originally estimated, she may try to add extra charges. Before hiring an attorney on a flat-fee basis, find out exactly which of her services are covered by the flat fee and what her fee schedule will be for any additional work.

Whether you hire an attorney on a flat-fee basis or at an hourly rate, ask her to draft a fee agreement detailing all fees and charges. It should include an estimate of how long your project will take, along with a provision that requires her to notify you when she has spent a specified number of hours on your case. Such a provision will help you to monitor your costs.

Not all attorneys automatically supply written fee agreements. In some states they are only required for certain kinds of cases, such as those taken on contingency.

You should also ask whether the lawyer charges for services such as telephone calls, photocopying, and postage. Many lawyers bill these as separate charges (over and above the hourly rate), and you can often save money by doing some of them yourself. For instance, a copy shop will probably charge you much less for photocopies than a lawyer will.

Do not hesitate to ask the lawyer to reduce her fee if you think it is too high. Legal fees are open to negotiation, and some lawyers do try to accommodate the different financial situations of their clients.

HELPING YOUR LAWYER HELP YOU

Once you have decided to hire a lawyer, there are some things you can do that will help make her job easier (and that usually means less worry and fewer costs for you).

◇ *Be candid.* Lying or withholding information about your case from your lawyer never helps. If you do, sooner or later the truth may be revealed, and you will have damaged your lawyer's credibility as well as her ability to represent you effectively.

◇ *Keep your lawyer up to date.* Tell her about any new information you receive or any contact you have had with the opposing party, if there is one. If you can suggest a helpful witness or locate a misplaced document, let her know.

◇ *Don't expect immediate answers.* Your lawyer will not always know the answers to your questions right away. She may have to do some research. Be wary of a lawyer who tries to give you instant advice on a matter that is complicated.

◇ *Don't hound your lawyer*. Remember that she has other clients and she cannot devote all of her time to your case. Keep phone calls and office visits to a minimum. Calling every day or every week for a progress report is usually not necessary (some cases take months or years to resolve) and can be expensive (most lawyers will charge for phone conferences as well as for visits).

PAYING YOUR BILL

Even if you feel you have been overcharged, always pay your lawyer's bill on time. A lawyer who has not received payment can place an automatic lien, or claim, on your case file, documents, and other materials. If she does this, you will then be obliged to hire another lawyer, who, because he does not have the original documents, will probably have to duplicate the work that has already been done. Moreover, the original lawyer can sue you to recover the sums you owe her.

If you have a dispute, first try to negotiate a settlement with your lawyer. If she refuses to negotiate, pay the bill under protest with a letter that makes clear your disagreement with the charged amount. Then you may call or write your local bar association and lodge a complaint. In some states the bar association has set up a fee-arbitration panel which may help you settle your dispute.

Finally, if nothing else works, you can file a lawsuit seeking reimbursement for the amount you feel the lawyer has overcharged you.

CHECKLIST

What You Should Expect From a Lawyer

When hiring a lawyer, remember that you are the boss. As such, you should expect the following from your lawyer:

❑ **COMPETENCE.**
If your lawyer lacks the skills to handle your case, you have the right to know this as soon as possible. You then should have the option to allow the lawyer to work with someone who does have the needed skills, or to find another lawyer.

❑ **RESPECT.**
Your lawyer should speak to you as an equal, take the time to explain strategies he proposes in a way you can understand, answer all of your questions to the best of his ability, and return phone calls promptly. The lawyer's staff should also be respectful and courteous toward you.

❑ **PROGRESS REPORTS.**
Although this does not necessarily mean a daily or even weekly update, you do have the right to expect reasonable progress reports, immediate notification about any unexpected developments or settlement offers, and copies of documents filed by your attorney or your opponent's.

❑ **REGULAR, DETAILED BILLING.**
You should be sent an itemized monthly statement that clearly states what the lawyer did, when he did it, and how long it took. Your bill should also itemize all fees for photocopies, messenger and delivery services, long-distance calls, filing fees, and other costs you are expected to pay.

❑ **THE TRUTH ABOUT YOUR CHANCES OF SUCCESS.**
If your case is a long shot, your lawyer does you a disservice by telling you that it is a sure thing, and he may be padding his own pocket by keeping a case alive when it would be better to settle or even abandon it.

PROFESSIONAL CONDUCT

In order to be admitted to the bar, lawyers in every state must swear to observe certain codes of professional conduct. These codes are usually established, interpreted, and enforced by the state's highest court.

Although codes of professional conduct for lawyers vary slightly from state to state, they are usually based on standards established by the American Bar Association in its Model Rules of Professional Responsibility. A lawyer must swear to represent her clients to the best of her ability, to preserve client confidences, to deal fairly with the opposing side, and to uphold the law.

Suppose that you have hired a lawyer to negotiate the sale of your house. She does not have the right to reveal to potential buyers the lowest price you will accept for your house. This information is considered privileged—that is, a private matter between client and lawyer.

MALPRACTICE

A lawyer who fails to observe the rules of professional conduct is guilty of malpractice—an unethical or illegal act committed in a professional capacity. For example, a lawyer who misappropriates her clients' funds for her own personal use is guilty of malpractice, as is an attorney who so neglects her clients' cases that they suffer as a result. An attorney can also be accused of malpractice if she displays an unreasonable lack of skill. Although incompetence is often hard to prove, certain failings are obvious—for example, if a lawyer does not take depositions, interview witnesses, file documents, or meet deadlines.

A lawyer who is successfully prosecuted for malpractice may be disbarred or prohibited from practicing for a period of time. Sometimes complaints are kept on file by the state attorney disciplinary committee in the event that similar or more serious grievances are lodged against the same lawyer. See also DISBARMENT.

STEPS TO TAKE WHEN YOUR LAWYER HAS ACTED IMPROPERLY

If you feel you have been damaged by your lawyer's incompetence or unethical conduct, you may consider taking the following steps:

1. Discuss your concerns with your attorney and give her a chance to justify her actions. If you still have doubts, get a second lawyer's opinion.

2. Make a written complaint to the state bar association or the attorney disciplinary committee of your state's highest court. Be as thorough as possible in describing why you feel your lawyer is incompetent or engaging in unethical practices. In most situations an investigator will be appointed to handle your complaint.

3. If you believe your lawyer has stolen money from you or committed some other criminal act, inform your local district attorney's office. There may be good reason to prosecute her in criminal court.

4. Consult with an attorney who specializes in legal malpractice cases for advice about using arbitration or filing a civil lawsuit. Although suing is time-consuming and expensive, it may be the only way that you can receive financial damages or other compensation. See also LAWSUIT.

LAWYER, ACTING AS YOUR OWN

Everyone in the United States has the legal right to act as his own lawyer in a legal proceeding, from a small-claims case to a murder trial. Most states have small-claims courts where people can act on their own behalf in lawsuits involving relatively small amounts of money. In fact, attorneys are often not allowed in these courts.

Similarly, you can perform a number of other legal tasks without a lawyer. You can sign a lease or sales contract, make credit purchases, and apply for loans without consulting an attorney. If you have a relatively small amount of property, you may sometimes be able to prepare your own will without a lawyer's advice.

In many situations, however, you should give careful consideration before acting as your own lawyer. By obtaining legal advice before you make important decisions about financial arrangements, trusts, contracts, wills, and the like, you avoid legal problems. In addition, many legal proceedings, such as a lawsuit over personal injury or a class-action suit, call for a lawyer's expert training and knowledge. See LAWYER.

LAYAWAY PURCHASE

Many stores offer their customers the opportunity to purchase merchandise through an installment contract known as a layaway plan. Under such a plan, the customer pays a small down payment and then makes additional payments until the full purchase price has been paid. The store keeps the merchandise until it is paid for.

Suppose you want to buy an expensive coat at a department store, but you cannot afford it right now. You decide to use the store's layaway plan, which lets you take up to six months to pay for the coat. After making the down payment and four monthly payments, you are laid off from your job and are unable to make another payment until after the six-month period has expired. Will you lose the coat or your money, or both?

There may be a grace period for redeeming the coat. If so, it will be spelled out in the contract. If there is no grace period, and the store sells the coat to another customer after six months have passed, you will probably receive most of your money back. But depending on the terms of your contract, the store may keep some of your money as a restocking charge or as compensation for a lost sales opportunity.

Suppose you change your mind after making three payments and decide you do not want the coat after all. Depending on the terms of the contract, you may receive a greater or lesser proportion of your money back. Be sure to read the contract before you buy anything on a layaway plan if you think you might have a change of heart.

As with any other contract, a court can enforce a layaway agreement. If, for example, the store mistakenly sells the coat to someone else and you have been making your payments on time, you could file suit against the store because they have breached their contract. But in most cases your damages would be limited to the money you had already paid and whatever additional amount you had to pay for a similar coat elsewhere. See also CONTRACT.

LEADING QUESTION

During a trial, a lawyer may sometimes ask a witness what is called a leading question—one that is phrased to prompt a particular response, usually a yes or a no. For instance, a lawyer may ask, "Isn't it true that at 8:15 P.M. on October 25 you were standing outside the jewelry store at the time the robbery took place?" The question seems to imply that the witness saw the robbery or that he perhaps was a lookout. By contrast, it would not be considered a leading question if the lawyer asked, "Where were you at 8:15 P.M. on the evening of October 25?"

In both civil and criminal trials, leading questions are generally prohibited during direct examination because testimony is supposed to come voluntarily from the witness, not the lawyer who is asking the questions. However, a lawyer may ask leading questions during cross-examination because the witness has already presented his testimony in his own words and the lawyer is now free to shape it in the way that best serves his case. See also CROSS-EXAMINATION; EVIDENCE.

LEASE

A lease is a real estate contract that creates a landlord and tenant relationship and establishes the rights and the duties of both. A written lease is important evidence in the event that a dispute arises between the parties, and in many states it is required by law.

A carefully worded lease can offer legal protection to both landlord and tenant. The form it takes may be standard for housing in your area, or it may be tailored to suit particular circumstances. But at a minimum, your lease should:

◇ Give a clear description of the premises that are being rented. If you are renting an apartment or an entire house, the address will suffice. If the lease is only for a single room or part of a larger space, the lease should describe the space carefully. If storage space, outdoor space, or garage space is included, the lease should say so clearly.

◇ State the amount of rent to be paid, the date that payments are due, and any penalties for late payments or for bounced checks.

◇ State the amount of a security deposit being charged and the conditions for its return. Security deposits are governed by state laws, which vary widely. See SECURITY DEPOSIT.

◇ Include the names of adult tenants who will live on the premises. The lease should state that they will be "jointly and severally" responsible for the rent. This means that if one tenant cannot pay his share, the others will be responsible.

◇ State the number of tenants who are permitted to live on the premises. Sometimes tenants invite friends or relatives to move in with them, adding to the wear and tear on the property. The landlord has a right to set limits.

◇ Spell out who has the responsibility for paying utility bills, removing trash, and maintaining the property. If a tenant is expected to mow the grass, shovel snow, or take care of any other upkeep, the lease should state this.

◇ Limit the tenant's right to sublet to someone else. The lease should either require the written permission of the landlord in advance or prohibit subletting entirely. See SUBLEASE.

You may find standard leases at stationery stores. For a sample residential lease, see the EVERYDAY LEGAL FORMS section of this book, beginning on page 552. See also EVICTION; LANDLORD; TENANT'S RIGHTS.

LEGAL AID

Often supported by government and private funds, legal-aid offices provide free or low-cost legal services to those who cannot afford to pay for them. Most legal-aid offices handle a variety of cases ranging from divorces and landlord disputes to immigration cases and juvenile court hearings. Some also provide public defender services for defendants in criminal cases, and others specialize in the needs of particular groups, such as the elderly.

QUALIFYING FOR LEGAL AID

Legal-aid offices follow strict guidelines when screening an applicant to verify that he truly cannot afford to hire a lawyer. If you apply for legal-aid assistance, you must be prepared to give detailed information about your income, other financial resources, and expenses. The restrictions that apply to applicants' income may not be as stringent in a specialized legal-aid office that receives its funding from a private individual or organization.

Legal-aid offices do not usually take on personal-injury or workers' compensation cases because lawyers who are in private practice are often willing to accept such cases on a contingent-fee basis.

PRO BONO WORK

To help people who do not qualify for legal aid but nevertheless cannot afford a lawyer, the American Bar Association and state and local bar associations encourage their members to provide some legal services on a "pro bono" basis, or free of charge. (*Pro bono* is from the Latin phrase *pro bono publico*, "for the public good.") Even if you do not qualify for free services, your local bar association will usually try to help you find a lawyer who will provide services at a price you can afford. See also DUE PROCESS OF LAW; LAWYER.

LEMON LAW

You have just bought a new car that looked like a peach in the showroom, but after a few weeks you begin to suspect that you have bought a lemon. You have taken it back to the dealer again and again, but after several visits the "friendly" service department does not seem quite so friendly and the car still has not been repaired properly. Although your warranty covers the repairs, you are tired of your car breaking down. What can you do?

Most states have lemon laws designed to protect consumers who buy defective automobiles, light trucks, or motorcycles. A defect is typically defined in lemon laws as anything that substantially impairs the use, value, or safety of your vehicle during the first year or 12,000 miles you own the car, which the dealer has tried to repair at least four times to no avail, resulting in your car being out of service for at least 30 days. Under most state lemon laws, such a defect entitles you to a refund or a replacement of the vehicle from the manufacturer. For more information on making a lemon-law claim, see the feature at right.

New cars also come with written warranties that are covered by the federal Magnuson-Moss Act of 1975. This is good news if you live in one of the two remaining states that do not have lemon laws, because the act allows you to sue an auto maker for compensation and, in some cases, even your legal fees. The act also authorizes class-action lawsuits if 100 or more car owners want to sue a car manufacturer over a common defect. See CLASS ACTION; MAGNUSON-MOSS ACT; WARRANTY AND GUARANTY.

LIABILITY

The term *liability* is generally used to indicate a legal responsibility, duty, or obligation. For example, if you take out a loan

ABC's OF MAKING A LEMON-LAW CLAIM

If you suspect that your new car or other vehicle is a lemon, heed the following advice:

- ❑ Keep the documents that show when you purchased the vehicle, since that will be the date your warranty begins. Return the registration card, if any, to the manufacturer.
- ❑ Keep all maintenance records as proof that the defect was not the result of your failure to maintain the vehicle properly. Many warranty claims are rejected because of claims that the owner abused the vehicle or failed to maintain it as required.
- ❑ Be sure to notify your dealer of problems as soon as you become aware of them. To take advantage of the remedies that lemon laws provide, you must give the warrantor a chance to repair your vehicle.
- ❑ Keep a log of all telephone conversations you have with the dealer about the problem, and keep copies of all the correspondence that relates to the situation.
- ❑ Keep accurate records of all repair work done to the car. Include information regarding the type of defect, the dates the vehicle was in the shop, and the amount of time the vehicle was out of service. Save all work orders, receipts, invoices, and warranty information.
- ❑ If the manufacturer's warranty allows for alternative dispute resolution (such as arbitration), make a written request for it and follow the procedure set forth before filing a lawsuit.
- ❑ If informal dispute resolution is not available or does not work, find a lawyer who handles lemon-law claims. Ask her about the relative advantages of filing suit in state or federal court (state laws may give you more rights), and whether you should seek a refund or replacement. You should also discuss the possibility of recovering your legal fees and costs from the manufacturer.

to buy a home, you are liable for the debt that is created by the loan. Liability is also created when a person or his property is harmed as a result of someone else's negligence. If your reckless driving causes an accident, for example, you can be held liable for the resulting injury or property damage.

The concept of liability takes a number of different forms under the law, the most important of which are discussed below.

PRIMARY AND SECONDARY LIABILITY

Primary liability is a term used to designate the person who will first be held responsible. For example, when you sign a loan agreement to buy a car, you have the primary liability for the loan. This means that you are responsible for fulfilling the terms of the contract, including making the loan payments on time.

Secondary liability creates a duty or obligation only when the person who has primary liability fails to fulfill her responsibilities. Suppose you ask a relative to cosign, or guarantee, your car loan agreement. If you do not meet your obligation to make timely payments, the loan company can turn to the cosigner for payment. See also COSIGNING.

JOINT LIABILITY

Joint liability applies to situations in which more than one person may be held responsible. Because both acted together in causing the damage, each wrongdoer (known as a tortfeasor) shares responsibility for some portion of the loss.

In some states, tortfeasors may be held jointly and severally liable, meaning that the person who has been harmed may sue more than one wrongdoer or just one. For example, if Ed is driving a car owned by Andrea when he injures you in an accident, you may be able to sue both of them together, sue only Ed, or sue only Andrea.

However, if you only file suit against Ed, the amount that you recover from him if you win would represent your full and complete payment for the suit. You cannot later file another suit against Andrea, because that would constitute a double payment for a single wrong. Therefore, you may be advised by a lawyer to sue them both together and individually. See also DAMAGES; TORT.

STRICT LIABILITY

Strict liability is often applied in product liability cases. At one time manufacturers were held responsible for injuries or damages caused by a product only if negligence could be established. Today manufacturers can be held liable without proof of negligence.

Suppose a pesticide manufacturer puts a new pesticide on the market after testing indicates that the product is safe. A few months later, numerous users complain that they developed serious rashes after using the pesticide. If they sue, the manufacturer will be held strictly liable, even though he had thoroughly tested the pesticide before selling it. The very fact that an unreasonably dangerous product is put on the market is sufficient reason to impose liability on a manufacturer. That is why pesticides and other products that are potentially hazardous carry prominent warnings on the package labels. See also NEGLIGENCE; PRODUCT SAFETY AND LIABILITY.

VICARIOUS LIABILITY

Vicarious liability means that one party can be held indirectly responsible for the actions of another party. For instance, an employer may be held vicariously liable for the actions of his employees. Suppose you make a delivery to the Tyler Tool Company and an employee accidentally runs into you with his forklift, injuring your hip. If the accident is due to the worker's negligence, the Tyler Tool Company may be held responsible for your injury.

Similarly, some states have laws governing parental liability. When parents fail to control their child, they may be held responsible for damage caused by the child's actions. See also PARENTAL-LIABILITY LAWS.

LIABILITY INSURANCE

Liability insurance pays for injuries or damages caused by the policyholder. Suppose that while visiting your home, your neighbor is seriously injured by a falling ceiling tile. The money she is awarded by a court to cover her medical treatment and any additional damages will likely be covered by the liability portion of your homeowners insurance policy.

In general, liability coverage is the most expensive component of an auto, business, or homeowners insurance policy. However, coverage is limited. Many experts suggest that in today's litigious society you should consider purchasing an umbrella liability policy in addition to your other coverage.

Umbrella policies are relatively inexpensive (costing as little as $100 per year), and they provide as much as $1 million in coverage. The reason the cost remains low is that the policy becomes effective only after you have exhausted your primary insurance. Suppose the neighbor who was hit by the falling ceiling tile takes you to court, where she is awarded $700,000 in damages. Your homeowners policy offers the basic liability coverage up to $500,000. An umbrella liability policy would probably cover the remaining $200,000.

If you are buying an umbrella policy, be sure that it also covers legal costs, which can be substantial in liability cases. See also UMBRELLA INSURANCE.

LIBEL AND SLANDER

Libel and slander are different (but related) forms of defamation. Libel is a false statement about a person's character or reputation that is communicated to others in writing or in some other visual, permanent form. Slander is verbal defamation. For a more detailed explanation of defamation, see DEFAMATION. See also TORT.

LICENSE

A license is the permission granted by a government agency allowing a person or a company to engage in an activity that the government wants to regulate. Many activities require a license. For example, if you want to operate a barber shop, practice law or medicine, drive a taxi, open a liquor store or restaurant, become an insurance or real estate agent, hunt, fish, marry, own a dog, or drive, you may first have to obtain a license from the appropriate regulatory authority.

The government has an interest in protecting the health, safety, and welfare of its citizens, and the right to do so (its police power). By requiring a license, the state can provide some assurance that a licensed person or business meets certain standards in conducting its affairs. Licensing is also an important source of government revenue, sometimes costing licensees several hundred dollars a year.

OBTAINING A LICENSE

In order to obtain a license, you must first meet the qualifications imposed by law. You will need to complete the required application forms, pay the fees that have been set by the agency, and perhaps provide references or even post bond. For instance, if you want to get a beautician's license, you must complete the number of hours of education in cosmetology required by your state. In order to become a real estate or an insurance agent, you must complete courses that have been approved by the state and perhaps be sponsored by someone who already has a license.

REVOKING A LICENSE

A license is a privilege and can be revoked by a regulatory body if you ignore regulations or violate the law, but you are first entitled to notice and to a hearing. Depending on the type of license you hold (if, for example, you are a doctor or lawyer), a formal hearing may be required—a process much like a court trial. If a licensing board revokes or suspends your license, you are entitled to appeal its decision.

FILING A COMPLAINT AGAINST A LICENSE HOLDER

If you have a complaint to make about a licensee, call or write the licensing board responsible for overseeing the licensee's activity or profession. (Many licensing authorities require the complaint to be in writing.) Unfortunately, licensing boards are often underfunded, understaffed, and overworked. For example, the California Board of Real Estate receives more than 10,000 complaints each year. Because of the volume, boards often cannot process all the complaints they get and must concentrate on the most serious cases or those that involve a large number of complaints about the same person or business. As a consequence, your complaint may simply be forwarded to the licensee with a request for an explanation. See also DRIVER'S LICENSE; REAL ESTATE AGENT AND BROKER.

LIE DETECTOR TEST

Also known as a polygraph test, the lie detector test has long been used by police departments and other government authorities in an effort to determine whether a person is telling the truth. A lie detector device measures a subject's bodily—and largely involuntary—reactions to stress. To perform the test, galvanized electrodes are attached to a subject's skin. These measure and record changes in blood pressure, pulse rate, respiration, and electrical resistance.

The person who is conducting the test first asks neutral questions, such as the subject's name and age, in order to help the subject relax and to see how he generally responds to this kind of questioning. When questions that are pertinent to the inquiry are asked, the lie detector indicates any changes recorded by the electrodes.

RELIABILITY

The accuracy of lie detector tests is still being debated, and lawyers usually cite the unreliability of these tests when the opposing side uses them as evidence. Although a polygraph machine definitely measures the physiological reactions to stress, the chance for inaccurate results is high if the machine is not properly operated and the test is not properly conducted. In an effort to improve reliability, at least 27 states require that polygraph examiners be licensed.

USE IN CRIMINAL PROCEEDINGS

Because of the chance for inaccuracy, courts generally do not allow lie detector results to be admitted as evidence. Even when test results are admitted, the jury is told that the results in themselves are not conclusive of guilt or innocence, but just one factor they should consider when trying to reach a verdict. See also CONFESSION.

USE BY EMPLOYERS

In 1988 Congress enacted the Employee Polygraph Protection Act (EPPA). This federal law has three major objectives. First, it prohibits most private employers from requiring, requesting, or even suggesting that a job applicant or employee take a lie detector test. Second, the EPPA makes it illegal for employers to ask applicants or employees about results of previous lie detector tests or to accept or use the results of any such test. Third, the EPPA prohibits dismissing, disciplining, discriminating against, refusing to hire or promote, or threatening applicants or employees on the basis of test results or the refusal to submit to a test.

Exemptions

The following categories of employers are exempt from the Employee Polygraph Protection Act:

◇ Federal, state, and local governments.

◇ Employers engaged in counterintelligence work for the federal government.

◇ A private employer who is investigating a case of theft, embezzlement, sabotage, or other criminal act that causes economic loss or harm to the company. The employer can only test reasonable suspects, and it must be explained to each employee why the test is being conducted. For example, a bank employee who had access to property that has been stolen from safe-deposit boxes might be asked to take a lie detector test.

◇ Companies that provide security personnel, such as department store guards.

◇ Companies that manufacture, distribute, or dispense controlled substances. See also DRUG; DRUG TESTING.

Violations

Every employer who is subject to the EPPA must display an EPPA poster detailing its provisions in a noticeable location. The U.S. Department of Labor enforces the EPPA, and any violation should be reported to the nearest regional office. Job applicants or employees who have suffered harm as a result of an EPPA violation may be hired, reinstated, or promoted, and they may also recover lost wages and benefits. Legal fees and reasonable costs may be assessed against the employer. In addition, an employer who has been found to be in violation of this act can be fined up to $10,000.

LIEN

A lien is a claim that is placed against property for the purpose of securing a debt owed by the property's owner. A lien gives the lien holder (the person who obtained the lien) the right to force a sale of the property in order to satisfy the debt. A home mortgage is one of the most common types of lien.

TYPES OF LIENS

Liens can take several different forms; the three most common are equitable liens, statutory liens, and mechanic's liens.

Equitable liens

An equitable lien may be either created by a sales contract or imposed by a court out of fairness. See also EQUITY.

Liens created by a sales contract are called express equitable liens. They are secured by the property you are purchasing. For example, when you borrow money to buy a home or car, the lender who gives you the loan obtains a lien according to the terms of the contract, with the house or the car serving as the collateral for the unpaid amount. If you do not make your payments as specified in the contract, the lender has the right to repossess your property and sell it to recover the money he lent you. See also MORTGAGE; UNIFORM COMMERCIAL CODE.

Liens imposed by courts are called implied equitable liens. Suppose Steven sells Frank his boat for $1,000. Frank agrees to make monthly payments of $200, but stops paying after three months. Steven asks the court to impose a lien on the boat. This lien allows him to reclaim the boat or to sell it in order to recover the amount he lost in the deal. It also prevents Frank from selling the boat to someone else without first paying Steven what is owed him.

Statutory liens

A statutory lien is created by law. Generally, statutory liens automatically go into effect when someone does something to improve another person's property or add to its value, and has not yet been paid. Suppose you take your car to the local garage for repairs. Until you pay your bill, the garage may have a statutory lien on your car (depending on where you live), and is not required to return the car until you have paid the bill. If you do not pay, the garage may ultimately be able to sell the car to recover the value of its services, in addition to expenses such as storage charges, court costs, and attorneys' fees.

A lawyer has a statutory lien on documents belonging to her client while they are in the lawyer's possession. If a lawyer has not been paid, she need not return the documents until such time as the bill is settled.

Some statutory liens require the lien holder to obtain court approval before he can sell a debtor's property. Others require only that the lien holder notify the debtor of the date and place of the proposed sale.

Mechanic's lien
A mechanic's lien is a type of statutory lien. However, with this type of lien, the property remains in the debtor's possession while the lien is in effect. The most common example of a mechanic's lien is the claim made by a building contractor when bills for improvements he has made go unpaid. The contractor may be able to foreclose on the property to collect the money owed him. For a full discussion, see MECHANIC'S LIEN.

FILING A LIEN

By filing a lien, you give notice of your claim against property to anyone who might have reason to know of it, such as someone who wants to buy or lease the property. In most states liens that are created by contract (such as through a mortgage or by retaining a security interest in a car or other personal property) require that a financing statement or a security agreement, or both, be filed in the appropriate state office. For mortgages, the office is usually that of the county recorder of deeds. Documents related to other kinds of property are usually filed in the office of the secretary of state.

DISCHARGING A LIEN

A lien is discharged, or ended, when the debt is paid or when the lien holder agrees to waive it. In some states a lien holder must take action within a specified period of time—often six months or one year—to enforce the lien. Failure to do so may mean that the lien will be lifted automatically.

Liens may sometimes be discharged if the property they secure is destroyed. For instance, if a contractor has a mechanic's lien on an uninsured house and the house burns down, the lien may be discharged. However, if the house was insured, the insurance company may be directed to pay the lien holder.

If property you own is subject to a lien, you should always be sure to receive a release of the lien in writing from the lien holder after you have paid him. Otherwise, you may face a foreclosure action or repossession if he later claims that he was not paid, or that the payment you gave was insufficient.

A sample lien is included in the EVERYDAY LEGAL FORMS section of this book, beginning on page 552. See also DEBT; DEFICIENCY JUDGMENT; JUDGMENT.

LIFE ESTATE

A life estate gives a person the right to use and enjoy property, but only during her lifetime. A person who holds a life estate may not sell or give the property away to another or pass it on to her heirs. For example, Neil and Ruth were widowed with grown children when they met. After a few years, Neil asked Ruth to move into his house, and she agreed, selling her own home in the process.

They never married, but Neil wanted to be sure that Ruth would always be able to live in his house, even after he died. He also wanted to be sure that his children, not hers, would ultimately be the owners of the family home. To ensure that Ruth's interest would be protected, Neil left Ruth a life estate in the home when he made out his will. When Ruth dies, the property will belong to Neil's children.

If the house is mortgaged, Ruth is responsible for making the payments as long as she lives in the house. If she cannot make them, Neil's children may arrange to do so. Depending on the circumstances, Neil's children may also choose to sue Ruth if she does anything to endanger the value of the property in which they have a future interest. See also ESTATE PLANNING; WILL.

LIFE INSURANCE

Life insurance is a contract under which you pay a sum of money (usually in installments called premiums) to an insurance company. In return for your premiums, the insurance company agrees to pay a specified amount of money when you die (known as a death benefit) to whomever you name as the policy's beneficiary. Life insurance can be an important component of your estate plan, and it serves as a way to provide for your dependents in the event of your death. But buying life insurance can be a dizzying experience because many kinds of policies are offered for sale. You should evaluate several policies carefully and not allow yourself to be pressured into buying one that is not appropriate for your needs.

THE FOUR KINDS OF LIFE INSURANCE

The four basic types of life insurance are: (1) term life insurance; (2) whole life insurance; (3) universal life insurance; and (4) variable life insurance.

Term life

Term life insurance is the least expensive kind, designed to protect your family and your estate during your working years. If you outlive the term of the policy, you and your heirs receive nothing.

Term life premiums are low when you are young, but they gradually increase as you grow older. For example, a company may sell a $100,000 term life policy to a 40-year-old, nonsmoking male for an annual premium of $175. When he reaches age 60, his annual premium may be about $400. Most term insurance plans increase their rates periodically—usually each year or every five years.

One kind of term insurance, known as credit life insurance, is frequently offered to consumers when they buy an automobile or a home. If you buy a credit life insurance policy, in the event of your death, the remaining balance on your loan will automatically be paid in full. Generally, it is cheaper to buy additional term life insurance than to buy a credit life insurance policy.

Most credit life policies are what is known as decreasing term insurance; as your debt decreases, the amount of insurance coverage also decreases, although your premium payments remain the same. In the last year of a five-year car loan, for example, you may be covered for only a few hundred dollars. Because the car will be worth more than this amount, you may be better off dropping the insurance and assuming the risk yourself.

In most states lenders cannot require you to buy credit life insurance in order to be eligible for a loan, although some lenders, especially car dealers, may leave you with the opposite impression. Never allow yourself to be talked into buying a credit life policy from an auto dealer's finance office. You are certain to obtain less expensive protection elsewhere.

Whole life

Whole life insurance policies carry much higher premiums than term life policies, but the premiums remain constant for as long as you own your policy. The premiums are higher because the policy builds up a cash reserve, or cash value, against which you may be able to borrow at a relatively low interest rate, or which you may obtain in cash if you cancel your policy. In essence, your premiums become a kind of savings plan. At the same time, you are providing insurance protection for your beneficiary in the event of your death. See also CASH SURRENDER VALUE.

Whole life policies, however, do have disadvantages. The money you pay in premiums, which is held in an investment account, does not pay a high rate of interest, and a large sales commission will be part of your first year's premium. Also, you cannot adjust the amount of the premiums. You may be able to pay the high premium ($1,700 or so for $100,000 of coverage at age 40) when you buy the policy, but the premium cannot be lowered if you suffer a financial setback. If you cannot pay the premiums, you will have to downscale the policy or use the cash value for reduced coverage.

Universal life

To overcome some of the disadvantages of whole life insurance, and to give policies more flexibility, insurance companies have developed universal life insurance, which provides insurance coverage while also allowing you to build up savings. The interest on universal life policies comes from short-term financial investments, such as corporate bonds. Interest rates on such instruments vary: when interest rates go up, their cash value builds up faster, and when interest rates go down, the cash value will build more slowly. In addition, you have the flexibility of increasing or decreasing your premiums as you like, and you can make withdrawals of cash value without having to forfeit your insurance coverage.

Despite their advantages, universal life policies are much more expensive than term insurance policies because the sales commission applies both to the insurance and to the investment elements of the first year's premium.

Variable life

Variable life insurance policies require you to pay a fixed annual premium, part of which is put into investments that you select from a choice of mutual funds. The rest of the premium is used to purchase life insurance coverage. If these investments are successful, the cash value and the death benefit of your policy can grow quickly. If the fund performs poorly, the cash value and death benefit decrease; however, the death benefit cannot drop below the amount you initially purchased.

The basic form of variable life is gradually being replaced by variable universal life, which combines the flexibility of universal life with the investment options of variable life.

INSURABLE INTEREST

In order to buy any life insurance policy, you must have an "insurable interest"—that is, you are expected to benefit if the insured person lives and suffer a loss if he dies. You have an insurable interest in your own life, and you have an insurable interest in the lives of your spouse and children. Children have an insurable interest in the lives of their parents, and as a result they can take out a life insurance policy on their parents' lives.

Other relationships may lead to the creation of an insurable interest as well. The partners in a business may have an insurable interest in each other's life, and a corporation may have an insurable interest in the lives of key employees who are essential to the conduct of the corporation's business.

ELIGIBILITY FOR LIFE INSURANCE

To determine your eligibility for life insurance, your insurer will ask you questions about your age, gender, health, and occupation. If you want a large amount of coverage or you are middle-aged or older, you may be asked to take a physical examination. If you have a serious physical problem, you may have to pay a higher premium or even be denied coverage. Likewise, if you work at a hazardous occupation, or if you have hobbies that involve placing yourself in physical danger (such as skydiving or drag racing), you may be charged an additional premium or be considered ineligible for coverage.

Hiding or misstating significant facts on your application constitutes fraud and allows an insurer to deny you payment of benefits (although the insurer would be required to refund your premium payments). However, most states require an "incontestability clause." This prohibits an insurer from turning down a claim after the policy has been in effect for a specified period of time, normally two years, even if it was obtained by the policyholder's misrepresenting the facts when filling out the application.

Some policies restrict the amount of benefits you can receive during the early years of your coverage. For example, a policy issued to an older person might not pay a reduced death benefit for the first two or three years if the insured died of a disease (although it may pay a death benefit if the death was due to an accident). Moreover, if the insured commits suicide within a specified period after buying the policy (typically two years), the payment is explicitly limited to the return of previously paid premiums.

LIFE INSURANCE AND YOUR ESTATE

When you buy a life insurance policy, you should name a primary beneficiary to receive the policy's death benefit. If you name your children as beneficiaries when they are still minors, you may want to name a trustee to manage the money for them until they reach the legal age of adulthood.

It is also a good idea to name a contingent beneficiary, who will receive your death benefits in case the primary beneficiary dies before or at the same time you do. Without these provisions, the death benefit may be included in your probate estate, and thus payment may be delayed. See also PROBATE.

As the owner of a life insurance policy, you generally have the right to change your beneficiaries, increase or decrease the death benefit, or cancel the policy in order to collect any outstanding cash value. But if you live in a community-property state, your spouse has an equal interest in any life insurance you buy after your marriage, and you cannot change the beneficiary on the policy without your spouse's permission. See DIVORCE.

Life insurance benefits are not considered taxable income when they are received by the named beneficiary, but they can be subject to estate taxes.

LIFE INSURANCE AND THE LAW

The regulation of life insurance companies is left to the individual states, which set insurance rates, establish standard forms, and examine the financial stability of the companies doing business within their boundaries. If you have a question about a life insurance company's stability or a complaint about its sales practices or customer service, you should write or call the office of your state insurance commissioner.

In recent years several large life insurers have had financial trouble that prevented them from paying benefits to their policyholders. Fortunately, nearly all states have a guaranty fund that reimburses customers of failed companies.

Insurance company failures have led to closer scrutiny of insurers and their investment policies. In fact, several private analytical firms rate insurance companies for safety and make their findings available to the public. See INSURANCE.

LIMITED-LIABILITY COMPANY

When someone starts a business, one of the important decisions that he must make is to determine what type of business organization it will be. The three main choices have been, until recently, sole proprietorship, partnership, and corporation. This decision is crucial in terms of the tax consequences, the authority given to individuals associated with the company, and potential liability (that is, the financial responsibility) for each person connected with the business.

In 1977 Wyoming was the first state to enact a law authorizing a new type of business organization, the limited-liability company (LLC). By early 1993, at least 10 states had authorized the establishment of LLC's, and another 10 states were actively considering similar legislation.

There are some restrictions on the types of business that you can set up as a limited-liability company. For example, in Wyoming and Florida, a bank cannot be organized as an LLC; also, in Wyoming an insurance company cannot be an LLC.

Limited-liability companies share some of the advantages of both corporations and partnerships without the disadvantages of these two traditional forms of business.

CORPORATIONS

One of the advantages of a corporation is that stockholders and officers in the business are not personally responsible for its debts. The law recognizes the corporation as a separate legal entity and any claims that are made against the corporation can only be paid from corporate assets. Furthermore, a stockholder can sell his interest in the company without first getting the approval of other stockholders. Another major advantage is that a corporation can continue indefinitely even when investors or owners quit, die, or declare bankruptcy.

The rate at which corporations are taxed by the federal government is a major drawback to this type of business, however. The federal tax code requires a corporation to pay taxes on its income before any distribution is made to owners. These individual owners must then pay tax on the income they receive from the corporation. Thus, in essence, corporate income is taxed twice. The maximum tax rate for a corporation is higher than the rate paid by individuals. See also CORPORATION.

PARTNERSHIPS

Forming a partnership also has its benefits and disadvantages. A partnership is less complicated to set up than a corporation, and this form of business avoids the double taxation to which the higher-taxed corporations are subject.

A major risk inherent in a partnership arrangement, however, is that each partner can be held personally responsible for the debts of the partnership. Another problem is that most state partnership laws provide that when one of the partners dies, quits, or declares bankruptcy, the partnership is then dissolved, jeopardizing the continuity of the business. See also PARTNERSHIP.

FEATURES OF LLC'S

Although the LLC acts adopted by the states contain different provisions, they do have some common features. Each LLC law establishes that individual members will not be personally liable for debts or other obligations of the company. Like a corporation, an LLC is a separate legal entity that can sue and be sued, and it can own property. An LLC must file its articles of organization with the state's secretary of state and must designate a registered agent who is located within the state. At least two members must initially be involved in forming the LLC (note that a "member" may be either an individual or a corporation).

An LLC cannot be in operation more than 30 years. During that time, however, the death, withdrawal, expulsion, or bankruptcy of one member does not necessarily represent the end of the LLC. If all of the remaining members agree, the LLC can continue. And in Florida and Kansas, the business can continue without the consent of all of the remaining members. If a member wants to sell or transfer his interest in an LLC, the other members must agree. See also SMALL BUSINESS.

LINEUP

When the police either arrest or detain a suspect for a crime, they may legally compel him to appear in a lineup—a group of people who are literally lined up for a witness to view. Those who are grouped in the lineup may share physical characteristics, such as race, approximate age, height, and weight. Sometimes the police might have all participants in the lineup wear clothing that is similar to that described by the witness. Or, if the witness reports that she heard the suspect's voice, the people in the lineup may be asked to speak, perhaps saying the same words that the witness remembers hearing. If the witness identifies a suspect from a lineup, her identification may be sufficient evidence for the police to charge him.

If a suspect is not available for a lineup, the police may ask a witness to look at photographs of suspects. This is known as a photo lineup.

A lineup must be conducted in a way that does not lead a witness to select a particular member of the lineup. Suppose a woman reports that a bearded man attacked her. It would be improper for the police to put one bearded suspect in a lineup with clean-shaven men.

A criminal suspect has the right to have his lawyer present during a personal lineup.

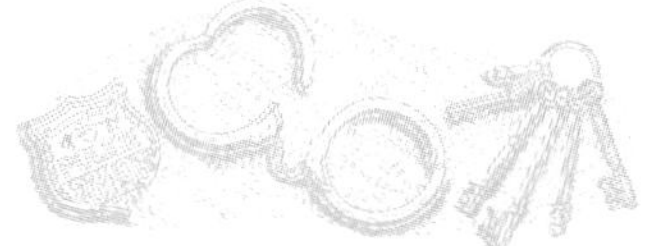

LIVING TOGETHER

Today more and more couples are choosing to live together without marrying. But living together (cohabitation) has a number of legal implications that you should consider if you are trying to decide whether to move in together.

First you should understand that living together is not the same thing as entering into a common-law marriage. Even in the states that recognize such marriages, you must have the intent to be married and hold yourselves out to the world as husband and wife in order for the marriage to be valid. See COMMON-LAW MARRIAGE.

Living together outside of marriage is not illegal, even though some states still have rarely enforced laws that prohibit sexual relations between unmarried persons. However, many communities do have zoning regulations that require the occupants of single-family homes to be "related persons." In rare instances these regulations have been used to prevent unmarried persons from living together in such communities. If successfully enforced, regulations such as these could result in an unmarried couple's being forced to move from a home they have already rented or purchased. Therefore, it is a good idea to check the zoning regulations in your community for any potential problems. See also ZONING.

CHILDREN

A child is not considered legitimate unless his parents are married or the father acknowledges paternity. The mother may have to bring a suit against the father in order to establish a child's paternity. Without this status, the child may not be covered by his father's work-related benefits, nor may he have inheritance rights to his father's estate. However, children are eligible for such rights and benefits from their mothers. See ILLEGITIMACY.

PROPERTY

Property ownership and inheritance can also be a problem for couples who live together without marrying. For example, a married person is entitled to a share in her spouse's property when he dies, no matter what is contained in his will. But there is no such protection for an unmarried partner. If your partner dies and leaves everything to his mother or his best friend, no law will allow you to overcome the provisions of the will.

Similarly, Social Security and other pension benefits will not be given to an unmarried partner, even if your partner was the primary source of income for your household.

A WRITTEN AGREEMENT

Finally, because you and your partner are not married, either of you is free to leave if you should choose to do so. If your partner owns the residence in which you live, he can require you to move out. You do not necessarily have the right to continued support or housing, although your children would be entitled to support if their paternity has been established. Although it is sometimes possible to argue in court that you and your partner had an unwritten contract for continued support, proving such a contract is often difficult because the court can rely only on one partner's word against the other. See also PALIMONY.

The most reliable way to protect yourself from such uncertainties is to create a written agreement about the terms of your cohabitation. Such agreements are generally enforceable, provided that nothing in them makes them illegal. For example, a provision that one partner will support the other in exchange for sex would be illegal, because it is against the law to exchange sex for money. Such a provision might also invalidate everything else in the agreement. For a sample cohabitation agreement, see the EVERYDAY LEGAL FORMS section, beginning on page 552.

LIVING TRUST

A living (or *inter vivos)* trust lets you transfer legal title of your property to a trustee, who manages it for you during your lifetime. When you die, he distributes your property to beneficiaries named in the trust.

By law, you can name yourself as the trustee, and name one or more cotrustees to take over if you become incompetent. A living trust may be revocable or irrevocable. Most are revocable; that is, you may be able to cancel or revise it at any time, adding or removing assets as you see fit. When you die, the assets belong to the trust, not you, and they are not subject to probate. See TRUST.

CONSIDERATIONS

A living trust is not for everyone. It is of main benefit to persons who own large estates and wish to minimize probate costs and delays and to persons who do not want the disposition of their estate to become public knowledge (as it does with a will). However, although probate is often expensive and time-consuming, especially when the estate is complicated, many states have informal, inexpensive probate procedures. Moreover, revocable living trusts do not avoid federal estate taxes or state estate and inheritance taxes. See ESTATE TAX.

Setting up a living trust is not a simple matter, and it can be very expensive. You must change the title on your bank accounts, automobiles, and deed to your home to reflect the new ownership of the property. You will have to make an inventory of all your property, complete transfer forms at banks and with your stockbroker, execute and record quitclaim deeds, and pay transfer fees or taxes. If you decide to name a financial planner or a bank or other institution as trustee, you must pay annual fees for their services.

A living trust does not eliminate the need for a will, since you may have assets that you do not wish to include in the trust or that you receive after it is established. A will may also be necessary if you want to make specific gifts to your family, your friends, or some charitable organization.

If you are considering a living trust, first talk to an attorney or estate planner to determine if it is right for you. Be wary of accepting advice from anyone who would profit from serving as your trustee, such as a bank or law firm that promotes living-trust seminars. Also ignore any promise that you can create a valid living trust on your own. State laws on living trusts vary, and a mistake in filling out the forms or a misunderstanding of the explanatory material could be costly. See also ESTATE PLANNING; WILL.

LIVING WILL

A living will is a written document that informs your family, friends, and physicians of your wishes in the event that you are incapacitated by serious illness. Generally it states that you do not want to be kept alive by artificial means or heroic measures if you are suffering from a terminal condition and your death is imminent.

In 1990 Congress passed the Patient Self-Determination Act, a law that requires hospitals, health maintenance organizations (HMO's), nursing homes, and home health-care providers to inform patients of their legal right to make decisions about accepting or rejecting treatments intended to prolong life. Patients may make their wishes regarding such treatment known through a durable power of attorney for health care, a health-care proxy (a person appointed to make decisions on the patient's behalf), or a living will. See also POWER OF ATTORNEY.

A living will instructs doctors and hospitals to withhold or withdraw life-sustaining procedures, taking only the steps necessary to provide for the patient's comfort and minimize any pain as he proceeds toward a natural death. A living will is also meant to relieve families of the burden of making a decision about continuing medical care if a patient is incompetent or otherwise unable to communicate his wishes.

Physicians and hospitals are legally bound to honor a living will. A physician who does not want to honor a valid living will must call in a doctor who will abide by it. A living will may be rendered invalid, however, if a woman is pregnant when her condition becomes terminal.

MAKING A LIVING WILL

Although an attorney can prepare a living will for you, nearly every state has its own form for creating such a document. You can buy a blank copy of your state's form in many stationery stores. Senior-citizen centers often have information about living wills, as does the organi-

REAL LIFE, REAL LAW

The Case of the Dying Daughter

In 1983, 25-year-old Nancy was badly injured when her car hit a patch of ice and skidded off the road, flinging her some 35 feet into a ditch. When she was taken to the hospital, Nancy was in a coma. She was diagnosed as being in a persistent vegetative state and was kept alive only by means of a feeding tube.

Three years went by. During that time Nancy's parents kept hoping she would recover, but they finally realized that she would not. Since Nancy did not have a living will—a document formally stating her desire not to be kept alive artificially without hope of recovery—Nancy's parents had to go to court to ask for an order terminating the feeding and allowing Nancy to die. The trial court granted their request, but it was opposed by the state attorney general, who appealed the decision to the state supreme court. The supreme court overruled the lower court on the basis of the state's "unqualified interest in preserving life at all costs." In lieu of "clear and convincing evidence" that Nancy would have wanted the feeding to stop—evidence that would have been provided by a living will—the court ordered the tube kept in place and Nancy to be kept alive.

Her parents appealed to the U.S. Supreme Court, which upheld the state supreme court's decision. It held that each state has a general interest in preserving life, and each state is free to set its own guidelines as to when this interest may be set aside.

Nancy remained in a vegetative state for the next seven years. Finally, in 1990, a new hearing was granted in the original trial court. This time, several of Nancy's friends, who had not testified at the original proceeding, came forward to say that Nancy had told them that she would not have wanted to be kept alive in her present condition. The court ruled that this met the state's standard of clear and convincing evidence, and ordered the feeding stopped. No appeal followed, and Nancy was allowed to die.

zation Concern for Dying, 250 West 57th St., New York, NY 10019. In addition, some government programs funded by the Older Americans Act will provide free or low-cost legal services to the elderly, including advice on how to make a living will. These programs are often administered by local legal-aid societies. A representative living will is found in the EVERYDAY LEGAL FORMS section of this book, which begins on page 552.

When you prepare a living will, you must follow the instructions exactly. At least one state, Mississippi, also requires you to file your living will with the state department of health. Failure to do so may render it invalid. Similarly, if you move from one state to another, you should execute a new living will in accordance with that state's requirements.

Be sure to give a copy of your living will to members of your family, to your physician, and to any hospital or health-care facility where you expect to receive treatment.

REVOKING A LIVING WILL

A living will only comes into effect when its author is diagnosed by his doctor with a terminal condition and the patient is no longer able to communicate his wishes about life-prolonging treatment (a second medical opinion may also be required, depending on the law in your state).

A person may revoke his living will at any time, regardless of his physical or mental condition. He may do so orally, by tearing the will up, by writing the words *canceled* or *void* across it, or by making some physical sign to his doctor indicating that he would like the will revoked. If circumstances permit, a formal, printed document may be used to revoke a living will.

A few states, among them California and Georgia, require that you re-execute your living will every few years to indicate that it still reflects your wishes.

LOAN SHARK

A loan shark makes loans at exceptionally high rates of interest. His clients are often persons who cannot get a loan from traditional sources such as banks, credit unions, and finance companies. Despite federal and state credit laws (which are designed to protect consumers from illegally high interest rates, threats and intimidation from collectors, and other questionable lending practices), loan sharks continue to thrive. That is because they are often the only source of loans for the poor, recent immigrants, small-business owners, and many others.

Loan sharking is a crime, and a borrower who falls prey to a loan shark need not fear that he will go to jail if he does not pay. However, it is likely he will be threatened with physical harm by the loan shark's "collector." If you are threatened by a loan shark or his collector, call the police immediately. By doing so, you have a better chance of avoiding harm, and you may help rid your community of this dangerous predator.

A TYPICAL TRANSACTION

Suppose Luis needs to borrow money to start a new business. Because of a poor credit record and no previous business experience, he has not been able to obtain the money he needs. He sees an advertisement offering loans "for good causes" and promising no credit check.

Luis answers the ad and is given an appointment to meet the lender at an address in a seedy section of the city. When Luis arrives for his appointment, the lender agrees to let him have $1,000, but Luis must pay back the lender $1,500 within one month. Luis is not asked to provide any references or credit information, and there are no papers to sign. The lender says, "It's all a matter of trust, after all." Luis gets his money, but the interest being charged is 50 percent, which translates into an annual interest rate of 600 percent!

When Luis fails to deliver the money at the end of the month, the lender sends a large man called Buddy to "remind" Luis of his obligation. As a reminder, Buddy gives Luis a bloody nose and promises that his next visit will not be so polite. If Luis is lucky, he may be able to come up with the money or obtain police protection. If he is not, he may have to suffer a further visit from Buddy.

STEPS TO TAKE

If you are looking for a loan and encounter someone who you suspect may be a loan shark because of the exorbitant interest rates he charges, be cautious, and consider dealing with the situation by taking the following steps:

1. Ask the lender if you can see his state license. (Finance companies and private lenders are licensed by each state.)

2. Ask if he will give you the names of other borrowers who have used his services.

3. Ask for a written promissory note and loan agreement that you can have your accountant or attorney review.

4. If you are still suspicious, call your local district attorney and convey your suspicions.

Lost and Found Property

Lost property can be defined as an item that the owner did not intend to give up but can no longer find, owing to neglect, carelessness, or a mistake.

If You Find Lost Property

Suppose you find a purse in the street or a shopping bag full of merchandise in a department store dressing room. You cannot legally claim the property as your own—at least not immediately. Your right to eventual ownership is subject to the owner's right to reclaim it, and you have an obligation to make an effort to find the owner.

In some instances it may be easy to locate him. A purse or wallet, for instance, usually contains the owner's name and address. A shopping bag may include a sales slip or price tag with the store's name on it. If you return merchandise to a store, the manager may be able to trace the property's rightful owner through, for example, a credit card number on the sales slip, the cashier's recollection of a familiar customer, or the customer's inquiry.

When there is no information to help identify the owner of lost property, contact the local police. Many states, including Florida, Illinois, and Michigan, have laws detailing the steps you must take to locate the property's owner, and if you do not follow them you may lose any right to claim the property as your own.

In general, you are required to turn lost property over to the police for a specified period of time, during which the owner may claim it. You may have to file an affidavit with the police describing the property and stating when and where you found it. See Affidavit.

In some states the clerk of the local court is required to publish a notice about found property in local newspapers. Depending on local law, the owner then has from 90 days to a year to reclaim it. If no owner comes forward, the finder usually becomes the owner.

Steps to Take When You Lose Something

If you have lost an item that you wish to find, here are some suggestions that may help you track it down:

1. If you lose the item while you are shopping, return to the stores you visited. Leave your name, address, telephone number, and a description of the item with the manager, security office, or cashier.

2. If you lose something during or after your stay in a hotel, notify the hotel management as soon as you miss it.

3. Call the local police and inform them of your loss. Ask about the procedure you must follow to reclaim your lost item if it is turned in.

4. If all else fails, run an ad in your local newspaper that describes the item, tells when it was lost, and (if appropriate) offers a reward.

5. Keep in mind that if a dispute over ownership should arise between you and someone who has found the item, it may be necessary for you to go to court to resolve it. See also Abandoned Property; Reward.

Lottery

State-sponsored lotteries are one of the more popular forms of legalized gambling. Not only are they popular, they raise a great deal of money for state treasuries.

The odds of winning the top prize in a lottery drawing run from about 1 in 3.5 million to 1 in 6 million, depending upon the state. But even if you do beat the odds and win the top prize, most states do not pay you all the money you have won in a lump sum. Because lottery commissions finance their prizes through the purchase of annuities, they will instead pay the jackpot over a period of 20 years or more. A few states will allow you to take the cost of the annuity in a lump sum, but the amount is much less than that of the announced jackpot.

In some cases groups of lottery ticket purchasers will pool their money in order to buy more tickets and thus increase their chances of winning. If you are involved in a lottery pool, make out an agreement in writing and have everyone who is a pool participant sign it. In general, the state considers the person who signs the lottery ticket the winner. Without such an agreement, if one of the pool participants signs the ticket and claims the money, the others may have to launch a costly lawsuit to get their winnings.

The winners of large lottery prizes are often the target of requests for money from charities, long-lost "relatives," and scam artists of every description. To avoid this kind of predicament, some lottery winners have their attorneys create a trust or a corporation to receive the prize.

Finally, remember that state lottery laws give you a limited period of time, ordinarily six months to a year, during which to claim your prize. The time limit in your state is printed on the ticket. If you fail to come forward before it expires, you will have to forfeit the money you won.

States are not alone in holding lotteries. Charities and religious organizations frequently obtain state permits to conduct raffles and other lottery games to raise funds. For information on how the law affects games of chance, see RAFFLE.

MACE

A chemical irritant that is typically packaged in a small spray canister, mace is used for self-defense. It causes temporary blindness when sprayed into a person's eyes, in some instances allowing a potential victim to disable an assailant long enough so that she can escape. Because mace causes only temporary discomfort, it is not usually classified as a dangerous or deadly weapon. Most states allow a person to carry and use mace in self-defense.

Be advised, however, that in many situations mace has been more of a hindrance than a help to the person who is wielding it. Attackers have been known to wrest a can of mace out of the hands of a defender and then use it against her. You can buy mace at drugstores and other retail outlets or through mail-order catalogs. See also SELF-DEFENSE; WEAPON.

MAGISTRATE'S COURT

If you have ever contested a traffic ticket or been involved in a small-claims suit, the proceedings may have taken place in a magistrate's court.

Every state sets up its own judicial system, and in some states, magistrate's courts handle both civil and criminal matters. However, these are courts (or a division of a court with wider authority) with "limited jurisdiction," which means they are permitted to hear only certain types of cases.

Generally, the purpose of a magistrate's court is to make decisions about cases concerning small amounts of money or property. In addition, these courts hold preliminary hearings to determine whether a crime has been committed and whether there is sufficient evidence to prosecute the case in a higher (criminal) court.

The federal court system also has magistrates, but they do not preside over their own courts. They handle certain judicial matters, such as hearing pretrial motions or trying misdemeanor cases for the federal district courts. See COURTS.

MAGNUSON-MOSS WARRANTY ACT

Today most consumer products come with warranty cards or brochures containing clearly written statements about the product and the steps you can take if it proves defective. This was not always the case. In the past, the language used in written warranties was often confusing or even misleading.

To standardize written warranties, in 1975 Congress passed the Magnuson-Moss Warranty Act, a law that established procedures allowing consumers to make claims for breach of warranty. The act is regulated and enforced by the Federal Trade Commission.

PRODUCTS COVERED BY THE ACT

The Magnuson-Moss Warranty Act defines consumer products as "tangible goods purchased for personal, family, or household use." This definition applies to a wide array of goods—clothing, appliances, motor vehicles, toys, and even mobile homes are all considered consumer products. (In contrast, insurance policies and farm machinery are not.) Products must cost more than $5 (and in some cases more than $15) before the act applies.

THE WRITTEN WARRANTY

A written warranty is a promise that the manufacturer's description of the quality of workmanship and materials used in the product is true. The Magnuson-Moss Warranty Act requires the manufacturer to repair or replace a product that is defective or that is not as described in the warranty. If a product does not come with a written (express) warranty, the consumer may still be protected under state law by an implied, or unwritten, warranty. For a full discussion, see WARRANTY AND GUARANTY.

A written warranty must be stated in simple terms and displayed in a noticeable place. Sales tags, stickers, packages, and product packaging may have the full warranty statement printed on them. If the manufacturer decides not to include the warranty with the product, it must be made available to retailers, who can then pass it on to customers when they buy the product. Retailers may also display a poster or sign in their stores that gives the full details of the warranty.

Products that are sold door to door and by mail order are also covered by the Magnuson-Moss Act. Door-to-door salespeople must either tell their customers about warranties or give them a copy. Similarly, a statement must be included in mail advertisements sent to potential buyers. Mail-order catalogs must contain a product's full warranty or a statement indicating that a copy of the warranty will be sent upon request. See also COOLING-OFF PERIOD; MAIL-ORDER SALES.

TERMS OF THE WARRANTY

According to the Magnuson-Moss Warranty Act, any written warranty for a consumer product must do the following:

◇ Include a description of the product, parts, or components covered by the warranty.

◇ State when the warranty comes into effect (usually on the date of purchase) and how long it will remain in effect.

◇ Explain to whom the warranty is extended. It may be the original buyer only or it may be anyone who owns the product during the warranty period.

◇ State what the manufacturer will do if the product is defective. For instance, he may repair or replace the product or pay for repairs done by someone else. The warranty must state any recourse available to the consumer if a disagreement arises with the manufacturer over a defective product.

Often manufacturers include "warranty" cards that you are asked to fill out and mail back to them, giving your name and address and where you bought the product. These are marketing tools and have no bearing on your warranty. Your protection when you buy a product with a warranty is the sales slip, which you should keep in your files.

FULL VERSUS LIMITED WARRANTIES

Another feature of the act is the requirement that the warrantor of a product that costs $15 or more must clearly state whether the warranty is "full" or "limited." Failure to specify means that the warranty is considered full.

With a full warranty the warrantor agrees to correct any problem without charge within a specified time, or a reasonable time if none is stated. If the warrantor has made a number of unsuccessful attempts to remedy the problem, the consumer has the option of getting a replacement without charge or recovering a full refund of his money.

A limited warranty sets certain restrictions on the manufacturer's responsibility for repairing or replacing a defective product. With certain products, for example, a limited warranty may extend only to the original purchaser.

Some products carry a full warranty on only some parts or components and a limited warranty on others.

Used-car dealers must comply with special warranty regulations. The types and duration of warranties available must be written on a window sticker on each used car. If there is no mention of any warranty, the customer must assume the car is being sold "as is." See also AUTOMOBILE PURCHASE.

RESOLVING DISPUTES

The Magnuson-Moss Act encourages prompt, informal resolution of consumer problems. If you have a complaint about a product, you should write to the manufacturer or the manufacturer's representative, whose name and address should be in the warranty. The information you need to provide and the time limit, if any, within which you must make your complaint should appear on the warranty or in other product literature.

The manufacturer must usually respond within 40 days of receiving your complaint. This response should explain what action the manufacturer proposes to take and outline your legal options if you are dissatisfied with that action.

LEGAL ACTION

If your dispute is not resolved to your satisfaction, you can file a lawsuit against the manufacturer for breach of warranty. If you win, the manufacturer may be required to compensate you for the cost of repairing or replacing the product or to refund the purchase price, as well as to pay your legal costs. See also ALTERNATIVE DISPUTE RESOLUTION; ARBITRATION.

MAIL

It is a federal crime to interfere with the delivery of mail, and violators can be punished by fines and imprisonment. Mailboxes, particularly those in apartment buildings, can be targets for thieves looking for checks, cash, or goods.

As with any crime, prevention is better than prosecution. One way to avoid having your checks stolen is to ask any individual, company, or government agency from whom you regularly receive checks to deposit them directly into your bank, savings, or credit union account. The Social Security Administration, for example, urges all recipients to enroll in a such a program.

Another precaution is never to send cash through the mail. Recently, the U.S. Postal Service arrested a mail handler in Denver and accused him of rifling through mail for greeting cards in order to steal any cash that they contained.

If your mail has been stolen, report the theft to your local postmaster right away so that Postal Service inspectors can investigate. Although their resources are limited, the inspectors have succeeded in apprehending a significant number of mail thieves. See also OBSCENITY; PORNOGRAPHY; SCAMS AND SWINDLES.

MAIL-ORDER SALES

Selling merchandise through the mail is big business. In 1990 more than 63 billion pieces of third-class mail were sent to U.S. households, including catalogs, sweepstakes offers, and advertising circulars for countless products. That figure constitutes nearly 40 percent of all the mail that the U.S. Postal Service delivered that year.

Buying merchandise by mail is convenient, but there are pitfalls. Packages can be lost, damaged, or stolen, and sometimes the goods you receive are not what you expected. Major companies with national reputations are less likely to be a source of problems, and they may be quicker to resolve them than smaller companies. If you are tempted to buy something from a company of unknown reputation, make your first purchase a small one and charge it to a credit card. If you encounter a problem with delivery of the goods, you can often ask the credit card issuer to intercede on your behalf. See DAMAGED MERCHANDISE.

Be wary of illustrations and product descriptions in mail-order brochures and catalogs. Some companies are deceptive or downright fraudulent in describing their merchandise. For example, one company advertised electronic pianos for sale at "the incredibly low price of

ABC's

Of Removing Your Name From Mailing Lists

If you are annoyed by the amount of junk mail you receive from mail-order companies, advertisers, and other sources, try taking the following steps to make room in your mailbox:

- ❑ To get your name off several lists at once, write to the Direct Marketing Association (DMA), a professional organization of direct-mail marketers. Indicate the companies from which you do not wish to receive direct mail; they may be DMA members. Or ask the DMA to remove your name from its complete list. The address is: Direct Marketing Association, Mail Preference Service, P.O. Box 9008, Farmingdale, NY 11735.
- ❑ Write directly to companies from whom you receive the most so-called junk mail and request that your name be removed from their lists.
- ❑ To protect yourself further from unwanted mail, send a letter to Equifax Option, P.O. Box 740123, Atlanta, GA 30374-0123. This division of the giant credit-reporting agency will forward your request to every mail-order company that subscribes to its services.
- ❑ To stop mail that consists of erotic or sexually explicit material, go to your local post office. There you can obtain a form that orders the makers of such materials to stop sending them to you. Companies that disregard this order may be subject to penalties and even legal action by the U.S. Postal Service.

$10." Thousands of consumers ordered the pianos, only to find that the instruments were actually battery-operated toys. Worse yet, the toys were available at novelty shops for $2.

Mail-order companies are required by federal law to fill your order within 30 days of the date you placed it, unless a longer period is indicated in an advertisement or catalog. If a delay is expected, the company must notify you, giving you the option to cancel your order and receive a full refund.

When it comes to mail orders, remember this: Any offer that seems too good to be true probably is. See also CONSUMER PROTECTION; FALSE ADVERTISING; SCAMS AND SWINDLES.

MANSLAUGHTER

A category of homicide (the killing of one person by another), manslaughter can take one of two forms. Involuntary manslaughter is the unintentional killing of another person resulting from the killer's gross negligence. A drunk driver who runs his car into a tree and kills his passenger is guilty of involuntary manslaughter.

Voluntary manslaughter is committed when a person is provoked to the degree that he acts on impulse and kills his provoker. Suppose you find a burglar in your home and see that while opening drawers, he has knocked over an antique vase that was a precious family heirloom. Enraged by his act, you attack him, and he is killed in the ensuing struggle. This is voluntary manslaughter.

Whether involuntary or voluntary, manslaughter is always a felony and is punishable by imprisonment. See also HOMICIDE; MURDER.

MARITAL PROPERTY

Marital property is defined as anything acquired during a couple's marriage, such as automobiles, boats, real estate, bank accounts, certificates of deposit, or stocks and bonds.

OWNERSHIP

There are two ways a couple can jointly own property they acquire during the course of their marriage: through tenancy by the entirety or through joint tenancy.

Tenancy by the entirety means that the marital property is owned in common by both spouses, and neither can sell it without the other's permission. When one spouse dies, the surviving spouse automatically owns the property regardless of the stipulations of a will or of any claims by the heirs of the deceased.

Joint tenancy also offers this right of survivorship, with the difference that either spouse can dispose of the property without the other's permission. Both forms of ownership prevent the property from going through probate court. See also JOINT TENANCY; PROBATE; TENANCY BY THE ENTIRETY.

MARITAL PROPERTY AND DIVORCE

During a divorce, the court often has to determine how a couple's marital property is to be divided. In some states, called community-property states, the court has the power to dispose of all of the couple's property acquired during the marriage, no matter who acquired it. In other states the court will consider only property that was acquired jointly during the marriage. Property owned before the marriage or property that was inherited by a spouse during the marriage is excluded in all states. See COMMUNITY PROPERTY; DIVORCE; EQUITABLE DISTRIBUTION.

MARRIAGE

The institution of marriage grants a couple special legal and tax status, confers certain obligations, and affects the ownership of the couple's property and inheritance rights.

The law recognizes two different types of marriage: ceremonial and common-law. A ceremonial marriage is one in which a couple's exchange of vows is presided over by someone the state has authorized to solemnize their marriage, such as a member of the clergy, a justice of the peace, or a judge. In contrast, a common-law marriage is one in which a couple privately agree to live as husband and wife and present themselves to the public as married. Only 14 states and the District of Columbia recognize common-law marriages. See COMMON-LAW MARRIAGE.

Although few people can be prevented from marrying, there are some exceptions. Persons of the same sex are not recognized as legally married, even if an authorized person performs the ceremony. If you are already married, you will not be granted a marriage license. And persons who are mentally incompetent may be prevented from marrying on the grounds that they are not capable of understanding the nature of the institution. See also BIGAMY; INCOMPETENCY.

You cannot marry a close relative, including the members of your immediate family, your grandparents, or your aunt or uncle; in some states you may also be prohibited from marrying your in-laws, your cousins, or a stepparent or stepchild. Your county clerk can tell you about the limitations on whom you can marry in your state.

In most states the legal age at which you can marry is 18, although some states allow minors as young as 15 to marry.

PROCEDURE

You do not have to be a resident of a state in order to marry there, but you do need to obtain a license from the place where you wish to marry. To get the license, you must usually produce identification, proof of the dissolution of any previous marriages, and in some states you must take a blood test for venereal disease or rubella or undergo a physical examination. You will have to fill out an application and pay a fee, and there may be a waiting period after you have filed the application before the license is granted.

If everything is in order, a clerk will grant you a marriage license that is valid for a limited period of time. If you do not marry within that time, you will have to reapply for a license before you can marry.

After you have been married by an authorized person, the license must be filled out and signed by each spouse, the person who performed the ceremony, and usually two witnesses. The marriage should be recorded with the county clerk. Unless you get an annulment or a divorce, your marriage will remain legally binding. See also ANNULMENT; DIVORCE.

FINANCIAL CONSIDERATIONS

Usually, the property that a couple brings into a marriage belongs to each of them individually. However, property that is acquired during a marriage generally belongs to both spouses. This joint ownership can become an issue during divorce proceedings, when marital property must be divided according to the laws of that state. Some states have community-property laws, which stipulate that spouses have equal ownership of any assets acquired during their marriage. Other states follow the equitable-distribution rule, which considers the contributions and needs of each spouse. See also MARITAL PROPERTY; PRENUPTIAL AGREEMENT.

Spouses are required to provide for each other the "necessaries of life," such as food, clothing, and shelter. Similarly, they are expected to provide necessaries for any minor children of their union, both during their marriage and after its termination. See also CHILD SUPPORT; NECESSARIES.

One spouse is not always held responsible for debts incurred by the other spouse, however. For example, if your spouse obtains a credit card without your signature and then charges $5,000 on it, which he cannot repay, you are not liable for his debt. Or if you can prove that you signed a joint federal tax return without knowing that it misrepresented your tax obligation, you may not be held responsible for the penalty owed to the IRS.

Usually, spouses inherit each other's property. Even if one spouse tries to disinherit the other, the state may order at least some of the inheritance to be distributed to the surviving spouse. See WILL.

MARTIAL LAW

In times of dire emergency, such as civil unrest or natural disaster, Congress and the state legislatures are empowered to order martial law, or government by the military. Under martial law, the military commander appointed by the civilian government has absolute authority to suspend civil law and use whatever force is necessary to restore order and preserve the peace. For example, in 1968 limited martial law was declared in Detroit after the assassination of Rev. Martin Luther King, Jr.

Once the emergency has passed, the commander must cede his authority to the civilian government as soon as possible. A civilian whose assets or property were used by the military during martial law can file a claim for compensation.

MATERIAL WITNESS

A material witness is someone whose testimony is essential to the success of a legal action. Typically, a material witness is ordered by the court to appear at a trial and testify against the defendant. If his testimony would implicate him in criminal activities, he may be granted immunity from prosecution. Should his testimony place him in danger, he may have to enter a witness protection program. See IMMUNITY; WITNESS PROTECTION PROGRAM.

MECHANIC'S LIEN

A mechanic's lien is a legal claim against property made by someone who has worked to build, repair, or improve it. Suppose you enter into a contract with Hugh to have your family room renovated and new windows installed. After the work is done, you pay Hugh, but he fails to pay his supplier, Leo, who provided the windows. You may then find that a mechanic's lien has been placed against your home for the sum of money that Hugh owes Leo for the windows.

Mechanic's liens are authorized by all states. They permit anyone who provides materials or labor for the construction, repair, or improvement of real estate to make a claim against the property owner for the money due. See also LIEN.

Under some state laws, you will be responsible for paying subcontractors even though you paid the general contractor in full. If you must pay a subcontractor for work for which you have already paid the general contractor, you will have to sue the general contractor for reimbursement.

Other states recognize that it is unfair to hold a property owner responsible for the actions of a contractor. In these states a homeowner can have a mechanic's lien lifted if he can show that the general contractor was paid according to the terms of the original contract. A canceled check, a credit card receipt, or a bill marked "Paid in full" can all be considered evidence that the bill was paid.

In most states a supplier who files a mechanic's lien against your property must take action to enforce the lien by filing a lawsuit against you within a specified time, such as six months or one year. If he does

REAL LIFE, REAL LAW

The Case of the Crooked Contractor

When Steve and Kathy decided to add a large family room to their summer home at the lake, they hired a general contractor to handle the project. They paid the contractor half his fee in advance. He hired several subcontractors and began work on the new addition. Steve and Kathy remained in the city, but they kept track of the work's progress by telephone calls to the general contractor.

One day they were unable to reach him. Further investigation revealed that he had left town for parts unknown, leaving his work incomplete. Worse yet, he had not paid the subcontractors for their work or materials. To recoup their losses, the subcontractors filed liens against Steve and Kathy's vacation home. One of the subcontractors, trying to gain an advantage over the others, filed a lien against Steve and Kathy's city home and threatened to start a foreclosure action unless his bill was paid first.

Steve and Kathy went to court to challenge the lien on their city home. The court stated that a mechanic's lien can be placed only against the property that was worked on, and not against other real estate. Because the subcontractor had not worked on the city home, the court ordered that the lien be removed. The mechanic's liens against the lake home, however, remained in effect, and Steve and Kathy had to borrow money against their city home to pay the liens.

not do so, his claim will expire.

A mechanic's lien can affect your credit rating and prevent you from selling your property. In an extreme case it can result in the forced sale of your property in order to satisfy the debt. See also FORECLOSURE.

STEPS TO TAKE

To avoid having a mechanic's lien placed on your property, take the following steps:

1. Deal only with general contractors whose reputations are established.

2. Require the contractor to obtain a surety bond—a guaranty that a third party will pay for any obligations the contractor refuses to honor.

3. Ask the contractor to give you a list of his suppliers and subcontractors.

4. Ask the contractor to give you copies of any receipts that prove he has paid all suppliers and subcontractors.

5. Obtain a copy of a statement from each subcontractor showing that he has been paid in full for his work.

6. Have the contractor give you a notarized affidavit of completion, acknowledging that all bills have been paid.

7. Do not make final payment to the general contractor until you have proof that subcontractors have been paid.

For a sample of a mechanic's lien, see EVERYDAY LEGAL FORMS, beginning on page 552. See also CONTRACTOR; HOME IMPROVEMENT AND REPAIR.

MEDIATION

It is not always necessary to turn to the legal system to resolve a dispute—even one that concerns a legal matter. Mediation is one method used as an alternative to a trial or other court proceeding, or as a way to speed up resolution of issues connected with a court proceeding. Mediation can be useful in resolving personal-injury lawsuits, business disagreements, neighborhood and community conflicts, and divorce cases, particularly those involving children.

For instance, although a couple may have agreed to dissolve their marriage, they may not agree about child custody or support and visitation rights. Rather than bringing these issues to family court, the couple may turn to mediation. Some states now require child custody and visitation disputes to be submitted to mediation before they can be brought to court. According to experts, mediation brings about agreement in approximately four out of every five cases.

HOW MEDIATION WORKS

In mediation, an impartial person is called upon to help the parties to a dispute reach an agreement. Like arbitration, another method of alternative dispute resolution, mediation offers privacy and informality. Moreover, although each side may retain a lawyer, especially in divorce cases, mediation may be less costly than going to court. In addition, mediation often reduces the tensions and acrimony that can prolong court proceedings. See also ALTERNATIVE DISPUTE RESOLUTION; ARBITRATION; CONCILIATION.

ROLE OF THE MEDIATOR

The parties to a dispute choose the mediator, whose role varies depending on the case. Some mediators prefer to be actively involved and may suggest ways to resolve the matter—for instance, by proposing terms for a settlement or trying to persuade one side to make concessions. Other mediators take a less active role, trying instead to create an atmosphere that fosters communication and allows the parties to reach their own agreement.

Regardless of the mediator's role, the ultimate decision rests with the people involved in the dispute. Unlike an arbitrator, a mediator has no authority to make the participants reach an agreement or accept her solution. Each party may withdraw from mediation at any time. If the parties resolve their differences, they may present their agreement to the court.

STEPS TO TAKE TO FIND A MEDIATOR

Whether it involves a dispute among neighbors or a battle over child custody, mediation can avoid costly legal battles. Here are some tips on finding a qualified mediator in your area:

1. Ask your county clerk to give you the names of qualified mediators in your area. You can also get referrals from the Academy of Family Mediators, P.O. Box 10501, Eugene, OR 97440. This professional organization can give you names of specialized mediators near you. In addition, you can find mediators listed in the Yellow Pages of most telephone books.

2. Interview several mediators before deciding on one. Be sure that she has experience in mediating the type of dispute you are involved in and that her personality is compatible with your own.

3. Check the mediator's references. If she declines to provide them, stating her clients' confidentiality as a reason, you can suggest she ask a few of her former clients to waive their confidentiality. Let her know that you are not concerned with the details of the cases, but rather with her skills.

4. Although lawyers and former judges often serve as mediators, you should think twice about using them. There is no requirement that mediators have legal training, and sometimes a lawyer or a judge may be a bad choice, especially if he is used to lawsuits and other adversarial proceedings.

MEDICAID

Medicaid is a government program that helps people with low incomes and limited assets to cover their health-care costs. Medicaid is funded jointly by federal and state governments and is usually administered by a local department of social services, health, or welfare. The federal government has issued broad guidelines for Medicaid, but within them, each state formulates its own regulations on eligibility, coverage, and benefits.

ELIGIBILITY

When you apply for Medicaid, an eligibility worker will take up to 45 days to determine whether you are eligible to receive benefits. He will make that decision based on your income and assets. Your eligibility will be reviewed periodically, and your coverage can be dropped if you cease to meet state requirements.

In general, Medicaid classifies income as money that you receive from any source, including Social Security, the interest on savings or investments, and money from rental property, wages, pensions, and annuities.

Medicaid considers as assets any money that you have in checking and savings accounts, savings bonds, the cash surrender value of life insurance policies, stocks, bonds, and IRA's, as well as some real estate and motor vehicles. If you are married and live with your spouse, his or her assets and, usually, income are also considered to be your assets. (Special rules will apply, however, if one spouse is in a nursing facility.)

Income and asset limits vary greatly from state to state. But in general, to be eligible for Medicaid, a single person's monthly income can be no more than $400 to $500, and a married couple's can be no

MEDICAID ALLOWANCES

Nursing home residents whose fees are paid by Medicaid may keep only a portion of their monthly income for their personal needs. Although these amounts are revised periodically, the most recent ones for each state are shown below.

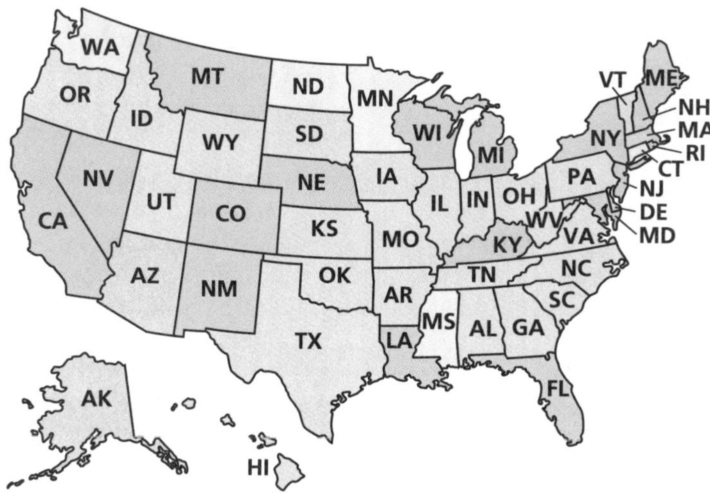

Residents are allowed to keep $30 or less per month for personal needs.

Residents are allowed to keep from $30 to $40 per month for personal needs.

Residents are allowed to keep from $40 to $50 per month for personal needs.

Residents are allowed to keep from $60 to $75 per month for personal needs.

more than $600 to $700. Depending on the state, an applicant may be eligible for Medicaid even if his assets include a home, a car valued at up to $4,500, a wedding ring, household goods, a life insurance policy with a cash surrender value of no more than $1,500, and additional cash and assets of up to $2,000 ($3,000 for a married couple). An applicant for Medicaid is also permitted to have set aside limited funds for his own burial expenses and a cemetery plot.

In many states a person can qualify for Medicaid if he is eligible for certain government income-assistance programs, such as Supplemental Security Income or Aid to Families With Dependent Children. Women who are pregnant and children up to age one who do not qualify for an income-assistance program but whose income is no more than one-third higher than the state poverty level may also qualify for Medicaid. See AID TO FAMILIES WITH DEPENDENT CHILDREN; SUPPLEMENTAL SECURITY INCOME.

Some states will also make Medicaid coverage available to people whom they consider to be "medically needy." These are people whose incomes and assets are above state eligibility levels but are being reduced, or spent down, by their large medical expenses. Some states, however, do not have this spend-down provision. Known as income-cap states, they deny Medicaid coverage if an applicant's income is even $1 over the limit.

MEDICAID PROVIDERS

Medicaid recipients have the right to choose their health-care providers, including doctors, hospitals, clinics, and laboratories. However, the providers must participate in the Medicaid program. Although participation is voluntary, a health-care professional who wishes to participate must be certified by Medicaid, and he must accept Medicaid's reimbursement as full payment. Providers must comply with Medicaid regulations—if a doctor fails to offer an appropriate standard of care, for instance, or files a fraudulent claim, his medical license can be revoked and he may face criminal charges.

MEDICAID PAYMENTS

Health-care providers bill their local Medicaid office for services they have rendered to Medicaid patients. The patients themselves generally do not pay any fees. Some states, however, may require those persons who have been designated as "medically needy" to pay monthly premiums and co-payments. Some states also require a copayment from Medicare recipients for particular medical services.

SERVICES COVERED

All state Medicaid programs are required to cover mandatory services, such as physicians' care, necessary ambulance service, laboratory tests, X-rays, home health care, outpatient hospital care, and inpatient nursing home or hospital care.

In some states Medicaid will also cover so-called optional services, such as care provided by dentists, optometrists, chiropractors, and podiatrists; eyeglasses, prescription drugs, speech and physical therapy, and rehabilitation; diagnostic testing and preventive screening; and inpatient psychiatric care for patients 65 and over.

Sometimes Medicaid will cover amounts that have not been covered by Medicare or private insurance, including copayments and deductibles.

In the future, Medicaid services may be handled by "managed care" programs, such as health maintenance organizations (HM0's). See HEALTH MAINTENANCE ORGANIZATION.

NURSING HOME CARE

Medicaid will pay for long-term hospitalization and nursing home costs, as long as the care is medically necessary and the patient is eligible for Medicaid. For those who already receive Medicaid benefits, entering a nursing home poses few financial problems.

For persons who are not already eligible for Medicaid, however, careful financial planning in advance of the need for long-term care can ensure that your income and assets do not disqualify you from Medicaid coverage. Otherwise, you could spend your life savings on nursing home care before Medicaid began to pay the bills.

Suppose doctors have determined that Uncle Jack, who is 76 and in failing health, needs to be placed in a nursing home. Uncle Jack's only income is a monthly Social Security check of $400, which falls within his state's income limits for Medicaid. Jack also has assets: a house, a car, and $50,000 in a savings account. The Medicaid rules in his state permit Uncle Jack to own his home and a car. These are considered "exempt assets." However, the money in his savings account exceeds his state's $2,000 limit on assets.

To qualify for Medicaid, Jack will first have to spend $48,000 of his assets ($50,000 in savings minus $2,000 allowable savings) on nursing home costs. Then his Social Security check will go toward the cost of his nursing home, with Medicaid paying the remainder of his monthly nursing home fees. Jack will be able to keep only between $30 to $75 out of each monthly Social Security check for personal use.

In this example Jack is single. If he were married, special regulations would apply. Jack's spouse would be allowed to retain all of her own income. However, if more than half of the couple's income was in Jack's name, his wife would be allowed to keep only a portion of their income—up to a maximum of $1,700 per month. She would also be permitted to keep any of their assets up to $70,000 (excluding the home).

In the hope of preserving as many of their assets as possible, many elderly people transfer their money or property to relatives or place their money in a special trust fund. However, you must transfer your assets 30 months before applying for Medicaid benefits.

There are also a number of short-term strategies you can use if a nursing home stay is imminent. For example, you can buy a home, a car, or an annuity for your spouse and avoid a Medicaid penalty, provided that she does not transfer these assets for 30 months. Because these strategies and Medicaid rules are complex, consult a specialist, such as an elder-law attorney or accountant who knows Medicaid eligibility requirements, before you begin to transfer or divest yourself of your assets.

Many people feel uneasy about moving money and property around to increase their Medicaid eligibility. Others fear that they may be affected by subsequent changes in the law and that it is not worthwhile. But keep in mind that it is certainly legal to take advantage of these strategies.

DENIAL OF ELIGIBILITY

If a person receiving or applying for Medicaid is denied benefits, he has the right to appeal the decision. Appeals procedures are governed by state regulations, which vary widely. If you appeal, your Medicaid coverage generally continues during the appeals process, but if the final decision goes against you, any benefits you received must be repaid.

A decision will be made within 90 days of your appeal. If you are not satisfied, you can request that it be reviewed by a court. The notice denying benefits will indicate how long you have to request a review, which will be handled by either a federal or a state court, depending on whether the denial of benefits was based on federal or state Medicaid regulations.

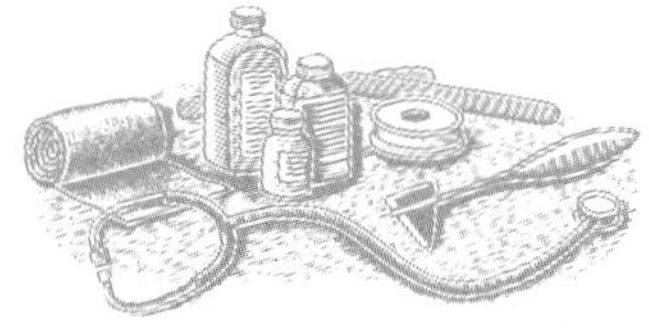

MEDICAL MALPRACTICE

When you become ill or are injured, the physician who treats you must make a diagnosis and administer appropriate care. But because medical science is not precise, and every situation is different, doctors can never be sure that the care they give will be successful or that unanticipated side effects or other complications will not develop. The law therefore recognizes that physicians cannot always be held responsible if a treatment is unsuccessful. However, if a patient is injured because a physician or other health-care professional does not meet minimum standards of care, the patient or her family can file a lawsuit against the practitioner for medical malpractice. Because of the costs involved, these suits are often settled out of court, but they sometimes proceed to trial.

DEFINING MALPRACTICE

Because physicians cannot guarantee the results of medical treatment, a patient's malpractice claim is not valid just because his treatment was not successful. Clear instances of malpractice include cutting off the oxygen supply during surgery, misdiagnosing an injury because routine tests and procedures were not followed, or prescribing an illegal drug or one not approved for the patient's condition. Also, if a physician does not obtain a patient's informed consent before proceeding with treatment, he may be guilty of malpractice, even if the patient's condition does improve. See INFORMED CONSENT.

NEGLIGENCE

Most medical malpractice cases are based on the concept of negligence—that is, the patient was harmed because the physician failed to meet the required standards of skill and care. A patient must prove four things in order to recover damages: (1) that the physician owed him a duty, (2) that the physician did not fulfill that duty, (3) that the patient has suffered an injury, and (4) that there was a causal connection between the physician's breach of duty and the patient's injury.

Duty owed

To prove that a physician owed him a duty, the patient simply has to demonstrate that a typical physician-patient relationship existed. Once this has been established, a doctor has an ethical and legal duty to give his patient medical treatment that meets an acceptable standard of care. The physician's agreement to treat the patient would serve as proof of this relationship.

Breach of duty

The second element of a malpractice case requires the patient to prove that the medical treatment he received from his doctor fell below the standard of care he could reasonably expect. For years the courts have struggled to define this concept of "standard of care," but generally a medical professional's conduct is judged in comparison with that of similarly trained professionals in the United States.

If the physician in question is a specialist, the standard of care is higher than that required of a general practitioner and is evaluated in comparison with other physicians practicing the same specialty. Likewise, if the defendant in the case is a hospital, its administrative procedures and standard of care will be compared to those of other hospitals.

Injury and cause

Establishing the third element —that the patient has been injured—may not be difficult if the results of the alleged malpractice are readily apparent. For example, if a patient is rendered blind, disfigured, or paralyzed, the injury is obvious. More difficult to prove is the fourth element, that the injury is directly related to the physician's failure to provide appropriate treatment. Suppose that Theresa claims she developed

REAL LIFE, REAL LAW

The Case of the Plastic Surgeon's Promise

Alice was a professional entertainer who decided to have plastic surgery on her nose. She consulted a plastic surgeon, who told her that the surgery would reduce the prominence of her nose and make it more harmonious with her other features.

Three operations later, Alice's appearance was changed—but not for the better. Her nose, which had been straight, was now bulbous, flattened, and actually broadened. Alice sued her plastic surgeon for malpractice and breach of contract. She told the court that the surgeon's promise to improve her appearance and her reliance on it constituted a legally enforceable contract, and her disfigurement was a breach of that contract.

In response to the charge, the surgeon argued that he had followed accepted medical practices and therefore could not be found guilty. He also argued that his promise to improve Alice's appearance was not legally enforceable, but merely the kind of assurance that a doctor would ordinarily give a patient.

Although the court did not find the surgeon guilty of malpractice, it did find him guilty of breach of contract. It held that the doctor's promises went beyond a statement of opinion. Alice was awarded damages to compensate her for the cost of the surgery, the worsening of her condition, and for her pain and mental suffering.

an infection because her surgeon left a sponge in her stomach after an operation. Theresa must prove specifically that the presence of the sponge, and not some other cause, was the source of her infection. Without expert testimony or other medical evidence that proves this causal connection, Theresa will not be able to win her case. See EXPERT WITNESS.

FILING A LAWSUIT

If you think that you are the victim of medical malpractice, first consult an attorney who specializes in medical malpractice cases. He can tell you if he thinks you have a potential claim. He will also consult medical experts to help determine the merits of your case. When you meet with the attorney, take along medical records, bills, any notes you have made, and any other documents that relate to your care or injury.

Lawyers often accept medical malpractice cases on contingency—that is, they receive a percentage of any money awarded to the plaintiff. See also CONTINGENT FEE.

If the attorney agrees to file a lawsuit against your physician, both he and the physician's attorney will conduct discovery procedures to learn as much as possible about the case. You may be questioned extensively by the physician's lawyer about the circumstances surrounding the alleged malpractice and other aspects of your health and personal life. A pretrial hearing may be held in which both sides present their cases before a judge. This is somewhat like a rehearsal for trial and is used to encourage both parties to reach an out-of-court settlement. If you cannot reach an agreement, your case will proceed to trial. See also DISCOVERY; LAWSUIT.

TIME TO FILE

Each state has a law, known as the statute of limitations, that designates the time period in which you should file a medical malpractice claim. The purpose of the statute is to ensure that a claim is made while information relevant to the case is still available. The deadline may be from one to seven years from the time the treatment was given or from the time the patient knew (or should have known) of the alleged malpractice. In the case of a minor, the statute of limitations may not begin until the minor turns 18.

DAMAGES

Damages in a medical malpractice suit may be awarded for medical expenses, pain and suffering, lost wages, and other costs related to the malpractice. Additional, or "punitive," damages may be awarded if the physician was grossly negligent or incompetent. See DAMAGES.

In recent years the awards given in medical malpractice

cases have averaged in the hundreds of thousands of dollars. This rise has created a corresponding increase in the cost of liability insurance for physicians and other health-care providers, and in turn to the rising cost of medical care. As a result, some states now limit the amount of money a patient can recover in a malpractice case. California, for example, has a $250,000 limit on damages (money awards), such as lost wages, missed business opportunities, and pain and suffering. Indiana limits a plaintiff's total recovery to $750,000, and a doctor's personal liability to $100,000, if he agrees to come under the provisions of the state's Medical Malpractice Act and contribute to the state compensation fund. The state will then pay any amount exceeding $100,000 that is awarded against the doctor.

CHECKING A MALPRACTICE RECORD

You can try to find out whether or not a practitioner has been sued for medical malpractice by asking your state medical licensing board or by checking at the county courthouse for any lawsuits filed against the physician. However, not all licensing boards will release this information to the public, and your county courthouse will not list actions that were filed in another district.

If you do discover that your doctor or other health-care provider has a record of malpractice cases, ask him about them. Many doctors have had at least one lawsuit filed against them (particularly high-risk practitioners, such as obstetricians). However, a repeated history of such lawsuits could indicate that the doctor has in fact been negligent.

ALTERNATIVES TO TRIAL

Because of the rising cost of litigation and the time it takes to conduct a trial, some states require the parties to a medical malpractice lawsuit to explore other means of resolving the case. Indiana, Montana, Pennsylvania, and Virginia, for example, require that medical malpractice cases appear before a neutral pretrial panel composed of members of the medical and legal professions, the general public, and representatives of consumer-rights or other groups.

Pretrial panels interview the parties involved and review medical records and other relevant evidence. Sometimes they give conclusions about the merits of a case, in the hope that such an evaluation will persuade the parties to reach an agreement without going to trial. If the case goes to trial, the conclusions of such panels are generally admissible as evidence, but this evidence will not be the deciding factor in the case.

MEDICAL RECORDS

Jonathan was hospitalized with a bout of pneumonia and a bronchial infection. Although the doctors have answered all of his questions about the diagnosis and prognosis, Jonathan would like to review his medical chart himself. Is he within his legal rights?

RIGHT TO ACCESS

In at least 20 states you have the right to see your medical records—whether they are kept by your personal physician or by a health-care facility. But check your state's medical records statute, available at your local law library, for any special conditions. For example, a few states allow you access to your hospital records only after you have been discharged from the hospital.

If you live in a state that does not allow you access to your records, your doctor, dentist, or hospital staff can refuse to show them to you.

RIGHT TO PRIVACY

Medical records are considered private information, and both federal and state laws forbid their unauthorized release. Even parents can be denied access to their minor children's medical records. A person whose records have been inappropriately released may file a lawsuit against the parties that released them, seeking monetary compensation for breach of contract or for invasion of privacy. See PATIENTS' RIGHTS.

However, not every unauthorized release is an invasion of privacy. In some cases the law requires medical personnel to report certain medical information to the appropriate authorities. For example, a gunshot wound or signs of suspected child abuse must be reported to the police. And because public health officials need to monitor the spread and prevalence of communicable diseases—such as measles, AIDS, or hepatitis—health-care workers must report such cases to state health agencies. However, in many states this information need not identify the infected individuals. Some states do require identification so that they can notify others who may be infected to seek medical attention. See also AIDS.

EMPLOYEE FILES

Medical information is also kept in an employee's personnel file and other records. Affirmative action plans, for example, may contain facts about the mental and physical condition of disabled workers. Although such information should be accessible to the company's medical staff, employers must make sure that no one else sees it.

Some companies offer employee assistance programs to provide counseling for employees' personal problems. These programs are usually administered by an independent consultant, and the records are kept confidential. However, nonidentifying information may be given to the employer for statistical purposes only.

As with hospital medical records, in most states an employee does not have a right to see his personnel file, including the medical information it contains. However, the Occupational Safety and Health Administration, a division of the U.S. Department of Labor, has issued regulations that employers in certain industries must give their employees the results of annual tests for exposure to toxic substances.

WAIVING PRIVACY

In some instances, individuals may authorize disclosure of their medical records. Health insurance companies, for example, usually require you to obtain a statement from a doctor before they will reimburse you for a medical bill. If you sue someone for personal injury, you will be required to disclose as much of your medical history as is pertinent to the case. And if you join the military or participate in certain sports, you may be required to disclose your medical records as a condition of acceptance.

MEDICARE

Medicare is a two-part health insurance program run by the U.S. Department of Health and Human Services but administered by the Social Security Administration. It is designed to help pay for the health-care costs of people aged 65 and older, regardless of their income or personal assets. Certain people under the age of 65 are also eligible for Medicare coverage.

Part A of Medicare covers hospitalization and is funded by Social Security taxes. Both employers and employees pay a tax of about 1½ percent of the employee's gross income to finance Part A of Medicare, while self-employed workers pay about 3 percent of their gross income. No premiums are due from persons who receive Part A of Medicare.

Outpatient medical coverage, or Part B of Medicare, is financed by premiums paid by the insured and tax money collected by the federal government. Both Part A and Part B have various deductibles and coinsurance, which reduce the program's outlay.

ELIGIBILITY AND ENROLLMENT

Certain groups of people automatically qualify for Part A of Medicare. Although they do not have to pay any premiums, they must pay a yearly deductible. These groups include: (1) people who are 65 or older and who are entitled to Social Security benefits (because they have paid into Social Security for the required amount of time), (2) individuals under the age of 65 who have qualified for Social Security disability benefits for 24 months, and (3) persons suffering from kidney failure who need kidney dialysis or a kidney transplant.

You must enroll for Medicare at your local Social Security office, either at the same time that you enroll for your Social Security retirement benefits or three months before your 65th birthday. (It takes about three months to process an application.) Because 65 is the age at which you become eligible for Medicare, even if you retire at age 62 and receive Social Security benefits, you cannot be enrolled in Medicare until you are 65. You do not have to be retired to receive Medicare, but if you do not apply for it with the Social Security Administration, you will not automatically receive it.

If you are automatically eligible for Part A coverage, you will

CHECKLIST

Buying a Medigap Policy

Before you buy private insurance to supplement your Medicare coverage, keep the following tips in mind:

❑ **SHOP CAREFULLY.**
Talk to several insurers to compare the costs and benefits of their policies.

❑ **LOOK FOR EXCLUSIONS.**
Most private insurance companies will not pay for existing conditions or illnesses, or they may impose a waiting period before treatment is covered.

❑ **ASK ABOUT RENEWAL.**
Policies that renew automatically offer the most protection.

❑ **CAN YOU SWITCH POLICIES?**
Owing to waiting periods or exclusions for preexisting conditions, your coverage may be limited if you decide to switch to another policy at a later date.

❑ **BEWARE OF CLAIMS OF GOVERNMENT SPONSORSHIP.**
The federal government never sponsors or sells policies that supplement Medicare, and an agent or broker who claims that his company's policy is endorsed by the U.S. government is mistaken or lying. If you think an agent has deliberately misrepresented a policy to you, inform your state's insurance commissioner.

❑ **BUY ONLY WHAT YOU NEED.**
Buying more than one policy will simply duplicate your coverage. It is illegal for an insurance company to sell you a Medigap policy that duplicates any coverage for which you are eligible through Medicare, Medicaid, or other private insurance.

also be eligible for Part B. To participate in Part B, you must pay a premium, which is deducted from your monthly Social Security check. You may decline Part B by notifying the Social Security office that you want only hospitalization coverage (Part A). If you subsequently change your mind, you can apply for Part B during any enrollment period (the first three months of each year), but you will be penalized. For every year that you wait to enroll after you become 65, your premium will be increased by 10 percent.

If you are over 65 and have been a citizen or legal resident of the United States for at least five years, but are not eligible for Social Security, you can still obtain Medicare insurance. You can get Part A coverage by paying premiums, which in 1993 were $221 per month. When you voluntarily enroll in Part A, you are enrolled in Part B, which also has a deductible and monthly premiums. (Although you can only get Part A coverage in combination with Part B, you can enroll for Part B only.) In 1993 the monthly premium for Part B was $36.60, and the monthly premium for both Part A and Part B coverage was $257.60, amounting to $3,091.20 per year.

HOSPITALIZATION: PART A COVERAGE

Part A covers services for patients who are hospitalized, persons who require post-hospital inpatient care in an approved skilled-nursing facility (SNF), and those who receive post-hospital home health care or hospice care (for the terminally ill). While you are hospitalized, Medicare covers the cost of a semiprivate room, meals, X-rays and laboratory tests, intensive or coronary care, blood transfusions, and regular nursing services. But you must pay a deductible for each hospital "benefit period." In 1993 the deductible was $676. A benefit period runs from the time you enter the hospital until 60 consecutive days after you are discharged from the hospital or an SNF. If you remain in the hospital for longer than 60 days, you must start paying part of the daily cost. In 1993 this amount came to $169 per day for days 61 through 90 and $338 per day for days 91 through 150. After 150 days, you are responsible for the entire daily charge.

Medicare will pay for all services for the first 20 days of a patient's stay in an approved SNF; after that, the patient must contribute to the cost (in 1993, $84.50 per day). After 100 days in an SNF, the patient is required to assume the entire cost through private income or insurance, or Medicaid. See MEDICAID.

Medicare does not pay for a stay in a custodial nursing home—that is, one whose patients require assistance with daily tasks (such as feeding themselves or dressing) but not nursing care. For a patient with a terminal illness, Medicare will pay the full cost for up to 210 days of hospice care given at an approved facility or at the patient's home.

MEDICAL SERVICES: PART B COVERAGE

The second part of the Medicare program, Part B, helps pay for doctors' services and outpatient hospital care as well as other services not covered under Part A. These include oral surgery, ambulance transportation, home dialysis equipment, mammography, artificial limbs and eyes, radiation treatment, and outpatient psychiatric services.

As with Part A, the patient is asked to help pay for some of the cost of his treatment. There is a yearly deductible ($100 in 1993), after which Medicare will pay 80 percent of any approved charge for a covered service—that is, the amount Medicare considers reasonable for that service. If the doctor's fee is over Medicare's limit, the patient is responsible for the amount that Medicare does not pay. Some doctors accept "assignments"—they charge only the amount that Medicare has deemed reasonable for a particular procedure or service. They may also bill Medicare directly, rather than making the patient responsible for the payment and for seeking reimbursement from Medicare.

EXCLUSIONS

Even though the Medicare program has broad coverage, many services and supplies are not included. Routine checkups, dental care, nonprescription drugs, hearing aids, eyeglasses, and cosmetic surgery are not covered.

Medicare covers medical services, including emergencies, only in the United States. If you travel abroad, you should purchase additional insurance. An exception can be made if you are in the United States and require the services of a doctor or hospital but the closest facility is in Canada or Mexico. Your local Medicare office can tell you more about services that are not covered.

FILING CLAIMS

The Social Security Administration has designated private insurance companies to process Medicare claims. The name of the insurance carrier can be found on the claim form or by calling your local Social Security office. As with any insurance, you may have to pay for services directly and then seek reimbursement from Medicare, or the hospital or doctor will bill Medicare directly and you will then have to pay the deductible and copayment amounts (the 20 percent that Medicare does not pay).

You must file your Medicare claims no later than December 31 of the year after the year in which you received treatment.

APPEALING

You can appeal a decision that was made concerning your Medicare coverage or a claim that has been rejected by contacting the Social Security office. If this fails, you can request that your claim be reconsidered. Social Security administrators will then review your case file. Depending on the service or the amount in question, you can also ask for a hearing before the Appeals Council of the Social Security Administration or before an administrative law judge or a federal district court judge.

ALTERNATIVES TO MEDICARE

You can, of course, decline Medicare coverage. If you have private health insurance, compare its cost and coverage to that of Medicare. Federal law requires an employer with a staff of 20 or more to offer his employees over age 65 and their spouses the same group hospitalization coverage he gives to any younger employees. When comparing policy costs, note that all Medicare premiums and copayments are adjusted annually and that you will have to pay a 10 percent penalty for every year after age 65 that you do not enroll.

Medigap insurance

Even if you have Medicare insurance, you can purchase private health insurance for items and services Medicare does not include, as well as for Medicare deductibles and coinsurance. Such policies are known as Medicare supplemental insurance, or simply Medigap. To prevent fraud and duplication, federal law limits Medigap policies to 10 standard plans, which are variously available in different states. Your state department of aging can give you specific information about Medigap policies in your state. See also NURSING HOME; PREFERRED PROVIDER ORGANIZATION.

QUALIFIED MEDICARE BENEFICIARY PROGRAM

Because Medigap insurance is too costly for many low-income individuals, Congress authorized the Qualified Medicare Beneficiary (QMB) program. To qualify for this program, a person must both be eligible for Medicare and have an annual income that falls below the national poverty level. (In Alaska and Hawaii the income guidelines are somewhat higher.) The beneficiary's assets, such as stocks, bonds, and bank accounts, cannot exceed $4,000 for a single person or $6,000 if he is married. If you qualify for the program, your state will pay the deductibles and coinsurance for both Part A and Part B of Medicare.

The QMB program is administered by the state agencies that provide Medicaid assistance, and specific eligibility rules vary from state to state, as they do for Medicaid. If you think you are eligible, apply to the state Medicaid office. See also MEDICAID.

MINIMUM-WAGE LAWS

The minimum wage that can be paid for most jobs in the United States (both full time and part time) is regulated by federal and state law. The federal Fair Labor Standards Act (FLSA) establishes the minimum wage for companies that engage in interstate commerce. Companies that do business in one state need to comply only with that state's minimum-wage laws, which may differ from those of the federal government. In April 1991 the federal minimum wage, which is adjusted periodically, was raised to $4.25 per hour.

COVERED EMPLOYEES

The FLSA's minimum-wage requirement applies to workers who are paid hourly, weekly, monthly, or annually, or who do piecework. Suppose Mary is offered a job as a receptionist at the rate of $100 per week for a 40-hour week. Her prospective employer would be offering less than the minimum wage, because Mary would be making only $2.50 per hour ($100 divided by 40). If Mary took a job as a seamstress and was paid $5 for each blouse that she produced, she would be making more than the minimum wage if she made a blouse every hour, but not if it took her two hours to make a blouse.

If employees receive tips as part of their total compensation, no more than 50 percent of their tips can be counted as part of the minimum wage.

Exemptions

Certain employers are exempt from meeting minimum-wage requirements. Among them are operators of training and rehabilitation programs for the handicapped, employers of students in such jobs as newspaper delivery, and school-related training programs. See also CHILD EMPLOYMENT.

Some state minimum-wage laws do not cover part-time workers. If you have any questions about minimum-wage laws in your state, contact your state department of labor.

VIOLATIONS

If an employer pays you less than the mandated minimum wage, you can file a complaint to make him comply with the law. You should refer any complaints about federal violations to the Wage and Hour Division in your regional office of the U.S. Department of Labor, and report violations of state minimum-wage laws to your state's department of labor.

If you discover that you have been working for less than the minimum wage for some time, you can sue your employer for back wages and possibly additional money damages. However, you must file your claim within two years of the time that the violation took place. You should consult an attorney who has experience in labor law. If you win, your employer may also have to reimburse you for court costs and legal fees.

MIRANDA WARNINGS

"You have the right to remain silent. Should you give up the right to remain silent, anything you say may be used against you in a court of law." Anyone who has ever watched a police show on television knows those words; but why do the police always recite them when they make an arrest?

A LANDMARK CASE

These words are part of the Miranda warnings, which are named for *Miranda* v. *Arizona*, a 1966 landmark case in which the U.S. Supreme Court overturned the conviction of the accused, Ernesto Miranda, on the grounds that he had confessed without any knowledge of his constitutional rights. The court decision established specific guidelines for the arrest and interrogation of suspects. Today, if the police do not follow these guidelines, anything said by an accused person in response to police questioning will become inadmissible as evidence in court.

YOUR RIGHT AGAINST SELF-INCRIMINATION

The Supreme Court based its Miranda decision on the Fifth Amendment to the Constitution. The amendment states that no person in the United States (even someone who is not a citizen) can be compelled to incriminate himself. This means that no one who has been arrested or is otherwise in police custody can be forced to make a statement, and no defendant in a criminal case can be forced to testify.

Many people either are not aware of the protections of the Fifth Amendment or do not readily think of them when questioned by law enforcement officers. Thus, under the Miranda guidelines, when the police arrest or detain someone they suspect of committing a crime, they must inform him of his right to remain silent—that is, he may refuse to answer questions. He must also be told that if he does choose to speak to the police, his statements may be used against him in court. The police must inform the suspect of his right to have an attorney present during questioning and tell him he will be provided with an attorney if he cannot afford to hire one.

EXCEPTIONS

Law enforcement officers are not obliged to give Miranda warnings when interviewing someone who is not a suspect. But if his voluntary statements during the interview lead the police to focus on him as a suspect, they must then give him the warnings.

If a suspect speaks to the police without first being questioned, his statement can be used against him even if he was not given Miranda warnings. Suppose Anthony is in a traffic accident. When the police arrive, Anthony blurts out the information that he ran through a red light before he collided with the other automobile. The police can later repeat Anthony's incriminating statement in court.

Although evidence obtained in violation of the Miranda rules cannot be admitted at a trial, failure to give Miranda warnings does not automatically invalidate an arrest, nor does it mean that a defendant will be acquitted. If there is enough other independently obtained evidence to support a conviction, the police's failure to give Miranda warnings is irrelevant. See also ARREST; CRIMINAL LAW; CRIMINAL PROCEDURE; FIFTH AMENDMENT.

MISSING CHILDREN

Established by Congress in 1984, the National Center for Missing and Exploited Children has compiled the following distressing statistics: from 1984 to 1989, almost 24,000 children were reported missing from their homes. Of this number, about 10,000 ran away, 13,000 were abducted by relatives, and 500 were victims of abduction by strangers.

INTERFERENCE WITH CHILD CUSTODY

The most typical child abduction is undertaken by parents during a custody battle. There have also been cases of grandparents disappearing with their grandchildren. A noncustodial parent who fails to return his children after they visit him, or a custodial parent who vanishes with his children and does not leave word of their whereabouts, is guilty of parental kidnapping, which in some states is called interference with custody rights.

Parental kidnapping is a crime, and it should be reported to the police immediately. The abducting parent, when found, may be charged with kidnapping under the Parental Kidnapping Act. For more information on what to do if a parent abducts a child, see "Steps to Take," on page 360.

RUNAWAY CHILDREN

In contrast to the official figures, some studies have estimated that from 1 million to 1.5 million children run away from home each year. Because a runaway is simply defined as a minor child who is away from his home for at least one night without parental permission, it is possible that many cases of runaway children are not reported. Fortunately, the majority of runaways—nearly 75 percent—return home within a week. Those who do not return, however, can face danger and great hardship.

LEGAL STATUS

When a runaway child is located, she may be referred to the juvenile court system. Being a runaway is a "status" offense—a condition rather than a delinquent act. Status offenders may be taken under the jurisdiction of juvenile court and placed in a temporary shelter, foster care, a group home, or even a detention center.

Most runaways leave home because of abuse, poor family communication, or a family crisis. Before returning a child to such a home, social workers with the juvenile court will try to help family members deal with the problems that caused the child to run away. They will interview parents and siblings and may recommend family counseling to help get the family back together. However, if they suspect that a child has been abused at home, social workers are obliged to make other living arrangements for her until the matter is resolved.

ABDUCTIONS BY STRANGERS

The abduction of a child by a stranger, although rare, strikes fear in parents everywhere. To help find a kidnapped child, parents must cooperate with the police, although they may also act on their own to distribute information through the media or hire private investigators. For a discussion of kidnapping laws, see KIDNAPPING.

Occasionally a newborn is abducted from the hospital. If the kidnapping is due to poor hospital security, the parents can file a lawsuit against the hospital and may recover money damages for their loss and mental anguish. Similarly, if a child is abducted from a school yard or day-care center, the parents may be able to sue the institution for failing to take steps to safeguard their child.

STEPS TO TAKE

If your child runs away or is abducted, you should immediately do the following:

1. Report your child's disappearance to the police. Give them a photo and detailed description of the child and ask that it be entered in the FBI's National Crime Information Center computer. After the police have compiled their report, ask them to issue a statewide missing-person bulletin right away. (If your child has run away, some police departments might wait, since they know that most runaways come home in a day or two.)

2. Describe the abductor, if you can, and state where he might take your child.

3. If your child has not returned or been found after 48 hours, double-check with the police. If they have not yet notified the FBI, call the nearest FBI office yourself.

4. If your child has been abducted by a custodial parent, have an attorney start court proceedings immediately to transfer custody to you.

5. If you are sure that the abducting parent has fled the state, ask a district attorney to apply to the local U.S. attorney for an "unlawful flight to avoid prosecution" warrant. Once this is done, the FBI can actively search for your child.

6. If your child is found with his parent in another state, send a certified copy of your custody decree to the family court in the town or county where they reside. Ask the local police to enforce the decree and return your child.

7. Get the names and addresses of local support groups for parents of missing children by calling the National Center for Missing and Exploited Children: (800) 843-5678.

8. If your child is returned from an abducting parent, consult with a lawyer about obtaining a restraining order limiting future contact between the child and his other parent. A family court may suspend or terminate visitation, or allow it only under supervision. See TEMPORARY RESTRAINING ORDER.

MISTRIAL

A trial that ends before a verdict has been returned by the jury or a judge is called a mistrial. The decision to declare a mistrial is made by the presiding judge. She may sometimes do so even before all the evidence has been presented. In other cases, the jury hears all the evidence but fails to reach a decision.

When a judge declares a mistrial, the party who brought the case (the plaintiff in a civil case or the prosecutor in a criminal case) must decide whether to take the case to court again. A mistrial has no legal effect on the parties; it is as if no trial had ever taken place.

HUNG JURIES

In most criminal cases jurors must reach a unanimous decision. Jurors in a civil case may also be required to reach a verdict that is unanimous or nearly so—for example, 10 or 11 out of 12 votes. If all the members of a jury cannot agree, they will notify the presiding judge. The judge may then remind the jury of the importance of reaching a verdict, due to the time, effort, and expense involved in trying the case. If the jurors nevertheless remain hopelessly deadlocked, the judge will be forced to declare a mistrial and the jury will be discharged.

OTHER GROUNDS

A judge may also declare a mistrial if there is a serious error in the trial proceedings that cannot be corrected. For example, in many courts the jury is not permitted to know whether the damages in a civil case will be covered by the parties' insurance. If this type of information is revealed to the jury and the judge feels that they could not be expected to disregard it, she may declare a mistrial.

Other grounds that may lead attorneys to ask for a mistrial include biased behavior on the part of the judge, jury tampering, the sudden death or severe illness of a juror or one of the lawyers, or a natural calamity, such as a flood, that interrupts the trial. See also JURY DUTY; JURY TAMPERING.

MITIGATING CIRCUMSTANCES

Events or facts that can reduce the level of blame for a person's act, but that are not enough to excuse it, are known as mitigating circumstances.

Suppose Jeff went to his dentist to have a tooth extracted. The procedure went awry and Jeff ended up in the hospital for six weeks, fighting a life-threatening infection. When he recovered, he sued the dentist and filed a claim against him with the state board of dentistry. Although Jeff's dentist did not dispute that the procedure had been mishandled, he claimed that personal problems at the time of the procedure—including his mother's death and the serious illness of his daughter—had impaired his professional skills. He provided evidence that he had undergone psychological counseling to help him overcome these problems and pointed out that Jeff's complaint was the only one brought against him in more than 20 years of practice.

By introducing this information to the court, Jeff's dentist was able to reduce the severity of the punishment that the board of dentistry imposed upon him, and instead of being suspended from practice, he was merely reprimanded.

Mitigating circumstances are not enough to exonerate a defendant, but they may convince a judge to reduce his punishment to smaller money damages, a reduced fine, or a shorter prison sentence. See also HEAT OF PASSION.

MOBILE HOME

With the cost of a traditionally constructed house averaging about $100,000, some Americans choose instead to buy less-expensive mobile homes (sometimes referred to as manufactured homes). Although mobile homes have come a long way since the original 14-foot-wide trailer models, there are still some disadvantages to buying one.

Unlike a traditional house, a mobile home generally depreciates in value over time. Because mobile homes tend to suffer significant damage from fire and high winds, insurance rates are generally quite high. Interest rates on loans to buy mobile homes are usually higher too—in fact, loans for mobile homes generally resemble automobile loans rather than standard mortgages.

BUYING YOUR HOME

If you decide to buy a previously owned mobile home, be sure to have it inspected first, just as you would if you were buying any other house. See HOME BUYING AND SELLING.

If you purchase a new mobile home, you should get the following documents:

◇ A certificate from the manufacturer declaring that the mobile home conforms to the National Mobile Home Construction and Safety Standards Act of 1974.

◇ The manufacturer's written warranty on the home.

◇ A bill of sale and copies of any manufacturers' warranties for plumbing, heating, and air-conditioning fixtures.

◇ A title (which is much like the title to an automobile).

◇ Copies of all documents regarding your loan.

FINDING A HOMESITE

When you buy a mobile home, you will probably put it either on your own lot or on a lot in a mobile-home community. Before installing the home on a lot of your own, check local zoning laws; some residential areas prohibit mobile homes. Your installation costs will include fees for constructing a pad or foundation, having utilities installed, and putting in a septic tank or a connection to community sewer lines.

If you decide upon a mobile-home community, you will pay a monthly fee for the lot and perhaps for maintaining common areas, charges for connecting utilities, and the cost of installing a skirt around the base of your home. You may also be subject to rules limiting or prohibiting your ability to own pets, hold garage sales, or have visitors for more than a few days unless you pay a fee.

MONEY MARKET ACCOUNT

A money market account is a type of mutual fund that invests in highly liquid assets (those easy to turn into cash), such as short-term corporate bonds, bank certificates of deposit, and U.S. Treasury bills and notes. You are allowed to write checks on a money market account, although some funds require that checks be above a certain dollar amount (such as $500) or that you write no more than a specified number of checks per month.

At one time, only stockbrokers and investment companies offered these accounts, which attracted customers because they paid higher interest rates than bank savings accounts and because checks could be written on them. But today most banks and savings and loan institutions offer them too. (See the box on page 363.) Because of their minimum-balance requirements and limitations on withdrawals, bank money market accounts usually pay higher interest rates than do savings accounts in the same institution.

Although there is no legal minimum deposit, banks and brokerage houses normally require a relatively high initial deposit, usually $1,000 or more. Then, if you keep a minimum balance, you will probably not have to pay a monthly fee or service charge. Many banks now also give their money market account customers an automated teller machine (ATM) card, which makes deposits and withdrawals convenient.

Money market accounts offered by banks and savings and loan associations are usually covered by Federal Deposit Insurance Corporation (FDIC) insurance. Those offered by brokerage firms are not FDIC-insured but offer a higher interest rate than FDIC-insured accounts do. See also BANK ACCOUNT; CHECK; MUTUAL FUND.

MORTGAGE

A mortgage is a loan agreement by which your home serves as the security for the money you borrowed to buy it. Because very few families have the financial resources to pay cash for a home, nearly everyone who wishes to buy a house is obliged to seek a mortgage, and the sale of a home is usually dependent on the buyer's receiving this financing.

A home buyer can obtain a mortgage from a friend, a family member, or even the seller of the house, but most often the lender is a bank or savings and loan institution. Because there are a bewildering number of home-financing options available, you should always take the time to shop around. All mortgages, however, work in essentially the same way.

In his mortgage contract, a mortgage holder agrees to make regular payments for a specified time. For the first several years, these payments cover interest and a very small amount of principal; only gradually does the amount of princi-

ABC's

Of Choosing a Money Market Account

If you think you would like to open a money market account, ask these questions of a few financial institutions—perhaps a bank, a savings and loan association, and a mutual fund company:

- ❏ What kinds of investments does the institution currently make?
- ❏ What minimum deposit must I make to open this account?
- ❏ What minimum balance must I maintain to avoid service charges, and what monthly fees do you charge if my balance falls below this amount?
- ❏ Are there any limits on the size and number of additional deposits I can make?
- ❏ After my balance rises over a certain amount, will I earn a higher rate of return?
- ❏ How are interest rates set, and how often do they change?
- ❏ How is interest compounded and paid? (The best money market funds compound interest daily and pay it monthly.)
- ❏ How many checks may I write every month, and are there restrictions on the amounts of each check?
- ❏ Will I receive an ATM card for depositing or withdrawing funds in my account?
- ❏ Is this account insured by the FDIC? If not, do you have other insurance?

pal repaid begin to increase. A mortgage holder may, of course, make additional payments to reduce the principal and shorten the life of a mortgage. (If you decide to do this, make sure that your lender permits prepayments without charging a penalty fee.)

If a homeowner cannot meet his mortgage payments, the lender can take possession of the property by foreclosing on it. See also FORECLOSURE; HOME BUYING AND SELLING.

FIXED-RATE MORTGAGES

The traditional fixed-rate mortgage is still a popular option for many home buyers. Although the initial interest rate for this kind of mortgage is usually higher than for other kinds, you have the security of knowing that it will not fluctuate over the life of the loan. Fixed-rate loans are offered for a variety of time periods, most commonly 15- and 30-year terms. The shorter the term, the larger the monthly payments, but you will save many thousands of dollars in interest charges with a shorter term—and you will own your home sooner.

A fixed-rate loan is a good choice if you are planning to stay in your home for more than a few years, because it provides you with stable payments and protection against the possibility of rising interest rates. But interest rates can also decline, as they did in the early 1990's. If they fall far enough, you may wish to refinance your mortgage.

ADJUSTABLE-RATE AND CONVERTIBLE MORTGAGES

If you are planning to buy a home and stay in it for only a few years, if you expect that your income will increase in the future, or if you think that interest rates will remain low, you may want an adjustable-rate mortgage, or ARM. The interest rate on an ARM rises and falls, depending on general market conditions and inflation. An ARM usually begins with a lower interest rate than a fixed-rate loan, and the interest can go up by no more than a stated amount (6 or 8 percent) above the initial rate. For example, an ARM that starts out at 7 percent may be "capped" at 14 percent—that is, you will never pay a higher rate of interest than 14 percent. Your payments can be adjusted to reflect interest-rate changes every year (although usually the interest rate can go up no more than a specified amount and usually no more than once a year). Some lenders offer an initial fixed rate for a period of three years.

Be sure to ask your lender to explain in detail how new payments are calculated. If you suspect that your lender may have miscalculated your payments, ask your lawyer or real estate broker for the name of a company that will double-check the lender's calculations for a small fee. If you have an ARM and interest rates go up significantly, try to refinance your loan and obtain a long-term fixed-rate mortgage.

Similarly, many lenders now offer convertible mortgages, which combine the benefits of an ARM (a low initial rate for the buyer and adjustability for the lender) with the option to convert to a fixed-rate loan in the future. The chief benefit of a convertible loan is that the conversion usually costs a flat fee of several hundred dollars and involves very little paperwork. By contrast, refinancing expenses may come to 4 to 6 percent of the borrowed amount, and the volume of paperwork involved is typically the same as it was for the original financing.

ABC's

Of Applying for a Mortgage

Applying for a home mortgage requires more than simply filling out a form and writing out a check for a credit report. To complete a mortgage application, you will need the following items, many of which the lender will help you obtain.

- ❑ A current appraisal of the property, made by a certified appraiser.
- ❑ A credit report from a reputable credit-reporting firm.
- ❑ Verification of bank accounts and investments.
- ❑ Verification of employment and your annual salary .
- ❑ If you are self-employed: signed financial statements, statements of income and expenses, and federal tax returns for the past two years.
- ❑ Approval of any government or private mortgage insurer.
- ❑ The sales contract.
- ❑ The preliminary title report or title insurance commitment.
- ❑ If you are buying a condominium or a cooperative apartment, copies of any financial statements of the condo or co-op association.

BALLOON MORTGAGES

Another option is the balloon mortgage, which allows the borrower to make equal monthly payments of principal and interest for a set period, usually from three to five years. At the end of this period, however, the outstanding balance of the loan is due in a lump sum, and the borrower may have to refinance her mortgage if she does not have enough cash on hand. Balloon mortgages are most often used by people who expect a future increase in income. See Balloon Loan.

SHARED-EQUITY MORTGAGES

If your income is too low for you to make the monthly payments necessary for the home you want, you might consider a shared-equity, or shared-appreciation, mortgage. With this type of mortgage, the lender or an independent investor pays a percentage of your down payment and monthly mortgage payment, in return for an equal percentage of any increase in the value of the property. If the equity sharer makes half of these payments, for example, he is entitled to half of the profits when you sell the property.

Although such a loan can help you obtain a more expensive house than you might otherwise be able to afford, you should consider carefully before deciding upon it. In some shared-equity mortgages, the equity sharer has the right to ask for payment of his portion of the equity after a given period of time, even if you do not want to sell the house. You may have to refinance the loan in order to pay off his share, and if you are not able to do so, you may be forced to sell.

BUYDOWNS

A popular mortgage option, especially for buyers of newly constructed homes, is the so-called buydown. With a buydown, you receive a fixed-rate loan, but the first and second years of the loan carry an interest rate one or two percentage points lower than the institution's current fixed rate, while from the third year onward you are charged a slightly higher rate. Home builders often make arrangements with lenders to provide this kind of loan as an incentive to buyers. The lower interest rate (and consequent lower monthly payments) during the initial years makes it easier for a home buyer to qualify for a loan. A buydown can be appropriate if you expect your income to grow significantly within a few years.

BIWEEKLY MORTGAGES

With a biweekly mortgage, you finance your home over a 15- or 30-year period, but instead of making 12 payments each year, you make 26 payments, one every two weeks. These payments are equal to one-half a standard monthly payment; so you actually make an extra monthly payment each year.

A biweekly mortgage can save you thousands of dollars in interest charges over the life of your mortgage, because by making the extra payments you can sharply reduce the length of the loan. In the case of a 30-year loan, the length would be reduced by nearly a third. Depending on the interest rate on your loan, you could save up to $80,000 or more in interest on a $100,000 mortgage.

A biweekly mortgage is attractive, but you can accomplish the same purpose with a traditional monthly mortgage by making an extra payment each year or by making an additional payment of principal to reduce the length of your loan. Either way, you are not locked into a series of higher payments at times when you might not be able to afford them.

Beware of companies that offer to help you shorten your mortgage if you make biweekly payments to them, which they then forward to your lender. Most of these companies capitalize on consumer confusion by making the process seem more complicated than it is, and they almost always charge a fee for doing something that you can easily do yourself.

THE PROBLEM OF POINTS

No matter what kind of mortgage you get, when you apply for the loan you will probably be told that you will have to pay "points" to obtain financing. A point is 1 percent of the total amount you want to borrow. The number of points you have to pay varies with the loan and will be included in the costs you pay at closing. See CLOSING, REAL ESTATE.

If you are buying from an eager seller, he may be willing to pay some of the points the lender requires. You can also try to negotiate with the lender, particularly if you are a long-time depositor at the institution and have taken out other mortgages or loans there. But often when points are reduced, the interest rate is raised. Like most other mortgage interest charges, points are tax deductible, although under certain circumstances, they must be deducted in equal amounts over the life of the loan, rather than all at once.

DOWN PAYMENTS

If you purchase a home with money obtained from a conventional mortgage, you will most likely have to make a down payment of at least 10 to 20 percent of the home's total price. For many families, that kind of money is hard to come by.

Fortunately, there are several federal programs that can be of help. You may be able to insure your mortgage through the Federal Housing Administration, or if you served in the armed forces, through the Department of Veterans Affairs. With such insurance, a lender may accept a down payment as low as 5 percent or even less.

Some state and local governments have programs that provide loan insurance to first-time home buyers. However, the terms and availability of these programs may change. Ask a savings and loan institution or a mortgage company for details about local programs.

Many younger home buyers must rely on the generosity of their parents, who may give them some or all of the down payment on a home. However, if you opt to do this, the mortgage lender will probably ask your parents to sign an affidavit stating that the amount they gave you is in fact a gift and not a loan. (If it were a loan, it would affect the total debt you were carrying, and you might therefore not qualify for the mortgage.) Under federal law, each of your parents can give you, your spouse, and each of your children up to $10,000 apiece in a single year without incurring any gift-tax liability.

OTHER COSTS

In addition to your down payment, you must also be prepared to pay a fair number of costs throughout the mortgage-approval process and at the time the purchase of the house is completed. These are called transaction, settlement, and closing costs, and they can add up to thousands of dollars. They include fees for the mortgage application, credit report, property appraisal, inspections, title search, and a survey of the house and land. There are also attorneys' fees and state transfer taxes. When you apply for a mortgage, federal law requires your lender to provide you with a copy of a booklet entitled *Settlement Costs*, published by the Department of Housing and Urban Development. If the lender does not give it to you at the time you make your loan application, he must send it to you within three business days. You can also obtain the booklet from the Federal Information Center. See FEDERAL INFORMATION CENTER.

QUALIFYING FOR A MORTGAGE

In order for you to qualify for a mortgage, your monthly payments—which include the mortgage payment, property taxes, and home insurance—cannot exceed 25 to 28 percent of your gross monthly income. The mortgage lender will also examine your credit history for any record of missed payments or excessive debt.

A mortgage application may be rejected because the lender thinks your property is worth less than the price you are paying or because you are asking to borrow more than you can repay. If your mortgage application has been turned down, you have the right to know the reason. If an inaccurate credit report or other mistake is to blame, you can correct it and then ask the lender to reconsider your application. If your credit rating is the reason, you can look for a lender who will assume the risk by charging you a higher interest rate.

Some banks apply different lending standards in order to deny mortgages to applicants who live in areas that are considered bad economic risks, such as poor urban neighborhoods. This practice is known as redlining, and it is illegal.

REVERSE MORTGAGE

A reverse mortgage is a loan that is intended to help homeowners, particularly the elderly, remain in their homes even as their incomes drop.

For example, although Ruby owns her home outright, she has only a small monthly income from investments made by her late husband. Concerned that Ruby does not have an adequate income to cover her living expenses, and knowing that she does not want to move, her neighbor Josephine suggests that she obtain a reverse mortgage from a local bank. With this type of mortgage, Ruby will receive either monthly payments or a line of credit to draw against as needed, and she never has to repay the loan. When she moves or dies, the mortgage is repaid through the sale of the home. It is also possible for either Ruby or her relatives to repay the bank and reclaim the home.

The Federal Housing Administration (FHA) allows lenders to make this kind of mortgage loan under a special program. Plan participants cannot be forced out of their homes, even if the amount they owe on the mortgage eventually exceeds the value of the property that secures it.

The Federal National Mortgage Corporation (Fannie Mae) has encouraged lenders to issue these reverse mortgages by making a commitment to purchase at least 25,000 of them through November 1995. A borrower in the Fannie Mae program can receive her payments in a number of ways:

◇ She can receive monthly payments of a fixed sum for up to 10 years.

◇ She can use the mortgage to establish a line of credit.

◇ She can combine a line of credit with the fixed-payment option. For more information about this reverse mortgage program, contact your bank, a savings and loan association, or the FHA office in your area.

STEPS TO TAKE

Applying for a mortgage can be stressful and time-consuming. Here are ways to make the process a little easier:

1. Plan ahead. Before you apply for your mortgage, obtain a copy of your credit report and check it for any errors or information that could affect your ability to get a mortgage. For more information, see CREDIT BUREAU AND CREDIT RATING.

2. Before you begin your house hunting, check with several lenders to learn how much they would be willing to lend you. Many mortgage companies and savings and loan associations will "prequalify" borrowers. When you know how much you can borrow, you are in a better position to negotiate. You will also avoid the disappointment of finding a home that you like but later learn you cannot afford to buy.

3. Once you have made an application, keep tabs on its progress. In most instances you can expect several weeks to elapse before you find out whether your loan has been approved. Meanwhile, do not call the mortgage lender or broker every day to find out what is happening.

4. Do not try to hide credit problems or make false statements about your income or work record. It is a crime to attempt to obtain a mortgage under false pretenses.

For more information, see HOME EQUITY LOAN; REAL ESTATE AGENT AND BROKER.

MORTGAGE INSURANCE

Some lenders require borrowers to obtain mortgage insurance, particularly if they are making a down payment of less than 20 percent. This insurance is in essence a life insurance policy that is equal to the amount of the mortgage. If the borrower dies, the proceeds of the policy go to the lender to pay the remainder of the mortgage. Mortgage insurance is similar to a term life insurance policy in that no cash value builds up. But although the face value of an ordinary term policy stays the same, the face value of an ordinary mortgage insurance policy declines as the total amount of the mortgage declines, even though the premiums do not.

If your lender requires you to get mortgage insurance, you will have to pay an initial premium at the closing. The size of the premium will depend on the size of the mortgage, but it could range from .3 to 1 percent of the mortgage amount.

Even if the lender does not require you to get mortgage insurance, you should have some form of life insurance that will pay off your mortgage in the event of your death. In families where both spouses work and help to pay for the mortgage, each should have insurance so that the survivors do not face the loss of their home.

MOTOR VEHICLE BUREAU

Your state's motor vehicle bureau, or department of motor vehicles, is the agency authorized by the state legislature to enforce regulations regarding the operation of private motorized vehicles on state roadways. Generally, states require the following documents if you own or operate a motor vehicle:

◇ *A valid driver's license.* To obtain a driver's license, you must be the legally required age, meet minimum vision standards, pass a written examination about the rules of the road, and pass a test of driving skills. See also DRIVER'S LICENSE.

◇ *A valid certificate of registration for the vehicle you own.* To obtain this certificate, you must pay a fee, which often varies according to the value of the vehicle being registered. You may also have to prove that the vehicle has passed safety and pollution inspections.

◇ *Proof of liability insurance for your vehicle.* When you register your car, most states require you to sign an affidavit stating that you have at least the minimum amount of insurance required by law, or they require you to post a bond to serve as compensation to anyone you injure in an automobile accident. Other states may not require such proof until you are actually involved in an accident or the police stop you for a traffic violation. If you get into an accident without insurance or a bond, you will be required to pay for any damages out of your own pocket, and you can also be charged with a criminal violation of the state's financial-responsibility laws. See also AUTOMOBILE INSURANCE.

MOVING

Most Americans move seven times or more during their lifetimes. Whether across town or across the country, moving can present problems with legal ramifications, including delays in pickups and deliveries, damage to property, and overcharging by movers.

References from friends and coworkers can be extremely helpful in finding a reliable moving company, but before you sign a contract with any company, check its reputation with the local Better Business Bureau and your state's consumer-protection agency. Do not sign an agreement with a company that has a history of consumer complaints. Make sure that any moving company you consider is licensed and insured. If your move is within the state, the movers should be licensed by the appropriate state agency, such as the commerce commission, transportation department, or the public utilities commission. If you are moving out of state, the mover should be certified by the federal Interstate Commerce Commission. The ICC has published a useful booklet entitled *When You Move: Your Rights and Responsibilities.* It explains the federal regulations and laws affecting movers. Ask your moving company for a copy, or write to the ICC, 12th Street and Constitution Avenue NW, Washington, DC 20423.

ESTIMATES

Interview two or three moving companies and obtain written estimates for the move. A low initial estimate does not always turn out to be cheaper in the long run. Some moving companies will give a free, but artificially low, estimate and then charge more money later.

Your best bet is to get a binding estimate from the mover. Although he may charge you an initial fee for such an estimate, the mover cannot afterwards demand an additional payment beyond the original estimated cost.

THE CONTRACT

Make sure that your contract with the mover (called a bill of lading) contains the following information: the pickup and delivery dates; the total cost (including extras, such as having the movers do the packing and unpacking and the cost of containers); an inventory of possessions being moved; and the amount of liability insurance. The bill of lading should also note any existing damage to furniture or other items and set out the terms of the mover's responsibility. It should state, for example, whether it is the mover who will be responsible for storing your goods, or if the company will allow someone other than the owner to accept delivery if you are not at the destination. Be sure to keep the contract and take a copy with you when you move.

ICC rules allow movers to limit their responsibility for damage to your property to 60 cents per pound, and most states do the same. Therefore, if the mover drops your antique grandfather clock that weighs 80 pounds, you will be entitled to only $48 as reimbursement, regardless of its value. You can, however, buy one of two additional kinds of insurance from the mover. Added-valuation protection will pay for the value of a damaged item, minus depreciation. A better, but more expensive, choice is full-value coverage, which will cover the full cost of repairing or replacing an item regardless of depreciation. With this kind of insurance, if your 10-year-old 19-inch color TV set is dropped and destroyed, you are entitled to a new 19-inch color set with similar features. Added-valuation coverage typically costs 50 cents for every $100 of insurance, while the average cost for full-value coverage is up to 75 cents for every $100 of declared value. These amounts vary depending on the company and the amount of the deductible, so ask the mover's agent for a quote.

MOVING DAY

If you are moving to a new home in the same area, you may be able to pay the moving company by writing a personal check, but interstate movers demand payment in cash or by certified check, travelers checks, or perhaps a credit card. And with an interstate move, you may have to pay the full amount before the movers will unload a single piece of furniture.

When moving day arrives, you should go over the bill of lading with the movers. You will also have to be ready for the movers at the new house, or pay added charges if they have to store your furniture and boxes temporarily. As the movers unload, check each item off the inventory list on your bill of lading and note any obvious new damage. Do not sign a release until all damage has been noted by both you and the movers.

If your property has hidden damage that you discover only after the movers have left—such as a television set that no longer works when you turn it on—you may not be reimbursed for it unless the movers

ABC's
OF MOVING

Moving can be costly, time-consuming, and stressful. By following these tips, you can help reduce the difficulties you are otherwise likely to encounter.

❑ Get at least three written estimates before selecting a moving company. Try to get a binding estimate to prevent the mover from adding charges before your belongings are unloaded.

❑ Do not schedule your move for the day your lease expires or the day the buyer of your current home takes possession of it. Bad weather, auto breakdowns, or other unforeseen events could delay your move. Likewise, avoid moving into your home the same day the previous occupants are moving out.

❑ Check your homeowners insurance policy to see if it covers your possessions during the move. If not, talk to your insurance agent about buying coverage that may be less expensive than that offered by the mover.

❑ When the driver picks up your items, carefully check his inventory sheets. All entries should be legible. If you disagree about the condition of an item, make a note on the inventory sheet about the difference of opinion.

❑ Make sure the mover can reach you while your goods are in transit.You are entitled to know about any delays or problems, but if the mover cannot find you, your possessions could end up in storage at an additional cost.

❑ If you do have a claim for damage, file it within nine months of the day your goods were delivered. Keep records of any correspondence or telephone calls made concerning the problem. Interstate Commerce Commission rules require the mover to acknowledge receipt of your claim within 30 days and either deny or settle the claim within 120 days.

packed the item. If they did, the company is generally responsible unless their contract states otherwise.

MOVING TO A NEW JOB

If you are moving because of a job transfer, your employer may cover most of the moving costs as well as transportation, meals, and temporary-housing costs for you and your family. Your employee handbook may tell you which costs the company will reimburse, and you may have to negotiate with your employer for any extras you want, such as reimbursement for house-hunting trips or your real estate agent's commission.

If your employer does not pay all costs, or if you are moving to a new job, you may still be able to recover some of your expenses. The Internal Revenue Service gives a tax deduction to some people who must move to a new job location and residence. If you qualify, some of your unreimbursed moving expenses may be deductible, including the cost of hiring a moving company. (Beginning in 1994, however, indirect costs which were previously deductible, such as expenses associated with house-hunting trips, can no longer be deducted.) To qualify, you must meet two requirements:

First, your new workplace must be at least 50 miles farther from your old home than your former workplace was. Thus, if you used to travel 8 miles to work, you meet this requirement if your new job is located at least 58 miles from your present home.

Second, during the first 12 months after you move, you must work at least 39 weeks in the vicinity of your new job site, even if you change to a different job. If you are self-employed, you must work at least 78 weeks out of the 24 months following your move to be eligible for the deduction.

MURDER

The killing of one human being by another, under any circumstances, is a homicide. Some homicides are legal and justifiable, or excusable; others are criminal. The killing of an enemy soldier in war or the execution of a convict under the valid sentence of a court is a legal homicide. An example of a justifiable homicide would be the killing of someone in self-defense or to prevent a violent crime. Killing without such legal justification or excuse is known as illegal or criminal homicide. Depending on the circumstances, criminal homicide ranges from criminally negligent homicide, or manslaughter (the least serious) to first-degree murder (the most serious). See also HOMICIDE; MANSLAUGHTER; SELF-DEFENSE.

The traditional definition of murder is the killing of one human being by another with malice. Malice is the element that distinguishes murder from manslaughter. A killing done with malice is an intentional killing without a valid legal reason (such as self-defense) and without any extenuating circumstances (such as extreme provocation or the heat of passion). See also HEAT OF PASSION.

There are two categories of malice under the law: express and implied. Express malice, or malice aforethought, exists when a person deliberately plans to kill another and then carries out his plans. Implied malice characterizes the action of a killer who did not deliberately plan the death of his victim but acted with wanton disregard for her life.

MURDER IN THE FIRST DEGREE

Express and implied malice form the bases for the two degrees of murder: first degree and second degree. The crime of first-degree murder is murder with malice aforethought, or premeditated murder. It is considered a heinous crime and is punished with great severity, sometimes by execution. See DEATH PENALTY.

The premeditation or deliberation necessary for murder in the first degree does not require that the killer mulled over his plan for a long time. It simply means that he intended to kill another person and that he had sufficient time to think about the act before committing it. In fact, a very brief time may elapse between premeditation (conceiving the thought or desire to kill a victim) and the actual time when the murderer puts his plan into action. Suppose Walt decides that he wants to kill Fred, and then immediately draws a gun and does so. Since many courts would hold that there need be no significant length of time between Walt's forming his intent to kill Fred and his carrying out that intent, his crime would be judged premeditated.

In some states certain types of killing are automatically classified as first-degree murder. For example, under some state statutes, killing by poison, torture, or ambush is murder in the first degree. In fact, killing by poison or torture may be first-degree murder even if the person who administered the poison or the torture did not intend for his victim to die.

In many states any killing that is committed in the course of a felony is also classified as first-degree murder, whether the killing was intentional or accidental. See also FELONY MURDER RULE.

MURDER IN THE SECOND DEGREE

A killing committed with implied malice, and without the extent of provocation that would reduce the charge to manslaughter, is considered to be murder in the second degree. Second-degree murder is not premeditated but results from the murderer's extreme recklessness and a heartless indifference to human life. An example is someone who intentionally fires a rifle into the stands at a crowded baseball game without regard for the lives of those sitting there.

DEFENDING A MURDER CHARGE

The defenses to a charge of either first- or second-degree murder include self-defense and the defense of others. But if you kill a person to protect yourself or someone else from death or serious bodily harm, you may use only the force necessary for your protection. You could not plead self-defense if you used deadly force against someone who had given up his attack and was attempting to escape, if you killed someone in "mutual combat" (a fight in which both people agreed to participate), or if you provoked the assault in the first place.

It is not a defense to a murder charge to claim that the victim consented to his own death or that the killing was necessary in order to relieve the victim's suffering. Many states have specific statutes that outlaw assisted suicides, and no states allow "mercy killings."

Insanity, delusions, and irresistible impulses are "complete defenses" to a charge of murder, meaning that you cannot be convicted of the killing or of any crime related to the killing if you can prove any of these situations in court. Another complete defense is diminished capacity, by which the killer is not considered legally insane but has significant mental defects that hinder her ability to premeditate a murder. "Voluntary" states of insanity or diminished capacity, such as those that accompany the deliberate use of drugs or alcohol, are not a complete defense to a murder charge. However, involuntary intoxication—if, for example, you go to a party and drink some punch that someone else had surreptitiously spiked with a hallucinogen—can be a complete defense to a charge of murder. See also INSANITY PLEA.

MUTUAL FUND

A mutual fund is a means by which you can invest money in a variety of different securities selected and managed by professional investment managers. The money you invest buys shares in the fund, which in turn invests your money in the stocks and bonds of other companies. A well-managed mutual fund will usually give you returns that exceed those you can get elsewhere (at a bank or savings and loan association, for example). But not all funds are well managed. You could end up earning less interest and even losing some of your initial investment if the fund's managers make unwise investment decisions.

The money-market funds offered by banks and savings and loan associations are FDIC-insured and therefore safe. But note that banks now offer a variety of other investments to their customers, and these are not FDIC-insured. See also MONEY MARKET ACCOUNT.

HOW MUTUAL FUNDS WORK

Different mutual funds have different objectives and therefore different risks. For example, some funds seek high returns by investing in the stocks of small companies that they hope will grow quickly, but that have a higher risk of failure. Other funds are designed to provide steady, reliable income by investing in stocks or bonds of large, stable companies or in government securities.

Mutual funds may be open- or closed-end. Most are open-end funds—that is, they can issue shares in unlimited numbers as investors buy into the fund. Closed-end funds have a fixed number of shares.

Many sources of information are available to help you choose the mutual fund that best suits your investment needs. Financial magazines report regularly on the performance of the various mutual funds. In addition, your local library may subscribe to one of the detailed mutual fund reports, such as the *Lipper Mutual Fund Profiles,* published quarterly.

COMMISSION AND FEES

Before you invest in any mutual fund, read its prospectus—the document that describes the fund's investment objectives, identifies its managers, and discloses its charges. A "no-load" mutual fund charges no up-front sales commission, while a "load" fund gives the salesperson a commission of about 5 percent, which is deducted from your initial investment. Some mutual funds charge a redemption fee, or a "back-end load," when you sell your fund shares. Generally, the longer you hold the shares in the fund, the lower this fee will be. Be wary of a mutual fund that charges additional sales commissions when you reinvest the dividends you earned through the fund; such fees can greatly reduce your investment.

Every mutual fund charges a management fee to compensate its managers and to pay administrative costs. In most companies this fee is 1 percent or less annually. Some funds may also charge what is known as a 12-b-1 fee, which pays for its advertising and marketing costs.

TAX CONSIDERATIONS

When you sell your mutual fund shares and make a profit, you have realized capital gains, on which you must pay income taxes. But you can offset capital gains taxes by taking a tax deduction when you sell investments at a loss. You must also pay income taxes on dividends or interest you receive from your investment, unless the investment is in an Individual Retirement Account (IRA). See CAPITAL GAINS TAX; INCOME TAX; INDIVIDUAL RETIREMENT ACCOUNT.

FROM NAME CHANGE TO NURSING HOME

NAME CHANGE

You might wish to change your name for any number of reasons. You may have just married or divorced, converted to a new religion, or entered show business. Although all states have a recognized procedure for name changes, most do not legally require you to follow the procedure, often simply assuming the new name is sufficient. However, in a few states (for instance, Alaska, Hawaii, and Oklahoma), you must go through court proceedings to formalize a name change. Some financial institutions may also require evidence of a court order before they will recognize your new name.

If you change your name, you should notify your employer, the post office, banks and other financial and credit institutions, and any businesses with which you deal. Government agencies such as the voter-registration office, the Social Security Administration, the Immigration and Naturalization Service, the Internal Revenue Service, and the motor vehicle bureau in your state should also be notified. Send them a letter stating that from now on you will be using a new name and would like all transactions and correspondence addressed to that name. If an institution asks for legal proof of your name change, provide a copy of the court order that granted the change.

COURT PROCEDURE

Before you petition for a name change, check with your state's bureau of vital statistics to see whether there is a residency requirement that you must fulfill. Then file the petition with the family or district court (your county clerk can tell you which court handles name changes), stating your original and new names, age, address, and why you wish to make the change. The court will then set a hearing. At the hearing, the judge may ask whether anyone objects to the name change. If no one does, you will be granted the new name, unless the judge deems it inappropriate.

In general you can choose any name you like, and you can choose any number of words in your name (a name is legally defined as the words that identify a person). However, you cannot choose a name that is obscene or consists merely of numerals. If a judge believes that you are changing your name in order to commit fraud or to confuse people, he may refuse to allow the change. Suppose you wanted to take on the name of a well-known politician and then run for office using your new name. The judge might refuse to grant you the name change on the grounds that voters could be confused by the name.

MARRIAGE

Traditionally, a woman who married would voluntarily change her maiden surname to that of her husband. However, many women now keep their maiden names or use a hyphenated form consisting of both surnames. Few states require a woman who decides to retain her maiden name to go through any special formalities. But in two states a woman must formally choose her surname when she marries. In Hawaii a woman must decide on a surname at the time of her wedding. In Iowa a woman must sign the marriage license with her future surname.

If a woman takes her husband's name when they marry and later decides to go back to her maiden name or use a hyphenated name, she can generally do so without any formal proceeding. Notifying the institutions named above is sufficient. Exceptions exist in those states where any name change must be formalized.

CHILDREN

Children also have reasons for having their names changed. A child's name may be changed when he is adopted or when he wishes to take the name of a new stepparent. The requirements for changing a child's name depend on state law, but approval is always required from one or both parents. A child cannot petition for his own name change; it must be done by one of his parents or his legal guardian. If there is a dispute between the parents about the child's name, the courts consider the child's welfare as the primary factor when ruling on the name change.

Suppose Susan and Anthony divorced, and Susan received custody of their 14-year-old son, Joshua. When Susan remarried, Joshua decided to change his name to that of his new stepfather, with whom he had developed a close relationship. Anthony had seen very little of his son since the divorce, but when he was notified of Joshua's desire to change his name, he objected. Nevertheless, the court decided that Joshua had a right to change his name, given his relationship with his father and stepfather.

However, if Susan had wanted Joshua to change his name just so that he would have the same surname as her new husband, the court would probably not consider that a sufficient reason to approve the change, especially if Anthony opposed it. See also ADOPTION.

NATIONAL LABOR RELATIONS BOARD

Created under the National Labor Relations Act, the National Labor Relations Board (NLRB) is an independent federal agency established to regulate management and labor relations. The NLRB has two principal functions. The first is to prevent or halt unfair labor practices by employers (such as preventing their employees from organizing a union) or by employees (such as staging an illegal slowdown). The second function of the NLRB is to conduct and monitor elections by groups of employees (known as collective-bargaining units) to determine whether or not they will be represented by a labor union. If the employees vote in favor of union representation, the NLRB gives that union the sole authority to be their representative. An employee can file a complaint with the NLRB if she believes that her union is not representing her adequately. See also COLLECTIVE BARGAINING; LABOR UNION.

NECESSARIES

The items needed to maintain a minimum standard of living, such as food, clothing, and shelter, are known as necessaries. Other items, such as expenses for medical care and burial, can also be considered necessaries, depending on state law and the circumstances. Necessaries usually become a legal issue when a couple gets divorced or separates and when spousal and child support are determined.

State laws make the spouses in a marriage responsible for providing necessaries to each other. Depending on the financial circumstances of the particular couple, the extent to which items are considered to be necessaries can vary.

For example, a young working couple with no children would be considered to have few requirements, so that a modest apartment, hot dogs and beans in the refrigerator, and clothes from discount stores might meet the legal requirements for necessaries.

At the other extreme, some courts have required a divorcing spouse to provide for the other spouse such things as maid service, luxury automobiles, and a lavish entertainment budget, if the couple have been accustomed to them while married.

Parents are required to provide necessaries for their minor children. In most states, if one parent buys necessaries for a child, both parents can be held responsible for payment. When a couple get divorced, child-support payments fulfill the noncustodial parent's obligation to provide necessaries. See also CHILD SUPPORT; DIVORCE; GARNISHMENT.

NEGLIGENCE

When someone injures another person or his property by taking an unreasonable action (or failing to take a reasonable action), he is guilty of negligence. Although negligence is often difficult to determine, it is the decisive factor in most personal-injury and property-damage lawsuits.

NEGLIGENT BEHAVIOR

To bring a lawsuit against someone for negligence, you must show that the person failed to meet the standard of care that a reasonably prudent person would have met under the same circumstances. This usually means that the negligent person was inattentive, careless, or thoughtless, and that his actions caused your injury or distress.

Negligent behavior is neither deliberate nor accidental. If Sam injures Elizabeth because he knocks her down while trying to steal her purse, he has willfully committed a criminal act, not a negligent one. Likewise, if Sam accidentally makes Elizabeth fall, his behavior would not necessarily be considered negligent unless he failed to act in a reasonably prudent manner. If he was barreling along the sidewalk on roller skates and knocked Elizabeth down, Sam might be found negligent, since a reasonably careful adult would not roller-skate fast on the sidewalk. See RECKLESSNESS; TORT.

In some circumstances you can be found negligent even if you did not participate directly in the incident that led to the charge of negligence. For instance, the owner of a car with faulty brakes can be found negligent if he lends his car to a family member or a friend who then causes an automobile accident. See also ACCIDENTS; AUTOMOBILE ACCIDENTS; FAMILY-CAR DOCTRINE.

DETERMINING NEGLIGENCE

Suppose Richard and Carolyn decide to go out to dinner on a Friday night. They arrive at a restaurant named Chez Pierre and park in the restaurant's rear parking lot. The lot is dark and the pavement is in poor condition. As Richard gets out of the car in the dark, he stumbles over a crack in the asphalt, spraining his ankle and tearing his slacks. If Richard sues Chez Pierre, the restaurant's management could be found negligent for failing to provide proper lighting and repair the pavement, and Richard could probably recover monetary damages to cover the medical expenses for his injured ankle.

After Richard picks himself up and limps into the restaurant, he finds there is a wait for a table, so he and Carolyn decide to have a drink at the bar. While they are enjoying their cocktails, another restaurant patron knocks over his beer glass, and a shard of glass cuts Carolyn's hand. In this case Chez Pierre probably would not be found guilty of negligence, since no restaurant employee failed to exercise reasonable care. But if the counter was slippery or the beer glass had a crack in it, the bartender (and the restaurant) might be considered at fault. Or the restaurant might be held responsible if the customer was obviously intoxicated when the bartender served him. Had the other patron in fact been negligent and Carolyn seriously injured, she could have sued him for monetary compensation for her injury.

After Richard and Carolyn are escorted to their table, they order spaghetti primavera as a first course. When their pasta arrives, Richard is dismayed to find a large dead insect in the sauce. In this situation the restaurant is negligent, since it has clearly failed to do what a reasonably careful restaurant would do—that is, serve food without insects in it. In some states Richard could sue Chez Pierre for the distress he suffered when he found the insect.

Their meal having ended prematurely, Richard and Carolyn leave the restaurant, find their car, and drive out of the parking lot. Because they are discussing the evening's horrors, Richard is distracted and collides with the rear fender of the car ahead of him.

As a driver, Richard did not exercise reasonable care when he chatted with Carolyn while leaving the parking lot. As a consequence, his negligence caused damage to the other car, and Richard will probably have to cover the cost of repairing the damaged fender.

ASSIGNING BLAME

Sometimes a person who is accused of negligence argues that the victim's negligence was the cause of the injury and that the defendant is therefore not responsible. This theory of contributory negligence is applied in some states. For instance, Chez Pierre might argue that Richard's carelessness caused him to fall in the parking lot (if he ignored a sign warning of the broken pavement, for example). If Richard lived in a state that followed this theory and the jury agreed with Chez Pierre, Richard would not be compensated.

Other states follow the rule of comparative negligence, by which a plaintiff's compensation is reduced by the degree to which his own negligence contributed to his injuries. Suppose Richard seeks $10,000 in damages from Chez Pierre. The jury decides that he should have been more careful and that he was 40 percent responsible for his fall. They award him $6,000. In some states, if you are found more than 50 percent responsible for your own injuries, you cannot recover anything at all from the other party. See LAST-CLEAR-CHANCE RULE.

You may also be prevented from collecting damages for injuries if you have voluntarily assumed a certain risk, particularly if you participate in a hazardous activity. For example, when Natalie decides to go horseback riding in Colorado, she signs a consent form releasing the stable of any liability for injuries she might suffer. Natalie assumes a risk, and if her horse throws her, she will probably be unable to receive compensation from the stables.

However, even when a person who knowingly engages in dangerous activities assumes a risk, she may still collect damages if her injuries resulted from another person's carelessness. In such cases the jury must decide whether or not the injury occurred in the ordinary course of the activity. Suppose that a stable employee sets off firecrackers and frightens Natalie's horse, which throws her off, breaking her leg. Because Natalie could not have anticipated such an event, she would be entitled to compensation from the riding stable for her broken leg. See also SPORTING EVENT.

NEGLIGENCE BY PROFESSIONALS

When you pay someone to perform a service in exchange for money, he has a particular duty to you. If you are injured as a result of a professional's negligence, you may be entitled to sue the person for malpractice. In general, juries try to determine whether the person acted according to accepted standards of professional behavior and competence. See CONSENT FORM; LAWYER; MEDICAL MALPRACTICE.

Businesses have a duty to their customers and the public in a number of ways. A business that is open to the public, such as a store or hotel, has an obligation to maintain its property so that customers or passersby are not hurt. In addition, employers are responsible for the negligent actions of their employees. See ACCIDENTS IN PUBLIC PLACES; LIABILITY.

The various levels of government are responsible for maintaining the areas under their jurisdiction in reasonably safe condition. For instance, the Department of Transportation is required to repair potholes on highways; local government offices are required to keep their floors safely uncluttered; and the Department of the Interior is responsible for maintaining safe conditions in federal parks. If you are injured in an accident involving government property, you may, in some cases, be able to bring a lawsuit against the government. See ACCIDENTS ON GOVERNMENT

REAL LIFE, REAL LAW

The Case of the Reckless Rafter

When Fred decided to go white-water rafting on the Arkansas River, the rafting company's operator required him to sign a release form. The form stated that white-water rafting is a dangerous activity, and that the operator disclaimed responsibility for any injuries participants might suffer.

The raft on which Fred was riding overturned. Fred was seriously injured and required extensive physical therapy. He sued the rafting operator, who disclaimed responsibility by pointing to the release form that Fred had signed.

Evidence introduced at the trial, however, showed that the guide in charge of Fred's raft was relatively inexperienced and had drunk several bottles of beer just before the accident. The guide's lack of experience was not disclosed to Fred when he signed the consent form, and Fred had no way of preventing the guide from drinking. As a result, the operator was not released from liability by the consent form. The court held that the company had a duty to monitor and supervise its employees, and that in failing to do so it had been negligent.

PROPERTY; ACCIDENTS ON PUBLIC TRANSPORTATION; ROADS AND HIGHWAYS; SOVEREIGN IMMUNITY.

NEGLIGENCE AND MINORS

Because children may not be able to recognize the dangers inherent in a situation, they are often not held responsible for their negligent acts. This is especially true of very young children. Furthermore, the law holds that adults have a greater responsibility to children than to other adults.

Suppose two-year-old Andrew is playing with a cigarette lighter in his neighbor's garage. If he sets the garage on fire, he will not be responsible for the cost of rebuilding it. On the contrary, the garage might be considered an attractive nuisance (dangerous property that attracts children), and if Andrew were hurt, the owner might be held responsible. See ATTRACTIVE NUISANCE.

However, the negligent acts of older children are treated differently. For example, if Andrew had been 16 years old, a court might require him to pay for the damage he caused. Because court judgments remain enforceable for many years, Andrew could end up paying for his negligence once he gained sufficient assets or began working.

In some instances parents can be held liable for their children's negligent acts. See PARENTAL-LIABILITY LAWS; TORT.

INSURANCE

You can buy liability insurance to protect you if you are sued for negligent behavior. Homeowners liability insurance protects you from a lawsuit by anyone who is injured on your property; likewise, automobile liability insurance covers you if you are in a car accident.

Businesses should also carry liability insurance to protect them against claims made by customers or employees. See AUTOMOBILE INSURANCE; CASUALTY INSURANCE; HOME BUSINESS; HOMEOWNERS INSURANCE; LAWSUIT; LIABILITY INSURANCE.

CRIMINAL NEGLIGENCE

In some cases a person's behavior can be so negligent that it becomes criminal. For example, a parent who fails to provide adequate care for his children may be charged with criminal child neglect. If the child dies as a result of such abuse, the parent can be prosecuted for negligent homicide, or manslaughter.

Or suppose that Stewart is involved in an automobile accident that results in the death of several people. Witnesses to the accident testify that they saw Stewart speeding and weaving his car from lane to lane on the highway without signaling. It is apparent that Stewart's reckless driving caused the accident and subsequent deaths. Stewart is convicted of negligent homicide and sentenced to several years' imprisonment.

NEIGHBOR

Whether you live in a high-rise apartment building or on thousands of acres of property, you have neighbors. Although there is no strict legal definition of who your neighbors are, anyone who lives near you, or who owns or lives on property adjoining yours, is considered your neighbor.

Neighbors have a responsibility to each other that must be balanced with their own enjoyment and use of their property. For instance, you cannot store dilapidated cars, trash, or other unsightly material that lowers the value of the surrounding property. Any construction work or landscaping that you do to your property should not adversely affect a neighbor's property or her enjoyment of it. Neighbors must also respect the boundary lines that separate their properties.

Although light, air, and views are pleasant, you are not automatically entitled to them. If your neighbor wants to build a new extension that will block your view of the sea, there may be nothing you can do to prevent him. See also BOUNDARY LINE; FENCE BUILDING; NUISANCE; QUIET ENJOYMENT; TRESPASS.

Problems between neighbors can vary from the relatively insignificant (such as a neighbor who lets his fallen leaves blow into your yard) to the extremely serious (someone who sells drugs from the house next door). Many of the disputes that occur between neighbors involve local ordinances or regulations. In addition, if you live in a planned community, condominium complex, or an area with a homeowners association, there may be additional prohibitions against certain kinds of behavior on your deed or lease. It is best to learn about such ordinances for or restrictions on your property, which may concern the following:

◇ In addition to being a public nuisance, making excessive noise is often against the law. See NOISE.

◇ In many places homeowners are expected to keep their property in good repair so that it does not constitute either a danger or an eyesore to others in the neighborhood.

◇ Many communities forbid homeowners to accumulate hazardous or smelly refuse or that which may attract vermin. In some cities, for example, you can be fined for putting your garbage out at any time other than on collection day.

◇ If you have pets, you may be required to keep them enclosed or otherwise restrained. You may also be required to clean up after them. See also ANIMALS; DOG LAW; PET.

◇ You may be required to keep your lawn and garden free of excessive growth, including weeds. If your trees overhang public property, the local utility company or government may require you to trim the branches or may do the trimming themselves. See also TREE.

◇ If you live in a neighborhood that has been given historic landmark status, you may be restricted in the type of construction or additions that you can make to your home. See also LANDMARK.

◇ You may be responsible for keeping the sidewalk in front of your house in good repair and free of snow and ice. See also SIDEWALK.

SOLVING NEIGHBORHOOD DISPUTES

In order to resolve minor disputes between neighbors, some communities have established dispute-resolution boards. These boards generally consist of elected members of the community, who listen to the arguments of each neighbor and attempt to mediate a solution without resorting to a legal contest. If you live in an area that is regulated by a homeowners association, it may also be able to assist you in resolving disputes. See also MEDIATION.

STEPS TO TAKE

If you have a problem with a neighbor, try the steps below. Sometimes a simple solution can be found.

1. If you are not sure whether your neighbor is violating a local ordinance, consult your local library or county clerk's office. Then, before doing anything else, talk to your neighbor about the problem. He may not know that he is breaking the law, and you may be able to work out a solution. Keep a record of your conversations or correspondence with your neighbor. You may need it if the matter ends up in court.

2. If this approach does not work, explain the problem to your landlord, tenants association, homeowners association, or condominium or cooperative board. Such organizations often help mediate disputes between neighbors.

3. Take your problem to a community dispute-resolution board, if there is one where you live.

4. If your neighbor is violating a local zoning law or other ordinance, report the violation to the appropriate government department. It then becomes the city's responsibility to persuade your neighbor to correct the problem.

5. If you are seeking a relatively small amount of money damages from your neighbor, consider filing a suit in small-claims court.

6. If none of these measures works, you may need to hire an attorney and go to court.

7. If you believe your neighbor is carrying out criminal activity from her home, report the problem to your local police department or district attorney's office. See also SMALL-CLAIMS COURT; ZONING.

NO CONTEST

In many criminal courts, a defendant who does not wish to admit his guilt can plead no contest, or *nolo contendere* ("I will not contest"). This is usually done when there is incontrovertible evidence against him. When a defendant makes this plea, he submits himself to the punishment of the court.

A no-contest plea has the same effect as a guilty plea in a criminal case. It only remains for the judge to hand down a sentence. However, there is a significant difference in its effect on any related civil lawsuits. A plea of guilty can be admitted as evidence of the defendant's culpability in a civil lawsuit, but a *nolo contendere* plea cannot. Therefore, the plaintiff in the civil suit will have to prove the elements of his case without being able to point to the defendant's criminal plea—a more difficult task.

Although a criminal court is not obliged to accept a no-contest plea if the judge believes that justice will not be served, in practice the courts often do accept such pleas because they help alleviate the burden on the court system.

NO-FAULT INSURANCE

States that have no-fault automobile insurance laws require anyone who is involved in an accident to seek compensation for his injuries and sometimes for property damage from his own insurance company. Under the traditional fault system, the driver who causes the accident and his insurance company must reimburse the other driver for such expenses as medical bills and lost wages.

The no-fault system was established to provide a way for accident victims to be compensated for their injuries without delay. For instance, Marlene, who lives in the no-fault insurance state of Kansas, was driving to work, obeying all of the traffic laws, when another driver swerved into her lane. The resulting collision left her with an $1,800 medical bill and $800 in lost wages during her recuperation. The damage to her car was $4,000. In Kansas Marlene can seek recovery for these expenses from her own insurance company, rather than waiting for the other driver's insurance company to decide upon her claim. However, in states with no-fault laws, you must sue the other driver to receive personal-injury compensation that exceeds the no-fault limit. And since no-fault laws prohibit payment for pain and suffering, you must sue to obtain such compensation.

If Marlene had had an accident while she was driving in another state, her coverage might be limited. Ask your insurance agent whether your no-fault insurance policy applies in all cases. See also AUTOMOBILE INSURANCE.

NOISE

Noise that disturbs you and deprives you of the use or enjoyment of your own property, or that diminishes its value, is considered a private nuisance. You have the right to call the police to have such noise reduced or halted. Anyone who creates noise that exceeds specified legal limits can be found to have created a public nuisance and can be fined.

Many communities have laws that limit the amount of noise permitted in residential areas or around such facilities as hospitals or nursing homes. Not only is the level of noise regulated, but also the type of noise and the time of day when it occurs. For instance, letting your son's rock group practice in the garage may be acceptable at 4 P.M. on Saturday, but not at 2 A.M. on Friday. The law often specifies a decibel level that is considered acceptable, and the police may measure it with noise meters.

If you live in a city, you are likely to need a higher tolerance for noise than if you reside in a quiet suburban neighborhood. In every community, however, there are people and agencies charged with creating or enforcing legislation against excessive noise. Landlords, co-op and condominium boards, homeowners and tenants associations, and the municipal government may all impose penalties on violators of noise regulations. Some communities even have special units that deal only with complaints about noise.

Barking dogs, yowling cats, and other raucous pets often prompt noise complaints. To deal with them, some local laws specify when and how long a dog can bark, for example, before its owners are obliged to stop the noise. If the dog barks continuously, the owners may be ordered to muzzle it or keep it indoors, and they may also be subject to fines. See also DOG LAW; PET.

DEALING WITH NOISE

Suppose the peace and quiet of your suburban neighborhood has been diminished greatly in the past few weeks by a new neighbor's late-night tuba practice. Together with several of your neighbors, you have already asked him to restrict his playing to a more reasonable hour, but he refuses. You call the police and ask them to visit your neighbor and order him to stop. Nevertheless, the next night your neighbor plays his tuba again. The police will once more come if you call them, but this time they may issue your neighbor a summons to appear in court. There he can be fined and ordered to cease his musical annoyance.

If you plan to have a party, do construction work on your house, or otherwise create excessive noise for a limited time, tell your neighbors. If they are forewarned, they may be less likely to call the police or file a complaint against you. See also NUISANCE.

NO-KNOCK LAWS

According to federal and state law, a law enforcement officer must "knock and announce" her presence before entering a residence. Even if a police officer has a search warrant, it is illegal for her to enter a dwelling without first identifying herself as a police officer and then giving the occupants time to open the door. Only if they refuse to admit her may she break open a door or window. If knock-and-announce procedures are not followed, the officer's entry is considered unlawful, and any evidence seized in the home may not be admissible in court.

In some situations knocking and announcing are not necessary—for instance, when the building or residence is unoccupied, or when the announcement would allow a suspect to escape or destroy pertinent evidence. Such "no-knock" searches often take place in drug arrests, because it is relatively easy for a suspect to dispose of evidence if the police are required to knock and wait for admittance. See also SEARCH AND SEIZURE; SEARCH WARRANT.

NONCONFORMING USE

Nonconforming use is a legal exception to zoning laws. Zoning laws dictate the purposes for which particular areas of land can be used—typically for residential, agricultural, industrial, or commercial purposes. If you notice a small tailor shop operating in an area that is zoned for residential use, it may be that the shop was established before the residential zoning ordinance was passed and that it has obtained a nonconforming use.

A nonconforming use runs with the land. This means that the use is not a personal right but transfers with a change in ownership. Thus if the tailor sold his store to another tailor, the second tailor could continue to operate the store.

A local zoning committee does have the right to cancel a nonconforming use if the owner substantially changes the existing use of the business (if the tailor shop becomes a video store, for instance), if the building is severely damaged or destroyed (so that the tailor has to rebuild his store), or if the owner discontinues the nonconforming use. Check with your zoning board to find out what actions can jeopardize the continuing legal recognition of a nonconforming use. See also VARIANCE; ZONING.

NONPROFIT CORPORATION

A corporation that does not distribute any of its income to shareholders but instead donates it for charitable or benevolent purposes is a nonprofit corporation. In most states a nonprofit corporation can be established and licensed for one of many reasons. It may be organized for public education; for scientific, agricultural, or medical research; for civic, political, or patriotic purposes; or to serve the members of a profession or trade.

Not every nonprofit organization chartered by the state is granted tax-exempt status by the Internal Revenue Service, allowing donors to obtain a federal tax deduction for gifts to the organization. To achieve this status, a nonprofit corporation must meet strict IRS guidelines. Always ask about an organization's tax-exempt status before making a donation, or ask for a copy of its IRS notice of qualification. You should also ask to see its financial statement, which will tell you how much of its income is used for such things as administrative expenses. For more information on assessing nonprofit corporations, see CHARITABLE DONATION.

Setting up a nonprofit corporation is similar to setting up a regular corporation. You must apply through the secretary of state's office in your state, which will grant you nonprofit status if you meet legal guidelines. State agencies monitor nonprofit corporations and can take away their status for such abuses as using funds for purposes other than those stated in their corporate charter. See also CORPORATION.

NOTARY PUBLIC

A notary public (sometimes simply called a notary) is someone authorized by state law to administer oaths and attest to the authenticity of documents and signatures. (In Maine a notary public is also authorized to perform marriage ceremonies.) Sometimes banks or savings and loan institutions have a notary public on staff as a service to customers.

To become a notary public, you must be an adult and you are usually required to pass a state examination. When you receive permission to practice in your town or within a certain area, you may be asked to post a bond to protect the public in case you fail to perform your duties. You can charge fees for your services at rates set by the state; however, notaries rarely make a living from their services.

A notary cannot be held responsible for the accuracy of documents that she notarizes; she merely verifies the identity of the person who presents them to her. Suppose Walter buys a car from a stranger. The seller signs the bill of sale before a notary public, who puts her seal on it—no questions asked. Later Walter learns that the signature on the ownership papers is a forgery. In fact, the car was stolen, and the police tell Walter that he must return the car to its original owner. Walter can sue the notary public because she should have required identification from the seller to prove that he was the person named on the title to the automobile.

If a notary public does not perform her duties, the state can revoke her authority.

NOTICE

In its most common legal usage, a notice is the warning given to someone to inform him of a legal proceeding in which he has an interest, such as a lawsuit for breach of contract or a divorce.

Actual notice occurs when you give information to the opposing party or when he is aware of the availability of the information. For example, before proceeding to court against your former husband in a child-custody dispute, you must give him notice of the impending legal action so that he will have the opportunity to respond in his own defense. The notice may be hand-delivered, sent by mail, or placed as a public notice in a newspaper, depending on whether your ex-husband's whereabouts are known.

Without actual notice, a person's constitutional guarantee of due process of law is violated. If, for instance, one party to a lawsuit does not appear in court to defend himself, a default judgment may be brought against him. However, if he can show that he did not receive notice of the court proceedings, the judgment may be invalidated. See also DEFAULT JUDGMENT; DUE PROCESS OF LAW.

Another type of legal notice, known as constructive notice, is the knowledge that you can reasonably be expected to have. Suppose you are sued for climbing over a fence and trespassing upon someone's property. You cannot claim that the charge should be dismissed because the property owner failed to post a "No Trespassing" sign. The court presumes that any reasonable person knows or should know that trespassing is illegal. In other words, you have had constructive notice that trespassing on the property is not allowed, even though there was no sign that specifically prohibited it.

NUISANCE

Any activity or condition that is unreasonable or illegal or inconveniences, offends, or annoys another person may be called a nuisance. A nuisance is also an activity or condition that causes damage to property. And anything that interferes with another's peaceful enjoyment of his property, home, or life can also be a nuisance. For example, unreasonable noise, foul odors, and disorderly conduct are all nuisances. Certain dangerous conditions that are especially tempting to children are called attractive nuisances. See also ATTRACTIVE NUISANCE.

Nuisances are usually classified as either public or private, or a combination of both.

PUBLIC NUISANCES

A public nuisance is a recurring or continuous activity or condition that is deemed to be harmful to the health, morals, or peace of the community. The harm must be substantial, but it does not have to affect every person in the community. For instance, a garbage heap where flies and vermin breed and generate disease can be a public nuisance (as well as a violation of sanitation laws).

The classic example of a public nuisance is a "bawdy house" where illegal gambling, drinking, and prostitution occur. A current example is a "crack house," maintained for the illegal sale of drugs, which has a continuing deleterious effect on the community. Many public nuisances are also violations of the law and are punishable by fines. In some states a person who is maintaining a public nuisance may also be prosecuted as a criminal. See also DISORDERLY HOUSE.

PRIVATE NUISANCES

A private nuisance is one that interferes with another person's private rights to the use and enjoyment of his own property. Maintaining a private nuisance is not a crime, but someone who is affected by a private nuisance may sue to end the activity or to change the condition. For example, it is not illegal to put up elaborate Christmas light displays on your property and play Christmas carols, nor is this offensive or dangerous to the public at large. However, suppose that by Thanksgiving, Graham's neighbor William has decorated his house for Christmas with such a tremendous number of Christmas lights that the sky is illuminated and Graham's bedroom is brilliantly lit all night. In addition, William plays "The Twelve Days of Christmas" continuously over a loudspeaker. Cars from surrounding communities are starting to drive up and down Graham's street, admiring the lavish display. Graham has grounds to sue William to end this private nuisance, though he should first try to convince William to end it of his own accord. See also NEIGHBOR.

To sue someone for a private nuisance, you must show both that the person committing the nuisance intended to do it and that his behavior substantially interferes with your enjoyment of your property. The jury will also be asked to decide whether his behavior conformed to a standard of reasonableness. For instance, if you want to prevent the women who live next door from sunbathing in bikinis because you find it offensive, you will probably not win your case. Sunbathing with appropriate attire is reasonable behavior.

NURSING HOME

Advances in medical technology and an improved standard of living have resulted in an increase in the older population of the United States. There has also been a corresponding increase in the number of residential and medical-care facilities for the elderly, including nursing homes, which are regulated and licensed by the state. According to the U.S. Department of Health and Human Services, more than 40 percent of all people over 65 are likely to be in a nursing home at some point; at any given time, 5 percent of older Americans reside in one. The stay can be brief, as for a convalescence, or it can become permanent for someone who is chronically ill.

At their best, nursing homes are pleasant places run by competent, caring staff. At their worst, they can be depressing, lonely institutions staffed by unqualified employees. Before entering a nursing home or committing a relative to one, you should carefully assess your needs and thoroughly evaluate the home.

DETERMINING YOUR NEEDS

The term *nursing home* describes several kinds of facilities. A skilled-nursing facility (SNF) provides 24-hour nursing care, including rehabilitative therapy, diet supervision, and the trained observation of the residents by nurses and other staff. A physician is on call and available for emergency care. Someone who requires professional nursing care following a hospitalization or accident should go to an SNF.

An intermediate-care facility (ICF) provides supportive care and nursing services for persons who suffer from chronic conditions but do not require the level of professional care given at an SNF. Rather than having registered nurses on staff, an ICF may have nurses aides or practical nurses, and physicians may not be on call.

A third type of nursing home is a personal-care home, which does not offer nursing care but caters to residents who may require help with daily activities, such as bathing or dressing. Individuals who live in personal-care facilities are in need only of a protective home environment.

Often a physician will be the first to recommend a nursing home. But be aware that there are other options for care and housing of the elderly, such as home health care and senior-citizens housing. If you are unsure whether to enter a nursing facility, ask a professional, such as a hospital social worker, about the level of care you may need. The following questions should be considered in determining the best level of care:

◇ Are you ill or planning to undergo surgery that will disable you for a period of time?

◇ Are you making a permanent living arrangement, or do you merely need a place to stay during a convalescence?

◇ Do you have relatives and friends near the home who will be able to visit you?

◇ Do you live alone? If not, do you have a family member who depends on you for care?

◇ Can you cook for yourself at home and organize your own finances and other household affairs?

◇ Do you have financial resources that are sufficient to pay for a nursing home? Are you eligible for any financial assistance that would provide you with alternative care?

If someone is under your guardianship, such as an elderly patient, you have the authority to place her in a nursing home. It is a good idea, however, to discuss this option with your relative before she becomes incapable of making the decision herself. See also Guardian and Ward.

SELECTING A FACILITY

To find a nursing home, ask your state licensing office for a list of the facilities in your area. For information on long-term care, ask your state's agency on aging. Be sure to consult your doctor and the social services departments of local hospitals for recommendations, and check with friends, church groups, and veterans or seniors associations.

Then visit several homes to get an idea of their services and general character. Make a checklist of important criteria, including the following points, and compare the different homes to see which offers the best combination of services.

◇ Is the home equipped with a fire alarm system and a sprinkler system? Has it posted an evacuation plan in case of emergency?

◇ Is the facility homey? Are residents allowed to decorate their rooms and bring in personal belongings?

◇ Do the residents seem to enjoy their surroundings, and would they recommend the nursing home to others?

◇ Is the staff courteous and cheerful?

◇ Does the facility specialize in certain conditions or illnesses, such as Alzheimer's disease? Would you feel comfortable around other residents who are suffering from such a condition?

◇ Is there a schedule of daily activities in which you can choose to participate?

◇ Does the food look appetizing and nourishing? Are the kitchen and dining areas clean?

FINANCIAL CONSIDERATIONS

Living in a nursing home costs about $30,000 per year, which is usually payable in monthly installments. Always ask the administrative staff which services are included in the basic fee and whether there are extra fees. Find out whether you must give the nursing home an initial deposit, and what procedure must be followed to get it back.

If you are paying privately for a nursing home, medical expenses that exceed 7.5 percent of your adjusted gross income are tax deductible. Despite this tax break, your entire estate can be depleted by long-term care costs before you become eligible for financial assistance through Medicaid. If you have a spouse with adequate resources, she can be held responsible for your nursing home or other medical fees. Your children cannot be forced to pay the expenses of your medical care unless they have agreed to do so—for example, by signing a contract with a nursing home.

If Medicare or Medicaid benefits will be covering your ex-

ABC's

Of Buying Nursing Home Insurance

The popularity of long-term nursing home insurance policies, which can help protect your financial security when you retire, has soared in recent years. These policies are designed to provide funds for costs that exceed your coverage through private health insurance, Medicare, or "Medigap" insurance, but you must choose your policy carefully. The following suggestions will help you evaluate and analyze a nursing home policy.

❑ Buy from an agent or broker whom you trust, and from a company that is financially stable. Some insurance agents have told potential customers that premiums for nursing home insurance are tax deductible or that benefits will be tax free. Neither statement is true.

❑ Plan to pay for the premiums with money from your income rather than savings. If you cannot afford the policies now, there is little chance that you will be able to afford them after you retire.

❑ Compare the policies offered by several reputable companies. Often the benefits can vary significantly, even when premium payments are similar.

❑ Ask whether the premiums are likely to increase as you age, and by what amount. Some companies increase their premiums by thousands of dollars after just a few years.

❑ Find out whether you will be able to switch to another policy and pay premiums based on your age at the time you purchased the initial policy, rather than the age you made the switch. You may be able to lower premiums by switching, since intervening rate increases may have been substantial.

❑ Visit several nursing homes to determine which would suit you if long-term care becomes a necessity. Then compare the cost of obtaining care from that home with the amount of coverage offered by the nursing home policy. Remember that the difference will have to come out of your savings or pension.

❑ Ask whether the policy permits you to enter a nursing home directly from your own home, or whether it requires that you spend time in a hospital first. Also ask whether it covers home health care as well.

❑ See if the policy has a waiting period before it will cover preexisting conditions. Six months or a year is a reasonable time; if you become ill earlier, you may lose benefits if a current health problem worsens.

❑ Try to find a policy that will adjust its benefits for inflation or allow you to purchase additional benefits if you need them.

❑ Find out about the insurer's cancellation rights. The best policies are noncancelable—that is, the company agrees to provide coverage for as long as you pay your premiums.

❑ Do not be disturbed by a 20-day deductible in a policy. Medicare will pay nursing home costs for up to 20 days after an operation or serious illness.

❑ Look for a policy that is written in plain English. Many states now have laws that require insurers to avoid complicated jargon and ambiguous terms when writing policies, but if you do not understand a term in the policy you are considering, ask for a written clarification from the insurer.

❑ Learn if your state has a Health Insurance Counseling and Assistance Program (HICAP) to help consumers evaluate different policies.

penses, you must find out whether the nursing home is approved by these agencies. If you are eligible for Medicare, it will pay for care in an approved SNF, but only if you are admitted to the home within 30 days of a hospital stay of three days or more. Medicare pays for the full cost of care during the first 20 days of your stay. For longer stays, Medicare will pay only a percentage of the costs up to 100 days. After that, you are responsible for the entire cost.

CHECKLIST

Your Rights as a Resident

Federal and state regulations require all licensed nursing homes to guarantee residents certain rights. These include your right:

❑ To know your medical condition and participate in decisions about your medical treatment.

❑ To manage your own financial affairs (unless a guardian or conservator is appointed).

❑ To be informed of services available in the facility and any extra charges for them.

❑ To have a safe, clean, comfortable environment.

❑ To be free from physical, sexual, or mental abuse, including corporal punishment, isolation, or restraints.

❑ To send and receive personal mail unopened.

❑ To associate and communicate privately with others.

❑ To participate in social and religious activities.

❑ To receive advance notice if you are to be moved to another room or facility, or if you will be getting a new roommate.

Medicaid will pay for care in either an SNF or ICF for people whose financial resources cannot cover the cost. Check with your local social services office to find out about Medicaid restrictions in your state. See also MEDICAID; MEDICARE; VETERANS BENEFITS.

PRIVATE INSURANCE

If you or a relative is concerned about the cost of nursing home care, consider buying nursing home or long-term care insurance. Generally, you purchase these policies as an individual, although some employers now offer them as an employee benefit. The advantage of such a policy is that you will not need to divest yourself of your assets in order to qualify for Medicaid assistance. See the "ABC's of Buying Nursing Home Insurance" on page 383.

RESIDENTS' RIGHTS

Nursing home licenses are issued by the state regulatory agency (usually the department of health) only if the facility has complied with minimum standards for construction, staffing, diet, and nursing procedures. In 1990, federal legislation went into effect to improve the quality of nursing homes, in particular to control such dehumanizing practices as restraining patients or sedating them to control their behavior, and to prevent the eviction of residents with limited funds.

When you enter a nursing home, you sign a contract. If you are mentally competent, you should be able to leave the nursing home at any time. The home may reserve the right to remove a resident who is not receiving Medicare or Medicaid under certain specific circumstances (such as violent behavior). It is much more difficult for a nursing home to evict a patient whose fees are paid by Medicare or Medicaid.

NEGLECT AND ABUSE

Even with laws that prohibit abuse, residents of nursing homes are at times placed in restraints, medicated unnecessarily, or neglected to the point where they suffer from malnutrition, bedsores, and other illnesses. If you have a complaint about nutrition, sanitation, or the health or safety of a resident, notify the nursing home administrator at once.

State laws require licensed medical professionals to report suspected cases of abused nursing home patients. If you suspect abuse that has not been reported, contact the nursing home ombudsman at your state's agency on aging and department of health. If the accusations are warranted, the licensing agency can fine the home or take away its license. For cases of abuse that present an immediate threat to the patient's safety or well-being, or that involve theft of a patient's money, Social Security benefits, or personal property, call the local police. In extreme cases, if battery, abuse, or assault has taken place, criminal charges may be filed against the nursing home. If you feel that the nursing home has been negligent, you (or your guardian) can file a lawsuit against the home.

FROM

OATH AND AFFIRMATION

TO

OVERTIME

OATH AND AFFIRMATION

A witness who testifies in court must first swear an oath to tell the truth. Someone who assumes public office swears an oath to fulfill the duties of the office. The oath is made on a Bible with the acknowledgment that if it is not upheld, the person who broke the oath will be answerable to God.

At one time people who refused to swear an oath to God, either because they did not believe in God or because their religious beliefs did not permit taking an oath, could not testify in court or hold public office. Today federal and state laws allow them to make an affirmation instead—a solemn declaration that contains no reference to God.

An oath or affirmation may be written or oral, but in order to have legal effect, it must be made before an official authorized to administer an oath or affirmation, such as a judge. See also PERJURY.

OBJECTION

In its commonest legal sense, an objection is a motion made by one of the parties to a lawsuit or criminal prosecution, protesting that some testimony or ruling of the court is improper and should not be allowed. Questions by attorneys, testimony on the stand, or rulings of the court may all be cause for an objection. When a judge agrees with the objection being made, it is said to be sustained; an objection that is not accepted by the judge is said to be overruled.

An objection can serve as the basis for an appeal, provided it is made during the course of the trial. Suppose a witness testifies about something he heard another person say. An objection that the testimony is hearsay must be raised at once. Otherwise, the party injured by this testimony cannot later claim in an appeal that it should have been excluded. See also EVIDENCE.

OBSCENITY

Defining obscenity in legal terms (in order to pass laws prohibiting it) is a challenge that has eluded lawmakers for decades. In its broadest sense, obscenity is any material that appeals to a prurient interest in sex, nudity, genitalia, or excretion and that has no socially redeeming literary, political, scientific, or artistic value when judged by an average person applying community standards.

DIFFERENCES

One problem with this definition is that community standards vary considerably. What might be found obscene in a small town in rural Mississippi or Nebraska could conceivably be considered a work of art by the average resident of a city like New York or Los Angeles.

Another problem with this definition is the requirement that the material in question have no redeeming social value. Some pornographers overcome this hurdle by placing political messages in their material or calling it a "scientific study."

Even if material is found to be obscene, it is not illegal for consenting adults to have it in their homes. Obscenity laws apply to the distribution or sale of material, not to possession.

Faced with these obstacles, many local prosecutors have given up the fight to prevent the distribution of obscene material to consenting adults. Rather, they concentrate on limiting access to the materials by restricting the locations of adult book and video stores and theaters that show pornography. Many zoning laws prohibit such establishments within a specified distance of schools or churches, or require businesses that want to open such stores to obtain the approval of neighborhood residents.

OBSCENITY IN THE MAILS

In recent years, however, the U.S. Department of Justice has begun to prosecute persons who distribute obscene materials by mailing them from one state to another. Similarly, the federal government and the U.S. Postal Service have been very aggressive in their efforts to stop the distribution and possession of child pornography. See PORNOGRAPHY.

Under federal law, you have the right to ask the Postal Service to order a company to stop mailing you materials that you find offensive. Then if the company continues to send you the materials, a federal court can issue an order in support of the Postal Service. Continued violations of this order place the company in contempt of court. Ask your local post office for more information. See also CENSORSHIP; PRESS, FREEDOM OF; SPEECH, FREEDOM OF.

OBSTRUCTION OF JUSTICE

The orderly resolution of disputes in our civil courts and the fair administration of justice in our criminal courts is of fundamental interest to everyone in the United States. Acts that undermine people's confidence in the justice system are therefore prohibited by a variety of laws, both state and federal. Acts prohibited as crimes are witness tampering or intimidation, influencing a judicial officer, giving false information, and hindering a police officer.

YOUR PROTECTION AND DUTY AS A WITNESS

It is essential for people with information relevant to an issue before the court to present that information to the judge or jury. If you are or may be a witness, you should immediately report:

◇ Any effort to influence your testimony through bribes, threats, entreaties, or intimidation, including offers of money or threats of violence aimed at persuading you to commit perjury (lie under oath) at a court proceeding.

◇ Any request that you hide or destroy documents or other objects that are, or may become, evidence in a case.

◇ An attempt to convince you to fail to appear in court, to leave the court's jurisdiction, or to hide to avoid being served with a subpoena.

◇ Acts or threats of retaliation after you have given your testimony.

Under the Fifth Amendment to the U.S. Constitution, you cannot be required to give testimony that would incriminate you. Therefore, it is not an obstruction of justice for another person, such as your lawyer, to advise you to refuse to answer questions that may subject you to criminal prosecution. See also FIFTH AMENDMENT.

JUDGES AND JURORS

Like witnesses, judges and jurors are also protected from interference. It is an obstruction of justice to attempt to influence a juror by bribing or threatening him. See also JURY TAMPERING.

Similarly, communications with judges will be scrutinized closely. Judges are allowed to solicit expert information or opinion regarding a case, provided that information is entered into the court record, and persons involved in a case may request to speak with the judge if they think they have some information that he requires. However, unsolicited communication that is off the record is not allowed. Accepting money or other favors from someone in return for using your personal influence with a judge is also an obstruction of justice.

POLICE

When a police officer is performing his official duties, it is illegal to try to prevent him from carrying them out. The following acts are all considered obstructions of justice and are punishable by law:

◇ Giving false information or concealing or withholding information to help someone avoid detection or arrest.

◇ Using or threatening to use force against a police officer.

◇ Refusing to provide identification when an officer requests it.

◇ Running away or hiding from a police officer. That means, for example, that you must stop your car when directed to do so.

You have the right to question an officer, but always use moderate language. It is not illegal to criticize a police officer, but you are obstructing justice if your language actually hinders the officer in the performance of his duties—for example, if you incite an angry crowd of bystanders to interfere with him.

Similarly, you are allowed to observe the arrest of another

person as long as your activities do not interfere with the police officer's ability to carry out his official duties.

Occupational Safety and Health Administration

The federal agency in charge of worker safety is the Occupational Safety and Health Administration (OSHA). OSHA is part of the Department of Labor and is responsible for implementing the Occupational Safety and Health Act, a 1970 law that protects the health and safety of certain private-sector employees. Among OSHA's duties are the development of safety and health standards for private employers and the inspection of workplaces by compliance officers to determine whether those standards are met. In addition to OSHA, states also have statutes governing the safety of people in the workplace.

SCOPE OF AUTHORITY

Some industries, such as the airline and nuclear-energy industries, are exempt from OSHA requirements because they are covered by other federal legislation. In addition, some employers are not required to comply with every regulation issued by OSHA. If the business employs fewer than 10 people, it may be exempt from some safety or health requirements. Family-owned and operated farms and self-employed individuals do not have to comply with OSHA, nor do federal, state, and local government agencies (although other state or federal statutes may apply to them).

Inspections

An OSHA compliance officer may inspect a workplace at any reasonable time, but he must have a warrant unless the employer voluntarily agrees to the inspection. Complaints alleging imminent danger to workers are given the highest priority. During an inspection, employees may be questioned, records inspected, and photographs and samples of hazardous materials taken. If a violation exists, a citation will be issued describing the violation and the monetary penalty being proposed. The Department of Labor then decides whether the penalty will be imposed.

COMPLAINTS

OSHA has its headquarters in Washington, D.C. There are 10 regional offices and over 70 area offices. There is at least one area office in every state except Delaware, South Dakota, Vermont, Virginia, and Wyoming. To find the nearest OSHA office, call the Federal Information Center. See FEDERAL INFORMATION CENTER.

If you think your workplace is unsafe, you can file a complaint with OSHA. Under federal law, you cannot be fired for filing a complaint if it is based on inaccurate information. Willfully reporting inaccurate information, however, is fraud.

If you believe that your employer is discriminating against you because you filed a complaint, you can file another complaint alleging discrimination, but you must do it within 30 days of the date you discover that retaliatory action was taken against you. See also WHISTLE-BLOWER.

ADMINISTRATIVE PROCEEDINGS

An employer has the right to challenge a citation or resulting penalty to the Occupational Safety and Health Review Commission (OSHRC), a body that operates independently of the Department of Labor.

The usual procedure is to have an administrative-law judge (who can rule for governmental agencies) hear the challenge. The judge's decision may then be reviewed by the OSHRC if at least one of its members so orders. Based on either the judge's original decision or the review, the commission will decide to uphold, modify, or overturn the citation or the penalty.

Odometer Statement

Jacquie was reading the classified ads one Saturday when an ad caught her eye. A 1965 Mustang was being offered for sale at a very reasonable price, especially since the ad claimed that the car had been driven only 20,000 miles. She arranged to see the car at a used-car lot. The car did look reasonably new, but she still found it hard to believe the low mileage.

Jacquie was wise to be skeptical, since many used cars are

sold with false odometer readings. To combat this problem, federal and state laws now require the sellers of used cars to provide purchasers with an odometer statement, which must say whether the mileage is accurate, whether it has been altered, or that the seller is unsure about its accuracy.

Anyone who deliberately misrepresents the mileage on an odometer can be held liable to the buyer for the loss in the car's value due to the higher actual mileage. For example, if Jacquie is told that a car has only 20,000 miles on it, but a mechanic finds that it has been driven over 100,000 miles, she can recover the resulting difference in the value of the car.

Federal and state laws also make it a crime to disconnect or tamper with an odometer with the intention of defrauding a buyer. Anyone who tampers with an odometer must pay the purchaser of the car $1,500 or three times the loss she incurs, whichever is greater, as well as the buyer's attorney fees.

If you are selling a used car, complete an odometer statement, which in many states is printed on the back of the title to your automobile.

STEPS TO TAKE

If you are buying a used car, take these steps to check the odometer reading.

1. Examine the brake and gas pedals for wear. The more worn they are, the higher the mileage is likely to be.

2. Check the odometer. The numbers on altered odometers are often misaligned.

3. Have the car inspected by a qualified mechanic who is not associated in any way with the seller. He can tell you if the wear and tear on the engine and transmission are consistent with the mileage shown.

4. If you believe that you have bought a car with an illegally altered odometer, report it to your local district attorney's office. If you bought the car from a dealer, also file a complaint with the board that licenses dealers in your state.

OPTION CONTRACT

Ray sees an antique dining room set advertised. After he looks at the set he decides that he likes it, but he wants a few days to think about it. How can he ensure that nobody else buys the set before he decides?

One way is for Ray to offer the seller, Joan, a small sum of money in exchange for her promise not to sell the set to anyone else for a given time. If she agrees, Joan and Ray have created an option contract—a legally enforceable agreement under which one party promises to honor an offer to buy or sell something for a specific price within a set time. In exchange, the second party pays a sum of money, or option fee. The second party then has the option to complete the deal within the specified time but is not obligated to do so. If Ray decides not to buy the furniture, Joan can keep the option fee because she upheld her part of the agreement.

On the other hand, if Ray decides to purchase the dining set and then finds out that Joan has sold it to Charles, he is entitled to get the money back. Depending on the circumstances, the holder of an option contract may also be able to sue for breach of contract and recover any financial losses he suffered because of the breach. In rare instances—when the item for sale cannot be duplicated, for example—it may be possible to file a lawsuit to have the sale rescinded.

Option contracts are also used in the sale of real estate. See also BREACH OF CONTRACT; CONTRACT.

ORDER OF PROTECTION

An adult victim of domestic violence may seek protection against her abuser. The court may issue an order of protection, stating that the abuser must keep away from his victim. Unlike a temporary restraining order, an order of protection applies only to cases of domestic violence—that is, abuse by a spouse, boyfriend, or girlfriend. If the abuser violates the order, he will be immediately jailed for contempt. See also BATTERED WOMEN.

If you are being abused and you wish to obtain an order of protection, you should fill out a petition at your county courthouse, setting forth the reasons that you need the court's protection and the type of relief that you need. Some courts can recommend a crisis counselor or victim's advocacy group to help you fill out the petition; your lawyer can also help you. Some states have a filing fee, but that can be waived if you cannot afford it.

A judge will conduct a hearing at which only you, or you and your lawyer, are present. Your abuser need not be notified of this hearing. You will tell the judge about any previous abuse and why you have reason to believe that your abuser may hurt you or your children. If the judge is convinced that you are in danger, she will issue an order of protection and set a date for another hearing, at which you, and possibly your abuser, will appear to present more evidence. When appropriate, the court may issue orders for the custody and support of your children and temporary spousal support.

The order of protection will be delivered to the abuser. It will usually state that he must stay away from your home and your workplace. If you own your home jointly, he may be allowed to remove his belongings under supervision. He will also be notified of the next hearing.

If your abuser violates the order of protection by approaching you at home or at work, you should call the police, who can take him into custody. In some cases it is a violation of the court order if the abuser telephones you.

At the subsequent hearing, the judge hears both sides of the story and decides either to continue the order of protection or to dissolve it. An order of protection can stay in effect indefinitely. See also TEMPORARY RESTRAINING ORDER.

REAL LIFE, REAL LAW

The Case of the Terrified Spouse

For more than eight years, Louise had been the victim of her husband David's abuse, including beatings so severe that she had to seek emergency medical care and take refuge in a shelter for battered women. When Louise told David that she was going to divorce him, David said he would kill her if he was served with divorce papers. Fearing for her life, Louise went to court to seek an order of protection to keep David away from her. Incredibly, the judge denied her petition. He held that an order of protection was available only to someone in "imminent fear" of an immediate threat, and that since David had not beaten Louise for seven months prior to his threat, and she had not served him with divorce papers, she was in no immediate danger.

Fortunately, Louise was granted an order of protection from another judge, but because the first judge's ruling was potentially dangerous to others, the Utah Court of Appeals took the unusual step of hearing an appeal on a case that was technically moot (a dead issue). Reversing the judge's decision, the court held that under Utah law, David's threat to kill Louise was more than enough evidence to support an order of protection, and instructed the state's lower courts that in similar cases in the future, an order of protection must be granted.

ORGAN DONATION

Owing to improved technology and an increased number of donors, medical organ transplants have become a fairly common occurrence. Although the sale of body parts for transplantation is illegal, the procedure for donating your heart, liver, eyes, or other organs for medical research or transplants has become very simple.

Under the Uniform Anatomical Gift Act, which has been enacted in every state, all that is required is for you to sign a donor card stating that you are willing to leave all or part of your body to medicine at the time of your death. The card must be signed by two witnesses. In many states this donor card is on the back of your driver's license. If you do not have a license, you can use a Universal Anatomical Gift form, which is available at the hospital or your doctor's office. Give a copy of the form to your physician. If you change your mind about donating your organs, all you have to do to revoke the anatomical gift is to cross out your signature on all copies of the forms or simply destroy them.

When you become a donor, the recipient pays the cost of removing the organs from the body. In some states, if a person dies in a hospital without an anatomical gift form, a member of the hospital staff is required to ask family members whether they wish to donate the deceased person's organs for transplantation. However, the family is under no legal obligation to consent.

OVERTIME

For most employees, the typical work week is 40 hours long. But occasions arise when a deadline has to be met or production must be expanded to meet client or customer needs. Usually, you cannot be forced to work overtime, although in some cases refusing to do so can be grounds for dismissal. If your employer asks you to work more than 40 hours in a week, you may be entitled to overtime pay.

FEDERAL LAW

The Fair Labor Standards Act (FLSA) is the federal law that sets basic requirements for overtime pay for some, but not all, employees. Eligibility for overtime pay depends on the type of work you do, the number of people that your company employs, and whether your employer does business within the state or across state lines.

For instance, if your company employs fewer than 15 people, the FLSA does not apply. Retail or service companies that conduct business within one state are also exempt from FLSA requirements.

The law also excludes various categories of workers from overtime coverage, including managers; railroad and airline workers; professionals, such as lawyers, teachers, and doctors; newspaper delivery employees; some limousine and truck drivers; most agricultural workers; and certain employees working on a commission basis.

OVERTIME RATES

Under the FLSA, an employer must pay covered employees at least one and a half times their regular rate of pay as overtime compensation. If you are employed on a piecework basis, your overtime rate is calculated by taking your total earnings for the week and dividing it by the number of hours worked to arrive at an hourly rate. Your overtime is then one and a half times this rate.

WORK WEEK

For most employees covered by the FLSA, any hours worked in excess of 40 hours per week must be paid at the overtime rate. This does not mean that you get overtime pay when you work more than eight hours on a particular day or have to work on a weekend or holiday. The federal law looks at the standard of 40 hours for the week as a whole, regardless of which day those hours are worked.

For some occupations, the FLSA uses different criteria to determine overtime. Hospital employees, for example, may have overtime calculated on the basis of hours worked in excess of an eight-hour day.

COMP TIME

Although most employees are paid for their overtime hours, some public-sector employees (such as firefighters and police officers) are given the option of time off for overtime, sometimes called compensatory time, or comp time. If your employer provides this option, you must receive one and a half hours of time off for every hour of overtime worked. Generally, comp time is granted during the same period in which you worked the overtime. If that is not possible, you are still entitled to your comp time.

STATE LAWS

Most states have their own laws that cover groups excluded under the federal law. The state rate for overtime is the same as the federal rate, with two exceptions. In California, covered employees receive twice the regular rate when they work more than 12 hours per day or more than 8 hours on the seventh day of work in one week. And most employees in Puerto Rico receive double wages for overtime work.

If you have questions about overtime pay, call your state's department of labor or other agency in charge of monitoring wages. At the federal level, contact the Wage and Hour Division of the Department of Labor. Union members can ask their union representatives about special overtime provisions in their labor contract. See also EMPLOYEE WORKING CONDITIONS.

PALIMONY

TO

PYRAMID SALES SCHEME

PALIMONY

Support that is paid to a former live-in partner is sometimes referred to as palimony. The term, which combines the words *pal* and *alimony*, entered the language in 1977 during a landmark court case involving actor Lee Marvin and the woman he had lived with for six years, Michelle Triola. Claiming that she had given up her own career to become Marvin's homemaker and that she and Marvin had an oral contract entitling her to one-half his income, Triola sued Marvin for a large share of his assets.

Triola lost the lawsuit, but the case established an important precedent. The California Supreme Court ruled that a contract between unmarried partners who are living together is valid. By such a contract, one party agrees to provide financial support, and in return the other party agrees to run the household, serve as a social companion, or manage financial affairs. If the court decides that this type of contract exists, the couple may be required to share their income and assets if their relationship ends.

To avoid a possible lawsuit in the future, you and your partner would be wise to draw up a cohabitation agreement, a written contract that spells out your obligations to one another during the relationship, as well as each person's rights if the relationship ends. Such an agreement will minimize disputes and protect you from the unfounded claims of an embittered ex-partner. A cohabitation agreement is especially important if one of you has substantial assets, or if the living arrangement requires one of you to make a major sacrifice, such as giving up a job or moving a long distance. For a sample cohabitation agreement, see the EVERYDAY LEGAL FORMS section of this book, beginning on page 552. See also LIVING TOGETHER.

PARALEGAL

A paralegal is a person who performs some legal tasks under the supervision of an attorney, but is not licensed to practice law. Although paralegals are trained legal personnel,—sometimes referred to as lawyer's assistants, legal technicians, or paraprofessionals—they may not give legal advice. Their duties include maintaining records, researching legal issues, and drafting or reviewing legal documents.

Paralegal programs are available nationwide and are open to anyone with a bachelor's or associate's degree or a certificate from a vocational school. If you want to enter a paralegal program, look for one that is "ABA approved." This means that the program meets the standards set by the American Bar Association.

PARDON

A pardon is an official action by the president of the United States or the governor of a state that exempts a person from punishment for a crime he has committed. The power to pardon is exercised when such an official decides that the public welfare is better served by lifting a sentence than by carrying it out.

A pardon may be full or partial. A full pardon absolves the person from all legal consequences of his actions and restores all the rights and privileges of citizenship. A partial pardon removes only a portion of those consequences.

In some instances, a pardon can be issued even before any criminal charges are filed. This was the case when President Gerald Ford granted a full, unconditional pardon to his predecessor, former President Richard Nixon, who resigned from office in 1974 as a result of the Watergate scandal. The scandal grew out of an illegal break-in at the Democratic National Headquarters. In effect, Ford's pardon prevented criminal charges from being filed by prosecutors. In most cases, however, a pardon is not granted until after a conviction.

Parental-Liability Laws

When a minor injures someone or maliciously damages or destroys property, most states impose some financial responsibility on the child's parent. Without parental-liability laws, persons injured by a child's actions must wait until the child becomes an adult to claim his wages or property.

In most instances a parent will be held responsible for his child's actions only if he has legal custody of the child. In a few states, however, a noncustodial parent may also be held liable. Several states make parents liable for all civil wrongs committed by their children, even if they resulted from negligence rather than malicious or willful misbehavior. Most states limit parental liability to an amount specified by law, typically no more than $15,000.

Parental-liability laws usually do not apply if the child is younger than the age specified in the state's statute. For example, in most states the parents of a six-year-old child are not responsible if the child injures another person or willfully destroys someone's property. And in some states a parent is not responsible unless the child's act is also a crime under state law (such as arson). See also LIABILITY; NEGLIGENCE; TORT.

Parking Garage

You drove your brand-new car into town this morning and parked it at Fred's Friendly Garage. But when you returned to pick it up, you learned that it had been stolen. What should you do, and who is responsible for your loss?

Before you do anything else, you should report the theft to the police and to your insurance company, as you would do with any other kind of theft.

The way in which the car was parked will determine who is responsible for its being stolen. If you parked the car yourself and kept the keys, the garage owner will probably not be held responsible, since he just rented you the space. If you were required to give your keys to an attendant, however, you created what is known as a bailment—that is, you entrusted your property to another person's care. In that case, the garage owner would be required to exercise reasonable

Parental-Liability Laws

If an underage child damages property or injures someone, his parents may be held liable, depending upon state law. Degrees of parental liability in different states are shown below.

care to safeguard your car while it is in his possession. If he failed to do so, he might be held liable. See BAILMENT.

If a car parked by an attendant is damaged, the garage owner is responsible. But if the damage occurs in a garage where you park your car yourself, the owner will probably not be liable.

If your car is insured against theft or damage, and your insurance company determines that your car was stolen or damaged as a result of the garage owner's carelessness, the company will pay your claim and then take action against the owner for reimbursement. But if you do not have the appropriate insurance, you will have to sue the garage on your own.

If you leave your car at a garage that requires attendant parking, make sure that the person to whom you give your keys is actually an employee. Ask to see identification, especially if the garage is one you do not use regularly. There have been a number of instances of car owners accepting receipts from young men dressed in official-looking jackets, only to discover later that the receipts were counterfeit and the "attendants" were members of an organized car-theft ring. See also AUTOMOBILE ACCIDENTS; AUTOMOBILE INSURANCE; LAWSUIT.

PAROLE

After serving part of a prison sentence, a convict may become eligible for parole—that is, he may be released, but only under certain conditions. Parole helps the offender reform by giving him time to readjust to society before his sentence has expired. Parole is a privilege—not a right—and not every eligible prisoner is paroled. A prisoner's age, mental health, behavior record, and the nature and severity of his crime are some of the factors that can influence the parole board's decision.

A convict "on parole" is supervised by a parole officer to make sure he observes the conditions of his parole. For example, he may have to visit his parole officer once a week, make an effort to find a job, and avoid contact with former criminal associates. If he violates these conditions, he may be returned to prison for the remainder of his sentence. See also PROBATION.

PARTNERSHIP

A partnership is an association of two or more persons, known as general partners, who act as co-owners of a business and operate it for profit. The other two major forms of business are a sole proprietorship and a corporation. See also CORPORATION; LIMITED-LIABILITY COMPANY; SOLE PROPRIETORSHIP.

Since each state has specific laws on the formation and dissolution of partnerships, as well as laws regarding the legal responsibilities of each partner, business owners are well advised to consult an attorney and a tax accountant before establishing a partnership.

ADVANTAGES AND DISADVANTAGES

A partnership is relatively simple to establish and does not require the same amount of record keeping as a corporation. Another advantage of a partnership is that income is taxed only once. By contrast, most corporations are taxed twice—they pay taxes on their income, and if there are shareholders, they in turn pay taxes on the share of the corporation's income that they receive as dividends.

Partnerships need only file an information return (a form indicating the partnership's income, expenses, and profits or losses) with the Internal Revenue Service, but the partnership itself does not pay taxes. Each partner pays federal, state, and local taxes on their income from the partnership as if it were personal income. See also STOCKS AND BONDS.

The chief disadvantage of being a general partner is that you can be held personally responsible for another partner's negligence or carelessness. This means that if your partnership is unable to meet its financial obligations, you may have to use your personal assets to pay off debtors, even though you personally may not be at fault. If the partnership defaults on a loan, for example, the bank has the right to sue any general partner to collect this debt. If you own a car or a home, the court may order you to sell that property and turn the proceeds over to the bank. (If you and your spouse own the property jointly, the bank is entitled to only one-half the proceeds).

Another disadvantage of a partnership is that if one partner decides to sever the business relationship, then the partnership generally dissolves. The bankruptcy or death of a partner usually results in the end of the partnership.

PARTNERSHIP AGREEMENT

Once you and another person have decided to form a partnership, you should prepare an agreement. If you plan to be in business for more than one year, the agreement must be in writing. If you are planning a short-term business venture, an oral agreement may suffice, but it is still best to put everything down on paper to avoid potential misunderstandings and disagreements. Your partnership agreement should include the following:

◇ The name of the partnership and the names of each of the partners.

◇ A general description of the type of business that will be conducted.

◇ The powers and duties of the partners, including any limitations or restrictions.

◇ The financial contributions each partner will make.

◇ How profits and losses are to be divided.

◇ How partners can leave the business and how new partners can be added.

◇ What steps must be taken to dissolve the partnership.

LIMITED PARTNERSHIPS

If you and another person have all the necessary business skills but insufficient capital, you might be better served by a limited partnership—a business made up of one or more general partners and one or more special partners with limited liability. Unlike a general partner, who is personally responsible for all debts and obligations of the partnership, a limited partner can lose only the amount of capital he has invested in the business.

A limited partner has relatively little power within the partnership because he is not allowed to be actively involved in the management of the business; he is merely a financial contributor. Nevertheless, he has the right to be informed of all business matters relating to the company and to share in its profits. (His profits, like those of a general partner, are treated as personal income for federal tax purposes.) If a limited partner starts making management decisions, his status immediately changes to general partner, and he becomes personally responsible for any business debts.

ENDING A PARTNERSHIP

After a partnership is dissolved, the partners are no longer authorized to conduct business together. To formally end the partnership, they must discharge all business obligations to creditors and divide all assets and any remaining profits among themselves.

PART-TIME WORK

If you are employed as a part-time worker—one who works on a limited schedule—you will probably not be eligible for the benefits given to full-time employees, and you may not be covered by laws regarding minimum wages or unemployment benefits.

MINIMUM WAGE

Before you accept a part-time job, you should check both state and federal minimum-wage laws to determine whether part-time employees are entitled to the minimum wage. Federal law not only excludes certain categories of work but also permits a lower-than-minimum wage for trainees, apprentices, or students in work programs approved by the Department of Labor. Your right to be paid the minimum wage, therefore, may depend on your job category rather than the number of hours you work. State laws vary; some exclude employees who work "at irregular times." See also MINIMUM-WAGE LAWS.

COMPANY BENEFITS

Part-time workers may also be ineligible for participation in group health, life, or disability insurance plans. An employer's contract with his insurance company defines "eligibility" or "employee." It also states the minimum number of hours per week and the number of days of continuous service a person must work to qualify for coverage. A typical policy may limit coverage to employees who work at least 20 or 30 hours per week with 90 days of continuous service.

Ask your prospective employer about the kind of insurance he offers. You may be eligible for group health coverage but not for long-term disability, for example. Note that the fact that one employer has a plan that covers part-time employees does not mean that other employers offer the same protection.

PENSIONS

As with insurance plans, pension plans require that part-time employees work a certain number of hours before they can qualify for plan participation. If the plan specifies 1,000 hours, therefore, those who work 25 or more hours per week become eligible for coverage after 40 weeks.

WORKERS' COMPENSATION

One benefit available to both full-time and part-time employees is workers' compensation. If you are injured on the job, the laws in your state will determine how much compensation you will receive and for how long. The amount of compensation will be affected by whether you worked full or part time, since one factor used in calculating your benefit is how much you would earn if you could continue working. If you work for a small company, whether full or part time, you may not be eligible for benefits at all, because some state laws require a company to have a certain number of employees for workers' compensation to be mandatory. See WORKERS' COMPENSATION.

UNEMPLOYMENT COMPENSATION

Eligibility for unemployment benefits is also determined by state law. If you are fired from a part-time job, you may not be eligible for unemployment compensation, or the benefits you receive may be reduced. In some states, benefits are calculated according to your base pay. If your compensation is less than the minimum amount, you will not qualify.

DISCRIMINATION

Your protection against job discrimination is determined not by the number of hours you work, but by the number of people who work for your employer. Title VII of the Civil Rights Act—which prohibits discrimination on the basis of race, color, national origin, sex, or religious beliefs—applies to private employers who have 15 or more employees working every day for 20 weeks. Even if you work only 3 hours each day during a 20-week period for a company with at least 15 employees, you are still counted as an employee and are protected against discrimination.

PASSPORT

Issued by the U.S. State Department, a passport is a document certifying that its holder is a U.S. citizen. It serves as identification for citizens traveling abroad and asks the host country to grant the bearer legal protection. A passport does not ensure that the foreign country will admit him, however. For this, he may need a visa. See VISA.

GETTING A PASSPORT

You can obtain a passport application at the main post office in your community, or you can visit the nearest office of the Passport Agency of the U.S. State Department. Along with the completed passport application form and fee, you will have to provide: (1) proof of U.S. citizenship—either a certified copy of your birth certificate, naturalization papers, or an expired U.S. passport; (2) two forms of identification, such as a birth certificate and a driver's license; and (3) two identical black-and-white or color head shots (two inches square), photographed within the last six months.

It usually takes a number of weeks to process an application. During the spring and early summer the wait can be especially long because of the volume of applications. If you need to obtain a passport in a hurry, call the U.S. Department of State's Passport Office in Washington, D.C. This office can help expedite your application, and you may be able to receive your passport within 24 hours.

Your passport is valid for 10 years from the date it is issued. However, if you are charged with a serious crime, the court may ask you to surrender your passport before granting bail, to ensure that you will not leave the country.

PROTECTING YOUR PASSPORT

U.S. passports are highly prized on the foreign black market, so guard yours carefully while traveling. Before your trip, make two photocopies of your passport; leave one at home and put the other in a separate section of your luggage. To avoid theft, carry your passport separate from your money—preferably in a front inside coat pocket or in a document pouch strapped under your shirt or blouse. Don't leave your passport in a hotel room; if you do not carry it with you, store it in the hotel's safe-deposit box and get a receipt.

REPLACING A LOST PASSPORT

If you lose your passport while traveling abroad, immediately notify the local police and the nearest U.S. embassy or consulate. These offices can help you obtain replacement documents that will allow you to continue your travels and return home. If your passport is lost, stolen, or destroyed in the United States, call the police immediately and send a written notice to Passport Services, Bureau of Consular Affairs, Department of State, 1425 K Street NW, Washington, DC 20524. See also CITIZENSHIP; IMMIGRATION.

PATENT

To promote the progress of science, the U.S. Constitution authorizes Congress to grant inventors an exclusive right to their inventions for a specified period of time. This right is called a patent, and it gives the inventor (or his heirs) the right to exclude others from making, using, or selling his invention. If someone infringes on this right without the inventor's permission and without compensating him, the inventor is entitled to sue that person.

Because patent law is complex, you should consult an attorney who specializes in the field if you want to obtain a patent. If the attorney believes that your invention has merit, he will first conduct a patent search to determine whether it is substantially different from existing patents. Keep in mind that almost 5 million patents have been granted by the U.S. Patent Office, and 90,000 or so are issued each year. If your invention is similar to one that already exists, you will not be able to obtain a patent. But if it is truly unique, the attorney will prepare a patent application for you to sign and submit to the U.S. Patent Office, along with the application fee.

Patents fall into one of two categories: mechanical and design. A mechanical patent is granted for a machine, process, device, or even genetically engineered material. This patent gives the inventor the exclusive right to his invention for 17 years. A design patent is granted for a new, original, and ornamental design for such items as fabrics, furniture, jewelry, and industrial equipment. The design must be in some tangible form—ideas alone cannot be patented. A design patent offers protection for 14 years.

ABC's OF APPLYING FOR A PATENT

To apply for a patent, the first thing you or your lawyer will need to do is write to the U.S. Patent Office and ask for complete instructions and application materials. Address your request to the Commissioner of Patents and Trademarks, Washington, DC 20231. Your application, once you have completed it, will generally consist of the following:

- ❑ A transmittal form (available from the address above).
- ❑ A description of the invention, including its title, a summary of its specifications, and an explanation of how it is made and used and what makes it unique.
- ❑ A notarized statement attesting to the fact that you are the original inventor.
- ❑ A drawing of the invention that shows its unique features.
- ❑ A filing fee.

Patents are the personal property of the inventors who receive them, and thus they can be assigned or licensed to others. In fact, most inventors do not have adequate financial resources to bring their creations to market; they usually sell or license their patents to companies.

Generally, before a company agrees to a licensing or purchase agreement, it will ask for a prototype—a working model of the invention. Depending on the nature and complexity of the invention, creating a prototype can be costly. Before you invest a lot of money in a prototype, you may want to have your patent evaluated for its marketability. Many universities critique inventions for little or no charge, and some private companies are in the business of assessing the commercial potential of inventions.

Be extremely wary, however, of companies that offer "development contracts," promising to market your invention for a large evaluation fee. In many cases these firms provide little assistance in relation to the size of their fees. See also COPYRIGHT; TRADEMARK.

PATERNITY SUIT

An unmarried mother can compel the father of her child to provide financial support for the child by bringing a paternity suit against him. Generally, the evidence—which often includes blood tests of the mother and alleged father, as well as testimony about their relationship at the time of conception—must show that the defendant is more likely than not to be the child's father. This is called establishing a preponderance of evidence. See also BURDEN OF PROOF.

Sometimes a state welfare department may file a paternity suit in order to remove a child from public assistance programs. See also BLOOD TESTING; CHILD SUPPORT; ILLEGITIMACY.

PATIENTS' RIGHTS

When you are sick or injured, you generally must trust in physicians or hospitals to give you the proper care. However, you should recognize that you are in charge of the treatment you receive and, as a patient, you have certain rights.

CONSENT

Your most basic right is that of consent. Your physician must fully inform you of all the options available for treatment and the risks and benefits associated with each. This is known as the doctrine of informed consent. A doctor who explains only the treatment she wants to provide has not fulfilled her responsibility, and the patient's consent will therefore not be valid. In some instances a doctor may be allowed to limit the amount of information she gives to the patient. For example, she may withhold information that could have an adverse effect on the patient, or the patient himself may not want to know the truth about his condition. In these situations the physician may keep family members fully informed about the patient's illness.

Before medical personnel begin any form of treatment—from a simple laboratory test to major surgery—they must obtain your consent. If they do not, you may be able to sue them for assault and battery. If you are too ill to give consent, they must ask the permission of a family member before beginning any procedures, unless a delay would be life-threatening. See CONSENT FORM; INFORMED CONSENT.

RIGHT TO REFUSE TREATMENT

Certain health-care facilities have a duty to advise patients of their right to refuse treatment. The federal Patient Self-Determination Act of 1990 requires hospitals, nursing homes, health maintenance organizations, hospices, and home health-care businesses that receive funds from Medicare or Medicaid to ask patients about their willingness to accept life-sustaining medical treatment. In practice, this law affects virtually all hospitals.

These federally funded medical providers must also inform patients that they have the right to specify which life-sustaining measures can be taken should they become terminally ill and incapacitated. Sometimes the patient may have executed a living will, a health-care treatment directive, or a durable power of attorney for health-care decisions. If he has not done so, medical personnel may be able to help him complete one of these forms. For an example of a living will and a durable power of attorney for health-care decisions, see EVERYDAY LEGAL FORMS, beginning on page 552. See also LIVING WILL.

CONFIDENTIALITY

As a patient, you have a right to confidentiality. Unless you agree to have medical information released, your doctor is not permitted to give it to anyone—even family members who may want to know about your condition. If you have a communicable disease, however, your doctor is obligated by law to notify the public health department and, in some cases, anyone close to you who might be at risk.

The issue of confidentiality is often raised when the patient is a child. Generally a parent must grant permission for medical treatment, because the child is not considered mature enough to make such a decision. In many states, however, teenagers are allowed to give consent for treatment involving pregnancy, drug abuse, alcoholism, or emotional problems without notifying their parents. Depending on state law, the physician may be prohibited from discussing the patient's condition with his parents unless he first has the child's consent. See also ABORTION; CHILDREN'S RIGHTS.

PATIENT'S BILL OF RIGHTS

When you check into a hospital, you may receive a copy of "A Patient's Bill of Rights," developed by the American Hospital Association to inform patients about standards for the care they are entitled to receive. Under these guidelines, you have the right to:

◇ Sufficient medical information to allow you to give informed consent.

◇ Information about hospital rules and regulations that apply to you.

◇ Complete, up-to-date information about your condition, treatment, and prognosis.

◇ Information about any experimental procedures that are performed on you.

◇ Considerate and respectful care.

◇ Privacy during consultations, examinations, procedures, and treatments.

◇ Confidential treatment of your medical records.

◇ Information about how care will be provided after you have been discharged.

◇ An opportunity to review your bill and an explanation of its contents.

STEPS TO TAKE IF YOUR RIGHTS ARE VIOLATED

If you believe that your rights as a patient have been violated by your caregiver, consider taking the following actions:

1. Express your concern to the doctor, nurse, or other caregiver. A frank discussion will usually resolve what may be a simple misunderstanding.

2. Call the hospital administrator, who may investigate the problem and order corrective action.

3. Write or call the state licensing authority (usually the department of health).

4. You may also want to notify the nursing board or board of medical examiners if you have a complaint about a nurse or doctor.

5. If the problem persists, call a lawyer.

PAWNBROKER

A pawnbroker is someone who makes loans using personal property as collateral. Pawnbrokers differ from banks in that they charge higher interest (up to 10 percent per month), are willing to lend smaller sums of money, and are more flexible about what they will accept as collateral. Borrowers pledge items of personal property, such as jewelry, musical instruments, electronic equipment—even automobiles—to secure their loans.

Because pawnbrokers are often lenders of last resort, used primarily by people with poor credit ratings who cannot get loans elsewhere, they lend their customers only a fraction of the value of their collateral—10 to 50 cents on the dollar is not unusual. For this reason, and because of the high interest rates, you should consider other avenues for borrowing the money you need before you go to a pawnbroker.

Collateral that you leave with a pawnbroker remains your property as long as you meet the terms of the loan agreement. The pawnbroker is prohibited from using the property or doing anything that would diminish its value. But if you fail to repay the loan, the pawnbroker can legally sell your property to recover the amount of your loan, plus interest (and sometimes insurance and storage fees). Whether he must return any remaining money to you depends on your agreement with him and the laws in your state.

Because pawnbrokers were once commonly used by burglars to obtain cash for stolen goods, every state now has laws that strictly regulate pawnbrokers' activities and require them to keep careful records of their clients' identities. If a pawnbroker knowingly or unknowingly accepts stolen property and the true owner can prove it is hers, the pawnbroker must return it without being compensated for his loss.

PEDESTRIAN

A pedestrian is a person walking or standing on a public thoroughfare. What constitutes a pedestrian figured in one famous case, in which an insurance company denied payment to a policyholder who was injured while standing on a street corner. In court, the company argued that its policy provided coverage only while the policyholder was traveling on foot, and that since the man was standing still when he was injured, he was not a pedestrian within the terms of the policy. The court disagreed, however, and ordered the insurer to pay the claim. Today the legal definition of the word *pedestrian* includes people in wheelchairs, on roller skates, on crutches—even on stilts!

PENSION PLAN

A program that provides retirement income for wage earners is called a pension plan. It may be sponsored by a government, private corporation, union, the employee himself, or a combination of these. The federal government has pension plans for its employees, as do state and local governments, which fund pensions for teachers in their public school systems, police officers, and other public servants. For information about individual retirement plans, see INDIVIDUAL RETIREMENT ACCOUNT; KEOGH PLAN; RAILROAD RETIREMENT.

Although many corporations offer pensions so that they can attract and keep good employees, no employer is legally required to provide pensions for its workers.

For many years, pensions, when provided, were largely unregulated by the government. Often companies offered pension plans to attract employees but then deprived them of their pensions by firing them just before they retired. If a company went bankrupt or used pension funds for other purposes, retirees were often left in the lurch because their funds were not protected. To end such abuses, Congress enacted the Employee Retirement Income Security Act (ERISA) of 1974 , the Retirement Equity Act of 1984, and sections of the Tax Reform Act of 1986. These laws set minimum standards for pension plans in private industry as well as regulating all "qualified" pension plans—plans that are officially set up by companies and for which the company takes a tax deduction when it makes a contribution. The legislation mandates that:

◇ Age and length-of-service requirements for eligibility must be reasonable.

◇ The pension plan must pay at least some benefits to all employees who have worked for the amount of time specified in the plan.

◇ Plan funds must be handled and invested prudently.

◇ The pension fund must contain enough money to pay benefits as they become due.

◇ Employees must be informed of all their rights to payments under their plan.

◇ The spouses of pensioners must be protected by provisions for joint-and-survivor benefits.

◇ The pensions of participants in defined-benefit plans (see below) must be insured by the Pension Benefit Guaranty Corporation, to provide benefits in case the company ends its plan or cannot meet its pension obligations.

TYPES OF PLANS

Private pension plans are divided into two categories: defined benefit or defined contribution.

Defined-benefit plans
A defined-benefit plan pays participants a fixed income from the day they retire until the day they die. The amount is related to the employee's length of service and earnings. Defined-benefit plans have become increasingly unpopular with employers, however, because they require that regular payments of specified amounts be made to retirees, regardless of the rate of return on the invested pension money. If the investments happen to do well, the employer can keep the profits; if they do poorly, the employer must make up the difference.

Defined-contribution plans Under a defined-contribution plan, your employer agrees to put a specified sum into your retirement fund every year. Unlike a defined-benefit plan, it does not promise you a fixed income at retirement. Rather, it offers a fixed annual contribution to your retirement fund.

The contributions are invested, and your retirement income will depend on how well those investments do. The investments must be reasonable and prudent, and the employer (or the plan's trustee) is legally responsible for managing the funds wisely. You can choose among several investment options in some defined-contribution plans.

Another choice available to you with a defined-contribution plan is that when you retire, you can take the pension either in monthly installments or in a lump sum.

There are several kinds of defined-contribution plans:

◇ A *401(k) plan* (named after a section of the Internal Revenue Code) allows a participant to place a portion of her wages in her pension fund, where the money and the interest it earns remain tax-exempt until she begins making withdrawals. The sum the employee places in her account each year reduces her income by that amount. If she earns $35,000 and contributes $1,000, her taxable income will be $34,000. The employer may or may not contribute to the 401(k) plan.

◇ In a *deferred profit-sharing plan*, the company decides how much money will go into the plan when profits are declared each year. This amount is divided among the accounts of all participants by a formula that is usually pegged to wages. Federal law prohibits employees from withdrawing money from their profit-sharing accounts until they retire, but there are a few exceptions, such as medical emergencies.

◇ A *money-purchase plan* is based on fixed contributions from the employer—generally a certain percentage of the employee's earnings.

◇ A *target-benefit plan* uses a formula to set a target pension benefit for each employee and calculates contributions accordingly. Unlike a defined-benefit plan, there is no firm guarantee that the benefit goal will be reached. Your eventual monthly pension could be more or less than the target, depending on how accurate the company's calculations were and how well the pension fund performed.

Other retirement plans Federal laws also regulate pensions for workers who are not employed by private companies. Employees of educational, charitable, and religious institutions may have a 403(b) plan (also named for the section of the Internal Revenue Code that authorizes it). This plan allows them to make tax-deferred contributions. While the rules for contributing to the plan are somewhat complicated, the law generally allows employees to contribute up to 25 percent of their annual income, but no more than $9,500.

State and local government employees are covered by Section 457 plans. The limit on contributions to these plans is generally $7,500 or 33 percent of their annual income (subject to certain exclusions), whichever is less.

Federal government employees can participate in the Federal Thrift Savings Fund. The rules for participating in this plan are virtually identical to the rules for 401(k) plans.

WHO QUALIFIES

Although the exact specifications can vary, the typical employee pension plan allows you to participate if you are at least 21 years old and have completed one full year of service, or two years if the plan provides for full and immediate vesting. Generally, a year of service is a 12-month period during which you have worked for at least 1,000 hours. However, some employers are permitted to use an "elapsed time" method, which uses the total number of days you came to work, not the number of hours spent on the job. For more information about eligibility and vesting, see EMPLOYEE RETIREMENT INCOME SECURITY ACT (ERISA).

WHEN YOU WILL GET YOUR PENSION

You will begin to receive benefits when you reach the age specified in your plan. This is usually age 65, but each plan contains its own specified age. Check the summary description of your plan, available from your employer. Some pension plans allow participants to retire before age 65, if they have worked a given length of time. If you retire early, your monthly benefit will be lower, since the pension will be paid out over a longer period. Some plans pay an employee retiring at age 55 half of what a 65-year-old retiree would receive.

EARLY RETIREMENT

In recent years, some employers have offered early retirement to employees to reduce overstaffing in general or in specific job categories. In these instances, the employer may offer employees nearing retirement age financial incentives to retire, such as bonuses or pension payments larger than those due to the employee. These offers are legal, unless certain employees are singled out to receive such offers because of their age, sex, or for other prohibited reasons.

Before accepting an offer of early retirement, be sure to weigh such factors as your ability to obtain other employment, whether you will lose company-sponsored medical insurance, and the length of time between your early retirement and your eligibility for Social Security.

MONTHLY PAYMENTS VERSUS A LUMP SUM

Suppose you are about to retire with $100,000 in your pension fund, which is a defined-benefit plan. You are told that you can take the money either in monthly payments or as a lump sum. What should you do?

Monthly payments

If you do not want the responsibility of handling a large sum of money, you may prefer to take your pension in monthly installments. But before you make this choice, be sure that your company is financially stable and that your pension plan is insured by the Pension Benefit Guaranty Corporation. You can obtain a copy of your company's Form 5500 by writing to the Pension and Welfare Benefit Administration, U.S. Department of Labor, 200 Constitution Avenue NW, Washington, DC 20210.

You can also find out about your company's financial stability by reviewing its quarterly and annual reports if the company is publicly traded. Other valuable sources of fiscal information are the trade journals, newspaper reports, and your company's own communications to its employees.

Lump sum

Some retirees take their pension in a lump sum because they want to use the money for a specific purpose, such as purchasing a new home, or because they want to reinvest it themselves. Keep in mind that you will pay income taxes on the lump sum in the year you receive it unless you take advantage of one of the following options, which you should discuss with a tax adviser:

◇ *Income averaging.* Although income averaging nearly always reduces your taxes, it is no longer available to every retiree. If you are more than 59½ years old, you can average the $100,000 over five years—that is, pay taxes at current tax rates as though you were receiving $20,000 per year for five years. If you were born before January 1, 1936, you can take a 10-year income average using 1986 tax rates.

◇ *Rollovers.* You can put all the money into a qualified individual retirement account (IRA) and pay taxes only on the money you withdraw each year while the rest of the money earns interest that is tax-exempt.

Unfortunately, rolling your money over into an IRA, a popular option, is not as simple as it once was. If you retired in 1992 or earlier and requested your pension as a lump sum, your company would have given you a check for $100,000 and you would have had 60 days to decide what to do with it. But a new law that took effect in January 1993 put an end to the 60-day waiting period. Unless your company sends your pension to a qualified IRA directly (making what is called a trust-to-trust transfer), it must withhold 20 percent of your pension money and send it to the IRS.

In view of the new law, you should be sure to roll over your IRA before you leave your job. Ask your employer to send the money to the bank or other financial institution you have chosen. See INDIVIDUAL RETIREMENT ACCOUNT.

GOVERNMENT PROTECTIONS

Three agencies of the federal government are responsible for safeguarding your pension.

◇ The Pension Benefit Guaranty Corporation insures the defined-benefit pension plans of businesses that run into financial trouble, although it will not necessarily replace retirement benefits dollar for dollar. In 1993 the maximum pension a single 65-year-old pensioner could receive was approximately $27,000 per year. The PBGC adjusts the maximum amount every year to account for inflation.

◇ The Department of Labor makes certain that all pension plans are managed in accordance with the requirements of ERISA and other federal pension laws.

◇ The Internal Revenue Service oversees pension-plan funding and vesting requirements and makes sure that plan administrators comply with federal tax laws. Employers must notify the IRS of their pension funds' assets and liabilities, show how the money is invested, and indicate whether the company is current on its payments into the pension fund. Most important, your employer must tell the IRS if it is considering terminating its pension plan.

PERSONAL BANKRUPTCY

If you file for bankruptcy, the trustee who becomes responsible for paying off your creditors will try to use your pension money unless it is classified as exempt property under federal or state law. ERISA-qualified pensions are classified as exempt property under federal rules. Some state exemptions are more generous than the federal ones. Before you declare bankruptcy, get a lawyer's help to make sure your pension is protected from creditors. See BANKRUPTCY.

IF A PARTICIPANT DIVORCES OR DIES

The Retirement Equity Act of 1984 generally prohibits a pension-plan participant from assigning benefits to someone other than his spouse. But this prohibition does not apply to an order by a state divorce court that awards a portion of a worker's pension as part of a spousal-support or child-support order. An order from a divorce court can require the plan to pay benefits to the former spouse or child beginning on the date when the worker reaches the earliest retirement age permitted under the plan. Suppose a pension plan permits workers to begin taking pension benefits at age 55. The divorce court could order the pension plan to make distributions to an ex-spouse when the worker reaches that age, even if the worker does not retire but continues working for another 10 years or more.

Suppose a plan participant dies before he or she retires. In this situation, ERISA and the Retirement Equity Act require the plan to pay the surviving spouse a survivor's benefit, unless both the spouse and the worker chose not to have the joint-and-survivor benefit for the covered worker.

The rules for obtaining pension payments after a divorce are complicated, but divorced persons should be aware that they do have rights. Ask your former spouse's employer for detailed information about how these rules apply to your rights to your former spouse's plan.

PLAN TERMINATIONS

Employers are legally entitled to replace their pension plans with new ones or to end them altogether. If your company merges with or is acquired by another company and issues a new plan, it must offer employees benefits equal to the old one. If your company decides to terminate its pension plan, the administrator must notify you in writing at least 60 days in advance and then give you your money in a lump sum.

In the event of a company bankruptcy, the PBGC may declare a "distress termination" of a pension plan in order to decide how much of the promised benefits the company can provide. If there is not enough money to pay at least the value insured by PBGC, the PBGC takes over as trustee of the plan and uses its own insurance funds to make up the difference to the pensioners.

FURTHER INFORMATION

The best way to find out what your pension will be is to check the summary of your plan's annual report. There you will find general information, such as the amount by which your benefit is reduced if you are married and elect to take a joint-and-survivor benefit, or what will happen if you take a leave of absence and return at a later date.

Regarding leaves of absence, ERISA has rules that prevent workers from losing their pension benefits because of a break in employment. But these rules are complicated and depend largely on when the break takes place and how long it lasts.

For more specific information about your pension, you can turn to your annual statement, which companies provide for each employee. See also SOCIAL SECURITY.

PEREMPTORY CHALLENGE

A peremptory challenge will allow an attorney who is in the process of jury selection to refuse a potential juror without giving a reason for dismissing him. If a juror reveals that he has a bias for or against one side, the attorney for either party can remove him "for cause." But if an attorney wants to remove a juror but does not have a legally acceptable cause, he can make a peremptory challenge.

NUMBER OF CHALLENGES

To ensure that a jury will be impartial, most states allow an unlimited number of challenges for cause. But they limit the number of peremptory challenges, with the result that attorneys first try to remove a juror they do not want by challenging for cause, rather than by using a peremptory challenge. Under most statutes both sides get the same number of peremptory challenges, although in some states the prosecution gets only half as many as the defense.

In federal courts the defense for a defendant charged with a capital crime (one that is punishable by death) is entitled to 20 peremptory challenges, as is the prosecution. If a crime carries a prison sentence of a year or more, the defense has 10 challenges and the prosecution has 6. For less serious crimes, each side may have 3 challenges.

DISCRIMINATION

Peremptory challenges play a vital role in jury selection. In most cases neither of the opposing attorneys will object to the peremptory challenges made by the other. However, the U.S. Supreme Court has ruled that peremptory challenges may not be used by prosecutors solely to exclude members of a criminal defendant's race. If the prosecutor is challenging only potential jurors who are of the same race as the defendant, the defense can object and the prosecutor must show that there was a "neutral" reason for the challenge—for example, that the potential juror was inattentive. See also JURY.

PERJURY

Perjury is the crime of intentionally lying under oath. Sometimes known as false swearing, perjury can occur in any proceeding in which witnesses are required to give sworn testimony.

Because perjury can result in a serious obstruction of justice, courts tend to view charges of perjury very seriously. Perjury is a felony that may carry a prison sentence of 10 years as well as possible fines.

EXAMPLES

The following are some common examples of perjury.

◇ Deliberately lying on the stand in a trial or hearing.

◇ Giving false testimony in grand jury proceedings, if the testimony is material—that is, related to matters that the grand jury is investigating.

◇ Giving false testimony to a congressional committee.

◇ Lying while giving a deposition (a procedure for conducting discovery or collecting evidence for a trial). See also DEPOSITION.

If your religious convictions prevent you from taking an oath and you affirm that you will tell the truth, this does not affect your duty to tell the truth under the perjury laws. See OATH AND AFFIRMATION.

EXCEPTIONS

In some situations false statements that are made under oath are not considered perjury. Such instances fall into the following categories:

Fifth Amendment
Under the Fifth Amendment, no one can be compelled to incriminate himself. For example, if Edward is forced to testify in a grand jury proceeding and lies under oath to avoid self-incrimination, he cannot be prosecuted for perjury. But if Edward has been granted immunity from prosecution for a particular offense, he cannot then give false testimony about that offense.

The Fifth Amendment applies only to criminal activity—misdemeanors as well as felonies. If Edward's testimony might subject him to civil penalties (typically fines), he cannot refuse to answer, since the Fifth Amendment does not extend to civil cases.

Ignorance
If you make a false statement under oath but do not know or believe it to be false, you have

not committed perjury. False statements due to mistake, forgetfulness, or misunderstanding the question are not considered perjury.

Irrelevance
To qualify as perjury, a false statement must be about the matter at issue, whether in a court or on a document. For example, if a witness testifying at a murder trial lies about her age, she would probably not be prosecuted for perjury.

Opinion
A mistake or an incorrectly held opinion is not perjury. If you say, "I thought that the driver was drunk," when in fact the driver was having a fainting spell, you are not committing perjury because you are testifying to your opinion, not fact.

PERJURY IN WRITTEN FORM

The crime of perjury is not limited to courtroom testimony. You can be prosecuted for perjury if you sign your name to a legal document that you know deliberately contains a false statement, as in the following situations:

◇ If you sign false pleadings—written statements regarding a lawsuit.

◇ If you make a false statement when applying for a marriage license (in some states).

◇ If you sign a false affidavit in connection with a lawsuit or with an application for a professional license or permit.

◇ If you sign your income tax return knowing that it contains fraudulent information.

REAL LIFE, REAL LAW

The Case of the Perjurer's Penalty

Michael DeMan testified at the trial of a business associate who was accused, along with DeMan, of bribing a state official. Because his testimony was so important, the prosecutors gave DeMan immunity, agreeing that they would not punish him for his role in the bribery scheme even though his testimony would be self-incriminating. Despite this guarantee, DeMan gave false testimony under oath and was charged with perjury. He was found guilty on seven counts of perjury and sentenced to four years in prison on each count. The sentences, however, were to run concurrently, rather than consecutively.

DeMan appealed his conviction, claiming that the sentences handed down by the court were excessive. In his defense, he pointed to his lack of any serious prior criminal record, his college education, and his long and stable work history as evidence of his ability to be a productive member of society. In addition, he noted that the state probation department had recommended less severe punishment.

In reviewing the case, the court of appeals cited that DeMan had misused business funds for personal expenses and that a presentencing physical exam had detected cocaine in his blood. Most important, however, it noted that DeMan committed perjury even though he would not have been subject to prosecution had he told the truth. The court emphasized that one of the reasons for prison sentences is to deter others from committing the same offense. Also, since perjury is classified as a felony punishable by as much as 10 years in state prison in some states, the court upheld DeMan's sentence, maintaining that the 4-year sentence was not excessive.

PERMIT

A permit is a document issued by a government agency that authorizes a person or entity to carry out some activity that would not otherwise be allowed. For example, you may need a permit from the local building department to add a deck to your home. Likewise, the piece of paper a customs official gives you after inspecting your baggage is a permit that allows you to remove your property from the customs area and take it home. See also HOME IMPROVEMENT AND REPAIR; LICENSE.

PERSONAL RECORDS

From the moment of birth, Americans begin to accumulate documents and personal records. Many of these, such as birth certificates, marriage licenses, real estate deeds, and insurance policies, should be retained for legal reasons.

WHAT TO THROW AWAY

Good record keeping means not only putting papers you need to save in places where they can easily be retrieved, but also discarding papers that are no longer useful. For example, there is no need to keep the following:

◇ Passbooks or checkbooks from bank accounts that you have closed, after you have reconciled them with your final bank statements. (Be sure to tear up or shred any unused checks, so that they do not fall into the wrong hands and so that you cannot accidentally write a check on an account that is closed).

◇ Warranties from products you no longer own.

◇ Paycheck stubs (once you have received your annual W-2 form from your employer and have compared it to the amount shown on the stubs).

◇ Credit card agreements for cards that you no longer hold.

◇ Expired passports (once you have received a new one).

WHAT TO KEEP

Certain records should be kept for a limited time.

◇ Canceled checks and bank statements that provide substantiation for income tax deductions and credits should be retained for seven years to protect you in case of an income tax audit.

◇ Credit card statements provide proof of the price you paid for major items and can bolster your case for certain tax deductions (such as business gifts) and should be kept for seven years, in case your tax return is audited.

◇ Statements of the sale of investments from your brokerage firm should be held for seven years. If you are audited and you have misplaced these documents, your broker can probably duplicate them.

For a list of records you should keep permanently, such as wills or deeds—and where you should keep them — see the Personal Records Inventory in the EVERYDAY LEGAL FORMS section of this book, beginning on page 552. See also FINANCIAL RECORDS.

PET

Along with the rewards and pleasures of owning a pet, you assume certain responsibilities when you take a dog, cat, or other animal into your home.

SELECTING A PET

Before you buy a pet, make sure that you are allowed to own it. If you live in a town or city, you need to find out about restrictions on the types of animals allowed within city limits. Most municipalities prohibit what they call dangerous animals, such as wolves, alligators, or poisonous snakes. Ordinances in your city may limit ownership to domesticated dogs and cats, canaries and other birds, rabbits, hamsters, gerbils, and mice.

State laws place further limitations on the animals that can be kept as house pets. For example, some people like to adopt animals they find in the wilderness and domesticate them. Since animals living on public property are generally considered to belong to the state, simply taking home a wild animal (even one that is not dangerous) may be a violation of the law. Your state conservation department can give you information about the status of wild animals that may live in your area.

LICENSING

States and municipalities may have licensing requirements for pet ownership, usually for dogs and cats. A typical municipal ordinance requires owners to obtain a license each year and pay a small fee. To obtain a license, the owner must provide written proof that the animal has been immunized against certain diseases, such as rabies and distemper. This licensing requirement serves two purposes: (1) it safeguards the public against animal-borne disease, and (2) it helps ensure that the pet will be returned to its rightful owner if it gets lost.

CARE AND LIABILITY

You are responsible by law for taking care of your pet. If you leave a pet unattended without adequate food or water, you may be reported to the local police for cruelty to an animal. If found guilty, you could face a fine or several months in jail.

Most cities and towns have leash laws that prohibit owners from allowing dogs to run around at large. If you do not keep your dog properly restrained, the police may impound it. At the pound, the dog may be made available for adoption or destroyed if you do not reclaim it within a period of time specified by law. In addition, you may face criminal penalties for violating the leash law, as well as a civil lawsuit if your pet causes an accident or injures someone while running around loose.

In most states the general rule is that you are not responsible for your pet's actions unless you were already aware the pet had antisocial tendencies. For example, if you know that your cat will not tolerate being handled by children, you can be held liable if it scratches or bites a toddler. Owners are usually not held responsible for a pet's action if its behavior was unpredictable. See also ANIMALS; DOG LAW; VETERINARIAN.

PET CUSTODY

Because people become attached to their pets, a beloved dog or cat can become an issue in a divorce case. Couples who quarrel over the custody of a pet should keep in mind that it is in their interests to settle the matter between themselves, just as they should try to agree about sentimental keepsakes or other personal property, such as furniture or cars. They can take the matter to court and the judge will make a decision, but judicial intervention will cost both parties a good deal of time and money.

WILLS

Suppose you leave $1 million to your dog, Fido, and only $1,000 to your only child, Sue. Sue could contest your will successfully, because you cannot leave property to property (legally, that is what a pet is). Sue would have less success if you made what is called a conditional gift to another person—for example, "I give my friend Jeff $1 million, provided he cares for Fido as long as Fido lives." Or you could put the money in trust for Fido's care, designating a beneficiary for any money that remains when Fido dies. Sometimes a pet owner requests in his will that upon his death his pets be destroyed. Most courts would find that this provision violates public policy, but occasionally a court allows it.

PETITION

A formal written application requesting that specific action be taken is known as a petition. A petition is the first step in civil litigation, for example. A spouse seeking a divorce must first file a petition with the divorce court in order to begin the divorce proceedings.

Another form of petition is a request made to a public official. For instance, to place a candidate's name or an issue on the election ballot, you must usually file a petition with the secretary of state of your state. It will be rejected if it is not filed in accordance with statutory requirements—for example, if it does not have enough signatures. Petitions may also be made to such governmental bodies as state and city landmark-preservation commissions. See also LANDMARK.

PHARMACIST

A pharmacist is a health-care professional who has been trained to prepare and dispense medicines, known as ethical drugs, which require a doctor's prescription.

RESPONSIBILITIES

The pharmacist's responsibilities are not limited to putting the prescribed number of pills or amount of liquid into a bottle and handing it to the customer. She must certify the prescription order by deciding whether the dosage is correct and the medication is appropriate for that patient. The pharmacist checks the safety of the dosage as well as legal requirements for dispensing the drug. Finally, she must make a record of the prescription, price charged, and the date dispensed.

As of January 1993, a new federal law went into effect giving pharmacists an even greater role in patient care. The law requires pharmacists to inquire about other medications their customers may be taking in order to avoid adverse drug interactions and other potential problems. The pharmacist must also offer to counsel customers on the safest use of a prescribed drug—for example, that it must be taken on a full stomach or with a glass of water. Although the federal law applies specifically to Medicaid patients, some states have passed legislation expanding the law to cover anyone receiving a prescription medication.

If you have questions about a prescription, ask your pharmacist before you have it filled. She can tell you about possible side effects, how and when to take the medication, whether generic drugs can be substituted to save money, how to store the medication at home, and whether the prescription is refillable.

POTENTIAL LIABILITY

Dispensing prescription drugs requires a high degree of care, because mistakes can result in injury or even death. If a pharmacist fills a prescription with the wrong medication or the wrong dosage or refills a prescription that was written by the physician as nonrefillable, the pharmacist can be subject to a lawsuit for negligence. A pharmacist may have her license suspended or revoked for a serious breach of professional duty.

Pharmacists also must comply with laws and regulations about storage, record keeping, and other administrative duties related to prescriptions. Failing to keep drugs in their original containers, which indicate lot numbers and expiration dates, or selling drugs that have been marked as professional samples "not to be sold," can lead to revocation of the pharmacist's license. Also, a pharmacist is required by federal law to keep complete and accurate records of his stock of "controlled substances," such as codeine, phenobarbital, and amphetamine. These are drugs that have such a strong potential for abuse that the government has established guidelines to monitor their use. See also DRUG.

PHYSICIAN AND SURGEON

Individuals who have received the required professional training and have been licensed to practice medicine are called physicians, or doctors. Those physicians who perform operations on the human body are called surgeons.

LICENSING

To practice medicine in a particular state, a physician must be licensed (or certified) by the state board of medical examiners. Each state dictates the qualifications needed for a license. They may include not only the necessary education and training but also personal characteristics such as honesty and good moral character.

Practicing medicine without a license is a crime in all states. In Georgia, for example, falsely representing oneself as a licensed physician is a felony, punishable by a fine of up to $1,000 or imprisonment for two to five years, or both.

Every state government has a regulatory or supervisory board of medical examiners, which oversees the medical profession. This board investigates complaints about physicians, such as unprofessional conduct or malpractice. After receiving a complaint, the board notifies the physician of the charges and gives him an opportunity to be heard. If the board finds that the charges are true, the physician's license may be suspended or revoked. See also MEDICAL MALPRACTICE.

CONFIDENTIALITY

The physician-patient relationship is built on trust. To diagnose a condition and treat a patient properly, the physician must receive honest answers to the questions she asks. To give patients the assurance that their answers will remain private, the legal system recognizes a so-called physician-patient privilege, under which a physician generally cannot be required to reveal any communications she has with a patient during the course of treatment.

If a physician is called as a witness in a criminal trial, for example, she has the right to refuse to answer questions about a conversation she had with her patient, but she can reveal the patient's condition. However, in a civil suit — such as a malpractice or personal-injury suit in which the plaintiff's mental or physical condition is an issue that relates to the case — the plaintiff (and his doctor) may have to waive the privilege. The privilege may also be waived when a person applies for insurance.

Physicians who breach the confidential relationship with their patients face disciplinary action before the state regulatory board. In addition, a breach of confidentiality might give the patient a basis for suing the physician for infliction of emotional distress, invasion of privacy, or malpractice.

In rare cases, a physician may be forced to violate the privilege—as when a patient threatens to harm another person. Then the doctor's duty to warn the intended victim outweighs her obligation to keep the patient's communications confidential. See also PRIVILEGED COMMUNICATION.

PICKETING

When people gather in an area in order to publicly announce a dispute or to gain support for a cause, the practice is known as picketing. Picketers usually carry signs or voice slogans related to their cause.

Picketing has been recognized by the U.S. Supreme Court as a form of expression protected by the First Amendment to the Constitution. As with other forms of expression, however, the right to picket is subject to certain limitations. In a labor dispute, for instance, a union may picket to let the public know that it believes an employer is conducting an unfair labor practice, such as hiring nonunion workers. This is known as informational picketing, and it is legal. But when a union sets up a picket line to harass an employer into accepting the union as the employees' bargaining agent, the employer can obtain a court order to stop the picketing after 30 days.

Picketers who interfere with people who want to go to work or who harass them by threats of violence can be charged with false imprisonment or assault and battery. An employer can ask the court to order a stop to this kind of picketing. Likewise, if picketers make untrue or defamatory statements about an employer, a court may order them to stop.

Picketing is not limited to labor disputes. Political figures are often confronted by pickets at rallies and other public gatherings, and even outside their homes. As long as these picket lines are on public property, they will generally be permitted. But just as in a labor dispute, the picketers can be subject to arrest and prosecution if they interfere with or threaten those who wish to cross their line. See also LABOR UNION; SPEECH, FREEDOM OF.

PLEA

A plea is a defendant's response to a criminal charge brought by the state. A defendant can generally choose from one of three pleas: guilty, not guilty, and no contest, or *nolo contendere* (Latin for "I do not wish to contend").

Contrary to popular opinion, a defendant cannot plead "innocent," because the purpose of a criminal trial is to find out whether the defendant is either not guilty or "guilty beyond a reasonable doubt." A not-guilty verdict does not necessarily mean that the defendant is innocent—although that may be the case—but rather that the state failed to meet the burden of proof that is required for a conviction.

When a defendant pleads *nolo contendere,* he neither admits guilt nor challenges the charge. He is subject to the same punishment he would have received if he had pleaded guilty or had pleaded not guilty and was convicted. But he is not prevented from denying the charge in another legal proceeding. See also CRIMINAL LAW; NO CONTEST.

PLEA BARGAINING

The vast majority of criminal charges filed in courts across the country are never tried before a judge or jury. Most are resolved through a process called plea bargaining. The bargain is that the defendant is treated more leniently, while the prosecutor gets a conviction without having to spend the time and money needed to conduct a trial.

Although plea bargaining is the subject of much criticism, especially from the victims of crimes and from victims'-rights groups, it is essential to the orderly administration of criminal justice. If every criminal defendant exercised his constitutional right to a trial, the criminal justice system would collapse under the weight of the constant litigation, because there are not enough judges, prosecutors, or courtrooms to handle the number of trials that would be required. Plea bargains are also used to encourage criminal defendants to cooperate with law enforcement officials in the investigation and prosecution of other crimes.

In a plea bargain, the prosecutor may dismiss one or more

REAL LIFE, REAL LAW

The Case of the Plea Bargainer's Plight

To avoid a sentence of three years in the state penitentiary, Vaughan King agreed to enter into a plea bargain with the prosecuting attorney. In return for his guilty plea, the prosecutor said he would suggest that King receive a sentence of only six months to be served in the county jail.

At the sentencing hearing, however, the judge presiding over King's case rejected the plea-bargain arrangement and sentenced him to 18 months in the state prison.

King appealed the conviction and sentence. He argued that he should have been given the opportunity to withdraw his guilty plea when the judge decided to reject the sentence recommended by the prosecutor. In fact, the evidence showed that the prosecutor had told King that he would have the right to change his plea if the judge refused to honor the plea bargain.

The state appeals court ruled that King should have been permitted to withdraw his guilty plea once the trial judge decided not to follow the plea-bargain arrangement. It ordered the judge to do one of the following: accept the terms of the original plea bargain; allow King to withdraw his plea and proceed to trial; or allow King to enter into a new plea-bargain arrangement that was acceptable to both King and the judge.

---

charges that were filed against the defendant or refrain from filing all the charges that could be made against him. In return, the defendant pleads guilty to the remaining charges. Or, in return for a guilty plea, the prosecutor may offer to reduce the seriousness of the charge filed (for example, lowering a first-degree murder charge to second-degree murder), and, therefore, recommend a lighter sentence to the judge.

Although a prosecutor can make a recommendation regarding sentencing, the judge is generally not obligated to follow it. If she does not accept the recommendation, in some states the defendant is allowed to withdraw his guilty plea. In others, he must accept whatever sentence is imposed.

Sometimes prisoners who enter into plea bargains and then receive harsh jail sentences claim that they were coerced into accepting the plea bargain because of the threat of more severe punishment if they asked for a trial. Such attempts to undo the bargain are usually unsuccessful. But if a prisoner can show that he was misinformed about the consequences of the plea bargain, that he was tricked into accepting it, or that the prosecutor did not keep his promise, then the prisoner may have grounds to appeal his sentence and ask that his guilty plea be set aside and the case go to trial.

PLEADING

A pleading is a formal written statement made to a court by the parties to a lawsuit that spells out not only the issues, but also the positions of the parties to the lawsuit. Pleadings consist of the plaintiff's complaint, the defendant's answer to the complaint, and the answers to any counterclaims and cross-claims. If a third party is named in the lawsuit, a third-party complaint and answer will be included, too. Normally, pleadings limit the issues that will be contested during the lawsuit. For example, a spouse filing for divorce cannot raise the issue of his spouse's cruelty unless he first made such a claim in the pleadings. See LAWSUIT.

PLEDGE OF ALLEGIANCE

An affirmation of loyalty to the United States and its flag, the Pledge of Allegiance is an oath that is taken by citizens of the United States when they salute the flag at public gatherings.

For most Americans, reciting the Pledge of Allegiance is a patriotic and honorable thing to do. But for some citizens, it is a violation of religious principles. Jehovah's Witnesses, for example, do not recite the Pledge of Allegiance because they believe it violates the biblical commandment against bowing down to "graven images." Atheists sometimes object to the recitation of the pledge because, since 1954, it contains the words "under God."

A legal problem arose in West Virginia when children who were Jehovah's Witnesses refused to recite the Pledge of Allegiance and were expelled from public school. As a result, they were considered juvenile delinquents, and their parents faced fines and imprisonment for failing to supervise their children.

The parents filed suit against the West Virginia Board of Education. They claimed that by requiring their children to recite the pledge, the board violated their constitutional right of freedom of religion. The board argued that by refusing to recite the pledge, the children disrupted the order and discipline of the classroom, which the board had a responsibility to maintain.

The U.S. Supreme Court ruled in favor of the Witnesses. It held that the expulsion of the children was an unjustifiable intrusion into their religious freedom and an attempt by the government to censor their religious beliefs. See also FLAG, U.S.; STUDENT RIGHTS.

POLICE

A division of state and local government, the police are responsible for protecting the safety, health, and morals of the public, and enforcing the law. Today some communities prefer to use the terms *public safety officer* or *law enforcement officer* when referring to a police officer.

JURISDICTION

A police officer usually has jurisdiction, or authority, in a defined geographical area. A state trooper's jurisdiction may extend over hundreds of miles, whereas that of a local police officer may not go beyond his city limits. Police officers generally cannot operate outside their jurisdictions.

However, police officers from different jurisdictions are required to work together to enforce the law. For instance, if a state highway patrol officer stops you for speeding, he may run a background check on your license number. If the officer finds that you are wanted for an offense in your hometown, he must notify your local police department that you are in custody.

QUALIFICATIONS

Each municipality or state sets its own requirements regarding the selection and training of police officers. Typically, a candidate must be a U.S. citizen, live within the jurisdiction of the police department, have a high school diploma and a driver's license, and be of legal age. Many police departments set upper age limits on their new recruits.

Police departments usually require recruits to pass physical and written examinations. Because of the rigorous physical demands of police work, disabled persons may be refused a job with a police department. However, a woman may not be denied a job because of her gender. Although the physical requirements, (for instance, the minimum height and weight) for female police officers differ from those of male officers, once on the force, there are no duties from which female police officers are exempt.

The methods of training police officers vary, but they almost always include learning the use of firearms, criminal investigative techniques, and some aspects of the law, such as the rights of the accused and the extent of police powers. Increasingly, police officers are required to take interpersonal training programs to increase their sensitivity toward minorities and women.

POLICE PROCEDURES

Because of their duty to protect the public, police officers are granted a wide range of powers. If they have sufficient cause, for example, they may temporarily deprive people of their rights, as when they take someone into custody. For the most part, however, in the course of their job, they must protect the constitutional rights of all people. To this end, police officers must follow proper procedure when they stop a car, make an arrest, or conduct a search of private property.

Because police work is dangerous and events often happen quickly, police officers are not always able to follow procedure to the letter. Nevertheless, they must observe it as closely as possible. For example, when a police officer sees a person committing a crime, he has the right to give chase and apprehend him, using reasonable force if necessary. Once he has apprehended him, the officer may disarm and search the suspect. But before questioning him, the officer must notify him of his constitutional rights (known as the Miranda warnings). If the officer fails to give these warnings, any statements made by the suspect may not be used as evidence against him in court. See also ARREST; MIRANDA WARNINGS.

Similarly, during a criminal investigation, police officers must follow certain procedures when obtaining evidence. If they do not, any evidence they acquire may be inadmissible in court. Telephone wiretaps, searches, entering a suspect's home, and other intrusions on a suspect's privacy must first be authorized by a judge in the form of search warrants.

Body searches must be conducted properly too. A woman who is suspected of concealing a weapon or drugs on her person usually can be subjected to a strip search only by a female police officer. Conversely, a female police officer is not allowed to strip-search a male suspect. However, if a male or female police officer has reason to believe that a suspect of either sex is concealing a weapon, the officer may perform a "pat down," or frisk—a quick, external search of the suspect. See also SEARCH AND SEIZURE; STOP-AND-FRISK LAWS.

USE OF FORCE

An officer may, and often must, use force to defend himself or to apprehend and secure a suspect, but he may not use unnecessary or unreasonable force. If a suspect does not resist arrest, the officer has no right to use violence. If the suspect is resisting arrest, the officer may use only enough force as is necessary to overcome the resistance.

Police officers may use deadly force—that is, any force that could cause a life-threatening injury—when necessary and reasonable to apprehend and secure a person who is believed to have committed a serious crime, or felony. Deadly force cannot be used against a person suspected of committing a less serious crime, or misdemeanor. However, if a police officer feels his life is threatened, he may use whatever force is reasonably necessary, including deadly force, in self-defense. See also POLICE BRUTALITY.

A ROUND-THE-CLOCK JOB

When a person becomes a police officer, he takes an oath to protect the public at all times. Essentially this means that police officers are on duty 24 hours a day. They are generally permitted to carry their weapons at all times and to use them if necessary.

Suppose that Doris and her husband Mike, both police officers, attend a hockey game on a day when they are both off duty. While sitting in the stands, they notice that several spectators are becoming rowdy. If the rowdiness turns to violence, with the spectators taking swings at each other, then Doris and Mike are legally required to break up the conflict. In doing so they must identify themselves as police officers. They can make arrests and hold the rowdy spectators in custody until police reinforcements arrive.

Some police departments allow police officers to "moonlight" (take on additional jobs when they are off duty). Often they work as security officers. Others do not, however, out of concern that the officers' on-duty performance will be affected by fatigue or additional stress. A police officer who moonlights illegally will be subject to disciplinary action.

YOUR DUTY TO THE POLICE

The public has an obligation to cooperate with the police during criminal investigations. If you refuse, you can be charged with a misdemeanor. For example, if you are a witness to a crime and the police question you, you must answer their questions to the best of your ability or face misdemeanor charges. See also OBSTRUCTION OF JUSTICE.

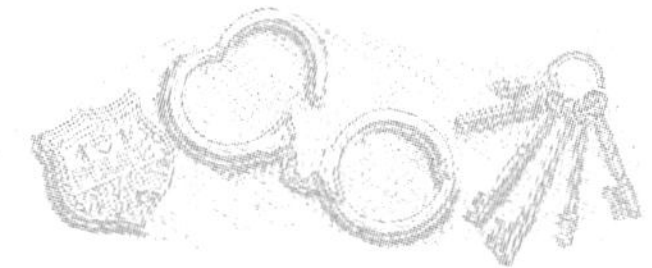

POLICE BRUTALITY

A police officer can be held responsible in civil and criminal courts if he uses unnecessary or excessive force against a citizen in the performance of his duties. He can be prosecuted as a criminal or sued for any injury or harm he caused.

EXAMPLES OF EXCESSIVE FORCE

Courts have found that the following acts exceed a police officer's authority to use necessary and reasonable force:

◇ Shooting and killing a motorist who refused to stop for an officer who wanted to arrest him for drunk driving.

◇ Handcuffing and forcibly placing a citizen in a police car during an unlawful arrest. (Since the arrest was illegal, any force used to effect it was unreasonable.)

◇ Using "third-degree" techniques, such as beating or punching, in order to extract a confession from a suspect.

TAKING LEGAL ACTION

If you feel that you have been the victim of police brutality, you should call the police department and ask to speak with the person who handles civilian complaints against officers. The department will investigate and, if necessary, will take disciplinary action, such as reprimanding, suspending, or even dismissing the officer.

Criminal charges

In addition, you can ask the local prosecutor or district attorney to file criminal charges against the officer for excessive force. If she feels there is sufficient evidence, she will present it to a grand jury, who will decide whether to indict the officer. The charge may be assault and battery or aggravated (more severe) assault.

Civil lawsuits

You may sue an officer in civil court for assault and battery or for wrongful death (for example, if you believe a relative was wrongfully killed by police). Your lawyer may suggest that you also file a suit against the police department or sheriff's office, as well as the municipality or state that employed the officer. As a result of your lawsuit, you may receive compensatory damages for medical expenses, lost wages, pain and suffering, disability, and the like, as well as punitive damages (monetary awards in excess of the actual harm you suffered). See also DAMAGES; LAWSUIT.

Since a police officer is an agent of the state, if he uses excessive force against you, he may be violating your civil rights. If so, you may also sue in the federal courts and receive compensation for the same offenses as in a state court lawsuit. In addition, the U. S. Attorney General may bring federal criminal charges against an officer who violates a person's civil rights through the use of excessive force.

FACTORS THE COURTS CONSIDER

Each instance of alleged police brutality is considered individually. In reaching its decision, a judge and jury will take the following questions into account:

◇ Was the victim committing an offense at the time of the purported assault, and if so, was the offense, such as a rape or armed robbery, inherently dangerous to the victim, the public, or the police officer, or was it a minor offense, such as shoplifting or vandalism?

◇ Did the suspect resist arrest, and if so, how? Did he threaten the officer with a weapon or shoot at him? Or did he simply have words with the officer?

◇ Was the officer's life or that of anyone else in danger, or did he have reason to believe it was? If a suspect, for instance, reached into his jacket and pulled out a gun, the officer may have believed his life was in danger, even if the gun later turned out to be a toy.

◇ Did the officer give the suspect a chance to surrender peacefully?

◇ Was there any way other than the use of force to apprehend or subdue the suspect?

POLITICAL ACTION COMMITTEE

An organization of individuals that share common interests and make political contributions to federal candidates is known as a political action committee, or PAC. For example, a PAC may be formed by small-business owners, by members of a labor union, or by trade associations and professional organizations.

A PAC pools the contributions made by its members, enabling it to make a larger contribution than is permitted from any single individual. Each PAC can donate up to $5,000 per candidate in a single election, while individuals can give only up to $1,000. Hence

PAC contributions can add significantly to a candidate's funding, and the PAC hopes that its support will influence the candidate to take positions favorable to the PAC's cause.

PAC's have been criticized for buying influence in the U.S. House of Representatives and Senate. They support incumbents by a ratio of 4 to 1, and sometimes make contributions to unopposed candidates.

Supporters of PAC's contend that they allow like-minded individuals and organizations to legitimately advance their interests in a way that prevents political payoffs to individual persons or companies. They argue that because PAC's must disclose the amounts of their contributions and the names of candidates who receive them, the public can decide whether a PAC's influence is too great.

If you want to know whether a PAC has contributed to a particular candidate, ask for a list of contributors from the candidate's campaign headquarters. See also ELECTION LAWS.

PONZI SCHEME

Named after Charles Ponzi, a swindler and confidence man who operated in Boston during the 1920's, a Ponzi scheme is a type of investment scam. It purports to offer big returns to investors, when in fact no investments are ever made.

Typically, the swindler recruits participants through social contacts, seminars, or church activities. He offers large returns on a specific investment, such as an oil well or a diamond mine. The first investors receive some money the swindler collects from the next investors, and the swindler pockets the rest. These investors in turn receive money from newer investors, and so on. Eventually, Ponzi schemes collapse, since the number of people whom the swindler can persuade to invest is finite. If no more new investors can be enlisted, then there is no more money to pay to participants.

A warning signal of a Ponzi scheme is an investment that shows high initial returns. For instance, one Ponzi scheme was based on selling shares in a nonexistent oil well drilling operation. For every $1,000 invested, the promoter's clients received $500 in interest every three months—a 200 percent annual return. Before long, hundreds of people had invested large sums of money in the supposed oil drilling company. But then the investors stopped receiving their interest checks. Calls to the promoter went unreturned. Finally, a group of investors visited the promoter's office, only to discover that it was vacant, and that he and their money had disappeared.

STEPS TO TAKE TO AVOID BEING SWINDLED

Even financially sophisticated investors such as brokers, lawyers, and accountants have been duped by Ponzi schemes. To avoid becoming a victim yourself, consider the following advice:

1. Look into the background of the individual making the offer. Verify his employment claims by calling his previous employers; check his claims to membership in professional organizations; contact the Securities and Exchange Commission or your state attorney general's office about his previous investment offerings. You might consider calling your local police department to see if there are any outstanding warrants against him.

2. Be wary of odd or exotic investments in precious metals, oil or gas leases, diamonds, or commodities, especially when they promise you enormous returns. Any investment offer that sounds "too good to be true" probably is.

3. Get the advice of an independent attorney or accountant before you put money in an unfamiliar investment. See also LAWYER; STOCKBROKER.

PORNOGRAPHY

Pornography is notoriously difficult to define and perhaps even harder to regulate; thus, the laws concerning it are constantly evolving. Generally speaking, pornography—when viewed by the average person applying "contemporary community standards"—is any material that appeals to prurient interests or depicts sexual conduct in a patently offensive manner lacking serious literary, artistic, political, or scientific merit or value. See OBSCENITY.

Pornography is legal provided it does not depict children (boys and girls under 18) and is not sold to children. Persons who create, sell, or possess child pornography, knowing the models to be underage, are

ABC's OF BATTLING PORNOGRAPHY

If you are concerned about sexually explicit material being spread in your community, here are a few suggestions on how to control it:

- From your local zoning authorities, find out if there are community ordinances that govern adult bookstores, nightclubs, and movie theaters. Ask if they are being enforced. Many cities have zoning laws that prohibit such businesses from operating within a specified distance from homes, churches, or schools. Others require that nearby businesses and residents consent to the opening of a business that sells pornography.
- If you have heard or seen obscene or pornographic materials over radio or television, including cable television stations, write a letter of complaint to the station and send a copy to the Federal Communications Commission (FCC),1919 M Street NW, Washington, DC 20554.
- To prevent an unwanted channel from being broadcast to your home by your cable television service, ask the cable company to block reception or to provide a blocking device that you can install.
- If you receive offensive materials in the mail, tell your local post office. At your request, the Postal Service is legally required to order anyone who sends you such mail to stop.
- Write or call the U.S. Attorney General's Task Force on Obscenity, 10th Street and Constitution Avenue NW, Washington, DC 20530; (202) 514-2041 for information about the federal government's efforts to eradicate obscene materials, and ask how you can participate.

guilty of a felony punishable by a fine, imprisonment, or both.

In one recent case the star of numerous erotic videos revealed that she was under age 18 throughout most of her career. Videos that she had made which could not be immediately censored became illegal, and video stores nationwide had to remove them.

To maintain the safety of the community and to protect children from being exposed to pornographic material, many communities have passed zoning laws that limit the locations where pornographic materials may be sold. The federal government works together with the U.S. Postal Service to stop the distribution of child pornography through the mail. See also FEDERAL COMMUNICATIONS COMMISSION; MAIL; PRESS, FREEDOM OF.

POWER OF ATTORNEY

A power of attorney is a written document stating that one person (known as the principal) delegates authority to another person (called an agent or attorney in fact). The agent undertakes to perform certain functions on behalf of the principal, such as handling financial matters, making decisions about medical care, or simply standing in for the principal during a legal proceeding.

GENERAL AND SPECIAL AUTHORITY

The authority granted to the agent may be very broad or quite specific. Broad authority is given through a *general power of attorney*. This kind of document may, for example, designate your spouse to make all financial or medical decisions for you should you become incapacitated.

A *special power of attorney*, in contrast, is used to authorize a particular person to take action in one or more specific ways. Suppose Martha is about to go on a long-awaited trek in Nepal. A few days before she is due to leave for the airport, her real estate agent calls to inform her that the couple who wish to buy her house have finally agreed to her price. Despite Martha's protestations, the closing will have to take place while she is out of town. Martha's real estate agent suggests that she designate someone to sign the papers on her behalf. Martha then gives her sister Anne specific power of attorney to attend the closing and sign all necessary papers on Martha's behalf. Anne's signature is as legally binding as if Martha had signed the papers herself.

Combinations of general and

special powers of attorney are also possible. For instance, if Martha had not yet found willing buyers for her house, she could create a power of attorney authorizing Anne to handle only those negotiations necessary to achieve the sale of her house while she was away. Thus Anne could act on Martha's behalf to a great extent, including reaching an agreement on the price and conditions of sale, and even closing the sale, without consulting Martha at any point. But she would not have a general power of attorney over all of Martha's financial affairs. Obviously, you must be extremely careful how you word a specific power of attorney, because allowing someone to make important decisions for you can have significant consequences.

In addition to making clear the kind of authority granted, a power of attorney should also state when the power goes into effect and when it ends. For instance, Martha may give power of attorney to Anne to be her agent in a real estate closing effective upon the date of her departure to Nepal and ending on the day she returns home. Or she may strictly limit her sister's authority to the particular day when the buyers plan to close the sale.

DURABLE POWER OF ATTORNEY

Generally a power of attorney expires automatically when the principal becomes mentally incompetent, under the theory that the agent can act only to the extent that the principal could act for himself. However, an individual may appoint an agent to act on his behalf in the event that he becomes incompetent or incapacitated. This special grant of authority is known as a *durable power of attorney*. It ends only when the principal dies or again becomes legally competent.

A durable power of attorney may give the agent the immediate authority to act on the principal's behalf, or it may be designed to take effect at a specified time, such as upon the incapacitation of the principal. The latter case is known as a *springing power of attorney*, because it "springs" into effect only when a specified event takes place — for example when an agent has medical corroboration that a principal can no longer make decisions about his medical care.

A common springing power of attorney is the *durable power of attorney for health care*, which authorizes the agent to make decisions on the principal's behalf concerning the principal's medical treatment, including the administration of life-sustaining procedures. This power of attorney is often used in conjunction with a living will and authorizes your agent to make decisions consistent with your living will. For an example of this type of durable power of attorney, see the EVERYDAY LEGAL FORMS section of this book beginning on page 552. See also LIVING WILL.

REVOCATION

To revoke a power of attorney, you can write "revoked" across the document or simply tear it up. You should also notify the agent that you are revoking his power of attorney. Agents may also relinquish their authority to act under the power of attorney. If there is any disagreement over ending the power of attorney, see a lawyer.

If any interested party wants to challenge a power of attorney, he can do so in court. For instance, if the family members of a principal feel that she was coerced or misled into granting a power of attorney, they can ask a court to revoke it.

PROS AND CONS

By selecting whom you wish to stand in your stead, you can avoid the need for a government or court to choose an agent for you in an emergency. Since you can designate the amount of authority you wish to convey and the circumstances under which the power should be revoked, you will have a greater degree of control over your affairs than you would otherwise.

Never underestimate the magnitude of the power of attorney. Once in effect, the right of the agent to act on your behalf is virtually absolute, and you are legally bound by the actions of the agent. As principal, you should choose your agent very carefully. It must be someone who has your complete trust and enough knowledge of your affairs to handle them competently.

You should not accept a power of attorney without first understanding what may be expected of you. Just as the law recognizes the authority granted by a power of attorney, so does it impose a duty on the

ABC's

Of Preparing a Power of Attorney

Suppose you have decided to give your power of attorney to an agent who has agreed to act on your behalf. Now you have to draft the document so that it will be legally valid. If you carefully follow the advice below, your power of attorney should be free of problems.

❑ For legibility, write the document on a typewriter or word processor, although a handwritten version will probably be valid. If you prefer, you can obtain a blank power-of-attorney form from your stationery store or bank. For samples of various power of attorney forms, see Everyday Legal Forms, beginning on page 552.

❑ Clearly identify yourself and your agent (or agents), using full legal names and addresses. Note any relevant information about your relationship to the agent—for example, whether she is your spouse or a sibling.

❑ Describe, in plain but precise language, the authority that you have conveyed. Indicate whether the power is general or special. State any limitations on the agent's authority.

❑ If you intend to give a springing power of attorney (one that takes effect in the future), indicate what event will "spring" it into effect—for example, if you become incapacitated by illness and you wish the power of attorney to continue during your incapacity.

❑ If you are granting the power to take part in a real estate transaction, include a legal description of the property on the power-of-attorney document. A simple description of the property may be sufficient, but some states and financial institutions require the standard legal description that is used in drawing up deeds.

❑ Specify when the power of attorney is to become effective and when it will end. State how and when the power of attorney may be revoked, such as by notifying the agent in writing that you are terminating the agreement and tearing up the original.

❑ Both you and your agent should sign and date the document. If you have designated more than one agent, each agent should sign and date the document. The signatures should be notarized.

❑ Some states require two witnesses to be present at the signing. If so, be sure the witnesses are of legal age.

❑ Before you have signed, notarized, and recorded your draft, you may wish to have an attorney review it (even though this is not required by law). Unless major changes are required, the attorney's review should be relatively inexpensive.

❑ Some states require a power of attorney to be recorded at the local courthouse. This is advisable even if it is not required by law, because it strengthens the authenticity of your power of attorney.

agent to be careful and judicious in upholding the wishes of the principal. You can be held financially responsible to the principal for any mistakes you make as the principal's agent. Bear in mind that you are under no obligation to accept the authority of power of attorney granted to you. You can simply decline to sign the form that authorizes it.

Preferred Provider Organization

As an alternative to traditional health insurance and health maintenance organizations (HMO's), some insurance companies now offer preferred provider organization programs, or PPO's. They are organizations composed of doctors who have agreed to provide lower-cost medical services in return for becoming the exclusive healthcare providers for an insurer or other sponsor, such as an employer. Since PPO doctors have all agreed to a reduced-fee schedule, PPO's help employers and insurers control health costs.

Unlike HMO doctors, PPO doctors do not work exclusively for the PPO or under a single roof. When you join a PPO, you can go to any doctor listed on its roster to be treated and your insurer will usually pay most or all of the costs of your visit. If you use a non-PPO doctor, however, your insurer may reduce your reimbursement or reject your claim.

Some PPO's are quite large, giving you a wide choice of doctors. If you are considering joining one, ask the sponsor for a list of the physicians available and their credentials.

Be sure to read your PPO policy carefully, especially in regard to emergency treatment or the services of a specialist. Some plans require that your primary-care physician obtain permission from the insurer before admitting you to the hospital or referring you to a specialist. If you do not get advance permission before entering the hospital, or if you choose your own specialist, you may receive reduced benefits.

Like other health insurance plans, PPO's are usually regulated by state insurance departments. See also HEALTH INSURANCE; HEALTH MAINTENANCE ORGANIZATION.

PRELIMINARY HEARING

When a person is accused of a serious crime, a preliminary hearing is held in court to decide whether there is strong enough evidence for the case to go to trial. The hearing is a procedural safeguard against a person's being subjected to a criminal prosecution based on insufficient or improperly obtained evidence.

At the hearing the prosecutor must show that he has reasonable grounds, or "probable cause," to believe that a crime has been committed and that the suspect committed it. The prosecutor is not required to prove his case beyond a reasonable doubt.

The defense will try to counter the prosecution's claims or will raise arguments about whether the evidence is sufficient or was properly obtained by the police or the prosecutor. If the judge determines that there is no probable cause, the case will be dismissed and the prosecution terminated, at least until the prosecutor and police can obtain enough evidence to show probable cause, which may result in another hearing. See also CRIMINAL PROCEDURE.

PREMEDITATION

The plan or decision to commit a crime before one actually commits it is known as premeditation. The plan does not have to be elaborate, and the decision does not have to be made far in advance of the criminal act. Suppose a husband sees his wife standing at the top of a long flight of stairs. The couple had been arguing and it occurs to the husband that if he pushes his wife down the stairs she will be killed. If he acts on his thought, even just a moment later, his act is premeditated. Premeditated crimes carry greater penalties than identical crimes committed without premeditation. See also MANSLAUGHTER; MURDER.

PRENUPTIAL AGREEMENT

A prenuptial (or antenuptial) agreement is a contract, entered into by a couple planning to be married, which specifies their individual property rights throughout the marriage and if their marriage should end. The agreement must be in writing, signed by both parties, and in some states, signed before witnesses and entered into the court records.

All states have laws that give a widow or widower a minimum interest in the other's property when his or her spouse dies, regardless of what the will says. But when a couple enter into a prenuptial agreement, they do so before either of them has a legal claim to the other's property by virtue of marriage. They are therefore not subject to state laws governing the division of property when the marriage ends, whether by death or divorce.

A prenuptial agreement takes effect when the parties marry. It may be revoked or altered at any time, provided both parties agree.

DECIDING WHETHER YOU NEED A PRENUPTIAL AGREEMENT

A prenuptial agreement may be a wise choice if you find that your situation is similar to any one of the following:

◇ If you have children from a previous marriage and are entering a new marriage with assets that you wish to keep for them. A prenuptial agreement can stipulate that your spouse may make no claim to those assets in the event of a divorce or upon your death.

◇ If your spouse has substantial assets. A prenuptial agreement can ensure that you receive support during the marriage and in the event of your spouse's death. Your prenuptial agreement may provide that certain property be transferred to you upon the marriage or left to you in a will when your spouse dies. It may also provide that your spouse carry life insurance for your benefit. And it may arrange for support, or limitations on support, in the event of divorce.

◇ If you have inherited property or expect to do so. A prenuptial agreement can stipulate that your spouse shall make no claim on these assets and will allow you to give them to other family members or to whomever you choose.

OTHER CONSIDERATIONS

If you are considering writing a prenuptial agreement with your future spouse, or if you are asked to sign one, note that the law does not condone such agreements as a method of avoiding marital duties. Both parties, therefore, must fully inform each other of the nature and value of their property. A prenuptial agreement is not valid without such disclosure. A court will invalidate the prenuptial agreement if it later comes to light that one party hid his assets from the other. For that reason, many prenuptial contracts contain a list of the property that each party is bringing to the marriage.

Make sure that you and your future spouse understand the meaning and the terms of the agreement. A prenuptial agreement that is signed through coercion, ignorance, or trickery can be declared invalid. Both parties are required to act in good faith. If one party is at a disadvantage because of youth, inexperience, or other circumstances, a court may not enforce the agreement. To be on the safe side, have your lawyer review the agreement.

Make sure that your future spouse will be adequately provided for when the marriage ends (whether through death or divorce). The courts do not favor one-sided prenuptial agreements that leave one spouse destitute or encourage divorce or dissension by unduly enriching one partner if the marriage ends. For a sample prenuptial agreement, see EVERYDAY LEGAL FORMS, beginning on page 552.

If you are looking for a lawyer, you may want to consider a prepaid legal-services plan. Such plans, which are offered by a number of independent marketing companies and law firms, provide a menu of basic legal services for an annual fee of several hundred dollars. With a prepaid legal plan, you will be able to get legal advice over the phone as well as in a lawyer's office. Most plans also offer the services of an attorney to review legal documents like wills and real estate contracts before you sign them. In addition, some plans provide a lawyer to write letters on your behalf, represent you in traffic court or in criminal cases, and draft contracts and leases. These services are often free once you have paid the annual fee, but some plans require you to pay additional fees for special services.

Some plans provide coverage in the event of a lawsuit, regardless of whether you are the defendant or plaintiff. A prepaid plan serves its members best, however, when their legal problems are simple and straightforward. It may not be suitable for complicated cases such as contested divorces or bankruptcies, which may need more time than the plan's attorneys can provide.

Many employers now offer a prepaid plan as an employee benefit. Prepaid plans are regulated by the state, and not all plans are available in all states. To obtain information about the plans offered in your state, send a self-addressed stamped envelope to the following address: National Resource Center for Consumers of Legal Services, P.O. Box 340, Gloucester, VA 23061.

CHECKLIST

Choosing a Prepaid Legal Plan

If you are thinking of joining a prepaid legal-services plan, here are some questions to consider before you sign up.

❑ **WHAT IS THE PLAN'S ANNUAL FEE, AND WHAT SERVICES ARE PROVIDED?**
Prepaid plans vary widely in their costs and services. A good plan includes unlimited telephone advice, the preparation of a simple will for husband and wife, the review of legal documents and letters, and telephone calls from an attorney to third parties with whom you may have a dispute. Avoid paying for services you may not need, such as patent or copyright advice.

❑ **ARE DISCOUNTS AVAILABLE FOR THOSE SERVICES NOT INCLUDED IN THE PLAN?**
Some plans require participating attorneys to offer a discount of 25 percent off their regular hourly fee for legal services that are not covered in the plan, such as patent and trademark work or a contested divorce, while other plans require lawyers to offer a lower hourly rate.

❑ **HOW DOES THE PLAN CHOOSE ITS ATTORNEYS?**
Some plans accept almost any attorney who applies, while others have fairly strict standards. Plan attorneys should have several years of experience in the areas of law that the clients are most likely to need, and they should be in good standing with the courts in the areas where they practice.

❑ **WHAT KIND OF CUSTOMER SERVICE DOES THE PLAN OFFER?**
Look for a plan that will give you another attorney if you are unhappy with the one you have been assigned. However, plan administrators cannot interfere with a lawyer's professional judgment or force a lawyer to take a case she believes is without merit.

❑ **DOES THE PLAN OFFER A MONEY-BACK GUARANTEE?**
Many plans give new members a 30-day trial period and a full refund if they are not satisfied.

PRESS, FREEDOM OF

The freedom to write and publish information without government interference is guaranteed by two amendments to the U. S. Constitution. The First Amendment prohibits the federal government from censoring most printed material before it is published, whether by prohibiting its publication or by deleting portions of its contents. The 14th Amendment ensures that no state or local agency can do so without due process of law.

As with other constitutional rights, freedom of the press is not unconditional or absolute. For example, writing and distributing material that defames another person, endangers national security, or is deemed obscene is not necessarily protected by the First Amendment. In such instances the government may have the right to seize the material before it is published or shown to the public. This exercise of power is called prior restraint. See Prior Restraint. See also Defamation; Obscenity.

RIGHTS OF JOURNALISTS

In the course of reporting a story, journalists frequently use "confidential sources"—people who might not speak to the press if they were identified. Because such sources are critical to the news-gathering process, their anonymity is protected. Legal problems can arise, however, when a journalist reports a story about a crime or a criminal, because the journalist's First Amendment right to publish without government interference can clash with the court's right to know.

If a reporter writes about a crime using information from an unnamed source, a court of law can compel him to reveal the name of his source. A reporter may also be forced to testify before a grand jury if he has background information relevant to a particular crime. If he refuses to reveal his sources or to hand over notes that are pertinent to a case, he may be found in contempt of court and fined or imprisoned.

A few states have so-called shield laws that protect journalists who refuse to reveal their research or the names of their confidential sources. However, shield laws do not offer absolute protection. The court still has the authority to decide whether the defendant's right to have access to the reporter's information about his case outweighs the reporter's right to protect the confidentiality of his sources.

INVASION OF PRIVACY

A free press is vital to democracy, but the press does not have the right to invade a person's privacy. Although publishing the truth about a person's private life is not considered libel, it can be an invasion of privacy, which may be grounds for a lawsuit. Such cases are hard to prove, however, because the right of the press to print true and accurate information usually far outweighs the right of a person to keep the same information private. See also PRIVACY RIGHTS.

PREVENTIVE DETENTION

Prisons and other places of detention are not occupied just by persons convicted of a crime. Some men and women are detained there without being found guilty of anything. Held under what is called preventive detention, these people fall into two categories: those awaiting trial who are denied bail because they pose a threat to the public, and those who are involuntarily committed to psychiatric hospitals because they are a threat to themselves or to others.

PRISONERS

Most subjects of preventive detention are people who have been denied bond or had their bond revoked. The courts have the authority to deny or revoke bond to prevent another crime or the obstruction of justice—for example, if a defendant who is awaiting trial threatens to commit still another crime, if it appears that he may flee the area, or if he threatens to harm or intimidate a witness. See also BAIL.

Some states invoke preventive detention by prohibiting the courts from granting bail to people accused of offenses that carry a sentence of death or life imprisonment. For less serious offenses, however, a defendant's right to bail is absolute, unless the court has a justifiable reason to impose preventive detention.

Most people in jail awaiting trial, however, are there because they are unable to come up with the money needed to meet the bail amount, or bond, set by the court. These defendants are not the subject of preventive detention since, in their case, bond has been set but cannot be met.

THE MENTALLY ILL

Some mentally ill persons may be forced into a hospital against their will through civil commitment proceedings. Only those who the court finds are a danger to themselves or others can be forced into preventive detention in this way.

In a civil commitment procedure, a petitioner—usually a friend, family member, doctor, or law enforcement official—presents evidence to the court that someone is likely to cause harm to himself or others because of his mental illness. In some cases a person suffering from alcoholism or drug addiction may be the subject of a civil commitment.

The petitioner must prove that the person she is seeking to have committed poses a "clear and present danger to self or others." The fact that he was dangerous in the past or might become dangerous in the future will not justify a preventive detention through civil commitment proceedings.

PRICE FIXING

When businesses in the same industry agree upon a price that they will all charge for the same product, they are engaged in price fixing, a practice that is prohibited by federal law. Similarly, a company that requires retailers to sell its products at a set price is also guilty of price fixing.

Price fixing is a difficult accusation to prove. The mere fact that companies charge the same price for the same goods or services is not enough to prove a charge of price fixing.

Sometimes you may notice that all the service stations in town appear to be charging the same price for gasoline, and you may wonder whether the station operators are engaging in price fixing. When service station operators are accused of this, they reply that the practice is "price leadership," not price fixing. This means that one operator sets a price, and the others independently adopt that price in order to compete. As long as there is no agreement among the operators to stick to a uniform price, the law upholds their contention that there has been no price fixing.

PRIOR RESTRAINT

When the government prevents the publication or dissemination of books, movies, or other materials to the public, it is using prior restraint. Such an action is prohibited by the First Amendment's guarantee of freedom of expression on the grounds that the right to speak and write is worthless unless there is also an opportunity to be heard and published. Thus, any state or federal law that requires a person to submit materials to a government agency for approval before publication, that denies a person the right to speak out on public issues, or that prevents a person from distributing handbills is unconstitutional and therefore unenforceable.

However, the Constitution allows the government to use prior restraint if it can show that the materials in question (1) present a clear and present danger to the country, (2) are obscene, or (3) unduly invade a person's privacy—causing, for example, irreparable harm.

The concept of prior restraint applies only to federal, state, and local governments. Private individuals, publishers, and distributors who refuse to publish, distribute, or sell certain materials are not guilty of prior restraint. See also CENSORSHIP; PRESS, FREEDOM OF; SPEECH, FREEDOM OF.

PRISON

A prison is a place where persons accused of crimes are kept until trial, and where convicted criminals are confined until they serve the sentence imposed upon them.

There are several types of prisons. A maximum-security prison is one that holds criminals who are likely to try to escape or who are guilty of violent crimes such as rape or murder. A medium-security prison is one in which burglars and nonviolent thieves are confined. A person who is convicted of a nonviolent crime such as embezzlement or forgery is usually placed in a minimum-security prison. The state's prison board or the Federal Bureau of Prisons evaluates each prisoner before assigning him to a particular facility.

REAL LIFE, REAL LAW

The Case of the Diet Doctor Videotapes

The syndicated television program *Inside Edition* was interested in doing a story about Dr. Stuart M. Berger, who was nationally known, and also criticized, for his diet program. In gathering information for the story, one of the program's producers went to Dr. Berger's office posing as a patient. Unknown to the doctor, the producer used a hidden camera and videotaped him engaging in allegedly unethical behavior and medical malpractice. The program later informed Dr. Berger that it intended to use the tape in its broadcast of the story about him.

Dr. Berger sued the producers of the show in federal district court, claiming invasion of privacy and making other charges. He also asked the court to order *Inside Edition* not to use the tape in their report, claiming it would irreparably harm him. The court issued a temporary restraining order preventing the airing of the footage taped in the doctor's office.

The producers appealed, claiming that the order violated the First Amendment right to freedom of the press because it prevented the broadcasting of the information. The Court of Appeals agreed. It stated that no matter how inappropriate the methods used to make the tape may have been, the right to disseminate information is protected by the First Amendment and ruled that the district court's order was an impermissible use of prior restraint. Although the court recognized that Dr. Berger might be embarrassed by the tape, it would not cause him irreparable harm. Once the video was broadcast, the doctor could sue for defamation or invasion of privacy.

Maximum-security prisons have high walls and heavily armed guards. They are built in isolated locations. Medium-security prisons may be located in more populated areas and may allow the prisoners more access to visitors. A minimum-security prison may resemble a college campus and may not even have a fence around it.

Prisons are usually built and operated by the government, but some states are turning to private companies to build and run them. These companies often can run a prison more efficiently than the government can, and they are able to earn a profit from the fees the state pays them. Privately run prisons must follow the same laws regarding prisoners' rights as publicly financed prisons. See the box on page 423.

Prison Sentence

When a defendant is found guilty, the court imposes its punishment, called a sentence. The sentence typically consists of a specified period of time in prison, or a fine, or both. Sentencing for felonies (serious crimes) does not take place immediately after the verdict; it is usually done several days or weeks after the trial.

PROCEDURE FOR SENTENCING

Most states have laws that determine sentences for felonies. Often a presentencing investigation is conducted to review the defendant's personal background, health, the circumstances under which the crime was committed, and the impact the crime had on the victim. (If this information was divulged during the trial, an investigation prior to sentencing may not be necessary.)

The findings are then considered at the presentencing hearing by the same judge who heard the case. The hearing is similar to a trial in that the defendant has the right to be present and to have a lawyer represent him. Both the prosecutor and the defense attorney may present evidence affecting the sentence, and the defendant has a right to make a statement regarding any mitigating circumstances.

In some states the victim of the crime has the right to be present at the hearing, to tell the judge about the impact the crime has had on his life, and to make recommendations to the judge, who considers them but does not have to accept them.

SENTENCING RESTRICTIONS

Every sentence—whether a fine or imprisonment—must fall within certain parameters for the crime, as set by law. For example, burglary in some states is punishable by a minimum of 1 year to a maximum of 10 years in prison. When a person is convicted of the crime, the judge decides how many years within that range he should serve.

It is rare for a higher court to overturn a sentence that is within the limits set by law. In a few cases, however, higher courts have found that a judge in a lower court abused his discretion. For example, in Rhode Island, a judge imposed a 15-year prison sentence on a defendant convicted of possessing marijuana. Because it was a first-time offense, the higher court ruled that the sentence was excessive and overturned it.

If a sentencing statute calls for either a fine or imprisonment, the court may not impose both. If it does so, the prisoner may be released once he pays the fine. However, some statutes allow the court to impose both a fine and a prison sentence.

Usually a defendant who was imprisoned because he could not make bail while awaiting trial is entitled to receive credit against his sentence for the time already served.

TYPES OF SENTENCES

A sentence is intended to fit the crime. When a defendant is convicted of several different crimes, he may receive several sentences. If he does, the court must decide whether they will run consecutively or concurrently. When sentences are consecutive, one must be completed before the next begins. Concurrent sentences are served simultaneously. The more serious the crimes are, the more likely that the sentences will be consecutive.

Indeterminate sentences For certain crimes, some state laws stipulate indeterminate sentences—ones that range between a minimum and maximum term of imprisonment, as set by the judge. For example, a judge may sentence someone guilty of breaking and entering

ABC's OF PRISONERS' RIGHTS

State and federal laws give every prisoner the following rights, which have been upheld by the courts:

- The right to send and receive letters without undue restrictions or unnecessary invasion of privacy. But in the interest of security, prison officials may censor a prisoner's mail.
- The right to privacy when talking with an attorney or spouse.
- The right (in some states) to private conjugal visits with a spouse or other person.
- The right to medical care. Prisoners also have the right to sue if they are the victims of medical malpractice.
- The right to regular periods of exercise, wholesome food, clean clothing, and showers.
- The right to bring a complaint and file a lawsuit against the prison when a prisoner believes his constitutional rights have been violated. To that end, he has the right to consult legal books and, in most cases, to have a lawyer assist him with his complaint.
- The right not to be psychologically intimidated or physically abused by prison guards. However, guards have the right to use necessary force to protect themselves and to preserve order in the prison.
- The right to practice one's religion, to have access to religious books and other materials, and to be visited by a member of the clergy.

to two to five years. This means that the offender must serve at least two years, but if he shows he has rehabilitated himself so that he can function again in society, the parole board may release him early. It is up to the state or federal parole board to determine whether or not the offender will serve the maximum number of years.

Enhanced sentences
Crime does not pay, especially for repeat offenders. State and federal laws called Habitual Criminal Acts allow sentences to be increased for offenders with a "record." For example, if a defendant with a record of previous crimes is convicted of a crime that carries a one-year sentence, the judge may double the sentence to two years.

Mandatory sentences
Some crimes carry mandatory sentences. Regardless of the circumstances under which the crime was committed, the judge is required to issue the sentence required by law. In some states, for example, if someone is convicted of an offense during which he used a firearm, he must serve a five-year minimum sentence, even if it was a first offense.

Many states have passed mandatory sentencing laws for drunk driving. There are federal mandatory sentences for certain felonies, such as trafficking in illegal drugs. State and federal parole boards can sometimes shorten mandatory sentences if circumstances permit.

PROBATION AND PAROLE

When the convicted defendant is a first-time offender, the judge may decide to place him on probation rather than sentence him to prison. On probation, the defendant remains free but is under supervision for the length of the sentence. Depending upon the nature of the crime, he may also have to meet certain conditions, such as taking periodic blood tests for a conviction. If he violates the terms of his probation, he will be sent to prison.

A judge may sentence a convicted defendant to a prison term, followed by a period of probation, as long as the two terms together do not exceed the maximum sentence allowed by law for the crime.

Parole, or the release from jail after serving only part of a term, is granted by a parole board, not a sentencing judge. A parole board grants parole to those prisoners who show genuine rehabilitation. See PAROLE.

APPEALING A SENTENCE

A defendant may appeal his sentence as well as his conviction. Usually he must serve his sentence while awaiting the outcome of the appeal. Ordinarily, the right to bail applies only to first-time offenders. Some states, however, have laws allowing defendants with a record of prior convictions to remain free on bail. See also APPEAL.

PRIVACY RIGHTS

Although there is no mention of the right to privacy in the U.S. Constitution, it is implied in the Bill of Rights, which guarantees freedom of association and prohibits unreasonable searches and seizures. The right to be let alone is a cherished one, but some aspects of this right continue to be hotly debated. For example, the right to privacy has become part of the debate surrounding a woman's right to obtain an abortion.

INVASION OF PRIVACY

Invasion of your privacy by private individuals or companies is a tort, or civil wrong, and you can sue for any damages you suffer. In order for an action to be considered an invasion of privacy, one of the following must have occurred:

◇ *Public disclosure of private information about you that is offensive or objectionable.* Suppose you are late in making your car payment and the lender sends you a letter of reminder. But on the outside of the envelope the phrase "PAY UP, DEADBEAT" is printed in large red letters for anyone to read. Your privacy has been invaded, and you may sue for any damages that happen to result, such as pain and suffering, lost wages, or some other misfortune.

◇ *Being portrayed in a false light.* Suppose your local television station decides to do a story about insurance swindlers. To illustrate the story, it uses a videotape of you at your insurance office. The implication is that you are one of the swindlers talked about in the broadcast. This puts you in a false light.

◇ *Use of your name or likeness for a commercial purpose without permission.* For instance, a cosmetics company cannot use your picture in a magazine advertisement without obtaining your permission in advance. If it does, you may sue for compensation based on the profits the company made by using your picture.

◇ *Unreasonable intrusion into your private life.* You do not have to endure people peeking in your windows, tapping your telephone lines, or going through your personal belongings without the legal authority to do so.

PRIVACY LAWS

According to federal and state laws, certain kinds of invasion of privacy are criminal offenses. For example, it is a federal crime for anyone to open your mail without your approval.

The Privacy Act of 1974 states that information pertaining to individuals kept by a government agency can be used only for the purpose for which it was obtained. Thus information about you or your family that was collected by the

REAL LIFE, REAL LAW

The Case of the Stolen Voice

Although actors, singers, and models are often in the public eye, they are nonetheless entitled to their privacy. In one recent case, the Ford Motor Company was sued by singer Bette Midler for violating her right to privacy when it used her vocal styling in a commercial without her permission. The lawsuit claimed that Ford had hired one of Midler's former backup singers to imitate her voice and vocal style while singing one of Midler's hit recordings, "Do You Wanna Dance?" Ford claimed that although the styles were indeed similar, there was little likelihood that the version of the song used in the commercial fooled the public or that Midler had been damaged in any way.

A federal court disagreed, however, and held that Ford and its advertising agency had misappropriated Midler's voice and used it without her consent. The court awarded the singer several hundred thousand dollars in damages, and ordered Ford to discontinue any use of the song in its future commercials.

Census Bureau can be used only by the Census Bureau and cannot be used by the IRS or anyone else.

Another federal law, the Family Educational Rights and Privacy Act of 1974, protects the privacy of student records and requires schools to keep a record of all requests to see a student's files.

Banks, savings and loan associations, and other financial institutions must meet strict legal requirements before releasing any information about your accounts. Unless a bank is responding to a court order or subpoena, it may not disclose the amount, number, or sources of funds deposited in your accounts without your permission. However, a bank may indicate to any creditor whether you have an account there and whether there is enough money on deposit in your account to cover a check drawn against it.

See also CREDIT BUREAU AND CREDIT RATING; FREEDOM OF INFORMATION ACT; PRIVILEGED COMMUNICATION.

PRIVATE CLUB

Federal civil rights laws prohibit discrimination based on race, sex, color, national origin, or religion in public restaurants, hotels, and other facilities, but they do not apply to private clubs or other private establishments.

WHAT MAKES A CLUB PRIVATE

Although civil rights laws exempt private clubs, they do not actually define what a private club is. Thus, in order to determine whether a club is private, the courts have used the following criteria:

◇ *Whether the club is publicly or privately owned and funded.* Private funding and ownership by club members increases the chance that the club will be found to be private.

◇ *Whether or not formal procedures and screenings are conducted before a person is admitted as a member.* If the admission procedure is selective, a court is more likely to rule the club private.

◇ *Whether the club solicits members through public advertising or by nomination from another member.* If the club uses public advertising to solicit new members, it is more likely that the courts will deem the club public.

CIRCUMVENTING THE LAW

After the Federal Civil Rights Act of 1964 was passed, groups organized private clubs for the sole purpose of circumventing the law. Federal courts, however, have consistently held that these clubs were not private clubs but public facilities.

An early case applying to private clubs involved the Lake Nixon Club, a recreational facility near Little Rock, Arkansas, which offered swimming, boating, picnicking, and other facilities to whites only. As soon as the 1964 Civil Rights Act was passed, the owners began to refer to it as a private club and required those who used the facilities to pay a seasonal membership fee of 25 cents. Evidence showed that more than 100,000 whites but no African-Americans were admitted to membership and that the club was advertised in magazines, newspapers, and on two local radio stations. Based on this evidence, the U.S. Supreme Court ruled that the Lake Nixon Club, though privately funded, was in fact a public accommodation subject to the provisions of federal law. See also DISCRIMINATION.

PRIVATE COURT

Because the public courts are clogged with cases, businesses and individuals who are involved in civil disputes are increasingly turning to private courts. These courts, which are created by private corporations, hear lawsuits for breach of contract, personal injury, and property damage, as well as other kinds of suits heard by public courts. When a suit is brought before a private court, both parties agree to be bound by the court's decision and waive their rights to take any further action or appeals.

Private courts usually hire retired state or federal court judges to preside over cases. The parties agree in advance to split the costs of the proceedings, which can be either a flat fee or an hourly fee. Sometimes the trial is formal and the usual rules of evidence are observed, but most cases are handled more casually—with a settlement acceptable to each party being the primary goal.

Although private courts can

offer a quick resolution to a problem, they can be costly. They are too expensive to be of much use in typical consumer or landlord-tenant disputes, for example. For alternatives see ARBITRATION; MEDIATION; SMALL-CLAIMS COURT.

PRIVATE INVESTIGATOR

Private investigators offer a number of services, from looking into the backgrounds of prospective employees to locating missing persons. Only about half the states have laws that apply to private investigators. Some states require investigators to be licensed. Others require them to complete law enforcement training courses or have experience with a law enforcement agency.

If you decide to hire an investigator, bear in mind that you could be held responsible for any misconduct on his part committed during the course of his investigation. For example, if a private investigator breaks into your neighbor's house and removes an item he believes is yours, you could be held liable for any damage he does. You might also be charged as an accessory to burglary if you knew about the investigator's action before it took place.

STEPS TO TAKE WHEN HIRING A PRIVATE INVESTIGATOR

Before hiring a private investigator, be sure to inquire into his background and expertise. Consider the following:

1. Find out whether the investigator is licensed by your state and check his credentials with the state's licensing board. Using an unlicensed investigator in a state that requires licensing can lead to serious problems, such as charges of invasion of privacy.

2. Ask whether the investigator carries liability insurance. Get the name of his insurance company and check to be sure his policy is in effect.

3. Inquire about the investigator's background. Ask about his training, experience, and whether he has ever been sued as a result of an investigation.

4. Check references. Don't be fooled by an investigator who says he cannot reveal the names of current or former clients out of respect for his clients' privacy. A client can always waive confidentiality. If the investigator refuses to give you references, look elsewhere.

5. Get a written agreement about fees and request that all bills for services or expenses be submitted in writing. Private investigators usually charge by the hour, and their fees vary widely. To be safe, draw up an agreement limiting the number of hours the investigator can spend on your case without obtaining additional approval from you.

PRIVILEGED COMMUNICATION

Private communications between you and someone in an advisory position, such as a doctor, lawyer, or clergyman, are considered privileged communication. Neither you nor the professional you consult can be forced to reveal the contents of your oral or written communications, nor can they be used as evidence in court.

In certain instances the law allows the person who sought the professional advice to waive his right of privileged communication, both in and outside the courtroom. For example, during a visit to your minister you confide the details of your husband's infidelity. Your husband later files for divorce. In order to claim your right to alimony, you ask the minister to testify about your conversation with him. The minister cannot refuse to testify since the privilege is yours to assert or waive. However, if the minister were to disclose this information without your prior authorization, you would be able to sue him for any harm you suffered as a result. See also LAWYER; MEDICAL RECORDS; PRIVACY RIGHTS.

PROBABLE CAUSE

Simple suspicion that is not corroborated by facts or circumstances is not enough to support an arrest or to justify most searches and seizures. Police officers and judges must have probable cause—that is, reasonable grounds to believe that a person has committed a crime or is about to commit one —before they can take serious action against a suspect. The proper use of probable cause is vital to good law enforcement, and is applicable at several stages in the course of criminal proceedings.

SEARCH WARRANTS

The Fourth Amendment protects citizens and their possessions from random, unjustified searches. Thus law enforcement officials may not search civilians or their homes without a search warrant. To obtain a search warrant for a home, office, garage, barn, storage facility, or car, the police must convince the judge that they have probable cause—sufficient information from other sources — to believe that a crime has been or is about to be committed and that evidence of it may be found at the place to be searched.

Before physically searching, or "frisking," a suspect, a police officer must have probable cause to believe that the suspect has the "fruits or instrumentalities of crime"(such as illegal drugs or a gun) on his person. If such an item is in plain view, an officer can arrest a suspect without a warrant. And once a person has been placed under arrest, the police officer has the right to search him for other evidence. See also STOP-AND-FRISK LAWS.

ARREST WARRANTS

A similar procedure must be followed before a law enforcement officer can obtain an arrest warrant. The officer cannot just tell the judge that she believes that the suspect is guilty. She must state the facts and sources of information that led her to that belief and thus provide probable cause.

Warrants are issued for specific places and persons. If it turns out that a warrant for a search or an arrest was not based on probable cause, or that the search or arrest was improperly conducted, then any evidence obtained in the search or arrest cannot be used in court. In the case of an arrest, the charges will be dismissed and the person will be allowed to go free.

PRELIMINARY HEARINGS

Probable cause plays a key role in determining whether a court can detain a suspect. For felonies and other serious crimes, some jurisdictions require a judge or magistrate to conduct a preliminary hearing to decide whether there is probable cause to go forward with a criminal trial. See MIRANDA WARNINGS; PRELIMINARY HEARING; SEARCH AND SEIZURE.

PROBATE

Probate, which comes from a Latin word meaning "prove," is the process that establishes the validity of a person's last will and testament. It is also the legal term that refers to the settling of the deceased's estate.

Probate allows for the transfer of assets from the deceased to his heirs, as stipulated in his will. But if the transfer of ownership was made before the person died—for example, by placing property in joint tenancy, naming a beneficiary to a life insurance policy, or establishing a living trust—then those assets do not have to be probated.

The will certifies the transfer of assets from the deceased to his heirs. The person in charge of handling this process is the executor, who is named in the will. The executor's first duty is to present the will to the state probate court. See EXECUTOR AND ADMINISTRATOR.

Once the will and probate petition are filed with the probate court, the will becomes public record. The court issues a notice of the filing to interested parties and arranges for a hearing. In some instances the date of the hearing is published in the local newspapers so that creditors can come forward to make their claims.

The probate hearing provides a chance for anyone to contest the validity of the will. There are only two grounds on which a person can contest a will: (1) that the will does not comply with state law, or (2) that the person who wrote it was legally incompetent (unable to make rational decisions about the disposition of his property). See COMPETENCY.

At the probate hearing the witnesses to the will may be asked to swear that they witnessed the signing of the will by the deceased and the other witnesses. In states that provide for self-proving wills, witnesses are not required to appear in court. See WILL.

Depending on the size of the estate, probate can be expensive and time-consuming. The total cost of probate, including attorneys' fees, court fees, and money paid to other professionals, such as appraisers and accountants, can be as much as 5 to 8 percent of the gross value of the estate. (These fees are in addition to estate and inheritance taxes.) From start to finish, probate can take as long as a year or more.

Many states have probate simplification laws, which allow only nominal fees to be charged for probating small estates or those that pass everything to the surviving spouse. And about 15 states have adopted the Uniform Probate Code, which makes the process so simple that it can often be done without lawyers or the courts.

Living trusts, life insurance trusts, and joint tenancy accounts eliminate or reduce the assets transferred through a will so that, in some cases, probate costs may be reduced, if not avoided altogether. See also ESTATE PLANNING; LIVING TRUST; WILL.

PROBATION

A form of conditional release, probation allows a person who is convicted of a crime to avoid a jail sentence or have it reduced and instead places the person under the supervision of a probation officer. See also PAROLE; PRISON SENTENCE.

PRODUCT SAFETY AND LIABILITY

When you go to the store to purchase toys, household products, or appliances, do you consider the safety features of the various brands and styles? Do you notice the warning labels and special packaging included by the manufacturer? These safety features are the result of product-safety legislation. Starting in the 1950's, uniform safety standards were enacted into law for a variety of consumer products in order to limit the risk of injury or illness. These laws protect citizens not only from defective products but also from false advertising and misleading or confusing disclaimers.

CONSUMER PRODUCT SAFETY ACT

The Consumer Product Safety Act was enacted in 1972 to safeguard the public against unreasonable risks of injury from the use of consumer products. The term *consumer product* applies to a wide range of items, from products used for recreation to items used in and around the home and school. Among the products covered under this act are toys, appliances, lamps, lawn-care equipment, snowblowers, and even pet turtles. Products that are not covered include cars, boats, prosthetic devices, and cosmetics, which are regulated under other laws. Additional laws address specific hazards.

◇ The federal Flammable Fabrics Act sets standards for clothing, furniture, and goods made of fabric and other materials, such as plastic, rubber, or synthetic foam.

◇ The Poison Prevention Packaging Act of 1970 mandates special packaging for products that might cause serious injury if accidentally ingested. Pesticides and other hazardous substances, and fuels used in cooking, heating, and refrigeration systems made for home use, must comply with these regulations.

◇ The 1958 Household Refrigerator Safety Act was passed in response to the numerous deaths of children trapped in refrigerators. Under this law, refrigerator doors must be operable from the inside when the refrigerator is upright. Most states have laws that require that the door be removed before the refrigerator can be discarded.

◇ The 1960 federal Hazardous Substances Act requires packages containing hazardous substances intended for household use to carry uniform cautionary labeling, such as "Caution," "Warning," or "Flammable." Manufacturers must also include instructions for handling and storing the product and first-aid treatment. An amendment to this law specifically bans the sale of toys or other children's products that contain hazardous substances or have sharp edges, surfaces, or openings, or moving parts that could cause injury. See also TOY.

CONSUMER PRODUCT SAFETY COMMISSION

The Consumer Product Safety Commission is the agency that enforces safety standards for consumer products and sets requirements for the warnings and instructions that come with them. If the commission finds that a product does not meet safety standards and poses a substantial risk of injury, it may order the manufacturer to take steps to make the product safe, to notify the public and known purchasers about the problem, and then either replace unsafe products with safe ones or give buyers a refund. If a product presents an immediate danger, it may be seized by the commission following a hearing in federal court. Manufacturers who violate safety acts are subject to imprisonment or fines or both.

STRICT LIABILITY FOR CONSUMER PRODUCTS

At one time, the law held that consumers could not sue manufacturers of defective products because they had not purchased the items directly from the manufacturer. This was called the doctrine of privity. But that doctrine has been abandoned, and today courts recognize that manufacturers have a duty to warn users of their products.

If you are injured by a product, you can sue the manufacturer, the seller, or sometimes both. The responsibility of a party to pay for harm caused by one of its products is called product liability.

Under the law, defective products fall into one of three general categories: (1) a product that has been manufactured with certain defects built in (for example, a chair whose legs are fastened with aluminum bolts rather than stronger steel ones), (2) a product that was poorly designed (like the Ford Pintos that were subject to fatal explosions and fires because of the location of their fuel tanks), or (3) a product that does not offer users adequate instructions and warnings about its safe use (for example, by failing to warn users not to stand on the top platform of a stepladder).

Although at one time consumers received little legal protection when they were injured by a defective product, today it is usually easier to receive compensation for property damage or personal injuries suffered from a poorly designed or defective item. Owing to newer, more sophisticated, technology, the average consumer cannot determine for himself whether a product is safe. As a result, the doctrine of "strict liability" has evolved in order to help protect purchasers who must rely on the assurances of the manufacturer that a product is safe. See also LIABILITY.

Under the doctrine of strict liability, a consumer who is injured by a defective product may collect damages from the manufacturer without having to prove that the manufacturer was negligent. All the consumer needs to prove is that he was injured as a result of a defective product marketed by the manufacturer. The doctrine is based on the premise that paying out compensation for injuries or damage resulting from a defective product is part of the manufacturer's cost of doing business. Although the manufacturer will have to raise the price of his products to cover potential claims, the additional cost to each consumer when spread out among the many hundreds of thousands of purchasers of his products is negligible.

Not every state has strict-liability laws, however. In states that do not—including Delaware, Massachusetts, Michigan, North Carolina, and Virginia—you must prove that your injuries or damages resulted from the negligent, reckless, or intentional misconduct of the product's manufacturer.

FILING A PRODUCT LIABILITY SUIT

If you have been injured by a defective product, you may have to sue not only the manufacturer, but the distributor, wholesaler, and retailer of the product too, since each of them contributed to placing the defective product in the marketplace, and any of them might have caused the defect. For example, suppose the Hi-Ho Hammer Company manufactures hammers and sells them to a wholesaler, MiddleMan Marketing. MiddleMan stores the hammers in a warehouse, where they are allowed to get wet and rusty before being delivered to Deuce Hardware, the store where you purchase one. The head of the hammer is fastened to the handle by a staple that has deteriorated because of the rust. When you use it, the hammer head flies off and strikes you in the face.

In this situation any of the parties involved—the Hi-Ho company, MiddleMan Marketing, or Deuce Hardware—might be held liable for your injuries. Hi-Ho might be liable for using a staple that rusted away too easily, MiddleMan could be liable for allowing the hammers to remain in a place where they could rust, and Deuce could be liable for failing to notice that the hammers were in an unsafe condition when they were put on sale. It may seem daunting for a single consumer to take a large manufacturer to court, let alone the wholesaler and retailer. Bear in mind that lawyers often accept product liability cases on a contingent-fee basis.

STEPS TO TAKE

If you are injured by a product or suffer property damage because of a product defect, here are some steps you can take:

1. Keep the product and any pieces that have come loose or separated. For example, if you have a coffeemaker that overheated and caused a fire, keep the coffeemaker and the glass carafe (or the pieces of the carafe if it was broken).

2. See an attorney experienced in product liability law. She may be able to find out if other consumers encountered similar problems and determine whether it is possible to file a successful claim.

3. Get legal advice promptly. In some states the time limit for filing a claim begins to run when the product is first sold, not when your injury occurs. See STATUTE OF LIMITATIONS.

4. Notify the appropriate government agency about the problem. You can write the Consumer Product Safety Commission, Office of the Secretary, Washington, DC 20207, or call its hotline at (800) 638-2772, ext. 999.

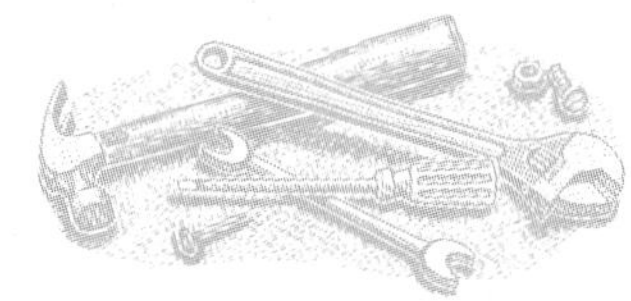

PROMISSORY NOTE

A written document by which one or more persons (known as the "makers") unconditionally promise to pay a specific sum of money to another person or persons (the "payees") at a specified time is called a promissory note. It is used when the payee has lent money or given something valuable to the maker in return for the promise of repayment. When you borrow money from a bank to purchase a car or a home, you will have to sign a promissory note.

Promissory notes are strongly advised when you lend or borrow large sums of money. A promissory note protects the maker from an unscrupulous payee who may demand more money than was originally loaned. The maker is obligated to pay back only the amount set down in writing. To be effective, a promissory note must state the amount to be paid, including the interest rate, if any, and when payment is due, and be signed by the maker. If the note is written to be payable on demand, the maker may redeem it at any time. If the note has a specific date for payment, the maker can collect only on this date.

If the maker dies, a promissory note serves as evidence of the debt, and the maker's estate is obligated to pay it. An example of a typical promissory note can be found in the EVERYDAY LEGAL FORMS section of this book, beginning on page 552. See also FAMILY LOAN.

PROPERTY TAX

If you own a home or other real estate, you must pay property taxes imposed by the town, county, and state in which you live. Some states and cities impose a property tax on personal property, such as automobiles and boats. These taxes help finance schools, roads, and other public services.

Generally, property taxes are determined by the tax rate (set by the town, city, or state) and the assessed value of the real estate. Property assessments are made by an official local body—the board of assessors. To arrive at a value for a property, the board evaluates the home's size, age, acreage, condition, and the value of comparable property in the area.

Depending on state law, real estate is reassessed regularly, sometimes as often as once a year, and when it is sold. Whenever your property is assessed, the board must tell you what the assessment is and how it was determined. If you do not agree with the assessment, you can challenge it.

FAILURE TO PAY

If you fail to pay your property taxes, the government can place a lien, or claim, on the property. A lien requires you to pay all past-due taxes and penalties before you can sell it. If you do not pay for several years, the government can foreclose on its lien and force the sale of your property to recover the money owed. See also FORECLOSURE.

PAYING TAXES

Homeowners with mortgages often do not pay their taxes directly to the government. Instead, a portion of the tax is included in their mortgage payments and placed in a tax reserve or escrow account. The bank or lender then forwards the payments to the tax office. The amount you pay for property taxes may be indicated on your mortgage coupon. If it is not, the lender will tell you what it is.

Recent studies suggest that some lenders require homeowners to pay more into their tax reserve account than necessary. Generally, you should not pay more than 110 percent of last year's tax into this year's reserve. The extra 10 percent takes care of increases in tax rates or reassessments. If you are being asked to send more money than this, write to your mortgage company for an explanation. In some states the law requires the company to make a reduction, or the lender may do so voluntarily. See also MORTGAGE.

PROSTITUTION

Prostitution, or the exchange of sexual relations for money, remains a serious social problem despite strict local and state laws that make it illegal. In the past, law enforcement efforts were aimed at arresting prostitutes and sending them to prison. Today many communities arrest the customers too.

Prostitutes are at high risk for contracting and transmit-

ABC's OF CHALLENGING PROPERTY TAX ASSESSMENTS

The amount of property tax you pay on your home or other real estate is based on a subjective evaluation of what your property is worth. If you believe this assessment is too high, you have the right to challenge it. To increase your chances of a successful appeal, here are some tips to follow.

- ❑ When you receive an assessment you believe is too high, contact the board of assessors as soon as possible to initiate your appeal. In some states, instructions for making an appeal are on the tax bill itself; in other states you must ask the board of assessors for instructions.

- ❑ Whatever the instructions are, follow them to the letter. If you must make your appeal in person, do so. If there are forms you need to complete, fill them out. Many tax-assessment challenges are rejected because the taxpayer failed to comply with the rules.

- ❑ Look for obvious mistakes in the appraisal of your property. For example, your home may have been listed as having three bedrooms and two baths when it actually has two bedrooms and one bath. Mistakes of this type are fairly common, and you will almost certainly get a reduction in your tax bill if you point them out.

- ❑ Assemble the evidence you need to support your case. This may mean securing a private appraisal of your property or obtaining information about comparable properties that have sold in your neighborhood in recent months. In some places an affidavit from the appraiser is sufficient evidence to present before the board; in others, the appraiser may have to appear before the board.

- ❑ Attend a hearing before your own case is scheduled. You will learn not only about the board's procedures but also the kinds of arguments that persuade the board.

- ❑ Tell the board in advance what evidence you intend to present, such as photographs of your property and comparable properties nearby, maps of the area, and the names of witnesses who will appear on your behalf. You may also want to provide copies of your original sales contract to show the price you paid for the property.

- ❑ Present your case briefly and clearly. Do not get long-winded or argumentative. Claiming you do not have the money to pay your taxes will not help your case.

- ❑ If you are still not satisfied, consider making a further appeal. The board of assessors must tell you what your appeal rights are and how much time you have to file an appeal. You will probably need an attorney at this stage of the process.

ting the Human Immunodeficiency Virus (HIV), which causes AIDS. In some communities convicted prostitutes who have AIDS and who knowingly exposed their customers to the virus, have received longer prison sentences.

PSYCHIATRIST

A psychiatrist is a physician who specializes in the study, diagnosis, treatment, and prevention of mental illness.

Psychiatrists are in a special position of trust and confidence with their patients, who may be in a precarious emotional state. Consequently, psychiatrists often face ethical challenges that other kinds of doctors rarely encounter.

For example, when a patient confides his secrets, the psychiatrist cannot ethically reveal them to others without the patient's consent. In the past, if the patient revealed information about criminal acts he had committed, the psychiatrist had to decide whether to give this information to legal authorities in order to protect potential victims from the patient.

Now, however, new laws in most states require psychiatrists to disclose to the police the facts about patients who are planning to do harm to others in order to protect potential victims. In one such case a psychiatrist was successfully sued by his patient's intended victim (who survived being stabbed by the patient) for not revealing to the police his patient's intent to kill her.

PSYCHIATRISTS AND SEX

Numerous reports have come to light of psychiatrists who have had sexual liaisons with their patients. Even though the American Psychiatric Association condemns such behavior, patients often do not bring suit because to do so, they would have to waive the doctor-patient privilege, thereby allowing the details of their personal lives to be revealed in court. When they do sue, psychiatrists often allege that the patient filed the suit in retaliation for his rejection of the patient's sexual advances.

OTHER MENTAL-HEALTH PRACTITIONERS

In addition to psychiatrists, there are other qualified therapists, namely psychologists and social workers, who practice in the mental-health field and are subject to state licensing procedures and laws.

In some states, however, almost anyone, regardless of training or background, can set up a "counseling" or "therapy" practice. To protect yourself from untrained counselors, be sure to check their credentials and membership in professional organizations. Be aware also that most health insurance companies do not cover counseling from therapists who are not licensed. Call or write your state department of health and the state board of medical examiners to find out whether the therapist is licensed and whether any complaints have been lodged against him. See also MEDICAL MALPRACTICE; PRIVILEGED COMMUNICATION.

PYRAMID SALES SCHEME

Employment ads for Koskot Interplanetary, Inc., sounded too good to be true. No experience was required, and the ad assured prospective salespeople that within a year's time they would make $100,000 annually. When eager candidates dialed the number of Koskot Interplanetary, they learned that they only had to pay a one-time fee of $5,000, which entitled them to distribute Koskot products and earn a 40 percent commission on each sale. Moreover, if a salesperson recruited other salespeople, he would receive $3,000 of their $5,000 start-up fees, as well as a percentage of their sales.

In a classic pyramid scheme, such as the one offered by Koskot, the first participants are paid with money from those who buy in later. In order for the later salespeople to make money, they have to recruit more distributors and so on, until millions of people must be made distributors in order for the previous distributors to make their profits. Those at the bottom of the pyramid will never get their money back. In fact, from the first level of the pyramid to the sixth, the program must have 5,461 participants in order to meet the profits already promised to the first through the fifth level.

Not all sales programs that resemble pyramid schemes are against the law. Many reputable companies, such as Amway and Mary Kay Cosmetics, use a form of the concept, which they call multilevel marketing. As long as a marketing program's primary goal is to sell products and not distributorships, multilevel marketing is legal.

Koskot Interplanetary Inc. was eventually forced out of business by federal and state government prosecutors, but similar pyramid sales schemes continue to surface.

STEPS TO TAKE

Do not buy into a pyramid or multilevel marketing plan before you take these measures:

1. Ask how much you can expect to earn. In reputable distributing companies, most participants earn $200 to $300 per month or less.

2. Investigate the company's product. Is the price reasonable when compared with similar products sold elsewhere? Does the company stand behind its products with a warranty? Will you be liable if a customer is harmed by the product?

3. Ask whether the company will require you to buy large quantities of their products, and whether you will be able to return unsold products.What out-of-pocket expenses will you incur if you are a distributor? What expenses will the company pay for?

4. Evaluate the company's payment schedule. If it has sales quotas, ask what yours will be. Find out how many distributors you will have to recruit in order to earn bonuses. See also PONZI SCHEME; SCAMS AND SWINDLES.

FROM QUIET ENJOYMENT TO QUITCLAIM DEED

QUIET ENJOYMENT

The right to use and enjoy your home without being disturbed is called quiet enjoyment. It protects you not only from trespassers but from nuisances created by neighbors, such as loud music or foul smells. To enforce this right, you can bring a lawsuit against your neighbor to prohibit such activities. See also NOISE; NUISANCE; TENANT'S RIGHTS.

QUIET TITLE

Harry Windsor had lived in his house for five years when he received an alarming letter from an attorney. The letter claimed that Harry's purchase of the house had been invalid, and that the attorney's client, Sam, was the true owner. As proof, the attorney provided a photocopy of an old deed that seemed to give title of the property to Sam several years before Harry's purchase.

When an unexpected claim is made against a property owner, it is referred to as a "cloud on the title." The owner should take steps to remove the cloud —that is, to have any invalid or fraudulent claims dismissed— so that there is no question regarding the legitimate ownership of the property.

To do this, the owner must file a lawsuit to "quiet title." In this proceeding the court examines the evidence presented by everyone who claims an interest in the real estate and then decides which claim prevails. When the court renders its judgment, it issues an injunction against persons whose claims are invalid, ordering them not to interfere with the true owner's right to use or dispose of the property. See also TITLE INSURANCE.

QUITCLAIM DEED

A quitclaim deed transfers whatever interest the grantor (or owner) has in a piece of property but does not guarantee that no one else has an interest in it. A quitclaim deed offers a buyer the least protection of any form of deed and allows the possibility that his ownership will be challenged later on. Before accepting such a deed, consult an attorney experienced in real estate law. A sample quitclaim deed is in the EVERYDAY LEGAL FORMS section, page 552. See also DEED.

Raffle

A raffle is a kind of lottery, a game of chance in which you purchase a ticket for a chance at winning something much more valuable than the price of the ticket. Many charitable organizations sponsor raffles for fund-raising. Because raffles are a form of gambling, they are strictly regulated by state laws. In most states only recognized charities may conduct raffles, and they must obtain a permit from the state to do so. Laws may limit the number of tickets sold as well as their cost. They may also prohibit the sponsoring organization from canceling the drawing if it fails to sell as many tickets as expected.

When you buy a raffle ticket, be sure that the raffle is sponsored by a legitimate charity. Keep your ticket stub, because you may not be able to claim the prize without it. If you belong to an organization that wants to hold a raffle, ask your state's department of revenue for information about the best way to proceed. See also GAMBLING; LOTTERY.

Railroad Retirement

More than 5 million retired railroad workers as well as their spouses and survivors have received retirement benefits, Medicare coverage, and disability payments from the Railroad Retirement Board, an independent federal agency that administers the Railroad Retirement Act and the Railroad Unemployment Insurance Act. The board was created in the 1930's to establish a retirement benefit program for the nation's railroad workers.

The Railroad Retirement Board is distinct from the Social Security Administration, although the two systems are similarly structured. Under the Railroad Retirement Act, retirement and disability annuities are paid to railroad workers with at least 10 years of service in the industry. Full benefits are available to persons with 10 years of service at the age of 65, or to persons with 30 years of service at the age of 62. Workers may also receive disability payments. Divorced and surviving spouses of retired workers, as well as the unmarried children, grandchildren, and dependent parents of deceased workers may be entitled to receive annuities.

If a railroad employee has less than 10 years of service at the time of his retirement or disability, credits earned by the worker under the Railroad Retirement System are transferred to the Social Security program, where they are treated as Social Security credits. If an employee or his spouse is entitled to payment under both systems, the Social Security Administration determines the amount due, but payment is made by the Railroad Retirement Board in the form of a combined-benefits check.

For more information about benefits available to railroad workers and their dependents, write to the U.S. Railroad Retirement Board, 844 Rush Street, Chicago, IL 60611. The board also has a number of regional offices throughout the United States. For the office serving you, call the Federal Information Center at the telephone number given on page 225. See also RETIREMENT PLANNING; SOCIAL SECURITY.

Rape

The crime of rape is committed if a man has sexual intercourse with a woman without her consent. A woman can be considered the victim of rape even if she does not resist her assailant, especially if resisting him would put her in danger of physical harm or death. Conversely, a man can be found guilty of rape even if he did not use physical force; the mere threat of physical violence or intimidation is enough to support a rape conviction. A woman is also considered a rape victim if she was not able to give her consent to intercourse because she was inebriated, drugged, mentally incompetent, or a minor. See also AGE OF CONSENT; STATUTORY RAPE.

Sexual intercourse is recognized by law as an essential part of marriage, and couples may divorce or have their marriages annulled when sexual relations are denied without good cause. But a husband's right to force his wife to have sexual relations with him is no longer recognized, as it once was. In most states a husband who has intercourse with his wife without her consent can be charged with rape.

In every state, rape is a felony punishable by imprisonment. A rapist who causes severe physical injuries to his victim or who rapes a child can be charged with aggravated rape and receive a more severe sentence for his crime.

PROSECUTING RAPE

Rape victims often do not report the crime or press charges out of fear that their past behavior will be scrutinized, that their moral character will be called into question, or that they themselves will be held responsible for the attack. To encourage victims to prosecute rapists, many states have repealed laws that require the testimony of a witness or proof that the victim made "earnest resistance" to the rape. So-called rape shield laws prohibit the defendant's attorney from questioning the victim about her prior sexual conduct—a form of questioning that can effectively turn a victim into a defendant.

Victims often fail to report a rape immediately because they suffer from emotional trauma. Because such a delay may cast unwarranted doubt upon the case, some courts allow the prosecution to show that the victim's delay was due to a disorder known as rape trauma syndrome, and the case is permitted to continue.

STEPS TO TAKE IF YOU ARE RAPED

If you take these steps and precautions should you be raped, you will help law enforcement agencies prosecute the rapist:

1. Report the crime to the police as soon as possible. In most communities a female police officer or victim's advocate will be available when you make your statement.

2. If possible, do not shower or bathe until after you have been examined by a doctor. A physical examination can provide crucial evidence to support your contention that you have been raped and may help identify your assailant.

3. Give the police the clothing you were wearing at the time of the rape.

4. Answer questions from the police truthfully and carefully. However, if an officer should suggest to you that you instigated the attack, ask for a victim's advocate or ask that the officer's supervisor be present. Then answer no more questions until your request is granted.

5. Call a rape victim hotline or community health center for counseling and emotional support. It is common for rape victims to experience periods of trauma that last for months or even years. Early counseling can help you to resume a normal life. See also DATE RAPE.

REAL ESTATE

The term *real estate,* also known as real property and realty, refers not only to land but to everything permanently below it (such as minerals, gas, and oil) and permanently above it (such as trees and buildings). Like all property, real estate may be bought, sold, inherited, leased, or given to someone as a gift. State laws regulate the manner in which real estate may be obtained or transferred. In all states, specific documents must be completed and filed with the appropriate local government agency in order to record a change in real estate ownership. See also DEED; GIFT; HOME BUYING AND SELLING; LEASE; MORTGAGE.

REAL ESTATE AGENT AND BROKER

People who sell real estate are often called real estate agents, but there are actually three different terms that apply to these salespeople. A real estate broker is someone licensed to sell real estate in exchange for a fee. A Realtor is a real estate broker who belongs to the National Association of Realtors, a nationwide trade association. A real estate agent is a person who sells real estate under the authority of a broker or Realtor but is not allowed to earn a sales commission on her own. Agents and brokers must be licensed by the state in which they work. To obtain a real estate broker's license, a person must take a course in real estate transactions and pass a test administered by the state real estate commission. If a broker or agent engages in fraudulent or unethical business practices, her license can be revoked.

IF YOU ARE SELLING REAL ESTATE

Real estate brokers are usually employed by people who want to sell property. The broker's primary duty is to locate a buyer who can meet the price and conditions set by the seller. If she succeeds in this endeavor, she receives a commission from the proceeds of the sale.

Listing agreements

Before you work with a real estate broker, you should have a written contract, or "listing agreement." Some states require a broker to have such an agreement in order to receive a commission. The agreement should be signed by all owners of the property. If you are married, your spouse should sign it, whether or not his or her name appears on the deed. The listing agreement should specify:

◇ The property that you are authorizing the agent to sell, as well as any items not included in the sale, such as your antique chandelier or built-in microwave oven.

◇ The period of time for which the agent has the right to list the property.

◇ The amount of the commission. (The average commission is 6 percent of the selling price.)

◇ The listing price of the property.

You should also be aware of your obligations under the contract. Many agreements call for an exclusive right to sell, which entitles the agent to a commission if the house is sold during the period of the contract—even if the agent did not find the buyer. The courts usually enforce these clauses. If you find a buyer on your own, you can avoid paying a commission by waiting until the time period specified in the listing agreement has passed before you sign a contract with the buyer you found. But if, after the contract has expired, you sell to a buyer whom the agent found, you will probably owe the agent her commission. Most contracts contain a "protection clause" that entitles an agent to her commission under these circumstances—but only for a limited period, such as six months after the end of the listing agreement.

Market analysis

One reason you pay an agent a commission is to benefit from her expertise in pricing property. Ask her for a market analysis that shows how similar property—comparable in size,

REAL LIFE, REAL LAW

The Case of the Broker's Commission

When John was ready to sell his home, he signed an agreement with Royal Realty. In the agreement was a clause that gave the real estate company "the exclusive right and authority to sell" his house. Soon after, John was approached by Helen, who wanted to buy John's house. With no assistance from Royal Realty, John and Helen came to an agreement, signed a contract, and closed on the house. Royal Realty sued John for their commission, arguing that under the terms of their listing agreement, they were entitled to be paid. John argued that he should not be forced to pay the commission when he had done all the work in handling the sale himself.

The court disagreed with John, pointing to specific language in the listing agreement, by which John agreed to refer to Royal "all inquiries of Realtors or others interested in the property." The court said that Helen was one of the "others interested in the property" described in the contract. Since John had failed to abide by this term in the contract, he had deprived Royal Realty of the opportunity to earn its commission. The court ordered John to pay Royal the commission.

Depending upon the way your listing agreement with a real estate broker is worded, you may end up owing him a commission even if he never does anything to help you sell your house.

condition, and location—is selling and at what prices. This will help you to establish a selling price for your home that is reasonable under current market conditions.

Seller's rights

As a seller, you have the following rights:

◇ You do not have to list your property at the price suggested by the agent.

◇ Your agent is required to bring you all offers, whether or not she thinks they are acceptable. Unless you specifically authorize her to accept or reject offers, that decision rests with you. However, if the agent brings you a buyer ready to pay the full listing price at the time and place specified by your agreement, you may be obligated to pay her the commission even if you reject the offer.

◇ Although most agents prefer an exclusive listing, you may request modifications. For example, you can have a provision stating that if you find the buyer yourself, the commission is reduced or eliminated.

◇ You are not required to show your home at times that are inconvenient for you, to place a "for sale" sign on your property, or to conduct an open house.

◇ Your agent must actively search for buyers—by advertising the property, putting it in multiple listings, or holding open houses. If she does not, you have the right to terminate your agreement.

IF YOU ARE BUYING REAL ESTATE

If you give a real estate agent a deposit on a home, she must keep those funds in an escrow account and must follow your instructions regarding their use. Keep in mind that in most instances, the real estate agent works for the seller, and that is the person to whom she owes her loyalty. For a full discussion of real estate purchasing, see HOME BUYING AND SELLING.

REBATE

As a way to boost sales, the manufacturers of everything from aspirin to automobiles often offer a rebate—a refund of part of an item's purchase price. When you respond to a rebate offer, you enter into a contract with the company offering the rebate. Like other contracts, a rebate offer is legally binding and can be enforced by a court; but since rebate amounts are usually small, they are seldom worth the expense of pursuing a court action. Nevertheless, there are measures you can take to persuade a company to honor its rebate contract.

Companies that offer rebates are permitted to place restrictions on their offers, but these restrictions must be clearly stated in advance. For example, a rebate offer may require you to buy more than one product or to send the company a copy of your sales receipt as proof of purchase. The company can limit the rebate offer to one per household or to a specified period of time.

Rebates for automobiles and other expensive items may be sent either to the consumer or to the dealer, who uses it to reduce your purchase price. Although the dealer cannot require you to assign your rebate to the dealership, you may not qualify for financing without it, since your down payment will be lower.

STEPS TO TAKE TO COLLECT A REBATE

If you are entitled to a rebate, do the following:

1. Be sure to read the terms of the rebate offer carefully and comply with all the proof-of-purchase requirements.

2. Keep a copy of the rebate coupon and your proof of purchase, and record the date on which you responded to the rebate offer.

3. If you do not receive your rebate payment within the time period indicated by the manufacturer, write to the company at the rebate address. Be sure to include a copy of the original documentation.

4. If you still do not receive a response, write to the president or chief executive officer of the company at its headquarters. You can find the address at the public library or by calling the company. Be sure to indicate a date by which you expect a response.

5. If all else fails, write a letter to the consumer protection division of your state attorney general's office. Send a copy to the company's president.

RECEIVERSHIP

A court order that places someone's property under the control of an independent person charged with preserving it for the benefit of concerned parties is known as a receivership. When a lawsuit is under way to determine the rightful owner of property, or when a person appears to be unable to meet his obligations as the owner of a business, the court may appoint an independent person, or receiver, to manage the property so that its value is not unduly reduced during that period. Suppose Hector is seriously injured in an accident, and as a result his business falls into debt. Hector's creditors could file a lawsuit asking the court to appoint a receiver.

The courts are usually reluctant to appoint a receiver, because the action takes property out of private ownership and places it under the court's supervision. The receiver does not serve as the representative of the property owner but as an officer of the court, and he must obey the court's instructions in running the business. A receiver who fails to preserve the property entrusted to him can be liable for any losses and can be removed and replaced by another person.

RECEIVING STOLEN PROPERTY

"Hey, buddy," a stranger calls from an alley. "Wanna buy a watch? Only fifteen bucks." He shows you an array of expensive-looking wristwatches. You ask where he got the watches and how he can sell them for such a low price. "They're hot," he replies, using the street term for stolen merchandise. If you buy a watch and get caught, can you get into trouble? The answer is yes.

Someone who knowingly accepts stolen property is guilty of either a misdemeanor or a felony, depending on the value of the goods involved. The fact that you paid for the watch is not a valid defense. If you knew it was stolen when you bought it, you can be found guilty. Nor can you claim in self-defense that you bought the goods in order to return them to the owner.

RECIPROCITY

When states receive privileges from and extend them to citizens of other states, they are said to engage in reciprocity. For example, reciprocity may be given in regard to driver's licenses. A driver with a valid license who relocates to another state may obtain a license without having to pass another driving test. Similarly, a person whose license has been revoked in one state may be prevented from obtaining a license in another.

RECKLESSNESS

Rash, irresponsible, or uncaring behavior that shows disregard for the possibility of injuring another person or damaging property is known as recklessness. Suppose John is driving down the street when he spots Elizabeth at the curb. To impress her, he takes both hands off the steering wheel, leans out the window, and whistles at her. Because he has taken his hands off the wheel, the automobile veers into the curb and hits Elizabeth. John is guilty of reckless driving. Although he did not intend to hurt anyone, his actions showed that he had no regard for the risk of injuring others. See also NEGLIGENCE.

REFERENCE, EMPLOYEE

An employment reference is a statement about the qualifications of a former employee. If you are seeking a reference from a former employer, you may find that he will only verify your dates of employment, your salary range, and your job title. Information that is not requested by the new employer may not be included.

Your former employer may refuse to give information on the telephone and insist that inquiries be written on your prospective employer's letterhead. If an employer gives out a false or defamatory reference that causes you to lose a job opportunity, you may be able to sue him. Suppose you are laid off at your company because of a slump in sales. When you ask the reason for your dismissal, you are told that it is due to your "insubordination" to your supervisor. You may be

CHECKLIST

If You Are Asked to Give a Reference

If you are an employer or manager, sooner or later you will be asked to give a reference for a former employee. You will want to consider the following before you agree to do so.

❑ **BE TRUTHFUL.**
When firing an employee, give the reason for her dismissal. If the reason is her poor job performance, don't say that it is a downturn in the company's sales.

❑ **OBTAIN PERMISSION.**
Have the employee sign a form giving her consent for you to release accurate and truthful information to the personnel department of a company where she applies for work.

❑ **PUT IT IN WRITING.**
Don't transmit uncomplimentary references by facsimile or telephone; you cannot be sure who else may have access to the fax machine or who may be listening to a speaker phone or on another extension.

❑ **ENSURE PRIVACY.**
Be careful that no one sees the reference except the person for whom it was intended. Address the envelope to the person making the inquiry, and seal it yourself. Do not leave it in an "out" box or anywhere that someone else could pick it up.

❑ **BE CIRCUMSPECT.**
Don't divulge any information that is not requested by the new employer.

❑ **FOLLOW THE RULES.**
If you are a manager, be sure to follow your company's policy if you are asked to give a reference. Failing to give references in the manner set out in company guidelines could jeopardize your own position.

able to sue your employer for defamation, even if he never gave the false reason for your firing to anyone but you.

Most companies ask departing employees to sign a form giving their consent to release accurate and truthful information to prospective employers. Be aware that by signing such a form you waive your right to sue the employer when this information is released.

Note that employers in sectors such as the health industry and the securities field are legally bound to ask a job applicant about many aspects of his background. If they fail to do so, they could be found guilty of negligence in hiring a person unsuited or unfit for a particular job. For example, a nursing home that fails to check the background of a newly hired orderly who was dismissed from his previous job for physically abusing patients can be held legally responsible for any injuries that the orderly inflicts at his new workplace. See also BLACKLISTING; WHISTLE-BLOWER.

RELEASE

A release is a contract under which one person agrees to give up a legally enforceable claim against another. Like other contracts, a release must be supported by consideration—something of value given up by the party obtaining the release in exchange for the other party's giving up a claim. Once a release is signed and goods or money are exchanged, no more claims can be brought.

You are most likely to encounter a release when you are involved in an accident—either as a victim or as the cause—and your insurer or the insurer of the other party asks you to sign a form before it pays you a settlement.

Before you sign a release form, be sure to read it carefully. If you do not understand what it says, get the advice of an attorney. If you think that the amount the insurer will pay will not cover your injuries or damage to your property, do not sign the release or accept the insurer's check.

Sometimes medical problems may linger or not even show up until weeks or months after an accident occurred. If you sign a release form before you find out the full extent of your injuries, you may be barred from seeking further payment that you would otherwise have been entitled to receive. For a sample release form, see EVERYDAY LEGAL FORMS, beginning on page 552. See also ACCIDENTS IN PUBLIC PLACES.

Religion, Freedom of

The First Amendment to the U.S. Constitution protects a number of our most cherished civil rights, among them freedom of speech, a free press, and peaceful assembly. The very first right it addresses, however, is the freedom of religion. The amendment begins with these words: "Congress shall make no law respecting an establishment of religion, or prohibiting the free exercise thereof." Known as the establishment clause, this brief but important clause is the foundation of American religious freedom. Among other things, it prohibits federal, state, and local governments from making any laws that promote or hinder any individual's freedom of religious worship.

The U.S. Supreme Court has defined religion as a person's views about his relation to his Creator and the obligations of reverence and obedience to the will of that Creator. Religious freedom also includes the freedom not to believe in or hold views about a Creator.

Church and State

The concept of the separation of church and state is based on the First Amendment, in that the government is forbidden from aiding any particular religion to the exclusion of others or imposing burdens on one religion that it does not impose on others. The government may not finance any religious group or provide religious instruction. In addition, the government cannot punish an individual for his religious beliefs or lack of religious beliefs.

Beliefs Versus Actions

Although the government may not interfere with a person's religious beliefs, it may restrict his actions in furthering those beliefs if the actions are contrary to the prevailing morals or threaten the well-being of society. For example:

◇ Religious freedom does not allow a member of one religious group to instigate violence against the members of another group.

◇ No person has the right to spread infectious diseases out of religious conviction. For example, a parent cannot use the First Amendment as the basis for avoiding compulsory vaccination laws for children when there is an epidemic.

◇ A parent may not justify the violation of child-labor laws (such as compelling a child to distribute religious leaflets on the street) on the grounds of the free exercise of religion.

◇ Polygamy may be (and is) outlawed, even though the practice is officially authorized by certain religious groups.

◇ The use of illegal drugs, the practice of prostitution, or the handling of dangerous snakes as part of a religious rite cannot be justified by the First Amendment.

Violations of Religious Freedom

Issues involving religious freedom have been vigorously contested in the courts, which have found that the following practices violate the First Amendment guarantee of religious freedom:

◇ Mandatory chapel attendance for students at federal military academies.

◇ A 19th-century law (reflecting fear of the papacy) forbidding federal employees from attending mass or doing missionary work.

◇ Exclusion of members of a particular religious group (the particular case concerned Jehovah's Witnesses) from the practice of law.

◇ Denial of welfare benefits on the basis of a recipient's affiliation with a particular religion (in this case, Catholicism).

◇ A city's use of public tax money to maintain a Christian cross in a municipal park.

◇ A Tennessee law prohibiting the teaching of evolution.

◇ A Minnesota state law granting tax credits or cash reimbursements to parents who paid tuition for their children at private schools, including parochial schools.

Laws Allowed by the First Amendment

Not every government act or law will be invalidated because it happens to benefit a religious group. If it can be established that the legislation has a secular purpose, the law can stand. Here are some examples:

◇ Leasing a hospital built with public funds to a religious charity.

◇ Giving federal aid in the form of construction grants to an institution of higher learning affiliated with a religious group (the grants were for the construction of buildings with secular purposes).

◇ Spending public funds to put on a St. Patrick's Day parade.

◇ Holding a public school graduation in a church.

RENT CONTROL

In an attempt to keep rental housing affordable, some cities have passed rent-control ordinances. By limiting the maximum amounts for annual rent increases, these laws protect long-time tenants from excessive rent hikes.

Most rent-control ordinances provide that if a landlord can demonstrate that rent control is causing him to lose money, he can appeal for larger increases. Moreover, if a tenant moves out and the apartment is rented to a new tenant, the landlord may be permitted to raise the rent to whatever the market will bear. Rent-control laws are generally applied only to apartment buildings with more than a specified number of units, often six or more. To find out if your community has rent-control ordinances, call your city housing department.

RENT STRIKE

Suppose you and the other tenants in your apartment building have spent months trying to get the landlord to maintain your building, all to no avail. The trash pickup has stopped, and garbage is piling up. The lights in the hallway have burned out and need replacement. Some of the tenants are talking about staging a rent strike, but you are wary about joining them. You are not sure that a rent strike is legal.

Your concern is a reasonable one. For years, all rent strikes were unlawful, and a tenant was obligated to pay rent even if the landlord failed to keep the premises in good repair or to provide services tenants could reasonably expect, such as water and electricity. Today, however, more and more cities and states are permitting tenants to jointly withhold rent from landlords who fail to properly maintain rental units.

There are usually strict requirements that must be met before a rent strike is legally permissible. It is not enough for an apartment to be merely unpleasant to live in. The fact that your apartment needs a paint job or that the appliances are old does not justify a rent strike. Nor can you stage a rent strike if you or the other tenants created the condition you object to, as by breaking windows or piling trash in hallways when receptacles were provided. Conditions must be such that the apartment or building is not fit to live in.

If a rent strike is justified and permitted by law where you live, tenants still must pay rent. Usually they must pay their rent into a court-supervised fund or to a court-specified receiver. The landlord will get the money only after all necessary repairs are made, or the court may order that the money be spent to make the repairs. After the apartment building is brought into a habitable condition, rent payments to the landlord must be resumed.

STEPS TO TAKE BEFORE A RENT STRIKE

A rent strike should always be a last resort. Before beginning one, you should be sure to take the following steps:

1. Provide the landlord with a clear written statement of your complaints, and give him a chance to correct them. Keep copies of all correspondence you send or receive.

2. Keep a careful record of the dates and times of any telephone conversations you have with the landlord, and make notes about what he said.

3. Photograph or videotape the problem. Nothing could be more effective in helping you make your case than a video of mice scurrying around.

4. Ask your local housing department to inspect the building. If inspectors find that the premises are not up to minimum standards, the department can declare the building a public nuisance, and the city will order the landlord to correct the problems.

5. If the problems pose a threat to tenants' health, get in touch with the local health department, which can start legal action against the landlord.

6. Make sure you have solid legal advice that a rent strike is permitted in your community. If you cannot afford to hire an attorney, contact the Legal Aid office in your area. Some communities have tenant organizations that can also provide legal help. See also LANDLORD; LEGAL AID; TENANT'S RIGHTS.

REPAIR SHOP

When Jacques's two-year-old power saw broke down, he read through the warranty for the saw and decided to telephone the manufacturer, even though the warranty had expired. The manufacturer could not give him the name of a store in his area that repaired his make of saw. That left Jacques with the difficult job of finding a repair shop by himself.

Since almost anyone can open a repair shop, finding a business qualified to repair your appliances or electronic equipment can be a daunting task. Moreover, many appliances today are designed to be disposable. It is often cheaper to replace a broken hair dryer, shaver, or coffeemaker, for example, than to repair it. In fact, many companies do just that when you send an item in for service under warranty. The decision whether to repair or replace an item under warranty belongs to the manufacturer, not you. See also AUTOMOBILE REPAIR; CONSUMER PROTECTION; WARRANTY AND GUARANTY.

STEPS TO TAKE WHEN CHOOSING A REPAIR SHOP

Here are some suggestions on choosing and dealing with repair shops.

1. Look for shops that have been authorized to repair major brand-name appliances. Manufacturers will have already checked to be sure that the shop's repair staff meets their minimum standards. You may pay a little more, but you will have fewer problems, and you may be able to get the manufacturer on your side in the event of a dispute.

2. Ask about the shop's policy regarding estimates. Some shops provide free estimates, while others charge a fee. Either way, be sure you know in advance whether the estimate is binding, and tell the shop to obtain your approval before undertaking any additional work beyond the estimate.

3. Find out what warranties the shop provides. Ask for warranties in writing, and be sure you learn whether they cover parts, labor, or both.

4. Always get a written receipt or claim check when you leave merchandise at a repair shop, and check any terms it contains before you leave the premises. For example, some claim checks may give you a time limit for claiming your merchandise, after which the shop will not be responsible for it. If you do not like the terms, take your item elsewhere.

5. Get a date by which the repair will be completed. If there is going to be a delay in getting parts or diagnosing the problem, make sure that the shop will notify you and give you a new completion date.

6. When your repair is complete, get an itemized receipt that shows the charges for parts and labor.

7. If the repair is defective, return the item to the shop and give it a chance to make good on its warranty. But if repeated efforts to fix the item fail, you may want to take it elsewhere. If the item can be repaired at another place, ask the first shop to reimburse you for additional costs. If it refuses, you can seek reimbursement in small-claims court.

REPOSSESSION

You are a few months late on your car payments, but you expect to pay them off by next week. As you are getting ready for bed one night, you look out the window and see your car being hooked up to a tow truck. You race downstairs in your pajamas and explain to the tow truck operator that you are going to make all your overdue payments next week. He takes your car away just the same.

Repossession of items that are collateral for a loan is governed by state law. In some states the lender does not have to notify you of your default or tell you that he plans to repossess your car. When you sign your loan agreement, your car is pledged as collateral. This gives the lender a security interest in your car; if you default, he can repossess it without giving you the chance to pay what you owe. In other states, lenders must give you notice and the opportunity to pay your debt.

States also have laws that limit the rights of the lenders. Some states prohibit repossession of a vehicle parked on private property or breaking into a car parked on a public street. Most state laws forbid a repossessor, or "repo man," from entering your locked garage to repossess property or taking any action that would disturb the peace or cause a confrontation. For the latter reason, most repossessions take place at night, when the delinquent borrower is likely to be asleep.

Once the car or other item is repossessed, the lender has the right to sell the item to pay off the loan. If the price he realizes is less than the outstanding amount of the loan and repossession costs, he can seek a deficiency judgment against the borrower for the remainder of the money. On the rare occasion that the lender sells the item for more than the borrower owes, the excess goes to the borrower. See also COLLATERAL; COLLECTION AGENCY; DEFICIENCY JUDGMENT; SECURITY AGREEMENT.

RESCISSION

Rescission is the cancellation of a contract by the mutual agreement of both parties or by one party who has the proper grounds to cancel (such as breach of contract).

Suppose you buy an expensive gold necklace for your wife's birthday at a jewelry store that offers a money-back guarantee. When your wife opens the gift, she is flattered but tells you, honestly, that she likes silver better than gold. When you return the necklace, you receive a refund. You have rescinded your contract, and you and the store are back where you started, as if the contract never existed.

But suppose the store refuses to honor its money-back guarantee. You can go to court to seek a rescission, since the store has breached one of the terms of the contract, giving you proper grounds. If you win, the court will order the store to return your money and take the necklace back.

Besides breach of contract, other grounds for rescission include fraud, duress, a mistake in the contract, and the mental incapacity of one of the parties. See also BREACH OF CONTRACT; CONTRACT.

RESIDENCY LAW

A state or local residency law determines the places where you can go to school, vote, pay taxes, or go to court and requires you to live in a certain area for a specific length of time before you can do so. Residency laws are often called residency requirements.

ACCESS TO THE COURTS

Where you live and how long you have lived there can determine your access to the courts. For example, if you wish to file for divorce, you must generally do so in the state (and county) in which you or your spouse resides. But you may not be allowed to file until you can prove that you or your spouse has been living in the state for the period of time set by state law, often 60 days.

If you are involved in a dispute over child custody, you may be subject to the Uniform Child Custody Jurisdiction Act, which has been adopted in many states. The act requires that legal actions involving custody be filed in the child's home state, which is generally defined as the state in which the child has lived for the previous six months. (This requirement may be waived in emergencies.) See also CHILD CUSTODY.

If you enter into guardianship proceedings, you must do so in the state and county in which the proposed ward lives. See also GUARDIAN AND WARD.

PUBLIC RIGHTS AND DUTIES

State and local governments can set reasonable residency requirements for the exercise of public rights and duties, such as the following:

◇ A state may require proof of residency when you register to vote.

◇ A municipality may require its employees to live within the city limits.

◇ A school district may limit enrollment to students who reside in the district.

◇ A state may require candidates for state and local office to have resided in the state or municipality for a specified period of time.

◇ State colleges and universities may set higher tuition rates and stricter entrance requirements for nonresidents than for residents.

DETERMINING YOUR DOMICILE

Domicile is a legal term that is often used interchangeably with *residence*. However, the two are not exactly synonymous. A residence can be a permanent, temporary, or part-time abode—a house from which you commute to work, a summer cottage, or even a hotel room you are using on a business trip. But a domicile is the one place that you consider your permanent home. You may have several residences, but you can have only one domicile.

A domicile is generally defined as the place where you normally reside and to which you intend to return when you are away. If you have more than one residence, a court may be called upon to determine which one is your domicile. In doing so, the court will consider the following factors:

◇ Where you pay personal property taxes.

◇ Where you go to church.

◇ Where you are a member of civic or social organizations.

◇ Where your spouse and children live.

◇ Where you vote.

◇ Where you have maintained a residence for the longest period of time.

◇ Where your job is located.

The court's decision about the location of your domicile may have important legal consequences. For example, it may determine the state in which you must pay taxes or the state in which your will is administered. See also DOMICILE.

RESTAURANT

A restaurant is a business that serves prepared food and drink to the public for immediate consumption, and as such it is subject to federal, state, and local regulations.

Federal laws prohibit restaurants from discriminating against their patrons on the basis of race, color, national origin, sex, or religion. They also require restaurants to make reasonable accommodations for handicapped customers and employees. State and local laws regulate sanitation and food-handling procedures, the serving of alcoholic beverages, and other details of day-to-day operations.

CONTAMINATED FOOD

One important aspect of the law regulating restaurants concerns a restaurant's responsibility when foreign materials are found in a meal or beverage it serves. All states have laws that prohibit selling contaminated or unwholesome food, but what constitutes contamination varies.

If you are served food that you believe is contaminated (food that is spoiled or contains foreign matter), you will have to show that you were actually injured in order to collect damages. The injury does not have to be physical, however—serious emotional upset may be enough. In one case a customer who was eating a banana split bit into something hard, which turned out to be shards of glass. Convinced that she had already swallowed some of the glass, she became very upset and called her doctor, who told her to eat some bread and take a sedative. When she visited the doctor the next day, his examination revealed no physical harm. Even so, she sued the restaurant, and a jury awarded her substantial damages.

The restaurant appealed, but the appeals court upheld the jury's decision, ruling that a restaurant offers an implied warranty that the food it serves is fit for humans to eat. See WARRANTY AND GUARANTY.

KEEPING CUSTOMERS SAFE

Restaurants have an obligation to maintain reasonably safe premises by keeping the floors and stairs clean and free of debris and the tables and chairs in good repair.

A patron who suffers an injury because there was a dangerous condition on the premises may be awarded compensation if he can show that the condition was created by the restaurant operator, or that the operator knew or should have known about it. For example, if a restaurant employee wet-mops a floor without letting customers know that the floor may be slippery, a patron who slips and hurts himself can sue the restaurant operator. But suppose a customer drops an ice cream cone on the floor and another customer slips on it immediately afterward. In this instance the restaurant is not responsible, since it did not cause the spill and had no time to clean it up before the accident occurred.

Restaurants are also obliged to keep their patrons reasonably safe from the actions of other patrons. For example, if a restaurant operator allows unruly or drunken patrons to remain on the premises and they injure another customer, the operator may be held responsible for that customer's injuries. See also ACCIDENTS IN PUBLIC PLACES; ALCOHOL.

RESTRAINING ORDER

A restraining order is a court order prohibiting a party from taking some action until a hearing can be held to determine whether the action is lawful. For example, a historic preservation committee can seek a restraining order to keep an owner from razing his building until a court can determine whether the building should be saved. Restraining orders are also known as temporary restraining orders, or TRO's.

RESTRICTIVE COVENANT

A provision in a deed to real estate that puts certain restrictions on the owner's use of the property is known as a restrictive covenant or—in real estate jargon—CC&R, which stands for covenants, conditions, and restrictions.

Restrictive covenants are not the same as zoning regulations, which are created by the government. Covenants are often put in a deed by the seller when he sells a part or all of his property. Enforcement of restrictive covenants is generally left up to the owners of neighboring land, whose property values, as well as the enjoyment of their own real estate, are affected by violations of the covenant.

Suppose that you own 1,000 acres of farmland, and a developer wants to buy half of it. A restrictive covenant prohibiting him from creating lots smaller than five acres can help to preserve your remaining property's value and to maintain the rural nature of the area.

Restrictive covenants are often found in deeds for residential real estate. Typically, they limit the use of property to a specified purpose—a single-family home, for example. In some situations, they may also do the following:

◇ Limit the height of fences.

◇ Restrict the construction of outbuildings, unless they meet certain standards.

◇ Limit the types of construction materials used.

◇ Limit the number and types of animals kept on the property.

◇ Prohibit planting trees that block a neighbor's view.

◇ Require landscaping and mowing.

◇ Prohibit basketball backboards and hoops.

◇ Prohibit parking on the street.

◇ Require garage doors to be closed.

◇ Regulate interior lighting and exterior paint colors.

Restrictive covenants are usually created by the seller as a part of the new owner's deed; therefore, your neighbor may not have the same kinds of covenants in his deed as you do, or any at all. To find out, you have a couple of options.

FINDING OUT ABOUT YOUR NEIGHBOR'S COVENANTS

If you and your neighbor both live in a planned subdivision with a homeowners associa-

REAL LIFE, REAL LAW

The Case of the Kiddie-Care Covenant

Mrs. Zinger operated a licensed day-care center out of her home, even though a covenant in her deed restricted the use of her property to "residential purposes." The homeowners association in Mrs. Zinger's community went to court to enforce the covenant and to obtain an injunction prohibiting her from operating the day-care center.

The trial court granted the injunction, but the court of appeals reversed the lower court's decision. It noted that Mrs. Zinger cared for only seven children at a time, no more than might be found in a large family. In fact, the sole indication that the home was used for day care was the slight increase in traffic as parents dropped their children off in the morning and picked them up in the afternoon.

The court also pointed out that the state, by passing legislation allowing day-care centers in private homes, encouraged such centers as a matter of public policy.

tion, you can check with the association's office to find out which covenants apply to your neighbor's property.

Another way to discover the covenants in your neighbor's deed is to visit the office of the county clerk, where deeds are recorded. You will need to provide the address of the property and the owner's name, if possible, because most deeds are filed by name. If you do not have the owner's name, the recorder may be able to locate the deed by the address. In any event, call the recorder's office before you go to find out exactly what you will need in order to get a copy of the deed.

ENFORCING A NEIGHBOR'S COVENANT

Trying to enforce a restrictive covenant in your neighbor's deed by filing a lawsuit against him can be difficult and expensive. Before you consider taking legal action, you should do whatever you can to avoid such a confrontation.

It is possible that your neighbor is simply not aware that he is violating a covenant, and bringing it to his attention may be all it takes to resolve the problem. If you live in an area with a homeowners association, chances are that the association can provide mediation services or will help you to enforce the covenant.

If your neighbor refuses to cooperate, and the issue is important enough to you, a lawsuit may be your only recourse. For more information, see HOME BUYING AND SELLING; HOMEOWNERS ASSOCIATION; NEIGHBORS; ZONING.

RETIREMENT PLANNING

Too many Americans find themselves approaching retirement with inadequate financial security. With no pension or individual retirement account (IRA) to provide them with income, they rely on payments from Social Security. But Social Security benefits were not meant to cover all retirement needs, and retirees should not count on them exclusively.

The time to begin planning for retirement is early in your working life—the earlier the better. Federal laws allow employers to establish pension plans and 401(k) tax-deferred savings plans for their employees, and employees can establish individual retirement accounts. The self-employed can set up Keogh plans and IRA's, which allow them to build up tax-deferred savings.

Many articles in this book will be useful to persons who are approaching retirement or have already retired. See AGE DISCRIMINATION; EMPLOYEE RETIREMENT INCOME SECURITY ACT (ERISA); ESTATE PLANNING; FINANCIAL PLANNER; INDIVIDUAL RETIREMENT ACCOUNT; KEOGH PLAN; LIVING TRUST; LIVING WILL; MEDICAID; MEDICARE; PENSION PLAN; SOCIAL SECURITY; TRUST; WILL.

REWARD

A reward is sometimes offered by a person, organization, or law enforcement agency for information leading to the arrest and conviction of a suspected criminal or for the return of stolen or lost property. The reward may be offered to a particular individual or to the general public by posting or publishing an announcement.

OFFER

An offer to pay a reward is like any other contract offer, in that it may be withdrawn at any time before it is accepted. Generally, an offer of a reward is accepted when a person knowingly performs the steps required to collect it, unless a government agency or official has offered the reward. Suppose you provide information to the police that leads to the arrest and conviction of a drug dealer and later find out about the reward. Depending on the way the reward was authorized, you may be entitled to collect even though your actions were not prompted by the reward offer.

TIME LIMIT

If a reward offer does not specify when it will expire, it will generally be considered to remain open for a "reasonable period of time." But what constitutes a reasonable time varies from case to case. Suppose a reward is offered for information leading to the identification, arrest, and conviction of a person who committed an armed robbery. If the statute of limitations for armed robbery is five years, it would be considered reasonable for the offer to remain open until the statute expired. Similarly, a reward for information leading to the identification, arrest, and conviction of a murderer might remain open indefinitely, since there is no statute of limitations for murder.

PAYMENT

One interesting facet of the law is that until the reward is paid, the person who recovered missing property has a lien, or claim, against it for the amount promised. Suppose you lose your college class ring and put an ad in the newspaper offering a $100 reward for its return. David calls you to report that he has found your ring and he wants to collect the reward. If you have a change of heart and offer David only $50, he has a legal right to keep your ring until you pay him what you originally promised. If David returns the ring and you refuse to pay him $100, he can sue you for the money.

ADVERTISING A REWARD

Keep in mind that if you want to advertise a reward for something you have lost, it is usually a good idea not to specify the amount you will pay. For example, if you say "generous reward offered," a person who finds your property cannot keep it if he happens to disagree with you about what constitutes a generous reward. See also ABANDONED PROPERTY; LOST AND FOUND PROPERTY; STATUTE OF LIMITATIONS.

RICO

When you ask lawyers why there has been a litigation explosion over the last 20 years, many of them will point to something called RICO, the federal Racketeer-Influenced and Corrupt Organizations Act of 1970.

The intent of the act was to provide a way for legitimate businesses to be compensated for damages caused by the illegal activities of organized crime—namely, extortion, murder, and mail fraud. In practice, however, the act was written in such broad language that trial lawyers have used RICO to file lawsuits in divorce cases and real estate foreclosures. The incentive for filing a RICO claim is simple: if you win, you are entitled to recover triple the amount of the actual damages that were suffered, as well as court costs and attorneys' fees.

Between 1986 and 1988, more than 3,000 civil RICO lawsuits were filed, but the vast majority were filed against accountants, insurance companies, and banks. Moreover, civil RICO suits have been used as a club in disputes that would otherwise have resulted in minimal damage awards. For example, suppose Jack and Diane are separated and are getting a divorce. If Jack calls Diane more than once to tell her that she "better not expect to get any money" out of him, Diane's lawyer could conceivably file a civil RICO lawsuit against Jack, claiming that his phone calls established a pattern of threats and extortion that falls within RICO's definition of racketeering activity.

Challenges to RICO's misuse have generally not been successful. In 1993, however, the U.S. Supreme Court ruled that business advisors, such as accountants who do not exercise control over a company's activities, cannot be sued under RICO. See also FORFEITURE.

RIGHT-OF-WAY

The term *right-of-way* applies to situations involving both real estate and automobile traffic. In real estate, an easement, or right, granted by a property owner allowing another person to travel over a portion of the property is a right-of-way. For example, a property owner might grant a right-of-way to the city allowing it to construct a road over his or her land. See EASEMENT.

In traffic situations, right-of-way applies to a person's or vehicle's right to proceed, to which others must yield. Emergency vehicles, such as ambulances, fire trucks, and police cars, for example, have the right-of-way over all other vehicles while they are responding to an emergency with their lights and sirens on. If you are driving and become aware of an emergency vehicle approaching, you must pull your car over to the right side of the road, if possible, and stop until the vehicle passes.

A vehicle traveling on a highway has the right-of-way over cars entering the highway from an on-ramp, and a car traveling on a through street has the right-of-way over cars entering or crossing the street from a side street or driveway. At an intersection with no traffic light or stop sign, or one with four-way stop signs, the right-of-way belongs to the car that reached the intersection first; if two cars arrive at the same time, the right-of-way belongs to the car on the right.

Pedestrians have the right-of-way when they are crossing a road at a crosswalk, provided they have started across before any traffic light or walk signal has changed against them. See also AUTOMOBILE ACCIDENTS; PEDESTRIAN; ROADS AND HIGHWAYS.

RIGHTS, INDIVIDUAL

The 10th Amendment to the U.S. Constitution provides that "the powers not delegated to the United States by the Constitution, nor prohibited by it to the States, are reserved to the States respectively, or to the people." The rights reserved "to the people" are individual rights, and they are numerous. Your individual rights consist of the powers and privileges that are provided to you by statutes and by the U.S. and state constitutions, as well as the rights to which you are entitled as a human being (sometimes called your natural rights). The Declaration of Independence identifies a person's natural rights as life, liberty, and the pursuit of happiness.

The rights you hold because of your citizenship or legal residence in the United States are called your civil rights. These include the right to marry and divorce; to enter into contracts; to buy, sell, and own property; and to choose your own religion. The rights to speak out freely about political issues, to vote and run for public office, and to associate with whomever you choose without fear of government interference are your political rights.

When you have a legal or constitutional right, you also have the legal power to enforce it in the courts or by your own means when necessary. For example, you have the right to defend your life and the lives of others when they are threatened. So if a robber points a pistol at you, the law does not require you to go to court to obtain an injunction prohibiting him from pulling the trigger. Instead, the law allows you to take immediate steps to protect yourself. Such steps may include disarming the gunman or even shooting him first. See SELF-DEFENSE.

In situations that do not pose an immediate danger, however, the courts frown on self-help solutions. For example, if you rent an apartment to a tenant who refuses to pay the rent when it is due, the law does not let you forcibly remove him, throw his possessions into the street, and change the locks on his door unless you first obtain a court's permission to do so. Similarly, if you enter into a contract with your neighbor to sell him your lawn mower for $100, and he then fails to pay you, you cannot simply take the money from his wallet or bank account. A court must hear the case, and if it rules in your favor, it will order him to make payment.

Despite all its imperfections and delays, the American system of civil and criminal justice provides a workable method for enforcing individual rights with a minimum of disorder. See also BILL OF RIGHTS; CIVIL RIGHTS; CONSTITUTION OF THE UNITED STATES.

RIGHT-TO-WORK LAWS

When you start a new job, you may be faced with the question of whether or not to join a union. In some states and for some jobs, the decision may already have been made for you. Because of an agreement between an employer and a union, you may be automatically added to the union's rolls. But in more than 20 states, you make the decision. These states have enacted right-to-work laws, which prohibit employers from requiring union membership as a condition of getting or holding a job.

LABOR LAW

The typical right-to-work statute prohibits any requirement that employees join or remain members of a union in order to keep their jobs. Some laws also forbid employers to require nonunion workers to pay union fees or dues as a condition of employment. Although unions have attacked right-to-work statutes as unfairly restricting their organizing activities, the courts have upheld their constitutionality.

UNION SECURITY AGREEMENTS

Right-to-work laws may prohibit the types of labor agreements that are known as union shops and agency shops.

In a union shop all workers

must join a union within a specified period, usually 30 days, after they are employed.

When a collective-bargaining agreement calls for an agency shop, workers have the choice of either joining the union or paying its dues and fees without becoming members. Employees who decline membership do not have to follow a union's orders. In the event of a strike, for instance, nonmembers who cross the union's picket line cannot be threatened with union sanctions.

The closed shop, which requires one to become a union member before being hired, is prohibited by federal law.

ENFORCEMENT

Because right-to-work laws are state laws, the authority to enforce them is somewhat limited. Employers who operate within a right-to-work state are subject to its law, even if the business crosses state lines. But the law is not applicable if the principal job site is outside the state. Right-to-work laws also cannot be enforced on federal property.

Right-to-work laws do not apply to railroad and commercial-airline workers. A special federal law, the Railway Labor Act (RLA), governs labor-management affairs for these two industries. The RLA permits union-shop agreements, and it cannot be superseded by any right-to-work law of the state.

If you live in a right-to-work state and have been denied employment because you will not join a union or pay its dues, you may be able to file a lawsuit in state court or present a claim against the union and the employer to the National Labor Relations Board. See also LABOR UNION.

RIOT

In 1992 the city of Los Angeles erupted in riots after a jury acquitted four police officers accused of beating Rodney King, a driver who allegedly resisted arrest after a high-speed chase. Hundreds of businesses were looted and burned, innocent passersby became victims of vicious beatings, and dozens of people were killed.

In law, a riot is defined as a disturbance of the peace by a group of people (which can be as few as two or three, depending on state law) who band together to terrorize others in a violent manner. Persons who participate in a riot can be charged with a number of offenses, depending on the nature of their actions.

For example, a person who engages in words or conduct meant to encourage others to riot is committing the crime of "inciting to riot," even if no riot ever takes place. Or when a group of people gather to commit a crime or even to take a lawful action in a way that creates a breach of the peace, they are guilty of "unlawful assembly," which is also a crime. Protesters who block the entrances to women's health clinics or the offices of foreign countries, for example, are often charged with unlawful assembly when they refuse to follow police orders to disperse. Although the protesters have a legal right to express their opinions, they do not have a right to physically prevent anyone from entering the clinic or office building.

Local and state governments have the legal responsibility to suppress riots as quickly as possible. Therefore, local authorities may call upon the governor to activate the National Guard when it is clear that they cannot control a riot. As soon as the local police can control the situation by themselves, the governor must withdraw the National Guard.

If you are charged with the crime of riot, you cannot challenge the charge by arguing that not everyone who rioted was arrested. The very nature of riots allows many of those who participate in them to escape prosecution.

ROADS AND HIGHWAYS

Roads and highways are the responsibility of local, state, and federal governments, who both build and maintain them and make the laws for driving on them.

RULES OF THE ROAD

Because traffic laws are enacted by state and local governments, they may vary in minor ways from one place to another, but they are essentially the same throughout the country, as are the penalties for violating them. For example, the law in every state requires drivers to stay on the right side of the road, and in the right-hand lane of multilane highways, except when passing another vehicle or while preparing to make a left turn.

PASSING

Passing on the right is permitted when a vehicle in the left-hand lane is preparing to make a left turn, or it may be permitted on a multilane highway. Passing or driving on the shoulder of a highway is prohibited. You may not pass another vehicle on a two-lane road when you are within 100 feet of an intersection, bridge, tunnel, or railroad crossing. Nor may you pass a vehicle when doing so would require you to cross a solid yellow line on your side of the road or when passing is prohibited by a highway sign.

You may not pass a school bus in either direction when it is loading or unloading passengers and its red lights are flashing. Even after the bus door closes and the red lights are off, you must wait until the children have crossed the street before you resume driving.

STOPPING

You are required to come to a complete stop at a stop sign or at a red traffic signal. When the light turns green, you may proceed after being sure that cross traffic has stopped or is able to stop. A yellow (or amber) light means "caution." If a traffic light turns from green to amber when you are within an intersection, you may continue through the intersection. If it turns yellow before you enter the intersection, you should prepare to stop if you cannot clear the intersection before the light turns red.

SPEED LIMITS

You must obey all posted speed limits, and you are presumed to know the maximum legal speed even in areas where no speed-limit signs are posted. Although speed limits vary, generally you may drive no more than 55 or 65 miles per hour on highways, 30 miles per hour in residential areas, 45 miles per hour on rural two-lane roads, and 25 miles per hour in business districts. See also SPEEDING TICKET.

TURNING

When making a turn, you must signal your intention at least 100 feet before reaching the intersection. You must make a right turn from the extreme right-hand lane and a left turn from the lane closest to the center line unless a sign permits use of another lane.

If traffic signals indicate that you may turn on a green arrow, you may do so only if oncoming traffic has stopped and it is safe to proceed. At some intersections you may be permitted to make a left turn only when the left-turn arrow is green; at others, a left turn is allowed either on a green arrow or a green straight-ahead signal, provided you can do so safely. In most states it is now legal to make a right turn after coming to a complete stop at a red light, but this may not apply in some cities or at certain intersections. See also TRAFFIC TICKET.

ABC's OF CONTRIBUTORY NEGLIGENCE ON THE ROAD

If you are injured or suffer property damage on a public highway or road, your claim could be reduced or even denied if your actions contributed to the accident. This is known as contributory negligence, and it includes:

- ❑ Driving too fast for conditions, as on a wet or snow-covered road or during fog.
- ❑ Driving without your headlights on at dawn or dusk, or whenever conditions would require them.
- ❑ Driving on the shoulder of the road, except in emergencies.
- ❑ Driving a vehicle that is overloaded.
- ❑ Driving a vehicle with defective brakes.
- ❑ Driving on the wrong side of the road.
- ❑ Driving on a road when signs indicate it is closed for repairs.

HIGHWAY CONSTRUCTION AND MAINTENANCE

The building and maintenance of public roads are financed through federal and state taxes on gasoline, diesel fuel, and motor oil, and to a lesser extent through tolls and general tax revenues. States may also issue bonds to help finance road construction and maintenance of bridges, roads, and highways.

State and local governments have a duty to maintain roads, highways, and other public thoroughfares in a reasonably safe condition. If your car is damaged or you are injured because of a poorly designed or maintained street, you can usually sue the government.

You must act quickly and follow the steps required by law for filing a claim against the government. In some areas the local government must have received written notice of a potentially dangerous condition before it can be held responsible for resulting damages. So if you hit a pothole and break a wheel bearing, you may not be able to collect any compensation unless the city was already notified that the pothole existed. In other areas, however, the law holds the city responsible if it should have known about the pothole because the hole had been there for a long time. Under these laws, knowledge of the pothole is not necessary.

You may also be required to file a written notice or claim of damage with a government agency within a specified number of days after the accident.

STEPS TO TAKE

If your automobile is damaged or you are injured because of a poorly maintained or designed road, you can take these steps:

1. As soon as possible, contact the government agency responsible for maintaining the road, and report the incident. If you were on an interstate or state highway, contact the state highway department; on a county road, the county highway department; in a city, the department of streets.

2. Ask the agency to send you any forms that are required for filing your claim.

3. Meanwhile, send the agency a letter confirming the incident. Include the date and time of your initial contact with the agency, the name of the person you spoke to, and the name of the person who agreed to send you the claim forms.

4. Obtain at least two estimates for repairing the damage to your car. For personal injuries, obtain a medical report from your doctor.

5. Complete the claim forms promptly. Send them by certified mail, return receipt requested, so that you can prove that your claim was delivered to the agency.

6. If your claim is denied, you may have the right to appeal, which will be explained in the denial notification. You may want to consult an attorney about proceeding further if your claim is denied. See also ACCIDENTS ON GOVERNMENT PROPERTY; AUTOMOBILE ACCIDENTS; SOVEREIGN IMMUNITY.

ROBBERY

Robbery is a crime against property because it is a type of theft, but it is also a crime against a person, because it involves violence, either threatened or real. A robbery occurs when someone takes property by using force or threatening to use force.

Robbery is considered more serious than other types of theft because of the use or threat of violence.The property may be on the person, such as a wallet or a piece of jewelry, or it may be in the person's presence, such as money in a safe. If the robber ties up a person in another room or locks her up while he takes the property, his action is considered to be a theft in the person's presence, although it occurs elsewhere. See also ASSAULT AND BATTERY.

The property taken in a robbery may be almost anything—money, credit cards, keys, even dentures. It does not have to be something of intrinsic value, as long as it has value to the person from whom it is taken. Nor does it have to belong to that person.

Taking property that belongs to you or that you honestly believe is yours is not robbery, but you could still face charges of assault or battery if you use force when you take it.

For a robbery to occur, a theft must be against the victim's will, by violence or intimidation. Suppose a thief steals property from your house while you are asleep. In the legal sense, he has not robbed you, because you were not subject to violence or the threat of violence. Instead, he has committed the crime of burglary.

Whether pickpockets and purse snatchers are robbers depends on the circumstances. If someone is able to steal your property without your knowledge and without using force, he is a thief but not a robber.

ARMED ROBBERY

Under the laws in many states, a robbery committed with a gun or other deadly weapon (such as a knife or blackjack) is armed robbery, a more serious crime that is punished more severely than ordinary robbery. An object not normally considered a deadly weapon, such as a baseball bat, may become one if it is used to cause or threaten serious bodily harm.

Laws regarding unloaded guns are not uniform. In some states a robber is considered armed even if he uses an unloaded gun; in others, the fact that a gun was unloaded or inoperable can be used as a defense to a charge of aggravated or armed robbery. In either case, a robber who uses an unloaded pistol as a bludgeon may be charged with armed robbery.

BANK ROBBERY

Robbery is typically punished in the state courts under state laws, but it can be a federal crime as well. The federal Bank Robbery Act makes the robbery of any federally insured bank, credit union, or savings and loan institution a federal offense, allowing the FBI or other federal law enforcement agents to pursue robbery suspects across state lines.

ROOMMATE

When you decide to share your home with another person, you run the risk of winding up in serious disputes, especially over money. This is true whether you found your roommate through an ad in the newspaper or she has been your best friend since kindergarten. When a roommate does not live up to obligations, the dispute can end up in court.

RESPONSIBILITY FOR BILLS

Perhaps the most common problems that arise between roommates involve responsibility for household bills.

Your rent or mortgage
When you and your roommate sign a lease, it probably will not specify how the rent is to be apportioned between you. It will merely state that each of you has agreed to see that the entire amount due is paid each month. If your roommate does not pay her share, you will have to pay the entire amount to avoid eviction. See also LEASE.

If you own a house or condominium and are paying a mortgage, you are, in effect, your roommate's landlord. You are obligated to make the full monthly payment, whether your roommate pays or not, but you can evict her if she refuses to pay. Similarly, if the lease is in your name alone, the responsibility for paying the rent is yours. Of course, always check that your lease permits you to have a roommate.

If you and your roommate own the property jointly, you are both responsible for seeing that the entire payment is made each month. If you pay your share but your roommate does not, the bank or other lender can foreclose.

REAL LIFE, REAL LAW

The Case of the Roommate Robber

Calvin and William were roommates when the police came to the door of their boardinghouse. William was a suspect in a robbery case, and the police asked Calvin for permission to search the room he and William shared. Sure of his innocence, Calvin consented, and the police found money taken in the robbery hidden in a closet.

At William's trial, his attorney objected to the use of the recovered money as evidence. The police did not have a warrant when they searched his room. And though Calvin had consented to the search, the lawyer argued, the room where the money was found was William's room as well, so his permission would have been needed to conduct the search without a warrant.

The court disagreed. It held that when more than one person legally occupies a residence, any one of them can voluntarily consent to a police search, and the evidence found can be used against any of the other occupants. William's objection was overruled, the evidence was admitted, and William was convicted of the robbery.

Utilities
Bills for electricity, gas, water, cable TV, and telephone service will probably be addressed to only one of you. Even if the utility company puts both your names on the bill, be sure that the entire amount is paid each month. If a bill is in your name and goes unpaid, the service to your residence will be cut off, your credit rating may suffer, and you might have a problem obtaining utility service in the future.

Deposits
You may be required to make a deposit before moving into your apartment or to start utility service. Your landlord or the utility company is required to return the deposit to the person who signed the check or is named on the receipt, even if some of the money came from someone else. If the deposit is returned to your roommate and part of the money is yours, you—and not the landlord or utility company—are responsible for getting your share from her. Also, the landlord can apply the deposit to money he is due for damages to the apartment, or the utility can apply the money to an unpaid bill, no matter which roommate originally failed to pay it.

Getting what you are owed
Even though your creditors do not have to honor agreements that you had with your roommate for the payment of household bills, you have the right to reimbursement from her. If she leaves you holding the bag for a telephone bill or more than your share of the rent, or if she departs with your share of the security deposit, you can take her to small-claims court. To do so, be aware of the following:

◇ When you file your claim, be sure you know where your roommate can be found. The clerk will need to arrange for your complaint to be mailed or delivered to the defendant.

◇ When you go to court to argue your case, take a copy of the lease, the rental agreement with your roommate, copies of unpaid bills, canceled checks and receipts showing what you paid, and if available, a written agreement with your roommate regarding payment of the bills. If anyone else can give the court information about your claim, ask him to come with you.

◇ If you win your case and the court gives you a judgment against your former roommate, you may enforce that judgment by garnisheeing her wages or bank account. See COMMON-LAW MARRIAGE; GARNISHMENT; LIVING TOGETHER; PALIMONY.

STEPS TO TAKE TO KEEP THE PEACE

Before problems arise, you can minimize the potential for conflict over money matters by taking the following steps:

1. Make a written agreement with your roommate regarding responsibility for bills.
2. Keep accurate records of payments made by all the roommates on all the bills.
3. Make a fair arrangement for buying household supplies, such as food and cleaning products, as by taking turns.
4. Try to keep personal bills separate whenever possible—for example, by buying your own snacks and toiletries.

SAFE-DEPOSIT BOX

The best place to store many hard-to-replace documents and small valuables is in a safe-deposit box. Most people who use safe-deposit boxes rent them at a bank, but some states have special safe-deposit companies. These private companies offer the advantages of more space, privacy, and accessibility, but their rates may be higher than those of banks.

RESPONSIBILITY

When you rent a safe-deposit box, either from a bank or a safe-deposit company, you create what is known as a bailment—that is, you entrust your property to the care of another person. In exchange for a rental fee, the bank provides a safe place for your valuables. Because each party in this relationship receives something of value, the bailment is considered to be of mutual benefit. The bank is therefore required to exercise only ordinary care —such as minimizing the risk of theft or damage—in safeguarding your property. See BAILMENT.

The level of responsibility that a bank or safe-deposit company can be held to, however, depends on your contract with the institution. Some agreements state that the provider of the safe-deposit box is responsible only for willful acts, such as theft, of its employees or agents, and not for ordinary negligence, such as failing to identify someone properly before giving him access to the box. Before signing the agreement, read it carefully. If the terms are not acceptable, ask to have them changed. If your request is denied, you may want to go somewhere else.

In addition to terms regarding liability, the rental agreement should include the following: (1) the names of the bank or safe-deposit company and the renter, (2) the rental fee, (3) an explanation of how to terminate the agreement, and (4) the rules for access.

ACCESS

If you rent a safe-deposit box in your name only, no one else will be allowed to open it. To gain access to the box, you must bring your key (which is used in conjunction with another key held by the bank) and proper identification. For further protection, you will be asked to sign an access ticket.

Because there may be times when you cannot go to the bank personally to deposit or retrieve items, it may be a good idea to authorize a member of your family to have access as well. It is not enough simply to give your key to that person or write a note to the bank granting your permission. The bank requires a signature form from each authorized co-renter. But having two or more names on the rental agreement does not always mean that a co-renter has access to the box if another co-renter dies. In some states, a safe-deposit box is sealed upon the death of a co-renter.

CONTENTS

Because your safe-deposit box may be sealed upon your death, keep any documents that your family will need immediately—such as the originals of your will, cemetery-plot deed, and life insurance policy—in a safe place at home or with your lawyer. All other important documents can go into the box: birth, adoption, marriage, divorce, and death certificates; citizenship papers; mortgages and real estate deeds; stock, bond, and savings certificates; military service records; automobile and homeowners insurance policies; a copy of your will; and an inventory of your personal property. Make a list of the contents of the box and give a copy to a relative or trusted friend. Update the list periodically.

If you have seldom-used jewelry or a valuable stamp or coin collection that you want to keep in your safe-deposit box, first check your homeowners insurance policy to see if it covers items placed in a safe-deposit box. If not, ask the bank if it offers insurance for the contents of a safe-deposit box.

When you rent a safe-deposit box, title to (ownership of) the contents remains with you. If you fail to pay the rental, you may risk losing them. Strict procedures dictate that the bank send you a written notice to remove the contents or pay your back rent. Typically, one or two years must pass before the bank can sell the contents.

SALE PRICE

You can barely believe your eyes. According to the newspaper ad, a $395 cappuccino machine is on sale at the local department store for only $49.99. Before you race to the store, though, there are some things you should know about the sale price the store has advertised.

SUGGESTED RETAIL PRICES

According to the ad, the cappuccino machine's "suggested retail price" is $395. Suggested retail prices are set by manufacturers, but they usually bear little relationship to the price the retailer will charge for the item. Almost the only time you will pay a price approaching the suggested retail price is when you shop at a very exclusive store or order from certain mail-order catalogs.

ERRONEOUS ADS

When you rush to the department store to buy the cappuccino maker, the salesclerk informs you that the $49.99 was a typographical error. The advertised price should have read $249.99. Can you compel the store to sell you the item at the advertised price?

Probably not. If the price in the ad was the result of an honest error, the store would not be required to honor it. If, however, you can show that the ad was a lure to bring customers into the store, a court might order the store to honor the sale price. To prove your case, you would probably need to show that the store has a history of deceptive practices or that its management knew of the error and took no action to correct it after the ad was published. But if the store required the newspaper to run a correction or posted a corrective notice in the store, you would have a hard time proving that the low price was an intentional misrepresentation. See also BAIT-AND-SWITCH; FALSE ADVERTISING.

A similar situation exists when merchandise is tagged incorrectly. Suppose you find a designer dress with a price tag of $24.99. When you take the dress to the register, however, the clerk tells you that the actual price is $249.99. Because anyone can make an honest mistake, you cannot force the store to sell you the dress at the lower price, unless you can show that the tag price was an intentional deception.

STEPS TO TAKE

If you think a store is engaging in deceptive sales practices, this is what you should do:

1. Take your complaint to the manager. A reputable merchant will appreciate being told about a mistake in its advertising or an item that is tagged incorrectly.

2. If an ad contains an incorrect price, check with the advertising department of the newspaper to see whether the store filed a correction. If merchandise is incorrectly tagged, visit the store again later on the same day to see if the price has been corrected.

3. If you suspect that the store is intentionally misrepresenting its prices, notify the consumer-affairs division of your state attorney general's office. You may be asked to file a written complaint; if possible, provide copies of ads and the names of store personnel with whom you spoke.

SALES TAX

A sales tax is a tax that is assessed by state and local governments on goods sold to consumers. Sales taxes are "pass-through" taxes; although they are assessed against the seller and are collected from him, they are charged to the buyer. State tax laws may exempt some kinds of goods from sales taxes. Groceries and prescription medicines, for example, are often exempt.

Sales taxes have become an important source of revenue for state and local governments —so much so that states have attempted to collect taxes on goods sold to their residents by companies located in other states. In 1992 the U.S. Supreme Court ruled that Congress could authorize the collection of state sales taxes on goods sold by mail to the residents in one state and mailed to them from another state without violating the due process or commerce clauses of the U.S. Constitution. Until Congress enacts such legislation, however, a state cannot collect sales taxes from companies that have no physical presence (such as a store or warehouse) within its own borders. Several states have imposed "use taxes" on items that were bought in another state. But except for purchases that require in-state registration, such as cars and boats, these taxes are difficult to collect.

SAVINGS AND LOAN ASSOCIATION

Savings and loan associations (S&L's) are specialized financial institutions whose original purpose was to provide loans for home buyers.

CHARTERS

All federal savings and loan associations are chartered and supervised by the Federal Home Loan Bank Board (FHLBB). They are required to belong to the Federal Savings and Loan Insurance Corporation (FSLIC), which insures depositors' accounts. States may issue charters to state savings banks and building and loan associations, which have a similar purpose.

CHANGES IN PRACTICES

For more than 40 years, the business operations of federally chartered S&L's were restricted. Checking accounts could not be offered, limits were placed on interest rates, and loans were restricted to long-term residential mortgages offering a low return. These restrictions led depositors to move their funds from S&L's to other financial institutions that provided checking accounts and higher interest.

In an effort to help the S&L's, Congress removed some of the restrictions on S&L business practices. In 1980, for example, Congress repealed the law that prohibited S&L's from offering interest on demand-deposit accounts, such as checking accounts. Interest rate limitations were lifted, and FSLIC insurance coverage was raised to $100,000.

Two years later, another law gave the S&L's authority to make commercial loans for shopping centers, office buildings, and even undeveloped land. S&L's were also allowed to invest in high-interest, high-risk corporate bonds, known as junk bonds.

In 1983 the FHLBB relaxed a regulation that limited S&L loans to a percentage of the appraised value of property and permitted them to lend 100 percent of a property's appraised value. As a result, developers and speculators could buy undeveloped land without having to put up any of their own money.

THE S&L CRISIS

With these new rules, S&L's experienced a rapid growth in deposits and therefore had more money to lend. But their employees were inexperienced in evaluating commercial-loan applications, and there were no federal regulators trained to spot potential problems. When investments in land deals and junk bonds began to sour, the outstanding debts of many S&L's far outweighed their deposits, and the FSLIC, which insured their deposits, did not have enough money to cover the funds.

THE BAILOUT

In 1989 President George Bush signed into law an act that overhauled the regulation of federally insured S&L's. The FHLBB was eliminated, the Office of Thrift Supervision was established, and responsibility for FSLIC insurance funds was transferred to the Federal Deposit Insurance Corporation.

The Resolution Trust Corporation (RTC) took over the management of hundreds of savings and loans and began to sell foreclosed residential and commercial properties to recover some of the money that had been lost. In addition, some S&L's were themselves sold. See also BANK FAILURE; FEDERAL DEPOSIT INSURANCE CORPORATION; FORECLOSURE.

BUYING RTC PROPERTIES

In order to recover some of the money lost by failed savings and loan associations, the RTC often conducts auctions of assets they hold. These assets include not only residential and commercial real estate but also items of personal property, such as artwork, cars, and office equipment. In many instances the items are sold for only pennies on the dollar of their original value. You can find the phone number of the Resolution Trust Corporation office in your telephone directory and ask to be put on their mailing list to receive notification of future auctions. A real estate agent will also give you information about homes, land, and other real estate being sold by the RTC in your area.

CHOOSING AN S&L

Because savings and loan associations may now set their own rules on account fees, interest rates, and service charges, consumers need to shop for the S&L best suited to meet their needs. You should consider the following guidelines in choosing an S&L:

◇ Is the S&L covered by FDIC insurance? If so, your deposits will remain safe up to the $100,000 limit per depositor. See BANK ACCOUNT.

◇ What interest rates does the S&L offer on its accounts?

◇ How are interest rates compounded and paid? Does the interest rate vary with the size of the account?

◇ What are the charges for stop-payment orders, automated teller machine (ATM) transactions, and other services? Are any charges imposed on accounts that fall below a minimum balance?

Keep in mind that some savings and loan "no-fee" checking accounts also pay no interest, no matter how large your balance is. Find an account that pays interest on deposits over a minimum balance, and be sure that you keep enough money in your account to avoid any service charges.

SCAMS AND SWINDLES

Thousands of con artists are waiting to prey on the unwary, with perhaps just as many types of scams and swindles. This article discusses some of the most common confidence games, but you should also refer to the following: EMPLOYMENT AGENCY; FRAUD; HEALTH CLUB; HOME IMPROVEMENT AND REPAIR; MAIL-ORDER SALES; PONZI SCHEME; PYRAMID SALES SCHEME.

THE PIGEON DROP

The most frequent targets for the pigeon drop are elderly people and newly arrived immigrants. The scam works like this: Harriet is walking down a busy street when she is approached by a younger woman who holds up a bulging billfold and asks her if she has dropped her wallet. Harriet says that the wallet is not hers, and the two women start talking about what they should do, since the billfold does not contain any identification.

At this point an accomplice enters the scene—Roger, a well-dressed man who offers to help the flustered women. When the con woman, Barbara, shows Roger the wallet, he claims to work for a lawyer and offers to ask his boss what the women should do. Roger disappears for a while, then returns with an elaborate plan. The money, he suggests, should be put in a safe-deposit box at a local bank, and an ad should be placed in the lost-and-found column of the local newspaper. If no one claims the money in 30 days, he says, Harriet and Barbara will be able to keep it. But there is one catch. As a "sign of good faith," each of the women must put up a sum of money (usually $1,000 or more) and store their funds in the safe-deposit box along with the found money.

The two swindlers accompany Harriet to her bank, where she withdraws the necessary amount. The man posing as a lawyer's clerk then takes the money from Harriet and Barbara and places it with the found money "for safekeeping." At about this time, Roger excuses himself to make a telephone call to his boss to set up the safe-deposit box. He promises to return in a few minutes. After a while Barbara, pretending to be concerned about Roger's long absence, goes to look for him. Of course, neither she nor her accomplice ever returns, and by the time Harriet realizes she has been tricked, the two swindlers have disappeared for good.

THE DEAD MAN'S BIBLE

For the scam known as the dead man's Bible, a con artist reads newspaper obituaries to find the name of a recently deceased person. Then he visits the home of the grieving family and claims to be delivering a box with merchandise that the deceased person had ordered to be paid on delivery. (In one common version of this scam, the merchandise is an inexpensive Bible which the con artist says is very valuable.) Because the family is usually too upset to ask questions, the con artist walks away with cash or a check for the "merchandise." Sometimes the box contains only a brick and some shredded newspapers.

THE BANK EXAMINER

In the bank examiner swindle, the con man stands behind his potential victim in a teller's line to learn her address, or he takes a peek at someone's mail to learn where she keeps her bank accounts.

The con artist then telephones or visits the person, identifying himself as a bank examiner who is investigating a bank teller suspected of dishonesty, and asks for the victim's help. All she has to do, he says, is withdraw some money from her account (again, usually around $1,000), place it in an envelope, and take it outside to the "bank examiner," who will then inspect the money for fingerprints or suspicious serial numbers. He promises that the money will be returned as soon as the investigation is completed, but of course it never is.

THE LONG-LOST RELATIVE

The long-lost-relative scam is often carried out by mail or telephone, although it can also be done in person. The victim is

CHECKLIST

How to Avoid Scams and Swindles

A healthy dose of skepticism is the best vaccination against a scam or swindle. Here are some tips:

❑ **BE WARY OF STRANGERS WHO ASK YOU ABOUT MONEY.**
If you are approached by someone who claims to need your advice about found money, a winning lottery ticket, or some other windfall, chances are you are being set up for a swindle. Call the police immediately.

❑ **BE WARY OF PEOPLE WHO CLAIM TO BE POLICE OFFICERS, BANK EXAMINERS, OR OTHER OFFICIALS.**
Don't be fooled by swindlers who give you a telephone number to call to verify their identity. The call will, of course, be answered by an accomplice. If you are suspicious, call the police or your bank at the number listed in the directory, not the number the alleged official provides.

❑ **BE WARY OF BYSTANDERS WHO SEEM TO BE STANDING A LITTLE TOO CLOSE TO YOU IN LINE AT THE BANK.**
Con artists can obtain a great deal of information from your deposit slips and checks that will help give them credibility later on.

❑ **DESTROY UNUSED OR INCORRECTLY COMPLETED CHECKS AND BANK SLIPS.**
If you spoil a deposit or withdrawal slip at the bank, take it home and dispose of it there.

❑ **REMEMBER THAT IF AN OFFER SEEMS TOO GOOD TO BE TRUE, IT PROBABLY IS.**
It is better to take a little time to investigate and ask questions than to fall victim to a savvy swindler.

notified that he may be the only living relative of a person who recently died without a will in a faraway state, leaving an estate worth millions of dollars. In order to investigate further, however, the con artist asks for a fee of $50 or more to cover the expense of the investigation, process the necessary paperwork, and protect the victim's claim to the estate. The con artist may even provide some information about the victim's background that helps lend credibility to his story.

The victim mails the "fee" to a post office box in another state. Several weeks pass, and when the victim calls or writes the "investigator," he learns that the telephone has been disconnected (or never existed under that name) or that the post office box has been closed.

IF YOU ARE THE VICTIM OF A SCAM

If you are swindled, here are some actions you can take:

◇ Notify the police immediately. Too many victims of con artists never report the crime because they are embarrassed about having been so gullible. The sooner you tell the police about the swindle, the greater their chance of recovering some or all of your losses, and the sooner they can protect others from falling prey to the same scheme.

◇ If you were swindled through the mail, or if you mailed money to a suspected con artist, inform your local postmaster, who will ask the postal inspectors to launch an investigation. If you are lucky, they may be able to track down the swindler and recover at least some of your money.

SCHOOL ATTENDANCE

Many Americans take the right to a free education for granted, assuming that it is guaranteed by the Constitution or the Bill of Rights; but there is actually no constitutional right to a public education. Nevertheless, all 50 states now have laws establishing public schools funded by the taxpayers. The Constitution requires that once a state law establishes the right to a public education, that law must be applied equally to everyone.

SCHOOL CHOICE

As a rule, a student is required to attend the public school in his district. The student's parents do not have the right to choose which school he will attend; only the school board has the authority to assign students in the district to particular schools. A school district may deny a student admission if he is not living in the district with a parent or legal guardian, or if it appears that he has established a temporary residence for the sole purpose of attending school in that district. To help achieve court-ordered racial balance, school districts sometimes allow nonresident students from adjoining districts to attend their schools. The child's parents or the district in which the child resides may be required to defray the cost of his education. A child may be denied admission if he is not of school age or has a contagious disease, but not because he is an alien, whether legal or illegal. Unwed mothers may not be denied admission to school solely because they are unwed mothers.

COMPULSORY ATTENDANCE

All states have laws regarding compulsory school attendance. The parents or guardians of school-age children are required by law to see that their children attend school. However, the U.S. Supreme Court has ruled that the states cannot require students to go to public schools. As a parent, you have the right to enroll your child in a private school, and in most states you may have your child "home schooled"—that is, educated at home. If you do not send your child to a public school, however, you must make sure that the education provided by the private school or tutor (such as yourself) meets the minimum standards set by your local school district and state authorities. See also HOME SCHOOLING.

If you fail to enroll your child in school or otherwise provide for his education, you may face prosecution in a criminal court. Furthermore, state welfare authorities may charge you with neglect in a juvenile or family court. You can be fined, and your children may be placed in foster care.

A child may be excused from attending school because of illness, dangerous conditions in the school, bad weather, or lack of transportation. But if your child refuses to attend school, he may be charged with truancy in juvenile court. If the child is found to be a truant, the court may impose restrictions on him or remove him from your home and place him in a foster or group home.

ATTENDANCE LAWS AND FIRST AMENDMENT RIGHTS

In some instances parents may keep their child out of school if complying with mandatory attendance laws would interfere with their religious beliefs. For example, children in the Amish community have been excused from complying with compulsory-attendance laws past the eighth grade. The Supreme Court has ruled that the children are exempt, since to require their further schooling in public schools would endanger or destroy the free exercise of Amish religious beliefs. However, the Supreme Court limited this ruling to "traditionally discrete and isolated communities." In contrast, a Florida court ruled against parents who refused to enroll their children in public school on the grounds that having their children mingle with children of other races violated their religious beliefs.

Private and parochial schools must comply with the minimum standards set by the state school authorities for private schools, even if these standards conflict with the religious beliefs of parents. For example, a private school can be required to teach mathematics, even if the parents believe such teaching to be a satanic activity.

Public school children may be absent from school for limited periods of time to receive religious instruction, as long as the instruction does not take place on school grounds. See also JUVENILE OFFENDER; SCHOOL PRAYER.

SCHOOL EXPULSION AND SUSPENSION

Public school boards and individual schools have broad powers to establish reasonable rules and regulations for primary and secondary school students. These rules generally cover such behavior as truancy, tardiness, plagiarism, inappropriate language, alcohol and drug use, and weapon possession. The regulations may also extend to off-campus events, such as class trips or other extracurricular activities.

Sometimes students are expelled for their parents' behavior—for example, when a parent physically or verbally assaults a teacher. However, a student may not be suspended or expelled for refusing to perform actions that violate his religious beliefs, such as dancing in a coed gym class or standing up while the national anthem is played.

SCHOOL AUTHORITY

If a student refuses to abide by the rules, school authorities may take disciplinary measures. Usually the school will try to counsel a student who misbehaves, but for major transgressions, or in cases of consistently disruptive behavior, the authorities may be compelled to suspend or expel the child. Suspension is a temporary punishment, but expulsion is permanent; both suspension and expulsion are entered on the student's permanent school record.

In most public school systems the principal has the right to suspend or expel students, but the school board or the district superintendent of schools may review and overturn her decision. A student who is expelled may be assigned to a special school, or if the matter is brought to a family court, a judge may order him to live in a group home or other facility.

Private schools are not subject to the same due process requirements as public schools and therefore have greater latitude to suspend or expel students.

STUDENTS' RIGHTS TO DUE PROCESS

The U.S. Supreme Court has found that laws allowing suspension or expulsion of a student without a hearing are unconstitutional. Schools must establish and comply with fair procedures, known as due process, to determine whether a student is guilty of misconduct.

◇ The student must be given written or oral notice of his alleged misconduct. The notice should indicate what the student is being accused of, why he is being accused, and by whom.

◇ The student has a right to a hearing at which he can refute the accusations. If the suspension is for 10 days or less, the hearing can immediately follow the notice. If the hearing does not take place at that time, it must be held before the student is suspended. However, students who pose a continuing danger to persons or property or cause an ongoing classroom disturbance may be removed from school before the hearing.

◇ If the student is likely to be suspended for more than 10 days or expelled, he must be given adequate time to prepare for the hearing.

◇ The student has the right to have an attorney represent him at the hearing, but only at his own expense. The school principal, the student, any teachers or other students who are involved in the matter, and usually a guidance counselor or school psychologist will also attend. After the hearing, the principal decides upon the punishment and the student is formally notified.

◇ A student may appeal his suspension or expulsion to the school board or district superintendent or even take the matter to court. If a court finds that a student has been wrongfully suspended or expelled, it can order him reinstated. Under some circumstances a student may file a lawsuit for damages if he has been wrongfully denied the right to attend school.

SCHOOL PRAYER

Over the last 20 years the role of prayer in public schools has been hotly debated between people who think that prayer has a legitimate role in fostering moral values and those who believe that allowing prayer, even voluntary prayer, in public schools violates the Constitution's provisions for the separation of church and state.

To date, the latter argument has prevailed. The U.S. Supreme Court has ruled that laws requiring or permitting prayer in public schools are unconstitutional. Religion may be taught in an educational context, but Bible readings and other religious activities are prohibited on public school premises during school hours. Outside school hours, extracurricular religious groups may be allowed to meet on school premises, but in allowing such meetings the school administration cannot favor any one group over another.

To circumvent the laws against prayer, some schools have tried to set aside a daily "moment for meditation" during which students could silently pray. However, the Supreme Court has held these to be unconstitutional as well.

In 1992 the Supreme Court

extended the ban on school prayer to invocations by clergy at public school graduation ceremonies, ruling that the state cannot require a student to sit through a religious activity as the price of attending graduation. In 1993, however, two federal court decisions permitted prayer at graduation provided it was delivered by students.

Since religious instruction is prohibited during school, parents may be permitted to take their children out of school during the school day to attend religious instruction elsewhere. Parents also have the right to educate their children in parochial rather than public schools, but they must do so at their own expense. See also HOME SCHOOLING; RELIGION, FREEDOM OF.

SCOUTING

For many children, part of growing up involves belonging to clubs and organizations, including the Boy Scouts and Girl Scouts, or their junior counterparts, the Cub Scouts and Brownies. Unlike most other youth groups, these organizations were established through federal legislation.

STRUCTURE AND AIMS

In 1916 Congress enacted legislation creating the nonprofit corporation known as the Boy Scouts of America, whose stated purpose is to teach boys about scouting, patriotism, self-reliance, and courage. In 1950 the nonprofit Girl Scouts of America corporation was established to promote loyalty, truth, helpfulness, and the highest ideals of character and patriotism. A national council was created and given the authority to establish a constitution, bylaws, a board of directors, and officers.

Both the Boy Scouts and Girl Scouts have the exclusive right to the emblems, badges, descriptive marks, and words or phrases used in the scouting program, including the terms *Scout*, *Boy Scout*, or *Girl Scout*. This means that the Scouts can sue anyone who tries to use material proprietary to the Scouts.

Regional scouting councils across the country set qualifications for the men and women who run individual Scout troops. Because of their special status with the federal government, the councils must make annual reports to Congress about events and proceedings over the previous year.

LIABILITY

If a Scout is injured during a scouting activity, he has the right to sue the national or regional council. But to win his case, he has to show that the council had some direct control over the activity.

If the Scout's injury was due to the leader's negligence, the lawsuit should be filed against him personally, unless the organization was negligent in selecting him as a Scout leader.

Suppose your son Bobby's Scout troop goes on an overnight hike in the Appalachian Mountains. During the hike the Scouts become separated, and Bobby falls and hurts himself. If you find out that the Scout leader had no wilderness hiking experience, you could probably sue the scouting council, arguing that it had the duty to make sure that the leader was qualified to take children on such a trip.

DISCRIMINATION

With the enactment of federal and state legislation to prohibit religious and racial discrimination, the admission and membership policies of both Boy Scouts and Girl Scouts have provoked lawsuits. In areas of the country where there are scouting troops only for boys or for girls, members of the other sex have challenged the rejection of their applications to join. Teenagers who were dropped from scouting because of their homosexuality have also sued.

Whether a lawsuit for discrimination succeeds may depend on the wording of the statute that was used as the basis for the suit. For example, a lawsuit based on Title IX of the Educational Amendments of 1972—a federal law that prevents discrimination by educational institutions—was rejected because Title IX specifically excludes social organizations like the Scouts.

The success of these suits also depends in large part on the state in which they were made. A girl who challenged her rejection as a Cub Scout under Oregon's Public Accommodation Act lost her case because the court decided that a Scout troop did not fit the definition of a "place of public accommodation." The court interpreted the act as applying only to businesses and commercial establishments.

In California, however, a Boy Scout who had been expelled from the organization because of his homosexuality won his discrimination claim because it was based on a state law that prohibited businesses from discriminating when providing services to the public. The court found that the Boy Scout organization was a "business establishment" because it has exclusive rights to its uniforms and emblems and derives benefits from franchising these items to retail stores and from the publication and sale of scouting books. See also PRIVATE CLUB; SEX DISCRIMINATION.

SEARCH AND SEIZURE

The Fourth Amendment to the Constitution states that "the right of the people to be secure in their persons, houses, papers, and effects, against unreasonable searches and seizures, shall not be violated, and no warrants shall issue, but upon probable cause . . . and particularly describing the place to be searched, and the persons or things to be seized." The amendment protects each person's privacy against arbitrary invasion by the police or other government agents, stipulating that they may not search your person or property unless they have first obtained a warrant from the court. However, the Fourth Amendment does not guard against intrusions by private individuals, including private investigators, security guards, or store detectives. See SEARCH WARRANT.

WHERE THE AMENDMENT APPLIES

The Fourth Amendment protects citizens and noncitizens alike in areas generally considered private—not only in their homes but in offices, hotel rooms, automobiles, and in some cases the grounds surrounding a building. But it does not apply to public places, such as restaurants or shopping malls, or places where no privacy can reasonably be expected, such as in a prison, military barracks, or hospital.

Sealed mail in transit within the United States cannot be opened by law enforcement officials, nor can mail that is sent over international boundaries into the United States. For example, if customs officials want to open a piece of mail because they suspect it contains drugs or other illegal items, they must either obtain the permission of the addressee or get a search warrant. If a package appears to present an imminent danger—for instance, if customs or law enforcement officials believe it contains explosives—they do not need to obtain a search warrant before attempting to dismantle or destroy it.

The Fourth Amendment does not apply to items that are discarded. Moreover, the police may seize illegal items or evidence of wrongdoing that is in plain view, provided that the officers had a right to be on the premises.

Electronic surveillance also falls within the purview of the Fourth Amendment. Law enforcement officials cannot "bug" your office, rooms in your house, or your telephone unless they have obtained a legal warrant to do so. In the majority of states, however, conversations on cordless phones are not protected.

UNREASONABLE SEARCH AND SEIZURE

To obtain a search warrant, a law enforcement officer must give a judge or other magistrate information that gives her probable cause to believe that the search or seizure will produce evidence of wrongdoing. Judges decide upon these requests as they are made, determining whether a reasonable person would find the information convincing.

Any evidence seized by an officer without a warrant will not be admitted in court. This is known as the exclusionary rule, and it protects the guilty as well as the innocent by barring any evidence, no matter how valuable, that has been obtained through a violation of a defendant's rights.

For instance, Fred, a police officer who had held a grudge against his high school classmate Tom for many years, went to Tom's home, demanded entrance, and searched the premises. Fred had no reason to believe he would find evidence of a crime, and he did not have a search warrant. Tom did not consent to the search but was afraid to protest. When Fred found a plastic bag full of marijuana in a bedroom drawer, he arrested Tom.

At the preliminary hearing, Tom's lawyer asked that the evidence be suppressed on the grounds that it was found during a search that violated the Fourth Amendment. The judge agreed and ordered that the marijuana be excluded from evidence, leading to the dismissal of the case because there was no other evidence against Tom.

When illegally obtained evidence leads to the discovery of still more incriminating evidence, that evidence is also inadmissible. Suppose Fred had found a hotel key when he searched Tom's home. He took the key and went to the hotel, where he found a stash of stolen money. Neither the key nor the money could be used as evidence in Tom's trial for robbery.

BODY SEARCHES

A strip search, for which a suspect is required to remove his clothes, or a complete body search, in which the suspect's hair and body cavities are searched, may not be conducted without a good reason. The justification for a body search must be a "clear indication" that a person has concealed something. Suppose a police officer, as he approaches a suspect to arrest him for drug dealing, sees the man slip something into his mouth. The officer would be allowed to do a complete search of the suspect, including his mouth.

State laws stipulate who may legally perform body searches; generally a suspect cannot be searched by a law enforcement officer of the opposite sex. Not only is the evidence obtained during an illegal body or strip search inadmissible at a trial, but the victim can file a civil rights lawsuit against the officer who performed it.

EXCEPTIONS

Evidence that is inadmissible in court can sometimes be used to determine whether a suspect should be indicted or whether a witness or defendant is perjuring himself. For example, if a defendant in a burglary trial denies that he ever met his codefendant, the prosecution could use his address book, containing the codefendant's name, to cast doubt on his credibility.

Some states have enacted laws prohibiting private individuals from snooping on each other, but in other states evidence found by private individuals may be admissible in court. In one case, a man videotaped his neighbors engaging in sexual activity and charges were brought against them for lewd and lascivious behavior. Although the people were in their own home and the tape was made through their partially closed blinds, they were convicted of a misdemeanor on the basis of the tape, because their previous and ongoing behavior had caused their expectation of privacy to be reduced.

For a list of the situations in which search warrants are not ordinarily required, see the checklist on page 464. See also STOP-AND-FRISK LAWS.

SEARCH WARRANT

Before a law enforcement officer can search you or your home or car, he generally must have a search warrant issued by a judge or magistrate. When applying for a warrant, an officer must make an affidavit, or sworn statement, that he has probable cause to believe that he will find a suspect or evidence of a crime at the location to be searched. Mere suspicion of criminal activity is not enough to convince a judge to issue a warrant—there must be facts or convincing circumstantial evidence. Secondhand information, such as statements from a reliable informant, may be enough.

Because warrants are sometimes needed urgently, the procedure for getting one is not complicated. In an emergency a warrant can be issued almost immediately, even if a law enforcement official must rouse a judge from bed.

A search warrant must describe in detail the person or place to be searched and the type of evidence that is being sought. Also, the police must limit their search to the scope of the warrant. For instance, if a warrant authorizes the police to look for a rifle at a specific address, they may open closets, cabinets, drawers, and other areas in the house where a rifle could potentially be concealed—but not a purse or shoe box. Under certain circumstances, however, evidence not specified on the

CHECKLIST

When a Search Warrant Is Not Required

Most searches are conducted only after the police have obtained a search warrant, but the police can legally conduct a search without a warrant in the following situations:

❑ **IF AN OBJECT IS IN PLAIN VIEW.**
No warrant is needed if a piece of evidence or an illegal item is easily visible. For instance, if the police walk by a car and see a sawed-off shotgun lying on the backseat, they may seize the weapon.

❑ **IF AN INDIVIDUAL CONSENTS.**
The police can conduct a search without a warrant if a person voluntarily gives permission, but they may not coerce or trick someone into consenting. The person who gives consent must be authorized to give it—a landlord, for instance, may allow a search of public areas in his building but not of private apartments—and he may withdraw his permission at any time.

❑ **DURING AN ARREST.**
When a suspect is lawfully arrested, the police may conduct a search without her consent. The search is limited to the suspect and the areas within her immediate vicinity, however.

❑ **TO SEARCH A VEHICLE.**
Because cars, boats, trucks, and other vehicles could be moved while the police obtain a search warrant, they may be searched on the spot if the police have probable cause to believe evidence of a crime will be found.

❑ **DURING AN IMPOUNDMENT.**
Police may conduct a warrantless search of a vehicle or other property they have seized during the commission of a crime. An inventory is taken both to protect the owner's property and to alert the police to dangerous items, such as explosives.

❑ **WHEN A PERSON IS A SUSPECT.**
A police officer may temporarily detain someone whom he suspects of committing or planning a crime. If the officer suspects danger, he may conduct a patdown search of the suspect for weapons.

❑ **IN AN EMERGENCY.**
Police may follow suspects into a building and search for contraband or weapons immediately if there is a risk that the evidence will be destroyed or hidden.

❑ **IF THE POLICE ARE IN PURSUIT.**
Suppose an officer arrives at a crime scene, sees someone running into a house, and is told by witnesses, "That's the guy who knifed that woman." The officer does not need a warrant before demanding entry to the home and searching the suspect.

❑ **AT A BORDER CROSSING.**
At an international border crossing, you and your luggage and vehicle may be subject to a complete search. However, customs officials must have strong suspicions before they can subject you to a body or strip search, even at a border crossing.

warrant may be obtained during the search. For an example of these circumstances, see the checklist at the left. See also NO-KNOCK LAWS; SEARCH AND SEIZURE; STOP-AND-FRISK LAWS.

SEAT BELT LAWS

For more than 20 years, federal regulations have required car manufacturers to provide seat belts for as many passengers as a given car is designed to carry. In the past decade so-called passive restraints, such as air bags and motorized shoulder belts, have also been mandated. But in spite of these regulations and the mounting evidence that seat belts save lives, many Americans still neglect to buckle up.

Today most states have laws against driving without using a seat belt. Generally, the police may cite a driver for failing to use his seat belt only after they stop him for some other traffic violation, but in at least seven states, police may ticket the driver even when no other violation is charged.

In some states the driver is responsible for seeing that the passengers wear seat belts as well. In most states, however, this is not the case, and a passenger who is injured in an accident cannot collect damages because the driver did not insist that he wear a seat belt.

Most states now require that children up to the age of four or five ride in specially designed car seats. In a number of areas throughout the country, parents who are unable to afford such car seats may obtain them free of charge through programs sponsored by hospitals and state agencies.

Courts in some states have held that failure to wear a seat belt amounts to contributory negligence in a car accident. If you live in one of these states and are injured in an automobile accident, you may have any potential compensation reduced or denied if you were not wearing your seat belt when the accident occurred. See also NEGLIGENCE.

Passenger seat belts are not usually required equipment for most public transportation vehicles, such as buses, trains, and subway cars. Airport shuttle buses and taxicabs usually must have them, although the driver is normally not responsible for seeing that passengers use them.

One immediate advantage to owners of cars equipped with the new passive-restraint systems is that insurance companies may charge them lower premiums. If your car has a motorized shoulder belt or an air bag, ask your insurer whether you are eligible for a discount on your premiums. See also AUTOMOBILE ACCIDENTS; AUTOMOBILE INSURANCE.

SECOND MARRIAGE

Remarriages of widowed or divorced men and women can proceed more smoothly if both parties are prepared to deal with such legal issues as financial responsibility, adoption, and estate planning.

PRENUPTIAL AGREEMENTS

People who are marrying for the second time often own substantial amounts of property. To avoid disputes arising when the marriage ends, whether through death or divorce, it is advisable for both parties to enter into a prenuptial, or premarital, agreement. This contract defines how the couple's property will be divided, and states how spousal- or child-support payments will be determined. See PRENUPTIAL AGREEMENT.

SPOUSAL AND CHILD SUPPORT

A divorced person who is receiving support from a previous spouse generally loses it when she remarries. If a person paying alimony remarries, he may be able to have the payments reduced if he can prove that his new marriage reduces his ability to pay.

Child support is generally not affected by the remarriage of either parent. However, a judge may decide to revise child-support payments if the financial circumstances of either parent change. See also CHILD SUPPORT.

ADOPTION

A new stepparent may wish to adopt the children from his spouse's former marriage. If both biological parents are alive, generally both must consent to the adoption. An exception can be made if a biological parent is unfit or has not acted upon his parental rights. Suppose Darlene's former husband, Stewart, has failed to pay support for their two children, never visits them, and shows no interest in their welfare. Darlene has remarried, and her new husband wants to adopt the children. Stewart is notified that there will be a hearing to decide whether he should continue to have parental rights. He fails to appear at the hearing and, after listening to the facts of the case, the family court terminates Stewart's parental rights. The court no longer needs to obtain Stewart's consent for the adoption. See also ADOPTION.

If a stepparent adopts a stepchild, he is responsible for supporting that child. A number of states require the stepparent to help support his stepchild even if he has not adopted her. Other states, including Alaska and New York, require the stepparent to provide support only if the child would otherwise need public assistance. See also STEPPARENT.

ESTATE PLANNING

Remarriage will affect the distribution of your estate. You and your new spouse should review your wills and specify what property you want to leave to each other and what should go to children or other relatives and friends. In many states, if you do not revise your will when you marry, your existing will is rendered invalid. If you die, your property will be distributed as if you had no will. See DYING WITHOUT A WILL.

Your new spouse has inheritance rights, but your stepchildren will generally have no claim to your estate if you do not adopt them. If you want them to inherit, you will have to so specify in your will. If you do adopt your stepchildren, they will be treated in the same way as biological children and have the same rights to a share of your estate.

SECTION 8 HOUSING

If you are looking for a house or apartment to rent and your income is low—or if you are a landlord looking for tenants whose ability to pay rent must be subsidized — you may want to investigate Section 8 housing, a program that provides federal dollars to help low-income families to rent safe, clean apartments and homes. It was created by Section 8 of the Housing and Community Development Act of 1974.

The program works as follows: A local public housing authority (PHA) enters into a contract with a landlord to rent properties to an eligible tenant, with the understanding that the federal government will pay part of the rent. The government payment varies, depending on the tenant's resources.

PEOPLE WHO QUALIFY

To qualify for rental assistance from the Section 8 housing program, an applicant must meet income guidelines, which are based in part on family size and location. In the Midwest, for example, these income limits in 1993 ranged from $13,600 for one person to less than $26,000 for eight people.

If you think your family is eligible for Section 8, you should apply to your local PHA office. Once you qualify, you can look for appropriate housing. When you find a place you want to rent, you must give the landlord information from the PHA explaining the Section 8 program, along with a form for him to complete.

HOUSING THAT QUALIFIES

Houses or apartments must meet standards of quality, and the rent must fall within PHA guidelines to qualify as Section 8 housing. A PHA housing survey in the community determines the fair market rental value of apartments and homes of various sizes. This information is available from the PHA.

WHAT LANDLORDS MUST DO

Each Section 8 landlord must give detailed information about the apartment—room size, utilities, rent, and appliances, for example—to the PHA staff, which will determine whether it meets federal guidelines. The PHA will then conduct an inspection, and if the rental unit is approved, the landlord will be asked to sign a one-year lease with the tenant and a one-year contract with the PHA. Processing the application and conducting the inspection may take up to two months.

RENT PAYMENTS

A Section 8 tenant pays no more than 30 percent of his adjusted gross income for rent. The PHA pays the landlord the difference between that amount and the full rent. For example, if a tenant's adjusted income each month is $800, he is required to pay only $240 (30 percent of $800) for rent. If the apartment rents for $300, the housing authority will pay $60 directly to the landlord.

OBLIGATIONS

All the parties to this arrangement have responsibilities.

◇ The tenant must provide the PHA with accurate income and family information and must allow the authority to inspect the residence periodically. He cannot transfer the lease to someone else.

◇ The landlord must maintain the rental unit in a safe and sanitary condition and permit annual inspections.

◇ The PHA must make sure that federal regulations are enforced and that tenants who are no longer eligible for assistance are removed from the program. If a tenant does not pay his rent, the PHA is not responsible to the landlord. The tenant's participation in the program is terminated, and the landlord can evict him.

Before the PHA can end its assistance, the authority must notify the tenant in writing of its reasons and of the tenant's right to an informal hearing before an impartial examiner. The examiner will issue a written decision, which the tenant may appeal if he wishes.

Securities and Exchange Commission

The Securities and Exchange Commission (SEC) was established by Congress in 1934 to protect investors from dishonest dealings in securities trading, such as those that preceded the stock market crash of 1929. Consisting of five members appointed by the president, the SEC regulates companies involved in interstate commerce that sell stock to the public.

Before a public offering of stock can be made, a company must register the stock under the provisions of the Securities Act of 1933. This act requires a company to fully disclose information about its business, management personnel, the type of stock that it is offering, and any risks that face investors who purchase the company's stock. The SEC also requires publicly traded companies to file an annual report detailing company activities and profits and losses. The SEC does not give opinions about the merits of any stock.

The SEC also regulates the activities of a publicly traded corporation's officers, directors, and advisers, such as lawyers and accountants, who handle the company's stock. It prohibits them from buying or selling the stock on the basis of information that has not been revealed to the public, a practice known as insider trading. See INSIDER TRADING.

Stockbrokers and investment advisers who have 15 clients or more must register with the SEC. The commission prohibits fraud in giving investment advice and selling stocks. See also BLUE-SKY LAW; CHURNING; STOCKBROKER; STOCKS AND BONDS.

Security Agreement

When you borrow money to make an expensive purchase, such as an automobile, jewelry, or a major appliance, you will almost certainly be asked to give the lender what is known as a security agreement. The agreement is usually a part of your sales contract, although it is sometimes a separate document.

The agreement states that if you do not adhere to the terms of your sales contract, the lender can repossess your purchase and sell it to recover any money you owe. The agreement creates what is known as a secured transaction—the lender's money is "secured" by his right to the property if you default on your payments. If the lender has to resort to this procedure, and the sale of the item does not pay off your entire debt, you can be held responsible for the balance. See also DEFAULT JUDGMENT; DEFICIENCY JUDGMENT.

Recording a Security Interest

State laws require lenders who keep a security interest in someone's property to file a form known as a UCC-1 (named for the Uniform Commercial Code), which becomes part of the state's records. By filing this document, the lender gives public notice of the interest he is retaining in your property. Once it is filed, a UCC-1

CHECKLIST

Property That Can Be Subject to a Security Agreement

The Uniform Commercial Code, which has been enacted in some form in all 50 states, lists nine types of property that can be subject to a security agreement.

- ❑ Consumer goods used for family or household purposes.
- ❑ Farm products.
- ❑ Business inventory held for sale to others.
- ❑ Business equipment, such as office and manufacturing machinery.
- ❑ Financial instruments, such as stocks, bonds, and promissory notes.
- ❑ Bills of lading, warehouse receipts, and other business documents.
- ❑ Leases on personal property, known as chattel paper.
- ❑ Accounts receivable.
- ❑ General intangibles, such as trademark, copyright, and royalty interests.

remains in effect for five years.

If the lender wants to keep a security interest longer than five years, he must file a form known as a UCC-3. If he fails to file one or the other document, he may lose his right as a creditor if you file for bankruptcy, as well as his right to repossess the item if you sell it to someone who does not know about the lender's security interest. See also BANKRUPTCY; CHATTEL MORTGAGE; DEBT.

SECURITY DEPOSIT

When a landlord rents an apartment or house to a tenant, he assumes a risk that the tenant may damage the property or move out without paying all the rent. To guard against this possibility, landlords routinely require tenants to pay a sum of money, called a security deposit, before they move in.

AMOUNT

The amount a landlord can demand as a security deposit may be controlled by state law. Typically, he can ask for one month's rent if the dwelling is unfurnished and additional money if it is furnished or if pets are permitted.

PURPOSES

The rental agreement as well as state law will specify the purposes for which a security deposit can be used. Sometimes the landlord will designate separate portions for a pet deposit, a cleaning deposit, or a default on the rent. The lease may also specify that some portion of the deposit is nonrefundable. These stipulations are important, because they regulate the landlord's use of the money. For example, if your lease says that a sum of money is to be used in the event that you do not pay your rent, but your landlord later attempts to deduct routine cleaning expenses when you move out, you may be able to challenge this deduction and get it back.

USE OF THE MONEY

State laws differ about how a security deposit is handled while it is in the landlord's possession. Some states consider the money the landlord's property and allow him to use it as he pleases until it is returned to the tenant. Other states, such as New York, consider the money the tenant's property and may require the landlord to keep it separate from other funds and even to put the deposit in an interest-bearing account, with the interest going to the tenant.

RETURN OF THE DEPOSIT

To get your security deposit back when you move from the apartment, make sure you have complied with all the conditions in your lease. First, note whether the lease specifies that you must give notice of your intent to move, and how far in advance the notice must be given. Second, make sure that your dwelling is clean. Walk through it with the rental manager so that he can inspect its condition, and ask for a checklist indicating the condition of each room. If you have any reason to believe that you may not get all of your security deposit back, take pictures of the premises.

Some states require landlords to return a security deposit within a specified time after a tenancy has ended, usually from two weeks to two months. If the landlord is going to keep some of the deposit, state law may require him to send you an itemized list of his deductions. If he fails to do so, he may lose the right to keep any of the money.

SMALL-CLAIMS COURT

If you and your landlord cannot come to an agreement about the amount withheld from your deposit, you can pursue the matter in small-claims court. Copies of your lease; check-in and check-out lists of the rooms, appliances, fixtures, and their condition; and pictures of the apartment or house will be useful when you present your case to the judge. See SMALL-CLAIMS COURT.

SELECTIVE SERVICE

Although the United States has not conducted a military draft since the early 1970's, federal law still requires all male citizens and legally admitted aliens to register with the Selective Service when they turn 18. Failure to do so is punishable by a fine and imprisonment. You can register at your local post office by filling out a short form.

To ensure that young men register, Congress enacted legislation that prohibits any male born after January 1, 1960, from receiving federally subsidized student financial aid unless he has registered. The Selective Service maintains computer lists of registrants, which are checked against lists of financial aid applicants. See STUDENT LOAN.

Women are currently under no obligation to register for the draft. The U.S. Supreme Court has refused to find that this release from duty violates prohibitions against sex discrimination. See also ARMED SERVICES.

SELF-DEFENSE

Late one night Harold and Maude were awakened by the sound of glass breaking downstairs. Harold grabbed the baseball bat he kept under the bed and headed down the darkened staircase. In the front hallway he encountered a burly figure, who swung a crowbar at him. Harold ducked, the crowbar missed, and Harold struck the intruder on the knees with the bat. The man fell to the ground, and Harold stood watch over him until the police arrived and took him away.

Under other circumstances Harold might have faced a charge of battery and been held financially responsible for the injuries he caused. But the law recognizes that people have a right to protect themselves when they are in danger. Because Harold acted in self-defense, he was not subject to criminal charges.

The law allows people to use reasonable force to defend themselves and others when they believe they are in jeopardy. Generally, what constitutes reasonable force depends on the circumstances of each case. Suppose that Harold had armed himself not with a baseball bat but with a gun, and the figure he encountered was busy loading the family silver into a cloth bag. Harold would not be justified in shooting the burglar, since neither his nor any family member's life was threatened. See also BURGLARY.

Suppose that Harold is not at home, but shopping at the local mall, when he sees a man running toward him with a large knife. Harold struggles with the man and wrests the knife away, and the man falls to the pavement, cracking his skull. Under these circumstances Harold could reasonably believe that the attacker was attempting to kill him (or someone else) and has the right to use as much force as necessary to prevent this from happening. Even if the man died as a result of the fall, Harold would not be guilty of murder.

SELF-EMPLOYMENT

At one time or another in your life, you have probably dreamed about "being your own boss." But turning that dream into a reality requires some careful planning. Important decisions must be made—not only about the type of product or service you will offer, but also about such matters as licensing, zoning, insurance, financing, taxes, and retirement planning.

LICENSING AND ZONING

People who decide to go into business for themselves often find that they cannot simply set up shop and begin selling a product or service. For example, if you want to start a bakery, you will probably find that you must have a permit for handling food. If you want to operate a liquor store, you must obtain a liquor license.

You should also check your local zoning laws. If you plan to operate a business out of your home, you could be violating a zoning law that prohibits business enterprises in residential areas. See also HOME BUSINESS.

LIABILITY INSURANCE

Many small businesses start out as sole proprietorships because they are easy to set up. But as a sole proprietor, you may be held personally responsible if someone is harmed by your product or injured on your premises. All of your personal property, bank accounts, and other assets are in jeopardy if someone sues you and is awarded a large amount of money. Check with your insurance agent about adequate coverage for your business. You might also consider forming a corporation or a limited-liability company. See CORPORATION; LIABILITY INSURANCE; PARTNERSHIP; SOLE PROPRIETORSHIP.

LOANS

If you need a loan to start up your business and cannot get one at a bank, you can apply to the Small Business Administration (SBA), a federal agency that currently guarantees more than $3.5 billion worth of financing for businesses that are unable to get conventional loans. The SBA's General Business Loan Program guarantees between 80 and 90 percent of business loans below $750,000. A similar program is now offered for businesses starting up in inner-city and rural areas.

SOCIAL SECURITY

If you have worked for an employer, you know that a percentage of your gross salary is deducted for Social Security tax. In 1993 employees paid 7.65 percent of their salaries, and their employers contributed an equivalent amount.

When you are self-employed, however, you act as both the employer and the employee. Instead of having a certain percentage deducted from your salary, you pay a lump sum to the federal government. If you are self-employed on a part-time basis, you may have to pay once a year—in April, when you file your income tax return. If you are self-employed full time, you must make quarterly estimated payments.

In 1993 the tax on self-employment was 15.3 percent—2.9 percent for Medicare and 12.4 percent for Social Security. If you are self-employed part time but earn the maximum taxable amount at your regular job, you do not have to pay additional Social Security tax. In 1993 the maximum earnings subject to the Social Security tax were $57,600, but the Medicare tax was assessed on earnings up to $135,000.

If your net earnings from self-employment are $400 or more and your wages from a regular job are lower than $135,000 (in 1993), you must fill out Schedule SE of your federal tax return (Form 1040). Although you must pay the entire 15.3 percent tax yourself, you will get a deduction for half this amount—an acknowledgment by the government that your tax burden is heavier than that of salaried employees. This deduction is reported on Form 1040 under "Adjustments to Income."

UNEMPLOYMENT AND RETIREMENT BENEFITS

If you are self-employed and operating as a sole proprietor, you do not have to pay an unemployment tax. Only people who hire employees—as defined in unemployment compensation laws—pay such a tax. If your business fails and you become unemployed, however, you will not be able to collect unemployment compensation benefits.

If you are self-employed, two retirement savings options available to you are Keogh plans and individual retirement accounts, and you may elect to have one or both of these retirement plans. See also Individual Retirement Account; Keogh Plan.

TAXES

When you start your own business, the number of tax forms you need to file will increase. As a sole proprietor, you must complete Schedule C, "Profit or Loss From Business," and attach it to Form 1040. Schedule C gives the Internal Revenue Service information on the type of business you have and its income for the year. You enter your expenses for such items as advertising, rent, supplies, utilities, employee wages, and pension plans. You can deduct these expenses from your gross income to determine your business's net profit or loss.

If you have property that depreciates in value, you should complete Form 4562, "Depreciation and Amortization." Computers, vehicles, and other equipment may be depreciated, thereby reducing the tax owed on your business profits. Depreciation on equipment costing less than $10,000 may be deducted entirely in the year of purchase.

To find out whether you need additional tax forms for your business, get the advice of a tax accountant, the Internal Revenue Service, and state and local tax authorities.

Because you are working for yourself, you may have to pay quarterly estimated taxes. The estimated tax includes both income tax and self-employment tax. IRS Publication 505, "Tax Withholding and Estimated Tax," explains how to determine whether you should make quarterly payments. Failure to file estimated taxes or to pay a sufficient amount each quarter can result in a penalty. See also Income Tax; Independent Contractor; License; Limited-Liability Company; Partnership.

SEPARATION

When married people decide they can no longer live together, they usually go to court to get a divorce. But some couples decide that although they do not wish to stay together, they are not ready to take the final step of dissolving the marriage. Such couples have two options: they can agree to separate voluntarily and draw up a formal separation agreement that covers spousal and child support, or one or both spouses can petition the court for a legal separation (sometimes called a judicial separation), and the court will impose the separation agreement.

A court-ordered separation is common when one spouse refuses to leave the family home voluntarily. In such instances, a judge may set the terms of the separation agreement as well as spousal and child support.

AFTER A SEPARATION IS GRANTED

Whether the separation is voluntary or involuntary, the people involved are still considered legally married and are therefore prohibited from marrying again—unless, of course, they get divorced. Nevertheless, both spouses are free from the duties and rights of cohabitation. The couple will remain legally separated until: (1) one of the spouses dies; (2) there is a reconciliation; or (3) they divorce to end their marriage.

If they reconcile, the parties must notify the court in writing to have their court-ordered agreement set aside. Couples who have made their own informal separation agreement should tear up the document when they are reconciled.

QUESTIONS OF PATERNITY

A child conceived after a legal separation has been ordered is considered illegitimate. Unless the father acknowledges the child as his, generally the mother must file a paternity suit against her legally separated husband. This action, if successful, legitimizes the child and allows him to inherit the father's property.

LEGAL ENFORCEMENT

A voluntary separation agreement is legally binding, but it does not have the force of a judicial order—that is, if one party does not honor a voluntary agreement, the other can sue only for breach of contract. But if a spouse violates a court-ordered agreement, he or she may be found in contempt of court and subject to fines, imprisonment, or both. In some states spousal support may be automatically canceled if a couple resumes marital relations after a court-ordered separation.

A separation agreement is not a divorce agreement; that requires further legal action. In some states a couple need only file a request to convert the separation, or limited divorce, into an absolute divorce. In others they must file a divorce suit. The terms of a separation agreement are often incorporated into the divorce decree.

If you are being sued for divorce, you may enter a counterclaim for a legal separation. Or if you are sued for a separation, you may ask the court to grant an absolute divorce instead.

STEPS TO TAKE TO OBTAIN A COURT-ORDERED SEPARATION

Prior to obtaining a legal separation, couples are often advised to try marriage counseling. If that fails and separation is advised, you can take the following steps:

1. Before taking any action, hire a lawyer who specializes in marriage and divorce law. Do not move out of the marital home without a legal agreement. Your spouse could claim desertion, change the locks, and refuse you permission to collect your personal belongings. To gain access to your belongings, you would have to file a petition in district or family court, in addition to filing for a legal separation.

2. Through your lawyer or on your own, negotiate the terms of your separation. The terms should address the division of property and debts; child custody, visitation rights, and support; and spousal support. Either party may waive spousal support, but if you do not claim the right to support at the time of the separation, you generally cannot ask the court to award it later.

3. You or your spouse must petition the court for a permanent order of separation.

4. The court will review the terms of the agreement and, if it decides that they are unfair, may insist upon further negotiation or impose its own terms. See also ALIMONY; CHILD CUSTODY; CHILD SUPPORT; DIVORCE.

SERVICE CONTRACT

You have shopped carefully for your new washing machine. You have read the consumer guides and compared prices at a number of local dealers. You are especially pleased with the manufacturer's warranty, which covers all parts and repairs for the first year of ownership, and parts for another three years. You are just about to write your check when the salesperson murmurs: "Of course, you will want to buy our super service contract, won't you?"

Today an extended service contract is available for almost every expensive appliance or piece of electronic equipment. Such a contract may provide for periodic inspections and cleaning and pay for repairs after the manufacturer's warranty expires. Depending on the cost of the item and the time period that the contract covers, the fee for this additional protection may range from a few dollars to several hundred dollars or more. Extended service contracts on automobiles can cost thousands of dollars.

How important is it to purchase an extended service contract? Despite the claims of salespeople (who earn a commission for each contract they sell), most service contracts are not necessarily a good value. A good warranty from a reputable manufacturer will cover all the costs of repair or replacement for a reasonable time. For example, typical warranties on personal appliances such as hair dryers and shavers provide for free repairs or replacement for 90 days to one year. On major appliances a one-year warranty is often the standard, and some manufacturers will guarantee the most expensive components for much longer periods. (For example, most refrigerator manufacturers will guarantee the compressor for five years.) Typical automobile warranties provide bumper-to-bumper coverage for at least 12 months or 12,000 miles, whichever comes first, and many now offer this coverage for three years or up to 36,000 miles.

Most service contracts merely extend the coverage of the original warranties, and some of them begin to run from the time of purchase, essentially duplicating your free warranty protection for that period.

Although much is made of the preventive maintenance features of these contracts, people who buy them seldom take advantage of the inspections and cleanings. Furthermore, the cost of a service contract is often disproportionate to the cost of the item itself. Buying a $200 service contract on a $300 VCR makes little financial sense.

Problems often arise when you try to file a claim. Most service contracts on automobiles and major appliances exclude coverage for problems caused by owner misuse, and many service-contract companies routinely reject claims on the basis of this exclusion. When that happens, the burden of proof shifts to you. Unless you have kept careful records of all maintenance procedures and can show that the item was never used in a way for which it was not intended, you will probably not win your case. See also LEMON LAW; MAGNUSON-MOSS WARRANTY ACT; WARRANTY AND GUARANTY.

SEX DISCRIMINATION

State and federal laws prohibit discrimination based on gender in many settings, from the classroom to the workplace.

EDUCATIONAL OPPORTUNITIES

Under federal law, all children in public schools are entitled to equal educational opportunities, regardless of their gender. School boards and districts cannot establish separate educational systems for boys and girls. They cannot exclude students because of pregnancy, childbirth, or the termination of a pregnancy, but schools may offer separate programs for pregnant students if participation is voluntary. The Supreme Court has held that a school system can establish a limited number of single-sex high schools if enrollment is voluntary and the district otherwise provides equal educational opportunities.

School sports

Schools are generally not required to allow girls to try out for boys' teams, or vice versa, in contact sports. But they must provide equal athletic opportunities for both sexes. In non-contact sports, such as golf, tennis, swimming, or volleyball, a school may establish separate programs for boys and girls if doing so is deemed necessary to offer equal opportunities.

Higher education

Colleges and vocational schools that receive federal or state funds may not allow gender to influence their admissions decisions. They may not rank applicants separately by sex or set quotas based on gender, nor can they use admission tests that are sexually biased.

The antidiscrimination laws work to the benefit of men as well as women. For example, the Supreme Court has ruled that a state-supported nursing school cannot deny admission to men.

Private schools have greater latitude in their admissions policies, but in general they cannot discriminate on the basis of sex if they receive any federal funds, such as tuition assistance for their students. However, some private schools, such as those sponsored by religious organizations, are not subject to laws prohibiting sex discrimination.

REAL LIFE, REAL LAW

The Case of the Teacher's Earring

When Mr. Strailey, who was in the habit of wearing a small gold earring to work at the Happy Times Nursery School, was fired from his teaching position, he filed suit in federal court. He charged that his dismissal was a violation of Title VII of the Civil Rights Act of 1964, which prohibits sex-based discrimination, and argued that he had been fired because the school administration thought it inappropriate for a male teacher to wear an earring, and that the school's stereotypical view that male teachers should have a virile appearance rather than an effeminate one was based on sex discrimination.

The federal district court dismissed Strailey's claim, and the federal court of appeals upheld the dismissal. The court pointed to previous decisions, which had all held that Title VII prohibits employment discrimination based on gender but does not protect employees against discrimination because of an effeminate appearance, just as it does not protect them from being fired because they are transvestites or homosexuals.

SOCIAL ORGANIZATIONS AND CLUBS

It is not against the law for fraternities to exclude women, or for sororities to exclude men, and the law does not apply to "voluntary youth service organizations whose membership is traditionally limited to one sex," such as the Boy Scouts, Girl Scouts, YMCA ,YWCA, and similar organizations. See also Scouting.

EMPLOYMENT

Federal law and many state laws prohibit employers from discriminating on the basis of sex when hiring and firing. Federal legislation protects pregnant women from employment-related discrimination. An employer may not refuse to hire a pregnant woman solely because she is pregnant, if she is able to perform the job. Moreover, an employer cannot fire a woman or force her to quit solely because of her pregnancy, although an employer may exclude pregnant women from certain jobs if their health and safety would be endangered by the work.

Employers with policies against hiring women with preschool-age children have been found guilty of sex discrimination. Under the law an employer may not prohibit a woman from using her accrued sick leave or vacation time in connection with pregnancy or childbirth. Refusal to grant maternity leave without a compelling business necessity has been found to be unlawful. Requiring a pregnant woman to take her leave on an arbitrary date, regardless of her health and ability to work, has also been found to constitute unlawful sex discrimination.

THE PREGNANCY DISCRIMINATION ACT

The special needs of expectant mothers are considered by a recent piece of legislation, the Pregnancy Discrimination Act of 1987. Under this law, if an employer provides short-term disability benefits, they must be granted to a woman for pregnancy and childbirth.

For example, if a company provides paid leave with job security for six weeks for an employee who has suffered a heart attack, it should provide the same type of benefit for a woman who becomes pregnant or has given birth. Under the same reasoning, if an employer grants employees time off for education and travel, similar provisions must be made for something as compelling as the arrival of a new baby. See also EMPLOYEE HIRING AND FIRING; EMPLOYMENT AGENCY.

SEXUAL ABUSE

The term *sexual abuse* can be applied to a wide variety of situations, but the common denominator is that one person is forced into having unwanted sexual contact with another. Typically, victims of sexual abuse cannot defend themselves because their abuser is physically stronger or holds a position of trust, as does a family member, babysitter, or professional caregiver.

The victims of sexual abuse are entitled to bring criminal charges against their abuser and can sue in civil court for money damages as well. If the abuse took place in an institutional setting, such as a nursing home or psychiatric hospital, the abuser's employers can also be sued. See also CHILD ABUSE AND NEGLECT; INCEST; RAPE.

SEXUAL HARASSMENT

Sexual harassment is prohibited under Title VII of the 1964 Civil Rights Act. Although employers often plead confusion and ignorance about what kind of behavior constitutes sexual harassment, the federal Equal Employment Opportunity Commission (EEOC) has established guidelines that describe it in precise terms.

Sexual harassment is obvious when an employee is made to understand that hiring, continued employment, or career advancement depend on submitting to unwelcome sexual advances. But another more subtle issue is what is known as environmental harassment—unwelcome sexual behavior that creates a hostile work environment. Any of the following kinds of behavior are considered to create a hostile work environment under federal law:

◇ Making graphic or degrading comments about an employee's dress, appearance, or anatomy.

◇ Displaying sexually suggestive objects or pictures in the workplace.

◇ Telling dirty jokes or making indecent gestures.

◇ Using such familiar terms as *honey*, *dear*, or *baby*.

◇ Asking questions about an employee's sex life.

◇ Offering descriptions of the harasser's own sexual conduct or experiences.

◇ Giving leering looks, whistles, or catcalls.

◇ Making unsolicited and unwelcome sexual advances or propositions.

◇ Making unwelcome physical contact, such as patting, pinching, touching, hugging, and kissing.

◇ Exposing genitalia.

◇ Committing physical or sexual assault, including rape.

Sexual harassment may be a much bigger problem in the workplace than many employers realize. Victims are often reluctant to file a complaint because they fear reprisals and ridicule. And in the majority of sexual-harassment cases the victim receives little more than job reinstatement and back pay, despite the fact that the Civil Rights Act of 1991 allows victims to sue for additional, punitive damages.

WHEN YOU ARE THE EMPLOYER

Employers are well advised to establish a clearly stated policy concerning sexual harassment. You should circulate a written list of unacceptable behaviors and outline the steps an employee can take to bring a harassment complaint to your attention. Every employee should know what punishment your company will administer to anyone who commits sexual harassment.

IF YOU ARE ACCUSED OF HARASSMENT

The burden of proof in sexual harassment cases lies with the person who brought the complaint. If she has little or no documentation or corroborating testimony, the case may become a "swearing contest"—one person's word against the other's. The best defense against a sexual-harassment charge is to behave in accordance with the EEOC guidelines and have witnesses who will testify that you do.

STEPS TO TAKE IF YOU ARE HARASSED

First of all, try to confront the offender directly and insist that he (or she) end the harassing behavior. He may not realize that you find the behavior offensive. Or write him a letter explaining your objection to his actions. If this approach fails, do the following:

1. Tell your supervisor. If the supervisor is the offender, take your complaint to his superior or your employer's director of personnel or human resources.

2. If the behavior continues, or if you are not satisfied with your employer's remedy, call the nearest office of the Equal Employment Opportunity Commission. You can find the telephone number by calling the Federal Information Center listed on page 225. Your state's civil rights commission may also be able to help you.

3. Be sure to document any instances of harassment. Keep a log of the dates and times that they took place. If other employees are being harassed or have witnessed your harassment, ask for their assistance in pursuing your claim.

4. If the harassment has caused you financial loss or great distress, consider filing a lawsuit against your harasser and employer. You should have the advice of an attorney experienced in labor law. See also DATE RAPE; EMPLOYEE RIGHTS.

ABC's

OF SPOTTING A SHOPLIFTER

If you are a shopkeeper or employee, be aware that the most effective way to combat shoplifting is through good customer service. Approaching as many customers as you can in a friendly way reduces theft, because shoplifters hate to be noticed. To spot a potential shoplifter, keep an eye out for shoppers who:

❑ Wander aimlessly around the store or drop merchandise on the floor. These "browsers" may be looking for an opportunity to conceal merchandise when no one is looking.

❑ Avoid sales personnel and other shoppers. It is easier to shoplift in isolated areas, and many shoplifters choose a time when customer traffic is slow and clerks are distracted by other duties, such as taking inventory.

❑ Wear loose-fitting garments or carry oversize packages. Be especially wary of shoppers wearing long or heavy overcoats on a summer day. Shoplifters may also use packages with spring-loaded false bottoms, which they can place over an item and carry out of the store. You can cut down on the use of these ploys by asking customers to leave their packages at the checkout area.

❑ Seem especially nervous. Shoplifters are always on the lookout for sales personnel, store detectives, and other shoppers. A shopper who spends more time watching others than examining the merchandise may be a shoplifter.

SHOPLIFTING

Jennifer was working at her part-time job as a sales clerk for a department store when she noticed a nervous-looking man near the jewelry counter. Jennifer was astonished to see the man place several pieces of costume jewelry in his jacket pocket. She quickly alerted a coworker, who notified the store's security staff. But before the security guards could arrive, the man headed for the exit.

Jennifer ran to the exit and closed the door to prevent him from leaving. Moments later the security guards escorted the man to the manager's office and Jennifer called the police. Despite the man's protests that he had intended to pay for the items, the police charged him with shoplifting.

While most states allow a shopkeeper to detain a suspected shoplifter, it is always better to have the assistance of the police, both for the safety of the store employees and to minimize or prevent later claims of false imprisonment or assault and battery.

In most states a person who

is discovered concealing store merchandise may be found guilty of shoplifting — even though he never left the store. All state laws require store owners to tell a suspected shoplifter why he is being detained. But the laws of some two-thirds of the states allow shop owners, employees, or security personnel to detain and question someone they suspect of shoplifting—even if he later proves to be innocent — without being held liable for slander, false arrest, false imprisonment, or malicious prosecution. If the innocent shopper sues the store, he has the burden of proving that the owner acted unreasonably.

In the remaining third of the states, the law favors the shopper, and the burden of proof falls to the shop owner, who must show that his actions in detaining the innocent shopper were reasonable. Check the laws in your state. See FALSE ARREST; FALSE IMPRISONMENT.

SIDEWALK

When a public sidewalk adjoins privately owned real estate, the private-property owner usually has several legal responsibilities. For example, she must report any damaged sections of the sidewalk to the city as soon as she notices them. She must also bear at least some of the cost of the repair, because the sidewalk benefits the property owner more than it does the public at large. In fact, homes in areas with sidewalks are usually valued somewhat higher than those in areas without them.

If you have a private sidewalk, such as a paved path that leads from the street or driveway to your front door, you must keep it in good repair. If you know that your private sidewalk is cracked or broken, you can be held responsible for any injuries a visitor may suffer, unless you put up a warning sign or place a barricade around the broken area.

Homeowners are responsible for clearing snow and ice from private sidewalks and walkways that are used by the public. In some states the law gives homeowners 24 hours after the snow has stopped falling to clear their sidewalks. If an owner waits longer or does a poor job and someone slips on her sidewalk, she will be held liable, even if she was out of town when it snowed. If you own property that is adjacent to a public walkway, it is a good idea to arrange for a neighbor or a hired helper to clear your sidewalk in your absence. See also ACCIDENTS IN THE HOME.

SIMULTANEOUS DEATH ACT

An airplane or automobile crash, an explosion, or a natural disaster may result in the death of a husband and wife or an entire family at the same time. One of the legal problems created by these situations is how to distribute their estates. For example, if a couple dies in a sailing accident with no surviving witnesses and no other evidence that one of them died after the other, the court must decide who died first in order to determine whose will takes effect first.

If the husband left his estate to his wife and the court rules that he died before she did, his estate would pass to his deceased wife, and her estate would then be passed along according to the terms laid out in her will.

In an effort to resolve the problem that arises when death appears to be simultaneous, almost every state has enacted legislation to cover simultaneous deaths.

As of 1993 every one of the states except Ohio, Louisiana, and Montana had adopted the Uniform Simultaneous Death Act (USDA). This act allows that in the case of simultaneous death the court will distribute the property of the deceased as if each person had survived the other. For example, John and Mary were killed together in an automobile crash. They had prepared wills leaving the bulk of their estates to each other, but like most people they had made no special provision for what would happen if they died at the same time. Thus, the court applied the USDA as follows: Since John was presumed to have survived Mary and Mary was presumed to have survived John, their individual property and one-half of their jointly owned property were distributed to other legatees designated in their wills.

See also COMMUNITY PROPERTY.

The USDA goes into effect only if there is no proof as to who died first. If the death certificates had indicated that Mary survived John by even two minutes, for example, the act would not apply.

To avoid any legal confusion or misunderstanding among family members, you can include a provision specifying what should happen to your property should you and your spouse die simultaneously. Similar provisions should be included in insurance policies, living trusts, and deeds. See also PROBATE; WILL.

SMALL BUSINESS

Today more and more Americans are working for small businesses or establishing their own. Whether you are an entrepreneur or you work for a small business, you will find the following articles useful and informative: HOME BUSINESS; INCOME TAX; INDEPENDENT CONTRACTOR; INDIVIDUAL RETIREMENT ACCOUNT; JOB DISCRIMINATION; KEOGH PLAN; LICENSE; RETIREMENT PLANNING; SELF-EMPLOYMENT; SMALL-CLAIMS COURT; SOCIAL SECURITY.

SMALL-CLAIMS COURT

Small-claims courts were created to help people with relatively minor disputes avoid long and costly litigation. In most states the maximum amount of money a small-claims court can award is between $1,000 and $5,000. From time to time these limits are increased; you can find out the limits in your state by calling the court. If your claim is only slightly above the maximum, consider reducing it to fit within the legal limit rather than hiring a lawyer and incurring the extra expense of bringing suit in another court.

Because the procedures in a small-claims court are far less complex than in regular courts, the parties to a lawsuit usually represent themselves. A decision is rendered after one short hearing, typically completed in 15 minutes or less. Appeal rights are limited, and judges tend to base their decisions on what seems fair in the individual case and not on legal technicalities or precedents.

The following problems are typical of those that you would be able to resolve in a small-claims court:

◇ Your landlord fails to return your security deposit after you move.

◇ The attendant in a park-

SMALL-CLAIMS COURT LIMITS

The maximum amount for which you can file suit in small-claims court is established by state law. To find out whether any of the limits listed below have changed, check with the county clerk at your local courthouse.

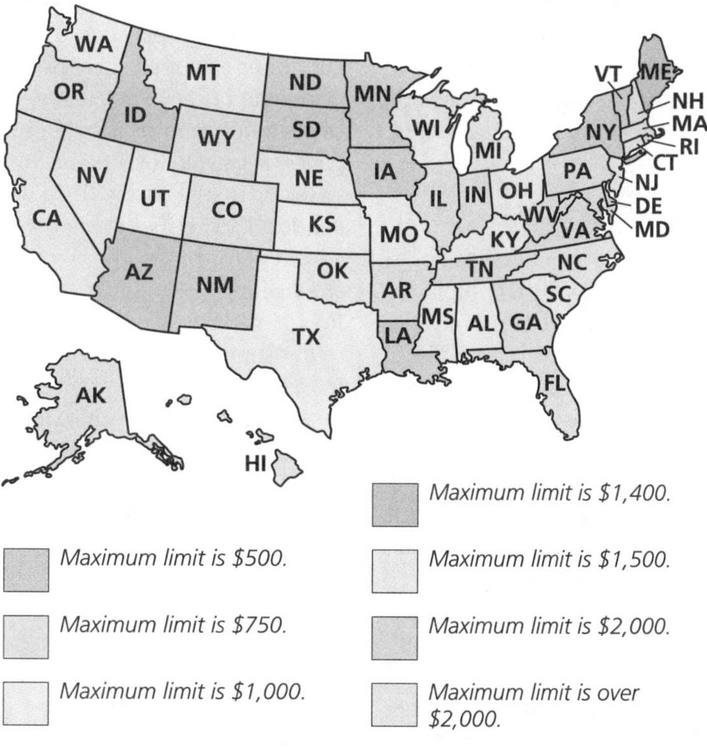

ing garage damages your car.

◇ A store will not replace a defective product you bought.

◇ A company owes you money for freelance work you did and will not pay you.

◇ You paid for auto repairs, but your car is still not fixed.

◇ You want your dry cleaner to pay for the suede jacket she ruined.

◇ You were bitten by the neighbor's dog and you want reimbursement for medical treatment.

JURISDICTION

Small-claims courts can usually order people to pay only money damages. They cannot order "specific performance"—that is, they cannot order the person you are suing to give you a particular piece of property or perform a particular act. Nor can small-claims courts grant injunctions forbidding an action. For these types of judgments, you must file a lawsuit in district court.

FILING AND SERVING YOUR COMPLAINT

To initiate a small-claims action, you must file a complaint, which you can obtain from the small-claims court clerk. The form is usually short and fairly straightforward. It asks for your name and address, the name and address of the defendant, the amount of your claim, and a brief explanation of your complaint.

If you have questions about completing the form, the court clerk can probably help you. Since small-claims cases are usually handled without lawyers, clerks are accustomed to dealing with questions about procedures.

File your claim as soon as possible, especially if you are bringing witnesses to testify for you. Every state sets limits on the period of time in which you can file a lawsuit, and if you exceed it, your claim may be dismissed. In California, for example, the time limit on personal-injury actions is one year from the date of the injury, while in Texas it is two years. Your local library should have information on your state's laws, or you can check with the court clerk to find out the statute of limitations in your state.

SERVICE OF PROCESS

An essential step in filing any lawsuit is notifying the defendant about the case so that he has the opportunity to defend himself. The notification consists of the complaint and a summons to appear in court at a specified time. The current trend among states is to allow process service for small-claims cases by mail. Usually the clerk sends it by certified mail, return receipt requested. You pay the mailing fee and the filing fee charged by the court.

In other states a sheriff or marshal will serve the papers, or you may be able to hire a private process server. Either way the fee for process service is usually around \$20. Some states allow any adult who is not a party to the lawsuit to serve the papers, but you cannot serve the papers yourself.

The rules about service vary considerably from state to state, so be sure to follow carefully whatever procedures apply in your court. You should be aware of some general rules:

◇ You must have the defendant served within a certain number of days before your trial is to be held. If the defendant gets less than the minimum notice, he is entitled to a postponement.

◇ The defendant must be served directly. The summons cannot be left with his spouse, child, or anyone else who answers the door.

◇ If the defendant is a corporation, some states allow service to an employee; others require service to a corporate officer.

◇ Out-of-state corporations must have a registered agent to receive service in every state in which they do business. Your state's secretary of state can provide the name and address of the agent for the corporation you are suing. Most states allow the agent to be served by mail.

IF YOU ARE THE DEFENDANT

When you are served with a complaint, usually all you have to do is show up in court at the specified day and time, prepared to defend yourself. A few states require you to file a simple answer stating whether you plan to contest the case and why.

As part of your response to the plaintiff's charges, you may wish to file a counterclaim, especially if you suffered any injury or loss in the same accident or other incident cited by the plaintiff. If you do not file a counterclaim, you may lose your right to sue your opponent at some later date.

CHECKLIST

Alternatives to Small-Claims Court

Before you decide to file a small-claims lawsuit, consider some of the following alternatives. If none of these methods resolves your dispute, a small-claims lawsuit is appropriate.

❑ **ARBITRATION.**
Arbitration programs have become the standard way of resolving attorney-fee disputes and claims against dry cleaners, stockbrokers, and others. The decision of the arbitrator may or may not be binding on either party. Today many business contracts require that any disputes that arise must first be submitted to arbitration.

❑ **CONSUMER ACTION PANELS.**
Consumer action panels, known as CAP's, are industry-run programs for resolving disputes. The largest are AUTOCAP, run by automobile dealers, and MACAP, run by appliance dealers. These groups contact the manufacturer when they receive a consumer's written complaint, and a review board then recommends a solution. The board's decision is not binding on the consumer but is sometimes binding on the manufacturer.

❑ **CONSUMER ACTION AGENCIES.**
All states and many local governments have consumer action agencies that investigate individual disputes and try to mediate a settlement. In most states, however, the types of matters these agencies handle and the amount of effort they expend are limited.

❑ **MEDIA PROGRAMS.**
Some television and radio stations and newspapers have consumer hotlines. These programs prefer to feature problems that have dramatic potential, and although they are unable to investigate all the cases brought to their attention, they can be of great help if they decide to report on your problem. The threat of adverse publicity can change a merchant's attitude about a consumer problem very quickly.

❑ **MEDIATION.**
Mediation programs are run by courts, nonprofit groups, and private profit-making organizations. A mediator tries to get the opposing parties to reach a solution between themselves. The fact that the parties themselves, and not an outsider, make the final agreement is especially advantageous when the parties must continue dealing with each other.

❑ **COURT PROGRAMS.**
Many small-claims courts offer optional arbitration and mediation programs as alternatives to a full-fledged lawsuit.

Be aware that if your counterclaim is for an amount larger than the limit for small-claims court, it may move the whole case to a higher court.

OUT-OF-COURT SETTLEMENTS

The defendant may offer a settlement just before your case is scheduled to be heard. This frequently happens when you are suing a business. If you decide to accept the settlement, be sure to obtain your money on the spot or get a written settlement statement from the defendant. A signed settlement agreement is a legally enforceable contract. If you are unable to collect the money as promised by the defendant, you can sue for it in small-claims court without having to prove your original case. All you need to prove is that the defendant has breached his written promise to pay you. Aside from listing the terms of the settlement, the statement should also say that if your opponent defaults, he will pay for your collection expenses. Then, if you have to use a lawyer to collect, your opponent will have to reimburse you for the attorney's fees.

STATING YOUR CASE

If your case goes to trial, arrive early so that you can familiarize yourself with the court's procedures and make an assessment of the judge's personality. In most courts the clerk will call the roll of cases being presented that day, and you can get an idea of the time the judge will hear your case.

You do not have to wear business attire at small-claims court, but being neat and conservatively dressed is an asset.

Remember that the judge and your opponent may want to question you or your witnesses. Be sure your witnesses are familiar with your claims and are prepared for whatever counterclaims you think the defendant might make. When your turn comes, state your case clearly and succinctly. Nobody expects you to be an expert on the law or have the presentation skills of a trial lawyer. The judge will ask you questions and guide you along to elicit the information she needs.

When you have presented your case, introduce any pertinent documents or witnesses that support it. Do not insist on covering points with which the judge already appears to be familiar. Be polite and do not interrupt the defendant or his witnesses. Be especially careful not to interrupt the judge.

JUDGMENT

In many small-claims courts a decision is not announced immediately. Instead, the parties are notified by mail within a few days. Most judgments are tax-free except for awards of lost wages, which are not. If the judge makes her decision in your presence and you are found at fault, you can petition her to be allowed to pay the plaintiff in installments. If the decision is to come in the mail and you fear that you will lose, you can ask the judge to let you pay the plaintiff over a period of time.

Decisions in small-claims courts are rarely appealed. Some states do not allow appeals at all, while others allow only defendants to appeal. An appeal usually results in a new trial in county or district court. In more than 20 states a mistake in the application of the law is the only basis for an appeal (for example, when the judge refuses to order the return of a security deposit to which you are legally entitled). Misunderstanding the facts of the case is not grounds for an appeal. Since there are no written transcripts in small-claims courts, and since judges do not write opinions explaining their decisions, it is very difficult to appeal on a matter of law. See APPEAL; COURTS; JUDGMENT.

SMALL-BUSINESS CLAIMS

Small-claims court is not just for individuals. Increasingly, such small businesses as painting contractors and retail shops are turning to the small-claims courts as a way to speed collections from customers who default on their bills. If you own a small business, you may want to consider using small-claims court as a way to reduce attorney fees and avoid the delays of filing suit in district court. However, if your business is incorporated, some states require that you have an attorney represent you, and some states limit the number of small-claims actions you can bring in a single year. In Kansas, for example, a plaintiff may file a maximum of five suits per year. Check with your small-claims court clerk for your state's specific rules for small businesses.

SMOKING

As medical research continues to expose the health risks of smoking, both to smokers and to people around them, the legal restrictions on smoking have multiplied. For example, the Federal Aviation Administration has banned smoking on all domestic commercial flights of less than six hours, and most states prohibit smoking in government office buildings, elevators, public libraries, and theaters.

Every state prohibits minors from purchasing tobacco products. Persons who are found guilty of selling or giving tobacco products to minors may be fined \$50 to \$500. Legislation has also been proposed to outlaw cigarette vending machines, which, because they are unsupervised, are a prime source of tobacco products for young people.

Because of rising health insurance costs, many employers now prohibit smoking in the workplace. Legally, smokers are not a "protected class," and the employer's right to limit or forbid smoking in the workplace does not violate constitutional guarantees against discrimination. Some courts have upheld employers who fired workers for refusing to obey a company ban on smoking. See EQUAL PROTECTION OF THE LAWS.

Some employers have even begun to require employees to give up their smoking habit altogether. Courts have held that employers may refuse to hire a smoker who will not quit without fear of being sued for unlawful discrimination.

SOBRIETY CHECKPOINT

As part of their efforts to curb drunk driving, many state law enforcement agencies set up

REAL LIFE, REAL LAW

The Case of the Smoker's Lawsuit

Rose Cippilone smoked several packs of cigarettes a day for years before developing lung cancer. When her disease was diagnosed, she filed a lawsuit against the manufacturers of the brands of cigarettes she smoked, claiming the companies knew of the dangers of smoking long before the government required warning labels on cigarette packages. The companies argued that by complying with the federal laws requiring health warnings on cigarette packages, they were immune from prosecution. Mrs. Cippilone died during the course of her lawsuit, but her heirs continued to pursue the matter. The trial court awarded $400,000 to the plaintiff, but that verdict was overturned on appeal, and the case made its way to the U.S. Supreme Court.

In a 7–2 decision, the Supreme Court held that the company's compliance with the federal labeling requirements did not protect it from a lawsuit based on claims of fraud, misrepresentation, or conspiracy. However, the court further stated that in order to win a lawsuit against a tobacco company, the plaintiff would have to prove (1) that she relied on the tobacco company's misrepresentations of the dangers of smoking, as evidenced, for example, in its advertisements or public relations campaigns, and (2) that the plaintiff was without personal fault for beginning and continuing to smoke—that peer pressure to smoke had been irresistible, for instance. After issuing these new legal guidelines, the Supreme Court remanded the Cippilone case back to trial court.

sobriety checkpoints, or roadblocks, usually on weekends and holidays. Sometimes the police announce that checkpoints are being set up without saying where they will be. Officers stop vehicles at the checkpoint area ostensibly to check driver's licenses and vehicle registration papers. While so doing, an officer can observe the driver's behavior for signs of intoxication. Stopping cars at roadblocks, however, raises the question of unreasonable search and seizure, which is prohibited by the Fourth Amendment. In reviewing sobriety checkpoint cases, courts look at such factors as how long each motorist was detained, whether the location and time interfered with the regular flow of traffic or created hazards for motorists, whether motorists were given advance warning that checkpoints were being set up, whether there were signs at the checkpoint explaining its purpose, and whether the police chose to stop the vehicles arbitrarily or according to a predetermined pattern, such as every second, third, or fourth approaching car.

The U.S. Supreme Court has upheld the government's right to make checkpoint stops. In reviewing a Michigan law authorizing sobriety checkpoints, the Court said that the slight intrusion on a driver's privacy was more than balanced by the government's interest in preventing drunk driving. But some state constitutions take a narrower view of the government's interest and prohibit sobriety checkpoints.

Generally most courts will admit evidence of drunk driving obtained from a sobriety checkpoint if the procedure to stop motorists was minimally intrusive. See also DRUNK DRIVING.

SOCIAL SECURITY

Established by Congress in 1935 in response to the financial ruin that many families experienced during the Great Depression, the Social Security Act provides retirement, disability, and survivors benefits for qualified workers and their families. These benefits are administered by the Social Security Administration. With 1,300 branches across the country, the agency also administers Medicare and Supplemental Security Income (SSI). In 1993 more than 40 million Americans received monthly Social Security payments, most of which were retirement and survivors benefits. See also AID TO FAMILIES WITH DEPENDENT CHILDREN; MEDICARE; SUPPLEMENTAL SECURITY INCOME.

FUNDING SOCIAL SECURITY

The funds for Social Security are provided by workers, who pay taxes on their earnings, and employers, who contribute Federal Insurance Contribution Act (FICA) tax for each employee. In 1993 the maximum annual earnings on which tax could be assessed for retirement, disability, and death benefits were $57,600. The maximum for Medicare was $135,000. In 1993 the Social Security tax rate for employees was 6.2 percent of earnings, with a maximum payment of $3,571; for Medicare, the rate was 1.45 percent, or a top annual payment of $1,957. An equivalent amount is contributed by the worker's employer. These taxes are adjusted annually by the Social Security Administration. Self-employed workers pay a higher rate than employees do because no contribution is made for them by an employer. See also SELF-EMPLOYMENT.

Most employees pay Social Security taxes. The only exceptions are (1) workers covered by the Railroad Retirement System; (2) federal employees hired before January 1, 1984, who are covered by the Civil Service Retirement System; (3) some employees of state and local governments who have their own retirement programs; and (4) workers who have earned less than $2,350. See also RAILROAD RETIREMENT.

SOCIAL SECURITY NUMBER

Every person working in the United States is required to have a Social Security number. It is through your number that the Social Security Administration tracks your contributions and benefits. The Internal Revenue Service also requires that any dependents (that is, anyone for whom you provide primary financial support) listed on your income tax return must have a Social Security number. You should secure a number for each of your children no later than the end of the year they celebrate their first birthday. If you do not show this number on your tax return, you can incur a $50 penalty.

To obtain a Social Security number for the first time, apply to your local Social Security office and complete the application (Form SS-5). You will need to provide original documents showing your (or the child's) identity and age, and citizenship, immigrant, or nonimmigrant status.

ELIGIBILITY

In order to obtain insured status—that is, to be eligible to receive benefits when you retire or are disabled, or for your family to receive survivors benefits upon your death—you must accumulate 40 work credits. In 1993, a worker received one credit for each $590 of earnings. The maximum number of credits you can receive in one year is 4, no matter how much money you earn. For most workers under age 62, it takes about 10 years of work to earn 40 credits, although the work period may be interrupted. Having more than 40 credits will not increase the amount of Social Security benefits; that is calculated on the basis of the total amount of money you earned in your lifetime. Therefore, a company executive who has worked for 55 years and a part-time beautician who has worked sporadically but has still accumulated 40 quarters will both have insured status, but they will not receive the same benefits.

You will also be granted insured status if you have earned one credit each year since 1951 until you are 62. Thus, if you turned 62 in 1984, you need have accumulated only 33 work credits, as long as you earned at least 1 credit each year.

RETIREMENT BENEFITS

You can begin to collect limited retirement benefits at age 62, but you must be 65 before you can receive full benefits. In the year 2000 the age at which full benefits will be paid will rise gradually, so that by 2025 you will need to be 67 to receive full benefits.

The size of your monthly retirement benefit is based on the length of time you worked and paid into the Social Security program and the amount of money you earned during that period. However, there is a limit on benefits. In 1993 the maximum was set at $1,128 per month for an individual or $1,692 for a couple—even if both had insured status.

Your Social Security payments are not affected by any other income you receive from investments, savings, or insurance policies. However, your benefits are reduced if you earn wages above a certain maximum amount.

In 1993 retirees under age 65 could earn $7,680 annually without a reduction in their benefits. But for every $2 you earn above that amount, your benefits are reduced by $1. In 1993 retirees between the ages of 65 and 69 could earn up to $10,560 without having their Social Security payments reduced. For every $3 earned above that amount, Social Security payments are reduced by $1. Retirees who are 70 and older may earn as much as they like without any reduction in benefits.

If you are divorced from a worker who earned insured status during your marriage, and your marriage lasted 10 years or longer, you may be able to receive retirement benefits even if your spouse has remarried.

Social Security benefits became taxable for the first time in 1983. In 1992, if the total of your adjusted gross income—that is, your total income less adjustments for items such as self-employment tax and alimony—and one-half of your annual Social Security benefits exceeded $25,000 for an individual (or $32,000 for a couple filing a joint return), your annual benefits were subject to federal income tax, and in some states, to state income tax as well.

RECEIVING YOUR BENEFITS

It is a good idea to submit a Request for Earnings and Benefit Estimate Statement (form SSA-7004) to your local Social Security office every three years. You will receive your statement in about a month, and it will tell you what your Social Security benefit is projected to be and will show you the SSA's record of your earnings. Check your own W-2 forms or income tax returns to verify that the Social Security records are correct. If there happens to be an error, it can be corrected, but you must report it no more than 3 years, 3 months, and 15 days from the time you discover it.

With the benefit estimate statement, you will be able to calculate the relative advantages of taking your benefits at age 62 or 65. At present, if you begin to collect benefits at 62, your monthly payments will be 20 percent smaller than if you had waited until you were 65. Similarly, the longer you wait to retire after age 65, the larger your payments will be. If you turned 65 in 1992, for instance, your benefits would be 4 percent higher if you waited until you were 66 to retire. See also Retirement Planning.

SURVIVORS BENEFITS

The surviving spouse and the minor children of an insured worker can receive benefits when he dies, whether or not he reached retirement age, if he earned sufficient credits while working. Social Security provides a lump-sum payment of $255 to a deceased worker's spouse living with him at the time of his death or to children under 18. It pays monthly survivors benefits to dependents

ABC's

Of Your Social Security Records

To avoid delays when you apply for benefits, and to make sure you receive whatever benefits you are entitled to, make sure your Social Security records are up to date. Call or visit your local Social Security office:

❑ If you need to get a Social Security card for yourself or a family member or to replace one that has been lost, stolen, or destroyed.

❑ If a family member dies and you want to apply for survivors benefits.

❑ If you are now disabled, and you are likely to remain so for more than one year.

❑ If you change your name because of a divorce, marriage, adoption, or any other reason.

❑ If you are planning to retire. Apply at least three months in advance; if you apply later, you may have to wait several months before your first check arrives.

❑ Every three years, so that you can check Social Security's records of your income and estimated benefits.

who fall into one or more of the following categories:

◇ A widow or widower age 60 or older.

◇ A totally disabled widow or widower age 50 or older.

◇ A widow or widower of any age who is caring for a child under age 16 or a child who is disabled.

◇ Unmarried children under age 18.

◇ Children under 19 who are studying full time in an elementary or secondary school.

◇ Unmarried children 18 or older who are severely disabled, provided the disability started before the child was 22.

◇ Parents who depended on an insured worker for at least half of their basic support.

As with retirement benefits, even if you were divorced from a worker who has died, you may be eligible for survivors benefits if you are at least 60 years old (50 if disabled) and if your marriage lasted 10 years or more and the worker earned insured status while you were married.

If you are a dependent and you think you may be eligible for survivors benefits, contact your local Social Security office. You will have to provide a copy of the deceased person's death certificate and (to prove your relationship to him) a copy of your marriage certificate if you are a spouse or a copy of your birth certificate if you are a child.

DISABILITY BENEFITS

You may qualify for disability payments from Social Security if you suffer from a long-term or terminal illness, have a mental or physical disability, or are blind. Disability payments are also figured on the length of time you worked and paid into Social Security, as well as the amount of money you earned during that period. For a more detailed discussion, see DISABILITY INSURANCE.

RECEIVING YOUR BENEFITS

You should apply for Social Security benefits at least three months before you are entitled to start receiving them—it can take that long to process your claim. (If you are turning 65, apply for Medicare at this time, even if you are not going to receive retirement benefits.) Social Security will notify you by mail whether your claim for benefits has been accepted and the amount that you are entitled to receive.

APPEALING AN ASSESSMENT

If you disagree with the assessment of your benefits, you must file an appeal in writing within 60 days of the time you receive the notification. The Social Security Administration will notify you by mail whether your appeal has resulted in an adjustment of your benefits. If you are still unhappy with the decision, you can ask for an administrative hearing, which will be held at a Social Security office. As a last resort, you can hire a lawyer and take the matter to court.

DIRECT DEPOSIT

To avoid delays and to protect their checks from loss or theft, about one-third of all Social Security beneficiaries have their benefits deposited directly into their checking or savings accounts. To do so, you must complete form SF-1199 and ask your bank, savings and loan, or credit union to send it to the Social Security Administration. Once you are enrolled in the direct-deposit program, your bank is required to credit the deposit to your account on the same day it is received, and a record of the deposit will appear on your bank statement.

SOLE PROPRIETORSHIP

If you own your business, the simplest form of ownership is a sole proprietorship, even if you have employees. All you have to do to start a sole proprietorship is to obtain the licenses or permits required of any business by state and local laws. Then you must report business income and expenses to the Internal Revenue Service by completing Schedule C and attaching it to your form 1040. The business income will be taxed at the rate established for your filing status (depending on whether you are a single person, head of household, married filing jointly, or married filing a separate return). Usually you will have to file estimated tax returns and make quarterly payments to the IRS. In a few states you may also have to pay an unincorporated business tax, which is usually figured as a percentage of business income.

When you operate your business as a sole proprietorship,

you assume personal liability, or responsibility, for all of the activities of the business. For instance, if you borrow money for your business and cannot repay it, the lender will be able to obtain a judgment against you personally for the unpaid amount—that is, he may be able to attach your personal bank account or put a lien on your house. Similarly, if the goods or services you sell harm someone or damage his property, you may end up forfeiting your personal assets to compensate him.

To avoid this kind of liability, you may choose to form a corporation or a limited-liability company, which is permitted by law in several states. Keep in mind, however, that these business entities require more complex accounting and reporting procedures than a sole proprietorship. See also CORPORATION; HOME BUSINESS; INDEPENDENT CONTRACTOR; LIMITED-LIABILITY COMPANY; PARTNERSHIP; SELF-EMPLOYMENT.

SOVEREIGN IMMUNITY

Under the common-law system, "the king (or sovereign) could do no wrong," and the only way a person could bring a lawsuit against the government was with the government's consent. Needless to say, the state did not give up this "sovereign immunity" lightly.

Over the years, however, federal, state, and local governments have established procedures allowing individuals to bring suit against them in specific cases. Today a private citizen who suffers personal injuries or property damage at the hands of a government agency or its employees can usually file a claim.

Chances are that the procedure will be complicated, and the compensation you receive may be limited. Furthermore, many state and local governments allow only a short time for filing a claim, after which you lose your right to file.

Suppose Laura twisted her foot when she stepped in a pothole, injuring her spine. She wants to sue the city in which she lives for her medical expenses. However, to prevent endless lawsuits of this type, the city has a law stating that the city can be found negligent only if it received written notice of a pothole and neglected to repair it. If anyone had reported that pothole and the city had not repaired it within a reasonable time, Laura could have sued, but because no one reported the pothole, Laura cannot sue the city.

There are similar limits on the types of lawsuits that individuals can file against the federal government. Under the Federal Tort Claims Act, you cannot sue the U.S. government for libel, fraud, battery, or other intentional wrongdoings, although you can sue for negligence on the part of government employees. If you believe you are the victim of government negligence or intentional wrongdoing, consult a lawyer who practices in the field of tort law. See also ACCIDENTS ON GOVERNMENT PROPERTY; NEGLIGENCE; TORT.

SPEECH, FREEDOM OF

The right to speak freely and without fear of prosecution by the federal government is guaranteed by the First Amendment. Similar protection from state governments is offered by the 14th Amendment. In effect, freedom of speech means that a person may express his views in any forum he wishes without fear of government reprisal or censorship. For instance, if Noel wants to appear on television talk shows or give speeches condemning the government for its foreign policy in Central America, he is within his rights to do so.

The 1st and 14th Amendments apply only to the government. Private companies, foundations, and other nongovernmental bodies may restrict the free speech of others without violating these amendments. For example, if a corporation fires an employee for publicly speaking out against corporate policy, it is within its rights. Private companies can also require employees and contractors to sign confidentiality agreements as a condition of employment. See also WHISTLE-BLOWER.

EXCEPTIONS

The right to free speech is not absolute. Just as the government may legitimately prohibit the distribution of printed matter that is obscene, violates national security, or libels another person, it may also place restrictions on oral statements that people can make in public. See also DEFAMATION.

Students and prisoners, for example, are permitted freedom of speech only as long as their speech does not interfere with discipline and order in their respective institutions. Statements that slander another person are punishable under the law. Similarly, the government can prohibit speech that is obscene or that presents a "clear and present danger" to the public. For instance, a speaker at a public gathering who urges the crowd to attack the police there can be arrested. If, however, the speaker merely rails against police brutality, he is protected by the guarantee of free speech.

Individuals do not have the right to make statements that harm the welfare of a nation, such as those that breach national security or advocate concrete steps to overthrow the government, although they may support revolution in an abstract way.

The government may also restrict its own employees' right to speak to some extent. A government worker with access to sensitive documents—such as those concerning national security or containing trade secrets—can be prohibited from disclosing the contents of those documents in public. And an agency such as the CIA, which deals with issues of national security, can require former employees to refrain from discussing or publishing information they obtained during the course of their employment without the agency's approval. See also PRIOR RESTRAINT.

TEACHERS

A public school teacher's right to free speech is limited in some respects. In general, teachers may express their views on political or historical events. However, a teacher cannot present views in a classroom that deny known facts. He may not teach that the Holocaust never happened or that the United States was the first country to send a satellite into orbit, for example. In addition, a teacher may not make statements that disrupt the running of the school or interfere with the educational process.

COMMERCIAL SPEECH

State and federal governments can place reasonable limitations on commercial speech, such as that in television or radio commercials. For example, the Federal Communications Commission has banned television and radio advertisements for cigarettes and liquor.

However, unreasonable regulation is not permitted. For instance, state laws preventing a physician from advertising his fees have been disallowed. The court found that the public's right to this information outweighs the state's right to prohibit professionals from advertising, provided the advertisements are truthful.

SYMBOLIC SPEECH

The constitutional protection of freedom of speech is not limited to the spoken word. The U.S. Supreme Court has consistently upheld the right of individuals to symbolic speech, actions that communicate an idea. For example, at one time laws prohibited the display of red banners that symbolized the anarchist movement, but in the 1930's these laws were held to be unconstitutional. In 1992 the U.S. Supreme Court held that laws against the desecration or mutilation of the American flag were unconstitutional. Such activities, although they are offensive and abhorrent to many people, are nonetheless a legitimate form of symbolic speech protected by the Constitution. See also CENSORSHIP; FLAG, U.S.; LIBEL AND SLANDER; PRESS, FREEDOM OF.

SPEEDING TICKET

You have had a terrible day. Your alarm clock did not go off, and you overslept. Then, to make up for lost time, you drove 50 miles an hour in a 40-mile-per-hour zone on your way to work, and soon saw a flashing light in your rearview mirror. The speeding ticket you got is going to cost you three points on your driver's license and a $100 fine.

CALCULATING SPEED

Police officers calculate a car's speed using a radar instrument or a speed trap. A car's speed obtained by a radar instrument is considered reliable evidence by the courts, so if such evidence indicates you exceeded the speed limit, you will probably be found guilty of speeding.

In a speed trap, the police time cars as they enter and exit a measured section of road. By knowing the length of the section of road and the time the car took to travel across it, they can calculate the car's speed. Courts consider this method to be less reliable than radar.

CONSEQUENCES OF SPEEDING

The consequences of speeding vary from state to state, but they can be severe—particularly if you have a record of repeated offenses or have greatly exceeded the speed limit. At the very least, you will probably be fined, the offense will be entered into your permanent driving record, and you will have points assessed against your driver's license. Your insurance rates can also be raised, and eventually your insurer may cancel your coverage. See also DRIVER'S LICENSE.

If you are caught speeding repeatedly or have accumulated a certain number of points on your license, the judge may order you to attend driving school, or he may suspend or revoke your license. In addition, most states have reciprocity agreements, whereby out-of-state speeding violations are entered on your driving record in your home state.

When you receive a speeding ticket, you may either contest it or pay the fine. If you do neither, the fine will be increased and you will receive a summons to pay it. If you choose to ignore the summons, your car may be towed away and impounded, and a warrant may be issued for your arrest.

Finally, speeding or otherwise driving recklessly may increase your liability in an accident. See also NEGLIGENCE.

CHALLENGING A TICKET

It is seldom easy to challenge a speeding ticket, especially if you have no witnesses. An officer's word is more likely than yours to have credibility with the court. Challenges to speeding tickets are usually heard in a traffic court by a judge, rather than a jury. You do not need an attorney if you are challenging a ticket for the first time, but if you face revocation of your license or a large increase in your insurance rates, you should hire a lawyer.

One way to challenge a ticket is to discredit the way the police determined your speed. If the police officer used radar, for example, your lawyer might ask him about his training in using radar equipment, the working condition of the radar equipment, and whether there was other traffic between the radar beam and your car.

If your defense is that your car's speedometer was not operating properly, you should have it repaired before you go to court and present the mechanic's receipt to the judge. Although having a faulty speedometer is not a valid defense against speeding, you may be able to convince the judge to be more lenient. See also TRAFFIC TICKET.

RADAR DETECTORS

If you are tempted to install a radar detector in your car, be sure you know your state laws. In a few states you may be fined if you are caught with a radar detector.

SPORTING EQUIPMENT

The manufacturers of sporting goods have frequently been held responsible for players' injuries when their products proved defective. For example, a football-helmet manufacturer was held liable because a player was injured when he was struck in the chest by another player's helmet. Manufacturers have also had to compensate players for injuries suffered because the helmets did not offer the protection that could reasonably be expected.

If the coach or organizer of a sports event knew that the equipment used was inadequate, he too may be held liable for any resulting injuries. Today most sports equipment carries labels with extensive warnings about proper use.

SPORTING EVENT

When you are a spectator or a participant in a sport, you have certain rights and you assume certain risks.

SPECTATOR SPORTS

Jack has bought a good seat for a professional basketball game. Just as he is settling down, one of the players chasing a loose ball bounds into the crowd and crashes into Jack, who suffers a broken leg. Can Jack sue the arena operator? No, nor can he sue the player who crashed into him. The law presumes that when spectators attend sporting events they are assuming the risk of being injured at the game. This is especially true in Jack's case, since he bought a courtside seat.

When you attend a sporting event, the operator of the arena is not obligated to ensure your absolute safety from a game-related injury, but he is liable for injuries you suffer if reasonable precautions could have prevented them. That is why screens are erected behind home plate at baseball stadiums and shatterproof glass barriers are put up at hockey rinks. If the arena operator fails to provide such protection and you are injured, you can sue. See ACCIDENTS IN PUBLIC PLACES.

When you buy a ticket for a reserved seat at a sporting event, you have an enforceable contract. If someone else is sitting in your seat and refuses to leave, you can ask the arena management to move her. But if the management does not respond, you are entitled only to a refund of the price printed on the ticket, even if you bought it from a ticket broker at a premium. The same refund policy applies in the event that the game is canceled.

Many cities and states prohibit scalping—selling tickets for more than the box office price. If caught, scalpers can be fined or sent to jail.

PARTICIPATING IN SPORTS

When you participate in a sport, you assume the risk of being injured during the normal course of play. For example, you cannot sue the operators of your neighborhood softball league if you break your ankle while sliding into second base, nor can you sue the outfielder of the other team if his throw to the second baseman hits you in the head. But if the second baseman goes into a rage and punches you because your hit drove in the winning run, you can file suit against him for your injuries, since his behavior is not a natural consequence of your participation in the game and you could not have reasonably expected it.

MINORS

When young people participate in sports, their parents are asked to sign a waiver excusing the sports operators from liability. Generally these waivers have no real legal effect except to put the parents on notice of the potential injuries that their children could suffer. Coaches, operators, or sponsors are responsible for an injury only if it resulted from their negligence. Suppose your child told his coach that he had sprained his ankle, but the coach sent him back onto the field anyway and

REAL LIFE, REAL LAW

The Case of the Injured Goalie

Although participants in sporting events assume some risks, if a player is injured through another player's reckless conduct, he may successfully sue for damages.

Julian, playing goalkeeper for his soccer team, was kneeling in the "penalty area" in front of the goal when David, an opposing player, entered the area and kicked Julian in the head. Julian suffered severe and permanent head and brain injuries, and he filed suit against David. The trial court found that Julian had assumed the risk of being injured by voluntarily participating in the game and dismissed the lawsuit. Julian appealed this decision, and the appellate court overturned the lower court's ruling. The appellate court noted that the soccer game had been organized and supervised by trained officials and was being played under a standard body of rules. One of these rules prohibits a player from making contact with a goalkeeper in possession of the ball in the penalty area. Several witnesses had testified that Julian was holding the ball when David kicked him. The court held that Julian had taken ordinary care for his own safety and had no reason to expect that David would violate a well-known rule of the game.

Taking all of this into account, the appellate court held that players in an organized sporting event have a legal duty to every other player not to violate a recognized safety rule. The appellate court remanded the case to the lower court for retrial.

the sprain was aggravated. The league and the coach could be held liable, because no reasonably prudent person would knowingly let a child continue playing with a sprained ankle. Even if you had signed a waiver of liability, neither the coach nor the league would be relieved of responsibility. See CONSENT FORM.

PROHIBITED SPORTS

State and local governments have the right to prohibit certain so-called sporting events, such as bullfighting, cockfighting, or bare-knuckle prize fights, because these events violate public policy against cruel treatment of animals and extremely violent activities. Attendance at an outlawed event is a crime, and you can be subject to a fine, imprisonment, or both if you organize, participate in, or attend such an event.

STATES' RIGHTS

The 50 states of the United States have many of the powers that are held by an independent country. States have the right, among other things, to establish their own judicial courts; to set standards for doctors, lawyers, and other professionals; to provide police protection for their residents; and to enact zoning regulations to govern the use of property within their boundaries. However, the same document that grants states their rights and powers also binds them in an indestructible union. Each state must comply with all federal laws and regulations. Furthermore, the Constitution permits only Congress and the president the power to declare war, enter into treaties, or print currency.

The Constitution ensures that the rulings and actions of each state are respected by the others. Article IV of the Constitution declares that the official and legitimate acts of one state government must be recognized by every other state. Thus a criminal conviction by a court in Georgia must be recognized as valid by the government of Florida, Alabama, or any other state. Similarly, marriages and divorces, civil judgments, and other actions authorized by one state must receive official recognition from all other states. This reciprocity is known as "full faith and credit."

Article IV also requires states to extend all "privileges and immunities" they offer their own residents to the residents of other states. This means that a state may not prohibit the residents of other states from owning property within its boundaries or from bringing lawsuits in its courts, nor can it deny them the protections of state law.

Although the Constitution grants states the power to make their own laws, it limits that power through the "supremacy clause" found in Article VI. This provision states that federal law takes precedence over any contradictory laws enacted by a state. If a state enacted legislation establishing Hinduism as its official religion and prohibited Muslims from practicing their faith, the law would be unenforceable, since the Constitution guarantees freedom of religion to all U.S. citizens.

STATUTE OF LIMITATIONS

All the states and the federal government have laws known as statutes of limitations, which limit the time period within which a civil lawsuit or criminal charge must be filed. Failure to comply with a statute of limitations means that a plaintiff loses her right to file suit or that the government loses its right to prosecute a criminal suspect. There is one important exception: no statute of limitations exists for murder.

Every civil and criminal offense has its own statute of limitations, which can vary widely from state to state. In most states, for example, a civil lawsuit for breach of a sales contract must be brought within four years, but in others you may have as long as six years, and in Louisiana you have only one year. A charge of embezzlement must usually be prosecuted within three years, but this statute of limitations also varies from state to state.

One purpose of the statutes of limitations is to prevent potential plaintiffs from "sitting on their rights" while memories surrounding the controversy grow dim and witnesses move away or die. They also allow potential defendants to go on with their lives without having to worry indefinitely that a lawsuit may be filed as the result of some long-ago occurrence.

In the area of criminal law, the statute of limitations prevents prosecutors from conducting open-ended investigations of people whom they suspect of committing a crime, but whom they cannot formally accuse because there is insufficient evidence.

STATUTORY RAPE

Statutory rape is the crime of having sexual intercourse with a female under a certain age, even if she consents. The offense is called statutory rape because it is rape only by legal definition. Force is not an issue, because an underage child is not legally qualified to give her consent. In some states sexual intercourse with an underage male is not a crime. Although such laws may appear to be discriminatory, the U.S. Supreme Court has ruled that they are not.

The age of consent is set by state law. In some states it is as low as 10 years, while in others it is as high as 18 years. Some state laws also define statutory rape as having sexual relations with a woman who is mentally incapable of giving consent, regardless of her age.

Certain circumstances may absolve a man accused of the crime. If he can show that he made a reasonable mistake about the age of a willing sexual partner, the charge may be dropped in some states. But in most states, mistaking the child's age is not a valid defense, although a judge or jury might take the mistake into account in sentencing.

In some states, charges for statutory rape cannot be made if the minor had previously engaged in sexual relations, or in legal terminology, was not "of previously chaste character." See also RAPE; SEXUAL ABUSE.

STEPPARENT

Donna married Paul about a year after the death of his first wife. He had two small children, both under four years of age when they married, and Donna quit her job in order to be a full-time mother to them. Seven years later, when Paul filed for divorce, he told Donna she would have no visitation or custody rights over the children whom she had come to love as her own. Donna was devastated. Did she have any legal rights?

STEPPARENTS' RIGHTS AND DUTIES

Although there are millions of stepparent-stepchild relationships in the United States, many stepparents have no rights regarding their stepchildren if their marriages end, either by death or divorce.

In most states, when stepparents divorce, the legal parent is automatically granted custody of the children. If the legal parent abandoned the children or proved to be an unfit parent, the court might award custody to a stepparent, because that would be in the best interests of the children. However, it is not an easy task to prove that a parent is unfit, and the courts generally prefer to keep children with their biological parents to maintain the integrity of the family.

Similarly, a stepparent may lose custody of her stepchildren when her spouse dies and the surviving natural parent comes forward to claim custody. In such a case the stepparent must show that the surviving natural parent is unfit or has abandoned the children. Naming your spouse (the stepparent of your children) in your will as the children's legal guardian will have no effect if their surviving biological parent claims custody.

In the event of death or divorce, stepparents have more success when seeking visitation rights. Some states—including California, Kansas, Oregon, Tennessee, Virginia, and Wisconsin — have laws allowing visitation rights upon request, as long as this is in the best interests of the children. Courts in other states have granted stepparent visitation rights without such statutes, under their broad powers to execute orders that are in the children's best interests.

A number of states—including Illinois, Oregon, and South Dakota—require stepparents to help support their stepchildren. Other states—including Alaska and New York—require the stepparent to provide support only if the children would otherwise be receiving public assistance.

ADOPTION

Many stepparents adopt their stepchildren. When an adoption is final, the stepparent assumes all the legal rights and responsibilities of the relationship. If the noncustodial biological parent is still alive, the adoption ends his or her parental rights and responsibilities. The adoptive parent has a duty to support the child, even if the marriage later ends in divorce. See also ADOPTION.

WILLS AND PROBATE

Many stepparents have close and loving relationships with their stepchildren and wish to provide for them upon their death. If you are in this situation, you should be sure to specify what portion of your estate you wish to leave to your stepchild or stepchildren in your will. If you die intestate (without a will), your estate will be divided among your "heirs at law," and because stepchildren do not fall into this category, they cannot inherit from you. See also DYING WITHOUT A WILL; WILL.

SOCIAL SECURITY AND VETERANS BENEFITS

When a parent dies leaving minor children, the children are usually entitled to government payments, such as Social Security and veterans benefits. If you have stepchildren who reside in your household and depend upon you for support, they may be eligible to receive these benefits also. See SOCIAL SECURITY.

STOCKBROKER

If you want to buy stocks or bonds, you will probably have to use the services of a stockbroker—someone who acts as an intermediary for your purchases and sales of securities.

Before you do any business with a broker, check with your state's office of securities regulation to find out how long she has been licensed; how long she has been employed at her current firm; whether she or her firm has ever been sued or disciplined by a state or federal regulatory body; and whether her firm is facing any financial troubles that might influence her to sell you higher-risk investments or churn your account. It is advisable to do this even if the broker is working for a large, reputable brokerage house. See CHURNING.

Stockbrokers receive commissions on the sales and purchases of stock made through their services. Their fees range from about 1 to 5 percent. One way to pay lower fees is to use a discount broker instead of a full-service broker. Full-service brokers will advise you about market conditions, suggest when to buy or sell particular investments, and have a staff of analysts to help manage your portfolio. Discount brokers merely follow your instructions for buying and selling.

COMPLAINTS ABOUT STOCKBROKERS

Even if you choose a stockbroker carefully, problems may arise, especially if the broker's "sure thing" turns out to be a loser. In most cases any losses you suffer as a result of a broker's recommendation are yours to bear. But if the broker has violated the law or neglected his professional responsibility, you may be able to get some or all of your money back.

For example, if your broker has traded securities in your account without your permission or intentionally misrepresented an investment by failing to disclose information about a potential risk, she may be liable for your losses. Similarly, if your broker puts your money in high-risk investments when your investment needs dictate a safer, less risky portfolio, the broker might also be held responsible.

Most stockbrokerage agreements require you to use arbitration to resolve disputes with your broker. Although you do not need a lawyer to represent you in an arbitration hearing, if the amount of money at stake is considerable, you should probably hire an attorney experienced in alternative dispute resolution. Many lawyers accept such cases on a contingent-fee basis.

STEPS TO TAKE

If you have a complaint about the way your stockbroker has handled your account, follow these steps.

1. Talk to the broker immediately and notify her of your complaint. Keep detailed notes about the telephone conversation you have with her and any follow-up conversations about the complaint. Ask her to put her explanation in writing.

2. Follow up with a letter of your own summarizing your discussion. State the actions you expect her to take to remedy the situation, such as making good on any losses created by unauthorized trading in your account. Include a deadline for a response, such as two weeks, and send a copy of the letter to the broker's manager.

3. If you do not get a reply, write to the president of the firm. Restate your complaint and the actions you want taken, and include copies of your previous correspondence.

4. If you still do not receive a response, or if you are dissatisfied with the response you do receive, contact the Securities and Exchange Commission and your state's office of securities regulation. Enclose copies of your correspondence with all the parties involved.

STOCKS AND BONDS

Buying stocks and bonds is a traditional way of diversifying an investment portfolio. But before you make any purchases, you should be aware of the legal, as well as the monetary, considerations of these financial instruments.

STOCKS

When you buy stock in a corporation, you become, in effect, a part owner of the business. That is why stocks are often called equities; when you buy them, you obtain equity, or ownership, in the company. As a stockholder, you participate in the company's success or failure in proportion to your investment. Most stockholders own only a minute interest, or share, in the business. Nevertheless, all stockholders are entitled to vote (in proportion to the amount of stock they hold) on major issues that affect the company's management. They may also receive a

CHECKLIST

Stocks, Scams, and Swindles

Although the vast majority of stockbrokers and brokerage firms are honest and diligent in serving their customers, some brokers take advantage of an investor's trust. The following stock scams and swindles might affect you:

❑ **FALSIFYING YOUR NET WORTH.** When you open your brokerage account, you will be asked to provide personal financial information. If your net worth—that is, all the assets you have free of debts—is low, ethical brokers will not consider investing your money in risky investments such as junk bonds, options, or penny stocks. Be sure to fill in all the blank spaces on your new-account form. It is possible that a dishonest broker could falsify your net worth on your new-account form, and could put your limited funds into risky investments, which often earn him a higher commission. Be sure to review your new-account form for inaccuracy.

❑ **STEALING FROM YOUR ACCOUNT.** A broker who is in personal financial trouble may succeed in circumventing the many security safeguards to gain access to your account. Be sure that you carefully read your account statement each month and bring any discrepancies to the attention of the branch manager of the brokerage firm immediately.

❑ **CHURNING—MAKING FREQUENT, UNNECESSARY TRADES.** Brokers earn a commission whenever they buy or sell a stock. Therefore, the more stock trades they make, the greater their commission. Beware of brokers who call frequently advising you to make trades, particularly if they will generate little profit for your account. See CHURNING.

❑ **OTC PRICE MANIPULATION.** Because over-the-counter (or OTC) stocks are owned by broker-dealers, it's possible that a dishonest broker-dealer could create intentional increases or decreases in an OTC stock price by aggressively trading it. If he convinces you to buy at the inflated price, the broker-dealer can take his profit, then sit back and watch as the stock value falls back to its real worth. He may then begin the process all over again. If you suspect a broker-dealer of manipulating the price of a stock, contact the National Association of Securities Dealers and your state's office of securities regulation for information about filing disciplinary proceedings against a broker.

portion of the company's profits in the form of a dividend.

Common stock

Corporations may issue two kinds of stock, common and preferred. When you buy common stock, you are entitled to receive a proportionate share of any dividends the company may pay, but you are not guaranteed any specific return on your investment.

Many profitable companies pay regular dividends to their common-stock holders, but they are not legally required to do so. The decision to pay dividends is made annually by the company's board of directors. If the company has had a bad year, it may decide to reduce dividends or eliminate them entirely. Even if business is booming, the directors may decide to reinvest the company's profits rather than pay them out as dividends.

Preferred stock

Sometimes a company may try to attract investors by offering preferred stock, which entitles shareholders to dividends at a specified rate. Holders of preferred stock will receive their dividends before any are paid to the holders of the company's common stock. Furthermore, if the company should fail, the holders of preferred stock can receive—ahead of those who own common stock—any assets that may remain after the company's debts have been paid. Sometimes preferred stock is "called" by the company. See the discussion about called bonds on pages 494-95.

Buying stocks

Although a few companies sell their stock directly to the public, most make their shares available through a stockbroker who works for a brokerage house. When you buy stock, the corporation will issue a stock certificate, which can be held either by you or by your stockbroker. See STOCKBROKER.

The stocks of publicly traded companies are bought and sold on three different exchanges: (1) the New York Stock Exchange (NYSE), which handles the stocks of the largest and most-established companies; (2) the American Stock Exchange (AMEX), which handles the stocks of mid-size firms; or (3) the "over-the-counter" market (OTC), which lists the stock offerings of small, new companies.

The NYSE and AMEX each have a central exchange board, which posts the asking and selling prices of their various stocks. OTC stocks are not traded through a central exchange, but are instead traded over computers by registered broker-dealers who create a market for these stocks for resale to other broker-dealers or to other brokerage houses. The prices of many OTC stocks are quoted in newspapers under the heading NASDAQ—an acronym for National Association of Securities Dealers Automated Quotation. Other OTC stocks, such as penny stocks, are listed on "pink sheets," which are daily publications that give the previous day's stock price ranges.

SIPC insurance

If you buy stock from a broker and the broker holds the stock certificate for you, make sure that his firm is insured by the Security Investors Protection Corporation (SIPC). The SIPC is a federally chartered, nonprofit membership organization that affords investors protection if brokerage firms go bankrupt. If an SIPC member firm should fail, a customer's holdings in stock are protected up to $500,000, and his cash accounts are protected up to $100,000. Many large brokerage houses have private insurance to cover larger accounts that exceed the SIPC's half-million-dollar limit.

Legal protection

As an investor, you are protected from unscrupulous stock market dealings by both federal and state governments. All companies offering stock for sale to the public nationwide must register the offering with the Securities and Exchange Commission (SEC). Companies must disclose information that enables a purchaser to evaluate the stock's worth and stability.

The SEC also requires publicly traded companies to publish financial information about their operations on a quarterly and annual basis. These reports, which are available from your broker, give investors a detailed accounting of the corporation's activities and financial performance. Be sure to review them carefully before investing in a company.

On the state level, regulatory agencies enforce what are known as blue-sky laws, which set out the requirements that must be met for issuing and selling stocks within a given state. See also BLUE-SKY LAW; SECURITIES AND EXCHANGE COMMISSION.

BONDS

Another way to invest in a company (or a government or governmental agency) is to buy its bonds. When you buy a bond, the issuer promises to pay you back the money you have invested in it, along with a specified rate of interest. As a bondholder you are a creditor. If the issuer is a corporation, it must pay the interest it owes you before it makes any payments of dividends to stockholders. Also, if the issuer should go bankrupt, you as a bondholder have priority over stockholders in receiving your share of any assets.

U.S. government bonds

The best-known government bonds are U.S. Savings Bonds, which are issued by the federal government and sold through federal reserve banks. To buy a savings bond, you must complete a purchase form, available at banks, savings and loan associations, and credit unions. After filling out the form, mail it to the appropriate federal reserve bank. Once your application has been processed, the bank will mail your bond to you or someone you name.

Savings bonds are a good investment for several reasons: (1) they are guaranteed by the U.S. government and can be replaced without charge should they be lost or stolen; (2) you can purchase them in installments through your employer; (3) you can redeem them at any time after six months; and (4) they accumulate tax-free interest before they are redeemed, and they are exempt from state and local income tax after they are redeemed.

There are two types of savings bonds. The Series EE bonds range in denominations from $50 to $10,000, and pay interest through a process called discounting. The buyer purchases the bond for half its face value. Provided the bond is held for at least five years, it earns variable market-based interest at a rate that is 85 percent of the average return on marketable five-year Treasury securities. Since March 1, 1993, a minimum rate of 4 percent is guaranteed.

Series HH Savings Bonds, available in various denominations from $500 to $10,000, are sold at their face value. They pay interest at a fixed annual rate of 6 percent through a check mailed to the owner semiannually. You cannot buy Series HH bonds; these bonds can be obtained only through the exchange of matured Series EE bonds.

State and municipal bonds

State and local governments and their agencies also issue bonds. The chief advantage of municipal bonds is that the interest they earn is exempt from federal income tax. If you happen to live in the state or city that issues them, they are also exempt from state and local taxes.

Like U.S. Savings Bonds, municipal bonds are available in many denominations. The interest they bear is related to prevailing interest rates and to the safety of the bonds, which depends on the fiscal health of the municipality that issues them. For an evaluation of bond safety, you should consult such publications as *The Bond Buyer, Credit Week,* and *Moody's Bond Survey*—all available at the public library.

Corporate bonds

Many corporations sell bonds —usually in denominations of $1,000—to raise money for expansion or to spread their existing debt among a greater number of buyers. Although the interest on corporate bonds is not tax-exempt as on municipal bonds, and although they are riskier than U.S. Savings Bonds, they promise regular interest income twice a year and may be redeemed for their full face value upon maturity.

How bonds are valued

The face value, or par value, of a bond is the amount you will be paid when the bond matures. But the amount that you actually pay for the bond (known as its market price) may be different from the face value. For example, a bond with a face value of $10,000 may be salable for only $9,000 if interest rates have risen sharply since the bond was issued. On the other hand, if interest rates have fallen since then, the bond will usually sell for more than its original issue price. The market price can fluctuate widely from the time a bond is issued until the day it matures. As a rule, a bond with a high interest rate is a riskier investment than a comparable one with a lower rate.

When bonds are called

When interest rates drop, businesses and municipalities often call, or redeem, bonds before their maturity dates. (Federal bonds are not callable.) Essentially, a call means that the issuer has decided to redeem its older bonds paying high interest rates and refinance its debt through new bonds issued at lower rates. To attract and keep investors, some bond issuers promise not to call their bonds for a given period of time, such as five years. The earliest date at which a bond can be called is specified in the bond contract.When a call is issued, you have no choice but to surrender the bond. You will receive its face value and perhaps a small bonus payment, plus the accrued interest owed on the bond.

Stop-and-Frisk Laws

As a rule, police officers are violating the Fourth Amendment of the U.S. Constitution if they do not have a search warrant when they search you, your car, or your home. An exception is the stop-and-frisk rule. Under the appropriate circumstances, a police officer is authorized to detain (stop) someone and pat down (frisk) the outer surfaces of his clothing to search for a weapon. See also SEARCH AND SEIZURE; SEARCH WARRANT.

In order for a warrantless stop and frisk to be legal, the police officer must have sufficient evidence to justify it. For example, if he sees two men loitering in front of a store, he may suspect that they are about to commit a robbery. If his suspicion is reasonable, he would be justified in stopping and questioning them, but not in searching them. If the officer spots a bulge under the coat of one of the suspects, however, he has reason to believe that the men are armed and dangerous, and he would be justified in frisking them to protect himself and any bystanders.

A few states have enacted laws that give a police officer the authority to stop and frisk individuals under specific circumstances. In Massachusetts, for example, the police may stop a person if they suspect he has some unlawful purpose in mind, and they may frisk him for a weapon if they suspect they are in danger. A police officer in Rhode Island may temporarily stop a person to ask him for his name, address, business, and destination. If he does not answer these questions to the officer's satisfaction, the police may detain him, but for no longer than two hours (to conduct a further investigation).

The typical stop and frisk occurs because a police officer suspects someone of wrongdoing. But law enforcement authorities may sometimes lawfully detain a person temporarily and frisk him even when they have no suspicion of illegal activity. Some courthouses, for example, require all visitors to pass through a metal detector and submit to a frisk if the metal detector is activated. At least one court has ruled that the constitutional protection against unreasonable search and seizure is not violated in such a situation, because the risk of harm to innocent bystanders outweighs the inconvenience of having to walk through a metal detector. The same reasoning has been used by courts when challenges have been made to searches made at airports.

Strike

A strike is a work stoppage staged by the employees of a company or industry in order to pressure the management into granting concessions, such as higher wages or benefits. At one time strikes were illegal, and an employee's only recourse against an employer was his freedom to quit his job. It was not until the 1930's and the Great Depression that Congress and the courts granted American workers the right to strike under certain circumstances and paved the way for the growth of the union movement.

The right to strike is not extended to all workers, however, nor is it unlimited. For example, employees of the federal, state, and local governments are generally prohibited from striking unless a statute specifically gives them the right to do so. This prohibition is legally justified by the public need for government services and the fact that a strike by public employees can cripple, or even paralyze, government operations and endanger the public safety.

In the early 1980's, for example, the nation's air traffic controllers waged a strike against the Federal Aviation Administration. President Ronald Reagan ordered the striking workers to return to their jobs and fired those who refused to obey the order. Although the controllers' union and individual controllers challenged the dismissals in court, the firings were upheld.

Federal laws also prohibit a strike designed to force changes in an existing labor agreement unless the strikers have given 60 days' notice before beginning the strike. During this period, an employee who goes on strike may be fired and replaced by another worker.

TYPES OF STRIKES

The law recognizes several kinds of strikes and treats each of them differently. Typically, employees strike for one of two reasons: (1) to force an employer either to increase wages or benefits or to prevent him from reducing them (called an economic strike); or (2) to force an employer to redress employee grievances about such matters as firing workers or disciplining them for union activities (called an unfair labor practices strike).

The legal protection strikers receive depends on the type of strike that is staged, regardless of whether or not workers are unionized. In an economic strike the employer may hire replacement workers while the strike is underway. When the strike ends, striking workers may not be able to get their jobs back unless a vacancy occurs, or a provision in the new contract requires that striking workers be rehired. In an unfair labor practices strike, however, the striking workers are entitled to return to their jobs as soon as the dispute is settled.

There are also certain types of strikes that relate only to unionized companies. A wildcat strike, for example, is one that the union has not authorized. Suppose the United Auto Workers union enters into a national agreement with all of the nation's auto manufacturers, but the workers at a single plant refuse to abide by the terms of the agreement and stage a walkout. Their action is called a wildcat strike, and their jobs would not be legally protected since wildcat strikes are prohibited by most union contracts.

A sympathy strike is conducted by workers to lend support to a strike being waged by a related union. Suppose a glassmakers' union strikes for a pay raise. Workers in the same plant who belong to the pipefitters' union may decide to stage a sympathy strike. Unless sympathy strikes are prohibited by their collective-bargaining agreement, they may do so.

An intermittent strike is a work slowdown, in which workers may stay on the job but reduce their productivity. Slowdowns are illegal, and any workers who participate in them can be fired.

UNEMPLOYMENT BENEFITS AND STRIKING WORKERS

In most states strikers are not entitled to receive unemployment benefits while on strike, since technically they are not unemployed. However, if you want to go to work but fear for your safety if you cross the picket line, you may be entitled to receive unemployment benefits. Usually a portion of union members' dues is placed in a special fund for workers who participate in a strike authorized by the union. Your union representative can give you the details about your union's strike fund. See also LABOR UNION; NATIONAL LABOR RELATIONS BOARD.

STUDENT LOAN

In this era of skyrocketing tuition, few parents can afford to send a child to college without some kind of financial assistance. With the annual cost of a private college averaging $16,000 and that of a state college averaging more than $7,000, financial aid has become an absolute necessity for most families.

APPLYING FOR FINANCIAL AID

By January of the year your child starts college, you should have completed a form from either the College Scholarship Service or the American College Testing Program. This form, available from your child's high school guidance counselor, asks for such data as your income, assets, household expenses, and family size. The information you provide is used to determine the amount you will be expected to contribute to your child's education. The remainder you will need to obtain through student loans or other kinds of financial aid, such as scholarships, grants, or work-study programs.

TYPES OF LOANS

The federal and state governments provide a variety of loan programs for college students.

◇ The Perkins Student Loan Program is a federally subsidized program available to students from low-income families. Unlike loans for which one must apply, a Perkins loan is awarded by the college as part of a financial aid package. While the student is in school, the federal government pays the interest on the loan. Once the student graduates or leaves school, he must start making payments on the loan within nine months. Repayment can be extended over 10 years.

◇ The Stafford Student Loan Program is also federally subsidized. Like the Perkins program, the government guarantees payment of the interest for as long as a student is in school. To receive one of these loans, the student must apply to a bank, savings and loan association, or other financial institution.

◇ The PLUS (Parent Loan to Undergraduate Students) programs are available for parents whose children do not qualify for federal financial aid because their parents are able to support their education. The parents are legally responsible for repaying the loan. The SLS (Supplemental Loans for Students) are loans for students who cannot be declared dependent upon their parents—for example, married students. Under both programs, repayment usually begins within 60 days of obtaining the loan. Payment can extend over 10 years.

In 1993 Congress enacted new legislation offering financial aid to students in exchange for a period of national service. For specific information about these and other federal and state programs, contact your school's office of financial aid.

REPAYMENT AND DEFAULT

In cases of economic hardship, repayment of student loans may sometimes be postponed or even forgiven. To obtain a postponement, however, the borrower must appeal to the lender. If you simply stop making payments, you may be subject to severe penalties, such as having your income tax refund withheld by the IRS. Federal employees may have payments taken out of their paychecks. A loan payment default may also jeopardize your credit rating, making it difficult to obtain future loans. See also College Admissions; College Scholarship; Credit Bureau and Credit Rating; Selective Service.

STUDENT RIGHTS

Americans place a high value on individual freedom and education. But there are times when a public school policy conflicts with rights guaranteed by the Constitution. Over the years, students have taken such disputes to court, and some of these cases have made their way to the U.S. Supreme Court. The Court has looked to the First Amendment, which guarantees freedom of speech,

REAL LIFE, REAL LAW

The Case of the Censored Students

The school administration of a junior high school prevented a student newspaper from publishing articles about divorce and teen pregnancy on the grounds that the material was inappropriate and that it invaded the privacy of some students who were quoted in the articles. The students charged the administration with "prior restraint," or censorship, and persuaded the American Civil Liberties Union to help them file suit against the school's administrators. The U.S. Supreme Court rejected the students' argument. It ruled that school officials are allowed to exercise prior restraint over a student publication if there is a reasonable possibility that publication would disrupt normal school activity—for example, disturb classroom attendance. The court ruled that a school newspaper is not a forum for the general public, and, therefore, school officials may impose reasonable restrictions on its content.

freedom of assembly, and freedom of religion, in deciding the rights of students.

FREEDOM OF RELIGION

The establishment clause of the First Amendment forbids the government to establish or promote a religion. On several occasions students and parents have filed suit against public schools to end practices that violated their religious freedom. In deciding these cases the Supreme Court has ruled that prayer, silent meditation, scriptural reading, and posting of the Ten Commandments in the classroom are all violations of the First Amendment. The Court also struck down a Louisiana state law that mandated the teaching of "creation science," which bases the origins of the universe on the account given in the Book of Genesis. The court ruled that creation science is not a science, but a system of religious beliefs.

The Constitution not only protects students from having religion imposed on them but also protects their right to practice their religion. The Supreme Court has ruled, for example, that a publicly funded university may not deny a student group the use of its facilities for worship if it has granted space to other groups for other purposes.

FREEDOM OF SPEECH AND EXPRESSION

Students are entitled not only to religious freedom but also to some degree of freedom of expression under the First Amendment. The Supreme Court has ruled that a school may not prohibit students from expressing their opinions, unless such expression would interfere with school discipline or operations. In the case that led to this decision, the Court ruled that by disciplining students who wore black armbands to protest the Vietnam War, the school had wrongfully interfered with their right to freedom of expression. In another case, however, the Court ruled that a school must discipline students who engage in lewd or indecent speech.

The Supreme Court has also held that the right to freedom of expression includes the right to be free from "compelled speech" or "compelled belief." Hence it has ruled that a school may not require students to recite the Pledge of Allegiance.

FREEDOM OF ASSOCIATION

The First Amendment protects freedom of association. The Supreme Court has ruled that students may not be denied the right to form school clubs—even if they promote ideas opposed to those of the school's administration—as long as the clubs do not disrupt the academic environment.

ACCESS TO IDEAS

Exposing students to diverse ideas is an important part of public education. While school officials have the right to remove books and materials they consider harmful (such as a book that shows how to make a bomb), they may not ban books or materials solely because they do not approve of the ideas they contain.

CRUEL AND UNUSUAL PUNISHMENT

Although many school systems no longer permit corporal punishment, the Supreme Court has held that it does not violate the Eighth Amendment's prohibition against cruel and unusual punishment. The decision to allow or not to allow corporal punishment rests with the school system. See also CORPORAL PUNISHMENT.

DUE PROCESS

Students facing suspension or expulsion for breaking school rules are entitled to be notified of the infraction and the proposed punishment. They are also entitled to a hearing, at which they may try to refute the allegations. See SCHOOL EXPULSION AND SUSPENSION.

SEARCH AND SEIZURE

The Fourth Amendment to the Constitution prohibits unreasonable searches and seizures by law enforcement officers, but the amendment does not pertain to school officials. Although the police must have a search warrant to inspect a student's locker, school officials do not need one. They may search a student's property and locker as long as they can show that the search is justified.

SUBLEASE

Four months after moving into a new apartment, you find out that your employer is sending you to the West Coast for a three-month-long assignment. You signed a one-year lease

ABC's OF CHOOSING A SUBTENANT

Because you are responsible for property you sublease, you should select a subtenant very carefully. Essentially, you are the landlord to the subtenant, and you should follow the same procedure your landlord uses in renting to tenants. Before agreeing to let anyone become your subtenant, you should be sure to:

❑ Obtain a copy of the subtenant's credit history from a credit bureau such as TRW or Trans Union.

❑ Call the subtenant's current employer to verify his employment and salary.

❑ Ask the subtenant's previous landlord to verify his length of residence.

❑ Put the sublease in writing. State the length of the sublease, the amount of security deposit, and the amount of the rent and when it is to be paid, as well as fees for late payment. Include a clause specifying responsibility for damages and the length of time required for notice to terminate the sublease.

and would like to keep your apartment, but you do not want to pay rent while you are away. One option you may have is to sublease (or sublet) your apartment to someone else during your absence.

A sublease is a contract between the original tenant and a second tenant that gives the second tenant *part* of the rights granted in the lease. The original tenant may sublet the entire premises for a specified period of time, or he may continue to live there and rent out part of his leased space. For example, a restaurant may rent space in a mall and sublet part of it to an ice cream shop. Or a person might rent a house and sublet a basement room to another tenant.

In a sublease situation, the landlord's only legal recourse for unpaid rent or damages caused by the subtenant is against the original tenant, because the landlord is not a party to the sublease. But the tenant can sue the subtenant for any expenses he incurs.

ASSIGNMENT

If you transfer your *entire* lease to another person—that is, the new tenant "takes over" the lease—the transaction is not a sublease but an "assignment." Thus, the new tenant assumes all the rights and responsibilities that were stated in your lease.

When there is an assignment of the lease, the landlord can sue the subtenant if the property is damaged or the subtenant does not pay the rent. In addition, the landlord generally has the right to sue you, as the assignor, for unpaid rent or damage, even if he consented to the assignment.

RIGHT TO SUBLEASE

If you are thinking about subletting your apartment, be sure to check the terms of your lease. Landlords frequently include a provision that either prohibits subletting or requires the landlord's approval. In some states, however, a landlord cannot unreasonably refuse a subtenant, provided she is financially responsible and meets the appropriate criteria. Even if your lease or the law in your state does not require the landlord's written approval, it is best to get it.

If the landlord denies you permission, do not sublease the apartment. The subtenant may then be considered a trespasser, and the landlord could begin eviction proceedings against both you and the subtenant. If the subtenant has not moved in, the landlord may get a court order prohibiting her from doing so.

Because you are legally responsible when you sublet property, you should exercise caution when choosing a subtenant. Ask for references from employers, and check the person's financial record. For more tips on choosing a subtenant, see the box at left. See also CREDIT BUREAU AND CREDIT RATING; LEASE; TENANT'S RIGHTS.

SUBORDINATION

In real estate law, establishing priorities in the payment of mortgages, liens, or other claims placed on property is known as subordination. Suppose you want to buy a house for $200,000. You have $20,000 in cash for the down payment, but your bank will give you a mortgage for only $160,000, leaving you $20,000 short. The seller agrees to help you out by lending you the remaining $20,000.

The bank, in order to protect its status as your major creditor, will require that the seller's loan include a subordination clause, which states that the bank's loan must be repaid first if you default.

SUBROGATION

You are driving home from work one Friday afternoon when a van comes speeding out of a side street and slams into your car. Although you are unhurt, the car is badly damaged. When you find out that the person at fault is uninsured, you notify your insurer of the accident, and the insurance company agrees to pay for the repairs to your car. Before the insurance adjuster sends you a check, he asks you to sign a document called a subrogation agreement, which allows your insurer to attempt to collect from the other driver (by getting a court judgment to garnishee his wages, for example). The proceeds may reimburse some or all of the amount your insurer paid to you.

A subrogation agreement is a standard part of most automobile insurance policies. Under certain circumstances, as in the case above, you may also be asked to sign an additional subrogation agreement.

SUNSHINE LAW

Universal participation in government decision making is an important part of the democratic system. Sometimes, however, government agencies lose sight of the need for public participation and conduct meetings behind closed doors. Such a lack of disclosure has often led to corruption and the misuse of power.

Sunshine laws (also called open-meeting laws) require many governmental agencies to conduct their meetings in public. Typically an agency must announce when and where it will meet, make its agenda available to the public, and offer citizens an opportunity to comment on agency matters. Sunshine laws make exceptions to the open-meeting format when discussions involve internal personnel, trade secrets, or sensitive security matters.

If you believe that a government agency has violated a sunshine law, you can seek a court order requiring the agency to release information withheld in violation of the law. In some instances a court may delay or prohibit the execution of any decisions an agency makes in violation of the open-meeting law.

To find out whether a federal, state, or local government agency is subject to a sunshine law, ask your councilperson, your state representative, your congressional representative, or the agency itself.

SUPPLEMENTAL SECURITY INCOME

A federal program created by Congress in 1972, Supplemental Security Income (SSI) provides a guaranteed monthly payment to persons with a low income who are also blind, disabled, or over age 65. Although this program is administered by the Social Security Administration, it is not funded by Social Security taxes but by the federal government's general revenues. States may contribute to the program as well. As a result, the benefits available from SSI often differ from state to state, depending on the state's contribution.

The purpose of SSI is to provide every needy American with a guaranteed source of income. Before its enactment, state-run programs, "poor houses," and mental institutions were often the only alternatives available to the needy.

To provide a minimum income for people in need, the federal government measures a person's income against a poverty-level index. This index takes into account the cost of food and housing as well as the size and needs of the household. If a person's income falls below the poverty level, he may be eligible for SSI benefits.

WHO IS ELIGIBLE

Under federal law, to be eligible for SSI benefits you must:

◇ Reside within the United States or within the Northern Mariana Islands.

ABC's OF APPLYING FOR SSI BENEFITS

If you think you are eligible for SSI benefits, you should apply at your local Social Security office. You will need the following documents to complete your application:

❑ Your Social Security card.

❑ A certified copy of your birth certificate.

❑ Documentation of disability or blindness supplied by the doctors who treated you, the hospital administrators where you were treated, or copies of your medical records.

❑ Names and addresses of any social workers or welfare agencies that have knowledge of your disability.

❑ Data on your income and resources, including tax returns, bank account numbers, current payroll information, real estate deeds, car registration, and insurance policies.

❑ If you are an alien, proof of your legal residency in the United States.

◇ Be a U.S. citizen, a lawfully admitted alien, or an alien living in the United States who is in the process of receiving authorization from the Immigration and Naturalization Service to remain in the United States.

◇ Be 65 or older, blind (defined as having vision no better than 20/200, or a limited visual field of 20 degrees or less with corrective lenses), or be unable to work because of another physical or mental impairment (if your vision is poor but does not fit the above categories, you may qualify for SSI under this category). The impairment must be expected to last for at least 12 months or be terminal.

◇ Have income and other resources that fall below the poverty level.

INCOME

Income is defined as anything you can use to pay for food, shelter, and clothing. Included are cash, checks, and "in-kind" income, such as food and housing you receive, whether as a gift or in payment for services.

For those especially in need, SSI does not count some kinds of income, such as food stamps or assistance in the form of food, clothing, and housing from nonprofit organizations or government-sponsored programs. Disabled or blind persons can also deduct the cost of any essential medical devices, drugs, medical services, and other disability-related expenses from their income.

RESOURCES

As with income, not all of a person's financial resources are considered in determining the amount of SSI benefits. Real estate is considered, for example, but not the house you live in or the land on which it sits. Personal property such as cash, bank accounts, stocks, and bonds is considered, but not household goods or small life insurance policies. A car is considered, but only its value in excess of $4,500.

After deducting all the exceptions, your resources must be $2,000 or less if you are single, or $3,000 if you are married, in order to be eligible for SSI benefits. In 1993 the basic federal SSI payment for a single person was $434 per month, and $652 for a married couple. If you are under 18, the income and resources of your parents or legal guardians will be considered. See also SOCIAL SECURITY; WELFARE.

SUPREME COURT, U.S.

The highest court in the land is the U.S. Supreme Court. It was established by Article III, Section 1, of the Constitution, and the Court's functions and organization were outlined in the Judiciary Act of 1789. The Supreme Court initially heard cases concerning states' rights versus the rights of the federal government. Now, however, it hears cases ranging from freedom of the press to the rights of schoolchildren, as long as the question relates to federal law and the U.S. Constitution. The Court will hear some cases from the beginning and others only on appeal.

THE JUSTICES

Federal law dictates the size of the Supreme Court. In 1789 the number of judges (called justices) was set at six. Now there are nine. One is designated as the chief justice and the other eight are associate justices.

All the justices are appointed by the president and confirmed by the Senate. The Constitution does not set any specific qualifications for the position, but justices are usually attorneys who have sat as judges on other courts. Once a justice is confirmed, he serves on the Court for life or until he voluntarily retires. A justice can be removed only if impeached (accused of misconduct) by the House of Representatives and convicted by the Senate. A vacancy on the Court does not mean that cases cannot be decided—as few as six justices can render a decision.

COURT SESSIONS

The Supreme Court, which sits in Washington, D.C., is in formal session for 36 weeks each year, generally from the first Monday of October until the end of June. The chief justice can extend the session or call a session during a recess if an urgent issue must be decided.

TYPES OF CASES HEARD

The Supreme Court has both original and appellate jurisdiction, or authority, to hear cases. Original jurisdiction refers to those cases that are heard for the first time by the Supreme Court. They include: (1) cases between two or more states; (2) cases between the United States and a state; (3) cases involving foreign ambassadors, consuls, public ministers, or their staffs; and (4) cases filed by a state against citizens of another state, aliens, or a foreign country. Only a few of the cases heard by the Supreme Court involve original jurisdiction, and most of these involve disputes between states.

The majority of Supreme Court cases involve appellate jurisdiction—that is, the authority to review (or reconsider) decisions that have been made by another court. Such cases include: (1) those from a state's highest court when the issue involves a substantial federal question; (2) cases appealed from lower federal constitutional courts (the U.S. District Courts and U.S. Courts of Appeals); and (3) most cases appealed from federal legislative courts (for example, the Court of Military Appeals and the Tax Court).

HOW APPEALS ARE MADE

Most of the appeals that reach the Supreme Court are brought by a writ of certiorari. (A writ is a legal order, and *certiorari* is a Latin word meaning "to be informed of.") The writ is a certified record of a particular case that was tried in a lower court. Before a writ is "granted," four justices must agree that there are irregularities presented in the writ that warrant a review of the case by the Court.

The cases that the Supreme Court agrees to hear usually concern questions about the validity of a federal law or a treaty or the validity of a state statute that may conflict with the Constitution or federal law.

DECISIONS

Every Friday while the Court is in session the justices meet privately to confer about the cases heard, each justice explains his opinion of the case, and a vote is taken. The chief justice then assigns the case to an associate justice for preparation of the written opinion, or he may write the opinion himself.

The majority opinion becomes the opinion of the Court. Those justices who do not agree with it may write dissenting opinions. If a justice agrees with the majority decision for reasons that differ from those of the majority, he may write a concurring opinion.

The Court has several options in deciding a case. It may affirm the decision of the lower court, reverse it, or vacate it (declare the decision void). The Court may also modify the lower court's decision in some way, or remand it — that is, send the decision back to the lower court with instructions to reconsider certain issues.

The decision of the Supreme Court is final. If it is not acceptable to someone, the only way it can be overruled is by congressional legislation or a Constitutional amendment. In some instances the Supreme Court may hear another case on the same issue and, because of the facts of that case or new justices on the bench, vote to overturn its earlier decision. But generally the Court uses its earlier decisions as guidance for deciding later cases.

SURROGATE MOTHER

"Woman gives birth to own grandchildren!" It may sound like a bizarre tabloid headline, but such a phenomenon is now possible and has occurred in at least one highly publicized case in which a woman agreed to be a surrogate mother for her infertile daughter.

TYPES OF SURROGACY

There are two different kinds of medical procedures for becoming a surrogate mother: artificial insemination and in vitro fertilization.

The typical surrogate mother is a woman who agrees to be artificially inseminated with a man's sperm in order to bear a child for someone else. When the child is born, she gives it up for adoption to the biological father and his wife. In this arrangement the surrogate mother is considered both the biological and the genetic mother of the child. See ARTIFICIAL INSEMINATION.

In another procedure, known as in vitro fertilization, a woman's egg is fertilized with her husband's sperm in a petri dish. The fertilized egg is then implanted in the womb of the surrogate mother, who bears the child and then relinquishes custody. In this arrangement the surrogate mother has no genetic link with the baby but is legally considered the biological mother. See IN VITRO FERTILIZATION.

SURROGACY CONTRACTS

Arrangements for surrogate mothers are sometimes handled in an informal way — that is, without fees, lawyers, or contracts — between close friends or family members who want to help a loved one have a child. Usually, however, the surrogate mother has a contract with the infertile couple whose child she will bear. A typical contract provides that the surrogate will relinquish her rights to the child upon birth. She may also be required to refrain from smoking, drinking, or using drugs during her pregnancy. The couple agree to cover all expenses related to the pregnancy and to pay the mother a fee.

THE LEGALITY OF SURROGACY CONTRACTS

Only a few states have laws concerning the issue of surrogacy. For example:

◇ Arkansas law says that surrogacy contracts are valid.

◇ A Nevada law exempts surrogacy contracts from a law barring payment to a mother in return for her consenting to her child's adoption.

◇ Louisiana law declares that surrogacy contracts are unenforceable if the surrogate mother is paid, and in Michigan such payments are illegal.

◇ In any state, offering to buy or sell a baby is illegal. If the surrogacy contract is poorly written, a court might overturn it by ruling that any fee paid to the surrogate was in fact a fee to purchase a child. For this reason, representation by an attorney experienced with surrogacy contracts is essential.

IF THINGS GO WRONG

Of the thousands of surrogacy arrangements, only a few have ended up in court with the parties battling for custody of the child. In the Baby M case, in which the surrogate mother was also the genetic mother of the child, the court found her agreement to give up the child for adoption to be unenforceable. The court then proceeded to make a custody decision between the surrogate mother and the father in the traditional way, based on the best interest of the child. The court awarded the child to the father but granted the surrogate mother visitation rights. See CHILD CUSTODY.

A California case in which the surrogate mother was implanted with a couple's embryo was brought to court when the agreement broke down before the birth of the child. The court was asked to decide whether the surrogate mother had any legal rights to the child. It decided against her, finding that she was a "genetic stranger" to the child and therefore had no legal status as a parent.

SWEEPSTAKES

"You may already be a winner." That message and similar ones arrive in mailboxes across the country several times a year, as magazine subscription services and catalog companies offer prizes large and small to those who respond to the mailing. Fast-food chains, convenience stores, and other retail businesses also sponsor sweepstakes. They are popular promotional devices used to entice consumers to purchase the sponsor's product.

SWEEPSTAKES LAWS

A legitimate sweepstakes does not require a purchase in order for you to win a prize. If a purchase is required, then the sweepstakes is actually an illegal lottery, since federal postal regulations prohibit the mailing of lottery offers or lottery tickets. State laws also prohibit lotteries, except for those operated or licensed by the state itself, such as church raffles. See LOTTERY.

Although there are no federal laws that prohibit or regulate sweepstakes offerings, many states have enacted strict requirements. Often the sponsor must post a bond to guarantee that all of the prizes offered will be awarded. The sponsor must also disclose the dates on which the sweepstakes will close and the prizes will be awarded, reveal the approximate odds of winning any particular prize, and state whether eligibility to receive a prize is restricted. For example, a sweepstakes may legally refuse to award a prize to employees or close relatives of the sponsor and the company handling the promotion.

SWEEPSTAKES SCAMS

Although many sweepstakes are legal and aboveboard, various scams and swindles masquerade as sweepstakes. They typically work as follows:

You receive a postcard in the mail announcing that you have won a sweepstakes prize, but that the sponsor has not been able to reach you. This seems very peculiar, since you have a telephone answering machine, but you read on, tempted by the thought of winning a valuable prize.

To claim your prize, you are instructed to call the company at its 900 number. In small print you notice — or perhaps you don't — that you will be charged $5 per minute for the call. When you call, you learn that you have won a "major prize," but in order to get it you will have to pay a fee for shipping it or buy some merchandise, such as vitamins or office supplies. When you receive the merchandise, it is generally overpriced and of poor quality, as is the "prize."

Sometimes you may be told that your prize is a discount on merchandise offered through a company's catalog, again at highly inflated prices. In some instances you may be asked to provide a credit card number, "just to verify that you are indeed the winner." If you should be so naive as to do so, your next statement may reflect purchases you did not make or charges for a "membership fee" you did not agree to, and then you will have to contest these amounts with your credit card issuer.

CAUTIONS

Consumers lose millions of dollars a year by falling prey to phony sweepstakes offers. If you ever receive offers like those mentioned above, call your state attorney general's office immediately and notify your post office.

Never give your credit card number to verify your identity to anyone who calls you over the telephone. Never call a 900 number (one that charges a fee) to collect a prize. A legitimate sweepstakes will not ask you to do either of these.

Never agree to buy anything to obtain a sweepstakes "prize." If you did not mail an entry to a sponsor, it is not a true sweepstakes and you have not won anything. A "prize notification" from an unfamiliar company is probably a fraud. See FRAUD.

SWIMMING POOL

Swimming pools can be a source not only of fun but also of anguish—injuries, fatalities, and lawsuits. If you own one, you should know about your legal rights and responsibilities.

TAKING PRECAUTIONS

A swimming pool is known in legal terms as an "attractive nuisance"—something on your property that attracts children and may be harmful to them. See ATTRACTIVE NUISANCE.

By law, you must take special precautions to protect children—even those trespassing on your property—from injuring themselves in or around your pool. The best way to do this is to erect a tall and sturdy fence around the pool area, and keep the gate locked so that children will not be able to get in easily. If a child does climb over the fence and injures himself or drowns, you will usually not be held responsible.

When children or adults are using the pool with your permission, you must carefully supervise their activities. Prohibit rough horseplay, beverages in bottles or glasses, and diving (unless restricted and carefully supervised). Ask those who refuse to comply with your rules to leave. Limit or prohibit the use of alcohol; if a swimmer is injured or drowns, and evidence shows that you knew or should have known that she was intoxicated, you may be held liable.

GETTING INSURED

Notify your homeowners insurance carrier when you install a pool. Most standard policies do not protect you from liability claims unless you have added a special provision, called an endorsement, and have paid an additional premium. Also, since pool injuries and deaths can lead to large court awards, you should consider buying an umbrella insurance policy. See also UMBRELLA INSURANCE.

USING POOLS ELSEWHERE

If you are staying at a hotel that has a pool or are using the pool at a health club, chances are that no lifeguard will be on duty. In most situations, pool operators do not have to supply lifeguards, provided that a sign clearly notifies swimmers that no lifeguard is on duty and that swimmers use the pool at their own risk. If you are injured while swimming in the pool, it is unlikely that you will be compensated for your injuries, because you assumed the risk.

Similarly, most public pools have clearly posted rules governing their use. If you violate one of these rules—for example, by swimming after the pool has officially closed—you may not be able to collect damages if you are injured.

TAXICAB

Because taxicabs are a form of public transportation, state and local governments are permitted to regulate taxicab owners and drivers. They can require drivers to take special tests and pay special fees in order to be licensed, and they can require taxicab owners to post bond, carry adequate insurance, and submit their vehicles to periodic safety inspections. Governments may also set maximum fares and limit the number of available taxi licenses. Taxicab companies and drivers that fail to meet state or local regulations may be fined or prohibited from operating.

If a taxi driver has acted improperly — for example, by overcharging you or using an indirect route to reach your destination — you can file a complaint. Before you leave the cab, make a note of the driver's name and license number — usually posted on the dashboard. Then write to the taxicab company explaining what happened and asking for a response. Suggest a remedy that the company can take, such as refunding your fare or disciplining the driver. Keep a copy of your letter.

If you do not receive an answer or are not satisfied with the answer you get, write to your local taxicab licensing agency and include copies of your correspondence with the company. The agency will make its own inquiries, and if the company refuses to respond or has a history of dissatisfied customers, its license may be suspended or revoked.

Taxicab companies are legally obliged to ensure the safety of their passengers. For example, they may require their employees to submit to periodic tests for drug or alcohol use, and they can require passengers to enter and leave taxis on the curbside only.

TAX PREPARATION

Despite the federal government's attempts to simplify its tax forms, many Americans remain confused and intimidated by the prospect of completing their income tax returns. These taxpayers can choose from a variety of tax-preparation aids that are available.

FINDING HELP

The least expensive and most basic assistance consists of

books and personal-computer programs designed to help you complete your return on your own. The Internal Revenue Service itself provides such a book, entitled *Your Federal Income Tax* (Publication 17), at no charge. In addition, the instruction book that accompanies Form 1040 lists other publications for taxpayers, as well as a toll-free telephone number that supplies prerecorded information on many tax topics. In many communities, volunteer groups prepare simple tax returns for senior citizens at little or no cost. To find out if such programs exist in your community, ask your local department of the aging or senior-citizens center.

If you are willing to pay someone to prepare a simple return, consider an individual tax preparer or a large tax-preparation firm. Their fees start at $50 to $75 but can be much higher depending on the complexity of your return.

If you need help with a complicated return (for example, if you have capital gains or losses or depreciation or amortization deductions), you can use a certified public accountant (CPA), who will either charge you by the return or by the hour (at a rate comparable to an attorney's). Ask for referrals from friends with tax situations similar to yours. Lawyers and bankers may be good sources too, because they often deal with accountants. Other help is available from preparers called enrolled agents, who are tested and certified by the Treasury Department to represent taxpayers before the IRS.

CHECKLIST

Choosing a Tax Preparer

Before you entrust an accountant or tax preparer with your return, you should interview him carefully. Here are some questions you should ask.

❑ WHAT KINDS OF CLIENTS DO YOU HAVE?
A preparer who mainly does simple returns based solely on W-2 and 1099 forms is not a good choice if you have a complicated return with many itemized deductions, investment income, or other complex matters.

❑ WILL YOU DO ALL THE WORK ON MY RETURN YOURSELF?
Some firms divide returns among several preparers. It is preferable, however, to have one preparer do the entire return. A single preparer can better answer your questions or those of the IRS.

❑ WHAT KIND OF TRAINING AND EXPERIENCE DO YOU HAVE?
The most desirable background is a degree in accounting, but college credits and on-the-job training with a tax-preparation company can be adequate for straightforward returns.

Be skeptical of anyone who does not ask questions about your basic financial situation, such as if you have an Individual Retirement Account or Keogh plan, own your home or rent it, or have a home office. Beware of preparers who promise a refund or ask for a percentage of your refund as their fee.

YOUR LEGAL RESPONSIBILITIES

Be aware that you (not your tax preparer) are legally responsible for the accuracy of your income tax return.

Accuracy
If your income is understated or your deductions are overstated, the IRS may assess back taxes, interest, and penalties, and you will have to pay them. If anything on your return seems questionable, ask your preparer to explain it. If you do not understand the explanation, you may want to have the forms reviewed by another preparer. If a tax preparer promises to pay interest and penalties incurred by any errors on your return, ask for a written guarantee. Note also that although some preparers say they will accompany you to an audit, they may lack the qualifications to help you at higher-level proceedings with the IRS.

You can call the IRS for advice about your return. Note the date and time you called and the name of the agent who helped you. Remember that IRS advice may be inaccurate. If your return is audited or additional taxes are assessed, the fact that you consulted the IRS may not be a defense.

Filing
You are responsible for seeing that your tax return reaches

the appropriate IRS office on time or that your application for an extension (in order to file a late return) is mailed before the April 15 deadline. Always keep photocopies of the records that you gave your preparer. The U.S. Tax Court has ruled that a taxpayer is responsible for substantiating his deductions, even if his preparer loses his records. See also INCOME TAX; INCOME TAX AUDIT; TAX REFUND.

TAX REFUND

Perhaps the only redeeming aspect of the tax season is the refund check you may get from the Internal Revenue Service. But if the refund is large, it means that you have either had too much withheld from your paycheck or overpaid your estimated taxes. Either way, you have given the government an interest-free loan of money that could have been earning money for you in a savings account or investments.

CONSEQUENCES OF OVERPAYMENT

Under certain circumstances, overpaying income taxes may affect you adversely. The IRS can withhold all or part of a refund for any number of reasons. For example, if you owe child support, defaulted on a federally guaranteed business or student loan, or owe back taxes, penalties, or interest for a previous year, you may not get a refund at all.

To avoid overpayment, find out from your employer how many exemptions you now claim and ask for a new Form W-4. If you take additional exemptions, you will reduce the amount of tax withheld from your paychecks. But be sure that the new amount your employer withholds is equal to the tax you owed for the previous year or is at least 90 percent of the tax you expect to pay this year. If the amount is not in this range, you will be subject to penalties for underpayment. If you make quarterly estimated-tax payments, you can lower them by making similar calculations.

WHEN YOUR REFUND IS OVERDUE

Generally, the earlier you file your return, the sooner you will receive your refund. For example, if you file in early February, you will probably get your refund within three or four weeks. If you file your return by April 15 and do not receive your refund by June 1, the IRS must start paying you interest.

STEPS TO TAKE

If your expected refund does not arrive within 10 weeks, do the following:

1. Call the IRS's Automated Refund Information (ARI) number listed in the instructions that accompany your tax return. Be prepared to give your Social Security number, your filing status (listed on lines 1 to 5 on Form 1040), and the amount of the refund you expect to receive. The ARI service will tell you when your check will arrive.

2. If you do not receive your expected refund by the promised time, write to the IRS center to which you mailed your tax return. Include your name, address, Social Security number, and a clear, concise explanation of your problem. Remember to keep a copy of your correspondence.

3. If your tax refund still does not arrive, or if you are dissatisfied with the response you receive from the Internal Revenue Service, contact the IRS's Problem Resolution Officer (PRO) at the center where you sent your return. The PRO will investigate and report back to you within five working days. If your refund is being withheld for some reason, you will be told the procedure for contesting the withholding. See also INCOME TAX.

TEACHER

To teach in the public school system, a teacher must obtain a teaching certificate or license from the state. The state can establish minimum requirements for the education and student-teaching experience of its teachers, and local school boards may impose additional standards. Some states require licenses not only for public school teachers, but for teachers in private schools as well.

The criteria for becoming a teacher vary from one state or community to another. Applicants can be rejected if they have been convicted of a violent crime or are known to abuse drugs or alcohol, but other factors, such as obesity, have been challenged as discriminatory and have been overturned in the courts.

RESPONSIBILITIES TO STUDENTS

Because teachers occupy a position of trust, their conduct toward their students must be above reproach. Teachers who are accused of child abuse or sexual improprieties can be subject to felony charges beyond those that would be imposed on other adults.

Teachers must by law report suspected cases of child neglect or abuse to their principal or to state child-welfare authorities. A teacher who fails to do so can be subject to criminal penalties and civil liability. If a teacher makes a report of suspected mistreatment that proves unfounded, she is usually protected from being sued.

TEACHERS' RIGHTS

Most teachers have contracts for their jobs that are renewed every year. After teaching in a district for a number of years, a teacher may be given tenure—the right to hold her job until she retires or resigns, provided she performs her duties.

If a teacher is dismissed for incompetence, inefficiency, or immoral behavior, she can, in some districts, request an administrative hearing before the school board. If her appeal is rejected there, she can file a lawsuit, usually in the district or county court. If a teacher is dismissed for an illegal reason, such as her race or religion, she should file a complaint with the Equal Employment Opportunity Commission.

Many public school teachers are members of unions that represent them in bargaining with the school districts concerning wages, benefits, and working conditions. But in some states teachers are legally prohibited from striking, even though they are unionized. See also JOB DISCRIMINATION; STUDENT RIGHTS; TENURE.

TELEPHONE CALL

Unwanted telephone calls have long plagued homeowners, and the problem is receiving attention from lawmakers and law enforcement officers.

OBSCENE CALLS

Making an obscene, harassing, or threatening telephone call is illegal. If you receive such a call, hang up immediately. If the caller persists, record the date and time of each call and notify the police. Most local telephone companies provide a service that enables the recipient to identify the caller's number simply by entering a special code on a touch-tone phone after the call has been received. This number is then given to the police to help them apprehend the offender.

TELEMARKETING

A more common problem is unwanted telephone solicitations. In 1991 Congress enacted the Telephone Consumer Protection Act that authorized the Federal Communications Commission (FCC) to protect consumers from excessive or intrusive sales calls. The FCC now requires telemarketers to compile lists of people who do not want to receive unsolicited calls, and the telemarketers must not call them. In addition, no calls can be made between 9 P.M. and 8 A.M. local time. Most computer-generated calls, which cannot be disconnected until a preprogrammed sales pitch is completed, are now prohibited.

STEPS TO TAKE

If you want to stop unsolicited sales calls, do the following:

1. Write a letter of complaint to the Telephone Preference Service, Direct Marketing Association, P.O. Box 9014, Farmingdale, NY 11735. At your request, the association will notify its members that you do not wish to receive telephone solicitations.

2. Since not every telemarketing company is a DMA member, you may still receive some calls. Ask these callers to take your name off their lists.

3. If a particular firm keeps calling you, send a written complaint to the Federal Communications Commission, 1919 M Street, Washington, DC 20554.

4. Call your state government's general information number to find out whether your state has a telemarketing law. If so, send a letter of complaint to the agency that enforces this law. See also MAIL-ORDER SALES.

TEMPORARY RESTRAINING ORDER

A temporary restraining order (also known as a TRO) is an order issued by a court, often without a formal hearing, that forbids someone to perform a certain act until the court can obtain more information and make a decision.

A judge issues a temporary restraining order to maintain the current state of events, out of concern that if a change were made, it would permanently affect the petitioner in a way that could never be fully rectified. Ignoring a temporary restraining order may result in a charge of contempt of court, which is punishable by a fine or imprisonment or both.

Suppose Lumbermill Inc. planned to cut down several acres of a forest that is home to a rare species of deer. An environmental action group, fearing that the destruction of the animals' habitat would threaten the species, steps in and files a petition in court for a temporary restraining order to halt the felling of the trees. If the judge decides that the evidence in the group's petition shows that the deer would be endangered by Lumbermill's proposed forest clearing, he will issue a temporary restraining order against the company.

After a temporary restraining order has been issued, a hearing is held, during the course of which both sides can present their cases. The judge then rules whether to lift the temporary restraining order or make it permanent. See also ORDER OF PROTECTION.

TENANCY BY THE ENTIRETY

In about 20 states a married couple who want to own property jointly can use a form of ownership called tenancy by the entirety. Under this arrangement, neither spouse may sell or dispose of the property without the permission of the other. If you and your spouse hold a savings account as tenants by the entirety, for example, neither of you may close the account without the other's knowledge and consent.

Should one spouse die, his or her share goes automatically to the survivor without going through probate court. Moreover, the surviving spouse owns the entire property regardless of any contrary provisions in the deceased spouse's will. See also JOINT TENANCY; MARITAL PROPERTY.

TENANCY IN COMMON

In a tenancy in common, two or more people hold a separate and undivided interest in the same property. This means that each tenant has the right to the use of all the property, and no tenant has an exclusive right to a particular part of it. Property owned by more than one person is generally presumed to be owned as a tenancy in common unless the deed or other proof of ownership states otherwise.

A tenant in common must share in the cost of maintaining the property, but he does not have to pay for unnecessary improvements—such as central air-conditioning—unless he specifically authorizes them. All parties must refrain from any action that would diminish the property's value, or else they risk being sued by the other tenants.

Tenancy in common can be ended when one tenant abandons his interest or sells it to a cotenant or someone else, or when the tenants in common reach an agreement to divide the property among themselves. Also, an heir may inherit the interest of a tenant in common through a will or the laws of intestate succession. See also COMMUNITY PROPERTY; EQUITABLE DISTRIBUTION.

TENANT'S RIGHTS

You moved into your apartment three months ago after signing a one-year lease. A month later Hiram moved in across the hall. He works from 3 P.M. to 11 P.M., and when he comes home he plays his stereo so loudly that dishes on your kitchen shelf rattle. You have asked Hiram to turn down the stereo, but he refuses to do so. What recourse do you have?

USE AND ENJOYMENT

When you moved into an apartment, you probably signed a lease that spelled out your obligations regarding rent, security deposits, use of the premises, and the like. Your lease may also have restricted the hours of noise and stated that a violation of this rule constitutes a breach of the lease. If it does, you can notify your landlord that a fellow tenant is violating his lease.

Even if the lease does not contain specific rules against noise, the landlord-tenant laws of your state define your basic rights and responsibilities as a tenant, including your right to the "quiet enjoyment" of your home. If your landlord makes no attempt to help you, and you have to move out, you can sue him for not fulfilling his obligations under state law. You may be able to recover money for your moving expenses as well as any increase in your rent for a new apartment. See QUIET ENJOYMENT.

HABITABILITY

In many states, another major right you have as a tenant is called the warranty of habitability, which means that a dwelling must be fit for human occupancy. It should meet the local building and sanitary codes, and it should have adequate plumbing, lighting, and heating. The windows, walls, floors, and ceilings must be in good repair. You also have the right to expect that common areas of an apartment building or complex, such as hallways, stairs, basements, sidewalks, and clubhouse areas, will be kept clean and safe. Many leases also make the landlord responsible for pest control, garbage collection, and security measures, including locks and keys that work.

PETS

A lease may specify that pets are not allowed. If you defy the lease and bring a pet into your apartment, the landlord can sue you for breach of contract. If a lease does not mention pets, pets are allowed. But if an animal creates a nuisance (by barking too much, for example), the landlord can evict you if you do not remove it.

RETALIATORY EVICTION

Tenants must be allowed to enforce their rights. Suppose you report unsanitary or dangerous conditions to the health department and your landlord responds by changing the locks and ordering you out. Such action is known as retaliatory eviction and is illegal. If this should happen to you, consult an attorney about steps you can take to regain entry to your apartment and to seek damages from the landlord.

SECURITY DEPOSITS

When you move into a house or apartment, the landlord may ask for a security deposit to compensate him if you default on the rent or damage his property. The deposit may be equal to one or two months' rent and may also consist of a cleaning charge and a deposit for your keys. Be sure that your lease specifies the amount of the security deposit and exactly what it covers. See also SECURITY DEPOSIT.

ADDITIONAL RIGHTS

State and local laws may impose other responsibilities on a landlord. He may be required, for example, to install smoke detectors or window guards, or to provide emergency entry when tenants are locked out.

STEPS TO TAKE

The action you can take when your rights as a tenant have been violated depends on the seriousness of the landlord's violation and on state and local laws. But there are things you can always do if you think that your landlord is violating the law or the terms of your lease:

1. If the problem affects the immediate health or safety of the tenants, contact building inspectors or health-department officials.

2. If your dispute is over repairs, always put your request in writing. Keep a copy of your letters and send them by certified mail, return receipt requested, as proof that you have notified the landlord. Take photographs of the defects in question; they may later serve as evidence if legal action becomes necessary.

3. Give the landlord a reasonable amount of time to take care of the problem. In some states, statutes allow landlords two weeks to take corrective measures after they have been notified of a violation.

4. If the allotted time passes and the landlord ignores your requests, you may either move out or continue paying rent and sue the landlord for the difference between what you are paying and what the apartment is worth. See also LANDLORD; LEASE; RENT STRIKE.

TENURE

Tenure is the legal right to hold a job or public office for a specified or unlimited period of time. Tenure protects many teachers and certain government employees from arbitrary dismissal. For example, federal judges serve for life, contingent upon their good behavior.

Public school teachers are granted tenure through state law, whereas private school teachers have the terms for acquiring tenure spelled out in their employment contracts. To receive tenure, teachers must usually complete a probationary period, which can last for several years.

Tenure allows teachers to retain their academic standing and job security even if their personal views are unpopular. A teacher cannot be dismissed for his political views unless he expresses them in a way that is disruptive to the school—for example, organizing a student strike. Once a teacher has obtained tenure, he can usually be dismissed only for incompetence or serious misconduct, such as physical abuse of a student or conviction of a felony. See also SPEECH, FREEDOM OF; TEACHER.

TIME-SHARE

Carolyn and Tom, who live in Delaware, are considering buying a ski chalet in Vail, Colorado. But they are dismayed at the high cost of property there. Then they learn they might be able to purchase a time-share at that location. A time-share is the ownership or use of real estate for a specific time period. By purchasing or leasing this period, each buyer or renter gains the exclusive right to use the property during that designated time.

Developers make large profits from time-shares because, since the cost of a single property is borne by a number of people, they are able to get a greater price for the property than if they sold it to one buyer. Although time-shares may enable buyers to enjoy a vacation property that they could not afford to buy on their own, they should not be viewed as investments, as they are rarely resold at a profit.

HOW TIME-SHARES WORK

Most time-share units are located in vacation resorts. A unit may be an apartment of any size, a cottage, a chalet, a studio, or even a full-size house. Typically the developer of the property owns the entire community or complex of units. He may also have arrangements with developments in other areas so that owners in his complex can trade their time-share for a stay in a unit located elsewhere.

REGULATION

Since the 1980's, when the time-share business expanded rapidly, most states—including vacation meccas like Florida, Hawaii, Virginia, and South Carolina—have introduced regulations to eliminate problems and abuses in the industry. Furthermore, uniform legislation has been developed that can be adopted by all states. The Model Real Estate Time-Share Act, for example, has been used as a basis for legislation in Massachusetts, Rhode Island, and Wisconsin.

Many states now require developers to register their time-share offerings with the state securities or corporation commission, the attorney general's consumer-protection division, or the real estate department. State regulators also oversee the creation and termination of time-shares and the licensing of sales representatives. Most states also require a "cooling-off" period, during which a buyer who has signed a contract can change his mind. States also determine whether properties bought as time-shares are taxed through sales taxes, lodging taxes, or real estate taxes. See also COOLING-OFF PERIOD.

TYPES OF TIME-SHARES

Before you sign a contract, you should have an attorney who specializes in real estate review the developer's proposal. The terms of time-share ownership differ from one developer to another, and you should know what type of interest in the property you are being offered.

Some developers require you to buy your time-share property outright. Although the ownership arrangements differ slightly from one company to another, you will probably receive a deed and possibly a separate agreement that establishes your right to use the property during specific time periods. For example, you might buy the right to occupy Unit 25 every year during the third week in July.

Other time-share developers make similar provisions but do not convey any interest in real estate to the buyer. Instead

ABC's

Of Choosing a Vacation Time-Share

Before signing a contract to buy or lease a time-share, take a close look at the details and discuss the following issues with the salesperson and your attorney.

- ❑ Does the time-share contract offer a cooling-off period? If it does, how can you cancel the contract?
- ❑ What amenities are included? Do you have to bring your own linens, for instance, or arrange for maid service?
- ❑ Is the time-share property still under construction? If so, has the developer posted a bond for its completion?
- ❑ Are you able to trade your time-share unit with another owner for use of his unit in a different resort?
- ❑ Does your contract permit you to sell the time-share at a later date?
- ❑ What extra expenses, such as maintenance fees and taxes, will add to your total cost?
- ❑ If there is a monthly maintenance fee, are there limits on how much the fee can rise?
- ❑ Will you need to buy additional liability insurance in order to cover you for accidents that occur while you have guests on the property? (If the salesperson is unsure, ask your insurance agent.)
- ❑ Will you have to bear the cost of making repairs or improvements to the property?
- ❑ Are there restrictions as to children, pets, or the number of guests you may have?

they offer you one of the following options:

◇ A *vacation license*, which entitles you to use a particular unit for a specified period of time each year for a certain number of years.

◇ A *vacation lease*, which is like a vacation license, but also enables you to rent or transfer your time-share rights.

◇ A *club membership*, which allows you to stay at the resort at a particular time each year, but not at a specific unit. Sometimes a club membership offers you a flexible arrangement, whereby you can stay at different residences at different times each year.

OWNERS' RESPONSIBILITIES

If you own the time-share, you have an interest in the real property and you can deduct the appropriate taxes and interest payments. Ownership also entails some responsibility for maintaining and repairing the property. If you lease the property, however, you are not entitled to any tax deductions for it, nor are you usually responsible for maintenance or insurance costs. For information on evaluating a time-share, see the box at left.

COMPLAINTS

If the developer who sold you a time-share misled you about the terms, you may be able to break your contract. A number of federal and state laws may provide the basis for doing so. The federal Truth-in-Lending Act, the federal Interstate Land Sales Full Disclosure Act, state consumer-protection laws, and securities ("blue-sky") laws may offer grounds for declaring your contract invalid. An attorney can tell you which laws apply to your situation. The state attorney general should be able to give you the names of developers who unfairly or misleadingly advertise time-share opportunities. See also VACATION HOME.

TITLE INSURANCE

Among the closing costs you pay in a real estate transaction is a lump-sum premium for title insurance. This type of insurance, which is usually required by mortgage lenders, protects you if someone else claims ownership of your new property, or if there are any outstanding liens or debts against it. Such claims create what are known as defects in the title.

When you buy title insurance, the insurer agrees to defend your title to the property if someone challenges your ownership in court or makes a claim against it arising from a previous owner's debts.

Title insurance usually costs about 1 percent of the property's purchase price, and the coverage lasts as long as you own the property. In some instances the mortgage lender purchases the title insurance. Most policies will insure you for loss up to the full purchase price of the house.

Title insurance will not protect you against any defects in the title that occur after you own the property. For instance, if you fail to pay the roofer for his work and he puts a lien on the house, you alone are responsible for the debt.

The title insurance policy will specify how and when you must notify the insurer about a claim. When you make a claim, you are entitled to be reimbursed only for your actual loss. For instance, if a subcontractor had a lien against the property that the previous owner did not pay, title insurance would cover the amount owed to the subcontractor. Or, if an undisclosed easement reduced the value of the property, you may be paid the difference between what you paid for the property and what it is actually worth.

Even when a title search indicates that the title is clear, someone may still challenge your ownership rights. For instance, Stella bought a house from Stanley without realizing that he was a minor, and thus not old enough to transfer the ownership of the property to another person. Stanley's older brother took Stella to court to invalidate the sale, and the court returned the house to Stanley's brother. Stella's title insurer reimbursed her for her down payment and for other expenses that she had incurred in buying the house. See also EASEMENT; HOME BUYING AND SELLING; LIEN.

TORT

A tort is a civil wrong committed by one person against another person. A tort occurs when someone injures another person or causes damage to his property, whether intentionally or through negligence.

Torts form the basis for most lawsuits. In a tort case the individual who has been harmed in some way (the plaintiff in the civil lawsuit) seeks some sort of redress or compensation from the wrongdoer (the defendant).

If the plaintiff sues the defendant, a judge or jury decides whether the case has merit and determines the amount of monetary damages to be awarded.

The element of injury or damage is important, for without it there are no grounds for a lawsuit. Suppose Jeff unintentionally bumps into Laurie on a crowded bus. Technically, Jeff has committed the tort known as battery (the unauthorized touching of another), but because Laurie has suffered no injury, she cannot sue Jeff.

Since a corporation or government body is considered to be a person in the eyes of the law, it can be either the plaintiff or the defendant of a tort. See also DAMAGES; LAWSUIT; NEGLIGENCE; SOVEREIGN IMMUNITY.

INTENTIONAL AND NEGLIGENT TORTS

Any tort that is willfully committed is known as an intentional tort. There are dozens of such torts, among them false arrest and false imprisonment, battery, assault, invasion of privacy, theft, interference with property rights, defamation (including libel and slander), infliction of emotional distress, damaging or destroying someone else's property, embezzlement, extortion, trespass, and malicious prosecution.

Unintentional torts are generally referred to as torts of negligence. The standard for determining negligence is whether the wrongdoer took care to act as a reasonably prudent person would in similar circumstances. Suppose Lucy slips and falls on a store's recently mopped floor. Since there is no question that the store owner did not set out to harm its customers, Lucy would have to prove that the store had not taken reasonable care to keep the floor dry. See also NEGLIGENCE.

Courts usually award damages to the plaintiff based on her injuries. A victim of an intentional tort may also receive a further award, called punitive damages.

STRICT LIABILITY

In some states and in some situations, a plaintiff in a tort lawsuit does not have to show that the defendant was negligent or that he acted intentionally. When a person or business creates or maintains a product or property that is inherently dangerous, he may be held strictly liable for injuries suffered by others. The operator of a nuclear power plant, the owner of a pet python, or the makers of a poisonous chemical could all be found strictly liable for an injury someone suffers due to their premises, pet, or product. The fact that their premises, pet, or product poses a serious safety threat may make them strictly liable. See also DOG LAW; LIABILITY; PET; PRODUCT SAFETY AND LIABILITY.

MINORS

Minors can be held responsible for their torts, depending on the age of the child. In determining whether a child who committed a civil wrong did so intentionally, a court must decide whether the child knew that his behavior was improper. All states have specific ages below which a child is considered to be incapable of committing an intentional tort.

Almost all the states have laws that make parents responsible for intentional torts committed by their children, but in most states parents cannot be held responsible for their children's negligence.

Suppose 10-year-old Darlene and her friends are standing on a bridge throwing snowballs at the cars passing below, and one of the snowballs shatters the windshield of an automobile. In her state, Darlene has reached the age at which she can be held personally accountable for her actions. However, because she is still a minor, her parents are liable for the cost of the windshield and any injuries suffered by the occupants of the car. But suppose Darlene had merely been playfully kicking at various rocks on the bridge. If one of the rocks were to tumble off the bridge and strike a windshield, Darlene's act would be considered negligent, and Darlene, not her parents, would be held liable for any damage or injuries. See PARENTAL-LIABILITY LAWS.

Of course, minors usually do not have assets or insurance to compensate a person for his injuries or damages. But state laws generally allow a winning plaintiff to keep his judgment in force for many years. Therefore, the person who was injured by Darlene's negligent rock-kicking and was awarded monetary damages in court might be able to enforce his judgment years later, when Darlene is a legal adult who is earning income or has acquired assets. See also JUDGMENT.

INCOMPETENT PERSONS

Mentally incompetent persons can be held responsible for the torts they commit, whether intentionally or through negligence. If an elderly man suffering from Alzheimer's disease drives his car into your yard, damaging your fence and lawn, you can sue him in civil court. However, if he is found to be legally incompetent, he cannot be criminally prosecuted. See also INCOMPETENCY.

TOTTEN TRUST

A type of bank account in which one person deposits money in his own name but holds it in trust for another is known as a Totten trust. Unlike the creator of other kinds of trusts, the person who sets up a Totten trust is free to do anything with the money in the account. She does not have to be concerned about preserving the funds for the beneficiary's use or notifying the beneficiary of the trust's existence.

When the person who established the Totten trust dies, the funds in it automatically become the property of the beneficiary without having to be probated. Therefore, Totten trusts are frequently used to avoid probate. Ask your bank for information about establishing a Totten trust in your state. See also PROBATE; TRUST; WILL.

TOUR OPERATOR

A tour operator organizes travel arrangements for vacationers in a "package" that usually includes transportation, accommodations, and meals for one inclusive price. Typically, these packages are sold by travel agents.

Although the vast majority of tour operators are honest and conscientious, some make promises that they fail to keep: First-class hotels turn out to be rundown, the airline is in fact a small-time charter organization, or an "experienced" guide may know little more about the destination than you do. Since there is minimal government regulation of tour operators, protect yourself against such mishaps by careful shopping and investigation. See also AIRLINE CHARTER; TRAVEL AGENCY.

INDUSTRY REGULATION

Ask your travel agent or the tour operator whether the company is a member of the United States Tour Operators Association (USTOA). In order to become a USTOA member, a tour operator must have been in business for at least three years and must be able to provide 18 references.

Members of the USTOA must adhere to certain professional standards. For example, they must provide truthful and accurate information on prices, itineraries, and any other conditions associated with the tours they offer. They must also participate in USTOA's $5 million consumer-protection program that covers the deposits and payments of customers in the event that a member declares bankruptcy.

The USTOA also requires its members to carry a minimum of $1 million of professional liability insurance. If you have a problem with a USTOA member, write to the United States Tour Operators Association at 211 East 51st Street, Suite 12B, New York, NY 10022. The organization may be able to intercede on your behalf.

STEPS TO TAKE

Before signing up for a tour, do the following:

1. Get recommendations from your travel agent and people you trust who have had direct experience with the tour operator.

2. To determine the financial stability of a tour operator, ask if he is bonded or is a member of the USTOA. In addition, ask the tour operator how long he has been in business and make sure that he deals only with reputable air carriers and hotel chains.

3. Ask your state or local office of consumer affairs if there have been past complaints about the operator and whether they were resolved satisfactorily.

4. Find out exactly what is included in the price of the trip and whether you will have to pay extra charges for meals, tips, agent's fees, insurance, or transfers between hotels and airports.

5. Pay the smallest deposit you can, and use a credit card. If you do not receive all the services you were promised, or if you are dissatisfied with the quality of the travel arrangements, your credit card company may intercede on your behalf. For more information, see CREDIT CARD AND CHARGE ACCOUNT.

6. Read the terms and conditions of your tour carefully. Find out the tour operator's refund policy in the event that the company cancels the tour or revises the itinerary in an unacceptable way. Inquire also about the operator's policy if you cancel. Most will refund only a portion of your money, and if you cancel on very short notice, you may not receive a refund at all. You may have to purchase cancellation insurance in the event that you become ill or otherwise have to cancel the trip.

TOY

Like the manufacturers of other products, toy makers are subject to product-liability laws when a poorly made or defectively designed toy causes an injury to someone.

Suppose you buy your young nephew a string of wooden beads—the kind designed to hang in a crib. Unknown to you, the beads are strung in such a way that a child could pull them off the string. While playing with the beads, your nephew pulls one off, swallows it, and chokes. Fortunately, his mother is able to dislodge the bead, but the child still requires medical treatment.

In this example, the manufacturer of the beads has violated the warranty of merchantability—the promise made to a consumer that the product is safe for intended use. Because your nephew suffered an injury due to the faulty design of the beads, his parents could sue the manufacturer for compensation for medical costs related to the injury and for additional damages for your nephew's pain and suffering. If the merchant misrepresented the age at which a child could safely play with the toy, the parents could sue him for damages too. Keep in mind that you will have no basis to sue if you give your child a toy that is inappropriate for his age or if you do not adequately supervise him when he plays with it. See also CONSUMER PROTECTION; PRODUCT SAFETY AND LIABILITY.

SAFETY STANDARDS

The federal Consumer Product Safety Commission (CPSC) monitors the safety of children's toys, furniture, and other products. Manufacturers and importers must conform to the CPSC standards for the design and construction of toys. Toys that fail to meet these standards may be subject to a recall by the CPSC, and the manufacturer or importer could be held strictly liable for any injuries caused by the toys. CPSC standards state that:

◇ Toys may not contain toxic chemicals or materials, except for a limited amount of lead paint.

◇ Electrical toys must be constructed in a way that prevents the possibility of electrical shock or burn.

◇ Toys intended for children under three years old must be unbreakable and free of small parts that could present a choking hazard. Certain toys, including crayons, chalk, and balloons, are exempt from this provision, however.

◇ Toys made for children under eight years old must not contain any heating elements, nor may they have any sharp points or edges.

If the CPSC receives a complaint about a poorly made or defective toy or learns of injuries caused by the toy, it can order the manufacturer to recall the product and refund the purchaser's money. You can find out about product recalls by writing or calling the Consumer Product Safety Commission, at the address given on page 116.

In addition, the toy industry has established voluntary age and safety labeling standards for toy manufacturers. For instance, a cloth toy should have a label stating that it is flame-resistant, and a toy oven should have a label indicating that it is intended for use only by children over eight years old. When you buy a toy, look for these warnings and for the manufacturer's name and address, which should be clearly displayed on the product's packaging. Some manufacturers offer toll-free customer-service lines to answer questions about their products.

REAL LIFE, REAL LAW

The Case of the Golf Gizmo

The manufacturer of the "Golf Gizmo," a device designed to help novices improve their golf swings, included the following statement on its package and in its assembly instructions: "Completely Safe—Ball Will Not Hit Player." Although 13-year-old Fred erected the Golf Gizmo according to the instructions, his club went under the cord of the device, causing the golf ball to loop back and strike him on the head. Fred suffered permanent brain damage. A lawsuit was filed against the manufacturer, and the court found in favor of Fred.

The manufacturer appealed the lower court's decision. It reiterated that the statement on the box and in the instructions was not meant to be a guarantee of absolute safety. The company claimed that there are inherent dangers in playing golf, and that Fred had assumed those risks in using the device. It also claimed that Fred should not even have been allowed to bring the suit, since he had not bought the Gizmo himself, but had received it as a gift from his mother.

The California State Supreme Court rejected the manufacturer's arguments. It noted Fred's testimony that he had read and believed the statements concerning the safety of the device, and it held that those statements did not adequately warn consumers about the dangers inherent in golfing. Moreover, it stated that the fact that Fred had received the toy as a gift did not bar him from bringing suit. The court allowed Fred to be compensated for his injury on the basis of the manufacturer's false representation and breach of warranty.

TRADEMARK

A trademark is a distinctive symbol, character, sign, name, or device that enables consumers to identify a product. By associating a product with a trademark, the manufacturer hopes that satisfied customers will identify the trademark as a sign of quality and not only buy the same product again, but also buy other products with the same trademark.

For instance, after years of experimenting with different recipes, Jackie has finally perfected what she thinks is the world's best-tasting barbecue sauce. She hopes that this will be the first in a small line of food products that she will sell at local farmers' markets. To make sure that her customers know this barbecue sauce is hers, Jackie asks a designer to create a distinctive trademark that she can put on the bottles of sauce.

Jackie must choose a trademark that is not generic or simply descriptive of her product. For instance, she cannot trademark such names as Barbecue Sauce or Spicy Barbecue Sauce, but she can trademark Jackie's Spicy Barbecue Sauce.

Furthermore, her trademark must not make a false or misleading claim. If she named her sauce Jackie's Scotch Whisky Barbecue Sauce, the sauce would have to contain Scotch whisky. In addition, Jackie must make sure that no one else has a trademark like hers. Once Jackie begins selling products with her trademark, nobody else has the right to use it. See also HOME BUSINESS.

REGISTERING A TRADEMARK

If she plans to sell her product in interstate commerce, Jackie may want to register her trademark with the federal government by writing to the U.S. Patent and Trademark Office for a trademark application. She will be asked to enclose a facsimile of the trademark and a filing fee with her application. An examining officer will review the application, and if the trademark is distinctive (that is, it does not resemble another trademark), he will publish a notice in the *U.S. Patent and Trademark Official Gazette*. Then, if no one objects to the trademark within 180 days, the examiner will issue a certificate of trademark registration. See also COPYRIGHT; PATENT.

Once her trademark is registered, Jackie can display it with a symbol consisting of the letter "R" in a circle, or the words "Registered in the U.S. Patent Office," or "Reg. U.S. Pat. Off." Exclusive right to use the trademark is granted for 10 years, after which Jackie must file a new application.

Similar procedures are used for state trademark protection. If Jackie plans to limit sales to one state, she may choose to register her trademark in that state alone. She can write to the secretary of state's trademark department in her state for an application. An attorney familiar with patent and trademark law can offer advice about the best options for protecting her trademark.

Anyone can register a trademark; Jackie does not have to be incorporated or own a business in order to do so.

LOSING A TRADEMARK

In order to protect her trademark, even if it is not registered, Jackie must display it and continue to use it. Otherwise someone else may adopt and register the trademark.

The holder of a trademark has the right to sell or license it to someone else, but it is not necessary for the new trademark holder to buy the rights to the original product. For instance, if a large food manufacturer buys Jackie's trademark, the company can simply use it on its own sauce; the manufacturer does not have to buy the rights to her original recipe.

INFRINGEMENT

The holder of a trademark also has the right to file a lawsuit against anyone who infringes upon it—that is, uses it without his authorization. There is no infringement, however, if the use of the trademark does not confuse consumers or involve competing products. In addition, if products are sold in completely separate markets, two companies may use the same trademark.

FILING A SUIT

If a person or company successfully sues someone for trademark infringement, the court may issue an injunction against the infringing party to halt its use of the trademark. It may also award monetary compensation, or damages, to the trademark holder. The damages may be based on the profit and goodwill lost by the trademark holder as a result of the infringement.

Trade School

Trade schools provide career training in a variety of fields, such as truck driving, auto mechanics, bartending, cosmetology, medical technology, carpentry, printing, computer programming, and secretarial work. In general, the course of study lasts up to two years.

Trade schools can vary widely in the training and opportunities they offer. Some make claims about their students' job prospects that are unrealistic or simply false. Furthermore, they may ask students to sign contracts that require them to pay large tuition fees. Even if a student does not finish the course of study, he will be obligated by law to pay the full amount stated in the contract. For this reason alone, students should take care when choosing a trade school.

ACCREDITATION

Although trade schools are licensed by the state in which they are located, the licensing requirements may be relatively easy to meet. In some states a trade school needs little more than a name, a permanent address, and a few instructors. You can find out what your state's licensing requirements are and whether a particular school has a past record of complaints from your state department of higher education.

Some trade schools are accredited by a national or regional organization, although the standards set by these organizations also vary significantly. Nevertheless, accreditation standards like the teacher-student ratio or the number and variety of classes are good indications of a school's quality.

INFLATED CLAIMS

Some trade schools try to attract students by advertising that their students are eligible to receive state- or federally sponsored loans and grants. They do not mention, however, that financial aid programs are generally available to students at any licensed trade school and are no indication of the quality of a school. A student's ability to obtain this aid will depend primarily on his own financial need.

Find out whether the school has a placement office and whether prospective employers regard the school's programs as adequate preparation for the field. Note that many junior colleges and vocational-technical schools offer similar training programs, often at lower cost, and do not require you to sign a long-term contract.

BEFORE YOU SIGN

Review the school's admissions contract carefully. Some schools expect you to sign up for a full program of study; others will let you pay for courses as you take them. Be sure you know the school's refund policy in case you change your mind after you sign up.

Do not let an admissions representative pressure you into signing a contract. Many of these representatives are actually commissioned salespeople whose income depends on getting you to sign on the dotted line. If you do not understand something in the contract, do not rely on the admissions representative for an explanation. Instead, consult a lawyer. Also, ask school officials for the names of former students, and be extremely wary of a school that will not divulge them.

Traffic Ticket

Because Sharon was late for an appointment, she drove faster than the posted speed limit. A police officer pulled her over and, while writing up the speeding ticket, informed Sharon that one of her car's brake lights was not working and included a citation for that violation as well. Sharon finally made it downtown and luckily found a metered parking space. When she returned three hours later, there was a parking ticket on her windshield; the meter had expired a half hour before.

Sharon has been the unfortunate recipient of the three types of traffic tickets: a moving violation, an equipment violation, and a parking violation. A traffic ticket is considered a summons, and if Sharon does not pay the fine or appear in court to contest the charge, the court may issue a warrant for her arrest. She may also be unable to renew the registration on her car if she has outstanding traffic tickets.

MOVING VIOLATIONS

Speeding is the most common moving violation for which drivers are ticketed. Other violations include reckless driving, failure to yield the right-of-way, not restraining a young child in a car seat (if state law requires it), and failing to obey a traffic signal.

If a police officer signals you to pull over, you must do so. You should remain seated in your car with your hands in plain view, unless the officer orders you out of the car. The officer will ask to see your driver's license and, in some instances, proof of vehicle registration. Being pulled over does not necessarily mean that you will be given a traffic ticket. The officer may decide to give you a warning. For more serious offenses, such as driving while intoxicated, you may be asked to take a field sobriety or breath test and be taken into custody. See also DRUNK DRIVING; SPEEDING TICKET.

EQUIPMENT VIOLATIONS

When you operate a vehicle on public streets and highways, the law expects it to be in proper working order and in compliance with all the required safety standards. If your vehicle does not meet these standards, you may be given a ticket. Headlights, taillights, brake lights, and turn signals that do not work are safety hazards that could prompt a police officer to issue you a ticket. If you have the necessary repairs made before your court date, the judge may be willing to waive the fine if you can prove that the repair was made.

Depending on state law, other equipment violations include not having a windshield made out of approved safety glass, having materials or objects that obstruct the driver's view, or not having a muffler or tail pipe. Tickets issued for these violations usually order the driver to make repairs within a reasonable period of time or pay a fine.

PARKING VIOLATIONS

Your vehicle may be ticketed for being illegally parked on a local street or on a state or federal highway. Among the violations found in most cities are parking in restricted areas, such as spaces for the handicapped; parking during hours prohibited by a posted sign; and parking in a space after the meter has expired. Your city may also prohibit you from parking dismantled or unregistered cars in your yard and may limit the number of registered cars you can park outside your garage over a long period.

If you find a ticket on your windshield, read the instructions carefully. You may have the option of paying the fine by mailing in the designated fee or appearing in traffic court to contest the ticket. Ignoring a ticket can lead to further trouble. You may find a "boot" on your car—a metal device that locks around the tire to prevent you from driving the car away. You may also be arrested, especially if you have other outstanding tickets.

TRAFFIC COURT

Before you decide to contest a ticket in court, look at the facts of your case objectively. Do you have a valid reason for violating traffic laws or just an excuse? Being late for an important appointment will never be accepted by a traffic court judge as justification for exceeding the speed limit.

Your case will also be weak unless you have objective evidence and impartial witnesses to support it. Close friends and relatives are not considered impartial witnesses. Suppose you are ticketed for having defective taillights. You may avoid a fine if you can give the judge a receipt showing that you recently had the car in for that repair, but the mechanic apparently did not do his work properly.

If the potential penalty is serious, such as suspension of your license, you may want to have an attorney accompany you to court. For most other traffic violations, where you face only the prospect of a small fine, you can generally appear without counsel. The judge will ask you whether you want to plead guilty or not guilty. If you plead guilty, you may be given the opportunity to offer an explanation.

If you plead not guilty, the case proceeds with the presentation of the evidence against you by an attorney representing the prosecuting attorney's office. The police officer who issued the ticket will be questioned to establish that you did, in fact, violate the traffic code. You will then be given the opportunity to cross-examine the officer. If he is the only witness for the prosecution, the attorney will rest his case. At that time you may present any witnesses or evidence to support your own version of the facts. Once all the evidence has been

CHECKLIST

How to Fight a Traffic Ticket

When your receive a traffic ticket, the state bears the burden of proving your guilt. In some states your guilt must be proved "beyond a reasonable doubt," while in others the government need only show your guilt by a preponderance of the evidence. In any case, if the state cannot meet the burden of proof, you will not have to pay the ticket. For this reason, some experts suggest that you always contest a traffic ticket in court and require the state to prove its case against you. A traffic ticket can be dismissed for the following reasons:

❑ **FAILURE TO SHOW EVIDENCE.** Suppose you are charged with driving under the influence. Under the DUI law, the prosecution must make a prima facie case—that is, a case with sufficient evidence to show that you were the operator of the vehicle on a public road and that you were under the influence of alcohol or drugs at the time you were charged. If the prosecutor fails to produce evidence of any of these conditions, you can ask the court to dismiss the charge for failure to make a prima facie case.

❑ **LACK OF JURISDICTION.** Suppose you are stopped for running a red light by a city police officer, but the ticket shows that the light is in an unincorporated area of the county. You would argue that the officer was not authorized to write the ticket and that the court has no jurisdiction over the matter.

❑ **LACK OF PROSECUTION.** This situation occurs when the state is not ready to present its case at the time of your court appearance. It happens most often when the police officer who wrote the ticket fails to appear in court to testify. The first time he does not appear, the court is likely to grant a continuance. But if he fails to show up a second time, the charges are more likely to be dismissed.

❑ **MISTAKEN IDENTIFICATION.** A classic instance of mistaken identity occurs when you receive a parking ticket in the mail from a town that you have never been in. The reason for the error usually is that the police officer miscopied letters or numbers on the offender's license plate. In this situation you can often have the ticket canceled simply by notifying the police department that issued the ticket.

heard, each side may make closing remarks.

Even though traffic court is not as formal as other court proceedings, you should dress appropriately and be neatly groomed. Your appearance can help make a good impression with the court. Be respectful of the judge and any witnesses, such as the officer who issued the ticket, and be courteous when asking questions. Practice your presentation before you go to court to help you organize your thoughts and present a clearer explanation of your case.

PENALTIES

Whether you plead guilty or you plead not guilty and lose your case, the judge will impose a sentence, which may be a fine or imprisonment. A serious violation, such as driving under the influence of alcohol, could result in both a fine and imprisonment. If the violation is not an extremely serious one, some judges will give the offender the option of attending a driver education or improvement program. Other possible penalties are suspension or revocation of driving privileges and community-service work. If the judge imposes a fine, you must pay it on time or you can be found in contempt of court. The judge could then issue a warrant for your arrest and have you put in jail.

TRAVEL AGENCY

Travel agencies make travel arrangements for their customers. They make their living from commissions paid by the companies that provide the travel services, such as airlines, hotels, and cruise operators. Few, if any, laws specifically regulate travel agencies or their employees. Nonetheless, agencies have a legal duty to be honest and fair in their dealings with you. For example, a travel agent who intentionally overcharges you for a ticket can be sued for damages, and an agent who takes money from his customer but fails to forward it to the airline or hotel can be charged with fraud.

If a travel agent makes a mistake on your reservation, you may be able to sue him for breach of contract. Some travel agencies try to limit their liability for such mistakes by printing disclaimers on ticket envelopes and itineraries, but an agent might still be liable for civil charges.

Be careful when choosing a travel agency. Travel agents who are certified by the American Society of Travel Agents (ASTA) have taken a two-year course of study and have five or more years of experience. Certified agents often display an ASTA emblem on their office windows and on their business cards. Besides giving you the assurance of training, experience, and reliability, ASTA provides mediation services for disputes between its members and their customers.

You can ask about a travel agency's reputation by calling the consumer-affairs division of your state attorney general's office. See also AIRLINE CHARTER; TOUR OPERATOR.

TREASON

Treason is a crime committed against one's country. The Constitution defines treason against the United States as consisting "only in levying war against them, or in adhering to their Enemies, or giving them aid and comfort."

The key component of treason is a person's willingness to betray his allegiance to his country. For example, a U.S. citizen who willfully encourages U.S. troops fighting in an enemy country to surrender is committing an act of treason. However, merely speaking out against the U.S. government's policy toward its enemies or its conduct of a military action is not an act of treason.

If a person is forced into committing an act of treason by the enemy, his action is not considered treasonous. In the Persian Gulf conflict, for example, several captured American military personnel were coerced, after being tortured, into making statements criticizing Operation Desert Storm and U.S. leaders. These statements did not constitute treason, however, since they were not made willingly.

Treason, the highest crime in the nation, is punishable by imprisonment or death. In order to convict someone of treason, the Constitution requires that there be at least two witnesses to the act or an open confession in court by the defendant.

TREE

George was annoyed when he saw that branches from his neighbor's tree were extending so far over the property line that they could scratch his new car. George asked his neighbor to trim the tree, but his neighbor refused. What action can George take?

First George should find out whether his community has a homeowners association that can provide mediation services. If the covenants in his neighbor's deed require the neighbor to keep his trees trimmed, the association might be able to take action on George's behalf. If this fails, and if George lives in one of the few states that allow a lawsuit to be brought against someone whose tree is extending onto a neighbor's property, he might want to take his neighbor to court.

If George prefers to take matters into his own hands, he has a legal right to trim the tree branches back as far as the boundary line between his property and his neighbor's. He would also be allowed to cut back or block the roots of his neighbor's tree if they extend onto his property. But in most cases George would not be allowed to trim the tree simply because it blocked his view or cast shade on his lawn.

If George decides to do any major trimming, he should first check with his city's building or parks department to see if a permit is required.

If George damaged or destroyed his neighbor's tree in the process of trimming it, he could be held responsible and might be required to reimburse his neighbor for the value of the tree. In some states, a person who intentionally damages or destroys a neighbor's tree could by required by law to pay double or even triple the value of the tree. If George decides to trim his neighbor's tree, therefore, he would be wise to hire a professional tree-service company.

A tree may be damaged or destroyed as a result of vandalism, an accident, or someone's negligence. In any of these situations, check with your insurance agent. Most homeowners policies provide for replacement of a damaged or destroyed tree up to a specified limit, such as $500. However, if the damage exceeds the amount covered by insurance, you may need to file a lawsuit against the person who caused it in order to be fully compensated. See also HOMEOWNERS ASSOCIATION; NEIGHBOR; VIEW.

TRESPASS

Entering another person's property without permission or interfering with an owner's use and enjoyment of her property constitutes trespassing. Trespassers can be subject to both civil and criminal charges.

You can be guilty of trespassing even if you do not step onto the property. Suppose you are hunting on public land when you see a deer in a privately owned field. If you decide to shoot, bear in mind that the moment your rifle's bullet crosses the boundary of the private land, you are guilty of trespassing. This is true even if no harm is done.

If your trespassing results in property damage, you can be held financially responsible for it, even if the damage was unintentional. Suppose your shot had found its mark and you enter the private land to collect the deer carcass. In doing so, you inadvertently trample on a garden planted with rare flowers. You are responsible for compensating the owner for the damage to his plants.

Trespassing can be caused by objects as well as people. For example, if your neighbor's unsecured garbage cans blow into your yard and ruin your tulip beds, your neighbor is guilty of trespassing and may be held liable for damages.

PROTECTING TRESPASSERS

Although trespassing is illegal, a property owner may not use force to remove a trespasser who poses no threat of violence. If he does, he could be subject to civil and criminal charges. Instead the property owner should call the police to have the trespasser removed.

A property owner could also be held liable if he sets a trap for trespassers and someone is injured by it. For example, if you dig a hole in your yard solely for the purpose of injuring trespassers and someone falls in the hole and breaks his leg, the trespasser might be able to sue you for his injuries.

You may have different responsibilities to children who trespass. The law extends spe-

REAL LIFE, REAL LAW

The Case of the Frustrated Florist

George Wilson's flower shop had been broken into on at least six occasions, causing George's insurer to cancel his policy. In desperation, George rigged a spring gun—a shotgun wired to the shop's back door. If anyone opened the door, the gun would go off, shooting the intruder. George posted a sign by the door stating: "Warning—No Trespassing."

A few weeks later, the spring gun did its job, shooting an intruder in the chest and killing him. The police arrested George and charged him with voluntary manslaughter.

At the trial, George waived his right to a jury trial and told the judge that he had not intended for the gun to kill the intruder, but merely to wound him and prevent him from escaping. He also argued that, because he had posted a warning sign at the back door, the intruder had assumed the risk of being shot by the spring gun.

The judge disagreed. She held that the law clearly prohibits a property owner from using deadly force on trespassers. While she sympathized with George's plight, she could not condone his reckless disregard for the safety of others and found him guilty of voluntary manslaughter. George was sentenced to 42 months in prison, but the judge suspended all but 6 months of the sentence.

cial protection to children if something on your property might cause them harm but is too tempting for them to stay away from, such as an unfenced swimming pool. See ATTRACTIVE NUISANCE; TORT.

CRIMINAL TRESPASS

In a few states a person who ignores a "No Trespassing" sign posted on private property or a verbal warning issued by the property owner is subject to criminal prosecution. But in many states, criminal charges can be made only when a trespasser enters someone's property with the intention of actually committing a crime, such as burglary or arson.

POSSESSION VERSUS OWNERSHIP

In cases between owners and tenants, most courts rule that the party in physical possession of the property has the right to keep out everyone else, including the owner. For example, if your landlord enters your apartment without notice or without obtaining your approval beforehand, he may be guilty of trespassing. See also ADVERSE POSSESSION; EASEMENT; EVICTION; LANDLORD.

TRUST

A trust is a legal arrangement by which the assets of one person are transferred to another person or institution for the benefit of a third party. In a trust the person with the assets (known as the settlor) transfers ownership of his property to someone (the trustee) who promises to administer the property for a third party (the beneficiary) according to the settlor's wishes.

TYPES OF TRUSTS

Essentially all trusts fall into one of two basic categories: living or testamentary.

Living trusts
In a living, or *inter vivos,* trust the settlor transfers ownership of his property to a trustee who manages it throughout the settlor's lifetime. Upon the death of the settlor, the trustee distributes the trust to the beneficiaries in accordance with the settlor's instructions.

In most cases, the settlor of a living trust reserves the right to modify or revoke the trust as long as he lives. This type of living trust is known as a revocable trust. If you are creating a revocable living trust, you can name yourself as the trustee, but you will have to name a successor trustee to manage your estate if you become incapacitated and to distribute your assets when you die.

A major reason for creating a revocable trust is to pass property without the delay and expenses involved in probating a will. Living trusts do not have to be probated. See PROBATE.

An irrevocable trust avoids not only probate expenses but the often considerably greater expenses of estate taxes. To create an irrevocable trust, the settlor signs away the right to make any changes to the trust. Be careful if you are considering establishing an irrevocable trust. If your financial conditions change, for example, you cannot cancel the trust or amend it to obtain more of the trust's income or principal for your own support. Never make an irrevocable trust without the advice of an attorney who is experienced in trust and estate law. See LIVING TRUST.

Testamentary trusts
A testamentary trust is a provision of your last will and testament. It instructs a trustee regarding the use or sale of property that the creator of the will, or testator, has left to his heirs. In effect, it allows the testator to extend control over property after his death. Since a testamentary trust is part of a will, it must be probated.

WHAT TRUSTS CAN DO

In addition to avoiding probate expenses and in some cases estate taxes, trusts are established to serve a variety of worthwhile purposes. The trusts described below can be either living or testamentary.

◇ In a *spendthrift trust* the beneficiary receives income from the trust, but the trustee is prohibited from distributing any of the principal. As its name implies, a spendthrift trust is a good way to keep an irresponsible son or daughter from squandering his or her inheritance on foolish investments or luxury purchases.

◇ An *accumulation trust* is designed to provide a nest egg for a beneficiary. To build the nest egg, the trustee keeps adding the interest and dividends from the principal to the trust until it is distributed to the beneficiary at the designated time.

◇ To create a *life insurance trust* the settlor names an

adult trustee as the beneficiary of his life insurance. Upon the settlor's death, the trustee distributes the proceeds of the life insurance policy in accordance with the settlor's instructions. A life insurance trust is advisable if you have large amounts of life insurance coverage, minor children whom you have named as beneficiaries, and an ex-spouse whom you do not want to have control of the money. See LIFE INSURANCE.

◇ A *charitable trust*, unlike other kinds of trusts, which must by law eventually terminate, may continue indefinitely. It can thus provide benefits to a charitable organization on an ongoing basis.

TRUSTEE

A trustee is a person who is authorized by another person (known as the settlor of the trust) to take possession of and manage some or all of the settlor's property on behalf of and in the best interests of a third party, known as the beneficiary, and in accordance with the terms of the trust.

NAMING A TRUSTEE

Although the law generally permits any legally competent person to serve as a trustee, not everyone is able or willing to accept the responsibility. Trustees are entitled to be paid for their services out of the trust's assets, although family and friends who agree to act as trustees may waive this right.

In some situations a settlor may want to consider using a corporate trustee—a bank or other financial institution that is authorized by the state to manage trusts. Most corporate trustees, however, rarely take on trusts that are valued at less than $250,000, and they will charge a fee for their services based on a percentage of the estate's value, up to the limit set by state law.

If you do not know whom to select as a trustee, your attorney can probably help you find a qualified person.

DUTIES AND POWERS

A trustee is a fiduciary—that is, he has a legal duty to act in the best interest of the beneficiary and abide by the provisions of the trust, as described in the checklist on page 525.

A trustee's powers are extensive. They may be either express or implied, mandatory or discretionary. Powers that are specifically stated in the trust document are express powers. For example, a written authorization given by the settlor to sell or lease trust property is an express power.

Implied powers are ones that are not stated explicitly, but that are necessary to carry out the trustee's duties. Suppose your trust requires the trustee to manage your business on behalf of your beneficiaries. The trust may not specifically authorize the trustee to pay rent for the business's warehouse or buy insurance for its assets, but the trustee's authority to do so is implied, since without it the trustee cannot fulfill his responsibility to manage the business.

Mandatory powers are ones that the trust document requires the trustee to exercise. For example, if a trust instructs the trustee to sell a piece of vacation property and deposit the proceeds from the sale in a certificate of deposit, the trustee has both the right and the duty to do so.

Discretionary powers require the trustee to use his own judgment in distributing assets to beneficiaries. For example, a trustee would be permitted to distribute a portion of the principal or interest of the trust if he felt that it was in the best interest of the beneficiary to do so. Unless the trustee acts irresponsibly or in bad faith, a court will not interfere in his exercise of discretionary powers. However, the actions of a trustee are subject to review by the beneficiaries, who can sue for restitution of any lost value.

TRUSTEES FOR NONPROFIT ORGANIZATIONS

Colleges, churches, hospitals, and other nonprofit or charitable organizations often turn over the management of their business affairs to a board of trustees. A board of trustees for a nonprofit organization serves much the same function as the board of directors of a profit-making corporation, making decisions about the management of the organization's finances.

Like the trustees of a trust created by an individual, the trustees of a nonprofit organization manage the property entrusted to them for the benefit of others. For example, a church's board of trustees manages property for the benefit of the church's members, in

CHECKLIST

Your Duties as a Trustee

Serving as a trustee is a difficult task, one that has legal and financial consequences if you do not perform your duties properly. Think very carefully before agreeing to serve as one. A trustee's responsibilities include:

❑ **THE DUTY TO FOLLOW THE EXPRESS INSTRUCTIONS OF THE SETTLOR OF THE TRUST TO THE BEST OF YOUR ABILITIES.**
If you fail to fulfill this obligation—for example, by refusing to sell property as required by the trust—you could be sued by the trust's beneficiaries.

❑ **THE DUTY TO ADMINISTER THE TRUST SOLELY FOR THE BENEFIT OF THE BENEFICIARIES, RATHER THAN FOR PERSONAL PROFIT.**
If you invest trust property in your own business, for example, you may be guilty of a breach of fiduciary duty and even criminal theft.

❑ **THE DUTY TO PROTECT THE TRUST PROPERTY.**
You must take reasonable steps to ensure that the value of the property is not diminished through unwise investments or mismanagement, make necessary repairs, and buy insurance for tangible property such as automobiles and real estate.

❑ **THE DUTY TO FOSTER GROWTH OF THE TRUST PROPERTY.**
It is not enough to keep the trust property as it is when you receive it. You have an obligation to manage, invest, and reinvest trust property in the best interests of the beneficiaries. In most states statutes prohibit trustees from making risky investments, and some states even set forth the kinds of investments a trustee can make. Failing to follow these legal requirements can make you personally responsible for any losses.

❑ **THE DUTY TO MAKE PAYMENTS TO THE TRUST'S BENEFICIARIES ACCORDING TO THE PROVISIONS IN THE TRUST.**
For example, if a trust orders the trustee to make payments only of income, you cannot pay with both income and principal. If you do, a beneficiary could sue you for the amount you spent.

❑ **THE DUTY TO KEEP TRUST PROPERTY SEPARATE FROM YOUR OWN PROPERTY AND FROM OTHER PROPERTY THAT YOU MANAGE.**
For example, trust accounts must be kept separate from your own bank accounts, and you cannot commingle funds from more than one trust unless you receive prior approval from the settlors.

accordance with the authority granted to them by the church. Unlike the trustees of a private trust, who may serve for the life of the trust, trustees for a nonprofit organization usually serve for a limited period. Like other trustees, they have the responsibilities outlined in the checklist above.

SERVING AS A TRUSTEE

If you are asked to serve as a trustee, either for an individual or for an institution, think carefully before agreeing to do so. As a trustee, you will have the duties described in the checklist at left, and if you fail to fulfill them for any reason, the beneficiaries or the settlor could have you removed. If your actions result in losses to the trust, you could be held responsible. In some situations you can even be held liable for the actions of a cotrustee—for instance, if you fail to object to a risky investment. Before you agree to serve as a cotrustee, ask your attorney about the laws in your state governing your potential liability.

TRUTH-IN-LENDING ACT

When Martha needed to buy a new dishwasher, the salesperson mentioned that the store could finance the purchase. By law, Martha is entitled to know the exact amount of money being financed, the finance charge, the annual percentage rate, and the total amount of her payments. The salesperson is required to disclose all of this information before Martha signs the credit agreement.

These mandatory disclosures are a direct result of the Truth-in-Lending Act (TILA), a federal law enacted in 1968 as part of the Consumer Credit Protection Act. In 1980 the TILA Simplification and Reform Act made numerous changes in the original law.

SCOPE OF THE LAW

The Truth-in-Lending Act requires all lenders to disclose important credit terms in the same manner, so that consumers can understand and compare the cost and terms of various loans. The law covers several consumer transactions. Transactions in which a person receives money, property, or services for personal, family, or household use are all subject to TILA disclosure requirements.

Contracts for leases of personal property—such as furniture, a television set, or an automobile—for household, personal, or family use for a period longer than four months must include financial disclosures outlined in the act. The law covers leases up to a value of $25,000.

CREDIT INFORMATION

The finance charge and the annual percentage rate of interest are the two key figures that must be disclosed for consumer credit transactions. The finance charge is not the same as interest. It includes not only interest but all the charges you pay for obtaining credit, including a finder's fee, credit report fees, and carrying charges for maintaining the account.

The other figure that indicates which creditor offers the best terms is the annual percentage rate (APR)—the rate of interest you will have to pay on the balance of the debt. How the APR is calculated depends on whether you have open- or closed-end credit.

With open-end credit, you may use the credit repeatedly and pay a finance charge on the unpaid balance every month. More important, you can extend your monthly payments for as long as you like, provided you pay the minimum required payment. Revolving charge accounts at department stores and VISA and Mastercard credit cards are examples of open-end credit. The APR for credit cards can vary. Some companies charge 11 percent or even less, others as much as 20 percent or more.

You have closed-end credit when you borrow a specific amount of money that must be paid within a specified period of time. Automobile loans, home mortgages, and student loans are common types of closed-end credit. With closed-end credit, you will be told your total number of payments and their due dates. See also HOME BUYING AND SELLING; MORTGAGE.

ADVERTISING

Companies that advertise the availability of consumer loans for their products must comply with TILA requirements. Television commercials, for example, often inform consumers about the cost of monthly payments for a new car. By law, disclosure of one term of the loan obligates the car dealer to advertise other terms, such as the amount needed for a down payment, the number of monthly payments, the annual percentage rate, and the price of the car.

VIOLATIONS AND PENALTIES

Creditors who violate the Truth-in-Lending Act are subject to both civil and criminal penalties. Criminal enforcement falls under the jurisdiction of the U.S. Attorney General's office. Charges may be brought against creditors for failing to disclose required information, giving information in a misleading manner, or using tables or charts that understate the annual percentage rate. Violators may be jailed up to one year, fined up to $5,000, or both.

In addition, the consumer may file suit against the creditor who lied to or misled him. If he wins the case, the creditor will have to compensate the consumer and pay his court costs and attorney fees. The creditor may also be required to pay a penalty of twice the amount of the illegal finance charges it collected.

STATE LAWS

Most states have also enacted consumer-credit disclosure laws similar to the federal Truth-in-Lending Act. Call your state consumer-protection agency or the state attorney general's office for information about your state's law and the procedures for challenging a company's credit practices.

TRUTH-IN-SAVINGS ACT

The Truth-in-Savings Act (TISA), which went into effect on June 21, 1993, was created by Congress to force banks, savings and loans, and credit unions to inform consumers about their financial services in a way that is standardized and easy to understand. For example, before TISA, banks often described the interest rates on their accounts in a less-than-straightforward manner, causing customers to be confused or misled. Under TISA, banks must declare their rates in a standardized way, known as the annual percentage yield (APY), or compound interest rate. This enables consumers to comparison shop for money-market accounts, savings accounts, and certificates of deposit (CD's) to find those that offer the highest yield.

According to TISA, interest rates and yields on investments must be explained to a new customer in a clear and understandable way before he can open an account. The terms *interest rate* and *annual percentage yield* must be used, and the methods for calculating all rates must follow formulas outlined in TISA.

DISCLOSURES

Before opening an account, the bank must provide the following information:

◇ The annual percentage yield (APY), which represents the amount of interest paid on an account for one year.

◇ The interest rate and the length of time it will apply.

◇ How often interest is compounded; when it is credited to an account; and how it changes for variable-rate accounts.

◇ The minimum-balance requirements.

◇ The limits on the number of withdrawals allowed and the amount of each withdrawal.

◇ Fees imposed for writing checks, check printing, or using automated teller machines or other services.

◇ Whether a time deposit account, such as a certificate of deposit (CD), will automatically renew at maturity and the penalties for early withdrawals.

TISA also requires financial institutions to give advance notice of fee and interest changes. See also TRUTH-IN-LENDING ACT.

PERIODIC STATEMENTS

If the financial institution sends statements to account holders at least four times a year, each must include information about the transactions in the account, the interest earned, fees imposed, and annual percentage yield. For passbook savings accounts, however, this information is entered when the customer presents his passbook.

ADVERTISING

TISA requires financial institutions to observe certain standards when advertising their accounts. For example, if an advertisement states the annual percentage yield on a new account, it must also disclose minimum balances, fees, and other conditions imposed on the account. And a bank cannot advertise free checking if it imposes a fee on an account that falls below a minimum balance.

PENALTIES

If a bank or savings and loan fails to provide the information required by TISA, it can be subject to a penalty. If a consumer suffers any financial loss because of the lack of disclosure, the financial institution is liable for damages and a penalty ranging from $100 to $1,000.

UMBRELLA INSURANCE

Most insurance protects its owners against the everyday risks of life. But sometimes people may want to extend their coverage beyond the limits of standard automobile and homeowners policies. Umbrella insurance, which offers protection against almost every contingency, provides the most comprehensive coverage available. An umbrella policy (also called a catastrophe policy) provides two types of extended protection.

First, it covers risks that other insurance policies usually exclude. Most homeowners insurance provides personal liability protection if someone is injured on your property. But an umbrella policy insures you against risks not covered by homeowners insurance — for example, if you are sued for invasion of privacy, false arrest, libel, or slander.

Second, an umbrella policy pays for losses that exceed the limits of your basic insurance policies. Suppose you have automobile liability insurance that pays up to $500,000 to anyone injured as a result of your negligence. You can buy an umbrella policy that will insure against awards or settlements above that amount. The typical limit for an umbrella policy ranges from $1 million to $10 million.

An umbrella policy is a particularly wise investment for people who have extensive personal assets and therefore run the risk of substantial losses if they are sued successfully. See also AUTOMOBILE INSURANCE; HOMEOWNERS INSURANCE.

UNCONSCIONABILITY

When a legal contract is blatantly one-sided and unfair in its terms, it is said to be unconscionable. Suppose you purchase a home with a 15-year mortgage that requires 180 monthly payments. Suppose also that the terms of your sales contract not only allow the lender to repossess the home without foreclosure procedures if you miss a single payment (even the last one), but also permit him to keep the extra money if your home is then resold for more than the amount you owe.

If you missed a payment and the lender tried to enforce the contract, you could argue that the harshness of the terms made the agreement unconscionable. On those grounds, you could ask the court to order an alternative remedy—perhaps one that would allow you to make up the missed payments as well as interest, late charges, and attorneys' fees.

UNDERWRITER

In the early days of international shipping, wealthy businessmen sometimes used their own money to insure a shipment against loss of goods in transit. Before a voyage, each man who accepted a share of the risk would write his name under the amount he invested, thus becoming an "underwriter." If the goods were delivered safely, each investor was paid a premium. If not, the underwriter lost his investment.

The term *underwriter* is still used to describe someone who subsidizes a venture involving risk. Insurance companies employ underwriters to determine whether to accept applications for insurance and the terms and conditions under which each individual policy will be offered. In the securities industry an underwriter insures the sale of stocks and bonds to the public by promising to buy all those that remain unsold. See also INSURANCE; STOCKS AND BONDS.

UNDUE INFLUENCE

When your uncle dies, you learn that a year earlier he had signed a power of attorney authorizing his neighbor to withdraw funds from his bank account. But what really seems odd is that the account had a balance of $25,000 when the power of attorney was granted, and now it contains less than $200. Could your uncle have been subject to undue influence when he signed the power of attorney.

Undue influence occurs when someone tries to benefit himself by persuading another person to do something that person would not ordinarily do. Charges of undue influence are most often made in cases involving deeds, contracts, and wills. To determine whether undue influence has been used, the court considers (1) the age, health, or mental capacity of the person who was supposedly influenced; (2) whether there was an opportunity or motive for someone to influence him; and (3) whether there is evidence to suggest such influence.

Suppose your uncle gave his power of attorney to the neighbor while she nursed him through a long-term illness. If so, all three determining factors were present: your uncle was in a frail and dependent condition; the neighbor had much to gain by being granted power of attorney; and a large sum of money suddenly disappeared from your uncle's bank account. Under these circumstances, a court might hold that the neighbor exercised undue influence on your uncle.

Unemployment Insurance

If you lose your job through no fault of your own, unemployment insurance is your safety net. Coverage for this type of insurance is a joint responsibility of the federal and state governments, and is financed by taxes paid by employers.

ELIGIBILITY

Generally, you are eligible for unemployment compensation if you have been permanently dismissed or temporarily laid off by your employer because of business or economic conditions, such as the employer's need to cut expenses. You are also eligible if your employer dismisses you without cause. In some states you may be eligible if you are transferred to a distant location and traveling there poses a severe hardship.

If you leave your job voluntarily, or if you are dismissed for misconduct or failure to fulfill the terms of your agreement, you are not eligible for unemployment compensation.

In most states you can collect unemployment compensation if you leave for "good cause." Though the exact definition of good cause varies and is subject to interpretation, in most cases it means that you quit because your employer treated you in an illegal manner, such as refusing to pay you a commission you had earned.

DETERMINING BENEFITS

Although the amount of unemployment compensation you are entitled to receive varies from state to state, in all states it is determined by both the amount of pay you received during the previous one-year period and the average weekly wage earned by all workers in the state.

In some instances your benefit may be reduced if you received compensation from a pension fund or other compensation, such as severance pay. Usually, you can receive unemployment pay for no more than 26 weeks after you lose your job, but the federal government often extends this period during hard times. Once your benefits run out, you must work at a job and earn wages totaling at least 10 times the amount of your weekly unemployment pay before you will become eligible to collect again.

APPLYING FOR BENEFITS

To receive unemployment benefits, you must show that you are available for work and are actively seeking employment in your field. This usually means that you must make a weekly appearance at the local unemployment office and sign a sworn statement that you sought work during the previous week. In some states you may also be required to provide the names and addresses of companies to which you have applied.

If you are laid off or fired, apply for unemployment compensation as soon as possible because your application must be reviewed and accepted before you can receive benefits—a process that can take several weeks.

Your claim may be denied because your former employer has disputed the circumstances of your dismissal. For example, the company may claim that you were dismissed because of misconduct on the job or because you failed to appear for work. In such a case you are entitled to a hearing before an officer from the state department of labor.

At this hearing, both you and your employer are permitted to testify about the circumstances surrounding your dismissal. If the officer rules in your favor, you will be granted benefits from the time of your original application. If the officer rules against you, you have the right to appeal his decision. Since the process can get complicated, you may want to hire a lawyer if you decide to appeal. Ask your local legal aid office for advice; as an unemployed person, you may be eligible for free or low-cost legal services.

If your request for unemployment pay is denied, you should request a hearing—even if you are in doubt about your eligibility. Some employers routinely dispute claims filed by their former employees, but fail to attend a hearing on the matter. If the employer does not show up, the employee wins by default. See also Employee Hiring and Firing.

Unemployment benefits are subject to income tax, and the state will report the amount you receive to the IRS. See also Income Taxes.

Uniform Code of Military Justice

Because members of the military are expected to live by higher standards of duty and discipline than civilians, a separate body of criminal laws and procedures governs all five branches of the armed services. Historically, each branch had its own system of military justice. But in 1950 the different systems were modernized and combined into the Uniform Code of Military Justice (UCMJ), so that all military personnel would have the same rights and be subject to the same charges and penalties.

In addition to listing prohibited actions and appropriate punishments for violations, the UCMJ sets forth a variety of procedural rules that must be followed in administering military justice. This system of laws applies not only to individuals who serve on active duty, but also to reservists, students at military academies, and prisoners of war.

Crimes

Some offenses listed under the UCMJ, such as murder, arson, and rape, are also crimes under civilian law. But other offenses are unique to military service and often represent a challenge to the military's authority. These include showing disrespect toward a superior officer, failure to obey an order, and being intoxicated on duty. Some offenses, such as deserting one's post, are combat related, while others, such as "conduct unbecoming an officer," involve more general behavior. The most common offense is being absent without official leave (AWOL).

Procedural Safeguards

The UCMJ includes procedural safeguards similar to those provided by the due process clause of the U.S. Constitution. As do civilians, military personnel accused of a crime have the right to remain silent, the right to be represented by an attorney, the right to be informed of the charges against them, and the right to be informed of all the above.

Proceedings

Minor charges brought against military personnel are handled as an "Article 15" proceeding, or Commanding Officer's Nonjudicial Punishment. The accused person appears before his commanding officer, who hears the evidence and then decides whether the person is guilty or not guilty. The commanding officer also determines which punishment should be imposed. Article 15 proceedings are used whenever possible because they are more efficient than trials and do not appear on the military record of the accused person.

More serious offenses are handled by a court-martial, which is similar to a civilian jury trial. The members of the jury are military officers, but the defense attorney can be a civilian if the accused prefers not to accept the military attorney appointed by the court. If convicted, the serviceman may be required to forfeit his pay, serve a sentence in a military prison, or accept a demotion in rank. For severe offenses, he may be given a dishonorable discharge.

Appeals

A convicted serviceman is entitled to appeal the court's decision. His commanding officer is the first person who will hear the appeal. At the next level is the Court of Military Review, which reviews all appeals for serious offenses. The third level of appeal is the U. S. Court of Military Appeals, which hears cases involving capital punishment and those in which the defendant holds the rank of general. Other cases may also be appealed to this court by the judge advocate general of each branch of the service.

Uniform Commercial Code

The Uniform Commercial Code (UCC) is a comprehensive set of laws intended to provide uniformity and fair dealing in commercial transactions. Developed in 1952 and revised in 1958 and 1962, these laws have been adopted in whole or in part by every state. However, real estate transactions are an exception. They are governed not by the UCC, but by the statute of frauds and other state and federal laws. See also Contract.

The UCC is divided into subdivisions called articles, which address different aspects of business and commercial transactions. Topics include sales, letters of credit, commercial paper, bills of lading, warehouse receipts, bulk transfers, investment securities, bank deposits and collections, secured transactions, and contract rights. See Bill of Lading; Security Agreement; Stocks and Bonds.

Uniform Transfers to Minors Act

Enacted in more than two-thirds of the states, the Uniform Transfers to Minors Act (UTMA) allows a person who makes a gift of real estate or a large sum of money to a minor to appoint a "custodian," someone to manage the property until the minor reaches a specified age. Depending on the state in which you live, this age varies from 18 to 21, although California allows you to extend the custodian's authority until the beneficiary of the gift reaches the age of 25.

Among the powers granted to the custodian by the UTMA are the right to hold, manage, invest, and reinvest the property and to spend as much as the custodian deems necessary for the minor's use and benefit—all without court approval. The UTMA requires the custodian to keep records of all transactions involving the minor's property and to act in a reasonable and prudent manner when taking such actions.

Your attorney can tell you whether the UTMA has been enacted in your state and explain the exact provisions of the law. He can also advise you whether UTMA is the best way for you to bequeath a gift to your children or other minors. See also Estate Planning; Trust; Will.

Unordered Merchandise

Under federal law, a company that sends a consumer unordered merchandise through the mail must clearly mark the package "Free Sample" and is prohibited from billing the consumer for the merchandise. If you receive merchandise that you did not order, you are legally entitled to keep it and treat it as a gift. If the company attempts to bill you for the merchandise, notify your local postmaster or your state attorney general's office.

Recognized charitable organizations are legally permitted to send you small items—such as pins, address labels, or note cards—and request a donation. But even in these cases you are under no obligation either to return the items or to make a contribution.

These legal protections do not always extend to unordered merchandise sent to a business. If you are a business owner, you should closely monitor the products you receive and refuse merchandise sent by companies with whom you do not do business. See also Consumer Protection; Scams and Swindles.

Vacation Home

A vacation home can be a valuable investment as well as a personally enjoyable possession, but it can also be burdensome and expensive. If you decide to rent your vacation home (or "second" home) for part of the year to trim expenses and to take advantage of tax benefits, you should know the tax rules for second homes in order to avoid pitfalls.

Tax Considerations

If you use your vacation home occasionally, but rent it out at other times, the amount of time you occupy it determines how the Internal Revenue Service views it for tax purposes—that is, whether it is considered a personal residence or a business property.

Personal residence

The IRS will consider your vacation home a personal residence if you rent it out for no more than 14 days a year or no more than 10 percent of the time you occupy the residence yourself—whichever is greater. You do not have to report the rental income you earn on those 14 days, and you cannot write off any rental expenses.

As a personal residence, the federal Internal Revenue Code generally entitles you to take the same write-offs on your vacation home—for example, mortgage interest and property taxes—that you are allowed on your primary residence. However, you are not allowed to claim these deductions on a third or fourth home.

Mixed use

If you use your vacation house periodically and also rent it out for more than 14 days, you must include your rental income in your gross income. Depending on the number of days you rent it out, you can deduct a portion of your total expenses—for instance, mortgage interest and property taxes, as well as depreciation and overhead costs like repairs and utilities—as business expenses. But if expenses exceed your rental income, you may not deduct the loss from your other sources of income.

Business property

If you occupy the house for less than 14 days a year or less than 10 percent of the total time you rent it out, it is considered a business property. As such, its losses may be deducted against rental or personal income, provided that you actively participate in managing the property and your adjusted gross income does not exceed $100,000. You may be able to take a full deduction against your regular income for up to $25,000 of business-use losses.

There is an additional factor to consider: If your house is a business property, you can still allocate expenses between business and personal use. But the portion of mortgage interest attributable to personal use cannot be deducted at all.

PROPERTY INSURANCE

If you buy a vacation home, you will need to insure it. Because a vacation home may stand empty for much of the year, it is an easy target for break-ins, thefts, and vandalism. You may therefore find it more expensive to insure than a primary home of equal value.

If you rent the house to others, your liability insurance rates will also be higher. Be sure that you keep your rental property in top condition and make regular inspections and repairs. Failing to do so can lead to costly claims for injuries. You may want to buy an umbrella insurance policy to enhance your liability coverage. See also HOMEOWNERS INSURANCE; UMBRELLA INSURANCE.

FINANCING

Just as insurance rates on second homes are higher, the cost of financing them is often higher too. Many banks require larger down payments and tack on extra interest points on mortgages for vacation homes, because the rate of default on these mortgages tends to be higher than on mortgages for primary residences.

Sometimes the seller of a home may be willing to "carry the paper" on the property—that is, provide the financing for you. If the owner offers such an arrangement, you should hire a lawyer to draw up the mortgage papers or review the documents created by the seller, since a homeowner who provides financing to a buyer is usually not required to make the same disclosures to you as are banks, savings and loan associations, and mortgage companies. See also HOME BUYING AND SELLING; MORTGAGE.

VACCINATION

Most school districts will not allow children to be enrolled in school unless they have been vaccinated against certain diseases. Their refusal is not a matter of discretion, because local school boards or school officials that fail to enforce compulsory vaccination laws may be sued by the state.

Some parents have refused to have their children vaccinated, arguing that compulsory vaccinations are unconstitutional because they violate personal freedom. But the courts have consistently upheld state laws because of the importance of vaccination programs to public health. Parents who refuse to have their children vaccinated for personal reasons can be charged with child neglect and with encouraging truancy. However, a few state legislatures have passed laws exempting the children of parents whose religious beliefs forbid vaccinations.

In general, the courts are

staunchly in favor of compulsory vaccination of children and have held that in some circumstances, as in an outbreak of smallpox, the local board of health may require that all persons be vaccinated.

VAGRANCY

Traditionally, the law defined a vagrant as an idle person wandering from place to place, with no ties to the community and no visible means of support. Laws prohibiting vagrancy have been enacted at various times, on the theory that vagrancy leads to crime and to general lawlessness. Some of the acts prohibited by vagrancy laws include begging, loitering, trespassing, prostitution, and fortune-telling.

Because it is usually considered unconstitutional to punish a condition, as opposed to an act, courts will not uphold vagrancy laws that interfere with personal liberty. For example, a law that prohibited people from "lingering, lurking, or standing idly around" was struck down. But a law prohibiting loitering in an area where narcotics were habitually used was upheld. So was a statute prohibiting "loitering in a place, time, or manner not usual for law-abiding citizens, under circumstances which warrant alarm or concern for the safety of persons or property." For example, hiding behind a pillar in a deserted parking garage at 3 A.M. would be prohibited by this statute, since the only likely reason to do so would be to break into a car or attack a driver.

VANDALISM

In A.D. 455 the Vandals, a tribe of nomadic people, overran and sacked Rome. Their appalling acts of wanton and senseless destruction earned them a permanent place in our vocabulary. Vandalism, sometimes referred to as malicious mischief, is generally defined by statutes as the "willful and unlawful injury to or destruction of the property of another, with the intent to injure the owner." Any such act that impairs the use or value of property to its owner is vandalism.

The crime of vandalism may be a felony or a misdemeanor, depending on the value of the property destroyed or the amount of damage inflicted. Many acts of vandalism, such as scratching the paint off someone's car with a key, are classified as misdemeanors. But sometimes vandalism results in irreparable harm to the public at large. For example, a disgruntled art student who spitefully slashes a rare painting in an art museum is guilty of a felony, which carries a more severe penalty.

The right to freedom of expression does not extend to acts of vandalism. In one case a group was convicted of vandalism after pouring blood and ashes on the walls of the Pentagon to protest nuclear weapons. In another case protesters were convicted after defacing a B-52 bomber.

If you accidentally destroy or harm property through carelessness, however, or if you destroy property that you reasonably but mistakenly thought was your own, you have not committed an act of vandalism.

VARIANCE

Generally, a community's zoning laws are enacted in accordance with a comprehensive plan designed to ensure orderly and predictable development. In some situations, however, the local zoning board may allow an exception to a zoning law, known as a variance. Suppose you want to operate a home-based business, but the zoning laws in your community prohibit you from doing so. Or you want to keep a horse or a cow in an area where the zoning prohibits farm animals. To obtain a variance, you would apply to the local zoning board, which is responsible for enforcing zoning laws. The board will review your application and schedule a public hearing, at which you will be permitted to make your case for the variance. Other members of the community will also be heard. If there are few objections or none at all, your application will probably be approved.

If your application is denied, you can appeal, but keep in mind that appeals can be costly and time-consuming. Local zoning authorities are given considerable latitude in the decisions they make. Unless the board failed to follow its own rules, or its actions were clearly arbitrary and unsupported by the facts, its decision will probably stand. See also NONCONFORMING USE; ZONING.

VENUE

The place where a trial or other legal proceeding is held is called its venue. Venue is not the same as jurisdiction, which is the authority of a particular court to hear a case. For example, state courts have jurisdiction over most personal-injury cases. Suppose the plaintiff in such a case lives in one county, while the defendant lives in another one several hundred miles away. The court in either county may have jurisdiction over the case, but the venue will depend on such factors as convenience to the parties and the potential for getting a fair trial. Usually, venue is in the plaintiff's county. However, the defendant can petition for a "change of venue" if, for example, publicity in the plaintiff's county or a friendship between the plaintiff and the local judge would make a fair trial unlikely. See also COURTS; JURISDICTION.

VERBAL AGREEMENT

"A verbal contract isn't worth the paper it's written on." This quip, attributed to the legendary Hollywood mogul Samuel Goldwyn, underscores a popular misconception that verbal agreements are not enforceable. However, the law views them as contracts that, even unwritten, are valid as long as they do not concern real estate, the sale of goods over $500, and other contracts covered by the Statute of Frauds which by law must be in writing. See also CONTRACT.

The problem with lawsuits over verbal agreements is the matter of proof. Suppose you make a verbal contract with a handyman, who agrees to paint your porch for $200. You give him half the money in cash up front, but he never does the job. If you take him to small-claims court and he denies making the agreement, it will be your word against his. Unless you have a witness, the judge will have to make a decision based on two conflicting stories, each of which may seem credible. Because the burden of proof is on you as the plaintiff, chances are you may lose your lawsuit. See also BURDEN OF PROOF; EVIDENCE.

Unless the amount of money in question is very small, it is a good idea to put all agreements in writing. Contracts do not necessarily have to be formal; a simple letter signed by both parties will usually suffice. For more costly projects or purchases, however, a formal written contract that details the terms of your agreement is advisable.

VETERANS BENEFITS

Although the federal government has always provided benefits to veterans of the armed forces, it was not until 1930 that Congress created the Veterans Administration to supervise these various programs. In 1988 Congress changed the agency's name to the Department of Veterans Affairs (VA) and elevated it to Cabinet-level status. Today more than 27 million former servicemen and women and more than 46 million of their dependents are eligible for some kind of veterans benefits.

ELIGIBILITY FOR BENEFITS

Generally, any veteran who left the service with an honorable discharge qualifies for benefits. In some instances, even those who received less than honorable discharges — for being absent without leave, for instance—may qualify. In these situations, eligibility is based on a review of the facts of an individual's case by the Discharge Review Board of his branch of the service. A dependent's eligibility to receive benefits is based on the eligibility of the veteran.

Benefits are usually limited to veterans who served in the regular armed forces, but some groups, such as the civilian merchant marines who served during World War II, are also eligible for most benefits even though they were not members of the military. A complete list of eligible groups is available from your local VA office.

EDUCATIONAL BENEFITS

The Department of Veterans Affairs administers several educational benefit programs for active-duty personnel, veterans, and their dependents. For

ABC's

Of Burial in Arlington National Cemetery

Under current regulations, burial in Arlington National Cemetery is limited to the following individuals or their surviving spouses, minor children, and dependent adult children.

- Any person who died while serving on active duty in the armed forces.
- Recipients of certain military distinctions—namely, the Congressional Medal of Honor, Distinguished Service Cross, Air Force Cross, Navy Cross, Distinguished Service Medal, Silver Star, or Purple Heart.
- Retired military personnel who are on an official "service-retired list" and are eligible to receive compensation, such as retirement pay, as a result of their military service.
- Individuals who performed honorable military service and held elective office in the U.S. government, or who held office in the Supreme Court, the Cabinet, or in positions compensated at Level 2 of the Executive Salary Act.
- Veterans who were granted discharges from the military because of a 30 percent or greater disability before October 1, 1949, who also served on active duty other than training, and who would have qualified for retirement under current retirement provisions.

example, the Montgomery GI Bill (Active Duty) is available to certain active-duty personnel who enlisted in the service after June 30, 1985, while other provisions of the Montgomery GI Bill apply to honorably discharged veterans or members of the reserve forces.

Vocational rehabilitation programs and other educational funding programs, such as the Veterans Educational Assistance Program (VEAP) are also available to eligible veterans. The requirements for eligibility and the benefits offered under these programs vary. You can obtain information about these programs from any VA office.

VA-GUARANTEED MORTGAGES

Home-mortgage guarantees are available to eligible veterans and to the surviving spouses of military personnel who either died from a service-related injury or illness or were declared missing in action. Under this loan program, the federal government guarantees payment to commercial mortgage lenders if the veteran defaults on his loan. As a result, VA home-mortgage rates are generally lower than those for conventional mortgages. Furthermore, lenders typically require only a small down payment or no down payment at all. Before you can apply for a VA home mortgage, you must complete Form 26-1880 (Request for Determination of Eligibility and Available Loan Guaranty Entitlement), which you can obtain from any VA office.

MEDICAL BENEFITS FOR VETERANS

One of the most important benefits to which veterans are entitled is health care. The VA operates more than 700 hospitals, clinics, and nursing homes that provide free or low-cost care to hundreds of thousands of veterans annually. Among the many services they offer are home health care, treatment for alcoholism and drug dependence, and outpatient care for medical, dental, and mental health treatment.

While the VA offers health care to all qualified veterans, it gives priority to those whose illnesses or disabilities are service-related. It also serves those veterans who have a low income. If a veteran has an illness that is not service-related, he will probably be required to supply the VA with information on his income and net worth.

Depending on his illness or income, the veteran's eligibility for health services will be classified as either mandatory or discretionary. For example, hospital care is considered mandatory for a veteran who is single, has no dependents, and has an annual income of less than $19,000. If his income is higher, however, hospital care is considered discretionary, and he will have to agree to pay an amount for hospital care that is equivalent to his copayments under Medicare in order to be treated. See MEDICARE.

MEDICAL BENEFITS FOR FAMILIES

The VA also provides health care to the survivors and dependents of veterans who suffer from service-related illnesses or who died during active duty. This program, called the Civilian Health and Medical Program, or CHAMP-VA, helps these survivors and dependents pay for the health-care services they receive in the private sector.

DISABILITY BENEFITS

There are two types of VA disability benefits:

◇ *Disability compensation*, which is paid monthly to veterans who were physically disabled during their military service or whose disabilities were aggravated during their service. The amount of these benefits depends on the percentage of disability. In 1992, for example, a veteran who was 100 percent disabled was eligible for a monthly benefit of $1,680, plus allowances for dependents.

◇ *Disability pensions*, which are available to totally and permanently disabled veterans whose disabilities are not service-related but who served during wartime and are in need of financial support.

BURIAL BENEFITS

Any veteran who was not dishonorably discharged is entitled to be buried in a national cemetery, as are their spouses and most (but not all) of their dependents. Burial in Arlington National Cemetery, however, is subject to limitations (see the feature on page 535).

The VA authorizes one grave site in a national cemetery for each eligible veteran and his or her family members. The VA will furnish a headstone or grave marker. The VA will not pay for a headstone obtained from a private source, but it will cover the cost of shipping it. Nor will the VA pay for placing the marker on the grave in a private cemetery.

If a veteran dies as a result of an illness or injury that is not service-related, the VA will provide a burial allowance of up to $300 and a burial-plot allowance of $150—provided that the veteran was eligible for VA benefits or died in a VA hospital. If the veteran died of a service-related illness or injury, the VA will pay up to $1,500 for the cemetery plot and burial. The VA will also provide an American flag to cover the coffin at the funeral. At the end of the ceremony, the flag is customarily given to the spouse or children of the deceased.

APPLYING FOR VA BENEFITS

To obtain VA benefits, you must have official government documents that verify your eligibility. Generally, you will be required to provide separation or discharge papers. (If they are lost or missing, you can obtain copies from the branch of the armed forces in which you served.)

You will then need to obtain form SF-180 ("Request Pertaining to Military Records") from your local VA office. Then submit the completed form to the following address: National Personnel Records Center, [branch of service] Military Records, 9700 Page Boulevard, St. Louis, MO 63132.

To complete the form, you will need to provide your name, date of birth, Social Security number, military serial number, VA file number (if any), branch and dates of service, and the highest rank you attained.

VETERINARIAN

A veterinarian is a person licensed by the state to diagnose and treat sick or injured animals. To be licensed, a veterinarian must have received a Doctor of Veterinary Medicine (DVM) degree and passed his state's written test for veterinary medicine. Like physicians, veterinarians must abide by certain ethical principles. These guidelines, adopted in 1960 by the American Veterinary Medical Association, direct veterinarians to prevent and relieve the suffering of animals, provide proper medical attention, and treat medical emergencies to the best of their ability.

In the eyes of the law, a pet is considered the personal property of its owner. A veterinarian is therefore responsible for the pet while it is in his custody. This means that the animal must be properly fed, sheltered, exercised, cleaned, and protected from other animals.

Although veterinarians are not subject to the same malpractice laws that apply to physicians, they can be held responsible for the suffering, injury, or death of an animal if it results from: (1) a negligent diagnosis, (2) unskillful surgery, (3) unsafe or inadequate food or shelter, (4) neglect or abandonment, or (5) actions by an unskilled or negligent employee. If a veterinarian is found guilty of negligence, he may be suspended from his practice and subjected to civil penalties, such as a fine. A pet owner who successfully sues a veterinarian, however, can usually recover no more than the dollar value of the animal.

If your pet injures a veterinarian or one of his assistants while it is under his care, you generally cannot be held responsible for the injuries, because veterinarians treat animals with full knowledge of the risks of being scratched or bitten. If your pet is unusually vicious, however, and you fail to warn the veterinarian, you might be held liable for any injuries the animal inflicts on him or his employees.

In many states, a veterinarian is entitled to keep your pet as collateral (and charge you for boarding the animal) until he has been paid for his services. If you want to dispute your veterinarian's bill, the best course of action is to pay the bill in full and get your pet back. Then you can file a suit in small-claims court.

VICTIMS' RIGHTS

Under the Constitution, a criminal defendant is guaranteed certain rights to ensure that he is not unjustly convicted. Until recently, however, courts and state and federal legislatures gave little or no consideration to the rights of victims of crimes. Nowadays, thanks to strong advocacy by victims' rights groups, the law protects not only the defendant but the victim as well.

HARASSMENT AND INTIMIDATION

Sometimes a victim may feel threatened by a defendant or his family during the prosecution of a crime. The Federal Victim and Witness Protection Act of 1982 makes harassment and intimidation a crime and also tries to minimize the risk that such actions will occur. For example, the court may set aside a separate waiting area at the courthouse so that victims who are waiting to testify do not have to come into contact with defendants.

RESTITUTION

Some recently enacted laws provide for restitution—a policy that requires a convicted defendant to compensate the victim of the crime for her losses. At the time of sentencing, the federal courts may require the defendant to pay a sum of money to his victim or, if she is deceased, her estate. Restitution can include reimbursement for medical expenses, lost wages, funeral expenses, and personal-property damages incurred as a result of the crime. The offender may also be required to pay the cost of physical therapy or psychological counseling.

If the court decides not to impose restitution, it must state its reasons at the time of sentencing. Federal law prohibits a victim from being compensated twice; therefore, if she received an award through a lawsuit or collected compensation from an insurance company, the offender will not be required to make restitution. If the victim prefers that restitution be made to an organization, such as a charity, the court can order this to be done. When appropriate, restitution may also be made in the form of service, rather than money. For example, a court may order a convicted vandal to spend a certain number of hours performing cleanup work in his community.

VICTIM COMPENSATION PROGRAMS

If an offender cannot pay restitution because he is in prison or has no assets, a victim may still be able to receive compensation. The Federal Victims of Crime Act, passed in 1984, makes grants available to the states to fund programs for victim compensation and assistance. This money comes from fines collected in federal cases and from profits criminals receive from book and motion-picture deals, which must be forfeited under the federal "Son of Sam" law. (The Son of Sam law is named for the notorious killer who terrorized New York City in the late 1970's. The killer's real name was David Berkowitz.) In addition, some states have victim compensation programs to provide financial aid to crime victims.

To qualify for assistance,

ABC's
Of Victims' Rights

Supplementing the Federal Victims of Crime and Witness Protection Acts, most states have a "Victim's Bill of Rights," which often guarantees a crime victim the following rights and privileges:

- ❑ The right to be treated with respect and courtesy.
- ❑ The right to be provided with prompt, appropriate medical treatment.
- ❑ The right to have personal property returned as soon as possible.
- ❑ The right to have the case handled as promptly as possible.
- ❑ The right to be informed of the progress of an investigation.
- ❑ The right to be notified of the dates, times, or cancellations of important hearings.
- ❑ The right to inform the court about the impact and harmful effects the crime has had on his life (except in some cases involving the death penalty).
- ❑ The right to be in attendance at the trial.
- ❑ The right to be consulted if the prosecuting attorney offers a plea bargain.
- ❑ The right to be heard at sentencing and parole hearings.
- ❑ The right to be notified when the defendant will be released from custody.
- ❑ The right to be informed of all victim compensation and assistance programs.

most state and federal programs require that (1) the victim report the crime promptly; (2) the request for assistance be filed within a certain period of time; (3) the victim demonstrate financial need; and (4) the loss exceed a certain amount. The offender need not be convicted in order for a victim to receive assistance.

VIEW

When Andrew bought his home, one of the features that made it most appealing to him was the spectacular mountain view it afforded. But he has just heard from a neighbor that developers are planning to build a tall commercial complex on the property located directly across the road. The result, of course, is that his breathtaking vista will soon become only a dim memory. Is there anything he can do to stop the construction?

Probably not. Under common law, a property owner has no legal right to a view—scenic or otherwise. As long as his neighbors do not act maliciously—by putting up a fence just to spite him, for example—Andrew has no recourse when his view becomes obstructed.

In some areas, however, local laws protect landowners from having their views blocked. And in a number of development communities, covenants in landowners' deeds prevent them from erecting buildings or putting in plantings that would obstruct their neighbor's view. To find out whether you are protected by local laws, ask your county clerk's office. Your homeowners association will be able to help you determine whether your view is protected by a covenant in your neighbor's deed. See also FENCE BUILDING; HOMEOWNERS ASSOCIATION; TREE.

VISA

A visa is an endorsement, usually in the form of a stamp, placed by a foreign government on a U.S. passport to permit the bearer to visit that country. Some countries, such as Italy and Great Britain, allow a brief stay (several months, for example) without a visa, while others, such as South Africa and Australia, require visitors to secure a visa in advance.

If you are planning to visit a foreign country, find out well in advance whether a visa is required and, if so, how to apply for it. Call the nearest foreign consulate or send 50 cents for a booklet entitled *Foreign Entry Requirements* to the following address: Consumer Information Center, Pueblo, Colorado 81009. See also ALIEN; IMMIGRATION; PASSPORT.

WARRANTY AND GUARANTY TO WRONGFUL LIFE

WARRANTY AND GUARANTY

A warranty, also known as a guaranty, is a legally binding contract in which the seller or manufacturer of a product promises the buyer that the statements he makes about the quality of his merchandise are true and that he will stand behind them.

In 1975, Congress enacted the Magnuson-Moss Warranty Act. Although this law does not require manufacturers to provide an express (written) warranty, if a manufacturer chooses to do so, he must comply with the requirements set forth in the act. For example, warranties must be written in easy-to-understand language, and any limitations there may be on coverage must be clearly stated. See also MAGNUSON-MOSS WARRANTY ACT.

EXPRESS WARRANTY

An express warranty may be either full or limited. A full warranty obligates the manufacturer either to repair a defective item within a reasonable period of time without charge or, if he cannot do so, to give the consumer the choice between a no-cost replacement or a full refund of the purchase price. If a full warranty is restricted to a specified period of time (such as 90 days or one year), the manufacturer must so state at the top of the warranty.

A limited warranty gives the consumer less protection. It may cover only selected parts or require the consumer to pay shipping and handling or labor costs in order to obtain repairs. Under Magnuson-Moss, a limited warranty must carry a statement indicating that it is a limited warranty and clearly state the nature of the limitations and any costs the consumer must bear.

IMPLIED WARRANTY

An implied warranty is one that the law presumes to exist, even if it is not expressed in writing. For example, when a furniture manufacturer sells a sofa to a consumer, the law presumes an "implied warranty of merchantability." This means that the consumer has the right to assume that the sofa will be of the same general quality as similarly priced sofas made by other manufacturers. If the sofa falls below this standard—for example, if the frame cracks prematurely with ordinary use—the consumer has a right to have it repaired or replaced.

Implied warranties represent the minimum standards imposed by law, whereas express warranties allow merchants and manufacturers to proclaim their high standards and obtain a competitive advantage. Suppose two manufacturers offer similarly priced 19-inch color television sets. If one offers a 90-day parts and labor warranty and the other offers full coverage for a year, whose set are you likely to choose?

Another kind of implied warranty is the warranty of suitability for a particular purpose. Suppose that your car requires a new engine. If you tell the auto parts supplier the make and model of your car but he sends you the wrong engine by mistake, he has breached the implied warranty of suitability for a particular purpose. See also SERVICE CONTRACT; UNIFORM COMMERCIAL CODE.

In some cases an implied warranty can be excluded, but only if you are told of the exclusion in advance. However, some states prohibit or severely limit these exclusions. You can find out about the laws in your state from the consumer-protection division of your state attorney general's office.

WEAPON

Just about any object or substance can be used as a weapon, from a hatpin to a can of lighter fluid. Since the law cannot control everything that could potentially be used to commit a crime, it concerns itself primarily with items that are most commonly recognized as dangerous (likely to produce death or severe bodily harm) and criminal (likely to be used in a criminal manner).

Although the U.S. Constitution safeguards the right to "bear arms," state and federal laws can and do regulate the possession of weapons by individuals. Most states make it illegal to carry or conceal weapons such as handguns, sawed-off shotguns, switchblades, explosive devices, and martial-arts weapons. They also impose higher penalties on those who use such weapons in the commission of a crime.

In some situations the law may permit certain people—such as security guards, private investigators, or licensed collectors—to own dangerous weapons. For example, you can legally purchase and own a machine gun if you obtain the proper permit from the federal Bureau of Alcohol, Tobacco, and Firearms. See also ARMS, RIGHT TO BEAR.

WELFARE

Entitlement programs, such as Aid to Families With Dependent Children (AFDC), food stamps, and Medicaid, are known colloquially as welfare. To receive these benefits, you must qualify for them on the basis of need. (An exception is Social Security retirement and survivor benefits, which are not based on need.) See also AID TO FAMILIES WITH DEPENDENT CHILDREN; MEDICAID.

FOOD STAMPS

Authorized by Congress in 1964 as part of President Lyndon B. Johnson's "Great Society" reforms, the food stamp program offers low-income people government-issued stamps which may be used to purchase food items at authorized grocery stores. Food stamps may not be used to purchase tobacco, alcoholic beverages, household supplies, medicine, vitamins, or ready-to-eat foods.

Although the program is administered at the federal level by the Department of Agriculture's Food and Nutrition Service, state social services or welfare departments determine the applicants' eligibility and issue the stamps. All U.S. citizens and legally admitted permanent aliens whose income and assets fall below certain levels are eligible for food stamps, and some other legally admitted aliens may also qualify for them. The income and asset limits vary, depending on the state where the applicant lives, the size of the applicant's household, and whether disabled or elderly individuals are members of the household. In 1993, some 27 million Americans received food stamps.

In order to apply for food stamps, you must make a personal visit to the food stamp office where you live, although if you are unable to leave your home you may appoint someone to appear for you. You or the person who represents you will be asked to present the following items:

◇ Identification, such as a birth certificate or driver's license; or if you are not a native-born citizen, proof of naturalization or legal alien status.

◇ Social Security numbers of all the members of your household.

◇ Proof of earnings from employment, if any.

◇ Copies of Social Security, pension, and Supplemental Security Income (SSI) statements, as well as records of any investment income.

◇ Bank statements for accounts owned by all members of the household.

◇ Utility and rent bills.

◇ Receipts for child care and adult dependent care expenses.

◇ Unreimbursed medical bills for expenses over $35 incurred by members of your household who are disabled or over 60 years of age.

STATE AND LOCAL PROGRAMS

Although programs like AFDC, SSI, food stamps, and Medicaid are all mandated and funded (at least in part) by the federal government, determining eligibility and distributing benefits are the responsibilities of the individual states. In addition to the federal programs, state and local governments may offer other kinds of entitlement programs. For example, state-funded programs in a number of states assist eligible families and the elderly with the payment of heating bills, and other states fund "meals on wheels" programs for the sick and elderly. These programs vary widely in eligibility requirements. If you need financial assistance, contact your local department of welfare or department of social services for information about programs for which you may be eligible.

WELFARE RECIPIENTS' RIGHTS AND DUTIES

A person who receives welfare benefits is entitled to all the legal protection afforded to others under the U.S. Constitution and the constitutions of the states. For example, a welfare recipient cannot be required to submit to unreasonable searches and seizures as a condition of receiving welfare benefits. Thus, she cannot be forced to allow welfare officials or law enforcement authorities to look through her furniture for evidence that she is hiding income or using drugs.

Each welfare recipient has duties too. She can be required to participate in a government-sponsored job training program, or to appear in person to meet with welfare officials. She may also be required to let social workers into her home to confirm her description of her living situation. For example, a welfare program may provide benefits based on the recipient's claim that she is unmarried and does not know where her spouse is. A social worker may visit the home to determine that the husband is indeed absent. If the husband is found to be residing in the home, her welfare benefits may be terminated and she may have to reimburse the state for prior payments.

AVOIDING FRAUD

When you apply for any entitlement program, you must provide the federal government with information about your income and assets. If you underreport these amounts in order to receive more benefits than you are entitled to or to receive benefits for which you are not eligible at all, you can be prosecuted for welfare fraud. If there is a change in your family status — if you marry, for example—or if you get a job, you should inform your caseworker. See FRAUD.

WHISTLE-BLOWER

An employee who witnesses a crime, a health or safety hazard, or a breach of employment rules by other employees or by management is called a whistle-blower when he brings that activity to the attention of the employer, the media, or government officials.

Until recently, whistle-blowers were not shielded from reprisals, but now federal and state laws provide at least some protection. For example, if an employee reports a safety violation to the Occupational Safety and Health Administration (OSHA) in good faith, he cannot be fired for doing so.

The protections offered to whistle-blowers vary. Most federal laws protect only government workers, and some of these laws actually give whistle-blowers financial incentives to come forward. In contract cases with the federal government, for example, whistle-blowers who expose major fraud can earn sizable rewards.

Most states have statutes that protect whistle-blowers, but an employee must follow strict notification procedures or risk having his case dismissed. Some states still afford no protection to whistle-blowers who work in the private sector. Furthermore, in some states a whistle-blower who files a lawsuit for wrongful dismissal may be entitled only to reinstatement, back pay, and reimbursement for attorneys' fees; he cannot sue his employer for damages. See DAMAGES.

In most cases whistle-blower lawsuits are settled out of court. In return for reinstatement, a cash settlement, or both, the whistle-blower signs an agreement stating that he will keep quiet about the situation. This agreement, however, cannot prohibit the whistle-blower from reporting illegal activities to the authorities.

STEPS TO TAKE

If you believe that your employer is engaged in unethical or illegal business practices, consider taking the following steps:

1. Make sure your allegations are well founded. Before making accusations to anyone, check with a reliable source to confirm that a particular activity is, in fact, taking place and that it is unethical or illegal.

2. Record your observations and your conversations with fellow employees and supervisors. Keep a journal listing the day and time of each activity, as well as the management's response to each complaint.

State Statutes That Protect Whistle-blowers

Many states have statutes to protect workers who report a job-related crime, health violation, or breach of employment rules. Your state department of labor can give you further information about your state's whistle-blower law.

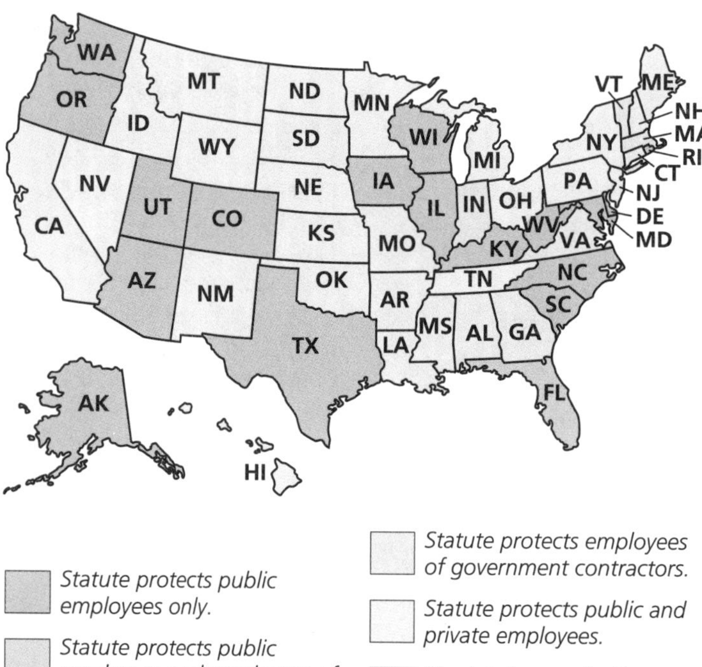

Statute protects public employees only.

Statute protects public employees and employees of government contractors.

Statute protects employees of government contractors.

Statute protects public and private employees.

No statutory protection.

3. Ask your state bar association for the name of an attorney experienced in employment law. Discussing your concerns with an attorney is not whistle-blowing; you are protected by attorney-client privilege.

4. If you do decide to blow the whistle, protect yourself by carefully following the steps required by law and outlined by your attorney. This may mean informing your employer of the wrongdoing in writing.

5. Do not talk to the media without your attorney's permission. By doing so, you could risk being sued by your employer for defamation.

Will

A will is a legal document that states how a person's property is to be distributed after his death. Countless words have been written about the importance of having a will, yet most Americans (70 percent, by one estimate) die without one. Many people never draw up a will because they think it will be too expensive or too complicated. But for most people a will is very affordable—as little as $100—and a simple will can often be done very quickly.

To make a valid will, you must be of legal age. You must also be "of sound mind"—that is, you must have a general understanding of the extent of your property and of the "natural objects of your bounty," such as your spouse, children, or grandchildren.

If you are married, you and your spouse should have separate wills, even if your assets are held primarily in only one of your names. It is possible to draw up a "joint will," but most attorneys discourage such wills because they can prevent a surviving spouse from making necessary changes after the death of the other.

Why You Need a Will

If you die without a will, your property will be distributed according to the laws of your state, which may not be consistent with your wishes. In most states, for example, if someone who has surviving relatives dies without a will, his spouse is entitled only to one-third to one-half of his property. In this event, the remainder of the property goes to the deceased person's children, parents, or brothers and sisters. See also Dying Without a Will.

A will is also important because it allows you to choose an executor to oversee your estate and to name a guardian for your minor children. If you do not have a will, a court will make these decisions for you.

Even if you own most of your property in ways that allow it to pass directly to your heirs without a will, such as in joint tenancy or a living trust, you need a will for other property that you own or that might come to you later, even after your death. Suppose your husband receives a large inheritance from his cousin Hilda shortly before his death, and he dies before he has the opportunity to put the property in joint tenancy or in trust. If he had no will, you would only receive the share allowed to you under state law, with the rest going to your children, grandchildren, or other relatives. See also JOINT TENANCY; LIVING TRUST.

NAMING YOUR EXECUTOR

To guide your estate through probate court and carry out the provisions of your will, you will need to name an executor. Most people choose a spouse, relative, or friend, but you can name almost anyone of legal age, even your accountant or attorney. Whoever the person is, he or she should be someone you can trust to carry out your wishes. Since your executor will be required to attend local court hearings and administer your estate, it is best to choose someone who lives nearby.

Serving as an executor requires a considerable amount of time and effort. Therefore, before naming someone, you should get her permission. You should also name an alternate executor in the event your first choice is unwilling or unable to serve when you die; otherwise, the court will have to name an executor. See also EXECUTOR AND ADMINISTRATOR; PROBATE.

NAMING A GUARDIAN

If you die while your children are minors, their other parent remains the legal guardian—unless he or she has been declared unfit for custody. If the children's other parent has died, or to protect against the possibility that he dies at the same time you do (or shortly thereafter), you should name a guardian in your will.

The guardian should be someone who can offer your children the kind of care and upbringing you yourself would give them. Usually, you will want to name a relative or close friend who is willing to accept the responsibility. You should also name an alternate guardian in case your first choice cannot or will not serve. See GUARDIAN AND WARD.

DISINHERITING A FAMILY MEMBER

If you want to disinherit a child, you should specify the child by name. If you fail to mention a child in your will, the law in most states assumes that this was an oversight, and the court may award the child the same share that she would have received if you had died without a will. In almost every state, the law makes it very difficult for you to totally disinherit your spouse—unless you have a valid premarital agreement that allows you to do so. Otherwise, no matter what you do, your spouse will usually be entitled to the same one-third to one-half share that he or she would have received if you had died without a will. See also DISINHERITANCE; PRENUPTIAL AGREEMENT.

SPECIFIC BEQUESTS

When you make a will, you can list specific bequests—gifts of clearly designated property, such as jewelry, furniture, specific amounts of cash, real estate, or just about anything else you own. However, if you no longer own the property at the time of your death, your designated beneficiary cannot claim the bequest. Suppose you leave your coin collection to your cousin Jim. Forgetting that you have made this bequest, you sell the collection. When you die, your cousin Jim cannot claim its monetary value.

YOUR RESIDUARY ESTATE

Your will should contain a clause relating to your residuary estate — that is, the remainder of your property after specific bequests have been made and the taxes and expenses of administering your estate have been paid. You must name a beneficiary for your residuary estate. If you fail to do so, your remaining property may be distributed as if you had died without a will, or it might even go to the state.

WITNESSES

For your will to be valid, it must be witnessed properly. Most states require two witnesses, but some states—Vermont, for example—require three. Louisiana also requires three witnesses, one of whom must be a notary public (someone authorized by the state to attest to the authenticity of signatures). Witnesses must be of legal age and should live nearby in the event they need to testify about the validity of the will.

Since witnesses are supposed to be impartial and have no financial interest in the estate, neither a beneficiary nor a spouse or child should serve as a witness. If you do use such a person as a witness, the validity of the will may be challenged or the beneficiary may be disqualified from receiving the bequest.

Today many states allow witnesses to sign what is known as a self-proving affidavit, which permits your will to be probated, or carried out, without requiring them to attest to the validity of your signature.

EXECUTING YOUR WILL

To execute your will—put it into effect legally—you must sign it in the presence of witnesses, and they must sign in your presence and in the presence of each other. Neither you nor any of the witnesses should leave each other's presence until the will has been completely signed and witnessed. If you are executing a self-proving affidavit, both you and the witnesses should sign in the presence of a notary public.

In some states you must "publish" your will for it to be valid. You must tell your witnesses that the document you are signing is your last will and testament and that you are asking them to serve as witnesses to it. They are not entitled to know the content of your will, only that it is your will.

You and your witnesses should also initial the margin of each page of the will, except the signature page. This is to prevent someone from changing your will by substituting a page with different provisions.

You should sign only the original of your will, but before doing so, you can make copies for your executor and others.

Keep the executed will in a safe place, such as a fireproof box in your home, or in your lawyer's office. If you intend to store it in a safe-deposit box, first check your state's laws regarding safe-deposit boxes. In some states a safe-deposit box will be sealed upon the owner's death until an inventory can be conducted by state tax officials, thus delaying the administration of your will by your executor. Be sure to let your executor know where your will is located.

REVISING YOUR WILL

You cannot revise a will by altering it. Corrections, erasures, or deletions can invalidate it entirely. There are only two ways to revise an existing will legally. One is to create a document known as a codicil—an amendment to a will that must be prepared, signed, and

CHECKLIST

Property You Cannot Will to Others

The law prevents some kinds of property from being passed to others in your will. The most common examples are:

❑ **JOINTLY OWNED PROPERTY.** Property you own with another person, such as a bank account, real estate, or stocks and bonds, automatically passes to the other owner when you die.

❑ **LIFE INSURANCE PROCEEDS.** Proceeds are paid directly to the beneficiary named in the policy. However, if you fail to name a beneficiary, the proceeds become part of your estate.

❑ **ASSETS HELD BY A TRUST.** Trust assets are distributed according to the terms of the trust.

❑ **PROPERTY UNDER CONTRACT.** Suppose you have a contract to sell your car, but die before the paperwork is completed. The buyer can enforce the contract, and the car will not be included in your estate. However, the amount of money received from the buyer as payment will be included.

❑ **COMMUNITY PROPERTY.** In nine states (Arizona, California, Idaho, Louisiana, Nevada, New Mexico, Texas, Washington, and Wisconsin), all property or income acquired during a marriage (except property acquired by inheritance or gift) is considered community property and is owned equally by both spouses. In these states you cannot leave more than your one-half share of this property to anyone.

witnessed in the same manner as a will. See also CODICIL.

The other way is to create a new will, which automatically revokes any previous wills and codicils. To avoid the possibility that your outdated will may be mistaken for a revised one, either tear it up, burn it, or write the word *revoked* or *canceled* across each page. It is also a good idea to state in your new will that it revokes all previous wills.

WHEN SHOULD YOU WRITE A NEW WILL?

Review your will at least once a year to make sure that it still reflects your property and wishes. You should consider making a new will if one of the following happens:

◇ If you marry. In some states a marriage automatically revokes an existing will.

◇ If a child is born to you or if you adopt one.

◇ If you get divorced. Although marriage may automatically revoke an existing will, a divorce does not. If your former spouse is named as a beneficiary, she will be entitled to any property left to her in your will, unless you write a new one.

◇ If you move from one state to another. Your will must be administered in the state in which you reside at the time of your death.

◇ If there is a change in your financial condition or that of your beneficiaries.

◇ If your spouse or some other beneficiary dies.

DOING IT YOURSELF

If your estate is relatively small, and if you plan to distribute it in a fairly straightforward manner, such as to your spouse and children, you may want to use a do-it-yourself will kit, available at many book and stationery stores, rather than hire an attorney. Keep in mind, however, that if laws change, or if you complete the forms incorrectly, your self-made will could be invalid, and your estate could be treated as if you had died without making a will. See also ESTATE PLANNING; ESTATE TAX; HOLOGRAPHIC WILL; TRUST.

For a sample will and codicil, see the EVERYDAY LEGAL FORMS section of this book, beginning on page 552.

WIRETAPPING

Wiretapping—using electronic devices to listen to or record private telephone conversations—is prohibited by federal law, with certain exceptions. Under federal law as well as most state laws, to wiretap a conversation legally you must have permission from one of the participants or a court order allowing you to do so.

THE FOURTH AMENDMENT AND WIRETAPPING

If the police or other law enforcement officials wiretap a suspect in a criminal case without a court order, any information that the wiretap reveals will be inadmissible as evidence, because wiretapping without a warrant violates the prohibition against unreasonable searches and seizures stated in the Fourth Amendment. See SEARCH AND SEIZURE.

To obtain a court order to conduct a legal wiretap, law enforcement officials must convince a judge that there is "probable cause," or sufficient reason, to believe that a serious crime such as murder, kidnapping, gambling, robbery, bribery, extortion, or drug dealing is occurring or is about to occur. The police must also show that only by using a wiretap will they be able to gain information about the crime because other investigative methods have failed or are likely to fail.

An order allowing a wiretap lasts for a limited period of time, and law enforcement officers must minimize the number of calls listened to or recorded. If it is clear that a monitored call is purely social and not likely to lead to information about a crime, the officers should not listen to or record it.

The police do not need warrants to intercept communications made over cellular or mobile phones that use radio frequencies, since the courts have found that the users of mobile phones have no reasonable expectation of privacy.

The courts have also found that tracing devices such as "pen registers," which record the telephone numbers from which calls have been placed, do not constitute wiretapping if they are used only to obtain the numbers.

PRIVATE WIRETAPS

Under federal law, you may tape your own conversations, since one of the participants—namely, you—consents to it. In some cases the tapes would even be admissible as evidence.

For example, if a reporter calls you for a quote and you record your reply, you might be able to use the tape as evidence in a libel suit if he misquotes you. However, in some states privately taped conversations cannot be used as evidence unless both parties have consented to the taping.

Listening in on a conversation as a third party with the intent of using overheard information against someone is considered an invasion of privacy. In one case, a husband had an extension to his home telephone installed in a closet in his office. He recorded all his home calls, expecting to find evidence of his wife's adultery. He did, but he was unable to use the recordings in court because the wiretapping law deemed them inadmissible. Ironically, the wife's boyfriend successfully sued the husband for invasion of privacy.

WITNESS PROTECTION PROGRAM

Witnesses to serious offenses, especially those involving organized crime, are often afraid to come forward and testify in court. In 1970 Congress addressed this problem by passing a law, the Federal Witness Protection Act, which authorizes the Attorney General to provide for the security of witnesses who assist in the investigation and prosecution of suspects believed to be involved in organized crime or other serious offenses. This law applies to both state and federal prosecutions.

The Federal Witness Protection Act allows the Attorney General to relocate witnesses and their families, provide for their security and living expenses, and establish new identities for them with the aid of supporting documents. The program also helps the witness to find employment and become self-supporting. The witness's new name and location remain a secret, unless they are requested by law enforcement officials who believe the witness has committed a crime.

The Attorney General is under no obligation to provide this type of protection, and a witness has no grounds for suing the Attorney General if he is turned down and is subsequently harmed.

RESPONSIBILITIES OF A WITNESS

Participation in the witness protection program is voluntary, and a witness may withdraw at any time. But while they are in the program, witnesses and their families must abide by the Attorney General's regulations and guidelines. For example, they must agree to testify and give information in all relevant proceedings; be careful to avoid detection by others; keep the government informed of their whereabouts; and cooperate with all reasonable requests of the government agents who are providing the protection.

Participation in the program does not give a witness the right to disregard the law. The Attorney General will cooperate in enforcing the terms of any civil judgments against the witness to the extent that the safety of the witness is not endangered.

WOMEN'S RIGHTS

A woman's right to vote became a constitutional right in 1920 with the ratification of the 19th Amendment. While women have made steady progress in obtaining equal property rights and access to education and employment, many still see the law as unfair to women.

PROPERTY RIGHTS

Under English common law, from which our American laws developed, women, especially married women, had little right to own property. For example, when a woman married, the husband and wife became one person in law, and the legal existence of the woman was suspended. Any real estate she owned, as well as her personal property, became the property of her husband. A woman could not enter into contracts, nor could she be sued. Any money she earned belonged to her husband.

It was not until the 19th century, when states enacted the Married Woman's Property Acts, that women gained the right to make contracts, own and manage property separate from that of their husbands, and keep money they earned from their own work.

Today, women have equal legal status with men in these areas and others, and this right is guaranteed in many state constitutions. See also COMMUNITY PROPERTY; DIVORCE; SEX DISCRIMINATION.

RIGHT TO EQUAL EDUCATION

Equality for women in regard to public education was not formally recognized until 1972, when Congress added gender to the list of factors that cannot be used to deny a child the right to a public education. School programs or activities that receive federal assistance are prohibited from discrimination on the basis of sex under the federal Education Amendments of 1972. This prohibition has been used in the courts to challenge sex-based discrimination not only in classroom education, but also in sports and other extracurricular activities. See also CIVIL RIGHTS; JOB DISCRIMINATION.

ABORTION

The U.S. Supreme Court has held that the right to privacy is implied in the Bill of Rights. Among other things, this right generally allows men and women to seek or refuse medical treatment. However, some aspects of this right do not always apply to pregnant women. Although a woman's right to obtain an abortion was given Constitutional protection in 1972, many state laws have sought to limit this right. See also ABORTION.

EQUAL RIGHTS AMENDMENT

In the eyes of many legal scholars, the failure of the Equal Rights Amendment (ERA) signaled a setback to women's rights. The ERA would have eliminated any discrimination based on gender. It was passed by both the Senate and House of Representatives, but in 1988 it failed to meet ratification requirements, when only 35 states ratified it rather than the requisite 38.

WORKERS' COMPENSATION

Jack was delivering bakery goods when his van was hit, and he suffered a broken arm. Thomas operates a punch press at a manufacturing plant and lost two fingers when the machine malfunctioned. And Marilyn had surgery on her wrist to correct an injury resulting from her continual use of a computer keyboard at work. Since all three workers were injured on the job, they can apply for workers' compensation benefits.

Workers' compensation is a system set up in every state to provide money awards to employees or their families when a worker is injured, becomes ill, or dies from a work-related activity. In the past, employees had to sue their employers in order to be compensated for job-related injuries. As plaintiffs, it was up to them to prove that the injury was the employers' fault. Employers often argued that employees assumed the risk of injury by taking the job, and the courts generally accepted this defense. Such rulings often left injured workers destitute.

To protect workers from financial loss due to work-related disasters, the first workers' compensation law was passed in New York in 1910. Today all 50 states have such laws.

Under workers' compensation an employer must compensate an injured worker regardless of how his on-the-job injury occurred. Generally, the only determinations to be made are whether the injury was work-related and the amount of compensation.

WHEN YOU CAN SUE

In return for workers' compensation, which is essentially a no-fault arrangement between workers and employers, injured workers generally forfeit the right to sue their employers. Some states, however, allow an injured employee to sue an employer over a work-related injury if the employer intentionally violated a safety standard or deliberately failed to inform workers about hazardous conditions.

Injured workers who receive workers' compensation may also sue a third party to the accident, such as the manufacturer of defective equipment. Since workers' compensation awards tend to be small, a worker seeking further damages should always consider suing the manufacturer.

ELIGIBILITY

By law, employers either purchase workers' compensation

insurance or contribute to a fund out of which benefits are paid to eligible employees. Some states will allow you to choose whether you want to participate in the program. If you do not, you must sign a waiver before taking the job.

State and federal laws determine which employees are covered by workers' compensation. Farm workers and household or domestic help are often excluded. Some employees are not covered because their companies have fewer than the minimum number of workers designated by the statute. Other categories of workers who may be excluded include temporary or seasonal employees, highly paid workers, executives, and management personnel. Depending on state law, volunteers and independent contractors (individuals who work for themselves) may also be ineligible.

ABC's

OF HIRING A LAWYER FOR A WORKERS' COMPENSATION CLAIM

If you have been harmed at the workplace and are filing a claim for workers' compensation, you have the right to be represented by an attorney, whose fees are generally set by law as a percentage of the benefits you receive. You should consider hiring a workers' compensation attorney under any of the following circumstances:

- ❑ If your claim for benefits is rejected.
- ❑ If your claim has been accepted, but you believe you are not receiving the correct amount of compensation.
- ❑ If you are fired, suspended, or otherwise disciplined for filing a workers' compensation claim.
- ❑ If you are asked to participate in a vocational-rehabilitation program, despite the fact that you believe you are not physically able to do so.
- ❑ If you are not satisfied with the medical treatment you are receiving from a doctor provided by the workers' compensation carrier.
- ❑ If you are released from medical care and ordered to return to work before you believe you are able to do so.

FILING A CLAIM

When you are injured on the job, notify your supervisor or employer promptly. Later you will have to fill out a claim form that asks for information about when, where, and how the accident happened; the extent of your injuries; and the medical bills for your treatment. You will then receive notification accepting or rejecting your claim. If the claim is accepted, weekly or monthly benefit checks will be sent to you.

If your claim is rejected or partly denied, you can appeal the decision. If the appeal board rules against you the decision can be appealed to a state district court judge.

BENEFITS

Every state has adopted an extensive schedule that is used to determine the amount and length of benefits per injury. When reviewing an application for compensation, the workers' compensation board looks at the severity of the injury, the prognosis for a full recovery, and the worker's salary. If you sprain your wrist, for example, your injury would be classified as a temporary partial disability, and you would receive benefits for the number of weeks allowed for that injury.

An accident that leaves you blind in one eye is an example of a permanent partial injury. Benefits for permanent disabilities are paid out until you have received the maximum amount set by state law. If the accident leads to your death, your family will receive compensation.

Receiving workers' compensation benefits does not disqualify you from getting benefits from other pension and disability insurance programs.

INJURIES NOT COVERED

An employee may be denied workers' compensation benefits if she lied about the condition of her health on her employment application. For example, if you lie about your bad back and the condition contributes to an accident, you may not receive compensation.

Some accidents or injuries

are due to the willful misconduct of an employee and are generally denied compensation. If you deliberately injure yourself, ignore safety instructions, fail to use safety equipment, or otherwise engage in willful misconduct, the employer is released from any obligation to provide benefits. For example, if you remove a safety guard from a piece of dangerous equipment in violation of company policy and then injure yourself, you probably will not receive workers' compensation.

Injuries resulting from a prank by a coworker may qualify for compensation. At one time claims based on pranks or practical jokes were not recognized, but today the laws are more lenient, and an employee might receive compensation for injuries if his employer knew he had no part in the prank.

Fights between coworkers may be excluded by state law, depending on the reason for the dispute. For example, if the fight was related to personal matters and had nothing to do with the workplace, the claim is likely to be rejected.

INJURIES OUTSIDE THE WORKPLACE

Workers' compensation provides coverage for injuries that occur "in the course of employment." Does that include going to and from work? The "coming and going rule" holds that an accident that occurs while a worker is traveling to and from work is not work-related. Exceptions have sometimes been made for salespeople who are injured while traveling to call on clients. If a salesperson is injured while combining business and personal errands, the workers' compensation board determines the primary reason for the trip. If it is business, the injury will be covered; if personal, it will be denied.

An injury that occurs during lunch hour may be covered only if the injured worker is on the company's premises. Injuries at company social gatherings and athletic activities are covered in some states if the events are part of the job, and especially if attendance is mandatory. Other states consider sports activities outside the scope of workers' compensation, and thus a worker may have to sue his employer to collect for any injuries.

WRONGFUL DEATH

When one person's intentional or negligent actions result in the death of another, a wrongful death has occurred. The spouse, children, or parents of the deceased may bring lawsuits for wrongful death against the wrongdoers to compensate for the loss of wages or other support they would have received had the person lived.

WHO CAN SUE

A plaintiff in a wrongful-death suit does not have to prove that he or she was completely dependent on the deceased for support, but only that the death results in a financial loss. For example, a woman whose husband dies in an automobile accident may have her own means of support, such as a job or an inheritance. But if she can show that her husband's income was put into a joint account and shared by them equally, she can recover for that loss. To help determine the deceased's potential income, the court will hear expert testimony from economists and statisticians.

In addition, some states—for example, Iowa, Missouri, Oklahoma, and Pennsylvania—allow the surviving spouse and children of a wrongful-death victim to sue for compensatory damages for the pain and suffering they experience as a result of their loved-one's death. Other states may allow the survivors to sue for the pain and suffering of the deceased. See also DAMAGES.

To win a wrongful-death action, the plaintiff must prove that the defendant's actions were the "proximate," or immediate, cause of the death. Suppose you carelessly run into a man with your car and knock him to the pavement. He picks himself up, dusts himself off, and continues on his way. Two weeks later, he dies of a heart attack. To find you liable for his wrongful death, a court would have to be convinced that the incident on the street was the cause of the heart attack, a connection that would be hard to make.

But suppose that, instead of getting up immediately, the man struck his head on the pavement and was knocked unconscious. He is ultimately revived, but dies from a brain injury several days later. In this case, the plaintiff would have a greater chance of proving the connection between the accident and the cause of death. See also JUDGMENT; LAWSUIT; LIABILITY; NEGLIGENCE; TORT.

WHO CANNOT BE SUED

Courts do not allow one member of a family to sue another for wrongful death. In common law, a government is also immune from wrongful-death suits, although many states now permit suits against the state government. Employers can be sued for causing a wrongful death, but their liability is generally limited by workers' compensation laws. See COMMON LAW; SOVEREIGN IMMUNITY; WORKERS' COMPENSATION.

FILING A SUIT

Wrongful-death suits are usually taken on a contingency basis — that is, the lawyer will take the case for a percentage of the damages awarded. But first the lawyer will determine whether the defendant has assets or liability insurance that he can use to pay any damages the court may order. Some people who are responsible for wrongful deaths are "judgment proof"—that is, they have no assets or insurance that can be used to pay compensation.

WRONGFUL LIFE

"I wish I'd never been born." Most people who say this do not really mean it, but some people have sued persons who, they claim, wrongfully allowed them to be born. These lawsuits, sometimes referred to as wrongful-life cases, are usually brought by or on behalf of severely disabled or disfigured children against physicians who allegedly were negligent in failing to prevent their birth.

Wrongful-life lawsuits are generally disallowed by the courts. Most courts have found that no person has a right not to be born, and therefore no person has grounds to sue anyone for not preventing his birth. Likewise, many courts have found that no one has the right to be born without defects. Thus even a child born with severe abnormalities may not sue a doctor for his birth and the pain and suffering caused by his disability.

Similarly, courts have rejected claims of illegitimate children against their parents, who maintain that they have been forced to suffer the stigma of being born out of wedlock. The courts have also rejected claims from people purporting to have suffered because they were born to irresponsible parents.

WRONGFUL PREGNANCY

Although courts generally rule that no one has legal grounds for complaint because they are born, in some cases parents may sue health-care providers, such as doctors or hospitals, when the provider's negligence leads to an unplanned and unwanted pregnancy. When the botched performance of a sterilization procedure, such as a tubal ligation or a vasectomy, results in the conception of a child, some courts will allow the parents to sue the doctor who made the mistake.

This is not a wrongful-life suit, but a wrongful-pregnancy suit, which is similar to many other types of medical malpractice claims. In these cases the parents may be compensated for the cost of the pregnancy and birth, the pain and suffering associated with the pregnancy and birth (as well as the failed surgical procedure), and the loss of the mother's wages due to the pregnancy and birth. In most cases, however, the courts will not grant any further awards, especially if the child is healthy.

WRONGFUL BIRTH

A wrongful birth is not a claim by the child that she should not have been born, but rather a claim brought by the parents against a doctor who allegedly failed to give them the option of terminating a pregnancy that resulted in an impaired child.

Courts that allow wrongful-birth claims do so on the theory that (1) couples have the right to prevent the birth of defective children, and (2) their doctors have a duty to provide them with the information necessary to make such a decision. For example, a doctor who failed to warn a woman that her use of Dilantin, an anticonvulsive drug, significantly increased the chances that her child would be born with severe deformities, could be sued for wrongful birth, as well as for medical malpractice.

If the parents of a child with birth defects sue for wrongful birth and win, they can generally recover the same type of damages allowed in a wrongful-pregnancy suit. See also LAWSUIT; MEDICAL MALPRACTICE.

X Mark

An X mark serves as a signature for someone who cannot write because he is either illiterate or physically disabled. This type of signature must usually be witnessed by a competent person who can testify that it is authentic.

X-Rated Material

In response to concerns about the language, violence, and sexual content of movies, the motion-picture industry established a rating system to indicate the suitability of films for certain age groups. Films are rated either G (suitable for audiences of all ages), PG (parental guidance required), PG-13 (contains matter unsuitable for children under age 13), R (restricted to persons age 17 or older unless accompanied by an adult), and NC-17 (no one under 17 admitted).

Although the X rating used for adult films has no legal definition, a theater or video store that allows minors to view or purchase X-rated materials may be charged with contributing to the delinquency of a minor or distributing obscene materials to a minor. See also Obscenity; Pornography.

Z Mark

A Z mark is used to fill in blank spaces on a legal document, such as a contract, to prevent an unauthorized person from filling in those spaces at a later time, thereby changing the terms of the contract.

Zoning

Virtually every city and county in the United States has enacted zoning ordinances to regulate real estate use.

Purpose of Zoning

Generally, zoning regulations are part of a comprehensive community plan developed to protect and improve the welfare of its residents rather than its businesses. For example, by prohibiting industrial development in a residential area, the city or county can minimize traffic and pollution that might endanger the well-being of residents. By prohibiting or restricting the development of shopping centers in these areas, a municipality can help preserve both the appearance and ambience of a community. Both actions may also maintain property values. To that end, laws limit the use of property in a particular area to agricultural, residential, industrial, or commercial uses, or to some combination thereof.

Zoning regulations may be general or specific. General regulations may prohibit buildings whose designs are inconsistent with the area's existing architecture. Specific regulations may establish a minimum number of off-street parking spaces for each newly constructed building.

Exceptions

Under special circumstances, certain uses of property that do not conform to current zoning plans may be allowed. If the property was used a certain way before current zoning regulations were enacted, that use may be allowed to continue under the "nonconforming use" exception.

Another exception may be made when a property owner wants to alter his property in a way that is not permitted by local zoning regulations. In this event, he may apply for a "variance"—official permission to use the property in a way that would normally violate the zoning laws. He may or may not receive permission, depending on the decision of the local zoning board. See also Variance.

Everyday Legal Forms

Contracts, deeds, notices, applications, wills, affidavits — the world of law is a world of paper. Designed to make something official by putting it in writing, these forms are often long and technical, and they can be daunting to the layman. But to lawyers they serve a valuable purpose: they simplify and standardize the legal process. On the following pages you will find some of the most common legal forms, 36 samples covering a wide variety of everyday situations, from buying a car to writing a will. Each form uses traditional legal terminology and is accompanied by clear instructions on how to fill it out and put it to use. Also, each form includes cross-references to related articles in case you need more information.

Although you can adopt some of these forms for your own use, you should do so with caution. Laws vary widely across the country, and the exact language required in your state may not match that contained in the sample provided. Moreover, some financial institutions will not honor forms that are not their own. For example, if you want to authorize someone to gain access to your bank account, your bank may require you to use its own power of attorney form. If a document has far-reaching consequences, such as a prenuptial agreement, be sure to consult a lawyer before signing it.

Whether you use these forms as working models or simply for reference, they will save you time and money. They will not only acquaint you with the language and content of formal legal documents, but will alert you to the information you will need in order to fill in the blanks. If you fill out a form before you see a lawyer, you will reduce the time he must spend explaining it to you and asking you questions, and you will therefore save money.

Perhaps most important of all, these forms will help you tidy up your legal life. If you are a tenant or a landlord, for example, you should know what information should be contained in a residential lease. If you are concerned about your credit rating, you should know how to check it and correct any errors. If you are considering granting someone a power of attorney, you should know about the different kinds that exist, and about the rights and duties of each. Filling out forms can be tedious and time-consuming, but the ones provided here will make the task much easier.

CONTENTS

Personal Records Inventory

An inventory of personal records can help you to keep track of important documents. It can also be invaluable to family members if certain items must be located in your absence.

My Personal Records

your name

Funeral Instructions: *location of documents*

Letters of Final Bequest: *location*

Anatomical Gift Form: *location; who has copies*

Will and Trust (s): *location; who has copies*

Living Will: *location; who has copies*

Power of Attorney: *location; name and address of appointee*

Insurance Policies: *location; names of insurance companies and beneficiaries*

Safe-Deposit Box Keys: *location of keys; name and address of bank*

Bank Passbooks and Checkbooks: *location; account numbers; names and addresses of banks*

Business Papers: *location; description*

Deeds to Real Estate: *location; list of property*

Mortgage Documents: *location; list of mortgaged property*

Stock Certificates: *location; name and address of brokerage firm; account number (s)*

Other Investment Certificates: *location; list of profit-sharing, pension, and retirement plans*

Social Security Card: *location; Social Security number*

Tax Returns: *location*

Birth Certificate: *location*

Marriage Certificate (s): *location; date and place of marriage (s)*

Prenuptial Agreement: *location*

Divorce Decree (s): *location; date and place of divorce (s)*

Death Certificates: *location; names of deceased*

Passport: *location; passport number*

Citizenship Papers: *location; date of issue*

Military Discharge Papers: *location; date of discharge*

Warranties: *location; description*

Other: *location; description*

❑ **Note:** Funeral instructions list the funeral arrangements you want. Letters of final bequest give instructions on the disposition of personal property not mentioned in your will. Update your personal records inventory periodically and keep it in an accessible place that is known to family members. For more information, see FINANCIAL RECORDS; PERSONAL RECORDS.

FUNERAL INSTRUCTIONS

Funeral instructions should state whether you wish to be buried or cremated, as well as where you want to be buried or where your ashes are to go. On either form, you can also include detailed instructions for the kind of burial or memorial service you would like.

Instructions for Funeral and Burial

I, ___*your name*___, hereby direct that upon my death my mortal remains be disposed of as follows:

1. It is my wish to be buried in ___*name and address of cemetery*___, Section No. ____, Plot No. ____ [if plot has been purchased]. The deed to this plot is with the original of these funeral instructions.

2. It is my wish that my funeral [or memorial] service be conducted at ___*name and address of church or funeral home*___. It is my wish that the following arrangements for my funeral [or memorial] service be honored:

[Instructions for service. For example, "I wish to have my funeral service conducted by the Reverend Peter Smith or one of his assistants."]

The fully executed original of my last will and testament can be found in ___*exact location*___.

___*your signature*___
Signature

Instructions for Cremation

I, ___*your name*___, hereby direct that upon my death my mortal remains be disposed of as follows:

It is my wish that my remains be cremated at ___*name and address of funeral home*___ and that my ashes be disposed of in accordance with the desires of my next of kin [or other instructions].

The fully executed original of my last will and testament can be found in ___*exact location*___.

___*your signature*___
Signature

❑ **Note:** Even if your will contains funeral instructions, prepare a separate document describing the funeral arrangements you want—a will often is not read before the deceased's funeral. Keep the instructions in a safe place and give copies to your family, executor, and lawyer. For more information, see EXECUTOR AND ADMINISTRATOR; FUNERAL AND BURIAL; WILL.

A Simple Will

This simple will is suitable for a married person with children. You should regularly review your will, and amend it by means of a codicil if needed. If you marry or become divorced, however, or after the birth or adoption of a child, you should execute an entirely new will.

Last Will and Testament

I, ______*your full legal name*______, a resident of the County of __*your county*__, State of ____*your state*____, being of sound mind and memory, and under no duress, hereby make, publish, and declare this to be my Last Will and Testament, revoking and canceling all previous wills and codicils made by me. It is my intention to dispose of all property, whether real, personal, or mixed, and wherever located, which I own or which I have the right to dispose of by will.

I. I am married to ____*your spouse's name*____, and all references to my spouse in this document are to the person named in this paragraph. I have __*number*__ children, whose names are:

[list names of children]

II. I direct my Executor to pay all of my just debts and the expenses of my funeral as soon as is reasonably possible after my death, and authorize my Executor to settle, compromise, and discharge any claims against my estate in his or her absolute discretion. I give my Executor full right, power, and authority to do any act in regard to my estate which I could do if living.

III. I hereby make and appoint ______*your executor's name*______ as Executor of this, my Last Will and Testament, to serve without bond. If my Executor is for any reason unable or unwilling to serve, then I make and appoint ____*your alternate executor's name*____ to serve as Executor, also to serve without bond.

IV. I give, devise, and bequeath to my spouse, ___*your spouse's name*___, my entire estate. In the event that my spouse dies before I do, or fails to survive me by thirty (30) days, then I give, devise, and bequeath my entire estate to my children in equal shares, per stirpes. If neither my spouse nor any children survive me, then I give, devise, and bequeath my entire estate to *name(s) of your alternate beneficiary (beneficiaries)*.

V. If I am survived by minor children, their other parent shall serve as Guardian. If the other parent dies before I do, or fails to survive me, I appoint *guardian's name* as Guardian. If the person named herein to serve as Guardian shall be unable or unwilling to serve, then I appoint *alternate guardian's name*, instead, to serve as Guardian. No person named in this paragraph to serve as Guardian shall be required to post bond.

IN WITNESS WHEREOF, I have signed and published this Last Will and Testament on this *date* day of *month*, 19___.

your name signed as it appears above
Testator

On the date written above, the foregoing document was signed in our presence by the Testator named therein, who declared it to be his/her Last Will and Testament, and at the same time, at the request of the Testator, in the Testator's presence and in the presence of each other, we have signed our names as witnesses. We attest that at the time of executing this Last Will and Testament, we believe the Testator to be of sound mind and memory, and under no duress, and that said Testator executed the foregoing Last Will and Testament as his/her free act and deed.

witness's signature	*witness's address*
Witness	Address
witness's signature	*witness's address*
Witness	Address

❑ **Note:** In order for your will to be valid, you must sign your name as it appears at the beginning of the will, in front of at least two witnesses. Some states require three witnesses. The witnesses must know you, but they cannot stand to benefit from your will. You may want to give unsigned copies of your will to the executor and guardian you have named in it, as well as to your spouse and children. Keep your original will in a safe place, such as a fireproof box, or with your lawyer. For further information, see CODICIL; EXECUTOR AND ADMINISTRATOR; GUARDIAN AND WARD; WILL (which includes an explanation of the term *per stirpes*).

ACKNOWLEDGMENT

In many states you can create a "self-proving" will with a notarized acknowledgment declaring that your will was properly executed and witnessed. The acknowledgment ensures that the witnesses will not be required to appear in probate court to attest to the authenticity of your signature.

State of ______*your state*______)
) ss.
County of ______*your county*______)

Before me personally appeared ______*your name*______, the Testator, and ______*witness's name*______, and ______*witness's name*______, as Witnesses, known by me to be the persons whose names are subscribed to this document, and having first been sworn, declared that the Testator signed and executed this document as his/her Last Will and Testament and did so as his/her free and voluntary act, and that each of the Witnesses, in the presence of the Testator and in each other's presence, signed their names to the aforesaid document as Witnesses. The Witnesses declare under oath that to the best of their knowledge, the Testator was of full legal age, of sound mind, and under no undue restraint or influence.

Subscribed and sworn to before me this _______ day of _______, 19__.

[SEAL] ________________________________
NOTARY PUBLIC

My commission expires: ___________

❑ **Note:** Fill in the blanks for your name and those of the witnesses. The notary will sign the acknowledgment and affix his seal to it. Then be sure to staple the acknowledgment to your will. For further information, see ACKNOWLEDGMENT; NOTARY PUBLIC; WILL.

Codicil to a Will

A codicil is an amendment to an existing will. You can use a codicil when you want to make small changes in your will. However, if you want to make extensive changes, such as when you marry, or if you have already made one or two codicils previously, you should execute a new will.

Codicil to Last Will and Testament of

___*your full legal name*___
Testator

I, ___*your name*___, residing at ___*your address*___, in the City of ___*your city*___, County of ___*your county*___, State of ___*your state*___, being of sound mind and memory, hereby make, publish, and declare this to be the first Codicil to my Last Will and Testament dated ___*date of your will*___, 19__.

I give, devise, and bequeath to ___*your beneficiary's name*___, the following described property:

[description of bequest]

IN WITNESS WHEREOF, I have signed and published this Codicil on this *date* day of *month*, 19__.

___*your name signed as it appears above*___
Testator

The foregoing document, consisting of ___*number*___ pages including this page, was signed, published, and declared by the Testator named therein as the first Codicil to his/her Last Will and Testament dated ___*date of your will*___, 19__. At the same time, in the Testator's presence and in the presence of each other, and at his/her request, we subscribed our names as witnesses this ___*current date*___ day of ___*current month*___, 19__.

___*witness's signature*___ residing at ___*witness's address*___
Witness Address

___*witness's signature*___ residing at ___*witness's address*___
Witness Address

❑ **Note:** This codicil adds a bequest, of either personal property or real estate, to a will. You can use codicils in other ways, such as to revoke a gift, name a new executor, or add another beneficiary to your estate. A codicil must be signed and witnessed just like a will. It should be stapled to your original will. For more information, see CODICIL; WILL.

LIVING WILL

A living will informs your family, doctors, and hospitals of your desire not to be kept alive by artificial means. It can be revoked at any time. Many states require special forms; your doctor or lawyer can tell you where to obtain the form used in your state. For more information see LIVING WILL.

Living Will Declaration and Directive to Physicians

Declaration made this __*date*__ day of __*month*__, 19__.

I, __*your full legal name*__, being an adult of sound mind, and emotionally and mentally competent to make this declaration, willfully and voluntarily make known my desires that my death shall not be artificially postponed, and hereby declare:

If at any time I should be diagnosed by at least two (2) physicians who have personally examined me, one of whom shall be my attending physician, as having an incurable and irreversible injury, disease, or illness, and that my death is imminent, where the application of life-sustaining procedures would serve only to artificially prolong the moment of my death, I direct that such procedures be withheld or withdrawn, and that I be permitted to die naturally, with only the administration of medication, food, or fluids or the performance of medical procedures deemed necessary to alleviate suffering and provide comfort care.

In the absence of my ability to give directions regarding the use of such life-prolonging procedures, it is my intention that this declaration shall be honored by my family and physicians as the final expression of my legal right to refuse medical or surgical treatment, and I accept the consequences of such refusal.

If I have been diagnosed as pregnant and that diagnosis is known to my attending physician, this directive shall be without force or effect during the term of my pregnancy.

I, my estate, and my heirs and successors will hold harmless any person, organization, or institution from any and all liability that may be incurred as a result of following the instructions contained in this declaration.

This declaration shall remain in effect unless and until it is revoked by me. I understand that I may revoke this declaration at any time. This declaration shall be governed by the laws of the state of __*your state*__.

Signed __*your name signed as it appears above*__
Declarant

City of Residence: __*your city*__
County of Residence: __*your county*__
State of Residence: __*your state*__

Affidavit

The declarant is personally known to me, and I believe the declarant to be of sound mind. I saw the declarant sign the declaration in my presence, freely and voluntarily, and I signed the declaration as a witness in the presence of the declarant. I did not sign the declarant's signature above for or at the direction of the declarant. At the date of this declaration, I am not entitled to any portion of the estate of the declarant according to the laws of intestate succession, or, to the best of my knowledge and belief, under any will of the declarant or other instrument taking effect at the declarant's death. I am not related to the declarant by blood or marriage. I am not the declarant's attending physician, nor an employee of the attending physician, nor am I an employee of or patient in the health care facility in which the declarant is a patient. I am not directly financially responsible for the medical care of the declarant. I am of sufficient legal age to serve as a witness to this declaration under the laws of the state of ____*your state*____.

____*witness's signature*____ ____*witness's address*____
Witness Address

____*witness's signature*____ ____*witness's address*____
Witness Address

NOTARY'S STATEMENT

STATE OF ______________)
) ss.
COUNTY OF ____________)

I, _________________________, a notary public in and for the state and county named above, hereby certify that on the _____ day of ______, 19___, personally appeared the declarant, and _______________________ and _____________________, as witnesses, and having first been duly sworn, each of them signed the above declaration in my presence and in the presence of each other, freely and voluntarily, and for the purposes described therein.

[SEAL] ______________________________
NOTARY PUBLIC

My commission expires: ___________________

❑ **Note:** The statement in the affidavit referring to intestate succession means that the witness is not someone who would be entitled to share in the declarant's estate if he were to die without having made a final will. This ensures that the witness is not likely to be someone who has an interest in the declarant's death.

Door-to-Door Sales Three-Day Cancellation Notice

Anyone who buys merchandise with a purchase price over $25 that is sold door-to-door, or at a location other than the seller's place of business, has a right to cancel the transaction. The seller must inform the buyer of this right as well as provide him with two copies of a cancellation notice.

You, the buyer, may cancel this transaction at any time prior to midnight of the third business day after the date of this transaction. See the accompanying notice of cancellation form for an explanation of this right.

NOTICE OF RIGHT TO CANCEL

date of transaction, **19 ___**

You may cancel this transaction, without any penalty or obligation, within three (3) business days from the above date.

If you cancel, any property traded in, any payment made by you under the contract of sale, and any negotiable instrument [such as a check] executed by you will be returned within ten (10) business days following receipt by the seller of the cancellation notice, and any security interest arising out of the transaction will be canceled.

If you cancel, you must make available to the seller at your residence, in substantially as good condition as when received, any goods delivered to you under this contract of sale; or you may, if you wish, comply with the instructions of the seller regarding the return shipment of the goods at the seller's expense and risk.

If you do make the goods available to the seller and the seller does not pick them up within twenty (20) days of the date of your notice of cancellation, you may retain or dispose of the goods without any further obligation. If you fail to make the goods available to the seller, or if you agree to return the goods to the seller and fail to do so, then you remain liable for performance of all obligations under the sales contract.

To cancel this transaction, mail or deliver a signed and dated copy of this cancellation notice or any other written notice, or send a telegram to the seller, *name of company*, **at** *address* **not later than midnight of** *date*, **19__.**
I hereby cancel this transaction.

your signature **Date: __________, 19 ___**
Buyer

❑ **Note:** The first paragraph must appear in bold type on the first page of the sales contract. The notice, also in bold type, may be part of the sales contract or a separate document. The seller fills in the transaction date, seller's or company's name and address, and expiration date; you sign and date the notice. Make a copy for your records. Send cancellation forms by certified mail, return receipt requested. For more information, see Cooling-Off Period.

Request for Credit Report

If you want to see the information in your credit file, you can write a letter such as this to make your request. Insert whichever paragraph in parentheses applies to your situation.

current date

credit reporting agency

street address

city state zip code

Re: Request for Credit Report

As provided for under the federal Fair Credit Reporting Act, I hereby request that you send me a full disclosure of my credit file. This should include the sources of information contained in my file, as well as the name and address of any person or organization that has received my credit report in writing, orally, or by any other means.

(As I have been denied credit in the last 30 days, I request that you provide me with this report free of charge in accordance with federal law.)

[or]

(I enclose my check for $*amount* as full payment for this request.)

Please feel free to contact me at the telephone number below with any questions you may have. Thank you for your prompt attention to this matter.

Sincerely,

your signature

your Social Security number

your area code and telephone number

your name printed

your street address

city state zip code

any previous name(s)

recent previous address(es)

❑ **Note:** Before mailing your request, call the credit bureau to ask what it charges for a report and whether it has any special instructions. Some bureaus require that requests be notarized. If you recently changed your name—because you married, for instance—or if you have been at your current address less than three years, you should provide the bureau with your previous name or address. For more information, see CREDIT BUREAU AND CREDIT RATING.

Correction to Credit Report

If you find that your credit record contains inaccuracies, notify the credit bureau immediately. You can use this form letter to be sure you have included all the necessary information.

current date ________

credit reporting agency ________

street address ________

city ________ *state* ________ *zip code* ________

Dear Sir or Madam:

A review of my credit file reveals the following erroneous or incomplete information:

[incorrect information as presented on your credit report]

This information is erroneous or incomplete because:

[facts explaining why information is wrong]

In accordance with the terms of the federal Fair Credit Reporting Act, I hereby request that you correct the erroneous information contained in my file.

Sincerely,

your signature ________

your name printed ________

your Social Security number ________

your street address ________

city ________ *state* ________ *zip code*

❑ **Note:** When you send this letter to the credit bureau, include copies of any documents that prove a mistake was made. You can also write to the source of the erroneous information (for example, the store that failed to credit your payment) to clear up any misunderstanding that caused the error. For more information, see Credit Bureau and Credit Rating.

Freedom of Information Act Request

The Freedom of Information Act gives everyone the right to examine many of the records held or maintained by federal government agencies. To obtain a copy of records that you want to see, send a written request such as this one to the agency or agencies that keep the records.

current date

Freedom of Information Act Request Staff

name of government agency

street address

city state zip code

Re: Freedom of Information Act request

Pursuant to the federal Freedom of Information Act, I hereby request a copy of all records held by *name of agency* pertaining to *information you are requesting*.

I will pay all reasonable costs associated with this request. However, if costs are expected to exceed $ *amount*, please let me know the amount in advance.

Sincerely,

your signature

your name printed

your street address

city state zip code

❑ **Note:** Your request should be as specific as possible. An agency can reject a request that is so unclear or broad that it would take an unreasonable amount of time to fulfill. The cost will depend on how difficult it is to find the records you want and how many pages must be copied. For further information, see FREEDOM OF INFORMATION ACT.

AFFIDAVIT

An affidavit is a document in which someone, who is called an affiant, makes a statement of facts under oath. Affidavits are used in business transactions and in legal proceedings and are sometimes required with applications for employment or for certain kinds of licenses.

STATE OF ___*your state*___)
) ss.
COUNTY OF ___*your county*___)

HAVING FIRST BEEN DULY SWORN, ___*your full name*___, the undersigned affiant, does hereby depose and say as follows:

[Your statement, for example: That on January 3, 1994, I was employed as the Vice President of Corporate Communications for the Temper Metals Company, and that the copy of the memorandum attached is a true and accurate copy of the memorandum that I wrote to John Jameson, President of Temper Metals Company, on that date.]

FURTHER AFFIANT SAYETH NOT.

Witness my hand under the penalties of perjury this ___*date*___ day of ___*month*___, 19__.

___*your signature*___
Affiant

NOTARY'S STATEMENT

State of ________)
) ss.
County of ________)

On this day personally appeared ____________________, who, having first been sworn, acknowledged the foregoing before me.

[SEAL]

____
NOTARY PUBLIC

My commission expires: __________

❑ **Note:** When making an affidavit, state the facts as you know them in a clear and precise way. If you believe something to be true but you are not positive, you should write in the affidavit that the statement is true "to the best of my knowledge and belief." Do not sign the affidavit until you have sworn before a notary or other qualified official that the statements you made are true. After you have signed it, the notary fills out the statement below your signature and affixes her seal to the affidavit. For further information, see AFFIDAVIT.

SUMMONS

If you are served a summons, it means that someone—designated as the plaintiff—has started a civil lawsuit against you — the defendant. Attached to the summons will be a document called a complaint, which gives details of the lawsuit that the plaintiff is making against you.

IN THE UNITED STATES DISTRICT COURT
IN AND FOR
THE DISTRICT OF KANSAS

Civil Action Number________

JOHN ROE,	)	
	)	
	)	
Plaintiff	)	
	)	
v.	)	SUMMONS
	)	
MARY DOE,	)	
	)	
	)	
Defendant	)	

You are hereby summoned and required to serve upon ____________, plaintiff's attorney, whose address is ________________________, an answer to the complaint which is herewith served upon you, within ______ days after service of this summons upon you, exclusive of the day of service. If you fail to do so, judgment by default will be taken against you for the relief demanded in the complaint.

____
Clerk of Court

[SEAL OF COURT]

Date: ______________

❑ **Note:** A summons is prepared by the plaintiff's attorney or another officer of the court and is mailed or hand-delivered to you. It tells you when and where you must respond to the charges on the complaint. You must respond to a traffic summons. If you do not respond to a summons in a civil lawsuit, you are not breaking the law, but your inaction will result in the plaintiff's winning his case. For more information, see DEFAULT JUDGMENT; LAWSUIT.

General Release

A general release is signed when one party agrees to give up all claims against another that resulted from a broken contract or an accident. For example, if you sign a contract to buy a home, and the seller later has a change of heart, you may be willing to accept monetary compensation from him rather than suing him for breach of contract. When the seller gives you the amount of money you both agreed upon, he will ask you to sign a general release like the one below.

Release

FOR GOOD AND VALUABLE CONSIDERATION, receipt of which is hereby acknowledged, the undersigned jointly and severally release, discharge, acquit, and forgive *name of person receiving the release* now and forevermore, from any and all claims, actions, suits, demands, agreements, liabilities, and proceedings of every nature and description, whether at law or in equity, arising from the beginning of time to the date of this release and more particularly related to an incident or claim that arose out of:

[Description of the accident or contract that is the cause of the dispute. For example: "A contract dated June 6, 1993, by and between the parties for the purchase of real property located at 1234 Albany Way, Chicago, Illinois 60617."]

This release shall be binding upon and inure to the benefit of the parties, their heirs, successors, assigns, and personal representatives.

Signed this *date* day of *month*, 19___.

witness's signature Witness	*signature of first party* Signature
witness's signature Witness	*signature of second party* Signature

❑ **Note:** For a general release to be valid, you must receive some kind of consideration, or compensation, in return for relinquishing your legal rights. Unless you are certain that you have been adequately compensated, do not sign a release of this type without first consulting a lawyer. For more information, see ACCIDENTS IN PUBLIC PLACES; RELEASE.

General Bill of Sale

A bill of sale is used when a seller transfers ownership of personal property (property other than real estate) to a buyer. It gives the buyer proof of ownership, and can be useful in obtaining insurance coverage for expensive items, such as electronic equipment or jewelry.

Bill of Sale

FOR GOOD AND VALUABLE CONSIDERATION, and in payment of the sum of $_*purchase price*_, receipt of which is hereby acknowledged, the undersigned Seller hereby sells and transfers to ________*buyer's name*________, Buyer, and his/her successors and assigns forever, the following described personal property:

[description of property]

The Seller warrants to Buyer that he/she has good and marketable title to and full authority to sell said property, and that said property is sold free of all liens, encumbrances, liabilities, and claims of every nature and description whatsoever.

The Seller warrants to Buyer that he/she will defend, protect, indemnify and hold harmless the Buyer and its lawful successors and assigns from any adverse claim made against the property.

The property is otherwise sold in "as is" condition and where presently located, and no warranties either express or implied are made regarding the condition of the property or its suitability for any particular purpose.

Signed this __*date*__ day of _____*month*_____, 19___.

_____*witness's signature*_____	_____*seller's signature*_____
Witness	Seller
_____*witness's address*_____	_____*seller's address*_____
Address	Address

❑ **Note:** The seller should not give the buyer a bill of sale until the buyer has paid the full purchase price. The bill of sale should include a full description of the property, including any model, serial, or identification numbers. A bill of sale may or may not include warranties of title, or ownership ("The Seller warrants to Buyer..."). When they are included it means that the seller declares that he owns the property free and clear, has the right to sell it, and promises that he will defend the buyer's right to the property against anyone who may claim to be the owner. However, in this example, the seller is selling the property in its present condition ("as is") and at its present location (he does not have to deliver it to the buyer), and makes no promise (warranty) regarding its condition. For further information, see Bill of Sale.

Bill of Sale for Motor Vehicles

This bill of sale transfers the ownership of a motor vehicle from a seller to a buyer. The seller should give the bill of sale to the buyer along with an odometer statement. Many states require a bill of sale; some have special forms that can be obtained from the state motor vehicle bureau.

Bill of Sale

FOR GOOD AND VALUABLE CONSIDERATION, and in payment of the sum of $*purchase price*, receipt of which is hereby acknowledged, the undersigned Seller hereby grants, sells, and transfers to *buyer's name* ("Buyer"), his/her/its successors and assigns, the following described motor vehicle:

Make: *manufacturer of automobile [e.g., Ford]*
Model: *name of model [Taurus]*
Year: *model year [1993]*
Color: *[blue]*
Vehicle Identification Number: *[number stamped on metal plate visible through windshield on driver's side]*

Seller warrants that he/she/it is the legal owner of said vehicle; that the vehicle is sold free and clear of all adverse claims, liens, and encumbrances; that Seller has full right, power, and authority to sell and transfer said vehicle; and that Seller will protect, defend, indemnify, and hold Buyer harmless from any adverse claims made against the vehicle.

Said vehicle is being sold "as is" and "where is," and no express or implied warranty is made as to its condition.

Signed this *date* day of *month*, 19__.

seller's signature	*seller's signature*
Seller 1	Seller 2
seller's address	*seller's address*
Address	Address

NOTARY'S STATEMENT

State of ________________)
) ss.
County of _______________)

Subscribed and sworn to before me this *date* day of *month*, 19__.

[SEAL] ______________________________
NOTARY PUBLIC

My commission expires: ________________

❑ **Note:** As with the general bill of sale, this bill of sale includes warranties of title but not of the vehicle's condition. The phrase "where is" means that the seller need not deliver the vehicle to the buyer. For a jointly owned vehicle, both sellers must sign the form in the presence of a notary. For more information, see Automobile Purchase; Odometer Statement.

Consignment Sales Agreement

A consignment agreement allows one person to place items for sale with another while retaining ownership of them until they are sold. The terms of the agreement are negotiable. While this one favors the consignor, another may favor the consignee. See also CONSIGNMENT; SECURITY AGREEMENT.

Consignment Agreement

AGREEMENT made this *date* day of *month*, 19__, between *name of consignor* with its principal place of business at *address* (hereinafter "Consignor"), and *name of consignee*, with its principal place of business at *address of business* ("Consignee").

1. Property consigned: *description of property*.

2. Property value: $*dollar estimate of value*.

3. Consignee shall hold the property consigned for the term of consignment in Trust for Consignor and for the sole purpose of selling the property. Consignor shall at all times retain title to the property consigned. Consignee agrees not to pledge, mortgage, assign, rent, lend, or otherwise encumber the property consigned.

4. Consignee shall pay to Consignor the value set forth above, within ______ days of selling the property consigned. A security interest in the proceeds of such sale shall vest in Consignor until Consignor is paid proceeds or the property consigned is returned to Consignor.

5. Consignor warrants that he/she/it has title to the property consigned, has the right to convey title to said property, and that the property consigned is free of all liens except those here noted: ______________________________. Consignor agrees to hold Consignee harmless for damages, including attorney's fees and court costs arising from any breach of said warranty.

6. The term of consignment for the property consigned shall be for _____ days/months from the date of this Agreement. When this period ends, each party may terminate this Agreement by giving the other party ______ days notice of the intent to terminate, in which case the property shall be made available to Consignor by Consignee.

7. Consignee shall insure the property against fire, theft, or other casualty loss during the term of consignment. Consignee agrees that he/she/it shall be fully liable for the above stated value of the property consigned if it is lost, damaged, or destroyed while in Consignee's possession. Possession of the property by Consignee shall begin at the time when the property consigned is physically delivered to Consignee or Consignee's employee or agent.

8. This agreement is evidence of the debt that Consignee is obligated to pay Consignor upon sale of the property consigned, and which is secured with a continuing security agreement in accordance with the laws of the State of ____________. Consignee shall have a priority interest in the property consigned, or the proceeds from the property consigned, in preference to any other claims or security interests of other creditors of Consignor.

IN WITNESS WHEREOF, the parties have executed this Agreement on the date first written above.

consignor's signature
Consignor

consignee's signature
Consignee

DEMAND PROMISSORY NOTE

When one person lends money to another, a promissory note is used to record the terms of the loan. A demand promissory note requires the borrower (the maker) to repay the full amount of the loan to the lender upon the lender's request. Two people must witness the maker's signature.

Promissory Note

FOR VALUE RECEIVED, the undersigned Maker(s) of this note promises to pay to the order of ____*name of lender*____, residing at ____*lender's address*____, the sum of ____*written amount of loan*____ ($ _*amount in figures*_) dollars, with annual interest at _*amount of interest*_% on the unpaid balance. The full unpaid principal and any earned interest shall be fully due and immediately payable UPON DEMAND of any holder of this note. Upon failure to make payment within _*number of days*_ days of demand, and should this note be turned over for collection, the Maker(s) shall pay all reasonable legal fees and costs of collection. All parties to this note waive presentment, demand, notice of nonpayment, protest, and notice of protest, and agree to remain fully bound notwithstanding the release of any party or any extension, indulgence, modification of terms, or the discharge of any collateral serving as security for this note. If this note is signed by more than one Maker, then each of them shall be jointly and severally liable under this note.

Signed this ___*date*___ day of ____*month*____, 19___.

____*witness's signature*____ Witness	____*maker's signature*____ Maker
____*witness's signature*____ Witness	____*maker's signature*____ Maker

❑ **Note:** In this sample, the borrower is responsible for expenses the lender incurs while collecting a late payment. To save time if collection is necessary, the lender is not required to follow certain procedures (demand and presentment, notice of nonpayment, and protest and notice of protest). And even if the lender voluntarily makes concessions (release of a party, extension, indulgence, modification, or discharge of collateral), the signers must still repay the loan. "Jointly and severally" means that each person who signs this note is responsible for paying the entire amount. The lender keeps the original document; the borrower should have a copy. When the loan has been repaid, the lender writes "Paid in Full" on the original, dates it, signs it, and gives it to the borrower. For more information, see PROMISSORY NOTE.

INSTALLMENT PROMISSORY NOTE

This type of promissory note is used to define the terms of a loan that is to be repaid in equal payments (installments) of principal and interest, in contrast to the balloon note on page 574.

Promissory Note

FOR VALUE RECEIVED, the undersigned Maker(s) promises to pay to the order of _____*name of lender*_____, or any subsequent holder of this Note, the sum of _____*written amount of loan*_____ ($_*amount in figures*_) dollars, together with annual interest of __*amount of interest*_% on any unpaid balance.

Payments shall be made in _*number*_ installments of $ __*amount*__ each, with a first payment due ____*date*____, 19___, and the same amount on the same day of each_*day/month*_ thereafter until the entire principal amount of this note and earned interest is fully paid. All payments shall be applied first to earned interest, and the balance to principal. The undersigned Maker may prepay this note in whole or in part without penalty.

This note shall be payable in full upon demand of any holder in the event that the Maker shall default in making any payments due under this note within _*number of days*_ days of its due date, or upon the death, bankruptcy or insolvency of any of the undersigned Makers of this note.

In the event of default, the undersigned Maker agrees to pay all reasonable attorneys' fees and costs of collection to the extent permitted by law. This note shall take effect and be enforced in accordance with the laws of the State of ___*lender's state*___. All parties to this note waive presentment, demand, protest, and all notices thereto, and agree to remain fully bound notwithstanding any extension, indulgence, modification, or release or discharge of any party or collateral under this note. If more than one Maker has signed this note, then each of them shall be jointly and severally liable for any and all obligations under this note.

Made this ____*date*____ day of ____*month*____, 19___.

____*witness's signature*____	____*maker's signature*____
Witness	Maker
____*witness's signature*____	____*maker's signature*____
Witness	Maker

❑ **Note:** Although it is similar to the other promissory notes in this section, this installment note not only gives the lender the right to demand repayment of the entire loan if a payment is late, but also in the event that any signers (makers) become insolvent, declare bankruptcy, or die. A detailed payment schedule to which the parties have agreed should be attached to this document. For further information, see PROMISSORY NOTE.

BALLOON PROMISSORY NOTE

This type of promissory note records the terms of a balloon loan. Like an installment loan, a balloon loan is repaid in equal installments for a specified number of payments, except for the final payment (the balloon), which is larger than the others and consists of all remaining principal and interest.

Promissory Note

FOR VALUE RECEIVED, the undersigned promises to pay to the order of _______*name of lender*_______, the sum of _______*written amount of loan*_______ ($ *amount in figures*) dollars, with annual interest at ___*amount of interest*___% on any unpaid balance.

This note shall be paid in ____*number*____ consecutive and equal installments of $ __*amount*__ each, with a first payment *number of days, weeks, or months* from the date of this note, and the same amount on the same day of each *week/month* thereafter, provided the entire principal balance and any accrued but unpaid interest shall be fully paid on or before____*date of last payment*____, 19___. This note may be prepaid without penalty. All payments shall be applied first to earned interest and then to principal.

This note shall be due and payable upon demand of any holder hereof should any payment due hereunder not be made within ___*number*___ days of its due date. All parties to this note waive presentment, demand, and protest, and all notices thereto. In the event of default, the undersigned agrees to pay all costs of collection and reasonable attorneys' fees to the extent permitted by law. If more than one person has signed this note as Maker, then each shall be jointly and severally liable under this note.

Signed this __*date*__ day of ___*month*___, 19___.

____*witness's signature*____
Witness

____*maker's signature*____
Maker

____*witness's signature*____
Witness

____*maker's signature*____
Maker

❑ **Note:** A balloon note has a payment schedule, and in this agreement, the lender does not have the right to demand repayment of the entire loan unless one of the payments is late. For more information, see BALLOON LOAN; PROMISSORY NOTE.

GUARANTY

A guaranty is an agreement in which a third party (the guarantor) promises a lender in writing that he will pay the borrower's debts if the borrower fails to do so.

Guaranty

FOR VALUE RECEIVED, and in consideration of and as an inducement for ____*lender's name*____ (hereinafter "Lender") to extend credit to ____*borrower's name*____ ("Borrower"), the undersigned jointly and severally and unconditionally guarantee to Lender the prompt and full payment, when due, of each and every claim hereinafter due Lender from Borrower.

The undersigned agree to remain fully bound on this guaranty notwithstanding any extension, forbearance, waiver, or release, discharge, or substitution of any party, collateral, or security for the debt, and hereby consent to and waive all notice of same. In the event of default, the Lender may seek payment directly from the undersigned without need to proceed first against the Borrower.

The undersigned further agree to pay all reasonable attorneys' fees and costs of collection necessary for the enforcement of this guaranty.

This guaranty is unlimited as to amount or duration, except that any guarantor hereto may terminate his/her obligations in regard to future credit extended after delivery of notice of termination of this guaranty to the Lender by certified mail, return receipt requested. Said termination notice shall not discharge guarantor's obligations regarding debts incurred up to the date said termination notice is received.

____*witness's signature*____
Witness

____*witness's signature*____
Witness

____*guarantor's signature*____
Guarantor

____*guarantor's signature*____
Guarantor

❑ **Note:** You should not guarantee a loan for someone unless you are confident of her ability to repay it. "Jointly and severally" means that each guarantor is responsible for paying all the borrower's debts. If anything in the borrower's loan agreement is changed, each guarantor is still obligated by the terms in this document. If the borrower misses a payment, the lender can demand repayment of the debt from the guarantor. Because it is "unlimited as to amount or duration," each guarantor is responsible for all future debts owed to this lender until the guaranty is revoked. If a formal revocation of the guaranty is sent to the lender, the guarantor is absolved from future debts, but not from debts the borrower owed before the revocation. For further information, see COSIGNING.

SECURITY AGREEMENT

A security agreement is signed when a borrower gives a lender collateral (a secured interest in personal property) of equal value to the borrower's debt. If the borrower (debtor) fails to repay the loan, the lender (secured party) can take possession of the borrower's personal property. The lender may either keep such property for his own use or sell it to recover the money he is owed.

Security Agreement

NOTICE: THIS SECURITY AGREEMENT OR OTHER REQUIRED FINANCING STATEMENTS MUST BE FILED IN THE APPROPRIATE STATE OFFICE TO PROTECT YOUR RIGHTS IN THE COLLATERAL AGAINST CLAIMS BY THIRD PARTIES.

BE IT KNOWN, that for good and valuable consideration, *borrower's name* whose address is *borrower's address* (hereinafter "Debtor"), grants to *lender's name*, whose address is *lender's address* ("Secured Party"), his/her/its successors and assigns, a security interest pursuant to Article 9 of the Uniform Commercial Code in the following property ("the collateral"), which shall include all after-acquired property of a like nature and description and the proceeds and profits thereof:

[description of personal property offered as collateral]

This security interest is granted to secure payment and performance on the following obligations now or hereinafter owed to Secured Party by Debtor:

[amount and date of loan]

Debtor hereby acknowledges to Secured Party that:

1. The collateral shall be kept at Debtor's above address and shall not be moved or relocated without the prior written consent of Secured Party.

2. Debtor warrants to Secured Party that he/she/it owns the collateral; that it is free from any other lien, encumbrance, and security interest or adverse interest; and that Debtor has full right, power, and authority to grant this security interest in the above-described collateral.

3. Debtor agrees to execute such financing statements as are reasonably required by Secured Party to perfect this security agreement in accordance with state law and the Uniform Commercial Code.

4. In the event of any default in payment or performance of any obligation for which this security interest is granted, or upon breach of any term of this

security agreement, Secured Party may declare all obligations immediately due and payable and shall have all remedies of a secured party available under the Uniform Commercial Code as enacted in Debtor's state. Such rights shall be cumulative and not necessarily successive with any other rights or remedies.

5. This security agreement shall further be in default upon the death, insolvency, or bankruptcy of any party who is an obligor to this agreement, or upon any material decrease in the value of the collateral or adverse change in the financial condition of Debtor.

6. In the event of default, Debtor shall pay all reasonable attorneys' fees and costs of collection necessary to enforce this agreement.

7. Debtor agrees to maintain adequate insurance coverage on the collateral as Secured Party may reasonably require, and Secured Party shall be named as loss payee.

8. Any waiver, express or implied, of any breach of this Agreement, shall not be deemed a waiver of any subsequent breach.

IN WITNESS WHEREOF, this agreement is executed this ___*date*___ day of ______*month*______, 19____.

______*debtor's signature*______
Debtor

______*secured party's signature*______
Secured Party

❑ **Note:** This agreement may accompany any loan agreement if the debtor agrees to put up collateral for the loan. The debtor declares that she is the owner of the collateral, and that no one else has an interest or claim in the property (it is free from lien, encumbrance, and security or adverse interest). She also agrees to complete the forms that are required by state law and the Uniform Commercial Code. These forms are filed with the state or county officials where the debtor lives, and they ensure (perfect) the secured party's interest in the collateral by making it a matter of public record. If any of the terms of this agreement are not met (default of payment or performance of any obligation), the secured party has the right to demand payment of the debt (declare all obligations due). Further, she can demand payment if the debtor becomes insolvent, declares bankruptcy, or dies. For more information, see COLLATERAL; SECURITY AGREEMENT; UNIFORM COMMERCIAL CODE.

GENERAL ASSIGNMENT

An assignment is a contract that transfers property, rights, or responsibilities from one person (the assignor) to another (the assignee). Usually it is property, or an interest in it, that is transferred.

Assignment

FOR VALUE RECEIVED, the undersigned hereby unconditionally and irrevocably assigns and transfers unto ___*name of person receiving property (assignee)*___, all right, title, and interest in and to the following:

[description of property]

The undersigned hereby warrants that he/she has full right, power, and authority to enter into this assignment and transfer, and that the rights and benefits assigned hereunder are free and clear of any lien, encumbrance, adverse claim, or interest.

This assignment shall be binding upon and inure to the benefit of the parties, their heirs, successors, assigns, and personal representatives.

Signed this ___*date*___ day of ___*month*___, 19___.

___*assignor's signature*___
Assignor

___*witness's signature*___
Witness

___*witness's signature*___
Witness

NOTARY'S STATEMENT

STATE OF _____________)
) ss.
COUNTY OF _____________)

On this ______ day of _____________, 19___, before me, a Notary Public, personally appeared _______________, known to me to be the individual described in and who executed the foregoing Assignment, and duly acknowledged it to me as his/her free act and deed.

[SEAL]

____
NOTARY PUBLIC

My commission expires: _____________

❑ **Note:** State laws vary regarding witnesses for assignments. Where they are required, the assignor signs the document in the presence of the witnesses, who also sign it. Assignments may also be acknowledged by the assignor in the presence of a notary, who completes the statement and puts his seal on it. If real estate is being transferred, the assignee must record the assignment with the recorder's office for the county where the property is held. For more information, see ACKNOWLEDGMENT; ASSIGNMENT.

MECHANIC'S LIEN

A mechanic's lien is a claim placed by a contractor (the lienholder) on a customer's property to collect any unpaid fees. Such a lien is on the entire property, not just the contractor's improvements to it.

Notice of Mechanic's Lien

Notice is hereby provided that the lienholder named below provided labor and/or materials relative to the construction and/or improvements on that real estate commonly known as:

address of property

city or town

state *zip code*

said real estate being more particularly described in Book or Volume *volume number*, page *page number*, of the *county where property is located* County Register of Deeds.

The owner of record of said property is: *property owner's name*.

This lien is filed to secure the balance of $ *amount owed*, plus such additional amounts as may be due lienholder in accordance with state law.

Dated: *date*, 19___

lienholder's signature
Lienholder
lienholder's address
Address
city *state* *zip code*

State of ________________)
) ss.
County of _______________)

Subscribed and sworn to before me this _________ day of ______________, 19__.

[SEAL]

____
NOTARY PUBLIC

My commission expires: ____________

❑ **Note:** To obtain a mechanic's lien, a contractor must show that he supplied materials or labor for home construction or other service but was never paid for them. Once a lien is placed, it will remain with the property until the property's current or future owner pays the debt or the contractor drops the claim. A mechanic's lien is usually recorded at the county clerk's office or the registry of deeds so that anyone interested in buying the property can find out whether there are any claims against it. For more information, see LIEN; MECHANIC'S LIEN.

PRENUPTIAL MARRIAGE AGREEMENT

Prenuptial agreements—also called antenuptial agreements — are made by couples before they marry. While these agreements can cover almost any matter, they are most frequently concerned with the way that property would be divided if the marriage ends either by divorce or death.

Prenuptial Agreement

THIS AGREEMENT is entered into this _date_ day of _month_, 19___, between _name of fiancé_ and _name of fiancée_.

WHEREAS, the undersigned parties contemplate marriage under the laws of the State of _state where marriage will take place_; and whereas it is their desire to enter into this agreement so that each of them will continue to own and exercise control over his/her own property; and whereas neither of them desires that their present separate financial interests should be changed by his/her marriage or the laws of this state regarding the division of property;

NOW, THEREFORE, THE PARTIES AGREE AS FOLLOWS:

1. All property, whether real, personal, or mixed, which belongs to each of the above parties shall be, now and forever, their personal and separate property, including all interest, rents, and profits that may accrue from such property, and such property shall remain forever free of claim by the other.

2. The parties shall continue to have the full right, power, and authority, in all respects the same as each would have if not married, to enjoy, use, sell, lease, give, and convey all property as may presently belong to him or her.

3. In the event of a separation or divorce, the parties shall have no right against each other by way of claims for spousal support, maintenance, alimony, compensation, or division of any separately owned property in existence as of the date of this Agreement.

4. In the event of separation or divorce, marital property acquired after marriage shall nevertheless remain subject to division, either by agreement or judicial determination.

5. In the event of the death of either party, the other party hereby waives now and forever any claim or interest in the deceased's property granted by statute, and agrees that the distribution of all such property shall be governed solely by the Last Will and Testament of the deceased party.

6. This Agreement shall be binding upon and inure to the benefit of the parties, their heirs, successors, assigns, and personal representatives.

7. Additional provisions:

[list any additional provisions here]

8. The parties acknowledge that they have entered into this Agreement after full disclosure of the property owned by each of them, and that each of them has been afforded the opportunity to have this Agreement reviewed by independent counsel.

9. This Agreement shall be enforced in accordance with the laws of the State of *state where couple will reside*. If any part or provision of this Agreement shall be found invalid or unenforceable, then the rest of this Agreement shall remain in full force and effect to the extent practicable.

Signed this *date* day of *month*, 19___.

witness's signature	*fiancé's signature*
Witness	Fiancé
witness's signature	*fiancée's signature*
Witness	Fiancée

❑ **Note:** A prenuptial agreement should be written in easily understandable language so that the parties cannot claim later they did not understand what they were signing. However, no one should sign a prenuptial agreement without consulting a lawyer. Each party should sign and keep a copy of the agreement. Each spouse should also write a last will and testament clearly stating how his or her property should be divided in the event that one spouse dies before the other. For more information, see MARRIAGE; PRENUPTIAL AGREEMENT.

Living-Together Agreement

Cohabitation, or living-together, agreements are useful for couples who share a home and expenses, whether or not they plan to marry. By putting their rights and duties in writing, they can avoid disputes over property or children if they separate. This sample is a typical agreement.

Cohabitation Agreement

THIS AGREEMENT is made this _*date*_ day of _*month*_, 19___, by and between _*first party's name*_ and _*second party's name*_, who presently reside in the County of _*name of county*_, State of _*name of state*_.

WHEREAS, the parties wish to live together, but do not wish to be bound by the statutory or common-law provisions relating to marriage, it is hereby agreed that the parties to this Agreement shall live together for an indefinite period of time subject to the following terms and conditions:

1. Property: Any real or personal property acquired by either of us during the relationship shall be considered to be our separate property. All property listed on the pages attached is incorporated in this Agreement by reference. The property now and hereinafter belongs to the party under whose name it is listed prior to the making of this Agreement. All listed property is and shall continue to be the separate property of the person who owns it. All property received by either of us by gift or inheritance during our relationship shall be the separate property of the one who receives it.

2. Income: All income earned or accumulated during the existence of our relationship shall be maintained in one fund, and all debts and expenses arising during the existence of our union shall be paid out of this fund. Each of us shall have an equal interest in this fund, and equal right to its management and control, and each of us shall be equally entitled to any surplus that remains after payment of all debts and expenses.

3. Termination: Our relationship may be terminated at the sole will and decision of either of us, expressed by a written notice given to the other.

4. Modification: This Agreement may be modified by an agreement in writing signed by both parties, with the exception that no modifications may decrease the obligations that may be imposed regarding any children born of our union.

5. Application of Law: The validity of this Agreement shall be determined solely under the laws of the State of ___*name of state where parties reside*___. If any portion of this Agreement is held invalid or unenforceable in a court of law, then the rest of this Agreement shall remain in full force and effect to the extent practicable.

6. Claims Waived: Neither of us shall maintain any action or claim against the other for support, alimony, compensation, or for rights to any property existing prior to this date, or acquired on or subsequent to the date of termination.

7. Free Act of Parties; Full Disclosure: The parties enter into this Agreement of their own will and accord without reliance on any other inducement or promise, and with full disclosure of the interest each holds in any and all property, real, personal, or mixed.

8. Captions: The use of captions in this Agreement is for convenience only, and shall have no bearing on the interpretation of the contents of the section to which they refer.

9. Right to Independent Counsel: Each party to this Agreement has had the opportunity to have this Agreement reviewed by independent counsel.

Signed this ___*date*___ day of ___*month*___, 19___.

___*first party's signature*___
First Party

___*second party's signature*___
Second Party

❑ **Note:** Cohabitation agreements should cover property rights, management of income, provisions for the termination of the relationship, and responsibility for any children that the couple have. Agreements can also include other topics that couples wish to add. Captions—the wording at the beginning of each numbered paragraph—make the agreement easier to read. A couple can usually write their own agreement, but it is a good idea for each party to have it reviewed by a lawyer before signing it. The couple should sign and date two copies, and each party should keep one copy. For further information, see LIVING TOGETHER.

GENERAL DURABLE POWER OF ATTORNEY

A general durable power of attorney is granted by someone who wants to place the management of her property and financial affairs in the hands of a person whom she trusts. This type of power of attorney remains in effect when the person granting it (the principal) becomes incapacitated.

Durable Power of Attorney (General)

NOTICE: THIS LEGAL DOCUMENT GIVES THE PERSON NAMED AS ATTORNEY-IN-FACT BROAD POWERS OVER THE PROPERTY OF THE GRANTOR, UNLESS LIMITED BY THE TERMS OF THE DOCUMENT ITSELF. THESE POWERS MAY EXIST FOR AN UNLIMITED TIME PERIOD UNLESS LIMITED BY THE TERMS OF THE DOCUMENT ITSELF. THE GRANTOR MAY REVOKE THIS POWER OF ATTORNEY AT ANY TIME. DO NOT SIGN THIS POWER OF ATTORNEY UNLESS YOU UNDERSTAND ALL ITS TERMS. CONSULT WITH AN ATTORNEY FOR ADVICE AND ASSISTANCE.

I, *name of person giving authority*, the undersigned Principal, hereby grant this General Power of Attorney to *name of person receiving authority*, as my attorney-in-fact.

My attorney-in-fact shall have full power and authority to do any and all acts on my behalf that I could do personally including but not limited to:

the right to sell, deed, buy, trade, lease, mortgage, assign, rent, or dispose of any of my present or future real or personal property;

the right to execute, accept, undertake, and perform any and all contracts in my name;

the right to deposit, endorse, or withdraw funds to or from any of my bank accounts, depositories or safe-deposit boxes;

the right to borrow, lend, invest, or reinvest funds on any terms;

the right to initiate, defend, commence, or settle legal actions on my behalf;

the right to vote any shares or beneficial interest in any entity;

and the right to retain any accountant, attorney, or other adviser deemed necessary to protect my interests generally or relative to any foregoing unlimited power.

The real estate covered by this Power of Attorney is commonly known as:

[list real estate covered under the general durable power of attorney]

My attorney-in-fact hereby accepts this appointment subject to its terms and agrees to act and perform in a fiduciary capacity consistent with my best interests as he/she in his/her best discretion deems advisable, and I affirm and ratify all acts so undertaken.

This power of attorney may be revoked by me at any time, and shall automatically be revoked upon my death, provided any person relying on this power of attorney before my death shall have full rights to accept the authority of my attorney-in-fact until in receipt of actual notice of revocation. It is my intention that this instrument be construed as a Durable Power of Attorney, and that it shall not be affected by my subsequent disability or incapacity.

A photocopy of this Power of Attorney shall be deemed an original for all purposes permitted by law.

NOTICE: DELETE POWERS THAT DO NOT APPLY

Signed this ___*date*___ day of ___*month*___, 19___.

___*principal's signature*___
Principal

I accept appointment as attorney-in-fact as granted by this Power of Attorney.

___*attorney-in-fact's signature*___
Attorney-in-Fact

NOTARY'S STATEMENT

State of __________)   ________________, 19___.
) ss.
County of ________)

Before me personally appeared ____________________ and ____________________, who having first been sworn, acknowledged the foregoing instrument as their free and voluntary acts, and signed the above instrument in my presence.

____
[SEAL]   NOTARY PUBLIC

My commission expires: ____________

❑ **Note:** The principal may delete any of the powers granted to the attorney-in-fact in this sample form. You can draft a power of attorney on your own, but never sign one without first consulting a lawyer. State laws vary on such issues as who may serve as an attorney-in-fact and whether special forms are required. The attorney-in-fact and principal should each keep several copies and give them to banks or other institutions with whom the attorney-in-fact will be dealing on the principal's behalf. A power of attorney can be revoked at any time by means of a notarized letter. For further information, see POWER OF ATTORNEY.

SPRINGING DURABLE POWER OF ATTORNEY

A springing durable power of attorney goes into effect only if the person granting it (the principal) becomes incapacitated. With this type of durable power of attorney, the principal retains full control over his own financial affairs until he is unable to do so any longer.

Durable Power of Attorney (Springing)

I, *name of person giving authority*, the undersigned Principal, do hereby grant a Durable Power of Attorney to *name of person receiving authority*, as my attorney-in-fact.

My attorney-in-fact shall have full right, power, and authority to do all acts on my behalf that I could do personally, including but not limited to:

The right to sell, deed, buy, trade, lease, mortgage, assign, rent, or dispose of any real or personal property; the right to execute, accept, undertake, and perform all contracts in my name; the right to deposit, endorse, or withdraw funds to or from any of my bank accounts or safe-deposit boxes; the right to borrow, collect, lend, invest, or reinvest funds; the right to initiate, defend, commence, or settle legal actions on my behalf; the right to vote (in person or by proxy) any shares or beneficial interest in any entity; and the right to retain any accountant, attorney, or other adviser deemed necessary to protect my interests relative to any foregoing unlimited power. My attorney-in-fact shall have full power and authority to execute, deliver, and accept all documents and undertake all acts consistent with the powers granted herein.

This Power of Attorney shall become effective upon and remain in effect only during such time periods as I may be mentally or physically incapacitated and unable to care for my own needs or make competent decisions as are necessary to protect my interests or conduct my affairs.

My attorney-in-fact hereby accepts this appointment and agrees to act in said capacity consistent with my best interests as he/she in his/her sole discretion deems advisable, and I hereby affirm and ratify all such acts as if they were my own.

This Power of Attorney may be revoked by me at any time, and shall automatically be revoked upon my death. Any person relying on this power of attorney shall have full rights to accept the authority of my attorney-in-fact until in receipt of actual notice of revocation.

IN WITNESS WHEREOF, I have executed this Power of Attorney this ___*date*___ day of ___*month*___, 19___, as my free act and deed.

___________*principal's signature*___________
Principal

I accept the duties of attorney-in-fact as described in the above Power of Attorney.

___________*attorney-in-fact's signature*___________
Attorney-in-Fact

NOTARY'S STATEMENT

State of __________) ____________________, 19___.
) ss.
County of _________)

Before me personally appeared ________________ and ______________, known to me personally as the Principal and Attorney-in-Fact in the Power of Attorney above, and having first been sworn, signed the above power of attorney as their free act and deed, in my presence, and for the purposes described therein.

[SEAL]

____
NOTARY PUBLIC

My commission expires: __________

❑ **Note:** Consult with a lawyer to find out what the laws of your state require for powers of attorney. Not every state recognizes a springing durable power of attorney. In states that do, it should be signed and notarized in the same way as a general power of attorney. Delete any powers in this document that do not apply, and review it periodically to be sure that it still reflects your wishes. Since a springing power of attorney does not go into effect immediately, the principal should keep the original document in a safe place that is accessible to the attorney-in-fact. For further information, see POWER OF ATTORNEY.

DURABLE POWER OF ATTORNEY FOR HEALTH CARE

A durable power of attorney for health care is used by someone (the principal) to give another (the attorney-in-fact) the authority to make medical decisions for him. This document helps ensure that if the principal becomes incapacitated, his health care wishes will still be carried out.

Durable Power of Attorney (Health Care)

I, *name of person giving authority*, the undersigned Principal, do hereby grant a Durable Power of Attorney for health care to *name of person receiving authority*, as my attorney-in-fact.

I hereby grant to my attorney-in-fact full power and authority to make health care decisions for me to the same extent that I could make such decisions for myself if I had the capacity to do so. In exercising this authority, my attorney-in-fact shall make health care decisions that are consistent with my desires as stated in this document or which I otherwise make known to my attorney-in-fact, including, but not limited to, my desires concerning obtaining, withholding, or withdrawing life-prolonging care, treatment, services, and procedures.

I hereby authorize all physicians and psychiatrists who have treated me, and all other providers of health care, including hospitals, to release to my attorney-in-fact all information contained in my medical records that my attorney-in-fact may request. I hereby waive all privileges attached to the physician-patient relationship, and to any verbal or written communication arising out of such a relationship. My attorney-in-fact is hereby authorized to receive and review any information, whether verbal or written, pertaining to my physical or mental health, including medical and hospital records, and to execute any releases, waivers, or other documents that may be required in order to obtain such information, and to disclose such information to such persons, organizations, and health care providers as my attorney-in-fact shall deem appropriate. My attorney-in-fact is authorized to employ and discharge health care providers including physicians, psychiatrists, dentists, nurses, and therapists as shall be deemed appropriate for my physical, mental and emotional well-being in my attorney-in-fact's sole discretion. My attorney-in-fact is hereby authorized to pay all reasonable fees and expenses for the provision of such services.

My attorney-in-fact is hereby authorized to apply for my admission to any medical, nursing, residential, or other similar facility; execute any consent or admission forms required by such facility; and enter into any and all agreements for my care at such facility or elsewhere during my lifetime. My attorney-in-fact is authorized to arrange for and consent to medical, therapeutic, and surgical procedures for me including the administration of drugs. The power to make health care decisions on my behalf shall include the power and authority to give, refuse, or withdraw consent to any care, treatment, service, or procedure to maintain, diagnose, or treat a physical or mental condition.

I reserve the right to revoke the authority granted to my attorney-in-fact to make health care decisions for me by notifying the treating physician, hospital, or other health care provider orally or in writing. Notwithstanding any provision herein to the contrary, I retain the right to make medical and other health care decisions for myself so long as I am able to give informed consent with respect to any such decision. No treatment shall be given to me over my objection, and no treatment or care necessary to keep me alive may be stopped if I object.

This Power of Attorney shall not be affected by my subsequent disability or incapacity. Notwithstanding any provision herein to the contrary, my attorney-in-fact shall take no action under this instrument unless I am deemed to be disabled or incapacitated as defined herein. My incapacity shall be deemed to exist when so certified in writing by two (2) licensed physicians not related by blood or marriage to either me or to my attorney-in-fact. Such certification shall state that I am incapable of caring for myself and that I am physically and mentally incapable of managing my financial affairs. The certificate of the physicians described above shall be attached to the original of this instrument, and if this instrument is filed or recorded among public records, then such certificate shall be similarly filed or recorded as required or permitted by applicable law.

My attorney-in-fact shall be entitled to reimbursement for all reasonable costs actually incurred and paid on my behalf under the authority granted in this instrument.

To the extent permitted by law, I nominate and appoint my attorney-in-fact to serve as my guardian, conservator, and/or in any similar representative capacity. If I am not permitted by law to so nominate and appoint my attorney-in-fact, then I request any court of competent jurisdiction that may be petitioned by any person to appoint a guardian, conservator, or similar representative for me to give due consideration to this request.

IN WITNESS WHEREOF, I have signed this Durable Power of Attorney this _*date*_ day of _*month*_, 19___.

*principal's signature*
Principal

State of ________________)
) ss.
County of ______________)

Before me appeared ________________, known to me personally to be the Principal named in the above Power of Attorney, and who, having first been sworn, signed the foregoing document as his/her free act and deed, voluntarily and under no duress, and for the purposes described therein, this ______ day of ____________, 19___.

[SEAL]

____
NOTARY PUBLIC

My commission expires: ____________

❑ **Note:** To make sure that you receive the health care you want, you can create both a living will and a power of attorney for health care. A living will contains instructions on the specific type of medical care you want. A durable power of attorney for health care authorizes someone to make decisions based on those instructions. You must be competent and of legal age to sign a power of attorney—otherwise it will be considered invalid and a court will appoint a guardian or conservator to act on your behalf. Many states require very specific language for a durable power of attorney for health care; ask a lawyer or your doctor about the form recognized in your state. This document should be signed and notarized in the same manner as a general power of attorney. The attorney-in-fact for health care should keep the original in a safe, accessible place. Both the principal and the attorney-in-fact should have several copies to give to the principal's medical care practitioners and facilities. For further information, see LIVING WILL; POWER OF ATTORNEY.

SPECIAL POWER OF ATTORNEY

A special, or limited, power of attorney is used when one person gives another the authority to perform one or more specific acts. For example, parents can use a special power of attorney to give a babysitter the authority to consent to medical care for their child in an emergency.

Power of Attorney (Special)

I, name of person giving authority, as Principal, hereby grant a limited and specific Power of Attorney to name of person receiving authority, as my attorney-in-fact. My attorney-in-fact shall have full right, power, and authority to undertake and perform the following acts on my behalf to the same extent as if I had done so personally:

[Description of acts for which authority is granted. For example, "To authorize medical treatment for my son, Ezra, and to obligate me for the cost of such treatment."]

The authority granted herein shall include such acts as are reasonably required or necessary to carry out and perform the specific duties granted to my attorney-in-fact. My attorney-in-fact agrees to accept this appointment subject to its terms, and agrees to act in said capacity consistent with my best interests as he/she in his/her sole discretion deems advisable, and I hereby ratify all acts so carried out. This Power of Attorney may be revoked by me at any time, and shall automatically be revoked upon my death, provided any person relying on this Power of Attorney before or after my death shall have full rights to accept the authority of my attorney-in-fact consistent with the powers granted herein until in receipt of actual notice of revocation.

Signed this date day of month, 19___.

principal's signature
Principal

I, ____________________, hereby accept appointment as attorney-in-fact for the above-named Principal, and for the purposes described.

attorney-in-fact's signature
Attorney-in-Fact

State of _________________)
) ss.
County of ________________)

Before me personally appeared ________________ and __________________, known to me personally as the Principal and Attorney-in-fact named in the above Power of Attorney, and having first been sworn, signed the above document as their free act and deed, voluntarily and under no duress, and for the purposes described therein, this ___ day of _______, 19___.

[SEAL]

____
NOTARY PUBLIC

My commission expires: __________

❑ **Note:** This document should be signed and notarized. The attorney-in-fact should keep the original, and the principal should keep a copy. A special power of attorney can be revoked with a notarized letter. For more information, see BABYSITTER; POWER OF ATTORNEY.

RESIDENTIAL RENTAL APPLICATION

Residential rental applications help landlords to determine who might make a good tenant. By asking applicants for information about such matters as family, pets, employment history, and income, and by checking references, landlords can minimize their chances of renting to tenants who are irresponsible or unable to pay their rent. For more information, see LANDLORD; TENANT'S RIGHTS.

Rental Application

Name ________ *applicant's name* ________ Telephone ________
Present Address ____ *street address* ________
City, State, Zip Code ________
How long at present address? ________
Social Security No. ________ Driver's License No. ________
Birth Date ________
Co-applicant's Name ________
Co-applicant's Social Security No. ________
Co-applicant's Driver's License No. ________
Co-applicant's Birth Date ________
How many in your family? Adults ______ Children ______ Any pets? ______
Name, breed, and weight of pet(s), if any ________
____

Current landlord ________ Telephone ________
Employer ________ Position ________
Number of years with current employer ______ Phone ______ Salary ____
Co-applicant's employer ________ Position ________
Number of years with current employer ______ Phone ______ Salary ____
Name of bank ________
____ Checking Account No. ________
____ Savings Account No. ________

Personal References

Name and Address	Relationship	Telephone

I represent that the information provided in this application is true and correct to the best of my knowledge. You are hereby authorized to verify my credit and references in connection with the processing of this application. I acknowledge receipt of a copy of this application.

Dated: ____ *current date* ____, 19___

________ *applicant's signature* ________
Applicant

________ *co-applicant's signature* ________
Co-applicant

Residential Lease

This sample lease contains the terms most commonly found in rental contracts. As with other contracts, a lease can be modified as long as both landlord and tenant agree to the changes.

Lease Agreement

LEASE AGREEMENT, entered into by and between ___*property owner's name*___ ("Landlord") and ___*renter's name*___ ("Tenant").

For good and valuable consideration the parties agree as follows:

1. Landlord hereby leases and lets to Tenant the premises described as follows:

[address of rental property]

2. This Lease shall be for a term of ___*length of lease*___, beginning on ___*date lease begins*___, 19___, and ending on ___*date lease ends*___, 19___.

3. Tenant shall pay to Landlord rent in the amount of $ ___*amount of rent*___ per month during said term, payable on the ___*day rent is due*___ day of each month in advance. Tenant shall pay a security deposit of $ ___*amount of deposit*___, to be kept by Landlord in accordance with state law, and to be returned upon termination of this Lease and the payment of all rents due and performance of all other obligations.

4. Tenant shall at his/her own expense provide the following utilities:

[list utilities tenant must pay for in addition to rent]

5. Tenant further agrees that:

a) Upon the expiration of the Lease, Tenant will return possession of the leased premises to Landlord in its present condition, except for reasonable wear and tear. Tenant shall commit no waste to the leased premises.

b) Tenant shall not assign or sublet the premises or allow any other person to occupy the leased premises without Landlord's prior written consent.

c) Tenant shall not make any material or structural alterations to the premises or change locks on the premises without Landlord's prior written consent.

d) Tenant shall comply with all building, zoning, and health codes and other applicable laws for the use of said leased premises.

e) Tenant shall not conduct on premises any activity deemed by Landlord in its sole discretion hazardous, a nuisance, or requiring an increase in fire or hazard insurance premiums.

f) Tenant shall not allow pets on the premises without the prior written consent of Landlord.

g) In the event of any breach of the payment of rent, or any other breach of this Lease, Landlord shall have full rights to terminate this Lease in accordance with state law and re-enter and reclaim possession of the premises, in addition to such other remedies which are available to Landlord as a result of said breach.

6. This Lease shall be binding upon and inure to the benefit of the parties, and their respective successors, agents, personal representatives, and assigns.

7. This Lease shall be subordinate to all present or future mortgages against the property.

8. Additional Lease terms:

[list any other terms to which tenant and landlord agree]

Signed this ____*date*____ day of ____*month*____, 19___.

____*witness's signature*____
Witness

____*landlord's signature*____
Landlord

____*witness's signature*____
Witness

____*tenant's signature*____
Tenant

____*co-tenant's signature*____
Co-tenant

____*co-tenant's signature*____
Co-tenant

❑ **Note:** Both landlord and tenant must initial any changes they make to the terms of the lease. The landlord and tenant should both sign two original documents, with each keeping one of the originals. For more information, see LANDLORD; LEASE; SECURITY DEPOSIT; TENANT'S RIGHTS.

Three-Day Notice to Vacate for Nonpayment of Rent

In most states, before a landlord can evict a tenant who is behind in the rent, he must first give the tenant an opportunity to pay the overdue rent. A notice such as this one is sent by the landlord notifying the tenant that he will be evicted if the overdue rent is not paid immediately.

Notice to Vacate

CERTIFIED MAIL — RETURN RECEIPT REQUESTED

date, 19___

TO: *tenant's name*
street address
city *state* *zip code*

AND ALL OTHERS IN POSSESSION:

You are hereby notified to quit and deliver up the premises you hold as our tenant, namely

[address of rental property]

within three (3) days of receipt of this notice.

This notice is provided due to nonpayment of rent. The present rent arrearage is in the amount of $ *amount of rent due*.

You may redeem your tenancy by full payment of this amount within three (3) days as provided for under the terms of your lease, or by state law. In the event you fail to make payment to bring your rent payments current or, in the alternative, vacate the premises, we shall immediately take legal action to evict you and to recover such rents and damages for the unlawful detention of the premises as are permitted by law.

landlord's signature
Landlord

landlord's name printed
Landlord's Name

❑ **Note:** The landlord should send his notice to the tenant by certified mail, with a return receipt requested. By doing so, he will have proof that the tenant received the notice. For further information, see EVICTION; LANDLORD; TENANT'S RIGHTS.

REAL ESTATE ESCROW AGREEMENT

Once a real estate sales contract is signed, the buyer's down payment is deposited in an escrow account. This agreement informs the escrow agent when the down payment can be released.

Escrow Agreement

AGREEMENT between _____*seller's name*_____ name (hereinafter "Seller"), _____*buyer's name*_____ ("Buyer"), and _____*escrow agent's name*_____ ("Escrow Agent"), made this __*date*__ day of __*month*__, 19___.

Simultaneously with the making of this Agreement, Seller and Buyer have entered into a contract ("the Contract") by which Seller will sell to Buyer the following property:

[address of property]

The closing will take place on the __*date*__ day of __*month*__, 19___, at __*hour*__ a.m./p.m, at the offices of _____*name of law firm, bank, etc.*_____, whose address is _____*address of law firm, bank, etc.*_____, or at such other time and place as Seller and Buyer may jointly designate in writing. As required by the Contract, Buyer must deposit $ __*amount of down payment*__ as a down payment to be held in escrow by Escrow Agent.

The down payment referred to above has been paid by Buyer to Escrow Agent, and Escrow Agent acknowledges receipt of $ __*amount of down payment*__ from Buyer. If paid by check, receipt is subject to collection.

If closing takes place as stated in the Contract, Escrow Agent at the time of closing shall pay the amount deposited with him/her to Seller, or as instructed by Seller in writing.

If no closing takes place under the Contract, Escrow Agent shall continue to hold the amount deposited until receipt of a written authorization for its disposition signed by both Buyer and Seller. In the event of any dispute as to whom Escrow Agent is to deliver the amount deposited, Escrow Agent shall hold the sum until the parties' rights are finally determined in an appropriate action or proceeding, or until a court orders Escrow Agent to deposit the down payment with it. If Escrow Agent does not receive a proper written authorization from Seller and Buyer, or if an action or proceeding to determine Seller's and Buyer's rights is not begun or diligently prosecuted, Escrow Agent is under no obligation to bring an action or proceeding to deposit the sum held by him/her in court, but may continue to hold the deposit. Escrow Agent assumes no liability except as that of a stakeholder.

Escrow Agent's duties are limited to those specifically set forth in this Agreement, and Escrow Agent shall incur no liability to anyone except as a result of willful misconduct or gross negligence so long as the Escrow Agent acts in good faith. Seller and Buyer hereby release Escrow Agent from liability for any act done or omitted in good faith in the performance of Escrow Agent's duties.

_____*seller's signature*_____
Seller

_____*escrow agent's signature*_____
Escrow Agent

_____*buyer's signature*_____
Buyer

❑ **Note:** An escrow agreement can be a separate document or it can be a clause within the sales contract. The escrow agent can be a bank, an attorney, or any third party who agrees to hold the down payment. However, the home buyer's lawyer is usually prohibited from serving as an escrow agent. For more information, see ESCROW.

Real Estate Binder

A binder is an offer to purchase real estate. It can be converted into a sales contract when the seller accepts the offer, as in the sample below, or it can require the seller and buyer to draw up a sales contract at a later date. For more information, see BINDER; HOME BUYING AND SELLING.

Binder

_____*buyer's name*_____ (hereinafter "Purchaser") offers to purchase from _____*seller's name*_____ ("Seller") the real property located at _____*address of property*_____ and which is more fully described in Schedule A, attached, together with all rights, privileges, easements, and all improvements, buildings, and fixtures in their present condition as are now on or affixed to the property ("the Property") on the following terms and conditions:

1. PURCHASE PRICE: Purchaser agrees to pay to Seller for the Property the sum of ___*written amount of sales price*___ dollars ($___*number amount*___) to be paid as follows:

(a) an earnest-money deposit in the amount of ___*written amount of earnest-money payment*___ dollars ($___*number amount*___), to be paid in accordance with the terms of this offer and to be deposited in escrow to a special or trust account and

(b) the balance of ___*written amount of balance*___ dollars ($___*number amount*___) to be paid at the closing of title in cash, or by cashier's check or certified check made payable to the order of Seller.

2. SPECIAL CONDITIONS:

[list any special conditions regarding the purchaser's offer]

3. TITLE: Seller shall give to Purchaser a warranty deed conveying such title as a reputable title insurance company would insure, free and clear of liens or encumbrances except for:

(a) restrictions of record and easements, reservations, conditions, and laws and governmental regulations affecting the use and maintenance of the Property, provided they are not violated by any improvements on or to the Property;
(b) zoning ordinances, if any;
(c) encroachments or projections, if any, of record;
(d) taxes and assessments not yet due and payable.

4. TITLE COMMITMENT: A current commitment for a title insurance policy in an amount equal to the purchase price shall be furnished Purchaser on or before five (5) days prior to the date of closing. Seller shall deliver the title insurance policy to Purchaser after closing, and shall pay the premium thereon.

5. APPORTIONMENT: The following shall be apportioned as of midnight of the day before the closing: rents as and when collected; interest on existing mortgages; premiums on insurance policies if transferred; taxes, water charges, and sewer rents; fuel oil or gas.

6. POSSESSION: Seller shall deliver possession of the Property to Purchaser on the date of the closing. If the Property or any part of the Property is damaged or destroyed before the closing, Purchaser shall, in its sole discretion, have the right either to a) receive any insurance proceeds, or b) cancel and revoke this Offer and the return of all money paid or deposited.

7. ESCROW AND CLOSING: The earnest-money deposit shall be deposited with and held in escrow by ___*escrow agent's name*___ within five (5) days of acceptance of this Offer by Seller. The closing will take place at ___*time of closing*___ a.m./p.m., on ___*date of closing*___, 19___, at ___*address where closing will take place*___, at which time Purchaser shall pay the balance of the purchase price and Seller shall present the deed in recordable form, all keys, and any and all certificates of occupancy or other permits required by law.

8. DEFAULT: If Purchaser shall default in paying the balance due at the closing, Seller shall be entitled to retain the down payment as liquidated damages. If Seller shall default, Purchaser shall be entitled to specific performance of the contract for sale by Seller.

9. ACCEPTANCE: Purchaser may revoke this Offer by written revocation at any time prior to its acceptance by Seller. Unless an accepted copy of this Offer is delivered to Purchaser on or before ___*time*___ a.m./p.m., on ___*date*___, 19___, this Offer will expire, and neither party will have any obligation to the other. Upon acceptance of this offer by Seller and payment of the earnest-money deposit by Purchaser, this Offer shall become a binding Agreement between Purchaser and Seller, containing all the terms and conditions necessary, and superseding all previous agreements, representations, and warranties, oral or written, all of which are merged herein.

___*purchaser's signature*___
Purchaser

___*purchaser's name printed*___
Purchaser's Name

____
Address

____
City State Zip Code

SELLER'S ACCEPTANCE OF OFFER

Seller acknowledges that he/she is the owner of the Property, consents to the deposit of the earnest-money payment in escrow with ___*escrow agent's name*___ and accepts the Offer to purchase the Property on the terms and conditions described in this Offer.

___*seller's signature*___
Seller

___*seller's name printed*___
Seller's Name

FULL COVENANT AND WARRANTY DEED

A real estate transaction is not complete until the seller (grantor) has signed a written description of the property (deed) and given it to the buyer (grantee). There are several types of deed; a full covenant and warranty deed offers the buyer the best guarantee against legal problems that might arise in the future as a result of judgments or claims by others against the property. If faced with such claims, the holder of a full covenant and warranty deed has the right to sue the seller.

Full Covenant and Warranty Deed

BE IT KNOWN, that ______*seller's name*______, Grantor, of ______*seller's address*______, County of ______*seller's county*______, State of ______*seller's state*______, hereby bargains, deeds, and conveys to ______*buyer's name*______, Grantee, of ______*buyer's address*______, County of ______*buyer's county*______, State of ______*buyer's state*______, and his heirs and assigns, for the sum of $ ______*selling price*______, the following described real estate in ______*name of county*______ County, State of ______*name of state*______, in fee simple:

[legal description of property]

along with all the tenements, hereditaments, and appurtenances belonging to the above property.

Grantor, for himself, his heirs and successors, hereby covenants with Grantee, Grantee's heirs and assigns, that Grantor is lawfully seised in fee simple of the above-described property and that he has the right to convey it; that the property is free from all encumbrances, except those listed in Schedule A attached to this document and incorporated herein by reference; that Grantor and his heirs, and all persons acquiring any interest in the property granted, through or for Grantor, will, on demand of and at the expense of the Grantee, or his heirs or assigns, execute any additional instrument necessary for the further assurance of the title to the property that may be reasonably required; and that Grantor and his heirs will warrant and defend forever title to all of the property so granted to Grantee, his heirs and assigns, against every person lawfully claiming the same or any part thereof.

Grantor obtained title to the above-described property by deed of ______*previous owner*______, dated ______*date of seller's deed*______, 19___, and recorded in the office of the Recorder of Deeds for ______*name of county*______ County in Book or Volume ______*number*______ at Page ______*number*______.

IN WITNESS WHEREOF, the Grantor has signed this deed this _*date*_ day of _*month*_, 19___.

*seller's signature*
Grantor

NOTARY'S STATEMENT

State of ________________)
) ss.
County of ______________)

The foregoing instrument was acknowledged before me this __________ day of ______________, 19____, by ____________________, as Grantor.

[SEAL]

____
NOTARY PUBLIC

My commission expires: ____________

❑ **Note:** All deeds contain a legal description of the property, which precisely defines its boundaries. In this deed the land, as well as any houses, buildings, or structures ("tenements, hereditaments, and appurtenances"), is conveyed to the buyer. The seller swears that he is the sole owner of the property ("is lawfully seised in fee simple"), that there are no encumbrances (liens or judgments) against the property, and that he and his heirs will defend the buyer's and his heirs' rights to the property if anyone challenges their ownership. If there are any encumbrances against the property, they should be listed on a separate page (here called Schedule A). The buyer should keep the property deed in a safe place, such as a safe-deposit box. For more information, see DEED; FULL COVENANT AND WARRANTY DEED.

Quitclaim Deed

A quitclaim deed gives a real estate buyer (grantee) the least amount of protection from any claims by others on the property. In a quitclaim deed, the seller (grantor) gives the buyer his interests or rights to the property, but gives no assurances that he has sole claim to the property.

Quitclaim Deed

BE IT KNOWN, that ____*seller's name*____ (Grantor), of ____*seller's address*____, County of ____*seller's county*____, State of ____*seller's state*____, hereby QUITCLAIMS and transfers to ____*buyer's name*____, of ____*buyer's address*____, County of ____*buyer's county*____, State of ____*buyer's state*____, for the sum of $____*selling price*____, receipt of which is hereby acknowledged, the following described real property located in ____*name of county*____ County, State of ____*name of state*____:

[legal description of property]

Grantor does not covenant that he/she is the lawful owner of any estate in the above-mentioned property, nor does he/she make any covenant regarding encumbrances, liens, or his/her right to convey the above-mentioned property. Nor does Grantor make any covenant, representation, or warranty regarding the quality or condition of the above-mentioned property. Grantor intends this deed to convey only whatever interest he/she may now have in the property.

IN WITNESS WHEREOF, I have signed this Deed this ____*date*____ day of ____*month*____, 19____.

____*seller's signature*____
Grantor

State of ____________)
)ss.
County of ____________)

Before me personally appeared ____________________, who acknowledged the foregoing as his/her free act and deed, this _____ day of ______________, 19__.

[SEAL]

____
NOTARY PUBLIC

My commission expires: ____________

❑ **Note:** A legal description of the property precisely defines its boundaries. The seller makes no promise (covenant) that she has lawful title to the property she is selling, or that there are no claims or judgments against it. Nor does she make any promises regarding the property's condition. Before accepting a quitclaim deed, consult an attorney about the possible problems you can encounter with this type of deed. You should keep a quitclaim deed in a safe place, such as a safe-deposit box. For further information, see Deed; Quitclaim Deed.

· GLOSSARY ·

The terms included in this Glossary should be regarded as supplementary to those that already appear as entry titles in the A-to-Z text. If you cannot find a word in the Glossary, look for it in the Index or in the text itself. To help the reader, many Glossary entries include cross-references to articles in the main text. But note that, in order to keep the main text free of legal jargon, terms that appear in the Glossary do not necessarily appear in the main text.

Abate To decrease, reduce, remove, or destroy. For example, to abate a bequest (a gift made to someone through a will) is to reduce it because there are not enough funds in the estate to pay the full amount. To abate a nuisance is to remove or destroy whatever causes it.

Ab initio (*ahb in-ISH-ee-oh*) A Latin phrase meaning "from the beginning." For example, to say that a marriage was unlawful ab initio means that the marriage was never valid in the first place.

Abrogate To abolish. A statute is abrogated, for example, if the legislature repeals it or a court declares it unconstitutional.

Abscond To flee from a court's jurisdiction (area of authority), or to hide within it in order to avoid prosecution.

Abstract of title A short history of the ownership of a piece of real estate, recording all its sales and transfers, its previous owners, and the liens and other liabilities against the property, as well as any other information a prospective buyer would need to know to be sure of its rightful owner. See CLOSING, REAL ESTATE; TITLE INSURANCE.

Action A legal proceeding, such as a civil lawsuit or criminal trial, held to enforce or protect someone's right, to redress or prevent a wrong, or to punish a crime. See CRIMINAL PROCEDURE; LAWSUIT.

Ad damnum (*ahd DAM-num*) A Latin phrase meaning "to the damage," referring to the clause in a civil complaint that states the amount of damages, or money, demanded by the plaintiff. See DAMAGES.

Addendum An item or list of items added to a document.

Ademption An act by which a person who has made his will sells, gives away, or uses up a bequest he has made to someone, so that it is no longer part of the will. Suppose your uncle leaves you his 1988 Buick in his will, but then sells it. This is an ademption and when he dies you cannot claim the car or anything else to replace it. See WILL.

Ad hoc (*add HOCK*) A Latin phrase meaning "for this," that is, for a particular purpose. For example, an ad hoc committee is one created for a specific purpose and no other.

Adjudication The judgment or decree of a court and the legal process by which the decision is reached.

Advocate A person who assists, advises, or pleads the cause of another person in court; a lawyer or counselor. See LAWYER.

Affiant A person who makes statements in an affidavit, and swears to the truth of those statements. See AFFIDAVIT.

Aggravated Severe; intensified. For example, someone who attacks another person with a dangerous weapon can be charged with aggravated assault. It is a more serious charge than simple assault, which involves simply striking another person.

aka An abbreviation for "also known as." Often used by police to indicate a criminal's alias, or alternate name.

Alibi From the Latin word for "elsewhere," referring to a defense by which an accused person tries to establish his innocence by showing that he was somewhere else when the crime was committed.

Allegation An accusation made by either party to a lawsuit, indicating what that party intends to prove. See LAWSUIT.

Amicus curiae (*ah-MEE-kus CURE-ee-eye*) A Latin term meaning "friend of the court," referring to a person or organization that, although not involved in a lawsuit, may be affected by the court's decision and is therefore permitted to point out information that might be helpful to the court in making a decision. Representatives of right-to-life and pro-choice organizations, for example, testified before the U.S. Supreme Court before it made its 1992 decision in *Planned Parenthood* v. *Casey*.

Amortization The payment of a mortgage or other debt in installments over a specified period of time. Amortization is calculated by adding the amount owed (the principal) to the amount of interest that will be paid over the life of the loan, and then dividing the total by the number of payments to be made. See MORTGAGE.

Appurtenant Belonging or attached to something else more important. For example, a garage is appurtenant to the main house. See HOME BUYING AND SELLING.

Arbitrary and capricious A term used to describe a decision of an agency or a court that is made with willful disregard for the facts and circumstances of the case and that is cause for an appeal to a higher court.

Attest To affirm that something, such as a signature or document, is either authentic or true.

Barratry The offense of repeatedly provoking quarrels or unnecessary lawsuits. A lawyer who tries to generate lawsuits for his own profit is guilty of barratry and may be disbarred.

Bearer A person who is in possession of a negotiable document, such as a bill, note, or check, that is payable to the person who holds it. See BOND; CHECK; COMMERCIAL PAPER.

Bench warrant An order that is issued by a sitting judge (hence the word *bench*) permitting law enforcement officials to arrest someone in order to compel him to appear in court. A bench warrant may be issued for a witness who has been subpoenaed, a suspect who has been indicted, or a person charged with contempt of court. See ARREST.

Beneficiary A person or organization designated to receive certain property or money, such as the proceeds from an estate or a life insurance policy. See LIFE INSURANCE; WILL.

Bequest A gift of money or other personal property (but not real estate) left to someone through a will. See WILL.

Bill of particulars A document listing the details of charges being brought against a defendant in a lawsuit or criminal trial. See CRIMINAL PROCEDURE; LAWSUIT.

Binding authority The relevant statutes and legal precedents a judge must follow when he rules on a case.

Bona fide (*BONE-uh fide*) A Latin phrase meaning "in good faith," referring to an action performed honestly, with no intent to deceive or defraud. See BAD FAITH; CONTRACT; GOOD FAITH.

Brief An attorney's written summary of the facts, arguments, and legal precedents he intends to use to support his case. See CRIMINAL PROCEDURE; LAWSUIT.

Bylaws A set of rules adopted by a corporation or other organization that governs the way it does business. See COOPERATIVE APARTMENT; CORPORATION.

Canon law The body of rules and religious doctrines adopted by a church to govern the institution and its members. Canon law has no relation to civil or common law, which affect the population at large.

Capacity The qualifications, such as age or competency, that are necessary for a person's actions to be legally permitted and recognized. Testamentary capacity, for example, refers to someone's legal ability to make a will. See COMPETENCY; WILL.

Causa mortis (*COW-za MORE-tis*) A Latin phrase meaning "because of death," referring to a gift given by someone because he believes he is near death. If the person dies, the gift takes effect; if he recovers, it may be revoked. See GIFT.

Caveat emptor (*KAH-vee-ott EMP-tor*) A Latin phrase meaning "let the buyer beware." It refers to the risk a consumer assumes when purchasing goods and his responsibility to be cautious. See CONSUMER PROTECTION.

Cease and desist order An order issued by a court or government administrative agency directing a person or business to discontinue an illegal practice. See FALSE ADVERTISING; FEDERAL TRADE COMMISSION.

Certiorari (*sir-shee-er-AHR-ee*) A Latin term meaning "to be informed of," referring to a writ, or order, from a higher court (usually the U.S. Supreme Court) to a lower one demanding a certified record of its proceedings in a case that is under review. See SUPREME COURT, U.S.

Chain of title The succession of transfers of a particular piece of real estate from its original source to its present owner.

Champerty (*CHAM-per-tee*) An arrangement in which one person, such as a lawyer, agrees to pay another person's expenses in a lawsuit in exchange for part of the settlement. Champerty is generally prohibited because it leads to unnecessary litigation. See also CONTINGENT FEE.

Chattel An article of personal property; property that is not real estate, such as money, stocks, jewelry, or cars. See CHATTEL MORTGAGE.

Civil law A system of law based on a legislated code rather than individual statutes and previous cases (precedents), which form the basis of common law. Because of its French and Spanish heritage, Louisiana is the only state that follows a civil law system. All other states follow common law. See COMMON LAW.

Claim A request or demand for some right or supposed right. Also, the thing that is requested, such as a piece of land.

Closed shop A business that hires only union members. See LABOR UNION.

Codification The act or process by which the laws of a state or country are systematically collected and organized into a body of rules, called a code.

Coinsurance A system of insurance that divides risk between the insurer and the insured. For example, if you have a health insurance policy that pays only 80 percent of hospital costs up to a specified amount, the 20 percent you have to pay is considered coinsurance. See HEALTH INSURANCE; HOMEOWNERS INSURANCE.

Comity The principle that the courts of one state or locality will give full acceptance to the laws and judicial decisions of another, not because of any obligation, but out of mutual respect. When a state court refuses to hear a lawsuit because the parties to it are involved in an identical suit in another state, for example, it is acting through comity.

Complainant The party that petitions the court in order to commence a legal action. In civil suits the complainant, or person who brings suit, is often called the plaintiff. In criminal cases the complainant is the state and is called the prosecution. See LAWSUIT; CRIMINAL PROCEDURE.

Concealment The act of hiding or withholding information. A party to an insurance contract, for example, is guilty of concealment if he fails to disclose or tries to suppress facts that he has a legal duty to reveal.

Confiscate To seize property from someone because he is using it illegally or does not own it.

Consanguinity The kinship, or blood relationship, between persons who share a common ancestor. Consanguinity is a consideration in inheritance rights and in eligibility for marriage (which is forbidden between parent and child, brother and sister, uncle and niece, aunt and nephew, and grandparent and grandchild). See also MARRIAGE.

Consortium The right of each spouse to the care, affection, companionship, and cooperation of the other. If one spouse is unable to provide these essentials because he is killed or injured by a third person, the other spouse can sue the third party for loss of consortium.

Contingent Dependent on a future event whose outcome is unknown. A gift left in a will, for example, may be contingent on certain actions or conditions, or a lawyer's fee may be contingent on the outcome of the case. See CONTINGENT FEE.

Contraband Goods that are illegal to import or export over national borders, such as narcotics or ivory.

Convey To transfer the title to (ownership of) property from one person to another, usually by deed. See DEED.

Coroner A city or county official who conducts investigations of unexplained or violent deaths and takes charge of unclaimed bodies. See AUTOPSY.

Corpus delicti (*CORE-pus de-LICK-tie*) A Latin phrase meaning "the body of the crime," referring to the physical evidence that indicates that a crime was committed, such as a body with a gunshot wound or cache of stolen goods.

Curfew A regulation issued by public authorities forbidding people to be on the streets at designated hours. See ASSEMBLY, FREEDOM OF.

Curtesy The right by which a man is entitled to a share in his wife's property after her death. See DOWER AND CURTESY.

Cy pres (*sigh PRAY*) A French phrase meaning "as nearly as possible," referring to the doctrine by which a gift or trust that cannot be administered according to the exact wishes of the deceased may be administered as closely as possible to those wishes. See EXECUTOR AND ADMINISTRATOR; WILL.

Debenture A document, such as a bond or promissory note, which acknowledges that a debt is owed and will be paid, usually without any collateral.

Deceit A trick, false statement, or pretense by which one person intentionally misleads another, who then suffers injury or damage as a result. See FRAUD.

Declarant A person who makes a declaration, particularly someone who makes a living will. See LIVING WILL.

Declaratory judgment A judgment that formally states the duties, responsibilities, rights, or status of the parties involved in a lawsuit without ordering any action to be taken. For example, a court may issue a declaratory judgment stating that a particular person is the true and rightful owner of a piece of real estate when its ownership is disputed.

Decree The decision of a court in a matter of equity, divorce, or probate. The terms *decree* and *judgment* are often used interchangeably.

Dedication A landowner's donation of private property for public use, as when he sets aside several acres of his land for a community center or park.

De facto (*day FACK-toe*) A Latin phrase meaning "in fact," referring to a government, corporation, or situation that exists but is not legitimate. A de facto government, for example, is one that attained power by means of an illegal overthrow of the legitimate government. The term is the opposite of *de jure*.

Defendant A person or organization that is being prosecuted for a crime or sued in a lawsuit.

Defraud To cheat, trick, or swindle a person; to deprive a person of his property, interest, or estate by deceit. See FRAUD; SCAMS AND SWINDLES.

De jure (*day JOOR-ay*) A Latin phrase meaning "by right," "legal," or "legitimate." The government of the United States, which was established according to a constitution and abides by it, is a de jure government. *De jure* is the opposite of *de facto*.

De minimis (*day MIN-i-mis*) A Latin phrase meaning "concerning minor things." The term is used to refer to a violation so insignificant that it should be overlooked in the interest of fairness and justice.

Demurrer A statement by the defendant in a lawsuit claiming that even though the plaintiff's accusations are true, they are not sufficient to compel the defendant to come to court to answer them. See LAWSUIT.

Dictum An incidental comment by a judge about some side issue that is not directly relevant to the case at hand.

Dismissal without prejudice The cancellation of an action or proceeding in a way that does not prevent the plaintiff from bringing another lawsuit for the same reason. See LAWSUIT.

Docket The list of cases scheduled to be tried before a court. The term is used interchangeably with *calender*. See CALENDER.

Ejectment The name of a lawsuit initiated to determine who owns a particular piece of land. The plaintiff claims ownership of the property even though the defendant currently possesses it.

Eminent domain The power vested in the government to take private property for public use (such as highways, parks, or telephone lines). The government can take the property without the consent of the owner, but the owner must be paid just compensation. See CONDEMNATION.

En banc (*on BONK*) A French phrase meaning "by the full bench (court)," referring to a court session attended by a full complement of judges. For example, a routine federal Court of Appeals case might be heard by three judges out of a possible five; all five judges would participate in an en banc hearing. En banc proceedings are usually reserved for important cases that establish far-reaching precedents.

Encumbrance Any outstanding claim on real estate that lessens its value or hinders its sale, such as a mortgage, mechanic's lien, or unpaid tax. See HOME BUYING AND SELLING.

Estate Everything a person owns or has a financial interest in; the property and possessions of a deceased or bankrupt person.

Estoppel (*es-TOP-el*) A legal prohibition that prevents a person from denying a statement previously made or changing an action already taken if it will cause loss or injury to another person who relied on that statement or action. Suppose that an insurance agent sends a policy application and fee to the company, which accepts them and issues a policy. The company later refuses to honor a legitimate claim, arguing that the agent was not authorized to sell that kind of policy. The company is estopped from making such a claim by its prior acceptance of the agent's actions.

Et al. (*et AHL*) An abbreviation for the Latin phrase *et alii*, meaning "and others." It is often used to indicate a number of defendants in a lawsuit, as in "*State of Georgia* v. *Williams et al.*"

Excise tax A tax imposed on certain types of goods, such as liquor and tobacco; on licenses to pursue certain occupations; or on corporate privileges.

Executory Designed to occur or be put into effect at some future time. For example, an executory contract is an agreement between two parties requiring one to perform a service for the other at a later date.

Ex parte (*ex PAR-tay*) A Latin phrase meaning "from one party only." The term describes a legal proceeding that takes place without the adversary party being notified. For example, when a court issues an order of protection for an abused wife without notifying her husband because he might harm her if he knew about it in advance, the order is called ex parte.

Expatriation The voluntary giving up of citizenship in one's native country to become a citizen of another.

Ex post facto Latin for "after the fact," referring to a law that makes an act punishable as a crime even though the act was committed before the law was passed. Ex post facto laws are unconstitutional.

Expropriation The taking of private property for public use, such as to build a park or railroad. See CONDEMNATION.

Expungement The process by which a criminal conviction is erased from official records. Expungement is usually available only for certain crimes, such as assault or breaking and entering.

Eyewitness A person who is able to give testimony about an act or event because he saw it take place.

Face value The amount printed on a bond, insurance policy, or note, representing its value at maturity, or when it is due. See STOCKS AND BONDS.

FICA An abbreviation for the Federal Insurance Contributions Act, the law that authorizes the federal government to withhold Social Security taxes from workers' pay. See SOCIAL SECURITY.

Fee simple Absolute ownership of real estate, giving the owner complete authority to sell or otherwise dispose of the property during his lifetime and to pass this authority to whomever he wishes upon his death.

Firm offer A written offer to enter into a contract, such as that made by a merchant who buys and sells goods. Such an offer usually states that it will remain open for a fixed period of time, during which it cannot be revoked. See CONTRACT.

Fixed asset Property (such as land, buildings, or machinery) that is held for the purpose of conducting business but is not used up in the operation of the business or sold for cash. Lenders consider the value of a company's fixed assets when deciding whether to grant credit. See SECURITY AGREEMENT.

Floating lien An agreement between a debtor and creditor in which collateral offered by the debtor as security for a loan will serve as security for any future loans from the creditor to the debtor. See LIEN; MECHANIC'S LIEN.

Forcible entry Taking possession of someone else's house or land without his permission and by means of violence or terror. The phrase is often used when a landlord tries illegally to evict a tenant. See EVICTION.

Foreman The member of the jury who is elected by the jury or the court to speak for the jury, preside over its deliberations, and communicate with the court on its behalf. See JURY.

Futures Contracts that promise to buy or sell standard commodities, such as grain, at a set price on a future date.

GI Bill Legislation enacted in 1944 that was designed to offer educational opportunities and other benefits to veterans who were returning to civilian life after serving in World War II. See VETERANS BENEFITS.

Grace period The brief period of time specified in a contract that allows a payment to be made after the due date. Generally, the term refers to the length of time an insurance policyholder has to pay the premium after its due date.

Holder A person in legal possession of a check, promissory note, or bill of exchange who is entitled to receive payment. See PROMISSORY NOTE.

Hold over To remain in possession after the end of a term, as an officeholder or a tenant. See LANDLORD; LEASE; EVICTION.

Housebreaking Breaking into and entering a home for the purpose of committing a felony inside; burglary. See BURGLARY.

Illusory promise A statement that appears to be the basis for a contract, but in fact is so vague that it promises nothing that is legally binding. A contract based on an illusory promise cannot be enforced. Suppose you buy an appliance with a service contract stating that the manufacturer will "replace or repair the item if, in the company's sole judgment, such action is within the terms of this warranty." With this type of wording, the company—not you—decides whether your appliance merits repair or replacement. Because there is no real warranty or promise, you cannot obtain satisfaction unless you take the company to court.

Impound To confiscate personal property, such as an automobile or document, as evidence or for safekeeping.

Inalienable right A right, such as freedom of speech, that cannot be bought, sold, forfeited, or transferred to another person. Someone cannot agree to become another person's slave, for example, because personal liberty is an inalienable right.

In camera A Latin phrase meaning "in chambers," referring to a case or portion of a case heard in a judge's chambers or in a private courtroom from which spectators are barred.

Inchoate Begun but not finished. For example, a contract that has not been executed by both parties is inchoate until both parties have signed it.

Indenture A deed, contract, or other written agreement between two or more parties that sets forth a certain mutual obligation.

Information An accusation similar to an indictment, presented by a prosecutor or an arresting officer rather than a grand jury. See CRIMINAL PROCEDURE.

Inheritance The property that someone receives from a deceased person, either through a will or as stipulated by law.

In loco parentis (*in lo-co pa-REN-tis*) A Latin phrase meaning "in the place of a parent," referring to the parental rights and obligations that are granted to a person or institution temporarily entrusted with a child, such as a teacher or school.

Inquest A court-ordered inquiry by a coroner or grand jury into the cause and circumstances of a sudden or unexplained death. See AUTOPSY.

In re (*in ray*) A Latin phrase meaning "in the case (or matter) of," used in the title of lawsuits or other legal proceedings in which there are no opposing parties. For example, an uncontested divorce might be identified as "In re the marriage of Smith and Smith."

In rem A Latin phrase meaning "against the thing," referring to an act or proceeding that involves a specific thing rather than opposing parties. For example, a probate court has "in rem" jurisdiction, or authority, over a deceased person's estate.

Insolvency The inability to pay one's debts as they become due, or the situation in which one's liabilities exceed one's assets. See BANKRUPTCY.

Instrument A formal, written, legally binding document, such as a contract, will, lease, or promissory note.

Insurable interest An interest in a person or property that gives someone reason to want to preserve that life or property. A husband has an insurable interest in his wife's life, for example, and can buy a life insurance policy on it, but someone who stands to benefit financially from the death probably would not. See LIFE INSURANCE.

Inter alia (*in-ter AH-lee-ah*) A Latin phrase meaning "among other things."

Interlocutory Temporary or provisional. An interlocutory divorce decree, for example, does not become final until a specified period of time has elapsed. See DIVORCE.

Interpleader A legal procedure used to decide the rights of rival claimants to money or property held by a third person who has no interest in it. Insurance companies often use interpleader proceedings when there are multiple claims upon a policy — for example, if the deceased person's heirs are fighting among themselves for the proceeds.

Interrogatory A written question, usually designed to obtain basic factual information, that is given by one party to the opposing party to a lawsuit before the trial begins. An interrogatory must be answered under oath. See DISCOVERY.

Inter vivos *(IN-ter VEE-vose)* A Latin phrase meaning "between living persons." An inter vivos gift, for example, is one that is given while the donor is still alive. See GIFT.

Intestate *(in-TES-tate)* The condition of having died without a valid will. The property of someone who dies intestate is distributed according to state law. See DYING WITHOUT A WILL.

Ipso facto *(IP-so FACK-toe)* A Latin phrase meaning "by the fact itself." When a person signs an insurance claim form, he gives up his right ipso facto to seek further damages (money).

Joinder The joining of two or more legal proceedings; the uniting of two or more persons (who are pursuing individual lawsuits) as plaintiffs or defendants in a single lawsuit.

Judgment-proof A person or company that claims insolvency or bankruptcy, and is therefore unable to pay the money damages that are awarded by a court. See JUDGMENT.

Judicial review The power of a court to review and revise the decision of a public administrative agency, such as the Food and Drug Administration, if someone affected by that decision petitions the court.

Jurisprudence The study of law and legal principles.

Laches *(LATCH-ez)* A defense raised by the defendant in a lawsuit alleging that the plaintiff has waited so long to file suit that the defendant can no longer defend himself.

Lapse The forfeit of a right or privilege due to a failure to perform some necessary act. For example, a lapse of insurance may occur if the policy owner fails to make premium payments.

Larceny Criminal theft; the act of taking someone's property without his consent.

Latent defect A defect that is not visible or apparent. A latent defect in merchandise or in the title to land, for example, is one that cannot be discovered by reasonably careful inspection.

Leasehold The property or land governed by a lease. If you sign a lease on a two-bedroom apartment, for example, the apartment is a leasehold for the time and conditions specified by the contract. See LEASE.

Legacy A bequest, or gift, of personal property left to someone through a will. Technically, the term refers only to personal property; real property is given by devise. However, when a will fails to make this distinction, the term legacy is usually understood to refer to both.

Legitimate Authorized or sanctioned by law; legal.

Lessee A person who is granted a lease. See LEASE.

Lessor A person who grants a lease; a landlord. See LANDLORD.

Letters of administration Documents issued by a probate court authorizing one or more persons to administer the estate of a person who has died without a will. See DYING WITHOUT A WILL.

Letters testamentary Documents issued by a probate court authorizing the executor of a will to perform the duties required by law and the terms of the will. See EXECUTOR AND ADMINISTRATOR.

Levy To impose or collect, such as a tax or fine.

Lewdness, public An act, such as removing one's bathing suit on a public beach or looking into women's bedroom windows, that offends the community's standard of decency.

Lex The Latin word for law; a collection or body of laws.

Licensee Someone who has been granted a license; also, a person, such as a mail carrier or delivery person, who enters someone's house or property with the owner's permission but without an invitation. See ACCIDENTS IN THE HOME.

Liquid asset Cash or anything else of value that can easily be converted into cash, such as stocks, bonds, or jewelry.

Liquidate To pay and settle a debt or estate. To liquidate a business, for example, is to pay off all creditors and put the company out of business. See PARTNERSHIP.

Litigation A lawsuit; a judicial contest.

Maim To injure seriously, as by mutilating or crippling.

Malfeasance The commission of a wrongful act, especially one that interferes with the ability of a public official to perform his duties. For example, a senator who conducts a smear campaign against his opponent is guilty of malfeasance.

Malice aforethought The intention to commit an unlawful act, in particular when the act results in the serious injury or death of another. Malice aforethought does not necessarily imply ill will or hatred toward the victim, but rather a conscious disregard for the life of another. See PREMEDITATION.

Malpractice Professional misconduct; the failure of a professional, such as a doctor, lawyer, or accountant, to follow the accepted standards of his profession in providing services to his clients. A lawyer who neglects to file a lawsuit before the time period allowed by law, for example, or a doctor who prescribes a medicine without first asking whether the patient is allergic, is guilty of malpractice. See LAWYER; MEDICAL MALPRACTICE.

Malum in se (*MAL-um in SAY*) A Latin phrase meaning "wrong in itself," referring to an act, such as cheating on a test, that is inherently wrong or immoral even though it is not prohibited by law.

Malum prohibitum (*MAL-um pro-HIB-i-tum*) A Latin phrase meaning "a wrong prohibited," referring to an act, such as driving faster than the speed limit, that is prohibited by law even though it is not inherently wrong.

Mandamus (*man-DAY-mus*) A Latin word meaning "we command." A writ of mandamus is a court order directing public officials or subordinate courts to do or not do something that is ordinarily within the scope of their official duties. If, for example, a city refuses to issue a parade permit when the law requires it to do so, the group seeking the permit could ask the court for a writ of mandamus ordering the city to issue the permit.

Marital misconduct Actions that would serve as grounds for divorce, such as adultery, cruelty, or desertion. See DIVORCE.

Marshal, U.S. A chief law enforcement officer for the federal court system, responsible for enforcing federal court orders, serving federal court summonses, and keeping the peace in federal courts and prisons. Each federal judicial district has one U.S. marshal, who is appointed by the president.

Mayhem The crime of intentionally maiming, disabling, or disfiguring someone.

Meeting of the minds The point at which both parties forming a contract come to an agreement on its terms. See CONTRACT.

Mental anguish The fear, anxiety, distress, depression, or emotional pain and suffering that may accompany a physical injury or result from a traumatic experience. If the plaintiff in a lawsuit can prove mental anguish, she may be awarded money damages in addition to those awarded for her physical injury. See DAMAGES; LAWSUIT.

Metes and bounds The precise boundary lines of a tract of land, usually measured and determined by a surveyor. See BOUNDARY LINE.

Mill levy An amount used by county treasurers to calculate a homeowner's annual property tax. To calculate the tax, the assessed value of the property is multiplied by the mill levy. A "mill" is one tenth of one cent. Thus, if the mill levy is 6.5 mills, the tax rate for each dollar's worth of property is $0.0065, and if your home is assessed for $100,000, your mill levy would be $650. See PROPERTY TAX.

Minor A person below the age (usually 18) at which he or she is legally entitled to the rights and privileges of an adult. See CHILD EMPLOYMENT; CHILDREN'S RIGHTS; JUVENILE OFFENDER.

Misdemeanor A crime punishable by a fine of $1,000 or less and a prison sentence of no more than one year in a county jail. See CRIMINAL LAW; PRISON SENTENCE.

Misfeasance The commission of an act that is wrong or improper but legal. For example, if a judge makes insulting remarks about a defense attorney during a trial, he is guilty of misfeasance.

Mistrial A trial terminated by the judge because of legal errors, disruptive behavior in the courtroom, or the failure of the jury to reach a verdict. See APPEAL.

M'Naghten Rule A standard used by courts in some states to determine whether a person was legally insane (that is, unable to understand the difference between right and wrong) when he committed a crime, and therefore not legally responsible for his actions. See INSANITY PLEA.

Monopoly The exclusive right or power to control the production, sale, or supply of a particular item. Monopolies are usually against the law because they are harmful to the general welfare by preventing competition and increasing prices.

Moot Open to discussion; undecided; debatable. A moot point of law is one that has not been settled by a judicial decision.

Moral turpitude An action or form of conduct, such as bribery or prostitution, that is viewed as highly dishonest or immoral because it is contrary to the accepted rules of society.

Motion A request made to a judge by one of the parties to a lawsuit asking for some action to be taken. For example, a defendant may make a motion to dismiss the case, claiming that the plaintiff has no grounds for a lawsuit. See LAWSUIT.

Motive The cause, reason, or incentive for a person's action or behavior, used most often in the context of committing a crime. See INTENT.

Mutuality of contract The principle that each party must take some action or make some promise in order to create a legally binding contract, since neither one is bound unless both are. See CONTRACT.

N.B. An abbreviation for nota bene (*no-tah BAY-nay*), a Latin phrase meaning "note well." It is used in footnoting legal briefs and writings.

Necessaries Things that are essential, proper, or useful for daily life, such as food, clothing, and shelter.

Next Friend One who acts for the benefit of a person who is not able to act on his own behalf in a legal proceeding, such as a child. See GUARDIAN AND WARD.

Nolle prosequi (*NO-lay PRAH-se-kwee*) A Latin phrase meaning "will not further prosecute," referring to the decision of a plaintiff or prosecutor not to proceed any further with his case.

Nolo contendere (*NO-lo con-TEN-der-ee*) A Latin phrase

meaning "I will not contest," referring to a plea by a defendant in a criminal prosecution that, like a guilty plea, subjects him to conviction, but without an admission of guilt. See NO CONTEST; PLEA.

Nominal Existing in name only; minor or trivial. For example, nominal damages are a small sum of money awarded by a court to compensate the plaintiff for a violation of his legal rights, even though he may not have suffered a significant loss or injury. See DAMAGES.

Non compos mentis (*non compis MEN-tis*) A Latin phrase meaning "not of sound mind," referring to a claim by a defendant in a criminal or civil case that he was mentally incompetent when he committed a certain act and should therefore not be held responsible. See INCOMPETENCY.

Note A written promise to pay a certain amount of money to a particular person at a specified time. See PROMISSORY NOTE.

Novation The substitution of a new debt or obligation for an old one, or of one debtor or creditor for another.

Nunc pro tunc (*nunk pro tunk*) A Latin phrase meaning "now for then," referring to an act that is given the legal consequences it would have had if it had been done at an earlier time. For example, a child born out of wedlock is no longer considered illegitimate if the parents get married.

Objection A formal statement used in court by an attorney, calling the court's attention to testimony, evidence, or a legal procedure that he considers improper or illegal.

Offer A proposal to make a contract that contains all the terms of the contract and becomes legally binding if the terms are accepted. See CONTRACT.

Officer of the court A court employee, such as a judge, bailiff, or attorney, who must obey court rules and regulations. See CONTEMPT OF COURT; JUDGE; LAWYER.

Ombudsman (*AHM-budz-men*) A government-employed investigator who resolves citizens' complaints against government agencies.

Open shop A company that hires both union and nonunion members. See LABOR UNION.

Opinion The official statement of a court after the completion of a case. It announces the decision the court has reached, outlines the facts of the case, and explains the laws and reasoning that were applied.

Ordinance A law enacted by a city government or other municipality. Ordinances regulate local affairs, such as traffic, parking, and business licensing.

Original jurisdiction The authority of a court to consider cases for the first time; distinguished from *appellate jurisdiction*, which is the authority to review cases on appeal. See JURISDICTION.

Overrule To reverse or reject. For example, for various reasons a judge may overrule a lawyer's objection during a trial or an appeals court may overrule the decision of a lower court.

Parens patriae (*PAIR-enz PAY-tree-eye*) A Latin phrase meaning "parent of the country," referring to a state's power to sue the federal government or one of its agencies on behalf of the state's citizens. The phrase also refers to a state's power to serve as a guardian for someone who is legally incompetent, such as a minor or a mentally ill person.

Parol Oral; expressed in speech rather than writing.

Parol evidence Oral evidence; testimony presented by a witness before a court. Under the parol evidence rule, a written contract takes precedence over any previous oral promise or agreement about the same matter. If Bob and Sue have a written contract that Sue will paint Bob's house and Bob claims in court that Sue had also agreed to "throw in" a paint job for the garage, Bob would not win his case under this rule. See EVIDENCE.

Party A person who takes part in a contract, transaction, or legal proceeding. In a trial, the parties are the plaintiff, or petitioner, and the defendant, or respondent. In an appeal, the parties are the appellant and the appellee.

Par value The value at which a stock, bond, or other security sells on the market. See BOOK VALUE.

Pauper A person who is so poor that he is legally entitled to receive public charity or to prosecute or defend a lawsuit at no cost to himself.

Pendente lite (*pen DEN-tay LEE-tay*) A Latin phrase meaning "pending or during suit," referring to an event that takes place while a lawsuit is in progress. For example, a court may require that a business be placed in receivership, pendente lite.

Pending Begun but not yet finished. For example, a pending legal action is one that is underway but is awaiting a court's final judgment, or decision.

Per capita A Latin phrase meaning "by heads" (by individual persons), referring to a method used to divide something into equal shares, such as the estate of a deceased person. See DYING WITHOUT A WILL.

Per curiam (*per CURE-ee-ahm*) A Latin phrase meaning "by the court," referring to an opinion rendered by an entire appeals court rather than one judge.

Peremptory challenge The right of the prosecuting attorney and defense attorney in a jury trial to reject a certain number of prospective jurors without having to give a reason. See JURY.

Permission slip A consent form used by schools to obtain permision from parents to have their child participate in some school-related activity, such as an athletic competition or field trip. It does not release the school from responsibility for its own negligence. See CONSENT FORM.

Personal property Anything a person can own other than real estate (known as real property).

Per stirpes *(per STER-pays)* A Latin term meaning "through the roots," referring to a method that is used by attorneys to divide someone's estate when a beneficiary or heir has died before him. For example, suppose Jim's will names his sons, Tom and Peter, to inherit equal shares of his estate, but Tom dies before his father and is survived by two daughters. If Jim's estate is distributed per stirpes, each of Tom's daughters will receive one half of their father's share of the estate. See WILL.

Plaintiff The party that initiates a civil lawsuit or criminal prosecution. In criminal cases, the plaintiff is a government entity, such as the state or the United States.

Police power The authority of government to make and enforce all laws and regulations it deems necessary for the good and welfare of the state and its citizens.

Post mortem A Latin phrase meaning "after death," referring to an autopsy or examination of a body made by medical authorities to determine the cause of death. See AUTOPSY.

Precedent A decision made in an earlier, similar case that a court uses as a guide in deciding the case at hand. Prosecuting and defense attorneys try to find precedents favorable to their case and present them in court.

Premeditation Prior consideration of a criminal act and the determination to commit it. A person who commits premeditated murder is subject to a higher penalty than a person who kills someone in the heat of passion, because he had enough time to consider the consequences of his actions. See MURDER.

Presentment A grand jury's written statement alleging that a crime has been committed and that there is adequate evidence to charge one or more persons with the crime. See GRAND JURY; INDICTMENT.

Pretermitted heir An adult or minor child who has been omitted from his parent's will. See HEIR.

Prima facie *(PRIME-uh FAY-shuh)* A Latin phrase meaning "on first sight," referring to evidence in favor of the plaintiff that is sufficient to present a convincing case against the defendant.

Primogeniture A common-law tradition (no longer valid) that the first-born son inherits all the real estate owned by his parent or other ancestor.

Principal A person who authorizes someone (called an agent) to act on his behalf. Also, an amount of money borrowed, not including interest and other charges. See AGENT.

Private property Any property that is owned by a person, association, or corporation rather than by the government.

Privity A relationship of mutual interest, such as that between a buyer and seller or two parties who make a contract.

Pro bono *(pro BONE-oh)* A shortened form of the Latin phrase *pro bono publico* ("for the public good"), referring to work performed by lawyers free of charge for clients who cannot afford their services. See LAWYER; LEGAL AID.

Process server A person authorized to serve a summons or subpoena to the defendant in a lawsuit. See LAWSUIT.

Pro rata *(pro RAY-tuh)* A Latin phrase meaning "according to a given rate, proportion, or percentage." Property taxes, for example, may be assessed pro rata between the buyer and seller of a home at closing.

Pro se *(pro SAY)* A Latin phrase meaning "for oneself," referring to a person who represents himself without a lawyer in a legal proceeding.

Prosecutor The public official, such as a district attorney, who files charges against a person suspected of committing a crime and acts on behalf of the government to get the person convicted. See CRIMINAL PROCEDURE.

Provocation Action or behavior by one person that invites another person to take some action in response. For example, if one man insults another man's wife, causing the husband to throw a punch, the man who made the insulting remark would be guilty of provocation.

Proximate cause The direct, primary cause of an injury or loss, without which the injury or loss would not have occurred. See LAWSUIT.

Proxy A document signed by one person authorizing another to act on his behalf in a specific circumstance, such as voting for officers of a club or corporation. Also, the person to whom such authorization is granted.

Public defender A lawyer employed by the government to represent criminal defendants who cannot afford to hire an attorney.

Public domain Belonging to the general public rather than an individual. A creative work whose copyright has expired is considered in the public domain, as is publicly owned land. See CONDEMNATION; COPYRIGHT.

Quasi (KWAY-sigh or KWAH-see) A Latin term meaning "as if," referring to a thing or situation that resembles something else even though there are essential differences between the two. For example, an administrative agency, such as the Environmental Protection Agency or the Social

Security Administration, acts in quasi-judicial capacity when, like a court, it holds hearings and issues rulings.

Quid pro quo A Latin phrase meaning "this for that," referring to the mutual exchange of benefits that makes a contract valid and legally binding.

Ransom A sum of money demanded or paid for the release of a hostage.

Reasonable and prudent person An adult without any physical or mental disabilities who is careful but not overly cautious. In negligence cases, the concept of a reasonable and prudent person is used as a standard against which the actions of the defendant can be judged. See LAWSUIT; NEGLIGENCE; TORT.

Recidivist A habitual criminal; one who continues to commit crimes even after being caught and convicted repeatedly.

Recognizance A written promise by a criminal defendant to appear in court at a later date, without posting bail, to answer charges against him. See BAIL.

Recourse A person's right to seek payment on a check from anyone who has previously endorsed it, even if the original issuer refuses to honor it. See CHECK.

Redlining The illegal practice by a bank of identifying a neighborhood as a poor lending risk and denying its inhabitants loans on the basis of their race or national origin.

Referee A court officer assigned to investigate a civil case, take testimony, decide matters of fact, and report his findings to the court, which will make the final decision.

Referendum The submission of a proposed law, such as one for a tax increase, to voters for ratification.

Reformation The revision of a contract by the court in a situation where the terms of the contract do not represent what was originally agreed upon due to a mutual mistake by the parties.

Registrar A government official responsible for maintaining public records, such as deeds.

Regulation A rule or order issued by a public administrative agency, such as the Federal Communications Commission (FCC), to supervise or control the operation of a business that affects the general public.

Remainder The assets of a deceased person's estate after all specific gifts have been made and all taxes and administrative expenses have been paid. Also, an interest in a piece of real estate that takes effect only after another's interest in the property ends. For example, suppose your father dies and in his will he gives a life estate in the family home to your mother, allowing her to live there until she dies. The will also states that upon her death, you will become the owner of the home. Your interest in the house is known as a remainder. See ESTATE; WILL.

Remand To return. For example, a criminal defendant may be remanded to jail after a preliminary hearing, or a case may be remanded to a lower court for retrial after being heard by a court of appeals.

Remedy The method by which a court compensates someone for a wrong that has been done to him, such as by awarding him money damages. See DAMAGES.

Renounce To abandon a right or privilege without transferring it to someone else. For example, when an alien becomes a U.S. citizen, he must renounce his allegiance to his former country.

Repeal The cancellation of an earlier law by a later one.

Repudiate To reject or refuse a right, privilege, or duty. For example, a party to a contract repudiates the contract if he decides not to honor his part of the agreement. See BREACH OF CONTRACT.

Replevin *(ri-PLEV-in)* A type of lawsuit used to recover property that has been taken illegally or borrowed and not returned.

Res *(race)* A Latin word meaning "thing," referring to the object of, or the subject matter of, a lawsuit. The res of a foreclosure proceeding, for example, is the property secured by the mortgage being foreclosed on.

Residuary clause The provision in a will that disposes of the remainder of a person's estate after all specific gifts have been made and all taxes and expenses have been paid. See WILL.

Res ipsa loquitor *(race IP-sah LOW-kwi-ter)* A Latin phrase meaning "the thing speaks for itself," referring to circumstantial evidence presented by the plaintiff in a lawsuit that indicates an event was probably caused by the negligence of the defendant. See EVIDENCE.

Res judicata *(race JOO-di-KAH-tuh)* A Latin phrase meaning "the thing judged," referring to a rule of law stating that when a court with authority over a matter renders its final decision, that judgment is conclusive, even though it may later be appealed.

Respondeat superior *(ray-SPON-dee-aht soo-PEER-ee-ore)* A Latin phrase meaning "let the master answer," referring to an employer's responsibility for any actions performed by his employees in the course of their work, including ones that may injure or harm another person.

Restitution Restoring something to its rightful owner; returning someone to the position he would have held if a contract had not been broken. For example, a court may order a convicted con man to make restitution to his victims by refunding the money he swindled from them.

Retainer The fee a client pays a lawyer in order to hire him; the act by which a client employs a lawyer and gives him the authority to represent him. See LAWYER.

Reversion A legal interest in real estate that a person keeps after transferring ownership of the property to someone else, which he may exercise at some point in the future. For example, suppose Fred sells property to Jeff, but includes a provision that if Jeff uses the property for anything other than a farm, it will be returned to Fred. Fred has retained a reversion in the property. See COVENANT.

Riparian rights The rights of a person whose property borders on a river or stream, which affect his use of the water. See FISHING RIGHTS.

Sanction A penalty imposed for violating a law or regulation.

Sealed verdict A signed jury verdict that is placed in a sealed envelope and secured until it can be delivered. It allows jurors to separate temporarily if they have reached a verdict when the court is not in session.

Seizure The forcible taking of property by a law enforcement official from someone who is suspected of having violated the law or someone who has neglected to pay a court-ordered debt. See SEARCH AND SEIZURE.

Service of process The delivery, either in person or by mail, of a summons to the person designated to receive it.

Setoff A counterdemand made by a defendant to reduce or defeat a plaintiff's demand in a lawsuit. It is unconnected with the plaintiff's cause of action, or basis for suing. See LAWSUIT.

Severability The ability of one party to a contract to force the other party to honor some of its provisions even though others have been found to be illegal or unenforceable. The unenforceable parts of the agreement are said to be severable (or separatable) from the whole.

Sheriff The chief law enforcement officer of a county, responsible for serving summonses and enforcing court orders.

Sine die *(SEE-nay DEE-ay)* A Latin phrase meaning "without a day," referring to the final adjournment (with no day specified for readjournment) of a court or legislative body.

Sine qua non *(SEE-nay kwah nohn)* A Latin phrase meaning "without which not," referring to a thing or condition that is essential or indispensable.

Solicitation The crime of asking or enticing another person to commit a criminal act. For example, a prostitute who approaches men on the street is engaging in solicitation.

Solicitor general The second-highest officer of the U.S. Department of Justice, responsible for representing the federal government in cases heard by the U.S. Supreme Court and the Court of Claims.

Solvency The ability to pay one's debts as they become due.

Specific performance A legal means of carrying out a contract exactly as the terms are written. It is ordered by a court when a contract has been broken and when money damages would be inadequate, as in the case of a broken agreement to sell a one-of-a-kind work of art.

Spousal support Regular payments made by one spouse to another during a separation or after a divorce. See ALIMONY.

Squatter A person who trespasses upon or occupies land that does not belong to him without the owner's permission. See ADVERSE POSSESSION.

ss. An abbreviation of the Latin word *scilicet*, meaning "to wit," or "namely." It is used in a legal document to state the venue (place) in which the document is executed.

Stare decisis *(STAH-ray di-SIGH-sis)* A Latin phrase meaning "to stand by the decided," referring to the policy of courts to base their decisions on those of similar previous cases, or precedents. See COMMON LAW.

Status offender Someone whose behavior is unacceptable to society but who has not committed a crime, such as a disobedient child or a truant. See JUVENILE OFFENDER.

Statute A law enacted by a legislature (such as Congress or a state legislature), as opposed to the common law, which is based on court decisions and precedents. Statutes prescribe and proscribe conduct, define crimes, levy taxes, create government agencies, and the like.

Statute of Frauds A law requiring certain types of contracts, such as those for the sale of real estate, to be in writing because they would be vulnerable to fraud if they were agreed upon orally. See CONTRACT.

Stay The use of a court order to stop a judicial proceeding or prevent a judgment from being carried out.

Stipulation An agreement between the parties to a lawsuit that is designed to speed up the settlement or reduce the costs. See LAWSUIT.

Sua sponte *(SOO-uh SPON-tay)* A Latin phrase meaning "of its own accord," referring to a court order made in the best interest of the court or of justice. For example, a court may move sua sponte to dismiss a criminal case if it believes there is not enough evidence to convict the defendant.

Subcontractor Someone, such as a plumber, who forms an agreement with a general contractor, such as a construction company, to do part of the job the general contractor was hired to do. See CONTRACTOR; HOME IMPROVEMENT AND REPAIR.

Subornation of perjury The attempt to persuade someone to lie under oath, which becomes a crime only if the person actually does lie under oath.

Subpoena *(suh-PEEN-uh)* A Latin word meaning "under penalty," referring to a court order commanding someone to testify in court on a designated date.

Subpoena duces tecum *(suh-PEEN-uh DOO-ches TAY-koom)* A Latin phrase meaning "under penalty, take with you," referring to a court order that commands a witness to bring to court a document that is relevant to a lawsuit.

Subsidiary A corporation controlled by another corporation which owns at least a majority of the shares—enough to control the subsidiary.

Sue To bring legal proceedings against a person, company, or the government in order to enforce one's rights or obtain compensation for some wrongdoing. See LAWSUIT.

Summons A document that notifies someone that he is being sued and specifies a date by which he must appear in court to answer the charges against him. See LAWSUIT.

Surety A person who agrees to be responsible for someone else's debt if she does not pay.

Surrogate court A court that presides over the execution of wills and estates. Also called probate court. See PROBATE.

Sustain To uphold, grant, support, or approve. For example, a judge in a criminal trial may sustain a lawyer's objection to evidence if he believes it is correct and appropriate.

Tariff A duty, or fee, that must be paid when merchandise is imported into the United States.

Tax sale The sale of a delinquent taxpayer's property by the government to collect payment for his unpaid taxes.

Tender A formal, unconditional offer of money or other property to satisfy someone's claim.

Tender offer An attempt by one or more investors to gain control of a corporation by offering to buy a certain amount of its stock at a specified price.

Testamentary Relating to, established in, or based on someone's will, such as a testamentary trust. See TRUST; WILL.

Title Ownership of property, entitling the owner to use, sell, lease, donate, or even destroy it. Also, the document that serves as proof of ownership for property.

Title search An examination of registered deeds to make sure that a piece of real estate can be sold without anyone else claiming a right to it. See HOME BUYING AND SELLING; TITLE INSURANCE.

Treason The crime of attempting to overthrow the legitimate government to which one owes his allegiance.

Treaty A formal, legally ratified agreement between two or more nations.

Truant A child who deliberately and repeatedly misses school without justification. See JUVENILE OFFENDER.

Ultra vires *(UL-truh VEE-rez)* A Latin phrase meaning "beyond the powers," referring to an act by a corporation that exceeds the powers granted by its charter.

Uniform law A law intended for general adoption by all the states.

Unlawful assembly A gathering of three or more people for the purpose of committing a crime or disturbing the peace. See ASSEMBLY, RIGHT OF.

Usury The crime of charging an illegally high interest rate on a loan.

Variance An official permit to use land or property in a way that does not conform to zoning regulations. See ZONING.

Video Piracy The crime of making unauthorized copies of commercial copyrighted videotapes for sale to the public. See COPYRIGHT.

Void Invalid; having no legally binding force.

Voir dire *(vwahr deer)* A French phrase meaning "to speak the truth," referring to the process by which prospective jurors are questioned by lawyers to determine whether they are qualified to serve on a case. See JURY; JURY DUTY.

Waiver The voluntary relinquishment of a known legal right or claim. An express waiver is one that is stated, such as the statement on a ticket to a sporting event that informs you that the facility cannot be held responsible for any injuries you might suffer. An implied waiver is one that is not stated, as when you allow someone to cross your property as a shortcut on a regular basis.

Warrant A written order directing someone to perform a specific act. For example, an arrest warrant issued by a judge authorizes a law enforcement officer to take a suspect into custody. See ARREST; SEARCH AND SEIZURE.

Writ A written order issued by a court that directs the person to whom it is addressed to take a specified action. A writ of habeas corpus, for example, orders government officials to present someone being held in prison so that the court can determine whether his imprisonment is lawful. See HABEAS CORPUS.

• SUBJECT INDEX •

For a quick guide to LEGAL PROBLEM SOLVER entries relating to major subject areas of everyday interest, use this handy thematic index to locate topics that might not immediately come to mind.

INSURANCE

MARRIAGE and FAMILY

NEIGHBORS

RETIREMENT

TAXES

TENANTS and LANDLORD

·INDEX·

A

B

C

D

F

G

I

J

K

L

M

P

R

S

U

XYZ